PRACTICAL
GODLINESS
A devotional exposition
OF THE BOOK OF
PROVERBS

KEITH WEBER

DayOne

© Day One Publications 2021

ISBN 978-1-84625-695-0

All Scripture quotations, unless stated otherwise, are from The Holy Bible,
New King James Version Copyright © 1982 by Thomas Nelson, Inc.
Used by Permission. All rights reserved.

British Library Cataloguing in Publication Data available

Published by Day One Publications
Ryelands Road, Leominster, HR6 8NZ
Telephone 01568 613 740
North America Toll Free 888 329 6630
email—sales@dayone.co.uk
web site—www.dayone.co.uk

Cover design by smallprint

Printed by 4edge Limited

PRACTICAL GODLINESS

A devotional exposition
of the
Book of Proverbs

KEITH WEBER

To Rhiannon,
my loving, godly wife and faithful companion
for over half a century

Commendations

For the most part, the nature of the book of Proverbs and its length does not lend itself to consecutive exposition. So preachers who major on that kind of treatment of other Bible books tend to dip in and out of it from time to time, perhaps as fill-ins between major series, or during the summer holidays when their congregations are coming and going. This may give Bible readers the impression that this particular part of it can be largely overlooked. But, of course, it is no less part of the inspired Word of God than John's Gospel or Romans.

This exposition reflects the thoroughness and thoughtfulness which I have come to associate with its author. After a helpful introduction to the book he explains and makes practical applications of each proverb and, where appropriate, its immediate context. It is clear that he has meditated on what might be particular areas and experiences of life to which we might apply them. In some cases he points to the way other Scripture passages illuminate their meaning and relevance.

Many of us who seek to read the Bible at home regularly are used to reading a whole chapter or at least a significant part of it. But this does not work well with Proverbs. One or two verses, more often than not, do not relate to the surrounding context. To benefit we need to focus and meditate on each one. So one way in which we might use this exposition profitably is to let it help us from time to time do just that, with or without moving on to a more substantial passage of Scripture. Or perhaps the very nature of an e-book, for those who have the book in this format, allows us to dip into it in the midst of a busy day via our smart phone or tablet.

This is a valuable resource for believers who want to get to grips with this very practical and down to earth book in our Bibles. At the end of the book there is a thorough word index and another of Scripture references.

Peter Seccombe, former pastor of Spicer Street Chapel, St Albans

Another explanation of Proverbs, and a large one at that! Keith Weber by God's grace has been walking as a Christian for more than fifty years. He has experienced raising a family, a robust working life, and very close involvement in at least two local churches. This lays the foundation for writing on such a practical book of the Bible. 'Wisdom does not merely acknowledge the truth of the statement, it probes deeper to understand why it is so, what the background factors are, and what is to be the best response to it. This should be the reader's objective in pondering the proverbs.' This is his own very profitable approach. For example, for the very first proverb of Solomon (10:1) he does far more than explain the words. He gets you to think of the adolescents themselves, the relationship with their parents, the difference in attitude of fathers and mother, the example of Esau, and the contribution of other proverbs to the topic. One danger of explaining an Old Testament book such as Proverbs is to write as if there is no New Testament, no gospel, no Jesus Christ. There are literally hundreds of references to the example, teaching and work of our Lord, as the revelation from God that completes Proverbs. I hope the book has a very wide readership and that the Lord will use it to impart that spiritual wisdom that we so desperately need.

Keith Underhill, former pastor of Trinity Baptist Church, Nairobi

The book of Proverbs is a treasure chest of wisdom. Keith's book, *Practical Godliness*, helps us to open up that treasure chest and to see the jewels within in all their beauty. Just like a jeweller's loupe it helps us to focus on, in much more detail, the priceless value of them and on the rewards of understanding and applying them to our lives. When it comes to writing a book to help us best navigate Proverbs, and to help draw every last nugget of wisdom from them, the job has been done and it could not have been done better. I wholeheartedly commend this book to everyone who wants to seriously study Proverbs.

Kevin Mason, Elder at Kidderminster Evangelical Church

Contents

Foreword

Since the time it occurred to me that perhaps I ought to put something from my studies on the Book of Proverbs into writing I discovered two things: firstly that there already exist a number of good and helpful commentaries on the book, and secondly that many people, knowing (or in some cases not knowing) what I had in mind, have said to me or in my hearing how underrated and neglected this book is. The latter was the spur to my writing, while from the former I have drawn deeply in putting this work together. Whether another commentary is really necessary time alone will tell, but if anyone benefits from the pointers this exposition gives to the One in whom are hidden all the treasures of wisdom and knowledge (Colossians 2:3), then the effort will have been well rewarded – to say nothing of the benefit it has been to the writer in the process, who has learnt much in pondering them.

The more I have studied this book the greater has become my appreciation of Derek Kidner's commentary [Kidner, D, Tyndale Old Testament Commentaries: *Proverbs*, Inter-Varsity Press, 2003], concise, insightful, always very much to the point. It has proved to be a real gem as a study aid.

KW
2021

Preface

Anyone who seeks to write a commentary on the Book of Proverbs of necessity has to address the problem of how to organise the material. Those who like to be systematic and to set things down in order would find, frustratingly, that this book is not really amenable to such treatment! The student of the book soon discovers that while there are certainly some basic themes running throughout the whole, its scope is exceedingly broad. It is aptly described as a manual of practical theology and has something to say about virtually every aspect of life.

The Book of Proverbs falls into the category of what is described as wisdom literature, along with the books of Job and Ecclesiastes. But whereas Job grapples with the question, 'Why?', in the context of adversity, and Ecclesiastes exposes and attempts to make some sense of the paradoxes of life, Proverbs is more concerned with the 'how' of living in the world as it is. Job and Ecclesiastes might be described as philosophical, but Proverbs is very much practical. All are theology, all acknowledge God as the fundamental reference point for every issue in life, but Proverbs is essentially practical in that it deals with matters relating to the conduct of ordinary everyday life.

Should the approach be verse by verse or thematic?

There are some parts that present no problem, such as chapters 1–9 and chapter 31.

For the most part of chapters 10 to 30 the question is whether the proverbs contained there are deliberately set out in random fashion or whether the context of some of them is significant. The answer appears to be that both aspects apply! It may be that the randomness of the way subjects crop up in the book deliberately reflects the similar way in which situations arise in life. Life issues tend to present themselves to us in random fashion. Situations requiring a response not infrequently come to us 'out of the blue'. We might be out in the car going to visit friends, with our minds largely on that, when we find our pleasant thoughts interrupted by an incident leading to an altercation with another motorist. We might be engrossed in work requiring our full concentration only to be called away by news that upsets everything. We might find some sudden situation sprung upon us that we don't know how to handle, and we find ourselves at least inwardly crying out for help.

If everything in life were tidy and systematic, and if we knew what was coming next, we would be better able to cope with it. But it is not like that. We cannot anticipate that when we come home from work we will be accosted by a troublesome neighbour, or we will discover an issue has arisen in school affecting one of our offspring. We cannot foresee the unexpected event that turns on its head all our careful planning. Along with the routine and orderly running of our lives there are also a host of disruptive happenings over which we have no control. Life is like that, and we need wisdom to conduct ourselves aright in both spheres. We need to expect the unexpected, to be prepared for the unforeseen event, and the Book of Proverbs helps equip us for just such eventualities by training us to think aright as we look out on life.

Life is not as tidy and orderly as most of us would like it to be, and we cannot apply an A-B-C approach to living it! So the book of Proverbs is not a manual of systematic wisdom to be worked through so that by the time we reach the end we have qualified. It does not work like that. The manner of its presentation is true to life. Application to wisdom requires extensive thought and effort. Any given area in which it is to be exercised needs to be revisited again and again. Perhaps for this reason any attempt to write an organised commentary on the book could be considered a self-defeating exercise!

As a few proverbs are repeated verbatim or almost so through the book, this is suggestive that context might be important in some way, though in what way is far from clear. Even though at first sight the majority of the proverbs appear to be quite randomly arranged, nevertheless there are groupings with similar themes or subject matter and there is evidence of system and order in the way they have been collated, and not infrequently it is found that one proverb has a bearing in some way on the previous one.

While a thematic approach might have its merits, in practice it is notoriously difficult to achieve, and to cover the whole book by such a method is virtually impossible. For while there are the big and obvious themes running throughout, such as wisdom and folly, righteousness and wickedness, the family, life and death, and so on, the range of subjects covered is so great and so embedded in the proverbs as to defy tidy classification.

If a thematic approach to these chapters were to be adopted it would be necessary to arrange the themes in some appropriate order and to trawl through the book to gather the information under headings. While there are some major themes which lend themselves to specific treatment (as Kidner has done in the 'Subject-Studies' in the first part of his commentary) the matters covered are so many and varied that they cannot all be captured in this way.

The reader engaging in serious study will want to be able to navigate a commentary, for whom it would be frustrating seeking comment on a particular verse and not being able quickly to find it because of its being embedded in a chapter on a theme.

Therefore for the reasons outlined above this exposition will proceed verse by verse as far as possible. As we do so, we will at the same time attempt to draw into consideration some other verses that have the closest bearing upon the matter in hand, or make reference to them. This should at least provide a limited framework of cross-referencing by subject. Although I have tried to be sparing with references to other parts of the Bible when considering each proverb, the Scripture reference index at the end is still quite extensive.

One problem this book, more than any other book of the Bible, poses for a commentator is the variety of words used in different translations. This exposition is based principally on the New King James Version (NKJV) because overall I believe it to be the best translation of the Book of Proverbs. Be that as it may, reference is frequently made to other renderings and it is hoped that those more familiar with other versions will have no difficulty following what is written here.

Also at the end is a word index covering chapters 10 to 31. This should be of service to those wishing to follow through a subject or theme.

Wisdom for life – this is what the book of Proverbs is all about. Wisdom is contrasted with folly throughout, and a great number of the proverbs flag up specific contrasting examples. Some themes are quite easily followed through. Here for example are just two, but the reader could easily add more.

Wisdom or foolishness in a son:

Ref.	Wise son	Foolish son
10:1	Makes father glad	Makes mother sad
10:5	Gathers in summer	Sleeps in harvest
13:1	Heeds father's instruction	Does not listen to rebuke
15:20	Makes father glad	Despises mother
17:25		Grief to father, bitterness to mother
19:26		Mistreats parents
19:27		Stops heeding instruction and strays
23:15	Causes father joy	
23:19	Guides his heart in the way	
23:26	Gives his father his heart	
24:13	Eats honey!	
24:21	Fears God and authority	
27:11	Upholds his father's honour	
28:7	Keeps the law	Shames his father by his conduct

The fear of the Lord:

1:7	The beginning of knowledge
1:29	Its absence contrasted with safety and security
2:5	Understood by earnest searching after truth, etc.
3:7	Linked with humility and the shunning of evil
8:13	Contrasted with pride, arrogance and evil conduct
9:10	The beginning of wisdom and compared with the knowledge of God
10:27	Prolongs days
14:26-27	A source of confidence, safety, and life
15:16	Of greater worth than riches
15:33	The instruction of wisdom
16:6	Accompanied by a departure from evil
19:23	Leads to life and satisfaction and protection from evil

Someone boasts about what they are going to achieve, and a friend quips back, 'Pride goes before a fall.' There are probably few people who are not familiar with that saying, even though most will be unaware that it originates from the Bible and the Book of Proverbs: 'Pride goes before destruction, and a haughty spirit before a fall' (16:18).

What is the use of proverbs? Of what benefit are they? The Book of Proverbs itself gives the answer in its opening statement, but this well-known one just quoted makes it clear that proverbs tend to stick in the mind (because they are intended to), with instant recall when an appropriate circumstance arises. I can be lying in bed in the morning, knowing I need to get up and get on with duties, and into my head pops that amusing but telling and unforgettable proverb: 'As a door turns on its hinges, so does the lazy man on his bed' (26:14). It rather robs me of my cosy feeling, goading me into the action I should have taken earlier. Proverbs can be like burrs which irritate and are not easily shaken off. Or, to quote the words of the preacher in Ecclesiastes 12:11 — 'The words of the wise are like goads, and the words of scholars are like well-driven nails, given by one Shepherd.'

So often we can be wise after the event. If only I had thought! If only I had seen this coming! If only I had recognised the symptoms. The Book of Proverbs helps us to be wise before the event, helping us to recall at the appropriate moments God's Word as it addresses various situations in life.

We may have good principles from God's Word yet fail through want of seeing their application at the proper time. Proverbs can act as a mental trigger. 'What a great business idea! That's the way for me – it will solve all my financial worries!' This triggers: 'There is a way that seems right to a man, but its end is the way of death' (16:25), placing caution upon undue haste, restraint from rushing headlong into something that might be bitterly regretted later on. Or take the example of gossip. Many a person who enjoys passing on a good story irrespective of its truth would do well to be acquainted with 18:8 – 'The words of a talebearer are like tasty trifles, and they go down into the inmost body' (repeated at 26:22). They would soon make such a one more wary in receiving and transmitting stories about others. Then there are people who are opinionated and quick to pass judgement. 'He who answers a matter before he hears it, it is folly and shame to him' (18:13). With that ringing in the ears, such a person might be shamed into being more careful to be thoroughly acquainted with a matter before venturing an opinion! And so we could go on with example after example.

Proverbs are a bit like pen sketches. They are caricatures. They illustrate types. They are word pictures, for the most part easily recognised, easily remembered, easily recalled, easily applied, relating to everyday life. Therein lies their value.

The Book of Proverbs is also a bit like a box of chocolates. There is variety. There is something there for everybody. It is when you bite into them that their individual flavour comes out.

The Book of Proverbs is, it would seem, rather neglected. Yet it provides an almost inexhaustible store for memorisation of Scripture. To memorise proverbs from this collection is generally much easier than memorising other passages from the Bible. When we consider the purpose of the book, we have every encouragement to delve deeply into it.

Here are some key words covering significant subjects in the Book of Proverbs (this is not intended as an exhaustive list): adultery, anger, authority, counsel, cruelty, death, desire, diligence, discipline, discernment, discretion, drunkenness, envy, faithfulness, favour, fear, flattery, food, folly, generosity, gentleness, goodness, gossip, greed, heart, hatred, honesty, humility, hypocrisy, immorality, integrity, interference, jesting, judgement, justice, knowledge, laziness, love, lying, mockery, oppression, partiality, perversity, poverty, pride, prudence, rebuke, riches, righteousness, scheming, scoffing, service, shame, stupidity, tongue, trust, truth, understanding, vindication, violence, virtue, wickedness, wife, wisdom, words, work, wrath.

The matter of adultery runs throughout the book. Temptation is enticement away from the commands of God, and to commit sin in the light of the knowledge of the truth is spiritual adultery.

The whole book is really a contrast between wisdom and folly – even a contest for attention from each. Short-term indulgence is set against long-term security.

Wisdom is the appropriate use of knowledge. Two people may be equally knowledgeable, yet one may be considered a fool while the other is esteemed wise. The reason is simply in the way knowledge is put to work and applied in life.

The major contributor to this book is Solomon, to whom God gave surpassing wisdom, the effects of which were seen in the administration of his leadership in Israel. After the introduction of the first nine chapters, there follow from 10:1 to 22:16 and from 25:1 to 29:27 (comprising two collections) the proverbs of Solomon, numbering about 500, presumably a representative sample of the three thousand we are informed in 1 Kings 4:32 that he spoke.

Most of the proverbs comprise two statements (though 29:5 has just one, 19:23 has three, 19:7 has four, and 25:6-7 and 27:23-27 are extended statements more akin to 'the sayings of the wise', the section which falls between the two collections of Solomon's proverbs, from 22:17 to 24:34, and which consists of pithy instructions and advice rather than proverbs as such, and covers a range of subjects). For these comparative statements in this exposition we will use the word 'clauses'. After these, in chapter 30 we have a specimen of the wisdom of Agur the son of Jakeh (about whom we know nothing else, nor can 'Ithiel' and 'Ucal' be identified, if they are people and the recipients of these sayings). King Lemuel in the concluding chapter has by some been identified with Solomon once again, though this seems unlikely. His identity is of no real importance. The name means 'belonging to God', or 'dedicated to God'.

Of the 'two-liners' which cover most of the proverbs, some are exact contrasts, some are relative contrasts, some are comparisons, some contain one idea expressed in two similar ways, the second clause reinforcing the first, some have the second clause as an outworking or consequence of the first (e.g. 22:6), some have the second clause as an observation upon the first. 21:25-26 is like two proverbs rolled into one and could arguably be considered as two. Both parts are concerned with the cravings of the sluggard. Some of the proverbs are paired in a chiastic structure (of which more later).

Here are some random examples:

Examples of a direct contrast (the 'but' kind) are: 'He who has a slack hand becomes poor, but the hand of the diligent makes rich' (10:4). 'The righteous will never be removed, but the wicked will not inhabit the earth' (10:30). 'Dishonest scales are an abomination to the Lord, but a just weight is his delight' (11:1). There are often variations in wording in such contrasts, as in 'The labour of the righteous leads to life, the wages of the wicked to sin' (10:16), or, 'The tongue of the righteous is choice silver; the heart of the wicked is worth little' (10:20). The majority of the proverbs follow this kind of pattern.

Examples of a relative contrast are: 'A gracious woman retains honour, but ruthless men retain riches' (11:16). The contrasts or comparisons here are more complex.

Examples of the use of simile (the 'as...so' kind) are: 'As a ring of gold in a swine's snout, so is a lovely woman who lacks discretion' (11:22), and, 'As a door turns on its hinges, so does the lazy man on his bed' (26:14).

Examples of cause and effect proverbs are: 'Train up a child in the way he should go, and when he is old he will not depart from it' (22:6); 'Cast out the scoffer, and contention will leave; yes, strife and reproach will cease' (22:10).

Examples of the second clause being an observation upon the first are: 'Whoever curses his father or his mother, his lamp will be put out in deep darkness' (20:20); 'Whoever shuts his ears to the cry of the poor will also cry himself and not be heard' (21:13). These are similar to the cause and effect kind, except that the result is not necessarily a direct consequence of the first action. 'The hearing ear and the seeing eye, the Lord has made them both' (20:12);

'There are many plans in a man's heart, nevertheless the Lord's counsel – that will stand' (19:21).

Examples of parallel statements in which the second reinforces the first are: 'The generous soul will be made rich, and he who waters will also be watered himself' (11:25); 'Mercy and truth preserve the king, and by lovingkindness he upholds his throne' (20:28).

Some proverbs make a thought-provoking comparison. The 'Better ... than...' proverbs fit into this category. For example, 'Better is a dinner of herbs where love is, than a fatted calf with hatred' (15:17).

Other proverbs do not fit neatly into any of these categories. For example: 'There is no wisdom or understanding or counsel against the Lord' (21:30).

In summary, the rich diversity of style in the proverbs adds to their interest and helps make them more memorable.

Structure is more than academic interest. The student of the book of Proverbs will be helped enormously toward a good understanding by giving close attention to the structure of each and the points of comparison in the clauses.

At one level many of the proverbs could be considered a matter of common sense and one does not have to be a believer in the Lord to recognise their relevance. In fact the section from 22:17 to 23:14 appears to draw extensively from the Egyptian *Wisdom of Amenemope*, while some other proverbs in Solomon's collection appear there also. In the ancient world there was a tradition of wisdom which is largely unknown in modern Western society. Many 'wise sayings' may have been in common circulation in much the same way as some of our maxims have been around so long that their origin is quite unknown. However, while wise sayings, or proverbs, may not be the exclusive province of God-fearing people, what we have in our Bible puts them in a context in which they can be properly understood and worked out. All people benefit from the goodness of God in countless ways. Created in his image and living in his world, it is to be expected that people will make contributions of all kinds to the benefit of society, even if they do not acknowledge the Lord. We would be churlish indeed if we dismissed out of hand words that came from a pagan simply because he was a pagan. As well as writing many of his own proverbs, Solomon collected them, and the criterion for their inclusion was their content, not their authorship. As believers, we may legitimately use anything and everything that comes out of the world without fear or censure, so long as we pass it through the sieve of God's Word.

To write on the proverbs borders on the inappropriate. If each proverb is there to be pondered, to be meditated upon, to be viewed from different angles, does any commentator have the right to do the reader's thinking for him? Is it not pretentious, even arrogant, to present one's thoughts and impose them on someone else? I hope that in what follows some small help may be given toward understanding and application, but what may be read in five minutes is not intended as a substitute for independent meditation but as provocation to spend time chewing it over. Then the reader, as the writer, will discover there are nuances of meaning and a range of applications encased in a few simple words. If these notes help the reader to think, well and good.

The proverbs are given for our instruction, learning and wisdom for life, and we must allow them to burn themselves into our thinking so that they find their outworking in practice.

Because the proverbs are intended to be personally applied, I have taken the liberty of challenging the reader from time to time rather than writing strictly objectively.

Part 1

Proverbs 1:1 to 9:31

The counsel of wisdom

Proverbs 1:1-7 – Introduction.

The first seven verses of the Book of Proverbs introduce us to what the book is about and what its aim is. It addresses us personally. If you have ever thought about subscribing to a course of learning you will have read up in its prospectus what the course requirements are, how much it will cost you and what its end benefits will be. You then decide whether you wish to proceed. Treat these verses in the same way. This course requires commitment and will be personally costly, but the end gains are to be considered carefully.

Just as the proverbs often address the reader very personally, so these notes often do the same. We need the personal challenge to stop and think, to think and respond.

1:1. Solomon's name at the head of this collection does not necessarily indicate all the proverbs originated from him; indeed it is clear from the content that though he himself may have contributed many, his role was more as a collector and editor, putting proverbs together from different sources to form a whole, and perhaps modifying some, to suit the purpose intended by God. Of all people Solomon was probably the best qualified, humanly speaking, to write it, God having given him wisdom surpassing that of anyone else until the coming of the Lord Jesus (1 Kings 3:12; 4:29; 10:6-7,23-24; Matthew 12:42).

The book was not compiled in its entirety by Solomon, for 25:1 indicates additions some two-and-a-half centuries later in the time of Hezekiah, and it may be then that under editors all the material was put together in its final form.

1:2-3. The purpose of the proverbs is stated here. From these verses four functions of the book may be identified. The first two (v. 2) are related, and concern the mind, what you know and how you think; the second two (v. 3) are also related and are concerned with the outworking of this knowledge in your life. The first two are concerned to 'get it into our head' and then to 'get our head around it'. The second two are concerned with taking it on board in life and practising it in its proper context.

The Book of Proverbs is intensely practical, and so it is important always to consider how you relate to what is written here. Therefore pause to consider how you stand in relation to these four functions. Take time to ask yourself – and perhaps write down – what impression the book is supposed to make on your mind, and what effect is it to have in your life, both personal and public. Such considerations are essential if the book is to be of any benefit.

1:2. To know wisdom involves recognising it for what it is. How do we have the capacity to observe, 'That was a wise decision', or 'That was well said', or 'That was well done'? How do we have the capability of speaking or acting with wisdom ourselves? This comes about only through being thoroughly acquainted with the matter of wisdom, and then to have the perception to appreciate what it is all about, that is, to be discerning.

1:3. For its application in life there are also two aspects: personal and public. First, there must be taking in. Wisdom is not innate, nor is it automatic. It must be received through instruction, and that instruction is more than mental: it involves training and discipline. The same word for 'instruction' ('discipline', NIV) appears in both verses 2 and 3. The word is concerned with disciplined and corrective training which often involves a measure of discomfort. If we have begun in wisdom we will recognise we stand in need of this training and will be prepared to submit to it. Our personal lives need to be re-formed in line with what God's Word teaches.

Learning for its own sake is arid and fruitless. It is all very well to acquire learning, but it will not benefit those who do not know what to do with it, nor will others receive any good from it. To hoard learning and yet to put it to no use is like the miser who lives like a pauper, benefiting neither himself nor others; it is like the buried talent. Paraded learning is equally fruitless, peacock's feathers merely drawing attention to the display – except that this is unjust to the peacock in whose display there is at least some beauty!

Wisdom ensures that learning, and the knowledge acquired, are put to work, harnessed for beneficial ends. Knowledge can be separated from wisdom, but not wisdom from knowledge. A wise man will be learned in the area in which he displays his wisdom, but a learned man may not be wise. Wisdom is about how you take on board the teaching. You are supposed, literally, to lay your hands on it, to grab it, and put it to use.

Justice, judgement (discerning between right and wrong) and equity (fairness) are the necessary outworking, the public face, of wisdom. It is these that are indicated as priorities in your relationships with others. Here are the most important life skills that are so often overlooked or neglected. These qualities which one expects to be found in the judge in the courtroom are the outworking of true wisdom, and should be characteristic of a man or woman in his or her dealings with other people in every context of life, whether in the home, or the workplace, or the social gathering, or wherever it may be. It is not surprising, therefore, to find the proverbs in this book are very extensive in their range, covering all manner of circumstances and all types of people.

1:4-5. For whom is the book written? Here we find two, or perhaps four, classes of people: two if those of v. 4 are considered of a piece and likewise those of v. 5; otherwise four.

If the proverbs are targeted at any one group of people more than any other, it would appear that young people venturing out into life are especially singled out, as v. 4 suggests and as much of the subsequent text confirms. The word for 'simple' is not a flattering term and it does not mean innocent! Underlying it is an inadequacy at every level, an ignorance that requires attention. The two clauses of v. 4 are in parallel, the second supplementing and expanding upon the first, and the implication is that by nature the young are in this category, lacking the vital life skills described by the words prudence, knowledge and discretion.

Nevertheless, the book is of equal value to those who have already attained to a measure of wisdom (v. 5). One is never too old to learn, or to benefit from instruction! On one occasion when my wife bought me a toy, even at my age I felt fully justified in accepting such a present, not just because it came from her and I trust her judgement, but also because on the box it said: 'Suitable for ages 8 to 108,' a category into which I fit very neatly! When it comes to learning from the book of Proverbs, we all fit very neatly into the categories it covers. It contains nothing that could be described as merely 'child's play'.

1:6. When we say that someone is speaking in riddles, we are indicating that we are being confused and made none the wiser by their talk. The riddles of the wise are mentioned in v. 6 almost as if what they have to say is inaccessible to ordinary mortals! Perhaps that is true to the uninitiated! Words of wisdom are very often not appreciated by their hearers, and the advice of a far-sighted person is frequently scorned. An enigma (parable, NIV) or a riddle is a saying concerning which either the meaning or the outworking may be obscure. An example of the latter may be found in 26:4-5. How do you respond to a fool when you are put on the spot? Should you give him a dose of his own medicine? Should you ignore him? Should you put him right? What should you do? For an example of the former (where the meaning may be obscure) see 30:15a.

This verse is not about being clever and 'seeing through' such statements. Rather, it is about coping with the many enigmatic, paradoxical, confusing or perplexing problems that we stumble across in life. It is an unhappy fact that many people live with bitter regrets because they did not have the wisdom to handle such things well. It may be that you can think of some examples in your life or experience.

The wonderful thing about the Book of Proverbs is that by meditating upon and absorbing its very practical observations on life both young and old can be equipped not only to cope themselves with life but also to contribute productively to the benefit of others.

1:7. Where does it all begin? There are many people who, conscious of their lack of wisdom, would be really enthusiastic about the idea of acquiring some. There are many people who would wish to better their lives much along the lines Solomon mentions in this introduction. Not all, though, like where it starts. 'The fear of the LORD is the beginning of knowledge.' When as a young man I was challenged by a friend after hearing the gospel several times, my smart answer, 'I am learning', was rebutted with: 'You will never learn anything until you submit to the Lord.' That was well said. 'The fear of the LORD is the beginning of knowledge.' That is where it begins, and that is how it continues.

The fear of the Lord is rather like the attitude an employee might have toward an exacting and watchful employer: not a hard, demanding taskmaster, but one who nevertheless expects all to be done carefully and properly. The conduct of a person who fears the Lord will be with a consciousness of being under his watchful eye, wanting to please him in everything. This fear is not terror, or anything like it, but is a sober respect for the perfection of his being and a desire to please him for who he is rather than for what may be got out of him! It involves awareness of the high privilege of being in the service of the King of kings and Lord of lords. The fear of the Lord is an absolute prerequisite for the wisdom of which Solomon writes, wisdom that can be obtained in no other way. For, even though the subject matter covers day to day living, this is not worldly wisdom, but spiritual wisdom. Proverbs may justly be described as a manual of practical theology.

If there are significant problem areas in your personal life, or in your relationships with others, it is possible that the real problem lies in your relationship with the Lord. Treat v. 7 with the respect it deserves, as God's word to you, to humble and help you.

At the conclusion of this introductory section is the first mention of the fool. The fool features prominently in this book because the fool features prominently in life. Our view of a fool may be someone who is silly, or a buffoon, or someone who has acted senselessly without proper thought or understanding. Any of these things may be true of the fool in this book, but underlying it all is a lack of regard for the Lord, so that in the fool in the book of Proverbs we observe spiritual and moral perversity. The fool is the subject of Psalm 14, a careful reading of which indicates that the majority of humanity falls under this description. The one who says in his heart, 'There is no God,' is not only the rank atheist but also the one who conducts himself *as if* there were no God. 'God is in none of his thoughts' (Psalm 10:4). Many a clever and erudite person may be a fool as described by this book.

When it says that fools despise wisdom and instruction, the implication is that they do not think it is worth giving the time of day to these things. They have better things to do to occupy their time; they are all right as they are and this kind of instruction is a burden to them.

James said that if anyone lacks wisdom he should ask of God, in faith, knowing that God gives generously and graciously to those who ask him (James 1:5). Many people take this to refer to wisdom in handling particular problems that arise in life, expecting an instant answer. That is far from being generally true. This is not slot-machine Christianity. There is something of the spirit of the Book of Proverbs in the manner in which James presents his material to his readers. It is true that we often become aware of our lack of wisdom when our way is blocked by some obstacle that we realise we do not know how to remove, or a situation arises that we do not know how best to handle. The answer to the problem rarely comes in the form of sudden inspiration about how to deal with it or what to do in that particular instance; more often it comes about by learning some important lessons in our relationship with God and, in consequence, with our fellow beings.

However, like so many of the proverbs which follow, 1:7 cuts both ways. Having presented the desirability of wisdom, and asserted that it begins with the fear of God, Solomon then adds that it is folly to turn away from it: '…but fools despise wisdom and instruction.' There is no middle way. You are a fool not to pursue wisdom; you are a fool not to fear God. The remainder of the Book of Proverbs exposes in a thousand ways the folly of those who lack wisdom, and in so doing tellingly reflects upon the godless society in which we live.

Because the matter of instruction, or discipline, is repeated in these verses (vv. 3,7), we must not soft-pedal the point but do justice to it and acknowledge it 'loud and clear'. Because the word in the original is also used of chastening and correction and involves the element of training, it reminds us that there are no gains without pains, and it is surely true that the greatest gains are worth the greatest pains. Wisdom comes neither easily nor comfortably, for by nature we are neither ready for it nor fit vessels for it. Paul mentions wisdom in 2 Timothy 3:15, and it is not without significance that the following verses refer to reproof, correction and training as essential functions of the Word of God in our lives. Hebrews 12:11 reminds us how unpleasant such things can be at the time. However, as the same verse goes on to explain, the rewards are great and more than worth the pains.

Wisdom comes through fearing God, one of the principal manifestations of which is heeding his Word. The vital importance of this cannot be stressed enough. What is the first thing that gets squeezed out of a busy Christian's life? It is the very thing the Christian needs in order to be able to function properly, as God intended, *in* his or her busy life!

1:8-9. The attraction of youth. Psalm 119:9-16.

Solomon now launches into his teaching. Notice to whom it is directed. He repeatedly addresses 'My son', or 'my sons' (or 'children') (1:8,10,15; 2:1; 3:1,11,21; 4:1,10,20; 5:1,7; 6:1,3,20; 7:1,24; 8:32) ... and who better to give such instruction than one whom God endowed with such wisdom? Given the nature of the book, though, inspired as it is by the Holy Spirit, you may rightly consider it addressed to you from an infinitely wise heavenly Father if you are his child. The time to begin to acquire wisdom is in the days of one's youth (v. 4). How many miss out on this, looking back on their misspent youth with regret! How blessed young Timothy was to have known the Scriptures from childhood, no doubt having been taught by his mother and grandmother (2 Timothy 1:5; 3:15)!

Never skip over the structure of the proverbs. This is the word of God, and every word is important. Each of these two verses has two clauses set in parallel. In v. 8, 'hear' is set alongside 'do not forsake'. Not only do we need to hear what is being said, but we need to keep a firm hold upon it and not let it go. Then, 'instruction' is set alongside 'law'. God's Word is intended to mould our lives; we are to be trained up in its teaching. Thirdly, 'father' is set alongside 'mother'. This training is placed by God in the hands of both parents, whose instruction and training come from different angles according to how God has made them and their position in life. One of the tragedies of fractured families is that it has a seriously detrimental effect upon the upbringing of children and their preparation for life.

Verse 9 draws attention to the benefits of instruction, emphasising it with parallelism. 'Head' and 'neck' are put together. Throughout history there has been a preoccupation with headdress, necklaces, chains of office and the like. These things draw attention to themselves and are intended to make a statement about their wearers. The 'graceful ornament', or 'ornament of grace' indicates the beauty and attractiveness of wisdom, and the 'chain' around the neck is like a badge of identity. For example, Daniel was promised, if he could interpret the writing on the wall, that he would be clothed with purple and have a chain of gold around his neck and be the third ruler in the kingdom (Daniel 5:16). Wisdom is a chain of honour.

The responsibility for imparting wisdom to the young is with their elders. Fathers and mothers should be instructing their children in practical wisdom for life, beginning with the fear of God (v. 7). Lack of maturity in the up and coming generation is not attributable to the perversity of youth alone, but also to the negligence of parents and other responsible people to provide wise instruction combined with a godly example – see 20:7 and 22:6,15 for example. This book, therefore, is not just for the young; it is as much for older people. It is for the instructed, and for the instructor. Those who teach must also be taught, and if you have responsibility over young people, to nurture and direct them in life, then you need to be adequately equipped. You can only give out what you have taken in.

From the outset the Holy Spirit through Solomon addresses the issues commonly faced by youth. Young people very often question parental authority, even if they do not necessarily rebel outright against it. In one sense this questioning is healthy, because they have to establish for themselves what are going to be true and right standards. There can be a lot of baggage with the rules and regulations laid down by parents and others in authority, and it is good for those growing up to distinguish between what is essential and what is simply accumulated junk. Here in the Book of Proverbs are presented pure, unadulterated essentials. Here is the kernel of the matter. Instructions and habits received from a wise father and mother, followed not slavishly or blindly but with understanding, will adorn the life of a young person, making him or her stand out from the crowd for worth and value (v. 9).

This is addressed to 'my son', but applies equally well to the daughter. Young men who want to succeed in life and still be there when the competition has evaporated will need the wise counsel of godly parents. Girls growing up, who so often think about looking their best, often fail to realise that what is most attractive to a man of worth is the adornment of grace built upon a substantial character. A relationship established upon anything else is likely to last only while those other ephemeral things last.

The problem for many young people is that the majority of their peers neither see nor think that way. Everything is for the here and now, and for what may be gained for oneself by whatever means without looking ahead to the consequences. The Book of Proverbs is for those who recognise the need to make sound, long-term investment, for those who want to stay the course in life. The wisdom it promotes will pay the dividends of honour, grace and glory (4:8-9).

A youth of sixteen was heard to observe how lacking in knowledge and understanding his father was. That same young man, at the age of twenty-one, commented favourably on how much his father had learned in five years! Parents may often suffer a negative reaction from their growing children who think they 'know better', who complain that their parents 'do not understand', or are 'old fashioned', or 'out of date', or 'stuffy', or whatever other descriptive term is in vogue at the time. Unfortunately, such descriptions sometimes have some justification. Parents need to understand what the problems are that face their children, and, though they may come in different guises, generally speaking they are much the same in every generation. The Book of Proverbs is no less relevant to today's society, even though it was written a long time ago and in a very different cultural setting. The opening chapters of the book cover the essentials very thoroughly.

God has ordained that the primary place for instruction is the home, within the family, and that the responsibility lies with parents in the instruction of their own children. This is not to be delegated to others such as church or school, though they may fulfil a helpful supplementary role.

By addressing his words to his 'son' we are not to suppose Solomon is excluding others of his offspring, but rather we are to understand that he is engaging his son 'man to man', on an individual, personal, basis. This is something that is so important. Parents sometimes have relationship problems with their children, especially when their children reach adolescence. We speak of the 'generation gap', and it is almost as if the things that concern the younger generation are so different from those that concern their parents that they have little common ground. For parents who have been accustomed to sharing their lives with their children with frankness and honesty, it will not be so difficult to continue doing so through the sometimes turbulent years of transition from childhood to adulthood. It is at such a time that such a relationship is so important.

Even though an element of warning or reproof is suggested by the word used for 'instruction', which is appropriate to what he is about to say, Solomon does not talk down to his son, speaking of things from the infinite distance of superior authority. He gets alongside him, and shows him things that affect him now and are going to continue to do so, things that his son will recognise and want to know about. What he has to say is timely, relevant and appropriate. He appeals to his son to heed not just his own teaching, but that of the boy's mother, too. What a privilege it is for young people who have God-fearing parents, where love and unity are to be found in the home! What an example is there, which makes it so much easier for instruction to be given and received!

It has to be recognised that this is not always the case, and there are many families where such a background to wise counsel does not exist, and you may lament that you are not in this happy position to instruct your son or daughter. One thing about advice, or instruction, coming from parents, though, is that it does not matter what may have been their own background, whether they had lived godly or ungodly lives, moral or immoral. A son or daughter who wants to find fault can do so from either angle: 'You have always lived such separated lives from the world that you are just afraid if I go out in it a bit and have the fun you never enjoyed.' Or, 'You did all these things when you were young, so why shouldn't I go out and enjoy myself by doing the same?'

What matters for you, if you are a parent instructing your children, is not where you were then, but where you are now. If you are living in the fear of the Lord now, you will be able to answer the objections of your children, or at least bear with them patiently. Better that, than their reproach for inconsistencies which charge you with hypocrisy! So, you want the best for your children? Then not only set them a good example, but instruct them in essential life skills founded on the fear of the Lord. You were once where they are now, and you want better for them than you experienced yourself. You want them to be well set up in life with qualities that will be of value to them and valued by others who recognise their worth. Then the best thing you can pass on to them is godly instruction in practical wisdom, which will adorn them all their lives (v. 9).

So from this point onward until the end of chapter 9 are a series of fatherly talks with a son, each covering vital aspects of life and conduct, each containing material that is of immediate relevance, value and importance to the young. Again, we see the wisdom of breaking it down in this way. The teaching is in short, powerful bursts, giving time to ponder and digest each bit before moving on to something else. Little by little, and systematically, a complete body of teaching is built up to provide the young person with all that is required for steering a safe course through the life ahead.

The exhortation of v. 8, then, is not simply for the benefit of domestic peace, as some cynics might suppose! Appended to it in v. 9 is a very wonderful promise which will stand young people in good stead for both the present and the future for everything worthwhile in life.

1:10. Peer pressure. It is not sufficient for parents to object to their children keeping certain company, doing certain things or going to certain places. If you are a parent you may not wish your son or daughter to spend evenings out with those you consider to be of dubious character. Unfortunately, sometimes parents flag up the wrong negative qualities and so rub their children up the wrong way and positively invite rebellion! Solomon has not pointed to superficial things, but has got to the heart of the matter, taking his son with him on a 'virtual tour' so that he can see what it is all about and use his own judgement from an informed perspective. This is what the book is all about: not handing down rules and regulations for life, but exposing the realities of life issues in order for sound principles to be established and right decisions to be made.

Solomon is well aware of what his son is up against: enticement. What is being offered has a strong appeal to the flesh. In all sorts of ways there is the tug to go along with it. It is going to be enjoyable, it is going to be fun, it is going to be lucrative ... it is going to give me just what I want!

It is important to recognise from whom this enticement comes. It comes from 'sinners', that is, from those who have no fear of God before their eyes, from those who have a completely different set of values from the believer. Everything in the Book of Proverbs boils down to this: Where are they coming from? Do they fear God, or do they disregard his law? Ultimately this enticement comes from the devil himself, who right from the beginning has deceitfully yet successfully made sin appealing.

1:11-16. Self-destruction. These verses paint a lurid picture which might find its place in gangland, but surely not in the average Christian home!

Bear in mind that Proverbs gives us thumbnail sketches, it paints vivid word pictures, it provides caricatures that stick in the mind, so that when the corresponding real-life situation is encountered its grotesque features are immediately identified behind the mask of innocence.

The picture is of young people, restless, full of energy, eager for action, banding together in some scheme by which they may better themselves, and recruiting others for that purpose (v. 11). Many a young person does not like to be left out of the action, or to be sidelined by his or her peers. It can hurt a lot. 'Come along with us' (v. 11) has a great deal of appeal, particularly if you are considered to be valued for something you can contribute. Young people often want to go where others go, see what they see, do what they do. So, especially for the young person brought up in a Christian home, maybe not yet converted, or even perhaps as a young Christian, there can be a tremendous pull from others at school or elsewhere to go along with them, and be 'one of the crowd'. 'Come along with us and you'll have a great time!' 'Never mind what your mum or dad think – what do they know about it?'

Here we see the pack instinct. This of course is very evident in our cities today, with young people roaming the streets in groups of ten or twenty, sometimes clashing with rival groups, often loud-mouthed, frequently intimidating others, saying and doing things in the security of numbers that few of them would dare to do alone. It is a safe way of self-assertiveness. Nearly always you will find that among such groups there are those who have been 'drawn in' through fear of being left out and who would never conduct themselves in the way they do if they had not been in the group, and it goes to prove the point that it is always the worst that comes out of such gatherings. How important is the teaching of this book!

See how these 'sinners' use their time and energy. Firstly, they lie in wait to shed the blood of the innocent (v. 11), and are even eager to do it (v. 16). Murder may be an extreme case, but it is often the case that there is a bravado among unprincipled and organised groups of young people that displays itself in disregard for authority and callous disdain for those it regards as weak and vulnerable. Robbery (v. 13) appears to be at the heart of their intentions, and violence its inevitable accompaniment. In a nutshell, what we are seeing here is gain at the expense of someone else.

Although the picture is painted at its worst in these verses, it is important to recognise that exploitation of others for the sake of personal gain can, and often has, degenerated into this degraded portrayal. What is at the heart of it? In a word, it is greed (v. 19). Solomon is identifying a temptation very common among the young. It may be a young person from a rich home, envious of the wealth and comfort of his or her parents, looking for a quick way to similar comfort and security. Or perhaps such a person with no shortage of money is simply out to use it to 'have a good time'. At the other end of the scale, it may be a youngster from a deprived home, despising the poverty all around him, anxious at all costs to break out of the rut. Whatever it may be, it is true that young people are often ambitious to gain possessions and set themselves up in life, and offers to do it quickly can have enormous appeal. Verse 14, 'Let us all have one purse', could be interpreted in a wider sense, 'Let us pool our resources.' The question is, with whom are you to pool your resources? What are you bringing to the group, and how is it going to be used? Not just your money, but your abilities?

So here we see two important questions any young person should ask before being drawn into anything with others. Firstly, who are the people who are encouraging you to join them; and secondly, what is their motivating principle? If they are questionable morally, then steer clear of them. If they are simply out to get gain without being too fussy about how they do it, keep away from them (v. 15).

1:17-19. Flying blind. Why are speed camera warning signs placed so prominently on roads? Clearly the intention is to deter people from speeding. Only the motorist driving furiously with eyes tight shut would get caught by such cameras (or so one would think!). If the cameras were hidden away out of sight without any warning signs, undoubtedly many more people would receive tickets – at least for a time until they got wise to it.

This verse highlights the ridiculousness of trying to ensnare a bird with a net deliberately placed in its line of vision. Only a bird 'flying blind' could possibly be caught in it. And here is the very point that Solomon is making. These young people motivated by greed, to get what they want at any cost, as long as it doesn't cost *them*, are in fact flying blind. Worse than that, they are actually making the net in which they themselves will ultimately be caught (vv. 18-19).

To the two important questions to be asked (who are the people, and what is their motivating principle?), a third must therefore be added: where will it all lead? Parents need to talk with their children about issues such as these. At the heart of it all are three key words: principle, motive, consequence.

Principle: godliness or godlessness? *Motive:* others or self? *Consequence:* fulfilment or disaster?

Verses 8-9 and then verses 10-19 have presented two courses of action and their consequences. The former is an encouragement to avoid the latter. The graceful ornament on the head, and chains about the neck of v. 9 are descriptive of status and dignity. Many seek status: they want to be someone, they want their presence to be felt. But they do not think about dignity. Like Absalom, who was splendidly good-looking and had a wonderful head of hair (2 Samuel 14:25-26), who set up a monument to himself (2 Samuel 18:18), these status symbols meant nothing when he suffered the indignity of being caught by his proud head in the branches of a tree and the consequences his self-centred conceit deserved.

Solomon was a man whose material wealth was fabulous. Yet throughout this book he lays the emphasis where it ought to be laid. Remember that God granted him the wisdom that he asked, though even then what was given was way above his asking; and in addition God granted him riches materially. The former was indispensable, the latter not. The adornments of v. 9 are the marks of the true wealth that pervades the book.

1:20-33. Psalm 73. Another voice: the voice of wisdom. Here, and again in ch.8 which opens in much the same way, wisdom is personified. Apart from the poetic or graphic effect, there is an appropriateness to this insofar as to possess wisdom is like having a lifelong relationship, a valued companionship. It does not have its origin from within the individual, it is not innate, but the wisdom stored up in the heart comes from the Lord (2:6).

This passage seems to take up the conclusion of the last, looking to the consequences of turning away from this voice. I remember as a 'poor' student somewhat resenting the approaches of an insurance broker trying to sell me life insurance. To my thinking he was attempting to take something away from me under the pretext that it would be of use to me if I lived to the grand old age of 65! My half-hearted attitude to that policy is the reason for its disappointing yield. The wisdom that comes from God is often regarded in a similar light, whereas in fact it yields the highest dividends, and not in the dim and distant future, either!

The enticing voice of sinners can without doubt have a heady appeal. Now we hear *another voice*. It is not enticing, it is not secretive. On the contrary, it is clear and public (vv. 20-21). This passage is in some ways reminiscent of open air preaching. The scene is one of hustle and bustle, of everyday noise, of the movement of traffic, of the activity of buying and selling, of animated conversation, and of everything else one may expect to find in a busy concourse. And there, on the corner, is *another voice*. It may be heard by those willing to draw near and listen, yet it is often ignored as having nothing to do with what is going on all around, as being incongruous to the environment (though it is anything but). The voice of wisdom, too, may be heard clearly and unmistakably by those willing to draw near and listen, in the often-times chaotic activity of life. Psalm 19:1-6 makes clear that the heavens declare the glory of God – the God who by wisdom made the heavens and the earth (Proverbs 3:19). Paul reminds us in Romans 1:19-20 that God has revealed himself in what he has made, to which we have an inner witness – *another voice*.

What is this other voice saying? Whom is she addressing? There is certainly no flattery here in v. 22! In general there is an amazing naïvete in the young which is often later burned out in the hard realities of life. Young people so often think they can indulge all sorts of fancies without suffering any ill effects. Maybe out to prove themselves, they get up to all kinds of things which, on sober reflection, were not such a good idea after all. In their growing bodies and minds they discover all kinds of emotions and passions needing an outlet, and pent up energy requiring activity. The problem is, these developing qualities by nature lack a guiding principle for their proper harnessing, and so are sometimes dissipated in ways that are not good. Wisdom is heard addressing this naïvete. The 'how long?' of v. 22 indicates that the hearers are already indulging in their supposed pleasures, and the call comes as a rebuke as well as an appeal. The sword of the Spirit is double-edged, and wisdom cuts both ways.

Many voices are saying, 'Come with us' (v. 11); this other voice says, 'Turn to me' (v. 23). It is a lone voice among many, and yet it is *the* voice that needs to be heard.

In these verses we see: *offer*, in the stretching out of the hand (v. 24); *advice*, or *counsel* (v. 25); and *rebuke* (v. 25). All these elements are essential in the 'instruction' of the young. Solomon takes up the consequences of failing to respond to any or all of these. Adverse reaction takes various forms: *scoffing*, or *scorning* (v. 22), which uses a variety of adjectives to justify disregarding the message as irrelevant; *ignorance* – for fools who hate knowledge are showing that they love ignorance; *rejection*, or *refusal* (v. 24), by which a deliberate turning away without consideration is intended – 'I've got other things to do'; *disdain*, or *ignoring* (v. 25) – 'I haven't got time for that stuff!'; *taking offence* at rebuke (v. 25). It all amounts to *turning away* from wisdom (v. 32; 'waywardness', NIV). The *complacency* (v. 32) of fools says, 'It won't happen to me.'

The consequences of ignoring the call of wisdom are described under the words: *calamity, terror, disaster, destruction, distress, anguish* (26,27,32). For many people, sadly, these words apply very fittingly. For others, they seem not to apply at all as far as their apparent success in the world is concerned. Nevertheless, things are rarely as they appear outwardly, and many such people live with dark secrets and bitter regrets. However, judged from the standpoint of wisdom, their full lives are really empty, and they live under an impending judgement too terrible to contemplate. The psalmist, during that period when he failed to see this, described himself as 'foolish and ignorant' (Psalm 73:22). Destruction and desolation await those who deliberately turn away from wisdom (Psalm 73:18-19).

Verse 26 must not be interpreted in the sense of vengeful glee. It is a vivid word picture poignantly describing the dreadful awareness of those who suffer the consequences of the folly they had been warned about and who had scorned the warning. The wisdom they had spurned now rises like a spectre to haunt them, at once intangible and inaccessible, to plague their minds. There comes a time when it is too late, when the opportunity is gone for ever, when the damage has been done, when the situation is irretrievable – rather like a driver who, having suffered terrible facial injuries in an accident through failing to wear a seat-belt, will suffer even more through the vain regret of 'If only...' from a law which mocks him every moment afterwards. But nothing can turn the clock back. We must not lose sight of the fact that Solomon addresses these words to the young. It is the young who stand in need of wisdom, not because older people have no need, but simply because the time to acquire it, or at least to begin to acquire it, is in the days of one's youth. It is only a half-truth that 'you can't put an old head on young shoulders.' The best way to acquire an 'old head' in this sense is to start young!

Verses 28-32 are very solemn. There is a point at which it is too late to retrieve a situation. Wisdom is personified here, but as it is God who is the giver of wisdom, those who do not choose the fear of the Lord (v. 29) when the Lord gave them the opportunity may find he has withdrawn the opportunity. Samuel warned the people who had foolishly demanded for themselves a king like the other nations round about them: 'And you will cry out in that day because of your king whom you have chosen for yourselves, and the LORD will not hear you in that day' (1 Samuel 8:18). We read of Esau that, having 'for one morsel of food sold his birthright ... afterward, when he wanted to inherit the blessing, he was rejected, for he found no place for repentance, though he sought it diligently with tears' (Hebrews 12:16-17). Paul writes of those who, 'Professing to be wise ... became fools' and 'even as they did not like to retain God in their knowledge, God gave them over to a debased mind' (Romans 1:22,28). In distress for fear of the enemy, 'when Saul inquired of the LORD, the LORD did not answer him' (1 Samuel 28:6). The reason was that Saul had consistently forsaken the Lord and gone his own way, and God had in the end forsaken him. Isaiah said, 'Seek the LORD while he may be found, call upon him while he is near' (Isaiah 55:6), the implication being that a window of opportunity was being given which would not remain open for ever. Proverbs 1:29-30, characteristic of those referred to above, led to the Lord giving them over to the consequence of their desires (vv. 31-32). For the ungodly to be allowed to have their own way is absolutely disastrous in the end. When wisdom calls, it is imperative to respond. When *God* calls, it is imperative to respond! He doesn't suffer fools gladly! There are grave consequences to spurning the gracious invitation from the King of the universe!

At the end of this stern and uncompromising warning there is one of the wonderful 'but's' of the Bible. In contrast to the dismal prospect from ignoring wisdom, there are *safety, security* and *confidence* for those who heed it (v. 33). Those who have rejected the fear of the Lord know nothing of these things. Fear, insecurity, anxiety, uncertainty about the future, often dog their footsteps. By contrast, those who have built upon a secure foundation, and especially those who have done so from an early age, have great peace, for the wisdom they have been granted through the fear of the Lord stands them in good stead to ride the storms of life and to guide them safely to their eternal haven.

2:1-4. Colossians 2:1-10. Prerequisites to the knowledge of God. So far Solomon has stated the nature of wisdom, where it comes from, and its importance. He has also drawn attention to two dangers: firstly to be enticed away from a wise course in life by the attraction of intoxicating pleasures appealing to natural greed; and secondly by complacent inertia which finds all manner of excuses to shut out the call of wisdom. In each case he has spelt out the consequences, leaving no room for any to imagine that somehow they might not be all that bad.

Those seriously listening to what he has to say should by this time be sufficiently sobered by the perils associated with a careless attitude to wisdom. Sometimes we think that wisdom is for the few. Though indeed few possess it, this is nevertheless a false conclusion to reach. The wisdom described in the Book of Proverbs is accessible to all, but on terms which do not appeal to all. We have learnt that knowledge and wisdom start with the fear of the Lord (1:7), and yet there are many who fear God whom one could not describe as being wise. They have made a good beginning, but why have they not progressed much further? We now learn that wisdom is not given on a plate to those who desire it. Some imagine that when Solomon asked for wisdom from God (1 Kings 3:5-14) he was granted it overnight. It did not happen like that, and here he is showing his son how he should be channelling his strength and energy. We learn immediately that there is a discipline involved.

Observe the 'If ... then ... for' in vv. 1-6, and start by considering the repeated 'If...' (vv. 1,3,4). There are conditions to be fulfilled. First of all there must be acceptance of the instruction given, recognising its true worth (v. 1). Then careful attention must be given to it (v. 1b) with ear (v. 2a) and heart (v. 2b). This exposes a sense of need (v. 3) which must result in unsparing effort (v. 4). When we consider the way these conditions are put, it is not so surprising that many acquire but little wisdom, regarding it as not worth the effort. Who enjoys painstaking study (vv. 1-2)? Who is willing to make a fuss in order to acquire something (v. 3)? Who is going to expend a great deal of time and energy to find what is sought (v. 4)? God never rewards casual attitudes or half-hearted approaches to him. But if we are in earnest, he says, he will reward our seeking (v. 5; compare Luke 11:5-13).

Whereas vv. 1-2 have a private aspect to them, observe that vv. 3-4 are more public. Verse 3 is a cry for help. It does not say to whom the call is made, and maybe deliberately so. Wisdom comes from God, and therefore the call must be made to him. But God uses means to give his answers, and so the call must go out to any who might be able to meet the need. Wisdom is acquired from many sources. The pursuit of wisdom does not artificially narrow its field.

2:5-6. Finding the knowledge of God. Verse 5 makes it clear that the pursuit of wisdom and the fear of the Lord cannot be separated, nor can wisdom itself and the knowledge of God be separated. The fear of the Lord is the beginning of knowledge (1:7), and the beginning of wisdom (9:10), but a beginning implies a continuance, and those who have made this beginning have set themselves on a lifelong pursuit of progress toward a fuller knowledge of God. It is wise for believers not only to review their progress but also to ask if that progress is being maintained.

Wisdom comes from God (v. 6); not only so, but it comes from 'his mouth'. We acquire wisdom by calling upon him and giving heed to his word. This is the combined operation of the Holy Spirit and the Word of God. Not the

Spirit independently of the Word, nor the Word independently of the Spirit, but, as Cowper wrote in his hymn, 'The Spirit breathes upon the Word, and brings the truth to sight.' What God has given us he expects us to use, for that is the reason he has given these things to us. What we need that he has not yet given us he expects us to apply for. We have his Word in our hands: that is what he has already given us, and he expects us to use it. But we need to understand it if it is to occupy its rightful place in our hearts, and that is where we have to apply to him, for it is the Spirit of truth who will guide us into all truth (John 16:13). Our unaided minds are darkened and will never properly appreciate God's Word except by the illumination given by the Holy Spirit. So study is not enough, important though it is; and prayer is not enough, essential though that is, too. There must be a combining of the two, submitting our minds to the influence of the Spirit of God to give us understanding, learning with discipline and with all humility. Study without prayer leads to pride and error; prayer without study is the vain prattle of one who is not prepared to listen to God who speaks through the Scriptures, which are his words.

We are shown further here that wisdom is inseparable from an 'upright' or 'blameless' life (v. 7), lived by those who have wisdom in their hearts (v. 10) as opposed to those whose minds may be well acquainted with the truth but whose hearts are untouched by it.

What are the 'ifs' of vv. 1-4 leading up to? Is it that: 'If you incline your ear to wisdom, you will find it'? 'If you cry out for discernment you will receive it'? 'If you lift up your voice for understanding you will be given it'? Verse 5 tells us: it is not *it* we are to seek, but rather *him* – finding the knowledge of *God*. Paul informs us that all the treasures of wisdom and knowledge are to be found in *Christ* (Colossians 2:3). This passage counters the lie Satan introduced in the garden of Eden (Genesis 3:4-6). Knowledge, understanding and wisdom are not found outside of God, or independently of him. Nor are they found simply by eating of the fruit of a tree or by any other 'magic formula'. Eve demonstrated for all posterity that the path to wisdom does not start there. If wisdom is to enter the heart (v. 10), it must be by application to God. There is no other way, for it is he who gives it (v. 6).

Though there are many 'alternative' forms of wisdom that are admired in this world, and though there are many learned men and women renowned for their knowledge and making their mark in the world, it has to be understood that these do not represent true wisdom, for they refer to this life only and hold no promise for the life to come.

Then is it worth the effort? How many people wish they had some assurance concerning the outcome of life! What is the meaning of life? Who am I? Why am I here? How can I know how to make the right choices in life? Is there a God? What is he like? Can we know the truth, if there even is such a thing as truth? What happens when I die?

It seems to many people that there are no real answers to the big questions in life because different people who purport to know tend to offer contradictory answers. It is amazing how many people consult horoscopes or employ equally fanciful 'techniques' in order to find their answers to some of these questions without considering the utter folly of doing so. Others think that by diligent application to religious observances and rituals they might find their way to an answer to these questions, or find their way to God.

Then is Solomon advocating a rigorous course requiring unsparing effort in order to discover the meaning of life? Not at all. In fact he tells us clearly that if we want to find the answer to the really big question, that is, if we really want to find the knowledge of God (v. 5), we must understand that this is something God alone gives. No one else gives it. All others who purport to give it are imposters. If we would know God, there is but one way: that he reveal himself to us. If the vast majority of humankind live and die without the knowledge of God, it is not because he is unwilling to make himself known to them, but that they are unwilling to seek him on his terms.

The promise, then, in these verses, is to understand the fear of the Lord and to find the knowledge of God. It is out of this that everything else flows. This is at the heart of this section. It is the 'then' part of the 'If ... then ... for.' The writer is following a simple argument. The *presupposition* is that we don't have the knowledge of God, we haven't found him. The *proposition* ('then') is that he may be found. The *prescription* ('for') is that he is the one who gives wisdom, knowledge and understanding, which originate in himself. The *condition* ('if') is that we be serious in our desire to seek such a high prize. Is anything to be compared with the knowledge of God? What price is to be paid for it? Ponder Jeremiah 9:23-24.

2:7-9. Benefits of the knowledge of God. Consider the benefits of the knowledge of God and the wisdom defined in this passage. They include protection, safety, and security. But underlying it all is the fact that righteousness and justice are to be prized for themselves. They accompany the knowledge of God. Notice the repetition of 'Then you will understand' in vv. 5,9. Those who do not have righteousness and justice at heart do not know God. As no person by nature really has these things at heart there is a problem. As has been said, the heart of the problem is the problem of the heart. It gives a poignancy to the need to cry out for discernment and to lift up the voice for understanding. There can be nothing casual about seeking after God, for the condition of man's natural ignorance of him is an absolutely desperate one. The crying out and the lifting up of the voice are like those of a drowning man: an urgent, unsparing cry for life to one who can save.

What kind of person is said to benefit from what the Lord offers, or rather, promises? Why is this? Some characteristics of such a person are described in Psalm 15. Spend a few minutes pondering each of these in relation to your own life. Having done so, look again at what it is that the Lord promises this kind of person.

Wisdom is inseparable from an 'upright' or 'blameless' life (v. 7), lived by those who have wisdom in their hearts (v. 10) as opposed to those whose minds may be well acquainted with the truth but whose hearts are untouched by it. Although v. 7 is variously translated, the idea of *accumulation* is present in the original. The storing up is an ongoing thing; the benefits to the upright in heart go on accumulating under the beneficent hand of the gracious Lord.

Righteousness and justice (v. 9) accompany the knowledge of God. They are prized for themselves by those who know God because they characterise God. It is not enough to desire righteousness and justice in the world at large, as many say they do. The writer's concern is about these qualities being found and operating in our personal lives as a mark of our relationship with God. It is therefore important to take the opportunity to think about these things, our attitude to them and their outworking in our own immediate sphere of life, and what we do about the inevitable shortfall.

Many might think of the benefits of wisdom being such things as honour, prestige and success in life. So it may be surprising to read that the benefits of the knowledge of God and the wisdom defined in this passage are those of protection, safety, and security (vv. 7-8). Why the Lord should promise these things in particular and not the other?

Do the words of v. 9 'ring a bell' in your mind? Solomon has now come full circle in his initial tour in which he has contrasted wisdom and folly. Just as 2:5 returns to the bare statement of 1:7, having firmly put the fear of the Lord into context, so in 2:9 he reiterates the life skills introduced at 1:3, having now shown us where their roots are and the soil out of which they grow.

2:10-22. The danger of enticement. Two specific dangers are highlighted in this passage, of which countless unwary souls have fallen foul. Note the word 'discretion' in v. 11. It is worth pondering the meaning of this word for a moment, and the negative form, indiscretion, will make an important point. A person who commits an indiscretion is one who says or does something at the wrong time or in the wrong way so as to cause social embarrassment. It often causes the offending individual embarrassment, too, often followed by, 'If only I'd thought...', or, 'If only I'd been aware....' It is all to do with discernment, being able to see hazards that may not be obvious on the surface, and hence to be able to steer a safe course round them.

This is very important in respect of the dangers outlined here. Though the Proverbs speak of 'wicked men' and 'the adulteress', for that is what they are, yet they do not necessarily immediately appear to be so; hence the need for discernment.

Both dangers are concerned with the effects of bad company. The first (vv. 12-15) is more particularly about the influence the wrong kind of company can have upon the mind. Again, it is a matter of being 'drawn in'. Young people brought up in a godly home have to mix with all manner of people who have not been nurtured in the same way, through contact at school or college, in the place of work, at recreational facilities, and so on. It is inevitable that friendships will form and that there will be a certain amount of socialising. While there is nothing wrong in this, it has to be recognised that the strong will lead the weak, and if the strong member is unprincipled then he will find ways of leading the weak along his unprincipled paths for the achievement of his own ends. Those who want to avoid becoming casualties of relationships that have moved in the wrong direction need to be able to see the signs in advance so that they do not get mixed up in something they will later come to regret. Relationships like this often start quite harmlessly, in which everything seems fine for a while; but as time passes someone gradually diverges from the straight and narrow, leaving the path of righteousness (v. 13), drawing others into compromise and questionable activities from which they then find it difficult to extricate themselves.

So often this happens little by little, until the unwary find themselves far removed from where they ought to be and wonder how they got there. The answer is that there were plenty of signs, but the victim failed to notice them, to read them, and so to respond to them. Because so many young people have fallen prey to the devious influences of unprincipled persons, we ought to recognise the importance of discernment and discretion. Discretion has its eyes open; it observes the potential, examines the possibilities, and selects the right course. *Without a clear knowledge of the Word of God this is quite impossible.* Many Christians have gone down blind alleys or worse simply because they have not applied themselves to wisdom – they have left the Word of God to one side in favour of other things. Like Abraham's nephew Lot, they have chosen for themselves on immediate appeal (Genesis 13:10-11) with reference to little apart from their own appetites or wishes.

The second danger (vv. 16-19) is of an entirely different kind, but equally powerful. This time the appeal is not to the mind but to the emotions and sexual appetite by women who have a way with words, dress and conduct and know how to use their charms to appeal to men. Again, it is little by little, by the use of plausible words and encouragement to let down one's guard and enjoy the way things are going. All sorts of ploys may be used, but the fact is that it is the woman who is calling the tune, and the man who simply allows this to happen has already committed an indiscretion! If you are to be kept from such influences then you will need a principle more powerful than your physical and emotional drive.

Many a man has abandoned himself to the pleasures of the moment only to regret it for the rest of his life. The guard against such flattery and seduction is the power of the fear of God, established upon a good understanding of his Word. How was it that Joseph was able to withstand the allurement of Potiphar's wife (Genesis 39:7-12)? For all we know she may have been a very attractive woman as well as a persuasive one. His answer to her was the model of discretion, and we ought to note that he did not say that her urging did not have a strong physical appeal. For a single man in his position very likely it did. He had encouragement and opportunity to indulge himself 'and no one would know'. However, his rational assessment of the situation, founded upon the fear of God, saved him. Many in his position would have succumbed with hardly a qualm. Joseph's answer was simply that the matter was non-negotiable, whatever his feelings and appetites might be. Observe that it was founded upon basic principles of trust, faithfulness and integrity, and he further demonstrated this by his subsequent behaviour toward her.

What kind of woman she was comes out all too clearly in the narrative which follows. Had Joseph given in to her enticement, he would have discovered this soon enough. People who get into such situations do not find it so easy to get themselves out afterwards. When they are in it 'up to their necks' the consequences are very bitter. This is just what Proverbs is saying in vv. 18-19. The long term consequences for evil men and wayward women is described in v. 22. Those who associate with them, or get drawn in, suffer with them.

Proverbs states unequivocally that there are dangers out there facing the young, and also the not-so-young. Now compare vv. 7-9 with v. 11 and see two sides of the same coin. In the former, it is the Lord who is a shield, who guards and preserves his people, while in the latter it is the believer's discretion and understanding that do this. It is very important to appreciate this. We may certainly, and we should, trust the Lord for his protection in life, but it is no use complaining if through neglect of what he expects of us we fall on our faces. People have said, when they have done something stupid or suffered the consequences of a rash action: 'Why didn't God prevent that from happening to me?' What a foolish question to ask, which amounts to blaming God for one's own negligence! He has given us all we need in his Word, and, having done so, he also requires us to give heed to it. People who ask such questions merely condemn themselves out of their own mouth. The chapter we have just been studying could not speak more plainly. All that is required is to take on board what it says.

Discretion brings its own reward. Wisdom, knowledge, discretion, understanding (vv. 10-11) not only deliver from the evils of being led astray in various ways by unprincipled men and women, they also hold promise for good (vv. 20-21). There are long term consequences for righteousness, too. Joseph was used as an example of one who resisted the powerful influence of sexual seduction. Though the short-term consequences for him were bad indeed, yet the eventual outcome more than vindicated him, and he himself was able to testify to God's hand having been upon him throughout for good (Genesis 41:50-52; 45:5-7; 50:19-21). There is particular poignancy in the last of these references: 'You meant evil against me; but God meant it for good.'

All the bad things that happened to Joseph were caused by other people, unscrupulous people who did not have the principles of conduct that Joseph had. Yet God looked after him throughout, and afterwards he could look back without bitterness and without regret. His discretion (v. 11) protected him in the furnace of trials, and he lived through the consequences to prove the truth of God's promises of vv. 7-8. Read Psalm 105:16-22.

Young people brought up with sound principles should not abandon them when the going gets tough, but should recognise that they will encounter difficulties in an unprincipled society. What else should they expect? They should be encouraged to take a long term view, understanding that God builds character through these things, that he is working out his purpose for good, and that the good promised is such that it is worth waiting for!

Do you have associations with other people, men or women, whose effect upon you tends to be morally or spiritually undermining? If so, consider some strategies, based upon the teaching of the Bible, by which you may be able to resist their unwelcome influence and instead exert a beneficial one yourself.

Have you had to suffer in some way on account of taking a stand upon the truth? If so, does it rankle? Do you feel sore about it? What is the remedy for bad feelings in this kind of situation?

Proverbs 3. Negatives and positives. Chapter 3 is full of 'Do not's' – in vv.1,3,5,7,11,21,25,27,28,29,30,31. The wisdom of 'Do not do this' or 'Do not think that' lies in the fact that to the prohibition is attached its positive counterpart. Our sinful nature is such that we need to be told what *not* to do because it comes so naturally to us. Our renewed nature requires direction for what we *are* to do. Our old corrupt passions are to be systematically replaced by new desires and wholesome conduct. Compare Colossians 3:1-17; Romans 12:2; Romans 6:12-13.

It is a good exercise to carefully read through the chapter and jot down the things that you are not to do, or to say, or think (there are about twelve occurrences), and then to go through these again and make a note of the positive aspect in each case. Finally, hold the negative and positive side by side and give some thought to the effects of each, considering what God promises in each case.

3:1-12. A sound heart. Are you one of many whose mind has been so fully occupied with other things that you have completely forgotten to keep an appointment and remembered it with embarrassment some time later? Distractions sometimes are so powerful as to divert us from our known and planned course of action. So when Solomon says, 'My son, do not forget my teaching,' we may admit that, however unlikely we may think it that we could do so, it can happen. Our minds can be so caught up with other things that we forget that God's Word is addressing us about the matter in hand; we can be diverted by some distraction to forget the proper rules of our conduct, as when a motorist's attention is drawn away from the proper business of driving and comes off the road, or worse. Consider Hebrews 2:1-4 in this context.

So we must acknowledge that this command is at all times as relevant and important as it is simple. One way we will avoid forgetting God's law is to acquire the habit of relating everything in life to it. This will be a feature of having his law in our hearts, which is its proper abiding place. If it is merely in our minds as a set of rules, we will very easily be distracted. If it is in our hearts, then we will quickly feel the discomfort associated with straying from it. The importance of the place of God's Word in the heart is mentioned three times in these few verses (vv. 1,3,5). In v. 1 we are told the heart is the place for God's commands to be kept.

Legalism follows the letter of the law of God, treating it as a set of rules and seeing little beyond 'Do this; don't do that.' Faith goes much further, following the spirit of the law, applying it in its widest sense.

3:1-2. An attentive heart. Probably most people, especially the young, regard a long and prosperous life as something to be looked forward to. The promise of v. 2 is appended to the condition of v. 1. Some object to this, saying that many God-fearing people have had their lives cut short through sickness, war, persecution or disaster. That of course is quite true, but it has nothing to do with what this verse is promising. One way of putting it might be that, other things being equal, obedience to God's commands will add years to one's life and bring peace (translated 'prosperity' in the NIV, but which must not be taken in the purely material sense). The psalmist said, 'Great peace have those who love your law, and nothing causes them to stumble' (Psalm 119:165).

To put it negatively, whatever your own set of circumstances may be, if you neglect God's Word you will cut your life shorter than it might otherwise have been, and give yourself trouble you might have been spared had you heeded it. This says nothing of the fact that the quality of life of the believer who treasures God's law in his heart, for however few years his life may last, is infinitely better than that of the unbeliever who may live for a century in ignorance of his Maker. What believer can look back with regret upon the life of faith and lament his losses when he has gained Christ and possesses everything in him? Long life and peace for the Christian has a dimension of which the unbeliever knows nothing! It is good for this life, and it holds promise for all eternity.

Read Philippians 4:6-7; Colossians 3:15-17.

3:3-4. A sensitive heart. The heart is the place for two principal attributes of God that he has revealed to us: mercy and truth (v. 3, NKJV), or love and faithfulness (NIV, ESV). The words in the Hebrew are rich in meaning and cannot effectively be translated by single words in English.

If you ask young people what they want from life, many will speak in terms of happiness, or security, or success, or perhaps of fame or power and influence. By and large the answers will be in terms of what they want *for themselves*. So what the Bible says at this point is worth noting. What really are the things worth having in life, to which young people should aspire? The answer is startlingly different, and yet it makes perfect sense. If you wear a tie, or a necklace, or some other ornament around your neck, every time you attach it let it be a reminder of the ornament of true worth, the chain bearing the twin gems of mercy and truth, of love and faithfulness. Not only does God value them, but they are also acknowledged by people (v. 4). Many a powerful man has been a curse upon the earth, many a rich man or woman has been bitterly unfulfilled and unhappy, many a person has experienced the isolation that is so often a side effect of success. Not so those who have understood the importance of mercy and truth. The young person wanting to get on in life should assess the worth of these two gems.

Mercy. What have we done to deserve God's love? If we recognise that the only answer we can give is, 'Nothing', this poses the next question, which is, '*Why* has he shown us his love?' The answer, inferred from Deuteronomy 7:7-8, may not satisfy us too well, but the thing we have to recognise is that the reason for his loving us is nowhere to be found in us, only in him. Think next about *how* he has shown his love to us. Of his own initiative and at his own cost beyond all measure he has sought and effected our highest good. He gave his Son for us, that through his death on the cross we might be forgiven, reconciled to him, and made heirs of heaven. So when God says that we are to bind *mercy* around our neck we are to understand that God has in view a response from us toward others of a similar kind to his response to us. Our attitude and our actions are to be intelligently and sensitively directed toward seeking the complete welfare of others, irrespective of whether or not we think they are deserving. Jesus reminds us that the world loves its own, but that our love is to be of a completely different order (Luke 6:27-36).

While it may be true that this kind of love is not something we should exercise for what we get out of it, we can still state that it is something that others will recognise and acknowledge and appreciate, even if they don't understand it. A reputation of this kind (v. 4) is worth acquiring!

Truth. This is the other gem. The word signifies truth not only in the objective, clinical sense but also in the way it is worked out in life. A 'true' friend is one who sticks by you through all circumstances, having the qualities of absolute reliability and unerring faithfulness. God's Word is the ultimate reference point for truth (John 17:17). When we turn to it we may depend upon it. There is no question about its reliability. It doesn't say one thing and mean another. It doesn't give with one hand and take back with the other. What God has said he honours. We are to be people like that in our conduct. People should not be able with any justice to accuse us of ambivalence. God has never spoken empty words, and neither should we. God has never spoken misleadingly, and neither should we. God has never promised anything and failed to fulfil it, and neither should we. Where our words and actions are concerned they should not be light on value. The standard set before us in this verse is integrity of speech and character based upon the Word of God and the character of God.

If we would know more of this then we should study the many passages in the Scriptures that tell us that God is a God of mercy and truth, of lovingkindness and faithfulness. The reasons God has been pleased to emphasise these two attributes in himself seem to be that we need to know that we can and must depend upon him, and that we should imitate him in these so that others may depend upon us as his ambassadors.

3:5-6. Psalm 37:1-11. A trusting heart. In v. 5 we are told that the heart is to be filled with absolute reliance upon God. God's person and his word cannot be separated. Those who say they love him but do not do what he says are deceiving themselves (Luke 6:46). Those who say they trust him but take a course of action in life that contradicts what his Word teaches have a mistaken view of what trusting God means. This command is especially relevant to young people, whose minds and imaginations are fertile, whose aspirations plentiful, whose energies abundant, but whose knowledge is as yet limited even though they may not be as aware of the fact as they might be! In the vigour of youth is the time to acquire the knowledge of God's Word, to store up his commands, to establish a basis for life. It is also a time when activity and enterprise and the exploitation of ideas can easily dominate and distort a proper perspective so that enthusiasm for one thing and another can squeeze out attention to God's Word.

The heart of the young person is susceptible to many influences. It is there that the habits of a lifetime take root. While many others will be seeking this and that in life, the young Christian should be learning to be an imitator of God (Ephesians 5:1 – and note in that context the reference to love and truth). Having observed the illustration of binding them about the neck, an adornment for all to see, there is the corresponding illustration of writing them upon the heart (v. 3b). When someone dies, the burial plot is called a *grave* on account of the stone *engraved* with some epitaph by which the person is to be remembered. In similar fashion we are to take the stonemason's chisel and use the stonemason's skill to engrave mercy and truth upon the tablets of our own hearts, to survive the wear and tear of our earthly lives. God will see what is in the heart, and approve; man will see what adorns the neck, and esteem. This is not self-praise. What God will see in the heart will be a likeness of what is in his own heart. That is why he will approve it. What men will see in the outward life and count of value are qualities that will reflect upon the love and faithfulness of God. So the favour and reputation we gain we may rightly enjoy with the gladness of heart that all is from God and to his glory.

Verses 5 and 6 are exceedingly well known among believers – though perhaps less well practised. They are particularly relevant to young people for a number of reasons. Firstly, on account of inexperience. Our own understanding (v. 5) is fallible at the best of times and we need a more reliable instructor, especially in situations requiring decisions. We are encouraged that we may trust God with all our heart. He is telling us that if we do so he will not fail us. Our own understanding may not be able to help, but he can. The two clauses in v. 5 are set in contrast to one another and one must be understood in relation to the other. We see elderly people leaning on a stick or a walking frame. In similar fashion we are to entrust the weight of our problems and decisions to the Lord. He will provide all the support that is needed. Some elderly people are too proud to be seen to be dependent upon these aids, and if they have them they like to be seen to be managing without them. 'They've insisted I have this thing, but I can get along well enough without it.' This must not be our attitude to our trust in God. We cannot get along at all well without him! The command of v. 5 is not an optional one. It is not advisory but mandatory. It is often taken as a promise, and rightly so; but it is also a command.

In v. 6 there is a second aspect to this, in which God is concerned for the honour of his own name. If we acknowledge him as we seek our course in life, then he will not allow us to fall flat on our faces. We make it publicly known that we are dependent upon God and are seeking his guidance and provision and by our lives we show that we mean it. How would it reflect upon his name if by so doing we ended up in a mess? 'I really trusted God in this situation, and look where it has landed me!' That is what some people have said, with apparent justification, through being premature to judge the situation. Joseph might have had cause to say this when he was chained up in prison after refusing Potiphar's wife! But we who know the end of the story acknowledge that God was in control all the way through and vindicated his name through his faithfulness to his servant from start to finish.

What a gracious command and promise he gives us here! He says we are to acknowledge him in all our ways, and that in whatever ways we do acknowledge him he will show himself to be faithful by directing our way, by making a clear way forward for us. God puts his reputation on the line for our sake! For him to fail in respect of this promise to us would be for him to fail himself. He never has, and he never will (2 Timothy 2:13)! He never will forsake those who trust him, or leave them high and dry. We should know that and act upon it. But Satan is a sinister tempter, and in just the same way as he tempted Eve in the garden so he tempts us to think that God does not really have our best interests at heart, that he is deliberately withholding something from us, that we have to take matters into our own hands if we are to succeed in life. However, these two verses provide a precious incentive to young people aware of their limitations, that God cares for them, and that their dependence upon him and the honour of his great name are inextricably bound up together.

3:7-8. Romans 12:9-21. A humble heart. Having been encouraged to trust in the Lord rather than depending upon our own limited understanding, v. 7 warns us in the area of pride. 'I can handle this myself!' 'I don't need anyone to tell me how to do it!' 'Who does she think she is trying to give me advice?'

When it comes to our course and decisions in life, whether big or small, if we proceed confidently without reference to God we are likely to end up regretting it. 'I don't need God's Word to direct me in this: the way ahead is obvious!' Unfortunately, though many of us would not put it so crassly, we have at times been guilty of proceeding in blithe ignorance of the implications of what we are doing. There was once a road safety advertisement circulated among motorists warning them of the importance of driving within the limits of visibility. It showed a driver speeding along on a clear road ahead who knew the road well and had travelled it hundreds of times. There were no hazards. Only *this* time, as we turned the page of the leaflet, a horse and rider were just round the bend ahead, out of the line of vision. Verse 6 says that God will direct our paths, provided we acknowledge him by staying within the limits of visibility. He is telling us to keep to the appropriate speed limits for the conditions which prevail. We simply do not know what lies round the next bend and need to proceed with caution with our eyes on him. Being wise in our own eyes is a sure way to wreak havoc and end up in hospital in the spiritual sense, where recovery may be slow and painful and the damage done irretrievable. What in one context might be said, 'Fear the law and ease your foot off the accelerator' is here stated with that much greater importance, 'Fear the Lord and depart from evil.' That is, if you would be healthy, strong and well-nourished (v. 8)!

The essential difference between the 'wisdom' of v. 7a and true wisdom is that the former has reference to self, whereas the latter has reference to God's Word. If the answer to 'How am I going to deal with this?' comes about by reference to our own resources and ideas, then the resulting action will demonstrate our being wise in our own eyes. That is the wisdom of this world which is coming to nothing (1 Corinthians 1:19). True wisdom looks to the fount of all wisdom and finds its answers there – in Christ in whom are hidden all the treasures of wisdom and knowledge (1 Corinthians 1:30; Colossians 2:3). When a man or woman is truly wise, it will be evident that he or she acts not on inward impulse but from the foundation of the fear of God and the principles of God's Word.

If the promise appended in v. 8 is not understood in context it will be misunderstood. Two people are lying next to each other in hospital beds, suffering from essentially the same malady, and both are in poor shape physically. One is a bombastic, self-centred individual, the other a godly person with a lifetime's experience of trust in God. Now consider how what is stated here continues to apply to the one, whereas it has never been experienced by the other. True well-being, though pictured in this verse in terms of physical health, actually extends far beyond it. Many a person in the midst of suffering has rejoiced in the grace of God when reflecting upon where they would otherwise have been. What a difference confidence in the Lord makes to those with long experience of implicit trust in him!

At the end of Romans 12:16 Paul says the same as v. 7a here. The context in which he says it gives us a good picture of the attitude and conduct of those who are not wise in their own eyes and it is worth pondering, point by point, what he says there.

3:9-10. Psalm 112. A generous heart. Each pair of verses of the chapter, up to and including this pair, take the form of a command and a promise. If you like, they are saying, 'This is what you should do, and these are the benefits.'

Verses 9 and 10 have been much misunderstood and misrepresented. If the thought in the back of one's mind is 'What's in it for me?', the likelihood is that this statement will be misinterpreted.

We have just been looking at mercy and truth (v. 3), two very precious and costly gems. In a similar way as it will deplete our resources to purchase and possess precious stones, so it will do to possess these priceless qualities. For those who possess mercy and truth are always opening their hearts and opening their hands and giving out, expending themselves for the good of others. Honouring God with their possessions and with the firstfruits of all their increase (v. 9) was commanded for the Old Testament people of God (Exodus 23:19; Leviticus 23:10-11; 27:30; Numbers 18:12; Deuteronomy 14:22; Malachi 3:10), and when we examine the reason (for there is a reason for all that God commands) we discover it is so that his grace might be made more widely known. It is, to use New Testament terminology, to prosper the cause of the gospel.

The tithes and offerings were for the upkeep of the priesthood and tabernacle and sacrifices, for the facilitating of the gatherings for celebration and worship on the prescribed occasions, for meeting needs where they existed in their society, for the poor, the widowed, the fatherless, the alien (Numbers 18:8-24; Deuteronomy 14:22-29; 26:10-13). The intention was for the dispensation of blessing, to rejoice in and share in the goodness of God with overflowing thanksgiving. A New Testament verse that is in line with this one is Matthew 6:33.

For those who seek to honour the Lord with all they have, he adds everything of which they have need. Whether visibly they have little or plenty is immaterial, for they will always have a sufficiency of all things (2 Corinthians 9:8). The poor widow at Zarephath who supplied for Elijah's needs had only a scrape in the bottom of her barrel and a little oil in a jar, but neither ran out throughout the time she provided for God's servant (1 Kings 17:8-16). His needs were met, and so were hers and her son's. Though they had little, it cannot be denied that they were plentifully supplied throughout the time of drought, for God provided for them.

It is all a question of our priorities and where our heart is. God does not require us to give everything away, but he does require us to honour him with what we have, and this will first be demonstrated with what we do with the first and best of our possessions. It is so that we can bless others before we think of our own needs. This is absolutely consistent with mercy and truth.

Look at that very moving statement made by Paul in 2 Corinthians 8:1-5 about the churches of Macedonia. It is moving because they were so moved by the needs of the suffering church in Jerusalem that their own troubles and their own poverty seemed nothing to them by comparison. If any church or individual had any cause for saying they could not afford to help, it was true of the believers in Macedonia, and yet they were the very ones noted for their overflowing generosity. Paul talks of their first giving themselves to the Lord (2 Corinthians 8:5). They were honouring God with their possessions, and we can be sure that God met all their needs, as indeed the apostle assured them in Philippians 4:19. In short, the promise God affords to people in Proverbs 3:9-10 is that he will supply every need of the generous hearted in order that they may continue in the same vein! Those who have this attitude need never worry that their resources will dry up. Many a wealthy person has ended up a pauper through squandering his resources, while those of lesser means, through honouring the Lord and his Word, have been instruments for accomplishing vastly greater good.

Young people setting out on life who often feel the pinch financially should take this promise to heart. Get your priorities right. Honour God with your possessions, return to him first from what he has given you, and leave it to him to look after the rest. It may be hard when you think of what you may have to go without through adopting this practice, but God is no man's debtor, and he is true to his word. What you have to go without will be no loss to you, and what you gain will be immeasurable in its benefit. Remember what the Lord said through Haggai when the people were feeling the pinch (Haggai 1:2-11). Their problem was that they were looking after their own interests and begrudged giving to God what was his due and consequently failed to meet the needs of the needy. Ironically, the more they tried to look after their own interests, the more difficult it became and the more uncomfortable things got. God honours those who honour him (1 Samuel 2:30). There is nothing wrong with looking after our own interests except when we put it in the wrong position in our list of priorities. If ever there was a church noted for its giving, that was the church at Philippi, yet Paul reminded them that each should look out not only for his own interests but also for the interests of others (Philippians 2:4). If that church needed such a reminder, then so do we.

3:11-12. A submissive heart: discipline. So far we have looked at the great principles of mercy and truth and how they are worked out in our lives. Some things are more easily said than done. To have good principles is one thing; to carry them through is another. To know how to do something in theory is fine, but to put it into practice often presents a problem. You can know from a book how to drive a car, you can understand the principles inside out. But get behind the wheel for the first time and the practice is embarrassingly unlike the theory! The same is true of most branches of learning.

'Do you understand this?'

'Yes.'

And this?'

'Yes.'

What about this?'

'Yes, I've got it.'

'Good! Now do this exercise.'

Then, after a few minutes:

'Help! I really can't see how to begin.'

The same is true in the spiritual realm. We have grasped some grand principles. Where do we go from here? The answer lies in the realm of *discipline*. The Lord has to do some work on us if ever we are to put into practice these principles of mercy and truth. This is probably the reason vv. 11-12 are placed here. There are times when the Word of God rebukes us by showing us some matter in which we are not conducting ourselves in accordance with what he requires of us. Sometimes to put such matters right involves personal inconvenience or discomfort and the natural response would be to dismiss it or defer action until another occasion. Except that we know that we cannot so easily put obedience to one side and we have to admit that another occasion more suitable for it will never come. Our slowness to respond sometimes means that he has to adopt more severe measures.

How we enjoy the caress of God's favour and shun the rod of his correction! However, we have cause to be thankful for the rod under which we are made to smart, because it is in the hand of a God who loves us and is promoting our highest good. There are times when he has to wean us off certain things in order that we might grow strong in him. Jesus spoke of his being the true vine and his Father being the vinedresser and pruning the branches in order to promote their fruitfulness (John 15:1-8). It is undoubtedly true that Christians need pruning if they are to be healthy and fruitful. If our heavenly Father cuts us back from dissipating our energies in unprofitable areas, are we to complain? He is the best judge of what is needed. We are to submit. The writer of Hebrews takes up this verse in Proverbs in Hebrews 12:5, acknowledging that suffering and pain are involved and the whole process can seem exceedingly unpleasant (Hebrews 12:11). What we need to grasp when such things happen to us is that God does it because there is something wrong with us that he intends putting right; that he does it because he loves us, and delights in us, and intends to do us good. There is a very real sense in which the pain is not of his inflicting, but is felt because of the trouble with us. If things were right there would be no pain, no need for discipline.

So our response should be to cooperate with him and not fight against him by asking hard and unreasonable questions like: 'Why has God allowed this to happen to me?' not because we want to know the answer but because we want to complain that his treatment of us is in some way unreasonable! Malachi had to contend with people who were full of complaints against the injustice of God's dealings with them. Malachi 3:10 is the culmination of a severe rebuke by God of the people called by his name who were giving him second best (if we dare call it that!). They knew what he required of them, for they knew what the law said, but they thought they could get away with cutting corners, bending the law to their convenience, somehow imagining that it didn't matter or that God wouldn't notice! However, God did notice, and because they were not heeding his word he had been inflicting the rod of hardship on them (Malachi 3:11). What is interesting and indeed alarming is that Malachi prophesied not long after the spiritual awakening and reformation that took place under Nehemiah, probably during the time when Nehemiah was back in Babylon for a few years. The spiritual backsliding that we can trace in this prophecy is so easy. We need God's chastening hand to be upon us to remove the dross and purify us, as much as did those of Malachi's day who gave heed to his word (Malachi 3:16-18).

...And more discipline! That discipline is necessary should go without question. What we need to do is to put it in its proper context. We know that the doctor who prescribes some unpleasant medicine does so for our good, or that the surgeon who operates does so with the intention of removing something which is doing harm to help restore the well-being of our body. They do so because it is their job. How much more should we accept with gratitude what our heavenly Father deems to inflict upon us for our eternal good (Hebrews 12:9)? See with what tenderness he speaks of its necessity, calling us his sons, reminding us that he loves us, and that he delights in us. In the trials of life let us 'do him proud' as the saying goes.

A problem we sometimes face is the inability to distinguish between trials – what is part of God's disciplining of us, what is the result of our own folly, and what comes from some other source. 'If I knew that this was God's discipline of me, I might feel the more able to submit to it, but I have no assurance that this is from him.' Such reasoning is not sound. It might be if he did not have his hand upon us at all times, or if his love and interest were sporadic, or if we could go off out of his field of vision or control and do our own thing. If I suffer for something stupid I do, even then there is no reason whatever for me to discard it as not being a part of my heavenly Father's training. Sometimes he allows us to 'learn the hard way' in order that we might thereby be spared something far more injurious. Then there are those occasions when we know perfectly well the source of our troubles, that they come from other people. There is no point in being bitter against them. Even what they do to harm us is still ordained by our heavenly Father for our good, and indeed maybe for the good of others too as a result, as the life of Joseph very clearly shows.

What happened to him illustrates these points rather well. To start with, the way as a young man he spoke about his dreams was not very wise, and he could on reflection have said with reason that it was his own fault he incurred his brothers' hatred. Then, he could have felt angry and resentful about their despicable act in ridding themselves of him in the way they did. In all, his analysis of the situation, when he found himself a slave on the way to Egypt for purchase by the highest bidder, would have been confused and without meaning. However, whether what happened was his own fault, or the fault of others, or a mixture of the two, subsequent history demonstrates beyond doubt that God intended it for good. He had a purpose in it all.

So it is with us. God shows no favouritism (1 Peter 1:17). He loves all his children equally and fully. He loved Joseph; he loves you. He disciplined Joseph according to his purposes and Joseph's need, and he disciplines you according to his purposes and your need. Because we are unable to see what is going on during times of adversity, are we going to despise the chastening of the Lord, or fail to recognise that he is fully in control of it?

The writer of Hebrews very wisely advises us what to do in such circumstances: we are, spiritually and practically, to look up, get up and get going, and not wallow in the mire of self-pity (see Hebrews 12:12-13). Adverse circumstances are rather like those pieces of a jigsaw that do not seem to fit anywhere. The reason we cannot make them fit is that other pieces relating to them are not yet in place. No one would be so foolish as to throw away such pieces of jigsaw while the picture is under construction just because they cannot see where they belong. They have their proper place in the picture and without them the picture can never be complete. So it is with trials. We need to learn to accept them, to examine them, and to keep them in view in the knowledge that they have their part to play and that one day we will understand their place as God's purposes for our lives unfold. They are all part of the picture, and ultimately they will fit seamlessly with everything else that God is doing in creating a perfect whole.

3:13-18. Ah ... happiness! Up to this point many benefits of the fear of the Lord have been mentioned, but here, after the rather sombre and maybe discomforting observations about discipline and chastening is the counterbalancing introduction of *blessing*. Verse 13 is probably best read as an exclamation. The word denotes happiness, but not that skin deep happiness that so many seem to understand by the term. This is a settled, deep happiness, a contentment, a joy. Like an iceberg, only a fraction of it may appear on the surface, but what is seen is indicative of a vast bulk beneath. This happiness is anchored deep within the heart.

These verses are a remarkable eulogy on wisdom. Personified as a woman, wisdom stands in stark contrast to the immoral woman of 2:16-19, and bears great similarity to the virtuous woman of 31:10-31. Finding wisdom (v. 13) is not to be regarded as a once and for all discovery. It is a bit like building a library of priceless books. It is a joy to be able to acquire and hold one precious volume, but there are more to be had, and as they are sought out and purchased so the pleasure increases and the value of the collection increases. Wisdom is to be acquired, and it is also to be added to. That the fear of the Lord is the *beginning* of wisdom indicates that more is to be added. We are to grow in wisdom. We are told of Jesus that as a child he was both filled with wisdom (Luke 2:40) and that he also increased in wisdom (Luke 2:52). How can this be? It is like a vessel whose fullness generates more capacity so that it may take yet more and still be full. Is it not true that as we study God's Word our capacity to understand increases? When we were babes in Christ his Word was precious to us and we were filled with joy because we had understood it. However, as we begin to understand him and obey him, so we get to understand him more fully, and as we obey him more fully so we grow in our knowledge of God ... and so it continues throughout our lives.

Not all believers can be described as happy, though, in the sense of v. 13, and the reason could be that they are trading in the wrong commodities. They have yet to find out what really matters in life and what is of lasting value. Their desire is for things of relatively little value. They may be things that are important to them, and it may be they are truly important in their own right; but set alongside wisdom, knowledge and understanding their importance pales and they do not matter so much. Many a believer is up against the problem of getting things into a right perspective and making the right choices in life. Many a believer lives an unfulfilled life through making the wrong choices.

Verses 13-18 describe a life that is enjoyed to the full. There is nothing so important as growing in our understanding of the Lord our God. Wisdom from heaven is needed for living on earth. Just think what you could do with an abundance of silver, or gold, or precious stones! Just think how you could trade with them, what you could acquire with them. Consider how you could improve your lifestyle, where you could go, what you could do – all the things you have wanted to do and never been able to. Let your imagination run along the lines of what would be accessible to you had you the means to purchase them. Yet, without despising the many good things you might get and be able to do, and how you might be able to benefit yourself – yes, and others too – the fact is that to possess and grow in the wisdom of God is of greater worth than that. You might be so poor as not to have two pennies to rub together, and yet have such unspoilt happiness in the true sense of the word that you lack nothing, because you are trading with the wisdom your heavenly Father provides.

It is sad that very many people in a materialistic society, surrounded by *things*, bombarded through the media with the 'must have' mentality, do not see this. They would say, 'I don't believe it.' Nevertheless, whatever they believe or do not believe, the power for happiness, for fulfilment, for personal benefit, for doing good to others, for surviving the course, for genuine contentment, lies here and here alone. As verse 15 says, there is simply nothing that can be compared with wisdom. Think of anything you desire, and then compare it with the knowledge of God and the understanding of his will, and where does that put it? You may still desire it, but it puts it in its proper place!

It should be clear by now that the blessings of wisdom are not for the self-seeking but for those who fear the Lord and seek to obey him. We know too that God is a rewarder of those who diligently seek him (Hebrews 11:6), and that those who ask will receive, and those who seek will find (Luke 11:9). The benefits of wisdom are described in vv. 16-18. Length of days involves time being stretched out. It is the opposite of time being cut short. There are many instances of the latter in the Bible. In his lament for lost blessings, Ethan the Ezrahite says of the king, representing the people, 'The days of his youth you have shortened; you have covered him with shame' (Psalm 89:45). God visited judgement upon many of the ungodly kings of Israel, terminating their reigns because they were wicked in his sight, others too being cut down in their prime. In Matthew 24:22 Jesus spoke of evil days being shortened for the sake of his elect people. By contrast, wisdom is seen to be extending her right hand with the gift of length of days. The gift is not intrinsic to wisdom, but is from God who gives it by the hand of wisdom. Whereas on the one hand the lives of fools are often cut short, on the other hand God is pleased to extend the life of usefulness of those who possess wisdom for the sake of his glory and the fulfilment of his purposes in the earth.

Wisdom is the gateway to a happy and fulfilled life, by which God will enable you to accomplish all that he has in mind for you. If he could make the sun stand still while Joshua defeated the enemies of the Lord and his people (Joshua 10:13), he can extend your day until the completion of the business he has for you to do in his service.

In that remarkable passage, Isaiah 53, it is stated in vv. 10-12 that the days of the Lord Jesus, described there as the Suffering Servant, are to be prolonged. This was to be *after* his death, *after* his making his soul an offering for sin, which clearly prophesies his life and activity after his death, which was subsequently witnessed to in his crucifixion and his resurrection from the dead on the third day. To what end do we read of the prolonging of his days? Study these verses, and you will see that it is in order that the great work for which he came into the world should be forwarded and brought to completion. It is that he should fulfil his Father's pleasure and obtain full satisfaction for the work he did (vv. 10b,11a); it is that he might enjoy the glory of the fruits of what he accomplished in his great victory upon the cross; it is that he might bring men and women down the ages into the benefits of the forgiveness of sin and of peace with God through his justifying work. In the light of this, what is your motive for wishing your days to be prolonged? To what end do you wish to live a full and fulfilled life? What do you wish to accomplish in it? Are your desires in harmony with the purposes of God, as were the apostle Paul's (Philippians 1:22)?

There are those who give with one hand and take with the other. Wisdom gives with both hands (v. 16). With the right hand she gives length of days, representing the principal gift for the service of God. With the left she gives riches and honour. Once again, we need to remind ourselves that these are not offered for self-indulgent use. It is all part of the provision God supplies for his service. Two men come to mind immediately when thinking of riches and honour: Joseph and Daniel. Both were men who were elevated in their respective kingdoms after a long period of suffering. Both served God faithfully with the wisdom and understanding he gave them, and both were rewarded with riches and honour. When we consider this, it becomes apparent that the riches and honour were the means by which their service was to be established and extended. The office they were given was necessary for them to accomplish what God wanted them to do. The riches and honour bestowed upon them, whether by Pharaoh or Nebuchadnezzar, were actually from God, channelled through the wisdom given them. While there is no hint at their using their position and wealth for self-gratification, there is plenty of evidence that they used them for the benefit of the communities they were called to serve. The principle, then, is that the riches and honour extended by wisdom are the provisions God gives in order for his purposes to be fulfilled through his servants. Anyone who thinks, 'Riches and honour – that will set me up for life!', have missed the point. It is not for them!

3:17-18. Delight. For the child of God the gifts of wisdom should be wonderfully appealing. Do you not have a longing to live a useful, fulfilled life, returning something to God by way of a thank-offering for the riches of his grace to you in Christ? He has done everything for you. What can you do for him? Through wisdom, God gives you both the time and the means. But then, he gives more. Remember David, who wanted to build a temple for the Lord (2 Samuel 7). His motives were good. He was looking at all the Lord had done for him, and how he was now living in comparative luxury, while the ark of God resided in a mere tent. He felt there was some disparity there, some injustice, something unworthy, and he wanted to rectify it by building what he saw as being worthy of the great God. Although it was Solomon who eventually built the temple, God did enable David to provide most of the materials (1 Chronicles 22). That was David's service. The point, though, which he himself acknowledged with wonder, is that while David spoke of building a house for the Lord, the Lord answered by speaking of building the house of David – and the blessings of the kingdom of heaven through the coming of the Messiah (2 Samuel 7:16). God rewarded David's concern with overwhelming comfort and encouragement.

As if it were not enough to have our days extended and the provision of what we need in the high privilege of God's service, verses 17 and 18 assure us that the way of wisdom is a delightful road to tread, and that those who walk in wisdom will find it truly pleasant and peaceful. There is certainly enough unpleasantness and strife in the world where self-centred thoughts generate heat and conflict in selfish actions resulting in pain and sorrow and bitterness. By contrast, wisdom promotes the opposite both in and through those who possess her.

It is, to understate the case, a sad fact that at the beginning Eve took hold of the fruit of the wrong tree. Although the tree of life was there in the midst of the garden as well as the tree of the knowledge of good and evil (Genesis 2:9), and although the fruit of the first was not forbidden, only that of the latter, yet she succumbed to the temptation to eat of the latter under the mistaken notion that, among other things, it would make her wise (Genesis 3:6). Thereafter, access to the tree of life was barred (Genesis 3:22). Is it not remarkable, therefore, that here in Proverbs wisdom should be described as 'a tree of life to those who take hold of her' (v. 18)? Men and women are still grasping after the wrong things, and what they hope for eludes them. Yet wisdom, this true wisdom from God, offers – and delivers – everything anyone could ever want that is worth the wanting. She is a tree of life to all who take hold of her. The original language indicates a purposeful, tenacious, and even passionate, grasping. For those who recognise her true worth, there is a 'must have' about wisdom which will not let her go! Happy are those who find her (v. 13), and happy are those who hold her fast (v. 18)! So begins, and so ends, this eulogy.

3:19-20. Creation and control. Many believe that the world came about by blind chance and ordered itself out of a process of random events. One might conceive of a tiny element of what we call order being found by chance in the midst of a chaotic universe, in just the same way as we might see a string of, say, ten consecutive zeros in a very large list of random numbers and think there was order there, except that by looking at the whole we recognise it to be just a natural product of randomness. When we consider our universe, order and system are found throughout, not just in tiny isolated pockets as might be the product of chance. Furthermore, the order is so complex, so intricate, that there is no conceivable possibility of its having arisen as a result of random processes. No 'blind chance' is involved, and the only blindness is in those who think there is. The truth is that 'the LORD by wisdom founded the earth; by understanding he established the heavens' (v. 19). It is all God's doing, and he knew what he was doing – and he did it right! Men are still trying to understand even the tiniest parts of what God's understanding has made. The universe declares the greatness of understanding of the God who made it out of nothing (see, for example, Job 9:8-10; Isaiah 40:26,28; Hebrews 11:3). The perfection of his understanding means that what he created was 'very good' (Genesis 1:31), which is quite unlike man's creativity which so often starts with a prototype, capable of and needing improvement. God did not start with the seed of an idea and modify his creation as he went along, changing this and having second thoughts about that. There was no process of evolution in his creative design, for it is by wisdom that he founded the earth.

The wisdom of God informs us that wisdom knows how to choose the best out of alternatives; it sees through the issues and has the ability to make the right choices. A small example of this is found in the counsel of Ahithophel (2 Samuel 16:23) whose advice to Absalom against David was absolutely sound, even though it was overturned by Hushai (2 Samuel 17:1-14). So then, why is the world as it is?

Verse 20 is taken by many to be a further comment on the original creation of the world. However, I am inclined to differ from this, for the following reasons. The breaking up of the depths is specifically and uniquely elsewhere mentioned in Genesis 7:11 of the act of judgement in Noah's time when the world was deluged with water, and it is difficult not to see this verse as a reference to that event. Furthermore, the word here for 'breaking up' is generally used of a destructive or judgemental act (as, for example, Numbers 16:31; Psalm 74:15; Micah 1:4; and even Isaiah 48:21 and 58:8 indicate dramatic events involving judgement). I see judgement and mercy in this verse: judgement in the sending of the flood; mercy in the provision of 'dew' from the rain. God's judgement is always tempered by mercy this side of the last day, that men might fear him and seek him. The flood upon the earth was not 'a natural disaster'. It was no accident, it was the judgement of God upon sin.

We will be wise to recognise that ever since then the disasters that occur upon earth, 'natural' or otherwise, happen within the design and control of God who orders everything according to the counsel of his own will and purpose. What kind of God is he who wiped out virtually the whole of humanity in one fell swoop? He is a God who must at length judge sin. Those who object to this fail to recognise the holiness of God and also fail to understand why Noah preached for 120 years prior to the flood (2 Peter 2:5; Genesis 6:3), or take into account that right until the last moment there was room in the ark for those who chose to escape the wrath to come. The aftermath of God's acts of judgement invariably reveals his grace, like the sun breaking through after a violent storm. Just because we could not see it did not mean it was not there before. In creation, in judgement, and in grace, God acts with wisdom, with understanding, and with knowledge. All his works and ways are perfect and glorious. All times and events are in his hands.

3:21-26. When troubles arise. New elements enter into the dialogue at this point: fear, trouble and danger for those who seek to walk in the way of wisdom. It is a fact of life that those who live in the fear of God, seeking to honour him and his Word, will for a variety of reasons find themselves in conflict with ungodly people. Because those who have no fear of God often use unscrupulous tactics there is always the danger of adopting their own methods to work against them. In some competitive ball games the cardinal rule is, 'Keep your eye on the ball.' Yes, be aware of what your opponent is doing, but keep your eye on the ball. Take your eye off the ball, and you will be caught unprepared, mis-hit it or miss it altogether and lose the point. It is easy to be distracted, and the opponent of our souls is a master of the art. The psalmist confessed to being foolish when his focus was too much on the apparent prosperity of the wicked (Psalm 73:22). Our assessment of everything, and in particular when we are dealing with adverse circumstances or unreasonable people, needs to be with the critical judgement that comes from a good understanding of God's Word. We are to keep our spiritual faculties trained on God's Word, retaining and using its instruction in every situation (v. 21).

To use the illustration of the ball game again, many competent players have lost games through lowering themselves to the standard of the opposition. We must never do that. Whatever tactics others may use, we are to play according to the rules. Just as a player in a game may expect the referee or umpire to give sound judgement in favour of the right, so we may expect the Lord to do the same for us when trouble comes, for he says as much in v. 26. Subversive conduct on our part is ruled out, however we might be tempted to it. We are not to attempt to beat people at their own game; it is not our business to 'get back at them', but to entrust ourselves to God who judges justly (1 Peter 2:23). The promises God gives here to those who 'play according to the rules' are life to the soul and grace to the neck (v. 22). These are the health and beauty of which God approves and which, furthermore, stand out and are taken note of in a corrupt society.

Most people know what it is to have disturbed nights and lose sleep through anxiety. Having a troubled conscience only makes matters worse. The further promise God gives here is that through keeping a single eye on sound wisdom and discretion he will give untroubled rest and refreshment (v. 24). 'Yes', he says, emphasising the point, for this is a very precious commodity. These verses reflect vv. 1-4, only this time in the context of adversity. In a murky environment it is a great thing to be adorned with such beautiful qualities, where their brilliance and worth will stand out the more. Trouble from the wicked (v. 25) is always around the corner. Those who desire to live godly lives will encounter it directly in one form or another sooner or later (2 Timothy 3:12) and there is no point in losing sleep over how it may manifest itself. Many a Christian has said, when considering others suffering for their faith, 'I don't know how I could cope in that situation.' The comment is understandable and valid in so far as it goes, only it doesn't go far enough. God himself has given, and does give, the resources for such circumstances, through his Word and by his Spirit, so that those equipped with heavenly wisdom will find the Lord to be their confidence to tread safely through the minefield of adversity without loss of dignity ('stumbling', v. 23) and without shame ('being snared', v. 26), and they will not come the worse out of it. The 'sudden terror' and 'trouble' indicate overwhelming devastation, a sort of worst possible scenario which people with lively imaginations often worry about and which rarely actually happens. If the worst does come to the worst, though, in just such a situation the promise of confidence applies. Many Christians who have passed through harrowing experiences have testified to being wonderfully sustained by the power of God.

We should carefully observe the difference between the Lord *giving you* confidence and his *being your* confidence. There is nothing triumphalist about this. It is not walking over adversity or opposition as if they did not exist. It is not the 'haven't a care in the world' kind of confidence. This is a confidence that is founded upon facts, not feelings. It looks at the problems fairly and squarely, assessing them for what they are, recognising their potential for harm, fully aware of their formidable and seemingly unassailable power, and seeing no solution. It is in that situation, when you have no resources left, when you cannot see your way through, that faith takes the place of sight and you know you may place your absolute reliance upon God, for he can see what you cannot, he is sovereign over all opposition, and he is working all things out for good for those who love him (Romans 8:28). Far from being what some disparagingly describe as blind faith, it is faith with the 20-20 vision of being founded upon the knowledge of God. These are very much the sentiments of Psalms 3 and 91.

A Christian who neglects his Bible and is not careful to maintain close fellowship with God is one who in such circumstances will encounter all manner of distress. He may cry to God, he may know that there is nothing else he can do, but he may well not be confident about the outcome, even though the outcome may be sure. The wise Christian has learnt to confide in God, developing a relationship of understanding and holy intimacy, out of which arises unshakable confidence in him. To those who do not know him such confidence may be scorned as foolish but, as Paul astutely observes, 'the foolishness of God is wiser than men' (1 Corinthians 1:25, perhaps playing upon the nuances of meaning of the Hebrew for 'confidence'?). It is interesting that the same word translated here as 'confidence' is rendered elsewhere as 'folly' or 'foolishness' (Psalm 49:13; Ecclesiastes 7:25), or as 'hope' in the positive sense (Psalm 78:7), or in the sense of misplaced confidence (Job 8:14; 31:24). Its meaning depends upon the context. Is your confidence wise or foolish? It all depends upon where it is placed. If not in God, it is foolishness, because it has no true foundation. If in God, it is wise, for it rests upon a rock. This reminds us of the wisdom of hearing and obeying the words of the Lord (Matthew 7:24).

3:27-30. Philippians 2:3-11. Doing good. This section represents a practical outworking of 'mercy and truth' (v. 3) which gains favour in the sight of man (v. 4). It concerns our relationship with our neighbours. When Jesus quoted the law, 'You shall love your neighbour as yourself', a man asked for clarification with the question, 'And who is my neighbour?' (Luke 10:27-29), wanting to satisfy himself that he was fulfilling the law. Doubtless the answer he got seriously disturbed his complacency. Proverbs 3:27 raises similar questions. To whom is good due? Or, following the NIV translation, who is deserving of what good I might do them? Is there someone to whom you owe a favour? Is that the meaning? Did the Samaritan who encountered the mugged Jew on the Jericho road owe him any favours? The more we look into this statement the greater the insight we gain into the meaning of mercy and truth (compare Matthew 9:13; 12:7).

Religious orthodoxy, attendance at all the meetings of the church, defence of the doctrines of the faith – all are a meaningless sham unless truth is accompanied with mercy. A heart of truth extends a hand of mercy. To whom, then, is good due? What is the good that is not to be withheld? To answer the latter question first, it is good in the widest sense of the word. It is anything by which you might benefit your neighbour. It might be a thoughtful word, a kind action, a loan of equipment, or even of money; it might be a listening ear, or the giving of advice. Whatever it is, it presupposes that you have sufficient interest in your neighbour's welfare to seek to be of use. This is the exact opposite of those who scheme on their beds to do harm to others (Psalm 36:4). Your attitude is to be different from those who say, with hostility or disdain, 'She deserves nothing from me.'

So, to the first question, to whom is good due? The answer stares up at us from this same verse. It is to anyone when it is in the power of our hand to do so. Your response to all the good that God has bestowed upon you, undeserving sinner though you are, should be to open your hand to others to do them good in whatever way is in your power.

Verses 27 and 28 concern two aspects of doing good: verse 27 with *failing* to do it, and verse 28 with *delaying* to do it. Spontaneous, ungrudging generosity is implied in v. 28. The law forbade a man taking a cloak in pledge from failing to return it before nightfall when its owner would need it for covering and warmth (Exodus 22:26-27). We are not to indulge in the perverse pleasure of allowing our neighbour we don't get on very well with, when we see him in some uncomfortable situation, to stew in his own juice a little longer before we give the help we know we can give, just to 'rub it in', or to 'give him a dose of his own medicine'. Nor do we hesitate to do good with the question, 'How much is this going to cost me?' James reminds us that to fail to do good when it is in our power to do so, is sin (James 4:17). As Charles Bridges so rightly observes on v. 27, 'Kindness is a matter not of option, but of obligation; an act of justice no less than of mercy.'

The saying goes, 'Tomorrow never comes.' Neighbours are not always welcome when they come knocking on the door (see 25:17)! Verse 28 presents two possibilities. One is that it presupposes someone coming to you for help in the hope and expectation that you may be able to do something to alleviate or relieve the situation. It is your neighbour who has taken the initiative. For what reasons might you put him off until 'tomorrow' (implying an indefinite period of time)? Are you a reluctant observer of the needs of others? Do you secretly hope the need will go away and so salve your conscience that you did not need to get involved after all? Perhaps you do not like your neighbour and do not wish to help him. Or it may be that you consider him to be a scrounger and not really needing what he has come to ask for, notwithstanding that his need is genuine. Maybe helping him is going to cause you personal inconvenience, and your own comfort is of greater importance than his present discomfort.

Another possibility of an altogether different nature presents itself from this verse, which is that you have borrowed something from your neighbour that he wants returned, and even needs back, but you keep hold of it with some excuse to make him think you cannot return it today, putting him off until 'tomorrow'. That would be an abuse of his generosity toward you.

Whatever the situation to which this applies, there is an element of selfishness in failing to do good on the one hand, or delaying to do it on the other.

Failing to do good (vv. 27-28) toward a neighbour is a mere step away from devising evil against him. Remember what Jesus said: 'Is it lawful on the Sabbath to do good *or to do evil?*' (Mark 3:4). The situation that gave rise to this question was the presence in the synagogue of a man with a withered hand. No one questioned the ability of Jesus to heal him. We might have argued that Jesus had the right to heal or the right not to heal. He was under no obligation to give attention to the man. Or was he? What did he say? 'Is it right to do good or to refrain from doing good?' 'Go away and come back tomorrow and I will heal you' (compare Luke 13:14)? His interpretation of the law was that to fail to meet his need *at once*, when it was within his power to do so, was to do evil.

So verse 29 of Proverbs 3 is of a piece with the verses that precede it. Withholding good from others is sometimes a means of preserving a kind of 'pecking order', of maintaining an inequality in which you are seen to be on top, superior, to be looked up to. Evil scheming and a contentious attitude (vv. 29-30) often serve the same ends, where one has an ego to preserve. Think of the help that Barnabas gave to Saul of Tarsus (Acts 9:26-27; 11:22-26), encouraging him, lifting him up and giving him opportunity for service, so that it was not long before Saul, or Paul, was occupying the limelight. Had Barnabas been thinking of his own prestige he might have reasoned: 'Now wait a minute, I've got to be careful here – if I give him too much opportunity he is going to usurp my position. I've got to make sure he appreciates I'm the one who had made all this possible for him. I must ensure I secure my dominance in this situation.'

There are many people in the world willing to help others so long as it secures their own ends. This is manipulative help, given for my own benefit as much as for the benefit of others. Or, if the truth be told, it would not be done for others if I did not benefit from it myself, for it is motivated by 'What's in it for me?' (which includes conscience salving!). It might have the appearance of 'doing good' to one's neighbour, but it is a far cry from what God commands his people. See Matthew 6:1-4.

Think about your 'neighbours', and consider their circumstances; and then, considering what God has given you, think about in what ways you might be an instrument of blessing to them.

The description 'control freak' is often heard these days. The Bible does not use such a term, but rather recognises the symptoms that may eventually manifest themselves in this extreme form. These verses of Proverbs actually identify a progression, where the withholding of good leads on to the manipulation of others, which eventually finds expression in outright oppression (v. 31). These negative qualities are much more prevalent in society than might at first sight be supposed. The reason there are not more 'control freaks' is probably that they have not been given the opportunity!

3:29-32. Oppression. Before we move on to a consideration of the oppressor, we need to observe something further about the 'neighbour' described in verses 27-29. If we assume we are considering here a neighbour who is in some ways in a disadvantaged situation, he or she is relying upon you for a measure of security. You are regarded as someone who can be relied upon in time of need. There is a tacit sense of trust (v. 29), the abuse of which is despicable. God often warned against the exploitation of the disadvantaged, writing into his law what our attitudes should be and stating that he himself would judge those guilty in this matter (see Deuteronomy 27:19), for he is a God who cares for the needy. Here are a few of the many scriptures which show this: Exodus 22:22-23; Leviticus 23:22; Deuteronomy 10:18; 14:29; 15:11; 24:17-22; Psalms 12:5; 68:5; 72:12; 146:9; Proverbs 19:17; 31:9; Isaiah 1:17; Jeremiah 22:3; Ezekiel 18:7; Zechariah 7:9-10; Malachi 3:5; James 1:27). Their very prevalence should indicate the seriousness with which the Lord regards oppression and the lack of proper regard for those in need. Sometimes it is easy to speak out against oppression and injustice in the world at large without seeing that it comes down to our own personal conduct within our families and our immediate neighbours and associates. God graciously gives us these commands for our own good as well as for the good of those who dwell securely with us.

There are those who take perverse pleasure in picking quarrels with others (v. 30). It is not that there is any real reason for contention, just that such people have a point to make, and to keep on making, about their ability, or strength, or prowess, and the only way they can do this is at the expense of others. Whatever I say, they are going to disagree with it. Whatever I do, they will find fault with it. Even if I bite my tongue and keep my counsel, they will still find fault. They will accuse me of causing offence, whatever I do or do not do, though I intend them no harm. Sadly, some of us will have met such people and know exactly the feeling of frustration they cause. Even more sadly, it happens in churches. Beware a contentious spirit! Beware the *cause* of a contentious spirit, which is a cold heart, a heart closed against the discomfort aroused by a sense of responsibility toward one's neighbour!

So what is there to envy in the oppressor (v. 31)? The NIV translates, 'violent man', but 'oppressor' probably captures the idea better, though undoubtedly violence is often a feature of oppression. Oppression is closer to the end in view, while violence is closer to the means of obtaining and securing that end. It is well known that there are techniques that can be used to one's material benefit which exploit others by taking advantage of their weaknesses or limitations and dependence. Involved are the intimidation and exploitation of others reinforced by thinly-veiled threats. The idea is that by keeping them in a state of dependence, by denying them the means to the freedom they might be striving after, those using them can enhance their own wealth. The threat, spoken or unspoken, hangs over those who are oppressed that things will be worse for them if they do not conform to the rules set them. It amounts to intimidation. The prospect of adding to one's wealth may be very appealing, but this verse warns against unscrupulous methods of doing so. Be careful whom you choose as your role model in life. There are all kinds of subtle variations of the principle of oppression, some of which have the appearance of being quite legitimate, but anything that ultimately violates the principles of vv. 27-28 is to be shunned. Do not let the appeal of riches, or power, or influence, close your mind to the abuse of the privileges or rights of others.

A perverse person (v. 32) is one who turns aside from what is good and right, abusing the goodness of God by rejecting the right use of what he has so generously provided for all to enjoy. If it would disgust you to see a gift you had made someone being used to harm others, how much more does it disgust the holy and just God to see his gifts so abused? If God turns away from such people, by contrast he turns toward those who are upright in heart and fear him, and there is this lovely statement here about his being intimate with them. See how God is always lifting up those who are dependent upon him and come to him. See how he is always good to them, generous toward them, open handed with them, working for their highest good! There are numerous references to the poor, the widow, the fatherless, and the foreigner (stranger, alien) and the many ways in which God expresses his care for those who are disadvantaged.

3:33-35. Grace and glory. What matters to you: your house, or your home? A deliberate distinction is made in v. 33. A house may comprise of people and possessions, but a home has the quality of intimacy and comfort and companionship and security. Those who are 'wicked', that is, who are morally bad, are under the curse of God. However well off they may be in the material sense, they cannot rightly be said to have a 'home'. Those whom God justifies have a home that is blessed. Even if you are alone as a believer in your natural family, yet there is the blessing of intimacy and security within the family of God's people. But very often, where the head of the natural family believes and is upright, blessing flows to its members. What is your relationship with those who live with you or near you? Is the blessing of the Lord upon you?

Verse 34 is quoted twice in the New Testament, in James 4:6 and 1 Peter 5:5, where the first clause is translated as 'God resists the proud.' God 'scorns the scornful' – that is, he deals with them according to their dealings with others.

As they look down on others, unjustly, so God looks down on them, justly. Their unrighteous subjection of others justifies God's righteous subjection of them to suffer according to the suffering they have caused. In quoting this verse James concentrates on the first clause, for the people he was addressing were in strife and needed humbling before they could appreciate and receive the grace offered. Peter, on the other hand, places the focus on the latter clause, for though he wanted his readers to be aware of the dangers of pride, his main emphasis was to encourage true humility of mind, in their relationships with others and in dependence upon God, knowing the sufficiency of his grace to see them through every circumstance. You will see in both passages how closely their arguments follow this section of Proverbs.

The section concludes in v. 35 with a wonderful promise towards those who are wise. Wisdom is not a passive grace, but very much an active one. We think of the oppressor plotting and scheming, but those who are wise do likewise, though in a very different sense! If you are wise, you will be actively engaged in promoting the qualities we read of here, for you will see that they are well worth working at. In every way wisdom is richly rewarded to those who love it and pursue it. We have already noted this in considering v. 13. But there is more, for God provides an inheritance for the wise. He always rewards those who love and obey him, for he delights in his people who follow his ways. Whether glory should be the *ambition* of any believer is debatable; rather, our ambition should be to live godly lives in this ungodly world. But surely glory is a wonderful *prospect* for those who struggle to keep themselves pure (1 Timothy 5:22c; 1 John 3:3) in the dingy environment of this life. All that they most earnestly desire will be granted them, and more beside! What a contrast this is with what happens to those who are foolish! In how different a sense will they be lifted up! They will be put on a pedestal of shame, for all will see that this is all they have been building all their lives.

4:1-9. The power of personal testimony. Being a recapitulation of what has gone before, much in this chapter provides the opportunity to restate and reinforce some of the essential points already covered. Here Solomon makes an appeal, and it is full of imperatives. This is the first time that he has specifically spoken of himself. Here he is giving testimony to his own experience. Personal testimony has so much more appeal than a lecture, even if the content is essentially the same. Little interest might be expressed in an advertised lecture on some major world event, but people would flock to hear someone who had been right there where it has taken place and been through it all. So Solomon, speaking of his own youth, makes what he has to say even more compelling. He has an affinity with his children that they can recognise. They can see he is passionate about this, that it comes from the heart, and that wonderfully reinforces what he has to urge upon them.

Now and again the writer slips into the plural, showing that the scope of his teaching is intended to cover all his 'children' in the widest sense (5:7; 7:24; 8:32). (Although translated 'sons' in the NIV, ESV, and generally used of such, the word can refer to offspring generally according to context – as for example in Genesis 3:16, or when referring to the 'children of Israel'. It is clear from the substance of these opening chapters of Proverbs that principally sons are being addressed with a view to the responsibilities they will be carrying in life. Nevertheless, much of the teaching is relevant to daughters, too. We have to consider what is gender specific, and what is inclusive of both.) For whatever other reason Solomon changes to the plural, at least it informs us that his teaching is not exclusive to any particular son. The teaching applies to all offspring of their father, but it is also to be applied to each one individually at the appropriate times in life. So although he says 'children', his mind is upon them individually rather than collectively, and he reverts very quickly back from the plural to the singular.

Quite likely we have here a son who is at that age when he is becoming more aware of the world around him, when he is on the verge of maturity, observing and asking questions about life and life issues. The time will come all too soon when he is 'on his own' so to speak, to take responsibility for his own life and to make his own decisions. The father has set before his son sound principles (v. 2), but now the time has come to urge upon him some imperatives (vv. 4-7) and to take a closer look at how things can turn out. Literally, to 'know' understanding (v. 1) indicates a level of understanding that extends to the perception of its significance and its application in practice. 'I understood all along what you were saying, but now I am beginning to see what it all means.' It is rather like understanding a piece of mathematical theory. I may know it inside out and be totally competent in repeating it and answering all sorts of theoretical questions about the mathematics. But my understanding will rise to a new and more significant level when I begin to appreciate the real life circumstances that gave rise to its development and then see its potential applications. This is what the father is aiming for in instructing his children where these spiritual issues are concerned. First he wants them to understand, and then he wants them to *know* they understand!

He is clearly a father who cares how his children develop and what happens to them in life, and he appeals to his children as a father (v. 1). Not to all people will the term 'father' have happy connotations: some will never have known a father, and others who have known one would rather they had not. The father who addresses his children in the book of Proverbs is one who loves them, cares for them, takes responsibility in his leadership in the home and accordingly instructs them in the way they should take. Filial affection and respect on the part of the children are assumed, as they will be in every God-fearing family.

Now let us see why. First of all, this father is not passing on simply the benefit of his own knowledge or teaching that he invented. Yes, it is 'his law' (v. 2b), or 'his teaching' (the word *torah* is used) insofar as he has taken it on board and made it his and owns it; and it is 'good doctrine' (v. 2a). But it did not originate from him. As far as his own recollections were concerned, it came from his own father (vv. 3-4). Probably his father would have said the same thing about the instruction he himself had received. Ultimately, this teaching, as with every good and perfect gift, is from above, coming down from the Father of lights (James 1:17). When Solomon says, 'Do not forsake my law', he does not intend us therefore to understand that it was invented by him.

Any father who tells his children to obey his instructions does not need to spell out every time where he got them from. There are times when it may be necessary, but on the whole it should be understood in a well-regulated and godly home that the principles of God's Word are being followed. Solomon gives us this insight into his own upbringing, that David his father urged upon him the imperative of wisdom and understanding. Of course there were times when David got it wrong and made a mess of things. His judgement was not always sound, and sometimes he went astray. In the light of this it may well be that Solomon, growing up in turbulent times in the life of his father David, could see even more clearly the importance of what his father was impressing upon him. His mother's teaching during his tender years was reinforced by his father's instruction. 'Get wisdom! Get understanding! ... Wisdom is the principal thing; therefore get wisdom, and in all your getting, get understanding' (vv. 5,7). Is it altogether surprising, therefore, when he was installed upon the throne and the Lord appeared to him in a dream and offered him what he should give him, that Solomon should ask for wisdom (1 Kings 3:5-9)?

If the first thing for the son to know is that the teaching did not originate from the father (vv. 3-4), the second is that its fruit is observable in the father. The wisdom of Solomon is proverbial. No one could question the benefits of wisdom in his own life. A son will respect a father's teaching when what he is teaching is evident in his own life.

Perhaps, though, someone reading this is not in that happy position. You find it difficult to instruct your children in this way because you never had such instruction from your own father, and your own life has been singularly lacking in wisdom. Take heart! You have a heavenly Father who now urges these same things upon you, and you have the right to urge them upon your own children, even though your life has been spoilt through ignorance or neglect of them. All those benefits into which you have lately come, through the love of your heavenly Father who has saved you and adopted you into his family, you may press upon your children to seek after. What they cannot see in the life you have wasted prior to your conversion they may observe now in the riches of the grace of God toward you. 'My son, my father never taught me these things and look how I suffered as a result. But now I have a Father in heaven who loves me and has taught me the right way to go, and has made such a difference in my life that I can now tell you that it is the right way for you to go, too. If you want to live (v. 4) in a way that I never knew at your age, then hear me now!'

4:6. Protection. Why is wisdom always personified as 'she' (v. 6)? And why are the womenfolk apparently left out of these instructions? The answer to the first question may be twofold. Firstly, there are qualities about one's relationship to wisdom that are paralleled in a man's relationship to a worthy wife. Secondly, the role of a wife is to be that of 'helper' (Genesis 2:18-23), and a wife who fulfils her role in her relationship with her husband is of inestimable value to him, to be cherished at all times. Wisdom is in some ways like that 'helper', bringing honour to a man.

There may also be a third reason, because wisdom is compared to folly who is likened to a morally loose woman. Just as wisdom will bring honour to those who embrace her (v. 8), so shame and disgrace fall upon those who embrace a harlot (2:18-19; 7:26-27). All these interrelationships complement and reinforce each other. Many a man's wisdom is attributable to the part played by a good wife. So the importance of wisdom devolves upon women too, which addresses the second question! While Solomon is specifically instructing his sons, daughters listening in will soon understand there is a role for them too in all this.

The pyracantha, or firethorn, may be an attractive shrub found in many gardens, but don't try handling it! Its vicious thorns provide a dense and very effective deterrent against would-be intruders, and so safe protection for those guarded by it. This is something of the idea of the protection offered by wisdom (v. 6). It is very important we should notice that protection is required in this life. Many young people grow up very self-assured, imagining they are in full control of their lives and can cope with any eventuality. It is not so. You have only to look at the middle-aged and consider what has happened in their lives to realise that! Life is absolutely full of pitfalls. There are troubles without number that are potential threats to those growing up. Parents are often anxious for their children, green and inexperienced, wondering how they will make out in life, whether they will sink or swim. However, they cannot run their children's lives for them. There comes a time when they have to loosen the reins. Children need a better protection than what their parents can offer, which is the very reason why Solomon instructs his children as he does. A wise son, inexperienced though he may be, who fears God and looks to him for protection and guidance, will not be disappointed in his expectations and will not be ensnared by temptation. Though human parents have influence over their children only for a time, they may entrust them to a heavenly Father who will care for them for time and eternity.

Furthermore, wisdom in a young man is, like the pyracantha, a powerful protector against 'friends' of the dubious kind who look out only for their own interests. Those who go about in crowds, who are out to have a good time and who have few scruples about how they will do it, will keep clear of those showing more sense who act on principle and exercise sound judgement. In other words, their wisdom will repel intrusions that would cause only harm. Those set upon by youths in our lawless society are invariably the lonely and vulnerable. If you are out in a dark place all alone and encounter a crowd of youngsters spoiling for a fight, you have cause to fear. How different the situation if you are in the company of someone who is obviously powerfully equipped and well able singlehandedly to deal with such thuggery. You know they wouldn't dare come near you! 'Do not forsake her, and she will preserve you.' If you leave wisdom behind, you make yourself a target for trouble – indeed, you positively invite it. Keep wisdom as your constant companion, and you are unlikely even to be approached by many temptations.

If you are a young person who trusts the Lord and find yourself isolated from peers on account of having godly principles, do not take it hard, but thank God for it. Those who avoid your company, who exclude you from their activities and leave you out of their invitations, are the kind of people whose companionship would not do you any good. Do not think of it as a mark of your exclusion, but of God's protection. Be patient, and he will reward you with far better company and an infinitely more fulfilled life. Seek out instead those who value what you value, and do not envy those whose pleasures are gaudy, short-lived and illusory.

This is one side to the protection offered by wisdom, that those who lack it tend to steer clear of those who love it. It acts like a spiritual insect repellent against parasitic individuals. The other side is how the application of spiritual understanding is always a protection against going astray, providing light for direction in dark and uncertain situations where one might otherwise miss the way or fall foul of obstacles. Those who really love wisdom will hold her close (3:18), and she will be a counsellor to whisper in the ear what is pertinent to any situation. If one side of the protection comes from how others perceive wisdom in you, the other side comes from how you are guided by wisdom. Wisdom will enable you to keep your head when others lose theirs and panic; wisdom will enable you to make the right decisions to clear your way in difficult situations; wisdom will open doors for you that are tight shut against others.

Little wonder, then, that the imperative is given (v. 7): 'Wisdom is the principal thing; therefore get wisdom, and in all your getting, get understanding'!

4:8-9. Promotion. Having spoken of *protection*, we now come to *promotion*. Many a young person never reaches this stage. They have been eliminated, as it were, in the preliminary rounds. They have failed the initial tests. They have excluded themselves from any possibility of promotion. They are the drop-outs of society who never heard or never recognised wise counsel, whose lives are a sorrow and a burden to others. Or if they survive, they are disillusioned with life, disappointed in how their starry-eyed expectations evaporated before their eyes. Their disappointment is as deep as their ill-founded hopes were high. Many, many people of middle age find themselves empty and unfulfilled; many have left a trail of destruction in their wake of broken relationships, bitter regrets, shameful actions, and so on. Even among those who have not, many go through the motions of life without really understanding its purpose, and lacking any real hope for the future. An observant young person might wonder, 'Will it turn out like this for me?' Well, that all depends, and it all depends on whether or not you are willing to receive and act upon the counsel given throughout the book of Proverbs.

Aspirations to glory are embedded in the hearts of so many young people. Some – very, very few – find it fulfilled in academic, sporting, or other achievements in which they attain a measure of fame; and even for them it is often of a temporary nature, to be eclipsed by someone else or something else. In the Roman games what was awarded for victors in the races was a laurel wreath. It was essentially a fading crown. The euphoria associated with such an achievement is temporary. It will not last all that long. Soon it will be a fond memory – appreciated, yes, but nevertheless of no present substance. This is not in any way to disparage some of the amazing achievements of men and women down the ages. They have their place and value and in cases beyond number they have been of enormous benefit to others. Neither is it wrong to aspire to achieve great things. However, the *principal* thing is wisdom! Recognise that, act upon it ('exalt her'), and she will promote you. Her reward is to bring you honour – not of a kind that may the next day be snatched from you by someone whose achievements put yours in the shade, but of a kind that is completely different from that of comparison with others, of a kind that is lasting and secure, having a beauty that does not fade with age, and a value that does not depreciate with the passage of time. This is not a trophy that is awarded for a year to be passed on to someone else the next time the competition comes around, for there is no competitive element in it whatsoever. Honour in the world is often seen in relation to other people, and not infrequently can be supplanted by others. The honour that wisdom promotes is of a completely different order. The ornament of grace and crown of glory are its features. Grace is what wisdom works in us, and glory is what wisdom provides for us.

We have encountered the ornament of grace twice already, at 1:9 and 3:22. It is undoubtedly true that the majority of young people growing up are concerned about their appearance. There are situations in which they want to look their best. Rather paradoxically, often they want both to blend in with others and to stand out among them and be noticed. The Word of God does not ignore this need or disparage it. While Solomon clearly uses imagery in this description, it is more than that. For the quality of character that spiritual wisdom produces in a young person is far more striking than mere physical appearance. It wonderfully enhances natural beauty. Lack of wisdom, on the other hand, disgraces it, as Proverbs 11:22 so pithily says! Both Paul and Peter mention the adornment of women, in 1 Timothy 2:9-10 and 1 Peter 3:1-6 respectively. Peter's comment arises out of the need for winsomeness in the context of a very difficult situation, and he points out that if anything is to win a man over it will be beauty of character. Neither is suggesting that attention is not to be given to outward appearance. They are simply pointing out that one takes priority over the other. True beauty will be seen in the godly character of a woman modestly arrayed where there is no need for pretentiousness!

Grace and glory are close associates. For both men and women, wisdom gained will serve to produce in their lives a bearing of conduct that will be recognised in the society in which they move. It will open the right doors to them and keep the others fast shut. It will direct them into beneficial relationships, guarding them from harmful ones. It will lead them into positions of recognition and respect in which they will be able to use their influence to promote what is good. It holds promise for the whole of life and not just the next few years. Indeed, it does more than that, for an imperishable crown, the crown of glory and of righteousness, is what its followers may look forward to at the end of this earthly life (1 Corinthians 9:25; 2 Timothy 4:8; Hebrews, 2:7,9; 1 Peter 5:4).

4:10-13. Staying the course. Though at first sight this appears to be a recapitulation of what has already been said at 3:1-2,21-23,18, it is more than mere repetition. Solomon keeps on coming back to his main theme, viewing the matter from different angles, giving different perspectives on it. The emphasis at 3:1 was on his son keeping the law in his heart and applying himself to mercy and truth, while at 3:21 it was on his keeping wisdom and discretion in view throughout his life. The emphasis here, though, is on the way wisdom will help give him a clear course through life.

Mercy and truth (3:3) are not easy to maintain in this world, and often involve personal cost. Discretion (3:21) requires close attention to the circumstances of others and thoughtfulness of their welfare before one's own. So here (4:13), instruction involves disciplined study. The writer clearly infers this it is not easy; it is far easier to slacken hold. However, instruction is a 'must have' for a wise Christian! So if you are feeling indifferent about any of these graces or qualities and what is required to develop them, look again carefully at the tremendous encouragements, incentives or promises, attached to each, and think again! If you are a parent, seeking to encourage your offspring in these graces, do they see from your instruction and example the value of what you are teaching them?

For many people, life is a discouraging obstacle course and they cannot see their way through it. Difficulties loom into view that they cannot get round, and things crop up that cause them to fall flat on their faces. Their life is like a path that looks good and promising at the beginning, but which before long narrows down and changes direction, becoming muddy and encroached upon by increasingly dense undergrowth, eventually disappearing and leaving them disorientated and distressed (v. 12a). Or it is like a runner enthusiastically and energetically setting out on a race that proves to be far tougher than he envisaged, suffering the embarrassment of his legs giving out from sheer fatigue well before he has finished the course (v. 12b). Whichever way it is, there is no easy track through life. What Solomon is promising is not that all the problems will miraculously disappear, which they never will in this life, but that wisdom will give the insight and foresight to see the way through and give the strength to pursue it. All this presupposes 'his son' being on the right way to begin with.

Many is the time a walker has mistaken the way, got lost, and had to backtrack to where he went wrong, either through a lack of signposts or through a failure to see them. Wisdom leads us in right paths (v. 11). We have already noticed many of the signposts to help us ascertain whether we are travelling them. The words of wisdom are rather like a map or a manual constantly to be consulted as we make our way forward. They help us to recognise the features on the landscape of life as they come into view, and understand what they represent. Wisdom is to life what a map is to a traveller in unfamiliar territory.

4:14-19. Psalm 1. Two paths. This is more about paths, involving a sharp contrast between the path of the wicked, and that of the just (vv. 14,18). There is a commonly held view that in order to be able to influence people for good you have to go along with them, do the things they do, and be as like them as you can. This is a gross distortion of the truth, and those who hold it, one suspects, do so because they think that by separation they may be missing out on something they would really enjoy were they not Christians!

For the young person, inexperienced in the ways of life, the question arises, just how far can he or she go along with others who have very different attitudes and moral standards? This takes all sorts of practical forms, for example attending parties where drugs may possibly be being passed around, where people may be 'letting down their hair' and engaging in practices that are immoral according to biblical standards. Or it may be in some very attractive moneymaking scheme the method of which is highly dubious when examined carefully. There are all sorts of enticements that make their initial appeal to the physical and emotional senses, to draw one in. 'It's all right, don't worry about it. There's no harm in it.' That is usually a cover for, 'Don't think too much about the implications.' However, God's Word shows us what is the right way to go in life and inculcates sound principles, and those who take them on board are taught to consider the consequences of their actions. We saw this before when we were looking at 1:10-19. All sorts of offers come our way, each with its own appeal. Any that conceal things that will prove a hindrance to living a godly life are to be shunned.

Solomon is unequivocal about association with those whom he describes as 'the wicked' and their 'way of evil', and so we must be clear about whom he is describing. The trouble is, we are unaccustomed to calling 'wicked' those whom the Bible describes as such. Those who are morally unprincipled, defined by the standards of the Ten Commandments, are wicked in God's estimation, and their practices are 'evil'. Some of them we may tend to think of as 'nice' people in spite of their views. There may be much about them that is likeable. But let us not for a moment imagine that this in any way casts doubt upon what God says of them. Before becoming a Christian I for one was regarded by many as an intelligent and respectable individual and was well liked on the whole. But God changed all that! He exposed the wickedness of my own sinful nature, saved me, and set me upon the right path. This brought me into conflict with some of my former friends, and brought me into friendship with some who formerly would have treated me with caution! Let us be clear that Solomon is not saying we should have no dealings with wicked people such as I used to be, or not associate with them (compare 1 Corinthians 5:9-10). What he is saying is that we should not enter their *path*. We are not to envy them, we are not to be enticed by any of the sinful pleasures they enjoy or the schemes they plan. We are not to enter it, we are not to walk along it or travel along it with them, we are to avoid it and turn away from it (vv. 14-15).

What could be clearer? In other words, our association with ungodly people should be absolutely clear-cut. We call the tune, not they. We set the standards, not they. We show them friendship which may be established upon our terms, not theirs. They may come our way, but we most certainly will not go theirs. What they have to offer may at times make its appeal to the flesh, but we have crucified the flesh with its sinful passions (Galatians 5:17,24). We are the ones who have our eyes open, theirs are still fast shut. We do them no favours by capitulating in the least to their demands, however they sweeten them. When v. 15 says we are to turn away and pass on, this is suggestive of making our escape. It will be far easier to turn away when we take a long-term view of where it will all lead, and it will likewise be far easier to pass on when we know we have other things that are altogether more profitable. If what they stand for and work for is to succeed, it will invariably result in harm to others. Their schemes are their food and drink; they know of no other kind of sustenance. It robs them of sleep to think their ways might be thwarted.

Wickedness and violence may seem to us to be excessively strong words for the kind of unbelievers most of us know. We must not, however, be deceived by the outward appearance, for God looks upon the heart, and this is his judgement, not ours. The wickedness and violence all around us that we recognise in society and which we deplore are in the main perpetrated by these very kinds of people. The sad truth, though, is that, if they are given their way, society will degenerate into a moral morass and all manner of destructive trends.

Now what of the other path? If we are not to enter the path of the wicked, the implication is that there is another path we should be walking on through life, the 'right path' of v. 12. This is the path of the 'just', or 'righteous', referring to everything the wicked are not. Those whom God accounts as righteous are those whom *he* has justified. The credit for any man or woman loving the commands of God is entirely God's. Knowing this path, seeing this path, and walking this path are solely attributable to the God who has told us about it, shown it to us, and placed us upon it. It is described by a wonderful picture of the dawning and development of a glorious day (v. 18). From the first light of dawn the way of the believer is attended with a light from heaven that grows ever brighter and clearer as the day of life progresses to its conclusion, or, we should say, its consummation in glory.

Solomon rounds off this section (v. 19) with the utter contrast of the darkness that is at every point attendant upon the way of the wicked. Should we then envy those who grope their way in life in spiritual darkness (v. 19), falling foul of all sorts of problems, yet still unable to see what the problems really are or know to what end they are heading? Far from envying what they seem to have, we should pity the terrible fundamental condition in which they live their lives and the conclusion to which it leads. If we really are concerned about their way and their end without Christ, then dalliance with them (which is what v. 14 is really all about) is the last thing we will want to indulge. Not only will it do us no favours, but it will obscure any light we might give them to show them the right way, thereby encouraging them in their ignorance. For that we will be held accountable at the last day.

4:20-23. Luke 6:43-45. Our heart. Each time Solomon addresses his son, he varies the words he uses. In respect of God's Word, he refers to instruction, law, commands, doctrine, reproof, sayings, words, and so on, indicating the broad scope in the way the Word speaks to us. In this respect it is similar to Psalm 119. In respect of how his son is to receive it, he says, 'hear', 'receive', 'keep', 'do not forget', do not despise', 'let them not depart', 'give attention', and so on. This is more than a didactic device. It is a demonstration that God's Word touches us at all points of our life and experience and that we are to respond to it at every level of our being: whatever our circumstances, whatever our activity, whatever our mood, whatever our thoughts and plans, the Word of God has a bearing on them all.

What Solomon said at 3:21 in connection with wisdom and discretion he now says at 4:21 in connection with his counsel in general. What is translated 'words' and 'sayings' (v. 20) is very broad in its scope. Solomon is passing on the breadth of his wisdom to his son, and it reminds us that God's Word is given in its entirety for our learning (Romans 15:4). The more selective we are in the reading of it the scrawnier spiritually we will be! For that is what he is indicating by implication in v. 22 in referring to 'life' and 'health'. There is a twofold aspect to this, 'life' indicating vigour and strength from the building effect of sound doctrine, and 'health' the curative and restorative effect of its teaching. There must be the 'pure milk of the word' for growth (1 Peter 2:2), and there must also be its influence for 'reproof and correction' (2 Timothy 3:16).

The reason for this counsel not departing from our eyes is that it should stay in our heart. One of the sad features about some people who have been knowledgeable in the Scriptures is that they have left off attending to them and gone astray. The purpose of reading God's Word with our eyes must be that we are seeking to store it up in our hearts for it to do its work there and have its outworking in our lives. It is not enough to say, 'Been there, done that.' We have to keep coming back again and again to the Word of God. To take up once more the analogy of music, one may come back to a piece of good music from time to time and find it not only just as satisfying as at first, but more so as its structure and form are better understood and appreciated (whether consciously or subconsciously). When we come back again and again to the Word of God we discover things we did not see at first, because last time we were not in a position to see them, whether through limited knowledge or limited experience. Our understanding of God, of ourselves, of the world in which we live, grows, and with it our ability to function in accordance with his will in these three areas.

What Solomon says here of the heart, that 'out of it spring the issues of life' (v. 23), Jesus took up when he said, 'Those things which proceed out of the mouth come from the heart, and they defile a man. For out of the heart proceed evil thoughts, murders, adulteries, fornications, thefts, false witness, blasphemies' (Matthew 15:18-19); 'Out of the abundance of the heart the mouth speaks. A good man out of the good treasure in his heart brings forth good things, and an evil man out of the evil treasure brings forth evil things' (Matthew 12:34-35). It is all a matter of what we have *in* our hearts, what we *are* at heart, and what we have a heart *for*. Every Christian knows what he or she was before being saved by the Lord. Repentance and faith involve a change of heart and a change of direction. The Holy Spirit uses the Word of God to outwork this fundamental spiritual change. Repentance involves a turn-around, but having turned we need to make progress in this new direction, and for this we need instruction. An appetite for spiritual instruction is an evidence of the work of the Spirit. We need to be sitting on the edge of our seats with rapt attention under the instruction of the Spirit; we need to be bending our ear (v. 20) to catch every last word lest we miss something important; we need to treasure it all up in our hearts (v. 21) because this is our life (v. 22). God's Word is to have the central place in our intellect, emotions, and will.

If we have such treasure in our hearts, it follows that we need to keep it where it is and not allow it to be plundered! We are exhorted not only to keep his Word in our heart (v. 21), but also to keep our heart in his Word (v. 23). What we know, we are to do. We all know about those 'unguarded moments' when we say or do things of which we are afterwards ashamed. We are 'caught off guard' when we are guilty of 'knee-jerk' reactions. In some ways that is the more straightforward of two problems the believer faces. The other one concerns those times when we are confused by enemy tactics, fail to realise what is going on and become spiritually disorientated. This is when we can 'drop our guard', and it usually results in our compromising ourselves in a way that we later come to regret. Our hearts need to be kept against direct, sudden attack and also against the subtle, subversive approach. The way to deal with both is always to relate our thoughts and actions to the guiding principle of God's Word. If Satan can't shoot us down, he will try to draw us off, but either way his objective is the same: to gain control of our heart and wreak havoc there.

4:24-27. James 3:1-12. A purposeful focus.

Our words. The advice given in these verses is clear and straightforward. It is about the focus of our words and ways. Each of vv. 24-27 has two clauses, the second reinforcing the first, so that the whole is emphatic. The way of wisdom is to redouble our efforts in these directions, and the need to do so is because by nature we are unaccustomed to it. While it is true that we need the grace of God working in our hearts for us to begin to do them, it is also true that he requires us to work hard at these things ourselves, or he would not have so commanded us.

There is no place for a slipshod attitude to growth in grace. There is great danger in carelessness. These verses are saying, be doubly careful in your words, and be doubly careful in your ways. Note the order. It may not have been the order we would have chosen. Remember what James reminds us of about the tongue (James 3:1-12). The tongue is the last thing that can be tamed, or brought into subjection, and so it is the first thing requiring our attention. The tongue is the vent for the fire in the heart, and it is when we think about the things we say that we realise the problem is a deep seated one. The advice is twofold. First, we are to 'put away' a deceitful mouth. That is, we are to resolve to have nothing to do with it and simply to decline from uttering anything that is less than the simple truth. Secondly, we are to distance ourselves from perverse speech.

There are a great many ways in which our speech can be perverse, or corrupt, or deceitful, or whatever word one wishes to use of it. Apart from the downright lie, one may economical with the truth, which involves putting things in such a way as to keep something covered up that one doesn't want out in the open. There are various forms of exaggeration and other kinds of distortion that are intended to enhance what is being described, or maybe to put on something the kind of slant that we intend. This is a sort of caricature of the truth. Someone may have a rather distinctive and prominent nose, and the artist cleverly exploits this feature to make it, and therefore its owner, instantly recognisable. People do this with words, so that a description of minor character traits can be so enlarged and distorted as to give entirely the wrong impression about the person concerned. In its extreme form it can be a kind of character assassination. Even the plain and simple truth can be told with a deceitful mouth by deliberately saying things in a context in which we know they may be misinterpreted or can only do harm. Gossip can fall into this category. Again, perverse lips can on occasion speak volumes by being kept tight shut. What we say or refrain from saying comes down to a matter of motive. However, it is not as simple as that, for some people are so accustomed to all forms of deceitful speech that it seems to pour out of them naturally. It may not be too serious, it may not even be malicious, but it springs from a kind of self-centredness that has never been examined and dealt with. In fact, most if not all of the kind of speech described in these verses is basically self-centred, and is concerned with the impression we wish to give from motives that are essentially our own. A deceitful mouth is also found in those who say one thing and do another.

We are not casually to give people our word and then fail to fulfil what we said or forget all about it, or even to say we were not being serious. Our word should be our bond, to be relied upon by those who receive it. In the sermon on the mount not only did Jesus commend straightforwardness and truthfulness in speech, he indicated where anything beyond it originates (Matthew 5:37). Again, perverse lips speak things that are not in accordance with Scripture. Promulgating one's own pet theories or ideas may fall into this category. The Word of God is the ultimate reference for truth. Once more, flattery is a form of deceitful speech because what is said, however true it may be (and often it is not), is designed to secure some selfish end. Much is said in the New Testament letters about what comes out of our mouths, covering a wide range of situations. Some of these are: Romans 16:18; 1 Corinthians 2:4,13; Ephesians 4:15,25,29,31; 5:4,6,19; Colossians 2:4; 3:8; 4:6; 1 Thessalonians 2:5; 1 Timothy 4:2; 5:13; 6:3-4; Titus 1:10; 2:8; 3:2; 1 Peter 2:1; 3:10; 4:11; 2 Peter 2:3,18; 3 John 10; Jude 8,16; Revelation 13:5.

Because these things are so, there is great need for us to examine our speech, and for every failing in this area to seek to cultivate the opposite quality. It is truly a matter of training and practice. If God commands it, should we not make the effort? Of the above passages, perhaps Colossians 4:6 is central: 'Let your speech always be with grace, seasoned with salt, that you may know how you ought to answer each one' — gracious, clean and cleansing, and appropriate to the situation. That is what should *always* proceed from our lips.

Our walk. What has been briefly stated about our words takes a long time and strenuous effort to work out in practice. Solomon now moves on from our words to our ways. This could perhaps be summarised as 'Look where you're going!' This imperative is usually made too late, when someone has already stumbled over something! Our walk, or our way, can be considered from two angles, the first being to look at the ultimate objective, and the second to look at how we are going to get there. This seems to be in keeping with the import of the verses.

It is particularly easy for young people to be bewildered by a great variety of choices in life. 'Which way do I go?' 'What choices should I make?' It greatly simplifies matters if one is singleminded about achieving a particular goal. Those who are not singleminded often fail to achieve what they might because they are distracted by all sorts of side interests along the way, and in the end they are disappointed in their expectations.

The advice of v. 25 is to be focused on the ultimate objectives of the kind that matter. Jesus said that the man who puts his hand to the plough and looks back is not worthy of the kingdom of God (Luke 9:62). He cannot steer a straight furrow ahead if he is looking over his shoulder at what he has left behind. He also warned on another occasion of the dangers of looking back, reminding us of Lot's wife (Luke 17:32). For the Christian, the danger may not be so much in looking back as in looking sideways! If we were to examine the ways by which some reach their destination we might suppose there were some drunken drivers on the road to heaven! What we need in the centre of our vision is, in a word, 'glory'. The writer of Hebrews takes up this idea in chapter 12, using a different illustration but making a similar point. Jesus, seated at his Father's right hand in glory, is the one upon whom our whole attention is to be focused in life.

The world is like a lively marketplace. But we are not here to do shopping, and this is no time to be sauntering through examining its wares. We are on our way to our heavenly destination. Glory is ahead of us, and glory awaits us. What has this world to offer by comparison? David was looking where he was going when he wrote: 'You will show me the path of life; in your presence is fullness of joy; at your right hand are pleasures forevermore' (Psalm 16:11).

The fact is that distractions along the way, when we allow our attention to wander from this glorious objective, do us no good. Often they give the appearance of providing satisfaction, of giving pleasure, of being good for us, but all they do is to impede our progress and leave us unfulfilled. These are the 'passing pleasures of sin' (Hebrews 11:25) that waste us. Moses, of whom this was said, 'had it made' for him in Egypt. So what kept him from lingering there? The writer gives us two reasons: he looked to the reward, and he endured as seeing him who is invisible (Hebrews 11:26,27). To prevent sideways vision and keep a horse's attention on the road ahead, its bridle would be fitted with leather side-pieces called blinkers. It is from that we get the expression of someone being 'blinkered', and it is usually used in a derogatory sense. People may well have described Moses as being blinkered, and the same may have been said of many of the great men and women of God. The truth is, though, that they were *focused*, not blinkered. They were well enough aware of all around them; it is just that what they had in the centre of their vision was of such surpassing worth that they had neither time to waste on, or appetite for, these other things. They were happy to use anything and everything legitimate in the pursuit of their objective, but nothing that might draw them off.

The other sense in which they were looking where they were going was in giving attention to how they were going to get there. 'Ponder the path of your feet, and let all your ways be established' (NKJV); 'Make level paths for your feet and take only ways that are firm' (NIV). The meaning of the original has to do with preparation. Few of us in our journeyings haven't seen road building in progress. All the big machinery is designed to excavate the ridges, fill the hollows, compact the surface, smooth out the rough patches, and create a durable, even surface for efficient travel. If we as Christians are to make good progress in our Christian lives, it is important that we give attention to where we are going and to remove obstacles in our way. This is the step by step element to our reaching our destination. Mountaineers in difficult terrain have no doubt about what they wish to achieve. They want to conquer the mountain and stand at the top. The summit is in their field of vision, and even when it is not so physically, it is mentally. Every move they make is toward attaining that objective as efficiently as possible, in the knowledge that any false move may deprive them of their goal. So every step is important, every step has to be tested to take the climber's weight securely, and every section has to be planned meticulously to ensure that there is a viable continuation of the route, avoiding all unnecessary risks. For the Christian, attention to detail is important in the consciousness that there are dangers along the way to be avoided. The prize is too valuable for us to be foolhardy about our progress along the way. Our map and guide is the Word of God, which is a lamp for our feet and a light for our path (Psalm 119:105). At all times it shows us both where we are standing and the right way to proceed, and to deviate from its instruction is to 'turn to the right or the left' with its attendant consequences for evil (v. 27). Mature Christians who have stood upright in life are those who have heeded this instruction. Others have had injurious falls with their crippling consequences.

5:1-6 Seduction. We have already been warned about the seductress at 2:16-19. Nor is this the last time we will hear of her, for Solomon takes up this matter again in chapter 7. Part of effective teaching is repetition. Just as variations on a theme give colour and richness to a piece of music, so repetition with variation reinforces teaching without its losing its edge, making it that much more memorable. Why make so much of this matter of immorality, though?

It is a sad feature of modern western society that the very notion of morality in connection with sexual relationships seems to have been relegated to a former age and deemed irrelevant. God, to whom we must all give account, declares otherwise. Need it be said that for many young men the opportunity for – and even nowadays the encouragement to – sexual promiscuity can be a very potent temptation? It plays upon powerful God-given emotions and capabilities, though in a perverse fashion to direct them contrary to his appointed way. In some circles people talk (casually) about 'casual sex'. The warning God's Word gives us is that there is nothing casual about it.

Hedonism is the principle that the highest good there can be is in the pursuit of pleasure, and it resists attempts to curb its activity. The pursuit of pleasure in a way that is contrary to God's commands is not only sinful, it is injurious, so that the consequences are both temporal and eternal. Paul warns that a man who commits sexual immorality sins against his own body (1 Corinthians 6:18). Quite apart from the danger of sexually transmitted diseases, tremendous psychological and emotional damage can be done by indulgence in sexual immorality, with far-reaching consequences affecting proper relationships with others in the normal course of events, as well as with one's marriage partner (even if the immorality is before marriage). All these points come out in one way and another in the narrative.

So Solomon introduces this subject again with an exhortation to listen carefully to what he has to say. This is not a matter to be allowed to go over the heads of his hearers. If you happen to overhear people nearby talking about you, then more than likely you prick up your ears and stretch them out to catch what is being said! For whether it is good or bad, you find there is an inner urge to know what it is all about. This is how, says Solomon, you are to give attention to him about the things of which he speaks (v. 1b). You need to have your wits about you in dealing with these temptations; you need to be canny and cunning if you are to overcome them. For the 'discretion' of which he speaks is not a passive quality, but very much an active one. It is both discerning and 'proactive' and not fooled by the outward appearance of things.

To get the force of v. 2 consider those who do the opposite and 'throw discretion to the wind'. That is, they act on impulse, against better judgement. Many have done this in the area of their sexuality, and it is precisely this the writer is warning against.

Now for the content of the warning. First of all, he indicates the power of the temptation. It is very simply stated (v. 3). 'The lips of an immoral woman drip honey, and her mouth is smoother than oil.' The picture is descriptive enough without requiring any explanation. She positively oozes her enticing charm, appealing powerfully to the full range of a man's natural desires toward women. It is not purely sexual, but is invariably complicated by a whole host of psychological aspects. However, it is essentially predatory, and the sweet, smooth words and appealing manner are really diversionary tactics to confuse the senses and mask the real issues. The reality of the situation could not be further from its appearance. The similes of v. 4 are at the other end of the spectrum from those of v. 3: bitter wormwood for sweet honey, a cutting sword for soothing oil. The influence of an immoral woman is like a poison, doubly dangerous because it is exquisitely enjoyable to the palate before it does its sinister work in destroying the body. The oil smooths and softens the flesh for the more effective entry of the blade. To become involved with an immoral woman is a soul destroying occupation (v. 5) with both short and long term consequences. Though verse 6 is not quite straightforward to translate, whether Solomon is warning his son or just describing the woman, the point is the same. Such a woman is totally adrift; her life has neither purpose nor meaning. No sense can be made of it because there is no sense to it.

5:7-14. Steer clear or become ensnared. Young people are sometimes given to overconfidence. Pride in their ability to cope with dangerous situations has brought many into trouble. Some even relish the challenge to do something foolhardy. One of the difficulties in dealing with such people is to get them sufficiently to understand the dangers to take them seriously. Many a parent on a cliff-top walk has said to a child, 'Keep away from the edge!' That has provoked many a child to dare the parent by trespassing as close as possible to the forbidden edge. As far as Solomon is concerned, immorality is a precipice to be avoided. He does not wish his children to go over the edge, and so he warns, 'Keep away!', and tells them what lies beyond. To change the image, the attractions of immorality are like a magnet. The closer you get to the temptation, the more powerful it becomes, until at last you are captured by it. Knowing that, the only safe course is to keep clear of its field of influence. This is what v. 8 is all about. When you begin to feel the tug toward compromise, that's the time to exert your strength to distance yourself from it.

He now examines a range of consequences of succumbing. To become enmeshed in immorality is to replace an honourable reputation with a dishonourable one, it is to sacrifice all that is noble and virtuous to what is shabby and shameful; it strips the glory from a man and robs him of his dignity; he loses the respect of others as well as his own self-respect. It brings him into bondage (v. 9). The beneficiaries of his indiscretion are those on whom he has squandered his passions (v. 10). As if to a blackmailer, he is always paying out, paying out, and receiving nothing in return. His resources are mercilessly squeezed out of him until he has nothing left (v. 11a). At the end nothing remains but bitter, vacuous regrets (vv. 12-13). 'Headstrong' is probably the best word to describe this man, who far too late acknowledges that he had scorned all the privileges and benefits that were his by throwing over every form of instruction, advice, command and warning. This self-recrimination, however, comes long after the damage has been done. 'Look where it has brought me!' he says at last (v. 14) as he views the wreck of a life that might have been well spent but instead ended in physical and spiritual bankruptcy. His conduct has eaten away at his life so that ultimately all that remains is a mere shell. The end of v. 14 is telling, reminding us among other things that immorality, however secretly conducted, is not a private thing and cannot be hidden away. It inevitably has a public face to it.

Its result is to bring one as near as one can get to total ruin (v. 14), which is a very sorry state to be in. For the Israelite, the community played a far more important part than we in our rather individualistic society may realise. Even in our churches we do not always have that sense of community that we ought. This man's predicament has the greater poignancy on account of the contrast between himself and others in the assembly of the people. We can draw some parallels with church life, for those who backslide, whether into immorality or in some other way, though they may be physically present at the meetings and give an outward appearance of involvement, are spiritually far away, withering away on the inside. If and when they come to their senses and they acknowledge this and repent of their backsliding, they will have suffering enough through an awareness of what they have lost.

Verses 12-14 are words put on the lips of one who has gone down this path of immorality and suffered the consequences. What this is doing is to underline the fact that the awareness of what has been lost and the reason for it never goes away. It is a mourning (v. 11a) for which there is relatively little comfort. The damage has been done (v. 11b). Verse 12 seems to have both a forward and a retrospective aspect. This man hated having to submit to instruction and the restraints it appeared to place upon him. Then, having thrown off such constraints he despised being told what he was doing was wrong and continued to go his own way (v. 13a). He was dismissive of sound instruction (v. 13b). In short, he did everything opposite to what he should have done. Notice how v. 13b repeats v. 1b, only negatively. He should have bent his ear to the understanding of his teachers, but he confesses at the end that that is exactly what he did not do.

There seems to be a bittersweet aspect to v. 14. To be on the verge of total ruin indicates having come short of it. One of the great blessings for such a person coming, albeit late, to his senses, is that the 'assembly' is still there, and he is still there in it. It may be that it is the very fact of the existence of the assembly that makes the difference between utter ruin and merely its brink. The company of God's people, concerned and caring, has prevented many a man and woman from 'going over the edge'. There is an interesting case in 1 Corinthians 5 and 2 Corinthians 2 concerning a man guilty of immorality.

Solomon has given a pen sketch of the consequences of immorality. He has pulled no punches. What promises fair in the eyes of undiscerning youngsters will ultimately take everything of worth from them. It is just one of the many variations on the theme of Satan's tempting of Eve in the Garden of Eden. The wisdom of this counsel from Proverbs is that it is utterly frank, hiding nothing. How many young people might have been spared the consequences of immorality had they had their eyes opened by teaching such as this! How careful are we to instruct our own children, or the young people in our churches, not merely declaring that the Word of God forbids immoral conduct, but showing them the effect it will have on their lives at every level and where it will lead them? There are plenty of public examples that can be drawn upon that exemplify this teaching, and why not, therefore, turn the folly of others to some beneficial end?

5:15-20. 'Enraptured with her love'. This, so far, is half the story. It is the negative side. Again, we need the wisdom to show our young people how their passions are to be directed. If we focus solely upon prohibitions, we can give the impression that God is out to deprive us our pleasures, whereas the truth is that he is good and desires only the best for us in every way. So Solomon now turns his attention to the positive side and to the delights of the proper outlet for our strength and passions. Here is a refocusing from the sordid and destructive to the beautiful and productive. He acknowledges sexuality and the emotions associated with it as God-given gifts. As such, they are to be valued and used and enjoyed as God intends, and not in the self-seeking impatience of lust. God has given marriage (v. 18) as the context for the sexual relationship (singular) and all that goes with it. Many a young person would be spared temptation and frustration if these things were made clear to them. Those who know them and trust God will be given grace to wait his time and his way for their fulfilment.

5:15-17. Water was a precious commodity in Israel, and the wealthier people had their own cistern, or well, from which to draw. Clear, clean running water was especially prized. The illustration therefore, euphemistic of sexual activity, is to value and enjoy what is rightfully yours, to use it for yourself, as is intended, and not to squander it on unworthy recipients. We are also reminded in v. 17 that there is an exclusiveness to this 'water'. The teaching is that sexuality is to be properly directed within the context of the marriage relationship alone. This not only excludes illicit sexual relationships but also flirtation, immodest dress or behaviour, and anything else that is intended to arouse sexual appetite outside of the sphere for which it was intended by God.

Solomon twice puts the matter to his son in the form of a question (vv. 16,20). He wants him to think about these things and to see that, as well as being wrong, it simply does not make sense to take that route. It is infinitely better to enjoy the gift of sexuality in the way that God has ordained and approves. To that end, with discreet poetic poignancy, he describes how the intimacy of the marriage relationship should be appreciated.

It is amazing how many men speak of their wives in a derogatory fashion, and though it is sometimes in jest yet it hints at a disrespect for the relationship. It is said that familiarity breeds contempt, but should that operate within the family? Should men treat their wives as mere chattels, to be taken and made use of or ignored at whim? There may be many individual reasons why men go astray and get caught up in adultery, but the underlying one is invariably that they have not been able properly to sustain their marriages – or maybe they never had a right understanding of marriage in the first place.

Firstly, he says, 'Let your fountain be blessed' (v. 18). Remember that he is addressing his son and expecting him to exercise initiative in this matter to help bring this about and sustain it. 'Young man', he implies, 'the success or otherwise of your marriage is largely in your hands: it will be what you make of it.' Any gardener will know that, given the best of soil and conditions, a garden will look good only to the extent that it is well tended. Paul intimated in another context that one sows, another waters, but it is God who gives the increase (1 Corinthians 3:6). The blessing of God in bringing the church at Corinth into being was the result of Paul sowing the seed of the gospel and Apollos watering it. Without Paul and Apollos doing what they were called to do there would have been no blessing. Now apply it to what Solomon is saying here to his son, and it will be apparent that a marriage neglected will become a wilderness, but one well-tended will be beautiful and a blessing. The first point, then, is that the man who values his wife and develops the relationship is the one who may expect to see blessing in it.

Secondly, in parallel with the first statement, he says, 'Rejoice with the wife of your youth.' Many men would do well to remember and dwell upon 'the wife of their youth'. When my wife lost a gem from her engagement ring I had once given her, I quipped to her that some of the sparkle had gone out of our marriage. I dared make such a comment because, thankfully, it was manifestly untrue. Had it been otherwise it would not have been taken in good part. The relationship has been built upon better and more valuable things than stones set in a ring! A marriage nurtured and blessed by God is a joyful affair! In this context, 'rejoice with' is probably better than 'rejoice in', for, though this is addressed to the son, it is a matter of intimate companionship. The happiness and joy are mutual.

He now uses an illustration from nature, of 'a loving deer and a graceful doe' (v. 19). In this verse the scripture speaks openly and approvingly of erotic passions and declares that they belong at home. The man is to see true grace and beauty in his wife, to value her attractiveness and responsiveness to his attentions, and to take his fill of pleasure, not *from* her, but *with* her, in mutual fulfilment. Note, too, that he says 'at all times', and 'always'. The intimate embrace and giving to one another are an essential part of a healthy marriage, and the man who responds to his wife's love so expressed by being, literally, intoxicated by it, will have neither thought nor time to devote his attentions elsewhere. His mind and heart will always be with her.

Compare that with the advances of a harlot, an adulteress, and the comparison exposes a sickening deficiency. The question of v. 20 needs no answer.

The man who enters upon an adulterous relationship, however it comes about, is one who has failed with respect to his own marriage, the responsibility for which must be laid at his door. When Solomon asks these questions, it is evident that a delusion is involved. The grass that is greener on the other side only appears to be from the present viewpoint. 'If things were different, then...'. But often things are as they are because we have made them like that. Those who forsake their marriage partner and take up with someone else, whether short-term or long-term, are merely advertising to the world their own failure and defeat, however they may brazen it out. Separation and divorce resulting from adultery are invariably accompanied by acrimony and lifelong bitterness. To state that 'things didn't work out' is a nice way of saying that the parties made a mess of what could and should have been a beautiful relationship.

But does all of this have anything to say to the unmarried? Certainly it does. It gives the young person who has no experience of these things something to look forward to and something to aim for as well as something to beware of. It is reassuring to know both that God has given sexual appetites and how he intends they should find fulfilment. It encourages patience as well as purpose to a man growing up and thinking about marriage or looking for a suitable marriage partner, that this is right and that he may look to the Lord for his provision. It establishes principles that are to be recognised before marriage so that they can be implemented and worked out when it is entered upon. It also guards against promiscuity before marriage, for who in his right mind would wish to spoil such a relationship before it is entered into?

5:21-23. Conclusion. Adultery is rarely advertised. It is entered into covertly with the intention that no one should know about it, and is covered with lies and deceit. To this Solomon makes two observations. The first is that nothing is hidden from God. When we look out on a large crowd, a sea of people, we see the crowd but fail to notice any individuals among them unless they stand out in some way or we are particularly looking out for them. It is easy to treat God's omniscience in this kind of way, as if he were not particularly interested in us or taking notice of us among so many. Nothing could be further from the truth, and v. 21 is at the same time disturbing and reassuring. It is disturbing when we have shameful things we are trying to hide, and it is reassuring when we acknowledge our need of God. This verse says that the ways of a *man*, not the ways of *men*, are before the eyes of the Lord. It is not impersonal and general, but personal and particular. What *each one of us* does is before his eyes, that is, it is in his full view. As the writer of Hebrews says, 'All things are naked and open to the eyes of him to whom we must give account' (Hebrews 4:13). You may see someone going down the road at an unexpected hour and question, pondering the matter, 'I wonder where she is going at this time?' However, when God ponders our ways, there is nothing about them that he does not know, there is no doubt in his mind about what motivates us or where we are going. He weighs them, he assesses their value, he sees their consequences. He is at all times as fully aware of you and as interested in what you are doing as he is of the person next to you in the crowd. Whether you are disturbed or reassured by this will depend upon your relationship with him at this present moment.

The second observation Solomon makes about this is that adultery reaps its own reward (vv. 22-23). In a sense there is no need for God to intervene or judge, for the man so conducting himself is actually disturbing an avalanche that will come down upon him to his own destruction. Sin has consequences, here and now. The web of deceit woven to conceal sin from the eyes of others only entangles the one who weaves it. It is sobering to note how often the scriptures associate adultery and death. To mess around with the sexual relationship, one of the fruits of which is procreation, is more serious in God's eyes than is generally given credit for, and the natural consequences, whether disease, or guilt, or strife, are of an order that exemplifies this. Paul confirms this in Romans 1:27. There is nothing clever, or smart, or noble, about immorality; there is nothing excusable about it, even if 'everybody is doing it'. Cheap pleasures are dearly bought. What you have now and discover to be worthless, you will pay for later with a high price. To sin in this matter is virtually the ultimate in folly.

Verse 23 speaks of death, and whether in a literal or figurative sense really makes no difference. And the reason? Simply for failing to heed instruction, or, perhaps more accurately, failing to accept reasoned reproof and restraint. The second half of the verse complements the first. 'Lack of instruction' is matched by 'the greatness of his folly', while 'die' is matched by 'go astray'. This latter word corresponds to being 'enraptured', or 'captivated' in verses 20 and 21. Such a man is drunk with his own folly: it has dulled his perception, clouded his vision, and desensitised him to the dangers. He is the man who, having drunk too much, gets into his car with heightened confidence in his own ability, and goes out onto the public road to destroy himself and others in the process.

As Solomon, by the Holy Spirit, enunciates these principles, so also should godly parents and teachers inculcate them into their children. Many a young person would have been spared distress and disgrace and instead found encouragement and help had he or she been instructed in these simple but far-reaching truths.

As a footnote to this section, it is curious that 5:18 should be penned by Solomon who multiplied wives to himself (1 Kings 11:3; compare Deuteronomy 17:17), accepted practice by powerful monarchs of the time. It just goes to show that even though he did such a thing, yet he knew what was right in the sight of the Lord. Further, it reminds us that it is possible to live by dual standards. Are you countenancing anything in your life that, though accepted in the world around you, is not in conformity to the will of God? How punctilious are you about taking your standards of conduct from the Word of God? It is easy to attach the word 'legalism' to scrupulous attention to detail as a sort of diversionary tactic to avoid facing up to uncompromising teaching of Scripture that does not suit us for all sorts of plausible reasons. Solomon's giving way in this area led to trouble from which he found it impossible to extricate himself.

6:1-5. A word for underwriters. A promise is a promise, and your word is your bond. Compare Psalm 15:4b. The subject crops up again in 11:15; 17:18; 20:16. This is more than 'helping someone out of a hole'. If a friend finds himself in financial trouble it may be right out of Christian compassion to do something to help. We are not to close our hearts to the needs of others, nor are we to hold back from giving such assistance as we can. We have already observed this in 3:27-28.

However, the situation Solomon is now describing is rather different. The idealism of youth or lack of discernment can lead people into compacts that they may later come to regret. For example, someone may have a brilliant business idea that needs capital, and a friend enthusiastically agrees to 'back it to the hilt' ... and they 'strike hands' in agreement. The problem is that this friend has not thought it through properly, and he realises that he could very easily be 'up to the neck' in trouble if things went wrong. In his eagerness and confidence he did not take the precaution to limit his liability. He may not actually have signed a contract, but the word he had given amounted to much the same thing. As has happened countless times in situations of this kind, the one providing the financial backing discovers it to be crippling as the entrepreneur comes back for more and more support while the pot of gold promised from the venture recedes further and further from view.

This is a monetary example, but there are other ways in which in all but name one may become surety for a friend, promising to support them in other ways, such as by using one's influence to give him access to certain privileges, or giving of one's time to look after certain of his affairs, so that in the end one is simply being taken advantage of. It is wise not to allow oneself to be talked into this kind of thing, but if it does happen, then any promise given must be clearly covered by safeguards. In the worst scenario like that set before us, when a rash promise has been made, then there is nothing for it but to go at once and admit the folly and negotiate a settlement with the person concerned. That person being a neighbour and a friend, or at least purporting to be so, there is reasonable hope that the matter can be resolved, even if it is at some cost. The last thing to do is to leave things as they are and hope the problem will go away. It usually doesn't, and grows into a millstone of anxiety around the neck.

We must never commit ourselves unconditionally to others. Even in marriage the commitment is subject to the condition of mutual faithfulness. The only one to whom we can and should unconditionally commit ourselves is God, because he is unconditionally faithful (see 2 Timothy 2:13).

Psalm 15:4 records that one quality of the person who may dwell in God's presence is that 'he swears to his own hurt and does not change'. What he promises he fulfils even if it proves more costly or troublesome to him than he might have supposed when he made the promise. He does not 'back out' with excuses when he discovers that it will turn out seriously to his disadvantage. So how are we to square this with Solomon's teaching in Proverbs 6?

The answer is really quite simple, for the two situations are completely different. Solomon is discussing a promise that should never have made in the first place. We are not in a position to offer ourselves as guarantors for others because we belong to the Lord. It is out of order because God does not approve it. The difficulty for the one pledging himself is that the other party made may not see it that way and may take offence, not accepting the prior claim on that person of the One to whom he belongs. However, there are many ways in which one may make promises to others that are right and which honour God. One might almost go as far as saying that they comprise an essential element in a well-ordered society.

To take an example of something that has happened many a time, someone agrees to sell his house to Person A for £x subject to contract, but some time later while the paperwork is being attended to Person B comes along and offers £$(x+y)$, where y is no small amount, and the seller withdraws from his commitment to Person A and transfers to Person B. A God-fearing person would not do such a thing but honour his original agreement, even at the expense of £y. After all, when he agreed to the sale, he had no notion that anyone would be coming along with a higher offer. It is not as though he had been cheated out of anything, but Person A would have every right to say he had been cheated if the agreement were withdrawn. I happen to know of a non-Christian who was offered cash payment far in excess of this who had promised his house to another, and though he could without doubt have benefited greatly from the additional sum he happily stood by his word and was honoured for it.

Other, less dramatic, examples abound in which we need to stand by our word. Our offers of help to others cannot be withdrawn at whim just because something else comes along which we would rather do, or because the commitment turns out to be rather more demanding than we expected. All these things, though, are a far call from the kind of situation Solomon is describing when he says, 'Deliver yourself like a gazelle from the hand of the hunter, and like a bird from the hand of the fowler.'

There is a striking example of one becoming surety for another in Genesis 43 and 44, when Judah stood as surety for his brother Benjamin, so that should any trouble befall Benjamin, Judah would substitute for him and bear the consequences for him. No doubt Judah was motivated at least partly by guilt because he was the one who had had the bright idea years before of selling Joseph to the Midianite traders (Genesis 37:26). In that case Judah was doing the right thing because it was a measure of the debt he owed.

This should remind us of our Lord Jesus Christ. He who owed us nothing, he who was motivated not by guilt or anything of the kind but purely by love for us in our lost condition, put himself up as surety for his people. He has first laid down his life that he might save a people for himself, and then to them he unconditionally binds himself to see they are provided for and do not fail. Hebrews 7:22 says that Jesus has been made the surety, or guarantor, of a better covenant. He has covenanted with his people to bring them to glory – and at what cost to himself! However, this is a covenant that cannot and will not fail.

Only he can make unconditional promises! We must not.

6:6-11. Laziness. If one area of potential snare for young people is immorality, another big area affecting them is laziness. Some are not used to work, having never had any training at home; others think they have the whole of life ahead and can afford to take things easy; yet others live under the delusion that in some way they are owed a living from society.

The writer has more to say on the subject later. Here, though is one of the unforgettable statements of Proverbs. 'Go to the ant, you sluggard!' It is a masterpiece of economy, power and irony. What a jolt this is to the senses, what a wake-up call! What is it that is going to motivate a lazy person? Where is such a person to be directed for advice? Maybe Mr Lazybones needs something big or dramatic introduced into his life to stimulate him into action and give him a sense of purpose. Perhaps he needs psychological counselling from someone with a string of letters after his name who has experience of dealing with this kind of difficulty. Not at all. Solomon takes off the gloves and delivers the blow where it is going to be felt the most. He classifies the condition by its true and unflattering name, demonstrating that the sufferer needs an object lesson and directing him to where he can find it!

In general it is unkind to humiliate people. However, laziness is one of those conditions for which an effective remedy, if there is one, is to be shamed out of it. Far too comfortable to take gentle advice seriously, an indolent individual needs a shock to the system to awaken him to his senses. Yet there is hope, and even the slothful person can become wise if he gets it from the right quarter. There are many different kinds of ant, but the one thing common to those seen in their natural habitat is purposeful activity. They have a job to do, and do they do it! They are a model of industry and their achievements are of monumental proportions. They need no serge-ant or command-ant to order them out of bed in the morning, goad them into action and direct or supervise their activity. There they are at all times, selecting building material and gathering the food they need to sustain their colony. In the world of men, too, it is often the 'little people' quietly, diligently, without ostentation following their God-appointed tasks, who get the work done that is so necessary for the sustenance and building of the church.

For now, though, observe that the ant gets on with the job without cajoling or coercion! Its activity is instinctive and necessary to survival. A lazy person could do no better than to spend some of his leisure time gazing at this little creature and thinking about what it is doing and where it is going and why, for he appears to have lost his own God-given instinct for work in the community both for his own benefit and the benefit of others, and the consequences threaten to be dire (v. 11). The ant by nature knows precisely when to be doing what (v. 8). The lazy individual, by lying in bed when there is work to be done, and by taking things easy when others are hard at it, or by saying 'later' (compare 3:28) when 'now' is the time, is acting contrary to the nature God gave him.

As one aspect of wisdom, Solomon repeatedly advises his readers to look to the consequences of any course of action, except that in this case it is a course of inaction. See how he so accurately describes laziness in vv. 9-10. The way he puts it underlines the fact that the sluggard is totally preoccupied with his present comfort zone in a sort of pleasurable semi-stupor. His analysis of the mind-set of the indolent person is incisively perceptive: 'how long?', a 'little' sleep, a 'little' folding of the hands. A delusion is involved in which he is only taking a little innocent rest and enjoying a little pleasure to which he is entitled, and there is plenty of time to do things later. In his view of things, it is only a small matter of no moment, and nothing to make a fuss about. However, tomorrow never comes, and the work of today never gets done.

The consequences of laziness are often exclusion from society and resultant poverty and need. Who is going to employ a person who cannot get up in the mornings, who might turn up at work or might not? Who is going to commit responsibility to one who cannot be relied upon? We learn to leave such people out of the reckoning when we make our plans and we get on and manage without them – they are more trouble than they are worth. Without looking ahead, without realising what is happening to him, the lazy person suddenly finds himself as destitute as if he had been waylaid and stripped by robbers (v. 11).

There is also a lesson in this when it comes to responding to the gospel. Those who give mental assent to the message of the gospel and yet who are at ease with their godless lifestyle and think, 'I will get round to these things some day, but not now,' are likely to be overtaken by judgement. Jesus told the story of a man whose attitude was, 'Soul, you have many goods laid up for many years; take your ease; eat, drink, and be merry.' And God's verdict? – 'Fool! This night your soul will be required of you' (Luke 12:19-20). The circumstances were different, but the point is the same.

6:12-15. Body language tends to tell a great deal more about people than they are aware of. It is interesting that traits of body language tend to span cultures with very different spoken languages. Solomon describes a person who is godless and who lacks real substance as far as his character is concerned (v. 12). In the Hebrew he is a 'man of Belial', and those so described in the Old Testament were dangerously unscrupulous, untrustworthy, without sensitivity and without regard for God or man. They can be found, for example, in Deuteronomy 13:13; Judges 19:22; 1 Samuel 2:12; 25:17; 1 Kings 21:10,13; Proverbs 19:28.

People of this calibre are not always immediately recognised for what they are because concealment may serve their ends. Yet the words such a person uses, the demonstrative way he uses his eyes, his feet and his hands reveals the kind of person he is. We can all identify this kind of person from this description. Even his manner of speaking, though, gives him away for what he is. He 'walks with a perverse mouth', or 'goes about with a corrupt mouth' (NIV). In keeping with the overall description, we might say that he 'talks out of the corner of his mouth'. Whatever he says has another side to it. Publicly he says one thing, but to those nearby he places his hand in front of his mouth and, speaking sideways for their ears only, puts an interpretation on it that means something quite different. There is a duality to his words which makes him essentially untrustworthy.

The winking of the eyes is a trait that confirms this, for it is a knowing look that attracts the attention of those for whom it is intended, as if to say, 'You know what I mean, even if they don't!'

The manner of his walking, the way he uses his feet, indicate his type, as do the gestures of his hands. There is often something just a little exaggerated in these things, just a bit too expressive to be true, just enough to give the game away that he is not what he would like people to think he is. His very plausibility is suspect. What he is not is straightforward.

This description is not intended to be an entertaining caricature, but a reminder that we need to train our young people to learn to recognise the signs and not be gullible in their assessment of character. It is important that they learn to weigh character by giving due consideration to *all* the evidence so that they do not fall foul of the wrong company.

The crookedness evident in the words and gestures of a godless person arise from the crookedness in his heart (v. 14). He behaves like this because this is what he is like. As a hen scratches around for food, so he is perpetually scratching around for something to satisfy his perverse nature, and, naturally, the result is trouble and strife. Far from picking up anything useful in the process, he is actually throwing up dirt. Where he is active, discord is the result.

Once more, Solomon speaks of the consequences. As with the lazy man, this one too will find himself suddenly and unexpectedly brought down. In his case, though, the judgement will be severer in proportion to the magnitude of his guilt. It won't just be poverty, but disaster; he won't just be left in need, he will be broken beyond mending.

We may debate why the wicked prosper. While it is true that some receive their just deserts in this life, others seem to 'get away with it', and it is they who trouble us when we wonder why God allows them to continue to speak and act as they do. This troubled the writer of Psalm 73 until he sought God about the matter, who gave him the same answer as Solomon gives here (Psalm 73:19). For the godless there will be an irremediable suddenness about the judgement, and it will be terrifying. When it comes, as it must and will, whether sooner or later, it will be swift and final. There will be no recall.

6:16-19. Philippians 2:1-16. 'Six … and seven' may be a poetic device (see also chapter 30 and the opening chapters of Amos), but when we look at the list that follows we may be in for a shock. The first thing to note is that this is not intended to be a comprehensive list. It might be more accurate to describe it as a representative one.

6:17. Pride. These things are so important that it is worth spending time on each one to try to see what is represented by each, and then consider what may be gathered from the whole. Every Christian has been called out of the world in which these principles operate and is now to live according to new, godly principles empowered by the Holy Spirit. Every Christian still has a sinful nature, and has to deal with it, and this is described in terms of putting to death the deeds of the body and earthly passions (Romans 8:12-13; Colossians 3:5), and of putting off the old man (Ephesians 4:22). So rather than look at this list and merely identify how bad things are 'out there in the world', let us use it to our own 'mortification', that is, to consider whether there are things still to be put to death in our own lives.

The previous verses have described 'a worthless person, a wicked man' (v. 12; or, as the NIV emotively translates it, 'A scoundrel and villain'), and vv. 16-19 seem to parallel vv. 12-15, picking up on the use of eyes, mouth, hands, feet and heart. These members of our bodies we are no longer to present as instruments of unrighteousness to sin, but rather as instruments of righteousness to God (see Romans 6:13 in context). A rehabilitation process is involved, in which our bodies and their members are retrained to function in a completely new way.

The first mentioned is 'a proud look', or 'haughty eyes'. This is body language again for the kind of person who considers himself or herself to be above others and therefore looks down on them. It is the very opposite of the attitude God requires of us and has demonstrated in his Son – see Philippians 2:3-8). Nobody is beneath us or unworthy of our notice or attention or concern. It is not surprising that this is something the Lord hates, that it is something he finds utterly odious, when he sent his Son into this world to befriend 'tax collectors and sinners' and to give his life for the lowest of the low. That we should arrogate ourselves to a position of pride of place above anyone is to esteem ourselves as being superior to him who 'humbled himself ... even to the death of the cross'. If we are tempted to this kind of pride toward anyone, let us consider how the Lord Jesus would view that same person, and then let us think again. To look down on anyone is to look down on the one who is exalted higher than the heavens (Hebrews 7:26).

The reason pride heads the list is because it is the essential characteristic of Satan: self-exaltation that stands in direct opposition to God who alone reigns on high. It is hardly surprising that the Bible is full of statements concerning pride, everywhere condemning it. Although Satan presents no real threat to God, yet the fruit of his pride has caused nothing but harm and anguish in God's world. In Ezekiel 28:2-15 and Isaiah 14:12-15, through the descriptions of the pride of Tyre and Babylon respectively and the pronouncements made against them we can see all that is essentially Satanic in its origin. While 'Lucifer', or 'Day Star', is actually an ironic descriptive term for the king of Babylon and should not be applied without qualification to Satan, the passage in Isaiah nevertheless gives by inference a fair representation of what Satan is like, what his ambition is, and what will ultimately befall him and his followers. The symbolic references to Babylon in the Book of Revelation confirm this. Power in the wrong hands so often leads to pride. Not only Tyre and Babylon, but other nations opposed to God's people are described in similar terms – Moab and Edom for example (Jeremiah 48:29; 49:16, and Egypt (Ezekiel 30:6,18).

Although Solomon at this point is speaking more on the level of relationships within society rather than of heads of state or rulers of kingdoms, the same principles apply. Pride, or self-conceit, in an individual of no consequence is of the same kind as pride in a person of influence. However limited its sphere of operation may be, pride is still opposed to God. The reason why so many dictators have caused untold misery is not that their pride was of a different order, but that their opportunity was.

The opposite of pride is humility. To the extent that a person lacks humility, he or she is proud. Consider Romans 12:3 which, if we are Christians, calls for sober realism in our assessment of who we are, what we have and where it comes from! It is a sad truth that the enemy of souls gets his foothold in many a church through infecting its members with pride. How appealing it is to 'be somebody', whether in the church or elsewhere, and how then that status is jealously guarded, even if it means (as often it does) treading down others or 'putting them in their place'. Church leaders, of course, have to be especially vigilant in this area, lest God-given authority is exercised from less than God-given motives and hence in the wrong way! Paul, writing to Timothy, mentions a danger in this area (1 Timothy 3:6). None of us has to guard his position: if God has appointed, he will uphold – end of story. Consider both the authority and the humility of the Lord Jesus, and observe how these blended together in perfect harmony.

6:17. Psalm 52. Deceit. The second on the list is a lying tongue. This is a matter of direct falsehood, of saying what is simply untrue. A lie presents falsehood as the truth. What cause might anyone have for doing this? After all, is it not simpler at all times to tell the truth? It is probably superfluous to give specific examples of lying. Suffice it to say that a lying tongue usually speaks in defence of its owner who has something either to cover up or to show off. Just occasionally it may speak on behalf of another for a similar reason or to counter an unpalatable truth.

For example, I recall a surgeon saying to a sick girl's parents that they were probably thinking the reason he had not operated was that she was not strong enough to go through with it, whereas he wanted to follow a different procedure. It came to light after her death that he had followed a different procedure precisely because she would very likely not have survived the operation. His lie had given hope where really there was none, and it left the grieving parents bewildered and upset, having deprived them (and their daughter) of the opportunity to prepare for the inevitable.

A lying tongue – God detests it! Just think what it would be like if God's Word could not be trusted, if he said one thing and did another, or if something he said was found out not to be true. We simply would not know what to believe! Jesus said, 'Your word is truth' (John 17:17), echoing the psalmist's declaration, 'Your righteousness is an everlasting righteousness, and your law is truth' (Psalm 119:142).

A lying tongue imitates Satan, for he is the father of lies (John 8:44). A lying tongue is very often found out, for, as the saying goes, 'Truth will out.' The result can be deep distrust, with doubts cast upon the truth of other declarations. Lying undermines relationships, promotes suspicion, destroys confidence, causes division. It does untold damage. If anybody reading this is guilty of a lying tongue, better to confess and sort the matter out with those concerned than suffer the consequences of being found out. The temporary embarrassment and humiliation involved in confession are far to be preferred to the lasting stigma attached to discovery and exposure.

6:17. Matthew 5:21-26. Murder. After these two rather searching 'abominations' we can relax over the third, for few readers will have innocent blood upon their hands. Or can we? Jesus said that the penalty for murder applied to those angry with others without cause, to those who show contempt for others, to those who declare others to be fools. The clear inference is that in his estimation character assassination is of the same order as murder. Those who have suffered from such treatment will know that mud thrown tends to stick. Enormous damage is done which in many respects is as serious as bloodshed. Anyone who has a heart to will someone else's downfall or destruction has hands that shed innocent blood.

However, there is another side to shedding innocent blood which is represented in sharp relief by James in his letter. He addresses rich oppressors whose disdainful treatment of their workers inflicts great suffering upon them (James 5:1-6). His conclusion is that they have condemned *and murdered* them. This is not necessarily to be taken in its most literal sense, though if some so deprived did die, the blood would indeed be on the hands of the oppressors. Unjust exploitation of others who have neither the strength nor the ability to resist and which causes them suffering, really falls into the category of 'hands that shed innocent blood'.

So whether it is out and out character assassination, or whether it is the systematic grinding down of others too weak to resist, God sees it in the same light as murder. We need to examine our attitudes and behaviour toward others, lest we harbour hatred, bitterness, envy, or simply, holding someone in contempt, fail to lift a finger to help them. Our treatment of others can lead to unforeseen consequences. Suppose, for example, person A is always running down person B, as a result of which person B suffers a nervous breakdown, or succumbs to depression, or even commits suicide. What would the verdict be at the bar of perfect justice? On whose hands would the blood be? This has some very serious things to say about our treatment of other people.

Jesus exposed the problem of heart attitude in the incident over the man with a withered hand in the synagogue (Mark 3:1-6). His question was, 'Is it lawful on the Sabbath to do good or to do harm, to save life or to kill?' We might have observed that this was a case of doing good or not doing good, and doing harm did not enter into it. Yet it did. The man, knowing Jesus had power to heal him, would have been positively harmed psychologically had Jesus disdained doing so. But what was the point of Jesus mentioning saving life or killing? Surely that was irrelevant to the case before him. Or was it? Verses 2 and 6 reveal that the religious leaders were not concerned for the life or welfare of others, only their own reputation; they were not interested in a Saviour, only in getting rid of him. Accusation and murder were in their hearts. In the end they cried out, 'His blood be on us and on our children' (Matthew 27:25). And it was.

6:18. 1 Samuel 25:2-35. Evil scheming. As we progress through this list it becomes clear how closely related all these things are. They are rarely if ever found in isolation. Those who are humble are not the kind of people who would be guilty of evil scheming in their hearts, for they would have no cause for it. On the other hand, a proud heart is very susceptible to this kind of thinking. Both Paul and the writer of the letter to the Hebrews remind their readers that God said, 'Vengeance is mine, I will repay' (Romans 12:19; Hebrews 10:30). Paul in particular is making the point that those suffering injustice are not at liberty to take the law into their own hands to get back at those who dealt unjustly with them. That is not justice, it is wickedness. Unfortunately it is an all too common trait that bad treatment at the hands of others rankles, and consequently all to common therefore to plan retribution.

There is only one kind of retribution that Paul sanctions, which he describes by using the nice irony (got from the book of Proverbs – 25:21) of heaping burning coals on the head of the targeted individual which, in a sense, is what the offended person wants, and then says it is achieved by repaying evil with good (Romans 12:20-21)!

When we suffer from mistreatment by others and when we experience that bitter inward burning sensation and our minds work overtime on what we are going to do about it, the answer is simple, but one we often overlook: we ponder what good we might do them! The trouble is, the temptation is very strong to let the problem go round and round in our minds which then come up with all sorts of subversive ways of setting the score straight! Christian, put that behind you! That belongs to your past, not the present. You are now motivated by higher, better principles, and those burning coals that you once would have wanted to pour down on the head of the adversary who is assaulting you to exterminate him, you now want instead to burn through a hard exterior to trouble the conscience and bring it to life through repentance and faith.

Peter reminds us of how the Lord Jesus repaid the insults he received in his earthly life: he worked for our ultimate good by suffering the death of the cross, bearing our sins in his own body on the tree (1 Peter 2:23-24). Yes, God approves scheming hearts. Let us lie upon our beds plotting people's good, using every trick in God's book!

6:18. Titus 2. Evil actions. So to the fifth detestable thing: feet that are swift in running to evil. Someone is in a tremendous hurry to get across a busy road to the other side. Head down, they 'go for it', unaware that they are actually running headlong into the path of an approaching lorry ... The picture is one of precipitate action which, once set into motion, cannot be reversed. The heart has made the plans, and now they go all out to fulfil them with unstoppable recklessness, regardless of the consequences.

This proverb speaks of running to *evil*. This word is very broad in its scope, including blatant wickedness on the one hand and doing harm on the other. Unfortunately, many people are unconscious of the fact that they are running to evil. For example, a great deal of harm can be done in a church by an ambitious person whose ambitions are not brought into submission to the Holy Spirit and the discernment of the will of God. Perhaps it is a person who covets some office in the church for himself, or herself, going for it with formidable determination. Perhaps it is someone determined to get his or her way in some other matter affecting church life, which is really nothing more than a cherished pet idea. Maybe it is an individual interpretation of a part of scripture that someone wants accepted, adopted and worked out in the church and he is perpetually canvassing his ideas. Examples can be multiplied. Churches have been divided by people who have forced their way through on particular issues. Sadly sometimes, even though the issue may be right and worthy of attention, it ends up being spoken evil of because of the way in which it has been promoted – and it has all happened because someone wants *his* way rather than the Lord's. Those already in positions of influence in the church need to be very careful about how they use their influence, that they are rightly motivated, especially in matters of policy. Those with strong personalities must be on their guard not to ride roughshod over others in the pursuit of their own aims.

Not to do good is to do evil; to be set on a course that is not in line with the will of God is to be running headlong into evil. Instead, let our feet be swift with the gospel of grace, and let not drag our heels when it comes to serving the needs of others.

6:19. Perjury. The sixth thing the Lord hates is a false witness who speaks lies. Here, specifically, is the intention to deceive, whether in defending the guilty or in condemning the innocent, or in other ways perverting the truth. Some notorious examples are on record in the Bible, including the many who testified falsely at Jesus' mock trial (Matthew 26:60-61). One is the incident of Naboth's vineyard (1 Kings 21) in which Jezebel chillingly used her manipulative skills with a town council to bring about Naboth's death so that Ahab could get his hands on the man's vineyard. It is not, however, only the two scoundrels mentioned (1 Kings 21:10,13) who bore false witness by speaking out lies about Naboth. The elders and nobles (there was nothing very noble about their conduct) were equally guilty by their doing as Jezebel said – no doubt for fear of the consequences if they failed to cooperate. Someone who fails to speak up in defence of the truth when occasion requires it is also every bit a false witness. There are those occasions when it may be personally 'convenient' to keep quiet, but a silent tongue may speak lies as loudly as one volubly perverting the truth. We should ask ourselves whether there have been times when we have kept quiet when we should have spoken, the result of which has been detrimental to the truth.

There are other ways in which false witness may be given, such as by diverting attention from one thing on to another – sidetracking from the main issue. Or it can be by placing an interpretation upon something that was said or done that was never intended by those words or that action. Satan, who is described as the father of lies (John 8:44), did both of these when he tempted Eve in the garden. With subtle plausibility he placed a false interpretation upon what God had said and upon what God had meant, and diverted attention from death to wisdom ... and Eve was taken in. He has been continuing the same successful tactics ever since to deceive the gullible. For example, God has said both that he created the world and given a clear outline of how he created it. However, Satan has flatly contradicted that and given false testimony in order to spread the lie of evolution. He has manipulated scientists, scientific ideas and the media to promulgate this deception worldwide in order to attempt to undermine God's authority over his creation and deny man's accountability to God, and he does everything he can to bring false testimony against those who, having knowledge and understanding, dare to contradict. They are often marginalised, shouted down or ridiculed to guarantee that what they have to say does not get heard or taken seriously. These are some of the tactics of false testimony, and the God of truth hates it.

It is not only in the area of creation that false witness has been given. In almost every matter where the Bible, which everywhere declares itself to be God's Word, speaks authoritatively the meaning has been questioned: 'It says this, but it really means that.' The consequence is always to undermine the authority of God, to tarnish the perfection of his being, the purity of his actions, and to make him out to be less than he is; and the end in view is to elevate man in his own eyes. It is therefore of the utmost importance that we should not be found guilty of bearing false witness by contradicting by speech or action what God's Word teaches. We need, perhaps more than we realise, to give ourselves to knowledge and understanding of the 'Scriptures which are able to make us wise for salvation through faith which is in Christ Jesus' (2 Timothy 3:15).

6:19. Discord. 'Six ... yes, seven.' The seventh in this list of what the Lord hates is something we need to be on our guard against in the church. One of the things about discord is that it is a pernicious weed that grows from seed and often finds the soil fertile enough for it to sprout up. Again, it is instructive to consider an example or two from Scripture. One notable case is Absalom (2 Samuel 15). Bitterly disgruntled because of the way his father David had treated him, he went out of his way to sow seeds of dissatisfaction, discontent and discord among those who were already troubled by matters of controversy they wanted to bring before the king for a decision. His intention was to rise to power himself and displace his father from the throne. His smooth words supportive of justice were no more than a front for his ambition, for he was actually undermining justice, destroying trust, creating ill-feeling, and dividing people. He was ultimately successful in wreaking havoc in Israel and precipitating his own downfall. It is instructive to read 2 Samuel 13 and 14 and analyse the contributory factors, which are various and complex. Those who sow discord often feel they have some justification for what they are doing.

Discord can spring up in all sorts of unexpected ways. A very straightforward case is found in Acts 6, where one group of people were suffering neglect and complaining against another because the latter appeared to be receiving preferential treatment. The complaint may have been just, but the quarter in which it was being voiced was probably not. On that occasion harmony was quickly restored by prompt and wise action on the part of the leaders of the church. The lesson we can learn from it, though, is that a complaint improperly expressed can cause division.

Another straightforward case is found in the church at Corinth, where personal followings led to envy, strife and division, and Paul told them, basically, that they needed to grow up spiritually (1 Corinthians 1:10-13; 3:1-3). What I like, who I like, how I like things to be done, what I think should be done... If we are vocal and forceful in displaying our personal opinions against those of others, damage will be done.

Gossip is one of the most common areas of life giving rise to discord among people because its half truths invariably set others in an unfavourable light.

In most cases, though (and this is really what Solomon is referring to), those who sow seeds of discord do so because they have a hidden agenda. Paul warns of such people in Romans 16:17-18, making it quite clear what their motives really are, and pointing to the need for watchfulness and discernment. The writer of Hebrews warns us to be watchful, 'lest any root of bitterness springing up cause trouble, and by this many become defiled' (Hebrews 12:15). Ambition and discontent are great handles to the temptation to stir up dissension. We need to be on our guard, examining the thoughts of our hearts and our motives, avoiding all causes of strife, at all times seeking harmony in the truth, promoting true unity in spirit and practice. The way to this is described by Paul in Ephesians 4:1-3, where he goes on to explain that the diversity of gifts is for the promotion of unity (Ephesians 4:13). The sad thing about sowing discord *among brethren* is that it divides those who should be united, tearing down instead of building up.

6:20-21. Deuteronomy 6:4-9,20-25; 11:18-21. Mother lays down the law! The repetition of address is familiar by now. Without doubt, Solomon did not overwhelm his son with all this teaching in one go! What we have in this book is a compilation comprising teaching on different subjects given at different times. Almost every new section commences with the introduction, 'My son...' or something equivalent. So it is here. Verse 20 is reminiscent of 1:8; v. 21 of 3:3. This is a reminder that the primary responsibility for godly training lies in the home, not the church, and that both parents are involved.

How is it that Timothy had known the Holy Scriptures from childhood (2 Timothy 3:15)? Without doubt, it is that his mother, and probably his grandmother, too, had instructed him in the Law of God (2 Timothy 1:5). Even if Timothy's father was not a believer (Acts 16:1-3), yet the instruction he received at home bore fruit when Paul came along and preached the gospel.

Throughout the books of Kings, when a new king came to the throne or died, there is a reference to his mother: '...and his mother's name was...' (1 Kings 11:26; 14:21,31; 15:2,10; etc.). Mothers exercise a tremendous influence upon their growing children, much of the training in whose formative years rests with them. What children learn on their mother's knee tends to stay with them through life. Her teaching and example are imbibed from the child's earliest days. So Christian mothers should be always talking of God and his Word, as they do of other things, even before they think their children understand them. They should be always directing their children to the Word of God, teaching it as they apply it in the everyday affairs of their children's lives, by which their offspring will grow up recognising the Bible as living and relevant. Godly living and godly instruction are the natural environment of a godly home in which everything, from the least to the greatest, is happily, comfortably and consciously placed under the authority of the Word of God.

The father's responsibility is in some ways more formal, but it is also to instruct, to train, to discipline; he carries the authority to command and expect obedience. He supports the mother's teaching and fulfils his role by ensuring as far as he is able that their children conduct themselves in a manner that is consistent with biblical principles.

In case someone should be wondering at this point, 'Shouldn't they rather be directing their children to put their personal trust in the Lord?', the answer is that the question indicates the point is being missed. The teaching, the training, the commanding, are all directing the children this way, who will know from their earliest recollections that the godly living required of them is bound up with a living faith which they needs must come to the Lord to give them. We know that our children will really take these things to heart only when their hearts are changed by the grace of God. They will only 'tie them around their neck' when they see that they are worthy adornments for their life. Parents must fulfil their God-given responsibilities, earnestly praying that God will do for their children the one and most vital thing they cannot do themselves.

6:22-23. 2 Timothy 3:14-17. Ever-present counsel. Many a parent has had misgivings when his or her son or daughter is about to leave home. 'Will he withstand the pressures of the prevailing lifestyle at university?' 'How will he make out at work?' 'How will she cope with her new life?' This will be the great test of the instruction given over the formative years. These verses give great encouragement to those who have indeed understood God's Word, taken it to heart and want to take it with them into the next stage of their lives. The Word of God is powerful. Those who have been instructed in it and received it have an enormous advantage in life over those who remain in ignorance or have been poorly taught, for it is the Word of God that the Holy Spirit applies to the mind of the believer. Christians who have received little teaching or those who have been negligent in the careful reading of the Bible often go through hard times and difficult experiences they might well have been spared had they been better taught. Thorough instruction and careful application result in the threefold blessing described in v. 22: guidance, protection, instruction. The foundation has been laid by parents, the teaching has been accepted by the son or daughter, and now God's Word may be relied upon to do its own work as the young person moves on to the next stage of life.

Note then the threefold blessing. Firstly, there is *guidance*. The NKJV translates, rather nicely, 'When you *roam...*'. It covers all aspects of being out and about and every variety of activity between getting up in the morning and going to bed at night, wherever one may be. God's Word covers all these aspects too, and the Holy Spirit brings it to mind in every situation to lead you in the right direction, so that your roaming is not aimless and unproductive, but purposeful and fruitful. There is a delightful statement made by Abraham's servant sent to get a wife for Isaac. He said: 'As for me, being on the way, the LORD led me...' (Genesis 24:27). This faithful servant had set out with many unasked and unanswered questions, with many uncertainties over details, reliant only upon the command and promise of God (Genesis 24:7). However, in the path of obedience he found that the Lord did indeed lead him. The young person setting out in life with such a dependent attitude may rely with all confidence upon God to lead by his Word and by his Spirit and by his ordering of all things.

Then there is *protection*: 'When you sleep, they will keep you.' This is the untroubled rest that the Lord gives to those who have his Word at heart. Those with guilt on their consciences or evil in their hearts are never free of the problems they bring, even in their sleep. Their minds, not under the conscious control of wakefulness, are often tormented subconsciously by troublesome nightmares. God's Word has a wonderful way of taking care of the unconscious mind, delivering it from irrational fears and providing real peace and refreshment. This is another angle on what we read at 3:24. On the other hand, even the sweetest dreams of a man under judgement mock him when he wakes up, as Isaiah graphically portrays in Isaiah 29:8.

Thirdly, there is *instruction*: 'When you awake, they will speak with you.' On a word of personal testimony, on the morning after my conversion I awoke with an extraordinary sensation: for the first time in my life my thoughts were toward God, and his Word addressed me. It had never been like that before, but it has been ever since. Morning by morning, God's Word has something to say to us to prepare us for the day ahead. David, in Psalm 139, was conscious of this. His knowledge of the Word of God was such that he could write: 'How precious also are your thoughts to me, O God! How great is the sum of them! If I should count them, they would be more in number than the sand; when I awake, I am still with you' (Psalm 139:17-18).

In v. 23 Solomon now picks up again the father's command and the mother's law of v. 20, explaining how they function. Psalm 119:105 says the same about the Word of God being a lamp to our feet and a light to our path. The lamp is like a candle or a torch, by which we can see where we are and cope with our immediate environment. The light, which is like the daylight, gives us a view of the wider scene to enable us to travel in safety. God's Word functions in both ways. We need to be able to recognise and attend to the matters that immediately concern us, where God's Word addresses us in particulars. We need also to be able to relate more widely to the world in which we live and move, and in this case God's Word addresses us with grand principles. As most, if not all, Christians know, the form in which the word comes to us is often by way of rebuke, correction and disciplined training. Paul, inspired by the Spirit, puts it so well in 2 Timothy 3:16, describing the way Scripture works: it first teaches us, then reproves us and corrects us, and continues by training us on in the discipline of righteousness. Here Solomon refers to this as 'the way of life', or 'the way to life'. The former is probably better, capturing the ongoing nature of this discipline. As long as we are in the flesh, we will still have need of this reproving and chastening operation of God's Word, as is explained for us in Hebrews 12:5-11.

6:24-35. Adultery. Applying what he has just been teaching Solomon once again returns to the matter of sexual immorality. Can we wonder at this, when the problem is all around us in the world? We are continually bombarded with temptations in this area which come upon us from all directions and all angles. We may be well defended against attacks from one quarter, but find ourselves weak in another area. Therefore the defences must be strengthened all round. The ones most at risk are those of the age Solomon is addressing. It is for this reason that he returns to the subject again and again. Women have been the downfall of many a man. God's Word says that woman was created to be a helper for man and to complement him (Genesis 2:18), so that they could find fulfilment as they lived and functioned together in the way that he ordained. Part of this involves sexuality and sexual desires which find their proper expression and fulfilment within the context of the marriage relationship. The troubles arise when these desires are excited outside of the context in which they are supposed to operate.

Solomon pictures a combination of three powerful factors that will draw a man after a woman, which women understand and know how to use. They can be rightly used, but here he gives an example of their wrong use, for it is an *evil* woman that he is describing. Any woman using this kind of influence without regard to the marriage relationship is acting wickedly because she is placing powerful temptations in the way of the vulnerable. First mentioned is her speech: smooth words to make him feel good and comfortable in her presence, to encourage his company and intimacy with her. Already she is out of order, for it is not proper that initiative should be taken by a woman in this way. Then there is her beauty. Whether this beauty is natural or achieved by artificial means is beside the point. The point is that she knows how to display and use her physical attractiveness to advantage. Thirdly is the way she looks at him, drawing him in with that unspoken, alluring invitation.

How will a young man respond to this sort of treatment? It depends upon both his principles and his resolve. He must be strong in both areas or he will very likely be in trouble. Solomon fires a warning shot across his bows: 'Do not lust after her beauty in your heart' (v. 25). That's what she's appealing to: cheap lust, nothing more. See it for what it is, and her flattering mouth and fluttering eyelids will give flight to her beauty. For, as all wise men know, true beauty in a woman involves a great deal more than form.

A woman who acts in this way is like a spider attracting a fly into the web. She has no interest in him beyond what she can get out of him. It is all purely selfish. Her designs on him from the outset are simply to use him and discard him. She will very likely survive the experience, but how he will come out of it is a very different matter.

A powerful antidote must be given to a powerful temptation. There is nothing like being thoroughly grounded in the Word of God to be able to cope with this kind of thing. Paul warned Timothy: 'Keep your head in all situations' (2 Timothy 4:5, NIV), the point being that Timothy was to have a sober awareness to see through all *seductive* teaching arising in the church and to respond appropriately (2 Timothy 4:1-5). The antidote to the allurement of a seductress is first to expose her for who she is, and then to take out every last twang of influence by seeing what would have happened had he succumbed. Such a woman would use him and continue to use her charm and attractiveness until that point at which he had nothing further to offer her. He would be impoverished according to every meaning of the word (v. 26). Three areas can be immediately identified: the material, the psychological, and the social. The woman who uses a man for gain also inflicts psychological damage that 'eats out his heart'. The illicit relationship also damages the man's standing in society, bringing him into dishonour, cheapening his reputation, destroying trust, undermining respect and limiting his usefulness.

So Solomon in effect is saying to his son: 'Keep your head when you see a beautiful woman who appears to be giving you encouragement. Look at the thing with hard-nosed objectivity, and let this be your guide. You know what God's Word says, and why it says so, and you have plenty of witnesses to the disastrous consequences of following that road. Is that really what you want? Even if the woman does not belong to someone else, know what kind of a woman she is and 'where she is coming from' before getting entangled in any way. If she is enticing you to any kind of illicit relationship then sever the connection!'

6:27-35. Just deserts. The illustration of vv. 27-29 is straightforward enough. Those who entangle themselves in an adulterous relationship are playing with fire. The questions asked require no answer. No one would think to do those things with fire because their clothes would catch light or their feet would be badly burned. The consequences of adultery are on a par with such behaviour and equally foolish and damaging, and yet there are people who are nevertheless enticed into it. It happens because objectivity is cast to the winds, the pleasures of sin for a season blinding a person to the long-term consequences. 'Whoever touches her' could be an intentional understatement, or a euphemism for lying with her. More probably, though, it is carrying through the idea introduced in the illustration about fire. Touch fire and you will get hurt; touch another man's wife and suffer the consequences. You don't play with fire, and you don't mess around with other men's wives. The least contact, physical or otherwise, that has any sexual connotations whatever goes beyond the limit of innocence (remember what Jesus said about this in Matthew 5:28). What some describe as 'a little innocent fun', or 'a little harmless play' will not be seen in that light either by the husband (v. 34) or by God. Such a person is accounted guilty and therefore liable to punishment on the day of accounting.

A different illustration follows on the heels of this one (vv. 30-31). An element of compassion is elicited for the poor unfortunate who, because no one provides for him, is reduced to stealing bread to keep body and soul together, accompanied by indignation against a society that fails to recognise the need or lift a finger to help to such a person. Pity is heightened for him when, however rightly, the law says that he must restore 'sevenfold'. In fact the law stated fourfold or fivefold or double, according to the circumstances of the theft (Exodus 22:1-4). This is not an exaggeration, contradiction or revision of the law. 'Sevenfold' is an expression which indicates full and complete restoration for what he has done, and in an extreme case it could cost him everything he has. 'Poor fellow' is the popular verdict in such a case.

The purpose of this illustration is the stark contrast between the thief stealing food to keep himself alive and the adulterer stealing another man's wife to satisfy his lust. The thief steals to satisfy (literally) his 'soul'; the man who commits adultery destroys his 'soul'. The thief is not despised (far from it), but the adulterer most certainly is. When the adulterer is found out, he will suffer wounds, disgrace and shame (v. 33), and people will say: 'Serves him right, he got what was coming to him!' His conduct will be regarded as despicable and will not be forgotten. Least of all will any compassion be shown by the husband of the woman toward the offender. Nothing can quench his anger (v. 34), and nothing can 'buy him off' (v. 35). In the eyes of the law (Leviticus 20:10), the offence has cost him his wife, for the price to be paid for adultery is the death of both parties, and the husband will exert himself to the utmost to see that the full price is exacted.

7:1-5. Closely guarded. Solomon returns to his introduction at 6:20. He is both rounding off what he has just been saying and leading into a further illustration. He has just been speaking of the soul-destroying nature of adultery, and shows his concern that by contrast his son should *live* (v. 2).

When we hear of people 'living it up', their activity usually indicates that they are really destroying themselves. Such is the deception of the evil one, and the writer is totally absorbed in the task of making his son wise to this and equipping him with every armoury against it.

Some of the things people most value seldom see the light of day. Precious jewellery may be locked away in a safe, or kept in a strong box in the vault of a bank, being brought out and worn only on special occasions and then returned again to its place of safe keeping. This is the thought behind 'keep my words, and treasure my commands within you' (v. 1). To 'keep' it is to guard it, and to 'treasure' it is to hide it. The psalmist uses the same word when he says: 'Your word I have *hidden* in my heart, that I might not sin against you' (Psalm 119:11). The point is that it is too valuable to be lost, and so must be kept somewhere where it may not be tampered with. The eyes of his mind turn inward upon his treasure, and the hands of his mind hold it, turn it, examine it, admire it, value it, clasp it.

That is how Solomon wanted his son to treat his commands. Certain plants and animals are so sensitive that they shrink away in self-defence the moment they are touched. One of the most sensitive parts of the human anatomy is the 'apple', the pupil, of the eye. Accordingly, we look after our eyes, and are very protective of this part of them. Anyone who has been struck by even a speck on the pupil of the eye knows how painful it can be. Solomon wants his son to be equally protective of his law, which is in fact God's law. It is too precious, too sensitive, too valuable, too useful to be tampered with. By analogy, the law will give him sight on life. The law represents the eyes of his understanding.

We have met the statement of v. 3 in various forms already – see 1:9; 3:3,22 (of mercy and truth); 6:21. The Israelites were expected to have a high regard for God's law, and to do all they could to ensure it was kept in sight in their everyday lives (Deuteronomy 6:8-9; 11:18-21). Solomon is reiterating this very important point. God's laws must be in the heart (7:3; 6:21) – that is, understood, valued and treasured; they must also be in the hands – that is, applied in everyday life; they must also be tied around the neck (6:21) – that is, they must adorn the life with the grace and beauty of godliness.

The young man has already been warned against involvement with the wrong sort of company (1:10). The kind of close company he *is* to keep is described in v. 4. He is to think of the closest family ties he has, and then think of being on as familiar and intimate a footing with wisdom and understanding. Perhaps he has a sister of whom he is somewhat protective. He is to look on wisdom as tenderly, and she will always support him and never fail him. Perhaps he has a brother he looks up to for his ability, knowledge, maturity. He is to look upon understanding, that is, a thoroughgoing knowledge of God's Word, with as much respect.

How earnestly Solomon desires his son to take fully on board in his life his commands, the law, and wisdom and understanding! How well we too would progress through life if we valued these commodities in the way he urges! Have these things, he says to his son, and you will be kept safe in life from seduction in every shape and form.

7:6-27. An object lesson. Solomon concludes with an object lesson for his son. It is immaterial whether he is relating an actual incident within his knowledge or describing a scene from his imagination, for the truth is that this kind of thing has happened countless times with endless variations in the history of mankind. We may very easily picture ourselves occupying a vantage point from which we can see everything that is going on, and follow the sequence of events as they unfold. First of all through the window we see 'the simple' (v. 7), identified as youths who are lacking in all the essentials of instruction, wisdom and understanding. 'Now watch', he says. 'That one there in particular – he is singularly devoid of understanding – look where he is going.'

He is probably the kind of self-assured young person who thinks he has the world at his command. You see him wandering along – perhaps swaggering might be a better word – as if he is looking out for someone, and as he moves down a particular street it becomes clear what he is up to. It's that woman he was 'chatting up' the other day. It's getting dark now and you need your night vision (v. 9). Suddenly there she is, 'dressed to kill' (never was a truer word spoken) (v. 10), and finds her quarry with no difficulty at all (v. 13). Turning on all her charm she tells him quite shamelessly that she had come out for the sole purpose of meeting him (vv. 13-15), using body, words and gestures to allure him, with abundant assurances that everything would be all right ('the man' was away – impersonally describing her husband), that all eventualities were covered, and that they would have a great time (vv. 16-20). She had no difficulty causing him to yield (v. 21), for that is what he had been looking for all along and couldn't believe his luck. One moment they are standing there talking intimately, the next he is being led to her house (v. 22) to indulge his sensual appetites and 'take his fill of love until morning' (v. 18).

Look at him now, who had the world at his command, being tamely led to destruction (vv. 22-23)! The ox is just as easily led by its owner on its last journey, unaware that this time it is to be slaughtered; the fool goes happily along in his ignorance, unaware that he is just about to be slapped into the stocks for his folly; the bird drops down for the tasty seed laid down for it, unaware that it is the one that is about to be a dainty morsel. So this ignorant youth who thinks so well of himself is about to forfeit his life and will not realise it until it is too late (v. 23).

It is interesting to note how contemporary it all is. It has a timeless quality about it. Even the description of the woman as being 'loud and rebellious', whose feet never 'stay at home' (v. 11) is so typical of the kind of girl who is seen in the company of young men in our city streets in the evenings toward nightfall.

Solomon wisely paints this picture knowing that his son can identify with the kind of sensations experienced by the foolish youth and recognise they have drawing power. Having warned, instructed, reasoned, and taught his son, and having given this example of ruinous folly, he fixes his children's attention (v. 24) with two imperatives (v. 25). The first is not to let the heart be drawn aside to her ways. This will happen only if one gets a very distorted view of things, but it can very quickly happen if principles are undermined by neglect and lost sight of. The second is not to stray into her paths. If you keep the right kind of company this is not likely to happen. However, opportunity sometimes gives rise to impulse that overrides reason, and the result is a sudden fall. Invariably the way this happens is via compromise with the claim, 'I can handle it', or, 'I am strong enough to withstand it.'

'No, you can't, and no, you're not', says Solomon decisively, 'for she has cast down many wounded, and all who were slain by her were strong men.' Note the 'many' and the 'strong'. This is no area for bravado or to underestimate the strength of the enemy. Reflect soberly upon what will happen to you if you are captured (v. 27), and then make absolutely sure it cannot happen!

If you have teenage children, are you as thorough and realistic as Solomon in instructing them in all the life matters covered in these chapters?

8:1-11. The real goods! Solomon now turns away from the sordid subject of adultery and the immoral woman to consider the beauty and excellence of wisdom, cast here as a woman who stands out in stark contrast to the loose woman of the previous section. 8:1-3 echoes 1:20-22, while 8:10-11 is reminiscent of 3:14-15. The question introducing this section seems suggestive of a contest between wisdom and folly, and this appears to be confirmed at the end of chapter 9 as this section closes. There is a lot of 'noise' in the world, with all sorts of things clamouring for the attention of the young, who often feel the thrill of the sights and sounds of the world's marketplace and are attracted to what is 'loud and lurid'.

As opposed to the clandestine activity of the immoral woman painted with artificial beauty and expressing herself with sticky, subversive attractiveness, this woman, as the personification of wisdom, takes her stand in full public view (v. 2), speaks plainly, clearly and openly with words that are straightforward, reasonable and open to examination.

Wisdom speaks, loud and clear (v. 1). The question, 'Does not wisdom cry out?' invites the questions, 'Does she?' and 'How?' The answers open out of the narrative that follows. Wisdom is said to stand in all the prominent places: on the heights (v. 2), along the way (v. 2), where the paths meet (v. 2), at the city gates (v. 3); and in each place the message is the same. The point seems to be that wisdom is neither hard to find nor difficult to hear. Indeed, the word used in v. 1 indicates that her crying out is personally engaging, as someone might hail you from across the road to attract your attention. Her standing on the heights speaks of her unchallenged supremacy and authority. 'Along the way' suggests her coming alongside people as they travel through life, while 'where the paths meet' might indicate that she is there when a choice has to be made about the way ahead from among a variety of alternatives.

In Israel, major cities having walls for security, the gates naturally became the focal point for any matters of importance. See, for example, Genesis 34:20; Exodus 32:26; Deuteronomy 16:18; 17:5; Judges 5:11; Ruth 4:1; 2 Samuel 3:27; 18:4; Proverbs 31:23,31; Isaiah 13:2; 29:21; Jeremiah 17:19; 26:10; 38:7; 39:3; Lamentations 5:14; Daniel 2:49; Amos 5:10,12,15; Zechariah 8:16. Her presence 'by the gates, at the entry of the city' therefore informs us that she is there where important discussions, judgements, and business and other transactions take place.

'Men ... sons of men' (v. 4) is a poetic device serving not only for emphasis but also to indicate that wisdom addresses men both individually and generally, both now and through every generation. (See also the use of this expression in Psalms 8:4; 80:17; 144:3; 146:3; Isaiah 51:12; 56:2; Jeremiah 49:18.)

Jesus said, 'I have not come to call the righteous, but sinners to repentance' (Matthew 9:13). These double-edged words, an offence to the self-righteous, were welcome to the 'sinners'. Likewise, the words of wisdom's address: 'O you simple ones ... you fools...' (v. 5), do not exactly flatter the proud, but are good news to those who recognise their need! By and large people are incredibly naïve when it comes to the major issues of life and death, and they progress through life shutting out from their minds the things to which they really ought to be giving their attention. Wisdom calls upon such men and women to display some intellectual backbone in the way they think about these things and adopt a more canny approach to life (v. 5). The whole verse is a bit of a wake-up call to the comfortably ignorant.

8:6-11. James 3. Read my lips! It is sometimes necessary to get a reaction out of one's hearers before it becomes possible to communicate the message one wants to get across. Those who are fast asleep have to be woken up before they can be got to listen! Now wisdom says, 'Listen!', in much the same way as we might address a child, commanding his close attention to what we have to tell him. 'Excellent things', 'noble things', 'worthy things' (v. 6a) – what wisdom has to say is eminently worth hearing. A former President of the United States of America famously used the words, 'Read my lips!' The expression caught on, but more often than not it became used in a sarcastic way of people, and particularly politicians, when their lips uttered lies and deceit. Not so here: 'From the opening of my lips will come right things; for my mouth will speak truth; wickedness is an abomination to my lips. All the words of my mouth are with righteousness; nothing crooked or perverse is in them. They are all plain to him who understands, and right to those who find knowledge' (vv. 6b-9).

What could be clearer? Whose lips are we going to watch and read? When we think about these terms there is a truly amazing contrast between the voice of wisdom and what we generally hear from others. Jeremiah frankly observed: 'The heart is deceitful above all things ... who can know it?' (Jeremiah 17:9). 'Out of the heart the mouth speaks' said Jesus (Matthew 12:34), and how true that is! Because there is something about the heart of man that is essentially unreliable, it follows that the words that proceed from his mouth are not necessarily to be trusted or depended upon. Consider the contrasts: our words are not always of such quality as to be worth hearing (v. 6a); nor are they always right, for they are sometimes mistaken (v. 6b); nor are they always truth, for they are mixed with much error (v. 7); nor is there perfect justice in them, for they are often uttered from impure motives (v. 8a); they are often convoluted and distorted, giving away the disorder and deviousness of our thoughts (v. 8b). In summary, they are far from plain and understandable (v. 9). If we are of an understanding heart (v. 5) we will acknowledge that all these things are true, giving us all the more reason to attend to the voice of wisdom in whom all the qualities so deficient in man are to be found in perfection and abundance.

Wisdom, then, first wakes us up, then appeals to our reason to see that we should give her our serious attention. She then tells us more about herself and what she has to offer. The ever popular 'What would you rather be...?' question invariably gives the choice between two alternatives each of which contains an unwelcome ingredient. For example, 'What would you rather be: fabulously rich but ugly, or stunningly good looking but poor?' The question is of course a hypothetical one. However, there are often strings attached to many of the attractive offers in life; so much so that when one comes our way we ask: 'Where's the catch?' So where is the catch in what wisdom offers? 'Ah, here it is!' says someone: 'What would you rather have – wisdom or wealth?' For v. 10 says, 'Receive my instruction, and not silver, and knowledge rather than choice gold.' This is the kind of way so many people think, but it is faulty. For one thing, it is not that kind of a choice, which a simple illustration will demonstrate.

Suppose a relative of yours dies and in his will has left you to choose whichever one of the two cars in his garage you wish to have before disposing of the other. On entering his double garage you see the two cars: one is an eye-catcher, gleaming and impressive, a real status symbol. However, the report from the service agent reveals that beneath the flashy exterior is a vehicle which will do nothing but let you down as well as being a pain to drive. The other car, however, though it may not turn heads, has an excellent service history, will 'go on for ever', and on examination has everything you could need or desire in a car. Armed with this knowledge, if you are looking for a reliable means of transport, though technically you have a choice, in reality you have none.

The choice between wisdom and riches is of the same order. People who are canny about cars are not always the same when it comes to life choices. To many people it is the money that gleams, the money that draws, the money that holds promise, the money that will give security, the money that will take them places (or so they think) ... and they do not give wisdom a second look. Times beyond number, riches without wisdom have brought only harm and disaster to their possessors. What Paul wrote to Timothy in 1 Timothy 6:9-10 is demonstrably true. There is actually no comparison between wisdom and riches. This is what the end of v. 11 is saying, and those with clear perception and know what they are about will not hesitate to choose wisdom above silver and gold. For wisdom has something of such far superior worth as to make money look cheap by comparison. Solomon himself sought wisdom over riches (read 2 Chronicles 1:7-12), and although God gave him wealth as well, it was his wisdom that established the nation and for which he was renowned.

8:12-21. Job 28. Wisdom's authority. Verse 12 encapsulates the intrinsic qualities of wisdom. Knowledge is the foundational element, which wisdom is ever searching out and building upon. Wisdom is knowledge applied in two areas in particular: prudence and discretion. Hence the figurative description of these qualities being wisdom's intimate companions. Prudence is really discernment of how to pick out what is relevant to a given situation. It involves a depth of understanding to be able to manipulate the essential elements to work toward a given objective. Discretion is a close relative, ensuring progress toward that objective without leaving a trail of destruction in the wake!

To give a trivial example, if you are going to climb a mountain, you could without any preparation set out and hope for the best. That would be foolish. Wisdom dictates that you should at least have some knowledge of what to expect when you start, what equipment is generally required, how long the climb is likely to take, what weather conditions are forecast, and so on. When you know these things, you are then in a position to decide that it would be prudent to set off at such-and-such a time, take appropriate footwear, a compass, suitable warm clothing and waterproofs, and some food, and let people know about your movements. Discretion advises you that you should check before raiding the larder that you are not depriving someone else of what they need, and if you don't possess a compass to ensure you borrow one from someone who is willing to lend it and not help yourself without asking; also to check you are not interfering with or encroaching upon the plans of others, and so on.

How much more important is it that we should have wisdom for the matter of living out our lives in God's world, which is so much more complex and challenging than a mountaineering expedition and has infinitely more at stake! Yet how many people drift through life totally unprepared for the hazards that await them, knowing neither where they came from nor where they are going, suffering blow after blow to which they have no idea how to respond, shutting their eyes against the inevitable, and demonstrating from beginning to end a singular lack of wisdom where it was most needed.

8:13. A necessary interruption. What is interesting is the relevance of v. 13 in this section, for if we were to read through from v. 12 to v. 21 omitting v. 13 it would make good sense; indeed, it would appear to read better. It is the kind of statement an editor would cut, arguing that it does not belong here and interrupts the flow of thought. However, we are not at liberty to edit the Word of God, and are obliged to note that this interjection intrudes upon our senses. In the middle of comfortable thoughts about the desirable qualities of knowledge, discretion, prudence, counsel, judgement, understanding and strength we are confronted by disturbing matters of evil, pride, arrogance, perverse speech and hatred. Furthermore, in the midst of a passage that is all about wisdom, suddenly there is a reference to the fear of the Lord.

What this verse is reminding us about – again – in the stark way characteristic of Proverbs is that wisdom and the fear of the Lord cannot be separated. All these admirable and desirable qualities are really inaccessible without the Lord being at the centre of one's thinking. This was stated at 1:7, and will be reiterated at 9:10. Many seek to be wise, many would like to be thought of as wise, but the wisdom of this world, even to such extent as it acknowledges the excellent qualities described in this chapter, is ultimately void if it does not have the fear of God as its primary motivating principle.

Furthermore, 'hatred' is not a word that it is 'politically correct' to use these days. Yet it is here as an essential accompaniment to the fear of the Lord. To fear the Lord is to hate evil. Do we fear the Lord? This can at least in part be revealed by the answer to the question, 'Do we hate evil?' What is meant by 'evil' is not only that wickedness that deliberately flouts God's laws (as set out in the Ten Commandments), but also the pervading indifference to what

God has said and what he requires, the consequences of which are evident throughout our world in a million ways. Wisdom does not dally with evil in any shape or form; nor is wisdom indifferent to it as if it were of no concern or relevance; nor does it turn a blind eye or a deaf ear to it. Wisdom *hates* evil, wherever it is seen, and however it manifests itself. Deep revulsion of it is a fundamental accompaniment of the fear of the Lord.

Pride and arrogance, words with closely related meanings, would seek to separate wisdom from the fear of the Lord – and say so, expressing themselves with perverse speech. Pride is voluble with alternatives to this uncompromising wisdom. But there is only one true wisdom, which starts with the fear of the Lord and continues in the fear of the Lord, submitting self-confidence and self-interest to him, loving what he loves, and hating what he hates. There is no hope for progress in wisdom for those who have either not reached this point or turned away from it.

Thus v. 13 interrupts us and makes us pause for serious self-examination. If we have the humility to honour the wisdom of God, then we will certainly benefit from what follows, heeding wisdom's counsel and submitting to her sound judgement (v. 14).

8:14. Wisdom's integrity. 'Counsel is mine' (v. 14a). Good advice comes from wisdom – but how? If wisdom is inseparable from the fear of the Lord, it is equally true that wisdom is founded upon the word of the Lord. Psalm 19:7 says, 'The testimony of the Lord is sure, making wise the simple.' It is what *he* says that matters ultimately, not what others may recommend. Eve was misled by the serpent's cunning, and having listened to his words she concluded that the tree was 'desirable to make one wise'. She took what God had said she should not take, having first taken the wrong 'wise' advice. The Word of God is the first and final word where wisdom is concerned. More, however, is needed than simply knowing the Word of God, and this again is a reason for the interjection of v. 13. We need the eyes of our understanding to be enlightened (Ephesians 1:18), because a right understanding of God's Word is not accessible to the unaided human mind, in just the same way as no prophecy of Scripture is of any private interpretation. The Holy Spirit who gave it is the Holy Spirit who interprets it. Paul made a similar point in 1 Corinthians 2:11-16. It is only through revering the Lord and humbly looking to him that we may truly understand his Word and become wise in our knowledge of him. We may *know* what God's Word says about this and that, but it will only *counsel* us when we bow to his lordship and wait upon his will.

'Counsel ... and sound wisdom.' The NIV translates, 'sound judgement', which probably brings out the shade of meaning as well as any other word. 'Judgement' here is the critical faculty that enables one to arrive at a balanced conclusion. Imagine yourself in a church meeting where discussion is taking place about an important matter. There are all sorts of contributions, people coming at the matter from various directions. Some comments are clearly relevant, others less so. Some make valid points that no one else has thought of. The minutes pass, and as they do so the discussion reveals that the issue is vastly more complex than was originally supposed, so that people are left wondering whether it will even be possible to reach a decision out of all the confusion. Finally someone stands up and makes some straightforward observations that touch the heart of the matter, revealing how all aspects of the discussion relate to it, and the fog clears and the way forward is seen. That person has clearly helped by making sense out of it all so that progress can now be made. A good example of this is found in Acts 15 when the early church was facing an issue that was far from easy to resolve, and a study of the problem and how it came to be resolved will reward anyone prepared to give it the time. Sound judgement is that aspect of wisdom that discerns how the Word of God is to be applied in complex situations in life, distinguishing what is relevant from a mass of often conflicting information, and using it all to work towards a just and satisfactory outcome. It is 'sound' because, unlike diplomacy, it never compromises on the truth and never yields on matters of principle.

'Understanding' is the next attribute of wisdom mentioned in v. 14. There are different levels of understanding, but that of wisdom can only be described as a full and perfect understanding. Pastoral problems in the church are not always resolved as they ought to be, and very often the reason is lack of understanding on the part of those trying to deal with them. It is one thing to know what the Scriptures teach concerning a problem that has arisen, but it is quite another to know how they should be applied in any given situation, which often depends upon a good understanding of the circumstances surrounding the problem as well as the human nature of the people involved.

Understanding is many layered, and every layer has its relevance. Suppose I plant a shrub, knowing all about the conditions of light and drainage it requires, and suppose I am competent in my knowledge of when and how to prune it. Yet for all my care and attention it remains weedy and sickly looking. I might conclude that it is just a poor specimen and needs to be ripped out and replaced with something better. However, one day someone, observing this shrub, says to me: 'What's that doing there? It will never do well in that position: it doesn't like an acid soil.' My understanding was good as far as it went. Nevertheless it was fundamentally flawed because it was deficient in one essential area and so could not be put to good use. The consequence was an incorrect diagnosis and a potentially disastrous solution as far as the plant was concerned. If in the church some of the members remain sickly and do not appear to grow in the faith the problem may just be a lack of understanding on the part of those responsible for nurturing them. The example of the plant, limited though it is, does demonstrate the very great need for wisdom and understanding on the part of leaders if they are to fulfil their role effectively.

Finally, from v. 14, is the 'strength' of wisdom. Of Stephen it was said, 'They were not able to resist the wisdom and the Spirit by which he spoke' (Acts 6:10). The wisdom he displayed carried all before it. His arguments were powerful, convincing, irrefutable, sweeping aside every obstacle his disputants put in his way (Acts 6:9). Such is its strength. Wisdom rules, having everything on its side except falsehood. It argues from the unassailable position of truth with the power of knowledge and understanding. See from Acts 7 how Stephen knew the Scriptures; see how he understood them; see how he perceived what God was doing throughout the history of Israel; see his insight into the relevance of the history of his people to what was happening at the present time; and see the masterful way in which he led his persecutors up to the devastating application that cut them to the quick.

8:15-16. The foundation for authority. The 'kings', 'rulers', 'princes', 'nobles' and 'judges' of vv. 15-16 cover every form of leadership and responsibility, while 'reign', 'decree justice' and 'rule' or 'govern' indicate the scope of their administration. This is not to suggest that all who are in positions of authority are endowed with wisdom or that it is by wisdom that they have established themselves. This would be to approach it from the wrong end. Wisdom is talking about *her* endowments, asserting that these people need to be endowed with heavenly wisdom if they are to fulfil their God-given responsibilities properly. Solomon himself on ascending the throne had recognised and expressed before God his need of wisdom to judge his people (1 Kings 3:6-9). There is no disputing that Solomon, given the wisdom of God, really reigned in the fullest sense of the word.

8:17. Provision for leadership. It is formidably disturbing to be placed in a position of responsibility and feeling totally inadequate to carry it out. For such people v. 17 should be a tremendous encouragement. This is confirmed by James who writes about the way God gives generously and without reproach to those who apply to him in faith (James 1:5-6). Notice carefully the way wisdom makes herself available. She says first, 'I love those who love me.' She does not love those who are merely infatuated with her, nor does she love those who are looking for a casual relationship with her! No young lady with her wits about her responds to that kind of approach from a young man; much less so lady wisdom to her casual admirers! The heart must ache for wisdom, the mind must crave for wisdom, the indispensable need for wisdom must be felt, the true worth of wisdom must be recognised.

The wonderful thing is that wisdom responds to an earnest suitor. Earnest? That is seen in the manner of pursuit of the suit: 'Those who seek me diligently will find me.' (The NIV translation is weak at this point.) The imagery behind this diligent seeking is that of being up at the crack of dawn in pursuit of some objective. So important is it to you that you do not leave it a moment later than you must and you are wide awake and fully alert to apply yourself to the task. I remember getting up ridiculously early one morning many years ago to undertake the long journey to visit my fiancée in order to be able to spend as much time with her as possible. Had I been as diligent in my pursuit of wisdom I might have been wiser than I am today! Wisdom loves those who love her, and rewards those who spend time with her. It is a relationship that is increasingly rewarding as it is given the opportunity to develop. This is a promise from God, to be accepted in faith, and to be depended upon when put to the test.

Those whom we recognise as possessing wisdom have usually come by it through necessity. They have gained experience by being put to the test over and over again in different ways. When you find yourself in situations of difficulty or perplexity, not knowing how to proceed, remember the promise of this verse as you apply yourself to understanding.

8:18-21. Wisdom's reward. Thus far we have been considering the need for wisdom in order to exercise responsibility for the benefit of others. In vv. 18-21 we are now told of God's overflowing generosity. These verses reflect Solomon's own experience. In response to his seeking wisdom in order to be able to govern God's people, God answered 'over-abundantly' by adding to him riches and honour (1 Kings 3:11-13). The verses before us in Proverbs make it plain that it is not material wealth that is principally in view here, for they speak of 'riches and righteousness' in the same breath (v. 18b), and of the fruit of wisdom being 'better than ... fine gold' (v. 19). Those with a hankering for material wealth may find this disappointing, but for those who have a true perspective on the value of things this in not in the least disturbing.

(Note: the NIV translates v. 18b as 'wealth and *prosperity*'. But the word in the original always has moral connotations and is invariably translated as *righteousness* or *justice*, and should be so translated here.)

The truth is that wisdom rewards *in every way* those who find her. They are the undoubted beneficiaries of the relationship. Material abundance may be included, indeed often it is, and certainly it was in Solomon's case, but it is not by any means the main thing. A person is rich who is amply supplied with all that is needed with some to spare with which to bless others, even though he may have a very limited income when compared with many. The life of many a millionaire has been filled with disappointment and heartache, emptiness and frustration. Not so for those who have embraced wisdom, from whom there is an inexhaustible supply to fill their treasuries (v. 21). The 'enduring' riches (v. 18b) are by definition not those of the kind that sprout wings and fly away (23:5).

Verse 19 enlarges on v. 11. Wisdom is better than rubies and better than fine gold because what she produces (her fruit) is superior to these things. She is also better because what she gives (her revenue) excels these things. The nuances of meaning are subtle, but we may draw parallels with what has just preceded, the fruit being likened to the prudence, knowledge, discretion, counsel, understanding and strength of wisdom, and the revenue to the riches and honour she bestows. The possessor of wisdom from God has much to give and everything to gain.

In v. 20 wisdom is indicating again where she is to be found. If you want to track down a woman in town you need to know her favourite haunts, for that is where you are most likely to find her, or information that will lead you to her. Wisdom haunts the way of righteousness and those looking for her will certainly not miss her if they are concerned for righteousness, technically, morally and personally, and if they pursuing a true course on the path of justice in their personal lives in their relationships with other people. This isn't for those on the edge of the action peering in but for those committed up to the hilt and fully involved. Those who are there with her and accompanying her are the ones who will receive to the full from her (v. 21). Those who love wisdom will have no fear of their resources becoming depleted, for she continually replenishes their treasuries from her inexhaustible supply.

8:22-31. Wisdom's credentials. What credentials can wisdom present to support her claim and demonstrate her ability to give all these things? These verses could be thought of as her *curriculum vitae*. At the same time they give some insight on the creation of the universe. It must be remembered that this passage is poetry, unlike the account at the beginning of Genesis which is prose. It is not a description of how creation came into being, but a statement of the part played by wisdom throughout the process. Firstly, wisdom was there 'before' everything. This passage looks back to before the foundation of the world and is set in the context of what God was about to do in bringing it all into being (v. 22). Before creation, beyond time itself, wisdom was with the LORD (v. 23).

Verses 24 and 25 speak of wisdom being 'brought forth'. This is no more being called into existence as the bringing forth of a child from the womb calls it into existence. A child in the womb plays no active part in this world; that starts at the moment of birth. Wisdom says, 'When there were no depths I was brought forth.' She was brought forth to play her essential active part in the work that was taking place, for the role she was to play in the way everything was to be made. And so, secondly, wisdom was there 'when' everything came into being (vv. 27-29). The unique qualities of her life were exhibited in every aspect of the heavens and the earth as they took shape: their design, their immensity, their order, their beauty, their abundance, their purpose – all exhibited then, and continue to reveal now, the hand of wisdom (v. 30). We could say that wisdom was there in the concept (vv. 22-23), there at the design stage (vv. 24-26), and there in its execution (vv. 27-29).

There is a strange irony that even atheists exploring and studying any aspect of the natural world find themselves using words like 'awesome', 'amazing', 'incredible', 'beautiful' of their discoveries when they see how everything works so wonderfully together. What they are witnessing, even if they fail to recognise or acknowledge it, is the wisdom of God pervading the whole. The NKJV nicely describes wisdom as the 'master craftsman' beside God and his daily delight. It is a pictorial way of describing what Genesis records, that 'God saw everything that he had made, and indeed it was very good' (Genesis 1:31).

Unadulterated joy is present here (vv. 30-31). Picture the happy, innocent laughter of a child having fun, the sense of unspoiled pleasure and complete contentment, and you have some idea of the kind of rejoicing of wisdom in the created world. Perfect and delightful, it was a pleasure to behold. More than that, though, the pleasure was supremely in its *life*. The world was made vibrant with life, and it was made, above everything else, with man in mind. Man was the pinnacle and perfection of God's creation, made with infinite wisdom and understanding as a being who would respond face to face with the eternal God.

Some see this passage as speaking of Christ. What is stated here is certainly applicable to Christ insofar as he is both eternal and perfect in wisdom and understanding. All things were created by him, through him and for him (Colossians 1:16). As wisdom is personified in this passage we may legitimately see parallels. Nevertheless this passage is speaking of wisdom, that wisdom which is found in its fullness in Christ (1 Corinthians 1:24; Colossians 2:3). 'The LORD by wisdom founded the earth; by understanding he established the heavens' (3:19).

This same wisdom involved in the creation of the universe through Christ is the wisdom delighting in men (v. 31), and giving to men. It reminds us of the power of God at work in Christians which is like the power that raised his Son from the dead (Ephesians 1:19-20).

8:32-36. Listen, watch, wait, find. Wisdom has told us who she is, on the basis of which she says, 'Now therefore, listen to me...'. We have every reason to listen to wisdom, and no reason not to do so. Not only so, but we also have every encouragement and incentive to listen to wisdom. There is blessing for those who follow wisdom (vv. 32,34). That is the way of true happiness. If we would be happy, let us be wise. It more than repays the effort!

Keeping to the ways of wisdom (v. 32) indicates giving close attention to being found in the places where wisdom may be gained. This has both positive and negative associations: our lives will be actively engaged in certain areas, and will actively avoid others. It involves making appropriate choices in life. It requires us to be hearing wise instruction (v. 33) in order to become wise. 'Do not disdain it.' This is not something to be ignored or neglected, or casually dismissed, or treated lightly as if it were of no consequence. There are some people we go out of our way to listen to, perhaps because they are celebrities and we don't want to miss their appearance, perhaps because they are great entertainers, perhaps because they have rich voices and a compelling style of speaking. What are they, though, to the voice of wisdom, and what have they to offer by comparison? There is blessing to those who listen to wisdom, who watch at her gates, and who wait by her doors. The words, 'listen', 'watch', 'wait' all have connotations of vigour. 'Listen ... hear ... listen...' (the same word is used in vv. 32,33,34). The word implies an intelligent and attentive hearing. 'Watching' is the kind of watching required of a man on guard at night, staying awake and alert for any sound of activity and being prepared to respond appropriately. 'Waiting' means observing closely for any signs of movement, as a reporter might wait outside a court room in an important case, ready to pounce as soon as the door opens in order to be the first to get the story. Is this how alert we are when it comes to *daily* (v. 34) reading from the Word of God? How serious are we really about acquiring the wisdom that comes from God? How blessed are we really?

Listening, watching, waiting results in finding, finding, finding (v. 35)! The blessing is in the finding. Think of the man who found hidden treasure in a field (Matthew 13:44). Bursting with joy over his discovery he sold everything he had in order to buy the field. Wisdom is hidden from those who are not prepared to look for her, but what joy there is for those who discover her true worth! There is Life with a capital 'L'! It is real life, true life, full life. Indeed, it is eternal life. Its concomitant is the favour of the LORD. What a wonderful thing it is to find acceptance with God, to be 'in his good books', to know that he looks upon you with pleasure and intends to prosper you!

By contrast (v. 36), there is an inevitability about the consequences of sinning against wisdom. What does it mean to sin against wisdom? Basically it means to disdain wisdom, to spurn her invitations, to turn away from her call. It is the sort of thing people are doing every day without giving it a second thought, and yet little do they realise they are actually doing violence to their own souls. If to love wisdom means life (v. 35), to hate wisdom spells death

(v. 36). To be without wisdom is to be without God, for it begins with the fear of the LORD. To be without wisdom is to place oneself outside of everything that God has made, because the wisdom of God is evident throughout his creation. Therefore to hate wisdom is, by both definition and implication, to put oneself into outer darkness (Matthew 8:12), the place of banishment from the presence of God, where there is no blessing but only weeping and wailing and gnashing of teeth. There is no other place to go, no middle way, no alternative, only the desolation of eternal ruin.

9:1-6. A great invitation. Jesus may have had in mind this last call to the house of wisdom when he spoke the parable of the great supper (Luke 14:16-24). No one on the day of judgement will be able to complain that there was no room in the kingdom of God or that they were not invited. The picture here is that wisdom has left nothing undone that needs to be done for anyone to be able to partake of what she has to offer. 'Seven' (v. 1) is a number of completeness, of perfection. The house of wisdom is elevated, strong and magnificent, perfect in every way. As such it is a place of habitation, a place of safety, a place of beauty. The picture continues (v. 2) by indicating that a great feast has been prepared: the animals have been slaughtered to provide the meat for the feast, and the wine has been 'mixed', probably with spices as was the custom, and therefore ready to serve; the tables have been laid in the lavish fashion appropriate to such an occasion. All that is wanting are the guests to come and partake and enjoy. This she attends to by sending out her maids, or maidens, who issue a call in her name in such a way that none can miss it (v. 3).

It may be stretching the imagery too far to try to identify the maidens. Suffice it to say that there are many and varied events in life that highlight the need for wisdom and point us in the right direction. But more to the point is: who are the guests? Verse 4 supplies the surprising answer that it is not the nobility, not the 'bigwigs', not the important people of the city, but the 'simple' and those who 'lack understanding'. In similar fashion Jesus called not the righteous but sinners to repentance (Luke 5:32, on the occasion of the great feast Levi gave in his honour in his own house). For those in need of wisdom and understanding this is a wonderful invitation.

In the same way that bread and wine are nourishment to the body, so wisdom and understanding are nourishment to the soul (vv. 5-6). 'Forsake foolishness' (v. 6) conjures up the image of a person living in a hovel, scraping together the bare necessities of life from the most pitiful of resources, being invited to leave it all behind immediately and to take up residence as a permanent guest in a mansion. Yet that is a poor image by comparison with the call to forsake the poverty of this world of sin for the riches of the kingdom of God.

From the foregoing a legitimate point may be made about the proclamation of the gospel. One of the reasons people don't listen to the gospel is that it is so often portrayed as being about things that are of no interest to them. For example, the life to come for them is a long way off, and they do not consider now is an appropriate time to think about it. Sometimes people think that if they accept the gospel they will be committing themselves to lifelong sensory deprivation! They see it as, 'You don't do this, and you don't do that' – a long list of negatives. That is the only concept they can understand. For others, the adoption of 'religion' would involve a denial of their intellectual faculty – a sort of 'blind faith', and the only way to accommodate it would be for it to occupy a separate compartment in their lives, rather like oil and water in the same container, incapable of mixing.

There are things we can learn about the way we present the gospel from these chapters. Looking through chapters 8 and 9, in answer to these things, first of all the immediate relevance of wisdom is seen all the way through. It is about *life*, without making any artificial distinctions between the present and the future, between the temporal and the eternal. It is of current and vital interest to people. Secondly, it is also about *fulfilment* in every sense of the word, without a hint of sensory or any other kind of deprivation. As Jesus said, 'I have come that they may have life, and that they may have it more abundantly' (John 10:10). This is what wisdom offers. There is not a negative to be found throughout the passage. Thirdly, it is, throughout, a lucid appeal to the intellect, it is altogether *reasonable*, without the need at any point for metaphysical gymnastics. At the same time, as we have seen, there is no hint of flattery, nor is there any disguising of the basic problem of man's natural and irrational aversion to these things. It is there as a matter of fact, as part of the complete picture.

The way in which wisdom is presented gives valuable insight into the way the gospel should be presented. There are principles here that are relevant and therefore useful in guiding us in our approach to speaking with people about Christ.

9:7-9. Giving and receiving. Wisdom, like the gospel, is so compellingly attractive that it is a matter of amazement that it should be rejected. There is a telling passage in C S Lewis' final book in the 'Narnia' series, *The Last Battle*, in which every presentation of what is good and delightful and valuable was shunned as foul and worthless by those to whom it was offered. The problem lies with men's corrupted perception of these things. Therefore to say that people will accept the gospel if its content is adjusted to suit their understanding or made more appropriate to their needs is starting from the wrong end. The gospel is perfect and entire as it is. If people do not accept it, that is because there is something wrong with *them*.

In these chapters the beauty and excellence of wisdom have been presented without the artificiality of embellishments to make her appear more attractive. Her perfection requires that nothing need be added or altered. Yet, sadly, no presentation will satisfy or change the minds of scoffers. Jesus said, 'Do not cast your pearls before swine' (Matthew 7:6). When you try to put right a certain type of person all you get in return is a volley of verbal abuse or, if they are particularly wicked, physical violence (v. 7). Human nature has not changed over the millennia! There are some people you have to leave well alone. Having made your point or presented them with the truth, to pester them with it afterwards will only prove counterproductive and harmful and breed enmity (v. 7a). If they are to be won over, it will have to be in a different way. Peter gives some wise advice in this respect to wives of unbelieving husbands (1 Peter 3:1-2).

'Rebuke' (v. 8) tends to carry with it negative connotations in our minds. However, the word has a positive as well as a negative aspect, for it does not say only 'Don't do that!' but also reasons to 'Do this!' It is a matter of seeking to put something right, not to put someone down! It should be done in a spirit of gentleness (Galatians 6:1). The manner in which rebuke or instruction are received reveals the wisdom or otherwise of the person to whom it is given. To be sure, reproof may hurt a man, but if he is wise he will acknowledge its justice and honour the person who has had the difficult task of administering it (v. 8b). It will be appreciated, because correction and instruction will augment his wisdom (v. 9); he will learn from it and it will be of real benefit to him.

Reflect therefore both on how you give reproof and on how you receive it. Most of us have things to learn in these two areas!

9:10-12. In conclusion. These verses form a concluding summary to the teaching of wisdom. Wisdom starts with the fear of the LORD. Upon that basis a relationship with the LORD, who is holy and to be revered, is developed. Understanding comes through knowing him (see Jeremiah 9:23-24).

The use of the word 'For' at the beginning of v. 11 virtually identifies the LORD with wisdom. We have already commented at 3:2 upon what is expressed in v. 11. Many people want to live a full life, and many live with a lurking fear of it being cut short in some way or other. It is a mark of wisdom to consider actually how *few* are our days on earth (see Psalm 90:10-12). Aware of the brevity of life, we should apply our hearts to wisdom, for it is only in wisdom's way that full use may be made of them. There is little point in living to 100 if in those years less is accomplished than could have been achieved by the age of 50 with application. A year of wisdom is worth more than a decade of ignorance! We must therefore understand the words of v. 11 in a meaningful way. Yet, as has already been observed, other things being equal, a wise person will enjoy a longer and fuller life than an unwise one (and, incidentally, the statistics confirm it!).

The comparison in v. 12 might be a little obscure if we come at it from the wrong angle. If I say, 'It's in your own interest to take my advice,' not only do I want you to take it, but I am assuring you that you will be the better for it; you will be doing yourself a favour; you will be doing it for yourself. Similarly, 'If you are wise, you are wise for yourself,' indicates that it is a very sensible thing for you to be doing! The NIV renders it: 'your wisdom will reward you.' On the other hand, 'If you scoff, you will bear it alone,' is indicating that you will be the one who suffers for it. The statement is not suggesting that others will not be affected either by your wisdom or by your scoffing. They will. But there are personal consequences to your course of action that no one else can share, for ultimately the responsibility will be laid at your door.

9:13-18. An empty offer. These verses very deliberately and dramatically mimic vv. 1-6. They remind us that there is continual contention for attention. Little can be said of folly (v. 14), for she has constructed no impressive dwelling, nor has she prepared a feast for anyone, nor does she have anything to give. She has no one to recommend her beside herself, and so she makes up for this by being noisy and thereby drawing attention to herself! Isn't that typical of the way of folly? It consists essentially in a lot of empty noise! She is certainly very prominent (v. 14) in our towns and cities with her colourful display. For some reason this attracts the attention of passers-by (v. 15).

Hordes of young people go after her, enticed toward her noise as a moth flutters toward a light. She gives them nothing because, unlike wisdom (v. 5) she has nothing to give. Instead she tells them they will get a kick out of what is unlawful (v. 17a) and a thrill out of clandestine activity (v. 17b). In this she speaks truth, but it is the sweetness in the mouth that turns bitter in the stomach (v. 18).

To turn aside to folly leads to indulging oneself at someone else's expense. No one is the gainer thereby. The one who enters her house, we are told, 'does not know' that the dead are there. Ignorance is the trading name of folly. Those who reject wisdom in favour of the strident tones of folly simply do not know what they are letting themselves in for. They bring judgement upon their own heads by scorning the voice of wisdom, reaping the fruit of their own choosing. They enter the company of the dead, those destined for hell (v. 18).

It is a tragedy of the first order that anyone should go that way when wisdom offers what she does. The Lord says, 'I have no pleasure in the death of one who dies. Therefore turn and live!' (Ezekiel 18:32).

The contrast is absolutely desperate, and should cause anguish to anyone contemplating the folly of those who listen to the wrong voice and go astray. If we have rightly understood these chapters of Proverbs, this conclusion to this first section of the book should make us recoil in horror. Perhaps it is here for this very reason.

Part 2

Proverbs 10:1 to 22:16

First collection
of proverbs from Solomon

The proverbs of Solomon, as stated earlier, are not all his own, but he was responsible in the first instance for their collection as a compiler and they were later added to in the time of Hezekiah (25:1 to 29:27).

This section starts in the same way as at 1:1. It is as if at the beginning the compiler is saying, 'I am presenting to you the proverbs of Solomon, but first let me tell you about the importance of wisdom.' Having now done that, at 10:1 he says, 'Here they are.'

The first nine chapters, which speak about wisdom in the fear of the Lord and the need for, and the benefits of, wisdom, are something of a preface to the proverbs proper. They are full of instruction, directly and personally engaging the reader and urging the reader to give attention to wisdom; they set out the purpose of the proverbs and why it is important to give thought to them. They are the context in which the proverbs are to be understood and received. From this point onward the exhortations cease and observations on life begin in the form of proverbs to be pondered and applied for the acquisition of wisdom for life.

10:1. Ephesians 6:1-4. Colossians 3:20-21. The opening proverb in this new section provides a fitting link with the long introduction in which Solomon has said, in effect, 'My son, be wise...' But it is also an appropriate introduction to what appears to be a random collection of wise sayings and observations, reminding us that these are things for the young to get fixed into their consciousness to help equip them for life. It also indirectly reminds us of the supreme importance of the family, the fundamental unit of society, and the bonds that exist when it functions as it ought and the troubles it produces when it fails to do so. What applies to the 'son' in the Proverbs will often apply equally to the 'daughter'. It may be that the son is singled out because of the leadership responsibilities he may in due course carry in the family and in society.

Wisdom and folly in a son are the subject of this proverb, and wisdom and folly more generally are the subject throughout the proverbs.

It is probably fairly characteristic of adolescents that they are little aware of the way their conduct affects their parents. They are probably preoccupied with their own independence and thinking about making their way in life. Good parents, on the other hand, though often thinking very much about the same things, are more concerned that their raw youngsters be adequately prepared for what they are going to face in life, and are potentially anxious for them. So the way children conduct themselves has a profound effect upon their parents. A good father takes pride in the achievements of his son; it is a natural and proper paternal response. He is happy for his son when he sees him getting on well in life and establishing himself. He always wanted and worked toward the best for his son, and now to see him maturing in wisdom is a great pleasure. A wise son will appreciate that and honour his father.

But this proverb is one of direct contrast and, as is typical of Proverbs, opposite aspects are faithfully presented. The focus immediately shifts to the opposite scenario. A good mother's tender and protective nature is deeply injured by a son who is foolish. Though by now he may be well beyond her influence, she still yearns over him in his waywardness, and every report of his irresponsible behaviour depresses her spirit and weighs heavily upon her mind. 15:20 indicates that a son of this kind not only disregards his father's instruction, he also despises his mother. 17:25 is very similar and indicates that grief and bitterness are shared by both parents when their son turns out to be a fool. 19:13 takes it even further, stating that a foolish son can have a ruinous effect upon his father. In such a case it may be, as has so often happened, that a father has had to bail out a wayward son who has got himself into financial difficulties, often out of relatively limited resources of his own. But, worse than that, a son who gains a reputation for folly actually tarnishes the name of his father: he disgraces the family name. 19:26 takes it even further still, envisaging a son who so despises his parents that, having exploited them to the full, he has no further use for them. This is the opposite of fulfilling his responsibilities as expressed in the Fifth Commandment. 23:24-25 express how things ought to be, bringing us full circle to the beauty and value of family relationships founded and built upon reverence for the Lord.

For parents, it is good to show to your children the pleasure it is to you when they do well, and to praise them for it. It is also right to show how much foolish behaviour causes grief. Family relationships should be warm, open and demonstrative, not cold, secretive and formal. Young people having left home, and perhaps having far less contact with their parents, should nevertheless be aware that the parental interest in their affairs continues to follow them. Good parents never lose this concern. Respect for one's parents (which is implicit in the Fifth Commandment, Exodus 20:12) will involve a consciousness not only of what they have *done*, but also of how they *feel*. Gladness and grief can each have a profound effect upon a person's well-being. If you are a young person about to leave home, what kind of effect are you going to have upon your own parents or, for that matter, upon any others who have a close interest in your development and progress? If you are older, are you aware these things still apply and will continue to do so throughout the life of your parents?

Sometimes young people assume that their life is their own business and that it is unreasonable for their parents to take such a close interest in what they 'get up to', especially at that period when they are emerging into maturity. They tend to view things that happen in terms of the effect they have on themselves more than on others. This somewhat self-centred attitude is perhaps partly attributable to living in an individualistic society, and perhaps partly also to the fact that young people have never experienced the emotions associated with long term commitment and responsibility. Individualism is remarkably destructive of a strong society. Parents do well who teach their children that they have a responsibility toward others and that how they conduct themselves is not only important to others but can affect them deeply. But they need to do this without employing the techniques of emotional exploitation. As well as inculcating sound principles, parents need to help their offspring think about in a straightforward manner and understand some of the ways their attitudes and behaviour affect others, whether for good or for bad. So in whatever ways might be appropriate, according to the situation, a father should be saying words to the effect: 'My son, if your heart is wise, my heart will rejoice – indeed, I myself; yes, my inmost being will rejoice when your lips speak right things' (23:15-16, and see also 23:24-25). Any son who respects his parents would find this an encouragement and incentive to wise conduct.

We find an example of singular lack of wisdom in Esau which must reflect at least partly upon his upbringing. He married two (not one, but two) Canaanite women who were a grief to his parents (Genesis 26:34-35). The reason no doubt is that these wives had no time for the faith of their parents-in-law. Too late Esau became aware of the displeasure of Isaac and Rebekah, and supposedly to make some amends he went ahead and married another woman, this time an Ishmaelite (Genesis 28:8-9), thereby revealing that he had not really begun to understand the nature of the problem. As a mature forty-year-old it had not even occurred to him that his parents would be, and how they would be, profoundly affected by these things. Proverbs 17:21,25 are indicative of the long-term and unremitting emotional pain foolish offspring have upon caring parents. It is a bitter thing indeed that many parents carry to their dying day. Many a godly mother and father, though enjoying the comfort of the Holy Spirit, nevertheless have been deeply troubled by wayward children, rather like a nagging pain of which one is sometimes more conscious, sometimes less, but which never actually goes away, depressing the spirits. At 27:11 we see another aspect of the way a son's wisdom affects parents. There is perhaps no better testimony to the character and integrity of a father than a son who has grown up wise. There are always reproach and contempt in the world, but a godly family, where the children fear the Lord and have good standing in society for their integrity and industry, are a witness to the validity of the standards set and followed and taught by the parents. Such parents can hold up their heads without fear or shame because the grounds for reproach are demonstrably empty.

Underlying this saying there is the care parents have taken in the upbringing of the son in question. Gladness and grief will be experienced in proportion to the time and trouble the parents have invested in seeking to inculcate wisdom in their son. If there is satisfaction when all the hard work involved in a child's upbringing has been fruitful, there can also be self-recrimination when a son or daughter turns out to be a disappointment. In begetting children parents are investing in the future of the community, and how the next generation turns out is largely their responsibility.

The wisdom or otherwise of a son will be recognised in connection with the fear of the Lord (9:10) and a response to what he commands (23:24; 28:7), respect and regard for his parents' instruction (13:1; 15:5), relationships with others and the company he keeps (28:7; 29:3), application to work (10:5), choices in life, and so on. Its basic principles have already been comprehensively set out in chapters 1 to 9.

This proverb, then, is about the emotional and psychological effects a son's conduct has on his parents. In one sense the statement of the proverb is self evident. Wisdom does not merely acknowledge the truth of the statement, it probes deeper to understand *why* it is so, what the background factors are, and what is to be the best response to it. This should be the reader's objective in pondering the proverbs.

Other proverbs or parts of Scripture will have a bearing on what is stated here, perhaps by way of explaining it or elaborating on it. We could ask, what characteristics mark out a son as being wise or foolish? We could further ask, how does it affect relationships within the family? Or, how does it affect the parents' standing in society? Indeed, a simple statement like this, when pondered, can raise a great variety of questions, and it is by bringing our minds to bear on these things that we ourselves may grow in wisdom.

Consider your personal responsibility: As a son or daughter, what positive or negative influences do you have upon your parents? How can you promote gladness and proscribe grief? Or, if you are a parent with growing children, what methods are you employing to seek to instil in them godly wisdom? Be practical and particular!

[Proverbs on wise and foolish son, or equivalent: 10:1; 10:5; 13:1; 15:5,20; 17:2,21,25; 19:13a,26; 23:15,24; 28:7; 29:3.]

10:2-3. 1 Kings 21. Righteousness, wickedness and reward.

These verses are taken together because of their chiastic structure: 2a relates to 3b, and 2b relates to 3a. When placed side by side and linked with lines, the lines form a cross, hence the term 'chiastic' from the Greek letter 'chi' which is in the form of an X, thus:

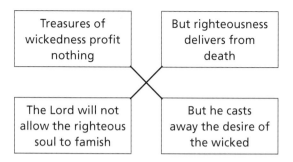

A number of the proverbs follow this pattern, though we will not repeatedly draw attention to it. They form a sort of 'sandwich' with a sharply contrasting filling.

Verse 2 comprises a stark contrast between wickedness and righteousness and the services they render, while verse 3 exposes the underlying reason why this is so.

The theme of these verses, righteousness and wickedness, closely associated with wisdom and folly, is one that runs through the whole book. In examining the usage of these terms it quickly becomes apparent that the writer is not concerned with comparative righteousness or comparative wickedness as if they were at opposite ends of a scale with various degrees of each between two extremities. Either a person is righteous or he is not; his deeds are either righteous or they are not. The notion of a sliding scale is foreign to the Scriptures. The question, 'How righteous do I have to be to meet the criteria of these verses?' is an invalid one. God does not compare our righteousness with that of our neighbour in order to determine how he will deal with us. It is essential to understand that wickedness and righteousness are terms that are defined by the law of God: a habitual law-breaker is a wicked person, while a law-keeper is a righteous person.

However, although the law is the objective criterion by which wickedness and righteousness are recognised, the ability truly to keep the law, or otherwise, lies in the heart of man. An evil heart which has no desire for the law will result in evil actions, that is, in law-breaking; while a good heart will be evidenced in a desire to keep the law. As Jesus so clearly stated in the Sermon on the

Mount, law keeping or law breaking operates at a much deeper level than that of the letter of the law. Behind the letter there is the principle, and so, for example, the law that says 'You shall not commit adultery' actually concerns itself with promiscuous desires as well as promiscuous behaviour. (It is worth noting that Jesus was not extending the scope of the law when he said this, but simply expounding the law and demonstrating that the law he gave is more extensive than the mere words.) So when in the book of Proverbs we read of righteousness or wickedness, while we must recognise these terms in relation to conformity to, or departure from, the law of God, we must also be conscious that underlying this is the fear of the Lord on the one hand or disregard of him on the other.

Throughout the Bible, righteousness is declared to be a matter of faith and imputation, even though the law is the objective standard by which it is recognised. For example, Abraham believed God, and it was accounted to him for righteousness. This was before the law was given through Moses. Abraham was seeking to live according to the standard of the law later to be given, because the law, though not as yet put into writing, was nevertheless in his heart (Genesis 15:6; taken up in Romans 4). All this is not to deny that there are degrees of righteousness, and also degrees of wickedness, in terms of conduct in the world. For example, God has testified that Lot was a righteous man (2 Peter 2:7-8), and so was Noah (Genesis 7:1), but in terms of their lives the righteousness of the latter was more clearly exhibited than that of the former.

So when in v. 3a we read that the Lord will not allow the righteous soul to famish, the reference is to a righteousness that has its roots in a heart right with God. It is not speaking of one who is merely trying outwardly to conform to the requirements of the law. It is a promise concerning God's care over those whose hearts are with him. Although the verse is couched in the material terms of the provision of food, it should be understood, partly by the nature of the comparison, but principally from the usage of statements of this kind throughout the Old Testament, that it is not limited to this. Rather, the very immediate and outward provision is given as a representation of God's care over his own at a far deeper level. Thus, for example, Isaiah 49:10 uses similar language in giving an overall description of the blessings of salvation.

The principle enunciated in v. 2 operates at two levels. There is, firstly, what might be called the earthly, or natural, level. Even at this level we often see how what is gained by wickedness serves those who amass it. Such people often suffer the consequences, sooner or later, and in one way or another, perhaps destroyed by their ill-gotten gains or brought down by others. Righteousness on the other hand often speaks up for those who find themselves in jeopardy, because they are recognised as people who can be trusted and so are spared the fate others might suffer. The reason this happens at the natural level is because we can never get away from the fact that man, however fallen, is created in the image of God, because of which the principles of righteousness and truth continue to operate, albeit in an impaired way, in the world. The best way to live is in harmony with God's creation and his intent.

However, the repeated use of the word 'often' in what has just been stated points to a problem. The problem is that from our perception of things this proverb is not universally true. It states a principle that is sometimes seen to operate, but it does not appear always to do so. Ill-gotten gains do seem to profit some people; righteousness does not always deliver from death. What is to be made of this? We might think it all very well to quote this proverb, but can it not be thrown back in our faces? How does righteousness deliver from death? Did Naboth's righteousness deliver him from death (1 Kings 21)? Did Stephen's righteousness deliver him from death (Acts 7)? What about the martyrs down the centuries? How do these things square with the statement that God watches over the righteous (for example Psalm 34:15,17, or Psalm 121)? This is why we need to look deeper than the outward appearance of things.

While we could look at the proverb from the other end and observe the problems people bring upon themselves who amass wealth by wicked means or seek personal security by ungodliness – in the form of fear of reprisal for example – this does not really sufficiently answer our questions. Many people live well without a care in the world who have gained wealth by less than honest means. On the other hand, many have suffered who have maintained a stand on righteousness and truth. Indeed, did not Jesus say that those who follow him will suffer trouble and persecution? (See, for example, Mark 10:29-30; John 15:18-21; 16:33; 2 Timothy 3:12.)

So we need to recognise that whatever appears to be the case at the superficial level, the principle set before us in this proverb operates at another level, a primary and fundamental one, because the Lord himself takes an interest in the matter. When we ask the question, 'How so?' to verse 2, the answer is returned in verse 3, which reveals to our view what is going on behind the scenes. God is protecting those he values and discarding those he finds worthless. That wicked people often appear to prosper can be a cause of offence to godly people. Psalm 73 is an example of this. Though many people have gained vast wealth by wicked means, this proverb nevertheless truly states that whatever is so gained is utterly worthless. To the materialistic mind, or viewed at the materialistic level, this may indeed seem nonsense. But when Asaph went into the presence of God (Psalm 73:17) he gained a proper perspective on the situation, including why the righteous often come in for a lot of suffering.

The book of Proverbs, like the rest of the Bible, goes deeper than the appearance of things and further than the short-term results. It deals with the *real* issues. The surface of a lake may be in turmoil and white with spray whipped up by a violent wind, when the waters below are deep and calm. The soul anchored in the depths of the love of God will not be unduly disturbed by what is happening on the surface. The wicked, incited by Satan, are always stirring up trouble and violating God's perfect law as if to give the impression that the law has ceased to operate. However, the long arm of the law – God's law – will catch up with them. What did Ahab gain by his ruthless acquisition of Naboth's vineyard except to add a nail to his coffin?

Treasures of wickedness profit nothing because God judges the wicked. Ill-gotten gains will be Exhibit A in the indictment against them in the day of judgement. In the same way that ill-gotten gains do not negate the law but only call it into operation, so the suffering of the righteous does not deny God's care but calls it into operation. Remember that it is *given* to some to suffer for the name of Christ (Philippians 1:29); also that it is a mark of all who wish to live godly lives (2 Timothy 3:12). We can be sure that Naboth, stoned as Stephen later was, experienced the same welcome at the hand of his God and Saviour (1 Kings 21:13; Acts 7:58).

What is expressed in v. 3, then, needs to be understood not in the immediate or short-term sense, for righteous people often do suffer hunger, and what wicked people crave they often do obtain, as in the case of Ahab just cited. Jesus himself suffered hunger when he was in the wilderness for forty days. When we are affected by such things we may be tempted to think that God has forgotten us, or that he fails to act justly. See for example Psalms 9, 10, 31, 44, 77, in all of which the psalmist was or had been troubled by circumstances that seemed to conflict with the care and justice of God on behalf of his people.

When everything seems out of control, God is still very much in control. The Bible makes clear that hardship and suffering, hunger and pain, trouble and perplexity, are the common experience of God's people; and yet, though this is the case, none of it denies the fact that God does care for them, or that at the last great day his perfect justice will be fully and finally vindicated. See Romans 8:31-39 and 2 Thessalonians 1:3-10. The God who will accomplish this is the same God who knows how to help and comfort his people in a timely fashion, as Paul makes clear in 2 Corinthians 1:3-11.

The theme of conflict between wickedness and righteousness runs like a thread through the Bible. Statements like this in the Book of Proverbs and many similar ones elsewhere serve as a continual reminder that God knows, God cares, God is just, and he is in control.

Those who do not have the fear of the Lord as the foundation for their lives, and for whom this life is everything, will be offended by this and many others of the proverbs, which will not make sense to them. However, what can the treasures of wickedness provide when it comes to the real issues of life? The desire of the wicked *will* perish (Psalm 112:10). Why? Because God casts them away with all their expectation. Jesus said, 'What shall it profit a man...?' (Mark 8:36).

[Related proverbs: 11:4; 21:6.]

10:4-5. Industry. The structure of these verses is similar to that of the previous two. 5a takes an example of 4b, while 5b does the same for 4a. Verse 4 is a simple, direct contrast, verse 5 is similar but more subtle. Once again, as with so many of the proverbs, these principles operate at more than one level. There is a sense in which v. 4 is obviously true. The word translated 'slack' or 'lazy' carries with it the meaning of deceit, treachery and falsehood, which indicates that there are underlying currents to idleness. A diligent person is one who has an incisiveness about him, not simply working because there is work to be done, but doing it intelligently, with purpose, and with an end in view. The 'hand' is referred to because actions are the evidence of sincere intentions. It is one thing to be 'well meaning'; it is quite another to translate this into 'well doing'.

Look again at this verse: Who is said to suffer from slackness? Verse 5 reminds us that there are particular times for purposeful activity, and the occasion missed is the occasion lost. 'To everything there is a season, a time for every purpose under heaven ... a time to plant, and a time to pluck what is planted' (Ecclesiastes 3:1-2). God has ordained that life should be ordered like this. There is a time for ease and rest, but it is not during harvest! The summer and the harvest require people to be busy gathering in the crops needed to see them through the leaner times ahead. It is not a task that can 'wait until another time' but one that has to be done when the conditions are right. The diligent farmer is watching both the crop and the weather to ensure that he gets the best he can from the harvest. Those who are thoughtful, careful and active about these things are the ones who are likely to do well, whereas those who are careless or casual are likely to be caught out by adverse circumstances. The hands of the diligent will be able to relax in due season, when the hands of the lazy will suffer the restlessness of frustration in their need.

There may be another nuance of meaning in the way v. 4 is expressed. The lazy person is the one who through his slackness will suffer for it. By contrast, the labours of the diligent person will enrich not only himself but others as well.

The mention of 'son' in v. 5 not only harks back to v. 1, but points to the social aspects of diligence and slackness. The son's responsibility in an agricultural society was to be available to shoulder responsibility, whether it be within his immediate family or in the wider community. Western society tends to be excessively individualistic and self-centred. So many people live to please themselves. 'My life is my own and I have a right to do what I like with it without interference from anyone else.' This statement is heard so often, and yet it is so manifestly false. Western society, which values personal independence and prides itself in upholding the rights of the individual, is actually remarkably vulnerable at this very point. Its very structure shows how dependent we all are upon one another, and how we cannot really live to please ourselves if we are to survive, let alone prosper.

The 'son', then, had a very important part to play in the welfare of the family, and the family in the community. His willingness or otherwise to fulfil his responsibilities would brand him as 'wise' or his conduct as 'shameful'. Though the structure of our society is so much more complex, these principles still apply even though they may be hidden beneath several layers. It may not be so obvious, but it is nevertheless true, that one who is slothful is impoverishing not only himself but also his community. It is equally true in the opposite sense of the one who is purposefully industrious. Our behaviour always impinges upon others.

Although the NIV describes the son sleeping during harvest as 'disgraceful', a term that tends to reflect solely upon the individual, the implication of the original is that of *causing* shame, and that not only to the son himself, but also to others. A parent can be filled with a sense of shame by the foolish behaviour of a son or daughter, just as much as they might be proud of a son or daughter who does well. Our conduct can have a profound effect upon those closest to us. How important are the concepts of responsibility and accountability and the recognition that we are mutually dependent upon one another in so many different ways!

Justice is not fully done to this proverb, though, by regarding it in a purely materialistic light. Just as verses 2 and 3 have a spiritual and eternal perspective, so do verses 4 and 5. What operates at the level of the material also does so in the spiritual realm. It applies just as much to the outworking of our relationship with God and our service in this world for his kingdom. Within the kingdom of God there are particular seasons for particular activities. God-given opportunities are to be recognised and taken hold of. There is to be purposeful activity of an appropriate kind in the church, labouring in God's harvest field, whether it be sowing, reaping, or praying for the increase in the period in between. We need to ask ourselves if we are doing what we ought in our life among God's people. Are we spiritually slack or sleepy? Do we give thought to what our abilities and responsibilities are? Are we exercising initiative to promote the welfare of God's people and the progress of his kingdom? Are we impoverishing or enriching the church by our presence in it? Are we a shame or honour to the cause of Christ? When it comes to our work in the church, are we lazy or diligent? Are we content to let others get on with the work, washing our hands of responsibility under various pretexts, or are we there in the action, doing what we can with a willing heart?

[Related proverbs: 6:6-11; 12:24; 13:4; 19:15; 21:5.]

10:6-7. Psalm 112. How are you remembered? These verses also form a pair, this time of linked observations about the righteous and the wicked: what proceeds from them, and how they are remembered.

The covering of the mouth may call to mind the plight of the leper who, according to the law, was to cover his mouth and cry 'Unclean, unclean' (Leviticus 13:45) in order that people would keep their distance from him for fear of contamination; or the mourner who would cover his mouth as a sign of his grief (Ezekiel 24:17,22). The word used here, however, is different, and indicates concealment in the sense of covering over or enveloping something. It is, for example, used of the covering of the mountains by the waters of the flood (Genesis 7:20), or of the cherubim covering the ark with their wings (2 Chronicles 5:8), or of being covered by disgrace (Jeremiah 3:25). The subjects of the two clauses are blessings and violence: blessings on the head, violence covering the mouth; one unashamedly open, the other damningly exposed. For here it is not a case of the wicked concealing violence in the sense of deceitfully speaking peace to cover violent intentions (which they may do), but of their mouth, that is, whatever they have to say, being covered over with violence, which is a clear demonstration of their intent whatever they may say. The mouth may be hidden, the words may not be heard, but their violence speaks for itself. It is, as the saying goes, 'written all over their faces'.

Blessings and violence are respectively attractive and repulsive. Blessing speaks of comfort and prosperity, violence of fear and ruin; blessing is concerned with the promotion of good, violence with the perpetration of evil.

Before proceeding, a matter of translation or interpretation arises in which care needs to be exercised. The first part of the verse could be thought of as blessing *coming to* the righteous, while the latter seems to indicate violence *proceeding from* the wicked, which seems to be a somewhat incongruous comparison. It may be because of this that the NIV translates the latter clause as 'violence overwhelms the mouth of the wicked', making a consistent comparison between the two in terms of what the righteous and wicked may expect. However, this translation seems forced, and translating the clause in this way only presents the same problem, except the other way round, at verse 11. It is more natural to view both verses in terms of what proceeds from the righteous and the wicked, in which case the first clause of v. 6 needs to be understood of what the righteous have to offer. There is nothing forced in looking at it in this way. One of the clearest results of the blessing of God upon his people is the way it overflows to others. The wicked have nothing to give except what is destructive. The righteous, living under and receiving the blessing of God so manifestly upon their head, are always in a position to be of blessing to others. This is exactly how God intends it should be. See how Psalm 37:21-22 and especially Psalm 112 exemplify this point.

We should think twice when we ask for God's blessing upon us: for whose benefit are we asking? However, note that the word is plural: blessings. Blessings are the individual tokens of the favour and kindness of God, expressed in so many different ways. When is the last time you counted your blessings? If you do so now, give thought to how you have enabled others to share in them.

This view of things leads naturally into the sentiments expressed in verse 7 and forms a fitting complement to what has just been said. What flows out from the righteous and the wicked determines how they will be remembered by those who have come under their influence. People are remembered for what they have done. The wicked, who have downtrodden others and made life a misery for them, thinking only of themselves and pursuing their own agendas, will be remembered only insofar as their lives may be held up as an example to arouse disgust, and no one will willingly or knowingly call their children by their name. This happens at all levels of society, whether the name be that of a tyrannical dictator of a nation or empire, or that of a tyrannical dictator within a family. The name stands for the person, and no one wishes to recall their deeds, desiring only that their name may rot.

On the other hand, the mark of a righteous person is not made by what he or she abstains from, but by how he or she contributes to society by the use of the blessings given by God. In this context consider Matthew 25:31-46, where the righteous (v. 46) are identified by what they did. By 'the memory of the righteous' is not intended only remembrance of a deceased person: it applies also to the living. There are people whose names are frequently and gladly brought to mind because their lives are, or have been, so attractive. It may be that you can think of some such people at a moment's notice. What is it about them that you find so appealing or of such value? One thing is certain: it will not be their gifts or abilities, or their prowess or personal achievements. Those things might arouse admiration or be the subject of hero-worship, but that is far removed from what is described here.

Now consider how others may think of you when they call to mind your life, not with a view to self-congratulation, but soberly in terms of how you have benefited them. Think, for example, of what was said of the Roman centurion at Capernaum (Luke 7:4-5) which, coming from elders of the Jews, was very telling; or of the reputation among the Jews of another Roman centurion, Cornelius (Acts 10:2,22). These men, though foreigners and representatives of an occupying force, were nevertheless respected, loved and well spoken of on account of the way they used their influence to promote the well-being of those under their authority. What influence do you have, and how are you using it? One final question on this pair of verses: if you desire God's blessings to be upon your head, what is the motivating principle behind that desire? Now look up and apply James 4:1-3 in this connection.

[Related proverb: 10:11.]

10:8. Humble hearing versus pompous prating. Look at the words that are set in opposition to each other: 'wise' and 'fool', 'heart' and 'prating' ('chattering', NIV), and 'receive commands' and 'fall' ('comes to ruin', NIV). Each of these contrast has something to say to us. Just as righteousness and wickedness are defined according to God's standards, so are wisdom and folly. Those who are wise and those who are fools exhibit give-away characteristics. In the book of Proverbs one of the prominent characteristics of the fool is his speech: he is disinclined to hold his tongue! He has plenty to say, but it is not worth hearing. 'Nobody is going to tell me how I should live my life', is typical of him. The wise man, on the other hand, is more ready to listen to what has worth and willing only to pass on what is of value. 'Fall' is a weak translation describing what will happen to the fool, because it gives perhaps the impression of his stumbling of his own accord, whereas the original contains the meaning of being forcibly thrust down. His empty, idle, self-opinionated verbosity will not be tolerated.

This proverb describes two types of people not in the privacy of their own homes but 'at large' in the society in which they move. Some people are very fond of expressing their own opinions, often formed without any substantial basis, and they are usually the kind of people who are at the same time very impatient when it comes to considering and weighing what others have to say on the subject. The reputation they acquire is such that people wish to put the lid on them! One of the marks of the wise in heart is that they are not too proud to listen to others to their own improvement, or to receive commands.

The word 'commands', however, is particularly used of the commandments of God. Supremely, the wise in heart will listen to God and receive his commands to their personal benefit. Notice this comes from the heart. They have a heart for God and his Word. It is what God thinks that matters to them, not what they think which they imagine matters to others. Thus in this verse we observe the wise in heart increasing in spiritual stature, while the prating fool, whose heart is not worthy of mention because it does not feature, is put down. Thus there is a spiritual dimension to this matter. What proceeds from the mouth of a prating fool is not just empty and worthless, it is positively harmful, examples of which are scattered throughout the Book of Proverbs, and the 'put down' will ultimately come from God, not men.

All these proverbs are intended to stimulate personal enquiry, relating as they do to real life scenarios. Many of us will know to our shame that we have been too ready at times to talk and have thereby revealed our ignorance or caused injury; also that we have been too slow to receive God's Word to our own and others' benefit. Often it is not easy to receive commands, especially when they reflect some failure on our part. The proverbs often touch us where it hurts, thereby revealing that we have a problem that needs attention from our heavenly Physician. We need to learn to welcome his probing fingers.

[Related proverbs: 2:1-6; 10:10,14; 13:1,13; 14:16; 17:10; 19:16; 29:11.]

10:9. See also 13:6; 28:18. No covering of tracks. It is safe to tell the truth. Those who don't, who find themselves trying to cover one lie with another, will get found out. This proverb, however, is about more than words, though integrity of speech is usually a mark of integrity of life, and in any case the life speaks even without words. Integrity is related to simple innocence and uprightness of character. No double life or dual standards are involved. What a person of integrity appears to be, he is; there is no cover-up to conceal some doubtful attitude or conduct which he guiltily wishes to remain hidden, as happened with David in the matter of Bathsheba. His 'walk' is his manner of life, the way he carries himself, and he is said to do so uprightly. He is not stumbling along, or hesitating, or deviating from the way, or shrinking away trying to remain hidden. Such a person 'walks' securely, and this time a slightly different but similar sounding word in the original is used.

To walk with integrity refers to character; to walk with security refers to progress. He makes progress in life safely, with assurance and confidence, without fear or anxiety on account of his conduct. Are there secret corners in your life? Are there things you are hiding from yourself, from others ... from God? If so, what are you going to do about them?

For many people there is a significant disparity between their public and their private lives, resulting in inner conflict and anxiety lest the private side should at some point be shamefully exposed. They are not 'walking' in integrity, they haven't 'got it all together', and therefore they lack the ability to 'walk' with the security and confidence of which this verse speaks. This is the natural condition of those dominated by their sinful nature.

We need to appreciate that this is not a person trying to put on an act. It is not a person making a great effort at integrity against the odds. This is the wonderful thing about the believer, who is now free to follow the way of truth with innocent simplicity. The unbeliever, living in ignorance of the true God, not having the life of God within, may possibly look upon integrity and uprightness as necessary standards to be striven after, but will always have a sense of guilt that they are not natural to him. Upright conduct will be seen as something artificial, something imposed, like a garment that does not sit comfortably upon a twisted frame. It doesn't look right, because it doesn't fit right. The frame first needs to be straightened. This is something only God can do. Many a person has been plagued by the bitter insecurity that comes from a crooked lifestyle. The straight road is the path of God's commandments, but the unbeliever finds it quite impossible to follow them, in much the same way as the drunkard cannot keep to a straight course but stumbles and lurches, and with a confused mind and eye cannot even properly see the way to follow.

But the believer has been forgiven and the past has been wiped out; the believer no longer has anything to hide; the believer has had the eyes of his understanding opened; the believer sees the way to go and has been given the desire and the ability to go that way. The believer has been given all his spiritual faculties together with a vigour for spiritual exercise. So for the believer, this proverb comes as a warning against backsliding as well as an encouragement to perseverance. There is no condemnation for those who are in Christ Jesus.

They may lift up their heads and step out without shame, clothed with the righteousness of Christ, their eyes set on the goal of the prize of their high calling in Christ. What a wonderful cause for thanksgiving!

As with so many of the proverbs, this has a temporal and an eternal aspect. Not all believers know security in this life, and for some their integrity will lead them into great difficulties. But that does not negate what this proverb is saying. Nothing can shake their security in Christ. Their walk will take them right into the presence of their God. Whereas the devious path of those who have perverted their ways will lead ultimately to exposure before the bar of divine justice and eternal separation from the presence of the Lord.

[Related proverbs: 3:23; 11:3; 13:6; 15:21; 28:6,18.]

10:10. Harmful silence, wholesome speech. We have met the winking eye before at 6:13, where we considered various gestures of worthless or wicked people. If the phrase is to be taken in the way we usually understand it, the winking eye involves a mutual understanding between two people about something from which a third party is deliberately kept in ignorance, invariably at that person's expense. It is done in the presence of the third party who remains unaware of what is going on and is about to suffer some unpleasant experience. In other words, it has malicious intent, frequently to the amusement of those in the know. Those who derive pleasure by promoting the discomfort of others are troublemakers. The winking eye is representative of a characteristic type. Some people do it 'to take others down a peg or two', but whatever justification they may find for their action, it has no warrant in scripture. It only causes trouble. We are only to promote people's good, not cause them shame or embarrassment or worse.

Alternatively, the winking eye may be taken as making light of things that should be taken seriously, as when one 'shuts one's eyes to what is going on under one's very nose'. This might fit in better with an alternative rendering of the second part of the verse. As it stands, it is a repetition of v. 8b, in which case it may be a comparison between two characteristics, indicating that one has more serious consequences than the other. It may be just an observation on life. If, on the other hand, v. 8b has been copied in here in error in an original manuscript, and instead we follow the Septuagint, translated in the RSV as 'but he who boldly reproves makes peace,' we have a very clear comparison between the person who for the sake of his own peace 'turns a blind eye' to unpleasant goings-on and thereby through his own inaction only promotes trouble, and the person who with courage exposes what is being done with a view to ultimately promoting peace. There are many situations in daily life in which it is easier to ignore wrongdoing than to take action about it. It requires wisdom to know when and how to act. However, it is wrong to close one's eyes when one has responsibility to provide correction, as for example in the case of a parent toward a child.

[Related proverbs: 6:13; 10:8; 16:30.]

10:11. It is interesting to compare this verse with James 3:10-11. 'Fountain' is a better translation than 'well'. Water was a precious commodity in Israel, and springs of fresh water were especially valued. This proverb is all about what emanates from the mouths of people. As with so many of the proverbs, the contrast is a stark and uncompromising one. Here are just two categories of people, the righteous and the wicked, not as opposite ends of a scale, but because ultimately every man, woman and child belongs to one or other of them. When they are true to type, these things are characteristic of them.

The picture here is of words issuing from the mouth of the righteous with life-giving effect. David said that with the Lord is the fountain of life (Psalm 36:9), while the Lord through Jeremiah twice described himself as the fountain of living waters (Jeremiah 2:13; 17:13). The lips are the mouthpiece for what lies in the heart, and we must observe with solemn realism that much that is written about this reflects the problem of the heart (Matthew 12:34-35; 15:18,19; Mark 7:21; James 3:1-12). If what proceeds from our mouths cannot really be said to possess life-giving properties, then we have to question our righteousness. There can be no room for pretence before God. He is the fountain of living waters, and it is only from his life active within that the mouth of the righteous can be a fountain of life. See John 7:37-39. This whole subject is worthy of a word study. Consider the gracious words which always proceeded from the mouth of the Lord Jesus.

The second clause of this proverb is identical to that of v. 6b, but whereas in the former case the emphasis was on what each has to *give*, here it is on what each has to *say*. We may profit from what others give us in a material sense, but we may also profit from what they give us in a verbal sense. In life it is arguable that a great deal more is done by people's words than by their actions. Our words may help or hinder others, may heal or harm them, may comfort them or cause them pain, may encourage or discourage them, may lift their spirits or crush their spirit, may refresh them or make them despondent, may give them hope or lead them to despair. Our words can give or take away so much. See Matthew 12:37.

Also in this proverb is the contrast between the openness of the righteous and the concealment of the wicked. This idea is evident again at v. 18. The conduct of the righteous is open, straightforward and clear, whereas concealment and deviousness and double meanings characterise the dealings of the wicked. What proceeds from the mouth of the righteous is fresh, clean and beneficial; what proceeds from the mouth of the wicked is murky and poisonous.

[Related proverbs: 10:6,31,32; 13:14; 15:2,4,23,28; 16:22; 31:26.]

10:12. James 5:20; 1 Peter 4:8. What price love? At first sight this is a simple commentary on the contrast between hatred and love and one area in which their effects may be seen. The second clause is quoted by both James (5:20) and Peter (1 Peter 4:8). Hatred and love are strong words. Both are active and powerful, and both must have their outlet. The hatred described here is like a fire burning in the heart which must find a way of destroying its object. Its visible effects are always harmful to its object. We are to hate evil (8:13; Amos 5:15; compare Micah 3:2), which means that as far as evil is concerned our intention must be its destruction. But, hating it, we will do our utmost to avoid it.

However, this verse is not dealing with that, but the effects of hatred and love towards others. Hatred and love always have a context and a motivation, and though none is mentioned here, it is probably best to think of both operating in the *same* context. One example will make a general point. Suppose someone seriously defrauds you. One very natural response to this would be to hate that person for it and to vow to get even with him. He has clearly done wrong and deserves what is coming to him. You could make the matter known as widely as possible so that people understand how badly you have been treated, to elicit sympathy and support in your drive to bring the offender down. However, the problem in all this is that the action is fuelled not by an impartial desire for justice but by the personal element, that it is *you* who have suffered, and it rankles. The expenditure of your energies in such a cause will inevitably lead to strife, as people take different sides. It simply adds fuel to the fire.

An example like this arose in the church at Corinth (1 Corinthians 6:1-8), and Paul declared that those letting their passions rule them into allowing disputes to become bitter to the point of taking them to court before unbelievers had already utterly failed in their Christian testimony. In fact he went as far as to say that they themselves were doing wrong and defrauding those against whom they had instigated such action. Paul advised that two things ought to have been done. First of all, there should have been Christians of sufficient maturity to be able to judge such issues and the matter should have been brought to them (v. 2). Secondly, their attitude to their brethren should have been such that they should rather have been willing to accept the wrong without complaint than to allow personal animosity to dominate their thinking (vv. 7-8). At no point did Paul suggest that wrong had not been done, but what he was saying is that there are proper ways of dealing with such things.

Observe what Jesus told the man who demanded that he tell his brother to divide the inheritance with him (Luke 12:13). Jesus replied that arbitration did not lie within his remit! But he did point to the real source of the problem, and the charge of covetousness was unmistakably laid at the door of the man who felt he was owed something. The man did not come to Jesus out of a concern for justice. Covetousness was eating away at his heart, and the veneer of a sense of fairness did not deceive the Lord. We could say that there was no love lost between the brothers. There was no love in the matter whatsoever. The sin in this case, if sin there was, could never have been covered while the underlying covetousness prevailed.

It is important that we beware those who are always harping on about how others have treated them. It is not a mark of love. In such cases we would be well advised to avoid taking sides, or we too will be caught up in the strife!

This, then, is the context of the proverb. Wrong has been done, sin has been committed, and suffering has resulted. Those who suffer, or their representatives, can react with hatred, in which case escalating trouble and strife may be expected; or in love, in which case there is some hope that the sin may be covered and reconciliation effected. Love does not ignore the sin, or say that the sin does not matter, nor does it make less of it than it ought by glossing over the wrong. The love described here is not a passive thing expressed as anything for the sake of peace, but an active power aimed solely at eliminating the problem and restoring harmony. It is a bit like the way you deal with a fire, putting a blanket on it to smother it. The blanket isn't there to hide the fire but to put it out! That is the object of love.

Notice, too, it says *all* sins, not just *some*. Love does not make exception for certain sins. 'I could forgive her anything, but not this!' The trouble is, human nature rebels against personal injustice, and as people are so often offending against one another in various ways it is hardly surprising there is so much hatred and therefore strife in the world. If there were more love, things would be different, but the lack of it exposes how great a problem man has. So when we read that love covers all sins, we ought to react by asking, what kind of love is this? As with all the other virtues mentioned in the book of Proverbs, it has as its foundation the fear of the Lord. This is a love that has its origin in God, and if it is found in man, that is because it has come from God. Not only does it have its origin in God, but it has been demonstrated by God (Romans 5:8). The love that went sufficiently far to effect reconciliation between sinners and a holy God is a love that has covered all sins. The apostle John confirms what Paul says (1 John 1:7,9).

[Related proverbs: 15:18; 17:9; 28:25; 29:22.]

10:13-14. What value knowledge? Verse 14 parallels v. 13, though the relationship between the two is complex. So wisdom features in vv. 13a and 14a, and folly in vv. 13b and 14b. However, speech features in vv. 13a and 14b, while vv. 14a and 13b refer to what is, or is not, stored in the heart.

The two people contrasted here are the one who has understanding and the one who lacks it. 8:5b says, literally, 'be of an understanding heart', and it is important to be aware that the heart involves the mind. Yet it is more than the intellect that is being called into play, but rather the whole being. The understanding spoken of in v. 13a is that of discernment involving the ability to distinguish between things which differ and to penetrate to the root of a matter and extract from it what is relevant. It doesn't come automatically, but (14a) through knowledge being added and stored up, as in a well stocked larder, to be appropriately prepared and served as occasion requires for the nourishment of others. The words of the wise are timely and edify the hearer. They may provide encouragement, or help, or rebuke, or correction, or instruction ... but whatever is said is intended for good. This is not knowledge stored up for its own sake, but in order that it might be usefully applied. It could almost be described as humanitarian research.

The other person is one who, literally, lacks heart (v. 13b). He has nothing in his heart; nothing of worth is stored there. He does not have the heart for wisdom; there is a 'can't be bothered' attitude to it; it is too much like hard work; it is not worth the effort. This is really another description of the fool. There is no fear of God as a proper foundation. Such a person will suffer as a result. He is not in a position to benefit anybody.

When we talk of people making a rod for their own back we usually mean those who take on tasks, perhaps unwisely, which cause them a great deal of trouble. The meaning here, though, is rather different. The person devoid of understanding will make a rod for his own back because he will frequently smart under the effects of his own foolish ignorance. The way this often happens is that he gives himself away by his talk (14b). Whether we see the rod as a direct or indirect result of his lack of heart makes little difference. By his whole way of life he is asking for trouble. He may have plenty to say but it is entirely worthless, at best benefiting no one, and at worst causing trouble and very likely to precipitate his own ruin (v. 14b). He condemns himself out of his own mouth.

Sadly, there are people like this all around us, who bring all manner of troubles upon themselves because they have no time for God, no desire for God, no sense of need of God, no reference to God's Word. They may talk big, but they benefit no one, not even themselves.

Verse 14 is similar to v. 4 except it operates in a different sphere. A person who stores up knowledge (the beginning of which is the fear of the Lord) is one who not only benefits himself but is also in a position to do good to others by means of wise and understanding counsel. 'Empty vessels make most noise,' and their sound soon jars the senses. What comes from wise people, though, is both edifying and satisfying.

How important it is to harness our minds to beneficial ends, to give time and thought to those things by which we may benefit others! Especially is this true when it comes to attending to the Word of God. The fear of the Lord is the beginning of knowledge; it all starts there. None will be truly wise who has not soaked his mind in the Scriptures. 2 Timothy 3:16-17 is relevant here. Note the range of influence of the scriptures, and the beneficial end not only to the man of God as he submits to their teaching but also to others who will be on the receiving end of 'every good work'. The spirit of wisdom and revelation is in the knowledge of the Lord Jesus Christ, and that is how the eyes of our understanding are opened (Ephesians 1:17-18). Nor is this a 'quick fix', for we must grow in the grace and knowledge of Christ (2 Peter 3:18). Paul's prayer in Colossians 1:9-10 runs much along the same lines, and in Colossians 2:3,6 he effectively confirms that effort is required on our part to acquire this knowledge and understanding. Is it worth it?

We are shown these two extremes because God would have us consider them carefully. Our speech betrays us, whether we are wise or foolish. These proverbs positively demand that we examine our hearts, our motives, our actions.

As we proceed through the book many subjects are revisited again and again, as we look at them from different angles and in different contexts, and all the time we are being led to look carefully at ourselves and others as God sees us. The questions for today must surely be, how much time do we give for God's Word to have its effect upon our minds and hearts, and how is this demonstrated by the kind of things we say to others?

[Related proverbs: 10:21; 14:33; 15:7; 18:6,7; 20:15.]

10:15. What type of security? The proverb is clearly about personal security. The facts speak for themselves. Those who are rich can usually buy themselves out of any trouble. Their money can secure their interests: it is a power base on which to build. They have the means to survive hard times, in much the same way as a well-stocked and fortified city would be able to withstand a long siege. By contrast, the first to suffer in times of economic stringency are those who are already poor, who have no resources, nothing behind them, nothing to fall back on. These things being so obviously true, why the proverb?

At the purely economic or material level, it dispels any romantic or ideological notions that there is any virtue in 'giving it all away' and living in poverty. But didn't Jesus tell the rich young ruler to give away all his money (Mark 10:21)? Yes, he did, but it was not so that the young man might live in poverty. There would have been a strange irony in his being required to give it all away to benefit the poor if he was thereby going to be reduced to the state of the need that he was relieving! This is not the place to expound that particular passage. Suffice it to say that Jesus was seeking to shift the young man's reliance from his personal security to the security that he, Jesus, would give him. Nowhere does the Bible make a virtue out of poverty, any more that it is disparaging of riches. However, it does have much to say about how to deal with poverty, and how to use riches.

As with so many of the proverbs, though, there is another, underlying level at which this needs to be understood. The theme of security of one kind and another weaves its way through this section of the book. It is seen in righteousness (vv. 2,3,16), diligence in work (vv. 4,5,16), integrity (vv. 9,17). Lack of security and its consequences are observed in wickedness (vv. 2,3,6,7,11,16), laziness (vv. 4,5), foolishness in its various manifestations (vv. 8,10,13,14,17,21). Wealth and poverty are measured in more ways than in money and possessions. So this proverb actually parallels v. 14. The wise have a wealth and security in store that money cannot buy, and the foolish are just as destitute and on the verge of ruin as are those who are penniless. So the proverb, situated as it is, is given to direct our minds to where real security lies, and away from purely material considerations. The material serves as an illustration of the spiritual. 'You know this from your experience of life,' says Solomon in effect; 'Now apply it to the weightier matter with which we are dealing.'

[Related proverbs: 14:20; 18:23; 19:7; 22:7.]

10:16. Where is it leading?

10:16. Where is it leading? What do people do, and what results from it? The people in question are the righteous and the wicked, assessed not by man's standards but by God's. The righteous are those who fear God; the wicked are those who do not.

The proverbs keep telling us to look at the consequences of certain courses of action. Where is it all leading? The words used about the gains of the righteous and the wicked are carefully chosen and have distinctive nuances. In the case of the righteous there is the element of activity, of labour, of work, with a view to reward for what has been done. By contrast, for the wicked the word used is the one for fruit in the sense of increase – what is produced or gained – but the idea of toil or achievement or reward is lacking.

There is a purposefulness in the work of the righteous, the work itself leading to that end. The righteous are not only working for the reward of life, but the work itself has life in its view. To put it in New Testament terms, 'Whatever you do, do all to the glory of God' (1 Corinthians 10:31); 'Whatever you do, work heartily, as for the Lord and not for men, knowing that from the Lord you will receive the inheritance as your reward. You are serving the Lord Christ' (Colossians 3:23-24, ESV). For the believer there is a dignity in work and a pleasure in its rewards.

For the wicked, they too may work, and they may make gains from it, but neither the work they do nor what they get from it has any ultimate purpose and so the tendency is to devalue the work and waste its proceeds.

This is not to belittle the much good that ungodly people have done in society or their notable achievements for the benefit of many. High principles have been shown by many in certain areas and some have been champions of worthy causes. None of this negates what this proverb is saying, for failure to acknowledge what God has given and what he has enabled them to produce is itself sin.

Life is contrasted not with death here but with sin (probably better than 'punishment'). See, however, Romans 6:23, where Paul reminds us that death is the inevitable consequence of sin, because sin demands punishment. In the meantime, though, sin works against life. It is harmful and destructive. Sin never produced anything good, only perverted self satisfaction at someone else's expense. Life is the result of the labour of the righteous, whereas sin is the result of the activity of the wicked. By what righteous people do, the reward of their labours works not simply for their own life, but for life in general. Their input in life promotes life. By what wicked people do, the results of their activity and what they may gain from it is only squandered. The result is sin.

This is patently obvious in society at the material level and is generally recognised. However, it needs to be recognised at a more fundamental level. For what are we labouring in life? What is it that motivates us? What are we sowing and reaping? Do we have a perspective on our activity that looks to the consequences, not simply for ourselves, but for society in general and God's creation in particular?

[Related proverbs: 11:18,19; 19:23.]

10:17. Reaction to discipline. This proverb may be linked with 2 Timothy 3:16. More than we may realise or be prepared to admit, we are all at fault in a great many ways. The evidence suggests that God invests a great deal of time in training us up out of our old ways and into his new ones.

Instruction (discipline, NIV) and correction are closely linked. Both incorporate the idea of chastisement, of reproof, of being put right where one is wrong. There are times when we all need this treatment which we find uncomfortable. The truth is that our need for correction offends our pride. When James says, 'We all stumble in many things' (3:1) he has teachers particularly in mind. For such, stumbling is a cause of greater embarrassment because everybody sees it! We can react in one of two ways to correction. One is to take heed, the other is to take umbrage! This is an area in which humility of mind, if it truly exists, is especially seen. We can all think of cases where wise counsel has been spurned, being regarded as unpalatable by those to whom it has been given, only to result in trouble. Regrettably, such cases are often more prominent than those in which wise counsel has been heeded. Somehow the benefits resulting from this often go largely unnoticed.

Asa and his son Jehoshaphat were great and godly kings in Judah. Fault was found with them over what they considered successful policies, and they each had to receive rebuke because they were in the wrong. It is instructive to consider how each responded to being corrected (2 Chronicles 16:7-10; 19:2-7).

The person keeping instruction, or heeding discipline, is one who does not just acknowledge the correction grudgingly, but gives the matter its proper attention so that it takes effect in his life. Adam was instructed to 'keep' the garden (Genesis 2:15), that is, he was to tend it, to work it, to make it productive. Abraham was instructed to 'keep' the covenant which God made with him (Genesis 17:10), and his descendants were told to 'keep' God's commandments with the greatest of care and attention (Deuteronomy 4:6). God promised to 'keep' Jacob wherever he went (Genesis 28:15). Do we regard correction as sufficiently important that we 'keep' it?

The one who refuses correction is said to go astray. The NIV and ESV say he leads others astray. Both aspects are true. To use a couple of well known expressions, correction keeps us on the straight and narrow, whereas if we refuse it we are all over the place. We are not to wander aimlessly through life, pleasing ourselves and ignoring others. Because we are sinful we need discipline which, we are reminded, is not pleasant at the time but is certainly beneficial when seen in retrospect (Hebrews 12:11)!

The Christian has to admit to having been at one time entirely in the wrong and needing forgiveness at God's hand and a new start in dependence upon him. A new believer is conscious of having much to learn and much to be corrected in his or her life. The danger is, though, that as time passes, the awareness that this is an ongoing process fades. Our own view of our progress as Christians, or our success in Christian service, can be a great hindrance to our willingness to accept the fact that we still go wrong, or to receive the correction we still need, especially when the instrument God uses offends our pride!

When corrected, does it make a difference to us from whom the correction comes, or how it is given? If so, the cross of Christ has lost its rightful place as the reference point for our Christian lives.

[Related proverbs: 3:11-12; 6:23; 10:8; 12:1; 13:1,18; 15:5,10,31,32; 29:17.]

10:18. 26:24-26; Leviticus 19:16-18. A 'catch-22' situation?

The word for hiding, or concealing, has been encountered at vv. 6,11,12. This proverb poses a very real dilemma where hatred toward another person is concerned. What is a person going to do with hatred in his heart? Should he conceal it, or should he give vent to it? If he conceals it, speaking in such a way as to give the impression it does not exist, he is guilty of a lying tongue. If on the other hand he does give vent to it verbally, he runs the risk of the charge of spreading slander, which is a very foolish thing to do. It is a no-win dilemma.

Are you harbouring hatred toward anyone? You might not put it as strongly as that. Are you harbouring ill will toward anyone, then? It amounts to the same thing. Is there anyone with whom you wish 'to get even' because they have wronged you? Hatred comes in various styles and colours and we do not always recognise it for what it is. It is easy for us to suppress it, or refuse to acknowledge its existence, because we know it shouldn't be there. But if it is there all the same, eating away at us inside, then we are deceiving ourselves and others.

It is a question not of what one should do *with* hatred in the heart, but what one should do *about* it. The solution is to deal with the problem of the hatred itself. God's Word says so clearly that we should not hate others. If there is a cause of provocation resulting in hatred toward someone, we need to follow Leviticus 19:17 (and see also the previous verse concerning slander), fulfilling a responsibility. It is so easy to recoil from facing up to our responsibilities to 'clear the air' with others, which usually only results in problems festering and growing out of proportion. 'Bottling it up' only makes matters worse, and speaking behind that person's back about it is both cowardly and foolish, because it has the effect of multiplying ill-will. See Matthew 5:43-44; Titus 3:3; 1 John 2:9,11; 3:15; 4:20.

We are told that God so loved the world that he gave his only begotten Son (John 3:16). Paul reminds us of how God demonstrates his love to us (Romans 5:8). In the light of this, for us to harbour hatred (or whatever euphemism we may care to substitute for this word) toward another is, in its most literal sense, ungodly. It exposes us as not knowing or obeying God as we may profess to do. Hatred must be dealt with, it must be removed, and the God who has loved a world at enmity with him is the God who can deal with the hatred in our heart. The fundamental remedy is found at the cross of Christ.

[Related proverbs: 10:12; 12:22; 26:24-26.]

10:19-21. The silver tongue. Here is a closely-linked triplet of proverbs about speech. When should you speak, and when should you hold your tongue? When you speak, are the words worth hearing? What is the purpose of your speaking? A great deal of our time is taken up with verbal interaction with others. Some people are naturally more talkative than others. Is v. 19 addressing them? The proverbs say quite a bit, at least by implication, about fools prattling on (10:8,14; 12:16,23; 13:16; 14:16,33; 15:2,14; 17:28; 18:6,7,13; 29:11). Fools tend to talk too much. Without being aware of it they reveal their ignorance. What they have to say is generally unwholesome or unprofitable. It is a waste of breath to the speaker and a waste of time to the listener.

It is probably best to understand v. 19 in the context of a circumstance that provokes a verbal response. When people get on their 'hobby-horse' they have a lot to say by way of expressing their own feelings and opinions and judgements. They get 'carried away', and it is precisely in such a situation they would have done better to hold their tongues. The more they say, the more impartial judgement is obscured, and they become guilty of sinful excess. When something burns inwardly and you are bursting to get it off your chest and speak your mind in no uncertain fashion, it is mark of wisdom that you exercise self restraint and confine yourself to saying only what is necessary and beneficial. This has nothing whatever to do with one person being naturally more talkative than another. The comparison is between pouring it all out and holding back. The first is usually rather self-centred, but the latter considers the implications for the hearer.

In this respect v. 20 follows on from v. 19. The value here is in the benefit to the one receiving the words. Picture yourself in a jeweller's shop with the privilege of being permitted to choose a few of the best items. Quality and value will be the primary considerations. The tongue of those whom God considers righteous is said to be like that. What proceeds from it may not be great in quantity, but it has quality and value. Choice silver is pure, without any admixture of dross; it is precious and not found in abundance. The value of the tongue of the righteous, however, is not to the owner, but to the listener. Do people in general benefit from what you have to say to them? Do they take your words away with them as important? Does your speech enrich them?

It should be observed that the comparison in v. 20 is between the tongue and the heart. We have noted before that 'out of the abundance of the heart the mouth speaks' (Matthew 12:34). The reason the wicked have little useful to say is that their heart is not right with God. One can give out only what one has taken in. The wicked take in what suits their ungodly temperament, and so it is hardly surprising that what proceeds from their mouth is much the same kind of thing. These proverbs serve as a reminder to us that we can benefit others only to the extent that we have given our hearts to storing up heavenly treasure. See Matthew 12:35; 6:19-21.

The figure of speech changes in v. 21, but the central idea is the same. So much of what people say is said simply because they want to say it, or because of the way it pleases them or enhances them in the eyes of others. However, we are often reminded in the New Testament that our words (and our actions) should be used for building up others (for example, Romans 15:2; 1 Corinthians 14:12; Ephesians 4:29; Colossians 4:6). Our verbal interaction with other people should be with a mind to doing them good. It should be more about them than about us. If we have not realised this before, this is a good time to start thinking about it and endeavouring to put it into practice. If this general principle were followed, relationships with others would be greatly enhanced.

Coming down to specifics, recognising that the ultimate source of nourishment is the Word of God (30:5; Deuteronomy 8:3; Matthew 4:4), our lips will feed others only to the extent that what we have to say is in accordance with God's Word. This is particularly important when it comes to giving advice, of venturing our opinion, or of seeking to help or encourage others. Our lips are not simply to speak our own words, declaring our own ideas, but rather to say in an apposite fashion what God's Word teaches, or is consistent with its teaching.

The wicked (20) and the fool (21) are one and the same, and which description is used depends mainly upon the context. These verses hark back to vv. 13,14 and really concern what is in the heart of people. The end of v. 21 may be taken in one of two ways. It says, literally, that fools die for lack of heart. It may be taken to mean either that, unlike the righteous who have over and above their own needs to nourish others, fools have nothing in their hearts to sustain even themselves, let alone benefit anyone else; or else that fools, having no heart for the food on offer to them by those who are righteous, perish as a result. Whichever way it is taken, the basic problem of the fool is exposed. Sadly, the lips of the righteous do not feed *them*, for they do not even recognise what the righteous have to offer.

In summary, in these three verses a number of comparisons are being made. Sin, the wicked, and the fool are set in parallel. The tongue which has most to say of worth is a tongue which is restrained. Even though restrained, it can do most good, for it feeds *many*.

[Related proverbs: 15:2,4,7; 21:23.]

10:22. Riches beyond measure. This is perhaps one of the better-known proverbs from the collection. Compare 13:7. The first observation, which is not clear in all translations, is that the emphasis in this verse indicates it is the Lord's blessing *alone* which makes one rich. At first sight this seems to be far from true. What about all those people who have no time for God and yet who are rich? Is that because God has blessed them? Then what about those who have accumulated wealth by unscrupulous methods? Surely they have not done so because of God's blessing upon them? That the wicked prosper is a problem which has already been encountered on a number of occasions. The man or woman of faith who knows the true value of things will have no wish to take issue with this proverb.

We know we are ultimately in the hands of God and look to him for every provision, right down to the basic necessities of life. Jesus made this quite clear when he said we should pray, 'Give us this day our daily bread' (Matthew 6:11). He also reminded us that 'Man shall not live by bread alone, but by every word that proceeds from the mouth of God' (Matthew 4:4; Deuteronomy 8:3). Without his blessing, that is, without his being generously disposed toward us, we remain in every sense in an impoverished state. We may be able to make ourselves rich in this world's goods and yet find, as so many wealthy people have done, that really we have nothing. True riches do not consist in this world's goods. The man who was offered treasure in heaven (Mark 10:17-22) was not being asked to forfeit all pleasure beforehand but was told to relinquish what stood between him and the Lord's blessing (Mark 10:21,29-30). He knew he lacked something, but he went away sorrowful. Which leads us into the second clause of this proverb.

Sorrows, or trouble, or pangs, do so often accompany the wealth that people accumulate. Perhaps, like the rich young ruler, they seem to have everything they could desire and yet are aware that they lack something of infinitely greater importance. Perhaps they do not know how to use their accumulated wealth, perhaps they abuse it and so harm themselves, perhaps they worry about guarding it or losing it; perhaps the lifestyle accompanying it becomes a millstone around their necks, burdening and dominating them; or perhaps they are conscience-stricken about how they have made it. In so many ways through what they have acquired they find themselves beset by the cares of this world. Contrast this with the blessing of the Lord, whether it takes material or any other form. From God's hand it is received as a gift, to be acknowledged with thankfulness and to be used in stewardship. It is not given with a sting in its tail, or with strings attached to restrict freedom.

This proverb extends far beyond material things. Every good and perfect gift comes from our Father in heaven (James 1:17). If we are living under the benevolent care of the Lord, then we are rich beyond measure. It more than suffices us to know that he loves us, takes care of us, provides for all our needs – so much so that his provision for us spills over to the benefit of others. Indeed, that is how we ought to see it. From his blessing upon us he would have us be a blessing to others; from the riches he bestows upon us he would have us enrich others. Here is Luke 6:38 in operation, that as we give according to how God has given to us, our resources, far from being depleted, are more than fully replenished. Even the penny-poor under the blessing of God have riches to share with others.

There is a saying, 'All good things come to an end.' That is generally true, and often particularly so of health and wealth. Here, though, is the grand exception. The blessing of the Lord makes rich. His is an inexhaustible supply. Compare Philippians 4:19. Compare also Psalm 23:1 – 'I shall not want.' Also Psalm 34:10. There is wonderful contentment under God's hand of blessing, as Paul said in Philippians 4:11. These are not benefits of the kind so often described as 'mixed blessings'. They are not blessings with drawbacks.

The reason Paul could say he had learned contentment in every circumstance was that he knew from experience what he encouraged the Philippians with at 4:19. Although the apostle experienced what we might describe as sorrows and all manner of troubles in his life, yet he would not have found fault with this proverb, but rather endorsed it, knowing that living under God's blessing and provision over-abundantly compensated for any hardship he might be called upon to endure, as he so powerfully asserts in Romans 8:35-39.

This proverb is wonderfully true, as all those who have learned to live in complete dependence upon God have discovered. The way this proverb is negatively expressed is to make us aware of just how true the opposite is. No, God does not augment his blessings with an unpleasant after-taste. On the contrary, to his blessing he adds blessing upon blessing so that the believer, having begun to drink of that well, will always be returning for more, and will be for ever satisfied with its unfailing supply. What a wonderful God he is who can make such statements in the knowledge that none can prove him wrong but only discover how true they are!

[Related proverbs: 10:6; 11:25; 28:20.]

10:23. Poles apart. 'It's no laughing matter' is the retort when someone has found amusement from another's calamity. To do evil is a matter of laughter, amusement, merriment, to a fool, who takes perverse pleasure in it. The NKJV, 'like sport to a fool' captures the sense well. It is like a game the fool plays. It is entertaining to see how much he can get away with. It gives him an exhilarating sense of achievement or gratification when he sees his schemes succeeding.

As with all the proverbs the second clause is related to the first, so that here, because it is not immediately obvious, we should be asking how. We should see it as contrasting with the first. The fool does not think beyond his own immediate pleasure or entertainment and has no regard for the implications for others (or even for himself, for that matter). The word for 'laughter' is understood to apply to both clauses (brought out in the NIV and ESV). What evil is to the fool, wisdom is to the man of understanding. He takes as much proper pleasure in wisdom as the fool takes perverted pleasure in evil. It is a cause of delight to him. This is something those devoid of spiritual enlightenment can never understand, how anyone can find true delight in the fear of the Lord and its outworking. For the man who understands the Lord and his ways, wisdom (and therefore to act according to wisdom in doing good) gives intense satisfaction. Thus there is a clean line of cleavage down the middle of this proverb, placing the fool and the man of understanding in two completely different categories.

Some people, and young people in particular, are given to the 'harmless' practical joke. Beware of such things, and consider that their intention is to have fun at someone else's expense, maybe by exploiting a weakness in that person. They do not always turn out as expected and have a habit of backfiring. People do not always see the funny side of others' pranks.

[Related proverb: 15:21.]

10:24. You've got it coming to you.

10:24. You've got it coming to you. Whatever the bravado shown by wicked men and women, there are things of which they are afraid. Beneath it all there is a lurking fear. With almost every evil deed there is a corresponding fear relating to it, usually suppressed but there nevertheless. This proverb informs us there will be no escape from the consequences. What they fear will inexorably pursue them and ultimately catch up with them. For some, and perhaps for many, it happens in this life; but if not, it will certainly happen in the day of reckoning. See Psalm 73 and the pivotal verse 17.

'Desire' in the second clause is at the opposite end of the spectrum from fear or dread. As an aside, this gives opportunity to mention one fruit of the amazing grace of God. It is only God who by grace can transform the wicked into the righteous. As intense as the dread of the wicked, so is the desire of the righteous. God by his gracious regenerating power replaces all the bad things once dreaded with good things to be longed after, with the promise that all these good things will be granted. Again, it may not happen in this life. But what is the loss in that, when there will be more than compensation in the life to come? It is a truly wonderful and liberating experience to have one's fears removed, and it is even more wonderful that in their place should be granted wholesome desires which generate a sense of yearning with the promise that it shall be satisfied.

Thus both the wicked and the righteous 'will get what's coming to them', the one dreaded, the other longed for. One shrinks from the judgement which will nevertheless overtake him; the other looks forward eagerly to the glory which has been promised (2 Peter 3:12-13).

[Related proverbs: 10:28; 11:23.]

10:25. Adrift or anchored? This echoes Psalm 37:9-11 and reflects the words of Jesus concerning the two houses (Matthew 7:24-27). The word translated 'whirlwind', or 'storm' or 'tempest' comes from a root word meaning to terminate, or bring to an end. The point about the whirlwind is its unexpectedness as well as its ferocity, uprooting everything in its path. Just as a vacuum cleaner picks up and removes the loose dust from the carpet, so the whirlwind of God's judgement carries away the wicked from the face of the earth.

There is a telling irony that in every generation, however much God's people are persecuted and downtrodden, they turn out to be the great survivors. In times of disaster they are still there, their help and advice are sought out, their influence is felt, because their life has a secure foundation. God is true to his word, and in every generation he preserves a remnant to be his witnesses and to proclaim the gospel. But again, ultimately, the righteous belong to the everlasting kingdom which shall never pass away. This proverb is also reminiscent of Hebrews 12:26-28. The security of the wicked lies entirely in this life, and so when his world is shaken – as it will be – he collapses with it. The world to which the righteous belong is the one over which the eternal, unchangeable God presides.

[Related proverbs: 12:3,7.]

10:26. What did you expect? The lazy man, or sluggard, features in a number of proverbs (6:6,9; 13:4; 15:19; 19:24; 20:4; 21:25; 22:13; 24:30; 26:13,15,16). Vinegar sets the teeth on edge, and smoke causes the eyes to smart; they induce intense discomfort. The trouble with sending a lazy person on an errand or entrusting any task to such a person is that one is constantly in a state of anxiety as to whether the job will get done. A person like this is a source of penetrating irritation. There are certain people to whom you give responsibility at your own risk. This proverb surely advises against employing the indolent on any matter of importance.

Let us also look at this from the other side, though, and ask ourselves about our attitude to responsibilities that are entrusted to us. Are we half-hearted or wholehearted about fulfilling them? Are we lazy where these things are concerned or are we diligent in getting on with the job? Is our attitude a cause of concern to others, or do they have cause for complete confidence in us?

When the Lord called for a messenger, Isaiah responded, 'Here am I! Send me' (Isaiah 6:8). What a faithful servant he proved to be, though his ministry was hard and unrewarding! When Jesus called Saul of Tarsus and he responded, 'Lord, what do you want me to do?' (Acts 9:6), on receiving his commission (Acts 22:21) he served with unremitting zeal (1 Corinthians 15:10) in spite of all the hardship and persecution he thereby experienced.

Whether 'sent' by God in the work of the gospel, or 'sent' by men in some mundane task (Colossians 3:22-23), our attitude should be the same, to be diligent, not lackadaisical, in whatever has been entrusted to us.

[Related proverb: 26:6.]

10:27-30. Stark contrasts. These verses continue the theme of vv. 24-25 in four dramatic contrasts between what the righteous and the wicked may expect. These verses feature the *fear* of the Lord (v. 27) – which is our attitude toward him and our response to him in recognition of who he is and also of his active involvement in the world and in our lives – and the *way* of the Lord (v. 29) which may be understood either as the way we are to follow, his commandments and the standard he sets for our living (as, for example, Genesis 18:19; Judges 2:22; 2 Kings 21:22), or as the way he is working out his purposes in this world (perhaps as in Ezekiel 18:25; 33:20).

10:27. Literally, it is 'days' which are compared with 'years', and maybe we are intended to see this comparison as deliberate. (However, compare 9:10-11.) Those who fear the Lord are content to live their lives one day at a time. They trust him for their daily bread. They know their times are in his hand (Psalm 31:15). They have no need to be anxious about tomorrow (Matthew 6:34), content in the provision of the Lord. Whereas those who do not know him often have their minds on the years ahead and their plans for those years.

The prolongation is an augmentation in the sense of adding more, the shortening is a cutting off, as in the harvesting of a crop, and is also used figuratively for discouragement (Numbers 21:4) or grief and vexation (Judges 10:16; 16:16; Job 21:4; Zechariah 11:8). See also Psalm 89:45; 102:23; Isaiah 28:20; 59:1; Ezekiel 42:5; Micah 2:7.

Through the fear of the Lord the righteous will get more out of life, will accomplish more and will enjoy fulfilment under God's blessing day by day, whereas the wicked, however long they live, will find themselves sold short.

10:28 compares hope with expectation (NKJV), or prospect with hope (NIV). The difference in meaning of the words is a subtle one and perhaps little should be made of it. However, it is worth observing that the hope of the righteous lies in what another, namely God, will provide, while the wicked have no expectation other than what they might obtain for themselves, either directly or through others. The hope of the righteous involves patient waiting and trust (Romans 5:4-5; 8:25), and it is a hope in which they can rejoice (Romans 5:2; 12:12). What can the wicked look forward to? Where is their hope? Any they might have is as short as their lives. In reality, they are without hope, for they are without God in the world (Ephesians 2:2).

Ultimately, we see the hope of the righteous embodied in the Lord Jesus 'who for the joy that was set before him endured the cross, despising the shame, and has sat down at the right hand of the throne of God' (Hebrews 12:2). Those who wish to live godly lives will suffer opposition and things may be difficult, as opposed to the ungodly who very often behave as if they 'hadn't a care in the world'. The righteous, however, out of this dark scenario have a sure prospect of unbounded, liberating joy in the fulfilment of all they hope for, because they are looking to the One who provides for them. By contrast, the expectation of the wicked is bound ultimately to perish, because they themselves will perish. While this is certainly true concerning life after death, its principle also operates in this life. The believer has everything to look forward to, unlike the unbeliever who really has nothing to look forward to.

[Related proverbs: 11:7,23.]

10:29. It is probably best to see both clauses as referring to the way of the Lord (as NIV, ESV). His 'way', or 'road' or 'path' is probably best understood in this context as his providential dealings with people. What God requires and what he does impinge upon the upright and evildoers in two totally different ways. The things being compared in this verse are a fortification and a ruin. For the one group, God is providing protection – protection from the intents of the wicked; from the other group God is removing any supposed protection they might think they have: their security is in ruins. Workers of iniquity have the way of God to contend with in decree and judgement. What is decreed will be enacted: in their case destruction – terror and total ruin.

God's ways embrace his works, which are studied by all who take pleasure in them (Psalm 111:2). The righteous find delight in God's creation, his laws and his providence. All that God has said and done are a source of comfort, encouragement and strength to his people.

10:30 is interesting insofar as though enormous efforts have been made to eliminate God's people over the centuries, and though the world continues in hostility to the truth, yet the church has spread throughout the earth and continues to this day. As long as the world continues, so long will the righteous continue on it. God will see to that. This is his world, and it is for his people.

Whether the territory in the second clause refers to the whole earth or to the land of Israel, the principle is the same. Israel dwelt in the land of *promise* – it was promised to the people of God, so long as they walked in his ways (Deuteronomy 28). When they did so, the righteous prospered and the wicked perished, in accordance with his promise. Also in accordance with his promise we look for new heavens and a new earth in which righteousness dwells (2 Peter 3:13). It will be the home of righteousness because it is the home of the righteous. It is their inheritance, and nothing will displace them. The earth is the Lord's, and all its fullness (Psalm 24:1), and it belongs to those to whom he has given it. This has always been true, and is true today. Satan is a usurper. Those who remain on his side are also usurpers. They do not belong here, and they will not stay here. The time will come when they are forcibly removed. See also 11:23.

This little group of proverbs, then, speak of the security, happiness and destiny of the righteous. They encourage objectivity by encompassing the whole picture. It is a very precious thing to be under the protection and provision of almighty God, and unspeakably comforting to be conscious of it.

[Related proverbs: 11:23; 12:3.]

10:31-32. Matthew 12:33-37. By your words... Note the chiastic structure of these two verses and the contrasts within them: 31a and 32b refer to the mouth of the righteous and the mouth of the wicked; 31b and 32a refer to the tongue of the wicked and the lips of the righteous.

The root meaning of the word translated 'bring forth' is that of germination, and carries with it the notion of fruitfulness. The fact that wisdom issues from the mouth of the righteous indicates that what the righteous have to say is beneficially productive. The tree that does not bear fruit is fit for nothing but to be hewn down and burnt to make way for something better; the branch of the vine which is unfruitful is cut out and committed to the flames in order to encourage more fruit in the productive part (Matthew 3:10; 7:19; John 15:2,6). The perverse tongue is like that, not only unproductive of anything good in itself, but positively hindering the growth of good elsewhere. The image recalls a barbaric practice and is not to be taken literally. But it does remind us that such people will be silenced, and although the means is not here stated, it is clearly under the judgement of God that it will happen.

In v. 32 the lips and mouth 'knowing' are obviously used for the heart and mind. But there is more to it than that, because by attaching knowledge to the lips we are being reminded that acceptable speech on the one hand, or perverse speech on the other, are almost unthinkingly automatic. The fingers of a pianist will dazzle an audience with their virtuosic skill, but it is largely because the piece has been practised and refined so many times that the incredible performance has become almost automatic. It wasn't like that at the beginning. That is just how it is with what proceeds from our mouth: it is out almost before we think about it, because we have been conditioned to it by long practice – a sobering thought!

What is acceptable, or fitting, is what meets with approval, or favour, and gives pleasure in the best sense. Surely one who comes before a king will be careful, even diplomatic, in what he says. The lips of the righteous know what is acceptable to the King of kings, and speak accordingly in lesser company as his representatives or ambassadors. The wicked, by contrast, have no such exalted principles, merely giving expression to the wickedness that is in their hearts, in whatever fashion it may spring forth. They 'know' of no better. Out of the abundance of the heart the mouth speaks (Matthew 12:34).

Consider what the word 'perverse' means, which occurs twice in these verses: a perverse tongue, and what issues from the mouth of the wicked. This is something which is so often in evidence, for it takes what is good and right and gives it a twist into something quite different. So for example it tries to give appeal to the opposite of the commands of God. Satan tempted Eve with a perverse tongue by making what was forbidden attractive. God said, 'You shall not commit adultery', but nowadays the pleasures associated with promiscuous behaviour are magnified out of all proportion to truth, the destructive side is played down, and so truth is turned into a lie. Or wicked people may describe righteous principles and behaviour as 'prudish' or 'outmoded' or by some other negative description in order to undermine and turn around what God has determined for the benefit of his creation. Even the word 'wicked' in recent times has been given a slant to turn its meaning around to something quite different from what it meant originally. A similar thing happened some time ago to the word 'gay'. Perversity, then, at its core, involves a twisting of what is good, right and true as God intended, to make the result – the perversion – acceptable to those who wish to discard the rule or influence of God in their lives.

11:1. Weighed in the balance. The first thing to note about dishonest scales is not that they cheat others but that they are an abomination to the Lord. He treats them with disgust. It is the word used about the attitude the Egyptians had to eating with the Hebrews (Genesis 43:32), the way the Egyptians viewed the pastoral way of life of the Hebrews (Genesis 46:34), and the way the Egyptians viewed the sacrifices the Hebrew people made to the Lord (Exodus 8:26). More seriously, it is the word used by the Lord about his attitude to homosexual conduct and the like (Leviticus 18:22-30), and also about his attitude to idolatry (Deuteronomy 12:31; 13:14). There is no point of contact between the two, no possible room for accommodation.

Why such strong language about weights and measures? The answer is that it involves a principle which reaches far deeper than cheating in trade (serious though that may be), going right to the heart of the perversion of justice. When we look at the law as stated in Leviticus 19:35-36, there we see the justice principle explicitly mentioned. Deuteronomy 25:13-16 deals with the same issue, only in this case condemning discrimination in favour of one against another by having two different sets of values – 'a law for the rich and a law for the poor'. Again, the Lord describes such attitudes as an abomination. God is a God of perfect justice, whose standards are maintained with unvarying exactitude.

By contrast with deceptive scales, a just weight is one having no deficiency. There was probably a royal standard for weights and measures (see 2 Samuel 14:26). In practice some variations would have existed in weights of a particular denomination owing to practical difficulties in accurate calibration. The proverb is not addressing such issues. For example, the monetary pound may purchase more of a commodity in one place than another for reasons which have nothing to do with inaccuracy in weights and measures or injustice with regard to their use.

What this proverb is about is the practice of deception in which the known and accepted standard is being substituted by something else with the intention to defraud, or curry favour, or in some other way to obtain something for oneself at someone else's expense. Viewed in this light, it becomes apparent that the matter has considerable ramifications. Do we treat different people differently on occasions simply because they are different? For example, do we put ourselves out for one person and deprive another on the basis of their social standing, or their connections, or their influence on our behalf, or some such factor which has nothing to do with the matter in hand? James has something to say on this kind of attitude (James 2:1-4).

When it comes to weighing out our love, or our time, or our resources, to others, do we hold dual standards, giving to one and withholding from another for arbitrary reasons which have no justification in God's book? Or do we measure ourselves leniently against the law while enforcing it rigorously on others?

This proverb challenges us over the standard of justice we exercise in our dealings with others and also with how we ourselves measure up to the standard set by God. This standard we all have continually to strive towards, and the incentive to do so should be that it delights God that we should be pursuing his standards of justice.

[Related proverbs: 16:11; 20:10,23.]

11:2. The ugliest feature of the human heart. There is a great deal about pride in the book of Proverbs, even though it may be explicitly mentioned on comparatively few occasions. Pride is a common problem. Like a weed, it keeps on cropping up and intruding where it is not wanted. Here it is linked to shame. In 13:10 and 28:25 it is associated with contention and strife; in 16:18 it is said to lead to destruction; in 29:23 it results in being brought low; 15:25 and 16:5 speak of God's judgement upon the proud. When we look at all these things, it becomes clear that the results of pride are the exact opposite of what the proud person intends for himself.

Pride and shame, or disgrace, are at the opposite ends of the spectrum. Shame is an awful mocker of pride. Pride elevates itself but actually achieves the very opposite of what it sets out to do. Why is this? Part of the answer can be seen in what happened to Nebuchadnezzar, which he himself so pithily summarises in Daniel 4:37. Pride in a person is often something that other proud people cannot stomach! However, it is God who will deal ultimately with this man-centred malady. There are many references to the fact that he brings the proud low, while he also exalts the humble (for example 2 Samuel 22:28; Psalms 18:27; 147:6; 149:4; Isaiah 2:11-12; Matthew 18:4; 23:12; Luke 1:51; James 4:6,10; 1 Peter 5:5-6). The reason is not (to put it crudely) that God wants to be 'top dog'. He himself displayed the virtues of humility by the Lord Jesus taking upon himself the form of a man, of a servant (Philippians 2:5-8). God is who he is. He has no need to defend his position or make out that he is something other than what he is.

Pride is the most self-centred of all character traits. Its root is in the heart of man. Pride is man thinking more of himself, of who he is, of what he is capable of, of what is owed to him, than he ought. Such is the conceit of pride that those guilty of it in general think too well of themselves to admit to being at fault in this area. So in relation to God pride fails to acknowledge the lordship of Christ; it does not recognise that we owe all to his grace; it may even say that God owes us something; or it may assert that we have no need of God and can get on very well without him (compare Psalm 10:4). In relation to man it compares and contrasts, elevating oneself above one's fellows. Both a sense of superiority and an acknowledgement of the same from others is meat and drink to a proud person. It is essentially presumption, bearing no relationship to the facts of the case.

The shame which is said to be the consequence of pride is such as speaks of acute personal embarrassment. It involves exposure to disgrace of the most uncomfortable sort. It is the mental and emotional equivalent of being stripped naked in public. What pride is so desperate to conceal will be shamefully exposed. The man who makes himself big will have his bubble burst and will be seen to be small.

The contrast, 'With the humble is *wisdom*', implies that pride is folly. Some people regard humility as a negative characteristic, almost as an affectation. A humble person is not always belittling himself, or parading his poverty of spirit or lack of ability or in other ways making out that he is a nonentity! That is just a perverse variation on pride! Nevertheless, humility requires effort and practice (see, for example, Matthew 18:4; 23:12; James 4:10; 1 Peter 5:6), the reason being that the sinful human mind has a natural propensity toward pride.

If pride makes us think of ourselves as more than we are, humility does not make us think of ourselves as less than we are. Rather, it makes us think of ourselves as less than we would like to think ourselves to be! It involves a realistic self-assessment. In so doing, and in relation to others, it has regard for others and esteems them in a way which it is impossible for a proud person to do. This comes out very clearly in Romans 12:3-10 and is a significant aspect of the outworking of a renewed mind which is bent on doing God's will. God himself displayed the virtues of humility by the Lord Jesus taking upon himself the form of a man, and of a servant at that (Philippians 2:5-8). We are to follow him!

The NIV translates, 'with humility comes wisdom', presumably with the intention of maintaining the comparison as closely as possible. Thus 'humility' is contrasted with 'pride' and the verb, which is not supplied, is assumed to be 'comes' as in the previous clause. Be that as it may, it is probably better to translate 'humble' or 'lowly' rather than 'humility', and the comparison would appear to be a little more involved. Pride is something which 'comes'. Once it becomes evident, it tends to grow to become prominent and results in being damagingly influential. That is in the nature of pride: it knows no bounds, and it is certainly not self-limiting. But disgrace follows hard upon its heels.

One might expect the comparison to be 'But with humility comes honour.' However, this is not the point this proverb is making. It would seem this proverb is more about the fear of the Lord, or the lack of it. Wisdom, especially in the Book of Proverbs, is closely associated with the fear of God, and the humble are those who have a right estimate of themselves in the sight of God. It is not a question of wisdom coming to the humble, or being the reward or outworking of humility, but rather that true humility of mind is a mark of wisdom. The humble, by virtue of their submission to God in all things, are displaying wisdom. They are not seeking to 'become somebody' or 'achieve something' which will elevate them in their own eyes, but rather are seeking to be what God wants them to be and do what he wants them to do, in order that what they become or what they achieve will reflect upon the one who is working in them and elevate him in the eyes of others. And here lies the essential difference between pride and humility.

[Related proverbs: 16:18; 29:23.]

11:3-6. A safe path through life. Direction and deliverance, destruction and death feature in this group of proverbs. Though they are connected, each has something to say in its own right.

11:3. Leading and following. The matter of guidance must rank among the most important things that concern the believer in life. How do we know how to make the right decisions about what we should do or the way we should go? So it is good before further comment on this verse to be reminded of bedrock principles. For the Christian, guidance is a matter of making the choices God wants us to make and going the way he wants us to go. It is, furthermore, about his leading and our following, rather like a shepherd leading his flock. Psalm 23 uses this illustration, leading and guidance being as much a part of the psalm as comfort and security. Psalm 77:20 also uses this illustration with the added dimension of the human element: God led the people, but it was by the hand of Moses and Aaron, indicating that his servants were instrumental in the process. Psalm 78 likewise concludes with David shepherding and leading God's people (and note there the integrity of his heart). In Proverbs 3:5-6 we are told that it is God who directs the path of those who trust him, while in 6:22 it is the commands and teaching of God's Word from godly parents which guide their son. In Psalm 32:8 God speaks emphatically of his directing his people in the way they should go, and Isaiah 58:11 refers to the Lord guiding them always.

But if the shepherd leads, the sheep must follow, and following means following *his* way. At 10:29 there is reference to the way of the Lord, which involves obedience to his commands. It is a wonder that the Israelites ever reached the point described at the end of Psalm 78, they had been so rebellious. Psalm 32:8 is followed by a caution against being 'mulish'. The guidance promised in Proverbs 3:5-6 presupposes trust in God and acknowledgement of him. Similarly, what was promised in Isaiah 58:11 was dependent upon true repentance and turning to the Lord. Psalm 119:105 declares that it is God's Word which shows the way we should take, and throughout the New Testament the Word of God is the guide for believers as they are enlightened by the Spirit of God, so that they might 'walk worthy' (Colossians 1:9-10; Ephesians 4:1ff; 1 Thessalonians 1:6; Colossians 3:16).

In this proverb it is said to be *integrity* which will guide 'the upright'. While it is perfectly true that God will direct them, it is equally true that, being on the right road, they will follow where that road leads. There is really no tension between the two. Choices will necessarily be restricted for those who have sound principles. Their course will be determined by their principles. Consider for a moment those who have no principles to govern their conduct. They may be enticed by a lucrative business proposition irrespective of whom it might be damaging on the way; or they may purely for personal gain make decisions which, knowingly or unknowingly, jeopardise their relationship with their family; or they may be seduced by pleasures which will destroy them physically or emotionally or psychologically. Examples could be multiplied, but the point is that if they lack the integrity which accompanies upright principles, they are 'all over the place', and are without means of guidance. The consequences which follow will be in accordance with the principles upon which their conduct is based.

So this and the verses which follow make some observations upon what these two groups of people may expect in life. It is in the nature of the upright to act with integrity, and by consistently doing so they will be led in a right way through life without the burden of anxiety about the choices they are making. It is in the nature of the unfaithful to act perversely, or treacherously, and this conduct will bring about their destruction. Like a treacherous cliff path which is not to be relied upon because it may give way without warning, so the perversity of those who are unprincipled will bring them to destruction. Cause and effect are operating in this verse, for God has established laws which operate in the moral world as well as the natural.

So if we are thinking about our path through life, and the decisions we need to make whether large or small, our first consideration should be whether we are acting with integrity: am I already following the Lord's way? Am I wanting his will to be done in my life? Is my path consistent with his Word? Am I respecting wise advice and counsel from others? If we expect to be guided onward in our lives we have to be in the right place to start with.

[Related proverbs: 10:9; 13:6; 28:18.]

11:4. Riches or righteousness? A 'day of wrath' is mentioned in Zephaniah 1:15, where it refers to the Lord's wrath, and v. 18 of the same chapter says, 'Neither their silver nor their gold shall be able to deliver them in the day of the Lord's wrath.' It graphically illustrates this proverb. Nebuchadnezzar was the human instrument the Lord used to bring judgement upon Judah. Righteous Jeremiah was certainly delivered from death in those terrible days.

The important thing to notice there is that behind the political and military manoeuvring God himself was in control. It was his wrath which was being displayed, even though the majority of the people saw only the human side of it. Ultimately, whatever the outward appearances, issues of life and death are in the hands of God, not of men. God cannot be 'bought off'. We see in the lives of Joseph, of Daniel and his three friends, and in the cases of others, that they were delivered on account of their righteousness and how it came about. There is also a remarkable statement in Hebrews 5:7 of application to the Lord Jesus. God does not treat the wicked and the righteous alike (consider Abraham interceding for Sodom, Genesis 18). He knows how to deliver the righteous (see 2 Peter 2:9). He makes a distinction between the righteous and the wicked (1 Peter 3:12).

It is also important to appreciate the context of the proverb and to read it the right way round. It is not saying that righteousness will always deliver from death. The context is the day of wrath, and a comparison is being made between the relative merits of riches and righteousness in that context. The ultimate day of wrath will be when Jesus returns. On that day only those clothed in his righteousness will be saved for eternal life. Absolutely nothing else will count.

[Related proverbs: 10:2-3; 21:6; 28:18.]

11:5. Conduct and consequences. This is reminiscent of v. 3, but whereas in v. 3 integrity focuses upon a person's mind and thinking, righteousness here has more to do with a person's conduct. This proverb is speaking about the road ahead for the blameless and the wicked. In v. 3 right thinking will enable right decisions for progress. Here, right behaviour will smooth the way ahead. The way of life for the blameless is made easier. Complicating factors are removed. It often wins the cooperation of others to pursue the right course. The wicked, on the other hand, are setting obstacles for themselves at every step, for their conduct wins no favours. Think in terms of character references. Two people may be equally competent when it comes to doing the job for which they are applying, but the way will be cleared for the one who has an impeccable track record as opposed to the other whose references raise all kinds of doubts about their reliability and relationships with others.

11:6. Character and consequences. This is about the snares of life and the context is temptation. Many of the things which entangle people are things they lust after, things they covet. Many people are held captive by their lusts, and not just alcoholics or drug addicts. Achan was captivated by the treasure he found (Joshua 7:21); David was captivated by the beauty of a bathing woman (2 Samuel 11:2-4); Adonijah was captivated by the idea of becoming king (1 Kings 1:5). In all these cases, and many others which could be cited, these people were lusting after what was not theirs to take and they suffered the consequences of the combination of lust and opportunity. The upright person has inward principles enabling him to avoid or break free from such sinister enticements, Joseph being a notable example (Genesis 39:7-12). Never underestimate the temptation to covetousness. It is at its most powerful, and you are at your weakest, when opportunity knocks. Look what happened to Ananias and Sapphira (Acts 5:1-11) who coveted the praise of men.

The spider negotiates the web in which the fly becomes hopelessly entangled. The spider is the master of the web, the web is the master of the fly.

11:7. Don't count on it. Because this proverb is framed in the context of expectation and hope, the thought may particularly be that of a wicked man dying, as we would say, 'prematurely'. Jesus told the parable of the rich fool in Luke 12:16-21 whose great plans for himself were brought to an abrupt and ignominious end. From this proverb which is about the ungodly, inferences by comparison may be made about the godly. For it says not, 'When a man dies...' but 'When a wicked man dies...' The righteous *do* have an expectation and a hope which will not perish (14:32; 23:18). Though most of the proverbs are framed in terms relating to this life, the eternal dimension is often there in the background. The tragedy of the wicked and unjust is that at the end they have nothing. Spiritually bankrupt, they enter into eternal punishment. The joy for the righteous and the just is that at the end of this life, whenever it may be, enriched by the grace of God, they enter into eternal bliss.

[Related proverbs: 10:28; 11:23.]

11:8. Deliverance. If the reference here is to trouble that the wicked by their scheming intend inflicting upon the righteous, the implication is that they fall foul of their own designs, that their plotting backfires upon themselves. Perhaps the classic examples here are those of Daniel's enemies who were killed by the lions they expected to devour Daniel (Daniel 6), and of Haman, who ended up being hanged on the gallows he had erected for Mordecai (Esther 8:9-10). David, in Psalms 7:14-16; 9:15-16, writes of the same kind of thing, making clear that both deliverance and judgement are from the Lord. Whereas in the previous verses we have seen how the righteousness of the upright or blameless works for them, in this verse it is different, for it is not his righteousness which delivers its possessor from trouble, because deliverance comes from another quarter. It simply says that the righteous is delivered. By what or by whom? The question is not answered. How are the tables turned? What unbelievers may attribute to miscalculation or chance mishaps or unforeseen events, the righteous wisely attribute to the unseen hand of God, unrecognised by unbelievers, who remains fully in control. See also 2 Thessalonians 1:3-10.

This proverb does not say the righteous will be *spared* from trouble but *delivered* from it. The trouble spoken of in this proverb is not general but specific. People have plenty of trouble that they have to live with, but this is the kind of trouble which speaks of urgent need for help. In Psalm 34 we find David in such a situation. At v. 6 by way of personal testimony he says: 'This poor man cried, and the LORD heard him and saved him out of all his troubles.' Then, at v. 17 he reflects, 'When the righteous cry for help, the LORD hears and delivers them out of all their troubles.' God's people have a heavenly Father on whom to call in their hour of need. The ungodly have no such help.

[Related proverbs: 11:6,21; 28:18.]

11:9. Words and the Word. The word rendered 'hypocrite' (NKJV) or 'godless' (NIV, ESV) refers to a morally corrupt person or an apostate. An apostate is one who has turned away from the faith he once professed. Some who have departed from the truth have by their plausible arguments led many astray, particularly those weak in the faith. Romans 16:17-18 and 2 Timothy 3:1-9 and other scriptures warn against people like this. 1 John 2:18-21 refers to the same kind of people. They existed in the early church, and they exist today.

This destructive influence is in the *mouth* of the apostate. His words, often pleasant and plausible, would lead others out of the way of truth, away from the path to life, into one of many different paths all of which lead to death. There are many ways in which his destructive work may be done, whether by misrepresentation, by distortion, by half-truths, or by outright lies. Satan is a master of such things. In the very beginning it was through the mouthpiece of the serpent that he deceived Eve, and it is through the words of his godless minions that he continues to work destruction right up to the present day.

How is the Christian to be aware of and combat such things? The proverb says that it is through *knowledge* that the righteous will be delivered, without specifying exactly what knowledge. If we consider how Jesus refuted Satan's temptations in the wilderness at the commencement of his public ministry (Matthew 4:1-10) it is evident that he not only knew the Scriptures but he also knew his enemy and knew how to apply the Scriptures to the situation.

Knowledge of God's Word and an understanding of how to use it are vital when it comes to deliverance from the cunning persuasiveness of those who have departed from the truth and who very often themselves, like Satan, have an acquaintance with the Word of God and will try to use it to their own ends. In each of the above quoted scriptures note how important a knowledge of the truth is to escape their influence. Romans 16:17 refers to vital importance of 'the doctrine which you learned'; 2 Timothy 3:7 refers to the 'knowledge of the truth' which the deceivers lacked; in 1 John 2:20-21 John indicates that his readers had a knowledge of the truth which not only distinguished them from the apostates but also gave them discernment.

Just as it is the weak of the herd which are most likely to succumb to predators, it is those weak in knowledge who are most vulnerable to Satan's devices. Christians should never underestimate the vital importance of knowing the Lord and knowing his Word. Such knowledge is an absolute essential in the warfare in which every believer is engaged (Ephesians 6:17). Young Christians in particular need to grow in the knowledge and understanding of God's Word as quickly as possible, in dependence upon the Spirit of truth to guide them into all truth. It is the particular responsibility of overseers to provide sound biblical and relevant instruction to strengthen the church against subversive elements (Titus 1:9-11).

This proverb speaks of destroying a *neighbour*, without reference to whether or not that neighbour fears God. The commandment says we are to love our neighbour as ourselves (Leviticus 19:18), again without reference to the kind of person that neighbour may be. Psalms 15 and 101:5 indicate how seriously God regards this matter.

Those who are apostates have in the past been close to true believers. It is these who are or have been the neighbours of believers, and it is these whose words are potentially most dangerous, who divide and destroy churches.

Once again we are reminded of the power of words, either for good or for evil, and it provides an appropriate opportunity to consider how we think and speak of others, particularly any who fall into this category of 'neighbour'.

[Related proverb: 12:6.]

11:10-11. Public influence. Kidner, commenting on these verses, drily states: 'However drab the world makes out virtue to be, it appreciates the boon of it in public life.' One suspects that the rejoicing in the city is not so much on behalf of the righteous themselves as on account of the resultant benefits they bring in terms of security, stability and general prosperity. There is an ambivalence among people in general who wish to enjoy the good things which accompany righteousness without what they see as its strictures. The truth is, though, that when ungodliness prevails, these blessings take themselves wings and fly away, leaving the curse of the opposite conditions.

There is a danger in thinking that godly people, especially when in a minority, can have little influence in society as a whole, whereas the fact of the case is that one Christian can have a greater influence for real good than one hundred who do not fear God. The Lord can save by many or by few (1 Samuel 14:6), and the principle behind Leviticus 26:8 remains in force.

'The blessing of the upright' can be taken in two ways, being either the blessing they receive, or the blessing they give. However, as has been pointed out before, the two are inextricably linked, for the blessing they receive overflows into the blessing they give. When the righteous prosper, everybody benefits in every good way. When the wicked prosper, everybody suffers in one way or another. That is why there is jubilation when the wicked perish.

There appears to be more than a hint at public administration in these verses. The city could be thought of as a centre for local administration. To a great extent cities were expected to manage their own affairs. Even today in our society local government is both important and influential. The blessing of the upright, in concrete terms, includes what God bestows upon them in the form of wisdom, skill and ability to serve the community in which he has placed them. We must never lose sight of the fact that the blessing God bestows upon his people is intended by him to be used for the good of others. Any society which is to prosper needs godly men and women in positions of influence and authority. When the dominant voice is that of those who have no fear of God – that is, the mouth of the wicked – one can expect only degeneration which if unchecked would lead to disaster.

These verses serve as a reminder of the great importance of having godly people as salt and light to bring cleansing and illumination in a world of corruption and darkness, and in particular to exercise influence in civic administration and civil affairs. Perhaps they should provoke us to ask to what extent we are making an effective contribution for good in our own society and whether there is more we can do. They should also prompt us to pray for those in authority over us, as Paul says in 1 Timothy 2:1-2. The church is the pillar and ground of the truth (1 Timothy 3:15): our presence and prayers make a difference. That is why God has placed us where he has, and why he would have us petition him on behalf of our leaders.

[Related proverbs: 14:34; 28:12,28; 29:2,8.]

11:12. Knowing when to keep quiet. The 'wisdom' which is lacking is the word usually translated 'heart'. It concerns the seat of understanding and affections. This is where the problem really lies, not with the neighbour. The picture here is of one who, by implication from the second clause, not only despises his neighbour in his heart, but also shows it by disrespect. The belittling of neighbours (making them look small) is all too common, expressing itself in a great variety of ways, verbally and otherwise. The result of such an attitude leads only to the fragmentation of a community through mutual suspicion and distrust.

The proverb exposes the real source of the problem. To be able to 'get on' with our neighbours we need to understand them and have a natural sympathy with them. This means giving them time and consideration. It is so easy to pick on the ways in which they are different from us, the things they do of which we might not approve, the things they say and the way they say them, their lifestyle, their tastes – in fact almost anything about them – and look down upon them as if in some way they were inferior to us. In this way we distance ourselves from them. Then we go and talk about them to others who give us a sympathetic ear, and so the damage we do spreads, and thus a person is demeaned in the eyes of others. There is a danger of equating 'different' with 'inferior' or 'unacceptable' when considering others, but anyone intelligent enough to think things through ('a man of understanding') will see the fallacy in this.

Even supposing there is more to it than a neighbour merely being 'different', and that there is evidence that this neighbour is truly foolish, or unprincipled, or conducts his affairs in a contemptible fashion, or is a nuisance, or whatever it might be, the proverb still holds true, that to despise such a person and *thus* to speak evil of him is 'heartless'. It still shows that the person doing so lacks both understanding and affection. Respect and consideration are still due to such a person, and an understanding heart will keep its counsel and seek a course of action which will promote the true welfare of the neighbour and properly address issues which require attention.

[Related proverbs: 3:29; 14:21; 24:28.]

11:13. Guarding the tongue. This is about more than being asked to keep quiet about something. The 'talebearer' or 'gossip' is one with malicious intent. The picture here is of a matter which is being considered behind closed doors. It may be a sensitive matter requiring close counsel or discreet attention, and certainly it is not something for public consumption or to be heard by the wrong ears. The person in view here is not just one who happens to have a weakness for divulging confidences, but one who is intent on picking things up in order to propagate them and so do harm. Treachery is involved. Perhaps it is someone who derives a sense of power from doing such things, finding perverse pleasure from the trouble he (or she) sees it causing others. He is compared to one who is of a 'faithful spirit'. Again, this is more than simply being trustworthy to keep a secret. It is having the desire to nurture what is good and cover what is evil. An example will make the point. Suppose someone commits an indiscretion which could have untoward consequences if not handled carefully. The talebearer getting hold of it will enlarge it, broadcast it and use it for the embarrassment and humiliation (or worse) of the person concerned. On the other hand, the 'faithful spirit' will feel for the person, and do everything for his sake to ensure that the damage done is contained and spreads no further. The talebearer puts a flame under it. The faithful spirit puts a blanket on it.

Talebearers find encouragement in a society which has an uncurbed appetite for the full details of every story which can be made into a scandal, who lap up with relish anything which is (or should be) revolting, promiscuous, or obscene. Do not encourage or imitate them!

[Related proverbs: 16:28; 20:19; 25:8-10.]

11:14 (compare 15:22). Seeking advice. This proverb has a very simple structure involving a direct comparison. The word translated 'counsel' (NKJV) or 'guidance' (NIV, ESV) is derived from a word for a rope of twisted cords. Perhaps it contains the idea of the strength of a number of people coming and working together, as together the woven cords of a rope give it strength and flexibility, or it may be the idea of ropes being used in, say, the guidance of a vessel. However it is understood, it is clear that a people – whether it be a nation or a smaller community – needs strong, coherent leadership for its security and prosperity. It is disastrous when this is lacking, as is evident from what happened to the nation of Israel from time to time during the period of the judges. A nation is also pulled apart by leaders with conflicting ideologies striving for supremacy. 'Safety' or 'victory' translates a word for deliverance, frequently used of the deliverance given by God from the enemy in times of war, but more generally of the salvation which God gives.

In the Proverbs we must never lose sight of the counsel of God which is always there, even if in the background. Deliverance and safety may come through the wisdom of many advisers, but their wisdom and advice are given them by God. Indeed, it could be said that the very existence or otherwise of such counsel is indicative of the blessing or judgement of God upon a people.

Whereas in this verse the focus seems to be at national level, 15:22 is more general in its application. We have probably heard the statement, 'It wasn't such a good idea after all,' when some plan has backfired or gone horribly wrong. Nearly always it has happened because of shortsightedness which could have been avoided had better advice been sought.

While it is true that we each have to take ultimate responsibility for our own actions, when important decisions have to be made it is better to seek out plenty of advice from trustworthy people than to act unilaterally. 'Plan A' may look very good to us and have strong appeal. But we need to see how much depends upon it and how serious the implications can be. Other people can bring different viewpoints on it, can raise questions we had not thought about, can provide insights which would never have occurred to us, can expose weaknesses in our ideas, can suggest alternatives or modifications. Even if there is some difference of opinion or there are some conflicting ideas, yet the sum total helps us to embark upon 'Plan B' with the greater confidence that it will succeed.

Many a bad relationship would have been avoided, many a bad business deal would not have been struck, many a heartache would have been spared, had the person had the wisdom to acknowledge the limits of his or her own understanding or ability and to be guided by sound judgement rather than headstrong determination.

But the social aspect of these proverbs should be recognised, that they cover plans which concern not just an individual but a company of people. There is strength and safety when many counsellors or advisers have reached a corporate decision, for the burden of responsibility is carried by many, and the decisions thus made are usually sound and are not easily overthrown.

There is an interesting and important example of the influence of many counsellors in Acts 15. It was a critical time for the church in terms of belief and practice and a wrong influence could have done untold harm by causing confusion among God's people. The dissension and dispute into which Paul and Barnabas were drawn in the church at Antioch (Acts 15:2) resulted in their being sent to Jerusalem to the apostles and elders, where clearly the dispute continued (Acts 15:7). The outcome, though, was a clearer understanding of the whole situation in which the body of men came to a unified conclusion. From Acts 15:28 it is evident that this was the will of the Holy Spirit, but his work did not bypass the minds of his people but worked through them. Because all were involved, and this was not the decision of just one man such as Peter, or Paul, not only was the matter clearly understood by the leaders, but the churches were confirmed in their faith and strengthened and encouraged (Acts 15:31-32).

[Related proverbs: 15:22; 20:18; 24:6.]

11:15. Up to your neck. Like the last, this proverb is a simple comparison. This subject was dealt with at 6:1-5 and it crops up several times in the book of Proverbs. It is of greater importance than at first meets the eye. The imagery is of a man in some way acting as a guarantor for another, but this is not so much a friend whom he knows intimately but one of whom he is less certain. It is going to cause him at least anxiety over how much he has let himself in for, and he may well suffer in other ways too. Unscrupulous people can use all kinds of plausible ploys to take advantage of the kindness and generosity of others, especially if they know they can get them to shoulder responsibility for them with promises they can't back out of. Even if it is a business arrangement, they can exploit partners who have unwisely committed themselves. There can sometimes be strong psychological pressures to give support to something one actually knows little about, for example out of loyalty to a friend who 'needs' their commitment and argues that to fail to do so is tantamount to betrayal. Many a person has suffered sleepless nights and endless worry over the potential cost of what turns out to have been a commitment to someone who proves less than utterly reliable and trustworthy.

The security of the second clause indicates confidence and freedom from care. Do you want to enter into something which could burden you down with anxiety and uncertainty, or are you going to steer clear and guard your freedom? After all, the decision is yours to make and you should not allow yourself to be swayed by coercion of any kind however convincingly it is presented.

There is another side to this proverb which may not be immediately obvious. People can pledge themselves to strangers by over-committing themselves financially for what they believe will provide them with a better lifestyle, through loans which turn out to be a millstone around their neck. They end up in bondage to unsatisfying luxury instead of enjoying a carefree attitude to things. They are making a pledge, they are promising to pay, and once committed there is no opt-out clause. They would have been far happier, far more secure, had they foregone their desire and not signed the form. As it is, they are held to ransom by those from whom there is no escape. Many suffering in the debt trap are experiencing the exact opposite of what they thought their foolish commitment would bring them.

There are many different ways in which people are encouraged to strike hands in a pledge, and in many cases it leads only to regret and self-recrimination. The lesson in this proverb is that one needs to be canny about committing oneself to anything, with hard-nosed objectivity, especially when the temptation of great returns is present. To commit oneself potentially beyond one's means, whatever shape or form it takes, is really a form of gambling. What is needed is a healthy abhorrence of this kind of thing in order to enjoy what matters most in life.

[Related proverbs: 6:1; 11:15; 17:18; 20:16; 22:26; 27:13.]

11:16. A valuable acquisition. The verb translated 'retains' or 'gains' is the same as that used at 3:18 and 4:4, and the thought is that of both acquiring and holding on to something. (By adding 'only', the NIV is interpreting rather than translating.) This proverb is about what two kinds of people keep hold of, what they retain (having been attained or acquired) as of importance to them.

Although some see the two clauses as being complementary qualities in men and women (tenderness and strength) rather than contrasting characteristics, the adjective describing the men is invariably used in a negative sense and the comparison does therefore seem to be between what is laid hold of and how.

Admittedly at first sight it seems strange that a gracious woman should be compared to ruthless men, though perhaps less so that honour should be compared to riches. 'Honour' is probably a better translation than 'respect'. It is often translated 'glory'. It is showing this woman to be a person of substance, to be taken note of, even to be revered.

The comparison is interesting and telling. A woman (singular) is compared with men (plural) (the word 'men', though not present, is implied). The woman is gracious (a reference to her character rather than her appearance), the men are ruthless. The comfort, security and confidence found in the woman are compared with the opposite qualities found in the men, who instil only fear. The woman is the weaker of the two and in that society less likely to be influential or to make a mark. The woman, it could be said, is worth her weight in gold, but the men are really worthless despite their great hoardings. The woman, being alone and having no natural resources or power, has, by the grace God has given her (always implied in the proverbs) attained far more than all the combined strength and scheming of wicked men.

All this makes a telling point about what is of true worth and how it is obtained, especially in a self-centred, materialistically orientated society in which people so often trample upon one another in order to get what they want. For the Lord's people it serves as a reminder that what is of inestimable value in the sight of God (compare 1 Peter 3:4) is not obtained by strength or influence, nor is it retained by might or power.

Honour sits well on a gracious woman, and her influence far exceeds for good anything that the accumulated wealth of wicked men can achieve. This should be a wonderful encouragement to Christians (whether men or women) who believe their resources and abilities to be very limited. The way to the top in God's sight is by means of progress in grace, and true godliness demonstrated in kindness of heart is infinitely more influential in real terms than riches.

Consider Romans 2:7-8 which in some ways mirrors the gracious woman and ruthless men of this proverb. Notice they both seek something. One, although seeking glory, honour and immortality, is actually doing good which, by implication, is seeking the good of others; the other, by contrast, is self-seeking which, by implication, is seeking the good of oneself at the expense of others. Each is rewarded by God accordingly.

[Related proverbs: 21:21; 22:1; 31:30.]

11:17-21. Punishment and reward feature prominently in this section which shows how they operate at different levels.

11:17. The benefits of righteousness. Kindness and cruelty bring their own rewards. There is no escaping the fact that there are natural benefits to living the way God intended and natural troubles to doing otherwise. It all operates according to the natural laws upon which God has structured his creation. A 'merciful' man is one who displays the faithful lovingkindness which is characteristic of God himself. He will certainly benefit others, but this proverb is saying that he will also benefit himself. His conduct toward others is to do them good and is not exercised with his own good foremost in his mind. Nevertheless, he does himself good. Firstly, he will have satisfaction from having been a blessing to others, and secondly he may also receive blessing from others. So there are both direct and indirect beneficial consequences. Furthermore, the benefit is to his 'soul', that is, to his whole being.

A cruel man, on the other hand, is one who inflicts pain and terror. The trouble he causes others rebounds upon himself. For example, he will often feel insecure, watching his back for fear of reprisal. There will often be a serious underlying discomfort because of the potential consequences of the way he has treated others. There will be psychological, if not physical, damage to himself resulting from his cruelty. It may be significant that the words used of the two kinds of men are different (a distinction not brought out in NIV, ESV): one benefits his own 'soul', the other troubles his own 'flesh'. The results are at the level of the action. While some people appear to get away with their cruelty and live in carefree disregard for what they do, appearances can be deceptive, and usually things are very different underneath. Quite apart from this, there is abundant historical evidence to show that the cruelty of cruel men eventually pays them a return visit. The word 'flesh' can also apply to 'kin'. A cruel man brings trouble not only upon himself, but also upon his relations or close associates.

[Related proverb: 21:21.]

11:18. Wages or reward. The question is often asked, 'Why do the wicked prosper?' Psalm 73 takes up this theme and reaches the conclusion stated in this proverb. The word for 'work' could be translated 'wages' (as in NIV, ESV). The idea is that what he gets out of what he puts in is deceptive. It is not what it seems. Contrary to appearances, it brings him no real reward at all. Even what he seems to gain will be taken from him, and his end will be moral and spiritual bankruptcy.

The exact opposite applies to the one who sows righteousness. The NIV follows the imagery through by supplying the verb 'reap'. Some think of righteousness as being a very sterile quality. The righteousness spoken of here is so far removed from that, that it is likened to a seed which is planted in the hope of yielding a harvest. Compare Hosea 10:12 and 2 Corinthians 9:10. To sow righteousness, therefore, is to promote it. In a world of sin, right thinking, right attitudes and right conduct stand out and are noticed. True righteousness exercises a very positive influence. Here the fruit of righteousness is described as a sure reward, where 'sure' contrasts with 'deceptive'. There is nothing deceptive, uncertain or ephemeral about it. The reward Asaph saw in Psalm 73 was to be kept, guided and received into glory by his God. Just as wickedness has both temporal and eternal consequences, so the same applies to righteousness.

[Related proverbs: 12:5,20; 13:13,21.]

11:19. The end of righteousness. This proverb sums up the preceding ones in terms of finality. It is very tersely put without any kind of embellishment: righteousness to life, evil to death. The only additional element is that of pursuit. Sowing righteousness and pursuing evil present two very different images. The latter conveys the idea of hastening the end. The wicked, by their running after evil, are only the more speedily bringing the ultimate judgement upon themselves. Their lives are truly cut short and cut off (Psalm 55:23). Now we see why.

[Related proverbs: 10:16; 11:23; 19:23.]

11:20-21. Detestation and delight; destruction and deliverance. Thus far we have alluded to some of the natural consequences resulting from good or bad conduct, but here we come to the Lord, the arbiter and judge of what is right and what is wrong. What he detests he punishes; what delights him he rewards. Consequences, whether they be seen to be natural or otherwise, are in his hands and under his control.

Verse 21 presupposed the question, 'Why do the wicked get away with it?' The answer is that they do not. They will be punished. This verse insists that there is no escaping punishment. The statement commences with, literally, 'hand to hand' (see also 16:5 where the same expression occurs), which is variously translated. If it is understood as of shaking hands on a promise, it could be a way of confirming that most certainly they will not go unpunished. Alternatively, it could mean that though the wicked join hand in hand, that is, though they strengthen themselves or become formidably powerful, nevertheless they will still be punished. Whichever way it is taken, there is a reassuring certainty that wickedness, of whatever form and from whatever source, will be dealt with ... by God.

The NIV says, 'but those who are righteous will go free'. The original, however, refers to 'the seed' or 'offspring' of the righteous being delivered, or escaping, and this is probably a deliberate pointer to the continuity of righteousness. The wicked sometimes seem so to have their way that the impression is given that righteousness will be exterminated. Not so, says the scripture. Wickedness will certainly be punished, but the line of the righteous will continue from generation to generation.

Elijah in his dejection thought that Jezebel had eradicated the righteous from the land and that he alone was left. But far from the righteous being driven to extinction, God was raising up a new generation of those who feared him, and it was Jezebel and Ahab who suffered God's judgement (1 Kings 19:14-18). At one point David cried to the Lord out of a similar concern (Psalm 12:1), but he was reminded that the Lord would preserve his people forever (v. 7 of the psalm). It has been the anxious concern of God's people from time to time throughout history, yet God is faithful to his promise. Time and time again seemingly impregnable ungodly ideologies have come tumbling down and the Lord's people have been delivered and have flourished.

These things have happened because God is in control. Until the great and terrible day of the Lord they serve as a perpetual reminder that the Lord detests those of a perverse heart and delights in those who are blameless in their ways. A perverse heart is a twisted, or distorted, heart. It is worth remembering that a self-righteous heart is also like this because it does not submit to the righteousness of God but puts something else – something very ugly – in its place! Those who are blameless in their ways are not those who display a rigid, formal rectitude of conduct, but are rather those whose lives exhibit grace, and the fruit of the Spirit (Galatians 5:22-23). There is an integrity, a wholeness, about them, whose righteousness is beautiful, a righteousness which exceeds that of the scribes and Pharisees (Matthew 5:20).

[Related proverbs: 12:7,22; 13:6; 15:9; 16:5; 17:20; 28:18.]

11:22. A head turner! What a wonderful image this is! It contrasts dramatically with v. 16. A beautiful woman can turn heads. But beauty is only skin deep. There is something which to the senses is offensively incongruous in a beautiful woman when it is discovered that her behaviour is anything but beautiful. The sense of offence is brought out by the first clause. A ring of gold is both attractive and valuable. The pig was, according to the Mosaic law, an unclean animal (Leviticus 11:7). The pig is not rendered beautiful by virtue of having a gold ring in its snout! Neither is a woman rendered beautiful by virtue of having a body which is perfect in form and enhanced by fine clothing and ornamentation – nose rings included (see Genesis 24:47; Isaiah 3:21; Ezekiel 16:12). In fact the outward appearance constitutes very little of the person. Peter makes this point in 1 Peter 3:1-6.

The proverb is actually very forceful, for the word 'like' or 'as' is not in the original, and so it is stronger than a simple comparison but rather indicating equivalence! We are intended to see the one in the other!

Proverbs 31:10-31 portrays the ideal wife, of whom no mention is made of her outward appearance except to draw attention to its irrelevance (v. 30)!

How unlike the images with which we are bombarded by the advertising media or by so many romantic books and films! This proverb presents to us the truth of the matter with a starkness which should give us a jolt! It ought to encourage women who are particularly self-conscious about their supposed lack of physical beauty, and on the other hand caution those who are very attractive, to focus upon real, lasting beauty. It should also remind men not to be shortsighted or shallow in their consideration of the opposite sex. God has made us the way we are physically, and our physical appearance has been largely inherited from our parents. There is little we can do about it, nor does God intend that we should. The work he does require of each and every one of us is that exercised in the realm of our character as we submit ourselves to him and as his Spirit does his sanctifying work in our lives. That is where true beauty can be formed, developed and displayed.

[Related proverbs: 11:16; 31:30.]

11:23. Those who seek will find. This verse has similarities to 10:28 but is viewing the picture from a slightly different angle. Desire and expectation have different nuances of meaning. 'Desire' in a negative sense can mean lust or a greedy longing, whereas 'expectation' includes more the forward look of hope (so translated in the NIV). The thing that fills the mind of the righteous, the matter that occupies his attention and directs his energies, is to do and encourage and promote what is good. Furthermore, it is *only* good. He cannot be bent on evil in one area and good in another. A good tree does not bear bad fruit ... a good man out of the good treasure of his heart brings forth good (Luke 6:43-45). Compare Philippians 4:8 where Paul fills out a description of what is good and what should engage the thoughts of the righteous.

It may be, however, that the proverb is speaking of the end, or the outcome, of the desire of the righteous, as it is of the wicked, in which case it is indicating that they will receive good in the end. Either way, it makes little difference, for each will receive according to his manner of life. Those who desire good will certainly be rewarded with good, while those who are wicked, with evil thoughts and intentions, will be rewarded accordingly with wrath from God. As with many of the proverbs, there is both a temporal and an eternal aspect to it. In this life there is often wrath against evildoers, and it is truly what they might expect from their behaviour, irrespective of what they will finally receive in the day of judgement.

The way 'desire' and 'expectation' are compared tells its own story. Righteous people have often been mocked or charged with hypocrisy for doing good only because they hope for 'pie in the sky when they die'. That is not the case. They do good because they delight in doing good, because it gives them pleasure, and not because of what might be in it for them. Of course they are looking forward to glory, but they do not see their works as a means to attaining it! It is true that people will be rewarded *according to* their works (Psalm 62:12; Romans 2:6; Revelation 20:12; 22:12), but it will not be *because of* their works. Their works testify to what they *are*. Works do not earn them any merit, and this is where the charge is demonstrably false.

Ponder how bleak the prospect is for the wicked. No wonder the atheist (who hasn't begun to experience the desire of the righteous) does not want there to be a God! What have the wicked to look forward to? Only what they are for ever trying to escape. What a hope!

[Related proverbs: 10:28; 11:19,27.]

11:24-26. Psalm 112. Giving and withholding. These three proverbs are very specifically about giving and withholding, about generosity and tight-fistedness. Compare Psalm 112:9.

They seem to touch upon a grey area in our responsibilities. When it comes to paying taxes, that is clearly defined by legislation. I do not have to consider how much I will 'give' in such a case. But when it comes to supporting the ministry of my local church, I do have to ask the question of how much I should give because it is not a clearly defined obligation. When it comes to my paid employment, if I am employed to work certain hours then I am obliged to work those hours. However, if I am in a profession, say as a teacher, then I do have to consider how much time I give in the service of those I teach. Likewise, in the church, if I am involved in any service, I need to think about what I give to it of my time and, possibly, my money.

So these proverbs probe into our attitude toward our giving not just of our money or our resources but of *ourselves* in various ways.

11:24,25. The word for scattering is not restricted to selective distribution but is very general, and in this sense it is unlike scattering seed sown for a harvest. In context it could almost be thought of as wanton generosity (though actually it is not that), giving freely for the benefit of others whoever they may be. This operates not just at a financial level. Something much wider is in view here. If you have something to give, then give it. It may be alms, but it may also be time, it may be advice, it may be experience, it may be knowledge, it may be expertise. If you have something of benefit to others, then do not keep it to yourself.

There are all sorts of reasons why people do withhold from others. Verse 24 speaks of a person holding back more than he should. That is, he is holding back on what he should be giving, and the tacit implication is that he is doing it for himself.

In each case the consequences spoken of are contrary to what might be expected. At first sight a generous person by his very generosity would appear to be impoverishing himself, while one who is frugal with his money would appear to be enriching himself. But, says this verse, it is not always like that. Granted that the proverbs view riches and poverty in a far wider sense than monetary or material terms, nevertheless even in this sense there are those who are exceedingly generous and yet grow only richer, while others, frugal though they may be, are seen to decline. Surely we are meant to ask why this should be?

What appears to be a contradiction at the natural level is seen in a very different light at the spiritual level. Behind the principles enunciated in so many of the proverbs is the unseen hand of God. These things happen not because of natural laws, but because of the higher laws which the Lord calls into operation as men honour him with their substance or keep for themselves what he has given to be used for the benefit of others. At the primary level is the matter of honouring God with what he gives us. At the secondary level is that of our blessing others with what he gives us. Haggai 1:2-11, Malachi 3:8-10 and Luke 6:38 are some examples of scriptures addressing these issues.

A church is enriched as all of its members are generous with the gifts God has given them. If God has given you a gift, it is not so that you should say 'Thank you' and use it for your own benefit, but that you should say 'Thank you' and use it as a blessing to others!

Water was a valuable commodity for the Israelites and it wasn't to be wasted. Verse 25 speaks literally of one who waters being himself watered. It is an image of satisfying the most basic needs of another. Just as in time of drought plants need water to survive and flourish, so there are people who know how to bring much-needed refreshment and sustenance to others. They are continually giving out, but they themselves do not 'dry up' because their reserves are being continually replenished from the fountain of the Spirit.

11:26. The principle of generosity is put to the test when circumstances are difficult. This verse appears have in view a situation of famine. Someone is well stocked with grain but for selfish reasons will not sell to those in need; or, the withholding could be seen in terms of keeping it back in order to hike the price, which would be an exploitation of the needy – 'kicking a man when he is down', as we would say.

While it might be considered that a person is entitled to use what he has gained as he wishes, and is not legally entitled either to sell or to sell at a stated price, yet morally he has an obligation toward his neighbour according to the law of God (Leviticus 19:18). From this it can be deduced that he has both a moral and a legal obligation toward his neighbour, and this is an example of how in the eyes of God law and morality are inseparable.

A curse is really an invocation for God to act in the light of evident injustice, but in its most general sense it is an expression of ill will and ill intent toward its object. Blessing is the exact opposite of this. This is seen in the life of Joseph, who sold grain not only to the Egyptians, but to people from other countries who came to him and, as far as can be seen, sold to all at an appropriate price to ensure the grain was not wasted and that life would be preserved. Certainly he was acknowledged as a life-saver (Genesis 47:25).

We too need to be wise with the use of the resources God has given us, displaying a generosity which is not squandering, to ensure as far as we can in responsible stewardship that our giving will be of maximum usefulness or benefit. This proverb does not speak of giving away grain, but of selling it. These proverbs invite us to give careful thought to how we are using the full range of resources God has given us. It could be argued that the provision promised as a result of the giving in Luke 6:38 is intended to be used for further giving, and so for the multiplying of blessing! How different this is from the 'health and wealth' gospel which is so self-orientated!

As an example of generosity in hard times consider the church at Philippi (Philippians 4:10-20 and 2 Corinthians 8:1-5). Philippians 4:19 was no empty sentiment but expressed Paul's confidence in the faithfulness of God to his promises.

[Related proverbs: 13:7; 19:17; 21:26; 22:16; 28:27.]

11:27. Seek, and you shall find. The seeker of good is pictured as being up early in its pursuit (the NIV is weak here). The picture is that of purposefulness, eagerness, determination, diligence. There are people who think it sufficient that they wish ill to no one and do no harm to anyone. That hardly commends them to others and is certainly no commendation before God. The finding of favour here actually intimates a seeking out of favour. The only people who will earn any commendation are those who are always on the lookout for what good they may do, for whom it is a habitual preoccupation. Psalm 34:12-14 presents the same point from a different angle.

By contrast (and note the stinging irony in the statement) those on the lookout for trouble will find it – it will rebound upon them!

This proverb presents an opportunity to check your focus has not drifted. Review what you desire and what you are seeking. What is the orientation of your longings and pursuits?

[Related proverbs: 12:2,14; 14:22.]

11:28-31. Resources sustained or squandered. The righteous flourish (v. 28); the unrighteous fail (v. 29); the righteous are fruitful (v. 30); the righteous are rewarded (v. 31).

11:28. Sustenance. Riches provide neither a satisfactory support nor effective security for life. God pronounces such a person a fool (Luke 12:15-21).

Much is made these days of environmental consciousness and of the importance of renewable and sustainable energy resources, and riches and righteousness could be compared to dead and live resources. Riches are a material resource, righteousness is a spiritual resource. Because man is a spiritual being, it ought to go without saying that to trust in riches to sustain life is fundamentally flawed, and yet this is just what people so often do who think of this life as all there is. Their misplaced trust impoverishes them. The righteous, however, draw upon the infinite resources God provides, and as they trust in him they will always be spiritually healthy and strong. Psalm 1:1-3 uses similar imagery, while Psalm 34:10 expresses the same thought in a different way. This proverb is not talking about what so many understand by life, or by falling or flourishing, but about the real things that 'money can't buy'. This proverb is a warning shot across the bows of those in the boat of materialism; it is a shot in the arm for those swimming against the tide.

11:29. Squanderlust. The comparison here is at first sight somewhat obscure. What is meant by one troubling his own house and in what ways might this happen? What is meant by inheriting the wind?

The two clauses of the proverb are parallels rather than contrasts. So he who troubles his own house is likened to a fool, while inheriting the wind is compared to servitude. The wise, literally the wise of heart, stands in opposition to the other two mentioned.

The one who troubles his own house is one who does so by foolish, or headstrong, or selfish unilateral action. He is often the one who says, 'I want...' at the expense of others or their sound advice. He is like the prodigal son of the parable Jesus told (Luke 15:11-14). This kind of thing is far from uncommon in families, and its consequences are usually such that 'inheriting the wind' is an apt description of them. What did they gain by it? What happened to their great ambitions? What success story did they bring home by way of compensation for those over whom they rode roughshod? It is only if and when, like the prodigal of the parable, they come to recognise what fools they have been, that there is any hope for them. Otherwise, they end up, literally, as bondservants. Just as wind cannot be grasped but passes through the fingers, so all that they hoped for through their misplaced ambition eludes them, and their hoped-for success ends in abject servitude – and notice to whom.

[Related proverbs: 11:17b; 14:19; 15:27; 17:2.]

11:30. Lasting fruitfulness. Outside the book of Proverbs, the tree of life is mentioned only in Genesis (2:9; 3:22,24) and in the book of Revelation (2:7; 22:2,14), where, using the imagery of one specific tree, it is symbolic of the provision of the full and continuing satisfaction of everlasting life and bliss in the presence of God. In Proverbs it is mentioned four times (here, and 3:18; 13:12; 15:4), where it is more a figurative expression, conveying the ideas of ongoing nourishment, provision, satisfaction, not so much in a material sense as in a fuller, spiritual sense.

So here in this verse the righteous are seen not as the forbidding and barren possessors of austere, cold and formal qualities – imagery which is so often portrayed by those who little understand what true righteousness is – but rather as possessing and imparting beneficial, life-giving qualities. Righteousness is often seen in the world as a curb to people's freedom, as having a stifling, killjoy influence, as taking the fun out of life, and so righteous people are often despised and excluded or even hated. However, when serious, impartial and unprejudiced consideration is given to the contribution made to life by the righteous it has to be said that it is all those good and lasting qualities which will only enhance life and will stand the test of time. A tree of life is a living, growing, flourishing thing. Such is the fruit, or influence, of the righteous.

The two clauses of this proverb, like the last, are in parallel. 'He who wins souls' is compared with 'The fruit of the righteous', and wisdom is compared with a tree of life. In 3:18 wisdom is stated to be a tree of life to those who possess her. To 'win' souls can be thought of as taking, or receiving, souls. As in taking a wife, or taking (capturing) a city, or receiving a bribe, there is the aspect of possession or even assimilation. The seductress is one who would 'take' or 'captivate' the unwary with her fluttering eyelids (6:25). Absalom deceitfully 'took' or captured the hearts of the people away from David (2 Samuel 15:6). Here the fruit of the righteous is seen in winning souls to righteousness, in capturing them, as it were, to a new cause and for a new purpose. It is literally a matter of turning people from death to life. Compare James 5:19-20.

In 8:10 the injunction is to take hold of the instruction of wisdom with a possessive tenacity, while in 10:8 the commands of God are received, taken on board, accepted, possessed, assimilated. Just as it is folly to lead souls into sin, so it is wisdom to win souls for righteousness. This proverb is indicating the righteous will be fruitful in the best sense of the word. Until the day of Christ let us pray with the apostle that we may be filled with the fruits of righteousness which are by Christ Jesus, to the glory and praise of God (Philippians 1:11).

11:31. Recompense ... when? This proverb is cast in the conditional form of 'If...then', inviting us to consider the case. It is about 'recompense', about receiving one's due, and in this case it is the recompense appropriate to the righteous or to the wicked. Thus in one case it could be considered reward, while in the other case it would be punishment.

What may at first sight seem unusual about this proverb is the reference to 'on the earth'. Do the righteous receive their due on earth? Are we not taught to understand that it is often not so and we are to wait for the day of judgement for the righteous to be recompensed? Is it not that which is intimated in Revelation 6:10, which also indicates that the righteous often do not receive their due on earth? Does not 2 Peter 3:7 say that the ungodly will be judged on that day and not before? As we consider the case, we might therefore run into a very real difficulty.

Very often in Proverbs we find broad principles expressed which operate even within a fallen world. We have seen this several times already. Thus, for example, in 10:27 the days of those who fear the Lord do not always appear to be prolonged, nor are the years of the wicked always shortened. Sometimes the wicked prosper and the righteous suffer. However, as a general principle, leaving aside those situations in which the Lord, according to his sovereign purposes, permits his people to suffer deprivation, the righteous do receive their due on earth. Righteousness brings its own reward with it. Righteousness leads to prosperity in every sense of the word, because it pleases God and because it is conduct in harmony with how God intended the world to operate. On the other hand, those who are ungodly, that is, morally corrupt, and those who do wrong, will suffer the consequences of living in the world in a fashion contrary to how God intended. According to natural laws they will suffer. When we further take into account the fact that even in this life God watches over the righteous and restrains or punishes the wicked (consider, for example, Psalm 34:15-17 and 1 Peter 3:10-13), we can see that this proverb is true.

However, there is another aspect to this proverb, because in 1 Peter 4:18 Peter quotes the Septuagint version of it. The context of Peter's argument is that of suffering, and he speaks of judgement, not only of the wicked, but of the righteous as well. It is difficult to find a suitable illustration to make the point, but one could think of a group of people in a vast open field with a great storm brewing. Some, fearing the worst, run for shelter and only just make it before the storm breaks, while others, who did not treat it seriously, find themselves stranded in the deluge. The righteous have fled to Christ for refuge (compare Hebrews 6:18) and are aware how narrowly they have missed the dreadful judgement. The ungodly, heedless of the danger, find themselves totally and hopelessly exposed. Peter's argument is to encourage Christians to commit themselves to God and to continue in doing good (1 Peter 4:19), fully assured not only that their persecutors will most certainly receive their due but also that they themselves have been spared only by the grace of God.

When we understand what we have received by grace in comparison with what we deserved by law, we will acknowledge we have received on earth nothing but good at the hand of our inscrutably wise and loving God.

12:1. Love it or hate it. Many of the proverbs link ideas which we would not normally put together, and so it is here. How do we take it when we are reproved, or corrected, or disciplined, or chastened? For that is the 'instruction' in the first clause and it carries with it discomforting aspects. Do we welcome it, or do we react against it? Do we take it well, or do we take it badly? Or does it depend on who it comes from?

Even a musical virtuoso will give careful attention to the advice of his or her mentor – who may not be able to play nearly so well – over small details in order to improve the quality of what is played in performance to please the audience. How much more should we be prepared to give attention to the details of correction we receive, from whomsoever given, in order to perform acceptably and with excellence for the Master whom we serve? Whether we love it or hate it reflects upon our pride, upon whether we are truly humble or conceited. Moses, who was the most humble man on the face of the earth, accepted corrective advice from Jethro (Numbers 12:3; Exodus 18:17). It would be foolish to fail to recognise and consequently reject a gift of value just because we don't like the hand which proffers it. But that is what so often happens!

The knowledge in the first clause includes understanding, that is, it is practical and not just theoretical knowledge; it is a thinking knowledge. By comparison the stupidity of the second clause is a brutish quality in which the mind is closed to, or unreceptive of, sound advice. It is as the psalmist confessed in Psalm 73:22, when he had lost his focus and taken offence at the prosperity of the wicked, especially as he himself was suffering chastening day by day (v. 14). Sometimes the discipline of the Christian life gets us down, but that is very often when our attention is shifted from the Lord and what he is intending to accomplish in us, to what is going on around us which has a more comfortable appeal. One of the principal characteristics of a hedonistic society is an unwillingness or inability really to think. Brainwashed by the attractions of this world, men and women act as brute beasts. They might well react against the charge of stupidity, but that is what it is.

King Asa acted out of character when corrected by the prophet Hanani (2 Chronicles 16:7-10). King Ahab acted in character when corrected by Naboth (1 Kings 21:3-4). How did their failure to receive correction affect (a) themselves, and (b) others? Give some thought to the same two questions in connection with correction you have either received or rejected.

[Related proverbs: 3:11; 5:12-13; 10:17; 13:18; 15:10,31,32.]

12:2. Goodness and favour. This comes as an encouragement after the uncomfortable realities exposed in the previous proverb. Note that the Lord sees the heart. It is the man of wicked *intentions* who will be condemned, the man who plans and intends to carry out things which are contrary to the law of God, irrespective of whether they come to fruition. We can be thankful that very often the plans of the wicked come to nothing, thwarted by God before they have a chance to do their damage. On the other hand, opportunities for good men and women for doing good are unbounded, and the knowledge that the Lord approves should be a wonderful encouragement and stimulus to get on with it.

What is a good man? When my parents admonished me as a small boy, 'Now be good while we are away,' what they really intended was that I should keep out of trouble and mischief. They equated being good with not doing bad things – hardly a rounded view of goodness! Maybe that was the very reason why I found it so difficult to comply! What is more demanding on a small boy than to have to keep his nose clean?

What makes a good man is not that he does nothing bad. That makes an insipid man. A good man is recognised by what he does, by his good deeds. Even then, we must not think it is they which make him good, or they which gain him favour from the Lord. Look at Barnabas when he visited Antioch and how he responded to what he saw (Acts 11:24). He wasn't good because of the way he responded. Rather, he responded as he did because he was good.

A good man is one who is good at heart, and Barnabas, we are told, was full of the Holy Spirit and of faith. 'Barnabas' wasn't the name he had been given at birth; it was bestowed upon him by others because he was a good man and because of the way his goodness manifested itself (Acts 4:36). Goodness is the fruit of the Spirit (Galatians 5:22; Ephesians 5:9).

We can obtain favour from the Lord only by what we are, not by what we do. His favour means acceptance – not grudging or partial or restricted, but glad and full and free. By nature we are bad, and only God is good (Mark 10:18). Therefore true goodness is God-given. This being the case, a good man has already wonderfully obtained favour from the Lord! However, the proverb is really speaking of ongoing favour. Christians will often testify to God's favour toward them as they see their needs being met, or their service for him prospering, attributing it not to their goodness before him, but to his goodness toward them.

But there is another side to this where God's favour, though real, is not so readily recognised. For example, Job was clearly a good man (Job 1:1-5,8; 2:3), yet throughout his suffering God's favour toward him seemed singularly lacking. In Psalm 73:13-14 Asaph, with more than a hint of inward rebelliousness, said in effect, 'What's the point in all the hardship involved in trying to live a godly life?' He was certainly not aware of obtaining any favour from the Lord toward him at that point.

Yet God was shielding Job in the furnace of affliction, and Asaph, when he took his problem to God and got his thinking straightened out, saw his own circumstances very differently (Psalm 73:23-26) and recognised the Lord's favour toward him and also the condemnation of the wicked. The Lord's favour is more than sufficient compensation for all the scorn of men against the godly. In neither case had the Lord's favour wavered for a moment. The Lord's favour provides a mighty incentive to persevere in doing good. See Romans 2:7, Galatians 6:9, 2 Thessalonians 3:13, all of which acknowledge that perseverance is not easy. Here, then, is a truth to rejoice in, a promise to lay hold of.

[Related proverbs: 8:35; 15:3.]

12:3. Foundations. We often hear of people wanting to establish themselves in life. What do they mean by that? They are usually thinking in terms of security, success, comfort, the ability to do the things they want to do, and so on. In the cut and thrust of life it does not do to have too many scruples. Get in there and go for it, and don't ask too many questions! What if making progress involves treading on some toes on the way? That's the way it is in life.

Is it? To leave God out as we seek to establish ourselves in life is actually morally wrong, for we are commanded to acknowledge him in all our ways (3:6). To use another word, it is wicked. This is not an 'over-the-top' way of putting it, it is plain and accurate, and, to follow on from the previous verse, it is under God's condemnation.

Over the years there have been many high profile cases of the rich and powerful being publicly disgraced because of 'irregularities' in their conduct. In many instances they had been the envy of others, strong and prosperous, with everything going for them. But underneath, where it mattered, were hidden corruption and decay, and in due course the cracks appeared in their lives and what they had built for themselves, and then things dramatically fell apart for them. They had got to where they were by 'bending the rules', or by 'exploiting the system', or by 'sharp practice', or by some other means, any of which the Lord bluntly describes as wickedness. Yet for each on whom disaster falls, there are many others seemed to continue through life unscathed.

Asaph in Psalm 73 recognised the truth expressed here, and it is a reassurance to God-fearing people that these things are true. In vv. 3-12 of the psalm his view of the ungodly was that they were secure and immovable, even right to the end of their lives, whereas later he saw that the very opposite was true (vv. 18-19). It was he himself who was absolutely secure with God (vv. 23-24). He had been looking at what they had built for themselves and for a while been alarmingly impressed. He had been intimidated by their scorn of his own scruples. When we look at others who seem to be well established in life, what do we see? Are we dazzled by things which are ultimately of no value? Do we allow these things to make us feel small, or even failures? Should we not rather *expect* them to mock and dismiss the eternal perspective of the Word of God? There is only one way to be established, and that is to build upon the right foundation.

All the way through the book of Proverbs we are encouraged not to look at life through the distorted lenses of the world's thinking, but to see things as the Lord himself does. As in the story Jesus told about the two houses (Matthew 7:24-27) it is the unseen part which is the most important.

Whether or not a plant can be uprooted depends both on its root system and upon the soil in which it is found. The righteous are grounded in the Word of God who himself does not change, nor does he change his mind. God's Word does not move, and if you are rooted there you cannot be moved. The deeper you are rooted in the Word of God, the more secure you will find yourself to be. Hebrews 6:13-20 uses a different metaphor to express the same security a believer has. As an extension of the idea, a root bears a shoot which produces fruit. Those who are the planting of the Lord will flourish to his glory (Isaiah 60:21; 61:3).

In Colossians 2:7 Paul writes of being rooted, built up and established, and it is all in Christ. In 1 Corinthians 15:58 he writes of being unmovable, and it is based on the glorious hope of the resurrection. We are secure in God, nowhere else. How slow at times we can be really to grasp this!

[Related proverbs: 10:25,30; 12:7,12; 14:11; 24:16.]

12:4. A woman's touch. On a number of occasions a wife is the subject of a proverb, before the eulogy of the virtuous wife of 31:10-31. See 14:1; 18:22; 19:13,14; 21:9,19; 25:24; 27:15.

However, it could be argued that it is not the wife, but the husband who is really the subject of this proverb. We can look at men in general and how they function in society and how they are regarded and give little thought to the extent of the influence, if they are married, of their wives. But, without apportioning blame, in how many public scandals involving men is there not a woman in the frame?

The adjective describing this wife is not easy to translate. (It occurs again at 31:10.) It embraces such qualities as resourcefulness, potential and strength of character. The same word is used of Ruth (Ruth 3:11) whose character shines out in the book bearing her name. Boaz may have been a wealthy and influential man and well respected in the community, but what she brought to him after their marriage is aptly described by this proverb. It is a remarkable description of the contribution a woman of substance can make to the marriage relationship and the functioning of the family in society. It echoes the role God gave to woman as described in Genesis 2:18-24, as a helper to complement him in the widest sense of the word.

A man with a good and virtuous and noble wife can lift up his head, in stark contrast to the bowing of the head by a man whose wife disgraces him. Notice that in each case it is not what the man does which elicits these responses, but the conduct of his wife. She may be the weaker vessel (1 Peter 3:7), but she has enormous potential for good or ill in the relationship.

It is worth noticing that her character and conduct reflect upon him, not the other way round. She has power to elevate him, she has power to disgrace him; or, to use the ideas here, to crown him or insidiously to decay him. She can enable him to lift up his head with dignity, or she can cause him to hang his head in shame. A man's performance in the world, as well as the world's perception of him, is influenced more than is generally recognised by the kind of wife he has.

A husband who properly cares for and values his wife will encourage rather than stifle those qualities in her which will enable her to bring strength and vitality to the relationship and so to his functioning in the public domain.

Embedded in this simple proverb are wonderful encouragements, incentives and advice for both husbands and wives for the fulfilling of their God-given potential.

[Related proverbs: 14:1; 18:22; 19:14; 31:10,30.]

12:5-7. The righteous and the wicked – three stark contrasts.

Verses 5 and 6 are chiastic in structure:

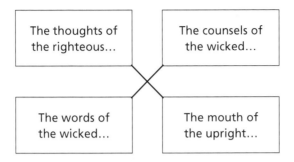

12:5. Consistency and inconsistency. There is some subtlety even in the most straightforward of proverbs. As the heart thinks, so the mouth speaks. Out of the heart come... (Matthew 12:34-35; 15:19). The reason for the thoughts, or plans (that is, what goes on in the mind with regard to intentions and relationships, etc.) of the righteous being right or just (that is, in a judicial sense), is that there is true righteousness in the heart, which can come about only through the operation of the Holy Spirit. This highlights the predicament of the wicked (that is, those who lack this moral, godly influence), because the way they steer their lives and those of others, whatever the appearance may be, is motivated by unsound principles and will lead to a bad end. Their heart is not right with God, their thoughts are not right with God, and so their counsel is not right with God.

Thoughts, or plans, invariably find expression in words and in action. For the righteous there is a consistency, a harmony, between the two. By contrast, the counsels of the wicked are *deceitful* because there is a fundamental inconsistency between their outward persona and their inward cravings. Many a Christian, looking back, can see the deceitfulness of the heart exposed in the uncomfortable conflict between action and thought.

12:6. Intention and outcome. 'Lying in wait for blood' is certainly a strong expression, and yet when we consider it we ought to be alarmed by its implications. The first person to do this was Cain, who said to his brother Abel, 'Let us go out into the field' (Genesis 4:8). Under the guise of these innocent-sounding words he brought his brother's blood to the ground. Likewise the words of the respected religious leaders in Jesus' time were aimed to bring him down, and they ended up literally crying for his blood. These were ostensibly righteous people, or at least they liked to think they were. But they killed the holy and just One. They wished him dead, and they accomplished their wishes.

For whose blood do the wicked lie in wait by their words – often unspoken words? Basically, for the blood of any who dare to cross them. The expressions of the hatred that is in the world today exemplify this proverb.

But now for the second clause. The speech of the upright may be referring to what they say when falsely accused or slandered. If anything is likely to deliver them in such circumstances it is a plain, gracious, wise, declaration of the truth. However, the import of the proverb may be more general than this, that their *habitual* speech is such that when it comes to a time of crisis it stands them in good stead against the evil intentions of evil people. When the officers were sent to lay hands on Jesus (John 7:32) they returned empty-handed saying, 'No man ever spoke like this man!' (46). Such were the grace and power of his words that they were completely disarmed. Is your mouth likely to deliver you in time of crisis?

[Related proverbs: 1:11; 14:3.]

12:7. Psalm 37. Collapse and continuance. This, taken with the previous verse, echoes what is stated in 1:18 as far as the wicked are concerned. They may be after the blood of others, literally or metaphorically, but the result is their own downfall. The evil they intend toward others rebounds upon themselves. The house of the righteous standing firm reminds one of the famous parable of the two houses (Matthew 7:24-27). The house of the righteous does not just stand, but it stands in the face of the fury of the wind and waves of the opposition of wicked people. Why so? Although we are not told here, we know from other scriptures that it is because God watches over the righteous for good but thwarts the intentions of the wicked (Psalm 1:6; 33:10,18).

[Related proverbs: 10:25,30; 11:21,27; 14:11; 21:12; 24:3.]

12:8. What we are and what we portray. Whether we like it or not, other people make their assessment of us, even as we do of them, and, generally speaking, we are known for what we are rather than what we would like to think we are!

Wisdom (the word here meaning understanding and good sense) is being contrasted with a twisted mind, and so one is straightforward where the other is devious. There are many men and women whom one would not describe as being particularly learned, yet who receive the approbation of others on account of their godly good sense and open conduct. This is real commendation as opposed to the shallow praise given to others on account of status, wealth or fame.

Perversity of heart may be hidden for a while but when it is exposed it will not be treated sympathetically. There is little which earns more contempt from others than those who try to make themselves out to be something better than they really are.

[Related proverb: 13:15.]

12:9. Things are not always what they seem. This links in with the previous proverb. Consider for a moment two people. One is very much working class in attitude and manner and is taken for granted – even thought little of; the other could be described as refined and upper class and is taken notice of. In our estimation we might suppose the latter to have all the advantages. There always has been, and still is, a tendency to regard people according to their status in society. There are those that people look up to, and those they look down upon. This proverb illustrates the vacuity of seeking to impress others or of craving to be thought well of. The one who is little thought of has a secure job, a stable marriage, a healthy bank balance, a contented lifestyle. The other, for all his 'airs and graces', is up to his eyeballs in debt, has no security, is on the run from his creditors and lives in uncomfortable uncertainty from day to day as to what might happen to him. Which really is the better off?

So this proverb really exposes the folly of the superficial attitudes so many people display. There are many ways in which people who want to be thought well of by others seek to achieve that goal, whereas only one thing really matters, which is our standing in the eyes of God who sees through all the posturing. The apostle Paul had some ironically revealing comments to make in this respect to the church at Corinth (2 Corinthians 6:4-10).

[Related proverb: 13:7.]

12:10. A caring disposition.
The man's animal was not a pet! It was a means of providing his livelihood – for example an ox for ploughing, or cows or sheep or goats for meat and milk – and stood in the same category as might our car or our work tools stand today as necessary for our business. It could be argued that he treated them well because his livelihood depended upon it. That may be true, but what is being said here is more than that. He cared for his animal beyond simply its usefulness to him. His treatment of his animal was not because he cared for himself but because he cared for it.

It is generally true that those who care for their own possessions will take equal care over the possessions of others. There are certain people to whom I would happily lend my car; there are others I would be most reluctant to allow to drive it!

This proverb, then, is not essentially about animal rights or animal welfare but goes far deeper than that and is really about intelligent sensitivity to the needs of others, whether man or beast. However, while on the matter of animals, there are a few scriptures which explicitly refer to giving due regard to their needs – for example Exodus 23:11-12 and Deuteronomy 25:4 (quoted twice in the New Testament, in 1 Corinthians 9:9 and 1 Timothy 5:18). See, too, Matthew 12:11 and Luke 14:5. Also expressed is God's care even for the birds of the air (Matthew 6:26). We should certainly have a responsible attitude toward our environment, for God commanded man in this respect from the beginning (Genesis 1:26-30).

The point about true righteousness is that it is not compartmentalised to certain parts of life. What a righteous man is to his wife and his children, he is also to his neighbours, to his animals, to his environment. He has a sensitivity toward what God has created because he is sensitive toward the God who has created it. This sensitivity expresses itself in taking time to know and understand the needs and requirements of others.

There is an oxymoron in the second clause. A wicked person, lacking this acknowledgement of God and his rights over him, also lacks this sensitivity, possessing something of a destructive streak. Self-orientated thinking will result in self-orientated behaviour. Perhaps the ultimate cruelty in the kindest acts of the wicked is the failure to give credit to the God whose kindness and tender mercies extend over all (Psalm 145:9; Luke 6:34).

12:11-12. Value added.

12:11. The 'something for nothing' mentality is very much all around us. There are people who seem to imagine that others owe them a living. There are those who dream of vast winnings on the lottery. Others, judging from the way they conduct themselves in their places of employment, seem to expect to be paid irrespective of how little work they really do. Paul had to rebuke some of the Christians at Thessalonica who, under a pretext of spirituality, were actually living in idleness (2 Thessalonians 3:6-13). It is a matter of simple common sense that there will be no harvest without labour and it is the height of folly to think otherwise. It is, as this proverb indicates, and as the NIV nicely translates, 'chasing fantasies'. There is irony in the text that such people are in hot pursuit of what isn't really there! No wonder it says they lack understanding!

The proverb speaks of the rewards of work. Generally speaking, those who work hard will be rewarded for their efforts, for the land is well able to support those who work it. Yet the work required is often painstaking. There may be times when the labourer grows weary and becomes discouraged and needs motivation to 'get on with it'. As with so many of the proverbs, this one points ahead to the consequences of a course of action. More than a mere observation of fact, it provides an incentive to keep going.

There are spiritual lessons in this, and Christians are reminded of both the dignity and fruitfulness of work. From the parable of the talents (Matthew 25:14-30) preachers often focus upon the reward and penalty. However, before ever the rewards were given observe the evident satisfaction of those who worked productively with what they had been given.

Psalm 126:5-6 and Galatians 6:7-10 draw from the natural sphere of sowing and reaping to illustrate the pains of spiritual labour and the promise of fruitfulness. [Related proverbs: 20:13; 28:19.]

12:12. This is another angle on productiveness. In the first clause two problems are highlighted. The first is that of gain by deceit. It refers to 'the catch of evil men', or, 'the spoil of evildoers'. Literally, it is the 'net' of evil men and the image is of what they have 'caught'. Such people by spreading a net for the unwary have made gain by deceit. They haven't earned it, but they have exploited others and enriched themselves at the expense of others.

There are many ways in which this happens, by 'borrowing' without returning, by petty theft and pilfering, by preying upon the goodwill of others, by dishonest trading, and so on, quite apart from the more extreme and overtly lawless cases such as robbery with violence. It is quite common for such people to boast of what they have acquired by underhand means.

When viewed objectively, however, there has been an overall loss. No one has really gained. Men and women who conduct themselves in this way for their own gain are only impoverishing society, taking out and taking out, but not putting in. Furthermore, they are a burden on society because they undermine what others are seeking to achieve by hard work.

The second problem is that of covetousness – 'The wicked covet….' This is not about their coveting what good men have earned but coveting what evil men have plundered. They want the same, and they envy those who by unscrupulous methods have acquired it. Their focus therefore is on evil and by their covetousness are bent on following the practices of evil people. Their attitude merely compounds the problem. Their covetousness doesn't even incline them to think about emulating the righteous, for they are looking in a different direction altogether. These people essentially are parasites, sucking the life-blood from their society, at the same time infecting it with the poison of their attitude. They may become materially prosperous, but they are morally and spiritually bankrupt.

By contrast, we are told very simply that the root of the righteous *yields*. The righteous are rooted and grounded in God and in God's Word. They draw upon his free provision and convert it into something from which they and others can benefit. There is an overall profit, through which not only they, but others have gained. They therefore enrich society, not just materially, but morally and spiritually. Christians are to be fruitful in every good work (Colossians 1:10) and are to produce the fruit of the Spirit (Galatians 5:22-23). This covers every aspect of their lives.

12:13. Giving testimony. This proverb and the next highlight the principle that people's words and actions tend to rebound upon them. Mordecai and Haman from the book of Esther are biblical examples.

The scenario before us here seems to be a situation of potential or real trouble, a time of reckoning or accounting, a time of judgement; maybe an occasion when accusations are made and people find themselves subject to scrutiny. Our words leave an imprint on others, and they are recorded in other people's memories so that they can be recalled by them. The speech of wicked men – deceit, lies, slander, flattery, or whatever it may be – returns upon them, so that the evil they have done by their words results in trouble for themselves. It is as if they have condemned themselves out of their own mouths. Jesus observed, 'Out of the abundance of the heart the mouth speaks' (Matthew 12:34). He reminded his hearers that a day of judgement is coming on which men will have to give an account for every idle word (v. 36), and when he goes on to say, 'For by your words you will be justified, and by your words you will be condemned' (v. 37) he is making clear that words will provide evidence enough one way or the other, quite apart from deeds.

The imagery is powerful and apposite. The more an animal struggles to break loose from its snare, the more harm it does to itself and the more painfully obvious it is that it is helplessly trapped. So the more the wicked say when called to account for things they have already said, the worse it will be for them. Their own words have entrapped them and there is no escape. That is exactly what happened to the wicked servant in the parable Jesus told (Luke 19:20-23). Our words unerringly reveal our hearts, however careful we may be to conceal the fact.

The reason the righteous come through trouble, or escape it, is that their words actually testify *for* them. That they have not sought trouble for others nor spoken to harm others nor boasted to elevate themselves, but rather the opposite, speaks for them.

[Related proverb: 5:22; 18:7; 21:6; 21:23.]

12:14. Rebound. This is the positive side of the previous proverb. It is a little difficult to translate, but it seems to be referring to a good man, and the idea seems to be that his good speech is rewarded with good, just as much as his hard work is rewarded with good. If bad speech rebounds in evil upon the one responsible for it, so good speech is rewarded with good upon the one in whom it is found.

Words are very powerful in their influence upon others, for good or for ill. Those accustomed to honest speech and who use their words for the benefit of others usually find that they themselves are also beneficiaries from others. It is as true of speech as it is of deeds. Words build relationships; words can have a powerful psychological influence; words can profoundly affect others and have long-term consequences. They will often be remembered after deeds are long forgotten.

[Related proverbs: 10:4; 11:27; 13:2; 14:14; 18:20.]

12:15. Folly goes public. 'When I want your advice I'll ask for it!' 'I can manage quite well enough without your help!' 'I don't need you or anyone else telling me what to do! I'll do it my way.'

There are people for whom it is an insult to their intelligence to suggest they are not self-sufficient or could benefit from the counsel or experience of others. They are so sure of themselves that it seems they are the only ones who do not recognise that they are fools. Then there are those who appear to listen to advice but who still, every time, appear to totally disregard it and simply go their own way. This proverb is about listening and pondering. 'There may be something in what you say' is carefully followed up and acted upon.

This proverb is not about always *following* the counsel of others, but about *heeding* it. There are an amazing number of situations in life in which we need to know what to do, the outcome of which is of importance. Some are big, such as taking a job, or getting married; some are small, such as when you might phone someone to discuss a matter. The fool acts with total disregard for others – either to listen to them or to be conscious of the effect his actions may have upon them. It is wise to be aware that the way we conduct our lives affects others as well as ourselves, and, that being the case, that we are answerable to others as well as to ourselves. It is part of considerateness toward others that we hear what they have to say.

Sometimes people are so sure they are right in their ideas or what they are doing that they immediately dismiss out of hand any suggestions others might make. Even if they are right, this kind of rebuttal can be insensitive and hurtful as well as giving a bad impression. And that is *not* wise.

[Related proverbs: 15:22; 19:20; 26:12.]

12:16. A knee-jerk reaction. Some people excuse themselves by saying they have 'a short fuse'. The second clause of the proverb is probably best understood as in the NIV: 'But a prudent man overlooks an insult.' The word translated 'shame' in the NKJV is the same word as in 9:7a and is perhaps not quite as we would generally understand it. It really indicates the intended effect of disgrace from a vituperative tongue – a belly-full of insult! Then the word 'covers' is used in a wide variety of senses, but its use here is certainly in line with 'overlooking'.

The scenario, then, is that of some kind of offence being given – whether intentionally or not, or whether justly or not, is immaterial – and the way one reacts to it. It is very common for people who have a strong sense of having been wronged to be always speaking about it, thereby drawing others into their grievances. This is foolish. Firstly, it does not help settle the grievance, and secondly it only promotes ill will. In this sense, 'cover' is better than 'overlook'. The person of sense and wisdom realises that no good is done by harping on about such things, and the sooner the matter is put out of the way – covered – the better. It often comes back to repaying evil with good, as Jesus commanded (Matthew 5:44-45).

This is very practical. Do you have a grievance over something someone has said to you? How have you reacted? How have you handled it? Have you taken it to the Lord to seek to cover the problem rather than to other people to seek to propagate it? Furthermore, how is it affecting your relationship with the person from whom you have received this abuse? Are you willing to see the sense in putting it behind you, not allowing a bitter or vengeful spirit to destroy the relationship on account of an isolated incident?

[Related proverbs: 20:3; 29:11.]

12:17. Truth and truth. This proverb of direct contrast may seem to be self-evident. But, as usual, there is more to this than meets the eye. When we speak, we are communicating with others. Thus every word we utter affects in some way those who hear us.

Taking the second clause first, when we speak what is not the truth, what we are saying is aimed to deceive others, because, for whatever reason, we are wanting them to believe something which is not true. If and when we are found out it immediately undermines their confidence in our words and damages our credibility. It destroys trust. For a person to say they meant well does nothing to alleviate the problem, and next time they won't be believed. False witness is nothing but damaging.

Consider what is involved in speaking truth. There is no incompatibility between truth telling and what is right. No conflict or tension are involved.

Truth and righteousness are partners. The argument which begins, 'I can't tell him the truth because...' is a false argument. But speaking truth involves more than the words used. There are different ways of speaking truth, and the word used here probably conveys more than the bald verbal declaration of truth to include the manner of its presentation. If truth is presented ungraciously, it only half fulfils what is expressed in this proverb. That is because, as has just been observed, speaking is communicating with others, and the manner of communication, as well as its matter, is important. What declares righteousness is this full-orbed truth which respects those to whom it is delivered.

It should be immediately obvious that one who speaks truth must be one who *habitually* speaks truth, and speaks it well. Otherwise there would be no declaration of righteousness, for it wouldn't be known when truth was being told and when it was not. Incidentally, the same argument applies to the Scriptures. Some people maintain that the Scriptures *contain* the truth, but are not completely true. If that were the case, to the extent they were not true, they would therefore be deceiving, and if they were deceiving in part, who would be able to trust the whole? Or if they were deceiving in part, who would know what parts were true and what were not? The Bible speaks true, both by its content and also by the manner of its presentation, and declares righteousness, and all who are concerned for righteousness testify to its truth.

The challenge for us is therefore twofold: firstly that we are consistently truthful in what we say, and secondly that we are truthful in how we say it.

[Related proverbs: 6:19; 12:17; 14:5.]

12:18-20. Words and words. These verses really enlarge upon v. 17.

12:18. How said. This proverb is concerned with the manner rather than the matter of what is being said. A different word is used here from v. 17 concerning speech. It denotes rash or angry outbursts, words which the speaker wants to 'get off his chest' for his own relief and are not intended for the benefit of the listener. Words thus spoken do no good whatever. They inflict pain and cause injury to the soul every bit as much as a sword thrust traumatises the body. By contrast, those who are wise will use their words not like swords but like balm. It is important not just *what* you say but *how* you say it. If you are going to use your tongue well you will be motivated by a concern to benefit your hearer.

[Related proverbs: 15:2; 16:24; 19:9; 25:18; 30:14.]

12:19. What said. This time a different word is used from v. 17 concerning truth. It is perhaps more objective, concerning the matter more than the manner. There could not be a greater difference between 'for ever' and 'for a moment'. On this scale of things we measure the difference between being truthful and lying. If we look back into history and consider on what our society (or any society) has been built, truth in all its manifestations is important. What is false is discredited and is useless. But this proverb is not concerned with truth and falsehood in a clinical sense, but rather with those who exhibit these characteristics, for it speaks of truthful *lips*, and a lying *tongue*. It is not just truth which will endure for ever, but truthful lips which shall be established for ever. With our New Testament understanding, we recognise that 'for ever' carries over beyond time and into eternity, whereas 'for a moment' indicates a time of limited duration, and however long it may be in this world's estimation, it is 'but for a moment' on the eternal timescale.

[Related proverb: 12:22.]

12:20. Why said. An interesting and perhaps unexpected comparison is here between deceit in the heart and joy. Devising evil is compared with counselling, or promoting, peace. There is a subtlety in the comparison in that the devising involves secrecy or concealment, keeping something in, whereas the promoting of peace is open and overt.

Give a little thought to what is involved in plotting evil of some kind, and in every case it involves secrecy and its outworking involves deception, for otherwise it cannot succeed. Then there is always the danger of being exposed with its attendant consequences. So devisers of evil generate anxiety within themselves and trouble for others.

All this is contrasted with those whose words (open) counsel peace, which embraces the well-being of others. The words are an expression of intent, and what has been going on under the surface is every bit as active as in the case of those who are planning evil. But there is nothing underhand about it, nothing sinister. The benefit to those following this course is joy: joy in the devising of it, joy in the execution of it, joy in the sharing of the benefit it brings to others. The happiest people are those who are always seeking to be instruments of blessing to others. The most miserable are those who seek their own benefits at the expense of others. When deceit is in the heart it is hidden and destructive; when joy is in the heart it bursts forth and energises.

[Related proverbs: 14:22; 24:2; 26:24.]

12:21. Psalm 91. Needed reassurances. In this topsy-turvy world the validity of this proverb might be questioned. Didn't great trouble overtake Job? Don't the wicked so often 'get away with murder', while the righteous seem to suffer at their hand? Is it not a theme running through history that the righteous suffer persecution from the wicked? Didn't Jesus himself say to his followers: 'In the world you will have tribulation' (John 16:33)? Then is this proverb offering false hope?

It would be foolish for anyone to expect exemption from trouble in this world. The proverb can hardly be suggesting such a thing. Who is the 'you' of Psalm 91:10 and what are the circumstances which make the statement there applicable? Do they apply to you?

Ultimately there will be a day of reckoning and deliverance for the righteous and condemnation for the wicked. Nevertheless, this proverb has validity in the shorter term, too, and may be considered as an incentive for the righteous.

Peter says: 'Who is he who will harm you if you become followers of what is good?' (1 Peter 3:13). Righteousness itself will never brings harmful consequences, but only good ones, upon those who live righteously. Peter is not saying that no harm will ever befall such people, for he continues: 'But even if you should suffer for righteousness' sake, you are blessed.' So trouble and suffering are not incompatible with blessing, and this is the testimony of countless believers who have suffered persecution. David could declare, 'Though I walk through the valley of the shadow of death, I will fear no evil; for you are with me; your rod and your staff, they comfort me' (Psalm 23:4). The valley of the shadow of death is a place of deep trouble. Yet this most dismal of places is viewed in context when God is present and providing comfort. How did Jesus finish the statement just quoted above about tribulation? 'But be of good cheer, I have overcome the world.' If he is with us, and he has overcome the world, then what harm can really befall us?

Righteous living promotes only good; evil living promotes only evil. The wicked can have no possible reason that they should not be filled with evil. Their way of life does them no real good, but only evil, short term or long. If the righteous suffer, it is not because of their righteousness, but because of the evil which is opposed to it. If the wicked suffer, it is because they are reaping the rewards of their own wickedness. They get what they deserve as it rebounds upon them. It does them no good. For the righteous, they know that nothing but good can come of their way of life, even if they find they have to suffer for it. Their very suffering indicates they are having some positive influence on the evil in the world. Therefore they have every incentive to pursue righteousness. Kidner says nicely of this proverb that its truth is 'cheaply held in prosperity, precious in adversity'.

[Related proverb: 11:8; 12:13.]

12:22. Treacherous words, truthful ways. The tension in the previous proverb, as well as the statement of v. 19, is resolved here. These statements about what the Lord detests and what he delights in are not given merely as information. There may be many things of which we disapprove over which we have neither will nor power to act. Not so with God. When we are informed of what he approves and disapproves, it is because we are to understand that he will act accordingly. What he abominates he will eliminate; what he delights in he will promote. Ultimately, all men are in God's hands and will be finally and irrevocably answerable to him. What happens today is not disregarded by him nor will be forgotten by him.

Lying lips are deceitful and conceal wicked intent, but nothing is hidden from God. Truthfulness is open for all to see, and God will certainly not overlook it.

This verse varies from v. 19 in that lying lips are not contrasted with truthful words but with truthful dealings, for truthfulness is a matter of action as well as speech. Furthermore, one of the principal benefits flowing from the grace of God is that the believer no longer has any guilty secrets to conceal, no show to put on to keep face before others, no lie to live because the truth would shame him before the world. Because Jesus has borne his people's guilt and shame, the believer is given the power to live truthfully, free to please him, free to delight him. See John 8:31-35. What a wonderful thing it is to be able to delight *in* God! What an amazing thing it is to be able to delight God himself! The one is necessary to the other, and combined they are an expression and result of the freedom the believer has in Christ.

[Related proverb: 12:19.]

12:23. Burying rubbish. A prudent person is one who has a measure of both insight and foresight, who thinks and considers the implications before speaking or acting. We sometimes describe a person like this as 'deep', because there is a lot more to him or her than meets the eye, and there is a lot going on beneath the surface. This is contrasted with the fool who cannot help but give himself away, who is known at once for who he is, having no discretion. However well he may think of himself and however eager to make it known, others immediately recognise him for who he is – a fool.

But there is an important aspect to this statement suggested by the word 'conceals' or 'keeps to himself'. The word in the original means to cover over. Under what circumstances would it be considered prudent to cover over some knowledge? Surely it would be in situations in which revealing that knowledge would be inappropriate, or untimely, or would do harm or cause unnecessary hurt. There are some things which, if we have any consideration for others, we do not 'blab' about. Others may consider such things juicy bits of gossip, or weapons to bring others down, but that is the way of the fool who is prepared to retail any bit of foolishness to make himself look big irrespective of the damage it might do to others.

Sadly, the media seems to have a preoccupation with sparing no effort in turning stones to discover and expose things which were better left hidden. But not only the media. When this happens it comes from the hearts of fools to feed the minds of fools. The foolish heart really is heartless.

A prudent person does not divulge confidences, does not trade embarrassing information, does not exploit or expose the failings of others for all to see. Instead, these things are properly regarded as private, to be buried, to be hidden from sight, to be put out of mind. Like an unexploded bomb some knowledge needs to be isolated from people, and then to be defused and rendered harmless.

Is there anything you know which you should be concealing? Are you doing so, and how are you doing it? It is no use leaving corners showing above the surface for people to tug at and say, 'What is this?' There is a great deal we see, hear or otherwise discover in life which is dangerous knowledge we should keep to ourselves. On the other hand, there is also much, too, which needs to be revealed, but which prudence recognises should be concealed until the appropriate occasion. It can sometimes do much harm to speak out of turn, or to say things before people are ready for it. If prudence conceals knowledge, it also knows when and how to proclaim it.

[Related proverbs: 13:16; 14:33; 15:2; 17:9; 29:11.]

12:24. Matthew 25:14-30. Due diligence. The diligence spoken of here involves more than hard work; it carries with it the sense of incisiveness. It is the 'get up and go' of the person who has something to aim for. People like this deserve to rule, or to carry authority, because in general they have an attitude which will motivate others and bring reward. They want to achieve something worthwhile, and in so doing lead by example and involve others in a usefully productive way.

The sad case at the other end of the spectrum is the person who is unwilling to exert himself to any effort, either for himself or for others. In the end he will find himself driven by others, obliged to do what he detests and from which he will derive no personal satisfaction or benefit.

[Related proverbs: 10:4; 12:27; 13:4; 21:5.]

12:25. The power of a good word. In western society the problem of depression has reached almost epidemic proportions. Anxiety of heart may not be the only cause of depression but it is certainly a major one. Many things can weigh heavily on the mind and heart and bow the spirit: overwork, or the inability to cope with finances, or circumstances, or a sense of being overwhelmed by difficulties, or fear of being unable to control or do anything about what is possibly going to happen, or guilt relating to the past, or health concerns, or the welfare of one's family … the list goes on and on.

A sense of insecurity and worthlessness very often lies at the bottom of the anxiety which leads to depression. The seat of the anxiety referred to here is the heart, the inmost thoughts which are inevitably bound up with inmost feelings. This being the case (as opposed to true clinical depression), the antidote is not in medication, not in antidepressants, but in what is described here as a 'good' word, for it is the heart which must be addressed. Indeed, it is often thoughtless, unkind words, or words calculated to harm, that crush the spirit of those who are struggling.

In v. 18 we read that the tongue of the wise promotes health, and this proverb highlights one specific example of it. Many people who suffer from depression do so because they lack friends who understand and who can respond with good, thoughtful and kind words; they feel isolated. In fact, the good word is really needed before full-blown depression takes hold. The good word is one which is appropriate to the need, it is good in the best sense of the word. It is not trivial, of the kind which says, 'Cheer up, everything will be all right,' but it touches in an understanding and kindly way upon the real issues. The problem is not just in the circumstances, it is in the heart. Addressing the circumstances may help a little, but dealing with the heart is what is really needed so that the sufferer can face the circumstances.

This proverb places a responsibility upon God's people to show sensitivity and understanding toward others, and not to leave them in isolation. A depressed person needs to recover the ability to face the present and the future, to come out of morbid self-withdrawal. It is worth considering what kind of 'good word' will be most appropriate in any given situation, but because 'none can cheer the heart like Jesus' the 'good word' will have him as its ultimate reference point.

There is significance in this proverb that the remedy is a good word rather than a good deed. Actions do not always speak louder than words. A depressed person does not primarily require practical help but the ability to face life. In fact, sometimes practical help can only make matters worse for the sufferer who has already withdrawn through a guilty sense of failure to cope. It can be tremendously helpful in such cases to be aware that God knows their problems really are bigger than they can cope with, and that it is a privilege he has given them that they might seek, find and experience his divine support. He would have them know where to take their anxieties, because he cares for them, and he is in overall control (1 Peter 5:7; Philippians 4:6-7; Matthew 6:25-34). They do not have to, nor are they expected to, bear their burdens alone (Matthew 11:28-30). Sensitive practical help may follow, but it will then be viewed very differently by both parties.

[Related proverbs: 15:13,15; 18:14.]

12:26. Relating to friends and neighbours. Though this proverb is variously translated, it is fairly clear that it addresses relationships. The word here is used of spying out, or reconnoitring, or making an investigative search, and so the first clause concerns the way a righteous person makes an evaluative assessment of another person. The second clause by contrast clarifies the meaning of the first, because there are people who would, given the chance, lead others astray.

Relationships don't just happen, they are formed. We cannot choose our neighbours as a rule, but we can choose our friends. Other people can have a considerable influence upon even the most strong minded, and so it is important that the people with whom we form any kind of close association are not going to be of the kind whose influence may be detrimental to our spiritual well-being.

Viewed in this way, this proverb is of particular relevance to young people leaving home, going out into the world of work or into places of further education. All people have a need for companionship of some sort, and so when they find themselves in a new environment they need to develop the kind of relationships which will be mutually beneficial. We may be amused by the quip, 'With friends like these who needs enemies?' yet the fact is that it has more than a grain of truth in it. Ill-chosen friends can prove to be a very harmful influence upon Christians. Many Christians have been led astray through forming the wrong kind of associations. One of the problems is that once a friendship is formed, very often a sense of loyalty obliges one to maintain it. So Christians need to have their spiritual wits about them right from the word go when they make new acquaintances, and they need to be aware of the rules which are to govern any friendship. At no point can the righteous afford to concede on principles, or they will be led astray, seduced into wrong ways. They should always be in strict control of the way a relationship develops.

Even if the proverb refers to relating to neighbours rather than forming friendships, the same principles apply. (In any case, all friendships start at the 'neighbour' level.) It is important to be able to assess another person's character in order to determine the kind of level at which a relationship is to be sustained. It is we who should be in control of the relationship, not the other person, for it is God who is our Master. In this way we will be able to set a good example to our neighbour.

Who is 'calling the tune' in your relationships with your neighbours and your friends? Is your relationship with any of them running ahead of your understanding of them? Are there any areas in which you need to exercise more responsibility?

[Related proverbs: 10:17; 16:29; 18:24; 22:5.]

12:27. Use it or lose it. Here we meet again the lazy and the diligent encountered at v. 24. There are some difficulties in translating this verse, and it has been pointed out that 'roast' is something of a guess. However, the image we have here is of a man who has gone hunting and caught something. But having caught it, he doesn't finish the job in terms of preparing it, cooking it, or preserving it, and so it largely goes to waste. The proverb is highlighting a characteristic of the lazy person, who may mean well, who may start well, but when it comes to practicalities it is too much of an effort to finish well.

Laziness is contrasted with diligence. Again, the precise meaning is unclear, whether the diligent person values what he possesses, or whether to be diligent is in itself a precious possession. Both senses are certainly true, and the latter encompasses the former, for those who are diligent will certainly make the most of every opportunity and will be careful not to waste precious resources.

This verse highlights the importance of using well the opportunities which come our way and the resources entrusted to us. Why some people prosper while others fail is very often down to how they used what they were given rather than inequality of opportunity.

Your abilities and circumstances are given you by God for a purpose. Regard the opportunities they provide with 'due diligence'. Take control of them, and use them for him and for others. For now, spend a few moments taking stock of what you have been given and how you are using it, and whether in all honesty your attitude is one of diligence or laziness and what you are going to do about it.

[Related proverbs: 10:4; 12:24; 19:15.]

12:28. The path to life. What a wonderfully encouraging statement this is! The second clause reinforces the first. In view here is a road, a path, or a track. One may stand on it, so that one is literally 'on' the way, or 'in' the way; but once on it, it is seen to lead somewhere, and so one finds oneself treading the road, tramping along it, travelling on it, 'on the way' toward a destination. The first clause of the proverb speaks of being on the road, and the second of then progressing along it.

In New Testament terms we understand that the Christian, being on the path to life, has life now. But the Christian is not static on this path, but moving along the path to life which ends in life everlasting in the presence of God. The proverb parallels 'life' with, literally, 'no-death' which the NIV boldly translates 'immortality'.

What kind of road is it? It is a way of righteousness, and only the righteous may be on it, and only the righteous may walk along it. The righteousness of Christ is *accounted to* the Christian, giving the right to *be* on the road (Romans 4:5, etc.), and the righteousness of Christ is *maintained in* the Christian, giving the right to *continue* on the road (1 John 1:9; 2:1, etc.).

Jesus said, 'I have come that they may have life, and that they may have it more abundantly' (John 10:10). As long as we follow the way of righteousness, as long as we remain on its pathway, we need have no fear of death.

Both life and death in the Old Testament are very wide ranging in their meaning. They refer to far more than our concept of physical life and death. We must remember that they are rooted in the events of the garden of Eden. Death entered by sin as soon as sin was committed, even though Adam and Eve lived for several hundred years after their disobedience. Life and death are inseparable from righteousness and sinfulness, and so both always have both temporal and eternal significance.

So there is no conflict between what the second clause of this proverb is saying and what happened to a righteous person like Abel whose 'life' was taken by his wicked brother Cain. Men may kill the body but, as Jesus implied, they cannot thereby really touch the life (Matthew 10:28). Entering into life is contrasted with being cast into hell (Mark 9:43); life is more than the body. Thus the proverb is a confirmation to the believer to follow righteousness, come what may, in the knowledge that in terms of the real issues of life and death there is total security. We have life in Christ now, and we will have life with Christ through all eternity.

[Related proverbs: 4:18; 10:2,16; 11:23,30; 15:24.]

13:1. Like father, like son. The words translated 'instruction' and 'rebuke' are closely related. The former is sometimes rendered as 'correction' in the disciplinary sense (for example 22:15; 23:13), and has to do with warning against error in order to follow the right way. 'Rebuke' is more applicable for someone who has gone astray and needs to be told so unequivocally. The words are appropriate to the parties involved. The first is a wise son. If he is wise, he will heed his father's admonitions without the need for stronger measures.

By contrast the one who is described as a scoffer is one who 'mouths at' the person rebuking him. This is the kind of person who in effect or reality pokes his tongue out at the person correcting him, a vulgar gesture indicating that he will do exactly as he likes whatever others say. He makes light of his actions and despises those who tell him they are wrong. He is beyond verbal instruction. This is often seen in society. It is impossible to reason with some people, who think only of themselves and what they want to do and have no time for any who would seek to correct them. This is the very antithesis of wisdom which listens to and weighs instruction.

Every man is someone's son. The Book of Proverbs gives some prominence to the father/son relationship. God's Word recognises the fundamental importance of the family unit. In this verse the vital connection between wisdom in the son and instruction from the father is made to stand out by the absence of the word 'heeds' in the original. A father is a unique role model for a son. His actions and words provide an example of a kind which will be found nowhere else. A son who turns out badly is often (though not always) found to have a father whose instruction has been deficient in some areas. A son who turns out well is usually (though again not always) found to have a father whose instruction has been thorough and consistent. Many a son is 'a chip off the old block'. How important it is, therefore, for fathers to be cognizant of their God-given responsibilities and to shoulder them faithfully, especially in a society which in general regards marriage lightly and fails to take parenting seriously.

Many fathers seem to leave all the parenting to the mothers, and many seem to assume their children's progress to maturity will somehow 'just happen' automatically. It is not so. Fathers, what pains are you taking to instil wisdom in your children? Do you teach them God's Word? In the midst of your busy work life, do you take sufficient interest in them to know how they are and to give them the kind of input which will encourage them in the right way? What are they learning from you as they observe your way of life? The primary responsibility rests on your shoulders.

The subject of this proverb, however, is the son. It is natural for sons growing up to want to become independent of their parents. But that does not mean ignoring or breaking away from their instruction. The son should always consider his father's instruction as relevant, even if he does not always think it is right. Wisdom does not dismiss instruction, it considers it. His father has years of experience of life, he has not. His father is likely to recognise weaknesses in him of which he himself is unaware. He needs advice from his father in many areas of life he is yet to encounter. He should respect the fact that his father has the desire to instruct him, for it is for his good.

[Related proverbs: 9:8; 15:12; 19:27; 23:19; 27:11.]

13:2. Eating your words. 'If anyone will not work, neither shall he eat' (2 Thessalonians 3:10). When Paul said this he was addressing those who were idle and sponging off others. As eating is fundamental to sustaining one's physical life, so working is the means for obtaining food, whether directly by farming or indirectly by providing services. So we should expect a man to eat well by the fruit of his *labour*.

The change of word transforms the whole into an image about moral and spiritual sustenance. Life is more than food and meeting the needs of the body (Luke 12:23). It is what you say, perhaps more than what you do, that will determine how well you live. The person whose speech is wholesome and directed to do good, and so is fruitful, will find it also does him good in every way. It will certainly dispose others well toward him. The first part of this verse is similar to 12:14a.

The other side of the picture is that those who are unfaithful, or, literally, treacherous, will themselves suffer accordingly. A treacherous path is one which looks all right but conceals hidden dangers, as for example a cliff path with sections liable to crumble away without warning. A treacherous person is one who acts covertly, covering over an intent for evil. If the picture is still about speech, his treacherous words will come back to him with a vengeance and he will suffer for them.

We have already noted in the previous verses that the tongue of the wise promotes health, and a good word makes glad one who is downcast (12:18,25); this verse is a reminder that such speech carries its own reward. It is a principle which God has built into the heart of man and into society, and even in the most corrupt of societies it holds good. It is for this reason that believers have so often suffered, having aroused the jealousy of others. It is those who speak from a good heart, and likewise do good, who in general enjoy good rewards.

[Related proverbs: 10:6,11;12:14a; 24:1-2.]

13:3. Slow to speak. This is reminiscent of 12:13 as well as having a connection with the previous verse. James speaks of the untameable tongue (James 3:8), and the psalmist cries for a guard to be set on his mouth (Psalm 141:3). What we do not say can be as important as what we do say. The expression 'opens wide' (NKJV, ESV) has lewd connotations. Here it could denote any form of vulgar or profane speech, and it has no restraint upon it. The people who indulge in it often derive a perverted sense of self-satisfaction from the exercise, unaware of the ultimate ruin to which it will bring them.

Comparing this with the last proverb, if good speech *promotes* one's life, by contrast restraint from bad speech *preserves* one's life. We need God's protection from a rash tongue. Whatever may be the *lingua franca* of the ungodly, they will be very quick to come down on godly people who slip into their kind of talk. 'Careless talk costs lives' was a slogan heading up a campaign launched in 1940 in the Second World War, warning the public against loose talk which might be overheard and be useful to enemy agents. How much more do Christians need to be aware that there are agents of the enemy of their souls who will exploit against them things they say in unguarded moments. So it is important to keep one's heart, and therefore also one's tongue, for only that which is beneficial, and to deal ruthlessly with thoughts which militate against it.

In the light of these two proverbs, are you getting a good diet and eating well? Consider how you can improve it! Are you safe? Consider ways in which you can improve your security!

[Related proverbs: 12:13; 14:3; 18:7; 21:23.]

13:4. Disguised sluggishness. It is actually the 'soul' of the sluggard which craves, and when we take this in its widest sense to encompass the whole of one's life – physical, moral, spiritual – the picture covers much more than the narrow material aspect. It is the whole person being addressed here.

In a materialistic society in which people work hard to do more than earn their living, so that they have plenty to spend on their comforts and pleasures, there is often a marked neglect in the moral and spiritual spheres. In these areas people are so often lazy, and whatever their deepest desires, they continue to be in want.

A student may enjoy a very full and active life socialising, but if he is neglecting his studies he can justly be accused of being lazy, because, after all, studying is what he is supposed to be doing, and no amount of craving for success will make the least difference. This illustrates the problem with so many people. Man is a spiritual being, created in the image of God, intended for a proper relationship with God. The perpetual sense of want experienced by so many results from neglect of their primary responsibility. They are very busy, but they are not doing what they are supposed to be doing. It is not that they have been given nothing by God, but that they have chosen to find fault with what they have been given, as well as with the giver, like the wicked and *lazy* servant of the parable (Matthew 25:26).

A Christian should be marked by diligence in every area of life. This does not mean frenetic activity but giving proper attention to things in their proper order of priority: being diligent in attention to the Word of God, diligent in maintaining upright behaviour, diligent in every form of work. It is all important, it is all worth doing well, and it will be well rewarded.

It is like the other people in the parable just cited: they acknowledged the giver, used what they had been given, and were well rewarded for their efforts (Matthew 25:14-23).

If by any chance you should be feeling lean and empty, it may be timely to review your priorities and consider whether your energy is being expended in the most profitable channels. Consider Hebrews 6:10-12 and Romans 12:11 and how you might best respond.

[Related proverbs: 10:4; 12:24,27.]

13:5. Personal righteousness. What is translated 'lying' or 'false' extends beyond mere words to anything that, figuratively, speaks falsehood, and this is the subject of both clauses. It is abhorrent to a righteous person that any impression should be given that things are different from what they are. The desire is for truth in action as well as truth in word.

The language of the original in the second clause is colourful, referring firstly and literally, to a stench, the kind of thing associated with putrefaction, and then to shame. It appears possible to take this in two ways. The first is looking at the *effect* of his speech, that the wicked person by the falsehood of his speech *causes* what is loathsome and shameful – that is, he generates and perpetuates it. Thus the words or works of the wicked have a disgustingly unwholesome and unhealthy effect. Alternatively, it could be referring to the *nature* of his speech, his speech itself being repugnant and shameful – reflecting upon him.

This proverb is a contrast, and it has in view the perpetuating of falsehood. This is what falsehood does. It savours of decay and rottenness and spreads. Overall, then, we are given a view of the righteous keeping themselves from morbid taint of deceit, in contrast to the wicked wallowing in it.

Do we see falsehood in its true colours? How easy it is to point the finger at what we see going on all around us, and to gloss over the fact that we often seek to put across to others things which are not strictly true! If we think about it, we should see we have a problem in this department. In Romans 7:7-24 the apostle Paul used himself as an example in acknowledging this problem (and he wasn't referring only to covetousness, but to every aspect of the law). Does this problem not trouble us? If it doesn't, then we really do have a problem! It should trouble us, as Paul was troubled. 'For what I will to do, that I do not practice; but what I hate, that I do' (Romans 7:15). We should hate falsehood in ourselves at least as much as, if not more than, the falsehood we see in the world around us, and that for the reason that it has no place in life of anyone the Lord accounts righteous. The very simple statement of this proverb should humble us to the ground and make us aware of the exceeding greatness of the grace of God toward us in Jesus Christ.

[Related proverb: 30:8.]

13:6. Ephesians 6:14. Personal protection. This is similar to

11:6. If you go into an area of contamination you may be expected to wear protective clothing to guard you against it. The person in view here is one of integrity, an upright person. This refers to the condition of his heart, and the outworking of it is righteousness of life. In what way does righteousness *guard* such a person? It certainly protects him in the sense that no just accusation can be levelled against him. But there is another aspect which is often overlooked: it keeps him from being exposed to many of the temptations which are often so appealing to those who have no scruples. An upright person, by virtue of the way he wants to live his life and therefore organises his affairs, is kept clear of so many of the things which snare others. He may not consciously be aware of it, he may not even think about it, but it is so. While it is true that the Lord preserves the righteous (2:8; Psalms 31:23; 97:10), it is equally true that righteousness has self-preserving tendencies. The contrasting clause makes this only too clear, for while it is true that the Lord will punish sinners, their own wickedness actually tends to their destruction.

[Related proverbs: 11:3,5,6; 12:7; 14:32.]

13:7. Appearance and reality. It is not quite clear how to take this

proverb, and maybe that is deliberate in that it certainly provokes thought. To translate 'pretends to be' is probably unduly narrowing down the intent of the original, for the very real possibility of self-deception should be considered. The question is whether a person really makes himself to be, or merely makes himself out to be, or thinks himself to be, rich or poor; that is, whether it really is so, or is but a façade to conceal the truth, the playing of a part for his own interests, or is a mistaken notion. Though the construction of the sentence tends to favour the playing of a part we will look at all aspects.

In the purely natural sphere there are people who wish others to think of them as more than they are because they crave prestige, or influence, or perhaps access to all the things they believe money can give them. On the other hand, there are people who give the impression that they have nothing because they shun the attention of others, or they are misers, or they fear that others will exploit them or make demands upon them. There are a host of reasons why people will conceal their true financial position from others.

This proverb, however, invites us to probe deeper than monetary considerations, because when we ask the question why it is so, we see that it is of wider application. For one thing, we cannot necessarily take people at face value or judge them by surface appearances. What they really have, and what they really are, may be far from immediately apparent. We may have had this experience in getting to know people, when our longer term knowledge of them has turned out to be very different from our first impressions – and that was even when they had no intention to deceive. How much more do we need care in assessing those who really are putting on a front. People are often not what they seem at first sight.

Now to consider the other possibility. A person may have or gain great wealth and yet be void of anything of real worth. Life is more than money. Some of the richest people in the world have been the most unhappy. But then there are those who are rich who appear to be enjoying life, and who may even think all is well with them and may be perfectly content, yet who in the eyes of the discerning are empty, void of any true value, having nothing which really means anything. They may be rich, yet they have nothing. The rich fool of the parable Jesus told was a case in point (Luke 12:16-21). This can be particularly true in a materialistic society.

Then there are those who through their generosity make themselves poor, for whom the welfare of others is of far greater concern than their own. This could be said of the churches of Macedonia, who were already poor, as they gave out of their poverty for the needy of Jerusalem (2 Corinthians 8:1-5). Jesus counselled the rich young ruler (Mark 10:17-22) to sell all he had and give to the poor, with the promise that he would have treasure in heaven. He was not advocating that the man should make himself poor, only that he should get rid of what was for him the obstacle which stood in the way of his gaining eternal life. It has been a characteristic of many Christians that they have gladly sacrificed many of the things they might have possessed in order to give to the Lord's work, and they have never begrudged it, rightly regarding the fact that they possess far greater riches in Christ.

So if there is some ambiguity in the precise meaning of this proverb, the different interpretations are not divorced from each other. What we have, or what we think we have, and how we view these things, will colour the way we conduct ourselves before others, and the impression we give.

[Related proverbs: 11:24-26; 12:9.]

13:8. The vulnerable rich.

'Rebuke' (NKJV) is also translated as 'threat' (NIV, ESV). The comparison in this proverb suggests this should not be taken only at its face value. Of course, a rich man may be held to ransom, in which case his riches can be used to buy him out; but that, surely would be the reason of holding him in the first place. Nobody puts pressure on a person who has nothing to offer because there is nothing to be gained by doing so.

It is the rich who so often are filled with care on how to guard their securities, who are concerned that their wealth is sufficient to cover the commitments which invariably accompany it. It is they who figuratively speaking may feel themselves to be held to ransom, or at least under threat, by those who seek to exploit their vulnerability in one way or another for their own gain. Such problems never come to the ear of one who is poor. Ecclesiastes 5:10-12 provides another view on this. This is not to commend poverty over riches, but simply to point out that those who are rich in this world have their own cares and anxieties and are not always as secure as they might like to think they are. 1 Timothy 6:17-19 provides good counsel. It is better for those who are rich to use their money for good rather than be held to ransom over it!

Jesus spoke of the cares of this world and the deceitfulness of riches (Mark 4:19), and he said they choke the word so that it becomes unfruitful. It is worth asking if your own riches (such as they are) are holding you to ransom, and whether your concern to guard what you have is having any choking effect on the fruitfulness of the Word of God in your life. Happy are you if you hear no threat (or rebuke) from this quarter!

13:9. Light and gloom. To say that the light of the righteous *rejoices* is a poetic way of expressing that it shines with life and energy. The light of the righteous produces an exultant joy. The word used for *light* here is normally used for broad daylight, and is contrasted with *lamp* which in general refers to a relatively dim, artificial light. You can't extinguish daylight! A lamp, on the other hand, burning oil from a wick, can easily be put out, and in any case given time it will die out of its own accord.

The truth is that the righteous have the light of life; their minds are enlightened by the Spirit of God. They can see clearly where they are going by this light without fear of either losing the light or losing their way. After the darkness they once were in, their whole attitude and outlook is now transformed. 2 Corinthians 4:6 expresses the wonder of this truth, including the dual aspect of the external light and the internal one. The Christian has the light within him, in his mind, in his heart, as well as from the pages of holy Scripture. This light enables him to pursue his course with energy, to live a productive, fruitful life, and to enjoy a glorious prospect at the end of it.

The wicked, on the other hand, are surrounded by perpetual gloom. They really are in darkness, and all they have is a lamp of their own making which flickers uncertainly giving everything it illuminates a sense of unreality. Worse than that, though, is that their light will in due course go out. Nor will it go out of its own accord, for the proverb says it will be put out. It is *appointed* to men to die (Hebrews 9:27); there comes a day when our soul is required of us (Luke 12:20); in that day our own light will be snuffed out. For those who have nothing but their own light it is a reminder of the outer darkness in which there will be weeping and gnashing of teeth, of which Jesus spoke on a number of occasions (Matthew 8:12; 22:13; 25:30). The wicked cannot really see where they are in life, and the light they have enables them to do nothing worthwhile. It is altogether a miserable existence, and they certainly have no view of where they are heading.

There could be no greater contrast between the prospects of the two classes. Believers are to let their light shine before men (Matthew 5:16), for it is a God-given light which will display his glory in the world. See also Matthew 6:22-23.

[Related proverb: 24:20.]

13:10. Sheer arrogance. There is some subtlety to this proverb. Each clause on its own makes sense, and yet though the two clauses are connected with a contrasting 'but', the relationship between the two may not be immediately obvious.

Two mutually exclusive attitudes are presented here. The 'well-advised' are those who have taken advice, as opposed to the proud who have not and will not do so. The word for pride in this verse is used of presumptuous arrogance rather than a sense of self-importance or grandeur, though it will often involve this. Pride has not received, and will not receive, advice. It is that attitude which refuses to consider, let alone concede to, the judgement of others but must have its own way. It describes that class of people with whom you cannot argue because they are always right. Their minds are closed against all other considerations.

It must not be supposed, though, that this attitude necessarily permeates a person's whole character, for often it displays itself only in certain areas. This is what makes it so dangerous. It can be observed sometimes in people who would not normally be described as arrogant, but who in some particular matter are so sure of themselves that they display a blinkered dogmatism and intolerance. Furthermore, we are all susceptible to this problem, especially when some of our cherished ideas are challenged and it is personally too costly even to consider the possibility of conceding that we might be wrong.

People have different viewpoints and needs, different attitudes and insights, various contributions to make with regard to what should be done, etc. When inflexible arrogance is encountered, no way forward can be found and strife is the inevitable result. There is always a way forward in any situation, no matter how difficult, provided good advice is sought and the parties have the humility of mind to consider it without personal prejudice.

This has nothing to do with compromising on the truth. Paul warned Timothy about this kind of proud spirit in the church and its alarming effects (1 Timothy 6:3-5). Rather than get drawn into this kind of thing, Timothy was to distance himself from it (1 Timothy 6:11,20). His emphasis was to be on teaching what accorded with godliness. He was to fight the good fight of faith, not strive with others over side issues.

Without wishing to impute the motive of pride to either party, nevertheless an example of strife occurred in Acts 15:36-40. Consider the situation. How might the parties have been advised with wisdom so that the problem could have been resolved peaceably?

Think, too, about situations you have known where strife has been in evidence, or in which you have been involved. Has pride been a part of them? Has wisdom been exercised in seeking to handle them and bring them to a satisfactory solution? If appropriate, consider this as a personal challenge.

Concerning the relationship between taking advice and wisdom, is wisdom the consequence of receiving counsel, or is the willingness to receive it a mark of wisdom? Surely both are true? But whichever way it is viewed, strife and the taking of advice have no common ground, nor do strife and wisdom. Why not?

[Related proverbs: 10:12; 12:15; 15:18; 16:28; 19:20; 20:3; 22:10; 28:25; 29:22; 30:33.]

13:11. Means tested. Although the NIV translates 'money', the word should be understood of wealth in its widest material sense. This proverb views two ways of accumulating wealth: at one's own expense or at the expense of others. The dishonest way, from whatever angle it is viewed, exploits the labours of others. Money acquired by gambling, for example, does this. So does stealing. So does anything which returns less for a man's labour than that of which he is deserving. It is true that some people amass great wealth by such means, which is almost in contempt of this proverb. The truth remains, however, that in the process nothing has really been gained, only redistributed, and in fact there has been a net loss. Life cannot be sustained on such a principle. Those who make such 'easy gains' lose credibility and respect, and they attract the hostility of those at whose expense they have enriched themselves (see James 5:1-6). In terms of true wealth, they are every time the losers.

The second clause is literally about gathering by hand. When we talk about doing something by hand we are usually thinking of a painstaking process involving personal effort and taking time. That is the image here. The only way in which wealth truly grows is by means of real labour, through the proper use of the resources God has given in the earth for our sustenance and enjoyment. The expression, 'an honest day's work for an honest day's pay' still applies. Not only will those who gather in such a way by degrees enrich themselves, but others will also benefit. Thus the one who works will reap a double blessing.

This proverb is patently not about the right way to make money and get rich. It is about true riches. It provokes us to ask how we have gained what we have gained, materially or in any other way. Are we putting in more than we are taking out? Are we contributing something worthwhile as we live out our lives? Who is being enriched by our presence in this world, and how?

[Related proverbs: 10:2; 20:21; 21:6; 22:16; 28:8,20,22.]

13:12. Some hope! 'Hope deferred', or hope long drawn out, is contrasted very directly with 'desire come'. One causes sickness of heart, the other a wonderful sense of well-being. The parallel is not exact, but the two who trudged the road to Emmaus were devastatingly downcast because they had hoped that Jesus was to have been the one who was going to redeem

Israel. After their arrival at Emmaus and their encounter with the risen Lord they immediately returned to Jerusalem with completely transformed spirits (Luke 24). What marked the difference between their outward and return journeys was not physical weariness and strength, but was purely psychological. Their manner of deportment was induced by a state of mind. So it is in this proverb.

Hope here should be taken in the sense of expectation rather than the vague 'might or might not happen' kind. It is perfectly natural for people to entertain hopes of all kind of things. There are things they look forward to in life with every expectation that they will materialise. Very often the hope is a stimulus to activity, to perseverance, and maybe to working toward the goal of the hope if it lies within one's power to fulfil it. Yet that works only to a point, beyond which discouragement can set in, especially if there are unexpected setbacks or delays over which one has no control. The expectation may still be there, but it may be accompanied by an element of pain, or anxiety of heart, or even doubt: 'Will it ever happen?'

It is against this background of delay, maybe of frustrating and seemingly interminable delay, that the materialisation of the hope is seen. In a sense, it is *because* the hope has been long drawn out that the fulfilment of the longing is found to be a tree of life.

For Christians, it is the expectant hope of the Lord's coming which enables them to persevere in faith. There are, however, many references to the fact that the coming of the Lord is seen to take a great deal longer than might originally have been supposed. It is easy to become discouraged, to become sick at heart, in a world of unbelief and scorn in which the hope seems to be receding rather than approaching. It is against this background of apparent prolongation of the hope of the Lord's return that Peter encourages perseverance (2 Peter 3), and by their conduct of anticipatory activity even to make the time pass more quickly (2 Peter 3:12). We know that when he does appear, it will be in the very fullest sense a tree of life for us.

In a lesser, though no less real, sense, many believers have had the experience of praying long in hope for something or someone, in the expectation of the Lord answering their prayers, and of being sick at heart because nothing seems to be happening. But then, often in an unexpected way (rather than unexpectedly!) the Lord has provided his answer, and that painful yearning has been replaced by an overflowing thankfulness and an inexpressible joy.

On many occasions the Lord and his apostles urge us to patience and perseverance in the light of the hope God has given us. This proverb is so true to life that it should encourage us in the things that matter, and to use sanctified imagination as we anticipate the fulfilment of all that we long for in Christ at his appearing, knowing that the fulfilment will actually far exceed the limits of our ability to imagine what it will be like.

[Related proverbs: 13:19; 18:14; 23:17,18.]

13:13. Psalm 19. The law of the Lord is perfect… 'The word' is translated 'instruction' and 'the commandment' is translated 'a command' in the NIV, making it very broad. However, the meaning of 'word' in the first clause should be understood with the parallel 'commandment' in the second, and as the latter is almost exclusively used of God's commandments (though occasionally referring to the command of an authority like a king – 2 Kings 18:36; 2 Chronicles 8:14,15; 24:21; 29:15,25; 30:6,12; 35:10,15,16; Nehemiah 11:23; 12:24,45; Esther 3:3; Proverbs 2:1; 3:1; 4:4; 6:20, etc.; Jeremiah 35:14), 'the word' must be similarly understood.

Therefore this refers primarily to what God has commanded, even though it may have a limited alternative application. It reminds us that God has spoken, and that his commands are living and active words. What was set in stone in the Ten Commandments was first of all heard from heaven (Deuteronomy 5) as God spoke to the people. If God has spoken, then those who treat his word with contempt are told unequivocally that they will suffer the consequences.

It is clear that the people who heard the commandments given on that occasion were in great fear. To fear the commandment here, though, is not so much to be afraid of it or of the consequences accruing to disobedience, but rather to treat it with reverence and with the utmost respect. It is a holy fear. The criminal may fear the law for obvious reasons. It is not that kind of fear which will be rewarded. But the law-abiding citizen may also fear the law, though for very different reasons and with a very different motivation.

The word translated 'rewarded' is used of restitution, or of rendering what is due. It is not to be thought that God rewards those who keep his commandments because they are deserving of it, or that he owes it to them on their own account. It is not that they have earned it. It is vitally important to understand that it is purely on account of his promise that God rewards those who fear him; it is because he has said he will graciously do so, and not because of merit in them. Note too that this verse does not say that those who *keep* the commandment will be rewarded, but those who *fear* it. There is a difference. No one can keep God's commandments. Some have no desire to do so and fail; others earnestly desire to do so and also fail. Therefore reward cannot be on the basis of merit.

This verse is all about our attitude to the Word of God, whether or not we will welcome and heed it. God has spoken of judgement and reward which hinge upon how we respond to it. Judgement is based upon law; reward is based upon grace.

[Related proverbs: 13:21; 16:20; 19:16.]

13:14. Deuteronomy 30:15-20. Life and death. There is a close parallel in 14:27, in which 'The law of the wise' is replaced by 'The fear of the Lord.' There is also a similarity with the first clause of 10:11 – 'The mouth of the righteous is a well of life' (NKJV), where 'well' there is translated 'fountain' here. This is prescriptive rather than proscriptive, encouraging what is right rather than merely prohibiting what is wrong, directing us into how we are to live our lives productively, fruitfully, beneficially.

The law of the wise is in complete accord with the law of the Lord. It could be said to be the demonstrative outworking of the law of God in one who has taken it to heart. To those for whom water is a precious commodity, for whom to find water at all is valuable, and to find fresh, clean, sparkling water in abundance is absolutely delightful, the expression, 'a fountain of life' speaks of luxuriant enrichment and enjoyment. The value of it is greatly enhanced by the comparison, 'to turn away from the snares of death'. Unlike the scribes and Pharisees and teachers of the law of Jesus' day, the wise will highlight not only by their words but also by their lives the benefits enshrined in the law and safeguarded by it, thus truly commending both it and the God who gave it, that sinners might turn to him from the concealed perils of lawlessness and its consequences.

The proverb is a mixed metaphor. We may be advised against mixing metaphors, but this one is effective. The fountain of life is clearly on display; the snares of death are cleverly concealed. The fountain of life has nothing to its detriment – quite the opposite; the snares of death have nothing to commend them – again, quite the opposite! The fountain of life is attractive; the snares of death are repulsive. The law of the wise by attracting people to God draws them away from the hidden dangers into which they are walking in life. The law of the wise is therefore of incalculable importance.

[Related proverbs: 10:11; 14:27.]

13:15. Know how to be useful. It is important to remember that the proverbs are intended to be very practical. This one is more than a theoretical statement but applies to particular situations. The ESV translates, 'Good sense', but we should be aware there is more depth in the word than in the way we often use it. However, it does bring out that under consideration here is the *exercise* of understanding. This is good understanding being exercised in a context. If we are to be of any practical use in the situations in life in which we find ourselves, then we need to have a good understanding of them. Elementary though this is, it is often overlooked. How many people are ready to give their opinion on matters of which they actually know very little, or their advice over something which they only very partially understand. Regrettably, all too often such people are unaware of their deficiency of understanding.

There are some difficulties in how best to translate this proverb. In the first clause good understanding either *gains* or *gives* favour. In the second, the way of the unfaithful (or treacherous) is said to be 'hard' – not hard on them but hard on those within their sphere of influence. But it has been suggested that there may have been a very minor copying error and that it should read 'not lasting'.

If we take it that a good understanding gains favour, it must be stressed that this is not the person on the lookout for favour. It is not, 'I must gain a good understanding of what is going on here or I am going to miss out.' Rather, it is, 'I must gain a good understanding of what is going on here or I am not going to be of any use in it.' Favour is not a selfish thing, but one which opens the door to useful opportunities for doing good. Many relationships, whether in the home, or in the workplace, or with neighbours, or even in the church, break down simply because no effort is made to understand one another and therefore to appreciate the undercurrents which affect people's thinking, moods, hopes and fears, and so on. Those with a good understanding are able to demonstrate it in sympathetic responses, and so gain the confidence of those with whom they mix, and as a result are often able to find a way in to be of real practical use. So whether it should be translated 'gains' or 'gives' is largely immaterial, because both apply.

People who gain favour are those who *habitually* exercises good sense. They can be relied upon to contribute helpfully and meaningfully in any given situation.

By contrast, the 'way' of the unfaithful indicates a very different course through life, and the word 'unfaithful' points to those who are unreliable, untrustworthy, even deceitful. There is something underhand about them. They are essentially self-centred without a true regard for others. They do not benefit others, they only make things difficult for them. They will therefore not gain favour; they will gain neither the affection nor the respect nor the confidence of others. They will not endure.

[Related proverbs: 12:8; 14:8; 16:22; 22:1.]

13:16. Know what you are about. This is a companion to the previous proverb. The word translated 'acts' carries with it a sense of purpose, or productivity, with definite consequences or results. This is action with something in view. When we say someone has got his head screwed on we mean that he really knows what he is doing, and is doing it well. You don't describe someone as prudent who trusts to blind chance or who hopes for a favourable outcome for what he does when the odds are stacked against him. A prudent person looks before he leaps. He wants to know where he is going, what will be the effect and outcome of his actions. He is careful of his facts, and makes sure he has all of them marshalled before he goes about his business. There is nothing rash about him.

While many people may try to be prudent in some of the big decisions that confront them in life, what we are looking at here is someone who carries that same attitude into everyday living. In some respects it resembles the last proverb in our interactions with others. The things we do affect other people, probably more than we are aware. We need to be careful to ensure the things we do and say are with knowledge and understanding and according to truth. This proverb is very similar to 12:23. Prudence cannot exist without knowledge but is utterly dependent upon it.

Contrast this with the conduct of the fool, because this proverb is comparing different people in the context of the same circumstances. There is something in his conduct which is pathetically – even embarrassingly – amusing. Clearly unaware of it himself, it is as if by his actions he is spreading out his hands and declaring openly to all, 'Look what a fool I am!' Others can so clearly see him for what he is. He not only fails to accomplish anything of any value, but his actions reflect badly upon himself.

Ultimately, though, we have to remember that the fear of the Lord is the beginning of knowledge (1:7); it is foundational. We can hope to be prudent in our dealings only insofar as we are humbly dependent upon him.

[Related proverb: 12:23.]

13:17. Isaiah 61:1-3. Putting it across. The messenger of the first clause describes one entrusted with conveying a matter of importance. The equivalence with the word 'ambassador' or 'envoy' in the second clause indicates responsibility beyond the mere conveyance of a message. Such a person would be acting on behalf of the one sending him, maybe in negotiating terms, brokering deals, and the like. It is the word also used of an angel.

We have a biblical example of a wicked messenger in the one who came to inform David of Saul's death (2 Samuel 1). It is likely that he compounded truth with error in conveying his message in order to further his own ends, but he certainly misjudged the situation, for he was executed for his troubles.

It has been suggested that the translation should be that the wicked messenger 'precipitates trouble' rather than 'falls into trouble'. It is a wicked messenger who either himself invents falsehood or who conveys a false message on behalf of others, as was the case with the messages from Sanballat and others (Nehemiah 6:1-14). They were certainly out to cause as much trouble as possible to the Jews at Jerusalem.

In short, a wicked messenger is just about as good as a man carrying in his body an infectious disease. He brings trouble to himself and to any with whom he interacts.

Trouble is contrasted with health, and wickedness with faithfulness, and it is reasonable to suppose it reflects upon the same person, either the one giving the news, or the one receiving it. It all depends on whether the translation of the first clause should be 'falls into trouble' or 'precipitates trouble'. Either way, what is highlighted here is that one conveying a message, especially one of importance, to another, must do so both accurately and wisely.

For example, suppose you are entrusted with the responsibility to convey some bad news to another person. How will you go about it? Will you tone down the message and make out that it is not as bad as it really is? Or will you relish the opportunity to deliver it dramatically, perhaps with embellishment, to make maximum impact on the recipient? Or will you faithfully stick to the facts? But even then, much more is involved than verbally transmitting bald facts. If you are to be faithful, you have to determine not only what you will say, but how you will say it, and that will have regard to the well-being of the recipient as well as to the accuracy of the message. Both elements feature in the task of the kind of messenger we are looking at here. We have another interesting biblical example in the way the news of Absalom's death was conveyed to David by two different messengers, neither of whom could be described as 'faithful' (2 Samuel 18:19-33).

The apostles were ambassadors for Christ (2 Corinthians 5:20). It mattered to the whole of the New Testament church not only what the message was that they brought, but also how they conveyed it. Likewise all Christians have an ambassadorial responsibility insofar as they represent Christ, and if we are to be faithful to our calling we too will take care not only in what we say but how we say it, remembering that not only was truth upon our Master's lips but also grace characterised his every word and action.

It is so important that we keep in view the right objectives. One would think by the conduct of some Christians that their primary ministry was one of judgement. It is not. That is God's prerogative. That is where Jonah went wrong. His message was one of judgement, but his ministry was one of mercy – or should have been. The true ambassador for Christ brings healing in the fullest sense, for that is precisely what Jesus did. The message entrusted to Christians is the message of the gospel – *good* news. It is imperative that it is neither watered down nor embellished but transmitted faithfully. Yet there are various ways of saying the same thing, and faithful transmission has regard for the circumstances and needs of the hearers, so that the pleasant as well as the painful aspects are presented with healing in view. This would apply particularly to the preaching of repentance.

[Related proverbs: 14:5; 25:13.]

13:18. How to take it. None of us enjoys being corrected! It is so easy to react against it with blind or even angry self-justification. On the other hand, when rebuked or corrected we can often feel humiliated and ashamed and become self-reproaching. So this proverb is remarkably encouraging when it tells us that the real shame attaches to the one who is dismissive of correction, whereas the one who takes it to heart and considers it is the one who is honoured.

The Bible is very realistic in showing us how often we go wrong in all kinds of ways, and that receiving correction is an essential part of progress. This aspect of 2 Timothy 3:16 has already been alluded to, and the end in view, in v. 17, should be noted. Rebuke is also an aspect of the discipline to which the Lord subjects us in life, and Hebrews 12:9-11 reminds us that God intends it for our good. No Christian, however mature, is exempt from this need.

That this proverb operates in the world is fairly self-evident. There are people so full of themselves that any suggestion, however gently put, that they are at fault in any way, only receives an adverse reaction. They are very soon accurately categorised! So are others, too, who simply fold in on themselves when corrected, which is invariably another way of avoiding the issue and which exhibits pride in a different form.

But those who are prepared to consider and do something about their faults when they are pointed out generally gain in respect as a result. Consider proud Naaman disdaining the waters of the Jordan for his healing (2 Kings 5). Yet he later heeded wise rebuke and counsel, even from his own servants, and he humbled himself and was restored. No doubt his household honoured him for it! Incidentally, the three 'messengers' of that incident – Elisha's messenger, Naaman's servants, and Elisha's personal servant Gehazi – provide a good illustration of the previous proverb.

Reflect dispassionately on some of the occasions on which you have been rebuked or corrected. How have you taken it? Have you benefited from the process? Have you learnt to view these things objectively and with justice and to respond accordingly? Are there still some items in the 'in tray' awaiting your appropriate attention?

By the grace of God this proverb applies in the spiritual realm, too, as well as in the world. The ultimate poverty and shame come to those who will not accept God's verdict upon their sinful condition and need, even though these truths be presented with love, kindness and concern. By contrast, those who do humble themselves under his mighty hand are in due course lifted up. But observe, too, that this humility, if it is genuine, will be accompanied by an attitude of humility toward others as well (1 Peter 5:5-6).

[Related proverbs: 1:23-33; 6:23; 10:17; 12:1; 15:5,10,31,32,33; 29:23.]

13:19. What do you want to achieve in life? This seems at first sight to be a somewhat disjointed comparison. What is the relation between the two clauses? The first refers to the very real sense of satisfaction people can get when something they have been working for, or working at, reaches its fulfilment. This, however, is not necessarily related to its intrinsic worth, for it may be only the achievement of a personal ambition which means nothing, or is of no value, to anyone else. Whatever it may be they have in their sights, they have got the bit between their teeth and they are going for it, and nothing is going to deter them until they have achieved their objective.

Have you ever heard someone say, when advised that what they are doing is not so good, 'I'm committed, there's no turning back now'? The nub of the matter is the drive of personal ambition. The further one progresses on a course of action the greater the incentive to finish, and the more difficult it becomes to stop.

The word translated 'evil' has wider than moral connotations. It includes what is regarded as bad in a wide variety of ways, such as bad circumstances (Genesis 19:9; Job 2:10), or a bad report (Genesis 37:2; Numbers 14:37). There is a subtlety in the wording of this proverb applicable to the case because it depicts the fool still on his headlong course even though the outcome will be bad. He may think that the accomplishment of his desire will be sweet to his soul, but the reality will very likely be far from it. True satisfaction attaches only to the fulfilment of those pursuits which are honourable and worthwhile, the bottom line of which is that they meet with the approbation of God.

The contrast in this proverb is indeed between the wise and the foolish. It is wise to bring one's ambitions under the scrutiny of the Word of God; it is wise to pursue what is good and right to its conclusion and not give up; it is wise to make that drastic and ruthless decision to turn back from following a course which, even if not overtly evil, has some dubious aspects to it. For if it is not truly good, it can hardly be anything but evil.

This proverb invites us to examine our objectives in life. Do you have longings for things you wish to achieve? Are you devoting time and energy to them? Have you considered whether what you are putting into these things represents a sound investment? Personal ambition no doubt has value as long as the goal is good. But suppose you are up to your neck in some project and have that very uncomfortable feeling that it is not as worthwhile as you once supposed? You have invested so much in it that to cut loose now would seem to amount to a confession of having wasted all that you put into it. But pursuing it to its end is only going to be a further waste of your resources. The prospect of losing face can be hard. Admitting to having been wrong or unwise can be humiliating. That is why some people go doggedly on though the end is only bitterness.

How much better it is not to get into such a predicament in the first place! David gives sound advice in Psalm 37:3-4. The only desires worth having are those which have come from the Lord and been given by him – and they are the only desires worth pursuing. It is *their* accomplishment which will truly be sweet to the soul. That kind of desire comes only as you trust in the Lord and delight yourself in him.

[Related proverb: 13:12.]

13:20. Choice company. The company you keep says a lot about you. Someone who said, when questioned about his association with friends who apparently held very different values from him, that he wasn't going to allow them to influence him, was already far more under their power than he realised. For one thing, the fact that he was expressing his own preference for that kind of company gave the message that beneath the standards he ostensibly held were others more in line with theirs. It was hardly surprising that after a little while he had become totally engulfed by their values and was now indistinguishable from them.

If a man consistently avoids the company of Christians, even though he makes an outward profession of Christianity, what conclusion will be drawn? Both the company he keeps and the company he avoids declare the truth, whatever his protestations.

While this proverb can be taken by way of advice, and rightly so, at the same time it is really classifying people into two groups, highlighting the fact that there is opposite polarity between those who fear God and those who do not. The believer is always subject to temptation, and this advice is good for him or her. Choose your company well. Mix and spend time with those from whose conversation and conduct you will benefit. Breathe healthy air. Just as a claustrophobic, smoke ridden atmosphere may do its damage long before the more sinister symptoms become apparent, so companionship with what the Bible describes as 'fools' (however clever they may be) is already threatening to reap its destructive rewards. The promise it holds for the future is utter destruction, and it will not renege on it.

It is vitally important for Christians to do all they can to strengthen their faith, and perhaps the most effective way of doing so is by means of association with wise friends and worthwhile social contacts. This does not mean, of course, severance from the company of unbelievers. This proverb is talking about companionship, not company. Company with unbelievers is for most people an inevitable part of living, as well as a useful opportunity for Christian testimony. At the same time, our companionship, our fellowship, is to be with those who are likeminded in faith in Christ. The bonds which united the early church were evident right from the beginning (Acts 2:42-47; 4:32) and their distinctiveness is seen from Acts 5:13. In 2 Corinthians 6:14 – 7:1 the apostle Paul had some strong words about those who were displaying the folly of worldly wisdom in the nature of their associations with unbelievers. If the fear of the Lord is the beginning of wisdom, its continuance will be seen in association with those who fear him.

Walking with the wise may be extended into other areas, such as the hobbies we pursue, or the books we read, or the television programmes we watch, or to our surfing the internet. We need to be walking with the wise in these areas, too.

[Related proverb: 14:7.]

13:21. What have you got coming to you? We might say that sinners pursue evil, and that would be true. Here is the flip side: evil pursues sinners. Evil here may be understood in a very wide sense, and it includes misfortune and calamity. This statement is true not only in the ultimate sense that final judgement awaits the ungodly. It is true all through life. Those who live at variance with the law of God are beset by the evils associated with their disregard of it. Most of the troubles which afflict society are directly traceable to deviation from the Word of God, and the troubles which afflict society are the very troubles which afflict each individual member who contributes to making up that society.

The description is the very graphic one of a chase, in which the one pursued is desperately trying to keep ahead of the pursuer. This so often happens in life, in which those who live contrary to God's laws are for ever trying to avoid the consequences. But it is a chase in which the pursuer will sooner or later overtake the one trying to get away. There is a morbid inevitability about it. Evil is a relentless predator!

What may be said of evil pursuing sinners has its counterpart in relation to good and the righteous. The NIV translates this as 'prosperity', but this perhaps unhelpfully narrows the meaning with its material connotations. When people are said to prosper, the implication is that they do well for themselves, or they get on well. But the righteous will not necessarily be rewarded with prosperity in this sense. The word used indicates good in its widest sense. Here, in contrast to the first clause, there is no hostile intent, but only a friendly one. The sinner is for ever on the run, looking over his shoulder at what lies behind threatening to catch up with him; the righteous has no such concerns but can look forward only to good. He may expect to be repaid in kind, that as he has done good to others, so others will repay him too with good.

At 16:7 we read that when a man's ways please the Lord, he makes even his enemies live at peace with him. This is a general principle, and as such recognises that even in a fallen world righteousness and the good which comes from it is respected. It is not of course universally applicable because of the basic antipathy between righteousness and wickedness. Peter says to his readers, 'Who is he who will harm you if you become followers of what is good?' (1 Peter 3:13), adding as a qualifier that suffering may come to the righteous. That, however, is not because of the good itself, but on account of the hatred of those who, for whatever reason, oppose them.

It is very important that we understand the distinction. The righteous have no grounds upon which to reproach themselves. Even if they suffer evil on account of their righteousness, they are blessed, as Peter affirms, and in this sense good is still repaid to them. One way or the other, they may expect only good to come out of their godly conduct. The Lord will see to it that the least service of righteousness will be rewarded (Matthew 10:42). This must not be thought of as payment in kind. It is nothing of the sort. Rather, it is the reward of grace. It is God's just acknowledgement of his own work in those he has accounted righteous.

What blessings attend the righteous! How wonderfully precious and liberating it is to be accounted righteous in God's sight, released from all the evils the ungodly fear, freed to do good and to live lives pleasing to him who loved us and gave himself for us!

[Related proverbs: 11:18; 13:13.]

13:22. Who gets it? From the good described in the previous proverb we move on to the good person. The word is the same. The assumption in the world is that it is the wealthy man who leaves an inheritance to his children's children, irrespective of his character. Not so, says this proverb, it is the good man who does so, irrespective of his wealth. The description 'children's children' is a deliberate one to indicate continuity in ongoing benefits down through the generations. In this connection compare Exodus 34:7 and Psalm 103:17.

In the contrasting clause we read of the wealth of the sinner. The wealth of the sinner cannot really be anything other than his material accumulation. This proverb reinforces the last. All ultimate benefits accrue to the righteous, who is identified with the good person. Who is it who gets the inheritance? The proverb is making the point that it is not the offspring of the sinner (that is, the one who persists in sin), but the offspring of the good person.

The image of inheritance is to be understood far more widely than in material terms. People often think of how they are going to provide for their children (or even grandchildren) and what they are going to leave their descendants, and they make their wills with this in mind. Without in the least disparaging this worthy consideration, it is of far less importance than the kind of inheritance in view in this proverb. Christian children brought up in godly homes with the solid background of biblical teaching and example from their parents receive an inheritance of far greater value than any material wealth they might expect to come to them on the decease of their parents.

Here is the outworking of the promises and warnings given in the law concerning the blessings or the curses relating to the offspring of godly or ungodly parents (see, for example, Deuteronomy 6:20-25 with its implications, and Exodus 34:6-7). For us this proverb lays its hand on our shoulder to remind us of the importance of providing the right kind of inheritance for the following generations. Malachi 2:15 refers to godly offspring. Some of the spiritual giants in history have come from homes of very limited financial means, and their stature owes itself to their upbringing in which God has blessed the way their parents nurtured them in the truth.

Are you a parent? If so, what are your children, and your children's children, going to inherit from you? Are you laying up for them now? But even if you are not a parent, just as you will have beneficiaries of your material things, so also you will have beneficiaries of your spiritual things. Make sure you have plenty to leave!

13:23. Use and abuse of resources. This is variously translated, but the meaning seems to concern the use of resources. The essence of it may be captured by imagining yourself looking out on to a piece of land. It is good ground, but it is lying there uncultivated. Seeing its potential, you might say to yourself, 'There's much food here.' But of course there isn't, because no use has been made of it. You happen to know that the owner is poor, and that may raise further questions in your mind.

A man may be poor not because he does not have the means to better himself but because he fails to use what is available to him. Did he but know it, or did he but work it, his fallow ground would be capable of producing a healthy crop for him.

Looked at more generally, we may not get on as well as we might simply because we fail to recognise or take advantage of the opportunities open to us. Thus the first clause could be alluding to the failure to use such resources as are available.

Another possibility is that the owner does not have the means to utilise his resource, pointing to injustice somewhere along the way. This leads into the second clause which seems to speak of the opposite problem to the failure to use resources, namely the tragic waste or destruction of resources either through injustice or because of lack of sound judgement. Man's amazing capacity for destruction is painfully felt at almost every point on our globe. Ironically, greed often lies at the back of it: the greed of the few at the expense of the many. Greed is a vice which is rapaciously destructive.

Without doubt there is tremendous wastage and destruction of earth's valuable resources simply because men lack the judgement to manage them wisely. Sometimes short term gain spells long term pain, and this operates at the individual level as well as the wider one.

For us this proverb can serve as a reminder to look carefully at our stewardship. On the one hand we are not to be like the man in the parable who buried his talent; on the other we are not to be like those who squander what God has given us on riotous living. Are we recognising and using what God has given us in a responsible fashion? Are there any areas of life that should be being cultivated? Are there resources that are being wasted? There is no need for the kind of poverty depicted in this proverb.

[Related proverb: 14:4.]

13:24. An uncomfortable but necessary responsibility. Take good note that the proper context of discipline is love. This is the context in Hebrews 12. Note too that the discipline has an objective in view, namely the well-being of the son (or daughter). Further, note that proper discipline is neither impulsive nor tardy, but prompt, or timely.

Impulsive discipline fails to take proper account of the circumstances and may do more harm than good. Tardy discipline is equally dangerous because it allows evil to go unchecked and shows an unwillingness to face the issues.

Effective discipline is both thinking and decisive. We should notice mention of the rod. Failure to discipline is not really an option for the parent who cares, but neither is feeble discipline. The language is strong here because there is so often a tendency to be soft on correction. For parents who care, being told that withholding proper discipline is equivalent to hating their offspring should provide the necessary incentive to overcome any natural reluctance to deal incisively with problems when they arise. It is sometimes necessary to inflict pain in order to curb behaviour which ultimately will result in far greater pain of a different kind.

Discipline which falls short of achieving its desired object is hardly worthy of the name. We note in Hebrews 12:6 the very strong word used, which is 'scourge'. God does not spare his children whom he loves with an everlasting love, and if we love our own children with a genuine godly love we will be prepared ourselves to suffer the necessity of disciplining them from time to time for their good. Where love is in evidence in family life there will be no danger of discipline being misinterpreted.

It is the angry, hasty punishment of children from parents and others who have lost control or who have unworthy motives which has produced such an adverse reaction to the concept of 'corporal punishment' in our society. The whole thing has got totally out of perspective. Discipline is an essential part of training up children (see also Proverbs 22:15 for one reason for this), and it is as uncomfortable for the one administering it as it is for the one receiving it! But it must be given. Failure to discipline leads to all sorts of evils, and we are seeing some of these in our own western society which has largely lost sight of the concept of biblical love. The rod in this proverb represents any mode of discipline which is *felt*, under which the recipient feels the smart. Furthermore, it is short and sharp, not long drawn out to run the risk of breeding resentment.

Loving discipline is intelligent discipline, appropriate to the situation and with an eye to the benefits for the recipient. God disciplines his children in order that they may be partakers of his holiness (Hebrews 12:10), which is the highest and most glorious end for them. Let us follow his example by training up our children not simply to curb their vices but to help them fulfil their God-given potential and enjoy his rich blessing.

[Related proverbs: 19:18; 22:15; 23:13-14; 29:15,17.]

13:25. Feasting the soul. Is this really about food? If we were to take the statement literally we would have to say it is not true, for Hebrews 11:37 refers to the destitution of many worthies of the faith, and history records how many Christians have suffered hunger and deprivation. However, there is every reason to understand it metaphorically, in which case we see an entirely different picture.

Eating and the stomach are often used in a metaphorical sense. We talk about being starved of love, or receiving a bellyful of abuse, or something being more than we can stomach, or of feasting our eyes, and so on. What we have in this proverb under the imagery of eating is an observation about true satisfaction and contentment. But when we ask *why* this applies we must see it in terms of God causing it to be so. It is certainly true in the ultimate sense. As David says, 'In your presence is fullness of joy; at your right hand are pleasures forevermore' (Psalm 16:11). But there is a sense in which it is already true. To quote David again: 'You have put gladness in my heart, more than in the season that their grain and wine increased' (Psalm 4:7). Isaiah uses the imagery of feasting (Isaiah 25:6) to illustrate the eternal blessing of the righteous: 'The LORD of hosts will make for all people a feast of choice pieces, a feast of wines on the lees, of fat things full of marrow, of well-refined wines on the lees.'

The believer has in Christ complete satisfaction and contentment. The unbeliever, though he may enjoy a measure of contentment in this life, can never have a true sense of satisfaction. There is a spiritual equivalent to enjoying a good meal and comfortably relaxing afterwards about which the unbeliever knows nothing. The apostle Paul could speak of personal contentment even when things were hard for him, the secret of which lay in his relationship with Christ (Philippians 4:11,13). He knew what he was talking about when he said to Timothy, 'Godliness with contentment is great gain' (1 Timothy 6:6). The writer of Hebrews likewise referred to believers being content with what they had in material things, because they had a Lord who would never leave them nor forsake them (Hebrews 13:5). The words of the hymn, 'Now none but Christ can satisfy...' are true. Real satisfaction comes through feeding upon Christ by faith (see John 6:51-58). The believer who does so can see how starved is the one who rejects Christ.

[Related proverb: 10:3.]

14:1. A proverb for women. Or is it? Who normally build or demolish houses? Men, surely? But this is not a matter of bricks and mortar but of a house in every other sense, including what makes a home a home, which in the majority of cases is attributable to the industry and creativity of a woman. This proverb is very picturesque. We are invited to consider the performance of two kinds of women that we will not find hard to identify in any society, and in thinking about them to look beyond them to the outworking of wisdom and folly. Perhaps we are intended to see wisdom and folly in personification here, as in chapter 9.

In God's design woman was created to be a helper to man (Genesis 2:18). In general in that society women were dependent upon men for their security and the wherewithal to live. The men were the 'bread-winners', the women the 'bread-makers'. It was the responsibility of the man to provide for the family in the sense that he went out into the field to farm, or followed whatever his employment was, and brought home the fruit of his labours for the benefit of his family. The women used what was given them for domestic management. With the home and family as the woman's principal sphere of operation, her influence there would be felt for good or evil in the way she provided for her household and trained up her children.

The same principles apply today, though the precise way they are worked out may vary from one culture to another.

If at one level we can think of this proverb as provoking women to consider how they are using what has been entrusted to them and how it reflects upon them, and although we may be able to recognise examples around us of wise and foolish women in the area of how they manage their homes, more particularly we are to be led to consider our own behaviour.

We are dependent upon God for our security and for all is required to live. He graciously provides all that we have need of, and it is our responsibility to use it well. What he gives is not for our selfish use but is entrusted to us in stewardship, for the benefit of others as well as ourselves, and in his honour.

We can look at this from two angles. One is to recognise that we need wisdom to be 'building' in a worthwhile fashion (see also 1 Corinthians 3:9-15). Solomon was given the kingdom and the wealth that went with it, but he humbly asked God for wisdom to manage the responsibilities entrusted to him (1 Kings 3:5-10). Likewise, we need wisdom from God to manage what he has entrusted to us. Do we view our resources in this way, acknowledging that we need his help and guidance in how to use them? By resources we mean not only material things, but also our gifts and abilities and even the circumstances of our lives.

But the other angle is to look at the effects our lives are having. What are we leaving in our wake? Is there debris where we have been? Have we left a mess behind us? In our marriage? With our children? In our church life? In our place of work or in our social sphere? People often complain about others when things go wrong in their lives and their relationships, but more often than not a large part of the problem is traceable to their own folly. The only real way to 'build' is upon the foundation which has been laid, upon Christ himself and upon his Word. By neglecting this the Corinthian church were falling apart and were in all kinds of trouble. That, too, is the trouble of so many who make a profession of faith but are not really serious about living accordingly.

God has put something very precious in your hands. Thank him for it, and wait upon him to help you use it for good.

[Related proverbs: 9:1; 24:3; 31:10-31.]

14:2. We give ourselves away. The order in each of the clauses is striking. The reverse order would appear to be the natural and logical one: 'He who fears the LORD walks in his uprightness, but he who despises him is perverse in his ways.' Yet it is not written like this. Why not? Aren't there some who walk in their uprightness who do not fear the Lord? Apparently not, and certainly not from God's viewpoint.

The expression, 'walking in uprightness' denotes a continued, ongoing, settled practice rather than sporadic activity. It is quite impossible to live an upright life without the fear of God, without holy reverence for him. There are some who may give an appearance of uprightness and yet in God's eyes they are crooked. There is something about the uprightness of a God-fearing man or woman which is unique and which bears the hallmark of divine grace. Only God can give true uprightness of heart and conduct, and so when it is seen it is an evidence of the fear of God which such a one possesses.

On the other hand, the person who is perverse in his ways is certainly a despiser of the Lord. He may not imagine himself to be so, he may not consciously be so, but nevertheless his behaviour demonstrates that he despises the Lord, for if it were otherwise he would not behave as he does. Whatever people say, and whatever they claim about being upright or God-fearing, if they are consistently disregarding his laws, then, whatever excuse they proffer, they are really despising him, whether or not they realise it.

It is as Jesus said: a tree is known by its fruit (Luke 6:44). A leopard is recognised by its spots. Our lives give us away. We cannot be what we are not. Those who are perverse in their ways might be able to create a fairly convincing impression for others, but it is no more than an illusion of piety. This is arguably the worst sort of perverseness, for it is devious and deceptive. In 2 Timothy 3:5 Paul wrote about those who have a form of godliness, a description which does not seem to sit well with what else he says of such people there. It is but a thin veneer covering what they really are.

People can tell about the state of our relationship with God by the way we conduct ourselves. We are more transparent than we might wish at times to be! If others can often see through us, how much more can God! Is there an uprightness we are trying to display, or a perverseness we are trying to hide? Let us not fool ourselves and make fools of ourselves!

It may be this addresses someone who has been walking uprightly but who has had a bad fall. There is a difference between falling, getting covered in mud, getting up again and going on, and falling and wallowing in the mire! To fear the Lord is to trust him, to hold on to him, to depend upon him for support and strength. How much more should we recognise this when we have let go our hold and suffered the consequences! The fact that we get up again with contrition and repentance and go on with renewed humble dependence upon him is in itself a testimony to the fear of God.

14:3. What is in your mouth? This is another of many proverbs about speech. The difference between a culvert and a sluice is that the latter has a gate to control the flow. It may be there is an element of this distinction in the comparison between 'mouth' and 'lips'. A fool lacks self control. What is in him comes out without regard to the consequences either for himself or for others. A wise person gives out or holds back as occasion requires.

So although 'mouth' is paralleled with 'lips' there may be significance in context in the choice of these words, insofar as the lips are like the door of the mouth and may be pictured as exercising restraint and control over what emanates from it (see Psalm 141:3), whereas foolishness pours forth uninhibited from the mouth of a fool (15:2). However, whether or not such a comparison is warranted, it remains true that the utterances of a fool, which are often uncontrolled and extravagant, are evidence of a heart which is too full of its own self-importance.

The translation in the NIV and ESV ('a rod for his back') is questionable, and although it makes a fitting comparison and is undoubtedly true, it does involve changing a word in the original. Where the phrase 'a rod to his back' does occur (10:13 and 26:3), two entirely different words are used from those here. Here the reference is to a 'rod of pride', and the word for 'rod' is that used in Isaiah 11:1 to describe a new shoot growing out of the stump of a tree which has been cut down rather than a punitive rod.

The shoot is like the stock: proud words come from a proud heart, for the mouth speaks from the heart (Matthew 12:34). When you open your mouth, others can see your tongue. When a fool such as the one described here opens his mouth, others can see there a rod of pride with all its potential for harm. The mouth of a fool gives him away. The pride of a fool is the root of all the words he pours forth, and his pride will be his downfall (16:18; 29:23). In the meantime, though, it ought to be observed that the outworking of his pride can cause others a lot of pain. Isn't it true that when we allow pride or conceit or arrogance to dominate our thinking, what we say and do is far from helpful to others? This is at least in part because we are thinking primarily of ourselves, and our talk is aimed more at self-gratification than the other's good. It is indeed a fool who is so taken up with himself as to be unaware of this.

A wise person, on the other hand, knows not only when to speak and when to keep quiet, but also knows *how* to speak. A slogan in World War Two was 'Careless talk costs lives.' There it was the lives of others. Here it is the lives of the talkers. It may not be 'lives' in quite the same sense, but in both the social and the spiritual sense it is true that their self-control in what the wise say provides protection for them. The proverb says their lips will preserve them. The 'them' probably refers to themselves, and self-control and thoughtfulness in what we say will certainly protect us from harm as we keep ourselves from saying things which will rebound adversely upon us. But surely wisdom extends beyond this notion of self-preservation, and we ought to be thinking of how, by what we say and how we say it, we may afford help and protection to others in a world where the damage caused by pride is only too evident?

Pride is subtle and insidious. When you engage in conversation, how much of what you say is about yourself – your interests, your activities, your achievements, your experiences, your problems, and so on? What will others take away with them from what you have said to them? How will it *benefit* them? How will it reflect upon you?

[Related proverbs: 10:32; 12:6; 13:3; 16:23; 21:23.]

14:4. What is in your barn? Picture a barn for animals. The trough, or manger, is empty, the stalls are deserted, and the whole has the appearance of having fallen into disuse. For the eastern farmer this picture would have had a tragic aspect, representing the serious situation of his means of livelihood no longer being there. His ox, or oxen if he was sufficiently well-off, were essential for his being able to work his land, to grow his produce and feed his family, and to prosper.

What does this have to say to us? Many people's lives are preoccupied with 'toys', and they sacrifice the things by which they will really prosper in order to gain the things which will give them temporary pleasure and then leave them empty and destitute – even sterile. The picture is not only that of the down-and-out eastern farmer, but also of the down-and-out materialist who has everything except what really matters. Surely we need to value what is important in life, to treasure and use what will build us up and not to squander our resources on what will ultimately bring us to destitution.

If the ox was the primary means by which a farmer could prosper, surely to invest in such an animal would have been of paramount importance, however difficult or costly in the short term. As with all the proverbs, we are to take a holistic view of what is being said, and this one applies not only to our material well-being but also to our spiritual. It extends from our personal lives to our church life where we need to invest in and value the God-ordained means for true prosperity and growth.

If we wish to enjoy a harvest at all it stands to reason that we must harness and work with the ox. There is the opportunity of an abundant harvest, if only we would invest in and use the means.

Give some serious thought to how this works out in your own personal and church life.

[Related proverb: 13:23.]

14:5. Faithful or false? This statement is so obviously true – is there any point in making it? How easy it is to overlook the obvious! How easy it is to *assume* the obvious without a second thought!

Stark and straightforward, note that this allows for no in-between category. A witness is either faithful or false. Here is someone giving testimony (not necessarily in a court of law, but in any situation), relaying what has been seen or heard, passing on received information, conversationally or formally, by spoken or by written word – reinforced by intonation and gesture and style.

So much of our communications with others can be classified under the heading of 'witness'. How challenging this is to us when we consider how easy it is to be economical with the truth, or to distort, or to exaggerate, or so to colour what we say as to give an impression other than that required by the strictest honesty. How easy, too, to forget matters of importance in our communications, or inadvertently to give the wrong impression through inability or carelessness.

No doubt the proverb here indicates intent on the part of a false witness to deceive, but it should prompt us to reflect upon how easy it is, even with the best of intentions (which often we do not have), to misinform or mislead. In short, the conclusion is that a faithful witness is hard to find!

Note that this proverb does not say, 'A faithful witness does not lie, but a false witness does not tell the truth.' The testimony of a false witness is discredited not because he tells the truth ninety-nine percent of the time, but because he lies the remaining one per cent. It is that which distinguishes him from a faithful witness.

With these things in mind, consider Jesus Christ, described as 'the faithful witness' (Revelation 1:5), and 'the faithful and true witness' (Revelation 3:14). His witness is faithful not only because he cannot and does not lie (Titus 1:2), but also because he is omniscient. He knows all things and observes all things; nothing is hidden from his knowledge or understanding, but all things are open and laid bare before him (Hebrews 4:13). On the one hand this truth is frightening for those who have something to conceal; on the other it is a great comfort and source of hope to those who have entrusted themselves to him by faith, knowing that all that he has said is utterly true, both in fact and in the manner in which it has been communicated, and may unreservedly be relied upon.

[Related proverbs: 6:16,19; 12:17; 14:25.]

14:6. 'Money can't buy you love.' There are certain things which are inaccessible to certain people, however much they might want them. Simon the sorcerer wanted to be able to communicate the gift of the Holy Spirit and thought to purchase the privilege with money (Acts 8:18-19). Wisdom and scoffing are totally incompatible. It is interesting, though, that the ungodly should sometimes see such things as sufficiently valuable as to desire them for themselves. Wisdom is attractive, because it comes from God – which is where the scoffer comes adrift through failing to make the connection.

As an aside, Christians often do not realise the impact their lives make on unbelievers. Paul wrote to slaves about their adorning the doctrine of God our Saviour in all things (Titus 2:10), indicating that even they, at the lowest end of the social scale, were able to display in their lives the beauty of the truth and make it attractive. Unbelievers often envy what the Christian has, but they cannot have it while they refuse the Giver.

To the one who understands that wisdom comes from God, there is no problem. If anyone lacks wisdom, let him ask of God, says James (1:5), which is the very thing the scoffer is not prepared to do.

Wisdom and knowledge are used synonymously in this verse. If you are looking for something, it helps to know where to look in order to find it. That highlights one of the problems when something is lost. The task is almost impossible if you have absolutely no idea where you lost it. By comparison it is easy if its location can be narrowed down to one or two small areas. It seems we are to understand 'easy' in this sense. The problem, instead of being insurmountable, is trifling. The proverb makes the point by highlighting opposite ends of the scale. That is not to say that wisdom is necessarily easily come by or that it requires no effort. There is a tremendous encouragement here, though, to all who fear the Lord. The fear of the Lord is the beginning of wisdom, and, having begun, God-given wisdom becomes accessible. Compare 8:9 in context. This is not a matter of erudition or academic or any other kind of ability, but that which comes through increasing acquaintance with the Lord through his Word and by his Spirit.

Colossians 2:3 says that in Christ are hidden all the treasures of wisdom and knowledge. However, as Paul makes clear in the earlier part of that letter, Christ's wisdom and knowledge are accessible to us through our relationship with him. What an amazing privilege it is to be in the position of knowing and understanding eternal truth, and hence seeing this life in its true light, because we who believe know the Lord of the universe and have had the eyes of our understanding enlightened (Ephesians 1:18)! This is something completely beyond the sharpest minds of unbelievers, too difficult for the most profound philosophers, and yet it is easy for the child of God. The fear of the Lord is the beginning of knowledge (1:7), and what knowledge this is! Value it, treasure it, use it!

[Related proverbs: 8:8-9; 18:15; 24:7; 28:5.]

14:7. Keeping your distance. There are certain people from whom we will derive no good. The foolish man is not necessarily one who is lacking in intellectual ability; the term rather has a moral and spiritual dimension, referring to one who has no time for God. To associate with such people is at best a waste of time, and at worst a source of harm. Sometimes such people can be easy company with engaging personalities and a sense of fun. Perhaps one of the areas in which God-fearing people particularly need to be careful is entertainment personalities on the television or other media. It is easy to become hooked into these and to imbibe their attitudes and ideas. But their influence is often subversive, which at the end leaves one empty, polluted and depressed. Sometimes it is physically difficult to go from the presence of a foolish man, but in a case like this the difficulty, if there is one, is ours alone, having insufficient motivation to press the 'off' button!

This proverb encourages discrimination of the best sort. We are not to prejudge people, but we are to assess them by the standard of God's Word, and then if we find they fall into this category of 'foolish' we are to walk away from the possibility of their compromising influence. Even if this is impossible physically, yet in terms of our attitudes and reactions we should make it clear that we are not 'with them' in that sense.

You have heard it said, half in jest, 'She's not with me,' (when 'she' has done something particularly embarrassing in company) as a way of distancing oneself from that disturbing individual! At times when it is not possible to avoid being in the presence of foolish people, we should, all the same, go from their presence in the sense of not wishing to be associated with them. Perhaps John 17:15-19 and 1 Corinthians 5:9-13 help us to a balanced view in this respect. If we are Christians we are not *of* the world, and therefore must not be identified *with* the world. But we are *in* the world, and have to rub shoulders with all kinds of people. There is, however, a difference between rubbing shoulders with people and putting your arms around them!

Give some thought to whether, or how, you are applying these principles in your relationships with other people.

[Related proverb: 13:20.]

14:8. The deceitfulness of sin. Two classes are compared: the prudent and the foolish, and this proverb points to characteristics which distinguish each: discernment and deception. What marks the wisdom of the one is that he is careful to follow a clear, intelligent, thought-out, straightforward and honest course in life. He not only knows what he is about but he knows where he is going and can give an account of himself. His way of life has no murky corners to be concealed from view at all costs. In the case of the fool, however, the very opposite applies, where things are not as they seem but have a fraudulent quality to them. Deceit means there are things which are being covered up or being presented in a misleading way. The deceit, or deception, involved is therefore that he endeavours to give an outward impression for which there is no corresponding inward reality. It may well be that he is deceiving himself as well as others.

The fool is the one who does not seek God but excludes him from his life (see Psalm 53:1-3). The man who leaves God, the ultimate reality, out of his life, by definition must be living a less than real existence. The folly of fools is their unwillingness to 'come clean'. They have too much to hide, for that is one of the effects of sin.

The believer should rejoice in the knowledge that sins forgiven and dealt with is wonderfully liberating, with no longer anything guiltily to conceal and with a clear way forward. The proverb is a reminder, though, to take stock of our course through life, to ensure we are not being deceived or sidetracked or confused or beset by useless clutter. Life can be full of distractions and people can lose sight of their way. How many people have found themselves on the wrong road and then asked the question, 'How did I get here?' The reason was inattentiveness. The signs were there but were not noticed. 'Understanding' our way in life, or 'giving thought' to it, or 'discerning' it, is not an occasional thing but a regular, ongoing one. It is like a map which we keep in our hands and consult at every turn to ensure we are still on the right way.

If you are a Christian, do you know where you are at right now in your 'pilgrimage'? Can you give a clear account of what you are doing and why you are doing it and what bearing it has upon your path through life and your eternal destiny?

14:9. Grace unmerited. The word in the first clause usually refers to the sin offering specified in the law. It was an offering made in acknowledgement of sin, recognising guilt, and to make atonement (for example, Leviticus 5:5-13). Prophesying of Jesus, Isaiah says, using the same word, that *his* soul was made an offering for sin (Isaiah 53:10). He is the antitype of which the sin offering was the type. Those who made light of the offering were therefore making a mockery of Christ's saving work upon the cross. By contrast, the 'upright' are those who take the sin offering seriously, and it is they who receive favour – from God.

The proverb by its construction links favour, or acceptance, with the guilt-offering. The link with the upright is secondary. It is not merited, or deserved, by the upright on account of their uprightness. The favour they enjoy is grounded solely in their recognition of the guilt-offering. We have earned no favour from God on account of anything we have done. Our acceptance before him, and the consequent pleasure he takes in us, is purely on account of the Lord Jesus taking our sins upon himself. Paul confirms this when he writes (Ephesians 1:6) that we are 'accepted in the Beloved' – 'accepted' there denoting God's wonderful favour toward us – and we read there that it is all of his doing and it is all down to his grace toward us based upon redemption through Christ's blood and the forgiveness of our sins.

This verse highlights an attitude to be found in fools, or perhaps an attitude which marks people out as fools, which is to hold a contemptible view of guilt, whether guilt toward God, or guilt in respect of their relationship with their fellows. Guilt involves accountability, and they (so they say) will be held accountable to no one. Sin is no big deal, they say: God does not see, meaning either that there is no God to see, or that, if there is a God, what they are doing cannot possibly have any consequences for them. To them, the very notion of having to answer to God is ridiculous. Nothing will happen to them. This attitude is consistent with what was observed in v. 8 about their deceit. Such being their attitude, they see no need to make amends.

In Ezekiel 8:12 and 9:9, the prophet was given a vision of people who were making a mockery of guilt and accountability. The Lord, for them, was nowhere to be seen, and so they continued in their abominable practices unaware of the imminence of the judgement from the Lord whose interest they denied. It was an object lesson that to make light of guilt is about the worst thing anyone can do. It is folly in the extreme. We must all appear before the judgement seat of Christ (2 Corinthians 5:10), who gave his life for sin and to bear guilt. How then will it be for those who mock at these things?

Favour, or goodwill, or acceptance with pleasure, is not to be found with such people, but it is found among the upright. The phrase '*among* the upright' indicates something held in common, a common bond. It echoes the declaration of the angels to the shepherds of the 'goodwill toward men' (Luke 2:14) which comes from God through his Son Jesus Christ and which results in goodwill in the horizontal relationship among its recipients. How unlike what is found among the ungodly, where so often there are suspicion, mistrust, envy, and every other evil! They can never begin to know what is experienced among the children of God. They can see the evidence of it, but they cannot understand it. This is goodwill to be prized, guarded and expressed!

Are you mindful of the sheer undeserved favour you and your fellow believers have received from God? Does your thankfulness for it express itself practically in your relationships with other Christians? How?

[Related proverb: 10:23.]

14:10. Glumness and gladness. Here are two emotions at the opposite ends of the spectrum: at one end bitterness of heart, and exuberant joy at the other. Though they are experiences common to all mankind, yet in each there is often, paradoxically, a sense of isolation. This proverb brings out that in the case of bitterness, it is the one suffering who is isolated, whereas in the case of joy it is the 'outsider' who is isolated.

These emotions are very personal, and very deep, to those experiencing them. People can be sorry for the one, or happy for the other, but that is as close as they can get. They cannot actually partake of either.

How does this address us? It is important that we should be sensitive toward those in the depths and not have unrealistic expectations of them or make judgements about them based on a partial understanding of their condition. Although bitterness of heart is experienced by most people at some time or another, yet when it is experienced the sufferer is very much shut in with a trouble which cannot lightly be dismissed. The failure of others to recognise this can be very hurtful. It might be well meaning to say, 'I know exactly how you are feeling,' but perhaps this proverb is reminding us that we do *not* know exactly how the sufferer is feeling, and our sympathy is better expressed in other ways.

Even if we have been through the same bitter experience as another so that there is a measure of empathy, there are often differences in circumstances and we need to be cautious in our expectation of how that person will respond. A quiet, understanding presence is more likely than words to touch the heart of the sufferer and open the way to providing real support. The nearest we can come is to 'weep with those who weep' (Romans 12:15), showing a genuine fellow-feeling for their trouble, showing we are with them. I recall one occasion when on receiving early news of the death in sad circumstances of the wife of a member of the church I went to visit him. When he opened the door to me I was suddenly so overcome with a sense of his grief that I burst into tears. I was so embarrassed, and yet he afterwards said this helped him more than any words could have done at that moment. Job's three friends were at their best when they wept and sat in silence with him (Job 2:11-13). They did not understand what Job was going through and they would have done well to continue to hold their tongues.

At the other extreme, for the one experiencing the heights of joy it is wise to be conscious that others will neither appreciate nor be helped by excess expressions of elation or the expectation that they should be feeling the same way. They won't. Insensitive exuberance is liable to arouse resentment and possibly even jealousy. Joy is best expressed in generosity, for others can definitely share in that. There is certainly something of a party atmosphere in Luke 15:6,9.

[Related proverb: 25:20.]

14:11. Psalm 72. Strength in weakness. A very deliberate contrast is here between 'house' and 'tent'. A house, considered materially, is a permanent structure; considered socially, it is a stable unit. The tent is a fragile, temporary structure, the habitation for a few only. So we think of a house as being strong, fixed and enduring, while a tent is flimsy, movable and vulnerable.

So what this proverb is describing is something which is contrary to natural reasoning: it is not what we would expect. So often the wicked seem to have it all their own way, and give the impression of being unstoppable in their expansive schemes. They are the secure ones, while those who are 'upright' look like being blown over and swept away. Yet, viewed in the longer term and seen in retrospect, it is evident that the wicked are the ones who come to ruin, while those who are upright in heart continue 'against the odds' and indeed flourish.

God's laws cannot be thwarted or suspended, any more than can the law of gravity. Whether or not his hand is actually seen in events, he is very much in control of them. His word and his promises prevail to uphold and strengthen and bless those who trust in him, and his same word and his same promises of judgement prevail to weaken and bring down those who oppose him. So this proverb gently reminds us not to judge by appearances.

A great cedar may be felled by a mighty storm, while a tender sapling survives it and lives on to flourish. Are we surprised? Not really, when we understand the laws of physics. Then should we be surprised that the true church, small and weak and vulnerable as it always has been, should continue to stand, upheld by the laws of him who said, ' "Not by might nor by power, but by my Spirit," says the LORD of hosts' (Zechariah 4:6) – and not only continue to stand, but to prosper? Has not God demonstrated a hundred times if he has done so once, that his strength is made perfect in weakness (2 Corinthians 12:9)? – that his armour is sufficient to enable the weakest to stand against the entire arsenal of the devil (Ephesians 6:11-12)? Jesus said, 'Do not fear, little flock, for it is your Father's good pleasure to give you the kingdom' (Luke 12:32). The weakest saint in the hand of God will flourish, while that same hand will bring to ruin the most powerful enemy of truth. See Psalm 37:34-38.

The 'house' and 'tent' are suggestive of another comparison, the house being a permanent structure and the tent a movable one. For those who have no knowledge or fear of God, this life is all there is and they are building here, whereas the godly are only passing through – they are 'pilgrims through this barren land' – looking forward to a more permanent dwelling in heaven. What is designed and built by man is imperfect and will not last; what God has prepared for those who love him is perfect and will endure for ever. See Hebrews 11:9-10,13-16.

[Related proverbs: 3:33; 11:28; 12:7; 15:25.]

14:12. Which way? This identical proverb appears at 16:25. It is one of a number of such duplications. Perhaps it indicates that context has some significance even in what appears to be a largely random collection of proverbs. Alternatively, perhaps the repetition is there simply because we need to be reminded of this truth!

Have you ever been out walking or driving and come to a confusing point of unexpected alternatives? 'I'm sure this is the right way,' you have said ... but some time later you have come to rue your choice! It looked right, but was in fact wrong! Your good sense misled you!

The first and most obvious observation to make from this proverb is, how wrong people can be if the way they consider to be right in life has such an end! God has said he will destroy the wisdom of the wise (that is, those who exalt their own wisdom above that of God – 1 Corinthians 1:19, quoting Isaiah 29:14). The message of the cross is central to the wisdom of God, and those who disregard it are by default signing their own death warrant. Proverbs 9:2 speaks of those who despise the Lord, and 14:9 of those who mock at sin. They think they know better (14:6), that their way is right. They are characterised by pride (14:3) and deceit (14:8). What is portrayed here is an attitude of godless self-sufficiency, of confidence in the rightness of their own ways, a man-made morality which is so very far removed from the standards God has set that its inevitable end under his hand will be death, for God will set a terminus point upon it.

A judicial blindness lies upon those who deliberately exclude God from their thinking, so that what they then believe to be right is completely wrong. As the fear of the Lord is the beginning of wisdom, so also does it teach us that we are sinful and in need of his grace and favour. This verse, depicting the way and end of the foolish, contrasts dramatically with the way of the wise, building (14:1) with integrity (14:2,5) and understanding (14:8), enjoying favour (14:9) and flourishing (14:11).

How important to learn to read and use the map!

[Related proverbs: 12:15; 16:25.]

14:13. Happy feet and a heavy heart. Behind their public image of laughter, jollity and fun it is well known that many comedians have lived acutely unhappy lives. This, coupled with the previous two proverbs, contrasts how things seem with how they really are. In v. 11 the house of the wicked seems strong and unshakable, and yet it will be overthrown; in v. 12 there is a way which seems right but that will end in death; and here everything seems to be happy whereas the reality is entirely otherwise and will end in grief.

Maybe this is an observation on the lives of so many people. Verse 10 says the heart knows its own bitterness, but often that is not noticed by others before whom a cheerful façade is presented. It is acting a part – an unreal part – because the truth is too painful to share and will not be understood. But this is what people do. Any way and every way, they conceal their real selves, with all their doubts and fears, with all their self-consciousness of weakness and mortality, with their craving for acceptance. They may be the life and soul of the party, but they are really lonely and lost. Their compensation for their fundamental insecurity leads only to a heightening of their sense of despair. They are 'having a good time', but underneath their heart aches. The 'morning after' effects which follow a party are but symptoms of this deeper malaise. The further people go from God the more widespread this problem becomes.

Heartache afflicts so many people because they know that grief inevitably lies before them. Having no effective means to face it, they try to bury it fathoms deep with things that give pleasure or satisfaction in the present. Look at the entertainment industry, how utterly trivial so much of it is, and yet like a giant magnet it draws its worshippers by the millions. It is 'the end' which people cannot and therefore will not face. Go into any social gathering and listen to the laughter and mirth. All seems well. But so often it isn't. There are deep undercurrents of a more sinister nature ... because there is nothing beyond 'the end' of grief for them.

Paul wrote to the church at Corinth concerning those who denied the resurrection of the dead, 'If the dead do not rise, "Let us eat and drink, for tomorrow we die!"' (1 Corinthians 15:32). In other words, let self-indulgence be a barrier to shut out the inevitable from the consciousness. Paul was quoting Isaiah 22:13, where God was calling people to face up to the surely coming judgement and turn to him in repentance, but all they did was brazenly to smother the warning with feasting and fun.

But the dead do rise! Jesus is the resurrection and the life. Those who trust in him may unashamedly laugh and may rejoice because he has suffered the bitterness of death for them. He has borne their griefs and carried their sorrows (Isaiah 53:4). The end for them is not grief, but rather fullness of joy and eternal pleasures at God's right hand (Psalm 16:11).

Are your laughter and mirth the real thing, or are you hiding things either that you do not wish people to see now, or that you are unprepared to face later? Look again to eternal realities, and consider what God has prepared for those who love him (1 Corinthians 2:9).

Christians should have a sensitivity toward the laughter of others and be aware that though it may often be simply a genuine expression of fun and enjoyment, sometimes it is desperately trying to conceal sinister undercurrents. We must not judge by appearances.

Furthermore, we need to recognise that causes for joy and celebration in this life can so easily turn to grief through unexpected events. For one example see Judges 11:34-35.

14:14. Have it your way, and see where it gets you. Expressed with the strictest economy of words in the original, this proverb is saying that the backslider in heart will be filled, or satisfied, with his ways, and that exactly the same is true of the good man. The 'payment' or 'reward' (NIV) is self generated rather than coming from an external source. In other words, it is about what we bring upon ourselves.

In the first clause we are looking at someone whose heart has turned back, and the implication is that this person has turned back to his own way from following the Lord. Those who spurn wisdom eat the fruit of their own way (1:31), but the case before us is much sadder. The classic Old Testament example is surely the tragic one of Saul who turned back from following the Lord (1 Samuel 15:11), and by whose pathological hatred of David only destroyed himself. Before that, back in Moses' time, after their amazing experience of the Lord's deliverance, the Israelites were at one point all for appointing a leader to take them back to Egypt (Numbers 14), so short-sighted were they and so distorted their view. Their faithlessness was repaid by their falling in the desert, never to enjoy what God had in store for those who trusted him.

Hebrews 6:4-8 seems to address a similar situation, showing just how far people can go in experiencing the power and grace of God only to fall away when, presumably, the going gets tough, and then to suffer the consequences.

In each case, instead of continuing in dependence upon God, these people rejected reliance upon him in favour of self-dependence. They were content only so long as God's ways suited them. Basically, they were unhappy about following God's commands and felt more secure in doing things their way even though this conflicted with what God required of them.

Many a Christian has backslidden at times, experienced the pain of it and come back again to the Lord in repentance, finding comfort once more in him. This proverb is not describing such people, but those who are backsliders *in heart*. Their hearts are hard, and even though they have witnessed the power of God and his works, they have not known his ways. See Psalm 95:7b-11, taken up with a warning in Hebrews 3:7-15. Shutting out God and relying upon themselves, it stands to reason that the fruit they produce in their lives will be of their own making – and it will be bitter.

The good man, following the logic of the proverb, is the man of faith, trusting God. He will be satisfied with the fruit of his ways, but the root or source of his fruitfulness is in God. The fruit he produces is not the fruit of the flesh, but the fruit of the Spirit. So, for example, we see the pleasure Barnabas derived from what he found at Antioch, and the fruitfulness of his life and the explanation for it (Acts 11:22-24).

Surely this proverb invites us to consider just what satisfaction we get from our way of life, as well as what motivates it? Suppose our own way of life is applied to us, that we 'get as good as we give' – how will this affect us? We need to be particular and specific about this. We bring upon ourselves the consequences of our actions, whether they are the 'natural' ones which operate throughout God's created order, or the 'judicial' ones as he declares his verdict. If we confess Jesus before men, he also will confess us before his Father in heaven, but if we deny him, he too will deny us (Matthew 10:32-33).

The laws or principles God has set in place in his creation carry with them their own rewards. God has created all things, whether physical, or moral, or spiritual, to operate according to the good laws he has built into them, abuse of which can only be harmful. So those who do abuse them, *per se* bring trouble upon themselves (and very often upon others); while those who honour them enjoy the benefits they are intended by God to confer. Yet God does not stand outside of his creation as a mere observer of what he has set into motion; he is active in his creation, for in his creation he intends that men should enjoy his presence and have fellowship with him. So a good man will find full satisfaction, enjoying the blessings of the provision as well as the blessings of the Provider.

[Related proverb: 12:14.]

14:15. **Something worth thinking about.** Some people are prepared to believe anything. By the 'simple' is meant the person who is naïve enough to take on board what he hears without question. This is not referring to one whose mental faculties are limited, but to one whose use of them is.

Many people believe what they want to believe. It suits them to believe it. They do not want to question their beliefs. They are content in their own comfort zone, and that is what matters to them. Others believe what the majority believe, again without question, using the argument that if most people believe it, it must be true, or right, or acceptable. They are letting other people do their thinking for them when they ought to be doing it for themselves. Yet others believe something on the strength of who said it: 'I heard it from so-and-so, so it must be true.' In every case they are making assumptions where they ought to be using their minds. It is mental laziness which is particularly dangerous because it affects the conduct of one's life. They cannot be bothered to question their ways (or maybe they are afraid to do so) and so they carry on as they are, regardless. This is actually a very serious problem, because it is virtually impossible to argue with one whose mind is closed.

The contrast here is with the prudent person, the one who is careful and discriminating and who gives serious thought to his *steps*. Note carefully this contrast between 'believing every word' and 'considering one's steps'. Things are not always what they seem. If you have ever had occasion to pick your way across a river you will know that a stone may not be stable and may move under your foot, or a boulder may be unexpectedly slippery, or unless you are careful you may make your way to a point from which you cannot continue. Every step has to be considered in order to get across without mishap. If we believe the next step to be safe, we will take it.

Christians should be thinking people, understanding that what they *believe* affects what they *do*, not just in the general sense, but also when it comes down to particulars. Christians should be being thoughtful and careful about the details of their lives, making the connection that what they believe impinges upon their conduct. This being the case, how important it is to believe the right things, for if our belief is wrong, our behaviour will be wrong!

This proverb raises some serious questions. For example, why do you believe what you believe? On what is your belief founded? By 'belief' could be understood anything ranging from your perception of something someone has told you about someone else, to what you believe about your standing before God. It is better to say, 'I just don't know what to believe,' with a desire for a better understanding, than to say, 'My mind is made up,' as a way of avoiding things which you fear may rock the boat of your security.

The Christian has nothing to fear by way of asking questions and wanting satisfactory answers. Truth can stand up to any and every falsehood. Probably one of the most serious errors people have unthinkingly taken on board is the teaching of evolution, the popularity of which is based not on truth or evidence or rational argument but on the fact that it is a convenient excuse to discount God – and the simple believe every word of it!

When someone says, 'Watch your step!', they are warning the person concerned that to follow their present course of behaviour is going to lead to trouble and something needs to be done about it. Steps lead somewhere, both physically and metaphorically. When hearing something of significance, it is prudent to consider where it will lead if heeded.

Concerning the steps of the prudent, consider the testimony of David: Psalms 17:5; 18:36; 37:23-24,31.

There is only one thing we may legitimately believe, and that is the truth. Concerning believing the truth and believing otherwise, follow Paul's argument in 2 Thessalonians 2.

14:16. There's nothing to be afraid of ... or is there? This

could be considered as an outworking of the previous proverb. The prudent person is wise, and his thoughtful attitude to his way of life leads him to fear. The NIV says, 'fears the LORD', and while this may be true, the original appears to make no reference to the Lord at this point. What, then, is this fear?

Surely there is a right fear of saying or doing what is wrong, and of the consequences accruing to it? For example, if you have to approach someone to discuss a delicate issue, you may rightly fear the possibility of mismanaging it, of saying the wrong thing and making matters worse. You may first need to consider your motives very carefully and think about how you are going to go about it. Or you may have to make an important decision about something, and you are afraid of making the wrong choice. Why does the element of fear enter into it? Is it not because you are conscious of a lack of confidence in yourself or your own ability?

Such fear is a good motivator, for it helps you to depart from evil, which needs to be understood more widely than just in a moral sense. If you are aware of potential dangers you will do your best to avoid them. Furthermore, because of a healthy mistrust of self, you will be the more inclined to look to the Lord for wisdom, help or guidance.

The fool by contrast crosses the line of prudence. This is the sort of person who climbs the stile onto the footpath across a firing range when the red flag is flying, confidently asserting, 'I can't hear any gunfire!' He trusts to his own judgement, making light of any warning signs that he might be wrong. Or he is sure of his ability to handle a situation and doesn't need anyone telling him what to do or how to do it. Often, when such a person is cautioned or challenged he reacts with angry self-righteousness. It is his defence mechanism by which he avoids facing up to the truth which would take him out of the comfort zone of his supposed self-sufficiency. It is a common trait among some of the more outspoken opponents of Christ.

Do you have this healthy sense of fear making you thoughtful and careful lest you bring harm upon yourself or others? Can you think of particular cases in your own experience where this fear has been in evidence and how it has worked out? On the other hand, can you think of examples where your over-confidence has led to trouble, and, if so, what valuable lessons you have been able to learn from it?

What David said in Psalm 56:3-4 in a dire situation is something we need to apply in *every* situation.

[Related proverbs: 3:7; 22:3; 27:12.]

14:17. Hot-headed or cold-blooded. A quick-tempered man is one who allows his feelings to stifle his thinking and cloud his judgement. He reacts because of the uncomfortable way things affect him, and in this sense he is like the person in the last proverb. His response is either unthinking, or very shallow in its thinking. In the extreme case it is all about his own perception of things and his exclusive right to it. He is right, they are wrong, and how dare anyone challenge him! Or, if he observes what he considers to be a fault in someone else, he reacts with self-righteous indignation. (Road rage would be an example of this kind of thing.)

Some may find this statement embarrassingly blunt! But note it does not say that a quick-tempered man *is* foolish, only that he *acts* foolishly. The reactions of the quick-tempered are foolish for two basic reasons: they are self-centred and they are intellectually unbalanced. There are probably few people at whom this proverb does not point the finger at some time or another! However, some people by disposition have a 'short fuse' and tend to explode prematurely, and, as with all such character defects, this problem needs attention.

When king David reacted in this way on one occasion, the Lord exploited it for his good (2 Samuel 12). Has he ever used your quick-tempered reactions to teach you valuable lessons? Have you remembered them?

If you are given to being quick-tempered, consider James 1:19-20 and how you might put this command into practice more effectively.

Most of the proverbs in this section comprise a contrast between the two clauses, linked in translation with the word 'but'. Although translated 'and' in this case, nevertheless a contrast is being made between two types.

The quick-tempered can be difficult to live with, and it may be easier to avoid them at times, but we must not misjudge them. In most cases it is just so much 'hot air' and nothing more, and we need to understand that. The storm blows over as quickly as it has begun, and the damage, though real, is rarely serious. However, there is an altogether different kind of person (and this is where the 'but' comes in): a man of wicked intentions – a schemer – who is far more formidable. This is the one who calmly plots to get his own way, for example meticulously planning retribution so as to inflict the maximum damage possible by way of revenge.

What we have represented here are two opposite ends of the scale in which a person might react to what is perceived to be an offence. If a quick-tempered man is one who allows his feelings to *stifle* his thinking and *cloud* his judgement, a person with wicked intentions allows his feelings to *direct* his thinking and *overrule* his judgement. It is still essentially self-centred. A person with sinister intentions attracts hatred.

For those of a proud, brooding disposition, beware! Those who have a tendency to be coldly calculating by way of response to personal injury, or to getting their own way, should consider the commands of Romans 12:17-21 and coldly calculate how they might put *them* into practice instead!

[Related proverb: 14:29.]

14:18. You've got it coming to you. This is the second of three proverbs which contrast the simple and the prudent. The other two are 14:15 and 22:3 (27:12 is the same as 22:3). All three indicate that one of the problems of 'the simple' is that they fail to think, or at least they fail to think about the things which matter. They are preoccupied with trivia, rather like the philosophers and others in Athens who considered themselves so wise (Acts 17:16-21).

The simplicity described here is not a neutral quality but a negative one. God has spoken to inform us and to make us wise. To ignore him is not a viable or acceptable option, any more than was the burying of the talent by the wicked and lazy servant of the parable (Matthew 25:14-30). The fear of the Lord is the beginning of knowledge, and the prudent will build on that. God sees all and rewards each man according to his work (Psalm 62:12; 1 Corinthians 3:8; Romans 2:6). The folly which the fool inherits, albeit of his own 'making', is nevertheless God's just judgement upon his lack of application to wisdom, for he lives in a world in which God's laws operate, whether or not he regards them. This is one of the things Paul had to point out to the Athenians, and he made it quite clear to them that true wisdom consists in seeking God in the light of what he had revealed of himself (Acts 17:22-34). They 'simply' were not thinking about the things which mattered.

Taken literally, both an inheritance and a crown are normally conferred by another, but the imagery here is pointing to what each will come into, what each may expect. The reward for those who live aimlessly, foolishly and uselessly is described as folly. That is what they are heaping up for themselves and therefore what they may look forward to. It is what those may expect who do not seek God, who do not consider their eternal destiny, who do not think seriously and objectively about who God is and who they are and their need of him.

On the other hand, the reward for the prudent is knowledge. The Bible refers to knowledge as an essential life skill, embracing understanding and wisdom and ability and the fear of God. Hence the description, 'crowned' with knowledge, because prudence gives a person real status.

In his commentary, Eric Lane says nicely of the two that 'one inherits the fool's cap (*folly*), the other the king's *crown*.'

There is also an eternal perspective on this. We are to 'grow in the grace and knowledge of our Lord and Saviour Jesus Christ', said Peter (2 Peter 3:18). By grace we have a knowledge base: the believer 'knows' the Lord. But there is more. Paul wrote, 'Now I know in part, but then I shall know just as I also am known' (1 Corinthians 13:12). Whatever knowledge we have now, and whatever benefits we enjoy from it, we will be crowned with knowledge when we meet Jesus face to face in glory. That is what the prudent are building towards. It is 'that I may know him' (Philippians 3:7-11).

[Related proverbs: 1:22; 8:5; 12:23; 13:16; 14:15; 22:3; 27:12.]

14:19. A happy ending. In a world in which wickedness seems so often to prevail, this proverb is a reminder that such a state of affairs is temporary and localised. It is the good and the righteous who occupy the high ground. Those who would have us think otherwise are imposters and usurpers. This is God's world and he is still in control of it!

Notice the tacit acknowledgement that the conflict between evil and good is still going on. The proverb is speaking generally and stating a principle. The time factor is not under consideration here even though some translations put it in the future. Evil cannot overcome or overpower goodness, it cannot conquer goodness. Goodness is unassailable. An evil person is never a match for a good one, and whatever damage he may inflict goodness blunts its effectiveness. However, the proverb clearly implies the ultimate triumph of good over evil, and of righteousness over wickedness. This happy state of affairs may not exist now, but in time it will.

Notice, too, the link between goodness and righteousness as well as that between evil and wickedness. The Bible makes it clear that those who do good are righteous, while those who do evil are wicked. There is no blurring of the edges. A person's conduct reveals the state of the heart. Disposition determines behaviour. The Pharisees of Jesus' day were widely regarded as righteous, but they were not in general recognised as good in the sense meant here. Goodness is an attractive quality, and by and large they certainly lacked that. Thus their lack of real goodness betrayed a lack of true righteousness.

Would other people describe you as good? Goodness is the beautiful outward display of the principle of righteousness. Evil is the ugly manifestation of the principle of wickedness. No one can hide his heart.

The context in which the second clause of this proverb (and perhaps the whole proverb) is set is 'the gates of the righteous'. The city gates were the place of the administration of justice, where the elders conferred to consider issues and reach their verdict. If the wicked are present at the gates of the righteous, are we permitted to ask what they might be doing there? It is not uncommon for ungodly people to seek to exert their influence upon believers, interfering in their affairs to promote their own agenda. We have the picture of Satan in the book of Job, having the audacity to appear before God in order to accuse God's servant (Job 2:1-5). We see the enemies of God coming under the guise of cooperation, offering to 'help' with the building of the temple in the days of Ezra (Ezra 4:1-5). Alexander the coppersmith was a powerful and persuasive opponent of the gospel in Paul's day (2 Timothy 4:14-15). In our time militant atheism is not content to leave the church alone but by all kinds of ploys seeks to undermine its business with a view to dismantling it. It is all contention at the gates of the righteous. The church is, as always, hard pressed by unfriendly and influential voices at its gates.

Bowing down denotes submission, or even defeat. When it was the king who sat in the gate, some of those who bowed down before him could expect execution. So it will be when king Jesus returns in glory and for judgement. Until that time, though, there will be many evil and wicked people who will bow in submission to Jesus as Lord (1 Corinthians 14:24-25), their allegiance changed for ever, and the work of the gospel will continue unabated in spite of the opposition.

In what ways should the truth of this proverb affect your attitude and reaction to:

(a) Personal injustice you experience?

(b) The troubles you see in the world around you?

14:20. The problem of poverty. We hardly need ask, 'Why so?', for the answer is pretty obvious! It can be framed in terms of giving or getting. To give attention to the poor and needy is going to prove to be a drain on one's resources, whereas to be in the company or favour of the rich has in it, if exploited well, every prospect of gain. A similar thought is expressed in 19:6,7.

Translated literally, the poor man is 'hated'. This is a form of hyperbole (as in Luke 14:26) and so must not be taken in its most literal sense. But it makes the point. There are certain people we will avoid because of the 'Oh, no!' factor when we see them on the horizon! The 'poor' often fall into this category because we know, unless we are completely callous, that we are going to have to help them out in some way. Nor does it seem to make much difference whether the poor person is a stranger or a friend or even a close relative, especially if we feel they are merely sponging off us and ought not to be in the condition they are in.

What is this proverb teaching us? Is it not that affections are often motivated by monetary considerations? The focus here is solely upon what a person does or does not *have*. If he has plenty, curry his friendship; if he has nothing, avoid him. It points to a marked lack of interest in people for who they are, only for what they have, and so reflects upon the selfishness of human nature. How contrary this is to the nature of God and what he requires of us! Consider for example Deuteronomy 15:7-8; Psalms 41:1; 82:3-4; 112:9; Luke 4:18; 14:13; Galatians 2:10; James 2:1-9.

[Related proverbs: 19:4,6,7.]

14:21. Callousness or kindness.

14:21. Callousness or kindness. Having made the observation of v. 20 and maybe elicited the impassive response, 'How true!', the writer now pulls this attitude apart! There are many reasons why one may despise, or look down on, one's neighbour. It is easy to show contempt for, or disrespect toward, the person who gets into financial difficulties through mismanagement, imprudence, laziness, recklessness, lack of self control, or whatever it might be. It is easy to despise a person whose personal life falls apart through the inability to sustain good relationships, whether with family or with neighbours. It is easy to look down on a person who seems to lack a sense of judgement and does foolish things to his or her own harm. But this proverb says that to despise such a person is wrong, it is sinful, however true it may be that their troubles have been of their own making.

Think about it: to despise others is to regard them as inferior, and by implication to regard ourselves as superior. Our attitude should rather be to show kindness, to be graciously disposed toward such people. The model for the Christian is the gracious way in which the Lord has chosen to bestow his favour upon us, utterly unworthy, foolish and hateful though we were, lifting us up and restoring our dignity and worth. To conduct ourselves in the way recommended does cost us, whether of our time, or of our money, or of our emotions. Yet, as the proverb implies, it will actually enrich us, for blessing attends such an attitude. This is clear enough from a consideration of those who have devoted their lives to the care of the needy. A serving heart seeks to lift up those who have fallen, whatever the cause of their fall may be. Whether it be their stupidity or circumstances outside their control will make no difference to *whether* help is given, though it may influence the *way* in which it is given. But the *motive* for giving it is that of mercy, in the recognition that such people are in need of help of some kind and there is a contribution we can make.

To despise one's neighbour is evidence of a singular heartlessness (11:12), and, ironically, the person doing so thereby impoverishes himself. Whereas the merciful, for all that it may cost them, are actually enriched, for they are blessed, and the blessing which comes ultimately from God is incomparable. 'Blessed is he who considers the poor ... he will be blessed on the earth' (Psalm 41:1-2).

[Related proverbs: 11:12; 19:17; 21:13; 22:9,22; 28:27; 29:7; 31:9,20.]

14:22. Plotting and planning. The same verb is used in both clauses. The contrast is between devising evil and devising good. It should be understood that evil and good are defined not by our own notions but by God's Word and are evil or good in his sight.

Much of our life is spent in making plans about what we are going to do, how we are going to spend our time, and so on. While at one level this is very mundane, at another it is helpful to remind ourselves that very often it does arise out of the disposition of our mind and heart. Thus if we are grieved, annoyed, or upset by someone or something, it might be that we plan vexatiously to do something about it which, if thought about dispassionately, will only do harm. This proverb is not dealing only with major issues which crop up now and again, but also with matters of daily living.

The first clause is framed as a question. It could have been given as a statement. Why, then, the question? Is it not for the reason that so often when tempted to devise evil (often to repay evil for evil), we fail to stop to ask and answer this fundamental question? In the heat of the moment, or in the heat of our emotions, we so often fail to pause to ask ourselves where it is all leading, and yet that is precisely what we need to learn to do. To devise evil, at any level, is to go astray.

The second clause gives some clarification. Mercy and truth are part and parcel of devising good. Where perhaps we are tempted to devise evil, we should be thinking rather in terms of mercy and truth, or love and faithfulness. Back at 3:3 we were reminded of the great importance of making sure we had mercy and truth always with us, inseparably bound to us. Our lives should be characterised by these two qualities. God is known for his mercy and truth (see, for example, the frequent references in the Psalms: 25:10; 57:3; 61:7; 86:15; 89:14; 98:3; 100:5; 108:4; 115:1), and these qualities are found among his people under his favour (Psalm 85:10). God is good, and he calls upon his people likewise to be good in all their thoughts and ways. Notice how this proverb reflects upon the previous one.

Once again this proverb brings out that it is not sufficient to think that we should be doing good. As with anything else worth doing in this life, it requires some forethought. People with a grievance give much time and thought to how they might get even with those who have crossed them. They set us an example! If it means so much to them to perpetuate harm, how much more should it mean to us to promote good and to occupy our minds and devote our energies to bringing blessing to others in the name of our Lord Jesus Christ! If we will do good, we must first devise ways and means.

When was the last time you gave serious and careful thought as to how you might bring some good into a bad situation? When might be the next time?

[Related proverbs: 3:3,29; 6:16,18; 12:20.]

14:23. No sweat. 'Blah-blah-blah', with the corresponding gesture, is a common derogatory reference to those who talk excessively but do little. There are many people who by their talk put the world to rights, but who themselves make no contribution whatever to that end. It is usually all about what other people should be doing! Then there are many people who make great boasts of what they intend to do, but never do it. It is so much easier to talk than to do. You can talk sitting in comfort in an armchair. But it won't achieve anything!

This proverb, then, is something of an ironical observation. The lunch hour gets extended over an animated conversation. Work in the office gets interrupted because someone has a juicy story to tell. The wielding of the tool gives way to the wagging of the tongue. Work is dropped as words are taken up. Passing the time in idle chatter results in the time passing in which useful work might have been done.

Statistics are available for the loss of productivity through sickness, but none for that caused by the at least equally debilitating malaise of idle chatter.

Real work done, however little it may be, is always profitable, whereas idle talk, however much it may be, is always pointless. This proverb is not saying that words are useless. Far from it – see 15:23. But it is commenting upon what is 'only so much talk' which is of little or no worth. The New Testament has its own observation on our talk. See Colossians 4:6; Ephesians 4:29.

The tongue, says James, is a little member and boasts great things (James 3:5). Read on to see what that boasting actually achieves! We need constantly to be on our guard against empty talk, for it impoverishes ourselves as well as others. In all labour there is profit, and this would include labour devoted to what we say and how we say it. Talk may be lighthearted, talk may be serious; talk may be about small things, talk may be about weighty matters; talk may be fun, talk may be sobering. But whatever it is, make sure your talk is *profitable*!

A few questions to answer:

What does your talk cost you in terms of effort?

What beneficial results have there been from things you have said?

What beneficial results are there in general from your talk?

14:24. Luke 12:13-21. Headdress. This is a comment not on the value of riches but the virtue of wisdom! There are many statements to the effect that riches in and of themselves are of no real value. See, for example, 11:4,28; 13:7; 22:1; 23:4,5; 27:24; 28:6,20; Ecclesiastes 5:12; Jeremiah 9:23; Micah 6:12.

This proverb is starkly contrasting the difference between wisdom and folly. Viewed from one angle, it gives another slant on the last proverb. Just as labour is productive, so is wisdom. Just as idle talk is unproductive, so is folly. Riches, though often referred to in a material sense in the Old Testament, need not be exclusively so considered. A wise person is enriched in every way. 10:22 speaks of the blessing of the Lord making rich, and we observed there that it is his blessing *alone* which makes rich, by which we infer that those who have become wealthy by other means are not truly rich in the sense described.

Jesus made this point in the parable of the rich farmer (Luke 12:13-21). Though the man displayed worldly wisdom he was described by Jesus as a fool because he was not rich toward God. God had blessed him materially, but he had not blessed God for such generosity or honoured him. What he had appropriated for himself was actually misappropriated and was about to be taken from him by his being removed from it.

Jesus spoke another very interesting parable about 'unrighteous mammon' and 'true riches' (Luke 16:11), commending the wisdom of the best use of what we have and concluding with the inability to serve both God and one's avarice.

This proverb is about true riches. A crown is associated with glory and is worn on the head, not hidden under clothing! The crown of the wise is a glory given them by God. They are made rich in the most meaningful sense of the word, and that is there for all to see. These are the true riches which cannot be taken away. Those who are wise may not 'make a packet' in life, but what they do acquire are true riches in the form of a crown of life.

Observing a wise person, then, one does not think of that person's material possessions or tot up their value, but one rather cannot help but notice the quality of life in terms of its meaningfulness, its value, its benefit, its fulfilment, its *richness*.

The contrasting clause, as has been observed, is something of a tautology. It very deliberately expresses the closed circle of folly. The fool is locked into a cycle of his own making and can never break out of it, like a dog endlessly chasing its own tail. It gets nowhere, it produces nothing except more of its own kind which is equally and absolutely useless.

Questions: How richly and gloriously are you attired? How do people see you in the management of your personal and public life? Are you exercising wisdom in your relationships within the family, in the workplace, in your social circle, or wherever you happen to be? Do you give as much attention to these things as to your personal appearance?

[Related proverb: 4:9.]

14:25. Truth revealed, truth concealed. This is related to 12:17 and 14:5 but looks at the consequences, and maybe is more closely related to conduct in a court of law, or perhaps, in that context, to dealing with disputes in the gate of the city. A witness in such circumstances is under oath (whether explicitly stated or otherwise) to tell the truth, and to tell it in such a way that it is clearly seen for what it is.

The truth never harms any except those who wish to suppress it. There are occasions when truth may hurt, and hurt deeply, but there is a world of difference between hurt and harm. The truth often exposes what is hidden, and that can cause a lot of pain and anguish, and sometimes people are afraid to declare the truth through fear of the trouble they think it may cause.

However, its declaration will always work for the benefit of the righteous, and will deliver the souls (or lives) of those who are falsely accused. Saving their lives needs to be viewed in the widest sense. For example, the testimony which clears a man falsely accused of corruption could be described as a 'life saver' in terms of what would have been the consequences to him otherwise.

A lying witness, which covers every other scenario including 'being economical with the truth' or lying to protect someone from harm, is not only deceitful in the sense that the testimony is aimed to deceive those who hear it, it is also deceitful in terms of the longer term consequences. It never really benefits anyone but, far from protecting anyone from harm, only produces harm. It encourages the one who 'gets away with' wrongdoing to continue in the same vein and so do more harm. It also harms the wrongdoer by hardening him in his ways, whereas being brought to justice might have a beneficial effect on him. Especially, it perverts the course of justice so that the innocent are frustrated and suffer unjustly.

Not only does this verse remind us that no harm is attendant upon absolute honesty of testimony, but that it is positively and significantly beneficial.

Are there occasions when you have withheld the truth, or part of the truth, through fear of its effect? If so, think again carefully about your motives, the justice of what you have done, and the wider consequences.

Questions: Has there been any occasion where, through your having failed to speak the truth, someone else has been affected? Would it still be appropriate to put matters right with that person? Are there any situations in your life in which you see being totally truthful is going to cause problems? What are you going to do about it?

[Related proverbs: 12:17; 14:5.]

14:26-27. Two benefits of fearing God

14:26. Security. There is security – great security – in living in the fear of God. This has two aspects to it. A person who jumps from a plane for the first time as a parachutist will be full of fear as he wrestles with what he knows in theory but has yet to experience in practice. But having done it on several occasions he will jump with confidence and even exhilaration. The parachute has been tested and found to be reliable in the security it provides, and accordingly the wearer places complete confidence in it. The man who fears the Lord does so with the assurance that the Lord will not fail him when the test comes, and will therefore be confident in the Lord. He is as solely and completely dependent upon him as the sky diver is solely and completely dependent upon his parachute.

The second aspect is that the promised confidence, or security, is not limited merely to the person of the one who fears the Lord, but graciously extended to those for whom he has responsibilities. Here we see at work the covenant love of God which is not limited, restricted or constrained. Almost certainly by 'his children' is not intended God's children but the children of the man who is assumed as the subject of the verse.

A man has responsibility toward his children. His fear of the Lord may lead to difficulties in his domestic life from children who have not yet come to place their trust in God. However, he will not let them go their own way, and in the fear of God will entrust them to him, for he knows that they too may have a place of safety, of refuge in the fear of the Lord. This is an encouragement for believing parents to conduct all their domestic affairs openly in the fear of the Lord, with unashamed reference to him and acknowledgement of him. God's covenant love is not to be assumed and neglected but recognised and depended on.

14:27. Satisfaction. The fear of the Lord provides not only security, but also incentive and direction for living – it could be said, *new* incentive and direction for living. In turning *from*, there is a corresponding turning *to*. The only loss through fearing the Lord is the loss of the bitter consequences, described as the snares of death. The fear of the Lord turns one from that, and it does so not just negatively, but positively; not just by repulsion but by attraction.

How little they know who imagine that being a Christian is dull, depriving and withering! They think in terms of what the Christian is missing in life, whereas the truth is the exact opposite. A fountain of life opens upon the fear of the Lord: a whole new delightful world, attractive, full of life, full of beauty, full of pleasure ... full of God! And therefore fully satisfying.

Questions: How often, within your family life, is the Lord acknowledged – for his provision, for his answers to prayer, for your need of dependence upon him ... for the way his Word addresses your or your children's personal circumstances? Is your home one which is confident, happy and secure in Christ, come what may?

[Related proverbs: 13:14; 19:23; 22:4.]

14:28. Wise rule. This is the first mention of kings and princes in this section of the book. When Baasha king of Israel saw large numbers of his people defecting and transferring their allegiance to Judah he built fortifications at Ramah to put a stop to this traffic (2 Chronicles 15:9; 16:1). He did what so many dictators since have done by one means or another by force to prevent their own downfall, and often it has resulted in the massacring of their own people. Their sense of insecurity turned them into ruthless oppressors and in many cases it also resulted in the very thing they were desperate to prevent.

But the principle operates at every level of society where individuals have authority over other people. If you want to keep them, you must value them and look after them and get the best out of them, and they will generally repay you in loyalty. At his height, Solomon ruled with wisdom in his kingdom, his people prospered, and he was held in honour. His son Rehoboam on the other hand, through his folly of rejecting the wise advice of the elders (1 Kings 12:7), nearly brought about his own downfall with the majority of the nation defecting from him. Look closely at the advice given him. He was advised to be a servant to his people, to listen to them and answer them with good words. Then they in turn would have been his servants forever. Bonds of solidarity rest on mutual service, and the lead must come from those in authority. Rehoboam was too proud to serve his people.

Look after 'number one', and that is all you will be left with!

Now look at the way the Lord Jesus Christ exemplifies what the elders advised Rehoboam. The manner in which he rules over his kingdom sets the pattern and example for any who have authority over others, whether in the church or in the world at large. He, the King of kings and Lord of lords, has so loved and served his people as to give himself for them; they, in return, have devoted themselves in everlasting thankfulness and praise to his honour and glory. He is king over a multitude no man can number, from every last member of which he receives unfailing and unfading adoration.

Questions: If you have a position of leadership, or have any responsibilities toward others, do you think of this in terms of your serving them? What is your response to the amazing example of Jesus Christ?

14:29. Cool it! A number of proverbs warn against hasty anger. Wrath may be aroused through personal affront, through righteous indignation, or through some other circumstance. But in every case, and even if there is some justification for anger, we are warned against an impulsive reaction.

Provocation to wrath is a bit like driving in a built-up area. A foolish person at the wheel of a powerful car may succumb to the temptation to let rip regardless, endangering both himself and others, whereas a good driver will restrain the power under the bonnet until such time and place as is appropriate to use it.

When provocative situations arise, very often there are far more factors involved than are immediately apparent, and the narrow focus of the heat of the moment fails to take in the overall picture. 16:32 graphically portrays the power of self-control under provocation; 19:11 gives honourable motivation to self-restraint; Ecclesiastes 7:9 provides a humbling check against volatile reactions; James 1:19-20 sets out what should be an all-round attitude when tempted to 'go off the deep end'!

The phrasing of this proverb suggests that slowness to wrath is far from common, for those who have it are said to have 'great' understanding. Many of us have known the humiliation resulting from 'knee-jerk' reactions to situations. This experience, and this and the other proverbs on the matter, provide a powerful and helpful incentive. We need to be conscious of the weakness of our own hearts. The power and dangers of wrath are only too evident, often leading to total loss of self-control and widespread and indiscriminate destruction which cannot be undone. The impulsiveness of one person in a volatile situation can act as the spark which sets others off, and all this does is to exalt folly, giving the action a status it should never have had.

If you are a person inclined to breathe fire, make sure you carry an extinguisher with you and learn how to use it! Keep understanding ready for every situation, and direct it upon the flames. Understanding will take a three hundred and sixty degree view of the situation and also consider the consequences of precipitate action.

If you are close to someone who is inclined to be short tempered, consider how you can be of real practical help.

[Related proverbs: 16:32; 14:17; 15:18; 19:11.]

14:30. An insidious worm. Many things have an influence on our health. 17:22 gives another example. Envy is contrasted with a sound heart. The word translated 'sound' ('at peace', NIV; 'tranquil', ESV) conveys the idea of health and wholeness. Envy undermines this. Its sinister desire gnaws away in the heart, producing discontent and even unhealthy physical symptoms.

Envy is often seen in resentment of others for what they have because we do not have it ourselves. For example, a woman may be envious of the good looks of another, little realising that it can have a one-sided souring effect on the relationship. Or someone may be envious of the success of another, or the praise of another, and that envy says, 'Why can't I be successful like that person?' and it produces unwarranted feelings of low esteem and may result in withdrawal which undermines not only a sense of well-being but also usefulness.

From whichever angle envy is viewed, it is self-destructive in a slow, sinister kind of way, as well as being harmful to others. It was because of envy that Joseph's brothers 'got rid of him' (Acts 7:9), and although Joseph undoubtedly suffered greatly as a result, it is arguable that the brothers had the worse end of the deal.

Envy was a problem in the church at Corinth where people seemed to be striving for superiority over one another (1 Corinthians 3:3). Paul warned against it in writing to the churches of Galatia, too (Galatians 5:26). James found it necessary to address this subject (James 3:14,16). We must be realistic and conclude from this that envy may exist in the church and needs to be guarded against. Envy produces strife and brings the worst out of people. It often works by putting others down in order to elevate oneself, which is the exact opposite of what Jesus taught and the example he set.

Envy is a form of covetousness, or it produces covetousness, which contravenes the last of the Ten Commandments. Whether recognised or not, or admitted or not, envy finds fault with God. It is a very common problem and has all kinds of untoward consequences. Paul, having mentioned envy as one feature of those who do not consent to wholesome words, goes on to say that godliness with contentment is great gain (1 Timothy 6:3-6). We are also exhorted to conduct ourselves without covetousness, being content with what we have, in the knowledge of the Lord's presence and provision (Hebrews 13:5-6).

Notwithstanding the physical ailments which can afflict us all, and the trials which Christians often suffer on account of their faith, on the whole they enjoy significantly better health than non-Christians. To be content in God and free from envy and strife is a very wonderful thing. Our relationship with God does affect our physical well-being.

We must not try to be what we are not, or hanker after what God has not given us. Rather, we should strive to be what God has made us for, and to use what God has given us, making our unique contribution for the blessing of others.

[Related proverbs: 15:13; 17:22.]

14:31. Psalm 72. Putting down or lifting up.

How can the poor be oppressed? The term 'poor' should be taken in a wider sense than just lacking materially. Oppression and exploitation go hand in hand. Oppressing anyone is to take advantage of that person in an area in which he is vulnerable and cannot defend himself. We see an example of this in the way the Israelites were subjected to hard labour by the Egyptians (Exodus 1). They had been living peaceably in the land and had no means to defend themselves against what was imposed upon them by the new Pharaoh who had no regard for the heritage Egypt had received through Joseph. So the Israelites were enslaved and put to forced labour. They were both oppressed and exploited and the regime did well out of them.

Materially, someone may be poor in the sense of needing to borrow money in order to start a business by which he would be able to sustain himself, but the person lending the money does so on terms which ensure the borrower pays back much more and for much longer than is just. Another example of oppression would be that of someone making sure for his selfish ends that a needy person is deprived the opportunity to better his circumstances, because he is of more use to him kept the way he is. There are so many ways in which the poor or vulnerable can be taken advantage of so that their sorry condition is perpetuated rather than relieved. Keep them ignorant, keep them from access to resources by which they might be enlightened and enabled to improve their lot. Keep them under, and they will have no opportunity to cause trouble – and by 'trouble' is meant trouble which would rebound upon the oppressor. Again, that is what was done to the Israelites in Egypt.

God has always commanded respect and help to be given to the needy (for example Exodus 22:25; 23:6,11; Deuteronomy 15:7,8; Proverbs 31:8,9), and so to oppress them is to dishonour God, their Maker. It is tantamount to denying that such a person has equal status and is due equal respect as one made in God's image. But it also reproaches God in another way, because it shows contempt for the God who in grace comes to relieve and deliver the oppressed through his Son. See Psalm 72:4,12-14 and Luke 4:18.

At 14:21 the one who has mercy on the poor is said to be happy; here he is said to be honouring God. In this verse there is a marked contrast between serving self and serving God, between self-interest and God-centred thinking.

Let us not be careful to justify ourselves in this matter, like the lawyer who wanted to know who his neighbour was. Consider the parable of the Good Samaritan (Luke 10:29-37) from the angle of this proverb. See also Matthew 25:31-46 in this light. If we withhold help from people who need it when we are put in a position to provide it, could it be argued that we are oppressing them?

One of the key marks of those who truly honour God is that they are sensitive toward any in need, their heart is moved toward them to show them kindness in whatever way is appropriate to their case. Every Christian has been needy and received mercy at the hand of a gracious God. If that does not move us to compassion and help toward others in need, what will? We will be kept tender if we keep our spiritual pores open to soak in the comfort of the compassionate love of God our Saviour.

[Related proverb: 17:5; 19:17; 22:2.]

14:32. Psalm 46. Safe and secure from all alarms. It is helpful to bear in mind that the Bible consistently divides people into two categories: the godly and the ungodly, or the righteous and the wicked; and while it may be true that there are degrees of wickedness, or even of righteousness for that matter, nevertheless there are only these two categories. Jesus spoke of separating sheep from goats, the former blessed and given eternal life, the latter cursed and sentenced to everlasting punishment (Matthew 25:31-46). There were no others who were not covered in the division.

Those who are wicked act independently of God, whereas the righteous live in dependence upon him.

The meaning of the first clause seems to be about what happens to the wicked when adversity or calamity comes upon them, and the answer is that they are overthrown, or brought down. They have no means of support, for they always rely upon themselves, and their way of life is such that when trouble comes there is no one else willing or able to lift them out of it. They are like a ship at sea without lifeboats, where everything is fine until the storm comes – and come it will. In Romans 1 there is the thrice repeated chilling statement concerning those who rejected God: 'God gave them up ... God gave them up ... God gave them over....'. They were determined to live without God, and God gave them what they wanted. As a result they suffered the consequences of their ungodly lifestyle. By rejecting God they had sown the seeds of their own destruction.

While this may be true generally, it should be noted that in this proverb 'wicked' and 'righteous' are both in the singular, and so it is true particularly and individually. The wicked individual is always insecure against any calamity, but the righteous person is always safe whatever happens.

The verb in the first clause ('banished', NKJV) can be translated as 'driven away', while the righteous of the second clause 'flee for protection'. It gives us a picture of two people moving in opposite directions, one against his will being thrust away from any hope of protection into calamity, the other being freely allowed to flee from calamity into welcome protection. This is exactly the situation in the parable of Matthew 25:31-46.

Most of the proverbs are observations on life in this world, but this is one which makes reference to life beyond death. It powerfully makes its contrasting point by observing that even in the last extremity, namely death, the righteous person has hope and refuge and safety in God in whom he trusts, for his God will receive him. A refuge is a place to which to flee in time of trouble. God is always there for the troubled believer, and he is especially there when death comes.

The wicked person fears the future, because he has no security against calamity, and whatever he may be able to avoid by careful manoeuvring, there is no escape from death and ultimate banishment. Man was made for fellowship with God, and the righteous person who seeks to walk with God by faith is able to rest easy, knowing that God is a refuge and strength, a very present help in trouble.

When wickedness appears to be on the ascendency, remember this proverb. The wicked will destroy themselves or be destroyed, but take comfort from the truth that God has the eternal security of his people at heart. If he is your refuge now, he will continue to be your refuge, even in death.

There is a very real danger to resort to mendacious sentimentality in the face of death. It is a subject on which God's Word is unequivocal and crystal clear.

[Related proverbs: 12:7; 24:16.]

14:33. Hidden depths. Translations vary, and the meaning depends on whether wisdom refers to both clauses or only to the first. Though the NKJV uses the word 'heart' in both clauses, the words are different and the second really means 'in the midst of', or 'among'. Note, then, that the first clause refers to a person of understanding in the singular, and what is in his heart, whereas the second refers to fools in the plural, and what is to be found in their midst.

How often and consistently the Word of God informs us of the importance of the heart, the seat of our understanding and emotions! So many people try to be what they are not and endeavour to present a public face which does not correspond to what they really are at heart. An understanding person is not like that. He does not have to make a special effort against his nature or compensate for his deficiencies in order to project an appropriate public image. He has no need to parade his knowledge, or draw attention to his cleverness. He does not need to put his wisdom on display for all to see. He has it in his heart, for he fears the Lord, and it is the settled principle upon which he conducts all his affairs. In much the same way as a familiar and comfortable jacket might rest upon his shoulders, wisdom rests in his heart – it fits naturally.

This proverb is also reminding us by its contrast that there is depth to a man of understanding and discernment. In this respect it is not unlike 12:23 or 13:16. The comparison is between what is not necessarily immediately obvious in the one and what is very evident in the other. By implication it would seem to be suggesting with some irony that foolish people, whatever their intentions, and whether they realise it or not, make it abundantly clear what they are like.

On the other hand, it is possible this proverb is indicating that wisdom may even be found among the foolish or made known to the foolish. There are times when foolish people together may recognise or exhibit wisdom – perhaps in matters which even they consider as of great importance – but the sad thing is that it does not come from their heart and it is not natural to them.

To whom do we turn when we are in need of counsel or advice? Consider a young woman in some kind of trouble. Will she turn to the circle of friends who are at least partly responsible for her predicament? 'You got me into this mess, now get me out of it!' If she has any sense will she not rather seek help from an older woman whose understanding and demeanour encourage confidence and hope? For what she has to give will not only be sound counsel, it will come from the heart.

Wisdom may rest in the heart of a man of understanding, but it does not serve him only, it also serves others. The supreme example of this is found in the Lord Jesus Christ and how he conducted himself in this world. He had 'the Spirit of wisdom and understanding, the Spirit of counsel and might, the Spirit of knowledge and of the fear of the Lord' (Isaiah 11:2). He had no need to shout about it (Isaiah 42:2). He could say, 'Come to me ... for I am lowly and gentle in heart' (Matthew 11:28-29). In him the grace of God has abounded toward us in all wisdom and understanding (Ephesians 1:8). It is to him we turn and it is on him we depend, for he is our mediator and advocate (1 Timothy 2:5; 1 John 2:1).

Do you have Christ dwelling in your heart by faith (Ephesians 3:17) – Christ, the power of God and the wisdom of God ... made wisdom *for you* (1 Corinthians 1:24,30)?

14:34. National honour and shame. This very well-known proverb declares a universal truth. What gives a nation status is not its material wealth or its military strength, or anything like that, but its moral high standing. National sin, on the other hand, is morally reprehensible, bringing shame and disgrace.

That this was true not only for Israel, God's chosen people, but for every nation, is evident from prophecies which were given concerning the nations. The universality of this principle is very clearly spelt out in the first two chapters of the book of Amos. It is also evident in Isaiah 13 to 24 concerning various nations and then the earth as a whole.

Comparing this proverb with 11:11 there is evidence of how important it is that God's people seek to influence national life, for if it is righteousness which exalts a nation, then it is the righteous who have a primary responsibility in this matter. It may safely be assumed that righteousness will not come about by any other means.

From Acts 17:26-27 it is clear that national divisions have their roots in God's appointment and that nations are therefore answerable to him. More particularly, this structure is in place so that men might be encouraged to seek after him. Furthermore, it is the will of God that the gospel be preached among all nations (Matthew 24:14; 28:19) and that his people will be called from every tribe and nation (Revelation 5:9; 7:9).

These things ought to impress upon us the paramount need to pray and act on behalf of individuals or organisations seeking positively to influence the leadership of our nation. In times of national confusion and corruption the need is even greater for Christians to make their voice heard – or rather, to make the voice of God heard by proclaiming his Word in the public arena as it addresses national life.

[Related proverbs: 16:12; 25:5; 28:12,28; 29:2.]

14:35. Influence in high places. This seems to corroborate what has just been observed. A king will recognise and value wisdom in a servant (or minister, or adviser), but he will not suffer fools gladly. We have a good example of this in the way the pagan king Xerxes honoured Mordecai but disposed of the troublemaker Haman (Esther 6 and 7). We have similar examples of the influence exerted by Joseph, Daniel and Nehemiah. By God-given wisdom in the realm of leadership, his people can influence kings and nations for good. Christians may be despised for their beliefs, yet their wisdom and ability can gain them entrance into positions of responsibility, authority and influence on which turn affairs of national importance.

There is often a danger that we worry about what will happen to Christians who dare to open their mouths publicly in defence of the truth when the majority voice seems to be against it. Perhaps we ought to worry instead about what will happen to a nation when Christians do not dare to open their mouths as they ought. Humanly speaking, Joseph, Daniel, Nehemiah, Mordecai were small fry and could have been dispensed with. Yet God gave them such wisdom and opportunity together with his protection that they gained the favour of the mightiest men on earth and influenced nations for good. Is anything any different today?

This is an incentive to pray and act in accordance with 1 Timothy 2:1-7.

[Related proverbs: 16:13; 22:11.]

15:1. 1 Samuel 25. Gentle might. The power of words is in evidence here, for good or for ill. Wrath is often displayed in fierce and threatening words. It would be natural to suppose that it can be countered only with something even more powerful and forceful, in much the same way as a great dyke is needed to keep at bay the pounding waves generated by a storm at sea. But no, wrath is turned away not by stubborn resistance but by a soft, or gentle, answer so that its fury ineffectually passes by.

At the other end of the spectrum, all may be calm and at peace, but just one ill spoken word (note the singular) can generate anger. It is like the small spark of which James writes which sets a forest on fire (James 3:5). Questions are sometimes asked about why some young people get such a thrill out of arson. Perhaps questions ought to be asked about this form of it! One volatile word is capable of starting a spectacular blaze.

There is a lot of anger in the world, with its inevitable destructive consequences. It is seen among growing infants, it is seen among leaders of nations, and it is seen at every intermediate level. In such situations fierce speech continually adds fuel to the fire to generate more heat and more destruction. Yet (barring the ignorance of the very young) most people would acknowledge the truth of this proverb. Why, then, is its truth not acted upon more often? Think of that when next you find yourself embroiled in a verbal conflict!

The answer which turns away wrath is said to be soft or gentle. It has that quality that wrath cannot cope with. Wrath depends on resistance, and its objective is to see and feel the resistance crumbling before it. But a soft answer neither resists nor crumbles. It *answers*, and in so doing turns wrath back upon itself.

An *answer* by definition addresses the issue in hand. A soft answer does not sidestep the issue, nor does it compromise, nor is it in any way dishonest. It is not soft in the sense of being feeble or obsequious. It is a bit like the sun in the fable, whose gentle and penetrating heat was effective in getting the coat off the man's back when the wind had spent all its fury in vain trying to do the same. When we are assailed by the kind of wrath which makes us retreat a step or two backwards, let it be not to give us space to kick back but rather to consider how with measured calmness we can get to the heart of the matter and from there disperse the heat. Consider how Gideon answered the Ephraimites in Judges 8:1-3.

We have an excellent example of both parts of this proverb in 1 Samuel 25. Nabal's harsh word (1 Samuel 25:10-11) certainly stirred up anger in David, but David's resultant wrath against the man and his household was turned away in a wonderful fashion by Abigail's carefully prepared and gentle answer. David came to realise that his wrath would not only have destroyed others, it would have had done him irreparable harm too. Abigail's words certainly reached his heart.

If you have been embroiled in verbal conflicts, think about your part in them and your motives in the light of this proverb, and how you might have conducted yourself differently. Think, too, about how this may help you to be prepared against the possibility of similar situations arising in the future.

[Related proverbs: 14:29; 15:4,18; 16:32; 19:11; 25:15; 29:22.]

15:2. Use and abuse of knowledge. This proverb is not so much about the value of knowledge as such, but more about how knowledge is used, and especially about how we speak from what we know.

A little knowledge is a dangerous thing, and those who have it, thinking that they know it all, invariably make up for their deficiencies in this department with an excess of zeal. There is a clear comparison here between a useful applying of knowledge and a useless parading of ignorance.

Again, Nabal and Abigail provide us with an illustration. They both had access to the same knowledge and understanding of David's situation but they reacted very differently to it. Nabal knew it all, didn't he (1 Samuel 25:10-11)? He had his answer off pat. He was true to his name: he was a fool (1 Samuel 25:25), and to a very reasonable request (1 Samuel 25:4-9) he reacted like a fool with his surly response of verbal abuse which is probably very much abbreviated in the text (1 Samuel 25:10-11). Abigail on the other hand, with the *same* knowledge as her husband, rightly interpreted the request, and her speech to David was a model of understanding. How well she used her knowledge of what had transpired in the way she addressed David!

So this is all about using knowledge well and doing good with it, about a considered and measured response to knowledge on the part of the wise as opposed to the unrestrained and ignorant gushing of the foolish.

What do you know, and how do you use it? There are so many situations in which knowledge may be used well or badly. Some people feel a need to parade their knowledge in order that others might think well of them, little realising that they are really pouring forth foolishness. It is all about *them*, *their* ability, *their* cleverness, *their* achievements, *their* superiority. Such a display of knowledge is useless. If they were wise they would be thinking about how to use what they know to benefit others.

Suppose someone (it might be a church member) does something very wrong and it becomes known so as to set tongues wagging. The tongue of the wise will speak responsibly, according to knowledge and understanding of the situation, with discretion and with a view to doing good. Those who eagerly relate the person's misdeeds to others, without due regard to the facts of the case, or consideration for the people involved, or concern to bring some good out of a bad situation, are simply gushing folly.

In general, how we speak of what we know – or what we suppose we know – will depend very much upon the state of our hearts and will reflect upon our motives. In another context, Paul said, 'Knowledge puffs up, but love builds up' (1 Corinthians 8:1, and compare 1 Corinthians 13:2). Paul added, 'If anyone thinks that he knows anything, he knows nothing yet as he ought to know.' This was to people who were making much of their so-called knowledge. Had they true knowledge, they would have used it very differently.

What motivated Nabal to answer as he did?

When you gain knowledge of other people, whether of their strengths or their weaknesses, how do you use this knowledge in the way you communicate with them or with others, and why?

[Related proverbs: 12:23; 13:16; 15:23,28.]

15:3. Watchfulness. This is one of many clear statements in the scriptures of the omniscience of God. He sees all; he misses nothing; he never turns a blind eye. He is, as it were, looking over your shoulder, but he is not breathing down your neck! He knows what you are doing, even why you are doing it, without necessarily interfering in its progress. The fact that he may not appear to be doing anything is often misinterpreted: sometimes by the righteous, that he does not seem to know or care (Psalms 10:1; 42:9; 44:23-24; 74:1; 88:14); often by the wicked, that he does not see or is impotent (Psalms 10:11; 94:7) – which in the latter case is promptly rebutted by withering logic (Psalms 10:14; 94:8-9). God does keep watch, he does know what is going on, and he watches not as a passive or helpless onlooker, but as one who knows exactly when and how to act – incisively, accurately, effectively.

A heron may stand in the water statue-like for a long time, its fixed gaze, for all its intensity, seeming to be one of reverie as if it were blind to its environment, a deceptive pose which is instantly shattered by a lightning and deadly strike to catch its prey. For all the time it was 'doing nothing', it was keeping watch. Had it not been keeping watch, it would never have caught its fish. God is not daydreaming, he is keeping watch, he is ready for action when the time is exactly right: no sooner, no later. As far as his enemies are concerned, it will be with deadly precision.

Furthermore, God's watchfulness is a discriminating one, for he is not said to be keeping watch on everything and everyone, but on the evil and the good – everything goes into just one of these two categories. The farmer who watches his wheat crop knows fully what is in his field, what is good and what is bad. His inaction is not inattention, it is deliberate, for his aim is for a good harvest. There will be action enough when the right time comes to sort out the good from the bad. Jesus made the same point in two of his parables (Matthew 13:24-30,47-50).

To make this more tangible and not just theoretical, think about the evil and the good in your own life. Think about the evil and the good in the lives of those around you. Think of the evil and the good that you hear about in the world at large. Sadly, it is so often the evil which makes a greater impact than the good. The result of your thinking about these things indicates that you are aware (and imperfectly at that) of just a very little of the evil and the good in a very few places. What *you* see is exceedingly limited in time and space. God sees all (2 Chronicles 16:9; Hebrews 4:13). Then, when you think about some of the evils which have come to your mind, you may be very aware that there is absolutely nothing you can do about them. Perhaps you experience a sense of frustration, even anger, that nothing is being done about them. Your observation of these things, then, is quite different from God's. You see it, but he is keeping watch. You see it and can do nothing, but he is keeping watch and will do something. In fact, he will do everything that needs doing when his time comes.

Not only do we often forget about the truth of this verse, but we fail fully to appreciate its significance. We should rightly fear such a God as this, but along with that fear we should also be greatly encouraged that the Lord knows 'what is doing'; he knows what to do, he knows how to do it, and he knows when to do it.

[Related proverbs: 5:21; 15:11; 20:12; 22:12.]

15:4. A tree of life – for whom? The expression 'tree of life' is encountered four times in Proverbs, here and at 3:18, 11:30 and 13:12, where it is preceded by the indefinite article: it is '*a* tree of life'. Other than that, it appears only in Genesis 2:9; 3:22,24 and in Revelation 2:7; 22:2,14,19, where it is *the* tree of life. In the latter cases the reference is to the benefits that accrue to taking from the tree of life.

In the Proverbs the emphasis is subtly different. The benefits we derive are related to our input. So for example, *wisdom* is a tree of life to all who take hold of her (3:18), but it is clear that serious application to wisdom is required in order to enjoy the benefits. Similarly, *the fruit of the righteous* is a tree of life (11:30), and again the benefits will be enjoyed only through righteous living. In Revelation 22:2 the leaves of the tree of life are said to be for the healing of the nations. Here in this proverb a wholesome, or a healing, or a curative tongue is said to be a tree of life. As with the other two proverbs just cited, the life spoken of is not only enjoyed by the subject, that is, by the one who grows in wisdom, or by the one who lives a righteous life, but it is also enjoyed by others.

If you work toward godly wisdom, it will certainly benefit you. But more to the point, it will benefit others too. If you live righteously, it will overflow into blessing for others. And here, if you have a wholesome tongue, it will certainly be a very real blessing to others.

One of the recurring emphases in the book of Proverbs is the way our conduct affects others. We are continually being directed away from self-centredness to consider other people. This is one such proverb. It is telling you that your speech has potential for incomparable good as well as for great harm. Many people speak according to what interests *them*, to what benefits *them*, to what enhances *them* in the eyes of others. There is in it a great deal of *self*. All too often very little real consideration is given to the effect it will have on others, unless it is deliberately to hurt them.

This proverb is given to be memorised and pondered. We can do far more with our words than we realise. A lot of people spend a lot of time thinking about what they might do for the Lord, how they might serve him. 'What does God want me to do with my life?' That is a good question, and yet it is not the most important one. God does not want you to be a great this, or a great that. He wants you to be a tree of life. He wants your speech to be such as will bring healing and health to others. Before he would have you train for the ministry, or train to be a missionary, or train for any other particular sphere of service, he would have you train your tongue for this kind of medical service!

Many a spirit has been broken or crushed not through overtly malicious words but simply by the weight of sheer selfish insensitivity in what is said. Paul said, 'Let your speech always be with grace' (Colossians 4:6) – and note that word 'always'! The Lord Jesus was known for his gracious speech (Luke 4:22). It was remarked upon. So too should we be, and so too should it be!

15:5. On being put right. The instruction, or discipline, spoken of in the first clause sometimes has a physical side to it which inflicts pain (see 22:15 and 23:13)! However, what is described here is reasoned and intelligent, not irrational or arbitrary. Here is a father exercising a corrective influence upon his son with his welfare at heart, with understanding of its importance. Surely it would be perverse to make light of that?

It is in the home and family where many of the important life skills are learnt which are then carried into the wider society. Those who will not accept parental discipline but instead despise it are showing themselves to be fools, and they will suffer a fool's reward when they are out in the big wide world.

Those who are growing up not only invariably make many mistakes but also consistently show themselves to be sinful, and reasoned discipline is needed. Quite apart from the particular issues which give rise to such discipline, the manner in which it is received and accepted and responded to is of far greater significance than many people realise.

People can react in a number of ways to correction. One is that of the fool who despises it by dismissing it or treating it with contempt. Equally foolish, though, is the one who overreacts by being cowed or humiliated by it, because to nurture a sense of hurt is just another more subtle way of spurning it.

The second clause speaks of *heeding* correction, which means looking it full in the face, examining it, understanding it and learning from it. Very often the people in life who are always right in their own eyes, or who are excessively critical of others but cannot take criticism themselves, are the people who never really learned this important life skill earlier on.

Even if it is painful physically when a youngster receives discipline, the physical discomfort is not the purpose of the discipline, but it is inflicted to reinforce the vital importance of where and why that person has gone wrong. If not physically so, it is invariably painful emotionally to be told one is wrong and to be put right. The ideal time to learn how to cope with these emotions in a proper way is in the formative years of life.

We go through life making many mistakes and going wrong in all sorts of ways. This is something we need to learn to accept and to be able to handle as an unavoidable part of life. Inability to respond properly to this is a common problem and leads to all kinds of troubles, not least in interpersonal relationships. No wonder it is said that to receive correction is evidence of prudence!

Some think it clever to trivialise parental correction. It is not being clever, but foolish, and such a reaction is detrimental to being able to cope with relationships in general. To be able to look at correction sensibly is a good investment for life.

This proverb raises questions for parents, asking them particularly if they are really training their youngsters for life with full-orbed instruction. It also raises questions for young people (and older ones!) concerning how they respond to correction in general. It is prudent to examine the reasons for the correction, and also the wider implications. Sometimes they will be obvious, but often they need to be thought about.

[Related proverbs: 3:11; 13:1,18; 15:32; 19:20,27.]

15:6. Treasure or trouble? There is a subtle contrast between 'treasure' and 'revenue' (or 'income'). Treasure is really worth something, whereas revenue is only of potential value, depending on how it is used. This proverb says nothing about the revenue which comes into the house of the righteous, for that is decidedly beside the point.

To appreciate the difference, a stately home may be open to the public to enable them to view and appreciate the many priceless treasures it contains. Some establishments of this kind find maintenance a real problem, though, and for their preservation are heavily dependent upon revenue coming in from the public and other sources. They are rich in treasure, though poor in revenue.

Now consider the house of the righteous, not in the bricks-and-mortar sense, but in the sense of character, and family, and security, and influence, and things like that. Can your own house justly be called a house of the righteous? If you think so, then what are its treasures? Where have they come from? Don't skip over these questions. Take time to make an inventory. If your analysis is a true one, money as such will not really feature in it. If you lay this house open for viewing, will others see things the same way that you do? The writer refrains from giving examples, for the proverb itself invites examination. Do you see your treasures as truly abundant? Does what you have, in the sense of true riches, reflect the blessing of the Lord upon you (10:22)?

By contrast, the wicked (covering all who have no fear of God) nearly always value what money can buy above other considerations. But lacking the principles of the righteous, whatever they gain yields no real satisfaction, and the more they gain, in general the more dissatisfied they become. Materially and physically they may be exceedingly comfortable, but their spirit is exceedingly uncomfortable. In terms of the real issues of life they are bankrupt. They are not rich toward God (Luke 12:21). 'The deceitfulness of riches' and 'the desire for other things' (Mark 4:19) so often fill the vacuum – or at least attempt to do so, though without success. The result is trouble. The ESV is not clear in its translation at this point. The NIV says that the income of the wicked brings *them* trouble, but the proverb does not limit it in this way. It takes only a moment's thought to see how much trouble is caused to others, too, by the lifestyle of the wicked. The misery which results from power being placed in the wrong hands is well known. In general, the wicked have no guiding principle on how to use the resources they come by, and so inevitably they misuse them. Spiritually, they have nothing. Their revenue is a source of trouble, not because it is bad in itself, but because it so often hinders them from finding true riches, and also because so often its use, or rather misuse, brings trouble. Very often people have a false expectation of revenue, and expect that it will give the things it cannot provide.

Again, give some thought to things you have taken on board in your life, maybe even have hoarded in your life, which are, if looked at dispassionately, really only a source of trouble to you. The question now is, what are you going to do about this?

Look at the rich young ruler who came to Jesus with such hopes of eternal life (Mark 10:17-22). He was rich, yet he had no treasure. See particularly how his riches got in the way of his receiving the treasure Jesus offered him. The exchange Jesus offered him cost him more than he was prepared to part with, and yet would have enriched him immeasurably. By retaining revenue on earth and rejecting treasure in heaven he brought trouble upon himself, for he went away sorrowful.

Have you a right sense of values?

The treasures in the house of the righteous are for others to enjoy, they are for the benefit of others as well as themselves. The one group, by self-seeking, bring trouble to themselves and others; the other, by seeking to honour God with their substance, bring good to themselves and others.

15:7. What are you spreading? Even the simplest and most obvious of proverbs is worth pondering. It is very easy to miss what is self-evident. The wise person and the fool are being compared here. What is on the lips of one and what is in the heart of the other are being considered. Because it is out of the abundance of the heart that the mouth speaks (Matthew 12:34) the comparison is natural. However, there is more to it than that.

Picture two fountains. They look the same, but from one is gushing a stream of water, while the other is bone dry. What is the problem? A blockage in the pipe? Lack of water? It turns out to be neither, for when the problem is traced back to its source it is found that its pump is defective. So it is here. The wise disperses, or spreads, knowledge. This is clear enough to all who will take notice. But when it comes to the fool, when one probes into the cause of the conspicuous absence of the display of knowledge, it is found to be his heart, that is, the seat of his understanding. It isn't that he has a communication problem, but it is far more fundamental than that. There is nothing of value to be got from him.

However, the significance of this proverb is not exhausted with this observation. It says the lips of the wise disperse, or spread, knowledge. That is what the wise do, in just the same way that when it comes to producing a jet of water, that is what a fountain does.

Perhaps, though, you consider the fountain analogy to be inappropriate in your case. You are not a speaker, there is nothing 'up front' about you, for you are a background person. Talking is not your strong point. Very well, change the picture to that of an irrigation system. Out of sight, and little by little, it provides essential moisture to enable and assist growth. Publicly or privately, all people talk!

One further point. The lips of the wise, literally, *scatter* knowledge. There is a kind of indiscriminateness about it. That is not to say that it is not specifically targeted at times. The point being made is that there is a habitual aspect to it, a generosity about it, from which any may benefit. The lips of the Lord Jesus were like this. Whether he was addressing the crowds, or speaking with his own disciples, or counselling individuals, or answering his critics – whoever he was with and whoever he happened to be addressing, words of knowledge were on his lips.

Can you really be considered wise if you are not habitually, generously and indiscriminately benefiting others in a productive way by your speech? 'Knowledge' in the book of Proverbs is a very positive thing, a vital ingredient for life. It is food for the soul. If you are dispersing knowledge, it means you are saying things which will nurture others in the best sense of the word, which will promote their spiritual well-being.

As Paul said, 'Walk in wisdom ... Let your speech always be with grace, seasoned with salt, that you may know how you ought to answer each one' (Colossians 4:5-6). Notice once again that word, 'always'!

So this proverb is really another take on what has been stated in vv. 2 and 4.

15:8-9. Abomination. Why would the wicked even think to offer a sacrifice? Even those who in general have no time for God often wish to safeguard themselves against the possibility of divine displeasure, either now or in the future. Whatever men and women may say, God is a formidable and inescapable reality, for man was created in his image.

This proverb clearly has in mind sacrifices prescribed by the Old Testament law, and yet it has a timeless application. There is a blind alley down which many even well-intentioned people have been led. This proverb is not dealing with well-intentioned people, though, but godless ones, people who are self-deluding, unaware of the way they are viewed by God. Some, while recognising that all is not well with their lifestyle, think they can make everything all right for themselves by offering some kind of sacrifice, rather like paying their insurance premium for another year.

In their minds, it is all about what they think they can *do*. There are some things which are non-starters where finding acceptance with God is concerned, and this is the supreme example. History has amply demonstrated that when people have wanted to be sure of gaining acceptance with God they have invariably believed that it is to be found in what they *do*. Likewise, when people's sins are exposed they imagine that they can make amends in some way by *doing* something by way of compensation. What they *do* in either case they think of as being a sacrifice, whether it be a religious performance or some kind of self-deprivation, and it is done on the assumption or hope that it will be of benefit to them before God. Samuel had some severe words from the Lord for king Saul who substituted sacrifice for obedience (1 Samuel 15:22-23). Saul was so full of himself that the rebuke came as a tremendous shock to him. Isaiah was given similarly severe words for the nation who thought they were doing so well in their religious observances, as if getting them right in the ritualistic sense counted for anything, whereas he showed them what they *should* be doing (Isaiah 1:11-20). Later, the people even complained that the Lord was not taking any notice of them when they were fasting and sacrificing (Isaiah 58:3). Jesus said there would be people who would think to find his favour by reminding him, 'Have we not done this, that and the other in your name?' (Matthew 7:22). Yet those same people he would remove from his presence.

Any religion which suggests that how you live does not matter as long as you perform the appropriate rituals at the appropriate times, is utterly false. Two people might have gone to the priest to offer exactly the same sacrifice, and one would have been accepted by God and the other rejected. Why? Because one thought that by his offering a sacrifice he gained acceptance, whereas the other saw that it was through the sacrifice itself that acceptance was to be sought.

Man sets great store by his performance, but God does not. Whatever man *does*, the real issue is not being addressed. God looks at the heart, and at the motives. If the heart is evil, then absolutely nothing can be done which will find favour with God. The only hope is that by genuine repentance the wicked heart will capitulate to the claims of God upon it and be changed by him. Man needs to get a new heart and a new spirit (Ezekiel 18:31), and these are God's prerogative to bestow. God abominates the sacrifice of the wicked, and little wonder when he sacrificed his own Son on the cross.

The *sacrifice* of the wicked (v. 8) is just one example of the *way* of the wicked (v. 9), it is just one aspect of his lifestyle. It is as godless as everything else about him, and it meets with the same reaction on the part of the Lord: he abominates it; it is disgusting to him. The fact that the best deeds of the ungodly are an abomination to God is a pill which sticks in their gullet. Isaiah had it right when he said, 'All our righteousness are like filthy rags' (Isaiah 64:6). God is angry with the wicked every day (Psalm 7:11).

Delight. From disgust and revulsion the proverb turns to delight and love. The upright person is one who could be described as 'straight' in God's estimation. There is nothing devious or crooked about him, there is nothing he is trying to conceal or make out as being different from what it really is. Such a person is said to follow righteousness, and this is no casual affair, for the word in the original indicates he is chasing after it, he is in hot pursuit of it. It is something he is determined to lay his hands on. It matters to him.

These figurative expressions are really quite challenging. They are characteristic of people who desire God (as in Psalm 73:25-26), and the reason they have such a desire is because God has given it to them. God is at the centre of their lives, and they want to live in his presence (hence their prayer) and live in his way (hence their pursuit of righteousness). We have an example of the pursuit of righteousness in what Paul wrote to the Philippian church (Philippians 3:9,12 in context).

Why does God delight in the prayer of the upright, or love him who follows righteousness? Is it not because this is the result of his gracious work in them, in transforming them from what they were before as ungodly people, to what they are now with a new heart and a new spirit? The Old Testament does not use New Testament terms, because the grand truths of salvation could be only imperfectly expressed before the full revelation when Christ came into the world. But here in these verses are the hallmarks of the unregenerate person and of the regenerate person.

The lesson for us is never to place any reliance upon anything we do, but total reliance upon what God has done for us. 'Nothing in my hand I bring: simply to thy cross I cling' (Toplady). What Jesus has done there is our sole and sufficient ground of acceptance. That doesn't change. It is as meaningful to a believer on his deathbed after a lifetime of service as it had been to that same believer on the day he turned from his sin to put his trust in the Lord.

God doesn't want a performance, but a prayer. God doesn't want our time, or our talents, or our money unless he first has our heart. Once he has our heart, then he may have all these other things as a great sacrifice of praise (Romans 12:1; Hebrews 13:15-16)!

Are our works self-motivated, or are they the result of God-given desires? The worship (if it can be called that) of the wicked is self-centred and hateful to God; the lifestyle of the wicked is self-centred and hateful to God. The worship of the upright is God-centred and delightful to him; the lifestyle of the upright is God-centred and seeks the righteousness which conforms to the character and works of God. The struggling believer should take great comfort from these words, finding wonderful reassurance that God delights in the prayers of one who seeks him, and the way of one who seeks his way.

[Related proverbs: 15:26,29; 21:21,27.]

15:10. Alternative route.

A driver decides, for reasons best known to himself, to leave the road to take a short cut along an unmarked track and pick up the road again later. Unknown to him the track turns out to be full of rocks and potholes and other hazards fully justifying the initial warning sign 'Unsuitable for motor vehicles.' The car is subjected to a punishing regime with which it is not equipped to cope, it is damaged in the process, and the driver suffers the frustration of delay, inconvenience, expense and self-recrimination.

God has not only set out a clear road for us to follow, he has placed equally clear warning signs on any superficially inviting turnings. 'The way' (a different word from that used in v. 9) is the way which he has provided and which is absolutely clear, not only by the signs he has placed along it but also by the tracks left by those who have already followed it. To be on that way and then to forsake it, for any purported reason, is to invite certain trouble. Many believers can testify to the very uncomfortable discipline they have experienced as a result of ignoring or making light of the warning signs. They can hardly complain that God ought to have made their own way comfortable for them when he has already provided the best route and warned them of the hazards associated with deviating from it!

There are people who have such antipathy for the warning signs that they are determined to flout them. They object to their restrictions, rebel against their subsequent strictures ... and suffer the consequences. Unlike believers who experience the harsh discipline which brings them back again onto the right road, these people never turn round, never repent, and are lost for ever in the way they decided to choose.

Have you ever thought to thank God for his great kindness in making things so hard for you, when you went astray, that you came back to him? A loving God will allow us to be distressed if that is the means by which we need to be restored to fellowship with him. Consider Psalm 25:16-18.

Have you ever thought, when enticed by sin, not to make hasty judgements but to read the signs very carefully? What may be attractive may not be good. To follow God's way is always – yes, always – best.

15:11. Exposed. The words in this proverb are 'sheol' and 'abaddon'. 'Sheol' is often translated as 'the grave'. It represents the place of the dead. 'Abaddon' has connotations of destruction, of perishing, and represents the place of the wicked after death. ('Abaddon' is the name of the angel of the bottomless pit of Revelation 9:11.) Sheol and abaddon are intimately connected with sin, death and judgement. Psalm 9:17 says the wicked shall be turned into sheol. Here the proverb seems to be indicating the place and the state of the ungodly after death, where they are banished by God to suffer everlasting destruction (two words which do not sit well together but which so powerfully express the terrible state of those who reject God's grace to their own ruin).

We speak of people turning in their grave when something outrageous is said about them. Job (26:5-6) speaks of the dead trembling when the truth is told about them, and of sheol and abaddon being naked and uncovered before God.

If the place of destruction to which God banishes the ungodly, whom we would therefore imagine to be out of his sight (compare Psalm 88:5), is 'before him', that is, is open to his view and full knowledge, and if what from our viewpoint is irrecoverably destroyed is still perceived by God in all its details, then does it not follow that the innermost thoughts of our hearts are equally open before God? All things are naked and open to the eyes of him to whom we must give account (Hebrews 4:13). See also Psalm 139:8. That famous statement of Samuel's in 1 Samuel 16:7 reminds us that the Lord does not see as man sees; for man looks at the outward appearance, but the Lord looks at the heart. Also, Psalm 139:16 speaks of God seeing what is as yet unformed, recorded even before its existence. God reads the hearts of (literally) the 'sons of men', a way of emphasising that this applies to the whole of humanity, past, present and future.

But why the comparison between sheol and abaddon and the hearts of the sons of men? What is the connection? It may well have something to do with the hidden recesses of the human heart, and in particular its depravity. People go about their lives as if God is unaware of their thinking; they imagine their private thoughts are truly private, known to none but themselves. 'Is there knowledge in the Most High?' (Psalm 73:11). Psalm 64 refers to the clandestine thoughts and activities of the ungodly, and it also makes clear that God sees every detail. Psalm 94 contains a withering refutation of the presumption of the godless that the Lord does not see or understand what is going on.

So this proverb is an encouragement to the Lord's people that he knows all that is going on right back to the innermost and most secret thoughts of men. It is also a caution against attempting to hide anything from him. See also Isaiah 28:14-15 and the nonsense God makes of it in the following verses 17-18. How does God make a nonsense of it? The answer is in v. 16. It is by Christ

Jesus, the 'precious cornerstone' and 'sure foundation' (1 Peter 2:6-8). God judges the secrets of men's hearts by Jesus Christ (Romans 2:16). If the living were so singularly unsuccessful in hiding the thoughts of their hearts from Jesus while he was on earth, how much less can our hearts be hidden from him who now sees us from heaven!

[Related proverb: 27:20.]

15:12. How to avoid the truth. The scoffer, or the mocker, represents a class of people with whom it is impossible to make any headway. Though they are in the wrong, yet they will not be told so, and any attempt to put them right will meet only with abuse. It may be for this reason that the treatment meted out to such people is described in terms of judgement (19:29), punishment (21:11), and exclusion (22:10).

There is irony in the way it is put, that the scoffer 'does not love' the one who corrects him (or, perhaps more accurately, he does not love to be reproved, or put right). Anyone who thinks to do so is only likely to get himself harmed in the attempt (see 9:7-8). However, the irony does remind us that correction and love are not necessarily disconnected: a wise man will respond with love to the one who corrects him, for he will truly appreciate the difficult service rendered toward him.

A scoffer needs correction but will not accept it. How frustrating it can be to have to deal with such people! There are some people with whom you can have an intelligent argument, or with whom you can discuss issues in a reasonable way. But no progress can be made with someone who merely responds with scornful dismissal. You can feel you have totally failed to get through. Very often, though, this is far from being the case. The scoffing is frequently a device to avoid facing up to uncomfortable truths. It is an evasive tactic. The day when the thoughts of men's hearts are revealed will probably show that some of the most vociferously scornful against the gospel have been those whose consciences have been most powerfully assaulted by its truth.

Why will the scoffer not go to the wise? It is because he is only too aware that he will not like what he hears. There is an interesting example of this in the encounter between king Ahab and the prophet Micaiah on Jehoshaphat's recommendation (1 Kings 22). Ahab was most reluctant to have any dealings with Micaiah, only he was virtually forced to do so. Although Ahab then scoffed at the prophet's words, there is more than a hint in the dialogue that he feared them. God judged the king by means of a 'randomly' shot arrow.

Let us make this personal. Are there any challenges to your way of life to which you respond with ridicule rather than reason? Are there any issues in your life which you are unprepared to share with people whose wisdom and judgement you respect? Are there people whose counsel or advice or remonstrance you have countered with mindless dismissal?

Or are you in the habit of seeking wise counsel, going to those who may tell you things you may find uncomfortable to hear, rather than associating with those who will unquestioningly approve all you say and do?

[Related proverbs: 9:7,8; 13:1; 16:22.]

15:13,15. Mood swing.

15:13. How our mood affects us. What creatures of mood we are! And it shows! Body language makes it obvious. The merry heart of v. 13 is one of exuberant joy, which bubbles up, or bursts forth, in outward displays of rejoicing. It invites the question, 'Why are you so happy today?' The contrasting sorrow of heart is the kind of grief over a circumstance which is seen as irremediable, and we ask, 'What has happened to bring you so low?'

A single event, a single item of news, can fill us with happiness and infuse us with strength ... or utterly shatter us. Circumstances over which we have no control can affect us as instantly as the flicking of a switch.

15:15. How our mood affects our view of our circumstances. One under affliction views his situation as only bad. His unhappy situation casts its shadow over everything else. While under this cloud of oppression he can find nothing good in life. The oppression smothers all and, while it lasts, as far as he is concerned the days are evil. For the other person, though,

life is good, and all is well with the world. Here the word 'merry' is a different one and denotes contentedness and satisfaction and that all is well. It is often translated 'good', as for example when God created the world and at the end of each day said what he had made was 'good', or when he described the land of promise as 'good'. The condition of this person's heart overrides any adverse effect some things might have had upon him had he been in a different frame of mind. He can find good where the other can find only bad.

Be sensible about your own situation. Perhaps these two proverbs subtly remind us of how fragile our condition is. We need not only to be realistic about the possibility of devastating news but also to give thought about how to avoid excess in the way we react to adversity. Look at it like this: Two people receive the same bad news or are affected by the same evil circumstance. One is able to bear it cheerfully, while the other goes completely to pieces over it. What is the difference? These proverbs do not, of course, give an answer to this question. We have to look elsewhere for that. We need to prepare ourselves as best we can against the 'evil day'. Consider the advice of Ecclesiastes 12:1 and Ephesians 6:13.

In the Sermon on the Mount Jesus encourages us to take the longer view (Matthew 5:11-12). A proper perspective on our situation is most helpful in the evil day. The writer to the Hebrews reminded his readers of their joy in adversity and their ability to cope with it (Hebrews 10:32-34).

Be sensitive about others' situation. Those whose spirit is broken through sorrow of heart should not in any way be despised. Far from it. Sympathy is more appropriate than scorn! The only effective way to deal with the problem is by helping in some way to alleviate the sorrow of heart, or the cause of the affliction. Psalm 147:3 says the Lord 'heals the broken-hearted and binds up their wounds' (or their 'sorrows', as here in v. 13). It takes only a moment to break a bone, but it takes weeks for it to be healed, and it will only heal properly if properly bound. The nature of the 'binding' depends on the bone which is broken and the type of break. But the idea is always to provide the best opportunity for healing and to protect the injury from further damage. So our sympathy toward those in the depths will in the first case direct them to the Great Physician who knows our hearts, and in the second case will be expressed through the kind of practical concern and action which the Lord says should be seen in those who follow him. As priests to God (1 Peter 2:9; Revelation 1:6) our help should be both spiritual and practical. [Related proverbs: 12:25; 17:22; 18:14.]

15:14. What are you taking in? In v. 7 the comparison was between the lips of the wise and the heart of the fool. Here it is the other way round. A further comparison between the heart and the mouth is found at 15:28.

The first clause is about a discerning person. People without discernment are often prepared to accept anything they hear. This is often the characteristic of gossip, where information, or more often misinformation, is passed on from one to another for its entertainment value with little regard for its accuracy or usefulness. There is a close connection between discernment and knowledge. Knowledge as it is used in Proverbs comprises more than mere facts, it encompasses the meaning and significance of those facts.

A person who 'knows his stuff' is someone who is an expert in his field. I may claim to know a piece of music, but I cannot pretend to know it like a conductor knows it. My knowledge is limited to my enjoyment of it, whereas the conductor seeks to know it in an altogether different way. If he is to be able to get the orchestra to perform the work well then he has to know it himself inside out, he has to understand it in its parts and as a whole, or else the orchestra will not be able to play it or communicate it in a meaningful way. That some performances of a work are far superior to others is invariably traceable to the knowledge of the work by the conductor and the way he is able to put this across to and through the orchestra.

The discerning heart does not seek knowledge purely for its own sake. All knowledge has application. This proverb is not dealing with abstract concepts. Nor is it to do with personal whims or ideas, such as 'I think I would like to learn a foreign language' purely for the intellectual stimulation it might give. The discerning heart is so called because it looks out on life with a discriminating faculty and recognises that it has to address issues intelligently and accurately. Each of us lives and moves among others and has his or her own contribution to make within our society. Each of us has responsibilities of one kind and another. To fulfil these responsibilities we need to know what to do. We ask ourselves, 'What should I do in this situation?' 'How should I decide whether to make this choice, or that one?' 'How can I best advise this person?' To equip ourselves to fulfil the obligations we meet in life we need to seek the knowledge which relates to those obligations.

Once again, as we probe the meaning of the proverbs, it is evident that the positive qualities they flag up invariably have a beneficial effect upon others, whereas their negative counterparts are either useless or harmful to others.

This proverb in both its parts speaks of taking in, but only the one is doing so to be of benefit of others. There are so many people who live essentially for themselves, whose life is an endless round of pleasure-seeking and entertainment and self-gratification. Their concern is for what they can get out of life, not what they can give to it. They are feeding on folly. Worse than those who exist on a diet of junk food, they will receive absolutely no benefit from their lifestyle, and they will certainly not contribute except detrimentally to the lives of others.

Can you improve your diet?

[Related proverbs: 18:2,15.]

15:16-17. Godliness with contentment is great gain (1 Timothy 6:6). This verse and the next are two of a number of 'Better ... than' proverbs. Others of a similar kind are found at 16:8; 17:1; 21:9; 28:6. Each represents a reversal of the relative values we would naturally put on things on account of the presence of an extra undesirable factor. In so doing it shows that the things themselves are indeed only of relative importance.

15:16. Money troubles. In the first of these two proverbs we are looking at the relative merits of having little of this world's goods – enough to live on

but not much more, so that we need to be careful managers of what we have – and of having so much that we don't know what to do with it.

Great wealth has its attractions, and there is nothing wrong with being rich. But to imagine that being wealthy means being carefree is something of a misconception. Almost always the rich discover that their riches prove to be at the back of many troubles they experience; they find themselves beset by cares and anxieties which the less well-off know little about. There is no question about the fact that they do not need their riches in order to be able to live. So has their money really given them the better life (as opposed to what is generally called 'lifestyle') they hoped it would?

But the parallel between 'the fear of the Lord' and 'trouble' is worth exploring. The proverb does not say, 'Better a little than great treasure with trouble.' The one who has little may experience trouble, for example the trouble associated with the constant anxiety as to whether and how he is going to continue to be able to provide for himself and his family. It is the fear of the Lord which makes all the difference. Those who fear the Lord, even though they may have little of this world's goods, may rest content because they trust in the Lord's promise that he will provide. They are given an inner peace. They do not have the burden of care which so often afflicts the wealthy. They can move through life easily and freely, not being encumbered by the armour that the wealthy carry with them for their protection. We need to learn to be content with what we have, and to recognise that those who desire to be rich (in the sense of striving after wealth) bring trouble upon themselves (1 Timothy 6:8-10,17; consider also Matthew 6:24-34).

There is also another aspect to this, which is often painfully evident in those who have made it into the higher earning bracket. Their wealth has not been bought cheaply. In many cases it has involved compromising principles and sacrificing relationships. Sometimes Christians upon the road to wealth have found that the time invested in its pursuit has squeezed out their relationship with God and their fellowship with his people. The aspiration which has dominated their thinking has proved to be a poor substitute for what they might have enjoyed had they learned contentment in their walk with him.

Few can handle wealth really well. The Lord does give it to some who will be faithful in their stewardship. Usually, those believers who are wealthy and use it well have not actually striven for it, whereas those who have worked hard to become wealthy are very often the ones whose lives are full of trouble.

In summary, the key here is the fear of the Lord. He is the source of contentment, and he is the guarantor of sufficiency. Note David's testimony in Psalm 37:25.

[Related proverb: 16:8.]

15:17 What flavours the food? This verse compares plain fare with a sumptuous feast. Once again, there is no question about the fact that no one needs to attend a feast in order to be able to live! Simple eating without any frills is perfectly adequate, though we may at times have a hankering after some mouth-watering extras!

The meal in view is a social occasion: there is company. Many a wedding reception and lavish banquet has been spoiled because of factions in the company who are at loggerheads with each other, whose conduct leaves a nasty after-taste. Doesn't this tell us that the company is therefore of more importance than the food? This proverb is set in the context of eating and drinking, and yet its application is wider. It is reminding us that the quality of our relationship with others is far more important than the environment in which that relationship is experienced. This will apply to any event. Supremely, where true love exists in the gathering and is expressed among its members, it is that which will be remembered long after the food and everything else has been forgotten.

So this proverb and the last put their finger upon absolute values as opposed to relative ones, and what is substantial as opposed to what is ephemeral. If you are invited into a partnership with great financial prospects, will you do so with your eyes open, and will your walk with God be an absolute and non-negotiable priority? If you are invited to a lavish event, will your decision whether or not to go be determined by who will be there and what the general spirit of the occasion will be like, rather than by what is laid on in the way of food, entertainment, or other such things?

These two proverbs gently warn us to guard the most precious things in life. For the believer, the fear of the Lord should be fundamental, central and determinative, and the benefits sought in life should be spiritual before material.

[Related proverb: 17:1.]

15:18. A short fuse or a slow one? The 'strife' of the first clause has the quality of disorderliness and of things being out of control, whereas the 'contention' of the second is more like a dispute or a quarrel which is amenable to reason. These words are fitting in connection with the characters and influence of the men contrasted here.

Mob violence on the streets is often experienced in areas where tension is running high, be it for a political, economic, ethnic, religious or any other reason. Frequently this is instigated by one or a very few, and very quickly it develops into a major incident. What happens in the public arena also takes place in other environments, too. Rhetoric from a hot-tempered person can incite the emotional sympathies of others into following his lead. Like a forest fire, it starts in a small way but expands with uncontrolled ferocity, destroying everything in its path. The wrathful man is one who may have a cause, but who fails to view it in a rational context. Like a bull at a gate he has his head down and goes for it. His own lack of balance and reason is then multiplied through those he inflames with his own passion. The obvious feature of the influence of a wrathful man is that it is indiscriminately destructive.

Some people by nature are more volatile than others. Some react instantly and heatedly to what they perceive as an injustice, and their reaction is often quite inappropriate, as sober reflection afterwards reveals. But more sinister is the smouldering wrath of one who has an agenda arising from his distorted view of things. One of the chilling things about the Jews' antipathy to the growth of the Christian church in the early days was that it was totally resistant to reason (see, for example, Acts 6:10ff). This resulted in the stoning of Stephen and the subsequent scattering of the Christians at Jerusalem. Another example of a wrathful man stirring up strife is found in Demetrius in Acts 19:23-41. Having fuelled and sparked off the wrath of his fellow craftsmen (Acts 19:28) the result was total confusion in the town, many of the people not even knowing how or why they had got caught up in the uproar (Acts 19:32).

Wrath in men and women is not uncommonly associated with a sense of insecurity. This was the case with the Jews and the Ephesian craftsmen just mentioned. It may also be prompted by a sense of injustice (sometimes in combination with insecurity). For ourselves, James warns us that the wrath of man does not produce the righteousness of God (James 1:19-20), that is, in itself it does no real good. Paul reminds us that we are to give place (not way!) to wrath, recognising that vengeance belongs to the Lord, not to us (Romans 12:19). It is helpful to train our minds to acknowledge that God is always in control, which will guard us against the temptation in anger to want to take control ourselves and thereby lose it! We need to beware of personal crusades, and consider what motivates them and what the outcome is likely to be.

Whether or not the man in the second clause is one of the parties involved in a dispute, contention, quarrel, argument, or whatever it may be, is immaterial, for the principle still applies. If someone flares up at you, there is always the temptation to react in like fashion. But actually to keep calm and show that you are considering or prepared to think about the matter has great potential for defusing the situation. It helps absorb the heat. Likewise, those who get drawn into disputes among others can by bringing calm reason to the situation help the parties to think more clearly what they are about. It is the person who is in control of himself, who is able and willing to examine things objectively, who is thereby setting an example for the disputants to follow. Such behaviour does not sweep problems under the carpet, but prepares the way for them to be addressed properly to the benefit of all involved.

There are so many ways in which people are divided, so many causes of friction and trouble at all levels, that close and thoughtful attention to this proverb will soon bring its rewards. The Christian, unlike any other person, has every reason for forbearance and patience, having a personal relationship with the Lord who knows, understands, and is in control.

[Related proverbs: 17:14; 26:21; 29:22.]

15:19. Road blocked … road clear. A lazy person is forever finding excuses for not doing what should be done. In this he is most industrious! This proverb can be taken in a number of ways.

Firstly, it could be that he perceives his way to be a hedge of thorns, seeing only painful obstructions to making any progress with his life. 'Everything is against me, so why bother?'

Secondly, it could be that he actually puts obstacles in his way because he doesn't want to move himself. 'I'm simply too tired to do this.' 'This is something beyond my ability.' 'If I embark on this it is going to involve me in a load of trouble.'

Thirdly, it could be that as far as others are concerned his way is a hedge of thorns. They know that to try to get anywhere with him is futile, that they are asking for the equivalent of cuts and scratches if they try to involve him in anything. Give any kind of job to a lazy person and you'll regret it: either it won't get done, or it will be done so badly that you'll have to do it again. It will be a painful experience.

Fourthly, it could be that the hedge of thorns is an apt picture of what has grown up round the lazy person through long practice of doing nothing!

We might have expected the comparison to be between a lazy person and an industrious one. But it is not. The fact that the lazy person is compared with the upright one indicates that laziness is morally reprehensible. It is not a neutral disposition. The lazy person is not simply a burden to himself, but is a burden to society. The lazy person does not simply not get his own work done, he is a hindrance to others doing theirs. Laziness is obstructiveness. Laziness is an attitude of mind, a selfishness which allows, even encourages, others do all the work. The lazy person is nothing but trouble. He should be playing a vital part in the company in which he moves, whereas all he does is to make life doubly difficult for others, first by failing to play his part in what needs to be done, and then by being a drain on their resources. The effect of a lazy person may be compared to a broken-down vehicle on a motorway, where the vehicle in question is not sitting unobtrusively on the hard shoulder allowing the traffic to flow freely, but is actually on the carriageway causing a tailback and frustration for hundreds of others.

An upright person not only makes progress himself in life, but he also facilitates the progress of others. His road is clear. He is trusting in the Lord and acknowledging him, and the Lord is making his paths straight (3:6). 'Upright' here and 'straight' in 3:6 have the same root meaning. Where it says here that the way of the upright is a highway, it indicates there that it is the Lord who shows the way ahead and clears and smooths it. For the lazy person it is too much trouble to seek God and walk his way.

[Related proverbs: 10:26; 21:25; 22:13; 26:13,16.]

15:20. Responsibility toward parents. This is very similar to 10:1. The first clause is the same, but the second is different. 10:1 may be looking more at the parents, and how wisdom or folly in their son affects them with gladness or grief. Here the focus may be more on the son, and what by his attitude he is doing to his parents. But however we look at it, we are reminded that there is point in repetition. In the Book of Proverbs we keep coming back again and again to the same topics. We can't say, 'Been there, done that' as if the matter is over and done with. Essential life skills need revisiting, they need to be looked at repeatedly in the light of growing experience and knowledge. Since we looked at 10:1 we have thought about many other matters, and now when we come back to this statement we may find we view it in a different light. Then again, we often need to be reminded of things which slip from our consciousness. For example, we may begin to take our parents for granted, we may begin to look down on them as they grow old and their faculties decline. We may need to ask the question: 'What am I doing to my parents?'

So what is the wise son doing? Whatever he may be doing as far as its details are concerned, in his overall conduct he is bringing pleasure to his father. Why is this? No doubt a large part of it is because his father has invested a lot of time and trouble in bringing him up and he is seeing the fruit of his labour. But more than that, the son is showing his appreciation of the training in life he has received, is conscious of to whom he owes it under God, and his consideration toward his father and his interest in his well-being make the father glad. Such is the attitude of a wise son. It is a positive attitude which actually looks out for ways of bringing joy to his father.

We now turn to a foolish man. Note this time the word used is 'man', not son, suggesting that this is one of more mature years who should be exercising responsibility toward his parents – for according to the law of the Lord family responsibilities continue throughout life.

In a different way from a father, a mother invests a great deal of herself in caring for and training her children, and she is likely to be far more emotionally involved in this than the father. For a man to despise his mother is the extreme in callousness in the light of the tender care and protection he had been afforded in his youth. This is *ugly* foolishness. A man should never forget what he cannot remember. If that sounds like a riddle, the reference is to the fact that before his conscious memory was fully functional, he was loved, fed, clothed, watched over and trained, and everything else a mother does was bestowed upon him for his proper development! A man who despises his mother is also likely to do a great deal of harm to others, for it indicates he has lost sensitivity in a critical area.

Someone reading this may have parents who have fallen very short in their parenting responsibilities and hardly deserve to be honoured. Yet the fifth commandment does not permit us to place restrictions on its scope. We are still to honour them by showing our care for them. If God so graciously did us unimaginable good though we did not deserve it, should we withhold ourselves from doing good where we have opportunity, not to mention responsibility?

[Related proverbs: 10:1; 17:25; 23:22,24,25; 30:11.]

15:21. Harmless fun? A couple are interviewed as they are discharged from the accident and emergency department of a hospital following an incident in a drunken orgy. They treat it as a huge joke, and no harm done.

That the emergency services had to be called out because the man suffered concussion and a nasty gash to his head which needed treatment seems to mean nothing to them ... A group of youngsters play an elaborate practical joke on a friend who is badly traumatised by the event and all they do is to smirk and shrug their shoulders ... Sitting with his feet up in front of his television, a man guffaws loudly at the cheap and empty jibes and gestures which are broadcast as popular entertainment ... A youth gets involved in a local riot, not because he is passionate for a cause, but because he gets a kick and a sense of power in throwing stones and bottles and getting one over on those in authority.

This kind of thing, with its endless variations, goes on all the time. It is perverse pleasure, because it is taking pleasure in what is wrong. The trouble is, often those who indulge in it do not look beyond the tip of their noses to see that there really is harm in it. They do not think about the consequences, or effects, of what they are doing. The word variously translated as 'discernment', 'judgement', 'sense', 'wisdom' in describing what they lack is the word 'heart'. This behaviour indicates there is something wrong at heart about them. There is a heartlessness in it. The reason for this is usually because they are thinking of no more than their own pleasures, and as long as they are enjoying themselves they couldn't really care less about how their actions affect others. It is irresponsible. Ironically, they fail to see, too, the effect their actions have upon themselves.

Now look at the person who uses his mind and thinks about these things. It says he goes on, or gets on, in a right or straightforward fashion. No mention is made in this clause of joy, or delight. Why not? It could be because it is a joy to him to live uprightly and this element is assumed from the first clause. Or it could be that personal pleasure is not the driving force of his life, and his life is lived not for his own benefit and satisfaction so much as for the good he might do others. Or it could be that living an upright life is considered to be of far greater value than any short-term personal delight. Yet surely all three are involved for the man of understanding. Even if his life gives him no thrills, he has far greater and more meaningful joy than that short-lived thing experienced by those who act foolishly.

Christians may be called killjoys because they neither approve of nor get involved in the mindless things in which others take pleasure. It is a cheap jibe from those who are ignorant! Peter takes up this point in 1 Peter 4:3-4. He says, 'We have spent enough of our past lifetime in doing the will of the Gentiles—when we walked in lewdness, lusts ... In regard to these, they think it strange that you do not run with them in the same flood of dissipation, speaking evil of you.' But it was these same Christians who greatly rejoiced, with joy inexpressible and full of glory (1 Peter 1:6,8).

What is the source of your joy? Where are you seeking it? Where your pleasures are concerned, are you consistently using your mind and conducting yourself with understanding? Escapism is not an option for the believer, nor will it bring any good.

[Related proverbs: 10:23; 26:19.]

15:22. In conference. This concept was encountered at 11:14, but whereas in the former proverb the focus was on the people, here it is on the plans, though of course the two are connected. It is a matter of common experience that when someone makes plans for something important, it is not unusual for the unforeseen to crop up so that the plans either fail completely or at least fail to work in the way intended. The lesson in this is: do not make plans unilaterally – at least not over anything of significance. It is wise to seek counsel over any intended course of action which is likely to be of importance. How often has one heard, when something has turned out disastrously, 'It wasn't such a good idea after all!', to which the reply comes, 'I could have told you that.' But he wasn't asked!

We often make our plans on the basis of what we would like, or what we think. There is not necessarily anything wrong in this, but we need to recognise we have our own limited perspective on things, and sometimes our ambitions are blinkered. A wise counsellor who says to us, 'Have you considered such-and-such?' is invaluable. Then there are occasions when some plan of action is necessary, but it can be worked out in different ways. If the matter is of some complexity, it is the kind of situation in which many advisers are needed, because though none has a monopoly of understanding and each may come at it from a different angle, their combined contribution will present a much fuller picture and so lead to a course of action which promises to succeed where the original idea would very likely have failed. Again, even if plans appear to work out, it may well be they would have worked out better had there been some counsel over them.

Counsellors are not there to rubber-stamp what we want to do but to help us reach an objective and well-informed decision. So a great deal depends upon our attitude and the kind of advice we seek. In 1 Kings 12 Rehoboam demonstrated this disastrously as he rejected the counsel of the wise and sought that of the young and inexperienced and foolish to confirm him in his own misguided intentions. Ahab likewise (1 Kings 22) rejected the advice of one man whom he knew deep down to be right, instead following that of his many ungodly counsellors – and that cost him his life.

These two examples show us that of paramount importance is to seek and to be willing to submit to the Lord. Such is our nature that this is sometimes easier said than done. It is not truthful to say we have trusted God over something if he has given us others to help us and we have ignored them. On the other hand, the advice of counsellors does not absolve us from personal responsibility. The seeking of counsel implies a willingness to modify one's ideas according to what one hears, which requires humility and flexibility.

Have you any important decisions to make before long in which others might have a useful input into your thinking? If so, you should know what to do: you should seek them out and hear them. Or perhaps you know of someone else in this position, and are conscious that you may have something relevant to say in connection with their plans. Do not regard your advice as interference and hold back, but act responsibly and give it graciously.

[Related proverbs: 11:14; 12:15; 13:10; 19:20; 20:18; 24:6.]

15:23. A word in season. A small boy in school was not very bright and by nature rather timid. On one occasion the teacher asked a question to which all sorts of answers were volunteered by others. Not satisfied, to his embarrassment she at last looked directly at him and said, 'And what do you think?' He stammered out a reply and to his amazement she said, 'That's exactly the right answer!' You can understand how he felt at that moment.

However, this proverb is not about giving the right answer to a question, or about boosting one's ego. It is more about the very real pleasure a person experiences who is able to respond verbally to a situation in a truly helpful way. Words are two a penny, but there are also words that are priceless.

At 15:21 joy, delight, intense pleasure, were encountered in a bad context. Some people derive perverse pleasure in the folly of destructive words. Here, though, is good, wholesome joy which comes with the knowledge that one has been able to say something particularly helpful at just the right time.

The two clauses in this proverb are not opposites or contrasts but are about the same thing looked at from two different angles: subjectively and objectively, from the angle of the giver and from the angle of the receiver. 'The answer of his mouth' ties in with the 'counsel' of the previous verse and yet is somewhat broader in its scope. This is a word appropriately spoken in response to some situation. It could be advice over someone's plans, but it could equally well be a word which defuses the tension in an argument, or a word which gives hope to someone struggling with doubts, or is just the right word to bring comfort to the broken-hearted. But whatever it is, the point is that it is timely, fitting and beneficial. As has been observed before, words have so much potential for good or for harm, and yet we often give so little thought to how we use them.

There is a reciprocal benefit to the word spoken in due season. It benefits the recipient, and it is this which in turn benefits the giver. Much better to know the joy of giving a helpful comment than to experience the shame of an inappropriate one! Those we most admire for being able to say just the right thing are usually those who best understand the characters of others and are most sensitive to their circumstances and needs. That doesn't come about without taking an interest in others, seeking to understand them and being concerned for their welfare. Haven't we ourselves had occasion to be profoundly thankful when others have so helpfully addressed an issue in our lives?

The proverb emphasises the timeliness of the word. This indicates that it is not only what is said that is important, but when it is said. In Acts 16 we read that Paul and his companions were forbidden by the Holy Spirit from preaching the word in Asia (Acts 16:6). That is not because God did not want the people in Asia to hear the gospel but that the time was not right. Later on, at the time God had chosen, so extraordinary was the ministry there that all who dwelt in Asia heard the word of the Lord Jesus (Acts 19:10). On the former occasion God intended the gospel first to be preached in Macedonia. In the prison at Philippi Paul was able to give a timely word to the jailer – a word which, if spoken earlier, would have fallen on deaf ears. As it was, it was a word of life to the man and his household.

These may be extreme examples, and yet we need to be sensitive as to when we speak as well as what we speak. We may think we have lots of things to say that others need to hear, and we may think they will benefit thereby, but to give advice, counsel, instruction and the like, when people are not ready for it, is not going to do any good. The word is good when it meets a person at his or her point of need – and for that we have to understand both the person and the need.

As an example of how both giver and recipient are the beneficiaries of the 'word in season', consider Abigail once again (1 Samuel 25). No doubt she personally derived joy from being able to give a wise answer to David's expressed intention to wipe out her family. But objectively, her timely word averted a disaster which could have reflected badly on David for the rest of his life. He would have had cause ever afterwards, whenever it came to his mind, to reflect how good that was!

But that is nothing compared with the joy of being able to give an answer to those who ask for a reason for the hope that is in us (1 Peter 3:15). How good was the word of the gospel when it came to us in such timely fashion!

[Related proverbs: 15:28; 18:13; 25:11.]

15:24. Upwards or downwards? Which way are we going? The word translated 'wise' in the first clause is not the usual one. This word has more to do with being prudent, acting intelligently and with forethought.

This proverb may be taken in two ways. In one sense it could mean that those who are wise are following a course in life which keeps them out of trouble – the ultimate trouble – preserving them from death. Thus, to take an extreme example, it is wise not to get involved in drink or drugs because to do so is a bit like signing your own death warrant: it is a quick way to the grave – to sheol, the place of the dead. So the wise person keeps himself above and out of the reach of these things. A lot of people have had the wisdom to see that they have needed to lift themselves above the prevailing attitude of their peers in order to be able to get on in life and avoid an early demise. Because the grave is the destiny of all mankind, it is argued that this proverb is about avoiding the inevitable for as long as possible!

However, this view of the proverb hardly does it justice! To the proverbs there is a spiritual dimension which we need to keep in view for a proper understanding. In *The Pilgrim's Progress* the route to the celestial city is depicted as a narrow, upward one involving effort and difficulty, reflecting Matthew 7:13-14. The broad and easy way is the one which leads to destruction.

There are many people whose attitude is to take things as easy as possible, to take every short cut to obtain what they want, and if possible to coast through life. Life is not like that, though, and one way or another they soon find themselves in difficulties, maybe even in the depths of gloom and hopelessness and down at rock bottom. They got there very easily – it simply involved them in no effort.

Now consider the mountaineer who not only enjoys the exhilaration of reaching the pinnacle but appreciates the increasingly breathtaking views on the way which make every step worth the effort that the upward journey requires. So it is for the wise. From the vantage point of his moral high ground he can see clearly. He sees where he has come from, and he sees where he is going to. He sees the route he has taken, and he sees the way forward. This, he can see, is indeed the way of life.

To 'turn away from hell below', or to 'keep [him] from going down to the grave', has in view the *consequences* of going there. It could be argued that we are all destined for the grave, but that is not the point. The point is: 'What then?' There is a hell to shun and a heaven to gain. There is death to turn from and life to turn to. Ponder Ezekiel 33:11 which is a call from the Lord to the wicked to become wise, to turn from their evil way which leads to death, to the right way which leads to life. The Lord was not addressing the Israelites in the Babylonian captivity about physical death or physical life, but about the *eternal* issues of life and death.

Like Christian in Bunyan's *The Pilgrim's Progress*, the wise person has left the city of destruction. Like Lot he has been delivered from the wickedness in the plains and escaped to the hills. We must not fail to notice that this is a way, or path, of life that the wise person not only sees but is actually on. Nor is it like so many mountain paths which seem to fizzle out half way. It is clearly defined, it is charted, signposted and navigable. God's Word marks it out and gives the directions. See Psalm 32:8; 37:23; Isaiah 30:21.

If you are struggling upward on the way of life, don't forget to enjoy the views!

15:25. Psalm 94. True security. The house of the proud represents what they have built and established for themselves. Consider Daniel 4:30 and the sequel. The boundary of the widow demarcated what had been allotted to her by divine right, for God had decreed that the land be divided by lot among the tribes inheriting it (Numbers 26:52-56). The boundary was protected by law (see Deuteronomy 19:14; 27:17, where 'landmark' is the same word as 'boundary' here).

There are therefore two aspects to this. The first is that God is able to protect what he himself has established, and the second is that he is able to protect the one for whom he has established it. In general a widow was a vulnerable member of society and had no protector. The unscrupulous are always ready to exploit the weak and defenceless. Boundary stones are much more easily moved than houses!

We see the power of God operating here at two different levels. The first is in destruction, and the second is in protection. Each has its time and place. The house of the proud, that is, those who lift themselves up against God and disdain his authority, will be torn out of their foundations. This applies to all who regard themselves as able to get along all right without God, it applies to every 'self-made' man or woman. They live in his world, they use the resources he has provided with the intelligence and abilities he has given them – and they say they have no need of him! What pride has established has no rightful place in God's creation. Wherever it exists, it does not belong there; it is there with neither right nor permission.

We may consider that we live in a very proud and arrogant society which is built upon principles contrary to the Word of God. It may look strong and secure. But it is not, because in the fullness of time God will uproot it. The Christian church may look very weak and insecure, seeking to live within the boundaries set by the Word of God. But it is not, because God will protect her where he has placed her. Her boundaries will be maintained where they belong, and no one will be allowed to encroach upon her territory.

Note this proverb is not suggesting any inherent righteousness or merit in the widow or her entitlement to any favour from God. Rather, it is about his interest in protecting his own, those who depend upon him, in a hostile world. His people should find encouragement in the knowledge that this is God's world and that ultimately it will be the way he wants it to be. He has power to remove wickedness and establish righteousness. The widow who entrusted herself to God could plead his promises (Luke 2:37-38; 1 Timothy 5:5; Deuteronomy 10:18). That is what every believer can do. God has set the boundaries of the church, which extend into every nation and every tongue (Revelation 5:9). However powerful the opposition, that is something we have a right to plead.

It is a fact that the house of the proud exists, and it is a fact that the boundary of the widow is under threat. This proverb is telling us both that things are not the way they should be and that in due course they will be the way they should be. It is telling us that God both sees and is in control of the situation. It is telling us, too, that power or impotence in man means nothing to God.

God will bring these things to pass because he has said so. For us that should be sufficient.

[Related proverbs: 22:22-23; 23:10.]

15:26. Not so secret. People like to think their thoughts are private. They are not! What goes on in the recesses of the mind is bound to come out in one way or another. God knows all about the root before ever the shoot appears. He discerns the thoughts and intents of the heart (Hebrews 4:12), and in this proverb 'thoughts' refers to intentions. In Genesis 6:5 there is the terrible indictment against men and women that every intent of the thoughts of their hearts was only evil continually. Even after the judgement of the flood things didn't seem to have changed much (Genesis 8:21), except to make it clear that it is only by God's grace that anyone is brought safely through judgement.

People may imagine that what goes on in the privacy of their minds bears little relationship to how they conduct themselves in public. That is pure delusion, as any impartial observation of society will demonstrate. In Genesis 6, God attributed the wickedness of man (Genesis 6:5a) and the consequent corruption and violence (Genesis 6:11) to what went on in his heart (Genesis 6:5b). In Matthew 5:28 Jesus addressed the issue of the thoughts of the heart, declaring equivalence with the act. That applied not only to adultery, but in every area. The Tenth Commandment (Exodus 20:17) is about what goes on in the mind before it is translated into practice, with the tacit understanding that thought inevitably leads to action.

Before a person has uttered a word or performed an action, God's judgement of him has already been made, for his thoughts, the motive power behind all he says or does, are known to God and identified for what they are (Psalm 139:4). This proverb is not suggesting that some of the thoughts of the wicked are bad, and some good. It is unqualified. The predicament of a person who is morally corrupt is that he is utterly incapable of a single thought which pleases God. If his thoughts cannot please God but rather are an abomination to him, how much more his every action and utterance. The wicked – those who are 'in the flesh' – *cannot* please God (Romans 8:8).

If the thoughts of the wicked are an abomination to the Lord, we need the reminder that he sees and knows every impure thought, and he knows where it leads even if we don't. A Christian disgraced in public for some sin did not fall suddenly into it almost by accident: the idea had already been entertained for some time in his or her mind. Playing with our thoughts in a careless fashion is a dangerous pastime. It is so important that we face up to the reality that our thoughts are before the Lord every bit as much as our actions. Our guilty secrets require his gracious attention.

In the second clause it is understood without the need for repetition that it is again *to the Lord* that the words of the pure are pleasant. (Note: the 1984 edition of the NIV makes no reference to 'words' though it is in the original; the latest edition reads: '...but gracious words are pure in his sight'.) Purity in God's sight is no mere outward thing. What pleases him comes only from what is pure, and what is pure in his sight can be only what he himself has purified. Notice how, when God commends his servant Job to Satan (Job 1:8; 2:3), each time Satan applies the reasoning of his own standards to the situation, as if Job's purity rested only on the surface of his character for whatever benefit he could gain from it. As Satan thinks, so the world thinks, having little or no concept of the direct connection between pleasant words and a pure heart.

The words of the pure are pleasant, delighting the Lord, because he understands the source from which those words come, a pure heart, a cleansed heart, a clean heart. They are pleasant to him because they are therefore good in themselves. They have a purifying effect, according with his will and purpose.

Have you made a rigorous check lately on the quality of your words?

[Related proverbs: 6:16,18; 11:20; 15:9; 16:24.]

15:27. Look at what you will get! Why the mention of bribes? People offer you a bribe when they want something out of you. It is usually about what they want, not what you want, but they offer sufficient inducement to 'make it in your interests' to satisfy their demands.

Basically, a bribe subverts justice, because it induces someone to give something where there is no proper entitlement, or to give it sooner than it is due. This proverb is all about the 'I want' mentality, and 'I will get it, no matter by what means I do so.'

Much of our modern, materialistic society, is based on the principle, 'Have now, pay later.' Modern marketing so often exploits this principle. They want something out of you, but they make it look as though you want something out of them. The seller with his slick marketing techniques is really offering the buyer a bribe – though, as with many a bribe, it is wrapped up in ambiguously 'innocent' language. 'You part with a little of your money now, and you will have all this! Look at what you have to gain!' So many fall for the superficial attraction, failing to see the hidden costs. Their greed for gain results in financial and emotional stomach ache! Countless families have ended up head over ears in debt, and family life has been torn apart, simply because of greed for gain fuelled by clever advertising. It is failure to recognise the principles presented in this proverb which has resulted in so much debt counselling.

We should never bribe anyone into giving us what we want, nor should we allow ourselves to be bribed by anyone into accepting anything which is not our due. The bribe works both ways in this proverb. Paul warned about the nature of the love of money (1 Timothy 6:10). Jesus made several references to greed for gain (for example Matthew 16:26; Luke 12:15; 16:13-14). The 'must haves' for the Christian are very different from those of others in the world around us.

Notice that it says that he who hates bribes will *live*. This really is a matter of life. Personal greed, however it manifests itself, really does undermine life. It certainly brings trouble to the family, who are often the first to suffer when the effects of greed become evident, for example in mounting debt and the inability to pay for the necessities of life. But greed is also a very selfish thing, and so it affects family relationships too.

Jesus said, 'Take heed and beware of covetousness, for one's life does not consist in the abundance of the things he possesses' (Luke 12:15). Observe his reference there to *life*. This proverb also contrasts covetousness and life. Covetousness is about what *I* want and *my* satisfaction; life is about what *God* wants and what is pleasing to *him*. They are in direct conflict, and so many people, with some recognition of this, arrive at the wrong conclusion. God is a killjoy, they say, he wants to take away what I have or deprive me of what I might have. But none who has sought him, and what is pleasing to him, has ever lacked any good thing or has ever gone away unsatisfied (Psalm 84:2,11). Not only do they live, but they are also the instruments of life for others too.

What is on your list of 'must haves', and why?

[Related proverbs: 1:19; 11:29; 28:16.]

15:28. Preparing your speech. Thoughts and words, heart and tongue, are often paired off in the two clauses of a proverb. There is the part that is seen, and the part that is unseen, but both are intimately connected. What goes on in the heart and what comes out of the mouth are both involved in the first clause here. The scenario is one of a question having been asked, or perhaps more widely, a situation arising which requires a verbal response of some kind.

A process of thought and meditation is to be found in the case of the righteous person – and for what reason? Although unstated it must surely be in order to respond in an accurate, appropriate and helpful way. When this same process is found in the wicked, it is with altogether different intent (6:14,18; 14:22; 24:2).

A righteous person acknowledges that words are important and have a power of their own for good or for ill (compare 18:21). Most of us have had the experience of blurting out something only to regret that we cannot recall the words once they have left our lips. The problem? We didn't think! It should be a characteristic of righteous people that they cultivate a habit of thoughtful speech which will benefit the hearers (Ephesians 4:29; Colossians 4:6).

An eminent theologian, when asked a question by one of his students, would often defer giving an answer. This was not always rightly understood because others imagined that he of all people should have the answer at his fingertips. He was a man with the humility of mind that wished to benefit his students rather than just give out his knowledge, and so he pondered how to answer. He was loved and respected as a result, for his words did so much good.

Many people will freely talk about the things that concern them or interest them with hardly a thought for the other person, and one suspects that in the majority of cases it is because their heart is excessively preoccupied with themselves and what *they* want to say. The heart of the righteous goes out to others, and therefore in all his communications he is thinking about how he may contribute to the other's welfare. Needless to say, an essential prerequisite to giving an appropriate answer is careful listening.

The situation with the wicked is obvious by comparison. So often their hearts are not constrained with any concern for the welfare of others, and so their words lack consideration for others. It all comes out regardless, and it is a bit like being in close proximity to someone with bad breath. Their speech is a mere vocalising of the moral corruption of their evil heart. Next time you have opportunity to listen in on the conversation of someone who clearly has no fear of God, instead of just listening to the words try to analyse the mind-set behind the words and think about the principles of godlessness operating there. It can be soberingly instructive. Where there is no reverence for God, there is no desire to acknowledge him in *any* of their ways, let alone *all* of them (3:6), and so any concern expressed for others lacks the essential spiritual element.

Are you a good listener? How much care do you exercise in 'answering' (in the widest sense)? Answer this question with reference to accuracy, appropriateness and helpfulness.

[Related proverbs: 16:23,27.]

15:29. Psalm 34. Far and near. In what sense is the Lord far from the wicked? It is certainly not in the sense of his having nothing to do with them, or leaving them to their own devices, for he is very active in their affairs. There are specific instances of this, for example in Joshua 11:20 and Judges 14:4, but the Bible is full of evidence that he limits and restrains their activity, and states quite clearly that he will judge the ungodly. Wicked men like Herod Agrippa who killed the apostle James are thwarted in order that the gospel may prosper (Acts 12:1-2,20-24).

We describe someone as 'distant' when something has come between them and us other than miles! The relationship is strained, or even broken, and something is wrong. This is exactly how it is between the Lord and the wicked. No intimacy or cordiality are found there. They are not on speaking terms. The wicked may not approach God or expect to be heard by him or expect to receive anything from him. In the day of their calamity he will not be found (Jeremiah 18:17) and they will be left cold and helpless, to face their terror alone. 'When they call, I will not answer...' (Proverbs 1:28, and see the context).

Godly people often complain that God is far from them, because of the opposition and oppression they experience at the hands of the ungodly. Why, the young church might have asked, did God allow Herod to kill James? The truth about a situation is, however, often very different from our perception of it. Compare Psalm 10:1-2 with v. 14 of the same psalm. While the earth exists, the wicked will persecute the righteous, and it may seem at times, because of what happens, as if God does not hear the prayers of his people. But however things may seem from our limited and often disturbed perspective, it is nevertheless true that God hears the prayer of the righteous. The very continuance of the Christian church in a hostile world is testimony to the fact.

Notice the singular and particular aspect of this: he hears the prayer of the righteous. If you are one of God's children, he hears your prayer. It is not that he hears in a vague sort of way the accumulated prayers of the church on earth and attempts to make some sense of it in order to respond. Not at all. He has given his word that he hears every specific prayer you, personally, make to him. With God, to hear is to attend, and to attend is to act. Your prayers are not in his in-tray to await his attention when he has the time. Your prayers are not in a queue, while a recorded message tells you that your call is important to him. Your prayers are not heard and dismissed as irrelevant. He hears them because he wants to hear them; he is listening before you open your mouth. The line is already open.

If the Lord is far from the wicked, the natural comparison would be that he is near the righteous. That God hears the righteous means he is near them.

Psalm 145:18-20 expands a little upon the second clause. God is intimate with his people. He is present with them. They have his ear, his concern, his interest, his action. The scriptures are full of examples of the prayers of the righteous in all kinds of situations, and they are equally full of God's answers to their prayers, for his hearing and his answering go hand in glove, as has been borne out in the experience of the saints to our present day.

The proverb tells us these things because God knows we need to hear them. In times of fear or of danger we need his reassuring word in our ear of how things really stand.

[Related proverb: 15:8.]

15:30. Psalm 34. Joy and strength.

15:30. Psalm 34. Joy and strength. Most people are susceptible to variations of mood, triggered often by relatively insignificant things. How we feel may have something to do with our general state of health, but very often it has more to do with the circumstances in which we find ourselves. There is a definite correlation between emotional and physical well-being.

It is uncertain whether 'the light of the eyes' refers to the bringer of good news, or its recipient. Probably both. Most of us know something of the encouragement received when we see the light in the eyes of someone who has come to bring us a good report about something, and most of us have experienced the elevating effect of good tidings which have made us want to jump for joy, or dance, or raise the roof! The news has brought health to our bones, and even if some say it is only psychological, it is nevertheless real for all that. In consequence it has brought light to our eyes as well. The two on the Emmaus road who returned to Jerusalem after their unexpected encounter with the risen Lord were undoubtedly infused with a new strength by the reception of the glorious news of the resurrection (Luke 24:13-35). They were 'all lit up' because they has been enlightened by it and by Jesus himself.

If we ourselves are conscious of how much these things mean to us, it should make us think about how our demeanour and words affect others, and therefore it ought to affect the way we conduct ourselves before others. A person who is depressed or wrapped up in himself and his problems can have a very discouraging effect upon others. On the other hand, one who is of a cheerful countenance and has a positive outlook on life can have a beneficial effect upon others.

When Jonathan went to find David when the latter was a fugitive from Saul, he 'strengthened his hand in God' (1 Samuel 23:16). For David the situation was pretty desperate, but Jonathan's coming to him injected the element of objective realism he needed, and even though the immediate news was not good, the prospect was, and he focused on that. Slapping him on the back with a vacuous, 'Cheer up my friend, things are bound to get better sooner or later,' would have done no good at all to David. If we are to strengthen others, it will not be by wishful thinking, but by ourselves being enlightened by the promises of God and the hope of eternal life, so that we can with joy point others to truths which will hearten them.

By drawing to our attention the effect great good news can have upon people, we are obliged to consider the substance of what we communicate to others, how we do it and the effect it has upon them. There are some people who do us good when they are around and they warm our hearts and lift our spirits. When we stop to think why it is, the reason is usually because of their sunny temperament and their wholesome conversation. The way they put things does us good. We are benefited by what they have to say. They see a side to things which others do not express. It is nothing to do with their being optimists while others are pessimists, but rather it is about their having a balanced, God-centred outlook on life, and a focus on those things which Paul enjoins upon believers in Philippians 4:8. Just to be with them is a tonic.

Above all, Christians are recipients of the good news of the gospel of Jesus Christ which they are entrusted to communicate to others, and it should make their faces radiant as they do so. Their demeanour and their conversation should be such as will bring help and joy to the heart and strength to others who believe and receive it. But the fact that Christians have experienced God's wonderful grace toward them should colour *every* aspect of their thinking, and *every* aspect of their relationship with others. Are you set on making the bones of others healthy?

Give some thought to how your presence can bring joy to others, and how your words can infuse them with strength. Are you a radiant Christian?

[Related proverbs: 13:9; 15:13; 17:22.]

15:31-33. Taking it on the chin. These statements are all closely connected. Verse 31 could be taken in two ways. One is that rebukes are part and parcel of life and are to be heeded; the other is that some rebukes can be life-giving. Both views are true to life. Throughout life we have a great deal to learn, and much of that learning has to do with correcting what is wrong in us. We have all inherited our father Adam's sinful nature, and so we all start off wrongly in life. Only the grace of God can put that right, but even when our sins are forgiven and we are born again by the Spirit of God, we still carry with us much baggage from the past, not to mention our often woeful ignorance of God and his requirements and how he would have us live. If these proverbs have application to unbelievers, how much more do they apply to believers! There is so much which is wrong in our lives, wrong with our thinking, wrong with our attitudes, wrong with our conduct. Pride would like to think that it is not so, but it is so. One of the essential functions of the Word of God as it instructs us is for reproof and correction (2 Timothy 3:16). As we are taught by it we learn that we are at fault in many ways. But it not only rebukes us, it also corrects us by pointing us in the right direction; and it not only corrects us, but it trains us so that we *proceed* in the right direction.

The words translated 'rebuke' and 'instruction' are very similar in meaning and have correction in view. The same phrase, 'hears rebuke' appears in both verses 31 and 32. In the context of the latter it is translated '*heeds* rebuke'. It is necessary not only to listen to rebuke but also to do something about it.

People can react to rebuke in all kinds of ways. It is easy to react angrily to a rebuke as a 'put down' and to reject it out of hand, or to turn upon the one giving it with some well-chosen epithet. Another reaction is to dismiss it lightly, with any kind of excuse as if to say that it really has no substance and a lot of fuss is being made about nothing. Another is to smart under it but then forget it as quickly as possible, so that nothing is learnt from it. Another is to brood resentfully upon it and to think of all the unreasonable aspects of it.

None of these reactions is the way of wisdom; all are ploys for fending off the impact. To listen, or hear, rebuke, means to give intelligent consideration to it *and* to submit under it. It subjects the emotional discomfort to the light of reason. It takes an objective rather than a subjective line on it. It is an essential aspect of true humility. People often imagine that to accept rebuke means to lose face, and that others will as a result think less of them. In fact the opposite is true. Such people are at home among the wise (v. 31); they gain understanding (v. 32); they are honoured (v. 33). Those who think it beneath them to give heed to rebuke or who think they will be despised if they do are, ironically, doing to themselves just what they fear others will do to them (v. 32). What would have been life to them they have set aside because they saw only harm in it for themselves.

It all comes down in the end to the fear of the Lord. Whereas 9:10 says the fear of the Lord is the beginning of wisdom, here (v. 33) it is said to be the instruction of wisdom. Wisdom does not just begin with the fear of the Lord, it continues with it. This is where king Asa went wrong. When he was young and humble he feared the Lord and obeyed his word, whereas when he was old and experienced he did not take kindly to Hanani's rebuke and suffered as a result (2 Chronicles 15–16).

Mature Christians with a wealth of experience behind them need to remember this. The 'instruction' of v. 33 is the same as the 'instruction' of v. 32: it incorporates the idea of correction, of restraint, of discipline, and the more experienced Christians are, the greater their need of true humility to accept the fact that they will never progress beyond the need of this kind of instruction. It is relatively easy for a young believer to acknowledge and accept the corrective instruction from God's Word, for it is all new and the need for change is often acutely felt. The real evidence of humility is in older believers who still receive the word with meekness. See James 1:21; 3:13.

[Related proverbs: 8:33,36; 15:5; 18:12; 25:12.]

16:1-3. Man proposes, God disposes.

16:1. Say-so. Although it does not say so explicitly, this verse hints at a possible disparity between what man plans and what God ordains. The preparations of the heart denote not casual intentions but carefully thought out purposes. The phrase, 'The answer of the tongue' indicates that the 'say-so' comes from the Lord. We could picture this as an individual or a group coming before a king to present a petition. They may have thought it out very well and have come with all their reasons, but at the end of the day the outcome rests solely upon the word of the king. Our God is an omnipotent as well as an omniscient King. He gives us as his subjects the ability and the right to think things out and to make our plans (so says the first clause), but we have to recognise that ultimately his word decides the issue (as says the second clause). It is therefore foolish to leave God out of the reckoning when we make our plans, for then they are almost certain to fail, and this is where vv. 2,3 come into play.

16:2. Scrutiny. This verse is not suggesting that men who act corruptly are not aware of the fact. What it is doing is showing that our understanding and integrity are limited. A student may submit a paper in an examination and believe he has done very well. But he is conscious that he is not the best judge of his performance, knowing that lies in the judgement of the examiners. They truly know how to assess the student's work, they understand and apply all the relevant criteria. So it is here. The Lord weighs the spirits. He is able to assess according to his own perfect standards, and he considers those aspects which often pass us by, those things which lie beyond our awareness. He probes the hidden motives, the unseen influences, the unconscious biases. Things which seem right and pure to us we may have to admit will be seen by God in a different light.

16:3. Submission. This verse therefore, gives us wise advice. It is reminiscent of 3:5-6. James also takes up this thought in his letter (4:13-16). At first sight this proverb seems the wrong way round. We might expect it to read, 'Commit your thoughts (or plans – what you devise) to the Lord, and your works will be established.' But it doesn't happen like that. There is of course a very close relationship between plans and works. What we do is intimately bound up with how we think in our heart. To return to the illustration of people petitioning the king, they have in mind an accomplished work and it is this they are presenting to him, even though it is at yet only at the drawing-board stage.

Let us now consider their petition. Why are they making it? Is this something which is purely in their own interests, from which they see themselves as the beneficiaries? Or is it something which they see as being in the king's interests, which will not only please him but from which all will benefit? Committing our works to the Lord really falls into the latter category. It is committing them *to* him in the sense that they are *for* him. When we are seeking to live for the Lord, to do those things which are pleasing in his sight, that is, when we are truly committing our works to the Lord, then on the whole, because of this, our plans, or intentions, tend to succeed. We don't get sent back with a flea in our ear to start all over again! Psalm 37:4-5 speaks along similar lines. Note there in v. 4 that while it could be interpreted that God will give us what we desire, it could be understood that he will actually give us the right desires themselves. When we seek to *go* God's way he enables us more and more to *think* his way.

Whose interests do you have at heart?

[Related proverbs: 3:5-6; 21:2; 24:12.]

16:4-5. Enduring vessels of wrath.

16:4. That the Lord has made all for himself is evident from Colossians 1:16 and Romans 11:36. At creation he observed that all he had made was 'very good'. But then sin entered, and its devastating consequences have corrupted and confused the whole situation as far as we are concerned. So a verse like this can be very disturbing. However, we can never get away from the facts: the fact that man fell into sin; the fact that sin is in the world; the fact that there are wicked men and women who are working against God; the fact that God will ultimately deal with all that is evil in the world and effect the reconciliation of all things to himself (Colossians 1:20).

But this verse is probably better rendered as 'The Lord has made all things to answer to his own ends...', in the sense that everything is under his control and will fulfil his purposes. In that sense the wicked cannot and will not thwart his purposes. The wicked are not an uncontrolled interference in the purposes of God. They do not in the least divert or thwart him. Their end is destruction, it is true, but while they are permitted to exercise their evil influence, they are still tools in the hand of God for the furtherance of his kingdom. The Chaldeans were called upon to overrun Israel and deport her people, but though they acted arrogantly and in a godless and ruthless fashion (Jeremiah 25:8-9; Habakkuk 1:6; Jeremiah 51:24) they fulfilled God's purpose which was to bring his people to repentance in a foreign land that they might be restored. Rather than being disturbing, this statement should be tremendously encouraging to God's people. The wicked cannot act outside of the purposes of God, and his purposes are those of grace in calling a people out to himself for his everlasting possession and for their everlasting joy.

16:5. One of the common features in wicked people is their arrogant pride. They think, speak and act contemptuously of God (Psalm 94:4-7). If they acknowledge there is a God at all, they declare that he doesn't notice, hear, or do anything (Psalm 73:9,11). So much for their view of God. God's view of them is described here, that he detests them. They are morally disgusting and abhorrent to him.

The translation of the second clause is unclear, but the phrase 'hand to hand' is suggestive of their joining forces, which is another common feature of the proud of heart in their attitude against the godly. Or the phrase could be figurative, indicating the certainty that they will not go unpunished.

In spite of all the evil in the world and the way in which wicked people seem to prevail, yet (as observed at v. 4) nothing is happening outside of God's explicit will and none can escape his promised judgement. These verses remind us that even though it has not yet happened, there is a time coming when for the wicked there will be a day of doom, a day of punishment, and none shall escape. But in the meantime, though their activity is intended to defy God and harm his people, yet it only serves for the advancement of his kingdom. As Joseph so memorably said, 'You meant evil against me, but God meant it for good,' and he continued with an explanation: '...in order to bring it about as it is this day, to save many people alive' (Genesis 50:20). The persecution of the church at Jerusalem was a prelude to the spread of the gospel through the world (Acts 8:1-4). The darkest deed of history served its own judgement in the triumph of the cross (Acts 2:23-24; John 19:30; Colossians 2:14-15).

Can you apply this to any specific situations in your own experience? [Related proverbs: 8:13; 11:21.]

16:6. Wonders of grace to God belong. 'Avoids evil' (NIV) gives rather the wrong impression, as if through the fear of the Lord one keeps out of the way of evil, as one might avoid bad company, or avoid exposing oneself to danger. But the problem is not one 'out there' so much as one in one's own heart. By the fear of the Lord a man *departs* from evil, that is, he cuts it out of his life, he removes it from him. He now deliberately and purposefully separates himself from what was once a part of him.

It is easy to see how unbelievers might misconstrue this statement. From their understanding, men might depart from evil only because they are possessed by the terror of the retributive wrath of God. Their motivation is craven fear. But the fear of the Lord is not like this. It is not a craven fear but a holy fear, not a terrible fear but a reverent fear, not an awful fear but an awesome fear, not a repulsive fear but an attractive fear. It is the result of the experience of the meaning of atonement for iniquity. (Again the NIV 'sin' is weak, because the word refers not so much to the offence itself as the moral perversity which results in it.) Typically, atonement was brought about by sacrifice. The wrath of God against iniquity was covered, he was appeased, reconciliation was effected, and the iniquity itself was purged away.

It is not the mercy and truth which provide atonement. But mercy and truth, or loving kindness and faithfulness, are nevertheless an essential accompaniment of the provision of atonement. The mercy and truth of God are frequently mentioned as being at the root of all the blessings he bestows upon his people (for example Genesis 24:27; 32:10; Exodus 34:6; Psalms 25:10; 40:10-11; 57:3,10; 85:10; 89:14; 108:4). Mercy and truth are the great foundational pillars upon which the reign of Christ is established (Isaiah 16:5). It is purely on account of his mercy and truth that God has provided atonement for the iniquity of his people. It is because of his great love for his people and his promise to them of salvation that he sent his Son into the world to die as an atoning sacrifice for sin. It is on account of his mercy and truth that he expects to see it reflected in his people.

Here in this verse we see the cause and the consequence. The great cause lies in the mercy and truth of God to purge away iniquity, and the consequence in man is that, being purged, he then departs from evil. How can anyone look at God's mercy and truth, or his love and faithfulness, steadfastly in the face and not feel thoroughly ashamed of every evil thought, or fail to be mightily motivated to live a godly life?

If anyone fears God and departs from evil, that is a sure evidence that God in his grace has atoned for that person's sins. One cannot depart from evil unless and until one's iniquity is atoned for. One cannot depart from evil unless one knows the fear of the Lord. One cannot have the fear of the Lord and not depart from evil. These things are linked in unity and cannot be separated. The work of God in man elicits a response from man. God's mercy and truth are all-conquering, and those they have conquered are ever afterwards willing and happy subjects.

'Give to our God immortal praise; mercy and truth are all his ways' (Isaac Watts).

[Related proverbs: 3:3; 14:22.]

16:7. Man pleaser or God pleaser? Those who fear the Lord will attract enmity. Jesus promised his disciples that the world would hate them for following him. He also promised them that they would be persecuted, and even killed for the faith (John 15:18 – 16:4).

This proverb does not sit comfortably alongside these facts. It is important to understand that many of the proverbs enunciate general principles rather than stating universal facts. They are given to prompt us to consider the principles. There are often times when one is tempted to be a pleaser of men rather than a pleaser of God in order to keep the peace or to avoid harmful consequences. The fear of man can cause us to tone down our testimony to the truth and to compromise (compare 29:25). This is often a very real and powerful temptation. To act in this way is to fail to recognise that God is in control; it is to suggest that man who is against us is more powerful than God who is for us (Romans 8:31).

Even Abraham compromised when in Gerah, fearing Abimelech more than trusting God (Genesis 20).

Now note that it says that '*he* makes', and the 'he' refers to the Lord. We may fear the consequences of godly ways in an ungodly world and what people might do to us. But that fails to take into account that God is well able to deal with this problem. We should be concentrating on living to please him irrespective of who is looking on or threatening us (either in our imagination or in reality). Those things we fear may well come to nothing, and our enemies may yield us grudging respect, and even be afraid to do anything to us on account of our stand for truth. Consider Psalm 105:12-15. When this happens we should acknowledge that it is God's doing, not ours. We should be getting on with the business of living for God and leaving the consequences in his care.

The things we might least expect, God is able to do, for it says he makes *even* our enemies to be at peace with us. That is not something we would expect of our enemies, is it? Even though Abraham's ways were not exactly pleasing to God in the incident in Gerah, yet God did indeed deal with Abimelech, abundantly demonstrating the truth of this proverb.

How often have Christians been surprised when those they feared might do them harm in some way have actually yielded them grudging respect or even been generously disposed toward them? It may not always be recognised that this is the Lord's doing.

By a man's 'ways' is meant a habitual way of life. This is not talking about individual actions (doing this or that to please the Lord) but continuous unbroken conduct. It therefore means not making exceptions for awkward situations. For example, Shadrach, Meshach and Abed-Nego (Daniel 3) might have used human wisdom and pandered to the king's whim over the golden image he had set up and bowed down to it like the many others there who disdained the idea but were not going to be incinerated for the sake of a small gesture. But to that point they had learned to live to please the Lord and honour him and they were not going to change now, for that would seriously dishonour God, invalidate their testimony at a critical point and do untold harm to others by casting doubt upon the truth (see Proverbs 25:26). The outcome exemplifies this proverb.

Likewise, Daniel might have deviated from his way because he feared the very real threat against him (Daniel 6:10), but he didn't because his way was to please God irrespective of the views or threats of men, and so he carried on with his worship of God regardless ... and God made even the ravenous lions to be at peace with him (Daniel 6:21-22).

Is pleasing God your great priority in life? If it is, you will make enemies. But...

16:8. Where your treasure is... This proverb can be linked with other 'Better than' proverbs, such as 15:16,17; 16:19; 17:1; 19:1; 21:9,19; 25:24; 28:6. This is another of the 'strings attached' type. It sets what is of greater worth against the lesser by means of an association we might be slow to consider.

Most people would far prefer to be wealthy than to be poor. One aspect of this was explored at 15:16. But here it is the moral aspect which is brought to the fore by setting riches in the context of righteousness.

Revenue without justice could be thought of as ill-gotten gains. 'Justice' here refers to the maintenance of a right standard. So revenue without justice implies a deviation from that standard. It implies making money by bending the rules, which is a euphemistic way of saying flouting the rules. In a world where money is universally coveted, people are often not too scrupulous about how they make it given the opportunity. Most people running a business will have encountered the deal whereby they might make a fast buck at someone else's expense or by concealing information. What is done 'under the counter' is certainly not 'above board'! Christians are not immune from temptation in this area, but if they succumb they compromise their consciences and soon discover they have made the worse choice. It is doubly worse, for not only is it worse for them, it is also worse for those they have defrauded.

Jesus said, 'Seek first the kingdom of God and *his righteousness*' (Matthew 6:33), which serves as a reminder that true righteousness is *his* righteousness, for God himself is righteous, and it is his righteousness we need, overriding and outweighing all material considerations. Jesus continued, 'and all these things shall be added to you'. What things? Things relating to what we regard as the essentials of life, such as food and clothing. Note the word 'first' in his command (and it is a command, not merely advice). The great priority for those who would be Christians is his kingdom and his righteousness. These are inseparable, we cannot have one without the other. If his kingdom and his righteousness are ours, then it will be unnecessary to worry about the necessities of life because we may trust God to look after such details.

Consider the poor widow back in Elijah's time (1 Kings 17:8-16). She was down to her last meal for herself and her son, and along came Elijah with a promise and a condition: a promise that she would be provided for by the Lord, and the condition that she *first* give her remaining food to Elijah. She could have taken him for a con-man, but she took him at his word, and was amply provided for from the little she continued to have throughout the drought. Likewise, Jesus promises us all sufficiency, but says that we must *first* give all that we are and have to him. If we do so, however little we may think we have, it will always be enough amply to see us through and provide for everything of which we have need ... and is it worth mentioning that we will have him present with us, which transforms the little into an abundance?

Revenue without justice will be called to account by a divine Auditor who examines the books and judges righteously. A little with righteousness is sufficient and irreproachable. Peace and a clear conscience are of far greater worth than any material possessions.

[Related proverb: 15:16.]

16:9. Getting directions. This proverb, though similar to v. 1 and also to 19:21, has an angle to it which should be a real encouragement for those who are seeking to live to please the Lord. Christians sometimes get into a tangle over their plans, especially over those which are likely to have significant repercussions. Am I making the right choice? Have I taken everything into consideration? Is there something I have overlooked? Am I being too hasty? What if I make the wrong decision?

The reasons for these anxieties are twofold. Firstly, our knowledge is limited and we cannot look into the future. But, secondly, we have sinful hearts and are not always sure of our motives, even though we may desire to please God. Is this the way God wants me to go, or is it just my own ambition? How do I know how to sort out the one from the other?

At some point we have to get beyond the planning stage and go into action, but even at that point we will not know all we would like to know.

We may spread a map out in front of us and plan a walk in the countryside. When we actually go on the planned walk we discover many things which were not indicated on the map in the form of unexpected hazards or misleading signs (or lack of them). We may also experience surprises and pleasures we hadn't anticipated. The map was fine and accurate as far as it went, but by its very nature it could only tell part of the story.

When we plan our way in life, in things great or small, we have only a limited amount of information at our disposal. It is good as far as it goes, but it is bound to be incomplete. No matter how careful and thorough we are in our preparations, there are factors we cannot take into account because we cannot possibly know them. But the Lord does know them, and he directs our steps. The expression is a strong one, meaning that he does not simply show us the way, but actually establishes us in the way he would have us go. We might hesitate with uncertainty, or proceed with trepidation, but God will take us on from there. Of course it is right to do our planning as best we can, and it is essential that we seek to do so according to the principles of Scripture, but it is also right to add our 'God willing' to our plans and to acknowledge our dependence upon him for their outworking, aware that we see only a very small part of the whole.

The Christian has a heavenly Guide. His presence may not necessarily be felt, but he is always there. Sometimes we can look back on the way we have taken in the outworking of our plans, and see very clearly how the Lord directed our way; and even if at the time we felt we were taking a step in the dark yet we have to acknowledge that he ensured our feet were securely planted.

But what if we have been out of the Lord's way and following our own independent course? Then our way must be a way of repentance, and very troubled, ashamed and confused we may be about it. Isaiah 55:7 is one of many statements which give great encouragement for those who forsake their own way to return to the Lord, who is gracious and compassionate and who will receive the repentant and direct them in his way.

[Related proverbs: 16:1,3; 19:21; 20:24.]

16:10-15. Aspects of rule. Not excepting v. 11, these verses refer to the function of kings. Although the context is that of a true monarchy, its application is wider and will extend to any authority structure, whether at the top is an individual or a group. Because these are the standards set by God, by inference they also inform us on the exercise of his own authority.

16:10,11. Authority – responsibility and justice.

16:10. Solomon himself as king sought wisdom from God in order to fulfil his responsibilities properly (1 Kings 3). In the same chapter is given an example of the ability God gave him to exercise wise judgement in a difficult case. Here in v. 10, 'divination' ('oracle', NIV, ESV) indicates his almost God-like power and authority and discernment. It is not only that his word is law, but that what he says must be seen to be right and authoritative in the fullest sense of the word, commanding respect for its weight and value.

The context in this case is the exercise of judgement, which requires discernment and discrimination. For a ruler to transgress in judgement would be to expose him as ineffectual, or a tyrant, or in some other way unworthy of the high office he holds. Throughout history there have been kings and dictators who have been bent on securing their own interests and safety and power against what they have regarded as a threat to their position. In a democracy, leaders are often accused of being more interested in pursuing their own agendas than in serving the people.

The reason that 'his mouth must not transgress in judgement' is not that he might otherwise lose face, but because he has an enormous responsibility toward those over whom he rules. He has not himself in view here but those he serves. Authorities are appointed by God (Romans 13:1) and are therefore answerable to him. So a king actually has a double responsibility because his authority has been delegated to him by God. The kings of Israel were required to be thoroughly acquainted with the law of God (Deuteronomy 17:18-20).

In any position of authority, those who are weakest are the ones who are looking out for themselves. Those who are strongest are the ones who have at heart the people for whom they exercise their responsibility and who speak and act in the interests of what is right. Think for a few minutes about any responsibilities you have. Can you honestly say you have a right attitude to them? In whose interests are you exercising them?

16:11. This reflects the Lord's demand for absolute and fair standards (Leviticus 19:36; Deuteronomy 25:13; Proverbs 20:10; Micah 6:11). Weights and measures were part and parcel of trading and there were those who were ready to abuse the system by having false weights and giving short measure. This verse is not so much about weights and measures as about true standards of justice, just as Micah 6:10-12 uses their false balances as an illustration of violence, lies and injustice.

To extend the illustration, the whole of the law of God represents his trading standards. Life before him, and life in this world, our relationship with him and our relationship with our fellows, are measured by this standard. Our standards are therefore to be the same as his standards. We are not to hold dual standards. Least of all was the king to set aside the standards God had entrusted to him in stewardship. Thus the law of God is placed at the very heart of the exercise of a king's responsibilities. It is exactly the same in the church. The standard for the exercise of responsibilities by church leaders is the Scriptures. They are to live by the Scriptures, teach the Scriptures, and rule by the Scriptures (2 Timothy 3:15-17; 4:2; 1 Timothy 5:17; Hebrews 13:7,17).

[Related proverbs: 11:1; 20:10; 29:4.]

16:12,13. Authority – responsibility and integrity.

16:12. Though the NIV says, 'Kings detest wrongdoing,' which ideally should be true, it seems more natural to read the verse as a reflection on the temptation to the abuse of power. 'Wickedness' is better than 'wrongdoing' here, because intent is involved. It is wrong for anyone to commit wickedness, but it is especially wrong for a ruler to do so. Of one to whom much is given, much will be required (Luke 12:48). It is bad enough for anyone to commit wickedness, but it is particularly abhorrent for one to do so to whom has been given the responsibility and authority to uphold righteousness, because it is a denial of his office.

This proverb points to the ever-present danger to abuse one's power. There are particularly strong temptations for those holding office and having influence. This, surely, is one of the reasons why we are urged to pray for those in authority over us (1 Timothy 2:1-2). The word translated 'established' here was used at v. 3, 'Your thoughts will be *established*', and at v. 9, 'The Lord *directs* his steps.' Security and stability are involved. What makes a throne secure is righteousness. What undermines it is corruption.

Corruption in high places is all too prevalent, and has been the downfall of many a regime. The media being what it is, these are the cases which are brought to our notice, while the righteous administrations continue to function smoothly without attracting any particular attention. There is a certain perversity in people luridly exposing the corrupt practices of those in authority when they themselves are actually no better. They may not do the same things because they do not have the opportunity, but often in their own lives they betray the same attitudes. A factory worker who pilfers from the shop floor is no different from the politician who makes false expenses claims. It is the same abuse of trust. Some of the relationships engaged in by leaders classed as scandalous are often just as much in evidence in the rank and file of society where they are accepted as the norm.

There may be a certain amount of hypocrisy in this pointing of the finger, and yet there is more to it than that, for there is a general acceptance that those in authority are supposed to be above such conduct. Indeed they are, and they will be held the more accountable before God, not because their sins are worse in themselves than those of others, but because they have knowingly misused what was given to them in trust. James refers to a stricter judgement for those who become teachers (James 3:1), because the office carries with it special God-given responsibilities.

[Related proverb: 25:5.]

16:13. Those in authority often have subordinates jockeying for position or favour. 'Spin' is put on words, counsellors and advisors often have their own private agendas which influence the way they present themselves, so that nothing is quite as it seems on the surface. Kings and rulers have to contend with all this and see through it, and the more intent they are on ruling justly the more important it is to them that they are not led astray by devious counsel. For them it is of inestimable value to be dealing with people who speak righteously, that is, according to God's standards, and who declare it straightforwardly without any bias through either selfishness or fear. Integrity is highly valued by good rulers. But again, these things filter down through every level of society. It is most important that what we say should be right and true, honest and straight, without it being modified or twisted through regard for how it will affect us. Sadly, a great deal of ordinary conversation does not meet these standards and often has much of self interest in it. And ours...?

[Related proverbs: 14:35; 20:28; 22:11.]

16:14,15. Authority – wrath and favour. Here we are shown two different extremes of a king's disposition, his wrath and his favour, with their association with death and life, under the images of darkness and light. When a storm is brewing we run for cover or suffer the consequences, for we have a healthy respect for the weather. When it brightens up afterwards we may venture out again.

16:14. The threat of death. The dark countenance, the wrath, of a king needs to be regarded with due respect. The scenario is probably one in which his wrath has been injudiciously incurred. We may have heard it said, when someone has offended a superior, 'If you've got any sense you will go and apologise.' Provoking the wrath of a king could incur the ultimate penalty, as in the case of Haman (Esther 7). There is no place for bravado. As Paul says, the governing authority does not bear the sword in vain (Romans 13:4), and it is wise to submit. There is also a lesson here for us, in that when it comes to offending one's superiors, the onus is upon us, not them, to put things right. They have the right to deal summarily with us when we step out of line. If we do, we will be wise to seek to appease them promptly and not suppose that the matter will simply blow over.

16:15. The promise of life. The other aspect of the king's countenance, the bright one, is his benevolence which augurs good and life for those on whom it is bestowed. The imagery of the cloud of the latter rain would have been well understood by an agricultural people who were so dependent upon the early and latter rains for the success of their crops. Their very livelihood depended upon them. So, on whom is it bestowed? Examples abound. Certainly not on those wise in their own conceits (such as Haman, Esther 6:6), but rather on those who serve intelligently and faithfully (such as Mordecai,

Esther 2:21-22; 6:2-3). Compare the attitudes of the recipients of the talents in the parable (Matthew 25:14-30).

Judgement and grace. Surely we ought to see in these things something of the disposition of the Lord himself, the King of kings, in the administration of his kingdom? Surely we ought to fear his wrath, which is a just wrath and not based on whim, and surely we ought to seek his favour by understanding on whom he is pleased to bestow it? When Haman pleaded for his life he went to the wrong person, to Queen Esther instead of the king himself (Esther 7). We can appease the righteous wrath of God only as we seek him in person and plead with him on his terms. He has given his Son, that whoever believes in him should not perish (on account of his wrath) but have everlasting life (on account of his grace). There is nothing to be gained, only everything to be lost, by going behind his back to secure our interests! God is not a hard taskmaster but a God of love, and all who will humble themselves before him will find this to be so. His love is a mighty motivator for the kind of life which will be rewarded by his approval.

There is that lovely blessing for God's people in the priestly benediction: 'The Lord bless you and keep you; the Lord make his face shine upon you, and be gracious to you; the Lord lift up his countenance upon you and give you peace' (Numbers 6:24-26). Do we not want the face of our King to shine upon us and to be assured of his favour? Is that not life to us? 'What is my being but for thee, its sure support, its noblest end? Thy ever smiling face to see, and serve the cause of such a Friend?' (Philip Doddridge).

[Related proverbs: 16:13; 19:12; 20:2.]

16:16. Exclaiming and explaining. The value of wisdom and understanding in relation to material riches has been considered in 8:10-11,19. Here, though, it is cast in the form of an exclamation rather than an exhortation. Why?

Why the enthusiasm? Two men with a passion for fell walking chanced to meet in a café. One, with the aid of a map and guidebook, was enthusing to the other over a walk he planned to do, only to discover a few minutes later that his new acquaintance already had first-hand familiarity with the area and could speak of it from personal experience. Both were enthusiasts, but only one could exclaim on its virtues.

So it is here. Here is one whose eyes have been opened to the true value of things, maybe one who now has some experience of the wisdom and understanding set out in this book, and who can identify with many of the things it says. It goes beyond the formal acknowledgement of the superior value of wisdom and understanding to the actual experience of their benefits.

Comparing the incomparable. Whether the person is rich or poor in terms of this world's goods, he or she can revel in the superior merits of wisdom and understanding. This is it! This is what matters! This is infinitely superior! This is to be chosen! It is an expression of gladness that one has had one's eyes opened to see just how wonderful the wisdom and understanding are which have their root in the fear of the Lord. 'How much better...' is a verbal comparison used to describe something incomparable. The child of God can declare, 'I would not have had it any other way!' There simply is no comparison between the kingdom of God and the things of this world.

What will you choose? Observe that a choice is involved. Two alternatives are before us: understanding or silver. Visualise a child in a toy shop with money to spend, hovering undecided between two boxes, not knowing which to select. Which is better? Some Christians seem to be like that when confronted with a choice between alternatives, one of which will be of benefit spiritually, while the other will be of benefit materially. Sadly, many have made financially lucrative choices which have taken them into a spiritual wilderness.

Take it from someone with experience that though there is a choice, there really is none. Understanding wins every time. The knowledge of God is supreme. Therefore always make life choices which promote this.

The attraction of material wealth can be painfully oppressive. Are the things of this world getting you down? Then maybe you are too preoccupied with them. We all need from time to time to receive encouragement from someone with experience.

[Related proverbs: 3:14; 8:10-11,19.]

16:17. On getting there safely. Highways and superhighways are a familiar concept in today's world. They are designed to help us reach our destination quickly and safely. Users of the internet will be aware that though they can usually navigate their way to what they want to find with relative ease there are often distractions along the way. In fact this superhighway is full of murky byways and cul-de-sacs.

Whether on the road or on the internet, it is essential to concentrate on the matter in hand and not become side-tracked with peripheral things. The highway of the upright is one which leads to a destination. It is both the way *of* life and the way *to* life. Along the route there are all kinds of enticements which will impede or halt progress, and if one gives in to these one will never reach the intended destination.

The highway of the upright leads through an ungodly world, and those on it should be well aware of the fact. They will be aware of the evils with their sinister and powerful attractions which seek to draw them away from their course, and so they will need to do two things. The first is that they will need positively to shun such evils. This requires effort and does not come automatically. For example, Paul says, 'Flee fornication' (1 Corinthians 6:18). Why such strong language? Because the enticement and opportunity are very powerful and believers need to put as much distance between them and it as quickly as possible. The second thing the upright need to do is to guard their way. That is, they need to give their full attention to what they are doing and to where they are going. They need to keep on track. In practice, for Christians these two clauses mean to keep away from evil and to keep focused on the Word of God. Both are vital.

On the subject of the internet, if you are a user, or a surfer, are you riding high or getting sucked down? So much is there which strongly appeals to the sinful nature which can be indulged in privacy at one's computer which one would never think of doing publicly. But God sees and knows. Are you doing the two things enjoined by this proverb and mentioned above, and are you seeking God's help in it as you would in any dangerous mission?

Flight from danger needs to be flight into safety. This proverb reminds us that we should have both in mind. If we are to depart from evil we need to be pursuing good (consider 1 Timothy 6:11; 2 Timothy 2:22). We are to run the race set before us, looking to Jesus, the author and finisher of our faith, and to pursue peace with all people, and holiness without which no one will see the Lord (Hebrews 12:1-3,14). By doing so we are actively providing ourselves with protection. It is like growing a hedge of thorns about our soul effectively to discourage unwanted intruders. If you value your soul, take practical steps to make it as difficult as possible for sin to compromise you at your weak points.

[Related proverb: 14:16.]

16:18. A humbling truth. Probably few people realise that our well-known saying, 'Pride goes before a fall' has its origin in this proverb. The imagination conjures up an image of someone strutting about with their nose in the air suddenly tripping over something, flying headlong and ending up with their nose in the dirt.

The picture may be sardonically amusing, but it does have its disturbing features. There is a telling irony in that proud people, who believe they should be looked up to, seldom are. People often like to quote the proverb in connection with others while altogether failing to apply it to themselves. People are quick to recognise pride and hauteur, particularly in their more extreme forms, in others and disdain them. Yet how slow we can be to identify and acknowledge similar traits in ourselves! Do we feel the rub when others display a superior attitude toward us? Why is this? Is it because of the way it reflects on us? If someone looks down on you, or treats you with a condescending attitude, you do not like it. Have you ever considered why this is?

Pride is one of the most invidious of sins. Pride does not keep itself to itself, it imposes itself upon others. Would it be an exaggeration to say that we all are to some degree guilty of it? Pride elevates self above its true status and those who are guilty of it deserve to come crashing down.

Kidner is well worth quoting in full on this verse: 'The special evil of pride is that it opposes the first principle of wisdom (the fear of the Lord) and the two great commandments. The proud man is therefore at odds with himself (8:36), his neighbour (13:10) and the Lord (16:5). *Destruction* may appropriately come from any quarter. See also 18:12.'

There are many examples of pride in the Bible – Nebuchadnezzar and Haman being but two whose downfall is recorded (Daniel 4:30; Esther 6:6) – and there are many exhortations and warnings against it (for example Isaiah 2:12; Daniel 4:37; Luke 14:8; 18:14; 1 Timothy 3:6; 6:3-5; James 4:6; 1 John 2:16-17). Complete humility is enjoined upon believers in the Lord Jesus Christ (for example Matthew 18:4; Romans 12:16; Ephesians 4:2; Colossians 3:12; 1 Peter 5:5). A consideration of how Jesus conducted himself on earth should prick the bubble in us and sober us to consider in turn just what our own attitude should be (Matthew 11:29; Philippians 2:5).

However, the image of pride produced by our minds may still be a very imperfect and inadequate one. The ultimate and universal expression of pride is to ignore what God has said or to fail to take him at his word. Isaiah 57:15 and 66:2b remind us of who he is and to whom he will look.

'God's Word says this, but....' We might not put it so crassly as this, but when our actions or our words deny or contradict what God has said, under whatever pretext or excuse, and when we rely upon ourselves and our own resources, or upon the words and ideas of others, and fail to tremble at *his* word, then we are exhibiting the pride which goes before destruction. We may call it by whatever name we will, but that makes no difference. We do not know better than God, nor does anybody else, nor does the accumulated wisdom of this world. God's Word has stood the test of time and will continue to do so. Any proud argument not in line with God's thoughts will in the day of testing be breached, it will fall apart; but the Word of God will stand forever (Isaiah 40:8).

[Related proverbs: 11:2; 18:12.]

16:19. In which circles do we move? This is a fitting companion to the previous verse. It is another of the 'Better than...' proverbs. As it goes against accepted thought, we ought to ask why the one is better than the other.

Dividing the spoil with the proud involves participating in what has been come by unjustly, showing off what has been gained supposedly by one's own power or ability. Spoil, or plunder, is what has been acquired at someone else's expense. That is nothing to be proud of, but rather something to be ashamed about. (It is true that on occasions God gave his people the right to plunder their enemies, but in every case this was an act of judgement upon the ungodly gains of those people, and the spoils were to be used rightly for God's honour and the welfare of his people. To analyse this requires some in-depth study for which this is not the place.)

The gambler who rakes in vast winnings has little sympathy or consideration for those who have thereby been impoverished. Maybe it is their own fault, but their weakness has been exploited and they are often despised for it. Burglars may have a great night out, returning in the morning with something to celebrate, but their gains are ill-gotten. Looters in riots may brag about what they have laid their hands on when they ought rather to be ashamed that they have taken advantage of others. But there are a thousand less dramatic and often unnoticed ways in which people make gains at the expense of others. The proud think only of themselves, and they preen themselves. But they will be brought down in the day of reckoning ... and that is one half of the reason why it is better to be of a humble spirit with the lowly.

To say that someone is in diminished circumstances is a euphemism for their finding it difficult to make ends meet and that life is a struggle for them. This proverb is asserting that it is better to be of a humble, or lowly, spirit in such a situation. It is better to be humble-minded with a hard, even a cruelly hard, life than to be a proud member of a criminal fraternity.

How easy it is to envy those who have more than we do! How easy it is to make light of the many 'little' ways people boast of as to how they have got to where they are or gained what they have! This proverb sets a check on such false thinking. True humility and absolute integrity are inseparable partners. Humility is not recommended simply because the humble cannot fall as the proud can, but because the principles of God's jurisdiction operate. If it were not so, then something might be said in support of dividing the spoil with the proud. But although it is not stated here, it is implicit that God opposes the proud but gives grace to the humble (1 Peter 5:5-7). Returning to Isaiah 57:15, God says not only that he dwells in the high and holy place, but that he is *with* those who have a contrite and humble spirit, to revive their spirit and heart – *and notice there how he makes it individual and personal.* That is the other half of the reason why it is better to be of a humble spirit with the lowly! For God to be with us is more than compensation for any hardships we might temporarily experience in this short life.

Better...? How much better!

[Related proverb: 29:23.]

16:20-24. This section focuses on words and communication.

16:20. Take heed how you hear. It starts with, literally, the 'word', and although this word can be variously translated the parallelism suggests that it is the word of God which is in view, that is, his instruction, and so it is all about how we hear (compare Luke 8:18).

There are many ways in which we can react to instruction, and many ways in which we can respond to the Word of God. This verse speaks of heeding *wisely*, and the meaning here is of giving intelligent thought to it. One might suppose it to be sufficient simply to heed the word and that the adverb is a superfluous extra. But God's word is free from embellishments. He says what he means. There are indeed different ways of heeding the word.

For example, concerning matters which God's Word raises, it is possible to heed them with a resentful spirit, so that we do what he says, but do so grudgingly and reluctantly. It may be obedience after a fashion, but our heart is not really in it. It is also possible to heed the word at face value only, and so we obey it to the letter but do not really think about its wider application and miss its spirit. In neither case can we expect to 'find good'.

What we really need is to give opportunity for the word to leave its mark on us; we must let it mould us, and that will come about only as we meditate upon it, thinking carefully about what it means and how it applies. This ought to happen as we listen to preaching, as we engage in group Bible study, and as we spend time privately reading the Scriptures. In what way will such a person 'find good' or 'prosper'? It may not be in any material sense, but it will certainly be in the sense that matters.

The true meaning of 'finding good' is one that dovetails with the sentiment of the second clause, which is the happiness or blessedness associated with trusting in the Lord. When we are intimate with people of substance and they with us, we tend to take what they say seriously and we trust them, and the relationship is strengthened. How much more so is it with the Lord. It is in seriously heeding his Word, without personal prejudice, and trusting him, that we become strong, we prosper in the truest sense of the word, and we enjoy the blessedness of real security in him, knowing that he loves us and will carry us through.

Trusting in the Lord is more than a comforting thought. You share yourself with people you trust. But also if you trust someone you will be placing yourself in their hands in cases of need. Furthermore, if you trust someone, then in circumstances which might question their word or their ability to do what they have said, you will continue to rely upon them. So if you are trusting in the Lord it means you will be confiding in him and exposing to him the secrets of your heart, it means you will be committing yourself and your needs to him, and it means you will not be moved from your reliance upon him when things look bad or when others call his word into question. This is a trust which will stand the test.

There is a strong emphasis in the second clause: it is an exclamation of happiness. It describes an incomparable happiness. Are you happy?

[Related proverbs: 13:13; 30:5.]

16:21. Putting it across. This verse is really all about the way the wise communicate their wisdom. The word translated 'learning' (NKJV) has really to do with persuasion – which involves making the hearer receptive to what is being said or taught. The wise in heart have a way of putting things so much more effectively and appropriately than others. This is often seen in difficult situations, when someone knows exactly the right thing to say, and we realise that they have seen through to the kernel of the issue and understand just what is involved, and their words are therefore 'spot on' and so helpful. What they have to say is worth hearing, it carries weight, it helps, it promotes understanding in the hearers and benefits them.

How wonderfully true this was in all of Jesus' teaching. His wisdom and gracious speech were noted by those who had known him growing up (Mark 6:2; Luke 4:22), and later the officers sent to arrest him returned empty-handed with the excuse, 'No one ever spoke like this man!' (John 7:46).

Many of us have been in a situation we have not known how to handle, perhaps where whatever we say or do is likely to be misconstrued or make matters worse, and someone has come along and addressed it so simply and so well, so gently and so disarmingly and so effectively, that we stand back in admiration at their discernment and ability. It is because they have been wise of heart in the matter concerned.

Think about how this comes about. There are two essential ingredients. The first is intimacy with the Lord. The second is understanding of people. Firstly, we must give time to the Lord, to his Word, to know and understand him better, to be enriched in our knowledge of him. But secondly, we must give time to people, to take an interest in them, to have their well-being at heart, to learn about them with a view to doing them good. Do these two things ring a bell? Read Mark 12:28-34. But the lawyer of Luke 10:25-29 was clearly more concerned about himself than about God and his neighbour and was given an uncomfortable lesson. Where do your interests lie in this matter, and how are they displayed?

[Related proverbs: 15:28; 16:23.]

16:22. Enlightenment. The 'wellspring (or fountain) of life' is a phrase which occurs at 10:11 where the mouth of the righteous is said to be a well of life, at 13:14 where the law of the wise is described as a fountain of life, and at 14:27 where the fear of the Lord is said to be a fountain of life. Here it is 'understanding' which is a wellspring of life. Putting these together we see how it all originates in, and comes from, the Lord. The fear of the Lord is the beginning of knowledge (1:7): it is by listening to his word that we gain understanding. The fear of the Lord is the beginning of wisdom (9:10): it is by learning from him that we gain wisdom. The fear of the Lord and understanding, knowledge, wisdom and righteousness are inseparable (2:5-9). It is through the fear of the Lord, and only through the fear of the Lord, that we can be channels of life to others.

Many people go through life without really understanding what it is all about. They exist, they go through the motions, but they do not really live in the sense indicated by these words. Two people are looking at a canvas in an art gallery. Both express appreciation of what they see, but it turns out in the course of their conversation that one of them not only is well acquainted with other works by the same artist and knows all about his techniques, but is an intimate friend of the artist himself, knows how the works originated, what they are intended to convey, and so on, and so he is able to explain and point things out to the other which unaided he would never have seen. The one had an understanding which the other lacked, and so the canvas 'came to life', so to speak. This is but a poor illustration of how understanding is a wellspring of life to him who has it. To know the Lord, to fear him, to revere his Word, to understand something of how he is working out his purposes, gives a whole new dimension to life. It is to be enlightened; it is to find meaning to life; it is to make sense of it all and to be able to appreciate it and benefit from it. The understanding spoken of here is much more than knowledge, or intelligence, but is the good sense which not only makes sense of life but can also apply that sense to its outworking.

Notice that it is to those who have it that understanding is said to be a fountain of life. It has an esoteric quality about it. It is something which 'none but his loved ones know'. Others can often see that Christians seem to have a secret source of life, but they cannot really make it out. It is an enigma to them. But even Christians need to use what is at their disposal in order to gain in understanding. Too many believers seem to live in the shallows and are afraid to 'launch out into the deep'.

In these five verses (20-24), v. 22b is the only clause which speaks negatively. The understanding which is the wellspring of life comes about only in the school of instruction and training and discipline. The word here translated 'correction' (NKJV), or 'punishment' (NIV), is frequently translated 'instruction' and has the associated meaning of chastisement and discipline. The NIV translation here is probably not the best. Here we are looking at the fool who utterly fails to receive such instruction. What he hears, which to the wise brings understanding and life, is to him folly. Instead of receiving it, he rejects it. It is the same instruction, which in the one by its reception produces understanding and life but which in the other by its rejection merely hardens him in his folly.

[Related proverb: 10:11.]

16:23. From the heart. This verse expresses very similar sentiments to v. 21. Whereas in v. 21 it was the wise in heart, here it is the heart of the wise. Whereas in v. 21 the lips increased learning, here learning is added to the lips. When people know they have something they need to say, no matter how difficult it is they will find a way of saying it. The understanding of the wise in heart makes it clear they have something vital to communicate to others, not because it is something they want to say but because it is something that needs to be said, and so they are guided by their understanding to formulate a way to get it across effectively.

The second clause seems to be suggesting that one result of this process is that it makes what is said that much more worth hearing. For example, a theologian may be very knowledgeable and very orthodox but his manner of expressing truth may be obscure and difficult to follow. If, however, he has a true understanding of it and sees its vital importance to others, a whole new dimension has been added. Then his heart will teach his mouth, and the learning will be added to his lips, so that he will make sure he communicates the truths effectively. It was the apostle Paul's intimate understanding of the gospel and its implications which made him such a fervent, persuasive and effective preacher (2 Corinthians 5:11). But it was not this alone, for he was always concerned to apply the message appropriately to each individual (Colossians 1:28).

The application of these two verses should be self-evident. If we are wise enough to see how they apply to us, we will be wise enough to see that we apply ourselves to what they say!

[Related proverbs: 10:21; 15:7; 16:21.]

16:24. Do you need a sweetener? Never underestimate the power of words. They can minister to both body ('bones') and soul. But what is meant by 'pleasant' words and their being likened to a honeycomb? Are they words which I want to hear? Is it when someone says something nice to me or about me which makes me feel really good? Are they pleasing words? Are they words which minister to my sense of well-being?

Junk food may taste pleasant, but that's about all that can be said for it. Good food is pleasant to the discerning palate and also does you good. These words are couched in the language of fortifying nourishment. If we have a taste for them they will be pleasant as well as doing us good.

In the context of the previous proverbs it is clear that they are words which have their origin, their rationale, in the word of the Lord. These are not flattering words, or entertaining words, or falsely comforting words, or words behind which anything unworthy is concealed. They have a beauty and grace of their own which do nothing but good. They speak the truth and commend what is good, doing it in such a way as brings pleasure to those who receive them.

The nature of this verse indicates that the substance of these words is important. Even though some of the things he said were very hard to receive, the Lord Jesus was universally noted for his gracious words (Luke 4:22; John 7:46), and Christians are urged to gracious speech (Colossians 4:6). There are many different ways of saying something. Some people pride themselves on being blunt and to the point, and although they seem to think it a very noble trait, it can nevertheless conceal a lack of sensitivity toward those to whom they speak. Maybe they could express themselves equally effectively and with more benefit to their hearers were they to think about how to be more agreeable about it! There is much to be said for giving a sweetener if thereby it helps down a bitter pill. For patients off their food serious thought has to be given to how best to get them to take the vital nourishment. Likewise there is much to be said for tenderness and compassion in putting across what might otherwise be an unpalatable truth. How we say something is as important as what it is we are saying.

Ultimately, it is the Word of God which brings sweetness to the soul and health to the bones (Psalms 19:10; 119:103; 107:20). God's Word is pleasant indeed, and our communication of it falls short if it conveys any other impression. The word may deeply wound, but always there is the balm to heal. The sinner may be crushed under the weight of condemnation from the law, but always there is comfort for the repentant in the cross of Christ.

This verse, then, shows us the importance of the way in which we communicate gospel truth. But also, on what we might think as a lesser level, it indicates that our speech in general should be pleasant, and be found to be sweet and strengthening and healing. So give some thought, with reference to specific occasions of praise, or rebuke, or caution, or advice, or exhortation ... or whatever it may be ... and ask yourself whether your words could truly and consistently be described as pleasant.

Consider James 3:11 in context.

16:25. You've already told me that! If this is what you are thinking, then at least you have remembered! This is a verbatim repetition of 14:12, and we hinted there at possible reasons for such duplication. How often we forget, though. Why is this? There can be a number of reasons. One is that we were not really paying much attention the first time. At the time it didn't seem to be relevant or all that important. Or we paid lip service to what was said but somehow it didn't seem to touch us in our circumstances. Or maybe we said, yes, this is important, but its significance was buried under what we considered other more pressing matters at the time, and so it remained at the bottom of the in-tray.

How many times people may hear the gospel of the grace of God, urging them to turn from their wicked ways, and yet at the time the realities of life and death are distant and remote to them. They deceive themselves into imagining that all is well. They are as good as the next person – or at least they are no worse than anyone else. They are essentially good people, and if anyone is going to win the approbation of a God of love, surely they are. On the general scale of things they are doing pretty well, they are 'doing all right' and there is nothing to worry about.

But then something happens, and all of a sudden they remember what they had relegated to the bottom of the pile. Matters of life and death loom large and clear with an awful reality, and what seemed all right at the time is now so obviously all wrong. And what has changed? Nothing – except their perception. How things seem and how they are can be so different!

So let this repetition be a reminder to us never to trust to our own judgement but to rely upon the Lord. He knows the way; we don't. He is our Guide. It is all too easy to forget this. It is often the most experienced of men who have made the most disastrous mistakes. Their judgement was impaired by a false sense of self-confidence.

There are some lessons in life we need to learn over and over again. We can think we've learned them, but as we grow in experience we discover on being reminded of them how little we really understood at the time. The thing takes on a whole new meaning in the light of what has happened in the meantime.

Then there are some truths we need constantly to be reminded of. It is insufficient to know them; they should be kept in the forefront of our thinking. This is one of them. Nothing relating to life and death should at any time be regarded as of little importance.

But isn't there something else lurking in this proverb? Isn't there something which you glimpse out of the corner of your eye but when you look again it evades you? Isn't there something which is playing hide-and-seek, doing its best to keep out of view? There is. It is pride, which clothes itself in an endless variety of innocent guises. In this proverb the voice of God is exposing the voice of pride.

Shortly before his death Peter wrote about people who had forgotten vital truths, using this sobering fact as an incentive to his readers to spiritual diligence. He admitted he was writing nothing new, but he was putting pen to paper because certain reminders are always in order (2 Peter 1:12-15; 3:1-3).

16:26. Motivation. Why do you work? Why does anyone work? In a highly developed society this might not be such a straightforward question to answer, but the underlying basic reason for most is that they do so in order to provide for themselves and their family. The bottom line is that those who do not work do not eat (and it should be recognised by those who *will not* work that they *should not* eat – 2 Thessalonians 3:10). In general, people need to work in order to keep body and soul together, though this elementary truth is rather obscured for the well-off.

This proverb brings us right back to basics. We have to eat to live, and we have to work to eat. There is both a necessity and a compulsion about it. It is a routine into which we are locked by a self-motivating principle. But as we think about it, it becomes apparent that something is operating here which extends way beyond the need to keep ourselves alive.

Many people, when asked the question of why they work, will think in terms of satisfaction. They have an appetite which drives them on, but it is not that of the knotted stomach craving food. It is something beyond this which they regard as equally compelling. They are working for a better lifestyle, or for some specific cause which they believe to be worthy of their efforts. It is all about motivation. Give them sufficient motivation, and they will work their socks off.

We talk about job satisfaction, and it is good that people should derive satisfaction from the work they do. Nevertheless, most people do not work because they enjoy it but rather because of what it will provide for them. Yet there is an elusiveness about both job satisfaction and the satisfaction of what it will provide which is nicely stated in Ecclesiastes 6:7-9. We eat to satisfy our appetite; we work to satisfy our primary needs. In each case, though, the satisfaction is only temporary. There is always a shortfall, especially to the one on the lookout for something better.

Now look at it from the opposite end of the one without this appetite. What about all those people whose lifelong ambitions are never fulfilled? They had the opportunity to fulfil them, and in a vague sort of way they wanted to fulfil them. But when it came to the point of getting down to the task there were too many distractions, and so the task was put off to a more opportune time. There was nothing to drive them on, no inner, inexorable, compelling motive. So the job never got done. One wonders just how many worthy projects which could have benefited countless people were never finished (perhaps not even begun) simply because those suitably equipped to do them lacked the motivation. If it had been essential to themselves it would have been done, but because it was only for others it got left.

Perhaps this verse should make us reflect upon what we do for ourselves, and why, and what we do for others, and why? Are we labourers for the Lord? Think of Colossians 1:29 and 1 Corinthians 15:58 in terms of motivation, and ask yourself whether you have it.

16:27-30. This is a group of proverbs about how godless people go about their work and the harm they do. Look at the imagery in vv. 20-24 and observe that all is sweetness and light, everything is open and clear and beneficial. Now look at vv. 27-30 and see how everything has a dark, underhand, secretive and destructive aspect to it. The godly and the ungodly live side by side in the world, and each has his influence on society. They are in a very real sense at loggerheads. One is constructive, the other is destructive.

Evil is best buried, but here is a scoundrel actually digging it up (v. 27)! Another is found out in the field sowing weeds to choke a crop (v. 28a). Another is quietly laying a minefield to blow apart inseparable companions (v. 28b). Yet another is enticing people into grave danger and taking pleasure in it (v. 29).

16:27. Exposing evil. Fire destroys. The 'ungodly man' or, better, 'scoundrel', is one who is thoroughly unprincipled. Two aspects of his activity are highlighted here: he exposes evil and he spreads evil. The reference to digging up evil (NKJV) or plotting evil (NIV, ESV) uses the same word as for digging a pit. It is a systematic and purposeful activity. The scoundrel is set on putting evil on display, making a trophy of it, making use of it, promoting it. It is on his lips, giving him perverse pleasure as he observes its destructive influence. He is a verbal arsonist, lighting a fire which is not as easily extinguished as a real one. Sometimes we see scoundrels working through the media. Sensationally they expose some of the viler aspects of society, not with the intention of dealing with them, but rather to influence as many people as possible with their lurid perversity. They have an unhealthy, morbid, fascination with what is evil and spread it as far as it will go. So they go into all the details, going to great lengths to pick out whatever 'juicy bits' they can which will then imprint themselves on the minds of others, infecting them and perhaps scarring them for life.

Let us beware the old news vendor's cry, 'Read all about it!' This is no area in which to let our imaginations work overtime in pondering unsavoury details. We are not to listen to such people, and if they try to push their unwelcome influence upon us we are to give them short shrift.

But let us beware something else, too. There are times when we are tempted to 'dig for evil'. Evil is evil. Think of the way radioactive substances are handled. They are dangerous materials, not to be played with, even though they may have some beneficial qualities. Evil is infinitely more dangerous, and it has no beneficial qualities. Every effort needs to be made to contain it, to neutralise its influence, to quench its fire, to remove its memory, to destroy it before it destroys us. What did the Israelites fail to do when they entered the land of promise? They failed systematically to destroy evil. They ignored Deuteronomy 7:25-26 and 12:29-32 and took a perverted interest in it. What happened? It destroyed them, just as God had warned.

It is possible to read these comments without realising that what they address includes a gossiping tongue. Give some consideration to how you should deal with gossip, either in yourself or in others.

[Related proverbs: 6:14; 26:20.]

16:28. How to perpetuate trouble. The greatest of troubles in any society are caused not by disease or natural disaster or any kind of unexpected calamity, but by strife in which people are at odds with one another. Individuals cease talking to each other, couples separate, families feud and fall apart, churches are split; and these things happen even though all the outward circumstances are conducive to prosperity and well-being. The reason why they happen is that people are unable to resolve their differences. So many families in our prosperous society experience profound emotional stress and deep unhappiness because members cannot live tolerantly side by side but are always arguing and fighting.

Invariably in such situations there are champions of causes who are more intent on running others down and speaking evil of them than maintaining and defending what they believe in an appropriate manner. This proverb addresses people like this. It is a mark of perversity to stir up and spread dissension. It never does anyone any good, and if the one responsible gains any satisfaction from what he or she has done, it is only a perverse one.

The second clause, however, addresses a really sinister aspect of this. The talebearer, or gossip, or whisperer, is master of the quiet undertone which says (privately, of course!): 'Have you heard...?', or, 'Are you aware that...?' as an introduction to a piece of information (very often misinformation) which will only do further damage.

Jesus gave instructions in Matthew 18:15-20 on how to deal with sins and offences between people. In the first instance it was to be kept private and to be dealt with privately between the parties involved. Only if it could not be resolved in this way was it to be brought out into the open and dealt with publicly. But in no case was there to be whispering behind people's backs. Whispering can do a great deal of harm, and it is said here to be capable of dividing close friends. The whisperer often puts on a plausible front of discretion: 'Don't let this go any further, but I think you ought to know....'

Sometimes a rumour is circulated about a person, and the person concerned is the last one to know about it. The first they become aware that something is amiss is when others start to look sideways at them or avoid them or in other ways act mysteriously toward them. Those who have been the object of malicious rumours know just how hurtful and damaging they can be, and sometimes people can believe the lies for years and the effects can linger painfully.

At other times one can hear a bad report about a friend which has all the hallmarks of authenticity about it because it is supposedly common knowledge, even though denied by the friend. Perhaps much later it comes to light that it was no more than empty and unfounded gossip originating from one individual. But by then the damage has been done and cannot be undone.

When accusations are made against church leaders, Paul in 1 Timothy 5:19-20 makes it very clear how they ought to be handled. Either they are to be summarily dismissed, or, if they have foundation, to be dealt with publicly. We should not be ignorant of Satan's devices (2 Corinthians 2:11). Within the church there is to be no place for the talebearer. We should neither tolerate nor encourage any communication which displays these underhand characteristics. Gossips need to be put down with a gracious ruthlessness!

[Related proverbs: 15:18; 17:9; 18:8; 26:20,21,22.]

16:29. Misleading the unwary. Wicked people rarely act on their own but find themselves in need of support of one kind or another. The 'violent' man of this verse is not necessarily one who is overtly physically violent. It could be one who has a cruel and heartless disposition, and one who is doing violence to the truth. Many a man who fits this description presents a public image which belies his true nature. A man of this kind has many ploys at his disposal to draw others, particularly the weak willed, into his schemes. The ringleader has his minions to do his dirty work for him. Notice the progression: he entices, and he leads. First he gets him on his side, and then he manipulates him to do what he wants. First there is a softening up process, and then he has him on a string. Where does he lead him?

It doesn't say he leads him in a bad way. Doesn't it mean that? Yes, of course it does. So why say 'not good' rather than outright 'bad'? There are two aspects to this. First of all, it *is* a way that is *not* good. People should be led in a way that *is* good, but the way this person is being led lacks this essential quality. Secondly, it is suggestive of the discovery along the way that it is not good, as if this person embarked on this course imagining that all was well only to realise after a little time that all was far from well. Sometimes people find themselves up to their neck in trouble and unable to get out of it, at the mercy of the unscrupulous who have a hold on them. Why? Because they were enticed in the first place and got involved for all the wrong reasons. What they naïvely imagined would be good for them turned out to be bad for them.

It is not so easy to back out again when one has succumbed to enticement. There are people who are very keen to make profit out of the weak willed and gullible. This proverb is not about gangland or anything as dramatic as that. People are daily being drawn into things which they later regret, whether in the form of relationships, financial commitments, business deals, or whatever, because they were seeing what they wanted to see, not what was really there. Whose fault was it that they were misled?

16:30. Without a word. There are some body gestures that are part and parcel of covert communication, intended to convey something to 'those in the know' without actually articulating it. It all speaks of subversiveness. But there could possibly be another side to this too, because, to use a well-known expression, people sometimes deliberately close their eyes to what they don't want to see in order to pursue their own agenda, and they keep their mouths shut when they ought to be speaking truth. So, when something wrong is done, on receiving his payment an accomplice might say, 'Remember, I didn't see it.' Of course, he did see it, but he is turning a blind eye to the action. He is also going to keep his mouth shut about it. He is thus perverting the course of justice and perpetrating evil.

We need to be exceedingly careful that we never resort to underhand tactics in order to avoid our responsibility in upholding the right. It is all too easy to adopt a compromising attitude for the sake of peace (our own, that is), behaving as if we hadn't seen something, or failing to speak out when we should. If we are doing that, are we not imitating the unprincipled and promoting their cause?

Or the pursing of the lips could be taken as an expression of deliberate malicious intent and purposefulness which speak louder than words.

Though there are various ways of interpreting the winking of the eye and the pursing of the lips, yet they speak clearly of underhand tactics. That is so often how the devil works.

In these verses picture the subversive activity of Satan. Under one of his many guises he entices, he draws in, he leads in a way that is not right. One sin leads to another ... and another. People who end up where they should not can often look back with regret and trace how they got there. The appeal to their passions or appetites was a cover for something far more sinister. Again we ask the question: whose fault was it that they were misled?

[Related proverbs: 6:12-14.]

16:31. Still bearing fruit in old age (Psalm 92:14).

Asked to what they attribute their longevity, the very elderly have given all sorts of answers, ranging from a strict diet, through an active lifestyle, to a carefree attitude toward life. That may very well be, but the Bible consistently makes just one meaningful association, namely with righteousness.

The original probably does not warrant the conditional 'if' inserted in the NKJV. As with many of the proverbs, this one is a general observation, expressing an abiding principle, and does not mean that it is universally true. That is, there might be some silver-haired rogues around! – see Ecclesiastes 8:12. There might equally be those who are righteous who never reach the age of silver hair. Outstandingly godly men like Robert Murray M'Cheyne and Henry Martyn died young. We have to look at this from the right end – this proverb is not concerned with one of the causes of longevity but one of the results of righteousness and the reason for it. How do you view aged believers whose life has been in the path of righteousness?

God promised to lengthen Solomon's days if he remained obedient to him (1 Kings 3:14). This was in direct confirmation of his word in

Deuteronomy 17:20 regarding kings. To what end was this promise given? Was it not to extend his usefulness in godly leadership? It was not merely for his own blessing, but especially for the blessing of others through him.

Deuteronomy 25:15 is set in the context of the maintenance of right standards and justice. The lengthening of days is associated with continuity and stability, the foundation for which is righteousness.

Long life was one of the promises for those whose hearts were set on walking with God (Psalm 91:16; Proverbs 3:2,16), which is the reason that it is said that the silver-haired head is found in the way of righteousness.

Job (12:12) asserted that wisdom and understanding were to be found with the aged. As has been observed throughout the Book of Proverbs, wisdom and understanding are inseparable from righteousness. But unlike physical strength, which grows and then declines, in general wisdom and understanding increase with age and experience.

Matters of judgement were entrusted to the elders of the people in Israel, not to the young and inexperienced. In general, the aged, especially those active in society, were respected for their experience and wisdom, and so the presence of a grey or white head was a mark of honour and regarded as a beautiful adornment (the sense of 'glory' here – see also 20:29). Leviticus 19:32 refers to honouring the elderly in the fear of God. Maybe it is with this partly in mind that Paul tells Timothy not to rebuke an older man but to accord him respect in the way he addresses him (1 Timothy 5:1).

It may be that you can without hesitation think of elderly people rich in grace and experience whose wisdom and counsel you have cause greatly to value. It is sad that in some churches the elderly are undervalued, whereas their company if sought out can be immensely beneficial. Just because they can *do* little does not mean they have little to contribute! Elderly saints can be some of the most important members of the church.

Are there elderly believers with whom you can share meaningfully in the things of God?

16:32. Self-restraint. Some comment was made on self-control at 14:29. In the Bible there are many references to the mighty and the honour accorded them (consider, for example, 2 Samuel 23:8-39), and the taking of cities is recorded in the book of Joshua and elsewhere. It is the mighty who find their way into our history books. People responsible for great exploits are rightly remembered; and yet, says this proverb, there are some who are better than them, who by and large attract no particular attention.

This is one of the 'better than' proverbs, and what an astonishing and uncomfortable comparison is made here! Look closely at what are being compared. In a nutshell, it is the restraint of power which is being compared with the display of power.

Why is it that someone who is slow to anger (the best translation) is better than the mighty? There are at least two possible answers to this. The first is that self restraint requires more effort than the display of power; the second is that it actually does more good.

This can be illustrated by the youngster at the wheel of a powerful car, surging past vehicles which are already travelling at a respectable speed, extravagantly weaving in and out of the traffic. Why? Is he in a hurry? Not at all. He is showing off and enjoying the exhilaration of letting rip! To restrain all that power is more than he can do! But he is probably making a nuisance of himself to other road users.

This proverb is not commending those of a placid temperament who would never be considered capable of accomplishing any outstanding feats, but rather addressing those who have it in them to react and act. It is highlighting the very real difficulty of exercising self control in the face of provocation.

The trouble with anger is that when aroused it tends to react before considering the whole picture, and therefore reacts inappropriately, doing more harm than good. Slowness to anger is learned often through bitter experience and the input of considerable effort. We need to learn to rule our spirit, to govern our temper. When we feel the temperature rising and the pressure building, we need to operate the safety valve of objective rationality. One way in which we can be helped not to react explosively is to cultivate the habit of immediately referring every issue that confronts us to the Lord. If we are in the habit of doing this automatically with relatively small matters, then when a big one arises we are more likely to be preserved from a volatile reaction. Another way is that we should be developing the habit of seeking the good of all with whom we come into contact, irrespective of how they treat us, our concern for them overriding our concern for ourselves.

Paul has something to say about this in Romans 12:17-21. When it comes to anger, we are to give place to him who really does have power and knows how to exercise it. Think about that passage in the light of this proverb, and consider not only the restraint of power but the power of restraint.

[Related proverbs: 14:29; 19:11; 25:28.]

16:33. A little about lots. If the expression 'into the lap' is to be taken literally it may simply reflect the method used for casting lots. But it could mean 'into the midst', in which case the picture is more of people gathered round to see what the outcome will be. Whatever may have been the details of procedure, the casting of lots was done in public as a means for reaching decisions and seems to have served two distinct purposes.

Firstly, in essence it was a random process, a device which would therefore ensure that decisions were seen to be free from bias. This seems to be its use in 18:18. In this spirit lots were cast for Jesus' garment (Psalm 22:18; John 19:23-24). The division of the land of Canaan was by lot (hence the terms 'allotted' and 'allotment'), presumably with the same intention of impartiality and to avoid argument (Numbers 26:55-56; Joshua 18:10 – 19:51).

Lots were cast for the two goats on the Day of Atonement, to decide which should be for the sin offering and which for the scapegoat (Leviticus 16:8) – illustrating two aspects of Christ's saving work. The first is that as a sin offering he died for sin. He was presented to God to bear before God the wrath which was due on account of the sins of his people. The second is that he carried their sins away, never to be recalled. Whichever way we look at it, Jesus has effectively dealt with the sins of his people, and the account is fully and finally settled. We might ask why it was necessary to cast lots for the goats, seeing that either would have served equally well for either purpose. Part of the answer must surely be that there was nothing remote or automatic or impersonal about Jesus' sacrificial death. His death was a matter of deliberate choice, in which both man and God were involved.

The second purpose behind the casting of lots is indicated in Joshua 18:6,10 in that the lots were cast before the Lord: it was a random process submitted to God for his guidance. This wasn't superstition, but done on the understanding that God was in control of all things, and that he would guide in respect of decisions which were beyond their knowledge or ability to make rightly and fairly.

Even unbelievers in the true God were known to cast lots for divine guidance, as in the case of the sailors transporting Jonah (Jonah 1:7). Whether or not in that particular case it was mere superstition, God overruled it for his own purposes.

In Joshua 7:16-18 the method of lots may well have been used to determine who was responsible for the trouble at Ai. Also, the Urim and Thummim may have had some connection with the casting of lots, though this was very specifically a means for seeking to know the mind of God in certain matters (Exodus 28:30; Numbers 27:21; 1 Samuel 28:6; Nehemiah 7:65).

Acts 1:26 records the use of the lot to discern the Lord's will as to who should succeed Judas Iscariot as an apostle. This is the last recorded case in Scripture of lots being cast to determine the will of God, and there is no indication that there is any longer a place in the Christian church for the use of such a method. Rather, it is assumed that now, having the full revelation of the inscripturated Word of God, his people will be guided by this under the influence of the Holy Spirit without the need to resort to the casting of lots or similar methods.

We should see beyond the literal act of 'the lot cast into the lap' to recognise that there is a part for people to play in seeking guidance from God. In most cases concerning God's guidance there are present both the human and divine aspects. For example, in Acts 15 in the council at Jerusalem the apostles were facing a fundamental issue and a great deal hung upon the outcome. The human aspect was evident in considerable debate, but the divine aspect was seen as God overruled the discussion, bringing scripture and recent experience in the growth of the church together to make clear what should be done.

The question sometimes arises, however, about how to choose between alternatives – sometimes very important ones – when one can clearly see arguments in favour of each but there are no obvious deciding factors. People can get into a mental tangle in situations like this with fears like: 'What if I make the wrong choice?' 'How can I be sure what is God's will in this matter?' It may not be a case of casting lots, but mentally it is very near it, being perceived as virtually a 'toss-up' between alternatives.

But do we not choose between alternatives almost every day about lesser things without batting an eyelid? This is because we do not perceive these matters as sufficiently important to warrant seeking God over them. So at what point do matters become sufficiently important that we need very specifically to know the will of the Lord?

There is no need to become neurotic about this kind of thing. Christians should be thinking in terms of doing the will of God at all times and in all situations with the awareness that their lives are in God's hands. James takes to task those who choose their course presumptuously (James 4:13-16). Whether the matter is little or big in our eyes, whether or not we are conscious of a clear need to seek guidance from God, by faith we may rest in the truth stated in this proverb, that every decision is from the Lord. He can and does overrule the thinking of those who truly submit to him and desire his will. We may choose course A when we might equally have chosen course B, but if we have intelligently committed our way to the Lord (which might include seeking counsel and advice from others – see 15:22 for example) we may rest assured that he has our decisions under his control. It may in the end have seemed a random choice for us, but it is not so with God.

So who is in control, and to what extent? This proverb informs us that the whole matter is under God's direction. People didn't cast lots for most decisions, only the ones for which the method was appropriate. For most of our decisions in life, the way is obvious and there is no need to seek special guidance. But when we are particularly in need of the Lord's direction and we therefore particularly seek him about a decision, maybe with a very real consciousness of our limitations of knowledge about what is involved, we may trust him implicitly to guide our steps, so that what may seem somewhat random from our point of view will actually lead us onward in the way he would have us take.

If you have any important decisions to make how will this proverb affect your approach to making them?

[Related proverb: 18:18.]

17:1. Having a good time? Feasting was normally associated with sacrifices at religious festivals (Leviticus 23), and the word for sacrifices is used here. While such festivals were intended as joyful celebrations of God's great goodness to his people (see also Deuteronomy 12), it was possible for them to be abused, especially when the occasion became a formality and the consciousness of God was lost (Amos 5:21-24; Isaiah 1:14-17). Then the feasting would become man-centred, and such occasions tend to be characterised by overindulgence and trouble. From the sacrifices of peace where God presided they turned into the sacrifices of strife where man held sway. A New Testament example of this is found among the church at Corinth in their abuse of the Lord's Supper (1 Corinthians 11:17-22).

A feast, of course, attracts a lot of attention. That 'there will be a good spread afterwards' will often persuade a person to attend a function who might otherwise stay at home. But there are more important things than food and drink and having a good time. People need to appeal to more than their appetites and ask what else is going on, what is likely to happen? Judging from the clubbers emerging from their night's indulgence one might wonder whether the drunkenness and brawling and vomiting and hangover were really considered in advance.

Another of the 'better than' proverbs, this one starkly asks us to examine the cost of our pleasures and luxuries. It goes without saying that we would prefer a feast to a dry morsel, but we would also prefer the quietness of undisturbed security to strife and trouble. When we look at the strings attached, which is the more important? Which will best minister to our overall well-being? When the question is asked, the answer is pretty obvious. The trouble is, the question is so often left unasked.

For the child of God, it is vital to look at the overall picture – not just in terms of food and drink which is the framework of the proverb, but in terms of material and emotional well-being when there might be doubtful implications. Many is the person who has been involved in what has appeared to be a very successful business enterprise, but who by choosing that particular path has become embroiled in bitter wrangling, legal battles, underhand practices, and the like, for whom these things have generated a great pall of misery overshadowing everything else. They have everything they could desire, but ironically they have nothing worth having. How they wish they could trade places with the person of limited means who is free from all these encumbrances and troubles and enjoys true contentment and security!

This proverb directs our minds to the choices we make in life. Do we make them with our eyes open? More importantly, do we make them with an acknowledgement of the Lord, valuing the things he values? We are not to go down the route where he has been forgotten and left out. Our supposed 'good time' will only have a very sour after-taste and leave us with bitter regrets. For those who know the quietness, the peace, the security, of resting in the Lord, even the dry morsel is as good as a feast!

[Related proverbs: 15:16,17.]

17:2. Wisdom and status. The idea of a servant ruling over any member of the family in which he serves appears to be almost a contradiction in terms. Does he serve, or does he rule? Surely he cannot do both ... or can he? A ruler serving is one thing, but a servant ruling is quite another.

A servant is one who has no rights of his own but is at all times required to attend to his master's wishes. If his master is good, he might enjoy a good life and have many privileges, as was the case with Abraham's servant. In fact, that man ruled over all that his master had (Genesis 24:2). It is also evident that he was a wise man, as the ensuing narrative reveals. Joseph, likewise, exercised wisdom in Potiphar's household and was made overseer there (Genesis 39:2-6). Yet those benefits could be taken away in an instant, as happened (unjustly) in Joseph's case. A man is likely to put up with a great deal from his son, but he will be less tolerant toward a servant who steps out of line.

The comparison here is between a wise servant and a shameful son. By birth, one has no rights and privileges while the other has them all and abuses them. One has no entitlement to an inheritance, whereas the other does. What this proverb is telling us is that one without entitlement may by wisdom gain what the other forfeits through lack of it. Wisdom is not constrained by the forces of rank and privilege. Wisdom makes its own way, whoever may be its possessor. Family, status, connections, wealth ... wisdom neither requires them nor depends upon them. Many a son has been a 'black sheep of the family' and disgraced the family name or squandered the family wealth, and many such have been tolerated and excused and forborne with for a long time. But ultimately, the wise servant is recognised and honoured and considered worthy of the place the unworthy son has sacrificed, even to the point of exercising authority over him and sharing in the inheritance reserved for the sons.

Here, then, are both encouragement and caution. The importance and value of godly wisdom cannot be overestimated. It is of supreme worth. On the other hand, natural privileges cannot be presumed upon. Consider the Jewish nation, who had everything going for them, for whom Paul wept because they, by unbelief, forfeited all that would otherwise have been theirs (Romans 9). Jesus himself spoke of the kingdom being taken from them and given to another (Matthew 21:43), and of the sons of the kingdom being thrown into the outer darkness (Matthew 8:12).

Wisdom and service go together. Are you involved in any kind of service? If so, there is usually scope for initiative and enterprise and a need for wisdom to fulfil the position responsibly. Potiphar would never have elevated his slave Joseph had he not observed wisdom in him. So think for a little while about whatever services you might be rendering, whether as an employee or in any other capacity. Are you merely fulfilling them to the letter, or do you give thought to how you might serve more effectively and really prosper those you serve?

Jesus says to those who have served him well, 'Well done, good and faithful servant; you have been faithful over a few things, I will make you ruler over many things. Enter into the joy of your lord' (Matthew 25:23).

[Related proverb: 11:29.]

17:3. Fiery trials. Silver and gold are precious metals, but it is not their ores which are put on display. Nor does anyone want to show off anything manufactured from these metals if they are contaminated with impurities. The silver and gold that are valued have passed through the refining process to ensure they are as pure as possible.

The 'heart' (not the physical organ) is the seat of man's thinking and emotions. What is it worth? The answer is that it is worth little if it has not been subjected to being tested by the Lord. Malachi 3:2-3 speaks of the Lord coming like a refiner to purify his people. The only heart which is of any value is that which has been purged and cleansed and purified by the Lord. His testing of the heart is anything but comfortable, for there is much dross to be burned off. The writer of Hebrews uses a different image to describe the way God's Word probes our hearts (Hebrews 4:12-13), and later he writes of chastening and scourging that we might be purified and made partakers of his holiness (Hebrews 12:5-11).

The proverb by its very comparison seems to indicate that the process can be an uncomfortable one. But it is also a worthwhile one. It presupposes there is something there of worth (unlike those addressed in Jeremiah 6:27-30). Christians may have renewed hearts, but that does not mean there is not much to be cleansed from them. Christians *do* have renewed hearts, and that means that the cleansing process is eminently worthwhile. So when we are subjected to fiery trials, let us remember 1 Peter 1:6-9 and submit with patience and faith. Invariably the Christians who are most used by the Lord in this world are those in whom his refining work has had most effect.

The refiner may test the metal and decide that it is still not fit for use. God may test our hearts and find us not yet fit for the purpose he has in mind for us. That means more refining. In the midst of the trials we may feel utterly worthless and we may wonder why the Lord is allowing us to go through them. However, the truth is that the Lord is not simply *allowing* us to go through them, but *ordaining* that we go through them, and not because we are worthless but because we are precious in his sight and he will make us vessels fit for his use. Surely it is not the will of God that impurities should mar our usefulness? Surely we have to admit there is still dross to be removed from our hearts? The Lord knows how he wants us to be and how we are to represent him – and who are we to question him? The end result is always worth the painful process.

There will be occasions in your life when you may be questioning the Lord as to why he is giving you such a hard and painful time. At such times you need to remember the words of the Lord Jesus: 'Blessed are the pure in heart' (Matthew 5:8). He is intent upon your blessing, and if the Lord is giving you a hard time you can be thankful that it is because you are in his hands and that the outcome is certain. Let us not live in denial concerning our 'impurities' but seek his face and his righteousness. See also Psalm 24:3-6.

[Related proverbs: 25:4; 27:21.]

17:4. 'Here! Just listen to this!' This section of Proverbs several times mentions the perversion of truth and justice. See also vv. 7,13,15,23.

Juicy scandal. This proverb refers to attention being captured and retained. Someone hears something which causes him to prick up his ears – his attention is grabbed. As he begins to listen, so he becomes absorbed in what he is hearing. This is the aural equivalent of an advertisement board, on which there is a large print caption to attract attention, and once the eye is directed where the advertiser wants it, it automatically moves on to the small print. The example in this proverb is the natural attraction of falsehood and malice to people whose minds are evil and whose motives are deceitful. They are attracted as wasps to jam by the heady scent and the sticky substance.

However hard they may try to hide it, people behave according to type. This is what wicked people and liars do, it is their food and drink. It is unrealistic to expect otherwise from them. Having eagerly absorbed what is vain, worthless and damaging, they then retail it to others.

A couple of applications from this are fairly obvious. The first is a caution to the God-fearing person, for ever present is the temptation to be attracted by the wrong things and to stretch out the ear to what will, at best, do no good and, at worst, prove to be a corrupting influence. It is worth giving thought to how one should react to the things one often cannot but hear. We may not be able to avoid hearing, but we can avoid heeding or showing any enthusiasm for such things.

The second application is that we need to know the person who is speaking before taking at face value what we are told. There are countless situations in which the very plausibility of a statement is belied by a knowledge of the character of the one making it. One should in general beware those who are in the habit of picking up and passing on juicy bits of scandal, or who have a flair for giving very colourful presentations of things they have heard, and consider what it says about *them* before giving any credence to what they have to say about *others*.

In particular, we need to be able to recognise the tell-tale signs in those who pass on falsehood under the guise of truth and speak evil of people under the guise of righteous indignation. One is the manner in which the matter is presented, and the other is the motive under which it is presented. In general, because of the attractiveness of what is sordid to those who are corrupt, we need to be exceedingly cautious about anything we hear which reflects badly upon others.

Christians are susceptible to listening to the wrong things, imbibing evil reports and making wrong judgements. The Lord's grace and power are needed to shun attitudes which are characteristic of evildoers. The words of a malicious tongue can sometimes stick like barbs in the mind. How are they to be dealt with?

[Related proverbs: 10:32; 24:2; 26:28.]

17:5. Two hard-hearted attitudes. Here are two situations within the experience of most of us. Both are offences against God, for in the latter case the implication is that punishment will be meted out by God. This kind of behaviour is often seen overtly in children, and it is also often a thinly veiled attitude among adults.

Oppressing the poor was considered at 14:31. Mocking them is but another form of oppression. The poor, as well as the rich, are created equal in God's sight. Both came naked into this world, and both leave it in the same way. What they possess in terms of this world's goods is irrelevant to their status as beings created in the image of God. But the term 'poor' covers far more than the lack of material possessions. It includes those who find themselves with specific needs through illness or adverse circumstances. It also includes those disadvantaged in other ways, such as those with physical deformities, or those lacking in some respects in their mental faculties, or those who stand out as being 'different' from others in other ways, who are therefore considered to be 'inferior'. Children often poke fun at them, either to their face or behind their back, thereby often further damaging them emotionally. But the attitudes of children are often carried through into adult life. Any kind of discrimination against the 'poor' is but a form of mockery. It treats them with contempt as if purely by their status they are not worthy of attention or consideration. This indictment stands against the mockers, that they are reproaching God. Even if some are 'poor' through their own fault, having abused what has been given them, yet to hold them in derision is, in God's eyes, contemptible, for those who do so are failing to recognise his own image in them – and nothing can change that.

The most serious form of mockery, however, is to give the poor some prospect of help only to withdraw it again. The law of God said to the Israelites, 'You shall open your hand wide to your brother, to your poor and your needy' (Deuteronomy 15:11). This law still applies to his people. If it is within our power and opportunity to help our neighbour who is in some way disadvantaged, and that neighbour has some reasonable expectation of help from us, then by withholding what we might do is equivalent to mocking.

The second clause is about those who are gleeful at the misfortunes of others. While it is true that some people take a perverted pleasure in seeing others suffer, it is probable that this statement is addressing something more personal. Suppose, for example, I have a neighbour whom I don't like (for whatever reason). If he falls ill, or his house is burgled, or some other disaster befalls him, am I to rejoice and say he deserved it? Again, whatever may have happened to him, and whatever his attitude may have been to me, I am still to recognise that God is his Maker, and I am to show him the respect which is accordingly due. Far from being right in my gloating that God is punishing him for what he is or what he has done, I am rather bringing punishment upon myself for my own sinfully superior attitude. It is to his own Master that he stands or falls; that is not my business, and neither do I have any right of judgement in the matter.

God is not only our Maker, but he is also the one who is in control of our circumstances. What we are and what we have we owe completely and utterly to his goodness and grace toward us. Our attitudes toward both ourselves and our fellow beings should reflect this.

[Related proverbs: 14:31; 19:17; 21:13; 24:17.]

17:6. Family as it ought to be. The preciousness of family life is in evidence here, a proper kind of pride which appreciates and values the bonds which exist within a stable and secure family unit, a closeness which has come about through a long and sometimes painful process of nurture, with discipline and advice, with encouragement and praise, with love and thoughtfulness and appreciation … and all the things which go to make up a whole person.

Above all, though, should be the acknowledgement of the kindness of God, for even if it is not stated in this particular proverb, yet the proverbs as a whole indicate that the fear of the Lord is essential to proper development in any area of life, not least that of the family. It should be noticed that the family bond spoken of here is one which not only spans generations, indicating continuity, but involves mutual affection and respect both from the elder toward the younger and from the younger toward the elder. God has made the family to be the fundamental unit of society. Where the love and security and trust implicit in what this proverb says are present, then society prospers. Where they are absent, it crumbles.

The literal 'children's children' is a better translation than 'grandchildren' (ESV) because continuity is being expressed here rather than limiting the statement to a particular generation. However, grandchildren can be thought of as the real starting point of that continuity, where values are seen to be being passed on from generation to generation.

What does it mean, that children's children are the crown of old men? A crown is symbolic of status, but the word is also used figuratively, as for example when we talk of a 'crowning achievement'. This is not describing sentimental doting of the elderly upon their grandchildren. It is the grandchildren who are the crown, not by their existence but by their conduct. When we consider all the instruction and advice and exhortation from father to son in the book of Proverbs, the evidence of its being heeded not only by children but by grandchildren is a mark of its success. The Word of God is to be passed down from generation to generation (Deuteronomy 4:9-10), and when its effects are observed in grandchildren then it is clear that this element of continuity is present. It is a reminder to us that we should not only be training our children to be obedient to the Word but showing them the principles contained within it. For when the rationale for obedience is understood, then it will be transmitted beyond its immediate present application.

The second clause speaks of the glory of children being their father. This can be taken in two slightly different ways. The NIV takes it in one way when it says that 'parents are the pride of their children'. We more often think of children who do well as being the pride of their parents. This is the other way round. Sometimes children are embarrassed about their parents, especially when they are in the company of their peers. It is a sign of a healthy family relationship when they can without reserve speak well of their parents. Usually it indicates a very open relationship between parents and their children, where no artificial barriers are set up, where all things can be talked about freely and respectfully.

The other way of reading this statement, that 'the glory of children is their father' (NKJV) is that it is the 'father' (both parents are included under this) who is responsible for what makes the children shine. When we see well-balanced children getting on well in life we can be pretty sure that in most cases it is largely on account of their upbringing. Good parenting lies at the back of it.

How open and God-honouring are your family relationships, and what are you doing to promote the principles behind this proverb?

17:7. Words are not always what they seem. The word used here for 'fool' is not the usual one in the Book of Proverbs but describes a worthless, profane person. The word is 'nabal', which may be familiar as the name of Abigail's husband who in a time of plenty churlishly refused David and his men provisions to meet their needs. We are told that Nabal was harsh and evil in his doings, and a scoundrel (1 Samuel 25:3,25). Abigail found it necessary to confess to David that as his name was, so was he. The same word is used at the commencement of Psalms 14 and 53, where the subsequent description fills out our understanding of the kind of person in view.

The reason why what is described here as 'excellent speech' is unbecoming in such a person is that it is not matched by quality of character. The kind of talk described here is 'over and above', or 'excess', and perhaps the notion is that of the fool having things on his lips which are beyond him. There is something intensely distasteful when a person of this kind speaks as if he were a paragon of virtue, or propounds high ideals, or makes great claims, or expresses noble ambitions. They are entirely out of character and have no hope of fulfilment in his case. There is a glaring disparity between what he says and what he is. Thus his words are totally inappropriate. Not only so, but such fine talk is often a tool for unworthy ends. It is a front in order to promote his own agenda.

Nabal himself is an example, with his high sounding words in 1 Samuel 25:10-11. Taken on their own and without regard to the circumstances it sounds very good. Looking at the whole picture, though, they were no more than a cover-up for his greed. He was concerned neither for justice nor for his employees.

At the other end we have a nobleman (probably better than 'prince', NKJV, ESV). This would be a person of status and influence in whom wisdom and understanding, integrity, honesty *and truth* are expected. If a fool's boasting may readily be dismissed on most occasions, when a person of influence practises deceit then trouble is in the wind. Much is expected from those to whom much is given. A fool 'talking big' can do relatively little harm, but a person in authority talking lies is likely to do much. Sadly this is not an uncommon problem among people in power when they are not rooted in good principles by which to operate. Power and corruption are proverbially linked in the pithy observation, 'Power corrupts; absolute power corrupts absolutely.' One of the principal ways in which such corruption is observed is in the covering up of unprincipled practices; in other words, in lying lips.

We have an example in Absalom (2 Samuel 15:1-6), whose fine words were lies designed to mislead the innocent, the outcome of which was civil war.

This proverb addresses us in two ways. Firstly, we need to consider whether any of our own words conceal dishonourable attitudes or practices. Secondly, we need to cultivate discrimination, because a person's words should not be understood in isolation from his or her character.

17:8. I'll make it worth your while. This isn't noting the true prosperity of a generous person but focusing on the dark side, for what is described here as a 'present' or a 'gift' (NKJV, KJV) is always used in a negative sense and essentially denotes bribery. It is a 'gift' purely in the selfish sense of its purchasing power. The very language used in this proverb should arouse suspicion. The 'precious stone', or 'charm' has connotations of subversive attraction. People are dazzled by it, their mental vision is impaired, their judgement is put to one side.

Two points are worth noting here. The first is that this proverb describes how a bribe is seen by its possessor, who seems to think that it can open any door to him. The second is related to it, that he thinks this way because it is so often true.

Such is the covetous nature of men and women that given sufficient incentive they will say and do almost anything. We have a striking example of this in the soldiers who witnessed the signs accompanying the resurrection of Jesus but who put their lives on the line, accepting a huge bribe to conceal what they knew and to tell a lie (Matthew 28:1-4,11-15). No doubt the chief priests and elders of the Jews were pleased (at least temporarily) with the result.

Bribery and corruption have always existed in the world, and always will as long as people have covetous hearts, and those who have the means to buy off others and pervert the course of justice will continue to succeed. But what they think or the success they seem to enjoy is only a very limited take on the situation. God's view is the one which matters, and his righteous judgement is the one which will prevail. Whatever may happen in the interim, the time will come when all will be put to rights.

Curiously, there are many who believe they can 'buy off' God, as if by their good works and acts of charity and the like they can appease him and gain his favour. Or they want to 'get him to do something' for them and imagine that they can make it worth his while by promising him something in return. Viewed from any angle, it is utterly ridiculous, reflecting man's high opinion of himself and his low opinion of God (see Psalm 50:21).

The 'free gift' enticement used as a marketing technique, and the 'offer too good to refuse', are but examples of the way covetousness is exploited by the covetous for the covetous! Beware of buying into it! If ever you are dazzled by the 'something for nothing' offer, remember it is not being done for your benefit at all but to prosper the one making the offer, and is appealing to, and encouraging, attitudes in you which ought rather to be put to death.

[Related proverbs: 15:27; 17:23; 18:16; 21:14.]

17:9. Bury or broadcast? This is a little different from 16:28, because here the context is actual transgression. People wrong one another in all kinds of ways, some small, some large, sometimes accidentally, often deliberately. This happens because we are all sinners, and even if saved by God's grace, yet there are still occasions when we sin against others. Very often it happens in the way we speak of others.

To take a very realistic example, suppose I blurt out something about a friend I ought not to have said which, if it reached his ears, would grieve him exceedingly. If the person to whom I said this sought love, he would probably rebuke me for my outburst and see to it that the matter was laid to rest, and so my friendship would continue as before. If, however, with self-righteous indignation or with malicious intent this person went to my friend and reported what I had said, maybe even harping on about it, it could have the potential for driving a wedge between us and our friendship.

The contrast here is between covering something to hide it from view, and exposing it for all to see and for making sure it is kept on display. One does his best to ensure that the wrongdoing is buried so that it is to all intents forgotten, whereas the other grabs it, duplicates it and distributes it to all and sundry. It is all a matter of motivating principle. One is love, the other pure selfishness whatever plausible 'reasons' are given to suggest otherwise.

We have the example of God himself in all this. The covering of transgressions features in the opening of Psalm 32, where we see that it is God himself who does the covering. The consistent message of the Bible is that God takes no pleasure of any kind in sin, nor does he take pleasure in its consequences in the death of the wicked (Ezekiel 18:23; 2 Peter 3:9), and if he exposes sin he does so with the intention that the sinner might see its enormity, repent of it, seek forgiveness and have it effectively covered once and for all by God (Isaiah 1:10-18). It is because God so *loved* the world that he gave his only begotten Son, that whoever believes in him should not perish but have everlasting life (John 3:16). It wasn't to condemn the world that he sent him, but that through him the world might be saved (John 3:17). It is the covering of transgressions, not the broadcasting of them, which promotes any good. Love among mankind is in short enough supply. If we really are seeking love, it will be seen in our attitude when dealing with the transgressions (real or imagined) that we see in others, whether they affect us directly or indirectly.

In the light of such love on God's part, the question which this proverb should leave hanging in our mind is, how do we talk about or deal with the faults and sins of others?

[Related proverbs: 10:12; 11:13; 16:28.]

17:10. Sensitivity to correction. The scenario of this proverb is the uncomfortable one of being put right when we go wrong. No one likes to be told he is wrong, and even less to be rebuked for it. Before we proceed, let us be quite clear that this proverb is not talking about other people, it is addressing us. It invites us to do two things. Firstly, we are to reflect on how we take rebuke; and secondly, we are to reflect on what our reaction to rebuke says about us.

The first person spoken of here is a person of discernment, one who is accustomed to giving thought to matters, and it is evident from what is said that even wise and discerning people sometimes need to be rebuked. James includes those who teach the Word of God to others – in whom we might expect spiritual maturity – when he writes of our all stumbling in many things (James 3:2). Even leaders have faults and failings ... in *many* things! Their reaction to correction needs to be exemplary. Sometimes when we stumble we need to be pulled up sharply. In 2 Timothy 3:16 Paul indicates one of the functions of the Word of God for *the man of God* is reproof and correction. We all need to be straightened out at times.

Think of times when you have suffered rebuke – perhaps from another person, perhaps from something heard in a sermon, or perhaps in your own private reading of the Bible. How have you reacted? Can you honestly say that the rebuke has been effective in your case? There are so many ways to react to it. You can ignore it, dismiss it, deny it, counter it, excuse it, resent it, be cowed by it ... the trouble is, all such reactions work against its proper effectiveness.

We should recognise that we do need correction from time to time, so that when it comes we react intelligently to it, which means giving objective and dispassionate consideration to it – something which is not easy when we feel the shock of it!

It is only the fool who sees no need for correction and who is therefore impervious to it, however severe a form it may take. He may feel a rebuke just as much as a wise person does, but all the same he has no *sensitivity* to the *rebuke*, only to his hurt feelings, and so he remains as he is. The proverb pictures the sterner measures required on account of his unresponsiveness. The blows he receives may be painful, but he will still not get the message. The law prescribed a maximum of forty stripes for an offence worthy of that kind of punishment. To exceed it would have been degrading (Deuteronomy 25:3). So the hundred lashes is really a way of saying that a fool is beyond remedy where understanding and accepting correction are concerned. Even degrading him will achieve nothing. But for an understanding and perceptive person all that is needed is for a word to be spoken and it will sink in, it will be felt, be taken to heart and acted upon.

[Related proverbs: 12:1; 13:18; 15:5,31,32.]

17:11. Tough justice. Those bent on rebellion can hardly expect clemency themselves. Ruthless people are very likely to be dealt with ruthlessly. They will get as good as they give. Absalom is a particularly unpleasant example of one who coolly rebelled against his father (2 Samuel 15). He was killed as he hung in the branches of a tree (probably caught by his splendid head of hair) in spite of David's plea that he should be dealt with gently (2 Samuel 18). Joab, who dispatched him, was himself something of a maverick character, taking his own way rather than submitting to authority, twice committing murder in cold blood, first of Abner, later of Amasa (2 Samuel 3:27; 20:9-10). In the end he was cut down as he himself had cut down others (1 Kings 2:28-35).

What has happened to individuals has also happened to nations. Habakkuk 1 describes the terrible judgement predicted upon the nation of Judah, that the Chaldeans were being sent by God against them, and they were indeed cruel messengers. But then in chapter 2 it is shockingly revealed that Judah would only be receiving in kind. As they had done to others, so it would be done to them.

The way this proverb is expressed in the original makes clear that 'evil' and 'rebellion' are intimately linked. Against whom, or what, is this rebellion expressed which is described as 'evil'? In the essential and fundamental sense it is rebellion against the authority of God, first witnessed in the Garden of Eden when Adam and Eve took their own way contrary to the clear command of God. So when it says that an evil man seeks only rebellion, it is indicating that his every desire and thought and expression is in rebellion against God. Not only is it against God in this primary sense, but it is also expressed against the laws God has given and the authorities he has ordained. Whether petty theft or grand larceny, both are expressions of rebellion against authority. The same is true of a murderous look or a murderous action. Rebellion is an expression of the desire to shift the centre of authority from where it ought to be to oneself. Joab was under David as his army commander; but in practice Joab tended to be a law to himself. Those who are a law to themselves are living in rebellion against God. It is not a case of rebelling because they see a better way, but rebelling because they want their own way.

This note started with those bent on rebellion, and we may have felt ourselves to be at some distance from such people. But if it means their being bent on getting their own way, maybe we begin to find this a little too close for comfort. The distinction has suddenly disappeared, and we should see there really is no difference. If we are determined to get our own way over something, we need to consider our motives and the warning of this proverb!

It is so often true, even in this life, that as we treat others, so we tend to be treated ourselves. Jesus said, 'Blessed are the merciful, for they shall obtain mercy' (Matthew 5:7). This is a promise from our heavenly Father to us, for he is merciful. Jesus also told the parable of the unjust steward who was treated in kind (Matthew 18:23-35). The last verse of the parable is a very solemn one, because God, who is rich in mercy, will nevertheless deal in kind with those who show no mercy, and especially who show no mercy in the light of his amazing forbearance.

17:12. The bear hug. If the comparison makes us smile, it is because it is one we would not have thought to make and it is a reversal of our perception of things. It nevertheless has a very serious side to it. Which is the more dangerous? Which has the greater potential for harm? The bear, obviously. No, says this proverb, that is the wrong answer. It is the fool in his folly.

This proverb teaches us the need to think biblically and to see things as God sees them. Unexpectedly to meet a bear in the woods would have been frightening enough, but to encounter one robbed of her cubs would have been dangerous in the extreme and the likely outcome would have been to be torn apart.

A fool in his folly, that is, one who is exercising his folly, has potential for doing untold harm. We are not talking about a harmless buffoon, but a person whose character is built up through the pages of the Book of Proverbs, the whole of which is seen to be something very sinister indeed.

Too many people get into a bear hug with fools and their fool ideas. Fool celebrities are worshipped and mimicked by admirers in their millions; fool politicians are never short of followers to help push through their own ideas; fool academics with their intellectual abilities persuasively influence others into adopting their philosophies of life. Too many people unthinkingly bask in the glory of fools.

In the unlikely event of your meeting a bear robbed of her cubs you will immediately realise what you are up against. The trouble with meeting a fool in his folly is that you may well be totally unaware of any danger. Are you being subversively influenced?

Now is the time to ask whether you have been emotionally or spiritually mauled by a fool in his folly? Are you carrying on your person deep wounds of anti-Christian ideas, ideologies or practices through getting too close to fools in their folly? Then come again to Jesus Christ and be healed, and drink in his wisdom.

We have seen that a fool is not amenable to reason (v. 10). When the door is shut fast against constructive dialogue and the fool is set on pursuing his own foolish agenda, there is only one thing to do. Some people and situations need to be given as wide a berth as possible, where danger lurks over which you have neither control nor influence.

If Solomon, wise as he was, gave way to folly in his later life, thereby bringing great harm upon the nation, we should be aware that the potential for folly lies in us all, which, if exercised, can seriously harm others. We need to keep close to Christ and to remember the words of 1 Corinthians 1:30-31.

[Related proverb: 27:3.]

17:13. The rewards of wickedness. Both David and Jeremiah complained to the Lord about those who rewarded their good with evil (Psalm 109:5; Jeremiah 18:20). It is one of the things godly people must expect to happen (1 Peter 3:13-14; 4:4,16-17) even as Jesus said it would (Matthew 5:10; John 15:20). One of the causes is that so often unbelievers misunderstand and misinterpret the conduct and motives of Christians, and very often it is because they judge them by their own standards. However, this in no way excuses them, but rather highlights the fact that they are evil-minded. For the Christian, the command is not to reward evil with evil but with good (Luke 6:27,35; Romans 12:20-21; 1 Peter 3:9), the very opposite of what so often happens to them. God's ways are diametrically opposed to the world's, and this is to be seen in the lives of his children.

So, pause to ask yourself, are you repaying evil with good?

Considering the second clause, we have to ask how this is so. Why will evil not depart from his house? As with so many of the statements in Proverbs, there are two sides to this. The first is the natural side. For one who so conducts himself, evil is already in his house. Evil never generates good (compare Romans 3:8), but only more evil, and so it stands to reason that so long as evil predominates, it will only perpetrate more of the same.

Yet this is not a sufficient answer. For one thing, the statement specifically relates not to those who are evil in their conduct, but to those who repay evil for good. That is, they are deliberately excluding the good, even trampling upon it, and so what else can be expected? If good will not be allowed in, evil cannot be got out.

But even this is not a sufficient answer either, and a consideration of Hebrews 10:26-31 suggests that underlying the statement is the judgement of God. This is God speaking, and if he says that evil will not depart from the house of such a person, we may be sure that it will be so, because he says so.

Although it is not an exact parallel, we see how sadly the house of David was afflicted after the Bathsheba affair (2 Samuel 12:10). The case has relevance to the proverb before us. We can analyse what happened to David from political and domestic and other points of view: that is, we can find naturalistic explanations for the events which followed in the wake of David's sin. Yet that is insufficient to account for what happened because God had already indicated this was his judgement (2 Samuel 12:11-12). So here, and in every other case, naturalistic explanations for what follows in the wake of evil are always insufficient. Evil conduct is always an affront to a holy God and is therefore subject to his judgement.

How is it with your house?

[Related proverbs: 15:3; 20:22.]

17:14. Plug it. It is a matter of common experience that many heated arguments start from very small beginnings. Look back on your own (assuming you have had any!) and consider whether this is not true? Disagreements tend to escalate. A sharp word elicits an even sharper response, and before you know where you are a full-blown argument has developed.

The picture before us is that of releasing water. The NIV translates that it is like breaching a dam. Once a dam or dyke is breached, even in a small way, the force of the water flowing through the gap erodes and widens it, so that a trickle soon becomes a torrent. Or if one thinks in terms of opening a sluice gate, once it is opened a great deal of water will flow through it before it is possible to close it again. It is much easier to open it than it is to close it again afterwards. Burst pipes can usually be mended, but often not before considerable damage has been done.

Who is this proverb addressing? The NIV translation seems to suggest it is the person starting the quarrel. Those who start quarrels, those who are inclined to be contentious, are doing a very dangerous thing. There are many reasons why quarrels start. Verse 19 refers to those who love strife, which we will come to in due course. Occasionally a quarrel will start on account of misunderstanding. More often it will be because one is out of temper or is nursing a grievance and is ready to 'let fly' given the least opportunity. But however the strife starts, very often it commences with an undermining statement or action which, by its very nature, is virtually demanding and expecting a response ... and that is where the danger lies.

The responsibility of containment therefore cannot be confined to the one party. In the last proverb we observed that God requires us to repay evil with good. We have to go on learning the need to avoid the self-centred 'heat of the moment' reaction to provocation. If someone picks a quarrel with you, it will only actually become a quarrel if you allow it to do so. Strife involves two parties, not one. That means the onus is upon you to deal with the situation, for which, bearing in mind your sinful nature, you need the grace of God.

If a breach in a dam is quickly plugged, disaster can be averted. Prompt and incisive action is always needed in the case of released water in order to limit the damage. And so it is with strife. It is natural that disagreements and problems in relationships will arise. What is important is the way they are handled. Quarrelling and strife usually, if not always, arise from self-centredness. Those who are serving the Lord are not to strive in the sense of being contentious (2 Timothy 2:24); but there is something they are to strive *for*, and that is peace with all men (see Romans 12:18; 14:19; Hebrews 12:14). Christians are to be peacemakers, which is to operate first of all in their own personal relationships before they ever exercise themselves with the problems of others!

Stopping contention before a quarrel starts is not a passive thing. This proverb presupposes that the water has begun to be released. That is not a situation you can simply walk away from. If you have started it, then you cannot leave the issue hanging, but have to put matters right. If the other person has started it, it is your responsibility to seek to arrest the flow and heal the breach in a gracious manner. Do not assume this will be easily done.

Often it will involve a great deal of effort and self-restraint and unless there is a genuine will for peace little will be achieved.

[Related proverbs: 15:18; 20:3.]

17:15. Upending justice. The NIV captures the terseness of the original: 'Acquitting the guilty and condemning the innocent'. A weak parallel would be: 'Calling the bad good and the good bad.' This proverb is highlighting a fundamental violation of the principles of justice. Each attitude (or action if it goes that far) is equally reprehensible: both are abhorrent to God. The question is, why would anyone ever think to do either of these things? Yet these things are often seen, albeit in embryonic form, at the personal level.

To fall in with someone who is set on doing something wrong, or to approve of what they are doing, is to justify them. The motive may be fear, or it may be greed. In the case of the soldiers who put out the story of the body of Jesus having been stolen, it was greed (Matthew 28:11-15). Many who have 'an eye to the main chance' and who see themselves as 'on to a good thing' will have few scruples about the source of their advancement. Ask yourself, who suffers as a result?

But simply to fail to speak up against what is wrong when the need arises for something to be said falls into the same category, and here the motive may be fear and self-preservation. However, we do not have a right to turn a blind eye to such things. If we are involved we cannot pretend not to be. It is not an option that God permits us. Give some thought to examples of the behaviour of those who are morally wrong who lie within your sphere of influence and ask if it could be argued that either by your complicity with them or by your failure to speak or act you could be charged with justifying them?

The other side, condemning the just, may also arise out of fear or greed. In craven fear Pilate attempted to wash his hands of responsibility as he condemned Jesus to be crucified (Matthew 27:24). But condemning the just is also seen in ill will toward those who speak out or act against injustice when their right words or actions are resented. The big issues often arise when the little ones are ignored for long enough. Not infrequently the real issues will be camouflaged in order to focus attention on irrelevant technicalities. Thus the Pharisees in their contention with Jesus repeatedly sought to use the law to condemn him, only they had concealed the real meaning of the law and twisted it to suit their convenience. The result was their condemning the innocent, as Jesus made clear to them (Matthew 12:7).

That justifying the wicked and condemning the just can be done without a word is illustrated in the encounter Jesus had with the Pharisees over the healing of a man with dropsy (Luke 14:1-6). In their case they wanted to justify *themselves* in their wickedness which they would not acknowledge, and to do so by condemning *him* in his righteousness which they would not acknowledge either. Their very silence (Luke 14:4,6) was an admission of their guilt. Their refusal to face up to what they were, and their refusal to face up to who he was, led to their ultimate travesty of justice by getting him crucified.

The principles of justice are enshrined in the law of God (see, for example, Exodus 23:1-7, Leviticus 19:15; Deuteronomy 1:17; 16:19), a law which people are often more ready to apply to others than to themselves. While people may recognise and applaud these principles to a point, when it comes down to their personal lives they often deny them, justifying themselves by trampling God's Word, and refusing Christ's rightful lordship over them, denying him place in their lives.

Amazingly, what God strictly forbids in us, he himself has done, for we read these extraordinary words, that 'God ... justifies the ungodly.' It is only through repentance and faith in Christ that this conflict is resolved. Give some thought to how God alone can with perfect justice justify the ungodly (Romans 3:21-26; 4:5), and why he should do so.

[Related proverb: 17:26.]

17:16. A question without an answer. This is one of only a few proverbs that directly pose a question. It seems to be cast in the form of a picture of someone buying merchandise.

Imagine yourself going into a bric-a-brac shop to snoop around, in the course of which you happen to notice what is to your mind a rather ugly vase. The price tag on it is within your means, but it is of no interest to you and you pass it by. Little do you realise that this same vase which you have disdained is actually a priceless antique and, had you bought it, it would have given you the means to be extremely rich.

This is how the fool treats wisdom, only his situation is worse because he has actually already been informed of its worth, and he still doesn't want it! To his mind it is ugly and of little value and he is not moved at all by the suggestion that the problem lies with his perception.

Consider the exhortation of 23:23 and the invitation of Isaiah 55:1. We have already seen at 9:4-6 that wisdom is available to all who will seek her – even to the simple and the foolish – for God gives ungrudgingly to those who ask him (see also James 1:5).

So the question is left hanging, to highlight one of the great paradoxes of life. Those who have wisdom value it; those who do not have no heart for it. Especially is this seen in the gospel invitation. Jesus Christ is the personification of wisdom. In him are hidden all the treasures of wisdom and knowledge (Colossians 2:3). Yet people do not want to know him and will not have him! Why? Why? we echo. Why remain ignorant, impoverished and hopeless? To those who have received him it makes no sense that others should pass him by.

But isn't that the position we once were in who now believe? How wonderful is the grace of God, for it is *of him* that we are in Christ Jesus, who became for us wisdom from God... (1 Corinthians 1:30).

[Related proverb: 23:23.]

17:17. Friend and brother. In card shops you will often find cards with witty and memorable captions. Here is one: 'A friend is someone who likes you even though they know you.' It prompts the question: Do you have friends? Real friends? This proverb, however, goes one stage further: 'A friend *loves* at all times.' Notice in this the twofold nature of true friendship. First of all, it is a commitment of *love*, a commitment of self-giving, a commitment to the other's welfare. Secondly, it is an *unconditional* commitment, because 'all times' covers both the circumstances and the temperament of the other. Many marriages have failed because they have been built on the shifting sands of romance rather than the bedrock of friendship.

There is a remarkable illustration of this proverb in the relationship of Ruth to Naomi (Ruth 1:14-22). Whereas Orpah was persuaded to look after her own interests, Ruth was determined to stay with Naomi through thick and thin. Throughout, the book illustrates Ruth's devotion to her even at the expense of sacrificing her own prospects and inviting hardship. What a friend she proved to be!

Yet even more remarkable are the words of Jesus in John 15:13-15. Jesus was accused of being a 'friend of tax collectors and sinners' (Luke 7:34). He also went as far as to call his believing people his brothers (John 20:17; Hebrews 2:11-12). Our proverb says a brother is born for adversity. How true this is of Jesus in delivering his people!

Consider just what this means. Jesus loves his people at all times – not simply those times when we suppose we may be worthy of his love, but those times when we show so clearly we are not worthy of his love, when we disobey, when we refuse to obey his word, when we act selfishly, and when we think or do all those other things of which we should rightly be ashamed. Jesus is with us in times of adversity. He came into this world for the very reason that he might deliver us from sin and then keep us close to himself, which in effect means his keeping himself close to us, never leaving nor forsaking us. The Holy Spirit who inspired these words in the book of Proverbs knew of whom supremely they spoke, and he who has called his people his friends shows unwavering loyalty in his love, even when his people wander away or, worse, deny him. Consider, for example, Jesus' friendship shown to Peter in going after him to restore him (John 21).

This proverb expresses true kinship. It speaks of real friendship as opposed to what we call 'fair weather' friendship; of brotherly love and not 'cupboard love'. It should make us ask questions about our relationships with others, and whether our friendships are really worthy of the name. The love the Lord has shown to us is unconditional. Is the love we show to him of the same kind, and what about the love we show to those we call our friends, or our brothers and sisters?

[Related proverb: 18:24.]

17:18. Intelligent commitment. Becoming surety for another has been considered at 6:1-5 and 11:15, and covers imprudent commitment to cover the costs or losses of another.

The phrase translated 'devoid of understanding', or 'lacking judgement', is used several times in Proverbs (6:32; 7:7; 9:4,16; 10:13,21; 11:12; 12:11; 15:21; 24:30). It is not a neutral phrase such as we might use of one who lacks understanding of some technical matter and who would not be expected to know about it, but rather a negative one of someone who most certainly ought to know better. This person is not only acting foolishly and to his own hurt, but he is also by implication doing no real service to the one for whom he is becoming surety.

We have heard the expression, 'throwing good money after bad'. This goes for resources other than money, too. Every form of commitment (the striking of hands) by which we promise something of ourselves to another person needs to be considered with due care. For one thing, we are stewards of what has been entrusted to us (Luke 12:42), and as such we are answerable to God for our stewardship.

Implied in striking (or shaking) hands in a pledge is a commitment to another person at least partly on their terms, giving them some right over you. Often people make pledges under the influence of emotional coercion and can be made to feel they are under some kind of moral obligation to do so. They are not.

The reproachful, 'I thought you were my friend,' is merely a form of exploitation, applying psychologically coercive pressure to give what true friendship does not and cannot give. This proverb warns against succumbing to it, reminding us that it is the course of someone who lacks judgement, maybe someone who is having the wool pulled over his eyes! Taken with the last proverb, it is not a mark of love to act in this way, even toward a friend or brother. Very much to the contrary, it can be an act of the greatest disservice to such a person because it is giving in to their weakness and perpetuating their problem. Giving timely help when it is needed is one thing; promising unqualified commitment is another. It is degrading for a person to keep coming back for handouts; it undermines their moral fibre. The greatest assistance we can render to people like this is to help them any way we can to stand upon their own two feet.

When our Lord Jesus Christ pledged himself to us there was no striking of hands, there was no deal, there was no pandering to our weakness. He understood us too well for that. He loved us too much for that. Thank God for that! We were broken by sin, and he caused us to stand upright. He is our role model in the privileges and responsibilities of our friendships.

[Related proverbs: 6:1-5; 11:15; 20:16,26.]

17:19. Asking for trouble. The NIV translates: 'He who loves a quarrel loves sin.' But the more natural rendering is to take both clauses in parallel, so that the first then reads: 'He who loves transgression loves strife.' Of course, no one loves strife, no one seeks destruction. And that is just the point we are being made to think about. We are being told that to act in certain ways is tantamount to doing this very thing. Those who get a thrill out of transgression (law breaking) and think it clever, those who despise God's laws and substitute their own which they regard as superior ... they are being told that they love strife. They might deny it, but there is an inescapable equivalence between the two.

The word translated 'gate' in the second clause is more commonly rendered as 'door' and is used of a door or a personal entrance rather than the gate of a town (translated by a different word). In Joshua 20:4, Ezekiel 8:3 and many other places both words are used together by way of making the distinction. The person who 'exalts his gate' (or 'makes his door high') isn't so much concerned about intruders onto his property as trespassers onto his superiority! His 'door' is an impressive façade by which he intends others will think of him more highly than is warranted. To conduct oneself like this is to court disaster! It is a variation of 16:18. Do not miss the strength of the language. It is not warning such a person that he will be brought down a peg or two; it is saying that he is inviting destruction.

By means of these expressions which make us sit up and take notice, namely loving strife and seeking destruction, the proverb makes us look at the *consequences* of transgression and pride. Few people really think about the consequences of their way of life, and few people who observe the consequences see them for what they are or give serious thought to the *causes*. The book of Proverbs is continually urging us to do both.

Plenty of examples of strife and destruction in our society exist which point back to transgression and pride. Likewise, plenty of examples of transgression and pride which exist in our society point forward to sinister consequences. However, before we look at society, we need to look first at ourselves. Have we not seen these principles operating in our own lives? Have there not been unwelcome repercussions to our own disobedience and to our own pride – not only for ourselves, but for others too?

The psalmist was wise when he considered the effect giving vent to his rebellious feelings would have upon others (Psalm 73:15). He thought about the consequences of his conduct for others and saw the harm it would do.

Peter gives us some good advice in 1 Peter 5:5-6. Consider these familiar words in conjunction with this proverb. They remind us that the proverb is not speaking simply of cause and effect in which we might suppose we have some control over the consequences, but that we are dealing with a mighty hand, the hand of God, a hand which resists, or puts down, or lifts up as the case may be. What is the case in your case?

17:20. Psalm 34 What good will come of it? Here is another proverb which speaks of consequences. The two clauses are in parallel. The second is the outward manifestation of the first, but together they emphasise a single truth. A perverse tongue is the puppet of the deceitful heart which pulls the strings. Falling into evil is the inevitable result of finding no good.

How little people consider the consequences of what they think or say or do! How many people live for now, almost as if that is all that matters! All they seem to want is to have a good time, or get on to a good thing, or pull off a good deal. They want what they perceive to be a good life. Principles seldom enter into it. And do they get what they want? Not at all. It turns sour on them. As this proverb says, they find no good. The deceitful heart has a twisted view of life, so that what it perceives as good is no good at all. The result is so often an intensified craving for that which cannot satisfy, for it is only real good which yields true satisfaction.

'Finds no good' is probably a better translation than 'does not prosper', for in the material sense many with a perverse heart do prosper. But they find no good from their deviousness. In a society where everything is on the surface and people are concerned about their image in every area of their lives, this sobering fact is easily missed. Good never comes out of perversity. Those who set out along that road simply do not realise where it will lead them. Even though the road is littered with casualties, they still vainly imagine they can steer their way safely through, with the illusion of security in the falsely comforting thought, 'It won't happen to me.'

For the 'perverse', or 'deceitful', tongue a word is employed which denotes turning and changing. It could apply to the person who is 'double-tongued', or to someone who says one thing and does another, or to one who lies, or to one who says different things to different people. It applies, in fact, to everyone whose words are not straightforward truth. People may be able to cover their tracks, but they are not able to recover their words. The consequences are invariably bad.

The proverbs are given for meditation. From your experience of yourself and your experience of others put these words under scrutiny. See if they are not true, and when you are satisfied that they are, consider what the remedy is, for this proverb paints a dismal picture for what is a very common human malady.

1 Peter 3:10, quoting Psalm 34:12-13, nicely reflects what this proverb says from a positive angle, and the two verses which follow provide both incentive

and warning. The remedy just mentioned will be found not by looking inward to find resources for reformation of life, but only by personal application to the one who is full of grace and truth, drawing on the resources freely provided by the one who is rich in mercy and rich in grace (John 1:14; Ephesians 2:4,7). They are words addressed to Christians, to those who have already sought the Lord, who have been heard, who have been delivered from sin, who have tasted that the Lord is good, who have put their trust in him. Unbelievers have no concept of these things. But the Christian has a secure foundation of grace, has found good in God who alone is good, and will never ultimately fall into evil.

[Related proverbs: 11:3,20; 28:18.]

17:21. A very unhappy man. Two different words are used in the original for the 'fool' of the two clauses. The first denotes sheer, inexcusable stupidity, and the second adds the element of moral perversion. Either way, a foolish son is a burden and a grief to his father.

While parents cannot guarantee that their offspring will grow up into mature and well-balanced adults, there may nevertheless be a warning here as to what might be coming to those who fail to train and discipline their children throughout their formative years. Even though the investment of godly training may not in the end result in wisdom in the children, that is no excuse for neglect in this area, for that merely invites a great deal of trouble in years to come.

The first clause speaks, perhaps provocatively, of 'begetting' a fool. It is suggestive of a father's causative and creative action. Possibly this proverb is saying, 'Look what your over-indulgence of your child, and your neglect of your responsibilities toward your offspring, are producing, and where it is going to lead you. You are going to look back with bitterness and sorrow, with heaviness of spirit, in the discovery that it is too late to do anything about it.'

It is inescapable that the subject of this proverb is the father. It is equally inescapable that he is the cause of his own depression. The fault is his own.

His easygoing, soft line toward his children for the sake of his own peace and to avoid rocking the boat has resulted in constant anxiety and trouble from which there is no escape. He has made his children into what they are.

Here is a warning to fathers that they cannot afford to neglect their responsibilities toward their children. They begot them, and therefore they are responsible for them. It is so easy to put off some of the more uncomfortable aspects of training and discipline to another time rather than to face them when they need to be faced. But neglect leads only to further neglect and the thing never gets done. Better to shed many tears now in dealing promptly with waywardness in the children and to have the subsequent joy of well balanced and mature sons and daughters, than to live later in dry-eyed remorse over neglected duties.

When we hear and witness so much of what is bad among the youth of our generation, to what do we attribute it? Are they socially deprived? Is their education lacking? Do they come from broken homes? Have they got in with the wrong group? Are they just 'letting off steam'? Whatever may be said by others, the Word of God places the responsibility – yes, the *responsibility* – firmly at the door of their fathers. Fathers, take a good look at the children of this generation, and resolve to take your responsibility with the utmost seriousness. This is not just in the area of discipline and training, but especially of ensuring you give of your valuable time to your children so that they will know just how much you value them, that you really do love them.

Take to heart the encouragement of 22:6 with the exhortation of Ephesians 6:4.

[Related proverbs: 17:25; 22:6.]

17:22. Psalm 42. How are your bones? It has long been understood that there is a connection between one's state of mind and one's physical condition. It appears that there is now clear scientific evidence confirming that a cheerful heart is indeed good medicine and that a broken spirit is deleterious to one's health.

What is to be learned, though, from this proverb, if it is admitted that the factors which contribute toward either condition lie largely outside our control?

Those who try artificially to induce a cheerful heart, whether by drugs or by partying or by self-indulgence or by giving themselves to any other form of enjoyment, invariably find it does them no good. On the other hand, there are people who truly possess a cheerful heart whose circumstances we might suppose ought rather to have the opposite effect.

Is this proverb hinting that we need to be looking out for the best in life and conditioning ourselves accordingly? Or is it telling us we should avoid anything potentially injurious to our spirit? Admittedly, there may be some things we can do to control, or at least influence, our circumstances, and it is true that we often have the choice as to how we view them, whether pessimistically or optimistically. Yet the real factors which determine our state of mind are not usually our circumstances but something far deeper within us.

Dry bones are dead bones, out of which the life has been taken. By contrast, 3:8 speaks of moisture, or marrow, being put into bones, that is, their being infused with life and strength. What takes the life out of the bones, and what puts life back into them?

A person whose spirit is broken is in a state of collapse, mentally and emotionally, if not physically. It is a person who has been reduced to a state of complete hopelessness. It may have been brought about by the sheer weight of the oppression of adversity, or it may have been through dashed hopes. But such a person no longer has anything to live for, anything to look forward to, anything to *hope* for.

We are spiritual beings, made in the image of God and made for fellowship with God. Joy in the Lord is something which every Christian should know (Philippians 3:1; 4:4), even in the most adverse of outward circumstances (Matthew 5:11-12). Notice how large hope features in these passages. The apostle Paul knew something of great sorrow (Philippians 2:27; Romans 9:2) and great trouble (2 Corinthians 1:4,8), and yet his spirit was not broken. He had learned in whatever state he was to be content, a contentment undergirded by the strength which Christ supplied (Philippians 4:11,13). The cheerfulness – or joy – of which this proverb speaks is not what the world usually understands by the term. It comes from what is in the *heart*, and those who have Christ dwelling in their heart through faith and who are therefore rooted and grounded in love (Ephesians 3:17) will surely experience something of true joy in their heart and know that it is medicine to their soul.

But to those in the depths, remember that Jesus will not break the bruised reed, and he knows how to bind up the broken-hearted (Isaiah 42:3; 61:1). He can bring help, and healing, and hope. If Christ is in you, he is the hope of glory (Colossians 1:27). He can revive your spirit and restore your strength. Give him your time, and place yourself in the hands of the heavenly Physician, who is faithful to all his promises.

[Related proverbs: 12:25; 14:30; 15:13,15; 18:14.]

17:23. Underhanded and subversive. There must be few who are not familiar with the phrase 'bribery and corruption'. The problem seems to be both timeless and universal. This verse describes one of the more common forms of bribery, which is to get someone to do something which is wrong and thereby pervert the course of justice. Consider the soldiers who were bribed by the chief priests to say that Jesus' disciples stole his body when they slept (Matthew 28:11-15). Doubtless the amount of the bribe was so overwhelmingly enticing that they took the money and did as they were told. Who could blame them? Countless others would have done the same in a similar situation. But consider how they perverted the course of justice by influencing many to believe their lie that Jesus did not rise from the dead. What a wicked act that was, allowing themselves to be bought off to protect the guilty and at the same time to hinder others from putting their faith in the risen Christ! To them the gold in their pockets was of far more value than the greatest, life-changing, event in history.

Whereas 17:8 looks at the bribe from the angle of the one offering it, this verse looks at it from the angle of the one receiving it. The one accepting the bribe cannot excuse himself by laying responsibility at the door of the one offering it. No one can take the money and then argue, 'It is not my affair; it has nothing to do with me.' It is the person accepting the bribe who is actually setting in motion the perversion of justice, not the one who is offering it.

Consider Judas Iscariot, who earlier had prompted and accepted a bribe from these same people in order to precipitate the greatest injustice the world has ever seen. Judas was certainly a wicked man and he knew what he was doing. He even admitted it afterwards (Matthew 27:3-4). This kind of bribery is invariably very private, but more often than not its results are very public. It is a wicked thing to accept a bribe, and a wicked person is willing to do so because he is more interested in what is in it for him than in the course of justice. If others suffer as a result, what is that to him?

Bribery also goes on in all kinds of subtle ways. If we are influenced by another person, in whatever way it may come about, to be less than strictly honest about something in order to advance our own ends, then let us call a spade a spade and acknowledge what this verse says, both that it is perverting the way of justice and that it is a mark of wickedness. 'If you keep quiet about this I will see that you are not the loser for it,' or words to that effect, should set clanging the alarm bells of conscience!

'Beware of covetousness,' said Jesus (Luke 12:15). A bribe is a direct appeal to covetousness, and this is a danger to us, for covetousness is one of the things we are to be putting to death in our bodies (Colossians 3:5).

[Related proverbs: 17:8; 18:5.]

17:24. James 1:2-8. What are your sights set on? Two people are standing side by side looking through binoculars. The first is intent on searching for something specific which he knows is there and which is of particular significance to him, and when he has found it he locks on to it, whereas the second is just scanning aimlessly and focusing from time to time on anything that happens to interest him for the moment.

This illustrates something of what is expressed in this proverb. What are you looking for in life? What really matters to you? What are your ambitions? What are you striving after? Where are you heading?

A person of understanding already has answers to questions like these. He has discernment enough to realise that certain things are worth aiming for, and therefore by implication that other things are best left behind as unworthy of any lasting attention. What he has in sight is described simply as wisdom. This can be taken in two ways, firstly that it is something he desires to attain to, and secondly that it is something actually within his reach.

For example, a young girl with real ability at swimming and recognised potential may have been given encouragement to set her sights upon becoming an Olympic gold medallist. At that time she had understanding enough to realise that such an objective lay many years down the road, but that did not deter her from singlemindedly working toward it. She had her sights set on it. Now, what she has for so long had in her sights may at last really be within sight as actually achievable.

No one will ever achieve anything worthwhile unless they have their sights set upon it. There may have been others of greater ability than the girl of the illustration who never even set out to realise their potential.

The pursuit of wisdom is a bit like this. It is not handed out on a plate. It comes in God's school of training. Solomon did not attain wisdom overnight. When James wrote of asking God for wisdom (1:5) he did not intend this as some kind of slot-machine approach where you put in your coin of request and out pops the wisdom you were looking for. Look carefully at the context of James' statement and notice the prominence of trials, patience and faith. If you are finding the going tough do not let that deter you. It is to be expected, and it is all part of the training. Be encouraged by the contrast with the fool of the second clause.

The eyes of the fool have no fixed objective. That they are on the ends of the earth again may be taken in two ways. Firstly, he may have his eyes on things totally unobtainable for him. Looking beyond the ends of the earth, he may be asking for the moon! But he will never get it! Or, secondly, his eyes may be roaming aimlessly from one thing to another, never settling on anything worthwhile, lusting after one thing after another and never getting satisfaction. He is 'fancy's fool', subject to every random whim. His life is full of fancies but void of focus.

[Related proverb: 15:14.]

17:25. The agony of disappointment in one's children. The grief spoken of here has overtones of provocation and anger, compared with the heaviness of sorrow mentioned in v. 21. In other words, a foolish son does more than depress the spirit of his father, he provokes in him a burning anger. When we view this in the light of v. 22 we can see just how damaging this kind of problem in a family can prove to be. It not only undermines relationships, but it is harmful to mental and physical health as well.

At v. 21 we considered the father's responsibility toward his offspring and the dangers of neglect. Whereas the father was the subject of v. 21, here it is the son. In a way it is a reminder that responsibility is rarely one-sided. A father has responsibility to train up his children. It is their responsibility to cooperate with godly submission (see Ephesians 6:1-4). This proverb is more than an observation of fact, and may be taken as directly addressing the son. Nor is it age-specific. It applies just as much to the son who has long since 'flown the nest' as to the one still under parental authority and influence. In fact it applies in a very particular way to the son of more mature years.

Young people rightly looking forward to their independence and making their own way in life have still to recognise that though their parents' practical responsibility toward them may to all intents and purposes have come to an end, their responsibility toward their parents does not cease at that point. The bond continues to exist. It just functions at a different level. Godly parents will continue to have a concern for their offspring throughout their lives, and how their children make out in life will affect them deeply.

Here the focus is on the negative side of this influence, where the conduct of children causes grief and bitterness. People grieve over what they have lost, and especially over a loved one. A son (or daughter for that matter) who is foolish has been 'lost' to the parents. Proper communication has ceased to exist. From the father's perspective, the cause of grief is that good training and advice over the formative years have been put to one side and been substituted with what is worthless. The investment of time and resources has failed and he sees a squandering of all he has put in. From the mother's point of view, the cause of bitterness is that her maternal love and tender nurture have been forgotten and replaced by a hardness of insensitivity.

A son or daughter who is unaware of the way their conduct affects their parents is indeed foolish. It should rather be their aim to make their parents proud of them, not ashamed, in appreciation for the upbringing they have received, and in thankfulness for what they have been given.

[Related proverbs: 10:1; 17:21.]

17:26. Not good. Kidner suggests that the 'Also' with which this proverb commences (see NKJV) may indicate it was originally paired with another such as 18:5; or, alternatively, that it could be translated 'Even' and that the second clause starts with an understood 'how much more'. Alternatively, as this proverb is concerned with the perverting of justice, Lane suggests it might be connected with 17:15 or 17:23. NIV and ESV omit the word.

Why put it in this negative way, though? One can understand God saying, 'It is not good that man should be alone' (Genesis 2:18), or Jethro saying to Moses, 'The thing that you do is not good' (Exodus 18:17), for in each case to use the word 'bad' might have seemed inappropriate or excessively strong. But here, surely, to say these things are 'not good' seems almost to be toning down their seriousness? However, to say that they are 'bad', true though this is, draws attention away from the vitally important point, which is that there *is* good that can and should be done.

'To punish' could be translated 'to fine'. The concept of fining for the purpose of making restitution was written into the law (see, for example, Exodus 21 and 22). The psalmist complained to God that he was required to pay back what he did not owe (Psalm 69:4). Examples of the righteous being punished in this kind of way abound in our world. Christians often suffer at the hands of unjust laws exploited by the wicked. To punish the righteous is bad, and that it should not be done is clear enough. We can look around our society and say, 'This is bad!' But we can also look around our society and say, 'This is not good!' – by which we mean that things ought to be done differently, that there is a better way. So it is here.

But what *is* good? What *is* the better way? Surely it is to reward the righteous, and to honour princes (or nobles, or persons of status) who conduct themselves in uprightness. To abuse such people represents a significant failure to do what ought to be done. It is not good for them, of course, but also it is not good for society. Sadly, where bad laws are passed, righteous people are sometimes punished for upholding biblical standards, thereby depriving society of their wholesome influence. Likewise, it sometimes happens that people of integrity in high places, if not actually struck, suffer the verbal equivalent when they attempt to use their influence to make a stand for truth. This proverb cogently addresses a society in which what is base in God's sight is not only allowed but encouraged. It is right to draw public attention to the mistreatment of people of godly principle, integrity, wisdom and ability, and to show that to put them down, by whatever means, is not going to promote the well-being of the community.

Get rid of the blight of religion, says the atheist, and all will be well. That is their philosophy, and it may be sincerely held. But whatever they believe, it is not good, either for them or for anyone else. They will receive no benefit from their purges, only the opposite.

How was Jesus treated when on earth? Why was he, the righteous one, punished? Why was he, the Prince of peace, struck? The history informs us of the pathological jealousy and hatred of the Jewish leaders toward him. But it was not only they who were guilty. The fact is that there was no room in a sinful world for a righteous Christ. But God informs us of the real reason these things happened to him (Isaiah 53; Acts 2:23). Amazingly, what was not good he turned into incomparable good for sinners.

How do we react when we are rebuked by righteous people? Do we seek to punish them for their treatment of us? How do we react when those in authority correct us? Do we seek to hit back at them in some way? Sadly, this happens sometimes in churches. When it does, do we need to be told it is not good?

[Related proverb: 17:15.]

17:27-28. James 1:19-20. The less said, the better. How do you react when provoked (to your mind, unjustly)? Do you fly off the handle? Do you let rip with a piece of your mind? How do you react when a situation arises which makes you hot under the collar? Do you wade into the fray? Do you have plenty to say about it? Do you harp on about it? Do you take every opportunity to air your views about it to all and sundry? Are you an animated recruiter of others to your cause? Note the warning of 10:19.

Do you ever stop to ask if this is the best way of carrying on? It is better to inform the mind before giving vent to the feelings. It is better to exercise the brain rather than the tongue. Knowledge and understanding will enable us to contribute in such a way as to do maximum good with minimum fuss. There is so much that does not need to be said, which is either beside the point or inciting. Better to say what must be said clearly and concisely, rationally and impartially, calmly and graciously, than to confuse the issue with irrelevancies or further provocation.

There are situations in which it is better to hold one's peace though one is sorely tempted to do otherwise! There are situations in which plenty might be said, but where in fact the more that is said, the more the harm likely to be done. There are situations calling for perception where there exist every encouragement for knee-jerk reactions. How many conflict scenarios are like this! How many get out of hand for want of people of the kind described here!

This proverb is all about verbal restraint and keeping calm under provocation. In such situations, as most well know, it is all too easy to say too much rather than too little, and so to add fuel to the fire. The knowledge spoken of here can be understood in terms of conscious awareness. There is often a danger in the heat of the situation to lose one's grip on the essentials, to allow emotion to override understanding and so depress consciousness of what are the real issues.

A proverb like this may come as both rebuke and encouragement. The rebuke aspect comes not only from the first verse, but also from the sting in the tail in the second! It reminds us of our foolishness when we have failed to maintain a calm rationality when provoked! But it encourages us as to a right approach, to remember, when things begin to get heated, that there is a right way of dealing with them. For the ungodly, provocation can act as a trigger for loss of self-control. The godly should want it to trigger the opposite. This is why it is so important to meditate on proverbs like this, so that these principles become deeply embedded in our subconscious. Maybe we recognise the value of self-control and acknowledge that it is a fruit of the Spirit (Galatians 5:23), but we need also to recognise that an important aspect of its acquisition is through discipline and training! So now is the time to think carefully and practically about what this proverb is saying, with reference to real-life examples close to your own experience.

The fool of v. 28 is not so foolish after all when he holds his peace and keeps his mouth shut! It is so uncharacteristic of such a person that one has to revise one's opinion of him! Maybe if we have been counted fools for our hotheadedness at times, there is yet hope for us!

[Related proverbs: 10:19; 14:17; 16:32; 29:11.]

18:1. Philippians 2:3-11. Going out on a limb. Though this proverb presents some difficulties of translation, yet some things are clear. It is about a man who isolates himself, and one who does that is certainly 'unfriendly' (NIV). The reason he isolates himself is in pursuit of his own ends.

Some people are 'loners' because they find it very difficult to socialise, but that does not appear to be the kind of person in view here. Here we have one who is so wrapped up in himself or his own opinions as deliberately to want to exclude others. It is essentially selfish. It happens at various levels. A man may isolate himself not universally but only from certain people. For example, some people consider themselves superior to others on account of their station in life, so that they adopt a snobbish attitude toward those they consider lower than themselves and have as little to do with them as possible. Others isolate themselves on account of their imagined intellectual superiority. Others will isolate themselves because they suppose others to be after what they have got. A miser would be one such example. At a trivial level, someone might isolate himself from another just because he doesn't like the look of the person. All kinds of examples might be brought forward, but the bottom line is that the person acting in this way is, in self-importance, cutting himself off from others. He does neither himself nor others any good by so acting. The proverb asserts that he is raging against all sound judgement.

Whatever the reason for people isolating themselves, this proverb says that it is both selfish and foolish. So why does it happen? Here are some more examples:

People can isolate themselves by making secondary matters primary. Christians can do this. They have particular views on certain secondary theological matters where there are clearly recognised differences of opinion humbly acknowledged by respected authorities. Nevertheless, they cut themselves off from all who do not dot their i's and cross their t's. This proverb says they are raging against all wise judgement. It is not only that in their own eyes they are right and everybody else is wrong, but by selfishly withdrawing they are failing to make the contribution they might otherwise be able to make for the benefit of the church.

Then some isolate themselves because they are disillusioned by others. They see all the faults in others. If this is what the church is like, they want no part in it. So they remove themselves. This proverb says that they, too, are acting selfishly. Their judgement is warped. They fail to see they are just as much at fault as others. They fail to see that what the church is like, they are like. They fail to observe the grace of God in others.

Some withdraw and isolate themselves from those who offer criticism. They will not countenance being told they are at fault or wrong and so they take offence and cut themselves off from the people concerned rather than objectively consider what is said. Their refusal to receive rebuke ruins a relationship.

Others isolate themselves because they feel unwanted, they have nothing to contribute, nothing to give. 'Nobody takes any notice of me, nobody wants me, and therefore I am going to withdraw.' Again, this is pure selfish introspection. It is raging against sound judgement, because every member is important to God, and every member has a part to play, however small, for the benefit of the whole body. By cutting themselves off they are actually harming the body by failing to function in it as God intends.

Some people isolate themselves because they think of themselves more highly than they ought and so consider others beneath their dignity. They are 'stand-offish' and have little or no time for others. Again, this is selfish and, for that matter, outrageous! They have yet to learn from Christ. Those most highly esteemed are invariably those who have time for others and who seek their welfare.

18:2. Revealing nothing. Many of the proverbs may be considered as caricatures, in which attention is drawn to some prominent feature. When we have portrayed for us a picture of pure self-conceit, the purpose is not that we should react with, 'I am not like that,' but rather that we should study it and consider whether and where it may have some resemblance to ourselves. If you had a twisted lip, a caricaturist in drawing you would undoubtedly exaggerate this feature. It would be no use looking at the drawing and denying your lip was twisted. If a caricaturist were able to sketch your *character*, what features would be emphasised? You might not like the result and complain about the distortion, but the drawing would have fulfilled its purpose in showing you things you might have been unwilling to notice!

In some respects this proverb is another angle on the previous one. It is amazing how many people in conversation are most willing to talk about themselves and their own affairs and concerns and yet show little or no initiative when it comes to asking after the welfare of the one with whom they are talking and fail to take a meaningful interest in others. They seem, perhaps, to expect the other to take this initiative. What it reveals is that they are rather self-centred, that their pleasure is in expressing what is in their heart more than in contributing something for the benefit of others. Furthermore, they seem to be giving no consideration to the fact that others may have something useful to say which will be of benefit to them!

This is uncomfortably close to the picture presented here of someone who is entirely self-absorbed. He is not really interested in what he might receive from others; he is not really interested in learning and acquiring understanding (not only in terms of knowledge but how to relate it to his dealings with others in life). All he wants to take in is what feeds his self-centred fancies, so that he can regurgitate it to others for his own entertainment and aggrandisement. Solomon depicts him with ruthless accuracy in Ecclesiastes 10:3. The only person who is unaware that the man is a fool is the man himself.

The irony in this is that though there is nothing in a fool's heart worth expressing and his opinions are worthless, yet he wants to reveal it for all to see! What is shameful he does shamelessly, embarrassingly exposing himself. His own high estimation of himself (for he finds no delight in understanding) and his opinions which he is eager to declare to others only expose him for what he is, and yet he is too blind to see it.

The Christian is one who should be Christ-centred. One of the principal ways in which this is displayed is in practical relationships with fellow believers. So, to mention but a few examples, we are to be kindly affectionate toward one another, we are to love one another, we are to receive one another, to admonish one another, to serve one another, to bear one another's burdens, to be kind to one another, to comfort and encourage one another and build up one another (Romans 12:10; 13:8; 15:7,14; Galatians 5:13; 6:2; Ephesians 4:32; 1 Thessalonians 5:11). We notice, too, that none of these has qualifying or opt-out clauses! It is our privilege, in view of the gracious attention our Lord Jesus has given us in saving us and setting us on the pathway of life, to reflect this in the way we view others and seek to be instruments of blessing to them. Let us make every effort to remove ourselves as far as possible from the fool of this proverb, and rather be imitators of Christ (1 Corinthians 11:1; Ephesians 5:1-2).

[Related proverbs: 12:23; 13:16.]

18:3. Genesis 19:1-12. An unwelcome visitor. There is something chilling about this proverb. First of all, even though this proverb may be indicating the effects of wickedness coming in, it is couched in terms of the coming of a wicked *person*. Wickedness is not an impersonal, abstract evil, but is represented in and expressed through people who are morally corrupt. Wickedness is introduced by wicked people. It does not come in any other way. It cannot be separated from its exponents. Furthermore, wicked people are but pawns in the hand of Satan himself, *the* wicked one. John reminds us that the whole world is under his influence (1 John 5:19). Jesus said of those outwardly morally upright Jews that they were of their father the devil (John 8:44) and therefore did his work.

If such people are allowed to exercise what they describe as their rights, what might we expect? The proverb uses three words variously translated, but all associated with aspects of shame.

The first mentioned is *contempt*. Contempt for what, and for whom? Contempt for everything and everyone not subscribing to their world view, and in particular contempt for Christians and Christian standards, making them objective targets as a way of venting contempt for Christ and his word. Thus Christians are ridiculed and vilified.

The next mentioned is *dishonour*, or *shame*. Whereas honour is due to those who live honourably and uphold the truth, the wicked bring such people into dishonour, seeking to shame them by bringing public opinion to bear against them.

The third thing mentioned, *reproach*, or *disgrace*, is what the righteous then suffer at the hands of the wicked, as judgement is passed against them.

All these ingredients are evident in the sordid incident at Sodom, and were it not for the Lord's intervention what might have happened to Lot and his family does not bear thinking about. The wicked always and without exception bring with them shame and degradation. We are to recognise this and also acknowledge our powerlessness to do anything about it. What we are to do is what the godly have always done, and that is to live godly lives and pray to almighty God for judgement and deliverance, following the example and reasoning of Jehoshaphat (2 Chronicles 20 – and note v. 12 there).

Peter writes of those who suffer for righteousness' sake, indicating that wicked people will defame Christians as evildoers (1 Peter 3:14-16). The Christian response is not to be that of retaliation or retribution, both of which are foolish and futile, but of consistent godly living and faithful testimony. There is nothing so undermining of wickedness as righteousness.

When an orchestra comes, so also does a lorry-load of musical instruments. When a circus comes, it is accompanied by all the paraphernalia relating to the circus acts. When the wicked (or wickedness) comes, in with it comes its own retinue, among which are disrespect, dishonour and disgrace. All these 'dis' words displace respect, honour and grace. What is good is replaced by what is base. How important it is that neither the individual nor society should give house room to such. Many people do not realise what they are letting through the door when wickedness comes, because it comes in disguise.

How willing are you to bear reproach for the name of Christ? Consider Romans 15:2-3, Hebrews 13:13 and 1 Peter 4:14.

18:4. Lurking in the depths. The comparison in this proverb is subtle. Observe first what are being compared or contrasted in the two clauses: the words of a man's mouth with the wellspring, or fountain, of wisdom; and deep waters with a flowing, or bubbling, brook.

If the words of a man's mouth are described as deep waters, the implication must be that there is much more beneath the actual words we are hearing. It is like standing on a bridge, looking down over the edge into a river the bottom of which you cannot see, wondering what is down there. It is clear enough what is moving on the surface, but what is beneath the surface? Deep waters are impenetrable, and whatever is down there is hidden from view in the murky depths. So the idea of concealment is present in the first clause (as it is also at 20:5 though in a different context). This contrasts sharply with the second clause where the image of a bubbling brook where nothing is hidden.

As deep waters are being contrasted with a bubbling brook, it is likely that the words of a man's mouth are being contrasted with wisdom, in which case the proverb is implying that in general man's words do not originate from wisdom and that they are often hiding something which the speaker would prefer not to be seen.

Have you ever been listening to the smooth flow of words of someone speaking to you, wondering what is at the bottom of it all? When we speak, we are disclosing what we want others to hear. It is very much on the surface. There are things down there we would not dream of dredging up for others to see. We want our words to display the presentable part of our nature. There are things we do not talk about and yet which nevertheless influence what we say.

But also, and perhaps more to the point, quite often the *motive* underlying what is said is hidden from view. There is more to what is said than the words themselves. The words are therefore *intended* to conceal as well as to reveal. The surface may look very appealing, but there are deceptive currents deeper down. Though politicians are often accused of being masters of this art, it has to be recognised that it is practised by all.

Furthermore, the words of a person's mouth may not be as pure as they sometimes appear to be; they may be permeated by unseen pollutants, and so their effect may be harmful.

Now to the contrast. The picture is of a pure mountain stream, sparkling, clean, cool and bubbling along, such as you would not hesitate to drink from. Its source is the wellspring (probably better than 'fountain') of wisdom. Its origin is clear and pure. The words which come from wisdom are like that. They are clear through and through, they have life-giving vigour, they are good and they do good. They have nothing to hide for there is no need to do so.

Finally the application. We all utter many words every day and do so for all kinds of reasons. Think about your communications with others, especially the more significant ones. Have any of them been influenced by the desire to conceal something? Why? Has there been any disparity between what has been said and what has been the intended outcome? Do you tell people what you want them to hear for reasons of your own?

Words of wisdom do not say one thing and mean another; they do not say one thing and intend another; they do not say one thing to conceal another. Like the bubbling brook, there is a sparkling transparency to them. What is said is clear, meaningful, truthful, helpful and will bear analysis. Enough said!

[Related proverb: 20:5.]

18:5. Psalm 82. Favouritism. This is reminiscent of 17:26 and also the perversion of justice encountered at 17:15,23. The word 'or' at the beginning of the second clause is not in the original and we should not allow ourselves to think that the two clauses are talking about two different things. Rather, showing partiality to the wicked is considered to be of a piece with overthrowing the righteous in judgement, one necessarily involving the other. Partiality to the wicked can be shown by means of bribery or threat (as happened at Jesus' trial – Matthew 26:60; 27:24; Mark 15:11; John 19:12). It is sometimes seen in the lobbying tactics of pressure groups, when what is right gets shouted down, and what is right gets pushed to one side in order to make entrance for the other. We should be aware that whenever partiality is shown to the wicked there is of necessity a turning aside of justice, and so an overthrowing of the righteous. Wickedness and righteousness cannot coexist. Wickedness is a usurper; furthermore, it is an aggressive usurper. It is like the fledgling cuckoo in the nest. It is not tolerant toward the rightful occupants to allow them nest room, but must edge them out and dominate.

Whereas 17:26 is about punishment, this is about judgement, both informal and formal.

What is stated in this proverb is 'not good'. Only great evil can come of it – and it will, unless something is done about it. It is the opposite which is good.

The term 'good' is to be understood according to God's definition. When he described his creation as good, this included not only *what* he had made but *how* he designed it to function and how man was to function in it. How far removed from that we are now!

Then, we need constantly to remind ourselves that terms such as 'wicked' and 'righteous' are also to be understood according to God's definition, not ours. (Incidentally, though the NIV uses the word 'innocent' in the second clause, the word uniformly means 'just' or 'righteous'.) If we knew exactly who God regards as wicked we might be surprised, even shocked. But that is because our perception is so imperfect. Who are the wicked? For 'the wicked' we should be thinking here of those who seek to conduct themselves and order their affairs in a manner contrary to what God requires, and 'the righteous' as those who seek to uphold what God approves and live their lives accordingly. Although wickedness and righteousness reflect what is in the heart of man, the objective standard by which they are measured is God's law.

When we say that we live in a sinful world, we mean that we live in a world of sinful people – ourselves included. In all people there is a natural bias away from the Word of God. Just as Adam and Eve, when they disobeyed God, hid from him, so ever since, as a result of disobedience, men and women seek to hide from God and shut out his Word. They regard neither him nor what he says with favour, and so as a consequence do not regard with favour those who by grace have received God's favour through repentance and faith and have come to love his laws.

Therefore by nature people will show partiality to the wicked, and this will have the inevitable consequence of adversely affecting the righteous. Only by God's restraining hand will things be otherwise. This proverb, however, is not presented to us in order that we can lament just how bad things are, but to provoke us to do something about the situation! We should see it as prompting us to work for good in this area where things are 'not good'.

This is to be shown firstly in our *personal* life, by ensuring that we do not show favouritism to unprincipled people for personal gain on the one hand or through fear of adverse consequences on the other. Also we are not to impose our own will against those who speak rightly when it makes us uncomfortable, but we are to honour them. Then it is to be shown in our *public* life, by speaking up when appropriate for those who are right whom others are seeking to put down for the wrong reasons. A witness who fails to come forward is perverting the course of justice just as much as one who tells lies, and so lying low when we ought to be standing up is not an option. If our personal lives are right then it will be evident that we have no hidden personal agenda when we speak out. Thirdly, it is to be shown in our *prayer* life, as we plead before the throne of grace for the righteous to be heard and respected and for the wicked not to be received with favour.

[Related proverbs: 17:15,23,26; 24:23; 28:21.]

18:6-7. Inviting trouble. These two verses are concerned with what the fool brings upon himself when he opens his mouth. In each verse the clauses are parallel. The repetition – lips ... mouth ... mouth ...lips – are suggestive of the fool's eagerness to speak, and yet notice the corresponding words: contention ... blows ... destruction ... snare. The verses are indicating that when he opens his mouth he is in trouble. His talk is going only to bring him into conflict and pain. While v. 6 indicates what he may expect in the present, v. 7 points to the infinitely more serious longer term consequences. Blows in the short term give way to destruction in the long term. Contention, or strife, in the short term give way to the soul being ensnared in the long term.

A fool entering into contention (NKJV) means bringing himself into it, and the ESV captures the essence of the meaning well when it describes the fool as walking into a fight by what he says. He could have held his tongue, but it is not in his nature to do so (see 12:23; 13:16; 18:2), and that is the cause of the trouble.

Once again, we must remember that in the Book of Proverbs a fool is a person who is devoid of the fear of the Lord. Though a different word is used there for 'fool', note what Psalm 53:1 says about him. Many very clever, erudite people are nevertheless fools because they exclude God from their thinking. Remember this when you consider your own position, and remember, too, if you are a Christian, that in spite of all your knowledge and ability you, like Paul with his great intellect, were at one time foolish (Titus 3:3), and that you owe everything to the kindness of God toward you that things are different now (Titus 3:4).

Contention and strife rarely arise without provocation, and what brings the fool into the realm of contention is not just that he has a wrong view of things and therefore says wrong things which warrant correction. It is that his words are also assertive, provocative, argumentative, and therefore stir up trouble. He is not interested in being corrected. The result is that he becomes embroiled in trouble of his own making.

The most fundamental cause of a fool revealing his folly is a self-centred ungodliness. His world revolves around himself, and because it does so his perception of everything else is skewed. In his self-importance, he believes that people should be listening to what he has to say, while he correspondingly belittles the judgement of others. He is essentially self-seeking, always wanting his own way. But because his own way is not God's way (for God is in none of his thoughts – Psalm 10:4), this leads to grievance and hatred. His understanding of others and of everything around him is born of his warped world view, and this leads to misrepresentation of both facts and people.

The words of a fool provoke more than merely a verbal exchange for two reasons. First of all, what he says is actually harmful; and, secondly, he will neither see nor listen to reason to curb his misguided passions. He is therefore positively inviting sterner measures to deal with his foolish talk and its consequences.

Even a beating, however, is insufficient to quieten him (see 17:10; 27:22). If arguing with a fool is futile, and beating achieves nothing, only one thing remains – destruction. The NIV refers to his mouth being 'his undoing'. While this may be the judgement of God upon him, nevertheless he has brought it upon himself because he would not receive correction (see 15:10). Like the wicked servant who ensnared his own soul by his foolish words (Luke 19:22), the fool condemns himself out of his own mouth.

These verses should give the Christian pause for sober reflection. We need to give attention not only to what our lips *should not provoke*, but also to what they *should promote*. Consider Ephesians 4:29 and Colossians 4:6.

[Related proverbs: 10:14; 12:13; 13:3; 19:29.]

18:8. Sweet to the taste, bitter to the stomach. (This proverb is repeated at 26:22.) Whether 'wounds' (AV) or 'tasty trifles' (NKJV) or 'choice morsels' (NIV) or 'delicious morsels' (ESV), the idea is the same, that the words of a talebearer burn themselves in and are not easily forgotten. These are words that have all the appeal the speaker can muster – easily heard, easily understood, easily absorbed – and yet they do indeed wound deeply. Like an embedded thorn, they are a constant source of irritation and discomfort.

Although it may not be edifying to recall such things, we can all think of stories we have heard about others presented in such a way as to cast a slur upon their character, often with a plausibility about them which it is not easy to check out. We would rather the words hadn't stuck, but they have; we would rather we had never heard what was said, but we have. Perhaps even now we wonder whether they had any truth in them.

The words of a talebearer, or gossip, are not intended to do good, but to be sensational without due regard to the truth, and often under the guise of innocence. 'Far be it from me to jump to conclusions, but have you heard that...?' So it is that a rumour is spread, or a piece of information isolated from its circumstances gets around, so as to give a totally false impression of what actually took place, and the consequence is that only harm is done to all the parties involved.

The imparted information implants doubts, or fears, or suspicions, in the hearer's mind which it is difficult or impossible to dispel.

It is helpful to bear in mind that the words of a talebearer would *always* be better left unsaid. Or even if something needs to be said, it would *always* be better said in a different way and from an entirely different motive.

The law God gave to his people strictly forbade this kind of conduct: 'You shall not go about as a talebearer among your people' (Leviticus 19:16). When we look at the context in which that prohibition was given we begin to see the seriousness with which God viewed it. What is sometimes described as 'a little harmless gossip', when it impugns the character and motives of other people is far from harmless. It is unjust, it is damaging, it stirs up trouble, and it does not serve the interests of righteousness.

This proverb with its powerful imagery should first of all impress upon us the need for care and consideration when speaking of others, especially when what we might say would reflect adversely upon them. Would we be prepared to say to their faces what we are inclined to say behind their backs? Is what we think to say strictly true, without bias or embellishment? Does it need to be said, and in this way, and to this person? Are our motives honourable? Will our words honour God? Will they do good and be for the benefit of others, especially the person about whom they are to be spoken?

These and other similar questions which should be asked, a talebearer never thinks to ask and in any case has no intention of asking.

But secondly, it should impress upon us the need for care when listening to others and to beware the sinister appeal of a juicy story. It is in our interests to do our best to refuse to listen to such people.

[Related proverbs: 16:28; 26:22.]

18:9. How to wreak havoc with very little effort. This proverb is not about working or not working, but about how work is done, indicates that bad workmanship can be worse than no workmanship.

There is often the temptation to downplay one's minor faults and think they are of little consequence. This proverb is a stark reminder that being slothful in work is not so very different from wholesale destruction. The two are directly related. Either way, something does not exist which should. Either way, someone is deprived of something. Slothfulness has its consequences just as much as does destruction. Perhaps when we are horrified by examples of vandalism we should reflect that those abusing their responsibilities in their places of employment by getting away with doing less than they should are achieving neither less nor more than the vandals.

This is a 'sit up and take notice' observation. The slacker is compared not with one who destroys, but with one who is a destroyer; and not just one who is a destroyer, but one who is a wholesale destroyer. To say the two are brothers is to indicate how close they really are.

The strength of the language is surprising. We may regard slacking at work as invidious because it means others have to carry extra burdens, but this proverb does not mince words as it declares that a half-hearted, lackadaisical worker is actually doing a great deal of damage. How so? When the work done is shoddy, careless, incomplete, it is bound to cause trouble to others.

For example, an irresponsible employee who contributes faulty or unfinished components at one stage of manufacture may be destroying a whole product, or a company's reputation, or may even be endangering lives, depending on the nature of what he should be doing but isn't. This kind of thing is far more common than is generally supposed. Even in a simple agrarian society in which every member was expected to pull his weight to ensure the land yielded its crops, a man slothful in his work could make all the difference between success and failure, between prosperity and hardship.

The difference between a slacker and a wrecker (to use Kidner's memorable description) is that the destruction the slacker does is insidious, whereas that done by the wrecker is obvious.

This proverb also applies in the area of Christian service, fulfilling the calling God has given. Would it be too much to suggest that a Christian who is slothful in his or her calling is not so far removed from those who are actually persecuting the church?

The Christian work ethic is very clear in the New Testament. Jesus encouraged his disciples to get on with their assigned task, saying that the worker is worthy of his food (Matthew 10:10). In this he himself set an example, for he had work to do, and it was his aim to do it and to complete the assignment his Father had given him (John 4:34), which he did (John 17:4). Paul used a telling illustration in 1 Corinthians 3:9-15, indicating that our workmanship will be tested. He also spoke of his working in order to provide for himself and promote the gospel (1 Corinthians 4:12; 9:6). See also Ephesians; 4:28; 2 Thessalonians 3:10-12; 1 Timothy 6:18; 2 Timothy 2:15.

In Romans 12:11 Paul uses an interesting expression concerning our service for the Lord when he says we are not to be slothful, or indolent, in our zeal, or diligence. By using these two words together which are virtually contradictory he powerfully makes his point. We are to be diligent in our service for the Lord, and anything short of that is slothfulness. If we are not doing what the Lord has gifted us to do, called us to do and enabled us to do, or if we are not putting our hearts into it, then does not this proverb convict us?

Application: 1 Corinthians 15:58.

18:10-11. Security – real and imagined. In these two verses, which so obviously go together and form a very interesting contrast, two pictures are presented to us. First of all observe some poor labourers working out in the open fields, and then transfer your vision to a rich man living in his own well fortified city. Now see a raiding party moving in to attack. The labourers run to a nearby tower for safety. The rich man just sits tight in the belief that he is protected by his wealth and that his money can buy him out of any trouble.

Under this imagery we are invited to consider the righteous and the wealthy. Why are we told that the *name* of the Lord is a strong tower, when it is the Lord himself who is the place of refuge? The 'name' of the Lord stands for his person. When we call upon his name we are calling upon *him*. The difference between saying that the Lord is a strong tower and that the name of the Lord is a strong tower is that the latter involves naming him! That is, it involves acknowledging him, and calling upon him.

The rich man imagines that his wealth will give him security and make him impregnable from any assault. This is what *he* has built, and it forms to his thinking a very effective barrier against trouble. In some ways he is like the rich farmer of the parable Jesus told (Luke 12:16-21). The rich man can *see* his wealth, but he only *imagines* that it provides security. The righteous cannot *see* the Lord, but in him he has *very real* safety. To quote Kidner again, who puts this so aptly: 'The world thinks that the unseen is unreal. But it is not the man of God but the man of property, who must draw on *his imagination* to feel secure.'

Many times did the psalmists say, and also find, that the Lord was their strength and security (for example Psalms 4:8; 16:8-9; 18:1; 21:1; 28:7,8; 40:2; 46:1; 55:18; 59:9; 68:35; 73:26; 81:1; 84:5; 86:16; 105:4; 118:14; 140:7). Such abundant testimony from experience puts the matter beyond doubt. The truth is, nothing man makes of himself is going to afford him ultimate security. Only God can provide that.

The name of the Lord certainly stands for his person, for who he is. But there is more to it than that. When we say someone has made a name for himself, we do not mean it literally but that his name has become well known on account of some achievement. The name of the Lord, as opposed to the names of all the other gods of the nations, was known and feared because of his mighty works, and in particular because of his deliverance and protection of his people (Joshua 9:9-11). Even the ungodly nations around Israel would acknowledge this years later (Deuteronomy 29:24-25). The promise of God's blessing upon his people is inextricably tied up with the honour of his name (Exodus 20:24).

Implied in mention of the *name* of the Lord is verbal acknowledgement. Declaration is involved. Look at Romans 10:9-13. To declare his name, to honour him before others, is a demonstration of genuine trust. It is not that you cannot be saved without confessing his name, but that failure to confess his name is evidence of a lack of true faith, for faith leads to confession. This somewhat akin to what James says about faith being demonstrated by works and faith without works being dead (James 2:18,20).

Thus, when the danger comes, the righteous exercise faith in Christ, they *run to him*, knowing that in him is true security, that in him is salvation; and thus they confess Christ before men as they invoke his name (Matthew 10:32, and note the context).

The world tends to ridicule people who actually *say* they are trusting in the Lord Jesus Christ when it comes to the practical matters of day to day living and assert that he will guide, he will provide, he will protect, he will meet every need. To their mind, it is foolish, it is fanciful, it is misguided, it is superstitious even, that Christians should say, let alone think, that Christ is their security and strength. True security, they imagine, lies in the visible things of money and possessions. If you are rich enough then you really are secure and you have no need of the artificial crutches of religion.

Being righteous and being rich are not incompatible. But trusting in the name of the Lord and trusting in riches are. Those who are rich in this world are warned not to trust in uncertain riches, but to demonstrate where their true riches lie (1 Timothy 6:17-18).

There is only one ultimate place of security, as will be evident in the final day of reckoning, and it will be for those alone who have called on the name of the Lord (Joel 2:32; Acts 2:21).

See also Psalms 20:7; 102:12,15,21; 124:8.

18:12. The lessons of history. At Wimbledon, tennis players are subjected to an interview after their matches when they are expected to talk about their victory or defeat, looking back and considering the contributory factors. In this proverb we are looking not at victory and defeat but at destruction and honour, and the word 'before' in each case is prompting us to consider the causative factors: what lay behind them.

There are some striking examples of destruction or honour in the Bible, among them Moses (Numbers 12:3-7), Sennacherib (Isaiah 36:20; 37:36-38), Tyre (Ezekiel 28:1-10; Isaiah 23:9), Nebuchadnezzar (Daniel 4:28-33), Haman and Mordecai (Esther 6:1-13), the Pharisees of Jesus' day (Matthew 23:6,11-12).

Although various agencies may be involved in either the bringing down or the lifting up, behind them is the hand of God. These things happened because God ordained them to happen, and this should serve to remind us that exalting ourselves is inviting destruction, but that by being truly humble we need have no fear of being downtrodden.

Why, though, does this principle operate? God is King over all, he is supreme and pre-eminent. Many may object to this, but it is his prerogative, his right. He justly holds the position of sovereign ruler. Satan is a usurper; his claim is false and, if given his way, he would bring ruin to the entire created order. Hauteur in man is a confrontation to God's just rule, and for the sake of good must and will be destroyed.

At the other end, true humility is an acknowledgement not only of one's limitations or dependence upon others, but of one's position in relation to the One who is holy, just and true. The honour he accords to such people enables them to exercise themselves in doing what pleases and honours God and in promoting what he approves.

Feigned humility is no more than a cloak for pride. The humility we are to show is not to be only skin deep. Nor is humility something which will be exchanged in due course for honour. Moses was a man who was greatly honoured by God, yet he *remained* humble. Humility has been the mark of many men and women who have received great honour in life, and this accords well with divine principles.

Jesus, observing people jockeying for position on one occasion, taught on the subject (Luke 14:7-11). There is a great tendency in this world for people either to think more highly of themselves than they ought, or to want others to think more highly of them than is just, and they will not miss an opportunity to promote themselves. It is often driven by an inner need for recognition to compensate for something they lack. Christians need to be reminded of such things for their own good (Romans 12:3,16; 1 Peter 5:5-6). Christians have a God who loves them, who cares for them, and that more than suffices! They have no lack. They have no need to give the impression of being what they are not, for they can be fully content with what they are by grace. The only status worth having is that which God gives. What greater status can there be than being beloved children of God? What more glorious prospect can there be than being like him and seeing him as he is (1 John 3:1-2)?

The first clause expresses the sentiment of 16:18, while the second clause repeats that of 15:33. The word for 'haughty' here is not often translated as 'proud'. It means to be lifted up, and so focuses particularly upon the way such a person lifts *himself* up to look down upon others. Alluding again to the parable of the Pharisee and tax collector, that is just what the Pharisee did in making his disdainful comment in prayer about the other. The word is used in Psalm 138:6 in comparison not only with the 'lowly', but also with the fact that the Lord is 'on high', from which position he regards not those who lift themselves up as if to say 'Look at me!' but rather those who bow to him with true humility.

If hauteur is to think more highly of ourselves than we ought, humility is not to think less highly of ourselves than we ought. The former overestimates self-importance and looks down on others, but the latter has a realistic attitude to both self and others. The honour of self is essential to the haughty person, but it is immaterial to the humble one. Haughtiness positively invites being brought down, because people in general cannot bear others to elevate themselves over them, at least partly because often they suffer the same malady!

Like the refining fire for gold, honour is a great test for humility. We can see this in the case of king Saul. See 1 Samuel 15:13-23. Physically, he might have been head and shoulders above anyone else in Israel, but he had started out as being small in his own eyes. After a period of time as king with the honour of some victories accruing to him, his successes went to his head and addled his judgement. Even godly Hezekiah (2 Chronicles 32:25-26), fell foul of failing rightly to attribute the bestowal of honour, lifting himself up. The Bible contains plenty of examples of those being brought low who have lifted themselves up, and of those being honoured who have lived with a humble spirit.

The way the proverb is expressed, it is virtually indicating the inevitability of destruction for the haughty or honour for the humble. Ultimately, God will bring it about. Only God is rightly and properly 'on high'. Those who resent this and lift themselves up in opposition will ultimately suffer destruction. It cannot and will not be otherwise. Those who have the humility to acknowledge that God is over all will ultimately enjoy the honour of a place in his kingdom and a share in his glory. In the meantime, though, the principle operates on a lesser level and in an imperfect way.

The tower of Babel (Genesis 11:1-9) supplies an illustration of the results of self-exaltation. The builders wanted to raise an enormous edifice for their own security – without God. That is what so many individuals, organisations and nations are doing today. They are elevating themselves and putting God down. But it is futile.

[Related proverbs: 11:2; 15:33; 16:18; 29:23.]

18:13. Quick to speak, slow to hear. The NIV paraphrases with 'answering before listening'. The original indicates there is a 'matter' or 'a cause' being presented, by which is meant something of sufficient importance that it *should* be considered. To say that it is folly and shame so to answer is suggesting attribution to, and consequences for, the one doing this. It is *folly* because a proper and just answer depends on hearing *and considering* the matter fully. It is *shame* because it shows up the person in a bad light. It does no credit to him, but rather has the opposite effect. It is shame, because it ought not to be done.

Here we have the opposite of James 1:19. Answering before hearing is not as impossible as it seems! Perhaps you have had occasion to hold up your hand

and say, 'Please hear me out,' when someone has jumped in prematurely with some kind of judgement on the basis of what they have heard so far. They were dying to interrupt with their own observation or advice before they had heard the half of what you were going to say.

Or perhaps someone has said to you, 'I told you, but you took no notice.' You had already made up your mind.

Here is someone who does not give due consideration to what is being brought before him, who answers with the kind of finality which does not do justice to what is being said. It reflects badly upon him, not necessarily because of untoward consequences, but because of what it reveals of his character.

Here are some causes (and often they will overlap):

Self-importance. I am not interested in the other person or what they have to say. It is of no concern to me, and the sooner I am rid of them the better. They are wasting my time. I do not know why they came to me in the first place. I may hear it with my ears but really fail to give the matter the thought and consideration it deserves. Someone complains: 'He didn't take the blindest bit of notice of what I said.' Yes, I heard it, but acted as if I hadn't.

A couple of times when I have had occasion to ask a question of, or make a complaint to, a company via the internet, a reply has been returned which reveals all too clearly that the respondent has failed to take the trouble to read it properly, and a matter of importance has been virtually ignored. Interest in 'customer satisfaction' has seemed to be lacking. That, perhaps has been precisely the problem: 'I'm not really interested in what this person has to say; let's get it over with as quickly as possible.' So, not only has a problem not been solved, there is now the additional element of frustration and annoyance.

Prejudice. This word means, literally, pre-judging. I have already made up my mind about the matter which is being presented, and so it is not worth wasting time listening to the other person. My answer is final and letting them have their say is going to make no difference. I am unwilling to consider or accommodate another view.

False assumption. Of the many reasons why we may jump in with an answer before we have properly heard what is being said, one is that we assume we know how to answer. I know exactly where the other person is coming from and what they are going to say, and so there really is no point letting them go on. I will make my decision now. In a competitive quiz programme a player might prematurely press the buzzer with an answer. The answer may, of course, be quite correct. But if is not right, hearing the rest of the question can be both a revealing and amusing observation on not jumping to conclusions. In real life situations, though, this can be both harmful and humiliating.

Impatience. I have far too many more important calls upon my time than to be bothered with this matter. I will give a short answer and that will have to suffice. I want to dismiss the matter as quickly as possible: 'Spare me the details, just do such-and-such.'

Shutting out the uncomfortable. What is being presented to me is not something I wish to hear because it puts me in a bad light. I will jump in (both defensively and aggressively) and give my answer to what it seems I am being accused of, and hopefully that will end the matter.

In each case (and in other cases which may come to your mind) something has been brought to me which is worthy not only of consideration, but of *my* consideration. Justice required me to hear it out, weigh it up impartially, and respond accordingly. The trouble is, I just would not listen.

How often we see these features when the gospel is presented. How many unbelievers answer before they have heard and so deprive themselves of the gift of eternal life! Nicodemus complained to his fellow Pharisees and got a short answer (John 7:51-52). It certainly was folly and shame to them.

Only God, who knows all things in advance (Isaiah 42:9), knows what we are going to say before we say it (Psalm 139:4) and answers before we speak (Isaiah 65:24). Even so, he still hears us (Psalm 34:4,6,15,17). How much more do we need to hear and to listen to what is brought before us, and have wisdom to respond appropriately and with grace!

Do any of the five causes cited, or others, resonate with you? If so, how are you going to remedy them?

[Related proverbs: 18:2,17.]

18:14. When things go wrong. Sickness of body is something even the most healthy will suffer from time to time, and adversity is something even the most privileged will experience occasionally. It is wise, therefore, to consider how we will react to these most unwelcome afflictions.

It is not clear whether the second clause also has sickness in mind. Perhaps not, for bearing with sickness is being compared with the inability to bear with a broken spirit. However, sickness can be very revealing of character.

In 1 Corinthians 2:11 ('For what man knows the things of a man except the spirit of the man which is in him?') Paul is alluding to the fact that a man's spirit is deep, and it is not generally known or understood by others. It is when unusual circumstances affect a person that aspects of his spirit otherwise hidden begin to be revealed. Outwardly, two people may seem to be very alike, but subject them to sickness and differences will soon show in how they cope with their affliction. The spirit of one may sustain him, while the other (as we might say) has little spirit and therefore suffers a great deal more than he might.

Maybe you have had close dealings with those sick in body or those sick at heart. Maybe you have seen at first hand broken health or a broken spirit. Coping with sickness is one thing, but coping with a broken, or crushed, spirit is quite another. You have seen these things in others. But what about yourself?

Of what sort of spirit are you? We have met a crushed spirit before, at 15:13 and 17:22, where we saw that sorrow of heart is a cause, and debilitation is the result. There are some people who are on top of the world when everything goes well, but the moment they are afflicted they come crashing down into the depths. Will your spirit sustain you when you are brought low by sickness or circumstances, or will your spirit be crushed by them? Neither you, nor anyone else, is able to bear the dead weight of a crushed spirit.

We sometimes think of affliction breaking the spirit, whereas this is probably more often than not looking at it from the wrong angle. The affliction will merely expose whether the person is strong in spirit or weak. It is not a case of the effect of the affliction upon the spirit but the response of the spirit to the affliction. We may have had the experience of being surprised when someone has crumbled under a test when we thought them to have been of a more robust spirit.

A broken spirit is not necessarily the same thing as depression, but the two are clearly related. Many people suffer from depression because their spirit has not been altogether right with God. Their spirit has not responded aright to the Spirit of God. We know just how difficult it is to 'bear' such a spirit. To bear, here, really means to support, or to lift up, or to carry. A broken spirit can be an unbearable burden, and it seems that nothing can lift it.

Sickness reminds us not only of our fragility, but also of our mortality. If our spirit is to sustain us it must be able to look these two things squarely in the face and have the means of coping with them. Consider 2 Corinthians 12:10. Probably very few could say they actually take pleasure in such things. So what was Paul's secret? How did his spirit sustain him? It was through his knowledge that the Lord's grace was sufficient for him. He knew that whatever happened to him, he was in God's care, kept by his power, given his strength in his own weakness so that he could go on living for him. This he had proved over and over again in his own experience. Paul looked beyond his weakness to see the power of God.

But what about his mortality? This he addressed in Philippians 1:20-23, and it was confirmed near the end of his life in 2 Timothy 4:6-8. He had an eager expectation of being with Christ. That is what mattered to him, and the only thing which he permitted to distract him from it was that for a little longer he might be able to serve others in Christ's name.

What will sustain you in affliction is not your natural disposition to 'get up and go'; it has nothing to do with your genes, or your conditioning of yourself to 'brazen it out'. Only a spirit in tune with God's Spirit will be able to cope realistically with these troubles. Only one anchored in the knowledge of the God of grace and certain of his rich promises can realistically expect to be carried through the darkest passages of life. 'Have you considered my servant Job?' said God to Satan (Job 2:3). We would do well to consider him from another angle: why his spirit was not crushed. Job was a man who walked with God when all was well, and that is how he had a spirit which kept him from sinking when he was in the depths.

Paul prayed for the church at Thessalonica – believers who were undergoing afflictions (1 Thessalonians 2:14; 3:3-4) – that their whole spirit, soul and body be preserved blameless at the coming of the Lord Jesus (1 Thessalonians 5:23). We have need for God to keep our spirit. We are to glorify God in our spirit (1 Corinthians 6:20). Hebrews 12:9 speaks of God as the Father of spirits. We need to submit our spirit to his and live! His training and discipline of us are to the end that we might be made strong.

[Related proverbs: 15:13; 17:22.]

18:15. A sound investment. The word 'knowledge' is repeated in this proverb. Many of the proverbs when repeating an idea use two different words of similar meaning, but there is particular emphasis here on knowledge. It is knowledge to be *acquired* and knowledge to be *sought*. The acquisitive aspect is stated before the seeking one, indicating that this is no once-and-for-all thing, but an ongoing one. Knowledge is never complete, and never can be in this life. The acquisition of knowledge is a lifetime's building project. What exactly, though, is this knowledge?

Remember, the fear of the Lord is the beginning of knowledge (1:7). True knowledge has the Lord as its reference point. Adam and Eve were misled into thinking that wisdom and knowledge were to be found independently of God (Genesis 3:5-6).

If we are to know the Lord we may learn of him through his *Word*, for that is the principal way in which he has communicated to us. Then, with his Word as a basis, we may gain in our knowledge of him through his *works*. Every study in this world thus undertaken will be enlightening and profitable, for it will deepen our knowledge of him. To what end is this knowledge? It is that we may live righteous lives – not what some perceive as an arid righteousness, but a productive righteousness, a fruitful righteousness ('fruits of righteousness' – Philippians 1:11).

Paul's supreme concern was: 'that I may know him' (Philippians 3:8,10), and that should be ours too. See the emphasis on knowledge in Ephesians 1:17-18; 3:19; 4:13; Philippians 1:9; Colossians 1:10; 2:3; 3:10; James 3:13; 2 Peter 1:2-3,5,8; 3:18; 1 John 5:20.

Of some tasks we say, 'My heart isn't really in it.' It isn't something we really want to do, and if we do it at all we do it reluctantly. The acquisition of knowledge certainly requires some effort. Is it worth taking the trouble to grow in the knowledge of God? Are there other things you would rather be spending your time on? Is your heart really in it? There should be two great motivating principles for the believer: love for God and love for one's neighbour. If we love God then we will want to know him and understand him. If we love our neighbour we will want to have that knowledge whereby we may be of better service to him or her.

It does not say that the wise will have their heads in books seeking knowledge, but that their *ears* will seek it. The emphasis here seems to be on having a teachable spirit (consider Psalm 78:1; Proverbs 2:1-6; Isaiah 50:4-5; Jeremiah 7:24-26). Principally, we are to listen to God, we are to give ourselves to *really* hearing his Word, as those prepared to take it in and act upon it – not giving half an ear to it, but taking the trouble to seek to know and to understand what he has to say to us. Time and effort are expected, and will be rewarded.

We may live in an acquisitive society, in which people believe they must have this, or must have that. Collectors focus upon acquiring certain things and are always seeking to add to their collections. Often as their collection grows so their heart becomes increasingly absorbed in the task, and they will do things they never at first dreamt of doing in order to acquire new pieces. This should be an object lesson to Christians, who have something far more important to acquire and to go on seeking out.

The knowledge spoken of here is that which is built up within the framework of the acknowledgement of God and reverence for him. In being told that the heart of the discerning acquires knowledge, we are to understand this to be a very active thing. The word for 'acquires' is often translated 'buys'. This kind of knowledge is worth the expenditure of time and effort. It is the kind of thing Bible students ought to appreciate, poring over the scriptures, working hard to improve their understanding of God and his work in the world. Does our world view have this kind of knowledge as its basis? Do we have a *heart* for it? If so, we will be investing in true knowledge and will be storing it up in our hearts.

Then there is the matter of what we listen to. The 'seeking' of the second clause is no half-hearted thing either. It is seeking and going on seeking until one finds. By nature, we tend to think of seeking as being an activity which uses mainly the eyes. Yet there is a seeking which uses the ears, as for example if one is trying to track down a missing person and asking people if they have encountered him or heard of him. When it comes to seeking knowledge, more is acquired through the ear than through the eye. We may see things with our eyes, but we tend to learn about them with our ears as they are explained to us. Do we have our ear to the ground where knowledge is concerned? Are we giving our attention to the right things? When we hear God's Word being expounded, are we eager to go over it again, ensuring we have understood its meaning and application? Do we listen as those seeking knowledge?

[Related proverbs: 14:6; 15:14; 22:17; 23:12.]

18:16. Want kudos? The 'gift' of this verse uses a different word from that with subversive connotations used in 17:8,23 or the second clause of 21:14 where the word 'bribe' might be used in each case. It is not necessarily a gift intended to curry favour, but clearly it is a gift which opens doors, and this is what we need to consider. There is nothing pejorative about the statement, it is simply expressing a fact.

It is the same word as is used in the first clause of 21:14, but there its context indicates that its use may still be on the borderline ethically! Questions have often been raised about politicians accepting gifts and the suspicion of potential corruption they may lead to. It has also been known to be a problem in churches in which wealthy benefactors have been permitted undue influence. For a gift really to be a gift, there should be no strings attached, either in the mind of the giver or in that of the recipient. Often, however, that is not the case. If a millionaire gives hundreds of thousands of pounds to a certain well known charity, he will almost certainly attract media attention, and the charity may well consider itself to be under some kind of obligation to him. He may then find himself in a position of influence as far as the policies of the charity are concerned, whether or not he sought it, because of the psychological effect of the gift on the recipient. His generosity is almost bound to open doors for him, and he may well be noticed or even honoured by the great.

But maybe this proverb is describing giving with the deliberate intent of exerting influence. In Genesis 32 we see Jacob, in fear of his brother Esau, sending 'gifts' on ahead of himself with a view to appeasing what he supposed was his brother's wrath. As he saw it, his gift was making room for him, so that when his powerful brother arrived his person would be accepted. In this case it is a gift with strings attached – rather like the 'free gifts' offered by companies who hope to encourage you to spend your money on their goods!

All of which should make us think very carefully when we 'give' to any cause, or even give to the church. What are our motives? Is there the least hint in our giving that we may thereby gain some opportunity of influence? Are we giving with a view to making room for ourselves?

There is something in most of us which craves recognition, which longs for a sense of being valued or the satisfaction of fulfilment. The trouble is, so many go about it in entirely the wrong way and from false motives. So many people are out for what they can *get* rather than thinking about what they can *give*. Yet, paradoxically perhaps, it is the latter which in every sense is the more rewarding.

When we look at the 'gift' of this proverb we need to consider it in its widest sense and not narrow it down to material things. The 'gifts' described in the New Testament as being given to God's people are very diverse – see for example Romans 12:6 in context; 1 Corinthians 12; Ephesians 4:7-12; 1 Peter 4:10.

God had gifted Bezalel and Oholiab (Exodus 31:2,6) with great artistic ability, and their gifts brought them to the notice of Moses, as a result of which their industry and skill brought them recognition throughout the community. In v. 6 there is a reference to 'gifted' artisans and it is significant that they were, literally, 'wise hearted'. Gifted men like Joseph and Daniel were brought before kings and served them.

Consider the woman who cast her two mites into the treasury. Her gift, meagre and insignificant though she may have thought it, brought her to the notice of Jesus (Mark 12:42). At the opposite extreme, the rich young ruler who had so much and wanted so much more, went away sorrowful because he would not give (Mark 10:17-22). No door was opened to him. Then there are the churches of Macedonia, so highly commended by the apostle Paul for their giving (2 Corinthians 8:1-7). Notice there that their generosity sprang out of their first giving themselves to the Lord (v. 5). The Lord himself has given them recognition throughout the history of the church for their example and generosity.

The Lord gives gifts to his people (Ephesians 4:8) and he intends these gifts to be used. No one can complain about not having any gifts. Every one is special and has his or her own special contribution to make for the growth of the church, and that is noticed by God himself and will be rewarded by him.

There is something wonderful about the fact that God should say 'Well done, good and faithful servant' when all we have done is to use what he has in the first place given us!

In Colossians 3:22-24 the apostle Paul encouraged those at the lowest end of the social scale, who might have felt they had nothing to offer, by indicating that their menial service, if done in the right spirit, would not go unnoticed by God but would be rewarded by him.

It is wrong to say there is nothing you can do, there is no contribution you can make, in your church. If you feel that way, it is probably because you are too self-absorbed and are not using what God has given you for the benefit of others. Your gift will make room for you in the right way if you take the trouble to use it as it should be used!

18:17. Avoid jumping to conclusions. There is something of a dispute, and one of the parties to it offloads her grievance and enlists your support. You are shocked by what you are told and filled with indignation at the unjust treatment this person has suffered. Of course you will take up her case ... or will you?

Most of us have experience of listening to entirely plausible and thoroughly convincing stories! Sometimes they are true ... sometimes they are not.

Our understanding of human nature should make it clear that we are not unquestioningly to believe everything we hear. There is a sense in which we need to cultivate a healthy scepticism. Regrettably, not all that we are told will be true. People who tell us things tell them from their own perspective. They include what they wish to include, leaving out what they wish to avoid our knowing. A personal bias is almost inevitable. They are seeking to make a particular impression and want us to believe what they say.

Our thoughts as well as our reactions need to be kept in check until we know the full story, which we will never know from only one account. We might be better placed if we have the opportunity to hear both sides of the argument, but again this can be hampered by both disputants presenting the issue from their own angles, and in any case this is not always possible. What we need is a second opinion. What is helpful is a fresh approach.

Someone else comes along and says, 'Did you mention such and such a matter?' 'What did you mean when you said...?' 'Did you explain exactly why the other person took the line they did?' 'Why in particular are you asking this...?' 'Why did you not point out that...?'

What this other person is doing is not just asking questions, but asking searching questions pertinent to the matter in hand. Weaknesses in the argument are being probed, gaps are being filled, a more balanced picture is being obtained, so that in the end there is a realistic possibility of providing a sound judgement. If the cause is right, it will be vindicated; if not, hasty and unwarranted action will be avoided.

We are told of Absalom that he stole the hearts of the people (2 Samuel 15:6). He did this by ensuring that they heard only his side of a case of his own invention and intention. It seems that people were gullible enough to be ready to revise their opinion of David as a result of the smooth words of a young upstart with a dubious reputation. The result was disastrous.

Shortly after Israel's entry into the promised land the Gibeonites had come to Joshua with a plausible story, on the basis of which a covenant was made with them (Joshua 9). They should have been subjected to a close cross-examination, which probably would have happened had Joshua and the other leaders brought the matter before the Lord.

This brings us to the most important point of all, and though it is not directly mentioned in the proverb a warning is implicit against trusting our own judgement. All such matters should be submitted to God, whose judgement is perfect, who knows all sides of every argument, whose has the wisdom to do right.

In summary, here is a warning about hearing only one side of an argument and being hasty in judgement. All arguments have two sides, and very often each side has some valid points. We may be completely convinced by what we hear from one side, but we should never consider ourselves to be so thoroughly sure that we are unwilling to hear the other side too. We have to beware thinking that we are acquainted with all the factors just because we cannot see any others. When someone else comes along with his own line of questioning we soon discover there were things which we had not thought about which have a bearing on the issue. This is a variation of the 'many counsellors' situation (11:14). It is because any individual's knowledge and perception are limited that there is benefit to others' help being sought, so that together a comprehensive picture may be built up on which to make sound judgement. It is worth asking how many of our opinions are formed on the basis of one-sided evidence.

18:18. Going to arbitration. Casting lots could be viewed as a random process. However, when everything is submitted to the Lord, one must trust that even such a process will be overruled by him. See notes on 16:33.

It is curious that the word 'arbitrary', which indicates something based on a random choice, and 'arbiter', which is a person who settles a dispute, should be derived from the same word meaning 'judge'. We would not expect a judge to be arbitrary in his judgement! At first sight the casting of lots may be viewed as an arbitrary process acting as the arbiter in a contention.

There are a number of recorded instances in the Bible of casting lots. In the case of the soldiers casting lots for Jesus' garment it was purely arbitrary (Matthew 27:35; Psalm 22:18). In the case of the sailors who had Jonah in their boat it probably had an element of superstition as a means of divination (Jonah 1:7). In Numbers 26:55-56 God himself had specifically ordered this method to be used as a fair and impartial means of apportioning the land of promise to the people. Thus Joshua submitted the process to God when it came to the division of the land (Joshua 18:6,10). Implicit in this was the understanding that God was in control of all things, and that he would guide in respect of decisions which were beyond their knowledge or ability to make rightly and fairly. It also forestalled the possibility of disputes over land in the future.

There are ways of resolving conflicts other than by fighting them out! There are cases when means independent of the contestants must be sought by which conflicts are resolved, yet by which the contestants are willing to abide.

It has to be admitted that sometimes disputes arise which are of such complexity that it seems impossible to unravel the rights and wrongs of the case. Some decision has to be made, or the contestants will tear each other apart and cause untold damage. Those involved in the dispute need first to recognise that it is in their best interests that something be done, and then to be willing to refer the matter to a third party whom they trust will act impartially and by whose judgement they will abide. Furthermore, this must be done publicly so that no one is left in any doubt about the outcome and that it makes a full end of the matter.

Sometimes disputes arise in churches and among Christians who feel strongly over certain issues. When this happens and there seems to be no other way of resolving the issue there is something to be said for the contestants acting according to the principle of this proverb, if not actually following the practice, by agreeing before God to abide by the decision of those they both trust, acknowledging in advance that one side will need grace to accept what from their point of view is an unfavourable outcome. The important thing here, though, is that both sides recognise it is done before the Lord and with a desire to honour his Word. With the Lord nothing is left to chance; there is nothing outside his control. When the Lord has been acknowledged, neither party then has any right to complain about the outcome. It stands to reason that whichever way a dispute is settled it is almost certainly going to appear to favour one of the parties. But that was the agreement in the first place. If it is accepted as the Lord's overruling it should be done graciously, not sourly following Adonijah's two-faced and altogether biased attitude (1 Kings 2:15). When the decision is reached, the 'losers' should be prepared graciously to acknowledge the Lord's sovereign overruling, even if they still think the decision was the wrong one! To be prepared to give way over an issue should be viewed as a mark of honour rather than an indication of defeat. If it comes to separation, an amicable parting is better than an acrimonious split!

[Related proverb: 16:33.]

18:19. Blood is thicker than water. Here is another proverb about contentions, but in this case it comes as a warning. The terse wording of the original is intended to make a strong impact.

In peace time, with the gates open, there would have been no problem about access into a strong city and doing business there. But should hostilities commence it would be a very different story for the gates would be closed and barred, the fortifications secured against entry, and there would be no easy communication or passage back in.

Think of what cost would have been involved in terms of time, expense, manpower and lives for an army to conquer a well fortified city. Think, too, of what the bars of a castle represented to one incarcerated behind them. Then ask, is it worth causing a breach with those closest to you? Or, if such a breach exists, do not suppose that putting things right is going to be an easy or trouble-free matter.

Under this imagery we are given a warning about the consequences of offending a 'brother', by which we may understand someone close to us. Restoring the peace is far harder than rupturing it, and the stronger the bond that is broken, the more difficult it is to mend it, which only underlines the importance of not breaking it in the first place! In the culture in which this proverb was set, mutual reliance, trust and loyalty were the marks of a relationship between brothers, and to cause offence amounted to a breach of faith. That not only hurt, it also did considerable damage.

Some of the most intractable problems are found within families. The most difficult relationships to repair are those within the family when there has been a rift. We must not underestimate the strength of family ties. Positively, the warning comes to remind us to value such relationships for what they are and to guard them as precious.

If natural family ties are intimate and strong, church family ties are (or ought to be) even stronger. The trust and intimacy involved here are at a deeper, spiritual level. Offences are therefore to be avoided at all costs. To be abused by outsiders, though uncomfortable, can be borne with relative ease. But to experience the same from those closest to us has an altogether different dimension, as David found to his deep dismay (Psalms 41:9; 55:12-14).

From this proverb we should certainly take warning against abusing our relationships with our brothers and sisters in Christ. What kind of things cause the offence of which this proverb speaks? Here are some: abusing intimacies, betraying confidences, denigrating brothers before others, trampling on feelings, rebelling against sound advice, acting selfishly without regard for the effect on others. You may add more examples. However, whatever specific matter might be the cause of division, the underlying cause is very often a headstrong attitude.

Family bonds need nurturing and protecting. A brother is not likely to be offended who is accustomed to your consideration and concern for his well-being. But take him for granted or take advantage of him, and his respect for you will be lost, to which there will be no easy return route. Where relationships are close there is so much more at stake. A breach of trust is a terrible thing in such cases. When a brother is offended, the one causing the offence should not suppose to dismiss it lightly, but should recognise it as being serious and requiring the utmost grace, wisdom, skill and patience in order to seek to deal with the damage which has been done in order to restore the relationship.

Cases of rifts within the family and rifts within the church are probably known to most of us. In many of these cases too little has been done to restore them. Where we see contention on the horizon, we are to do what we can to minimise its effects. To disagree over things is the common lot of mankind. Some disagreements may legitimately be held without creating a great commotion and certainly without causing offence. In other cases there is a very great risk of some being offended, and in situations like that the way the matter is introduced and the way the disagreeing parties are approached and respected will make a great difference to the outcome.

The more powerful the contention, the more the parties will fortify themselves against each other. Unless offences are settled promptly, a person who is offended in one matter by another person will very often find other causes of offence to add to it. This often happens when relationships break down, and the offended party trawls up from history a formidable array of real or imagined offences which might otherwise have gone unnoticed.

It is worth asking whether you have ever done any of these things, or if a breach with someone who was close to you has indeed occurred? If it has, restoring amicable relations is going to be far from easy. There are formidable barriers to be overcome. If you have been responsible for causing them to be erected, it may be beyond your power to get them removed again.

If you are in a situation where there is the potential to 'offend' a brother, it is wise to consider the possible consequences. You should think long and hard before causing offence which may do irreparable harm to the relationship. Rather, you should start from the position of valuing the relationship for what it is, to regard it as precious but fragile.

In Psalm 73:15 Asaph very wisely reflected that even to speak out what was on his disturbed mind would have been a betrayal against the people closest to him. His question was, 'How will it affect *them*?'

Suppose, however, that you are the offended one. Are you to keep your brother shut out? Consider Matthew 18:15-17 which is all about doing one's utmost to restore severed relationships.

In an individualistic society relationships are often greatly undervalued. The situation in the church should be demonstrably different.

Are there any cases when it would be right to offend a brother? There is possibly only one. Jesus would have been well aware of this proverb when he spoke of setting families at loggerheads and a man's enemies being those of his own household (Matthew 10:34-39). There is one thing more important than the ties of family, and that is the call of the gospel. Many people have held back from the faith because of the offence they perceive it would cause family members, and that is understandable. Nevertheless Jesus gives a warning which is even more powerful than that of this proverb, which is that none is worthy of him who puts family relationships first above love for and allegiance to him.

18:20-21. These are both about the tongue.

18:20. Are you satisfied with what you give out? Those concerned with healthy living are usually particular about what they eat. They are filled and satisfied with what enters their mouth. We might expect a man's stomach to be filled with the fruit of his *labour*, with the produce resulting from his hard work. Yet it is words, not work, which features here. This proverb strikingly turns logic on its head by indicating that satisfaction of the appetite comes not from what the mouth takes in but from what it gives out. Obviously the word 'stomach' is being used figuratively, but then we do that anyway when we say we have no stomach for something, or that we cannot stomach somebody's comments.

In a society which is so bent on finding satisfaction this proverb comes as a warning shot across the bows that most seem to be seeking it in entirely the wrong way. It is found not in what we get or acquire but in what we give out. There are some who seek satisfaction in their giving to charity or other worthy causes. This proverb is saying that satisfaction is not even found in giving from our material possessions. It is not going to cost us in the sense that we have to budget for it.

The focus here is on the quality of what we give out verbally, and the inference of this proverb is that what is more conducive to real health and well-being is connected with what we give out rather than what we take in. This is something we should think about carefully.

You may go into the supermarket and take great care in how you select from the fruit and vegetables on display to ensure they meet your exacting standards in freshness, ripeness, and appearance. You may also be careful what you put on your plate in the way of food, that it is both fit for consumption and will do you good. With this proverb in mind, do you give the same kind of careful attention to your words? Are you properly selective in what you say? Are your words designed to do good? Are they top quality? As you nourish others with your speech, so you nourish yourself. In the longer term people will almost certainly remember you as much – maybe more – for your words than for anything you do.

It is a fact that for most of us words tend to roll off our tongues with hardly a second thought. Have you noticed, though, how frequently people are categorised by their talk? 'She's a gossip.' 'She has a sharp tongue.' 'He's altogether too outspoken.' 'He's very fond of speaking his own mind.' 'He tramples on other people's feelings.' 'She's always got a good word for everybody.' 'She's such an encouragement.' 'He is always ready to listen and give helpful advice.' Examples abound. We tend to assess people by what they say rather more than by what they do, and we respond to them accordingly.

Someone who exclaims, 'That did me good!' when they put somebody down by giving them a real piece of their mind, is actually under a false impression. In the longer term it has probably hindered a relationship and may well rebound in painful fashion.

Jesus said, 'My meat is to do the will of him who sent me' (John 4:34). He also said, 'Life is more than food' (Matthew 6:25). Jesus also said that we are to do to others as we would have them do to us (Matthew 7:12; Luke 6:31) and that includes our speech.

What people say has enormous potential for good or ill, as v. 21 here indicates. Words can, directly or indirectly, benefit or harm others, can encourage or depress them, can lift them up or cast them down, can heal them or hurt them, can build them up or wear them down, can strengthen their resolve or undermine it. What we say *to* people, and what we say *about* people, affect them in one way or another.

But these verses are particularly about the way these things affect us, or rebound on us. If I am a grouchy individual, always finding fault with others, then my words are not going to do me any good or really give me any satisfaction. They will only further promote my bad feelings which in turn will very likely undermine my health. That is one aspect. The other one is that my words will affect how others relate to me, and as a consequence of my negative attitude toward others, they will not be inclined to respond positively to me, and so I will be doubly deprived of any benefit. There are many lonely, isolated, bitter people who have none but themselves to blame for their situation because of the things they have said.

The other side is the tremendous personal benefit of knowing that one's words have been instrumental as a blessing to others, that what we have said has really helped them. Simply the knowledge of it can provide us with profound satisfaction. But then, those who are like this also invariably find themselves the recipients of good from others, and so they have double satisfaction.

The questions remain: How satisfied are we in life? How filled? How nourished?

[Related proverb: 12:14.]

18:21. A matter of life and death. This follows on from the previous proverb. The schoolchild chant, 'Sticks and stones may break my bones, but words can never hurt me,' has a hollow ring, for the truth is that words can hurt deeply and do more lasting damage than sticks and stones.

Death and life are in the power of a dictator? Death and life are in the power of the elements? Maybe. But it is often overlooked that death and life are in the power of the tongue. Death and life being in the power of the tongue is not a reference to despots who can decree with a word who shall live and who shall die. It is a perfectly general statement and applies just as much to you and me. Maybe we would not for a moment imagine anything so dramatic as our words being instruments of death or life. Yet the very use of the words 'death' and 'life' should prompt us to reflect upon the possibility that what we say about others may have a far more profound effect upon them – and upon us – than we realise.

Those who love it ... love what? The tongue? The power? Perhaps both. Do you love that sense of power that your words can have upon others, the ways in which you can influence their thinking, their actions, their mood, and so on? Note the double-edged nature of this proverb. It is given as both a warning and an encouragement. Do we really consider how powerfully what we say can affect other people? Then know that the way you exercise this power will return to you. If you use your words to undermine or destroy others, they will work, too, for your own destruction. On the other hand, if you use your words to benefit others, to infuse life into them, they will work for your own life and well-being, too.

We are familiar with the statement: 'Do to others as you would have them do to you' (Matthew 7:12). This includes the way we speak of them.

There is a saying that those who take the sword shall perish by the sword (Matthew 26:52). Have you ever thought to apply it to the use of words? The tongue, like a sword, can cut both ways. One way it is deadly, the other way it is life-giving. James, using a different metaphor, refers to the power of the tongue (James 3:6) and he speaks of both blessing and cursing proceeding from the same mouth (James 3:10).

How easily words slip off our tongues! How easily we plan what we are going to say to people and how we are thereby going to influence them or affect them, little considering that in due course they will come back to visit us with similar influence.

Someone who is of a relentlessly critical disposition, always finding fault, always demanding the impossible, never praising, and so on, is actually destroying the one on the receiving end just as much as if they were committing cold-blooded murder. At the other end of the spectrum, someone who is always on the lookout to speak for the benefit and building up of another, who takes an interest in the person and shows kindness and consideration, even if it may at times involve some negative criticism, is in reality imparting to that person something as precious as life itself.

We see something similar in the message of the gospel, for Paul spoke of himself and other ambassadors for Christ as being an aroma of death to those who were perishing, but an aroma of life to those who believed (2 Corinthians 2:14-16).

18:22. 5:18-19; Ephesians 5:25-33. A lifelong blessing. The marriage relationship has come under considerable attack from various quarters, not least by example through being disparaged by those who have found it has not worked for them. It has been described as outmoded, restrictive, even irrelevant. Husband and wife jokes abound which reflect upon aspects of the relationship which do not always work in the way they should.

It was God who instituted marriage between one man and one woman in the beginning as part of the created order which was 'very good', an abiding truth which is reflected in the wording of this proverb. The writer of the letter to the Hebrews found it necessary to assert that marriage should be held in honour by all (13:4). If there is dishonour, it belongs to those who mistreat this precious gift from God. God, who instituted marriage, makes it quite clear here that it is an honourable status.

Observe carefully what is said and what is not said in this proverb. A wife is worthy of that name insofar as she fulfils God's intended role for her in life and in her relationship with her husband (Genesis 2:18,24). Many men have had marriage partners who have not lived up to the name of 'wife'.

Favour from the Lord is far more than a nod of approval! His favour is something for which there is ongoing evidence, even abundant evidence, and it should be clear from this statement that it comes through the instrumentality of the wife who proves to be a blessing to her husband.

Many a man has reason continually to bless God for having found a wife. Sadly, many a man has reason to rue a hasty choice. If these notes address a man who is not yet married and is thinking about it, if you are seeking a wife it is a good time to ask yourself dispassionately and carefully what you are looking for. Have you thought about the lifetime role a wife will play in your life and how the right kind of person will meet with the Lord's favour and lead to blessing for both you and your wife and any children you may have? Romantic notions may have a part to play, but they must equally be realistic notions. So important is this that it carries with it this singular promise from the Lord, that you will be blessed in making the right choice. How about making a list of priorities in what you are looking for in a wife, and comparing these with the list of priorities the Lord has for your own life?

Or, if you are a married man, how about reviewing these things in the light of your experience and, with a fresh appreciation of the Lord's goodness to you, seek to enhance your relationship? Never take God's favour for granted! Never take your wife for granted!

For women, this proverb rightly understood should be greatly uplifting. The apostle Peter reminds husbands to give honour to their wives (1 Peter 3:7), for in the sight of God a wife has a noble responsibility and a position of honour. She is a lifelong evidence and instrument of God's favour to the man who found her!

When God said, 'It is not good that man should be alone' (Genesis 2:18) he added, 'I will make him a helper comparable to him,' and he created woman. In the husband and wife relationship as God intended it to function there should be complementarity. This verse is a reminder that God ordained marriage, and that as he blessed Adam with Eve, so it is a mark of his favour that a man should find a wife. There are many men who for one reason or another avoid marriage. Maybe they think it will restrict their freedom and inhibit them. Maybe they worry that a side of them they would prefer to remain hidden will be exposed and, related to that, they do not think they could cope with having to share their lives with anyone. Maybe they think they simply would not be able to handle the responsibility. Many, sadly, go through life satisfied (so they think) with casual relationships with the opposite sex. This proverb, then, is reminding us of the importance in God's eyes of the marriage relationship, and that it is honourable for a man to seek a wife. Modern presentations of human relationships have greatly obscured this simple but profoundly important fact.

[Related proverbs: 8:35; 12:4; 19:14; 31:10-31.]

18:23. 2 Corinthians 8:8-15. Circumstances and speech. In this section of the book there is a spate of proverbs about the poor (see also 19:1,4,7,17,22). This one could be an observation on how the rich so often respond to the poor, or it could be a simple contrast between the general attitudes of one class toward the other. It is another observation on the use of the tongue and the way it reflects upon sinful human nature. Note that it is an observation, not a judgement.

By the poor is understood those with needs they cannot meet themselves. In a sense, they are reduced to begging. The NIV, 'pleads for mercy', while relevant, possibly narrows down the meaning too much. The poor have no choice in the matter. The poor may have everything to lose if they cannot obtain what they need and so are very careful to adopt an attitude and formulate words which they hope will succeed in gaining a favourable response from those who are in a position to help them. Their words are the one resource which they do have and which they tend to exploit to the full, often beyond what is just and true. Notwithstanding they may have genuine needs, their entreaties are often embellished and exaggerated in the hope that by adding such 'colour' to them they may be the more likely to obtain what they seek. If they can persuade you with their hard luck stories, with the injustice they have received, with the account of their broken health, with the dire condition of those they have to support, and so on, their appeal to your sympathy and generosity will be richly rewarded.

Our circumstances influence the way we speak. If you are in a position of need in which you find yourself dependent upon others, you will be careful how you speak to them, because in respect of that need you are poor. If your needs are not so dependent, you may be much freer in the way you go about meeting them. So for example, you may simply say that if you do not get what you want from one quarter you will go elsewhere to obtain it. You can do this because you are coming at it from a position of strength, and you are making it clear who is calling the shots.

Riches tend to breed a kind of callousness and insensitive indifference to the needs of others. Many who are rich, enveloped as they are with their comforts, may view the approaches of others for help with resentment, and may have no inclination to distinguish between hangers-on and spongers and the genuinely needy. The easy option is summarily to dismiss all calls for help and to look down on all who are in their eyes looking for a free hand-out. If people think they are a 'soft touch' then they are going to have to think again.

The rich can speak how they will. If they wish, they can trample upon the poor, and it will make no difference to them. If they wish, they can give others the rough edge of their tongue without it affecting their comfort zone. If they wish, they can regard their riches as entitling them to look down on others and treat them with disdain. Such attitudes, though not universal, are certainly prevalent in society, and the more secure a man thinks himself, the less he feels the need to concern himself with the troubles of others. More than that, the presentation of such troubles to him disturbs his ease, prompting him to react harshly. He considers he has to act in this way in order to guard himself and his riches.

The whole scenario smacks of insincerity and hypocrisy. The poor use words, perhaps fawning words, which they would otherwise never have used, and the rich, too, use words necessitated by their circumstances in order to guard their self interests. Both parties, in their own way, are out to secure their own ends. Truth and justice and equity do not enter into the matter. The law dictated that partiality was to be shown neither to the rich nor the poor (Exodus 23:3; Leviticus 19:15; Deuteronomy 1:17). That is because it is God's law, and his law is a reflection of his person, and he sees the heart. To him, there is no difference between the poor and the rich of this world. His grace is displayed toward all who call upon him with genuine humility. He is always sensitive toward true need, and he never turned any away who called upon him to meet their need.

The principle of equality (2 Corinthians 8:14) may be a noble one and widely acknowledged, but when it comes down to practice the opposite tends to operate.

Whether we are poor or rich, or somewhere between the two, our communications with others should not be self-centred and purely aimed at guarding our self-interest. The poor man uses entreaties in order to get what he wants; the rich man responds harshly in order to keep what he has. Neither has a genuine interest in the other. Now look again at 2 Corinthians 8 and see there that the principle of equality is founded on giving based on love, not getting based on rights.

As far as our relationship with God is concerned, in ourselves we are poor, but in Christ we are rich. God is rich, and in particular is rich in mercy and in grace, and so does not answer us harshly. We will never get a rough answer from God. So our approach to him need not be with uncertain or obsequious entreaties, but with the humble confidence that if we are able to ask in Christ's name we are sure to receive that for which we ask. The incident involving Jesus and the Syro-Phoenician woman is interesting in this respect (Matthew 15:21-28).

18:24. Friends, friends and a Friend. The first clause of this proverb is a play upon similarly sounding words of different meaning. So 'must himself be friendly' (NKJV), or the like, is probably incorrect. More likely it should be rendered something like: 'A man of friends may be ruined.'

There is also a play upon the word 'friend' because that used in the second clause is very different from the one in the first. This proverb is saying that there are friends and friends. There are the friends like those the prodigal son acquired in the foreign country (Luke 15:13), and there are the friends like Ruth was to Naomi (Ruth 1:16-17; 4:15). The first word is more casual and detached, the second is more intimate implying emotional involvement. Here is a case where quality is so much more important than quantity. There are some people who could be described as everybody's friend, yet who are actually extremely lonely and their personal lives are in a mess. That is because all their friends are of the first kind. To have had just one of the second kind would have made all the difference. Jeremiah 3:1 uses the first word of 'lovers' of the kind who are doing no more than satisfying their own lusts. Too many friends of that kind will very likely bring a person to ruin. This shows the importance of building friendships of the second kind. The cost of this kind of intimacy is far outweighed by its benefits.

So let us start by asking the question, who is the person who has no friends? A person without money? Look, for example, at 19:4,6-7. We will come on to that in due course, but the real answer has to do more with disposition than possessions. The person without friends is the one whose character repels others, and it is often these people who end up lonely and embittered.

The proverb is really looking at the quality of friendship. Think about your friends and the nature of these friendship and give yourself time to think about the following questions and answer them objectively. What is the substance of your friendships? How deep are they? On what are they based? In what ways do you contribute to the friendships to give them strength? What are they worth to you? Which of your friends would stand by you in trouble, and why?

There are such things as 'fair weather friends', who are friendly only when everything goes well, but who desert you as soon as trouble arises. If that is the only kind of friends you attract then something is wrong – not with your friends but rather with you yourself.

In the culture of Solomon's time family ties and responsibilities were far stronger than is generally the case today. Brothers stuck together, and 'blood is thicker than water' really meant something. It was unthinkable as far as the family honour was concerned that one should get into difficulties and be ignored by a brother who was in a position to help. So the friend who sticks *closer* than a brother is a friend of inestimable value, and invariably the ties are mutual. This raises the question of what kind of friend you are to others, and how far you will go for them.

Remarkably, Abraham was known as 'the friend of God' (Isaiah 41:8; 2 Chronicles 20:8; James 2:23).

Jesus called his disciples his friends (John 15:13-15) as well as his brothers (Hebrews 2:11), notwithstanding he knew them through and through, 'warts and all'. These friendships were based on love, faith, loyalty and obedience on their part, and divine love and faithfulness on his. We sing, 'What a Friend we have in Jesus, all our sins and griefs to bear.' He is the one who sticks closer than a brother. His friendship is to be cherished because it is unlike every other and will never fail. We read back in v. 19 that a brother offended is harder to win than a strong city. But the Lord Jesus is not so offended by the failings of his people that he will turn a cold shoulder to them. Though all may forsake us, he will never (Hebrews 13:5; compare Peter's statement to the Lord in Matthew 26:33).

A man may have many friends and yet still come to ruin. That will never happen if we cherish the friendship of the Lord Jesus Christ and nurture it. 'All may change, but Jesus never, glory to his name!' 'Earthly friends may prove untrue, doubts and fears assail; One still loves and cares for you, One who will not fail... Jesus never fails, Jesus never fails; Heav'n and earth may pass away, but Jesus never fails.'

[Related proverb: 17:17.]

19:1-2. Poverty and perversity. The 'Better... than...' formula is expressing a truth which may not be so obvious on the surface. Integrity of life is compared with perversity of speech, and one might wonder why it should be said that one is *better* than the other when one is clearly right and the other wrong. But in life the real issues are often buried layers deep and therefore overlooked. So we may see a poor person, struggling and downtrodden, side by side with another person not really so different but who appears to be doing rather well for himself. Our view suggests that the latter is better than the former. Only when we look into it more closely we discover that the second person has actually got where he has by devious means. Now who is the better off? We have to revise our opinion and say it is the former.

However, this proverb may not be comparing people in different circumstances but focusing solely upon the poor and the way they conduct themselves. Life can be hard for the poor, and being poor has many attendant difficulties as well as temptations which are peculiar to this class, dishonesty of various kinds for the sake of personal gain being among them. A poor person may find that a little deceit will open the door to bettering his or her circumstances. This touches for example on the matter of benefit fraud, but there are other examples. Also, many a poor person has been led into crime by others dangling the carrot of personal gain. It is interesting that the first clause of this proverb is repeated at 28:6, but there it is contrasted with perversity in the rich.

Whatever a poor person lacks, there is something he may and should possess, and that is integrity. Anyone who lacks this quality, no matter how well off he may be in other respects, is worse off than a poor man. A man of integrity is one whose life is consistently honest and open. He has 'got it all together'. He is not unravelling, nor are there loose ends of his personality out of control. The comparison is with a person who is perverse with his lips, which is one of the first ways in which lack of integrity is revealed. To be perverse means to twist what is good and right into something it should not be.

The addition of 'and is a fool' seems to be a commentary on the second person. Perverse speech marks one out as a fool. Perversity is folly, whether it be found in the poor or the rich. There is no excuse for it, and no allowances are to be made for it. Integrity of character and speech override every other consideration. Why is it better? The importance of having a clear conscience may be presented as a reason, but the real reason is that it is approved by the Lord and that perversity will be judged by him.

There are plenty of people in this world who 'have got it made for them' and display a rather condescending attitude toward others whose scruples have held them back from enjoying the same carefree existence. They look on them as being poor, and maybe in terms of this world's goods they could be considered so by comparison. Yet when it comes to what really matters, their integrity has deprived them of nothing, and they are truly better off.

The 'also' at the beginning of v. 2 (dropped by the NIV and ESV) indicates that verses 1 and 2 are connected (though see on 17:26). When we read of 'knowledge' in the book of Proverbs we must understand that it has its source in the knowledge of God (1:7). It starts with the fear of the Lord and with a relationship with him. This is where so many go so far wrong. True knowledge cannot exist in isolation. Without the fear of the Lord there can be no real knowledge, no real understanding, only information and ideas which ultimately do not relate to anything. The perversion of the lips and the hastening of the feet, and folly and sin, all arise from the sinful human heart, and unless something is done there the problem cannot be remedied, even though it may to a certain extent be masked.

Observe the contrast between *walking* in integrity in v.1 with *hastening with one's feet* in v.2. Walking in integrity indicates a measured pattern of life, as opposed to doing things in a hurry without thought and without principle. A person of integrity does not act on impulse, is not enticed into hasty decisions or actions but sets these things against the standards of God's Word and responds accordingly.

The person who hastens with his feet misses his way. He is in too much of a hurry pursuing his own ends to stop and consider what is the way God wants him to take. Consequently he 'sins' or 'misses his way'; he finds himself in the wrong way.

It is not good for a soul to be without knowledge, for integrity depends upon it. We must set a premium upon knowing the Word of God and upon understanding his will in order that we may obey it. This is something we cannot fast track. The time spent in this exercise may appear to leave us poorer in other respects, but it is better to be poor and to have this knowledge than to be busy in other pursuits, or to jump at any opportunity to 'get rich quick' by the dubious means often advocated in this world.

We have observed that saying one thing is better than another is a device for exposing what is good and what is not good. Here, something else is not good, and it is this lack of knowledge which sometimes is partly responsible for the wrong choices people make when they sacrifice integrity to the enticement to gain.

What is the connection between the two clauses of v.2? Perhaps part of it is that knowledge makes us cautious, and gives us criteria against which to assess certain courses of action. There is a saying, 'Look before you leap.' Hastening with the feet is a picture of a person in a hurry, and in particular a person in a hurry who is not really looking where he is going! People have been known to say, 'If I had known where this would lead me I wouldn't have touched it with a bargepole.' They lacked knowledge, and therefore they did the wrong thing. Integrity is one thing, but it needs to be combined with knowledge. Knowledge is absolutely essential to integrity, because the word for integrity denotes wholeness. It is a golden rule that we need to know what we are about before we embark on it. In life, if we are in too much of a hurry we are likely to find ourselves rubbing our noses in the dirt, spiritually speaking!

[Related proverbs: 14:2; 21:5; 28:6.]

19:3. 3:5-8. Who can I blame when things go wrong? How common this is in life. How many people blame God for what is wrong in their lives or for what is wrong in the world, when they have no one but themselves to blame!

A good workman will not take a hammer to a screw. That is sheer abuse of design and purpose. The screw may go in, and may even look all right, but it will not hold properly on account of the damage done beneath the surface.

Twisting one's way (NKJV), or ruining one's life (NIV), or bringing one's way to ruin (ESV), essentially means doing in one's life what ought not to be done, contrary to God's design. However it looks, however it appears to be, under the surface irreparable damage is done and it will not hold under strain. A man twists his way when he finds reasons for falsehood and deception instead of the simple truth; he twists his way when he covets what others have; he twists his way when he overindulges himself, whether in food or drink, or entertainment, or any other form of self-gratification; he twists his way when he makes himself the centre of his life, excluding God from it. He twists his way whenever and however he deviates from the design and purpose of God for him. 'Professing to be wise, they became fools,' declares Paul (Romans 1:22), for the abuse of God's design and purpose is sheer folly.

Then, having taken the hammer to the screw, when things fall apart in his life, with perverted logic he blames God. Having twisted his way and found all sorts of problems arising as a result, he attributes his troubles to God and boils up inside against him. Or he complains that God is wanting to deprive him of what is in his own interests and of what he imagines would do him good. The perversion in the heart of man is for ever twisting what the good God has provided, abusing both the gift and the Giver, and then complaining about it as if it were God's fault!

This fretting against the Lord comes from the heart, for it is the heart which is deceitful above all things and desperately wicked (Jeremiah 17:9). So where things are wrong with the world, or wrong in their circumstances, people so often ask the question as to why God allows such things, charging God with blame instead of facing up to the uncomfortable truth that almost all troubles can be directly attributed to man's folly (or at least lack of wisdom), and for those which cannot, that God himself has given adequate explanation traceable back to sin which is rooted in the heart of every individual.

Fretting against the Lord contrasts with being content in the Lord. The antidote to fretting against the Lord is submitting to the Lord. It is because he is who he is that we can do so and be content. It is as we commit our way (that is, both our way *of* life and our way *in* life) to the Lord that he makes our way straight (3:6). If people were in the habit of committing their way to the Lord they would find their lives much more straightforward than they do. The apostle Paul, for all the hardships he experienced in life, said he had learned, in whatever state he was, to be content. How? Through Christ who strengthened him (Philippians 4:11,13). His way was committed *to* him, and his way was looked after *by* him. The apostle James writes to a discontented people of the need to submit to God, with the promise of God's gracious presence for those who do so (James 4:1-10). The apostle Peter, too, writes of the need for a humble, submissive spirit under the hand of a gracious God who cares (1 Peter 5:6-7).

19:4. Fickle friendship. There is an irony in the use of the plural in the first clause and the singular in the second, and this gives the clue to the kind of friends in view here. It does not say that the wealthy make many friends, but that wealth does, and that is the give-away to what is going on here. The translation that wealth '*makes* many friends' (NKJV) could be a little misleading. '*Brings* many friends' is probably better, for these 'friends' are not so much the product of wealth as the parasites on wealth. They are those who are more interested in what is on offer, on what the people *have* and how they may benefit *from* them, than who they *are* and how they may be of benefit *to* them. The wealthy may have the power to hold on to such friends and enjoy their company for what it is worth, but what really is it worth?

The poor person, on the other hand, has no resources outside of himself to attract and hold friendship, and any 'friend' whose interest is chiefly mercenary will soon tire of him.

Now think about the kind of friendship Jesus was speaking of when he said that he called his disciples his friends (John 15:13-15). It was after three years of close acquaintance and a developing relationship (hence his expression 'no longer' – ' No longer do I call you servants') that he used this term of them. So the friendship was not trivial. It was based on a deep knowledge and understanding on his part. Furthermore, it was not based on what he could get out of them, for he was only too well aware of their weaknesses and failings, their slowness to understand who he was and the fact that they would desert him in his darkest hour. It was a friendship which had love as its basis, an intention to do them good, a purpose to draw them into a closer relationship with him for their own benefit.

We need to give thought our own friendships. Although friendship should really be a mutual, two-way relationship, rather than thinking about the friendship we *receive* let us consider for a moment the friendship we *give*. It is easy to call someone a friend on relatively slight acquaintance, but then, when things go wrong in their lives, to desert them and all but disown them. True friendship is of a different order. You cannot call someone your friend if you hold them at a distance or are reluctant to talk with them about things which affect them. Consider what God said about Abraham his friend before he destroyed Sodom and Gomorrah (Abraham's nephew Lot was living in Sodom). He said, 'Shall I hide from Abraham what I am about to do?' (Genesis 18:17). Likewise, Jesus said that a mark of his calling his disciples his friends was that all things he heard from his Father he made known to them.

Much friendship is casual, like that in the proverb before us. True friendship is committed, like that of 18:24. That is the kind commended to us and exemplified in Jesus Christ.

[Related proverbs: 14:20; 17:17; 18:24; 19:6,7.]

19:5. Something we cannot get away with. Here we are looking particularly at things said either about other people or which involve other people. Back at 6:19 we were informed of God's intense hatred of false witness. 'You shall not bear false witness' is the ninth of the Ten Commandments (Exodus 20:16). One aspect of this comes out in Exodus 23:1 where we read, 'You shall not circulate a false report' which, for one thing, means we need to be sure of the facts before passing on news, and if this were done it would put an end to a great deal of gossip.

Perjury is the offence of wilfully telling an untruth or making a misrepresentation under oath. There is a danger we may think of false witness as a lesser offence when it is not under oath or when it does not take place in a court of law. However, God makes no such distinction. When he commands 'You shall not bear false witness', it matters not what the circumstances are or where we are, for the command applies universally. Furthermore, it is God who requires it and we are effectively bound under oath whether or not we acknowledge it. False witness always perverts the course of justice; false witness always harms the innocent and often acquits the guilty.

False witness comes in various forms, ranging from out and out lies dressed up as truth, to truth combined with the withholding or distorting of certain information with intent to mislead.

False witness is given from various motives, from callous hard-heartedness and hatred at one extreme, through greed of gain, to cringing fear under threat of reprisal at the other extreme. Examples of each may be found at Psalm 27:12; Acts 6:13; 2 Kings 5:22; Genesis 26:7. See also Deuteronomy 1:17.

This provides an opportunity for us to examine our own motives about how we speak of others. Of people we particularly dislike, do we 'do them down' by our words? Do we take sides in an issue with the hope we will benefit from it? Do we fall short of honest testimony because we are afraid of the consequences of speaking out the truth?

Those who bear false witness do so with the intention that they will get away with it and not be found out. This proverb bluntly states that this will not happen. Absalom's false witness (2 Samuel 15:3) set off a train of events which led ultimately to his ignominious death. 2 Samuel 17:14 specifically informs us that this happened according to God's purpose. Whether our motives for false witness are callous, covetous or cringing, we may confidently expect to be called to account for them. It is better to deal with it now in confession and repentance before a forgiving God than to continue in concealment and denial only to be exposed later.

We may not know exactly what happened to the scoundrels who gave false witness against Naboth (1 Kings 21:13) or to those who gave false witness against Jesus (Matthew 26:60). What we do know is that sooner or later they appeared before the bar of divine justice.

Why does God speak with such severity against false witnesses? Surely it is because it involves a deliberate attempt to undermine or overturn his own justice which is based on truth. It involves 'malice aforethought'. They seek unjustly to bring punishment upon those undeserving of it, or to circumvent punishment for those deserving of it, flagrantly violating a fundamental principle upon which God works. There is a certain poetic justice in that God should justly bring punishment on those who seek unjustly to bring punishment upon others. His judgement is both a mark and a vindication of his justice.

[Related proverbs: 6:16,19; 12:19; 19:9; 21:28.]

19:6-7. Beware of covetousness. This proverb, reminiscent of v. 4, is focusing upon attitude toward money and possessions. To the usual two clauses of the proverbs is added a comment on how this so often works. It is making an observation upon one aspect of human behaviour. None of us can fail to understand or appreciate what it is saying. It is drawing our attention to something common enough in the world, with the intention that we should stop and look at it and ask what the underlying causes are and how they address us.

What do these verses say about human nature? For one thing, they hint at a dreadful, almost sickening superficiality which exists in so many human relationships, where wealth and prestige and connections are the things that talk.

Firstly, we see people running after those from whom they might hope to gain. 'Nobility' here could refer to status or it could equally refer to disposition. Either way, the reference is to those who might by one means or another be persuaded to give hand-outs. It is clear that the favour sought or the friendship nurtured is primarily for the gift and not for the giver.

A man who gives gifts (setting aside those who do so for dishonourable reasons) is one with a generous disposition. It is an abuse of his generosity to curry favour with him simply for the sake of what might be on offer.

People sometimes take this line with God, or they regard the church of God as a 'soft touch'. They want something for themselves, whether it be healing, or material provision when they are in trouble, or some other kind of help, but they have no real interest in God or his people, only in themselves.

Secondly, we see people running away from those to whom they might have to give. Why should I have to spend time, money and effort providing for a relative who keeps pestering me for help? These things are mine and they have neither right nor entitlement to them. If I give way I am going to have to do it again and again. Better to stand firm and shut them out; better to keep at a safe distance.

When it says that the brothers of the poor *hate* him, this is to be understood figuratively rather than literally, as in Luke 14:26. However, in respect of their conduct toward him, there may be little obvious difference.

In short, we see people grasping at what they might have to keep. In the Tenth Commandment God says, 'You shall not covet...' There is an inbuilt tendency for people to want what they haven't got and not to want to part with what they have got. To the extent that these desires are selfish they are covetous. No wonder Jesus warned, 'Beware of covetousness' (Luke 12:15)!

This proverb shows how covetousness cuts both ways and affects rich and poor alike.

In writing to Timothy Paul addresses both aspects. Firstly, he says that godliness with contentment is great gain (1 Timothy 6:6), upon which he enlarges in the verses which follow. The Christian has no need to chase after favours from anybody. Secondly, addressing those who are rich, they are not to ring-fence their wealth for themselves but use it wisely for the benefit of others. To those who understand Hebrews 13:5 these things are not a problem!

19:8. Have a heart! Although this is generally translated, 'He who gets *wisdom*', the word for 'wisdom' is really 'heart'. It might be a problem for translators, but it is not so difficult to appreciate what the proverb is getting at. We use the word 'heart' in all sorts of ways. We might describe one person as 'heartless', another as 'warm-hearted', another as having a 'hearty' disposition, another as being 'broken-hearted', and so on. We might encourage someone to 'take heart'. All of these expressions relate to what is at the very *heart* of a person's being!

The meaning of the word in this proverb is to be understood from the word in the parallel clause, 'understanding'. That is why it has been translated 'wisdom', or 'sense'. It underlines that wisdom and understanding are not cold, clinical things but pulsating, vibrant qualities. 'A man's wisdom makes his face shine' (Ecclesiastes 8:2). The acquisition of wisdom and understanding makes us into real, living people!

Do you love your soul? Then you will see to it that *at heart* you are right with God. Your heavenly Father says to you, 'Give me your heart' (23:26). Look again at 2:1-2,10-11; 3:1-2; 4:4,23. This is undoubtedly something which costs us trouble and effort, for the proverb speaks of *getting* heart, a word which is often used for purchasing something in order to possess it. This is reinforced in the second clause which refers to *keeping* understanding. People go to great lengths to protect their valuable property. They lock up their possessions in safes, or they build great walls around their properties, or they hire security guards to ensure they are not broken into.

The word here suggests you are to build a hedge of thorns around your understanding. Surely your understanding cannot be stolen? Maybe not, but it can be compromised or impaired if the unwanted intruders of temptation are allowed through. The understanding spoken of here is not just head knowledge but embraces wisdom, discernment and discretion. The most serious way in which understanding can be compromised is through succumbing to temptation. For example, many Christians have succumbed to the temptation to be unequally yoked with unbelievers (2 Corinthians 6:14) not because they did not understand what it means but because they did not guard their understanding, and the reason they did not guard their understanding is that they had not taken the pains to 'get' the heart of the first clause. Even Solomon fell foul of temptation because he permitted his passions and the common practice of the day to override his reason and ignored the clear teaching of the Word of God by taking many wives – wives who led him into serious compromise (Deuteronomy 17:17; 1 Kings 11:1-4).

In every case such people have found anything but good and have lived to regret their folly. How important it is, therefore, that our hearts should be dominated by, and willingly submissive to, our gracious God, who always and at all times has the good of our souls in view, and who always and at all times wants the best for us.

'Where your treasure is, there will your heart be also' (Matthew 6:21). Is the Lord Jesus still precious to you? Is he still supreme, pre-eminent, in your heart?
[Related proverbs: 15:32; 16:20.]

19:9. More on false witness. A number of proverbs are duplicated, but none are separated by so small a space as this one. It would be easy to dismiss this as having been covered at v. 5. Perhaps the duplication was a copyist's error? If so, surely it would have been picked up quickly and eliminated? There is a far more convincing reason for this being here.

Why do people repeat something to you? One reason is that you might not have been listening properly the first time! Another is that they return to it because it needs to be reinforced or because there is more to be said on the subject. You will notice that in fact this verse is not *exactly* the same as v. 5, for the ending is different. Verse 5 says what will *not* happen to those who speak lies, while this verse says what *will* happen to them. The difference is small but significant. This addresses two things false witnesses fail to reckon with or about which they have unrealistic expectations.

As well as bearing false witness about others, people can and do bear false witness concerning themselves, and this is worth thinking about, too. When you speak about yourself, is it strictly honest? The image you project of yourself to others, is it strictly true? If not, you are bearing false witness, for there is deceit in your bearing and you are living a lie.

Both verse 5 and this one make no distinction between the penalty for false witness and that for lies. Where man may wish to make distinctions God makes none. People may lie in order to cover up what they have done and so seek to escape the consequences, little realising that, whether in the shorter or longer term, this simply will not happen. Verse 5 says there is no escape. Just as the lies of a small child are transparent to a parent, so the lies of the sophisticated adult are transparent to an all-seeing God. What they do in the hope of escaping what might otherwise happen is not only futile, it also increases the offence. Those who hope to lie their way out of a situation are informed they will not succeed. A false witness has entered a blind alley and as long as he follows that route he will not get out.

Sometimes people speak of 'facing the music' when 'the game is up'. However, playing deceit is no game, and at the end of it there is no music. It is easy to make light of punishment for those who make light of the offence. This proverb says what the punishment is. God is a God of truth, and the only appropriate punishment for those who lie is that they should perish, and so they shall. Those who consider such a sentence unjust merely demonstrate their ignorance of the seriousness of the offence and their disdain of the holiness of God in their belittling of his commands.

Many of the proverbs indicate that judicial and natural consequences often go hand in hand. That this is the case is seen, for example, in Romans 1:18, where we read of the wrath of God being revealed from heaven against all ungodliness. This is indicative of his judicial action, and no one escapes the judgement of God. However, further on in the chapter we read of God giving the ungodly over to their sinful passions, one of the results of which is that they bring upon themselves disastrous natural consequences (Romans 1:27). Those who speak lies, for whatever reason, are bound to find themselves at odds with their fellows. Who will believe them? Who will trust them? They alienate themselves and lay themselves open to all kinds of untoward consequences.

Thus those who live in defiance of the laws of God will not go unpunished. In fact they will suffer in two ways. They will suffer the natural consequences of conducting themselves contrary to the Maker's pattern, and then they will suffer the eternal consequences under the judicial punishment at the bar of divine justice – they will be punished, and they will perish.

[Related proverbs: 6:16,19; 12:19; 19:5; 21:28.]

19:10. Inappropriate situations. That things like this happen in life is all too evident. Many a foolish person has inherited vast wealth and lived in the lap of luxury. As for servants ruling over princes, Solomon himself testified to having seen this happen, which he attributed to fault on the part of rulers (Ecclesiastes 10:5-7). In fact, Jeroboam son of Nebat was a servant of Solomon and he went on to rule over ten of the tribes of Israel (1 Kings 11:26-31).

This proverb is dealing with inappropriateness, and is suggesting that something is out of order when these things happen or are allowed to happen.

Let us take them in order. Under David, and particularly under Solomon, the nation enjoyed such comfort, security and wealth that in general they truly lived in luxury (2 Chronicles 9), a luxury which spoke of the enjoyment of rich benefits promised by God to those who feared him, followed him and honoured him (Deuteronomy 28:1-14).

One of the characteristics of a fool is that he does not acknowledge God. A fool who lives in luxury is enjoying the gift while denying the giver. Not only does he not deserve his luxury, but he is really a parasite living off others. His contribution to the prosperity he enjoys is nil, as is his contribution to others' well-being. In this latter respect it is not fitting that he has it, in that he does not know how properly to use it but rather lives in self-indulgence.

Jesus told a parable about a rich fool (Luke 12:13-21). In that man's case he may have worked hard, and he may even have considered that he had earned what he had obtained, though in fact it was in the providence of God that his fields had yielded so well. He had thought to live long in luxury, but God called him a fool. He was a fool not to acknowledge God, he was a fool to think only of himself, and he was a fool to expect to live in self-indulgent ease.

If you enjoy a measure of luxury, is it fitting that you should do so? What reasons can you give?

The inappropriateness of servants ruling over princes is of a different order altogether, for the proverb says 'much less'. It should be understood that this proverb is not appealing to outmoded class distinctions. Joseph had been a slave, yet he was elevated to second-in-command in Egypt. Later, Daniel was a servant (Daniel 1:4-5) yet he was raised to prominence in Babylon. When they were thus promoted it is true that they ceased to be servants, but the point is that they were through their circumstances both prepared and equipped for their high office.

What is being addressed here is the situation where the wrong people are in authority. Servants were trained to serve, and if they had aspirations to take the reins they were exceeding their authority and abusing their privileges. On the other hand, princes should have been brought up to hold office, to take a responsible lead and to set an example to be followed. Neglect on their part through wanton dissipation would open the door to a popular uprising and a take-over by those not suitably equipped for the job. Where rulers will not serve, servants may rule, and all will suffer.

There are many reasons why the wrong people end up holding office. It is not uncommon for unworthy people to occupy important positions while those who have all the gifts and abilities are sidelined or downtrodden. This would include people qualified for particular jobs being usurped by others for unworthy reasons. For example, many Christians have been prevented from fulfilling useful roles in society or in the workplace because of prejudice, others being put in their place who are far less qualified or able. The consequence is that things go wrong and injustice tends to prevail.

[Related proverb: 30:21-22.]

19:11. Longsuffering. The NIV 'gives him patience' is rather tame. This proverb is about anger, and one of the marks of aroused anger is a quickened heartbeat and rapid, hard breathing accompanied by a vigorous verbal or physical response. Taking a deep breath can help forestall both the symptoms and the reaction! The angry retort is invariably unbalanced and 'over the top', and even if anger is appropriate it is probably better expressed in a different way and at a different time. So it is that a person of discretion, or of good sense and judgement, will keep calm under provocation in order to consider the situation rationally. More often than not, anger is unnecessary. There are occasions when self-restraint will lead to the other party apologising where a vitriolic reaction would lead only to a more intense altercation. Furthermore, discretion will often indicate that there is no good reason to become angry at all because there is, on reflection, at least some justification for the so-called offence!

The second clause is striking and memorable, and we need to take it to heart! It is the little man who 'demands his pound of flesh'. He is thinking only of himself, of his rights, of his position, of his pride. Someone has wronged him, and he is up in arms about it! He is quick to make sure everybody knows about it and how he has been treated.

If we are sufficiently aware of what we have received from the Lord in spite of all our provocation of him, we will count it a great privilege to be able to pass by and dismiss offences we suffer from others. Love keeps no record of personal offences (1 Corinthians 13:5) and is more concerned with the welfare of others than to wish to inflict retribution upon them.

Of course there will be transgressions which must not be overlooked. This proverb is not concerned with those. It is concerned with the transgressions which may be overlooked – and that, for us, is most of them! It is a fact that people take note of those who are 'big enough' to overlook an offence. It is a sign of strength, not weakness. It is an adornment of beauty of character, it is a mark of honour. Such people are not despised for their acquiescence, they are esteemed.

Ultimately, though, it is not they who are our role model, but the Lord himself. Paul makes this clear in Ephesians 4:31-32. God's amazing grace toward us in forgiving us, when we had done nothing but provoke him by our godless lives, is set before us as a pattern of what our attitude toward others should be when our spirit burns within us. Paul upbraids the church at Corinth for the complete failure of some in this matter (1 Corinthians 6:7). Peter reminds us of how the Lord Jesus responded when he suffered the severest unjust provocation (1 Peter 2:23-24). For whom did he do this, and with what result?

Note, too, the priority where responding to offences is concerned. God makes this quite clear in Exodus 34:6-7. Observe the triple emphasis, that he is merciful, gracious, longsuffering. See how willing he is to forgive. See how this accords with his unchanging nature right up to the present time (2 Peter 3:9,15).

'Quick ... slow ... slow' – let us get the order right (James 1:19)!

[Related proverbs: 14:17,29; 16:32.]

19:12. Fear or favour. This is anger of a different order from that of the previous proverb, and we move out of the sphere of personal offence to the administration of justice in the public realm.

There is nothing so apt to inflict terror as the roaring of a lion. By that time its victim's fate is sealed.

Solomon, who wrote this proverb, knew what he was talking about! As supreme ruler in Israel, and with God-given wisdom, there were occasions when he had to be wrathful. We can see examples of this in 1 Kings 2:13-46.

However, in each case the men concerned had sealed their own fate by failing to take seriously the king's authority.

In a dry land dew on the grass is a real blessing, gladdening the heart and speaking of life and refreshment. We have an example of the king's favour in the way Solomon's father David treated Mephibosheth (2 Samuel 9). We are told little of how Mephibosheth felt about this, but it is not difficult to imagine his relief, his elation, his gratitude for such treatment, considering his situation and background and natural prospects.

Why the proverb? It is the utmost foolhardiness to provoke a lion! We are wise not to provoke any in authority who have power to harm us. We may not be in a position to seek their favour, but one thing is certain: there will be no favour for those who those who despise their authority, only for those who respect it. That is much in line with what Paul writes in Romans 13:2-5.

Peter writes about submission to the authorities in 1 Peter 2:13-17, concluding tersely: 'Fear God. Honour the king.' Note the order. If these statements concerning the wrath and favour of an earthly king or authority are to be taken seriously, how much more those of the King of kings and Lord of lords? How foolish is mankind in his ignorance of God, in his defiance of God, in his disdain of God! The Lion of the tribe of Judah will yet roar, and heaven and earth will pass away as all are summoned to the last judgement.

For those, however, who have bowed the knee to King Jesus, their experience is of nothing but favour – sheer, undeserved favour, day in, day out, through time and on into eternity.

To what extent do you value the riches of the kindness, forbearance and patience of the holy, omnipotent King of the universe? See Romans 2:4.

[Related proverbs: 14:35; 16:14-15; 20:2.]

19:13. Domestic troubles. The father-son relationship crops up time and time again throughout the book of Proverbs (see, for example, 1:8; 4:1; 6:20; 10:1; 13:1; 15:5,20; 17:6,21,25; 23:22,24,25; 29:3). We are left in no doubt about the importance of this relationship, how it develops, how it is to be nurtured, and the blessings and troubles which can attend it.

A foolish son causes his father sorrow (17:21) and grief (17:25). Now we have an even stronger term: ruin. We are not to suppose this means financial ruin (though it may include that – many is the father who has continually had to bail out a wayward son from trouble). Here we are looking at the calamitous consequences psychologically, emotionally and socially. In these senses foolish sons have so often destroyed their fathers – fathers who have wanted to take pride in their sons but who have been shamed by them; fathers who have neglected their sons and suffered the consequent public opprobrium. Like it or not, a son's character reflects upon his father, and it does so because in the public eye he is his father's responsibility. 'Like father, like son' goes the saying.

A troublesome wife features elsewhere in the Proverbs (21:9,19; 25:24; 27:15). It has been said that a woman's chief weapon is her tongue. The concept of the nagging wife is well-known and has been the subject of much satire. This technique seems to penetrate the toughest hide to create intense irritation, so much so that the man will often give in to his wife's demands for the sake of a bit of peace and quiet! But it won't be happiness; it is very far removed from wedded bliss!

This proverb merely makes these two observations without comment and without judgement. However, they are not made for us to observe that 'life's like that', or to evoke sympathy for the father or husband. Assuming the proverb is here for a reason (which it is), for whose benefit is it given? Is it aimed at sons, fathers or wives? If you fit one of these categories, what does it say to you and your relationships? What is your appropriate response in the light of its observations?

Ask yourself these questions: What is so often the principal cause of a son turning out badly? What is so often the principal reason for a wife nagging her husband? In the light of the answers you give, what are the appropriate remedies to these ills?

This proverb highlights two things that should not exist but that so often do. It therefore indicates serious relational dysfunction somewhere. Should you find this proverb touching a sore spot in your own life, remember that although God often permits us to suffer the consequences of our failures, he nevertheless gives grace to the repentant to provide comfort and to give hope for the future.

[Related proverbs: 10:1; 17:21,25; 21:9,19; 25:24; 27:15.]

19:14. Domestic comfort. Many a man has inherited a family fortune and has been able to live in the lap of luxury. Others might look on and think he has all that he could possibly want. Not so.

The way the comparison is set up in this proverb is striking. It is not talking about a man having the security of a roof over his head and money in his pocket, but of his having abundant wealth. It is then indicating that there is something more important and overriding than this. Relationships trump riches. In particular, a good wife is of far more value than all else that a man may possess.

Furthermore, the comparison here is between what the world has to offer (in this case material inheritance) with what the Lord gives (in this case a prudent wife).

When God said, 'It is not good that man should be alone,' he created from him and for him 'woman', with the consequent observation that 'Therefore a man shall leave his father and mother and be joined to his wife' (Genesis 2:18-24). This was God's original design for mankind, 'woman' being created to be 'a helper comparable to him'. A prudent wife certainly fits this description and therefore functions as God intended.

If the man of the previous proverb was wealthy then his nagging wife would certainly have spoiled his enjoyment of all that he had. If the man of this proverb inherited nothing from his father, yet a prudent wife would have more than made up for what he lacked in other respects. What comes from the Lord is incomparably more precious than what comes from the world. How important therefore to have a right sense of values!

Any man looking for a marriage partner would do well to take this proverb seriously, looking to the Lord for a worthy woman and seeking romance of substance. Similarly, any woman hoping for a husband should seek to adorn herself with those qualities which will be attractive to a man of discernment and integrity, one who will be looking beyond the physical appearance to the real person, one who values what God regards as precious. See 1 Peter 3:3-4.

This proverb also speaks to those who are married, especially to husbands, each to honour the wife the Lord has given him. See 1 Peter 3:7. How often husbands take their wives for granted, treating them almost as part of the furniture! If you are a man who has a wife who is intelligent and understanding, circumspect and diligent, caring and considerate, and whatever else may be captured by this word 'prudent', then you have cause daily to be thanking God for her, and treating her as your most precious, God-given asset.

The God-given marriage relationship is the most fundamental one in society, and therefore it is the one which comes most under attack from Satan. It is assailed from all directions. What is needed are relationships which are *from* the Lord, and which then are established and built up *in* the Lord and will therefore testify *to* the Lord.

[Related proverbs: 12:4; 18:22; 31:10.]

19:15. Zzzzzzzz. Have you ever been suddenly awakened out of a deep sleep and experienced a sense of disorientation and unreality as you gradually come back from far, far away? People sometimes talk of having been drugged with sleep, though that is usually when they have been disturbed out of it, when they find their brain and limbs do not seem to want to work properly and for a while they feel utterly useless and unable to get back into things. However, the proverb speaks of laziness *inducing* a deep sleep.

With this in mind think of the effects of laziness. We are not intended to think of a literal deep sleep here but rather to take it as a metaphor. For all his usefulness, the lazy person might just as well be in a deep sleep. However, the proverb speaks of laziness *casting* a person into a deep sleep. It is like a drug which works by disabling any appropriate response to stimuli. Perhaps you know how it is when you are sitting in comfort reading a book after a heavy meal on a warm day, and your eyelids become heavy. You have no will to fight it and before you know what is happening you are dead to the world.

In a spiritual sense, this is what laziness does. It renders one comfortably indifferent to stimuli which are urging one to get up and get going. What is laziness? It isn't the same thing as physical lethargy, and it isn't associated with tiredness. It is an attitude of mind. It finds an excuse for not doing what one ought to be doing at any given time until eventually all consciousness of the fact is lost. It is essentially self-indulgent.

It could be a work-out at the gym when one ought to be visiting a sick person. It might not be perceived by others as laziness at all, but that is what it is. The visit to the sick person can wait until another time. It can always wait until another time, for which reason it never gets done. It is the deep sleep syndrome. Laziness puts what I want before what God wants; what pleases me before what pleases the Lord.

It may be that there are many Christians who are in a deep sleep. The point of this exercise, however, is for us to determine whether or not *we* are in a deep sleep. Are you hearing the voice of the Spirit of God as you read the Word of God, and are you responding to it?

This proverb adds a corollary. Laziness is a hindrance to productive work, the natural consequence of which is deprivation. In the natural sense, a lazy person is not working to provide for himself, and therefore sooner or later finds himself suffering hunger. The spiritual equivalent is the profound sense of dissatisfaction Christians can suffer when they consistently excuse themselves from doing what the Lord is asking of them, or when they habitually refrain from exercising any initiative in this area.

Back in Haggai's day, after some opposition the Israelites had then for many years left off the rebuilding of the temple with the excuse that the time had not yet come to do the work (Haggai 1:2). It was a lame excuse. They had been very busy in building and embellishing their own dwellings while neglecting the house of the Lord (v. 4). As a result they suffered hunger and deprivation (v. 11). Their spiritual laziness had cast them into a deep sleep, and there they would have remained had it not been for their 'hunger' and the awakening word from the Lord.

Here are some verses to ponder: Ephesians 5:14-17; Romans 13:11-14; 1 Thessalonians 5:6.

[Related proverbs: 6:9-11; 10:4; 20:4,13; 24:33-34.]

19:16. Guarding what you possess. One of the greatest abuses of the grace of God is to argue that, being saved by grace, it does not matter how you live. Christians who suggest the law has been superseded by the gospel, or by love, and therefore say that the preaching of the law is irrelevant, have completely missed the point and confused two totally different issues. The law never was a way to salvation except insofar as it led us to Christ. This proverb is not talking about salvation, but about keeping, or guarding, what one has and the consequences of negligence. Throughout the New Testament *obedience*, the bottom line of which is equivalent to keeping the law of God, is urged upon believers, not as a means to salvation but rather as an appropriate response to what they are and have in Christ, and as their responsibility in safeguarding all they have received in Christ.

The NIV translation 'instructions' is weak at this point, for the word is used almost exclusively of the commandments of God. Keeping the commandment is said to be equivalent to keeping the soul. If you owned a priceless treasure you might wish proudly to advertise the fact and have it on display for others to see and appreciate. You would also take great care to see that it was guarded against theft or defacement, with multiple layers of protection such as glass cases, security alarms, locks and the like. You certainly wouldn't go to bed at night leaving the doors unlocked and the windows open.

We who are Christians do possess a priceless treasure. We have Christ in us, the hope of glory (Colossians 1:27), and we wish to advertise this fact by sharing the gospel with others, presenting Christ to them. There is nothing Satan would like better than to destroy or deface the image of Christ in us. Ultimately we are kept by the power of God (1 Peter 1:5), but in the meantime he has given us the means by which to protect what he has entrusted to us.

Paul urged Timothy to safeguard his Christian profession by godly living (1 Timothy 6:11) and to guard the message entrusted to him by knowing it, valuing it and using it (1 Timothy 6:20; 2 Timothy 4:2).

Neglect of the law of God among Christians has almost always resulted in trouble and disgrace. The more the Lord Jesus means to us the more we will wish to safeguard the relationship and the more we will wish to live to please him by keeping his word.

They are asking for their souls to be plundered who give scant attention to the Word of God, and for whom holiness ceases to be a priority (see Hebrews 12:10-15; 1 Peter 1:14-16). Keeping the commandment is contrasted with being careless of 'his' ways (not God's ways, but those of the person who is the subject of this proverb), indicating that the way of man is intimately bound up with the command of God. If you want to know if you are being careful of your ways, the answer can be found by considering whether you are giving careful attention to the Word of God with a view to obedience to what it commands. Consider Psalm 119:9-16,33-40.

Do you value the commandments? Do you value your soul? Do you value your life? How does it show?

[Related proverbs: 13:13; 29:18.]

19:17. Underwritten and guaranteed. A loan by definition is something to be repaid. Lending to the poor might seem like putting money into a bag with holes. Some people think of the poor as a useless drain upon a society's resources, and when help is given it is often given grudgingly.

This proverb, though about a loan in relation to the poor, does not refer to lending to them. Nor is it about free hand-outs. Nor is it about giving to salve one's conscience. It is not about giving to fob someone off or to get rid of a pestiferous beggar! In fact it is not necessarily about monetary giving at all. It is about kindness and generosity and about intelligent help – which will invariably not only involve initiative but will cost us in one way or another.

The word has to do with showing grace and favour toward one who has no right to it. This is not an obligation or a duty, any more than God was under obligation to be gracious toward us! In the priestly blessing we read: 'The LORD make his face to shine upon you and be *gracious* to you' (Numbers 6:25, where the same word is used). Such kindness and mercy are in his nature, and we are to be imitators of God as dearly loved children (Ephesians 4:32; 5:1).

Had this proverb not said so, whoever would have thought even of the possibility of being able to lend to the Lord? It is an astonishing statement. When we give help to the poor – and this can be done in a great variety of ways – we do not think in terms of receiving anything back because in general it goes without saying that they will not be able to repay us.

Our emotions are sometimes in conflict, and not seldom do many of us have doubts at times about the extent to which we can or should help those in need. So this proverb is a remarkable encouragement to be generous at all times.

If I knew that whatever I lent to someone would unfailingly be repaid, I would surely never hesitate to give help. Now doesn't this proverb say just that? Ah, but there's a catch somewhere, isn't there? Very well. What catch? Where is it? Am I suggesting that God does not mean what he says? Perhaps that he will not repay in an acceptable form? Or that he will not repay in a timely fashion? Is there some small print somewhere with terms and conditions detrimental to the statement as it appears on the surface?

God has made a statement here. Why has he made it? Surely not that I might question it! Why then has he made it? Is it not so that I can be generous with what he has given me in order to help meet the needs of others without my having to give undue consideration to how much it is going to cost me?

See how King Jesus responds to those who compassionately served those in need (Matthew 25:31-40) and how he repays them for their deeds. Do we suppose that those 'blessed by my Father' (Matthew 25:34) were in any way the losers for what they did? To say that God recompensed them with interest is to grossly understate the case!

God's concern for the poor is expressed very clearly in his law, and we might wonder why this is so. Look, for example, at Exodus 22:25-27; Leviticus 25:35; Deuteronomy 15:7,11. Notice that God there reminded the people that he had brought them out of slavery in Egypt. The equivalent for us is our redemption by the blood of Christ, delivering us from hell and bringing us into his kingdom.

If we really understood just how poor and needy we were and just how much God has freely given us we might be more ready gladly to open our hearts and our hands toward others in need.

[Related proverbs: 14:21,31; 21:13; 22:9; 28:27; 31:20.]

19:18. Hebrews 12:5-11. A painful experience.

Note that this proverb assumes the need for chastening, and that it has an end in view. Also implicit is that there is a time limit on it. It says that to ignore or delay is tantamount to wanting to destroy him. It also places responsibility in the hands of the parent.

We must not be intimidated by a society which indiscriminately disapproves of smacking and what it terms 'corporal punishment'. One should rightly react against unreasoned physical punishment arising out of uncontrolled rage. This proverb, however, is dealing with something very different.

Though it is not necessarily referring to physical blows but is more general, yet these are undoubtedly included. Furthermore, though the punishment element may be included here, the intention is not just to punish for wrongdoing but rather to make clear that wrongdoing will ultimately be punished by God and that he intends something better for those who put their trust in him.

This proverb is indicating that discipline, or chastening, takes place within the family, and is administered by one who loves. It is a mark of love that chastening is administered from time to time. Hebrews 12:6 tells us that God disciplines his children because he loves them, and the context informs us that it is because he has in mind their greatest good, and because they need it in order to bring it about. These are the things parents should have in mind when disciplining their own children. Thus chastening should not be seen as a harsh, repressive, cruel action, but as a necessary corrective to what is wrong with a view to producing something better. Indeed, the word translated 'chastening' has to do with the positive elements of instruction and correction. Chastening should remind its recipient that he has done wrong because he is sinful, that it is a serious matter, that something needs to be done about this sinfulness.

This proverb speaks of hope. Hope for what? Hope for salvation rather than destruction, hope for life rather than death. True, it is not guaranteed that the measures will achieve the desired end, but to fail to administer them is very much more likely to lead to destruction. A medicine prescribed for a serious condition may not produce the intended result but we don't refuse to take it just because there is a possibility that it might not work. We take it in the hope that it will work, and in most cases it does. Thus a parent chastens a wayward son with the very real hope that the measure will bring benefit.

Parents are here warned against being soft on discipline. This is so important that the warning is given in the strongest possible terms. Of course the heart of the parent would not be set on the destruction of his child. But that is exactly what failure in the area of proper discipline amounts to. It is selfish and cowardly of a father to fail to take robust measures just because he himself will be hurt by it. It is also cruel. A soldier sent out to war without rigorous training is being sent to his doom. How much more will a child growing up in this world without proper discipline be unprepared for life and eternity?

[Related proverbs: 13:24; 23:13; 29:17.]

19:19. Will he never learn? Kidner says nicely: 'An ungovernable temper will repeatedly land its owner in fresh trouble.'

A man susceptible to outbursts of uncontrolled rage will have to pay for it – over and over again. However often he says it will not happen again, yet it does. It has a destructive quality to it by which he does harm to others and consequently also to himself. Called to account, it can prove costly to him in every way – financially, emotionally, socially.

If a friend is able to bail him out or steer him out of trouble on one occasion, it will only be until the 'next time', for the problem will not have been solved. However many times he is extricated from the furore he has created, there is an inevitability it will happen again, and likewise inevitably he will suffer punishment for it. The one who attempts to get him out of trouble is fighting a losing battle.

Unruly passions lurk in the heart of man and need to be brought under the lordship of Christ. Some people are more prone to outbursts of anger and seem to have a predisposition to it by nature. However, this is no excuse for such behaviour. They have no right to say, 'Well, that's just the way I am.' If it is the way they are then there is an underlying reason for it and something needs to be done about it, as with everything else that is wrong and sinful in their lives. Even though God alone has the grace and power to deal with such problems, it is our responsibility to bring them to him in repentance and faith.

This proverb is probably addressing both parties: the offender and the rescuer. The offender is a compulsive one and cannot help himself; the rescuer is frustrated by the inability to produce a long term solution.

Perhaps this proverb reminds us how intractable are some of life's problems. We can sometimes be slow to recognise this. We like to imagine that we can handle these situations and find solutions. In the end we find ourselves having to acknowledge that the remedies are quite beyond us. Yet we may apply to an almighty and a gracious God who has the power to deal with such things. The God who can bring the dead to life is the God who can extinguish the anger and frustration which result in outbursts of rage, replacing them with something better.

19:20. Laying up for the future. The words translated 'counsel' and 'instruction' cover two aspects of the same thing. Broadly speaking, one says, 'Do this,' the other, 'Don't do that.' There is the way we should take and, by implication, there is the way we should not take.

Though counsel and instruction come from the Word of God, in practice they are often received through a great variety of channels and are presented in a great variety of ways. Notice the proverb does not specify the source of the counsel and instruction, which suggests that we are to listen and receive it from whatever quarter it may come. We are not to rebut it if the manner in which it is given is less than gracious, because it is not the manner but the matter which is the important thing. We need to listen and take heed without prejudice, always testing what we receive by the touchstone of Scripture.

Thus if an unbeliever gives us some advice or reproves us in some matter we should not dismiss it because of the person from whom it has come. This person may be the channel through whom God has something to teach us, and God may deliberately be using this means as opposed to the relative comfort of having another Christian instruct us.

We are told of Josiah, great king though he was, that when Necho king of Egypt advised him not to interfere at Carchemish, he 'did not heed the words of Necho from the mouth of God' (2 Chronicles 35:22). It cost him his life and was a disaster for the nation. It very much looks as if he had his own interpretation of the political scene and entered the fray when he should have stayed at home. Would it have been any different had he received the same counsel from the prophet Jeremiah? We do not know, but this incident warns us of the danger of prejudice when we are instructed.

Counsel and instruction are part and parcel of the training of the man (or woman) of God (2 Timothy 3:16), where we see again the positive and negative aspects and the end in view. It is all there in Scripture, and here we are obliged to answer the question as to whether or not we take the Word of God sufficiently seriously that we *listen* to its counsel (which means giving intelligent consideration to it) and *receive* its instruction (which means actively facilitating its influence in our lives). This is not a once-and-for-all thing, like passing an examination, but an ongoing process of learning and living: it is Coursework with a capital 'C', and its effects are cumulative! It is a characteristic of wisdom that it builds upon itself.

We are being told here about how we should be in the future. How we look ahead into the future which is unknown determines how we conduct ourselves in the present which *is* known. There are those whose lives say, 'Eat, drink and be merry, for tomorrow we die,' for whom today is the only thing which matters. But the believer should always be looking ahead, and in the light of the promises of God heeding the commands of God.

Most people are in the habit of laying up for their future financially, so that they have enough to live on when they retire and are unable to continue to earn a living through old age or frailty. It makes good sense to make such provision. What is not so common is for people to lay up for themselves reserves which will help them cope with the often unexpected things that life will present to them in the future. That is why so many people as they grow older cannot cope adequately with life itself, evidenced by the attitudes they display in old age, often as a result of neglect of receiving the Word of God with meekness (James 1:21).

This proverb is not, however, about preparing for old age but about being prepared for the future, and that includes tomorrow. Counsel and instruction given today, received and heeded today, are our provision for the needs of tomorrow.

[Related proverbs: 12:15; 13:10; 15:31,32.]

19:21. Not my will, but yours, be done (Luke 22:42). Jesus did not say these words because he willed anything differently from his Father. Rather it was because what was required of him was so horrific that any alternative, had there been one, would have been acceptable. From the human perspective, Jesus passed this ultimate test because his will was fully in line with that of his Father.

This proverb is a corollary to the last. The word 'counsel' appears in both. (In the NIV and ESV it is translated 'advice' in v. 20 and 'purpose' in v. 21.) It compares a man's will with the Lord's counsel and indicates which will prevail. We may take this as both warning and comfort. How many of our plans are really submitted to the Lord? James warns us against negligence in this area (James 4:13-17). If we have our own idea of what we would like to do, while in the back of our minds is some anxiety that maybe the Lord would not approve, then we need to sort out our thinking in his presence. Or if we have our own idea of what we would like to do, without any thought to what might be the will of God for us, then we need to sort out our *attitude* in his presence. So often we pay lip service to the concept that the Lord's will is best, while a voice from somewhere deep within us insists on having our own way. That is why it is so important to strive to live openly before God, desiring only that he might have his own way with us, overruling our unruliness when it raises its ugly head. His will really is best, despite what any other voices shout or whisper.

This proverb is addressing plans that a man has in his heart. We are not dealing here with some ideas which he is formulating in his mind which he may or may not decide to implement in the end. It goes deeper than that. We say about certain things that they are close to our heart. We mean that they are very important, they matter more than other things, and there is an emotional attachment and involvement. You might say that you have it in your heart to do something. That means you fully intend doing it and you will not easily be dissuaded. This is all very well, provided what you have in your heart is consistent with the counsel of the Lord!

Furthermore, there are *many* plans in a man's heart. He is full of what he wishes to do. He is not planning an event, he is planning his life. To varying degrees, this is what we all do, and indeed much of the time we need to do.

We can take comfort from this proverb in two respects. The first arises out of what has just been observed, for if we are sufficiently aware of our sinfulness, which we might describe here as our wilfulness in a direction different from God's will, it is comforting to know that he has ways of dealing with a problem we find so difficult to deal with. Secondly, though, when we think of the plans of men great and small as they are exhibited in the world at large, with fears of where they might lead, we know that God is fully in control, and his counsel will be worked out to the end he has in view, contrary to the end men have in view. That end for the believer is a glorious one and will not and cannot be thwarted by men or devils. We are looking for new heavens and a new earth in which righteousness dwells, in accordance with the promise of God whose counsel stands (see 2 Peter 3:13).

Let us therefore be the more eager to receive the Lord's counsel as we hear, read and study his Word. Paul urges us not to be unwise, but to understand what the will of the Lord is (Ephesians 5:17) – obviously with a view to living accordingly! If we have a heart for God, then our many plans are the more likely to be in line with his will.

[Related proverbs: 16:1,3,9.]

19:22. Lovingkindness.

The precise meaning of the first clause is a little elusive, but perhaps this does not matter greatly, for whether it is what is desired *by* a man or what is desired *in* him or *from* him makes little difference in the end. The word translated 'kindness', or 'lovingkindness', or 'steadfast love' is one which is rich in meaning. It is the word used of God's covenant love toward his people, a love full of mercy and compassion, undeserved, unbreakable, unchangeable, boundless and faithful, unfailing in its satisfaction; a love in which to rest and find eternal comfort and bliss.

Whether or not people realise it, all stand in need of this lovingkindness, and without it they live in a state of deprivation. How many people long deep down for stable, lasting, precious relationships as a foundation for security and a sense of being valued! How many people feel cheated when what they hoped for breaks down and their relationships fall apart!

Clearly if the key to understanding this word 'kindness' is found first of all in God and his grace toward his people, then it follows that only those who know the Lord will really know what it means in experience. Those who do know the Lord and have experienced (and go on experiencing) his lovingkindness have every reason to rejoice and be glad in the bond of love which is deeper and more enduring than that found in any other relationship. It also follows, however, that only they will really be able to show a similar kindness toward others. It may be of a different *order* to that shown by God, but it will be of the same *nature*, because it is what is received from God.

If you are a Christian, first and foremost this lovingkindness is what *God desires* in you in your relationships with other people. Jesus expresses this, for example, in Luke 6:35. See also Ephesians 4:32. In both cases note that a telling reason is appended.

Secondly, though, this lovingkindness is what *others need* from you. What is the basis of the relationships you form with other people? Is your heart in them? Are you committed to them in this kind of way? Do people say of you, 'He's a kind man,' or 'She's a kind woman' because this is a prominent aspect of your character?

As with so many of the proverbs a contrast is given. At first sight this contrast may seem incongruous. So let us put it this way: What so often is the first thing to undermine a relationship of love and trust? Is it not deceit? Is it not lies, or, perhaps, being found to be living a lie? How damaging and undermining it is when it is discovered that someone is not what he has made himself out to be! Whatever else he may be or may have means nothing when this happens, for a breakdown at this point is fundamental. What a person stands most in need of, and what formed the basis of a deep trust, has been compromised and there is no remedy. Hence a poor man is better than a liar. A poor person who can be trusted, a poor person who is kind, a poor person who has the capacity for love and faithfulness, is infinitely to be preferred to anyone who cheats and reneges on relationships.

Consider the principles of Matthew 10:8, Colossians 2:6 and 1 Peter 4:10 in the light of this proverb and the grace we have received from the Lord.

19:23. Psalm 25:12-15. From the God of all comfort. In the Book of Proverbs the phrase 'the fear of the Lord' occurs fourteen times, and other direct references to fearing him in another four places. It is declared to be foundational to wisdom (for example 9:10), its evidences are described in terms of the kind of life which attends it (for example 3:7; 8:13), and some of the benefits following on from fearing him are stated (for example 10:27; 13:3; 14:26).

This particular verse refers to three benefits accruing to the fear of the Lord, two things which will result, and one which will not. As with many of the proverbs, it is expressed with a strict economy of words, and these come out rather like sermon headings. The subject is the fear of the Lord, and the three sub-headings arising out of a consideration of this subject are life, contentment and security.

The fear of the Lord. We must never trivialise the meaning of this statement. The person who fears the Lord has such a holy reverence for him that he is always in his thoughts, consciously or subconsciously, aware that he is under his eye, but also that he is under his care. To live to please him is an overriding priority for those who fear him. Careless or self-centred living are a denial of the fear of the Lord; careful and God-centred living are a mark of the fear of the Lord.

1. Life. This is eternal life, understood not only in terms of its duration but also of its quality. It is God-given and of such a nature that those who do not have it have no concept of what it is like. They may think fearing God is stifling, restrictive, deadly. How little do they know! Jesus said, 'I have come that they may have life, and that they may have it more abundantly' (John 10:10). The apostle John confirmed: 'He who has the Son has life; he who does not have the Son of God does not have life' (1 John 5:12).

2. Contentment. 'Now none but Christ can satisfy,' testifies the hymn writer. People are always striving for satisfaction. True contentment in life is very elusive and few find it. Even those who have the most congenial of circumstances and surroundings often have an inner restlessness because they cannot find contentment in themselves. Nor will they, for true contentment comes only from God, and it comes through the forgiveness of sins, through his cleansing power, and through the knowledge that he has accomplished full and free salvation for those who fear him. The person who fears the Lord has nothing remaining to strive for in this area. The apostle Paul could write: 'I have learned in whatever state I am, to be content' (Philippians 4:11). The Puritan Jeremiah Burroughs produced a classic work entitled 'The Rare Jewel of Christian Contentment'. A rare and precious jewel it is, and it is given by God to those who fear him.

3. Security. The original says that the person who fears the Lord will not be visited with evil. We may think this untrue if we know some of the troubles which have afflicted those who without doubt fear the Lord. 'The angel of the Lord encamps all around those who fear him, and delivers them' (Psalm 34:7). Part of the reason for Paul's contentment was that the Lord always delivered him. His grace was always sufficient. We cast our cares upon him, for he cares for us (1 Peter 5:7). 'He who has begun a good work in us will complete it until the day of Jesus Christ' (Philippians 1:6). With such a God who cares for us, what evil can really visit us? Paul understood that when he wrote Romans 8:31-39. Do we?

[Related proverbs: 10:27; 14:27; 22:4.]

19:24. Too much like hard work. Does the mental image bring a smile to your face? The scenario is amusingly absurd, as if lifting the hand from the dish to the mouth is simply too much effort for the lazy person. It is an observation on laziness at its ridiculous extreme. We will be aware that some people live a hand-to-mouth existence, but this is something else! Here is a man whose hands are *buried* in the bowl as if to consign them to permanent uselessness.

This picture is cast in this humorous form for our instruction. Of course it is ridiculous, but laziness is like that. Let it invite us to ponder what laziness is really like.

The resources are there, but they are not used. If we stay with the imagery, who provided the food? Not the lazy man, that is for sure. There are those who receive every benefit, encouragement and help from others, and yet who make nothing of them. Plentiful provision is there and all that is required is a little application, but even that seems too much like hard work for them. It is really a slight on those who do so much to try to help them when even then they will not lift a finger to help themselves. Furthermore, it is a sheer waste of what has been given for their benefit.

The consequence of laziness is self-deprivation. Spoon-feeding a lazy person is the ultimate indignity. If he cannot be bothered to make use of what he is given, then he must suffer – and suffer he will. In every sense of the word, laziness is impoverishing.

Laziness neglects the essentials of life. Food on the table was for most people at that time (and is for many today) a precious resource not to be treated lightly. Thus this proverb addresses the matter not in the workplace, nor in the social sphere, but at the domestic table where it is of the greatest importance.

A challenge to Christians. 'Oh, taste and see that the Lord is good' exclaimed David (Psalm 34:8). 'How sweet are your words to my taste!' (Psalm 119:103). Peter, in his second letter, sets before us a bowl full of the promises of God (2 Peter 1:3-4) which are there for our vital nourishment. If we are to experience them and benefit from them we must imbibe them, which requires some effort on our part, for he continues with an exhortation to diligence (5) and even more diligence (10). To neglect spiritual growth through laziness in spiritual things is even more disgraceful than the sluggard of this proverb.

The important thing is not to sit week by week under good ministry from the Word of God, or to have an abundance of good Christian literature and other resources in the home, but to feed on these things and grow thereby. God's children are to consider the dish set before them, and then to feed themselves from God's abundant provision that they may become strong and useful.

[Related proverbs: 15:9; 20:4; 26:15.]

19:25. Measures appropriate to the case. Here are two kinds of people who receive two kinds of treatment. The first is a scoffer. This is the kind of person who treats verbal reproof with derisory contempt. No amount of reasoning or arguing will make the least impression on him or achieve anything. The only treatment which he might just understand is that which hurts him physically, which serves also as a reminder of the pain his attitude inflicts on others.

Sadly, it is true that this kind of treatment is necessary in some cases and on some occasions, whatever may be argued to the contrary. Note particularly who are the chief beneficiaries of it. The 'simple' are people who are inclined to be foolish, who are easily led astray, who might well look up to the braggart who so easily dismisses words of reproof. When they see this same person receiving painful blows it makes them think twice. Not wanting to run the risk of receiving the same treatment they take care to conduct themselves in a more appropriate fashion. The severity of the manner in which the scoffer is treated is therefore a wholesome deterrent to those who might easily themselves become hardened, and paves the way for a more reasoned approach to them.

No one is above reproof on occasion. Blows given to a man of understanding or discernment would be entirely inappropriate and would produce in others quite the wrong effect, for even the simple have sense enough to recognise it as harsh and unjust. A verbal rebuke is all that is needed which, because he has discernment and thinks about what he is told, will be effective in making him the wiser for it.

This proverb, then, looks at two extremes and what is achieved in each case. Between these two extremes are a great variety of situations where reproof or correction are required. We are told that the Lord disciplines those he loves (Hebrews 12:6), for we are all in need of reproof, correction and training. This being the case, we all ought to be able to think of occasions when we have been particularly conscious of the Lord's reproof, how it has come to us and how we have received it and responded to it.

Also, perhaps, we need to give some thought to how God's treatment of us has affected others. If we have at times smarted under his rod, it may be that others have been warned concerning the seriousness of the sin into which we have fallen and are therefore strengthened against similar folly. We should thank him for that. If on other occasions his Word has come to us with humbling reproof, again we have cause to thank him for the benefit it has been to us.

[Related proverbs: 9:8; 21:11.]

19:26. What kind of a son is this? The Book of Proverbs recognises the family as the fundamental unit of society, and the well-being of society depends very much on the well-being of the families which comprise it.

One of the most disgusting examples of a son mistreating his father is seen in the way ungodly Absalom treated godly David. He was out for his blood (in which he did not succeed), but in the meantime mistreated him in a number of ways which the reader can pick out from the narrative in 2 Samuel 15 and 16. It is instructive to consider from the historical account the personal and other factors which resulted in Absalom acting in this way.

As for a son chasing away his mother, we have to consider that in return for the nurturing a mother has given to her son it would be expected of him to play his part in providing for her, especially if her husband has died or been incapacitated in any way. To chase a mother away, denying her requests, ignoring her needs, would be an act of the utmost callousness.

The commandment which says, 'Honour your father and your mother,' is just as valid today as it was when it was given (Exodus 20:12; Ephesians 6:2). To its recognition was appended a promise. To its abuse was appended a severe warning, for the law also addressed those striking their father or mother, or cursing their father or mother (Exodus 21:15,17; Leviticus 20:20).

It was a commandment which the Pharisees and scribes through their selfish greed and power hunger set aside, to whom Jesus quoted this commandment in both its positive and negative forms (Mark 7:9-13). Do not miss the fact that Jesus quoted this commandment as relevant and applicable when they were 'merely' creating a loophole for reneging on material support to parents. Jesus showed on this occasion and on others that the commandments of God are more comprehensive and far-reaching than might be supposed at a casual reading.

That said, we should be prompted to consider, if we have living parents, what our attitude is toward them. All have a responsibility of respect and care, but believers especially so through their knowledge of the Word of God. If shame and reproach are the result of the kind of treatment spoken of in this proverb, then the opposite will accrue to those who carefully and thoughtfully honour the commandment.

Perhaps we could note, too, that the command applies even in the case of fathers and mothers who have not fulfilled their own responsibilities well. No disclaimer is written into the commandment. The honouring of parents is not dependent upon their being deserving of it. Even a son who has been abused by his parents still has a responsibility toward them. The treatment he has received is not to be reciprocated, but rather the abiding principle of Romans 12:17-21 applies.

Upon whom do the shame and reproach fall? The proverb does not say. Or does it? Is not the answer that shame and reproach stick to all concerned – to the son himself, to the parents who have been shamefully treated; but also to the community in which this disgraceful conduct has been witnessed? Shock and outrage ought to be felt by such heartlessness, and action taken.

19:27. Never close the book. This is probably best understood in the sense that those who stop listening to instruction will go astray. This fatherly advice to a son addresses a danger some young men have of a misplaced self reliance, a false confidence in their own ability to get where they want.

A particular post is pointed out across the other side of a field to a person who is instructed to note it well. That person is then blindfolded and instructed to walk to it. They know how to walk in a straight line, and they know where the post is. So it is not such a difficult task. However, when it has been completed and the blindfold is removed, they are astonished at how far wide of the mark they are. Lacking the corrective guidance of their vision, they followed a natural bias of their feet, a bias of which they were quite unaware.

So it is in our course through life. We may know where we are going, it may have been clearly pointed out to us, we may have understood what we are to do, and we may have confidence that we will get there all right; but without the continual corrective guidance of the Word of God we are bound to go astray. There are simply too many subtle influences in life for us to navigate our way safely through unaided and we need instruction every step of the way.

Nor is it sufficient that we should have a comprehensive knowledge of the Word of God. The word 'instruction' here has a corrective aspect to it, and the important thing is the application of the Word of God in our lives at any given time. We need to have our spiritual eyes open to see where God is leading us. The psalmist who said 'Your word is a lamp to my feet and a light to my path' (Psalm 119:105) obviously had his eyes open! We need to have our spiritual ears open to hear the voice of the Spirit applying the Word of God as he says, 'This is the way, walk in it' (Isaiah 30:21, and see the context).

Although this proverb is addressed to 'my son', the advice it gives continues through life. Even if we know and are established in the truth, we still need reminders (2 Peter 1:12). Until we reach our destination we need continual recourse to our navigation aids, those correctives to deviation which enable us to keep safely on track. There is a particular danger for those who are viewed as being 'mature in the faith' to become set in their ways, to become complacent in their knowledge and understanding, and even to become resistant to correction or resentful of it. A mark of true humility is to recognise that we have never arrived until we have arrived! Until that time we will continue to need the Lord's instruction through whatever chosen instruments he is pleased to use.

The 'know-it-all' knows very little! This is the second law of thermodynamics working in the personal realm. A battery will run down unless it is recharged. If we are to maintain our spiritual vitality we need to be plugged into the power source of God's Word, by his Spirit absorbing its life-giving application to our own situation.

[Related proverbs: 10:17; 22:17.]

19:28. Wronging the right.

What comes out. On the word of a witness a great deal can hang. We have already encountered the false witness at 6:19; 12:17; 19:5,9. Here, however, it is a witness who is a rogue; he is wicked and worthless. He is corrupt. If he is like this, we might ask why he is a witness at all. He may have been called upon to witness a legal transaction for subsequent corroboration should the need arise. Or, in a scenario similar to our legal court, he may have been called as a witness, or come forward voluntarily, to testify. Either way, there is a sharp incongruity about his presence, for he is in a place where justice is supposed to be administered, and yet justice is of no concern to him. What end is he therefore serving there? Clearly not the end of justice, which he despises, and so it must be his own end. In his own thinking, it is 'What might be in it for me?' or 'How can I bring this person down?' rather than 'How can I serve the cause of truth?'

There is a sinister side to this, for many a witness serving his own end has displayed all the marks of plausibility and has given the appearance of acting in the interests of justice, whose testimony has done untold damage.

We need not confine our ideas of witness to the court room or its equivalent, for people act as witnesses in all kinds of ways in daily life. In general, when you give an account to someone of something you have seen or heard, you are really acting as a witness. Much of this is inconsequential. However, there are times when, perhaps unwittingly, what we say can be influential for good or for harm, and it is only if we are in the habit of serving the interests of truth and justice that our words on such occasions will be right. So often there is the temptation to distort, exaggerate, embellish or otherwise corrupt the simple truth. Although the context is a little different, the principle is the same, and concerning verbal testimony Jesus put it succinctly in Matthew 5:37.

The most important witness we can render is to the gospel, and it is imperative here that our witness be true and rightly motivated. Paul said something interesting about some people preaching Christ with a view to making things more difficult for him (Philippians 1:16). How sad it is when unworthy motives influence testimony to the gospel of the grace of God. Even more sad is it when unprincipled people distort the Word of God to suit their own purposes. Incalculable damage has been done to the cause of truth in this area.

What goes in. What is food and drink to 'the wicked'? Not truth, not justice, not good, not what honours God. None of these things, but iniquity. What do people gather round to hear or see? Juicy gossip, a salacious story, a bawdy spectacle ... When people are not at work and are relaxing in a social atmosphere, these things and the like are commonplace and enjoyed. For this kind of thing people seem to have 'a continual lust for more' as the NIV puts it (Ephesians 4:19). If this is the kind of stock people are taking in, is it surprising that this is what is retailed on to others?

By God's grace alone the Christian has been redeemed and delivered from such a worthless way of life (1 Peter 1:18). That does not mean, however, that we are immune from temptation in these areas. How important therefore that we do our utmost to keep clear of such things! See Ephesians 4:20-24.

[Related proverbs: 6:16,19; 25:18.]

19:29. Too late to make light of weighty matters.

The tragedy in the judgements following all the prophetic warnings of the Old Testament which the people rejected to their hurt was that they might have accepted them to their salvation and blessing.

The judgement spoken of here is the administration of wrath, and the preparation indicates it is already in existence and merely awaiting its implementation. There are many references to the Lord executing judgement (Exodus 12:12; Numbers 33:4; 2 Chronicles 24:4; Ezekiel 5:10; etc.). These are all displays of God's wrath against sin. In none of these instances is it a case of unpremeditated action. The sentence given and the punishment meted out are strictly according to God's principles and unerring in their administration.

The scoffer we have met at v. 25 and his attitude at v. 28. People like this can sometimes upset us, making light of the Word of God and treating it with arrogant contempt. Why should they trouble us, though, as if they had everything on their side? It is not as if they can get away with it.

There is a very clear irony in this proverb. Judgements are *prepared* for scoffers. However much people may make light of the warnings, what they disregard and mock will soon enough catch up with them. The word has already be uttered, and the judgement has already been prepared. Their attitude can make not the least difference to what will actually happen. There will come that dreadful day when men and women, both great and small, will call for the mountains to fall upon them (Luke 23:30; Revelation 6:16), such will be their fear of the wrath of the one who might have been their Saviour.

The administration of judgement is in God's hands. This is seen clearly in Esther 6 and 7. Haman had prepared (same word) a gallows on which to hang

Mordecai (6:4), only what had been prepared for his enemy was used for him (7:10). Thus was he elevated in the sight of the people!

Stripes, or beatings, for the backs of fools appears to be of a slightly different order. It does not have the same finality about it. The beatings are intended to curtail or correct the folly. Many of the characteristics of fools are listed in Titus 3:3, and Paul says that we ourselves were once like that. In the verses which follow he refers to God's kindness, love and mercy. Not a few Christians have testified to the way God brought them into great trouble in order to bring them to their senses and to call upon him for mercy. Every blow was administered with love, with compassion, and with deep concern.

If you feel you are being 'beaten', if you are asking God, 'Why is this happening to me?' is there a possibility that he is seeking to deal with some folly you are indulging – or perhaps even to keep you from some folly you might otherwise be indulging? Remember Hebrews 12:5-7 and take note and take heart.

[Related proverbs: 10:3; 18:6; 26:3.]

20:1. Another one won't do me any harm. The 'mocker' here is the same word used in 19:25,29 for 'scoffer' or 'scorner'. This is not the place to discuss the merits or otherwise of wine. Suffice it to say that the scriptures indicate it has its proper place and proper use. What is being considered here is its improper use as an intoxicant.

This verse covers alcoholic beverages in general. Wine and strong drink are frequently coupled in the Bible (for example Leviticus 10:9; Numbers 6:3; Deuteronomy 14:26; 29:6; Judges 13:4; 1 Samuel 1:15; Isaiah 5:11,22; Luke 1:15), and when they are it is their abuse which is often in view, and even when not there is an underlying acknowledgement that they have power to befuddle the senses and lead to irresponsible behaviour.

It is often overlooked that it is not the alcohol itself which generates such behaviour. The alcohol has an effect on the brain and the brain generates behaviour which is normally restrained and controlled but which nevertheless is potentially there. It reveals one of the terrifying aspects of the dominion of sin and the way sin has permeated the whole of our being. 'Do not get drunk with wine,' says Paul (Ephesians 5:18) 'for that is debauchery, but be filled with the Spirit, addressing one another in psalms and hymns and spiritual songs, singing and making melody to the Lord with all your heart.' The song of the drunkard under the influence of alcohol is to be replaced by the song of the saved under the influence of the Spirit of God. Our renewed minds are to be transformed and saturated with his life-giving influence.

Consider for a moment what it means to be 'led astray'. Sometimes we hear of young people who have been led astray by their peers and become entangled in some illegal activity. More often than not, the fault is largely their own because they have not had the will to resist but rather have been enticed by the thrill of the activity which has overridden their conscience or reason. The same is true of wine and strong drink, and those led astray by it have really already led themselves astray. They have permitted, or even invited, the drink to take control over them – or, more accurately, to loose them from their control of their passions.

Many people seem to think it is quite all right to go out and get drunk from time to time, that it is quite acceptable to 'go on a binge', drinking to excess with the intention of 'having a good time' or getting 'blind drunk' and 'stoned out of their senses'. They regard it as liberating. God's Word is quite clear that this is not so. It is liberating only to their sinful passions. People who do such things are being led astray. The very expression, 'led astray', is in itself instructive. Those 'under the influence' of alcohol are, by that same influence, led astray. It takes them in the wrong direction. What makes it the more dangerous, though, is that it takes them in the wrong direction under the promise of bringing benefit to them.

Two words are used of the effects of the abuse of alcoholic beverages. It is a 'mocker'. It makes a pretence of giving what is sought and delivering on expectation, but in reality it takes, and binds, and destroys. It is seductively sinister. It always promises; it never delivers. The other word, 'brawler' indicates what is so often the result of those who pursue strong drink with the specific intention of getting drunk. The result is loud, unruly behaviour, often involving violence, leaving them much the worse for wear.

Why is refuge in drink said to be 'not wise'? Several reasons can be put forward, ranging from the adverse influence on behaviour to adverse influence on health, and from failure to deliver any good to actually delivering positive harm. Beneath all this, though, the question persists, if this is not wise, then what is? Obviously it is not wise to be led astray.

But what are the circumstances which lead to drink, what are the underlying factors, and what is the wise course of action in such circumstances? At one end, drinking may be for escapism, seeking relief from trouble and sorrow; at the other end it may be hedonism, seeking satisfying experiences. But whatever it is, the result is failure. Only the Lord can give relief from trouble and sorrow, and only the Lord can truly satisfy. It is wise to seek the Lord in any and every circumstance; it is not wise to shut him out and seek relief or satisfaction from any other source.

[Related proverbs: 23:29-32.]

20:2. 2 Peter 3. Underestimating omnipotence.

20:2. 2 Peter 3. Underestimating omnipotence. The first clause is similar to that in 19:12. However, this proverb involves not a contrast but a caution. If you are out in the English countryside and enter a field occupied by a bull it is likely you will proceed warily and with a watchful eye! If you were out in the wilds of the African interior and spotted a lion you would certainly keep your distance and look anxiously for a place of safety! It might look placid enough, but you would not be deceived if you knew something about the creature. This proverb speaks, literally, of the terror inspired by a king being like the roaring of a lion: a sound which carries with it the sentence of death!

The king of Solomon's day was a man with almost unlimited power and authority. He might appear benign and generous to his subjects, and kind in his administration. Any who thought to take advantage of this, assuming these things to be marks of weakness, would be making a grave mistake.

Mention is made in Revelation 6:16 of the wrath of the Lamb. He may look like a lamb, but he is King of kings and Lord of lords; he may look weak, but he is almighty (Revelation 17:14). Before him every knee shall bow (Philippians 2:10). Countless people over the generations have underestimated him; they have provoked him to anger (a recurring theme throughout the Old Testament), they have abused his rule, they have usurped his authority, they have done anything and everything to belittle him. The fact is, they have not known who they have been dealing with. They have sinned against their own lives, and the Lion of the tribe of Judah (Revelation 5:5), the blessed and only Potentate (1 Timothy 6:15), has roared.

Jesus taught about seeking to settle matters with an adversary while there is still time (Luke 12:58). From what he had just been saying it is clear that this was a parable about getting matters settled properly with God while he gave opportunity to do so. Many seem to regard his gracious forbearance as a mark of weakness or impotence (little realising that in fact it is a very clear indicator of his supreme power), and so instead of humbling themselves before him and pleading for his mercy and pardon, they continue to provoke him to anger. Peter reminds his readers of this fact for their encouragement and patience in the midst of a society of rank ungodliness.

Do not forget God's power to save or his power to judge (2 Peter 3:8-9).

[Related proverbs: 14:35; 16:14,15; 19:12.]

20:3. Giving in or giving up? There is a touch of wry humour in the NKJV translation '...since any fool can start a quarrel'. It is a bit of a put-down for those who are inclined to be contentious!

It may be this proverb is about it being honourable to *avoid* strife and keep away from it whereas the fool is attracted to it and becomes embroiled in it. Some people seem to be spoiling for a fight and go out looking for trouble. It is very easy to get drawn into a situation of strife, for example by being urged for support by someone against another's words or actions; or, more directly, by being tempted to react under direct provocation.

However, if this proverb is about *disengaging* from a situation of strife rather than avoiding it in the first place, a somewhat more demanding scenario comes to mind.

If two people are at loggerheads and neither is prepared to give way the strife is perpetuated and invariably escalates. The stakes get higher and higher, the complications and ramifications increase, and the loss involved in climbing down becomes too great to contemplate. This kind of thing is not uncommon, whether it be at the domestic level or on the international scene.

Now suppose in such a situation of strife one abandons the argument and no longer insists on being heard or understood or making his point or getting his own way. So he has lost, and the other contestant has won. That is how it might seem in the eyes of others. How it rankles to give such an impression! How personal pride is offended, especially at the gloating of the other party! How a grieved sense of personal injustice revolts against the idea of letting things go! What a mark of shame!

Not so, says this proverb, it is actually a mark of honour; it is an indication of strength of character, not weakness. Pride sends all kinds of false signals to the brain, but humility of mind will see things in their true light.

So, perhaps you have given up on a contention, and do you have reason to believe that others are left with a wrong impression of you as a result? Do you worry that they may therefore think the less of you for so doing? The opinions of men count for very little. It is whom God honours that really counts.

It is the fool who will not let things go, who will not desist but obstinately persists in having his say and having his way. He is so wrapped up in himself that he is completely insensitive to how things affect other people.

There are some things worth striving for: peace, for example! Read Romans 12:18 and observe how it continues by addressing the potential for strife. Romans 14:19 indicates that energy should be expended in the pursuit of peace rather than insisting on our own way at the expense of others. Ephesians 4:3 speaks of the bond of peace, the previous verse putting it in the context of lowliness, gentleness, longsuffering and forbearance! Hebrews 12:14 says that peace should be *pursued*, as does 1 Peter 3:11. In every case it is clear this is something to be aimed at and worked for.

Matters like this make it abundantly clear just how much we need to live in the fear of the Lord and seek grace from him to live lives which are so different from what the natural man craves.

[Related proverbs: 17:14; 26:17.]

20:4. Out of one's comfort zone. The occasion for ploughing is the very reason the sluggard puts forward for not doing it! He doesn't find the conditions conducive to ploughing ... the ground is too hard ... the weather is unsuitable ... the prospects are not good. Whatever it is, he has a reason ready at hand for not doing what needs to be done at the time it needs to be done; and whatever the reason, it is anything but the real one, which is that it is too much like hard work for him.

Whether it suits him or not to be hard at work is really beside the point. The point is, what suits the harvest he would like to see?

Psalm 126 talks about sowing in tears. 'Putting in' is hard, back-breaking labour with little to show for it in the short term. But it also talks about reaping with joy. The lazy person is so incredibly short-sighted in his self-centredness that he cannot see beyond his comfort *now*.

There is a basic principle that if you don't put in, you won't get out. In the second clause the verb means, essentially, 'ask'. When we ask too much of someone it means we are making unreasonable and unrealistic demands on them. The meaning in this case is probably not that the man will be asking, or begging, from others (though he may), but rather that he is asking too much of his land. Of course there will be nothing there if he has not done the preparatory work. Yet there are people who seem to expect something when they have no reason to do so. They ask for a good job when they have not bothered to train properly; they ask for a comfortable life when they haven't cared for hard work; they seem to have an expectation that things will be provided for them even though they have made no contribution themselves; they seem to think that others owe them a living. Come harvest time, when others are enjoying the fruits of their labours, they will have nothing.

Avoidance of doing what ought to be done manifests itself in all sorts of areas. Are there things you are not doing? For what reasons? The Israelites were not rebuilding the temple. The original reason had been that they had forcibly been prevented from doing so, but that reason had given way to a more comfortable indifference (Haggai 1:2-4). An historic reason had degenerated into a convenient excuse.

Questions: Should Christians ask for a harvest of souls if they haven't done the preparatory work and sown the seed of God's Word?

When Paul told Timothy to preach the Word and to be prepared in season *and out of season*, he must have had a reason. What was it?

Let us not grow sluggish. God's Word contains many incentives to be getting on with preparatory work. Consider 2 Corinthians 9:6-11 and Galatians 6:7-10. [Related proverbs: 6:6-11; 13:4; 19:15; 21:25.]

20:5. Plumbing the depths. The picture here is that of a well. The water is a long way down, hidden from view in the darkness. This is illustrative of what goes on in people's hearts.

A man who keeps his own counsel is one who keeps his thoughts to himself. He may have his own ideas about things, and his own plans and intentions, but they are his business and nobody else's. What goes on in people's hearts is often far from obvious, and if we say someone is 'deep' we usually mean that what eventually comes to the surface is unexpected and surprising.

The picture continues as we see someone with a long rope letting down a bucket into the depths and then carefully drawing up its contents. This illustration is not about getting advice from one reticent about giving it but finding out what is going on in the hidden recesses of someone's mind. What, though, is the point?

What comes up may be sweet and clear or it may be bitter and murky. If the former, we may benefit from it; if the latter, we may be in a position to do something about it. Anyone in a pastoral position needs to have this quality of understanding in order to be able to minister to others. It requires the ability to establish a rapport with people, to gain their respect, to win their confidence; it requires a patient, persevering interest in both them and their welfare. In some cases the rope on the bucket may need to be many years long.

If we are to benefit from others or to minister to others we need to be people of understanding. We need spiritual discernment. We need to appreciate what the heart of man is by nature and the things which influence it and how they do so. We need to understand the workings of the grace of God in the heart and recognise its manifestations.

We are told that the Word of God is a discerner of the thoughts and intents of the heart (Hebrews 4:12), and so we need to be appropriately equipped with his Word, first of all by his Word having worked deeply and effectually in us.

How ably did Jesus draw out the people he encountered! One has only to think of the woman at the well (John 4), or the Syro-Phoenician woman (Matthew 15:21-28), or Nathanael (John 1:47-48). How well he who was sinless understood human nature! How thoroughly did he penetrate the hidden depths of people's minds and have some teaching appropriate to them or others as a result (as for example in the case of the rich young ruler, Mark 10:17-31)! The things they said, the things they did, revealed to him the people they were. To what end? In order that he might bring the message of the gospel to them, to give them life and hope.

Are there people you feel a need to get to know better? Are you giving thought as to how to go about it?

[Related proverb: 18:4.]

20:6. Do not believe everything you believe.

What people say and what they are, are rarely the same thing. Furthermore, what people believe themselves to be, and what they are, are rarely the same thing. Witness Peter with his protestations of loyalty to Jesus (Matthew 26:35). The heart is deceitful above all things (Jeremiah 17:9).

This proverb is not simply informing us, it is positively emphasising that appearance and reality may be far removed from one another. There are two aspects to this.

The first is the way people wish to present themselves. In just the same way as people who 'blow their own trumpet' are not usually all they make themselves out to be, so it is here. Most people will take pains to give others the impression that they are good people, and caring, and virtuous, can be relied on, and so on. There may be more than a hint here that people often do this by comparing themselves favourably with others. Again witness Peter saying, '*Even if all* are made to stumble because of you, *I* will never be made to stumble' (Matthew 26:33). 'Unlike other people, I can assure you that I will not fail you....'

The second aspect is that people so often believe what they say about themselves. Peter certainly did. You couldn't accuse him of being hypocritical even if he was rather cocksure of himself. So, in addition to the impression people wish to give of themselves, the problem is compounded by the lack of true knowledge they have of their own hearts.

In his letter Peter talks about *faith* being proved genuine when it is tried (1 Peter 1:7), and here it is much the same with faithfulness. A person who not only means what he says but who will be true to his word is hard to find. More often than not, when such a person is found, he or she will be someone who has been put to the test in experience and who, furthermore, will not be forward about it. When Aaron and Miriam thought to elevate themselves by finding fault with Moses, we are told first about Moses' humility, and then about his faithfulness (Numbers 12:1-8; Hebrews 3:5), things which he had learned through many trials over many years in which God had changed him from the brash young self-confident prince expecting to do things his way (Exodus 2:11-15) to one who walked closely with God in complete dependence upon him.

It is interesting how the apostles write of their fellow workers in the gospel: 'Timothy ... faithful' (1 Corinthians 4:17), 'Tychicus ... faithful' (Ephesians 6:21; Colossians 4:7), 'Epaphras ... faithful' (Colossians 1:7), 'Onesimus ... faithful' (Colossians 4:9), 'Silvanus ... faithful' (1 Peter 5:12). These were all people who through trial had proved their worth as they had laboured with the apostles.

Faithfulness should be an essential characteristics of believers who are servants of Christ and have a sacred trust (1 Corinthians 4:1-2). This applies not only to the way we hold to the truth of the gospel but also to the way we conduct our relationships within the body of Christ.

[Related proverbs: 3:3; 25:14.]

20:7. Laying up for your children. What is the connection between the two clauses? Simply this, that the way of life of a father has a profound influence upon his children. This is a truth so obvious when one thinks about it and takes the trouble to observe it, and yet it is so little considered in real life. The negative side of this is only too evident in the many dysfunctional and broken families which undermine the stability of society. However, this proverb focuses upon the positive.

What is the best foundation a father can lay up for his children? A good education? Wealth and prosperity? Security? How many who consider themselves responsible fathers put things like these high on their agenda. They want their children to have the best opportunity in life, and to get the most out of life. They may want their children to have what they themselves never had, and may work long and hard to see they get such things.

While these things may be commendable, they only take a poor second place. The second clause of this proverb is something of an exclamation: 'How blessed they are!' This proverb should come like a breath of fresh air to believers being suffocated by the stagnant air of materialism or being pushed under by the forces of self-centred competitiveness. How many fathers suffer from a sense of inferiority because they cannot give their children what other parents give?

Many a child from a poor home has said, later in life, 'I did not have the things other children of my age had, but I had a godly father whose life and example meant more to me than anything else.'

If you are a young person from a Christian home reading this, do not let the false standards of this world deceive you into thinking you are in some way being deprived because your parents put godliness and integrity before material considerations. Get your thinking straight and focus on the things which really matter. The glitter of this world is fools' gold. The real treasure is being laid up in the home where Christ is honoured.

Likewise, fathers, never let the temptation to 'get on in the world' or 'provide better for your children' induce you to sacrifice the essential of spiritual integrity or to compromise on your responsibility to bring up your children in the fear and admonition of the Lord (Ephesians 6:4). A home which experiences a father's presence, love and instruction is of far more worth than one in which he is rarely seen, where his influence is barely felt, and where his example and leadership are singularly absent.

If you would be a blessing to your children and leave a blessing for them, focus on your relationship with God and your responsibilities before God.

[Related proverbs: 14:26; 31:28.]

20:8. Psalm 139. The God who sees. The throne of a kingdom is a symbol of supreme authority. Solomon's building projects included the Hall of Judgement (1 Kings 7:7) which housed the throne from which he judged. There, when as king he sat upon it, he would be acting as judge before a gathered assembly. Those present would not be in the least doubt about the extent of his power.

The function of a judge is to discriminate in favour of what is right and to punish the wrongdoer. It involves what could be considered as a kind of sifting process, and that is exactly what is described here for, literally, he *winnows* all evil. Winnowing is a process by which the chaff is separated from the grain after it has been threshed (see also v. 26). The husks are blown away and the grain remains.

Now notice how he does it: with his eyes. A king would not tolerate anything which was an affront to his rule and his senses would be finely tuned to the least thing that smelled of subversion. For a king who was ruling righteously, this meant anything evil. The heart of anyone riveted with those eyes would miss a beat if he had anything to hide. Have you ever had the experience of someone looking at you in that disconcerting, penetrating fashion, leaving you wondering what they know about something you would prefer to remain hidden? Now consider Psalm 11:4.

It was the king's business to know what was going on in his kingdom and to exercise the faculties of discernment and discrimination, seeing things which might not be apparent to others. Such was his knowledge, and such the intelligence in those eyes, that he really needed to say nothing, and those who were evil were (to continue the metaphor) blown away.

There is one who is ruler over the kings of the earth, whose eyes are described as being like a flame of fire (Revelation 1:5,14). When he draws the attention of the church at Thyatira to this fact, it is to remind them that he is the one who searches the minds and hearts and judges accordingly (Revelation 2:18,23).

The one who is King of kings and Lord of lords will one day sit on his throne of judgement. Because he sees, and knows, and understands, nothing being forgotten or overlooked, nothing being hidden or obscured from his penetrating vision, and because he judges righteously, there will be a great separating out of the good from the evil. John the Baptist said of Jesus that his winnowing fan is in his hand (note the present tense) and that he will thoroughly clean his threshing floor, gathering the wheat into his barn, but burning the chaff with unquenchable fire (Luke 3:17). To all intents and purposes the process is going on now. When he sits on the throne of his glory for judgement there will be no need for close questioning or cross examination, for all will be transparent both to him and to those standing before him on that great day. No words will need to be spoken as he separates one from another, any more than does a shepherd dividing his sheep from the goats, until he utters his verdict: either wonderful, 'Come, you blessed...', or terrible, 'Depart, you cursed...' (Matthew 25:31-46).

[Related proverbs: 16:10; 20:26.]

20:9. A question to leave us speechless. This is clearly a rhetorical question. No answer is required. However, asking it throws up a fundamental problem afflicting all humanity. While there is an answer to this question – though the answer is not required – man can find no answer within himself to the problem it raises – though an answer *is* required.

The proverb addresses each one of us personally, and if it does not expect an answer it certainly expects a response: 'I have a problem!'

Many people have overcome all kinds of problems and disabilities through sheer will power or determination or persistence. But here is one that no one has been able to overcome. Either a man has no will for a clean heart, or if he does, he finds he has no power to achieve it.

At v. 6 we observed that people wish to be seen in a good light. Yet lurking beneath the surface of how they would like to appear is the sinister truth that they are not what they seem. Man has an intractable problem. He cannot clean up his own mess. The heart is deceitful above all things and desperately wicked, says Jeremiah (17:9).

When the scribes and Pharisees brought to Jesus a woman caught in adultery and quoted the law to him, he responded by saying that the one without sin should cast the first stone. Each man's conscience convicted him that as a sinner he had no right to do this. Jesus, however, could later ask the question of them, 'Which of you convicts me of sin?' (John 8:7,46).

Cleansing and purity – these are the two aspects of this proverb. They point in turn to man's need for two things: forgiveness and regeneration.

David prayed, 'Create in me a clean heart, O God' (Psalm 51:10). That he couldn't do this himself he knew only too well. He also said, 'Wash me, and I shall be whiter than snow' (Psalm 51:7), recognising that God could make him both clean and pure. God himself reasons through Isaiah (1:18), 'Though your sins are like scarlet, they shall be as white as snow,' and he informs Israel through Ezekiel (36:25), 'I will cleanse you from all your filthiness ... I will give you a new heart and put a new spirit within you.' John declared, 'If we confess our sins, he is faithful and just to forgive us our sins and to cleanse us from all unrighteousness' (1 John 1:9). Later (Revelation 1:5) he ascribed praise and glory to Jesus, 'who loved us and washed us from our sins in his own blood'.

For every believer this is the never-failing cause of wonder, to have a cleansed heart, to be reckoned pure in God's sight, and to enjoy a relationship with the living God based not upon self-achievement which would have been totally impossible, but upon Christ's accomplishment upon the cross.

So this proverb is not given to mock man's helplessness in his failure, nor to say, 'Do better next time' and set him upon a course of self-improvement. Those who have taken that road have become either desperate or deluded. Its very asking of the question is a reminder of people's fundamental problem: their sin and their inability to do anything about it, try though they might. It is a profoundly humbling truth, but it is one that is intended to direct us back to God, and to Jesus his Son, who dealt with this very issue when he died for sinners upon the cross at Calvary.

20:10. Dual standards. Whereas 11:1 is addressing head on sharp practice with the intention to defraud, here there may be some subtlety, reflected in the repetition of the word for weights and the word for measures. It doesn't actually say 'different' weights, but, literally, 'weights and weights'. If I say, 'There are ways and ways of dealing with this' I am not simply indicating that there are different ways of dealing with it, I am saying I have my own special preferred way of dealing with it! Or if I say to someone, 'There are friends and there are friends,' it may be to reflect on the way they have been let down or given short measure by someone.

Though drawn from the area of trade, and though applicable in that area, the proverb is far more wide ranging. Jesus had something to say about this (Matthew 7:1-5), again using the measure as an illustration. At first sight in v. 2 he appears to be indicating that if we short-measure others we are likely to receive short measure ourselves from them, and if we are generous in our dealings with others, they are likely to be generous toward us. This may be true. From the overall picture, however, it is clear he is implying that all our conduct is open before God who knows and examines our hearts. Can we expect him to be generous toward us if we are mean-spirited toward others?

Actually, God is unfailingly generous in his dealings with us, notwithstanding our short-changing others, for that is his nature (see Luke 6:35-36). Even so, when it comes to the final reckoning, we can expect the punishment to fit the crime, a principle built into his law. What he urges upon us is the generosity of spirit described in Luke 6:35.

It is very easy to hold dual standards, such as expecting things of others that we would not expect of ourselves, or criticising others for faults we know we ourselves have. How often public figures are shamed by the rank and file who are just as guilty of the same kind of thing. Admittedly, there is some special culpability in those who are in the public eye, but nevertheless it reflects a duality of standard, a duality of measurement, which says, 'It doesn't matter if I do these things, but it does matter if someone else does them.'

The principle of Luke 6:35 raises another issue which Jesus has already touched upon in the previous verses. There must be a consistency in our dealings with all people, irrespective of who they are. Justice is required in all our relationships and the standard is that which is set by God himself and exemplified by Jesus. Thus in our dealings with two people in the same situation we are to be equally fair to each, even if one is our friend and the other our enemy.

This proverb is couched in terms of weights and measures. Not just one or the other, but both. It is not limited but comprehensive. We are not entitled to be generous with our weights but mean with our measures. It is insufficient to exemplify the principle of justice in one area of our life if we cheat in others. For example, you may be just, even generous, in your use of money, but are you equally just in the use of your tongue?

Perhaps this proverb ought to make us feel uncomfortable, for meditating upon it is likely to expose many shortcomings in our attitudes and conduct. Let us seek comfort from the God of all grace, and strength from him to live consistent lives worthy of his name.

[Related proverbs: 11:1; 16:11; 20:23.]

20:11. 'By their fruits you will know them.' 'Even a child...' – why 'even'? Is it suggesting this is something people might be inclined to overlook? What is true of adults is equally true of children. The term 'child' refers in general to those who have not yet reached maturity and perhaps the sense of responsibility and accountability which go with it. Many people like to think of children as 'innocent'. This proverb, as well as others (22:6,15; 23:13; 29:15) give the lie to this notion.

Discernment and recognition are being spoken of here: you can recognise what a child is like by what he or she does. Even though it may be displayed in a childish way, there is still a rationality about behaviour, so that behaviour is a true reflection of the child's nature. If adults, with all their layers of sophistication, cannot but reveal what they are by what they do, exactly the same is true of children in their simplicity. Sometimes we may smile at children's transparency because they have not yet learnt the art of sewing fig-leaves to cover their nakedness as adults have done. But it does not make them any different. Their knowledge may be different, and so their accountability may in some respects be different (see Luke 12:47-48), but they are not essentially any different from anyone else. 'By their fruit you shall know them' (Matthew 7:20) applies just as much to children as it does to adults.

This proverb is not addressed primarily to children, but to adults, and by implication it tells us two things. Firstly, it shows us that God is interested in children, in their deeds and what is in their hearts. Jesus himself showed an interest in children when others were inclined to dismiss them (Matthew 18:2-4; 19:13-14). No child may be considered too young to be within the reach of the grace of God. Secondly, it implies that adults have a responsibility toward children which they must not overlook. From their birth children need to be directed toward the fear of God and pointed by word and example to the Saviour. This was enshrined in the Old Testament law (Deuteronomy 4:9-10) and confirmed in the New Testament letters (Ephesians 6:1-2; 1 Timothy 3:4).

Even a child is known by his deeds ... even a child needs to know a Saviour's forgiveness and love. The assertion that 'all children go to heaven' is nowhere found in Scripture, and we must not allow sentimentality to cloud the issue and make us slack about our God-given responsibility. Their spiritual welfare is entrusted to their parents from their conception, through their birth, and on through their developing years, that they might give their hearts to the Lord Jesus and be clothed in his righteousness. Observe that this proverb admits of the possibility that a child may do what is pure and right. There is none too young to receive the grace of God with his life-transforming power.

We are encouraged to a realistic recognition of the nature and need of children, and from that to their nurture in the training and instruction of the Lord.

[Related proverb: 22:6.]

20:12. Psalm 94. Sense with our senses. The ears and the eyes
are the two principal organs through which most of us take in information,
unless our hearing or sight is impaired. This proverb looks at the case where,
physiologically at least, they are functioning as they ought.

There are at least two important points to be drawn from this seemingly
obvious statement. But by way of preamble, note it does not say these organs
evolved from any more primitive form by any accidental process over a long
period of time. They were made by fiat of almighty God in his act of special
creation of man made in his own image (Genesis 1:26).

The first important point was expressed by the Lord to Moses who was
looking for an excuse to get out of doing what the Lord was wanting him to
do (Exodus 4:11). It is also expressed by the psalmist in Psalm 94:9. If God
created our hearing ears and our seeing eyes it follows that he himself both
hears and sees. So many people conduct themselves and their affairs as if this
were not so (Psalm 94:7). They are charged with mindless folly (Psalm 94:8).
Psalm 34:15 gives the believer a wonderful encouragement about the Lord
who sees and hears.

The second important point is that if God created our ears and eyes (and
he did), then in a very real sense they belong to him and we are accountable
to him for the way we use them. These organs were created for a purpose.
This is implicit in the proverb, for it does not say, 'The ear and the eye', but
'The *hearing* ear and the *seeing* eye.' Recognition and response are involved.
For example, the Israelites so often *heard* the words of the prophets, but they
did not *hearken* to them, for their words fell on deaf ears. Similarly, after the
Exodus the Israelites had *seen* God's work (Psalm 95:9), but they did not see
it with *enlightened* eyes.

This means we are to hear and see in a responsible fashion. In some areas
we have control over what we hear or what we see. So we may avoid certain
conversations or we might purposefully attend certain talks, and so on.
Likewise, we may avoid watching certain things on television or reading and
viewing certain things on the internet. In other areas, however, we have no
direct control over what we hear or what we see, and that presents a problem.

When we are in public going about our ordinary business our senses are continuously bombarded with the sounds and sights all around us, many of which are harmless enough ... but not all. In this situation we have to train our ears and eyes, and have to learn with God's help to filter out what is undesirable.

What amazing and precious organs our ears and eyes are! Maybe we need to develop a more conscious recognition of the fact that God has given us our hearing and our sight, and seek to express our thankfulness to him by using them in a manner glorifying to him. Even a day spent in deliberate acknowledgement of this gift of creation's design might bring real challenges to us and heighten our awareness of the riches of God's grace toward us.

At 17:24 it is stated that the eyes of a fool are on the ends of the earth. They are everywhere except where they ought to be. Where is your spiritual focus? We are to have our spiritual eyes upon the Lord and his word and not on vain things (Psalms 119:18,37; 123:1-2). We have spiritual ears, and we are to use them to hear the word of the Lord (Mark 4:23; Revelation 2:7 etc.). So both our physical ears and eyes and their spiritual counterparts, precious gifts from the Lord, are to be trained and used in his honour. Let us glorify God with true thankfulness if he has given us ears to hear and eyes to see.

May the eyes of our understanding be enlightened (Ephesians 1:18).

20:13. Drowsiness. This, like so many of the proverbs, has both physical and spiritual aspects. We may rightly enjoy sleep (Psalms 4:8; 127:2) but we must distinguish this from the love of sleep which is a mark of indolence (6:9-10; 19:15).

This proverb is a warning. 'Coming to poverty' is an interesting expression. Picture a night watchman who is supposed to be on duty protecting a warehouse. But night by night, instead of doing what he is supposed to be doing, he has made his post comfortably warm and cosy and spends his time sleeping there. As this becomes known, little by little the warehouse is surreptitiously raided and its contents removed. Then one day he wakes up to the discovery that much of its valuable content has disappeared. Without his being aware of it, it has gone. Others have taken possession of it.

There is a spiritual side to this. A very real danger exists for mature Christians to become spiritually lazy, to leave off the study of God's Word, to become increasingly slack about prayer. Outwardly everything may look all right for a long time, but all the time their spirit is being silently and systematically plundered, and in time their spiritual poverty (as opposed to their being poor in spirit, Matthew 5:3) runs the risk of being dramatically exposed.

'Open your eyes and you will see what is going on right under your very nose.' That is what might be said to someone who is wilfully dismissive of a matter of importance. It is not an uncommon problem. People often close their eyes to what they do not wish to see. They do not want to acknowledge there are things in their lives they need to face up to and do something about. They are not taking the trouble to focus attention upon what their real situation is, and in the long term they are impoverished as a result. It is a shirking of responsibility and it has devastating results. This operates in the spiritual sphere just as much as in the physical.

If we are to survive – and more than survive – we need to be aware and alert and active. We need our wits about us spiritually. Again, the expression here is interesting. The clause in the original talks about more than merely being satisfied with bread, but of having food and to spare. The unspoken implication is of having not just sufficient for ourselves, but of having something extra with which to benefit others.

God's Word is consistent from beginning to end that we do not live for ourselves (Romans 14:7), and our eyes need to be open to this fact. The supreme expression of this truth is found in 1 John 3:16-17.

Consider 1 Peter 5:8 and Revelation 3:2-3 and Matthew 24:43.

[Related proverbs: 19:15; 24:33-34.]

20:14. Driving a hard bargain. 'Look what I picked up in the car boot sale today! I told the fellow I was interested but that he was asking way too much for it. I even managed to knock him down a bit, still complaining the price was exorbitant. In the end I handed over my money leaving him with the impression I had done him a big favour. I could hardly keep a straight face! Wow, what a bargain! The man hadn't a clue what he was parting with!'

Is this a case of keen but legitimate trading? Is it a case of deception with the intention to defraud? Is the buyer acting dishonestly, or is it a case of 'All's fair in love and war'? From this rather extreme example it can be seen that this proverb may raise some interesting ethical questions. Does a buyer have any responsibility to divulge to a seller that the 'agreed price' might be very much to the seller's disadvantage?

We have looked at some proverbs which address those who sell, warning them against false weights and measures. This one is about those who buy. Is the buyer defrauding the seller if he deliberately keeps the latter in the dark about the value of what is being sold? Consider the potential consequences when the full facts come out into the open. What should be the Christian's attitude to this?

Of course, it may be that here we are simply looking at normal trading in the marketplace where haggling was the custom and where in the end both seller and buyer were satisfied, even though to each other's face they would not be prepared to say so. People are out to get as much for themselves as possible. Is haggling a bad practice in which each party is out to get as much for himself at the expense of the other? Businesses which want to maximise their profits will ask as much for their goods and services as possible, though they would be prepared to accept less. Does this legitimise the buyer trying to knock down the price? In both selling and buying there is a distinct possibility that covetousness may play a part.

Even if we do not think that this proverb does actually raise any ethical questions, it nevertheless tellingly reflects on human nature. We have all seen children gloating over the loser when they have got their own way, in their own eyes 'the better end of a bargain'! Is boasting over an advantageous purchase any different?

Does this proverb not highlight a certain deceitfulness on the part of the buyer? What he says to the seller is what he wants the seller to think rather than what is strictly true.

If ever you are in a position to gain at someone else's expense, in whatever it may be, and however it may be, what should govern your thinking and action?

20:15. Something beyond value. The clauses of this proverb seem to indicate that it is the beauty of adornment which is under consideration here. It is deliberately drawing gold and rubies to our attention, as if to say, 'Just look at those jewels and their setting!' It then goes on to compare them with what proceeds from the mouth. If the bias of this proverb therefore tends toward women, it nevertheless applies to all.

On the subject of jewellery, many women have a fascination for it and love to be adorned with precious items which they can display (or show off?) in social gatherings. Whether it does anything for them is another matter, but at least it draws attention to them, and maybe makes people take note of what they are worth – in which case it is a kind of status symbol.

To fall into conversation with one so bedecked, the awe of the adornment is soon lost in the reality of the verbal exchange. The gold may still gleam, and the sparklers may still sparkle, but what is spoken becomes the important thing. Does what this person has to say in any way live up to the impressive exterior? For whatever reason, though probably from the impression they give, more tends to be expected from the rich than from the poor in their speech. A disparity at this point tends to grate uncomfortably and result in scornful disappointment.

It need hardly be said that the real value of a person is not in what is worn on the outside, impressive though this may be. It is when they open their mouths that people show what they are worth. 'Lips of knowledge', we must remember, in this context denotes spiritual wisdom rather than academic or worldly knowledge. This does not of course exclude academic or worldly knowledge provided it is properly harnessed and applied.

For the believer this should be a great encouragement. A Christian may legitimately seek to look his or her best, and there is nothing necessarily wrong with outward adornment or seeking to present oneself attractively, so long as it is borne in mind that what really matters is the quality of speech as it reflect the nature of the heart, whether what is said is full of grace and is edifying to the hearer.

Where women are concerned, Paul is quite specific about this in 1 Timothy 2:9-10, as also is Peter in 1 Peter 3:3-6, as they seek to encourage Christian women to display their true worth, where what they say and how they say it is included as part of the godly conduct enjoined upon them. Indeed, Peter echoes this proverb as he writes of such conduct being very precious in God's sight. What is precious to God will be recognised and acknowledged by those to whom the Lord Jesus himself is precious (1 Peter 2:6-7). If a woman has nothing to show except wise and godly counsel then she is already completely and beautifully adorned.

Let us set a true value on wisdom and gracious speech (Colossians 4:5-6).

20:16. Protecting people against themselves. 'Seductress' or 'wayward woman' may simply be translated 'foreigner', in which case the second clause is a variant of the first and reinforces it. This proverb is repeated at 27:13. Its meaning needs a bit of teasing out.

In Exodus 22:25-27 the law made it clear that the poor were not to be reduced to utter destitution. The garment was the last resort, and if taken was to be returned by sundown so that the unfortunate man could at least get some sleep. A very strong point is therefore being made here.

Unlike 11:15 and 17:18 this proverb involves a third party. It could be taken as a severe warning to a third party not to get involved! This kind of thing is not uncommon. Suppose someone comes to you and says, 'Will you help me out? I am committed to supporting so-and-so and am running rather low on resources at the moment.' What are you to do?

What you are *not* to do is comply with the request. What you *are* to do, in the imagery of this proverb, rather than giving anything, is to take the man's garment lest he lose all through his foolishly having put up security in a dubious cause. You help him by protecting him.

What he is asking of you is a sort of security by proxy in which you are at least one step removed from the actual situation. That being so, you are also at least one step removed from understanding the actual nature of the case.

Don't jump on the bandwagon! There are many who foolishly commit themselves to what is described to them as a 'good cause' without really investigating what they are supporting. The term 'good cause' is sufficient for them. Very often it is a 'bad cause'.

A person is taking a risk who acts as surety for a friend or a relative. One who so acts for a stranger is doing worse. To be prepared to support someone doing this kind of thing is a bad risk. There are some people who through weakness of character or resolve get involved in ruinous commitments. If they turn to us for help we should not simply allow them to drag us down with them.

While we are to be generous toward those in need, we are not to be blind and indiscriminate. Taking the garment indicates that any involvement is to be calculating and canny. It is intended to make the other see the seriousness of the position he is in and so work toward a solution rather than perpetuating an intolerable situation.

Although the context of this proverb is material things, it works in other ways too. The 'good cause' need not be a money-based one. People often seek support from others because of their personal and relational commitments and the problems they raise. What should set the alarm bells ringing is when it is 'support' they are seeking rather than counsel or advice. On the surface it may look plausible or even commendable, but it can be a bad risk and can result in ruined reputations. Don't go with such people on their terms, but make sure it is done on yours. That way you will not only spare yourself, but you may also be of real help to them.

[Related proverbs: 22:26; 27:13.]

20:17. Who are you deceiving?

At 9:17 we read of those who get a kick out of something which is unlawful at someone else's expense. They are enticed by folly and fail to think about the consequences. So it is here.

Bread is the staple food to sustain life. We may be thinking here of those who sustain their life not by hard work but by deceiving others. There may be something intrinsically satisfying to have tricked someone, however it may have been done. It boosts one's ego, and the more so if an element of risk has been involved. Or we may be looking at a one-off situation in which deceit has been employed for personal gain.

With regularity the proverbs direct our minds to look ahead to the consequences of any course of action. The sheer disgust of a mouthful of gravel can be appreciated only by experience. Who would bite into a delicious chocolate knowing that in the centre was something revolting which would leave a lingering and damaging after-taste? Yet this is what so many people do in their lives, attracted by the heady scent of easy money without a thought to where it all might lead.

Some questions were asked at v. 14 about ethics in trading. Here are some questions about ethics in work. How have you come by your 'bread' to date? Has it all been honest labour, or has some of it been at others' expense? Have you ever deceived anyone else for your own financial gain? Those who have been unscrupulous 'on their way to the top' have often in this life found themselves ultimately in deep trouble of one kind or another and life has become anything but sweet to them. Those who deceive others quickly make enemies. That aside, however, there is coming a day of reckoning, where each man will be rewarded according to his works (Matthew 16:27).

A pastor supported by his church may be lazy without anyone knowing it for a long time, and he may enjoy the comfort of his easy life. Such a man is gaining his bread by deceit. He should be labouring to feed others, while in reality he is allowing others to labour to feed him, giving them nothing in return. See Ezekiel 34 about false shepherds feeding themselves.

Similarly a workman who uses every trick up his sleeve to avoid doing an honest day's work for an honest day's pay may think what a sweet number he's got. He may think it's money for old rope, but the time is coming when the slippery eel will be reeled in and he will wriggle in extreme discomfort.

Deception is theft. Paul addresses this in Ephesians 4:28, that those who have been guilty in this area should, instead of working dishonestly toward what they might gain, work honestly toward what they might give. That advice is good enough for us all, and it will leave a sweet after-taste!

[Related proverb: 9:17.]

20:18. Collective wisdom. This subject has been visited before (11:14; 15:22) and will be again (24:6). No one has a monopoly on wisdom. The wisest people are those who are most aware of their limitations. Sometimes you hear it said, 'If that's what you are set on doing, don't listen to what anyone else says, you can do it. Just go for it.' This kind of advice is not sound. It may come from a fear that conflicting opinions may put a person off from doing what they are gifted for, but even so it is still the wrong advice. This proverb has two parallel clauses, one general, one more specific, but the same principle applies to both.

First of all, on a variety of matters in which they might be inclined to decide for themselves without any outside help, in general people would do better to receive advice and counsel. Surprisingly to many minds, marriage is one of them. Many have made bad marriages because they allowed their hearts to overrule their heads.

There are all kinds of important decisions dependent upon careful research in which it is advisable to consult experts in their own fields. But though this is obviously the case in large scale projects affecting many people, it is also the case for the individual who is seeking to plan with regard to his career, or his aspirations in life, or where to live, and so on. He doesn't have all the relevant information at his fingertips. There are others who can make useful contributions if he will but seek their advice. In the end there may well be some conflict in the advice given, some matters which he will need to resolve in order to make a decision. Nevertheless, he will be in a far stronger position to do things correctly if he has all this counsel to hand instead of relying solely upon his own judgement.

Secondly, the particular matter of war is mentioned. Maybe this can be broadened out into any situation which will involve conflict of some kind

– as when, for example, one has to 'fight for a cause', or one has to confront someone over something which is likely to involve a head-on collision. The cause may be just, but the way in which it is handled could be vital to its success. In situations like this special wisdom is needed for the effects of any action may be irreversible. In a sinful world conflict, and the potential for conflict, are a very present reality. Paul reminds us (Ephesians 6:12) that we are in a war, and it is not against flesh and blood – but it does manifest itself in conflict at the human level. The illustration he uses there is not of an individual but of an army, each individual fully equipped so that together they may effectively withstand the enemy. Just as the army needs to work together so in a situation of conflict we need to work together with others. This is no place for individualism or bravado.

One has to be very careful in situations where others might be hurt. The war scenario will be familiar enough to most of us, if only observing it or hearing about it from a distance. Seldom, it has to be said, has sufficient wisdom been exercised in its conduct. If you are involved in any way in doing things which may adversely affect others, get counsel from those whose reputation and expertise are unimpeachable before taking any action.

[Related proverbs: 11:14; 15:22; 24:6.]

20:19. Tittle tattle. The law specifically forbade going about as a talebearer, or gossip (Leviticus 19:16). Proverbs 11:13 contrasts such a person with a faithful one. A gossip belongs to the gutter press, wantonly parading things which would better be hidden. A faithful person knows when to keep quiet about things which if revealed would only do harm.

The word used here probably has a more brazen aspect to it than that used in 18:8. What we are looking at here is a scandal-monger. However, talebearers of any hue make it their business to wheedle out of people things they ought not to divulge – described here as secrets – and then to publicise them. No discretion is involved. Sensation is the order of the day. Those practised in the art have a way with them which encourages others to talk about matters which should only be discussed in circles where discretion is exercised.

Associating with people like this is inviting trouble. Quite apart from unintentionally opening the door for them to latch on to privileged information, they are likely to take liberties and make something out of nothing. A dirty mind will see dirt where there is none. A corrupt mind will readily distort what is pure. Paul warns against this kind of person and discourages association with such (2 Thessalonians 3:11,14).

Flattery is one of the tools of the trade for a talebearer, and it is often subtle. Everybody likes to be well thought of. However, if there is evidence of flattery, steer well clear of such people, for their intention is by one means or another to extract from you anything which will further their purpose. It will do you no good, neither will it do others any good.

We saw at 18:8 how deeply the words of a talebearer embed themselves in the mind. They are like barbs which enter easily but cannot be pulled out again. This is another reason for not associating with such people. Quite apart from what they might get out of you in an unguarded moment, they will also infect you with their poison.

We are each to speak the truth with our neighbour, and then only that which edifies (Ephesians 4:25,29).

20:20. Parents are to be honoured. Full stop. This proverb echoes Exodus 21:17 and Leviticus 20:9 and hinges upon Exodus 20:12. The appendage of the death penalty shows how seriously God treats the matter, for it strikes at the crown of God's creation (Genesis 1:26-28). Disobedience to parents is included in the list of practices listed by Paul as deserving of death according to God's decree (Romans 1:30,32). The severity of the judgement is because the family has been ordained by God as the basic unit of society and the principal place where godliness can be nurtured, and where family life falls apart so in due course does society, with disastrous consequences. Parents are to be honoured. To curse them is really the opposite of this. Little wonder, then, the judgement expressed in this verse.

One of the things we should take note of in the fifth commandment is that no qualifying statements are appended. It does not say we are to honour

our parents if we consider them worthy of honour, or if they merit honour. This in general is the world's attitude toward honour and respect. It is not the Christian attitude. The Christian attitude is far more demanding, that honour is to be given on the basis of position as well as merit. For example see Romans 13:7. Thus parents are to be honoured because they are parents, irrespective of how they have conducted themselves. On the subject of honour, 1 Peter 2:17 is very wide ranging! Husbands are to honour their wives – it is due to them (1 Peter 3:7). Christians are to honour those appointed to leadership in the church (1 Thessalonians 5:12-13). See also 1 Timothy 6:1 and Romans 12:10.

If we live in a society in which marriage and family values have been seriously eroded, or if we are personally in a situation in which we legitimately find it difficult to get along with our parents, this command may be difficult to obey. Yet obey it we must for, like the other nine, it is of abiding relevance and force.

Though a man shall leave his father and mother and be joined to his wife (Genesis 2:24) yet the requirement to honour parents continues throughout life. In one respect there is discontinuity, in another continuity. Though no longer under their authority, he is still under obligation to them.

What does honour mean in practice? In some cases it means obedience (Ephesians 6:1-2; 1 Peter 2:17-18); in some cases practical care (1 Timothy 5:3). In all cases it means giving the respect due to those created in the image of God, however they may have abused that image, and demonstrating that respect with appropriate action by endeavouring to speak well of them and do well for them.

Having looked at the positive side, we should see how heinous is the negative. To curse father or mother is to wish them dead, or to wish the worst for them. It is an expression of vengeful hatred. It is an expression of rebelliousness at its most basic level, a turning against those who have nurtured and provided for their child. It is an expression of pure self-centredness which, when it cannot get its own way because parents object (often with justification), retaliates with perverted insensitivity.

The extinguishing of his 'lamp' must be seen as God's judgement upon them and its terrible and hopeless finality emphasised here is reminiscent of Jude 13.

But what if parents have been notoriously bad in bringing up their offspring? What if they have abused their children? Even so, this should elicit pity and help, not cursing, in line with Romans 12:14 and Luke 6:28. In every way, believers are to show the world that they have the utmost respect for the place of the family as ordained by God, demonstrating it in the area in which it is most put to the test.

[Related proverbs: 30:11,17.]

20:21. I want it now. Grab what you can, when you can, and how you can. Implied in this proverb is the element of dishonesty. An inheritance was normally, though not always, received on the death of the testator. Thus in the parable of the prodigal son (Luke 15:11-32) the father was coerced into giving his younger son his portion of the inheritance prematurely. In the case of Ahab, he 'inherited' Naboth's vineyard by first getting rid of its rightful owner (1 Kings 21).

Then there were the kings of Israel who 'inherited' the throne by assassinating its previous occupants (2 Kings 15:10,14,25,30). These kings all met an unhappy end. By way of contrast consider David who, with all the promises made to him concerning the throne, refused to seize the opportunity to kill king Saul but waited the Lord's time. He was blessed in the end.

This proverb clearly stresses the beginning and the end. All those mentioned above (apart from David) wanted what they could get for themselves without considering the rights of the matter. They thought that by taking possession or by seizing power when they had the chance they 'had it made'. How short-sighted they were! Whatever they thought they had at the beginning, they certainly were not blessed at the end, for it all turned sour on them.

To want something before the proper time and to find a way to get it will never turn out for blessing, only for trouble. To be practical about it, a courting couple looking for fulfilment prior to marriage will live to regret it. It is an illusion from the evil one to think otherwise. A man who gets promotion and better pay by underhand methods likewise will sooner or later find himself in trouble. Examples could be multiplied, but it all boils down to covetousness and impatience. The courting couple should eagerly wait God's time for the blessing of the sealing of their relationship in marriage. The man seeking promotion should not do others down in order to get the position but should show his worth by his diligence, waiting for it to be properly recognised, trusting God in the process.

In anything we look forward to, we must learn to wait God's time, and do so in faith, believing that he knows, that his will is best, and that he is fully in control of the situation. The temptation is that we will miss out if we don't take matters into our own hands, force the situation and act now. Recognise temptation for what it is. It is by waiting upon the Lord that we will know if and when and how to act. In Psalm 37 note both the direct and indirect references to waiting upon God and the references to an inheritance. Learn and apply v. 4 there, and receive from the Lord what he gives, when he gives it, and how he gives it.

20:22. Retribution. There are two very clear and opposite examples of this in the life of David. The first was his long restraint while Saul was seeking to destroy him, even to the point of refusing twice to take vengeance when he had, as someone put it to him, a God-given opportunity (1 Samuel 24 and 26). The second, in the same period of his life, was his volatile reaction against Nabal who refused his men provisions (1 Samuel 25).

That the same man could act so differently to two kinds of injustice serves as a warning to us that there are some things we can bear while others get under our skin. Undoubtedly David was more tolerant in the grave situation, but it was the relatively trivial one which riled him, in which he did not feel constrained by the same principles.

We need to take this proverb in conjunction with 15:18. When we take retaliatory action against what we perceive as personal injustice the result is invariably to perpetuate strife. Family feuds (which are far from uncommon) bear eloquent testimony to this.

How often we have heard the sentiment expressed, 'I'll pay you back for this!', and not in appreciation for services rendered! The blood boils most fiercely when the heat of injustice burns most personally.

The exhortation of this proverb is given because, of course, the temptation *is* to say it! More than that, it is to *do* it! Now, why are we not to say it? Is it because we cannot carry out what we say? Is that the reason? Not at all. We are not to *say* it because we are not to *do* it. A so-called God-given opportunity is precisely *not* that, for the simple reason that God has never given anyone the right or responsibility for personal vengeance.

When we are insulted, threatened, endangered, suffer injustice and the like, one of the effects of this is to impair our judgement. We stand too close to the problem to be able see it objectively and impartially. Instead, the instincts of our sinful nature are aroused and complicate the issue.

It is noteworthy that this proverb is one which is alluded to several times in the New Testament – Matthew 5:39; Romans 12:17,19; 1 Thessalonians 5:15; 1 Peter 3:9. Need we ask why it crops up so often?

Peter sets before us the example of the Lord Jesus (1 Peter 2:22-23). When Peter says that Jesus 'committed no sin' he is not speaking generally here, true though that was. He is speaking into the particular issue of reaction to injustice. If it would have been sin for him, the sinless Son of God, to respond to personal injustice with personal threats, how much more so for the likes of us!

Jesus acknowledged that retribution was the prerogative of his Father who judges justly whatever the outward appearances, and so he continued to entrust himself to him, even in his extremity. Likewise we, whatever the appearance of things, should continue to wait for the Lord. If he alone is the righteous judge who retains this prerogative to himself, we can be sure that he knows what he is doing and will bring deliverance to us without our even thinking to take the law into our own hands!

It is a mark of faith to take God at his word, and this kind of situation requires that we do so.

[Related proverbs: 15:18; 17:13; 24:29.]

20:23. Our standards and God's. There are some lessons in life we are slow to learn, about which we have to be reminded over and over again. Having considered something very similar on at least two previous occasions (11:1; 20:10) it is tempting to gloss over this. 'Been there, done that,' we might say, not considering there are areas we need to keep revisiting because things have changed – and we have changed. Perhaps our weights have become damaged; perhaps our scales need recalibrating. Just as shoddy standards in business in the weights and measures department can incur severe penalties, so will careless, inconsistent attitudes and falsehood incur God's severe displeasure. God still says, 'Be holy, for I am holy' (1 Peter 1:16). That is the standard. We are to have no other.

Things are not always what they seem. Here is either a deliberate intention to deceive, or by implication a deliberate policy of exercising bias where there should be none.

Our society has made much of equality – equality for all – meaning a variety of things but including equality of opportunity and equality of treatment. It is very evident, however, that whatever people understand by this phrase, in practice there remains a great deal of inequality. People are often treated differently for no sound reason, only through prejudice. Personal bias is alive and well, and where this thrives in dealings with other people, some are going to get a raw deal while others receive preferential treatment.

This may be a good point to consider God's weights and scales and how he uses them. There are references in the law to maintaining a perfect standard.

We need to make it our business to calibrate our actions and attitudes against the standard which God has set, and to keep on doing so because of the natural tendency to drift away from the mark. In spite of what is often claimed, the world has very different standards, and being in the world so much of the time the temptation is always there to adopt its standards and use either them or God's standards according to which suits us at any given time.

At 20:10 we focused on consistency in our dealings with others according to the standard God requires. Now may be the opportunity to consider consistency in our dealings with ourselves in relation to others. Are the standards we expect of ourselves the same as those we expect of others? When we judge others do we judge ourselves by the same measure (Romans 2:22)? Are we hard on others but easy on ourselves?

Take it a step further. How does what we require of ourselves compare with what God requires of us in terms of our attitudes and standards? When God has given us his standards, do we then make our own and accept and use them, knowing they are different from his? If we excuse ourselves by saying, 'That is just how I am,' or, 'I cannot be expected to do better than this,' that is just what we are doing, replacing God's standard with our own. We are using false scales.

If, to take an example from everyday life, the road sign sets the standard at 30 miles per hour but we say that our standard is 40 miles per hour and drive accordingly, we can hardly argue that to be fined for speeding is being legalistic.

Neither is acknowledging and seeking to keep God's laws being legalistic. We do not depend upon them for acceptance, but neither do we set them aside or replace them with our own standards. We acknowledge that the law is holy and just and good (Romans 7:12). We are to rely upon his grace and enabling to live up to his standard, not set it to one side and seek to live in our own strength according to our own lesser standard.

When God says, 'Be holy, for I am holy', how can we be satisfied with less and say that it will do? How can we fool ourselves to say that it measures up?

Just as the Israelites needed to discard their idols from before a holy God (Joshua 24:19-23), so we need to rid ourselves of false standards.

[Related proverbs: 11:1; 16:11; 20:10.]

20:24. Who is in control in this world? This proverb is very general and ought to be very humbling. We are told that our times are in God's hands (Psalm 31:15). From the human perspective it might appear that 'time and chance happen to them all' (Ecclesiastes 9:11). Here, though, we are informed that our very steps are ordered by the Lord. Our comings and goings, and all that we do, are under his sovereign control.

If the whole of history is at every step of the way fulfilling God's ultimate purpose then we have no choice but to believe it. The coming of the Lord Jesus Christ into this world as promised and predicted in an enormous variety of ways throughout the Old Testament period, was fulfilled down to its last detail, and its fulfilment involved the 'steps' of a vast number of individuals from all walks of life over several millennia. Likewise the combined activities of all the people of every generation are working toward the fulfilment of what is yet predicted concerning the coming again of the Lord Jesus in glory and for judgement at the end of the age. What is happening on the grand scale of things is being effected at the level of the minutiae which make up the whole. Our history is *his story*. Your steps and mine are contributing toward the fulfilment of God's ultimate plan for the world.

Ultimately, it is not we who are in control of our lives, but God. We are perfectly at liberty to exercise our freedom of choice and decision, but it all falls within the compass of God's overarching authority. Kidner puts it memorably thus: 'Our improvising cannot compare with his composing.'

The unbeliever may rebel against such a notion, but that is because he does not want God to be in control of, or have any authority over, his life. This statement calls for submission, and yet to submit is the one thing he will not do. Then when things don't work out the way he would like them to and he doesn't understand what is going on, so often he finds fault with God.

How different it should be for the Christian, knowing he is called by the Lord, loved by him and kept by his power! We may at times not understand the way we are taking, and sometimes we may find ourselves taking a very different route from what we had imagined or planned. But to know that God is guiding our steps is wonderfully reassuring and comforting, and as long as we walk with him we will not go wrong. We are told very specifically not to lean on our own understanding – that is, not to rely upon it – but to trust in him, acknowledge him, and be led by him (3:5-6).

So if you are perplexed by the way things are turning out for you, if you cannot understand the whys and wherefores, do not be surprised by this. We may never understand the work and ways of God (Ecclesiastes 8:17) – and why should we expect to? But he knows your work and ways, and he says to commit your way to him, and he will direct your paths.

There are some things which are beyond our understanding. If it were not so, God would not be God, and we would not be mere mortals. Our recognition of who he is should draw the response from our hearts as it did from Paul's, 'To him be glory forever. Amen' (Romans 11:36).

[Related proverbs: 16:1,9; 19:21.]

20:25. On putting your head in a noose. The classic example of making a rash vow to the Lord is Jephthah (Judges 11:30-31). Without question he meant well, only there were factors he did not take into consideration, and probably could not have done. Though he fulfilled his vow, it cost him more than he had intended.

Other statements relating to making and keeping promises are found in Genesis 28:20; Deuteronomy 23:21-23; Psalms 15:4; 119:106; Ecclesiastes 5:4-5.

This proverb relates not to promises generally but promises made to God. How many people say, 'If God will do such and such for me, then I will do such and such for him,' only afterwards to forget or make excuse. Their heart was not in it from the outset. They only wanted to twist God's arm, as it were, under the mistaken impression that perhaps they could coerce God into doing something for them. There was no true devotion to him.

That said, sometimes in their distress people will believe themselves to be sincere, that if only God would act on their behalf they will respond with personal or practical devotion. The reality is that both their motives and their judgement are impaired by their circumstances.

On a bigger scale, the same is true of false professions of faith. Jesus strongly cautioned a man who avowed his intention to devote himself to following him (Matthew 8:19-20). There is need to count the cost (Luke 14:28). There is need to consider all the factors. There is need to know one's own heart and not be self-deceiving. Promises are to be kept; vows to the Lord are to be paid.

There may be some significance in this proverb following the last. Here is a statement of what I intend doing, but when it is made without due consciousness of my limitations and without an understanding of my own heart then it falls under the condemnation of being rash.

If we will be held to account for every idle word (Matthew 12:36), how much more for unfulfilled vows of devotion to God!

When Jacob made his vow to the Lord (Genesis 28:20-22) it was based upon what God had already promised him rather than on what he wanted God to do for him. Nevertheless we might wonder what would have become of his vow had God not first reminded him of it (Genesis 31:13) and then held him to it (Genesis 32:24-30). His fulfilling of his vow was attributable to God and not to Jacob!

Where vows to God are concerned, they are mentioned with the qualification of there being no necessity to make them. Deuteronomy 23:21-23 indicates that vows to the Lord should be realistic and be honoured, probably as deliberate expressions of thankfulness to him, and Ecclesiastes 5:4-5 reflects this and the folly and penalty of reneging.

If we are the Lord's, we are his, body and soul. Our devotion to him is to be total. We are pledged to devote ourselves to him as living sacrifices (Romans 12:1). We cannot vow to him anything extra! Even so, if we make specific promises before God, such as the Corinthian church did about providing aid to their brethren in Jerusalem (2 Corinthians 9:1-5), we must not do so lightly and we must be careful to fulfil what we have promised.

20:26. Purging evil from society. The imagery is that of the threshing floor. As in v. 8, the word for winnowing is used. The threshing wheel was a device for separating the grain from the straw by a combination of rolling and dragging. After this was done, the grain, still mixed with debris, was winnowed, often using sieves, to get rid of the remaining chaff and dust. It was a painstaking and thorough process.

This is a picture of what a wise king will do in dealing with every form of wickedness in his kingdom. Half measures will not do. If the kingdom is to be wholesome, it must be pure. Threshing was an energetic process requiring effort and time and trouble. As such it is an appropriate metaphor for this particular task of a king.

Wickedness is present in any kingdom and in any society, because it is present in the human heart. We have this on good authority, because it is God who says so (Jeremiah 17:9). One of the principal functions of rulers is to maintain within society a standard of conduct which is higher than what it would otherwise be given the nature of the heart of the individual. Needless to say, this calls for tough measures which will generally not be too well appreciated. There is almost an inevitability that any government will come in for criticism because of the curbs it puts upon the freedom of the individual, because of the scrutiny to which people are subjected, or because of the pressures which are brought to bear upon them. Few seem to realise that without this so-called interference or these so-called intrusions it would not be possible to separate the wheat from the chaff, to rid society of its unwholesome elements. Again, the metaphor is appropriate, because both the wheat and the chaff are together subjected to pressures and to being tossed about. It is not a gentle or a comfortable process. The godly may be subjected to considerable inconvenience and discomfort in a wise administration, but it is they who will come through the process unscathed.

What goes on at national level under the king also happens at the individual level under a heavenly father's discipline. The whole of life for the believer may be thought of as a process of winnowing, for there is much within us which needs to be prised off and blown away!

We are commanded to pray for kings and for all who are in authority (1 Timothy 2:1-4). We should pray that they will be wisely robust and diligent in their administration. Peter informs us that kings and governors are sent by God for the punishment of evildoers and for the praise of those who do good (1 Peter 2:13-14). This fact remains even though they may abuse their authority or fall short in the exercise of it. Anarchy is devastating. The health of a society is directly related to the health of its administration.

Note what John the Baptist said of the coming King (Luke 3:17). [Related proverb: 20:8.]

20:27. Know yourself. A great deal more goes on within our minds and hearts than we let on to others, or than others see. We sometimes refer to the 'dark corners' of a person's mind, indicating that things lurk there for shame of being exposed for others to see. There is an aspect of our essential being, called our spirit, which is sensitive to our innermost thoughts and what they are all about. We have a consciousness of what we are, of who we are, which goes deeper than rational thought. Rationally, we may wish to exclude parts of our lives from scrutiny or exposure. It is our spirit which prevents this from happening insofar as we cannot escape an awareness of what we are like.

Our spirit is said to be the lamp of the Lord. We were made in God's image and he breathed into man the breath of life (Genesis 2:7). 'Breath' and 'spirit' are the same word, serving as a reminder that we are as essentially spiritual beings as we are physical. The 'breath of life' is more than the capacity to sustain physical life from the air we breathe, it is the capacity to relate meaningfully to God who made us, for it was he who breathed into man the breath of life.

The lamp of the Lord is like a torch which is used to shine into all the dark recesses of our being, showing us what is there. Of course, most people do not seem to understand this, and it may be one of the reasons why so many people find it difficult to live with themselves or suffer various psychological problems. They have no means of coping with what they know they are and try to live in denial of what their spirit shows them.

What our spirit shows us is what God sees, for he has given our spirit to us to help us to see ourselves as he sees us. It is into this situation that God graciously speaks the word of the gospel, and when the spirit of man yields to the Spirit of God then the inner depths of the heart are cleansed and the fear of exposure disappears. The believer is 'light in the Lord' (Ephesians 5:8).

The apostle Paul makes a remarkable statement in 1 Corinthians 2:9-12. God has given us our spirit that we might know ourselves. Nobody else can know us in this way because they do not have our spirit. Neither can we know them in this way because we do not have their spirit. Paul applies this to God, saying that nobody knows the things of God except the Spirit of God. People often quote v. 9 out of context. But the amazing truth Paul is declaring here is that God has given his Spirit to his people that they might know and understand him – something which is totally inaccessible to the natural man.

This giving of his Spirit makes all the difference between a mere intellectual knowledge or theorising about God and an intimate understanding of who he really is, to know him, to love him, to trust him, and to find peace and eternal security in him.

'The Spirit himself bears witness with our spirit that we are children of God' (Romans 8:16).

20:28. 2 Samuel 7. Top qualities. At v. 26 we see the severe side of kings and rulers. In 1 Peter 2:13-14 we read of both punishment and praise from rulers – the punishment of evildoers and the praise of those who do good. What this proverb says, however, is in a different league. Here the word 'chesed' appears twice. In the NKJV it is translated first as 'mercy' and then as 'lovingkindness'. It denotes a responsible love for the people, a love which resolves to care for them and do them good, a love which exhibits itself in faithfulness and stability, in truth. It has to be said that these are qualities seldom seen in national leaders.

Two aspects of preservation are seen here: firstly of the king, secondly of the throne. We are told that rulers are sent by God (Romans 13:1-7). Here we are told how it is that they keep their position secure! Look at how Rehoboam by forsaking mercy nearly brought about his downfall, and his self-centred harshness certainly undermined his throne (1 Kings 12:14). Look at how many tyrannical rulers throughout history have been assassinated even though they have sought so carefully to protect themselves from the very thing they feared.

King David may have had his faults, but one thing stands out in his life, and that is the way he loved and cared for his people and in general (though not perfectly) maintained the truth. Not only did the Lord preserve him, he also upheld his throne with the promise that his throne would be established forever (2 Samuel 7:16), a promise fulfilled in great David's greater Son, the Lord Jesus Christ.

Furthermore, not only was the promise fulfilled in Jesus, but he is the great exemplar of this proverb. His love in dying for his people and his faithfulness in keeping them have established a kingdom which shall not fade away, in which he will receive honour and praise and glory from a people who worship him with eternal gratitude and love (Revelation 1:5-6; 5:12-13).

If it applies to kings and rulers, this principle of mercy and truth also extends to every other kind of administrative authority, including the workplace and including the church. Note especially what Paul wrote of Timothy and Epaphroditus (Philippians 2:19-30). Caring for their people before themselves characterised these two outstanding Christian leaders and servants of God, in true Christlike fashion.

Many a ruler has been brought down who has forsaken truth or integrity and given way to personal and political corruption. Both mercy and truth, or faithfulness, or uprightness, are essential to the security of any leader and government.

Whether or not we are in a position of authority, these two lovely characteristics should be in evidence in our relationships with others.

[Related proverb: 3:3.]

20:29. Recognising glory and splendour. This focus upon the young and the old is intended to make a point which covers those in between as well. The point is that every age group has its value and usefulness and should be appreciated. God has a purpose for his people, whether they be young or old or somewhere in between, and it is through fulfilling his purpose that not only will they find satisfaction but the whole church will be benefited.

The word used for the 'glory' of young men is not the same as that generally used for the 'glory' of God but is more akin to ornamentation and impressiveness, perhaps even with prowess. It is about what we see and recognise in young men in their prime.

The grey hair of old men is a clear indicator that, physically at least, they are well past their prime! It seems somewhat incongruous to compare the strength of young men with the grey hair of the old men. Strength can serve a purpose, but what purpose does a grey head have? The key lies in the word used to describe it: splendour. Dignity and honour are involved in this word.

Now it has to be said that there is no glory, there is nothing impressive, about a young man who misuses his strength; nor is there any honour in a grey-headed rogue! What we should be looking at here are the endowments the young and the old have received from God. God has given the young strength for a season and for a reason. God has given the grey-headed a lifetime of experience, and it is from such, rather than from anyone else, that wisdom may be sought and received.

What would we do without the young and their capacity for work and their ability to see things through fresh eyes? What would we do without hands to get things done or people with the strength to work?

What would we do without the benefit of the wisdom and experience of the elderly to help younger ones make right choices and get on in the best possible way? What would we do without the management and other skills of those knowledgeable in their specialised fields?

There is a great tendency to be critical of people for what they do not have instead of valuing them for what they do, to home in on blemishes instead of observing beauty. We need to harness the qualities with which God has endowed people and put them to good use. The young who can use their energies in beneficial ways will not only benefit themselves by doing so but will gladly give extra when their efforts are appreciated. The elderly who can give counsel and advice and who can relay their experience to the help of others will find the opportunity rewarding. All have a contribution to make who will make it all the better when they know they are valued.

Whatever the young may lack in experience and wisdom, they have a useful contribution to make by virtue of their youthful vigour. Whatever the elderly may lack in the way of strength and activity, they have an invaluable contribution to make on account of the knowledge and understanding they have gained over many years.

The church is endowed by the Lord with spiritual gifts (1 Corinthians 12; Ephesians 4:7-11). She is also endowed with natural abilities, so that all can and should gladly present their members as slaves of righteousness (Romans 6:19).

[Related proverb: 16:31.]

20:30. Ouch! To inflict pain on others is commonly regarded as sadistic or cruel, and in many cases it may be so. But not always. At 19:29 we saw that some people are deserving of punishment and beatings, while here there are some for whom a beating serves a very valuable purpose. It is sad when a ban is imposed on smacking and the like because so many abuse it, for there are occasions when this kind of treatment is appropriate and works to the long term benefit of the one who suffers it and also to others.

God is not cruel, and is the loving heavenly Father of his people, yet look what is said of him in Hebrews 12:5-6, quoting from Proverbs 3:11-12. He does it for our good, that we may be partakers of his holiness (Hebrews 12:10-11). Now of course God does not actually physically scourge his people, but this illustration is used for two reasons. Firstly, because there has never been anything intrinsically wrong with this form of punishment. An occasional physical beating was well understood as being an appropriate form of punishment and an effective deterrent to continuation of behaviour which would prove harmful. Secondly, because God sometimes brings his people through exceedingly painful experiences.

Though couched in physical terms, the principle in this proverb goes beyond this, for the proverb is not about corporal punishment but about cleansing away evil. Looking at it from the wrong end will lead to a wrong conclusion. The means is subservient to the motivation. What is the intention? It is to remove evil, and in the same way that a scourer is used to remove stubborn dirt from a pot where an ordinary dishcloth would have no effect, so some severity is required where lesser measures would act like water off a duck's back.

We have an expression which says that sometimes 'you have to be cruel to be kind'. What this means is that there are occasions when it is necessary to say things which are going to hurt because that person needs to hear them for their own good and for the good of others. You know they are not going to take kindly to the words, and they may even react against them initially, but all the same they must receive them if they are going to experience any benefit from them. It is a bit like taking unpleasant medicine or a painful course of treatment to counter disease.

Evil, wherever it is found, is directly contrary to holiness. If holiness is to be promoted, evil, where it is found, is to be removed. The trouble is, evil is often deep-seated. There are inner depths to the heart, and sometimes it is necessary to probe and pierce in order for things which lurk there to be exposed and removed. As chaff is not removed from grain without a beating, so there are some bad things which are cleansed away only by strong measures.

The most saintly people are usually those who have experienced and accepted the Lord's chastening. If you feel you are suffering severe affliction under the hand of God and ask the question why, although there may be no immediate answer to satisfy, at least remember that he intends it for good. There will come a time when you will have cause to thank him for his dealings with you. It may be helpful to remember your Substitute, that *he* was bruised for *your* iniquity, it is with *his* stripes that *you* are healed (Isaiah 53:5). He endured the cross for you (Hebrews 12:2-3): what are you going to endure for him?

[Related proverbs: 17:10; 19:25; 27:6; 29:15.]

21:1. Who is in control in this world? The simile becomes clear when it is understood that the word translated 'rivers' denotes a man-made channel cut for the purpose of irrigation. Thus in Psalm 46:4 we have the picture of a river from which rivulets were directed for the benefit of the city of God. In the same way as men might cut channels to turn the water from the river to irrigate their crops, so this proverb speaks of the Lord redirecting hearts of kings to flow in channels of his pleasing.

Was Solomon writing of himself? As king he may well have had some self-consciousness of the truth of this statement, but only as an example of its general application. Naturally we might expect this state of affairs to have applied to godly kings, like David, or Jehoshaphat, or Hezekiah, or Josiah for example, because their hearts were in tune with the Lord and they sought him to direct them.

Amazingly, though, it is also true of ungodly rulers who neither sought nor knew the Lord. Cyrus is one example among many recorded in Scripture. Read the remarkable prophecy of Isaiah concerning him (Isaiah 44:28–45:7), written long before his time, and the outcome in Ezra 1 where we read (v. 1) that 'The LORD stirred up the spirit of Cyrus king of Persia,' moving him to permit the Jews to return home from their exile.

A little less than a century previously God had spoken through Habakkuk that Nebuchadnezzar would shortly be in the ascendancy, in God's hand as an instrument of punishment upon an ungodly Jewish nation (Habakkuk 1:1-11).

In Romans 13:1-4 Paul asserts that such authorities as exist are appointed by God. He goes further to say that the authority is God's minister, or servant. The logical conclusion therefore is that exactly the same is true today concerning kings, rulers and authorities. As then, the nations still rage, even against God and against his Son (Psalm 2:1-2), but let us not be misled into thinking that somehow God has lost control of the situation. He is still working out his purposes so that the gospel can be taken to the ends of the earth and bear fruit until the King of kings returns in glory.

21:2. This is how I see it. This proverb is a variation on 16:2. So, what if we have heard it before? Perhaps we need to hear it again. It is not suggesting that we are not aware when we are deliberately doing wrong. What it is addressing is that when we imagine we are doing right we can be deceiving ourselves. For it is not only contrasting what we see with what God sees, it is reminding us that God is looking right into our hearts – something we are often reluctant to do ourselves.

What we need to be reminded of here once again is that doing the right thing is not enough: it has got to come from a right motivation. There are many people who will justify their actions and protest that they have done well. Isn't that good enough for God? I've always done my duty; I've always attended church; I say my prayers; I've given regularly to charity; I don't smoke, I don't drink, I don't swear. What more can God want? ... It may be that he wants your heart! Certainly it is the heart that he weighs. His assessment of you is based not upon your outward performance but the hidden springs which motivate it. 'My son,' he says, 'give me your heart' (23:26).

Would a rich man be satisfied with a wife who did all the right things simply because she was interested only in his money? Surely he would want her heart: he would want her to love him as he loved her. And does God who has loved us not want our hearts? Forget for a moment your good deeds, or your right living, and answer this simple question: Does it all arise from a heart which loves the Lord who has first loved you? That is what matters. Right living in God's eyes will follow out of a right heart relationship with him.

We sometimes seek to give corrective advice to people by asking them to look at things from the other person's point of view. They are sure they are right, but when they look at it through the eyes of the other person, then they see they have been at fault. So it is with our life before God. In our own eyes we may believe we are 'doing all right'. Maybe we are, maybe we are not. That is beside the point. What matters is not how we see things from our own perspective, but that we should be seeing them from God's perspective. What matters is not that we justify ourselves, but that he justify us. Let us therefore lay our hearts on his weighing scales!

[Related proverbs: 12:15; 16:2; 24:12; 26:12.]

21:3. A matter of comparison. This has a connection with the previous proverb. Self-righteousness arises from a heart that is stubbornly resistant to God's influence; true righteousness comes from a tender heart which welcomes it. When it says that to do what is right and just is *more* acceptable than sacrifice, it does not mean on the one hand that sacrifice alone was acceptable without righteousness and justice, or on the other that righteousness and justice in any way dispensed with the need for sacrifice. This proverb is addressing formalism, when the heart is not involved in the service and religion is merely a ritual performance. Without a true concern for living rightly and justly, the observation of religious duties is a complete sham. Jesus addressed the self-righteous Pharisees on this very issue (Matthew 9:13; 12:7; 23:23).

This is what God stresses in such passages as Isaiah 1:11-17, Amos 5:21-24 and Micah 6:6-8. Some have misinterpreted these passages, claiming they are saying that the sacrifices were redundant or irrelevant. They are not saying that. What they are saying is that the people were making a mockery of their religious observances and rendering them utterly meaningless because there was no corresponding righteous conduct in their lives. Similarly, it does not matter how faithfully people attend church, participate in the communion service, give tithes and so on if they argue it does not matter how they conduct themselves in the world.

In Old Testament times God prescribed in his law for sacrifices to be offered for atonement for sin. They were to be offered until the coming of the One they foreshadowed, the Lamb of God, the Lord Jesus Christ, who would atone for sin by the sacrifice of himself upon the cross. A sacrifice was supposed to have been a recognition on the part of the one presenting it that atonement was needed and provided, through forgiveness and cleansing, by another on his behalf. The sacrifice, truly offered, expressed need, dependence and thankfulness to be outworked in the life. How much more so is it for those who have come to Jesus Christ in repentance and faith, accepting his sacrifice on their behalf, henceforth to work out in their lives what he has wrought in their lives, living according to the Spirit and not according to the flesh (Romans 8:4)!

There have always been those who are dependent upon gaining acceptance with God by sacrifice under the mistaken notion that the sacrifice is what *they* offer, what *they* do, and that, having done that, nothing else is required of them. Sometimes they even think of their good works as being a sacrifice and that somehow these will gain them acceptance with God. The truth is that the sacrifice in which they need intimately to be involved is not one which they make, but one which has been made for them, on their behalf, because of what they could *not* do, and then that *everything* is required of them! A little sacrifice makes few demands; a great sacrifice makes great demands. That Christ laid down his life for me demands my soul, my life, my all, as Isaac Watts so appropriately said.

[Related proverb: 15:8.]

21:4. Look, thought and action. Unlike most of the proverbs, this one is a single clause. Three things are described as sin, and they are all intimately related. The third requires some explanation. What is translated 'ploughing' in the AV and NKJV should quite possibly be 'lamp', as in 1 Kings 11:36 and Proverbs 13:9. Even then the meaning may need teasing out. Unlike Psalm 119:105, the lamp of the wicked is certainly not light provided by God. It is not his word by which they are illuminated. The light by which they live is their own light, of their own making. If, however, 'ploughing' is correct, the furrow they plough is their own course through life, doing it their way, not God's. It amounts to the same thing whichever way we look at it: it is setting self in place of God, in which human philosophies, human wisdom, human ideas and ideals displace and take the place of God and his Word. Like Jeroboam's system of worship it may have many features which look deceptively like the real thing (1 Kings 12:25-33).

In brief, then, this proverb is describing the look, thought and action of the wicked: eyes, heart and feet in coordination. A haughty look and a proud heart are prominent characteristics of the wicked. The haughty look disdains others, it despises them, it looks down on them. That is especially true of their attitude toward the godly. It comes from a proud heart which has no need of God, which is self-sufficient, which rejects outside help, especially any advice, admonition or instruction from God-fearing people. They are more than able to make their own way in life, and their own success is testimony to their philosophy.

People like this can be intimidating, with their withering looks and pompous words, treating the godly as if they were infants, mocking Christians as pathetic for needing a crutch in life or for living in ignorance in some outdated scientific backwater; or even accusing them of narrow-minded arrogance.

God has one word for all this: sin. Those who begin without God and continue without God are living in sin, for sin is disobedience to God's Word. If they continue that way, they will end without God, and sin leads to wrath.

We all began that way, says Paul (Ephesians 2:1-3), who then switches focus to the amazing grace of God. Having thought about those things, this is what we now need to do: focus on the amazing grace of God. What do the Lord Jesus and his apostles repeatedly say should be the attitude of his disciples toward others? What should be the settled state of their hearts? According to what principles should they be conducting their affairs? Where are they heading?

Let us not become infected with the spirit of the world, but be filled with the Spirit of the Lord. This will show in humility of mind, in respect toward others and in a life which acknowledges the Lord at every point, including all the little things.

21:5. Don't be in such a hurry. At 10:4 diligence is contrasted with slackness; here it is with hastiness. If there are some things which are not easily come by, equally there are some things to which there is no short cut. The process of mining will provide an example. There have been not a few disasters in the past for those so eager to extract the earth's rich resources that they have tunnelled quickly and carelessly without 'wasting time' over the conditions, without bothering to shore up the tunnels properly ... for maximum gain at minimum expense. Maybe nobody could have faulted their enthusiasm or zeal, but the result was the precise opposite of what had been hoped for. Yet the riches were there for the taking – given the right approach. Studying the rock strata, judging where the ore is to be found, considering the best means for extracting it, investigating the various dangers and how to minimise them – all these things and others require painstaking effort and time, not to mention expense, before the work is even begun.

The 'get rich quick' mentality manifests itself in all sorts of ways. Impulsiveness is rarely rewarded. Feverish activity without stopping to think is a sure recipe for trouble. There is a saying that if something is worth doing, it is worth doing well. In the long run, quality is more important than quantity.

Yet again we have a proverb which provokes us to look ahead; indeed, to *stop* and look ahead. Do we want plenty, or do we want poverty? A silly question, but not when we think about how our present way of life relates to it. How many people in life are chasing after this and that, doing their utmost to keep up with fashions and trends and 'the Joneses', imagining that by so doing they will be better off. Life is one big round of frenetic activity ... and in the end it only impoverishes them.

The 'plans' of this proverb are not just ideas or aspirations, but concrete and well formed, like the plans for a journey. You know where you want to get to, and the plans you make take you from the starting point to the finishing point, due consideration being given to every point between. There can be nothing vague or haphazard or incomplete about these plans if you want to be sure of reaching your destination.

There are many areas in life in which people are inclined to be hasty. Relationships is one, especially romantic ones. Is it going to reward you or ruin you? Have you taken time to think about what you want from it? Have you taken time to prepare for it? Have you looked at the stages on the way from where it is now to where you hope it will ultimately be?

Business is another. A sound and thriving business will usually need careful planning. Rushing headlong into a business venture under pressure is never a wise move.

Beware of people who are out to sell you something by offering special incentives, supposedly in your own interests, putting pressure on to you commit yourself immediately. Never do it unless you have already thought through the whole thing. People have ended up head over ears in debt by succumbing to this kind of thing.

Take your time, do things well, aim for what is best for all involved. Above all, wait upon the Lord for wisdom and guidance.

[Related proverbs: 8:34; 10:4; 19:2.]

21:6. Avaricious deceit. The second clause is somewhat difficult to translate, but the NKJV seems to capture the meaning. An irony is involved. Suppose we say to someone, 'If you're looking for trouble, just go ahead and do it.' We understand well enough that the person is not looking for trouble, but to do what they propose to do amounts to it. So here, no one is seeking death, but to get treasures by a lying tongue is tantamount to their doing so. There is, however, a double irony, because what they believe to be a substantial gain turns out to be of no substance whatever. They clutch at it, and like a vapour there is nothing to it. It is a mirage: when they get there it is gone – it was never there in the first place.

Many use a lie as a credit card to gain something for which they do not have the means to pay. It will rebound upon them with interest.

A lying tongue is almost always involved in any unscrupulous method used for personal gain. At the bar of divine justice, if not before, liars will have to account for their words, and being found bankrupt of real riches they will pay the appropriate penalty. Even before this, though, there will very likely be disappointment, guilt, emptiness, a consciousness that their ill gotten gains have not even begun to deliver according to expectation. Many a fat exterior conceals a withered interior.

Gehazi lied in order to enrich himself at Naaman's expense (2 Kings 5:20-27) and as a result was struck down with leprosy.

Judas Iscariot gained his thirty pieces of silver with a lying tongue (he lied because what he said did not correspond with what was in his heart). How did that benefit him? It cost him his life (Matthew 26:14-15; 27:3-5).

The soldiers who witnessed the resurrection events gained a considerable sum of money by promising to lie (which they did, Matthew 28:11-15). What happened to them will be revealed in the last day.

What will happen to the 'health and wealth' gospel preachers who enrich themselves at the expense of others by lying in God's name? What about those who lie about their qualifications or experience or abilities, or even put down others, in order to secure a prestigious position? Or those who have a lie prepared to cover up the fact that they have stolen? Or those who are paid handsomely to lie in support of some criminal activity?

One of the saddest things for Samuel must have been that his sons, whom he appointed judges over Israel, took bribes and perverted justice (1 Samuel 8:1-3). They enriched themselves by taking bribes to declare the guilty innocent and, by implication, the innocent guilty.

What about those who are living a lie in order to enhance their prestige? Jesus was blunt and to the point in addressing such people in John 8:44. His words are very uncomfortable when their wider implication is considered.

How well is Ephesians 4:25 being worked out in your life?

[Related proverbs: 10:2-3; 11:4.]

21:7. Justice violated. Almost daily, if we follow the news, we read or hear of violent people who seem to get away with the most terrible deeds. It is in the nature of the news that we often hear of the atrocities which have been committed but not so often do we learn of what happens to the perpetrators. Thus we can get a biased view which fills us with alarm and leads us to ask the question, 'Is there no justice in the world?' Were we able to find out, we would probably discover that justice is served on far more of these people than we originally supposed, and we might be surprised about how it happened.

In Matthew 26:52 Jesus responded to Peter's rash action by saying that those who take up the sword shall perish by the sword. It was a foolish thing for Peter to do, and had he persisted it would have been only a matter of time before someone stopped him by thrusting him through.

Violence is only asking for a violent response, the more so when it comes from wicked people. As they destroy others, so they are in effect destroying themselves because of the outrage they precipitate against themselves. The language of the original is graphic, for it says that their violence will 'drag them off'.

However, a reason is given for this destruction coming about. It is because they refuse to do justice. Note it is not simply that they do not do justice, but that they refuse to do it. This implies they have been shown what is right and just and yet they will not submit to reason.

This is a sinister violence because it is not amenable to any kind of negotiation. It is violence which will not listen. It is violence which instils terror. This has been witnessed over and over again throughout history. It is certainly being witnessed in our day. The only answer to it is destruction. The only way left of dealing with such people is by force, and so inevitably they end up by suffering violence themselves.

So what is there here for us? Firstly, we should be reassured that though terror campaigns take place, they are ultimately self-destructive. Secondly, we should be warned by the general principle involved here that if we will not submit to reason over any matter, if we refuse what is just (whether or not physical violence is involved), that is, if we *violate* justice, we can expect to receive back in like fashion.

Another principle is related to this, when we look at the opposite scenario. There is blessing for the peacemakers, for those who do what is just and right, who heed God's Word. It is they who will receive the benefit of their way of life, who will find good reciprocated to them. God has put a wonderful new principle in the hearts of his people which leads only to good. It is that good which is not afraid of those who refuse to do what is right; it is that good which rains down burning coals on the heads of the violent; it is that good alone which can destroy the violence of the wicked in a constructive and beneficial way (25:22; Romans 12:20).

21:8. Crooked and straight. Of the two people being compared here, one is guilty, probably burdened with guilt, while the other is pure, or clean, without the stain of guilt. This proverb seems to be looking at the way guilt or purity affect our way of life.

For someone to be guilty over something means they are deserving of a penalty on account of what they have done wrong, irrespective of whether or not they are aware of it. More often than not, though, they will be aware of it, and their misdeeds will trouble them unless they are suppressed.

That is precisely what many people do when disturbed about their wrongdoings – they try to push them out of their minds, or to rationalise them, or in some other way to prevent their coming back to haunt them. Perhaps it means they avoid certain company, or certain places which would remind them; perhaps it means seeking escape from their thoughts through alcohol or drugs; perhaps it means trying to compensate for their secret or not-so-secret wrongdoing by virtuous activity. Whatever they do, however, there is no way they can really and effectively overcome their awareness of guilt. It lurks in the background like a spectre. It is seen out of the corner of the eye. It poses a constant threat from which there is no escape.

A guilt-driven life is all wrong. A person with what is popularly called a guilt complex thinks and acts in relation to the sense of guilt. It is described as perverse, or devious, because it is essentially selfish and in any case cannot deal with the root problem.

Jesus exposed the deviousness of the Pharisees in Luke 11:39 when they sought to maintain an outward purity while inwardly they were full of greed and wickedness. They were being called upon to yield their hearts to God and then, Jesus indicated, they would be pure.

For the pure, who have no guilt, they can get on with their lives and do their work (in the widest sense of the word) without having to look over their shoulder in case someone should catch up with them concerning their past. They can concentrate on their work, for the work's sake rather than their own, in the knowledge that they are doing what is right.

But who is pure? Have we not all inherited Adam's guilt? Do we not all by nature try to cover our guilt and impurity with such fig leaves as we can find? Then is it not an amazing thing that we can be made pure? When God makes a guilty non-Christian into a Christian through faith in Christ, the guilt is removed, for its cause is dealt with once and for all at the cross. Not even the shadow of guilt remains to trouble the believer. For the first time in their lives, new born Christians know what it is to be pure in God's sight, and to begin with delight to do works of righteousness.

Do you remember such a time of being released from guilt? Are you still living in the good of it? Are you still filled with wonder that God should account you pure in his sight? Are you continuing to enjoy the glorious freedom to do what is right?

21:9. Exclusion and discomfort. Some things bear repeating. This proverb is repeated at 25:24. The nagging wife syndrome is so well known that there is an almost endless variety of takes on it. On the humorous side, it is an ever popular subject for cartoonists. On the serious side, there is a great deal of advice on how to deal with it (much of which is thoroughly unbiblical).

This proverb, though not without its humour, is actually making a serious point. Although the proverb refers to a 'woman', the context would seem to suggest that a wife is principally in view here. A wife who is contentious or quarrelsome or argumentative (and this would include nagging) spoils everything for her husband and taints his whole environment. Bearing in mind that the typical house had a flat roof, the comparison is made between living up there in one corner exposed to the elements and living in the house with the comforts of its accommodation and the company of family members.

Or the reference may be to the servants' quarters. Either way, the sense of exclusion and discomfort is very evident in stark contrast to how things ought to be.

This is another of the 'better ... than' proverbs where the better is rendered the worse on account some unwelcome element. Obviously it is better to live in a mansion than a hovel, but what if there are strings attached? Is a contentious woman enough to drive a man to prefer the latter if only he can get away from her? The answer is in the affirmative.

For men, the lesson is that it is better to get away from such a woman than to suffer an attitude where nothing is right for her, for no discomfort compares to that. The quip, 'Never argue with a woman,' certainly has some truth in it in this context. To become embroiled in contention with her is very likely to cause things to escalate out of control. Escaping the scene of contention may be the only viable option.

For women, it is a reminder of the damage such an attitude can do to a relationship. A woman's chief weapon is her tongue and she needs to understand its destructive as well as its constructive power.

What this proverb does not address are the causes for contention, nor does it apportion blame. It does, however, indicate that a woman who is contentious takes the enjoyment out of everything. It is an attitude which blights the relationship and will serve only to drive away the other party, and so will do no good whatever.

Perhaps what makes the situation so intolerable for a man is that it flies in the face of his God-given responsibility of headship in the relationship (1 Corinthians 11:3-12) and in effect points the finger at his failure in this respect, rendering him helpless and frustrated. For the woman, her contentious spirit flies in the face of her God-given responsibility of being her husband's companion and helper (Genesis 2:18) and is insidiously destructive of her true beauty and usefulness (1 Timothy 2:9-12; 1 Peter 3:1-6). It is a no-win situation for both, which will prevail until the root causes are dealt with by both before God.

If you happen to be in the unhappy position of personally identifying with the proverb, what steps do you (not the other party) need to take in order to restore harmony?

[Related proverbs: 19:13; 21:19; 25:24; 27:15-16.]

21:10. What do you crave? What this proverb says that the soul of a wicked person has a *craving* for evil. It is a kind of intense longing which demands to be satisfied. Our trouble is that we tend to recognise evil only when we observe it in its grosser features. We are too familiar with the caricature to recognise the real face. We need to be reminded that any desire which excludes the Lord is evil. If we do not want God interfering with our pleasures, then our pleasures are evil. If we do a 'good deed' but think there is no need to bring

God into this because we did it of our own volition, then our good deed is evil, for it honours self rather than God, the giver of *every* good and perfect gift. If our heart excludes, rather than welcomes, God's authority over it, then we are replacing what is good with what is evil, because we should be loving the Lord with all our heart, mind, soul and strength (Deuteronomy 6:5; Matthew 22:37).

A wicked person, who has no argument with himself about his behaviour or motives, is in a position where he cannot but crave evil. It is a terrible condition to be in. Life is ultimately about himself, his own needs and his own aspirations (whatever impression he gives to the contrary). He boasts of the cravings of his heart and God is in none of his thoughts (Psalm 10:3-4). Neighbours are all right if they serve his purposes but not if they have needs: they are going to receive no favours from him.

'You shall love your neighbour as yourself.' So says the Lord (Leviticus 19:18; Matthew 27:37). But here is someone who could not care less about his neighbour.

Our neighbours, let us remind ourselves, are those with whom we have been brought into some proximity in one way or another. By and large, we do not choose our neighbours, and some we may find it rather difficult to get along with. This gives all the more force to the command. We are not given the privilege of choosing whom we will love and whom we will not, whose good we will seek and whose we will not. When people run down others of their acquaintance and do not have a good word for them they are actually violating this command. This kind of thing goes on all the time, sending a clear, unambiguous message about the people who do it.

What is your attitude to the colleague at work who has been taken ill, or the young mother you see at the school gates whose husband has just lost his job, or the elderly man you so often see in his garden across the road who has recently been bereaved, or that other family you know who are torn apart by relationship problems? Are they none of your business? Do you reason it is not in your place to get involved? Or are these thoughts just trite platitudes to give you the excuse to keep your distance? *Why* does God say, 'You shall love your neighbour as yourself'?

When David's soul craved water from the well in his home town of Bethlehem (2 Samuel 23:15), then in enemy hands, and his men risked their lives to get it for him, he was filled with alarm that to satisfy his desires he had endangered the lives of others. He placed the welfare of others before himself.

Can you honestly say you have a craving for what is good? This can come only as we have a longing for God, for his name, for his honour, for his judgements (Isaiah 26:8-9).

21:11. Two forms of instruction. What is expressed here is very similar to 19:25. There is a strange and sad irony here in that it is not the one who is punished who benefits but those who witness it. The one who derides God's Word is putting himself beyond the reach of remedy for his condition. Did he but know it, by serving himself he is doing himself the greatest, and disastrous, disservice. In so doing, however, he may indirectly be serving others. An example of this is found at Deuteronomy 21:18-21.

Both a contrast and a progression are discernible in this proverb.

The contrast. A scoffer receives instruction like water off a duck's back. It does not even make him wet. When a wise person is instructed, he is receptive to it and it soaks into him. Your resilience or receptiveness to the Word of God is an indicator of the type of person you are. A scoffer on the receiving end of punishment may curse at it, but it will not soften him up, whereas a wise person on the receiving end of a profitable word will be sensitive to it and respond rightly, whether that word be painful or pleasant.

The progression. Punishment, even of others, can sometimes prove to be a wake-up call to foolish and impressionable people – 'simple' people in this sense. It is an unhappy situation where the proud and arrogant (see v. 24) are not called to account for their conduct, because it encourages others – the 'simple' – to follow them. Punishment can have a remedial quality for a third party. How many foolish and ignorant people have been stirred out of their sinful complacency when they have seen judgements fall upon others, realising with alarm that the same could so easily happen to them? As Isaiah so rightly said, 'When your judgements are in the earth, the inhabitants of the world will learn righteousness' (Isaiah 26:9). These things sharpen people's awareness that they need to get right with God. They may be motivated by fear, but even fear, if it drives them to the Lord, is a good thing – 'Chosen, not for good in me, wakened up from wrath to flee' (M'Cheyne). From this awakening the simple become wise enough to begin to receive instruction, and so grow in understanding and increase in wisdom. In other words, they fear the Lord, and, fearing him, they listen to him, and, listening to him, they heed him.

Then, to contrast this, Isaiah adds (26:10), 'Let grace be shown to the wicked, yet he will not learn righteousness.' There are some for whom judgement and punishment are the only option, even though it will not do them any good. The apostle Paul, troubled by the arrogance of some in the church at Corinth, asked them how they wanted him to come to him, whether with a punitive rod or with a spirit of gentleness (1 Corinthians 4:18-21). Discipline was needed in that church, not toleration of the wickedness which was present among them. Dealing incisively with the problems would instil some wisdom in the others and then the church could grow again.

We live in a world upon which God has lavished his grace. When we see his judgements it is because a gracious God deems them necessary, and we are not to complain but to fear, to seek him, to give the closer attention to his Word and so to grow in wisdom and understanding.

[Related proverb: 19:25.]

21:12. Psalm 37. Omniscient assessment, omnipotent action. Although God is not actually mentioned in this statement, it must be he who is referred to. He alone is the 'righteous one' who has authority to bring judgement upon the wicked. Other than him, only rulers are given this right of judgement, as his appointed agents for the punishment of the wrongdoer (Romans 13:4), and yet the term 'righteous' hardly applies to the majority of them.

The 'house' of the wicked denotes not so much individuals as a confederacy. A group or organisation has so much more power, influence and security. This was the philosophy of the original builders of the tower of Babel, and has been the thinking behind many subsequent large projects in which pride and self-sufficiency often feature so prominently. So when wickedness, that is, godlessness, is on the ascendancy in organised form in society, the godly may become very alarmed.

We see 'the house of the wicked' around us in many forms, and we may sometimes think that nothing is being done about it. This state of affairs is not new, but to think that nobody of influence is taking any notice is simply not true. God still has his finger on the pulse. The psalmist's observation (Psalm 37:35-36) has been repeated countless times through the course of history. It is true that the wicked sometimes acquire great power and even seem unassailable and invincible. It is equally true that just as often they are cut off, often by surprising means. If the wicked were truly in control the world would be a very sorry place. But God is in control, and it is for this reason that the psalmist can encourage believers not to fret and can assure them that their inheritance, unlike that of the wicked, will be for ever (Psalm 37:1,18).

It does not come out in all translations, but this proverb informs us that, more than simply overthrowing the wicked for their wickedness, God does so on the basis of intelligent consideration of what they are up to. He knows exactly what is going on. That he should allow wickedness to increase, when wickedness is defiance against him, is actually an indication that he intends to confound it by using it for his own purposes, not that somehow he has lost control of the situation. For example, how many people have become Christians while hearing the gospel under evil regimes who might otherwise in their complacency have given no attention to the message?

In a world under sin and its consequences we must *expect* all sorts of evils to occur for which we have no adequate explanation. That does not mean, however, that there *is* no reason or that God has no influence over them. He is very much in control. With infinite wisdom he uses the materials at hand to craft what he is making (compare Romans 9:19-24), and in the end the wicked, who thought to overthrow the righteous, will themselves be overthrown, together with all that is evil, and what remains will be good and glorious, his masterpiece complete in Christ.

To use another illustration, God uses the wicked like a catalyst which facilitates a reaction but does not itself change. Their presence serves his purpose in what he is making, and having done so they are removed, for they have no place in the finished product.

How does 1 Peter 3:12 reassure you, and how does it address your conduct in the world?

21:13. Psalm 112. He who has ears to hear... Our attitude to the needs of the poor receives a lot of attention in the Scriptures. It is a subject frequently revisited. There must be a reason for this. What do you think it is?

What are earplugs for? They are used to block out unwelcome, disturbing or damaging noise. Some people use them at night in order to sleep undisturbed by troublesome nocturnal sounds. God has made our eyes so that we can close them naturally when we do not wish to see, but he has wisely made our ears so that we cannot close them naturally against what we do not wish to hear.

The cry of the poor is a cry for help. To respond to any cry for help will almost inevitably inconvenience us (as in the parable Jesus told of the friend wanting bread, Luke 11:5-8). It is often a cry for help because every other avenue has been tried and come to a dead end. As has been mentioned before (at 14:31), by 'the poor' we are not to understand the term just of those who are poor materially. It refers to those who are lacking in some way, just as we refer to someone as having 'poor sight' or 'poor judgement'. These are deficiencies which, without appropriate help, render them vulnerable.

A cry is something which attracts our attention. The cry of the poor is not to be taken with crass literalism, but to be understood in much the same way as 'This new car is just crying out to be put through its paces.'

In Matthew 25:41-46 Jesus uses a parable of poverty in its various guises. The respondents' claim 'When did we see you hungry...?' was a hollow one, for Jesus would not have accused them had they not been aware of the need. Amazingly, he speaks of *himself* having been hungry, and so on, arguing that their neglect of those in need was a neglect of *him*.

From this we may infer that God takes it personally when we turn a deaf ear to the needy. God, who has compassion on the poor and needy, has brought their cry to our ears. There is a personal element in it. This is a cry which has come to our ears because it was *directed* to our ears. It is a cry which has penetrated our mind because it was *intended* to do so. Why so? That we might ignore it? That we might say it is someone else's responsibility? Is it not rather that we might respond to God, and minister to them in his name?

In Matthew 10:33 Jesus spoke of those who deny him being denied by him before his Father. That was not a threat but a statement of the inevitable. Denying him was to exclude him, and to exclude him was to eliminate any possibility of a relationship. How then could Jesus own a relationship which did not exist? Similarly, this proverb is not a threat: 'Do this or else.' A denial of the needs of others which we know they have will result in a denial of our own needs which we may not as yet be aware that we have. If God justly writes off those who refuse to obey him in listening to *his* cry to them through the poor, they have shut a sound-proof door on themselves. Contrast Psalm 41:1-2.

In James 2:15-16 we are directed to our responsibility to the poor 'on our doorstep'; likewise in 1 John 3:17-18. What God commanded in Deuteronomy 15:7,11 requires tenderheartedness, sensitivity, compassion. Have you thought of late of God's compassion toward you?

[Related proverbs: 19:17; 22:9; 28:27.]

21:14. Making amends. A statement like this is not made to justify or commend bribery, for God strictly forbids such practices – at least in the area of administering justice (Exodus 23:8; Deuteronomy 16:19). Then why is this here, and what has it to teach us?

Notice first that the two clauses are in parallel. The second emphasises the first and is expressed in more forceful language. The word 'gift' in the first clause would be innocuous enough were it not coupled with the word 'bribe' in the second, and the air of secrecy about the transaction shows that there is more to this than meets the eye! Notice, too, that the concealment of what is done is essential to its success, quite apart from the fact of bribery being against the law. This is a far cry from someone saying 'Sorry' to someone they have wronged and bringing a token gift to show their genuineness.

Someone has done something to make another person angry – very angry. The offended party has every reason to take matters further against the offender. What is to be done about it? The offender, or maybe friends of the offender, can find only one solution: 'gifts' to soften him up, and 'bribes' to buy him off.

Some kind of moral offence is typical of what leads to this reaction. But the gift or bribe appeals not to moral justice but to covetousness. Everything is wrong about it, just as what Jacob did in seeking to pacify his brother Esau whom he had defrauded was wrong (Genesis 32).

But doesn't this proverb say that it works? On the surface, maybe it appears to. People can be bribed to keep quiet or take no further action. Bribery might have done the trick, but the unease is still there. The anger may have been tamed but the hurt is still there. The problem has not been solved. A tamed lion is still a lion, and the tamer cannot afford to relax.

If people can be 'bought off', God certainly cannot. When you sin against God and give him just cause to be angry, how do you deal with it? Do you entertain any secret thoughts of doing something extra special to try to win back his favour?

When you sin against another Christian and you realise the extent to which you have upset that person, how do you deal with the matter? Reconciliation is to be sought privately, not on the basis of gifts and the like, but on the basis of Christian love and forgiveness. Dealing with a matter privately is quite different from dealing with it secretly and involving subversion. Whether the matter is personal or more public, the same principles apply: repentance followed by forgiveness (freely given) and reconciliation. Restitution may be needed in some cases to put certain thing right, but this is a far cry from gifts intended to pacify.

When wrong has been done and anger has been aroused, there is only one effective way of dealing with it. On the part of the offender this is genuine sorrow and a plea for mercy and pardon; on the part of the offended an unconditional willingness to forgive. It depends upon the response of both parties. God has set the lead in this, for none has just cause like him to be angry for all our sins against him. Yet he is willing to forgive fully and completely any who call on him in true repentance. We do not need to pacify his anger, we need to be at peace with him.

Do you have any relationships to repair? What tools are you going to use? [Related proverbs: 17:8; 18:16.]

21:15. Joy and justice. The first clause may be taken in two ways, both equally valid. It could be saying it is joy to the righteous either to see justice done (as NIV, ESV) or to do what is right and just (as NKJV). The two aspects dovetail together.

This joy is something no non-Christian can really understand, for it is the fruit of the Spirit (Galatians 5:22). Unbelievers may see the need for justice, they may even be relieved when justice is done, but the kind of joy expressed here is foreign to them. When it comes to their 'doing' justice themselves, it may be a matter of necessity, and it may even give some satisfaction as a duty performed and make them feel better, but it is not the kind of activity which generates joy.

Justice is associated with the just. God is just, and as judge of all the earth he will do right (Genesis 18:25). God is just and the justifier of the one who believes in Jesus (Romans 3:26). It is only those whom God has justified who are just, and it is only they who really understand what justice is. Because they are at peace with God through faith in Christ, they not only understand what justice is, they also appreciate it, and love it, and rejoice in it. See, for example, in Psalm 119, the great variety of ways in which the psalmist, who has 'done justice' (Psalm 119:121), expresses his delight in it and longing for it.

The performance of justice has a bearing upon the workers of iniquity – upon evildoers. It is a token to them of their destruction. The strict application of justice is bad news to them because a different principle is at work in their hearts and the two are incompatible. So in the final analysis, justice is a terror to them, for if justice prevails then they cannot but be destroyed. Far from a mere absence of joy, they are pervaded with a dreadful sense of foreboding at the prospect that justice may catch up with them and measure out to them what they deserve.

How wonderfully liberating it is to be made just in God's sight! Have you thought lately about the implications of this? What used to be a burden to you, to do justice, is now a joy – isn't it? What used to be a cause of anxiety to you, to be on the receiving end of justice, is now a cause of profound and happy thanksgiving because you know that justice has been done and your sins have been dealt with, and you are free to live to please God. The wages of sin is death, but the gift of God is eternal life in Christ Jesus our Lord (Romans 6:23). God's justice prevails in both cases.

Read 1 Peter 3:18 and consider the joy to God and the joy to you at the administration of such justice.

21:16. Wanderlust. How many parents have had that heart-stopping experience of discovering their child has wandered off into a crowd in a moment when their attention was distracted, and is nowhere to be seen! The youngster, taken by some attraction elsewhere, is blithely unaware of the dangers all around while the parents' imagination runs riot. The only safe place is at the parents' side.

For the Christian, the only safe place is in the way of understanding at the Father's side. The way is described as the way of *understanding*. Some people treat faith and understanding as if they were in some way in conflict; so that some, claiming to be acting in faith, have been led – or have wandered – into all sorts of trouble. At the heart of faith is obedience to God's Word, which one must understand in order to be able to obey it. The word used for understanding embraces instruction and knowledge, intelligent consideration and wisdom. The way of understanding *makes sense*!

Another feature of the way of understanding is that it is well marked. It is not like some public footpaths which are clearly signposted only so far, after which the walker is left bewildered about which is the correct continuation. Those who follow God's Word will not be left in the dark or without direction. Quite the opposite, the further they follow, the clearer the indicators.

Therefore to leave the way of understanding involves a deliberate disregard of the signs. 'Wandering from' aptly describes the aimlessness which results in straying into uncharted territory. The attractions and philosophies of this world are a confusing jumble of conflicting signs. They appear to lead in all different directions, but whichever route is chosen the end turns out to be the same: death. The assembly of the dead denotes a large number of people. They have all come to rest in the same morbid place. A bit like vehicles of all kinds and in various states of decay in a breaker's yard, they have one thing in common: they are all dead. Unlike a breaker's yard, there is nothing salvageable. It is a graveyard of ruin, a depressing sight when comparing what they are with what they were, what they are with what they might have been.

How sad it is that any should wander from the way which the Lord has so clearly marked out for us, the way which leads to life. It does happen, though. Yet all is not necessarily lost. Like the parent who goes in search of the wandering child, we should with compassion and concern go after those who wander from the truth in the hope of bringing them back. Read James 5:19-20.

21:17. Self-indulgence. Wine and oil here are indicative of festivities. One interpretation of this could be that those who love partying will not be rich, though we should not narrow it down only to that.

Well, who is there who does not love pleasure, or joy and gladness? Doesn't the psalmist say, 'You have put *gladness* in my heart...' (Psalm 4:7), and (Psalm 16:11), 'In your presence is fullness of *joy*, at your right had are pleasures forevermore'? Haven't we just read, 'It is *joy* for the just to do justice' (21:15)? In each case it is the same word translated 'pleasure' here.

The Westminster Shorter Catechism begins: 'What is the chief end of man?' And the answer is, 'Man's chief end is to glorify God, and to enjoy him forever.' The order is biblical and significant: it is out of the aim to glorify God that we then find our enjoyment of him. Those who make it their priority to enter into the enjoyment of God, noble though that may seem, are likely to be disappointed, for more often than not it is no more than just another subtle form of self-indulgence with an emphasis on happy experience more than pleasing God. It is not by enjoying him that we glorify him, but by glorifying him that we enjoy him.

So it is with this proverb. Pleasure is not something to be sought for its own sake, for is contingent upon something else. The world is full of pleasure seekers, many of whom are as a result extremely unhappy. Many pursue 'the good life' (a misnomer if ever there was one!) only to discover that it does not satisfy.

The pleasures and luxuries of this world come with a price tag. Those who pursue them are systematically impoverished. The 'prodigal' son soon discovered how much his pleasure seeking cost him, and he never found true pleasure until he came to his senses and returned to his father (Luke 15:11-32).

The poverty referred to in this proverb is not just monetary. It is far more than that. Not only do those who chase after pleasure and luxury soon find these things do not deliver on expectation, but they also are made poor in other ways, being starved of the qualities of character and experience which would have enriched their lives had their priorities been different.

Returning to the psalms quoted above, the gladness David experienced was given by God and arose out of his concern for godliness and righteousness and from his trust in the Lord (Psalm 4), while the joy he experienced in anticipation in Psalm 16 had its foundation in his singleminded commitment to the Lord.

Seeking the will of God is more important than seeking pleasures, and laying up treasure in heaven is more important than indulging in luxury on earth. The fruit of the Spirit – love, joy, peace – given to those who walk in the Spirit, is infinitely to be preferred to anything this world can offer.

21:18. Paying the price. This isn't the easiest of the proverbs to understand. A ransom price is paid to free someone. So if terrorists take hostages they may demand a ransom payment as a condition for setting them free, in which case someone has to pay the price.

Extending the illustration, how often are the righteous held hostage to the wicked, either literally or metaphorically, their movements restricted, their liberties curtailed, their services exploited? How many are incarcerated for no other reason than that they belong to the Lord? Are their persecutors simply going to be allowed to get away with it? Not at all, says this proverb, for they shall pay the price for their deeds and the righteous will be freed. It is the Lord who will exact the price from them in judgement, and it is he who will free his people.

There are illustrations of this in the history of the nation of Israel. When God redeemed his people from slavery in Egypt, who paid the price? Was it not the Egyptians who had been their oppressors, who had unjustly enriched themselves at Israel's expense? It cost them dearly. God exacted the payment from them to free his people. Again, when he freed his people from the seventy year captivity in Babylon, God uses the language of ransom in Isaiah 43:1-4. Babylon paid the price under God's judgement for the people's liberation. God had raised up these powers, and he brought them down again. The wicked were raised up by God, and having served their purpose were removed (Romans 9:17).

The big difference between the wicked and the righteous is that the latter belong to God, every one is precious to him. Nobody touches the least of them with impunity. The wicked, on the other hand, are expendable. What they hoped to gain at the expense of the righteous they will lose. Whatever they demanded will be exacted of them. There will be a price to pay, and they will pay it in full – and then be forgotten; whereas the righteous will be held in everlasting remembrance (Psalm 112:10,6).

Admittedly, there is a tension between what now is and what will be. To outward appearances the wicked are the dominant force in the world. The righteous do suffer, the upright and godly are persecuted. This has been the case from the beginning of time. If it were not the case there would be no need for a proverb such as this. The two clauses express a single truth and so emphasise it. It is given to reassure God's people that he watches over them for good, and that *all* things work together for good for those who love him. In a world of wickedness, injustice and suffering in which the godly generally have a raw deal, it nevertheless remains that the wicked will end with nothing, whereas the righteous will end with everything. Paul expresses the ultimate reality of this in 2 Thessalonians 1:4-10.

The wicked being a ransom for the righteous might turn our minds to the extraordinary opposite scenario, in which our righteous Saviour gave himself as a ransom for unrighteous men and women, redeeming them for his Father (Mark 10:45; 1 Peter 3:18). To free us from the bondage of sin God has himself paid the price in full in the blood of his beloved Son.

21:19. A contentious matter. This is similar to v. 9. The woman of v. 9 is contentious; this one is also in a very bad mood! What an awful woman, to drive a man to prefer to live in the desert! Well, maybe, maybe not.

Whether this is a husband-and-wife issue, or is more general, anyone who gets in the way of a woman in such a mood is liable to receive a verbal lashing!

Even to comment on this proverb is liable to be provocative! The reader is invited to consider the truth or otherwise of what is written and to extract from it what may be of benefit.

As in v. 9, this proverb is making an observation, not apportioning blame. Yet, describing a situation which should not be, surely it invites the thinking mind to look into causes and cure? Genesis 2:18-25 sets out the fundamentals of the status and nature of the relationship and should form the basis of any analysis.

The saying in jest, 'Never argue with a woman', contains more than a grain of truth. It is more often than not a fruitless exercise. When a bone of contention arises, a man may accuse his wife of being unreasonable, while she in her turn accuses him of not understanding. This view of each on the situation merely demonstrates that they are on different wavelengths, and as in such cases so often they are, little progress is going to be made.

Why ever does this level of discontent develop in a woman that she should become like this?

Within the family, the man carries the responsibility for leadership (1 Corinthians 11:3; Ephesians 5:23) and for the care of his wife (1 Corinthians 7:33; Ephesians 5:25). If his wife is contentious or angry this may very possibly reflect upon deficiencies in his God-given role as husband. For him to 'dwell with' such a person, perhaps even with a measure of resigned acceptance of an unhappy situation, is a clear indicator of failure. The 'hen-pecked' husband is a remarkably common sight, and a sorry one at that, portrayed by cartoonists as a stoop-shouldered, small man! Unknowingly, how accurately they are depicting his spiritual stature!

Who wants to live in an arid wasteland? To use the wilderness as a comparison, describing it as better than a relationship which ought to be one of mutual comfort, respect and care, shows just how devastating is the state of affairs in which a woman rules with an unruly tongue.

So, does this proverb reflect badly upon the contentious woman? Maybe, maybe not. Might it not at least equally reflect upon a negligent, selfish, and irresponsible man? Will such a man take up the reins again and conduct himself like a man, the way God intended?

[Related proverbs: 21:9; 25:24; 27:15-16.]

21:20. The beauty of riches. While there are different ways of looking at this proverb, they all boil down to the same thing: the husbanding or wasting of precious resources.

The focus of this proverb is first on what is found in the place where the wise live: not just treasure, but desirable treasure, the kind of treasure which others recognise as of real worth. The mention of oil seems symbolically to indicate joy accompanying it (see, for example, Psalms 10:15; 45:7; Isaiah 61:3).

It is this *same* treasure which is said to be squandered by a foolish person. How so? How can someone squander what belongs to someone else?

At a purely material level, like the son in the parable Jesus told (Luke 15:11-13) many a foolish son has rapidly squandered the wealth his father had over a long period of time built up through hard work and careful management. Just as descending a hill is so much quicker and easier than ascending it, so valuable resources can be dissipated far more easily than they can be acquired.

A foolish man might look longingly on what someone else has come to possess by dint of careful economy and imagine what he might do with it. 'If

I had such comforts and possessions I would be set up for life.' Not so, for he does not know his own heart. They would not last for any time; they would be wasted on him, for he would have no idea how to manage them.

The wise look after their resources, using what is put at their disposal to increase and add value to what they possess. Psalm 112 has been visited several times in these notes on Proverbs. It describes a wise man, a God-fearing man, who uses the wealth with which he has been blessed by God (Psalm 112:3) to benefit others (Psalm 112:5,9). While it is encouraging to see some people really appreciating such kindness and using well what they have received, it is also sad to note that others take and waste what they have been given and end up no better off than they were before. However prudent and careful one is about giving to others, there is an inevitability that some of it will be wasted.

Behind the material cloak which garbs this proverb is a more substantial truth. The wise are in themselves an attractive depository of treasure, for having and living in the fear and knowledge of the Lord it is their delight to be able to share of this treasure with others in giving spiritual counsel and sound advice about living. This is their real treasure, this is what is of overriding value. There will be those who will benefit enormously from their wisdom by making good use of it, whereas there will be others on whom it is utterly wasted.

What do we do with wise, spiritual counsel? Do we set great store by it, treasuring it and using it well, or do we go our *own* way, dismissing as foolish what is wise? A cat may have nine lives, but if it has not learnt anything after eight close shaves its doom is near. A man who repeatedly squanders God-given opportunities to repent and receive the treasure of his Son will sooner or later stand bankrupt at the bar of divine justice.

Jesus, priceless treasure, source of purest pleasure. 'In him are hidden all the treasures of wisdom and knowledge' (Colossians 2:3).

21:21. Have you found what you are looking for? Note that this is the language of pursuit; there is nothing indifferent or half-hearted about it. This is not for the person who thinks of righteousness and faithful, committed love as nice ideas. It is as Paul wrote to Timothy, urging him to 'Flee these things [harmful lusts] and pursue righteousness, godliness, faith, love, patience, gentleness,' and to 'fight the good fight of faith' (1 Timothy 6:11-12). 'Flee', 'pursue', 'fight' are imperatives, not options.

A lot of people seem to desire there to be righteousness in the world with little consideration for personal righteousness in themselves. They are wanting others to be what they themselves are not. A lot of people seem to lament the fickleness of the world around them, the hatred, the lack of love, the general level of unfaithfulness, while they themselves are far from being paragons of virtue in these very areas.

Again, many people think of righteousness and love as being poles apart, one cold, formal and forbidding, the other warm, kind and gentle; as if to have the one excludes the other. These are not biblical righteousness and love, for in God's sight only the truly righteous *can* love, and those who are truly righteous *will* love.

Jesus used two other strong words in connection with righteousness: hungering and thirsting after it (Matthew 5:6).

To have desires like this is not natural. Paul quotes the Old Testament's terrible indictment of man's sinful nature in Romans 3:10-18, and it is a prelude to his introduction of a God-given righteousness through faith in Christ.

The believer, with an imputed righteousness by faith in Christ, will desire to conform to that righteousness in life and action; and being a beneficiary of God's unmerited and faithful love in Christ will desire to respond also to that love in life and action. God having given us all things pertaining to life and godliness, we are, *with all diligence,* to add corresponding personal characteristics (2 Peter 1:3,5-7). The life of a Christian should be one of striving to perfect holiness in the fear of God (2 Corinthians 7:1; Hebrews 12:14). The New Testament is full of exhortations to leave behind what we were and to be what we are by grace, and this requires all the energy, strength, determination and discipline we can muster, the Lord enabling us.

Is it worth the effort? Of course it is! God's Word is as full of encouragements as it is of exhortations. The life, righteousness and honour that are to be found are precious gifts of God. Jesus spoke about giving life (John 10:10), and truly there is nothing which begins to compare with the life he gives to those who follow him. Then, with the pursuit of righteousness comes the enabling by the power of the Holy Spirit to live righteously. The honour spoken of is primarily being honoured by God as we seek to honour him (see 1 Samuel 2:30; John 12:26). It will not necessarily involve being honoured *by* men, nor should we expect that; but it will involve being honoured *in the sight of* men. The greatest honour we can know is to be honoured with the presence of God in our lives.

My soul rejoices to pursue the steps of him I love, till glory breaks upon my view in fairer worlds above.

[Related proverbs: 8:18; 12:28; 15:9.]

21:22. Pulling down strongholds. There is a very literal scaling of a city in 2 Samuel 5:6-8. The Jebusites were very confident that no one could get into their city, regarding it as impregnable. Yet David conquered it, not by a show of strength but by subterfuge. It provides an apt illustration of the point this proverb is making. More is accomplished by the application of wisdom than the use of brute force.

Jonathan and his armour bearer used the wisdom of God to scale the enemy ramparts in order to defeat their over-confident enemy (1 Samuel 14:1-23).

'Not by might nor by power, but by my Spirit, says the Lord' – and look what was accomplished thereby (Zechariah 4:6-7). With the wisdom to rely solely upon God and to act accordingly, what seemed humanly impossible was achieved. In that case it appeared to be building the temple rather than bringing down a stronghold, though on closer inspection it becomes clear that a mountain of opposition and other obstacles stood in the way of achieving the objective and a way had to be found to overcome them.

In the world today there are many trusted strongholds which stand in opposition to the truth and have been erected in defiance of God: other religions with their millions of faithful devotees; materialism with its narcotic deadening of the spiritual senses; atheistic humanism with its powerful backing of evolutionary dogma and modern Western scientific thought. Are these to be left alone and permitted to extend their influence? Then how are they to be overcome? By a show of strength on the part of Christians? That would be laughably ineffective. We can trust neither in our numbers which are pitifully small, nor in any human champions of our cause, who would simply be downtrodden.

These, and others, are strongholds which need to come down. There may also be strongholds of opposition in our own personal lives. The apostle Paul writes about the weapons of our warfare to deal with all such things being 'mighty in God' (2 Corinthians 10:4-5). He earlier had to remind the church in Corinth that the foolishness of God is wiser than men, and the weakness of God is stronger than men (1 Corinthians 1:25).

It is the wise, with God-given wisdom, who will be enabled to break through the most stubborn resistance. Do not be intimidated by the strongholds of opposition which vaunt themselves in this world. They are not impregnable. Do not be cowed by their appearance of power or be brainwashed into accepting their philosophies. Look to the Lord and his wisdom and you will find that even if these things still appear to stand, they will no longer have any hold over you, and as far as your own life is concerned they are defeated enemies.

We need grace to use the truth wisely so that it will penetrate rather than bounce off those who oppose it. Truth always undermines error and every false confidence however firmly held.

[Related proverbs: 8:14; 24:5.]

21:23. Keeping and keeping. Something similar is said at 13:3. There are some things that do not come automatically, and controlling one's tongue is one of them. We should note that James states that no man can tame the tongue (James 3:8), and while he says that an unruly tongue ought not to be (James 3:10), in this section of his letter he is pointing out the extent of the problem without (at least on the surface of things) offering any solution. The psalmist, in asking the Lord to set a guard over his mouth (Psalm 141:3), in the same breath asks for his heart to be kept from evil inclinations.

The two things we can extract from this are, firstly, that we need the Lord's gracious power to be applied to us to keep us from speaking wrongly, and, secondly, that what we say comes from the heart.

Returning to James, it becomes clear that the remedy for the tongue lies in the heart. There is only one way effectively to deal with your tongue, and that is by dealing with your heart, by submitting to God, as James says (James 4:7-8).

This does not mean that we should not give specific attention to guarding our mouths and tongues (for this Proverb implies that we should). Nor is this proverb suggesting we should guard them by not using them. Rather, we should use them thoughtfully and responsibly.

Do not skip over this part! Suppose you think for a few minutes about those occasions when your words have led to trouble (whether for you or for someone else). Would it not be true to say that in most cases a fault is traceable to your heart? Let us make some suggestions: might it be because of self-assertiveness, or pride, or conceit, or wanting your own way, or thoughtlessness, or insensitivity, or disregard for what is appropriate, or misplaced humour, or a failure to take the trouble to understand another person, or self-justifying overreaction, or unwillingness to admit you are in the wrong? Or it might be because of bitterness, or an unwillingness to accept a situation, or intolerance, or a desire for revenge?

The list goes on. The point of the exercise, though, is to see that in nearly every instance an examination of the *motive* for saying things which turn out badly reveals deficiencies within our hearts, a very evident lack of sanctification in certain areas. We will never be able to guard our mouths and our tongues if we fail to trace the words back to their source, humbling ourselves before God and praying about the specific faults to which they point.

If we are too full of ourselves this will be clear enough (at least to others) in the way we talk. It will lead only to trouble for us. This proverb focuses upon the negative, but that does not mean we should not at the same time consider the positive side. If we are full of grace and of the Holy Spirit this also will be clear enough to others in the way we talk. Not only will it keep us from trouble, but more especially it will have the effect of doing good to others.

Perhaps the best way to keep your soul from troubles is to have it set on being a blessing to others. With this at heart, your mouth and tongue will be guarded, that is, kept, for good use.

[Related proverbs: 12:13; 13:3; 18:21.]

21:24. An unpleasant character. This man (or woman, for women can be just as guilty of these attitudes) is the very antithesis of the person of the previous proverb.

He is proud. That is, he thinks of himself more highly than he ought. Other people do not really matter. His principal preoccupation is with himself and his own ideas. The word intimates more than this though, because it is used of those who oppose the godly. For the godly are perceived as a threat to them and to stand in their way by reason of their having a totally different philosophy of life.

He is haughty. As he thinks, so he behaves. He lifts himself up, elevating himself above other people. His words and actions are designed to emphasise his superiority. This is sheer arrogance. He has no actual right to such a position but gets there by 'bully-boy' tactics. It is not sufficient that he should elevate himself, for it can be achieved only by means of trampling the humble.

He is a 'scoffer'. That is the name given to him as an appropriate description of his character. The word indicates an aggressively scornful attitude to any who dare to suggest there is anything amiss with his thinking or conduct. In particular, it is descriptive of one cocking a snook at God and his laws. This indicates the extent of his arrogance.

His conduct is designed to instil fear. Acting with 'arrogant pride' uses a word which is so often used of the wrath of God. Here is a man who lets it be known – and demonstrates – that he will not hesitate to come down with a heavy hand on any who do not support him and his cause. He rules by fear.

Quite clearly this is describing a godless tyrant, whether it be one who rules over a nation, or one who exercises unauthorised power in a family. This is symptomatic of the 'control freak' who will not tolerate any questioning of his self-assumed authority.

Because some of these characteristics belong to their former nature, Christians – especially those in positions of leadership – should beware the signs of their resurfacing in any shape or form. Remember Ephesians 4:1-2.

Christians must expect to be on the receiving end of abuse from power-hungry proud and arrogant people. Pain and suffering are bound to come in one way and another. What is to be done about it? Remember 3:34, referring to the same class of people, and apply its principles – 1 Peter 5:5-7. Resisting the proud is really in God's hands, not ours. Our part is to conduct ourselves with humble disregard for their threats and with sincere trust in God. A godly life is a powerful weapon in God's hands.

21:25-26. A death trap. These two verses comprise a single proverb and they are dominated by 'desire'. The repetition of the word in the second part indicates an intensity of desire, a craving which is rendered the more intense by virtue of its being unsatisfied.

'A little hard work won't kill you!' But apparently inveterate laziness will. What we have here is the picture of a person whose unremitting and unfulfilled avarice is eating away at his soul and destroying him. The irony is that he has the remedy but will not apply it; that is, he will not apply *himself* to it.

This extreme case which has a kind of pathetic humour to it points to an all too common malaise in human nature. How many people have an objective but discover on the way that it is too much like hard work to fulfil it. So they go through life unfulfilled and bitter, not because they were incapable of achieving what they set out to do but because they were unwilling to make the effort and face up to the discipline and perhaps pain which would have been involved on the road to accomplishment.

In this proverb a lazy person is contrasted with a righteous one, indicating that laziness is unrighteousness. God made us to work, and therefore not to work when we are able is sin. God has given each one of us particular capabilities to be developed and used. To neglect them is sin.

Observe two particular points of comparison here. The first is that the lazy man is preoccupied with himself and with satisfying his own desires.

His concern is with *getting*. The righteous on the other hand is thinking about others and meeting their needs. His concern is with *giving*. The second comparison is implied: the lazy man remains frustratingly unfulfilled, whereas the righteous one gains satisfaction from his giving (for he does not spare, or hold back). The lazy man is unsatisfied because of what he fails to get; the righteous one is satisfied because of what he is able to give. The former, through refusing to work, fails to meet his own needs; the latter, by his diligence, not only provides for himself but has plenty 'left over' (though he would not view it that way) with which to bless others.

Sad to say there are some professing Christians who hanker endlessly after God's blessing upon their lives yet live in a state of perpetual dissatisfaction. When one looks into it they are discovered to be spiritually bone idle. They do not study God's Word, they do not think about developing gifts God has given them or serving others. All they want is that comfortable 'feel good' experience. James has a pithy comment on this kind of attitude in James 4:1-4 – coveting in order to serve one's own pleasures.

Labour, or hard work, is commended in the New Testament (Acts 20:35; Romans 16:6,12; Colossians 4:13). Those mentioned worked hard not for reward but for the love of blessing others in the Lord's name. They in turn were amply blessed!

Reflect upon any unfulfilled desires you may have. Are they unfulfilled because they are wrong? Are they unfulfilled because you are unwilling to do your part in working toward them? Or are they unfulfilled while you are actively waiting upon God that they might be fulfilled?

Reflect upon your giving. What are your motives for giving? Are you working hard in order that you might be able to give something to be of benefit to others?

[Related proverbs: 11:24; 13:4; 19:24; 26:15.]

21:27. Buying God off. The notion of slaughtering an animal and offering it as a sacrifice may be foreign to us, but to the Old Testament Jew it was well understood as essential to being in favour with God (to put it rather crudely). Leviticus 4:27-31 gives some idea of what it was all about. From even a cursory reading of the Old Testament it is clear that sacrifices formed an integral part of national life.

Perhaps the nearest we come to it is in celebrating the Lord's Supper. Though this is not a sacrifice in itself, it is a remembrance of a sacrifice – that of Jesus Christ upon the cross for sin, the one sacrifice to which all the sacrifices and offerings of the Old Testament pointed. To come to the Lord's Table with a wicked heart is also an abomination. There are many who imagine that by simply partaking of the Lord's Supper their sins will be forgiven and they will be 'all right' with God. They come to the Lord's Table with a sense of compulsion that this is something they must do to gain acceptance with God and to keep in his good books. If they take communion regularly, their thinking is that all will be well for them. It does not matter how they live between times, so long as they avail themselves of this means of pardon and acceptance. This is blind superstition and a gross abuse of the Supper.

In 1 Samuel 3:14 we see there was nothing automatically effective about the offering of sacrifices. In 1 Samuel 15:22 we learn that there was something which must precede the offering of sacrifices if they were to be meaningful in God's eyes. In 2 Samuel 15:12 we observe Absalom 'going through the motions' to give a good impression while all along with wicked heart he was conspiring against his father. In Isaiah 1:10-15 God talks of the abomination of the people offering sacrifices when their hearts were dead set against his laws, as if they could appease him with these things and carry on regardless. Amos 5:21-24 speaks in similar vein.

There is always the subtle temptation to make what we *do* the means to gain acceptance with God. How many people talk of 'making sacrifices' (the word being used here in a completely different way) and imagine that this will earn them merit before God? They may not put it in those precise words, but it amounts to the same thing.

The only way the sacrifices of the Old Testament were accepted by God was when those offering them came with a right attitude, confessing their sins, with reverence and humility. Likewise, the only way the sacrifice of the Lord Jesus upon the cross is efficacious for any is when they come to him in true repentance, in submission, in faith, looking to him to do for them what they cannot do for themselves.

The sacrifice of the wicked is all about what they do to gain acceptance with God. That is an abomination. The only sacrifice acceptable to God is that of his Son upon the cross, and the only way we can be accepted by him is to acknowledge that it is all about what he has done, and not at all about what we can do. We must come with nothing in our hands, that we may embrace him by faith and then go on with him through life.

[Related proverb: 15:8.]

21:28. An enduring testimony. By adding the word 'him' ('the man who hears *him*') the NKJV introduces an interpretation which is probably unwarranted. In following a similar line the NIV translation seems to go even further out on a limb. This proverb is not concerned with a man who hears a false witness. Eric Lane in his commentary brings out the meaning clearly, and he does so simply by rightly focusing upon the points of comparison between the two clauses. The false witness is compared with the man who hears. The former is one who gives evidence on the basis of what he has *not* heard – he is a false witness; the latter speaks on the basis of what he *has* heard – he is a true witness. Then, 'perish' is compared with 'continuing speaking'. The false witness will perish, and his words will perish with him, but the words of one who hears and testifies accurately will endure.

So much for the meaning. What does it have to teach us? The ninth commandment says, 'You shall not bear false witness against your neighbour' (Exodus 20:16). The Ten Commandments were given by God as a fundamental and foundational expression of what he requires of the whole of humanity in relation to him and to one another. It follows that those who are found to be in breach of the ninth commandment will inevitably suffer his judgement and will perish. However, this also operates at a secondary level. Sooner or later, the testimony of a false witness is invariably discredited, and then he too is discredited. Often, sadly, his false testimony is found to have done much harm in the meantime, and then its exposure rebounds upon him with serious consequences. Ultimately, false testimony is universally recognised as undermining of any kind of trust, and it is treated accordingly.

A false witness is not concerned with the truth, only with what is of advantage to him (in the widest sense) when he speaks. Therefore whether by speaking or by keeping silent about something he is attempting to create an impression in other people's minds which suits him rather than seeking to express the truth impartially. There is a world of difference between 'I want them to think that...' and 'I want them to understand that...'.

It is those who are wrapped up in themselves who are most likely to give false testimony. People who are self-centred are on very dangerous ground. They are less inclined to hear accurately and more inclined to speak inaccurately. A little falsehood can undermine a lot of truth. By contrast, the person who has a genuine interest in the welfare of others is much more likely to listen and take the trouble really to hear what is being said. His reporting is then true and balanced, and as a result of his integrity he earns the right to speak and is more than willing to be heard.

There is an emphasis in John's Gospel on accurate testimony with the intention that people might believe in the Lord Jesus Christ (John 21:24; 20:31). But note in particular what Jesus says at John 5:30. His hearing was accurate (and therefore his judgement was right) because his concern was to do his Father's will. It is when our primary concern is to do the will of God our Father that we will hear in a proper way both his Word and what others say, on the basis of which we will speak and earn the right to go on speaking with none to shut us up!

[Related proverbs: 19:5,9.]

21:29. Psalm 37:34-38. Hiding nothing. As in the previous proverb, a careful comparison between the clauses brings out the meaning.

'Hardening the face' has really to do with putting on an impressive exterior. The NIV translates this nicely as putting up a 'bold front'. It is a bit like those big shop fronts seen from the street behind which is little more than a small shed. Others might be impressed by what they see, little realising what lies behind (or rather, what does not lie behind!). There used to be a popular panel game in which those taking part were required to provide the meanings of obscure words given them. A participant might not have the faintest idea of what the given word meant but would endeavour to bluff others with an eminently plausible definition. This is the way of a person who has no fear of God. He has no real idea of what he is doing or where he is going but does everything he can to present a plausible front.

The contrast is with the upright person who 'establishes' his way. The translation 'gives thought to' is weak. The proverb is presenting a strong contrast to the front put up by the wicked.

First of all, unlike the wicked, the upright person *has* a 'way'. He is on the narrow way which leads to life. The wicked person is going nowhere. He does not even have a 'way', for in his own mind he has no real destination. His life is all show and no substance. He has nothing behind him in the sense of backing him up, and he has nothing ahead of him for which ultimately to live, and in every sense he is living a lie. The way he hides this is by brazening it out.

Secondly, root, shoot and fruit, the upright person is *establishing* his way. He is grounded in faith in Christ, he is growing in knowledge and understanding, and his way of life bears out what he is in a consistent fashion. He has real stature, for his life is built not upon the empty philosophies and ideas of godless men but upon the truth as it is in Jesus.

Look at Psalm 37:35-36. Believers need not fear verbose and influential unbelievers who arrogate themselves against God. Nor need they fear their dogmas. For all their plausibility there is actually nothing behind them. They may be persuasive, they may shout about their knowledge and ability and scorn those who have other ideas. But never forget: whatever they think they have, they do not have the truth.

Kidner, concise as ever, says: 'The proverb shows that a bold front is no substitute for sound principles.' This applies to Christians, too. Some can be very persuasive in promoting their own pet theories, unwilling to subject them to close scrutiny.

How well are you established on the way that leads to life?

21:30. Romans 11:33-36. Effectively ineffective. For some this statement can be extremely disturbing, while for others it is inexpressibly comforting. Had this been written of anyone other than the Lord we would have genuine cause to fear. How many a dictator has put down with ruthless efficiency any wisdom, understanding and counsel which is a threat to him. The proverb, however, is not putting God on a par with those despots or indicating he will crush every form of opposition whatever its value.

We need to understand that there simply *is* no wisdom or understanding or counsel against him. Effectively it does not even exist. Believers need to be reminded of this constantly, living as they do in a world which is hostile to God and has created a vast array of intellectual weapons which are trained upon him and which often give anxiety to his people.

Wisdom. In Christ are hidden *all* the treasures of wisdom and knowledge (Colossians 2:3). Paul reminded his readers of that because there were deceivers with persuasive words. He was very well aware of their plausibility, but they achieved that by shifting the focus away from Christ and presenting a distorted view of life. That was the only way they could gain a following. In writing to the church at Corinth Paul, with scathing precision, cuts worldly wisdom down to size (1 Corinthians 1:21-25). There is no wisdom, no philosophy, no world view which can even begin to compete with the Lord, not because he will put it down but because it is false and contains the seeds of its own destruction.

Understanding. Isaiah declares of the Lord, 'His understanding is unsearchable (Isaiah 40:28). From v. 12 of that chapter he compares the sovereign creator of the ends of the earth with all the cleverness of man – or rather shows there is no comparison whatever. Modern western science contests this, claiming to have an understanding which denies that God created the world as he says he did. It is an understanding which is based upon false assumptions, and though it is continually being shown to be flawed nevertheless it has its followers by the million.

Counsel. How many people would like to tell God what he ought to be doing or how he ought to be going about it! They think they know better! We can be thankful to God that they will not prevail! One sinister way in which such counsel manifests itself is in opposing God's laws. For example, in contravention to the seventh of the Ten Commandments sexual experimentation is encouraged as a healthy thing to free people from 'unnatural' inhibitions, or a day devoted to the worship of God is discouraged as being a waste of time at best or as fettering people with narrow-minded notions at worst.

Isaiah prophesied of Jesus: 'The Spirit of the LORD shall rest upon him, the Spirit of wisdom and understanding, the Spirit of counsel and might, the Spirit of knowledge and of the fear of the LORD' (Isaiah 11:2).

Although anti-God wisdom, understanding and counsel may seem to prevail in this world, it will not do so against God. Like the bold front put on by the wicked (21:29), it may seem to be fearfully powerful and have countless adherents, but in reality it is devoid of substance. God is still in control of the world he created. The Word of God has stood the test of millennia and will continue to do so until the final showdown.

[Related proverb: 19:21.]

21:31. Preparation and providence. It was Cromwell who said, 'Trust in God and keep your powder dry.' Of much older origin is the saying, 'God helps those who help themselves.' Whatever we make of these and similar sayings, it is true that in any situation of conflict there is man's part and there is God's part, and for us to dispense with either is folly.

To take an extreme case, there is a famous 'battle' recorded in 2 Chronicles 20 in which Jehoshaphat and his army raised no weapon against the enemy which was routed by the Lord. Nevertheless the army were still required to turn out and confront their enemy in battle array and to be ready for action.

Throughout the history of Israel, it was when they trusted in the Lord that they enjoyed victory over their enemies, indicating that it was God's doing that they were successful. Back in David's time, Jonathan showed initiative and displayed wisdom and boldness in the use of his slender resources, trusting God to show him the way, and was thereby instrumental in achieving a great victory which would never otherwise have been dreamt of (1 Samuel 14).

The apostle Paul spoke in the same breath of his working and of God working in him (1 Corinthians 15:10-11; Colossians 1:29). Nevertheless, he attributed the success solely to God (1 Corinthians 3:5-7).

When Jesus fed the five thousand, he could have produced bread from stones. However, the lad with the five barley loaves and two small fish had the privilege of seeing what the Lord could do with the little he had to offer (John 6:9-13).

It is a principle of God's operation that he is pleased to use means. This proverb is not for a moment suggesting that because deliverance is of the Lord it is pointless preparing the horse for the day of battle.

This leaves us with a number of questions.

Firstly, we are all familiar with situations of conflict of one kind and another in our life and experience. Are we bringing to these situations both our plans and our prayers? One without the other simply will not do. Do we think carefully about how we might be able to resolve problems while earnestly relying upon God to see us through?

Secondly, are we exercising initiative in our conduct in a hostile world, seeking to confront the enemies of the gospel rather than ignore them; seeking to bring the gospel to those who are yet the enemies of Christ? God has equipped each of us for our part to play in this, and however inadequate we may feel it to be, it is sufficient in his hands for success and victory.

Thirdly, do we ever think, when problems arise, 'I can handle this myself'? Small difficulties can turn out to be surprisingly big when we think we do not particularly need to trust the Lord. At the opposite extreme, beware of the notion, when problems arise, that 'The Lord will sort this out' as an excuse for not using means he has placed within our power. We can hardly blame God when things go wrong, arguing that we have trusted him alone, when we have left in the stables the horses he has provided for us.

22:1. Bettering oneself. If you had the choice, what would it be...? We live in a world in which wealth and prosperity are eagerly sought and highly esteemed. God tells us not that these things are necessarily unimportant but that there are other things which take priority over them. Here in this proverb are two: a good name and loving favour.

But do we have any choice in the matter? Certainly we do. So many people intent to 'better themselves' think purely in monetary terms. They want to be 'better off', they covet things other people have and strive toward the position in which they can attain them. Even if they never achieve their goal, it is an energy-consuming preoccupation with them; and if they do, often they do not find themselves really better off than they were before.

Though you may never be in a position to be able to choose riches for yourself except in flights of fancy, when it comes to name and favour you do have a choice.

Name. Reputation is involved here, and, by comparison with the second clause, it is a good reputation. Everyone has a reputation of sorts. When your name crops up on other people's tongues, what is their perception of you and what is the part you have played in providing them with it? Let us make it more concrete with a couple of examples. Luke 7:1-10 records an incident concerning 'a certain centurion'. A member of the Roman occupying force, his situation would have had little to endear him to the Jews. Pick out from the narrative *three qualities* about the man which contributed to his good reputation among the Jews, and ask if these three qualities are in any measure to be found in you. Next consider Dorcas (Acts 9:36-43). You will have to read between the lines to understand why she was held in such affection from others. What part did her skills play in this?

Favour. To get a handle on this word (a better word than 'esteem', NIV), we read that Noah found favour, or grace, in the eyes of the Lord (Genesis 6:8). While on the one hand we could argue this was completely unmerited, on the other we see that Noah was responsive to God's word to him and persevered in obedience over many years in the face of the considerable discouragement of the unbelief all around him. In so doing he remained in God's 'good favour'. If you have received God's unmerited favour in saving you from your sins, are you responding by seeking to keep yourself in his favour by the obedience of faith to which he calls you, recognising this is of far greater worth than silver and gold or all this world can offer? Two connected evidences of this response are seen in 1 John 5:21 and Jude 21.

In the light of this, what principles apply to gaining and retaining the right kind of favour among men also? We read of Jesus, that he increased in wisdom and stature, and in favour with God and men (Luke 2:52). How did he do this, and in what respects are you making the same choices?

[Related proverb: 3:4. See also Ecclesiastes 7:1.]

22:2. God our Maker – whoever we are. The rich and the poor seem to have so little in common. They are usually poles apart in comforts, in status, in privileges, in opportunity, and often in dignity. The rich often neglect the poor, disparage them, look down on them, deny them, exclude them, blame them for their poverty and often consider it a waste of time and money to try to help them – in short, they oppress them. In the eyes of both there is a great divide.

There is a tendency among men for those who are well off consider themselves to be superior to those who are less well off, and, likewise, for those who are poor to consider themselves inferior to the rich. This has been reflected in all the distinctions of class which have plagued our society in the past and to some extent still do. The rich often possess a false self-esteem based upon what wealth has provided for them, while the poor often consider themselves worthless – attitudes which are damagingly detrimental to both. This artificial divide has always existed, and probably will always do so. With pithy irony James checks such attitudes (James 1:9-11).

Why does this proverb make a statement which is so patently obvious? Is it not because the obvious so often is overlooked or ignored? Is it not because its implications are not considered? At a stroke this simple statement cuts across all the distinctions made by men based on wealth or social status. It reminds us of a great fundamental truth which places rich and poor and everyone between on an equal footing. If the Lord is the maker of all, then in reality the rich and the poor have everything in common: both rightfully belong to the Lord and are answerable to him. In his eyes the richest and best educated people on earth are essentially no different from the illiterate pauper who is reduced to begging. We brought nothing into this world, and we can carry nothing from it. As we came into this world by the will of God, so we shall leave it according to his same will. If God does not esteem our wealth, neither should we.

It is not uncommon for people to kowtow to their superiors and kick their inferiors. What right have we even to think in terms of superiority and inferiority in the way so many do? We are not to measure people by the yardstick of earthly status, nor are we to conduct ourselves before them with this principally in mind. The tendency to partiality based on wealth can also afflict the church, and James warns against such an attitude (James 2:1-4). We are to give respect to whom it is due, likewise honour (Romans 13:7), but this is far removed from behaving as if they are somehow different from the rest of mankind.

It is on the basis of our common humanity that the law says we are to show no partiality in judgement (Leviticus 19:15; Deuteronomy 1:17; 10:17), and this embraces our attitudes to one another.

Christian responsibility extends toward rich and poor alike. All need to hear the gospel, all need to bow to the lordship of Christ. Some may be better off or worse off in the eyes of the world, but there is no difference in the eyes of the Lord, who looks not on the outward appearance, but on the heart.

[Related proverbs: 14:31; 17:5; 29:13.]

22:3. Have your eyes open. Out in the mountains a group are looking apprehensively at the subtle changes in the sky and agree with some reluctance that it is time to change their plans and head for shelter. Not far away another group carry on unawares until they find themselves enveloped in a fearsome storm…

Both groups should have known of the potential dangers of walking in the mountains, but only one took the matter seriously. Both groups should have been on the lookout for tell-tale signs of trouble ahead, but if the second group noticed anything at all they treated it with a foolhardy bravado.

People may go into hiding, or lie low, for all sorts of reasons, the most obvious being when they perceive their life to be under threat. They do not wait until they are face to face with the danger, for then it is very likely too late for them to do anything about it.

There was even an occasion when Jesus hid himself (John 8:59). Foreseeing the danger he slipped away through the crowd before the scene could turn ugly, for he still had work to do.

Fleeing and hiding are two related things. The element of flight is not present in this proverb because the evil, or danger, is recognised in advance so that it does not become an emergency situation.

For most of us there are no life-threatening dangers on the horizon. However, what is spoken of here is usually translated 'evil' and there are certainly many evils on the horizon. 'If I had seen this coming, I would never have...'. Evil often relies on the power of temptation, and temptation often relies on the element of surprise. 'Hiding' means keeping out of striking distance. With these things in mind, the proverb takes on a whole new dimension.

We all have areas of weakness, and where we are most vulnerable we need most to be protected, usually by shutting the door against temptation and keeping ourselves hidden from it. It is no bad thing breaking out into a cold sweat thinking about what could happen if that helps us keep out of harm's way. This could be applied to such things as friendships which could prove to be a bad influence; or the enticements of pornography; or illicit sexual attraction; or the dangers of alcohol; or the sinister effects of greed. All these things and others besides can have a ruinous effect upon life.

Think of occasions when you have been overcome by temptation. Could you have foreseen it? If so, how? Why did you not? Are there any areas of your life where you are vulnerable? (The answer should be in the affirmative!) In what ways are you being proactive to protect yourself? It may be you need to arm yourself against the dangers and face them. On the other hand, it may be better to follow the advice of this proverb and remove yourself as far as possible from the danger.

Trusting in the Lord is not incompatible with hiding. Often that is the way he would have us keep out of trouble. Sometimes when people fall, they ask why God did not deliver them. Usually one of two answers is patently applicable: either they didn't foresee the danger because they weren't keeping close to the Lord; or they did see it and should have had the sense to get away from it but allowed themselves to be enticed.

[Related proverbs: 14:16; 27:12.]

22:4. Inseparable companions.

Humility and the fear of the Lord are so closely connected that there is no 'and' in the original. One cannot really fear the Lord and not be humble. To know how great God is, to be aware of the perfection of his being, to recognise how dependent we are upon him, to have consciousness of the riches of his grace toward us in Christ – how shall this knowledge not instil in us a reverent fear and make us aware of our lowly, though greatly privileged, position? True humility not only abases self, it also exalts the Lord.

Neither can one be truly humble without the fear of the Lord. Humility defers to others in an appropriate fashion and properly esteems them. Then how can anyone really be humble without proper regard for the Lord who made them and without giving him due honour?

It has to be said that humility does not come naturally. Ever since the fall, people have been afflicted with a self-centred, self-sufficient, and self-assertive arrogance: they want the universe to revolve around themselves, they want to be independent, and especially independent of God's interference in their lives. Christians, though saved by God's grace and having new principles of conduct, have no reason to be complacent in this area. Perhaps this is why Peter says we are to be 'clothed' with humility (1 Peter 5:5), and why Paul says it is one of the things to be 'put on' (Colossians 3:12). People give thought to what they wear, and especially that they might be clothed appropriately for particular occasions. Humility is modest but serviceable garb. It does not draw attention to itself or, for that matter, its wearer. It may not be the height of fashion, but if others are going to be comfortable around you it is the best thing you can be wearing. It is also why Peter says we are to 'humble ourselves' under the mighty hand of God. It is something to which we need to give deliberate attention for the very reason that it does not come naturally.

In this topsy-turvy world riches, honour and life are not the things people would associate with humility and the fear of God. But in this topsy-turvy world people's concept of riches, honour and life are far removed from the biblical meaning of these words. Yet, as has been observed before, because we are living in God's world, the principles upon which he has established it can never be completely eradicated by wicked men, and so it is that even in this life godly men and women tend to prosper in every sense of the word.

However, give some thought to these words – riches, honour and life – and what they mean to Christians. Here are just a few random biblical references as pointers: Philippians 4:19; 1 Timothy 6:17; Hebrews 11:26; 2 Corinthians 8:9; 9:11; 1 Samuel 2:30; Psalm 112:3,9; John 12:26; Psalm 36:9; John 10:10.

To be rich in grace, to be honoured by God, to have life in his Son – are not these of incomparable worth to anything that goes by these names in this world? True riches, honour and life do not come automatically as an inevitable outworking of humility and the fear of the Lord, as if by doing certain things these results will follow. They are a gracious gift from the Lord, based upon his rich promises, received by faith, accepted with thankfulness, and rendered up again with praise.

[Related proverbs: 3:16; 8:18; 15:33; 18:12; 21:21.]

22:5. Avoiding two evils. Thorns tear and injure; snares entrap, bringing their victims into bondage. These are said to be in the way of the perverse. A number of words are used to denote a wicked person, but this one emphasises deviousness and crookedness. Perversity is a meaningless term unless there is a standard against which it can be measured. Crooked is not straight, and so straightness defines crookedness. The standard is God's law, whether written or natural. To deviate from such a standard is perverse. When people do away with God's laws, whether of commandments or nature, they have dispensed with the standard by which to regulate their lives. Having then no standard, they may object when others talk about perversity and they may say their lifestyle is just as acceptable as anyone else's. This is the situation which has come to prevail in much of the western world.

However, one thing remains unfailingly true for them: there is no escaping the thorns and snares. Perhaps in thorns and snares we should see two aspects of the harm done to the perverse.

Thorns were introduced at the fall (Genesis 3:18) and have ever since been a painful reminder of the result of man going his own way. Straying from the 'straight and narrow' way that leads to life inevitably means being torn by 'thorns', whether it is the sickness or disease caused by overindulgence or substance abuse, or the oppression of guilt caused by abusing others in some way. Thorns are the natural causes of affliction for perversity. In a sense, at least for people with their eyes open, these are fairly obvious.

Snares, on the other hand, are man-made devices, are usually well concealed, and are therefore the more sinister. Those who indulge in perverse practices sooner or later find themselves ensnared by other people and held mercilessly under their power. Others will use and abuse them. Threats may be held over their heads, or they may live in crippling fear over what others could and might do to them. While people are carefully negotiating the thorns, they often fail to see the snares.

A sign encountered in the woods reads, 'Beware! Traps have been set in the undergrowth for vermin. Keep to the right of way.' The right of way was the right way in any case, and to stray from it was the wrong way. So in a sense the warning was redundant. How graciously God has provided warning notices like the one of this proverb to remind us that there are dangers out there, even though we know we should never be straying 'out there'! Keeping to the right of way, walkers were completely safe, for although danger might have lain within just a few feet of them, being on the path meant they were so far from it that there was no possibility of harm for them. So it is for believers who walks by faith in the way marked out by God. Their soul will come to no harm. Having a healthy fear of what lies off the path will help keep them focused upon obedience to their Lord. Consider Deuteronomy 28:14 in context.

[Related proverb: 15:19.]

22:6. Preparation for life. Children grow up fast! The period from infancy to adolescence is often referred to as the formative years, and for good reason. Good parents will use the time to mould and influence their offspring in the way they should go, preparing them with principles and seeking to develop in them strength of character which will see them safely and productively through life. Training is a term which has both a method and an end in view. Lack of these on the part of parents where their children are concerned will leave them at the mercy of their own sinful nature and the harmful influences of an ungodly society.

The Proverbs lay great stress on the training of children, approaching it from all angles. Consider what is involved in training. Fundamentally, there is instruction (4:1-2). The teaching of the Word of God should permeate every aspect of a child's development, not just be left to a corner of the day with a 'Bible story'. Thus the Scriptures should be brought to bear naturally on a child's thoughts, attitudes, actions, questions, needs, circumstances, and so on – and always in a manner appropriate to their developing understanding. Love is at the heart of it, and although it is not explicitly stated in Proverbs, it is implicit in 3:12 and evident throughout. This gives context to the punishment aspect which recurs in the book (3:11-12; 13:24; 19:18; 22:15; 23:13; 29:15), showing that it is invariably a necessary part of training because 'foolishness is bound up in the heart of a child' (22:15). Because we are sinful by nature, corrective influences of all kinds are required, sometimes painful – and painful not only to the recipient but also to the one administering the correction. If God so deals with his own children in love (John 15:2; 2 Timothy 3:16; Hebrews 12:5-11) then we must not shirk this necessary aspect when the need arises. But corrective influences, if they are to be worthy of the name, must contain the positive element of instruction as well as the negative one of discomfort.

Another vital aspect of training is example. Parents provide a role model for their observant children; they lead by example (4:11). There can be no place for dual standards and unrealistic expectations. Good parental example tends to strengthen the family bonds and gives meaning and substance to the instruction which children will recognise and respect.

Then there is the time aspect to training. In short, it is *all* the time. Development is a continuous process, each stage of which presents unique opportunities. Obviously a young infant will not be able to respond to reason, but has to be shown what is right and wrong by physical influence, and the verbal instruction which may accompany this will be understood in due course. Reasoning follows later. There is always something new in a child's development, providing the occasion to bring appropriate instruction to bear. Above all, there should be a relationship in which the lines of communication are always open. The reason this rapport is so often lacking between parents and their children is that the earlier aspects of training have been neglected. It then becomes so much more difficult to remedy the situation.

This proverb is accompanied by an observation. Of course there are some children who will rebel against all that is good in their upbringing and go off the rails. But make no mistake, they are the exception rather than the rule. Nearly always the human cause of such disasters can be traced back to negligence in their upbringing. Again, nearly always the people who are outstanding examples of godly and productive living have come from homes where the Word of God has been held in high esteem and lived out and applied. They are living proof of the validity and importance of this proverb.

22:7. The power of money. The words used in this proverb are in the singular, focusing on individuals. This proverb is not concerned with government, though some of the principles involved extend to that. Consider why it is that a rich person 'rules' over a poor one, that is, why he exercises influence over his life and to some extent determines what the poor person shall or shall not do. Is it necessary? Is it just? Is it simply inevitable? What are the factors involved which cause it to be so?

It is good to ask questions like this in order to distinguish what is relevant from what is purely incidental. Why does one so often have to have money to have clout?

There are two significant factors (though there are others) which often play a part in this. They are *need* and *greed*. The second clause which parallels the first brings out the aspect of need and dependence. It is ironic that a poor person, who is the least able to repay, should sometimes have to borrow in order to provide for the necessities of life. He thereby places himself under obligation to the lender, which in the worst case scenario can end up as a form of slavery.

The greed (covetous) aspect can frequently be seen on both sides, for 'poor' people can sometimes bring themselves under obligation to 'rich' people in order to get something for themselves which they do not really need. This is often seen among the socially deprived who are up to their ears in debt because they must have the gadgets that their neighbours have. Covetousness can also be seen among the rich who take advantage of the weakness of others, exploiting it for their own self gratification.

Ecclesiastes 9:13-16 makes an interesting observation on how money often speaks louder than wisdom. It counts for more in the eyes of the world.

This proverb is stating a fact, not passing judgement. The verbs are neutral, not pejorative. Rule may be exercised in the interest of the poor, and the borrower, though servant to the lender, may be treated well. That, indeed, is how it should be, and the example should be set in public life. So Joseph, though he was elevated and enriched by Pharaoh (Genesis 41:42), did not allow his suddenly acquired wealth to influence him in his administration in Egypt. Neither did Daniel in a similar situation in Babylon (Daniel 2:48). Nevertheless, in the eyes of their kings, as well as in everyone else's eyes, riches were recognised as necessary accoutrements to their office and were the recognised symbols of esteem and influence.

The one place in which the rich are not permitted to rule over the poor is in the church of the Lord Jesus Christ. Here money is not to talk, and here deference is not to be shown to people on the basis of their worldly status. James, in his typically forthright manner cautions Christians about this (James 2:1-7).

There is no place for wealthy church members to use or withhold their money in order to exercise a personal influence.

Nor is money to play any part in the matter of rule and leadership is in the church. Elders are appointed and esteemed on the basis of spiritual gifts and abilities and service irrespective of their financial status (see for example 1 Thessalonians 5:12-13; 1 Timothy 3:4; 5:17).

22:8. Sowing to the flesh. The parallel between the two clauses is not immediately obvious. Sowing iniquity is linked with the rod of anger, and reaping sorrow is linked with failure. All the wrong kind of passions are associated with what is described as sowing iniquity. In a nutshell, it means being determined to do my will, not God's. Not only will sorrow and failure be the result for me, but others will be harmed in the process. For example, the Christian woman who becomes emotionally involved with an unbelieving man will not only be doing herself no good, but she will be bringing grief to others. She may be angry with God over his disapproval of what she perceives as being good for her, and she may continue to be angry when the expected benefit turns out to be bitterness and others are left to pick up the pieces.

It is a sad fact of life that there are many casualties from personal iniquity. If you rebel against God, many will suffer besides yourself. We are not necessarily talking about wholesale rebellion, for it may be in only one small matter over which you are set on having your own way, such as in a relationship, or over a hobby, or concerning a possession, or in some other matter of self-indulgence. You may not even think of it as being classed under the heading of 'iniquity'. The time and attention given to 'your thing', which you regard as your exclusive domain, will adversely affect your general outlook, will curtail the time and attention you should properly be giving to God or to others, and will cause you to react badly when you feel threatened in this area. Many a wife and children have suffered long term ill effects when the husband and father has indulged in activities outside the home which he would describe as 'legitimate' but which God might describe as 'iniquitous'.

Sowing and reaping are frequently used for illustrative purposes in God's Word. Although Eliphaz' application was false, his observation was true (Job 4:8), that trouble invariably follows on the heels of iniquity. Hosea 8:7 shows how things can get devastatingly out of control. The consequences of sowing iniquity are never productive but always destructive. Paul urges us not to be deceived in this matter (Galatians 6:7-8), the unspoken implication being that it is easy for us to allow ourselves to be led astray under the false supposition that 'there's no harm in it'.

Not only are there inevitable and natural consequences to indulging iniquity, but there are judgemental ones as well, as indicated in Jeremiah 12:13; Micah 6:15; Haggai 1:6.

Though beyond the direct scope of this proverb, there are some precious positive encouragements where sowing and reaping are concerned. Sowing what is worthwhile rather than what is vain may be hard and troublesome, but there will be wonderful benefits (Psalm 126:5-6). There is a way back into blessing for those who have strayed into iniquity (Hosea 10:12-13). Galatians 6:8-9 is reassuring and comforting that sowing to the Spirit and thereby doing good to all will be abundantly rewarded.

The wrong kind of sowing leads to trouble, emptiness and failure. The right kind of sowing leads to blessing, fruitfulness and fulfilment.

22:9. How observant are you? By saying 'a generous man' the NIV misses something significant. The original refers to having a good (or generous) *eye*. There may be many people who could be described as being generous, but there is something special about a person who is on the lookout for the opportunity to do good. Paul writes to the Galatians (6:10): 'As we have opportunity, let us do good to all.' Through Timothy, he urges the rich to do good and to be rich in good works (1 Timothy 6:18). This certainly does not mean waiting for opportunity to come our way; it means our going out and finding it!

There is another important aspect of the giving implicit in this proverb. It is the *personal* aspect. The proverb does not refer simply to giving to the poor, which can be done in an impersonal way (which is not to deny that such giving has its place). It is not a case of, 'What can I spare for a good cause?' Nor is this person giving his bread to the poor in a sacrificial manner and thereby depriving himself. (Again, there may be a place for such giving on occasions.) The text does not say he is giving his bread.

What it says is that he is giving *of* his bread to the poor. That is, he is inviting the poor to participate *with* him in the abundance he enjoys. In Luke 14:13-14 Jesus spoke about giving a feast and inviting the needy to participate in the good things provided at the table. He also spoke about a blessing attending such conduct. It is not about free handouts but about sharing. This is the significant point about having a generous eye, an eye for doing good: it is about drawing others into the blessings you enjoy. There is a double blessing in that!

Are you on the lookout to see how others can benefit and rejoice *with* you in the Lord's goodness to you? Such was the spirit of the Feast of Weeks and the Feast of Tabernacles in which all – the rich and the poor alike – gathered together and partook together of the good things provided – and rejoiced together in grateful acknowledgement of the Lord's goodness (Deuteronomy 16:9-15).

[Related proverbs: 14:21,31; 19:17.]

22:10. Oh for some peace and quiet! It is a fact that when certain people are around one can expect nothing but trouble. Some people have a knack of producing discord, having an argumentative spirit not amenable to reason. Described as a scoffer, or a scorner, or a mocker, this is the kind of person who is both arrogantly self-opinionated and singularly lacking in consideration for others, totally without sensitivity except perhaps where he himself (or she herself) is concerned.

Of necessity, many of the proverbs give little more than caricatures in a few words. There are all kinds of variation on this theme. In looking at the scoffer and the effect he has among others we should be prepared to ask ourselves whether there might be in us any evidences of similar characteristics. For example, am I inclined at any time to be dismissively disparaging toward anyone – perhaps unreasonably so? Or am I overly forceful in putting forward my own ideas and reluctant to hear the views of others? Am I the kind of person who insists on having his own way? Do I ever have a tendency to become angry or argumentative, or even derisive, when people oppose me? Am I ever the cause of discord and strife and division? Are there occasions when I have trampled on the feelings of others, or through insensitivity stirred up trouble in meetings?

The trouble is, the scoffer is the kind of person least likely to look objectively at questions like these. They will be dismissed as irrelevant. Sadly, even in churches there can be people with such a propensity for generating strife that it would be better if they were not there. Paul writes about *endeavouring* to keep the unity of the Spirit in the bond of peace (Ephesians 4:3). That is a very active word involving the utmost diligence. But look at the qualities which precede this exhortation and upon which it hangs.

For those who cannot take a hint, and for those who seek to impose themselves and their views on others, there is but one remedy – exclusion. Sometimes, just as a splinter in the flesh needs to be expelled, so the removal of a contentious person is the only way to peace. There may be times when it is necessary to tolerate an unwelcome presence in a meeting (whether formal or otherwise), but there are also times when such a person needs as graciously as possible to be told he is not welcome with his views and especially attitudes, so that without him harmonious progress can be made.

So when a contentious situation arises, whether it is in a social context or a formal one, whether it is in a group discussion or a business meeting – when the heat starts to rise, it is good to ask whether the cause is the issue itself under consideration or the attitude of a person or persons involved in it. Dealing with a divisive person requires wisdom, and no ground should be given for it to be construed as a personal matter. Paul gives some advice on this in 2 Thessalonians 3:6 and 1 Timothy 6:3-5; 2 Timothy 3:2-5; Titus 3:9-11.

[Related proverb: 26:20.]

22:11. How to make friends and influence people. See also 16:13. Read almost any history concerning rulers and governments and it will be apparent that power struggles and deceit are seldom far away. Biblical history does not hide this fact, and it can even be found in the church (Philippians 1:16-17; 3 John 9-10). At every level of society there are people who, finding themselves in a position to covet what they see as the top jobs, will not be too scrupulous as to how they advance themselves.

Whom can a king trust? With whom can he drop his guard? In whom can one in such a position confide? Who among his counsellors and advisors can he be sure will serve his interests and those of the kingdom rather than his own? In the scriptures we have an outstanding example in the person of Daniel, whose purity of heart and gracious speech shone out in his dealings with the king's servants in chapter 1 and with Nebuchadnezzar himself in chapters 2 and 4. In chapter 6 there is evidence that, years later, he had won the affection of king Darius. Daniel was undoubtedly a statesman of the first order, and yet what enabled him to break through the defences of kings was probably the quality of his character. Three times he is referred to as a man 'greatly beloved' (Daniel 9:23; 10:11,19, NKJV). This word, though not usually translated 'beloved', is appropriate for one in whom others delight and whose company is therefore appreciated and valued – in other words a true friend. This testimony was given on no lesser authority than that of God himself.

There is an obvious connection between purity of heart and gracious speech. The latter without the former is grotesque. Note, however, the presence of the word 'love' here. There have been many who have striven for purity of heart or who have put in a great deal of effort to be gracious in their speech and yet have failed miserably because love was lacking in the endeavour. Such love comes only to those whose lives have been touched by the transforming power of the grace of God and who are devoted to nurturing their relationship with him, for it is only they who find the purity and holiness of God compellingly attractive and their lack of the same utterly repugnant.

There is no thought in this proverb of seeking to make a good impression in high places. Rather, the emphasis is on the great value and usefulness of purity and grace, so much so that they are noticed and appreciated by kings (or others in positions of power).

People lay great store by learning and skills and gifts and abilities, and it is true that rulers look out for such things (22:29). But somehow this proverb shifts the focus to where it really ought to be. Ability plays second fiddle to grace. Grace makes way for gift. If you would really be useful in this world, here is the way, without neglecting the other. 'Take time to be holy, speak oft with thy Lord; abide in him always, and feed on his word ... Thus led by his Spirit and filled with his love, thou soon shalt be fitted for service above' (Longstaff). True, but it is also the key to being fitted for the highest service here below!

[Related proverb: 16:31.]

22:12. Vigilance.

'Will you keep your eye on my bike while I'm in the shop?' This watchfulness preserves the bike against the possibility of theft and will result in action should the need arise. This illustrates something of the thought behind this proverb. Knowledge is given by God, and he has not left it in the world to be plundered or perverted. Knowledge is intimately bound up with the truth and is too precious to be left to the mercies of the unscrupulous and unbelieving. He is watching over it, he is guarding it, he is preserving it.

Since the world began a battle has been in progress to usurp true knowledge and set up false knowledge in its place (which is not knowledge at all but mere supposition). False religions have competed for dominance over the hearts of men; false teaching has striven to undermine the veracity and authority of the Scriptures; false science with its unfounded presuppositions has sought to impose its atheistic world view on the masses: words, words, words – clever words – to lead people away from real knowledge and to keep them in the dark with regard to the truth. And people believe the lie because they have no desire to believe the truth (Romans 1:18-22; 2 Thessalonians 1:11-12).

Yet truth and knowledge remain in the world, and in spite of the most strenuous efforts of people who are faithless in the sense that they have no time for God, the Word of God stands. In each of the three areas just mentioned knowledge has been preserved and God's Word has been vindicated. He often uses his people to bring about the overthrow of the words of the faithless. So it is that Paul wrote: 'The weapons of our warfare are not carnal but mighty in God for pulling down strongholds, casting down arguments and every high thing that exalts itself against the knowledge of God' (2 Corinthians 10:4-5).

It is the *words* of the faithless that God overthrows. He does not necessarily overthrow the faithless themselves, or even disillusion them with regard to their words. Truth and knowledge are with God's people, and God will see to it that every attempt to take it from them is overthrown. Christians have nothing to fear in this respect from the words of the faithless. Christians can sometimes be deeply unsettled by the persuasive arguments of unbelievers, especially when it is put over that knowledge is on the side of their opponents. But it is not, and because it is not it cannot stand.

There may be times when knowledge seems to be eclipsed. An eclipse, however, is only temporary, and though we may find ourselves in the dark, our God is not. For him to see is to act. Falsehood is continually being overthrown for it has no secure footing, and one day it will be overthrown for good when the earth will be filled with the knowledge of the glory of God as the waters cover the sea.

22:13. Haggai 1. Not now...

Notwithstanding there were lions about at that time, the ludicrousness of the situation is meant to hit us. It presents to us an uncomfortably absurd scenario which is amplified in 26:13-16.

A lazy person will always be ready with an excuse, however far-fetched, to avoid doing what should be done.

It cannot be denied that being attacked by a lion outside was a possibility, though exceedingly remote. Yet here is a man whose willing imagination runs riot to the extent that in his mind's eye he actually sees the beast outside his door! He is not really afraid, he only wishes to give the impression that he is. Nor is he really in any danger.

Maybe we are intended to laugh at this ridiculous excuse ... and then turn our thoughts inward to reflect upon some of the excuses we have made in our time for avoiding doing what needs to be done. The trouble with excuses for laziness is that they are invariably based upon real possibilities which are deliberately magnified out of all proportion and then permitted to take on an unwarranted plausibility in the mind. Even busyness can be a cover for laziness.

Laziness has many faces but one heart – comfortable self-indulgence. To do this is going to take me out of my comfort zone. I'm sure I can find a good reason for not doing it. Whatever we come up with may impress us, but others will not be taken in. We may object to the word 'lazy' being used to describe the reason for our inaction, but what else can it be if for the sake of our own comfort and ease we will not do what is calling for our attention and which is seen as our responsibility?

When the people said, 'The time has not come that the Lord's house should be built' (Haggai 1:2), what was their reasoning behind it? What is there in the passage which suggests that laziness might have been the root of the problem? Are there any applications concerning our service for the Lord today?

[Related proverbs: 6:6; 26:13-16.]

22:14. What are you playing at? This subject has been extensively covered in 2:16-19; 5:1-23; 6:24-35; 7:6-27. But that was a long time ago. Maybe you were carefully taught about the dangers of immorality – but that too was a long time ago. Perhaps it is time for a sharp reminder.

Immorality is so prevalent in western society that it has virtually ceased to go by that name. Let us call a spade a spade. We are looking here at a woman who uses her sexual attraction to the full and out of its proper context, enhancing it with alluring words. Very often this is done not in a brazen fashion but in a very subtle way. Little by little the intended victim is enticed closer to the edge until suddenly he loses his footing and falls headlong. He is then well and truly trapped. That is the imagery here.

Women have a way with words, and in the case of immoral women they can be highly refined. Let us note that we are not dealing here with the harlot plying her trade. Very possibly it is not a woman whom we would brand as being 'immoral' at all. It may be a woman who is lonely; it may be a woman who has developed a 'fatal attraction' for a particular man. It may be a woman who is simply out for a 'good time'; it may be a woman who has allowed and encouraged romantic notions to arise out of an ordinary friendship and then exploited them.

Whatever the 'reason', the woman is immoral for she is using her influence in an ungodly way. She is bringing pressure to bear upon a man at his weakest point. How many respectable men – indeed, how many men in the pastoral office – have become engulfed in scandal through being drawn into an adulterous relationship? To be sure, there has been folly on their side, maybe a willing blindness to the way things were developing, but it was encouraged on by persuasive words.

The really chilling thing about this is in the second clause. Not only is it a trap, but it is one connected with the Lord's abhorrence for the man who falls there. It is his judgement. Here is a very solemn reminder of the terrible consequences of playing around with what God has sanctified for holy use. There seems to be a tendency today for people, even Christians, to treat the Ten Commandments as advisory rather than mandatory. God's words, 'You shall not commit adultery' (Exodus 20:14) carry the full force of his law as much today as they ever did, and there are both natural and judicial consequences for breaking his law.

The earlier chapters of Proverbs particularly addressed younger men on this subject. This verse addresses men at any stage of life. Notice that: the focus is upon men. It is the man who carries responsibility in this area and it is the man who bears the judgement. It is amazing how many older men have fallen into adultery who in their younger years were very clear and strong in their principles. Here is a subject where there is no place to play around.

The situation might have been somewhat different, but was David under God's wrath for taking his ease at home and being slack about obedience to God when he 'happened to see' Bathsheba (2 Samuel 11)?

[Related proverbs: 2:16; 23:27.]

22:15. A painful subject. This proverb may not be politically correct today, but it is the word of God ... and it is true! There is strenuous support of the innocence of children by nature, and vigorous opposition to the use of any form of corporal punishment. Both of these things are in outright contradiction of what God teaches *and requires*, and only add trouble to an already troubled world.

The proverb emphasises the nature of the problem when it says that foolishness is *bound up* in the heart of a child. It is this foolishness which, if left unattended, will manifest itself later in grosser sins.

For example, the foul language and insubordinate attitudes of many children in our schools today are a reflection not only of their foolishness but of the lack of correction at home from their infancy.

Because foolishness is bound up in the heart of a child, it requires strong methods to loosen its hold there. A child who exhibits disobedient behaviour, if not appropriately corrected, will continue to do the same. The rod of correction, properly administered, is likely to make that youngster think again before repeating the offence.

The ultimate expressions of wisdom and foolishness are in relation to God. By nature, no one is righteous, no one understands, no one seeks God, no one does good (Romans 3:10-12). That, essentially, is foolishness, and it manifests itself in behaviour which reflects the state of the heart (Romans 3:13-18).

While external influences may encourage expressions of foolishness in a child, there is in the first place already a natural propensity to it in a child's heart. The fact that only the grace of God can fundamentally change this unhappy state of affairs does not absolve parents from the responsibility to deal with foolish behaviour and tendencies. Indeed, not uncommonly it is the application of loving parental discipline which is used by God to awaken their offspring to their deeper need for God's forgiveness and love.

Correction is not cruelty. No doubt the 'rod of correction' is an umbrella term for all forms of correction which children need as part of their training, but it does include the use of physically painful measures on occasions. There are times when a painful blow appropriately administered is in every sense far more effective than long drawn out sanctions which can be emotionally scarring. A bruise lasts but for a short while, whereas some forms of emotional deprivation breed resentment because they are inappropriate to the offence.

Correction takes many forms, but the important thing is that it is intended to deal in the most effective possible way with the problem which has prompted it. The outworking of foolishness is far more damaging than the temporary pain experienced from correction. The rod of correction serves as a reminder of this. Unless attended to, foolishness will cause much deeper pain later on.

The rod of correction is not brutality, nor is it an expression of frustration or rage. Parents in their corrective dealings with their children should have ringing in their ears: 'Whom the Lord *loves* he corrects, just as a father the son in whom he delights' (3:12, quoted in Hebrews 12:6).

[Related proverbs: 13:24; 22:6; 23:13; 29:15.]

22:16. Poor returns. The economy of words in this proverb leaves room for differences of interpretation. One possible meaning is that it makes an ironic observation, namely that more is to be gained from the poor than from the rich. Oppressing and therefore exploiting the poor is an effective path to gain, whereas making gifts to the rich in the hope of currying favour and obtaining better returns is very likely to backfire.

The former is reprehensible and forbidden by the Word of God (Deuteronomy 24:14), and yet has been practised in every generation whether by child labour, slave labour, or by sheer suppression of any opportunity for advancement. The latter is plain folly on the part of those who are covetous and looking for a 'soft touch', and they merely get what they deserve.

The love of money is the cause of many troubles and sorrows (1 Timothy 6:9).

The other interpretation, more favoured though perhaps a less straightforward translation of the original, is that poverty will surely come to both classes. James (5:1-6) portrays this in graphic language, observing that the poverty to which rich oppressors will be reduced is altogether more terrible than financial ruin and is brought about under the judgement of God who sees all and hears the cry of the oppressed.

Whichever way we take it, the conclusion is that the returns of greed mock the avaricious. Ultimately no gain is to be found there, only total bankruptcy.

This proverb applies to us if in any way we are putting our own wealth before others' welfare.

Part 3

Proverbs 22:17 to 24:34

'Words of the wise'

22:17-21. 2 Timothy 3:16-17. This is for you, even you. After a long section on the proverbs of Solomon (from 10:1) there follows here, up to the end of chapter 24, a collection of wise sayings from another source. In fact it appears that much of this material had come from Egypt in the *Teaching of Amenemope* and was suitably adapted and incorporated into the Book of Proverbs. In general the style is somewhat different, yet the content is soon seen to be all of a piece with what has preceded.

This section breaks down into thirty subsections. This is consistent with the translation of a difficult word in v. 20 rendered 'thirty sayings' in the RSV, NIV and ESV, which in the AV and NKJV is rendered 'excellent things'.

Kidner's comment on these verses is so much to the point that we quote him in full. He heads it, 'The right use of proverbs', and continues: 'A series of proverbs demands much of the reader, if it is not to remain for him a string of platitudes. The present call to attention is salutary not only in its immediate context but beyond it, to enable the disciple to review his response to all Scripture. Does he read with alert concentration (v. 17)? How much is retained and ready for passing on (v. 18)? Does he receive it in the spirit in which it is given – to deepen his trust (v. 19), guide his decisions (v. 20) and strengthen his grasp of truth (v. 21)? Does he see himself as the virtual envoy (v. 21) of those whose knowledge of the truth depends on him?'

Notice how he extends the application beyond the proverbs themselves to the whole of Scripture. Familiarity with the text can dull our concentration. The proverbs, brief and punchy and sometimes unexpected, help to stimulate thought and direct the mind to other parts of God's Word with fresh insight and appreciation. Because the proverbs are short (though there are many of them!) they are quite easily memorised, and especially so if we spend a few minutes thinking into what they are really getting at and how they apply (v. 17). So 'passing them on' becomes relatively easy because they are appreciated and retained (v. 18) – not necessarily restricting ourselves to their exact words but rather conveying through their words their wider application.

In reading and thinking about these proverbs which touch upon every aspect of life and put everything into the context of the Lord who is over all, are you drawn closer to him, to trust him more implicitly (v. 19)? Looking out on life can be confusing and perplexing, but looking at it in this way helps clear the fog and brings what is blurred into focus.

When we begin to see things as they really are rather than how they are so often presented to us in this world, we become able to make right decisions – informed decisions – and avoid the pitfalls of ignorance (v. 20).

In the proverbs truth and error are so often set side by side, opened up for examination to be compared and contrasted. We are thereby encouraged to see the truth for ourselves, to be clear about it, to be absolutely certain (v. 21a).

Then, finally, we are equipped for service (v. 21b), ambassadors for the truth even as we are for Christ (2 Corinthians 5:20), with the precious truth on our tongues, having taken it on board in our minds, received it into our hearts, and welcomed it into our lives.

22:22-23. Exploitation of the vulnerable. Here is the first of the thirty sayings of this section, and it starts by addressing pure selfish, heartless covetousness.

Even the poor have something to lose. The key word here is 'because'. Because he is poor he is vulnerable and may be unable to defend himself against exploitation. Because he is poor he may have little opportunity for self-advancement. The poor can be robbed not only of the little they may possess materially, they can be robbed by being paid less than is their due simply because they cannot hope to find work elsewhere. They can be robbed of opportunity, robbed of dignity, robbed emotionally by being pushed around and ostracised – because they are poor. Some people are stigmatised for no other reason than that they are poor. They are degraded on the social scale. They may be in reduced circumstances, but that does not give others any right to demean them in their thinking. Yet such attitudes are prevalent in our world where material considerations and outward circumstances carry so much more weight than spirit and character and mercy and justice.

Some people want to have nothing to do with the poor because they are poor and are perceived to be a drain on their resources. Therefore instead of speaking up for them and giving them a helping hand they speak against them because they don't want them around on 'their patch'. 'The gate' was where some business transactions were carried out and, more particularly, where matters of justice were discussed and settled, and so oppressing the afflicted at the gate represented public opposition when they came with a cause or a plea. Some people are just not worth bothering about. Jesus told a parable of a poor widow pleading for justice, The judge in the story considered her a troublesome pest and wanted her off his back (Luke 18:1-8). Her cause was of no interest to him and taking it up would be of no advantage to him. He made his own comfort the criterion by which he decided whether or not to give her his attention, as is made clear in what happened. By contrast the Lord shows that he is concerned for full justice in a timely fashion. God does not believe in a law for the rich and a law for the poor. His concern is for justice for all on the basis of truth.

Righteousness and retribution. If God commanded mercy and justice for the afflicted (Deuteronomy 24:10-22), we can be sure he upholds his own law, both in providing help for the afflicted (Deuteronomy 10:18) and in bringing judgement upon the oppressors (Deuteronomy 27:19). Though the sheer scale of the problem is daunting, yet those who cry to him may be reassured of his help on the basis of his character and word.

Many of the proverbs in this section are concerned with things we should not do. In the case of this one, it should make us review our mental attitude toward disadvantaged members of our society and beyond. Are there things realistically we can do positively to alleviate the needs or afflictions of others?

[Related proverbs: 14:31; 17:5; 19:17; 21:13; 22:16.]

22:24-25. The chip on the shoulder. Quite a lot is said about anger in Proverbs (for example 14:17; 15:1,18; 16:32; 19:11; 29:22; and see also Ecclesiastes 7:9), but this one focuses particularly upon association with anger. Those who are all fired up over a cause can easily ignite others. When things get out of hand and a lot of ill feeling is generated in a group, more often than not there turns out to be a single instigator of it.

Christians are not immune from the temptation to anger, and Paul draws attention to this (Ephesians 4:31-32), as also does James (3:14-18). Nor are churches immune from problems in which anger can be aroused. Very often, when divisions occur in churches – often accompanied by a lot of heat – they too can be traced back to an individual, a 'champion of a cause' who has been more forceful than reasonable, with whom it would have been better to remonstrate than to listen to.

This proverb is indicating that there is a very real risk of becoming involved with the attitudes of an angry person, to become infected with that person's passion and then end up in trouble, caught up – snared – in a situation which was not originally of your making. It is simply asking for trouble.

Brooding resentment is a form of anger and, given opportunity, what is smouldering there will break into a flame. Friendship with an angry man only encourages his passion as he senses a measure of support: to his thinking, you are then on his side. This in due course emboldens him in his anger to apply himself with a will in giving vent to it.

The warning, 'Don't play with fire', is pertinent here. You do not want to be the combustible material to fuel the fire of an angry man. Friendship in the sense of linking your name with his, or expressing a fellow feeling with him, is the worst possible service you can render either to him or to yourself. A safe distance must be kept in order to contain the situation.

If you keep your distance, what positive contribution can you make to any volatile persons or situations? Or if you are closely acquainted with any volatile persons or situations are there any positive contributions you can make?

It is important to distinguish between someone who is rightly passionate for a cause and worthy of support and one who is merely vexed over an issue. The difference may not always be immediately obvious, and yet it will become evident in the attitudes displayed in the way it is worked out.

22:26-27. Do not be a soft touch. Here is another association from which one should steer clear. If friendship with an angry man is hazardous, friendship with a reckless one is likely to be ruinous. If you undertake to bale someone out of trouble the likelihood is that you will have to do it again ... and again.

This matter has been addressed before in Proverbs (see 6:1; 11:15; 17:18) and examined from different angles. Here the way it is put seems to suggest that there is a class of people who do this kind of thing. Perhaps the profit motive lies behind it as in the case of insurance underwriters, only in this case a more personal element is involved, indicated by 'striking hands'.

This proverb addresses what may really amount to a form of gambling which has the expectation of good returns but where the stakes are high.

Whatever the particular circumstances, God's Word consistently declares it to be a foolish risk. Promises to pay should never be made where there is a possibility of liabilities beyond one's means. It can lead to utter ruin, and not just financially.

To take a man's bed from beneath him is a graphic way of describing his being stripped of his last and most essential need: rest. Picture the bailiffs coming at night and removing everything else, finally hauling the bed from beneath the sleeper, giving him a rude awakening to the reality of his utter destitution.

How many people have said they have been unable to sleep because of worry? How often that worry has been a severe debt problem. Our comfortable western society has many buffers against this extremity, but, for many, to have their bed taken from under them would be disastrous indeed. Yet in reality, if only in the metaphorical sense, this is exactly what has happened to them.

This proverb probably also covers the lesser matter of not allowing others to sponge off you. People have been known to get into serious financial difficulties because they cannot bring themselves to say 'No' when others come to them with their hard luck stories using every trick in the book to apply psychological pressure for promises of help.

Never pledge yourself to someone over anything for which the outcome is uncertain and could get you into deep water. See how this proverb focuses upon the potential damage to you by asking you a pointed question. There is an irony in that the help you give to save someone else from ruin will probably fail in any case, and in the process it will also precipitate your own ruin. So in the end you will have doubly failed.

This proverb is couched in monetary terms. But are there other ways in which you could unwisely pledge yourself beyond your means to your own hurt?

[Related proverbs: 6:1-5; 11:15; 17:18; 20:16; 27:13.]

22:28. Setting the boundaries. This proverb is reinforced at 23:10-11. In Leviticus 25:23 we read that God declared the land to belong to him, and that the land was allocated by him to his people and termed the land of their possession. Furthermore, we understand from Numbers 25:53-56 that it was specifically allotted to the tribes and to their families. This is something which took place after entry into the land of promise. Thus it was intended that each family should have its allotment of land which was to be passed down from generation to generation. By the time of Solomon therefore these landmarks were 'ancient'. From the beginning the law expressly forbade the removal of a neighbour's landmark (Deuteronomy 19:14; 27:17).

If today a householder whose back garden bordered a farmer's field decided to extend his land by moving the boundary fence ... well, he wouldn't dare to do such a thing! He would have an outraged farmer bringing the full weight of the law against him. That is nothing compared with what 'removing the ancient landmark' meant. It would have been tampering with what God had set in place for the benefit of someone else. But even buying the land allocated to someone else was forbidden, and so, for example, Ahab was seeking to remove a landmark when he offered to buy Naboth's vineyard (1 Kings 21). It wasn't his to buy because it wasn't Naboth's to sell, and the encounter proved to be a head-on collision between ungodly and godly principles. From Ahab's angle Naboth was probably perceived to be churlishly turning down a good offer. From Naboth's angle what God had given him in trust was non-negotiable.

As this no longer applies today, we might ask whether it has any relevance to us. To answer this we have to think about what factors lie behind the specific prohibition. In short, we see the clash between motive and principle. The only motive for removing an ancient landmark would have been that of personal gain, often at the expense of someone else, and this falls under the general umbrella of exploitation in the bad sense of the word.

The Pharisees were guilty of exactly this in the matter of 'corban' (see Mark 7:9-13). They were 'bending the rules' to achieves what they wanted. They were interfering with the law of God. Examples of this kind of thing could be multiplied.

People interfere with the law of God because they do not want the law of God to interfere with their wish to do what he forbids or avoid what he commands. God has established certain inviolable principles, and to try to change them is a direct challenge to him. For example, some years ago a manufacturing company tried to impose on all its workers a ten-day week. It turned out to be a disaster not, as some said, because everything else worked according to a seven-day week and so it could not be made to fit, but because God has established a week of seven days.

More generally, everything that God has put in place could be considered to be landmarks, whether in the natural world or the written word. We are intended to live within the framework of his created order and his verbal laws.

[Related proverb: 23:10-11.]

22:29. Going far. Notice how this proverb invites observation and reflection. We probably all know of people who have proved themselves to be outstanding in some field. But then they tend to be few and far between. It is because they stand out from the crowd that we notice them. They do not necessarily make a lot of noise about it and rarely are they seeking honour for themselves. They are simply getting on with the job. Their ability is evident in the work they do and it speaks for them. They excel at their work irrespective of *for* whom they are doing it or *before* whom they are doing it.

Headhunting. If *we* see and take note of such people, we can be sure that in general kings and rulers will do so, who want the best, can afford the best, and will be on the lookout for the best, and lesser ('unknown') men will not be able to retain their services or compete against them.

Ambition. Because our focus is directed at the way opened up by the work itself, the matter of ambition seems conspicuous by its absence, for there are many who would covet and strive for the top jobs and the prestige associated with them.

When Paul reminds slaves that they are serving the Lord Christ (Colossians 3:22-24; Ephesians 6:5-8) and doing their work for him, that is an encouragement that their work is noted by the Lord and will be rewarded by him, whatever the treatment they receive from their earthly masters. He is not saying that it should in principle make any difference to the work they do. That is, they should not be doing it better because it is in service for Christ than if it had not been in service for him. He is saying that it should be done well in any case, and that it is the Lord who will be the judge of the quality. It is *this* King before whom we stand with respect to the work we do!

Service. When Joseph served Potiphar (Genesis 39:1-6), and later when he was in prison and served the prison keeper and the captain of the guard (Genesis 39:22 to 40:4), he served well. But finally, when he served Pharaoh (Genesis 41:40-41), he was able to put his gifts to their best use in the service of the nation and beyond.

In Joseph's case it was not his work which brought him before Pharaoh – or was it? Had he not been capable and diligent he would never have been in the right place at the right time to use the special gift God had given him. So, while admitting the singular providence of God in the matter, it was indeed his application to his work which resulted in his standing before the king, which then opened the door to his rendering his people a great service.

There is therefore something for each of us in this. Our focus should be upon doing good work, not climbing the social ladder. It is not he who commends himself, but whom the Lord commends, who is approved (2 Corinthians 10:18). Each of us has been given certain gifts by the Lord, which are to be used not for our advancement but for his, to commend him from whom we have received them, for there is nothing we have which we did not receive (1 Corinthians 4:7). Jesus said that faithful service will be rewarded by him (Matthew 25:20-23,29). If we are not content with that then our attitude is at fault.

23:1-3. So you've finally made it to the top. For the vast majority of readers the 'When' of this proverb is pure fantasy! But we can travel there in imagination, or observe from a distance, and see that the powers and privileges are not at all what they might seem at first sight.

To sit down to eat with a ruler would have been a mark of privilege and courtesy extended toward you. You would be there by invitation of the ruler, but the honour as such would not convey any rights or freedoms. There is emphasis in the phrase 'consider carefully', and it does not mean examine the food! It probably means you are to consider the undercurrents and implications of your presence there. Do not get carried away with any sense of self-importance (remember Haman! – Esther 5:9-14) or the idea that you are free to indulge yourself. This isn't a domestic table where you can relax and enjoy yourself. Your every move is being watched, your every action is being weighed. The honour bestowed upon you may be genuine, but it is also precarious and needs to be carried well.

There is more than a hint that it is better that you put a knife to your own throat than have somebody else do it for you! This is not an occasion for enjoying the food but for restraint and decorum! The food may be – undoubtedly is – excellent, but the reason it is deceptive is that it has not been put on the table for your benefit but for his (the ruler's).

The illustration here is telling us never to allow success to go to our head. We should never preen ourselves on our accomplishments, and even less on the social standing we have achieved. Nor should we use such things as an opportunity for self-indulgence.

For those who reach the top it is good that they be constantly aware that the position is unstable and every direction from there is down!

Jesus had something to say about this: 'Whoever desires to be first among you, let him be your slave' (Matthew 20:27). Now read on and see how he continued. He also said, 'He who is greatest among you shall be your servant' (Matthew 23:11). Again, read this in its context.

Baruch was a good man, but Jeremiah warned him from the Lord, 'Do you seek great things for yourself? Do not seek them' (Jeremiah 45:5). The greatest of Christians and those who have risen highest in society have been consistently characterised with humility and noted for their service.

23:4-5. 1 Timothy 6. Worthwhile labour. Here is another fantasy.

How many people are convinced that if they have enough money all their problems will be solved! How many people work, work, work to try to make their dream a reality only to discover that it is forever eluding them.

There is nothing wrong with working hard, and indeed diligent labour is commended in the right context. It is all a question of what you are working toward, what you have in mind when you take on extra work or go for that new job. Do you have your sights on a new this or a new that, or an extended holiday. Is that really what it is all about?

The proverb is so worded that it appears to be addressing those who are already working themselves to death, or in danger of doing so, with the wrong end in view. It appeals to our understanding. What are you getting so stressed up about? Relax! It is just not worth it. It is not going to achieve anything for you. It is all an illusion. A life exhausted in accumulating wealth is a life wasted. Unfortunately our understanding does not always master our passions.

The New Testament says that those who desire to be rich bring all manner of troubles upon themselves (1 Timothy 6:9-10). Paul talks there about what is certain (v. 7) and what is uncertain (v. 17). He is not advocating in vv. 6-8 that we do a minimum and take things easy. Far from it, for he has just been advising slaves who have believing masters to work well in order to benefit them and the church generally (v. 2), and later he exhorts the wealthy to work hard in using their resources for the good of others.

The knife to the throat is used to illustrate that 'making it' in society is deceptive. Here is an equally vivid image showing that a rich man's wealth is deceptive for those who set their eyes – and their heart – on it. Just picture those lovely crisp bank notes emerging from your wallet, unfolding their wings, taking to the air and soaring upward to heaven!

Jesus spoke of the fool laying up treasure for himself and not being rich toward God (Luke 12:21). He also spoke about not laying up for yourself treasures on earth, but laying up treasures in heaven (Matthew 6:19-21).

Riches are only really useful if they are really used. Our lives should be used to enrich others in every way, to be a blessing to others. We need to be rich in grace and fruitful in every good work (Colossians 1:10). We need to understand what are true riches.

23:6-8. Miserable company. As with vv. 1-3, eating with someone is really representative of involvement with them. In the best context it is an occasion for fellowship. But not here. Having such a head of the table completely transforms the situation.

Let us discuss it over a meal. The picture here could well be that of doing business with someone. At his invitation you are sitting down together for some such purpose and you hope to derive some benefit from the transaction. The proverb hinges upon the two phrases, 'his delicacies' and 'your pleasant words'. That is, he appears to be offering you something, and you are responding in an appropriate manner.

What is on the table? Here is yet another deception. First of all, what this stingy person says to you and what he is thinking are two entirely different things. Secondly, what you hope to get out of the contact is wasted; it will not do you the least good.

Whatever he might say, the parsimonious person resents every mouthful you take of his fare. His only interest is what he might get out of you. He says, 'Eat and drink!' inviting lavish participation, whereas in reality he is counting the cost of every morsel you consume and regarding the exercise as one of damage limitation. This is the opposite of the person who invites you to have a 'bite to eat' with the intention of generously giving you your fill.

The money motive. Overworking to be rich (4) will frequently result in miserly tendencies, where every act of giving to others is seen as working against the main objective, and so there is a very definite connection between this proverb and the last.

The illustration used this time is unpleasant, and deliberately so. Far from deriving any benefit from involvement with a miserly person, the result will be the opposite. You will not be able to stomach even the little you seem to have gained from the encounter.

This proverb is telling us that we should avoid doing business at any level with those whose sole preoccupation is with themselves, their self-interest and their own worth, who have a reputation for grasping and not for giving. However mouth-watering their offering, it will only result in food poisoning!

The service motive. Too many people in business seem to think only of their own profit margin. They are in it for what they can get. Sadly, this extends beyond business into life more generally. The miser is at the extreme end of the scale and is set before us as an example of where one-sided attitudes can lead. When we do initiate business meetings or their equivalent what we are offering others should be genuine, and our interest in their welfare genuine. Naturally the purpose is to benefit ourselves, but if that is the only, even the primary, consideration, then it is altogether unworthy. We are to serve others with what God has given us, and that extends to business dealings as to any other area of life.

23:9. Do not cast your pearls before swine. Do not speak 'in the hearing' of a fool (NKJV, ESV) is a bit misleading because this is concerned with direct address, not about being overheard. Indeed, it is suggestive of some intimacy (as in 'a word in your ear'), and it is probably in this sense we are to interpret the proverb.

A number of proverbs remind us that a fool is not receptive toward wisdom but hostile to it (for example 1:7,22; 14:9; 15:5; 17:10,16; 18:2).

The fool is consistently portrayed as one who is godless, who has no time for the things of God, whereas wisdom has its roots in the fear of the Lord. This makes for communication difficulties between the two. A fool may be erudite, but when it comes to the things of God they are foolishness to him (1 Corinthians 1:18).

This proverb is not suggesting we engage in no verbal interaction with fools. It has to be understood by the conditioning second clause. Because he is not receptive to wisdom, to attempt to share certain things with him will be a waste of time. Worse than that, it will incur his contempt. Jesus gave a similar caution when he said, 'Do not cast your pearls before swine, lest they trample them under their feet, and turn and tear you in pieces' (Matthew 7:6). In other words, indiscretion in this area can be positively dangerous.

This proverb is also allied with 14:7. There can never really be any kind of intimacy with those the Bible classes as fools. The type of conversation we can have is limited on account of their foolishness. We do not want to give such people a handle for scorning what we say through their not understanding our words or, because of their viewpoint, twisting them to mean something we did not intend. Christians do need to be careful about what they say to unbelievers, especially those who are clearly hostile to the truth. They need to think how their hearers will understand and respond to what they have to say. There is no way they can share holy things with them.

The apostle Paul said, 'What fellowship has light with darkness?' (2 Corinthians 6:14). It is impossible. The constraint placed upon communications with the ungodly should by contrast make us appreciate the more the kind of open fellowship we can have with fellow believers. The unity we have in Christ and the ways in which this can be expressed should be a cause of wonder and joy.

[Related proverbs: 9:7; 14:7.]

23:10-11. Ruth 4. Redeemed … with the precious blood of Christ (1 Peter 1:18-19).

This proverb takes up again 22:28, only this time it focuses upon the exploitation of the defenceless for gain. The fatherless are mentioned as representative of the vulnerable of society, the father being the breadwinner. On the death of the father the family might descend into debt. If a merciless creditor leaned on them with the threat of either taking from their land, or even taking their land itself, he would be lifting his hand against God who had allocated the land, for God had said, 'The land is mine' (Leviticus 25:23). Entering the fields would have been trespassing, and at the very least an act of intimidation. Their land was a vital resource for providing food for sustaining life, and so to place it in jeopardy would have been a display of heartless callousness.

There are people who are willing to break the law if they can get away with it. They see something of advantage to themselves, and though they are aware they can obtain it only at the expense of others they go ahead, showing little or no feeling for them. Very often their actions are covered with a thin veneer of plausibility which they know will not stand close scrutiny. If they knew the eyes of the authority were on them they would never risk what they were thinking to do.

One of the problems of the poor of that society was that they might have no relative to come and help, and they might be forced to sell their land temporarily (it could never be sold permanently – see Leviticus 25:10,15,23) and wait until the jubilee when it would return to them, or until such time as a relative (a 'kinsman') was able to buy it back for them (that is, to redeem it, Leviticus 25:25). Boaz was such a kinsman-redeemer for Naomi to plead her cause (Ruth 4).

In the context of this proverb 'redeemer' is the correct translation in the second clause and it is surely a reference to the Lord who is described as a father of the fatherless (Psalm 68:5), and who is mighty to act on their behalf (Deuteronomy 10:17-18).

The Lord made himself known as the Redeemer of Israel in bringing them back from the captivity of Babylon (Isaiah 43:14-15), for they were his inheritance (Isaiah 47:6).

We, too, have a mighty Redeemer. Satan had plundered us, but Jesus has come and pleaded our cause against him, presenting his own blood as the payment price to demonstrate that Satan has neither right nor claim upon us. For as believers we are God's people, chosen, redeemed, and his inheritance (Ephesians 1:4,7,18). Jesus has identified his relationship with the people he has saved by calling them his 'brothers' (Hebrews 2:11-12). He truly is their kinsman-redeemer.

The word 'cause' ('plead their cause') is being used here because of its being called into question or threatened or exploited or undermined. The basis of the cause of the fatherless was not that the land had been acquired by hard work, or that they had any intrinsic right to it. Their cause was solely that it was theirs because God had allotted it to them, and it is on that basis that they could appeal to him to plead their cause.

Similarly, that was the basis of the 'cause' of Israel in captivity. Through disobedience they had been removed from their homeland – the land *promised* to them by the Lord. Fulfilling the conditions, they could appeal to the promises. See Deuteronomy 30 and the culminating verse 20, and consider the cause presented by Daniel in his prayer to God in Daniel 9:16-19. Solomon in his prayer on the occasion of the dedication of the temple makes this very point – see 1 Kings 8:46-53.

Question: Do you have a 'cause' to plead, and on what is it founded that you should have any confidence that God will take it up?

[Related proverbs: 22:22-23,28.]

23:12. Back to basics. Some things are fundamental, and this certainly is. It was encountered several times in the introductory section of the book (for example 2:2; 4:20-21; 8:33) and it is a theme which has subsequently recurred over and over again in various shapes and forms (such as at 12:1; 14:33; 15:5,14,31-32; 18:15; 19:20), and most recently at 22:17. Yet how necessary is this reminder, and especially in a society which is preoccupied with frivolity and in which there are all manner of distractions. This is not advice, it is an imperative! Do it!

Apply your heart – you are to take your heart to the task, you are to put your heart into it with a sense of purpose. This is not for the half-hearted or faint-hearted, only for the whole-hearted.

Instruction – this is a word often used of chastisement and correction, in other words something which can be uncomfortable. But just as the discomfort of disciplined physical training strengthens the body and enhances skills, so purposeful application to instruction improves the mind, by which is meant more than mental faculties, but life skills in their widest sense.

Apply your ears – again, you are to take your ears to words of knowledge, and give ear to what is being said. It is said that a picture is worth a thousand words. This is true in only a limited way because pictures do not instruct like words do. Words give meaning to things. Jesus said, 'Take heed how you hear' (Luke 8:18), referring in particular to the teaching he had been giving. Not only do we need to hear the words of the Master, we need to hear intelligently.

By way of application, we need to take ourselves to where the Word of God is preached and applied faithfully. Sometimes the sermons and talks we hear are excellent, while at other times they can leave something to be desired. But always our ears should be receptive to knowledge and we should be listening with the appropriate critical faculty, not in the sense of finding fault but subjecting what we hear to a discriminating process: thinking about it, weighing the words, retaining what is of value. If we are to be wise we need knowledge, for the right kind of knowledge is a base for wisdom. We are not necessarily in control of *what* we hear, but we can control *how* we hear it.

Most knowledge at the time the Proverbs were written was acquired through listening to teachers. Today we have the added and enormous privilege of the abundance of the written word, and so reading can be subsumed under hearing. A good student working toward a degree in his or her speciality will not only attend lectures but will also do a great deal of reading around the subject. Surely a serious Christian will not only listen to sermons on Sundays but will be a student of the Word of God and be eager to read whatever will help toward growth in the grace and *knowledge* of the Lord Jesus Christ (2 Peter 3:18).

23:13-14. A painful but necessary responsibility. Severe discipline was considered at 22:15. What we have here should be viewed in the overall context of vv. 12-28 and beyond so that there is no misunderstanding. It is all about a father's deep concern for the welfare of his son.

The first thing to observe, in the exhortation 'Do not withhold', is that it addresses a natural reluctance to apply correction of this kind. If the use of the rod (or its equivalent) comes easily, something is very wrong. It should be at least as painful to administer the rod as it is to smart under it. Furthermore, it should be only with the proper end in view that it is ever administered. That is why we should read this verse in its context. There is no fury here, no loss of self-control, no cruelty, only an earnest desire for the child's highest good.

Next to notice is the counter to a natural fear. In saying 'he will not die', there is no suggestion that the child is to be 'thrashed within an inch of his life', or 'beaten black and blue'. That would indeed be a mark of vindictiveness or cruelty. But a parent might be concerned about harming the child, and this is reminding him that children are much more resilient than might be supposed. Discipline properly, and no fear need be entertained on that count.

Then v. 14 is effectively a command which reinforces 'Do not withhold' with 'You shall do it.' Not indiscriminately, of course, but when occasion requires it – which may be rarely, or may be more often, depending on the nature of the child. It must be done appropriately, which requires at least an understanding of the child, the circumstances surrounding the incident, and evidence that deliberate disobedience was involved.

What is the end in view? It is to 'deliver his soul from hell' (sheol). That is an indication of how important it is. We might argue that only God can deliver anyone from hell and that we are entirely dependent upon his grace. So we are, but he also places certain responsibilities in our hands. If he gives us children, he has shown us how he expects us to train them up in the way that they should go (22:6). If we fail to do what he requires of us, we can hardly complain if our children go astray.

There is almost an ambiguity in the phrase, 'will not die'. The first clause is negative: 'If you do not do that, something will not happen'; the second is positive: 'If you do this, something will result.' We could interpret the first statement thus: 'You do not want your child to die, do you? Then do not withhold correction.' The second statement reinforces it: 'You do want your child to be delivered, don't you? Then make sure you provide correction.'

Generally speaking, children grow up to respect the discipline they have received in an environment of love, accepting it as a necessary part of a wholesome upbringing. Far from turning the child away from the father, the mutual pain suffered in these occasional experiences often has the opposite effect of strengthening the bond.

In a society where there is so much cruelty to children in the form of physical abuse we should have some sympathy with legislation forbidding any form of corporal punishment, understanding the reasons for the concern. Christians should nevertheless not be intimidated by this but continue to obey the Word of God, demonstrating that right motives and right actions yield right results.

[Related proverbs: 13:14; 19:18.]

23:15-16. Heart to heart. Notice the repetition of 'heart' throughout this section: verses 12, 15, 17, 19, 26. Of course a father is concerned about the behaviour of his son, but it goes deeper than that: it goes to the heart. Outward conformity to his standards is not good enough. If that is all there is, there will be no joy or delight (15, 16, 24, 25). Nothing less than right heart principles will produce these emotions. How many a godly parent has grieved over an unbelieving son or daughter not because their offspring has been openly rebellious or anything like that but rather because there is no real fellowship, nor can there be, because the heart is not given to the Lord.

Eye service is not good enough. Look at Judas Iscariot. He did all the right things and was a 'look-alike' to all the other apostles. Yet in the end it was evident that his heart was not in it. It was all right so long as it suited him, but when he became disillusioned he went completely off the rails. A wise heart is a heart which is willingly and gladly surrendered in its totality to the Lord, a heart upon which his word is written, a heart which beats at the impulse of his love. What we read here about the father/son relationship is in some ways a picture of the relationship between the Lord and his children. There is joy in heaven over one sinner who repents (Luke 15:7,10,20-23). God himself rejoices over those whose hearts are given to him – given back to him to whom they belong in response to his yearning love.

We are all somebody's son or daughter, and some have parents who care more than others. No one has a father who cares like a heavenly Father cares for his children, and none rejoices like he – yes, he himself – rejoices when he sees wisdom in their hearts and its outworking in the 'telling' way of their speech.

How many people long for joy in their hearts and never find it. How few people think about giving joy to caring parents, and fewer still about giving joy to God!

A cynical view of this passage would suggest that it is all about the father – what the father wants of his children, what will please him. A rebellious son or daughter might say, 'What about *me*? What about what *I* want? What about what will bring *me* pleasure?' Sadly, that is the attitude of many towards a God whom they view as seeking to impose his will upon them, and it is a totally distorted view. So they see him as a ogre and rail against him because they do not find what they are seeking, as if he were set on depriving them.

How far removed this is from the truth! The father's concern is for the very best for his children, and his joy is in seeing it materialise. The most contented, the most satisfied, the most fulfilled Christian is the one who is bringing joy to the Father's heart.

[Related proverbs: 10:1; 15:20; 23:24-25; 27:11; 29:3.]

23:17-18. Hebrews 6:13-20. Is zeal abating? Don't let it happen. This exhortation is given because we can so easily let it happen. Living wisely in a world such as ours is not an easy task. It can seem like trying to run a particularly difficult obstacle course. Why do things the hard way? Why the need for this constant discipline? 'Sinners' – that is, those who have no scruples where God's law is concerned – often seem to have things all their own way. They do not have to worry about what God's Word says; they are not bound by principles of righteousness; they have no concerns about who they mix with; they have freedom to conduct themselves as they please and to do things in their own way; they are not answerable to anyone; they can concentrate on building a good life for themselves.

Even the godliest of people can fall foul of envy (see Psalm 73). This is most likely to happen in times of trial, when the going gets particularly hard, and when the mind becomes focused on all the difficulties of life. It is easy to look enviously at other people who seem to be getting on so well when you yourself are getting on so badly!

To address this temptation there is a 'but' and a 'for'.

But. Envy saps energy, or rather redirects it into different channels. The word 'zealous' (zealous for the fear of the Lord) has been supplied in the NKJV, NIV translations. Actually, we are to pick up on the word translated 'envy', which could also be translated 'jealous' or 'zealous', as applying to both clauses. We could put it this way: 'Do not be jealous of sinners but for the fear of the Lord.'

It adds, literally, 'all the day', or 'all day long'. There is a reason for this. The NIV translates, 'always'. That is true, but it is not specific enough. The point is, it is during the day that our senses will be assaulted with provocations to envy sinners. It is in the midst of this that we are to train our faculties jealousy to guard our hearts in the fear of the Lord. When there is danger of drifting off it is time to check and renew allegiance. We are to be vigilant in maintaining awareness that what pleases God is of far greater importance and value than what may be gained from the pleasures of sin for a season.

For. This is emphatic – 'for surely' – and it is given in the light of the very real temptations the godly will encounter. It leads us to take a longer view. Looking at the prosperity of sinners has an exceedingly narrow focus. Look at it in the overall context and in relation to everything else. However rosy the present for the sinner, there is neither future nor hope. However bleak the present for God's people, there is a future, and there is a hope (Jeremiah 29:10-11). If things are tough right now, it is a good time to take a hard look at what God has promised those who love him who are called according to his purpose. Do you believe his promises? How much there is to look forward to! How incomparably wonderful it will be, beyond comparison with anything we could possibly experience now, and certainly any present discomforts are not worth comparing with it (Romans 8:28,18).

This is no uncertain hope, and again it is emphasised. It is based upon a promise underwritten by God himself, effected in Jesus Christ who both speaks on our behalf and brings all the blessings of God to us through his sacrifice and intercession (Hebrews 6:19).

So: 'Do not grow weary in doing good' (Galatians 6:9; 2 Thessalonians 3:13).

[Related proverbs: 3:31; 11:7; 24:14,20; 28:14.]

23:19-21. Two ways to be happy. Take control, sort things out, and make things clear and straight and happy in your life. How? By hearing good advice and being wise enough to weigh it up and follow it intelligently (v. 19). This does involve self-discipline. Children are trained by their parents and others, but as they grow up they are expected increasingly to take responsibility themselves for their development and progress. The root word for guiding the heart includes the idea of making it happy. We may talk about a happy thought, or a happy choice, which lies behind something which has turned out well. The happy choices in life for the believer are made on the basis of hearing and weighing and following the word of our heavenly Father.

Furthermore, there is a difference between our heart guiding us, and our guiding our hearts. People who let their heart guide them often end up in a mess, because the heart is deceitful above all things (Jeremiah 17:9). Those who guide their heart are taking control of their lives and passions, maybe going against the grain of what their heart craves, and in due course bring their heart into the place where they enjoy being where they are. There is nothing so very mysterious about this. For the athlete on the podium, for example, the glory of achievement is more than worth all the self-sacrifice and disciplined and often painful training without which it would not have been possible.

The Christian life is one of self-discipline and self-control. The reward is infinitely greater (1 Corinthians 9:25). Self-control is one aspect of the fruit of the Spirit (Galatians 5:23). It was particularly urged upon believers living in a society in which people were in general ruled by their passions (Titus 1:12; 2:2,5,6).

Those who simply let their hearts guide them, looking for the easy way of the endless round of pleasures and going with the flow, mixing with those who are out for a good time, partying and drinking (v. 20), find themselves in a downward spiral under the illusion of being happy but actually being fundamentally depressed.

The drowsiness spoken of is one of the effects of an undisciplined life. Taking the easy way in a mindless fashion has a numbing effect upon the faculties. Try getting the partying person up in the morning for the day's work! The lyrics of *The Enemy*'s song, 'Be Somebody' say: 'Know the only thing that really makes us smile is a joke and a laugh and a night on the tiles.' This really is from 'the enemy', not from God, and is a sure way to knock the bottom out of anyone's life.

There is a biting irony at the end. You have yet to see in a shop window a tailor's dummy clothed with rags. Yet, metaphorically, many are frequenting that shop, being stripped of what they have and being fitted out with worthless, smelly rags. However, the real tragedy lies not in the way they are clothed but that they have sacrificed everything of inner worth: they are wraiths in rags.

By contrast, the virtuous wife, the embodiment of wisdom, clothes her household in scarlet (31:21) and the man who embraces her is inwardly clothed with dignity (31:22).

[Related proverbs: 6:10-11; 15:14; 20:13; 23:12,29-30; 28:19.]

23:22-23. Isaiah 51:1-2. 'Look to the rock from which you were hewn.'

The fifth commandment, 'Honour your father and your mother' (Exodus 20:12) applies throughout life and also has appended to it a promise of true prosperity applicable not only to Old Testament Israel but also to New Testament believers (Ephesians 6:1-3).

Not despising your mother 'when she is old' indicates this proverb is addressing a grown-up son (or daughter). The implication is that parents, even after the time of training of their children has long since passed, can still have a valuable contribution to make to their offspring in the way of advice and counsel born of experience. 'Listen to your father who begot you' is strongly suggestive that the father wishes to speak into the situation in which his son finds himself, or that the son should be actively encouraging his father to share his advice and experience. These things are marks of strong, well balanced family life.

Not all will be in the happy position of having wise and understanding parents who care. Nevertheless the principles apply universally. Children should have an appropriate respect and regard for their parents, and being prepared to listen to a father and showing concern for a mother is a mark of this and may keep the door open for doing them lasting good.

These words are also applicable in a wider sense. Israel's believers were exhorted to look to their spiritual roots in their 'father' Abraham, the man of faith, and their 'mother' Sarah who bore and nurtured them (Isaiah 51:2). In that sense Christians have fathers and mothers in the church from whom and through whom they have received so much. Paul could describe himself as a 'father' to the church in Corinth (1 Corinthians 4:15), and a 'father' to the runaway slave Onesimus (Philemon 1:10); likewise Timothy and Titus were both his 'sons' in the faith (1 Timothy 1:2,18; 2 Timothy 1:2; 2:1; Titus 1:4). In so addressing them he expected them to listen what he had to say.

We therefore need to have due respect for those through whom we came to faith in Christ. Furthermore, we need to value the nurture we have received through the church. 'Do not despise your mother when she is old' is of course applicable in its literal sense. It may, however be applied in another way. There can be an unhealthy preoccupation with for ever seeking something new, putting aside the old ways as outmoded and irrelevant. 'We do things differently now. We have a different view of things now. We don't believe things the way they used to.' Very often this is little more than an excuse for diluting faith and practice.

Verse 23 links closely with v. 22. Listening to your father parallels buying the truth. Not despising your mother parallels not selling the truth. Truth is truth for all time. Contrary to what is promulgated these days, truth is absolute, not relative, and does not change. Truth is to be exchanged for nothing, and truth is *not* to be exchanged for nothing!

Collectors passionate about works by a particular artist will always be on the lookout for opportunity to purchase further items and will be prepared to pay a high price for them in order to add to their collection. They will also closely guard what they have acquired and will not part with any of it because it is so precious to them. This is to be our attitude toward the truth. It should be the focus of our attention, and wherever we see it we should be buying into it.

Truth determines practice. Wisdom and instruction and understanding rest upon it, and these must never be compromised or forfeited.

Above all, we are begotten by God as our heavenly Father (1 Peter 1:3; 1 John 5:1) and we need to listen to him; and we are nurtured by the Holy Spirit whose leading we must not ignore or despise. He is the Spirit of truth (John 14:17); it is he who instructs us (John 16:13), and gives us heavenly wisdom (1 Corinthians 2:4) and understanding (Ephesians 3:16-19). There never comes a time when we can cease listening to the Lord to whom we owe our very lives and who will teach us old truths by way of reminder and new truths as we are able to receive them. There never comes a time, either, when we can dispense with the work of the Holy Spirit in our lives, when we do not need to depend upon him to apply the Word to us and guide us and help us.

[Related proverbs: 1:8; 4:5,7; 6:20; 18:15.]

23:24-25. A child to be proud of. Most parents know that their children can bring them a great deal of anxiety and heartache at times. Many also know that they can be a source of pleasure and joy and gladness. Parents invest more in their children than often they are aware of.

If we have good parents, do we appreciate that our conduct in life, the decisions we make, the relationships we form, the attitudes we display, all impinge upon them and affect them? No matter how old we are, if our parents are still alive they have an interest in us and we will bring them happiness or sorrow but rarely indifference.

This proverb comprises a statement and an exhortation based upon it, and so both are aimed at the children. It is natural for a father to want his son or daughter to do well in life and prosper, but the expectation of godly parents should be twofold, that above everything else their offspring should be both righteous and wise. Health and wealth is one thing, but this is quite another. These are considerations which completely override material prosperity. A wise son or daughter will recognise this.

The fundamental concern which permeates the proverbs is that children should fear the Lord. In many societies will be found the pressure to conform to certain standards, to be socially acceptable, to obtain a good education, or whatever it may be, and much parental energy can be diverted into these channels rather than upon what matters most. It is of paramount importance that children fear the Lord and put their trust in him, that through repentance and faith they become righteous in God's sight. The responsible way to go about this is for parents to honour the Lord in a natural way in big things and small in the day-to-day life of the family. Salvation may be of the Lord, but he lays certain responsibilities upon parents.

Then, it is insufficient that the children put their faith in the Lord. They then need to grow up in the Lord. That is, they need to acquire heavenly wisdom for their earthly life. So the training continues. This investment of energy is wonderfully conducive to strengthening the family bonds. To see the God-given fruit from such labour is more than a cause of satisfaction on the part of the parents, for it brings joy and delight.

It is only parents who have made this kind of training part and parcel of their family life who can justly give the exhortation of v. 25, if indeed it comes from them. Then the encouragement given is one which is based upon a sound family relationship. Children brought up in this environment will want to bring pleasure to their parents. Here is neither a negative threat of what they might otherwise lose, nor an incentive for what they might gain, but the prospect of the lasting pleasure they might contribute for the well-being of their parents.

Nevertheless, the exhortation is valid from whomever it comes and is to be received in its own right insofar as it is all part and parcel of the Fifth Commandment.

[Related proverbs: 10:1; 15:20; 23:15; 27:11; 29:3.]

23:26-28. Use your eyes. There are two particular areas in which young men can so easily come adrift. One is sex, and the other is drink (to which we might add drugs). Prowess in these areas is often considered a mark of manliness. For this reason the writer returns to these subjects.

There are two things a godly father wants his son to do. First of all, he wants his son's heart. Should he not rather want his son's independence? Some see these as contradictory. They are not. The heart of a godly and wise son will be with his father and for his father to whom he owes so much even though he is no longer dependent upon him. However, there may come times of heady temptation which disorientate his thinking, when a reminder is necessary.

The second thing, which is related to it, is that a father wants his son to take note of his example. A godly father should have nothing of which to be ashamed. His life should speak for itself. He need not remonstrate with his son with, 'Look at all your mother and I have done for you.' His life, and the fruit from his life, will be obvious to anyone who takes the trouble to look. Ironically, that might include his faults and failures, for even they have something useful to show to his son!

The inducement to sexual immorality can be powerful and the opportunity for it wide open at times. Many a man has lost his heart to a seductress and suffered the consequences. Many a man has shut his eyes to the reality of what he is letting himself in for.

The deep pit and narrow well both indicate being in a desperate situation from which it is very difficult to extricate oneself. Those who fall are well and truly mired. One of the problems for those who succumb to the temptation is that they are likely to become hooked and continue that way, held down by its dark, sinister appeal. Witness the alarming influence of pornography on the internet, a web into which even many Christians have been drawn.

Men brought under the influence of sexual sins by women who use their bodies to arouse them by whatever means are rightly described as 'victims', or 'prey' to robbery. They are letting themselves in not for a good time but for devastation or destruction. Such women cause no end of trouble, for unfaithfulness in this area arouses strong and dangerous passions which remain like poison in the system of society. Not a few Christian pastors have had their lives ruined and done untold damage to their churches, blinded by a fatal attraction instead of using their eyes.

Above all, God the Father wants the hearts of his children so that they can enjoy all the rich benefits his ways provide. Read 1 John 2:15-17. He wants their heart, and he longs for their obedience – doing his will. He is faithful to his word, and he wants us to be faithful too.

[Related proverbs: 2:16; 6:24-35; 7:5; 22:14.]

23:29-35. On the binge. We are given six clues from which to determine who is being described. This person has:–

Woe. This is deep distress of foreboding of a calamitous nature.

Sorrow. This is being in the depths of unhappiness.

Contentions. This indicates mindless brawling.

Complaints. Totally dissatisfied, everything is wrong for this person, which he expresses loud and clear (though perhaps not very coherently!).

Wounds without cause. He is battered and bruised, having picked a fight either with others or with the furniture!

Redness of eyes. The bloodshot eyes are symptoms of a deeper malaise.

Such are the well-known and incontrovertible characteristics of those under the influence of alcohol. Those are the 'benefits' with which the substance rewards them. So why do so many people go after it? Because, like the seductress, it has an addictive influence. Verse 31 points to its hypnotising appeal and short term 'benefits', verse 32 to its real effect. Verse 33 shows how it both addles the senses and loosens the tongue to perversity. Verse 34 shows how all judgement is lost, and verse 35 how all sensation is lost. When the hammer of the hangover has ceased pounding, this person goes back for more!

Reason asks, who could want such things? We have just looked at six things alcohol delivers to those who seek it. Now compare their counterparts for those who are led by the Spirit of God. They have everything to look forward to with an assured hope, they have joy, they have peace, they have contentment, they have well-being, they have soundness of body and mind. They have no sorrows to drown, for Jesus has borne them (Isaiah 53:4), they have everything to live for. They have nothing to shut out or escape from, they can face anything and everything, for they now live in the real world under the care of their heavenly Father.

For some young men there is a strong psychological pressure to go down to the pub – or to the nightclub – 'with the boys' and to prove that they are as good as the best of them. All they might prove is that they are as bad as the worst of them.

As far as the wine is concerned, do not let your eyes be drawn by its deceptive attraction (31). Do not be fooled. It will unerringly do for you what it has done for others.

Read Titus 2:11-14.

Abuse of sex and substance abuse are two prominent and common marks of lack of self-control and utter folly. They strip a man of his dignity and bring him into bondage, holding a power over him from which he is rarely freed, and, even if he is, often scarring him physically and emotionally *for life*.

'My son, give me your heart.' There is only one safe place for our hearts throughout life, and that is with our heavenly Father. Give him your heart, and let him keep it!

[Related proverb: 23:20-21.]

24:1-2. 'You shall not covet.' The further you read through the book of Proverbs, the more aware you will be that you are revisiting places you have been before. It is just the same in life. There are some areas in which we need constant reminders, and this is one.

Envy: this little word describes a monster. At 14:30 we are reminded of how in a sinister manner it eats away inside us if we allow it house space. Once again it raises its ugly head.

We are not to be envious at all, so why the reference to evil men? For we are reading here about evil men (or women), what goes on in their hearts and what they give voice to, namely violence and troublemaking. They sound a bit like gangsters, and surely no one reading these notes would be seeking that kind of company! So this proverb is not relevant to you, right? Wrong!

Many of the proverbs are like caricatures, emphasising features and drawing our eye to them. Or they hold up to our view something in its raw format before it is softened by cosmetics. Or they illustrate things by means of an extreme case with the intention that we should recognise them in their less stark form. So it is here. In certain instances we may not see evil or be aware of violent intentions or notice troublemaking until it is pointed out to us, and one of those instances is when our perception is clouded by envy.

A teenager may idolise a pop star or hero worship a footballer or some other 'personality' and do things and go places with others who are likeminded. What the person is really like, or what the other followers are really like, usually doesn't enter into the equation. But attitudes rub off, as shown by the memorabilia, the language, the company, and so on. Envy often features large in such cult followings.

When we start to look at people in terms of what they have got rather than what they are, we are going badly astray. This includes not just possessions but personality and gifts. We may think of one person who has tremendous charisma, and another who has stunning looks, or we may know someone else who is remarkably gifted in some way, and we wish we had those things and it rankles that it makes us feel so inferior. Perhaps it will add to our status if we are seen to be associated with them or their followers? In a subtle way their mind set influences our own thinking and behaviour. Yet what do these things really matter? It is what they are underneath these mere externals that matters. All the time that we are envious our perception is distorted and we are masking out the things we do not want to see or acknowledge. More seriously still, we are failing to consider how God has made us and what he intends for us personally, instead pouring our emotional energy into a bottomless pit.

This proverb bluntly tells us the reason for not being envious of evil men. It shouldn't be necessary, but it is because envy is so short-sighted. Some people who have gained a tremendous following have actually done untold harm to others by their lifestyle and example. Some in public are as smooth as butter who in private are vitriolic.

Envy begins where admiration ends.

[Related proverbs: 1:15; 3:31; 23:17; 24:19.]

24:3-4. Time for an internal inspection.

Visiting other people's homes, or going round stately homes, can be an interesting experience. It can tell you a lot about the people – their lifestyle, their standard of living, their passions and priorities, their hobbies and interests, the things they have done in life – and sometimes the things they don't like or can't be bothered with. It may even cause you to revise your opinion of them!

While a literal understanding of this proverb is valid, more likely we are intended to see in it a pictorial representation of the way people build their lives and the things they do. In this respect it is similar to the parable of the wise and foolish builders of Matthew 7:24-27. We may take these words to address our personal lives, and they apply equally to the building of a family.

Do you live in a house or a hovel?

Wisdom. This is the essential prerequisite to any project which is going to succeed, and it applies supremely to life itself. The question which must repeatedly be asked and answered is, are you hearing and obeying the words of the Lord Jesus Christ? Is every brick of your life fitting into his pattern? How about inspecting the brickwork now?

Understanding. Is your house strong and secure ('established'), or is some part of it in risk of collapsing? Following the Lord is not mindless, slavish obedience. It requires understanding and intelligent application. We are not to be foolish, says Paul, but to understand what the Lord's will is (Ephesians 5:17). Believers have renewed minds (Romans 12:2) and they are supposed to use them! In understanding we are to be mature (1 Corinthians 14:20).

Knowledge. Believers are to grow in the grace and knowledge of the Lord Jesus Christ (2 Peter 3:18), for in him are hidden all the treasures of wisdom and knowledge (Colossians 2:3) – hidden for us to search them out, a bit like mining! Knowledge is precious in wise and understanding hearts. Many people have knowledge and do not know what to do with it. Some in the church at Corinth were not short in this department (1 Corinthians 1:5) but they were abusing it (see ch.8 for example) because they were immature (3:1-4) and needed to grow up.

Beauty. Knowledge well used will ornament and beautify our lives and enrich the lives of others too. There is a comprehensiveness about v. 4. Many people's lives are cluttered with knick-knacks of no intrinsic worth. The general appearance is one of untidiness and disorder. Given the proper foundation mentioned above, knowledge of the Lord – his Word, his laws and commands, his grace and power, his promises, his ways, his purposes, his providence – and everything else there is to know of him – this knowledge will be found to be of immeasurable worth in both its parts and its whole, making your house an attractive repository of riches.

If you are a Christian, your body is a temple of the Holy Spirit (1 Corinthians 6:19-20). The temple of God should be filled with what is holy, with what is beautiful, with what is enduring, with what is best.

[Related proverbs: 8:18; 15:6; 21:20; 23:23.]

24:5-6. How to fight your own battles. In some ways this follows on from the preceding. A house exists for protection as much as for comfort. Life is not cosy. We need strength to be properly equipped for life. We have all seen lives swept away by the winds of temptation or destroyed by the storms of adversity. This causes as much distress to onlookers as to the people themselves. People ask, 'Why did this happen? How did it happen?'

24:5. Beware the danger of going it alone – you need the Lord. Your life may look good, whether in your own eyes or those of others. However, when the storms of life come – and they will – it is not appearance but strength which is important. Wisdom is unassailable. This is wisdom which has the fear of God as its root. Knowledge gives it its strength. This is knowledge which has the fear of God as its branch. These are concepts which are not popular today, which is why so many lives are in disarray.

As a good soldier understands how important it is to look to his commanding officer and follow his instructions. A member of an orchestra, however gifted, knows it is essential to take the lead only and always and completely from the baton. So a wise man understands the imperative of dependence upon the Lord and of understanding and obeying him. Says the Lord to Daniel concerning a time of great opposition: 'Those who know their God shall be strong, and do' (Daniel 11:32).

24:6. Beware the danger of going it alone – you need others.

We all have our own battles to fight, but that does not mean we fight them alone. We may be strong, but we may not be strong enough. It is not sufficient to say we are depending on the Lord if we fail to use the means he has put at our disposal. Imagine a soldier who has been told of the location of a cache of weapons for his use disregarding them and entering the danger zone without them. It would be suicidal.

In our Christian lives we need the support and counsel of others. This among other things is what the church is there for. It is not a mark of weakness but of wisdom to seek outside help when difficulties come along and we find ourselves under threat in some way. If we are to see our way through safely, we will have others to thank for it.

If you are a very private person, ask yourself whether this is right. It may be a mark of pride, it may be simple timidness. But it is also a great weakness. The attitudes of an isolationist society should not be carried into the church. We need one another. The weakest needs the strongest, and the strongest needs the weakest. Our brothers and sisters in Christ can be a blessing to us in our times of need. So let us have the wisdom to refer to them. It is also a blessing to be needed and to contribute to the help of others. So let us have the wisdom to do so with grace and understanding.

[Related proverbs: 11:14; 15:22; 20:18.]

24:7. Out of his league. A rather pathetic picture is portrayed here. A fool has nothing of worth to contribute when it comes to any matter of importance.

A certain unbeliever attended a meeting on the subject of Christian fellowship and was asked afterwards his opinion of it. He opened his mouth and no words would come out. Have you ever attended a meeting where you have felt completely and utterly out of your depth, when if you were asked to say something you wouldn't have known how to begin? This of course may not have been your fault.

This is the position of the fool in the gate, only in his case it is very much his fault. 'The gate' in this context is the equivalent of the court of law, the place where disputes were settled, or the place where issues of grave concern were discussed.

In the Bible the fool is never spoken of neutrally. This proverb is critical of the fool. The implication is that he ought to have a contribution to make but he cannot, not because he does not have the mental capacity or even knowledge, but because he is on the wrong wavelength. He is a fool. He has never troubled himself with what is important in life or what matters to others. The things of God are of no concern to him. Principles of righteousness and justice are things with which he has never bothered himself.

We all have an important contribution to make in life and in the society in which we live. An ungodly society is a very foolish one. So many people live as if having a good time and a comfortable life are all that matters and they hardly look beyond themselves. Of all people, Christians ought to be making their voice heard in the gate. Theirs ought to be the voice of wisdom in society, upholding what is right and exposing what is wrong with cogent arguments. Christians need to be aware of the issues confronting society, and especially (though not exclusively) those which challenge the Word of God; they need to be bringing to bear the voice of reason, demonstrating right concern, showing by right living and right speech the way forward.

Are there matters being discussed 'in the gate' – that is, at the higher levels of society – about which you are confused? Would it be appropriate for you to find out how God's Word addresses such matters? Would it help to be equipped to speak with others about such things where at present you feel, perhaps uncomfortably, obliged to hold your tongue?

24:8-9. Naming and shaming. The difference between those who do evil and those who plan to do so is that the latter are ten times more dangerous. The one described here as a 'schemer' is, literally, a 'master of evil plots'. That is what he will be known as, what he will be called. Some crooks are petty criminals working on their own. In other cases, behind criminal activity there is a mastermind who has it all worked out, the sinister figure lurking in the shadows, a controlling force who is feared and usually hated.

There are men and women of influence who have proved to be unscrupulous about achieving their own ends. They are the scheming individuals regarded with suspicion by others – and this verse is indeed about how they will be regarded. They gain a reputation for underhand dealings, for deception, for using their power to bend others to their will.

Verse 9 closely parallels v. 8. The machinations of the schemer, described here as the devising of foolishness, is sin. A person who does this is showing blatant disregard for truth and equity, and is appropriately called a scoffer.

We might expect such a person to be described as an abomination to God, but the point being made here is that he is also an abomination to *men*.

Wickedness in this world is tolerated so long as people think they benefit by it, but in the longer term it is recognised to be the scourge of society, and those who promote it, especially those holding public office, are often rooted out, exposed and disgraced, receiving plenty of media attention in the process.

The scoffer is also an abomination to men in a secondary sense in that the effects of his scheming only prove harmful. Any evil is always damaging.

Christians should be heartened by the fact that these things are so. Where public figures exert pressure to overturn laws that are based on the Word of God, deliberately suppressing evidence and ignoring known facts, any short term success they may enjoy will be to their detriment. Not only so, the effects of their measures will bring only harm. It will prove to be an abomination to men.

Sin is a reproach to any people; it is righteousness that exalts a nation (14:34). Truth can stand upon its own two feet, and no one need fear that it can be defeated. Deep down men know this, and that is why deception has to be employed in order to push any form of evil. Believers have an ally in the hearts of those who deny the truth. Truth does only good and can be promoted openly and freely.

Having looked at the 'big things' going on 'out there', give some thought to the 'little things' going on 'in here'. Are there any matters in which you are practising deception in order to get your way or what you want or where you want to go? How would others view it if they did but know?

24:10. The stress test. A man buys a fish tank, puts it on a table in an alcove, fits it out with its decorative features and proceeds to fill it with water. He has nearly finished this stage preparatory to introducing the fish when the table gives way and the whole thing is a spectacular disaster.

The table had looked fine, but its legs could not cope with the stress introduced by the weight of the tank of water, and it gave way.

People can be like this. They can look fine and can seem to be getting along fine. We might think of them as strong. 'She's a strong Christian,' we might say. Someone else we might have serious doubts about, but not her. However, the stresses of adversity can produce some unexpected results. Those we might judge to be strong sometimes fall apart when subjected to severe trials, while others bear much more than we would have thought possible.

We all fairly regularly suffer adversity in various shapes or forms throughout life. How do you cope with it? Or can't you? Do you tend to go to pieces when things go wrong? Do you crumple when others put the pressure on you?

Look back again at vv. 5-6. War involves adversity. It requires fighting. Giving in means losing. Strength is assessed not by appearance but by the wisdom which is the fear of the Lord, which relies one hundred percent upon him, and it is enhanced through the knowledge of him. Temptation likewise involves adversity. Temptation can introduce tremendous pressures. Are you going to yield to it? How do you know?

There is something of a paradox here. If you do faint in the day of adversity, it proves that your strength is small. At the same time, you need to understand and acknowledge that your strength *is* small if you are going to stand through it. Paul said, 'Let him who thinks he stands take heed lest he fall' (1 Corinthians 10:12). He also said, 'I can do all things through Christ who strengthens me' (Philippians 4:13), and God said to him, 'My grace is sufficient for you, for my strength is made perfect in weakness' (2 Corinthians 12:9). Our strength is that which is acquired through total reliance upon God. This is not in a mystical kind of way but involves intelligently applying his Word to the situations in which we find ourselves.

The trouble is, the pressures of adversity can have a distorting effect upon our thinking and we lose objectivity. We focus upon the adversity which pokes its ugly features in our face rather than standing back and looking at it in the light of God's Word.

Think about the times when you have reacted in a wrong way to troubles. Maybe something has gone wrong and you have 'blown your stack'. Or you have been subjected to a tirade of criticism and you have withdrawn into sullenly feeling sorry for yourself. Or you have suffered an injustice and all you can think about is how to get even over it. Examples could be multiplied, but they are all instances of *fainting* in the day of adversity. They all fail to ask and answer the simple question: how does the Word of God address this situation? We are to be strong in the Lord and in the power of his might (Ephesians 6:10). Then in the adversity we are to use the tools he has given us. Our strength is his strength, our weapons are his weapons. 'He gives power to the weak, and to those who have no might he increases strength. Even the youths shall faint and be weary, and the young men shall utterly fall. But those who wait on the Lord shall renew their strength ... they shall walk and not faint' (Isaiah 40:29-31).

24:11-12. Intervention and support. There are on record many notable acts of bravery in times of war in which men have risked their lives and personally suffered greatly in order to deliver fallen comrades from a certain death. In a day of adversity they have proved their strength and not fainted.

Not many of us would ever find ourselves in the literal situation described by this proverb. It is using an extreme example to illustrate a general principle, and all of us find ourselves in *that* position from time to time.

There seem to be two thoughts here. The first is being in the grip of something too powerful and being dragged down by it (11a), while the second is that of running out of strength and collapsing (11b). The first requires intervention to deliver; the second requires support to enable to go on.

Both are concerned with our responsibility toward our neighbour, irrespective of who our neighbour is. The parable of the good Samaritan is applicable here. Knowing the attitude of the Jews toward the Samaritans he could have turned the man over, recognised him as a Jew, given him a kick and gone on.

Some of the most remarkable acts of deliverance in time of war have been when men have found enemies in dire straits and have gone out of their way to help and restore them. Now, isn't that how God has dealt with each one of us? We were God's enemies, heading for death, stumbling to the slaughter, and yet his Son shed his own blood in order to deliver us (Romans 5:6-8) and then gave us strength to go on.

It is in the light of this that we should be very much aware that we have responsibilities.

This proverb seems to be addressing a situation in which people might think to make excuses, not wanting to get involved. It provides two incentives, one negative, one positive. Firstly, God weighs the heart. He knows all that is going on there. He can see through the excuse, 'I was no the other side of the road: I didn't see anything.' Secondly, God keeps your soul. Does that not mean anything to you? If God has shown such kindness to you, is it too much to ask that you show a little to others?

To say, 'I can't get involved in this,' when a serious need arises, is not an option. The fact that it has come to your notice and it is within your power to do something, automatically lays an obligation upon you. It may cost you.

God says, 'Do it!' It may be painful to you. God says, 'Do it!' You may be afraid. God says, 'Do it!' This is not a time to ask questions, it is a time to act.

The final clause asks a question. It may be taken as either a warning or an encouragement, depending on your point of view! The neglect of obedience will result in retribution. Obedience will result in blessing.

Further questions – if they need asking: Do you know anyone for whom intervention is essential if they are to survive some crisis? Do you know anyone finding it difficult to cope and desperately in need of support? How does this proverb address you?

24:13-14. A find for the faint and weary. There is no hardship involved in complying with this exhortation as there might be had the words been, 'My son, take this medicine because it will do you good, though it is bitter to your taste'! Honey is delicious to the palate, it brings a sparkle to the eyes of the weary and helps restore strength and energy.

King Saul's foolish prohibition from eating when pursuing the enemy meant that when his army came upon honey in abundance in the forest they were not allowed to taste it, and so their victory was unnecessarily hindered because of their faintness (1 Samuel 14:24-30).

The Bible contains numerous references to honey. For example, God described the land of promise as a good land, a land flowing with milk and honey (Exodus 3:8), a description which stuck. The manna he supplied for his people in the wilderness tasted like wafers made with honey (Exodus 16:31). In Psalm 81:11-16 the Lord said that had his people given him heed he would have fed them with the finest of wheat and satisfied them with honey.

Honey is not just exceptionally sweet, it has concentrated nutritional value and other uses. A little can be satisfyingly beneficial. Then as now it would be carefully gathered and stored. Even in a land flowing with milk and honey it was too precious a commodity to waste.

All this, says our writer, is illustrative of wisdom. He is really saying, 'My son, imbibe wisdom!' How foolish to reject such fare! How wretched to have no taste for it! God's Word is said to be sweeter than honey to those who feed on it (Psalms 19:10; 119:103). The wisdom which comes from God is restorative and strengthening. It is to be had for the asking (James 1:5). It clears the mind, revives the spirit, gives something to look forward to and renews hope.

This proverb speaks, literally, of an *end* for those who have found wisdom. This, however, is not an end in a negative sense, as for example coming to the end of one's resources or the end of life. Quite the opposite, for it is an end in the sense of fulfilment, of achievement, of satisfaction, and it is paralleled in the final clause with a hope which will not be cut off. Ultimately, there is only one such hope. Death sets a terminus point on every hope bar one, and that is the hope of eternal life.

Wisdom is sweet for time and for eternity. The fear of the Lord will never diminish into anything less than pure pleasure for those who have it. His Word will never cease to delight. As we grow in the knowledge of the Lord, so do we grow in our appreciation of him and his surpassing grace, and so are we continually refreshed as time progresses toward eternity.

If you are growing faint or are beset by weariness in your Christian life, go back again to the Lord and extract the sweetness from his Word, waiting upon him until he gives you the strength to go on again.

24:15-16. Psalm 94. Resilience and protection. This is a not so much warning shot across the bows of the wicked as a quiet assurance to the godly. History is full of examples of the wicked taking advantage of the vulnerability of those who live righteous lives in an ungodly society. Hebrews 10:32-36 records one such case (note v. 34) through which believers had passed.

These things happen literally in parts of our world today where extremists pillage and kill Christian communities living at peace without the defences to resist and with neither the desire nor the right to take up the kind of weapons their persecutors use.

Also implicit in this proverb is the acknowledgement that the righteous often do not have an easy time of it, for it speaks of the possibility of his *falling* 'seven times'. However, the righteous have something the wicked do not understand.

What is it that enables believers to get up and get going again when they suffer, sometimes repeatedly, at the hands of evil people? There are two intimately related aspects to this. The first is that they have the Lord watching over them, and the second is that they have a glorious hope beyond the troubles of this life which means that they can hold things lightly which others set great store by. These two factors also explain why the wicked fall calamitously, for they are without hope and without God in the world (Ephesians 2:12).

Psalm 94, already alluded to several times in these notes on Proverbs, expresses unequivocally that the Lord is well aware of the threats to his people and the plight in which they often find themselves. He knows how weak and vulnerable they are, and how fearful. Human impotence finds its comfort in divine omnipotence, for the Lord not only sees, he also acts. This does not mean, however, that the righteous are spared suffering at the hands of the wicked. On the contrary, Psalm 94:5-6 makes it clear that some in their helplessness are killed.

So alongside one another we see atrocities being committed against some and God providing protection and deliverance for others. People may ask, 'Why does a God of love allow...?' Or they may ask, 'If there is a God and he is as powerful as you say, then why doesn't he...?' The Lord Jesus spoke of wheat and tares being allowed to grow together (Matthew 13:24-30). Ever since Adam disobeyed God this world has been a battleground, and the Lord has made it abundantly plain that those who live godly lives will suffer persecution. What is also made clear is that his people cannot be destroyed (2 Corinthians 4:9). The wicked may regard believers like a pernicious weed to be rooted out and destroyed, but their root system is such that even if they are eliminated in one place they will in the meantime flourish in another and bear fruit to the glory of God!

The wicked have everything to lose, the righteous everything to gain. Ultimately, the righteous will rise again. Ultimately, the wicked will fall forever. Like the psalmist, we may cry, 'How long...?' Nevertheless we know it is only a matter of time.

'A sovereign Protector I have, unseen, yet for ever at hand, unchangeably faithful to save, almighty to rule and command' (Toplady).

[Related proverbs: 10:25,30; 11:21,23; 14:32.]

24:17-18. Yes! But no!

How often have we seen the hand raised, the fist clenched, and the lips utter a triumphant, euphoric, 'YES!'

This may have its place in the realm of sport and the like, but not here. Verses 15-20 hang together with reference to what will happen to the wicked and the righteous. It is interesting that the Lord is mentioned specifically only in this pair of verses and not in the others where we might expect it. Is it to give us a perspective on his character which we can so easily forget? God does not desire the death of the wicked (Ezekiel 18:20-25; 33:11-20; 2 Peter 3:9). Our attitude should be altogether different from that of the wicked who rejoice when the righteous fall. Romans 12:20-21 is not concerned with our getting vengeance upon our enemy. The 'burning coals' are for his conscience, that he might be led to repentance. That is how good overcomes evil! Remember the sons of thunder (Mark 3:17) wanting to command fire to fall on those who would not receive the Lord and the answer he gave them (Luke 9:54-56).

If our enemy stumbles or falls it is not our place to gloat. We are to show a different spirit – a *Christian* spirit. Jerusalem was destined for destruction. What did Jesus do? He wept over it (Luke 19:41; 13:34). He had already said his disciples are to love their enemies, to seek their well-being, to do them good and to pray for them (Matthew 5:44). No wonder this proverb speaks of the Lord being displeased with any finding pleasure in another's distress!

So when we see those who have been a particular trouble to us coming a cropper, we are not to say with gloating satisfaction that it serves them right. It would serve *us* right if the Lord turned his wrath away from them and allowed them to afflict us further!

The wrath of God displayed against the ungodly is never a source of pleasure to anyone. It gives God no pleasure, and so the last thing we should do is to delight in their misfortune. This side of eternity, it may be that mild displays of the wrath of God will lead enemies to repentance. After all, if it has happened to us in that when we were enemies we were reconciled to God through the death of his Son (Romans 5:10), then it should be our primary concern that those who are our enemies on that account should come to know the same Saviour.

Do you have any personal enemies who you know have fallen into trouble? Ask the Lord how in such a situation you can repay evil with good, and how you can be a blessing to those who are hostile to you.

24:19-20. Retain objectivity and perspective. The second clause of each verse parallels the first in such a way as to add emphasis to what is being said, while the second verse gives a reason for the injunction of the first. In so doing it acknowledges there are very real and powerful temptations in this area.

This is the third of three related proverbs commencing with 'Do not...' with an associated reason: 'Do not ... for...' (15-16); 'Do not ... lest...' (17-18); 'Do not ... for...' (19-20). Among other things, it reminds us that God's commands are always reasonable – there is always a reason for them. They are therefore to be followed not in blind faith but with intelligent faith.

Here are two things we are not to do.

We are not to fret. How easy it is to grow heated when we see evildoers getting away with their evil deeds. Why doesn't God do something about it? The situation gets under our skin, it irks us, and the next thing we know is that we are planning what we would do about it had we the chance. But it is not for us to take the law into our own hands. Or else perhaps we get angry because we feel something ought to be done about it but we ourselves are completely helpless.

Those who are for ever talking about and lamenting all that is bad in the world and carrying on about the perpetrators of evil have a negative and unhealthy bias. There are many things with which we can rightfully become preoccupied, but this is not one of them. It is not a good use of our time or emotional energy. We have better things to be thinking about and acting on.

We are not to envy. Why should they get all the perks? Why should I be the one to suffer? So we feel that they are in some way better off than we are, and it is just not right! So we either become sullen about it or compromise our principles to get in on what they have got. But this is covetousness. We are to be content with what we have. The reason? Because the Lord is the giver of every good and perfect gift. If we hanker after what he has not given, we are hankering after what is not good for us. We may think otherwise, but otherwise is not wise, it is other-wise.

Fretting and envying belong to the short-sighted who do not think to ask where these people are going. They are going nowhere, they have no prospect. What they seem to have is illusory, and even that will not last. It is a no-hoper for them. Back at v. 14 we saw that there *is* a prospect for those who have wisdom.

All that the wicked stand for, all that they work for, will come to nothing. With them, it will be plunged into darkness. By inference, the lamp of the righteous, though the wicked attempt to extinguish it, will go on burning. That is because God is able to keep it alight (compare Isaiah 42:3). He is the one who will extinguish the lamp of the wicked.

As with so many of the proverbs, we are exhorted to take the long view, which – let it be admitted – is not easy when the short view is so troublesome.

This proverb is concerned with what we are *not* to do. Now turn to Psalm 37 and consider its advice on what we *are* to do.

[Related proverbs: 3:31; 13:9; 20:20; 23:17; 24:1.]

24:21-22. Romans 13:1-7. Authority. Jesus said, 'Render to Caesar the things that are Caesar's, and to God the things that are God's' (Matthew 22:21). Peter says, 'Fear God. Honour the king' (1 Peter 2:17). Paul says of the governing authority, 'He is God's minister ... he does not bear the sword in vain' (Romans 13:4).

The Lord is the ultimate authority, but he has delegated authority to kings and rulers, whether they acknowledge it or not.

Once more, this proverb is addressed to 'My son'. Again, there is a 'Do not ... for...'. Whether the translation is 'Do not associate with those given to change', or 'Do not join with the rebellious', or 'Do not join with those who do otherwise', the central idea is clear. The idealism of youth often sees the instituted authorities as a hindrance to freedom and progress. As a result they want to take radical action to change things and this brings them into conflict with the powers that be. Almost every generation has its youthful champions of causes, with significant followings.

The warning here is that personal and popular crusades are liable to be put down with devastating consequences.

Anyone who has a just cause may raise it in the right way. There are two essential prerequisites to public life and public action. The first is the fear of God, and the second, arising out of it, is the fear of the authorities instituted by God. Where the fear of God is lost, loss of respect for his instituted authorities will not be far behind with its consequent anarchic tendencies.

Those who despise the Lord will be called to account at the last day. Those who despise instituted authorities will not have to wait so long! They will soon find themselves in all kinds of trouble and certainly will not receive a sympathetic hearing.

While there is no injustice with the Lord (though many people foolishly think otherwise), there often is much that is wrong with those wielding power in our society. Does this put a limit on the injunction of this proverb? Not at all! In fact, quite to the contrary. The proverb is remarkable in that it deliberately makes no distinction, placing the infallible Lord and fallible king on the same footing in relation to fear, as well as on the same footing in relation to retribution.

So, whatever may be wrong with our rulers, we are to 'fear' them. That is, we are to maintain a proper respect and show a robust deference for them, acknowledging and supporting what is right in their rule. It is common in a democratic society to find fault with leaders. To listen to some people talk one would think the government comprised a bunch of charlatans! The Christian attitude should be notably different.

We are always to recognise that they are there by God's authority, and also that they have power. To provoke them by rebellion will not further any cause, it will only bring swift retribution. If there are things that are wrong, or that need changing, the right approach is through a proper fear. Consider David's attitude toward Saul. He never lost his fear of Saul (and we don't mean his fear of being killed by him), even though he was unjustly hounded and hunted. His lament in 2 Samuel 1:17-27 was quite genuine.

24:23-25. An impartial view of justice. To the end of the chapter are some 'further sayings of the wise' covering some things not mentioned in the section starting at 22:17. They commence with a caution about violating a basic principle of justice.

A judge or jury member who knows well or is related to the accused is automatically disqualified from service in that case because of the very real potential for bias. All kinds of emotions can influence one's attitude in judgement (take a moment to think about each of these) – greed, fear, sympathy, hatred, jealousy – whereas the only and absolute criterion should be the law and the intent of the law, that is, the law rightly interpreted. This proverb speaks literally of 'respecting the face' in judgement. When 'who it is' interferes with 'what the issue is', or when self-interest plays a part, then partiality is entering into the picture and this is not good.

While 17:15 says that the Lord abominates those who justify the wicked and condemn the righteous, here we read of the reaction from society. This proverb is very wide in its application and is not concerned only with what goes on in a court of law. People are outraged when they see wicked people being treated as if they were righteous, and nations are outraged when they see perpetrators of evil in public office getting away with and even being approved for what they are doing. A sense of right and wrong still runs deep in the human heart.

Silence sometimes speaks louder than words. Inaction can be construed as tacit approval. To speak out against evil and to rebuke evildoers is every citizen's responsibility, painful and difficult (and even dangerous) though this may be. The 'delight' (v. 25) attendant upon this is not the feel-good factor of having put someone in their place, or of scoring a point against another. It is more to do with the satisfaction of having done what is right in God's eyes and for the general benefit of others. God promises a good blessing for such people.

Christians should be more vocal than others in this area, not because they are better than or superior to others, but because they have – or should have – a truer and fuller concept of justice through the knowledge of God and his Word.

This proverb raises certain questions about the place of the law in our minds and hearts and lives. Judgement is based on law – in this case God's law. Prejudice so easily enters into our relationships, colouring our views and clouding our judgement. In our circle of acquaintances, close or otherwise, are we approving or turning a blind eye to what others are doing when it is really our responsibility to speak to them about these things? Or are we more interested in our own comfort and security than to take a real interest in the welfare of others or the public good when under threat from evildoers?

Another personal application: The law which applies to others also applies to ourselves. Are we showing partiality to *ourselves* in judgement, allowing ourselves concessions where we should not? If others have occasion to rebuke *us*, how do we take it?

[Related proverbs: 17:15; 18:5; 28:21.]

24:26. Intimate honesty.

Compare 25:11. In thinking about a right answer it might be worth considering first what the question is! Broadly speaking, it is any situation in which a response is required and in particular to which a wrong response might so easily be given. It is in this kind of situation that a right answer has so much merit.

What is meant by a 'right' or 'honest' answer is one which is marked by straightforward truthfulness and integrity. It is apposite, it addresses the issue, not skirting round it or evading it, and it does so in an appropriate manner. For example, suppose a friend asks you for advice or your opinion about some matter and you realise at once that something has been touched upon which is going to cause hurt if the truth be told. The fear is that your friendship will be upset if you give the answer your friend needs to hear, and so you are tempted to settle for less than the whole truth for the sake of keeping the peace.

Without wishing to confine the meaning, consider an illustration. Your friend has fallen out with someone else and asks you what to do about it. You know that the real underlying issue, of which your friend is oblivious, is her lack of discretion and tendency to tell tales about others. It would be relatively easy to find a patch-up solution, but that would not address the real problem. How are you going to tell her this home truth? What you fear might sour your friendship (and it might indeed do so in the short term) will actually seal it in the longer term when your friend, having taken to heart your answer, recognises your integrity and your concern for her well-being.

Relationships which are cluttered with no-go areas and 'things we do not talk about' to avoid upsetting them are bound to remain stunted because 'right answers' are excluded. The kiss on the lips is a token of affection and intimacy, of acknowledging the bond in a relationship. By responding rightly you are showing this affection.

The exemplar of the 'right answer' is the Lord Jesus in his public ministry. Many came to him with all kinds of questions and with widely varying motives. The Lord's answers were always full of wisdom and understanding and pertinent to the listeners. In the case of the sincere young enthusiast who came to him with his question about eternal life (Mark 10:17-22) Mark specifically notes Jesus' love for the man as he touched on a sore spot. It was a kiss on the lips did the man but know it.

There are many questions in life to which there *appear* to be no right answers. That does not mean that there actually *are* no right answers, only that they are not so easily found. There may have been occasions when you have been at a loss to know how to respond to a situation. To give a right answer often involves wisdom and insight, tact and discretion. One thing is sure and it is that the ability to give a right answer depends upon two essential factors: love for God with soul, heart, mind and strength, and love for one's neighbour as oneself. Without the Lord the right answer will not be found, and without love for one's neighbour a right answer will not be given.

24:27. First things first. This proverb, though set in the context of a rural economy, is of general application. There are priorities in life. To 'build your house' in this context is probably figurative for marriage and starting a family.

Many young people have unrealistically ideal views of love and marriage, impatiently launching into a relationship with starry-eyed expectation that everything will work out all right. If love is blind, sooner or later it is going to run headlong and painfully into obstacles.

What are you going to live on? This proverb does not use the word 'responsibility', but it is there. How is a young man going to support and provide for his wife and family? Has he given it due consideration? Has the matter been properly worked out? Financial anxieties can impose great strains on marriage and lead to bitterness and recrimination with unhappy long term consequences.

A young man thinking of marriage should take a responsible attitude to it, carefully considering its practical implications. This proverb touches upon two areas for him. The first concerns a good work ethic, for it speaks of preparation and setting himself up and making things ready in his work life. So, is he industrious? Is he applying himself to provision or only to pleasure? Is he showing by the way he conducts his affairs now that he will be fit to support a wife and raise a family?

The second concerns a secure base. If his circumstances are precarious then he needs to give time to sorting them out before he gets involved in matters of domestic life. 'Happy go lucky' is nowhere on God's agenda for his people. Better to wait a year or two now and enjoy a secure relationship than to be hasty and suffer years of regret.

Other areas of application. Many people attempt to build their houses on debt instead of hard, self-sacrificing work. They must have the comforts and luxuries they cannot afford, and in the end it costs them more dearly than they ever imagined in anxiety and trouble.

Not a few people have built their businesses on unrealistic hopes and expectations, only later to find them crashing down around their ears in bankruptcy. Their preparatory work had been minimal and what they hoped for mere wishful thinking.

Jesus gave the illustration of a man setting out to build a tower without first having worked out the cost, and being mocked because he was unable to finish it (Luke 14:28-29). He had not done his preparatory work. His grandiose ideas (symbolised by the tower) far exceeded his means and dismissed all rational objections.

In the case of that illustration, Jesus was making the point that there is a cost to following him. How many people think to build a Christian life without due preparation, without having understood the essential prerequisite that it will first cost them everything? Only when everything has been given over to Christ are they then given everything they need to build upon him.

24:28-29. Tit for tat. If there is no cause, why would anyone wish to testify against his neighbour? The backdrop to these verses seems to be an acrimonious relationship. Neighbours do not always get along together as well as they might. Grievances, petty squabbles and disputes are all too common.

24:28. Making something out of nothing. 'Witnessing' here is a serious matter having a public aspect. People's minds can be so poisoned by bad feelings that they can make out a case against someone when there really is no case at all. Things are blown up out of all proportion, situations are exaggerated, so that when they are described they bear such little resemblance to the truth that they are deception.

The ninth commandment says, without qualification, 'You shall not bear false witness against your neighbour.' There are no ifs and buts. However you may feel about your neighbour, what you say, *and how you say it*, must be strictly according to the truth. If not, you are practising deception, poisoning other people's minds with your ill will.

24:29. Just recompense. Now suppose your neighbour is indeed an awkward individual who does things which he knows will annoy you and seems to go out of his way to make himself objectionable. Do you not then have cause against him?

First of all, notice the words, 'I will do ... I will render....' They savour of personal vendetta. You have no right to take things into your own hands. If there really is a cause, there is a proper way of dealing with it.

Secondly, you have no right to use his own tactics against him, 'just as he has done to me'. Giving him a taste of his own medicine will only lead to a feud. It will not solve a problem, only perpetuate it and deepen it.

There are so many damaged and broken relationships at all levels of society, and it is the Lord's concern to bring reconciliation and healing. Is it yours? This can come about only by bringing to bear upon situations the principles of his Word. We are not to repay evil for evil, but to return evil with good (Romans 12:17). There is so much in the Word of God about forbearance and forgiveness, about kindness and gentleness and self-control, all of which are beneficial characteristics directly opposed to the attitude displayed here.

When others act upon us like festering sores, we need to remember the amazing goodness, forbearance and patience of God toward us (Romans 2:4). It is love which wins the day.

[Related proverbs: 20:22; 25:18,21.]

24:30-34. An object lesson. If the man was sick, or if he had overriding concerns elsewhere, the condition of his land might be excusable. But no, we are told from the outset that this is the land of a man who is bone idle. There are many causes of poverty, but the one for which there is no excuse is laziness. It contravenes the first command God ever gave to man, to be fruitful and multiply, to fill the earth and subdue it (Genesis 1:28). Verse 30 says two things about this man. It says that he is lazy, and it also says that he is devoid of understanding; literally, that he lacks heart. He lacks the heart for work.

There is a 'behold' in the original of v. 31. Passing by this field, the observer's eye was drawn to this state of dereliction and he says he considered it well and received instruction. So as we take in this picture what does it have to say to us?

First, he observed it to be overgrown with thorns and nettles. These testify not only to neglect, but also to the land being good. Having good land is not enough. It has to be worked. Field and vineyard need to be tilled and tended. Otherwise they produce those plants which are a mark of the curse God placed upon man's disobedience (Genesis 3:18).

By way of inference, a lazy man's life is not barren. What it produces is unsightly and is a cause of nuisance, pain and discomfort to others. It propagates the fruit of the curse. Laziness is not just pathetic, it is reprehensible.

Secondly, the stone wall of the vineyard was broken down. Its presence indicated that once the vineyard had been productive. This man had inherited something valuable and allowed it to go to rack and ruin. Laziness is inherently destructive. Again by inference, we receive a great many good things from God, gifts which he intends we should develop and use and make productive and fruitful. Of course it requires hard work – disciplined, intelligent hard work. But it is eminently worthwhile.

There is a statistic which has never been published: the cost of laziness. How many people do not realise their full potential because of it? How many things are left undone simply because they can't be bothered?

Thirdly, the land had not produced anything of worth for some time. To neglect the means of livelihood pointed one way only. Verses 33 and 34 repeat 6:10-11. The lazy man was too comfortable to give his mind to where it was all leading. The suddenness of the descent of destitution is captured well with the imagery. People can live quite well while resources last, but when they run out it is a different story and very suddenly they find themselves in the grip of poverty.

Another thing is implied by the repeated use of the word 'little'. The word is not disparaging relaxation. What it is doing is using a biting irony. It is the excuse of the lazy person. He will do it later, or tomorrow, but not just yet. For now he has got his feet up and is just enjoying a little rest! Only tomorrow never comes.

Consider the spiritual equivalent of each of the physical aspects in these verses, treating it as you would a parable. What does it have to teach of importance as to how you are to live the life God has given you?

[Related proverbs: 6:6-11; 10:4.]

Part 4

Proverbs 25:1 to 29:27

Second collection
of proverbs from Solomon

25:1-3. Hide and seek. Something of a revival took place in the time of Hezekiah (2 Chronicles 29 to 31). At such times of deep concern for the things of God there is invariably a renewed interest in good literature, and it may be this which prompted Hezekiah's men to trawl through Solomon's writings and supplement his previously published work with some further gems.

The collection opens with a rather enigmatic statement. It is reminiscent of Deuteronomy 29:29. There are things about God and his purposes which in his wisdom he has kept from us, that we do not know and cannot know. Paul exclaims about the ways of God being past finding out (Romans 11:33) as he marvels at the wisdom and knowledge and judgements of God, and in doing so ascribes glory to him (Romans 11:36).

What we do not know and cannot know of God and his ways are more than a matter of his keeping such knowledge from us, for they are a mark of his majesty and greatness, his exalted nature which places such knowledge completely out of our reach. As Isaiah declares, 'As the heavens are higher than the earth, so are my ways higher than your ways, and my thoughts than your thoughts' (Isaiah 55:8-9).

The all-wise God knows what to conceal from us and what to reveal to us, and what he has revealed often requires our searching out, and it is so that we may better follow in the path of obedience. If this applies generally, it does so especially to kings and those who rule. God commanded that kings apply themselves diligently to his Word (Deuteronomy 17:18-20). It was essential to effective rule. (If only some of our leaders today understood this!) In addition to this, kings needed to search out and know what was going on in their kingdom. It was very much to their honour and glory if they were in touch with the people over whom they ruled and were thereby able to rule wisely and well. These things undoubtedly apply also to those in leadership in the church.

How different is God in heaven from the kings of the earth! He does not need to search out a matter, nor does he need counsellors to instruct him! He knows all and understands all and therefore is able to rule with perfect righteousness.

If in v. 2 there is a comparison between God and kings, in v. 3 a similar one is made between kings and their subjects. To a certain extent this applies to kings worthy of the name. By virtue of their appointment, their responsibilities, their privileges and opportunities they are in a unique position, having an understanding of the workings of government and an access to knowledge denied to the majority. As God in heaven keeps his own counsel with regard to the outworking of his purposes, revealing what is appropriate for his people to know, so kings do likewise in relation to their subjects. It is essential to their effective rule that they do not disclose everything within their knowledge about affairs of state, nor divulge their intentions which, even though good, may be better expressed at a time when the people are ready for it.

This verse is a reminder that it is so, and that it is rightly so. Our response should be one of understanding respect and proper support.

25:4-5. Malachi 3:2-3. Take it away! The first statement is obvious, clearly understood, and makes perfect sense on its own. It is used as an unexpected and powerful introduction to the second, making a far from obvious but telling comparison.

Silver, though valuable in itself, is worth little if it is compounded with impurities. The process of refining removes the dross, so that the precious metal may then have value added at the hands of the craftsman who fashions it into an ornament of beauty. Similarly in the case of a king, however worthy to reign he may be in himself, if he is surrounded by a mixed bag of advisors and ministers, some good, some bad, some indifferent, he is likely to make little impression in his kingdom or achieve anything of lasting value.

'Corruption in high places' is a phrase familiar to us all because, sadly, it exists. A throne established in wickedness has horrific and brutal consequences. We should be thankful when wickedness is exposed and dealt with, unpleasant though it may be, because when it remains active and unchecked it spells trouble for all, including the head of government, 'the king' in the political context of this proverb. If the king, or his equivalent, is not supremely concerned for righteousness in his kingdom, and if he tolerates or, even worse, values aides who are wicked, his throne will be far from secure, as has been demonstrated time and again in history, not least in the history of the latter days of Israel's existence (2 Kings 15:8-31).

People have all sorts of ideas about what makes for a secure and prosperous nation. Rarely among them is the truth voiced that it is righteousness which exalts a nation (14:34) and the place it must be found in order to be effective is at the hub of government.

Removing the dross from silver is not an easy process and it is not without its hazards. The reason it is done is because of the known value of the end result. Likewise removing the wicked from before the king was likely to involve considerable difficulty and potential dangers. Is that why David did not remove Joab, the commander of his army? (See 1 Kings 2:28-33; 2 Samuel 3:26-30; 20:9-10.)

This proverb echoes 16:12. There it says a throne is established *by* righteousness, which is the reason it is an abomination for a king to commit wickedness; here it says a throne is established *in* righteousness when wickedness is removed from before the king.

This should guide us in our praying for those in leadership over us, and especially for Christians in high position in government.

The kingdom to which believers belong is the church of the Lord Jesus Christ, built upon the foundation of the apostles and prophets, Jesus Christ himself being the chief cornerstone (Ephesians 2:20). He is the righteous King, and his ministers for the extension and establishment of his kingdom are and must be clothed in his righteousness and serve in righteousness. There is no place for impurity within the church of Christ. Daniel 12:10 indicates that both the believer and the Lord are intimately involved in the necessary refining process.

[Related proverb: 16:12.]

25:6-7. Honour and dishonour.

25:6-7. Honour and dishonour. This proverb still has something to say to us even if we are unlikely ever to come into the presence of royalty! It will bring to mind the parable Jesus gave when he saw guests choosing out the most important places for themselves (Luke 14:7-11).

Many people have too high an opinion of themselves. Like Haman, who thought the king would be pleased to honour him (Esther 6:6), so they imagine themselves more important than they are in the eyes of others. It is an image of themselves they find it hard to dispel!

In another parable, the Pharisee paraded his virtues before God. He obviously thought he deserved high standing in God's presence. As if this were not bad enough, he also put down the tax collector with his speech (Luke 18:10-14). Not only is there the danger of too high an opinion of ourselves, there is also a great tendency to compare ourselves with others and to imagine that we stand higher than they do in the presence of God.

Notice who does the talking. It is not what we think or say that really matters. The perspective of our own judgement is invariably flawed. In the proverb it is the king who makes the assessment, and he is probably a much better judge of worth and interpreter of body language than those around him suppose! Furthermore, he has his own understanding of what and who is important, and it is that which matters. Even more so God, who knows the thoughts and intents of the heart, will not err in the position he allots to us, working according to his own will and purpose.

Christians can sometimes act as if they think they ought to have more recognition than they do have, pushing themselves forward and being frustrated when they meet with resistance. Sometimes they see others being honoured before them and it hurts because they have made it clear that they feel themselves better qualified or more gifted in that department and it seems like a big put down. Lane says nicely: 'Humility is a grace but humiliation a disgrace.'

We need to remember that grace trumps gift. Greatness in the kingdom of God has nothing to do with status and nothing to do with gifts or abilities. It has everything to do with humble service. Jesus, our Lord and Teacher – and also our King – made this clear enough when he washed the feet of his disciples (John 13:3-17) who had not long since been discussing which of them was going to be the greatest (Luke 22:24-27). What is more important, to be somebody in the eyes of the world or to give your life in service irrespective of whether or not anyone notices it?

Those who are looking for honour ought first to learn what true humility is (15:33) and to be clothed with it (1 Peter 5:5). It is the apron of service which we should be proud to wear.

25:8-10. I saw it with my own eyes. It is likely that the last line of v. 7 belongs to v. 8, and is saying not to go hastily to court on the basis of what your eyes have seen. Things are not always as they seem, or how they appear on the surface.

This proverb has aspects strongly connected to the last. The desire to exalt oneself is invariably accompanied by a desire to put down others. Both are liable to rebound in disgrace.

It is not just hasty accusation which is being cautioned here. It seems that an undercurrent of ill will is being exposed in which the accuser is ready to think the worst of his neighbour and to act precipitately. Also there is a strong warning about talking behind the neighbour's back, which amounts to malicious gossip.

These words sound a warning in two areas: make sure of your facts, and make sure of your motives! Unsound knowledge and an unsound heart are going to have painful repercussions!

The first scenario is that of the matter being taken to court where the truth comes out totally discrediting the charge and exposing the accuser as both arrogant and foolish.

The second scenario is one of the matter being taken to a third party behind the neighbour's back who then puts the talebearer to shame as underhanded, ill-informed and of ill-intent.

Either way, the reputation which the accuser was so eager to enhance at the expense of another ends up in rags.

The apostle Paul gave a scathing indictment of those in the church in Corinth who were taking their brothers to law (1 Corinthians 6:1-11). They were displaying the self-centred and self-aggrandising characteristics which feature here that Paul exposed to their shame.

If it is true in the case of a genuine offence, how much more so is it here, that matters like this should always where possible first be approached with a face to face encounter, as Jesus taught in Matthew 18:15. Very often this requires grace, humility, tact and understanding. The absence of these qualities means it is so much easier to jump to conclusions and take the wrong kind of action. If a personal encounter is personally costly, failure in this respect will be far more so.

Anyone desiring his neighbour's well-being, seeing something to raise his eyebrows, would go to his neighbour and raise the matter with him (v. 9a), not go immediately to bring a lawsuit or go rushing off to someone else with a supposedly incriminating tale (v. 9b). Those out to damage the reputation of another are likely to find their own damaged with a vengeance!

25:11-12. A twenty-four carat word. The previous proverb was concerned with words *un*fitly spoken with malicious, or at least misguided, intent. The picture was not a pleasant one. What a contrast is here! Even though the precise translation of some of the words is unclear, there can be no mistaking the point being made, and we will not go far wrong if we concentrate on *value*, *beauty* and *benefit*.

Verse 4 referred to taking away the dross from silver, and maybe here we could think in terms of removing the dross from our speech, seeking to ensure that what we have to say is pure and of value! Yet more than this is required in the word that is fitly spoken because this proverb is focusing on how the word is received: it is precious and beautiful to the hearer. So the speaker must have sensitivity toward the hearer's temperament and circumstances. Two people may be in need of essentially the same advice, but the way it is given to each may be very different when these things are taken into account, and to do it wrongly in each case can be as bad as to do it rightly is beneficial. Wisdom and understanding are absolutely essential to the case.

If this applies to the giving of advice, it applies equally in administering comfort, and even in giving praise or encouragement. These things need to be done thoughtfully with a genuine concern about how the words will be received.

The proverb now moves on to what is perhaps the hardest area of all, the giving of a rebuke, the administering of correction. We all need to be put right at times and none of us enjoys being shown up where we are wrong. All the things just said apply to this difficult task. One giving wise reproof will look beyond the cause itself to the benefit to the recipient and will have his welfare at heart. If we have occasion to administer reproof, promoting what is good is at least as important as purging what is bad.

It is all too easy to reprove because I am offended or someone else has been hurt or the other person ought to know better, and so on. That may be so, but if these are the only things in mind the rebuke will not qualify for the description given here. Of the many ways of saying something, there will be one way which will be most appropriate and effective and worth its weight in gold. Look again at God's Word as it comes to us – 2 Timothy 3:16-17. See there the necessary elements of reproof and correction. But it does not stop there, for it goes on to show the right way with instruction in righteousness, and the end in view is maturity and usefulness.

Finally, is yours a listening, an attentive, an obedient ear? How well are you receiving reproof? – assuming of course that you need it! Are you appreciative of its worth, and is it something that you highly value?

[Related proverbs: 15:23,31.]

25:13. Cold comfort! Harvest is a time for working in the heat. Have you ever been labouring on a sweltering day and expressed the wish, 'Oh, for a nice cool breeze!' How comfortingly an ice-cold drink goes down a parched throat and you say, 'Ah, I needed that!'

This picture of physical longing and satisfaction expresses nicely the emotions which can be involved in entrusting to another an important errand. Will the message be delivered? Will it be put across accurately, without omissions or additions? Will it be given in the manner intended?

We can imagine the messenger returning to his master and giving a full account of what happened and how he has rendered his service, and a smile of relief and satisfaction spreading over the master's face as he recognises just how well the service has been performed. His spirit, ill at ease until this point, is refreshed by the report.

With the abundance of communication aids available to our modern technological society it is easy to miss just how important the messenger was to former generations. He would in fact be far more than our popular concept of a messenger. He would be responsible for carrying news, and even for transacting important business on behalf of another. Often he would be acting in an ambassadorial capacity. Abraham even sent his servant as a 'messenger' to find a bride for his son Isaac (Genesis 24)!

The prophet Haggai was described as the Lord's messenger (Haggai 1:13), while Malachi reminded the priests that they were messengers of the Lord (Malachi 2:7). John the Baptist was the Lord's messenger (Malachi 3:1; Matthew 11:10). They were all 'sent ones' with delegated authority and responsibility, and this applies equally to all who are both called and sent to proclaim the *message* of the gospel.

The prophet Isaiah responded to the Lord's call for a messenger, but only after his lips and his heart had been purified (Isaiah 6:6-8). Only thus could he serve faithfully.

Paul writes touchingly to the church at Corinth of how certain brethren acting as messengers refreshed his spirit and theirs (1 Corinthians 16:17-18). Later on, in writing to the same church, he refers to the way his 'messenger' Titus was refreshed, but no less so was Paul himself in learning of the accomplishment of a successful mission.

If we have a message to proclaim then it follows by definition that we are messengers. As we have opportunity to share the gospel with others let us do so faithfully, remembering that it is not our gospel but God's, not to be expressed in our way but in God's way.

But also in our lives we sometimes find ourselves acting on behalf of others, in which case we are to be faithful and not confuse what they have asked of us with what we want. We are not to be like the composer who sought to complete another's unfinished work after his death but ensured the closing bars were in his *own* style that he might have some honour from it. It should be honour enough to have brought satisfaction and refreshment to whoever sent us.

[Related proverb: 25:25.]

25:14. Does practice match profession? In a relatively dry climate dependent upon rain at its proper time, cloud and wind without rain were not only a disappointment, they also somewhat mocked the need. That is exactly the situation with those who promise to respond to a need and are in a position to do so but who fail to deliver.

We see this in false teachers who have plagued the churches down the generations. Peter writes of such people (2 Peter 2:18-19). They boast loudly. Their great swelling words are like big clouds full of promise. They promise so much but fail to give what they promise. Worse than that, promising freedom they instead deliver bondage (and compare what Satan promised to give Eve in the garden – Genesis 3:5). Jude has much the same thing to say about false believers in the churches, actually referring to them as clouds without water (Jude 12).

It might be said of Ananias and Sapphira (Acts 5:1-11) that they falsely boasted of giving insofar as they obviously wanted to make a favourable impression on the church. Indeed they did give. That was not the problem. They suffered judgement not because they did not give enough but because they wanted to give the impression that they had given in full when they had only given in part. It was deceitfulness from a very unworthy motive.

This does not apply only to monetary giving. It extends to any form of giving, including the giving of our time. Those who would have it known that they are fully occupied in the Lord's service who in fact in private spend much time in self-indulgent pursuits come under the condemnation of this proverb. Their big words are of little worth.

Anyone who wishes to look bigger than he is, to that extent is like a cloud without rain.

How do others see us? Do they see us as we are, or as we want them to see us?

What we have determined to give, let us give honestly, seeking no credit to ourselves. For what is our giving in the light of what the Lord has given us? In that light we should be ashamed even to mention it.

25:15. Pulling down strongholds. If things need to be changed at the top, the best way is not by making a song and dance about it, by hue and cry and loud protests. That is not to say that protests are always out of place. However, the most effective means of bringing about change, or of persuading the authorities in some matter, is that patient demonstration of what is right in the midst of what is wrong, until eventually it receives proper recognition.

Peter gives two examples of the truth of this proverb in 1 Peter 3. The first is the way a wife may by submissive and pure conduct win an unbelieving husband – which almost inevitably will involve considerable forbearance (1 Peter 3:1-2)! The second is the way believers by meekness and reverence can in the end cause those who revile them to be ashamed (1 Peter 3:15-16).

Force and vitriolic attack invite automatic resistance. How often we see that on the political platform! Aggressive techniques tend to put people's backs up.

Patient forbearance and quiet reasoning are part of the Christian's arsenal. Forbearance and gentleness are among the fruit of the Spirit (Galatians 5:22-23) in stark contrast to some of the more spectacular evidences of the works of the flesh (Galatians 5:19-21).

Forbearance and a gentle tongue are impossible to resist. You can push against an obstacle or fight against a strong wind, but forbearance absorbs all force of opposition and a gentle tongue is as inescapable as a whispering breeze.

The second clause is unexpected and dramatic on account of its implausibility. Of course a gentle tongue cannot break a bone. We all understand that. But it is speaking figuratively, and powerfully indicating what we don't always understand, which is that a gentle tongue can demolish an argument, it can crumble opposition. It can find its way into weak spots which no amount of bludgeoning would touch.

These Christian graces play an important part in the work of the gospel. Our tendency is to love high drama and to want quick results. It rarely happens like that. The opposition in the hearts of unbelievers is such that it has to be tackled with weapons it does not recognise. If you are becoming frustrated with the thought that your persistent, patient, quiet witness to someone is getting you nowhere, think again. It is surely doing an unseen and effective work of undermining the defences until, under God, no resistance remains and his word gains entry.

No adjective in God's Word is superfluous. Mere forbearance is not enough. It is *long* forbearance that is needed. What is forbearance? It is holding back from taking action, it is self-restraint. What is long forbearance? It is holding back even when things become painful or difficult beyond the bounds of comfort. It means self-restraint in the face of strong temptation to do otherwise. Have you ever said, 'How I wish I had waited a little longer!'? Had you done so, things would have turned out well, whereas your precipitate action spoilt what you were trying to achieve.

Bear in mind that but for the Lord's long forbearance toward us we would not be where we are now.

[Related proverb: 15:1.]

25:16. Enough is as good as a feast. Delicious honey! Yet the body can take only so much of it. Hence the advice. A couple of spoonfuls may be greatly enjoyed and be beneficial, but if that enjoyment entices us to eat a whole jarful then we are in for trouble!

Highlighted in this illustration is the tension between need and greed, and when it comes to something which gives pleasure the line of demarcation is not so clear. The enjoyment of something pleasurable is often accompanied by a natural tendency to want more of it. Yet there comes a point at which more is less and pleasure yields pain.

We see all around us the craving people have for pleasure. They can't get enough of it, but the more they have of it, the less it satisfies, until ultimately it turns bad on them. Paul wrote of the Gentiles of his day, 'Having lost all sensitivity, they have given themselves over to sensuality so as to indulge in every kind of impurity, with a continual lust for more' (Ephesians 4:19, NIV). This problem is still with us. When an idol is made of pleasure it invariably leads to impurity and perversity. It may start with legitimate pleasure which then leads to excess, and when that fails to satisfy it turns into different, unwholesome directions.

We should recognise that there is a perverseness in human nature for wanting more than is good for us.

So how are we to handle the pleasures of life? We are to enjoy them, but we are not to overindulge. We need to understand the difference between moderation and excess, and that the point comes at which the craving for more is bad appetite.

So where is the line to be drawn? That is the wrong question. It is where we *begin* which is important. When we experience the pleasures of life, great or small, they should be received with thanksgiving to God for his generosity and kindness toward us. The sweetness of honey to our palate should be inseparable from our delight in God the giver, so that we cannot enjoy the gift without the giver. Have you found honey? How good God is! That should be our automatic response. When the God of love gives us good things to enjoy they are to be received and enjoyed because they have come from him, so that our enjoyment of *them* is really our enjoyment of *him*, the response of our love to his love.

God gives us good things to enjoy, but he expects us to use them responsibly. If we have a tendency to overindulgence, what Paul writes to rich believers may help (1 Timothy 6:17-18). Having assured them of God's wonderful generosity, he then advises them about how to use their riches. What might have the potential of becoming an idol to them he urges them to make a servant, a blessing received turned into a blessing to be given.

[Related proverb: 25:27.]

25:17. Go away! Getting on with our neighbours is clearly important, for God says we should love our neighbours as ourselves (Leviticus 19:18), which means we have certain responsibilities toward them.

In saying we are to covet nothing of our neighbour's (Deuteronomy 5:21) God's law recognises that our neighbour has exclusive possessions and rights. This includes our neighbour's house, and so when we set foot in it we are standing on what is his property, something we must at all times respect. We have no automatic right to be there, only such rights as the neighbour may be pleased to grant us. Whenever we are in a neighbour's house, however welcome we are we should always be conscious that we are on foreign soil. We are there at the neighbour's pleasure, not our own.

This means we should be sensitive about the duration of our stay, bearing in mind the purpose of our visit, thinking of our neighbour's interests above our own.

It is better to be greeted with a cheerful, 'The door's open, walk right in,' rather than a silence which says, 'Oh, no! What is it this time?'

You may be on good terms with your neighbour. Your neighbour may even take pleasure in your company. Yet if you are in the house too much your neighbour may get sick of you. There seems to be a deliberate connection between this proverb and the last in the use of a particular word, brought out nicely in the NIV in the phrases 'too much of it' in v. 16b and 'too much of you' in v. 17b. You can 'have your fill' of honey and be sick of it, and your neighbour can 'have his fill' of you and be sick of you!

Be a neighbourly spirit, not an intrusive busybody. Respect your neighbour's privacy. Giving consideration to your neighbour's circumstances and needs. Think twice about going round. Note the key word 'seldom'. The same is true about other forms of intrusion into other people's lives. Make sure your influence is sweet, not sickly.

25:18-20. Three highly damaging forms of conduct.

25:18. False. False witness is forbidden by the Ninth Commandment (Exodus 20:16). The Lord, the God of truth, hates it (6:16,19). By false witness others are deceived (12:17). A false witness is easy about telling lies (14:5,25) and has no regard for justice (19:28). Punishment is assured for such a person (19:5,9; 21:28).

Take a look now at the damage it does. Would you go round to your neighbour and beat his brains out with a club? Would you drive a blade through his ribs? What a horrible and gruesome thought! This proverb does not spare our feelings of revulsion because it indicates that to tell a lie about a neighbour, to testify falsely about him, is in God's estimation every bit as bad as murder. Bear in mind the very apt description, 'character assassination'.

Although the context of this proverb may be a court of law, the nature of the comparison should be deeply sobering. Lies about others can stick and do irreparable damage. The words uttered take to the skies like the blown seeds of a dandelion, beyond recall, to replicate themselves in unexpected places. What we say about others should be strictly true. We should never pass on our prejudices or unconfirmed opinions or suspicions about others, or rumours, as if they were established facts. Witness concerns what we have seen and heard. If we pass on as fact what we do not know as fact then we are false witnesses releasing deadly arrows against our neighbour.

25:19. Faithless. The person described here is deceitful and treacherous. It is not clear from the original whether the confidence is that of the person himself, or someone else's confidence in him. Both senses are equally valid. The confidence of the wicked is certainly ill-founded. However, it is more likely that the proverb is referring to someone placing confidence in a person who turns out to be unfaithful.

It is in times of trouble that we feel vulnerable and are likely to be looking around for help and support, when we need someone in whom we can confide in the sense of placing our trust. We need to be careful about the people in whom we confide. One who lets us down in our time of need is only going to exacerbate our distress. An unfaithful man will betray confidences in more senses than one. We need to be careful about the people upon whom we rely. Just when you most need his support an unfaithful man will let you down. Never be intimate with people of less than proven worth.

The same word for 'confidence' is found in Psalm 118:8-9 where it serves as a reminder that the Lord is utterly faithful. The Lord will never leave us nor forsake us (Hebrews 13:5).

25:20. Frivolous. 'Sing us one of the songs of Zion!' taunted the captors of the Jews whose hearts were heavy and bitter (Psalm 137). They were in no mood either to sing or to be sung to. The taunts only accentuated their sorrows. In their case their tormentors were taking malicious pleasure in making matters worse for them.

However, it is equally possible to sing songs and make merry and generally think to jolly people along with no awareness that this method is no remedy for a heavy heart. It is rank insensitivity and produces the opposite of what is intended. Taking away a garment in cold weather only increases the sufferer's discomfort. Vinegar on soda produces useless froth and does good to neither. If you are in a mood to sing songs and make merry, think about whether it is appropriate. Paul says, 'Rejoice with those who rejoice.' He immediately adds, 'Weep with those who weep.' How can anyone with any sensitivity be full of joy in the presence of a believer who is in the depths? A heavy heart needs the warmth and comfort of genuine sympathy and fellow-feeling.

[Related proverb: 14:10.]

25:21-22. 2 Kings 6:8-23. Sweet revenge. There is an irony in this title. But so is there too in the proverb.

This proverb expresses more fully what earlier ones hint at, that our attitude toward others and our duty to them transcends what we may feel about them or how they treat us – see 24:11-12,17-18,29.

The law made clear that right was to be done toward all irrespective of who they might be. Thus if a man found something his enemy had lost he was to restore it, and if he came across his enemy in difficulties he was to resist the temptation not to get involved but was to go to his aid (Exodus 23:4-5).

In Matthew 5:43-48 Jesus corrected a misinterpretation of the law and enunciated a principle which followers of a heavenly Father should want to put into practice. His command demonstrated that Exodus 23:4-5 is still in force and extends to all people.

God's Word makes it quite clear that in the case of enmity we are to refrain from returning like for like. Consider Romans 12:14-21 in which Paul quotes this proverb. Do we want to perpetuate enmity by returning evil for evil, or to seek to vanquish it by repaying evil with good? It is the enmity which needs to be destroyed, not the enemy.

The incident in 2 Kings 6 gives a striking illustration of this proverb. The Syrians were at war with Israel, but their army, given over to the king of Israel by the Lord, were at his instructions treated with kindness and fed and watered and sent away. This turned out to be far more effective than bloodshed in putting a stop to the raids into their country.

The kind of treatment advocated here goes right against the grain of human nature. Note what Saul said when David spared him (1 Samuel 24:19). He recognised that it was not human nature which was operating here, but something far transcending it at work in David's heart.

Care and consideration for those who hate us may be misunderstood and misinterpreted by them, but it cannot be ignored. It baffles people, it upsets them, it touches them where it hurts. It raises questions which they cannot answer. The proverb puts it better: it heaps coals of fire on their heads.

As we have opportunity we are to do good to all (Galatians 6:10). That means all! When people treat us badly we are, as we have opportunity, to treat them well. We are likely only really to seize the opportunity if their well-being is already in our hearts.

The proverb speaks of the Lord rewarding the person who does this. Literally, it means he will make it up to the person, he will fully recompense the person, he will see the person does not lose out.

That God should require this of us is a reflection of his own character. Once again we come back to Romans 5:8. Reflect upon the good God did you when you were at enmity with him. What effect did this have upon you then? What effect does it have upon you now?

25:23-24. An ill wind. In Israel the north wind is associated with hot dry weather and is not regarded as the harbinger of rain. The AV translates that the north wind 'driveth away' rain, which would make sense except that the verb really means to bring forth. 'The north wind doth blow, and we shall have snow' is a line most of us will be familiar with from a very old nursery rhyme, but how many of us know anything more than that about it? Perhaps the observation of this proverb would have meant something specific to people of Solomon's time, and perhaps it originated from a particular location. Puzzler though it may be to us, we can be sure that Solomon knew what he was talking about and that the people of his time understood it. In any case, the application is clear.

Those who talk maliciously about others in their absence are likely sooner or later to have to answer in their presence for their words, coming face to face with those they malign. Backbiting is one of those practices which is recognised to be mean and low and it meets with general disapproval, and yet it often slips unobtrusively into general gossip. Never say bad things behind people's backs which you would not be prepared to say to their face.

Verse 24 is identical to 21:9 and similar to 21:19. Here it seems to be connected with v. 23 and the misuse of the tongue. There is nothing so unbecoming in a woman as a contentious spirit and there is nothing so degrading to a man as to suffer under it. It undermines the roles God intended for man and woman: the man to lead, the woman to help.

Just as a backbiting tongue does no good but only harm, so it is the same with a contentious woman, whatever the bone of contention may be. It arouses anger, it produces separation, it perpetuates whatever the problem is, it solves nothing. The harmonious relationship between husband and wife is so important that this kind of situation is intolerable. People will go without a great deal of the material comforts and pleasures of this life for the sake of love. Where love is eclipsed by contention no amount of such comforts and pleasures can compensate for it. It follows that relationships need to be preserved and nurtured.

What a lot of damage the tongue can do! It is just as James asserts (James 3). We all know this, and are we not all guilty? If this proverb today convicts you in any specific matter, then take words with you to heal and put things right. If your words have been a chilling blast from the north, bring them round from the south to minister warmth and comfort.

25:25. Closing the gap. How well an ice-cold drink goes down after hours of sweated labour! What a wonderful feeling it is after foot slogging on a blisteringly hot day at last to encounter a fresh stream and to remove your boots and let the chill water run over your feet! It quickly dissipates the weariness and invigorates the system in a way that nothing else can.

As the body cries out for refreshment in such circumstances, so the spirit feels the same way about lengthy lack of contact with loved ones far away. Though loved ones are not specifically mentioned in this proverb there is certainly the element of real personal concern, and surely a concern for loved ones dovetails with the sentiments expressed here.

In those times news from 'a far country' would take a long time to arrive, and that is the point the proverb is making. Our understanding is not to be confined to a literal reading. It is an illustration of lengthy and prolonged and anxious waiting.

If someone you love and are close to has gone on a long journey it is natural that you should be concerned for their welfare, the more so if there are potential hazards along the way or after arriving. How did the journey go? Have they arrived safely? Are things working out well for them? Are they experiencing any difficulties? You long to hear news, and the passing of time without hearing anything only intensifies the longing. What a relief it is eventually to hear that all is well!

Perhaps the most noteworthy biblical example of this proverb is the news Jacob received of his son Joseph being alive in Egypt after decades of believing him to be dead (Genesis 45:25-28).

The 'far country' may remind us of the parable of the lost son (Luke 15:11-32). In the father seeing him when still a long way off we should not miss the inference that he must have been constantly wearying his eyes looking out for him and longing for his return.

Many are weary in their soul with longing for good news concerning loved ones who are in a 'far country' spiritually, but equally many have been wonderfully heartened with news of those for whom they have been praying for so long coming to faith in Christ. There is no news like that news!

The apostle Paul wears his heart upon his sleeve as he says how greatly he was refreshed upon receiving good news from churches far away – churches for whom for a variety of reasons he had a great deal of concern (2 Corinthians 2:13; 7:5-7; 1 Thessalonians 2:17–3:8).

Are you in the position of being in a 'far country' in any respect? Do you have parents, or other relatives, or friends who have a very real concern for you while you are at a distance from them whether physically or spiritually? Are you keeping in touch with them, thinking of their concerns and not just your own? They need to hear from you. You need to be open with them. Sometimes it is said that no news is good news. Maybe so, but real news is better news! Are you refreshing the spirit of others by conveying a good report to them when there is the opportunity?

We may expect to hear from time to time from those serving the Lord as missionaries in other places, whom we think of as being in the 'far country'. That, however, is only our perspective. For them, it is 'back home' which is the far country. Have we thought of communicating more effectively with them? Have we thought how much they might appreciate receiving news from 'back home' and being refreshed in the midst of their labours?

In these days when communication is so quick and easy it is amazing how many people are lonely and weary. Is there no good news for them? Is there no messenger to deliver it?

[Related proverbs: 15:30; 25:13.]

25:26. Bitter disappointment. What the NKJV translates as 'falters' may be misleading here if we think only of hesitation, as in the faltering of an engine which then picks up again. Would that it were only that! It may be that in this sense we all falter from time to time, shaken by the strength of some temptation. It reminds us, and maybe others, of our weakness, and we learn to go on in more careful dependence upon God.

What is before us in this proverb is something more serious. More than a blip, it is a breakdown. It may start with faltering, but instead of picking up as expected, it collapses.

How would you react if you were to turn on the tap one morning and find water gushing out which was full of detritus? Would there not be a sense of disgust followed by dismay as you begin to consider the implications? The likening of a righteous person to a spring or a well is showing us just how vital a part such a person has to play where others are concerned. What we are looking at here are the murky waters of compromise.

It is sadly true that many men and women respected for their righteousness, instead of standing up to them have given way before the wicked for various reasons, with the consequence that those who have looked up to them and even depended upon them have been deeply disturbed. Instead of ministering to others as they should, they have done them harm.

Lot is an example of such a person. Peter affirms that Lot was a righteous man (2 Peter 2:7-8), but clearly Lot gave way before the wicked inhabitants of Sodom (Genesis 19:8). He comes across as a weak man. His problem stems from the fact that he 'chose for himself' (Genesis 13:11) instead of first seeking the Lord's will or considering (as he ought to have done) the welfare of others and giving due deference to his uncle Abraham. He serves as a warning to us that when the righteous do give way, invariably there has been an undermining process going on for some time. We are not to tolerate, suppress or leave unattended anything which might weaken our faith and afford the enemy opportunity to bring us down. Self-interest is dangerously undermining. It can also open the door to the acceptance of what amounts to a bribe which can be presented under all sorts of guises.

What might cause a righteous person to give way before the wicked? *Fear*, *doubt* and *weakness* are three notable causes. Fear of man and what men might do may lead to giving way if the fear of God is deficient. Doubting God's Word is another. It is exceedingly sad that so many have compromised by giving way to Satan's favourite ploy (see Genesis 3:1-4). Weakness in the faith, sheer ignorance of what the Word of God says, is another cause of giving way to the wicked, allowing their evil ideas and practices to hold sway. These things result in compromised life, example and teaching.

If we imagine ourselves safe in these areas, we should remember Peter's pride and self-confidence which led to his denying his Lord, and which he came with shame bitterly to regret. 1 Corinthians 10:12 serves as a reminder of our very great need always to rely implicitly upon the Lord and his Word for strength to stand.

25:27. Look at me! Honey is good. Too much honey is bad. Both v. 16 and this verse use this to make a point. Back at v. 16 it was observed that pleasure is good and beneficial, but that to chase after it and to seek it for its own sake is bad.

Here, honey is sweet and good, and so can honour and glory be to those who receive it. But as soon as any start to seek it for themselves and to promote their own glory, that is excess, which is not good.

Nebuchadnezzar had been informed by Daniel that his kingdom, power, strength and glory had been given him by God (Daniel 2:37), and when he attributed these things to himself as his own achievement he was struck down (Daniel 4:30-33). In between times it was very clear that he was orchestrating events to advance his own glory – with very unpleasant results.

How many people seek glory of some kind for themselves! They have a craving for recognition, something that will give them status in the eyes of others. It matters to them that others should know that they are wise, or powerful, or rich, or clever, or whatever it might be, and should honour them for it. They set great store by these things as if they matter, as if they are some kind of security (Jeremiah 9:23-24). In truth, what we are in the eyes of others matters little. It is what we are to God and our relationship with him that matters.

Twice Paul had to remind the church at Corinth that he who glories should glory in the Lord (1 Corinthians 1:31; 2 Corinthians 10:17). For a Christian to seek his or her own glory is like slapping God in the face. We should crave nothing other than his mercy, his favour, his love, which, having received, we should enjoy to the exclusion of all else.

Glory is only glory when it is bestowed, and the only glory really worth receiving is that which is bestowed by the God of glory himself. See Psalm 84:11. The glory which believers will one day enjoy will be the glory of God, to abide in his glorious presence. It will not be their own and will not reflect upon themselves. They will bask not in their own glory, but in God's. We receive grace, that we may ascribe glory to God now and look forward to the eternal weight of glory to come (2 Corinthians 4:15,17).

When athletes enjoy the glory of their achievements it is common for them to give a great deal of the credit to others who have coached, encouraged and otherwise supported them, without whom they would never have attained their status. How much more should we ascribe glory to God and honour him to whom *all* credit is due!

If you are accustomed to being praised and receiving honour, beware lest it develop into a craving on your part! The glory of man is ephemeral. The glory of God is eternal. The theme of all the men of God throughout the scriptures is to ascribe glory to God. The men who we might expect to refer to their glory are silent on the matter. The only reason Joseph spoke of his glory in Egypt (Genesis 45:13) was not to boast about it but to mention it as a matter of fact so that his father might be persuaded to join him. He had already attributed it to God and the furtherance of his purposes. Therein lies the lesson: whatever glory you receive, use it for God and for the blessing of his people.

[Related proverbs: 25:16; 27:2.]

25:28. When the battle is already lost.

No enemy would make his initial attack at the strongest point of defence. In surveying the land he would look for the weak points to make his first incursions. A city broken down and without walls would be a soft target. Their battle would be lost before it even began.

Just as much as a city needed walls for security and prosperity, so our spirit needs to be ruled. Ruled. That is a good word. There needs to be government, control, order, discipline. There is also maintenance work which needs to be done. *Laissez faire* will lead only to disorder and eventually to chaos.

This proverb may bring to mind someone who has an ungovernable temper or an unruly tongue and the trouble it gets them into, and yet there is far more to it than that. We have passions which wage war against the spirit (Galatians 5:17). Temptations entice the flesh. For example, sitting at the computer while on the internet, there are things available which will appeal to our sinful nature, and they are there at the click of a mouse. If we have no rule over our spirit there in secret, we are laying ourselves open to the enemy of our souls, and it will sooner or later come out into the open.

It is not legalism to say that we need to rule our spirit, subdue our passions and exercise strong self-discipline. The Christian life is a life of spiritual warfare and God's Word makes this very clear and what we need to do to 'fight the good fight'. Look how seriously the apostle Paul takes this in 1 Corinthians 9:27. The letters to the churches are full of exhortations in this area.

How are we to rule our spirit? How are we to strengthen our defences? We will confine ourselves to mentioning two fundamental factors which are both essential and effective in motivating us to do so, and they pervade the New Testament letters.

The first is to remember *where we have come from*. Any who can say, 'The Son of God loved me and gave himself for me' (Galatians 2:20) will know they have handed over the reins of their life to him that he should take control. As we remember his love and his sacrifice we will want to live as he pleases and will seek by his grace to rule our spirit in accordance with his Word.

The second great motivator is to remember *where we are going to*. We are told that Moses rejected the passing pleasures of sin, esteeming the reproach of Christ greater riches than the treasures in Egypt; for he looked to the reward (Hebrews 11:25-26). At the end of his life Paul could write, 'I have fought the good fight, I have finished the race, I have kept the faith' (2 Timothy 4:7). If we are going to finish, and finish well, we need to know there *is* a finish and what lies beyond it! In 1 Thessalonians 5:1-11 Paul sets forth the anticipation of the Lord's return as a great incentive to self-controlled living.

In Titus 2:12-15 Paul presents both of these incentives together that we might rule our spirit. Never lose sight of grace and glory. Jesus Christ came to save us; Jesus Christ will be there to receive us. He is the author and finisher of faith (Hebrews 12:2).

[Related proverb: 16:32.]

26:1. Popular idols. Snow in summer is almost an anachronism. Rain in harvest is unwelcome and damages the crop. Giving honour to a fool is at best totally out of place and at worst harmful. It gives him no credit nor does it reflect well on those who honour him.

Among the popular 'stars' of our day there are many whom the Word of God would class as fools, and yet they are showered with accolades, their opinions are sought, their conduct is mimicked, and the popular press is full of them and their doings. They are thought clever when they rise to new heights of lewdness. They are honoured when they have the audacity to step over the boundaries of decorum, and praised as if they were doing something great for mankind by introducing new freedoms of thought or expression.

There is a tendency, especially among the young, to idolise certain personalities in the areas of entertainment or sport. These people have their cult followings, and the honour they receive is often excessive and quite inappropriate and invariably they end up in an even worse state than how they began. Their devotees gain nothing from them, and more often than not it proves detrimental to their well-being too. It is often thought that 'following' these personalities is quite harmless and acceptable. It is neither. Giving honour to fools is a no-win scenario.

While fools are being honoured, those truly worthy of recognition are often overlooked or ignored. The Bible says we should give honour to those to whom it is due (Romans 13:7). So, for example, parents are to be honoured on account of the responsibilities they carry in the upbringing of their children and the fundamental importance of the family unity in society (Exodus 20:12; Ephesians 6:1); husbands are to honour their wives, giving them the love, respect and support they need in order to fulfil their vital role in the home (1 Peter 3:7); elders who rule well are to be counted worthy of double honour that they may continue to serve their churches faithfully and effectively (1 Timothy 5:7). In so doing everybody benefits.

In all these things, and in more besides, we are to honour God our Father and our Lord Jesus Christ, to whom all honour and glory are due (1 Timothy 6:16; Hebrews 2:9; Revelation 5:13).

Who are your role models in life?

[Related proverb: 26:8.]

26:2. Groundless fear? In some cultures a curse can be taken very seriously. A curse can cause misgivings, anxiety, fear. People may not be willing to live in a house because they have heard there is a curse on it, or they may not go near a certain place because of a curse. They imagine they may fall ill, or die, or suffer some other disaster by being brought under its influence. Even among those who regard such things as pure superstition there can still be a lurking suspicion that there may be something in it. People under a curse may be filled with fear, going to great lengths to try to prevent its fulfilment. They have a terror of some intangible power which is capable of bringing evil upon them.

A notable example of someone seeking to bring a curse without cause is Balak king of Moab who hired Balaam to curse Israel (Numbers 22–24). Clearly Balak thought that Balaam possessed supernatural powers and if he cursed Israel it would bring disaster upon them so that they would no longer pose a threat to Moab. But Balak was wrong (Numbers 22:6). The Bible makes it quite plain that the power of a curse lies in God's hands alone. So when men utter a curse against someone with intent to inflict harm they are really calling upon a power outside of themselves to act. In many cases this will be demonic power. Even so, demons are subject to God and have no power to implement the wishes of the likes of Balak. Israel was not under the power of Balaam, but Balaam was under the power of God. In short, the only one holding the power of a curse is God. It is his sole prerogative to bless or to curse.

Sometimes, however, on account of something they have done, people may feel themselves to be under a curse and may believe they are deserving of it. They may be fully persuaded that what is happening to them is not without cause and fear that something worse will settle upon them. Are they to receive reassurance, and, if so, from what source?

God himself has uttered curses. These are 'with cause'. He placed a curse upon the ground on account of Adam's disobedience (Genesis 3:17) so that throughout history the fruitfulness of the ground has been choked by thorns and thistles, and diminished by blights and pests. Furthermore, God uttered curses upon subsequent disobedience (Deuteronomy 27:14-26; 28:15-68). God also warned that but for a certain event he would strike the earth with a curse (Malachi 4:6).

We might rightly conclude that by nature we are under God's curse. How can we find that his curse is without cause in our case? Only when the cause has been removed. Only then can the curse be removed. That happens when the curse has been borne for us, when we have been redeemed from the curse of the law of God, when we know that Christ has become a curse for us (Galatians 3:13-14). The blessing of God pronounced before the curse at creation and at the giving of the law was made of no effect on account of disobedience. But because Christ has borne the punishment due to our sins by becoming a curse for us by hanging on the cross and bearing the wrath of God, so the curse is now superseded by blessing, and blessing is restored.

26:3-28. The remainder of the chapter comprises collections of proverbs related to the fool, the lazy, and the troublemaker.

26:3-12. Focus on the fool. These verses comprise a collection of proverbs about the fool by the men of Hezekiah (25:1). Before we look at them let us remind ourselves that the fool is defined as one who is devoid of the fear of God and who rejects the wisdom of God (1:7). In this section we see particular ways in which this is manifested.

26:3. Controlling the fool. There is no verb here. We could think of it more like a labelled display cabinet! The writer is pointing out three familiar objects. The first is a whip used to stimulate a horse into movement and the second is a bridle used to control the movements of a donkey. The third is a rod. What is that for?

See how the fool is being put on a par with dumb animals in that he requires physical correctives, that like brute beasts he is not amenable to reason to follow a right course in life. The Lord says we should be looking to *him* for our directions in life, and that when we are under his instruction he guides us with his eye (Psalm 32:9). We need to acknowledge and understand him, otherwise we are very much like the horse or mule which require physical constraints.

This is not being pointed out to us in order for us to feel any sense of superiority but rather to highlight the painful predicament of the fool. Paul reminds us that without God 'we ourselves' (emphatically including himself, you and me) were once foolish (Titus 3:3), and he elaborates on how this was evidenced in our thinking and behaviour. It was only God's intervention in our lives which changed all that, when we came under the sound and power of the gospel. This raises the question of how we engage with people who appear to have no time for God, and especially how we respond to the things they say.

[Related proverb: 19:29.]

26:4-5. Answering the fool. At first reading this is a conundrum and may leave us wondering whether it is even possible to answer a fool without either making ourselves look foolish or making him think too highly of himself. The scenario is that of someone who is a fool (which in this context means someone who deliberately has no time for God) who has provocatively raised a matter or asked a question which virtually demands a response. Do you respond, or don't you? If you do, how do you go about it? How do you deal with loaded questions?

Bearing in mind that ungodly people are not amenable to godly reasoning and that 'their foolish hearts' and 'understanding' are 'darkened' (Romans 1:21; Ephesians 4:18), the way we interact with them requires care. Jesus said we are not to cast pearls before swine. They will not appreciate their worth and will merely trample them (Matthew 7:6). So in our dealings with ungodly people and their foolish talk we cannot engage with them at the level of heavenly wisdom because it means nothing to them. But neither should we sink to their level and adopt their tactics in the way we respond to their provocations, because if we do we are conducting ourselves like them, which does us no credit.

On the other hand, if we respond in such a way as to show the fool where his attitudes and line of thinking are leading, for example by exposing his folly by using his own arguments against himself, then any self-conceit on his part will be quenched. This is the kind of argument that the apostle Paul employed in 2 Corinthians 11 and 12 to undermine the foolish attitudes some of the people there were entertaining.

Those entrusted with the ministry of the gospel need to be 'wise as serpents and innocent as doves (Matthew 10:16).

In his dealings with people, and especially in confrontation with his critics and those who were out to discredit him, Jesus never ignored them but always displayed consummate wisdom in the way he answered them, exposing their folly, or ignorance, or deviousness, or hostility, or arrogance, or whatever it may have been. His answers always addressed the real issues and were to the point and dignified. His answers never gave people opportunity to go away with either a superior view of themselves or an inferior view of him.

26:6. Reliance on the fool. Here is a fool's errand with a difference. Notice the strength of language here. Using a fool's feet would be as effective as cutting off your own. 'Drinking violence' indicates just how bad such a mission would be. By 'message' we are to understand far more than mere words. It is more like a business transaction. The thought here is that of sending someone to negotiate it who has no real understanding of what is involved and no interest in it.

The messenger in Solomon's time carried considerable responsibility. He was doing far more than merely conveying and delivering a written communication. He was more like an ambassador who was entrusted with the task of speaking for his master and often negotiating on his behalf. In any important matter the messenger would be carefully chosen, for it would have to be someone of integrity who was completely trustworthy and who could be depended upon to fulfil his commission in an honourable fashion. To make a mistake in this area could be disastrous. It was not just anybody, but his most trusted steward that Abraham sent with the 'message' to obtain a wife for Isaac (Genesis 24).

Perhaps this should remind us of the qualities God expects in those who are ambassadors for Christ. The prophets and apostles ensured they thoroughly understood God's Word and they proclaimed it in his name to others without embellishment or alteration. It is not our privilege to proclaim what we like or in the way we like in the name of the Lord. Where faithfulness to the truth in matter and manner is lost then evil is permitted to prevail.

26:7-9. The wisdom of the fool. The point about proverbs is that they are wise and significant sayings addressing matters of importance and are intended to make a relevant point in a concise fashion. Quoted out of context by fools who have no real understanding of their relevance and application, what should be strong and vigorous are rendered totally useless and ineffective and serve no purpose whatsoever (v. 7). Worse than that, though, is that a proverb in the mouth of a fool may result in abuse or trouble (v. 9). Even if the drunkard is so insensitive that the thorn in his hand fails to produce foul language, it will nevertheless produce a festering sore. Thus fools make sport of wisdom, using it out of context and lampooning it.

In just the same way as the proverb and the fool are incompatible, so too are honour and the fool (v. 8). To bind a stone in a sling is a nonsense because the purpose of the sling is to fling the stone. It renders a very effective weapon utterly useless. Giving honour to a fool is an effective way of rendering useless the wisdom of the proverb. It will never hit its target.

26:10. Employing the fool. The original of this verse is so uncertain that a great variety of possible meanings has been given. The NIV rendering fits well with the general import of these proverbs: 'Like an archer who wounds at random is he who hires a fool or any passer-by.'

The picture here is one of wanton damage. Imagine a gunman firing at anything and anybody in a random fashion. How fearful that would be! This is being equated to randomly giving important work to any irresponsible person. It is asking for trouble big time. Not only is the work likely to be badly done, but it will just as likely lead to trouble or harm in an unpredictable way. If the sense of responsibility is absent, then anything goes.

This vivid image may make us reflect that any significant service in the church should be done by responsible people suitably qualified and equipped and not just by anybody. See, for example, what is required of office holders in the church (1 Timothy 3:1-13).

26:11. The homing instinct of the fool. This proverb is quoted by Peter (2 Peter 2:22) to describe a situation so serious that we should give careful heed to it. It is so easy for people to deceive themselves, to imagine that they have reformed, or turned over a new leaf, or however they wish to describe it, only it has all come from within them, and they are merely trying to lift themselves up by their own bootlaces. Having had no real change of heart, in due course they return to their old ways.

In the absence of regeneration it is quite impossible for people to be anything other than what they are. It is quite possible for people to have a head knowledge of Christ, and to be so affected by the knowledge of the truth (for truth is compelling) that it results in a change of life for a time. However, the Christian life cannot be lived out unless the life of Christ lives within. Those who are in the flesh cannot (note that word, 'cannot') please God (Romans 8:8). It is not enough to approve of the commandments, nor is it enough to reform one's life by endeavouring to keep them and follow the teaching of the Lord Jesus. It falls far short of the very first command that Jesus issued on the commencement of his public ministry: 'Repent and believe the gospel' (Mark 1:15).

The mark of the fool is that, having heard the gospel, having been impressed by the truth as it is in Jesus, he bypasses this first command. 'Skip that bit,' he says, 'let's get on to the more serious stuff.' Such people are like the characters from Bunyan's *Pilgrim's Progress* who climbed over the wall onto the road instead of entering by the wicket gate (Matthew 7:14).

To repeat, to live out the Christian life, the life of Christ must live within. Repentance is fundamental, regeneration is essential. Without these there is no change of nature. The fool is one who is impressed by the truth but does not receive it in the way the author of truth requires. His foolish wisdom guarantees that he reverts to type.

The apostle Paul was deeply concerned that some in the church at Corinth had no true knowledge of God (1 Corinthians 15:34). He had come to that conclusion because some having professed faith were living no differently from those around them, and were even proud of it. With these things in mind he urged the people there to examine themselves, indeed to test themselves, whether they were in the faith (2 Corinthians 13:5).

What are your homing instincts? That of course will depend on where your home is. Do you examine yourself, and how do you do it? How do you test yourself? What will be the substance of the examination paper you present to God on the day of reckoning?

26:12. James 3:13-18. The ultimate folly. This is the sting in the tail of this section on the fool. The person in view here is being contrasted with a fool, which by implication means he is not one himself. Yet for all that he is acting as one.

I know it all. Note how the proverb is stated as a question, 'Do you see…?' Sadly, the answer is often in the affirmative. We are looking here at the self-opinionated, people who are full of themselves, certain of their opinions as facts, unwilling to entertain the possibility that they might be wrong; unwilling, too, to give consideration to what others have to say or advise. They are exasperating because there is no getting through to them, and there is no hope of making progress with anything when they stand in the way. From the previous verses we might think the condition of the fool to be pretty hopeless, but this beats all!

I've got it all. A form of this attitude was displayed in the church in Laodicea. Their imagined condition bore no resemblance to their real condition (Revelation 3:17). Sure and proud of their status, they were under the impression that they had arrived. They had no need of anything.

As soon as any Christian says anything like this we can be sure something is wrong. Beware of the conceit that we have all the answers! Beware of the notion that others should be listening to us, and not the other way round! The real experts in their field are those who know they still have much to learn. The wiser we are, the more acutely will we be aware that we have barely begun, and with true humility will have our ears and eyes and minds open to receive and consider, in order that we may be wise.

You listen to me. We see this conceit, too, in the Pharisee of the parable, with his superior attitude toward others (Luke 18:11-12). He even expected without question that God should listen to him! It was all about him and about his status in comparison to others. We must not suppose that Jesus was merely taking a swipe at the Pharisees. He was exposing an all too common mind-set.

Keep your distance. One of the characteristics of a person who is wise in his own eyes is a stand-offish attitude towards others. You can't imagine the Pharisee of the parable putting his arm round the tax collector, because there was a complete absence of either sympathy or empathy. Even in company with others such a person would wish to make it known by word or gesture that he was a cut above them. This contrasts sharply with the mind-set Paul commends in Romans 12:16, where there is to be mutual love and respect, genuine fellow feeling and true humility. The apostle had to address high-mindedness in the Corinthian church, pricking their bubble of conceit with: 'Knowledge puffs up, but love edifies. And if anyone thinks that he knows anything, he knows nothing yet as he ought to know' (1 Corinthians 8:2).

James asks, 'Who is wise and understanding among you?' To those who raise their hands he has some pungent advice. Note especially the qualities listed in James 3:17.

26:13-16. Some idle moments. We have met v. 13 before at 22:13, and v. 15 at 19:24, but here they are included in a collection of four ironically humorous statements about a lazy person.

26:13. The lazy man in fear for his life. Of course he isn't, but there is no limit to the excuses a lazy person will make to avoid facing the unpleasant prospect of getting down to work! There may not be a lion outside, but there is an elephant in the room.

For ourselves, are we in any matter making irrational excuses for failing to do something we should be doing, deliberately avoiding the very thing that requires our attention? It will do us no more harm than the imaginary lion waiting to pounce on us!

26:14. The lazy man's restless comfort. The hinges keep a door on its doorpost and restrict its movement. We picture a lazy person similarly constrained to his bed, turning one way and then the other but never able to get off it.

For ourselves, are we so rooted to any particular comforts that we are unwilling to forsake them for important things which should take their place?

26:15. The lazy man's self-neglect. The picture is intended to be utterly ridiculous, for it is showing us the ultimate in apathy. If food will not motivate him, nothing will. Here is a man who can find no enthusiasm for anything. For him nothing is worthwhile, nothing is worth the effort.

For ourselves, are there ways in which we are neglecting to feed ourselves? Do we open our Bible only to find it too much like hard work to read it and feed on it? Is it just to much effort to go where we might obtain spiritual nourishment?

26:16. The lazy man in conference. Here he comes into his own and holds his own. Here he has plenty to say. We cannot miss the sarcasm in this statement. Such is the inertia of a lazy man that it is going to take more than seven men to move him. He has all his ready-made excuses for not doing what he should be doing and can be extraordinarily inventive in producing more. He is more than a match for them.

For ourselves, are we making excuses for ourselves in order to indulge our comforts when we should be getting out of our comfort zone and serving others in the Lord's name? The task is too risky? It may get us into trouble? We haven't the time? It is not our scene? We need a break? We are fully involved in other things? It is not worth the effort? It is something someone else should be doing? The list is not difficult to extend.

26:17-22. Strife. These verses are about ways in which people can cause unnecessary trouble.

26:17. Meddling. Anyone who happens upon others involved in a dispute which is no concern of his and who wades in regardless is not only guilty of unwarranted interference but is likely to come off the worse for it. Anyone taking hold of a dog by the ears is asking for trouble! We have enough troubles of our own without making ourselves arbiters or judges in other people's affairs. It would serve us right to be told in no uncertain terms to go away, that it is their affair and is none of our business. We would very likely be attacked by both parties in the quarrel. When we take it upon ourselves to interfere in others' affairs without any real knowledge or understanding of the details or circumstances, we put ourselves in a no-win situation, for we invite trouble for ourselves and only make matters worse for others. Matters like this are not for the passer-by. The only people who might be of any help are those who are both intimate with the situation and sympathetic to the parties involved.

26:18-19. Provoking. Practical jokes have a habit of backfiring and are really a no-go area for Christians. We may think it only a bit of fun at someone else's expense, giving little thought to what it is really costing them. Any way in which we deceive others, whatever the motive, and however we excuse it when it is exposed, is both dangerous and harmful, as this proverb makes quite clear. If they have been caused fear, or anxiety, or sleepless nights, or unnecessary expense, or other trouble, they are not going to see things your way as a bit of harmless fun and the matter is likely to have serious repercussions. It is indeed madness to set out to deceive others even in jest. Never underestimate the potential for harm in this kind of conduct.

26:20-22. Gossip. Verse 22, which appeared at 18:8, is repeated here as part of a trio of proverbs on this subject. Gossips do a great deal of harm. The world would be a better place without them. It would certainly be a more peaceful place (v. 20). Have you any nice juicy stories to tell against others? Bin them or burn them before there is any chance of publishing them. Every story we tell behind someone's back which is intended to reflect badly upon them is a cause of strife. Invariably, the grain of truth it may contain is hidden in a mound of falsehood.

Gossiping about others is as bad as causing grievous bodily harm and should be considered a punishable offence. Have you noticed how unpleasant incidents or salacious stories tend to stick in the mind? Gossip enters the mind like barbs which go in easily but which cannot be pulled out again. Or, to use the imagery of v. 22, it burns its way into our innermost being.

Whether aware of it or not, a gossip is a contentious, or quarrelsome, person (v. 21) – certainly in the sense that he or she is spreading trouble and stirring up strife. Many a small fire has developed into a fierce blaze by heaping on the wood of gossip. Talebearers would have done better to have left well alone. They will have a lot to answer for.

Far better to learn to speak well of people as opportunity arises, for this goes along way to quenching the flames fuelled by gossip.

26:23-26. Hatred. What a lot of hatred there is in the world, and the reason for this is the amount of hatred which exists in the human heart. More often than not it is concealed or disguised and operates under cover. That is what these verses are all about and they are indicating we need to be wise about it.

26:23. A thin veneer. There was a time when you could buy 'genuine gold plated' watches and other items for a price which attracted the gullible. They soon learnt they had been taken for a sucker as the shine wore off and exposed the goods as cheap rubbish. In the example of v. 23 the impressive glaze produced by silver dross would soon give way to reveal the sham and what was really underneath. Fervent lips might persuasively say all the right things and make a good impression, but if there is a wicked heart behind them their vacuity will soon be evident to those deceived and taken in by them.

It is possible for people who harbour hatred in their hearts to speak graciously if by the pretence they can gain their own evil end. Verse 24 states a fact, verse 25 provides a warning, and verse 26 assures exposure.

26:24. Fact. Things are not always what they seem. People may speak well of you when their real intention is to find an opportunity to bring you down. That is exactly what the religious leaders intended to do to Jesus when they commended him (Luke 20:21). The Lord's people need to be aware that godly living generates persecution (2 Timothy 3:12).

26:25. Warning. Fair speech is not always to be believed. That is all very well, but if someone speaks kindly or graciously, how do we know whether or not to believe they are genuine? With the wicked there are invariably tell-tale signs which take the form of a disparity between what they say and what they do. We are not to be naïve in supposing that fair words indicate good character, or even reformed character. Something more is required. When we do not know a person we should not unquestioningly take what they say at face value. We need to be aware that words are merely a front, and we should be careful to know what lies behind them. Who is this person who is saying such fine things? How easy it is to be taken in! We are not to believe everything we hear. That is not to say we should have a suspicious nature or be unduly sceptical. However, we should have a healthy respect for the truth about human nature, and not judge a person on fair words alone.

26:26. Exposure. There is comfort in that however carefully hatred and wickedness are covered, almost inevitably in the end will be public exposure, for deceit is as unstable as truth is stable. Deceit is constantly needing to be propped up with more deceit, which only increases its instability. Like a tower of cards it will ultimately collapse.

26:27-28. Psalm 7. Hoist with his own petard.

26:27. Deceit rebounds. The pit would be carefully concealed by covering it over to make it look like the surrounding ground. The stone set as a trap would roll back when disturbed to seal its victim. These were customarily prepared for animals, and the imagery is used for the kind of plots people use for bringing harm upon other people. People's evil intentions toward others have a habit of being turned back upon themselves.

The religious leaders who hated Jesus repeatedly concealed traps for him, intending to entangle him in his words (Luke 20:20) or accuse him in his actions (Matthew 12:10). With consummate wisdom every time he turned the tables on them, exposing their hypocrisy, and they were the ones caught up in the snares they had prepared.

In Psalm 7 David prays for wickedness to come to an end (v. 9) and calls upon God to act in justice (vv. 6,11). He then speaks of trouble rebounding upon the head of those who perpetrate it (vv. 14-16). The question of whether this is divine retribution or the result of natural developments may be impossible to answer in any given case. In the end no answer is really needed if we believe that God is in control of all events and circumstances and that he is perfect in justice, for 'natural causes' are just as much under his direction as what we might describe as 'divine intervention'.

26:28. Deceit ravages. In the meantime, however, it has to be acknowledged that lying and flattery, just as intended, do a great deal of harm. While in the longer term we may be assured that justice will prevail, in the short term we must accept that there will be a lot of trouble and pain. Many people have been crushed when the lies and smooth words of others have found their mark.

By deceit those who hated Jesus brought about his crucifixion. He was bruised, or crushed, for our iniquities (Isaiah 53:5). If God permitted that for his Son in order to bring about our salvation, should we not accept that we might be crushed beneath the lies of those who hate us?

Hatred is a feature of this world. It never does good, only harm, for that is its intention. Yet it is never satisfied, even after it achieves its objective. It may crush and ruin others, but having done so the hatred will not in the least be diminished. The hatred exhibited against the Lord Jesus did not die when he died but has been perpetuated against his followers; nor will it die when they die. Their suffering will only intensify it. For hatred proceeds from the father of lies, the devil, and nothing can placate it. It is already an unquenchable fire in the heart of God's enemies.

Perhaps we are to take these verses as a warning against the temptation to underhand tactics or harbouring hatred.

If we are on the receiving end of hatred as in v. 28, we find small comfort in the retribution of v. 27. Do we console ourselves that they will get what is coming to them? Is that to be our attitude? Look at Saul of Tarsus. What did he achieve by his hatred of the church? The death of Christians, yes. But also the spread of the gospel which he was trying to quench. In that respect his hatred rebounded upon himself. Hatred of this kind, horrible though it is in every respect, cannot thwart the purposes and promises of God. But then, what happened to his hatred, and with what result? Therefore what should be our attitude?

27:1 'Man proposes, God disposes' (Thomas à Kempis).

Though this quotation may appear to fit more closely to 16:9 or 19:21, it serves as a reminder that the future is not only unknown to us (as this verse says), it is not actually in our hands.

We may be prepared to admit that in an uncertain world anything might happen to us or to our circumstances by the time tomorrow arrives to completely scupper our plans. However, James, who picks up on this proverb (James 4:13-16), goes beyond this, making it quite clear that what happens tomorrow is not a matter of chance or unforeseen or unforeseeable events but a matter of the will of God.

So it is not sufficient to qualify our plans with: 'Unless something unexpected happens I will do this or that,' as if we were subject only to random events in a world of chance and change. We are subject to the will of God. It is not what we will that will prevail, but only what God wills. Our intentions and plans should therefore be submitted to him, and in addition he should be acknowledged in them.

To make the point, look at what happened to three people:

Nebuchadnezzar boasted about tomorrow (Daniel 4:30) insofar as he assumed the continuing honour of his majesty. How mistaken he was, because he must equally have assumed the judgement pronounced upon him a year or more earlier was not going to happen.

The rich farmer of the parable (Luke 12:16-21) boasted of what he was going to do, making false assumptions not only about the next day but the coming years, little realising that he would not even see tomorrow. His heart attack (or whatever it was) was more than an unfortunate event which no one could have foreseen, for it was a predetermined appointment with the Judge of all the earth. Maybe it was only a story that Jesus told, but it is so true to life that it is a tragedy that anyone should dismiss it.

An officer of the king of Israel boasted foolishly against the Lord, denying what the Lord had predicted would happen on the following day (2 Kings 7:1-2). Tomorrow is in God's hands, right down to the last detail.

What we do not know, God knows fully.

What are your plans for tomorrow? What are God's plans for you for tomorrow? Are you ready for them?

[Related proverbs: 16:1,9; 19:21.]

27:2. Haven't I done well! Here is another aspect of boasting. The two clauses are so close that the second is almost a repeat of the first. That the repetition is deemed to be necessary tells us something we may be reluctant to take on board. Here is a truth which needs to be drummed into our unwilling minds!

The emphasis of 'another', and 'a stranger' is that praise is coming from someone who has no vested interest in doing so. It is totally impartial and objective.

Impressions of others. Does it matter to you what other people think of you? Does it matter to you what they say about you? Even though some people strongly affirm otherwise, surely this is only a cover-up, because it really does matter. We have an inbuilt need for acceptance, for being well thought of, for being valued. Praise is important to us.

Impressing others. If it is true that praise is important to us, we need to ask why it is so. This proverb certainly acknowledges that praise has its place and can be received in the right spirit. What would be wrong is for me to have such a craving for praise and a dependence on it that I do my best to engineer it, seeking to attract the attention of others to my praiseworthy deeds so that my craving will be satisfied. That would be to feed an overinflated ego.

Jesus spoke of those who did their good deeds in order to be seen by men (Matthew 6:1-2). The praise of men is all that such people had in mind. How fickle is that! No wonder those who seek such praise are never satisfied!

Worthless praise. Ultimately, what matters? The praise of fickle men or the praise of a faithful God? Jesus said of some of the leaders of his day that even though they believed in him they were not prepared to say so publicly because they loved the praise of men more than the praise of God (John 12:43). What an indictment! On another occasion he said, 'Woe to you when all men speak well of you, for so did their fathers to the false prophets' (Luke 6:26). This just goes to show that praise from men can be completely worthless (or worse). Keep quiet about Jesus and continue to receive the praise of men, or speak up for him and accept the consequences of a loss of popularity.

Worthy praise. Paul said that man's commendation or opprobrium are of little consequence, whereas what is of importance is what God approves and praises (1 Corinthians 4:5).

The apostle had unstinting praise for some of his fellow workers (for example Timothy and Epaphroditus – Philippians 2:19-30) and for some of the churches (see 2 Corinthians 8:1-5). How would they have reacted to knowing they were so praised? What would have mattered to them would have been who said it – they would have valued the fact that it came from Paul because they knew that praise from his lips was genuine. Primarily, though, what really would have mattered was the way it reflected on the Lord, as evidence of his gracious work in them.

Praise is not necessarily to be rejected, and yet we need to learn to receive it in a right spirit and respond rightly to it. Our first and heartfelt response should be one of thankfulness to God that he should have been pleased to equip us and make us useful in some way in his service.

2 Corinthians 10:18 sums it all up.

[Related proverb: 25:27.]

27:3. An immovable object. It is not just the sheer weight of stone or sand which makes them feel heavy. Managing them is difficult because of their shape or shapelessness. Stones and boulders can be formidable obstacles. Sand is a dead weight and one of the most difficult things to handle and even in a bag it seems almost to have a will of its own to be uncooperative!

Obdurate. Just so the fool. He is not amenable to reason. Often he has made up his mind about things and there is no moving him from his own opinions. His attitude can be very much like that of the lazy man of 26:16. In particular, he has made up his mind about rejecting the counsel of God. You will only break your back trying to shift him from his position. Any attempt to impose order upon him meets only with resistance. Trying to get a fool to cooperate with anything worthwhile is unrewarding hard work. He is only a burden, never a help.

Obstructive. This proverb refers to a fool's wrath, or perhaps more accurately, his provocation. Here is someone who is always in the way, hindering progress, interfering unhelpfully in what ought to be done, and there seems to be no moving him.

Obsessive. What do we have to learn from this? For ourselves, we are guilty of foolish provocation if we stubbornly entertain attitudes or views about things or hold on to traditions without being willing to scrutinise them in the light of Scripture, and especially so if we foist them upon others. Some people are like this because they fear they will lose their security, clinging on to what they have instead of relinquishing it for something better. That is a bit like a man at sea clinging on to his piece of driftwood unwilling to cooperate with someone trying to winch him up to safety. This would be typical of those who hold on to their false religion with all its associations and ties, afraid to cut loose and commit themselves to a Saviour even though they know he is true.

Obstinate. But others are provocative out of sheer pig-headedness that they are right and above being questioned about it. They are the fools with closed minds. They are the ones who reject God's Word out of hand, who refuse to consider it or even listen to it.

Open-minded. As Christians we have nothing to fear from opening our minds and being willing to listen, to ponder, to scrutinise, and to act accordingly. Nor do we have such complete understanding that we do not need to do these things. We must be willing to test all things, and then to hold fast to what is good (1 Thessalonians 5:21). God's Word, with the enlightenment of his Spirit, is our rock of security, our infallible and inerrant guide. In any respect to deviate from the book is foolish provocation, whatever the circumstances. To trust his Word and obey it, whatever the circumstances, is wisdom. Though some may scornfully say this is closing our minds, yet all the evidence is to the contrary and wisdom is justified by her children (Matthew 11:19).

27:4. Jealousy – bad and good.

Negatively. In this context, 'jealousy' is a more appropriate translation than 'envy' (AV). Envy is the intense 'I wish I had...' attitude toward what someone else has, and it invariably linked with covetousness. We may envy someone's prosperity, or be envious of their possessions, or their success, and so forth, because these are things they have which we don't, and we wish we did. But jealousy is of a different order because it aims to take away from others whatever it is we covet that we may have it for ourselves. A spirit of rivalry exists which is not satisfied unless and until it has got what it wants at the expense of the other person.

Positively. 'Jealous' and 'zealous' are words of similar origin. A jealous person, like a zealous one, is very active in pursuit of his objective. We often think of jealousy as a bad quality, and so it may be. But it may be perfectly just. Take the man who seduces another man's wife, violating the sacred marriage bond. The husband will rightly be jealous and nothing can compensate for the despicable deed that has been done or make amends for it (6:30-35). In a day when marriage is often held in contempt and a casual attitude to relationships exists it is still true that intense jealousy is aroused when someone 'steals my girl' or 'gets my man into her clutches', for which there are often bitter consequences. It belies the trivialisation of a relationship which is so fundamental to men and women.

Uncompromising. Wrath may often be appeased, and anger may abate, but jealousy is unquenchable. Jealousy arises over rivalry which should not exist, and at the level of human relationships we see its most powerful expression where adultery is committed. Yet there is a far more important aspect to jealousy, the divine aspect, for God has declared himself to be a jealous God who will brook no rival, and who even goes as far as to say his name is Jealous (Exodus 20:5; 34:14). God does not and cannot acquiesce in his people compromising their covenant relationship with him by any attraction which usurps his rightful priority in their lives. Idolatry on the part of his people always arouses his jealousy, because they belong exclusively to him.

This should both warn and comfort us. We can sometimes imagine the grass is greener on the other side, we can be tempted to forsake the fountain of living waters for broken cisterns (Jeremiah 2:13). And we will only suffer for it. God will rightly be angry with us, because when by faith we came to him we did so unconditionally, surrendering all to him. Then we knew and valued the genuineness and fullness of his love. Gladly and without regret we were his and his alone. Can we have forgotten, that our responsive love should have grown so cold as for us to seek to warm ourselves by another fire? God warns us that he is a jealous God.

We should be comforted because he is unwilling, and indeed refuses, to let us go. Our foolish flirting with the world arouses his jealousy because we belong to him by a covenant of love sealed with the blood of his own Son, for which reason he will never will relinquish us. Our self-harming grieves him intensely, for he wants us in the security of his care, to be safe and at peace, to delight in us and we in him. Surely therefore it is our comfort that God is a jealous God.

27:5-6. Hurt, or flattered?

An unexpected comparison. None of us likes to be rebuked, least of all openly, but sometimes it is necessary, as in the case of Peter and his companions at Antioch (Galatians 2:11). On the other hand, all of us like to be known that we are loved, and so it is bitter to us if we are given the impression that we are not loved, especially by those from whom we might expect it.

Then why is the one better than the other? Is it not because open rebuke, though painful, is beneficial, while concealed love, also causing pain, does no good whatever and, it can probably be argued, actually does harm?

Loving rebuke. Sometimes the mistaken notion is entertained that rebuke and love are in some way incompatible. Jesus, having delivered a stinging rebuke to the lukewarm believers at Laodicea, immediately added: 'As many as I love, I rebuke and chasten' (Revelation 3:17-19) as an incentive to their responding rightly.

Disciplinarian parents who carefully conceal their love for fear that it might work against the correction and training of their offspring only leave their children confused and bitter. Love is not meant to be concealed, and in this instance its expression, with the inevitable sharing of the pain of discipline, helps to promote understanding and respect and therefore intelligent compliance. Rebuke is a bitter pill which love sweetens and makes easier to swallow.

Again, some people can seem almost ashamed to express their love, whether by word or by deed, imagining that it might be misunderstood or even be rejected. Yet true love, which seeks the highest welfare of its object, is nothing to be ashamed of, and must find expression. It is love which wins hearts.

A painful purpose. We would not expect a friend to hurt us. When it happens, we accept it because we know from the friendship that it is done out of love and without any ulterior motive. The 'wounds' might take the form of rebuke, or even interference in our affairs. Though we may not take kindly to it at first, we understand that the friend is looking out for our welfare. David understood this when he wrote (Psalm 141:5): 'Let the righteous strike me; it shall be a kindness. And let him rebuke me; it shall be as excellent oil; let my head not refuse it.'

There is none so faithful as our heavenly Father. When we find ourselves experiencing pain and afterwards licking our wounds let us remember Hebrews 12:5-6.

Kiss of death. The kisses of an enemy may remind us of Judas' betrayal of Jesus (Luke 22:47-48), or of Joab's treachery toward Amasa (2 Samuel 20:9). There is, however, a side to this we do not always recognise. The enemy of our souls can lull us into a sense of false confidence, to believe all is well with us and to make us think too well of ourselves, so that we grow complacent and comfortable in the neglect of our spiritual well-being. A convincing liar, he can masquerade as an angel of light (2 Corinthians 11:14). We should not be ignorant of his devices (2 Corinthians 2:11).

Retain objectivity. This is not so easy with things that can so affect us emotionally. To be hurt or to be praised will offend or appeal to our wretched pride. Whether we are experiencing the wounds of a friend or the kisses of an enemy, we should always be objective and have the end in view: where is it all leading? Are the dealings faithful or flattering? It is the truth which matters, not how we feel about it!

[Related proverb: 28:23.]

27:7. More than is good for you. God has built into our bodies a remarkable mechanism which indicates to us when we have eaten enough. So we can stomach only a certain amount even of the best of food. This mechanism is sometimes overridden by greed, with the consequence that overindulgence leads to discomfort. But this mechanism also works at the other end, so that when really hungry we will eat with pleasure what we would normally disdain. From being satisfied, we build up an appetite as we work, and the longer and harder we work, so in proportion is our enjoyment of our next meal, whether plain or sumptuous.

This proverb is really an illustration of something not so readily recognised. The self-indulgent rich are among the most uncomfortable people in this world. Adding to their wealth only sickens them and they derive no pleasure from it. On the other hand, those who live in relative poverty find true delight in simple pleasures.

Taking in. Let us apply this to the Christian. The Christian who is always taking in, listening to good sermons, reading good books, always present at all the fellowship meetings and special events, and never giving out, is heading for big trouble. For these things, good as they are, will eventually become nauseating. It is good to have an appetite for these things, but not to the point where appetite turns to greed. The principle of 2 Corinthians 8:13-15 operates here. Dissatisfaction in churches often arises when there is too much taking in and too little giving out.

Giving out. Look at what you are taking in. Have you given serious consideration to what you might give out as a result? For that is one of the reasons for your taking in. From what you have benefited, how can you benefit others? You might argue that you have little to give, or that you cannot serve your simple fare on a golden platter. That is no argument, though, for there are people around who are hungry enough to benefit from, and find sweetness in, even what you have to offer and your limited way of presenting it. The more you give, and the more you are a source of nourishment to others, the better will your own appetite become and the greater will be your own appreciation of what you receive.

A bloated Christian is not a healthy Christian!

[Related proverb: 25:16.]

27:8. Ephesians 5:25–6:4. A man's place is... The comparison in this proverb is actually between a mother bird and a man. The picture is that of a mother bird producing and protecting her offspring until they fledge. If she wanders from (perhaps in the sense of being frightened off and having to flee) her nest either the eggs will grow cold and will not hatch or they will run the risk of being predated. If they have hatched, then the fledglings will not be fed properly or be kept warm and dry, and so they will die. It is the bird's God-given instincts to brood her young, and it is unnatural if she fails to do so.

Running away. This proverb, however, is not making a comparison with mothers, but with men. While it could refer to a man who has had to flee his place, losing everything, there is a comparison closer to home which bears scrutiny. It is a sad truth that in Western society the number of men who have wandered, or been frightened off, or fled, from their place has reached epidemic proportions.

Relinquishing responsibility. Such men have either suppressed or abandoned or lost all sense of their inbuilt God-given responsibilities. A man who 'wanders from his place' is one who, for whatever reason, has run away from responsibilities he ought to be carrying, even if he is sitting at home with his feet up! For example, he has a wife for whom he should be caring, being sensitive to her needs as the 'weaker vessel', supporting her, providing for her, giving her a sense of security, showing his appreciation of her and valuing her for the help she gives him. He has children before whom he should be setting an example of leadership, exercising discipline and training and encouragement. He should be setting an example for them of dignity and worth. He should be seen to be the man of the house in the proper sense of that word.

So many men seem to have abdicated these and other responsibilities. They leave it all to their spouses, absorbing themselves in their work, or their own interests and pleasures. At worst, they take up with other women and so multiply their irresponsibility. The fruit of all this is dysfunctional families with children growing up in an unstable environment, who have no bearings by which to navigate their lives.

Role model. Christian men would do well to review these things regularly. The principles may be understood well enough, but the practice requires much thought and close attention. For example, what is meant by bringing up your children in the training and admonition of the Lord (Ephesians 6:4)? It is more than instructing them in the things of God. 'Of the Lord' implies doing things in the way the Lord would have us do them. Think about how the Lord as our heavenly Father trains and admonishes us and all that is involved in this. Think about his love, his faithfulness, his perseverance, his understanding, his sensitivity to our needs and the appropriateness of all his dealings with us, especially in the light of the difficult material he has to deal with! He is the role model for the way in which fathers are to bring up their children.

Men, know your place and stay in it!

27:9. Aromatherapy.

In a hot climate one of the principal functions of ointment and perfume was to mask unpleasant odours. A room filled with fragrance was much to be preferred to the smell of sweaty bodies!

Counsel. The comparison is patent. The counsel of a good friend is like that. Firstly, earnest counsel, or 'the counsel of the soul', comes from the genuine, deep friendship of one who cares. It is a great privilege to have friends like that who are looking out for, and are concerned about, our welfare. Secondly, earnest counsel is more than casual advice. It is something which comes from the heart, something of importance which is meant to be heard, accepted, and acted upon. Coming from a friend makes it valued and appreciated, and even if it is intended to cover some unpleasantness, the manner in which it is given makes it eminently acceptable and makes compliance a pleasure.

Cover. On the matter of unpleasantness, there are many ways of dealing with it. One is by open rebuke (27:5), another is by making it hurt (27:6), both of which can in their own way be quite legitimate. However, here is a third way, by the introduction of counsel which will cover it up and remove it with its hardly being noticed. Some people have such a gracious and winsome way of giving their counsel that only afterwards do we become aware of how great a service they have rendered us and from what they have spared us. It was all done so pleasantly and smoothly.

Comfort. When we observe faults in others, even in our friends, we do need to think about how best to deal with them. Exposure is not always the best way, as the Lord's dealings with us abundantly demonstrate. It is true that he does sometimes deem it necessary to expose some of our sins to our view and make us smart on account of them. More often, though, he delights us with his Word, makes us feel his love, comforts us with his presence, and shows us the sheer pleasure of doing what he wants that we find ourselves leaving behind odious character traits and other sins without his having to bring them to our attention. Just think of what the effect on us would have been had he revealed to us all our faults! What a friend we have in Jesus!

Care. If we are inclined toward a critical spirit, even where our friends are concerned, let us make it a habit of taking with us ointment and perfume to use as appropriate! This proverb should make us think about the quality and substance of our friendships and whether we are using them for improvement. Do we really care, and will we really care? The New Testament word variously translated 'exhort', or 'beseech', or 'encourage' or 'comfort' (for example Hebrews 3:13; 10:25; Philemon 9-10; 1 Thessalonians 4:18; 5:11) expresses very well the kind of counsel spoken of here and can be exercised effectively only when there is a true fellow feeling which finds pleasure in the presence and counsel of our brothers and sisters in Christ.

27:10. What friends are for. In this proverb there are three kinds of people: friends, relations and neighbours; and an observation on how we interact with them in situations of personal difficulty, for the context here is that of some calamity. Calamities come in all shapes and sizes, invariably unexpectedly. They may come to you or to someone close to you, and suddenly some kind of outside help is needed.

Helping. The first clause can be viewed from two angles. The first is that of trouble befalling your own friend or a friend of the family and of your needing to be there to help. They are depending on you in a crisis and you owe it to them for the sake of the friendship to do all you can for them.

The saying, 'A friend in need is a friend indeed,' hints that there are friendships and friendships. Some people are fickle, only fair weather friends, and when they see they may be required to give help they disappear from the scene or make excuses. Some are even treacherous, using so-called friendship merely for personal gain, turning against the person for advantage, like Ahithophel turned against David (2 Samuel 15:12; Psalm 41:9). Judas Iscariot, when he saw there was no gain from being with Jesus, turned against him. The real test of friendship is when it becomes costly in some way to stand by the friend.

For example, your friend falls ill and is incapacitated. How much inconvenience are you prepared to suffer in order to give time to your friend with personal encouragement and practical assistance? Or your friend is the object of slander which you believe to be false though the rumours are popularly believed. Are you willing to be besmirched by standing by your friend in this time of need, when it would be so much easier to keep your distance?

Being helped. The alternative angle on the first clause is that of the suffering party forsaking their friend by going off to their relatives and inviting the question, perhaps with a justifiable reproach, 'Why didn't you come straight to me when I was right here at hand?' The proverb is not saying we should not go to our relatives in such circumstances, but rather is emphasising the importance, value and strength of friendships. Friendships need to be honoured and respected from this angle, too. The ties of friendship are strengthened by proper use.

Whichever way we take it, we have a reminder that friends are there for us when need arises, and if we are true friends we will be there for others when they need us.

Nurturing. Notice how friend and neighbour are treated in this context as virtually one and the same. Neighbourly friendship is an ideal which often is not realised! The reason for this, though, is that potential friendships are not cultivated. How well do you know your neighbours? What efforts have you made to develop relationships with them which will lead to friendship and respect? Would you be willing to ask them for help when you find yourself in difficulties of some kind? Sometimes doing this in small ways is a bridge builder. They feel honoured to be able to be of use to you, and this paves the way for you to be of use to them on occasion.

Friendship does not have strings of the kind which bind blood relations. [Related proverb: 17:17.]

27:11. Psalm 127. Wisdom loves to be a blessing. These are the words of a man who has poured his love, his time and his efforts – his heart – into his son's upbringing. While it is true that some people turn out well in spite of their upbringing, in the majority of cases it is because of their upbringing.

To caring parents, what happens to their offspring is of paramount importance and can have a profound effect upon their well-being. The connection between a wise son and a glad father has already been seen at 10:1 and 23:15,24. Here, however, it comes as an exhortation.

Motivation. We have the capacity to act wisely, and also to act foolishly. There are times when an exhortation is necessary, as for example when we are tempted to react hastily to a situation or are enticed by something with false appeal. A reminder to be wise when it comes to specifics will be accepted by a man who has reason to respect his father but will be treated with contempt by one whose father has never invested in wisdom himself. Furthermore, a son loved by wise parents will in general find pleasure in making them glad.

Rationale. What of the reason for this exhortation? At first sight it may seem rather self-centred. On closer examination it will be found to be entirely otherwise. Christian parents are often reproached by others for the way they bring up their children. They are accused among other things of being selfishly bigoted, narrow minded, indoctrinating, restrictive, depriving, denying their children the freedom of choice and pleasures that others enjoy. Whereas in fact they are bringing them up in the training and admonition of the Lord, instructing them in right and wrong, teaching them to think for themselves and make decisions according to godly principles, giving them the security of love and stability that is unique to a Christian home.

Result. Psalm 127 refers to the Lord building a house, by which we may understand a family, for the later verses speak of children being a heritage from the Lord. The scenario is that of a man bringing his affairs under the authority and direction of the Lord. God is the foundation for his life, and what is built is in keeping with that foundation. The psalm concludes with their not being ashamed but speaking with their enemies in the gate, by which we are to understand that their enemies have nothing to say against them which will stick.

The family is still and always will be the basic unit of society. Homes in which Christ is not honoured, in which the Word of God has no influence, are vulnerable to all kinds of unhappy influences. People from such homes, although they may scorn Christians, are very often conscious of the rock-like stability of Christian families in spite of all that happens to them, of the good order, of the high moral principles, and often of the ability and influence seen in their offspring.

The father of a wise son may answer a reproaching world without a word. The results speak for themselves. It remains true that God honours those who honour him. This proverb should be an incentive to Christian parents not to be intimidated by the voice of the world, but to listen to God for the upbringing of their children.

Is God your heavenly Father? Is it your desire to be wise and to make *his* heart glad?

[Related proverbs: 10:1; 23:15,24; 29:3.]

27:12. If only I had known. Because this is identical to 22:3 it is tempting to skip over it. God does not repeat himself without reason. This is something of which we need to be reminded. Perhaps we need to think again about it or look at it from a slightly different angle. If we see trouble heading in our direction it makes sense to take steps to avoid getting caught up in it. On the other hand, if we see ourselves heading for trouble we may need to take avoiding action. The one requires us to look ahead at what is coming toward us; the other requires us to look ahead and see what we are heading toward. So here we will take the telescope approach and deliberately look into the distance, not simply to see what is coming, but rather, what *we will be coming to* if we continue on our present course.

What lies ahead? Would it be better to take a different course? As we progress through life all sorts of things happen to us. We fall into a particular line of work, we develop hobbies, we become engaged in various kinds of service, we acquire various habits, and so on. As life goes on it tends to become increasingly complicated. On the whole we tend to 'run with it' unless some crisis intervenes. Some crises fall upon us unexpectedly and could not have been foreseen. But some are overtaken by us rather than our being overtaken by them, only we had not been looking ahead.

Where is your life leading you? Look at any given aspect of your life and ask yourself the question about what lies ahead. Is there potential trouble there?

For example, you might consider your eating habits. Are self-indulgence or excess involved which have the potential for health problems in the future? Or are you going to wait until it is too late and suffer the consequences?

Or consider your employment. Does your work have the potential to lead you into areas of compromise? If so, are there steps you should be taking now so that it will not happen?

Or your family. Where are you leading them? What will be the state of your family relationships if things go on as they are?

Or perhaps consider something you are *not* doing now and what the result could well be some time down the road of life. Are there areas of neglect which in all probability will bring trouble into your life later on?

In these contexts hiding yourself simply means recognising potential consequences and not exposing yourself to them. The troubles which afflict others will not touch you because you have looked ahead and seen them and removed yourself from them.

Prudence is proactive. It looks ahead. It thinks ahead. In the light of what it sees it takes avoiding action where potential evil is concerned. The simple are silly with their *laissez faire* approach, just taking what comes.

The Christian should always be looking ahead to the glory of being with Christ. John says that he who has this hope purifies himself (1 John 3:3). This necessarily involves looking ahead in our own lives, foreseeing evil and taking remedial action.

27:13. Guarding the last resource. This proverb, too, is a repetition, for almost identical words appear at 20:16.

The law of God made provision for the needs of the poor, so that no matter how, or how greatly, they were impoverished, they at least had a garment remaining so that they could sleep at night (Exodus 22:25-27). So if his garment was taken in pledge, it was to be returned by sundown.

The reasons for poverty are many and various, but the scenario before us seems to be the case of a person likely to be reduced to poverty through his own foolishness. Two classes of people are mentioned. One is the stranger and the other is a 'strange woman', or an adulteress. In the first case we are looking at someone committing himself up to his eyeballs in the dark to someone he does not really know, while in the second case it is someone committing himself through a sinful emotional entanglement.

The expression 'take his garment' can be viewed in one of two ways.

1. Cautionary. This view is simply to stress that anyone who makes himself unconditionally responsible for someone he does not know or for someone with a sinful reputation is in effect ruining himself. It is the extreme of folly. What he is doing is in effect allowing his garment to be taken from him, leaving him with absolutely nothing. You dare not make that kind of commitment with your eyes shut.

2. Compassionate. The second view is that the focus of this proverb is upon a third party – someone who has some dealings with a person foolish enough to stand surety for another without safeguards, and who maybe even feels some sense of responsibility toward that person.

What are you to do if you see someone undertaking a bad risk which may well ruin him? You are to 'take his garment', so that he does not lose everything. A pledge is a promise, and in this case holding it in pledge is a promise to return his garment to him by nightfall. How does this work out in practice in our very different cultural situation?

It can be very frustrating dealing with people who haven't the sense to see they are making bad investments which may very well ruin them. It can be exasperating dealing with people who cannot manage their affairs and squander what they have so that they are left with nothing. It can be emotionally draining dealing with people beset by sins which strip everything away from them.

Intervention. It may be that here, 'Take the garment' is pointing to intervention on behalf of someone who is running the risk of losing everything through imprudence or sin. But the intervention, if that is what it is, is not to *give* but to *take*. It is intervention with the aim of guarding a person's last resource, what is absolutely essential to him.

Thus this proverb is not suggesting giving people hand-outs or anything like that but rather letting them smart under their folly while protecting them from the ultimate indignity. There is a situation where the most appropriate help is minimal, where to do more would be detrimental. Even fools need compassion.

[Related proverbs: 6:1; 11:15; 17:18; 20:16; 22:26.]

27:14. A blessing which isn't. One morning you are just about to start on your day's work when someone calls, as effusive in apologies for disturbing you as in compliments on your being such a kind friend, declaring how thankful he is that you are so close at hand.

You could be forgiven for wondering what he is after this time! Whatever he says at that time of day when you've got work to get on with, his presence on your doorstep is a nuisance and anything but a pleasure. His blessing is a curse!

Give-away signs. We live in a world where things are not always what they seem, and that is especially the case when people want something from us for benefit to themselves without regard to ourselves. Bearing in mind that the proverbs are about wisdom for life, we need, as Jesus said, to be wise as serpents while at the same time being innocent as doves (Matthew 10:16). Exploitation has many faces. We need to learn to read them. In this proverb are two tell-tale signs.

Early in the morning. Early rising is generally commendable, provided it is for the right reason. The familiar saying, 'The early bird catches the worm,' is an indication that timely industry and application are rewarded where slovenly attitudes miss out. Here, however, is someone being over-forward with blessing or praise, who wants to make you feel good for no good reason. It is too early in the day for that. When we use that expression, 'it is too early in the day' for something, we mean that it is premature to make a judgement or a decision because we do not have all the necessary facts at our fingertips. So here is someone being premature in his 'blessing', and an impartial assessment of it suggests there is something phoney about it.

With a loud voice. This is the second give-away sign. The 'blessing' is over the top. He wants everybody to know what a good person you are. He wants you to think more highly of yourself than is just. Every day is new and the work of the day is just beginning. If 'blessing' is due, it was due either at the end of the previous day on account of what happened then, or is due at the end of the current day after the day's work is done and cause has been given for it. So, voluminous praise at that inappropriate time of day carries with it a huge cringe factor for any who are not conceited enough to be taken in by it.

If we are somewhat inclined to relish being praised, or even in danger of dependence upon being well spoken of, we need to be on our guard to recognise what is given in an untimely or inappropriate manner.

Friend? One of the features of true friendship is that fawning flattery and roundabout tactics are completely absent. Friends say what they mean and mean what they say, with consideration for how they say it to benefit. In that sense friendship has no 'airs and graces'. It does not resort to selfish subterfuge.

Real 'blessing' fully acknowledges the Lord from whom all blessings flow. Anything else is sham.

27:15-16. Never argue with a woman!

Will it ever stop? There is nothing like a gloomy day of incessant rain to dampen the spirits and raise the question, 'Will it ever stop?' There is a kind of helplessness about the situation in which one knows one can do nothing about it.

Will *she* ever stop? A contentious woman, or wife, says this proverb, is just like that. No matter what you say or do there will be no pleasing her, no making her stop. She will have an answer to anything you say, with words that get under your skin, and the gloom will remain.

What cannot be done. This proverb highlights the futility of attempting restraint. The very idea of restraining the wind or grasping hold of oil is ludicrous. Nor will you ever get a grip on this situation by any words you might use.

Like the other proverbs which mention a contentious woman (19:13; 21:9,19), this one passes no judgement. It merely makes an observation as to how things are. It informs a woman of the effect a contentious spirit has on those around her (and especially her husband). It informs a man that he cannot handle such a situation in the way that might come most naturally to him. The rather frustrated plea of 'Do be reasonable!' is one which will achieve nothing. He very naturally wants a bit of peace and quiet, he wants the woman to stop nagging and complaining, but to attempt to shut her up or restrain her is entirely the wrong way of going about it.

What *can* be done. When we see that things are not as they should be, we should ask *why* they are as they are (though often we fail to do so). When we understand that, we are then in a better position to address the symptoms. What is it which has led to the discontent? What are the factors which have contributed to the present dissatisfaction with everything and everybody?

In this situation a woman does not need to be subjected to cold rational argument. That only exacerbates the problem which is usually an emotional one. Have I been insensitive? Have I been thoughtless? Have I taken her for granted or ignored her needs? Have I allowed, or even required, her to take on more than she can cope with? Am I expecting her to handle things for which I should be taking responsibility? Have I allowed a distance to develop in a relationship in which there ought to be intimacy? Has something happened which has upset her equilibrium? She may be making a great fuss about everything except the one thing which is really at the bottom of it all.

Contentions rarely arise where love, and sympathy, and thoughtfulness, and consideration, and sensitivity, and openness are in evidence. When they do arise, these qualities usually quickly extinguish them. The question we should be asking is not how to *restrain* contention, but how to *disperse* it. If we ask the right questions, we are likely to find the right answers!

Though these notes principally address a man, it is hoped a woman may read them to advantage.

27:17. Cutting edge technology. The image is that of employing the friction of iron against iron to sharpen a tool to improve its usefulness, and it is used as an illustration of something that is achieved by the interaction of two people who are in some way associates on an equal footing, and hence the translation 'friend' in some versions. Certainly the idea of mutual recognition and respect is involved here. Sharpening 'the countenance' (NKJV) may be taken in a wide variety of ways ranging from clarifying his perception to improving his character or personality. In general it may be understood of making him a better, or more capable, person. It is part and parcel of loving one's neighbour (same word as that translated 'friend') as oneself (Leviticus 19:18).

One-sided. Job had three friends who sat with him in his suffering, and although they got it wrong it could be argued that what they said sharpened Job's thinking. Their friendship, however, lacked an essential ingredient, for they jumped to unwarranted conclusions, sure that they were right, and what they intended as a help proved to be only a hindrance. They were willing to speak their opinion – no doubt well meaning opinion – but they were unwilling really to listen to Job.

Double-edged. Really good friendship desires and encourages the best in the other person and interacts to that end. It is willing if necessary to rebuke or correct the other person without being judgemental and without there being any risk of detriment to the status of the friendship. Furthermore, it is as willing to receive as it is to give. 'Iron sharpening iron' is a two-way thing.

Testing the blade. Consider the status of some of your friendships. Are they stimulating and improving as well as enjoyable? They should be. What are you getting out of your friendships and what are you putting into them? Here are a few examples to set you thinking, and you will be able to think of many more.

Your friend is inclined to speak rather disparagingly of certain people, to your mind unfairly so. How are you going to address this situation to help your friend toward a better understanding and improved relationships with others?

You have an important decision to reach about a matter and share the problem with your friend. It is not so much their opinion you need as their input to help you make the right or the best decision. What kind of things could they say and how could they contribute to your thinking in a way that would be really useful?

A friend of yours has to broach a delicate subject with a mutual acquaintance and, not quite sure how to go about it, asks your advice. How should you most helpfully respond to the question, 'What do you think I should do?', in such a way as will 'sharpen' your friend?

Another friend is involved in writing on a certain subject and shares with you that they have rather dried up and lost impetus. How might you, with little knowledge of the subject, help them to get going again?

There is no short, set answer to any of these questions, but there is an underlying principle.

Read Hebrews 10:24 in the light of this proverb and see if it helps you in applying yourself to this noble task.

27:18. No gains without pains. A fig tree carefully tended will yield plenty of good, nutritious fruit. Neglected, it will disappoint. Compare Matthew 21:19.

Intelligent service. The verbs in the two clauses are very similar in meaning. The fig tree is guarded and protected in order that it may be fruitful. It is a task which requires dedication over a significant period of time. The servant's attitude to his master is similar in that he seeks, and goes on seeking, the best for his master. With careful watchfulness and intelligent consideration he guards and protects his master's interests. That is what Joseph did for Potiphar in Egypt, and later what he did for the prison keeper, and later still for Pharaoh. That, too, is what Daniel did for a succession of kings. They gave their time and their lives to the task.

Fruitful service. Many people do a job because it is a job to earn them money. Their thinking goes no further. So they do not think about how they might do it better, or look for ways of improving how they might serve their employers.

Honourable service. Some people look for honour by seeking to build their own little empires. Their view is not what they might give to others but what they might get for themselves. This is completely contrary to the principles God enjoins on his subjects and the example he himself has set, for Jesus came not to be served, but to serve, and to give his life a ransom for many (Matthew 20:28). He took the form of a servant (Philippians 2:7), and as a servant demonstrated what true service is all about. As a result he has been exalted to the highest place (Philippians 2:9).

Honoured service. Jesus illustrated this proverb in his parable about the talents (Matthew 25:14-30). Note how the faithful servants were working in their master's best interests with what they had been given – and clearly taking pleasure in it – and how in the end they were honoured.

Without doubt neither Joseph nor Daniel served the way they did in order to gain promotion or receive honour. Their sole concern was to *give* honour – to their God. This is the more evident in that when they were honoured they served with just the same diligence as they had before. It was a matter of principle with them to give of their best, and to give it for the best of others.

Only honour deserved is worth having. Most of us are in the service of others in one way or another, and in many cases there is someone to whom we are directly accountable. Is our service rendered in a manner consistent with seeking the best interests of these people, or only what we perceive as our own best interests?

As priest, Eli's responsibility was to wait upon the Lord with devoted service, something he failed to do because he put his sons first. The Lord said to him (1 Samuel 2:30): 'Those who honour me I will honour, and those who despise me shall be lightly esteemed.'

This promise applies to Christians, who are a 'royal priesthood' (1 Peter 2:9), called into the service of God, and one way in which this service is rendered, which is pleasing to him and in his interests, is in how we are to relate to our brothers and sisters in Christ. So we are to serve one another in love (Galatians 5:13), and in honour we are to prefer one another (Romans 12:10). We should count it an inestimable honour to wait upon our heavenly Master.

27:19. Self-examination. The absence of verbs in the original language of this proverb makes the correspondence more immediate and more complete. In a reflection no detail is lost. So likewise the heart of a man *is* the man.

Outward reflection. In Solomon's time people did not have glass and mirrors as we know them and so were unaccustomed to seeing themselves as they were. Still water provided them the opportunity of leaning over and seeing their face reflected (and that is about as much of them they would be able to see in this way, water surface being horizontal). We are so used to mirrors that we can see our reflections many times a day and know what we look like.

Inward reflection. A mirror, however, tells only a limited tale. It is accurate (apart from left-right orientation) in showing us what we look like on the outside, but it does little to reveal us as we *really* are.

Parents often notice with some amusement when their growing children begin to spend time in front of the mirror, having suddenly become self-conscious about their appearance and wanting to look presentable. They may want others to take notice of them, or they may want to make a favourable impression on others.

If people spend so much time and take so much trouble before a mirror to ensure that they look all right outwardly, would it not make sense that they should look inwardly, into their hearts, into themselves, with close self-examination to see what they are *really* like?

A person buying a car may want it to look good to impress his friends, but what is the point if mechanically it is falling apart? We may wish to look our best in company, but what use is that if we haven't the quality of character to gain acceptance – or to contribute meaningfully?

More than an overhaul. Inward self-examination is much neglected. A girl may spend a lot of time in front of a mirror looking for blemishes and considering how to deal with them, and generally on how to improve her appearance. As Christians, we should be prepared to examine our hearts, our personalities, in the light of God's Word. We will find many blemishes there, but the Word of God provides the means not just to conceal them so that they do not show but, far more than this, to remove them completely, to beautify us internally. Thus self-examination is not a morbid exercise but an eminently healthy one. The more and better this is done, the more people will see behind the face (or the façade) to recognise us as we really are by God's grace. The more too we will recognise God's grace toward us for what it is, and glory in him.

When was the last time you looked into a mirror to attend to your appearance? When was the last time you looked into your heart to attend to your character?

Unbelievers may repudiate the idea of self-examination, not knowing how to deal with what they find within themselves. But Christians should have nothing to fear, knowing already that by nature no good thing dwells there (Romans 7:18) but that by God's grace they are born again (1 Peter 1:23) and inwardly renewed (2 Corinthians 4:16; Colossians 3:10) and that God is at work in them (Philippians 2:13).

27:20. Never never land. The comparison is so striking, unusual and unexpected that one might wonder what the intended connection is. Take the first clause. Hell and Destruction (Sheol and Abaddon) represent the abode of the dead and what is experienced there, a solemn reminder that death is not the end of existence, only the beginning of a different one. We have mortal bodies, but we are immortal souls, a painful dichotomy brought about by the entrance of sin into this world.

Capacity. The house of the dead is never bursting at the seams. No one can ever think with relief, 'Perhaps there won't be room for me there'! It is an accepted fact that death is relentless and insatiable. Hell will take as many as come and there will still be just as much room as before. It doesn't need a sign saying 'Vacancies' for there will always be vacancies. There are always people crowding its portals, and the endless procession of new arrivals will make not the least difference to its capacity.

Now for the second clause. We could take it to mean that whatever and however much we see, there is more to be seen, and that in theory this is limitless. But there is more to the meaning than this. Look around you. What do you see? Are you satisfied with what you see?

Curiosity. Our eyes are our window on the world and we respond in all sorts of ways to what we see. So for example our curiosity may be aroused by something we see and we respond by looking closer, or by wanting to see more, or by investigating further. In that case we were not satisfied with what we saw at first. Curiosity, however, may be satisfied, and so on its own it does not fall within the scope of this proverb. Now take the case of a photographer looking for the perfect shot in relation to his particular sphere of interest. His eye is never satisfied because the perfection he is striving after is unattainable. He is constantly looking for that better picture.

Covetousness. This leads in to what is the root cause of the eyes never being satisfied. Curiosity often leads to covetousness. The eye is being constantly drawn to something which attracts closer attention, which arouses desire. There is invariably a measure of dissatisfaction in what the eye sees. In Ecclesiastes 4:8 we are informed of a person whose eye is not satisfied with riches. He sees what he has, but it isn't enough. He must have more. The eye is often covetous, seeing more and wanting more. It is for ever striving after the unattainable and, because it is unattainable, is never satisfied. However many 'must haves' he sees and acquires, there are always just as many to take their place.

In his sermon on the mount Jesus spoke of the eye being the lamp of the body (Matthew 6:22-23), and it was in connection with whether our sights are set on heavenly things or earthly ones. Earlier, he had spoken of the appeal of lust entering through the eye. Go down that route, and the eye is never satisfied, and so only drastic action will deal with it (Matthew 5:28-29). John likewise refers to the lust of the eyes (1 John 2:16) as being a feature of the love of this world. It is a lust which will never yield satisfaction, fuelled by eyes which are focused on an illusion.

Conclusion. So there is a very definite connection between the insatiable eye and the insatiable grave.

27:21. Applying the heat. The second clause should read, 'and a man according to his praise'. Once again, as in v. 19, there are no verbs in the original of this proverb, and so we have to think about the relation of silver and gold to the refining pot, and then about how praise and a man are related in some similar way.

The first clause is the same as 17:3, where we see the Lord as the refiner at work on our hearts. Here, however, we are looking at 'praise' in relation to the refining process.

The refining pot receives the ore, and the process 'tests' it to reveal if there is anything of worth there. We can identify at least two possible meanings here.

What are you worth? The first is concerned principally with the *value* aspect of the refining process. What we think of ourselves and our own worth is not necessarily an accurate evaluation. The praise accorded to us by others is a more objective and meaningful assessment.

You may take an item you consider to be worth something to an auctioneer to be valued. When it is auctioned what matters is not what you think it is worth, but the opinions of experienced bidders. You may be disappointed that the bidding does not even reach the reserve price; alternatively you may be elated that it goes under the hammer for far more than you imagined. It is the 'praise', or 'appraisal', of the bidders which is the all-important factor.

So it is that other people are better judges of you than you are of yourself. It is their appraisal which counts. This has echoes of v. 2.

Do you pass the test? A second meaning is concerned with the *testing* aspect of the refining process. A person is tested by the praise he receives. While to be constantly criticised can have a very demoralising effect, at the other end of the scale to receive much praise opens the door to the temptation to pride, conceit, self-congratulation, and generally thinking more highly of ourselves than we ought. To receive it in the wrong spirit can lead to an unhealthy dependence upon it. We can see something of this in Saul and David (1 Samuel 18:7-8). Notwithstanding the chant was very insensitive, it nevertheless exposed serious flaws of jealousy and fear in Saul's character.

How do you handle praise? When you receive accolades or lesser honours, what effect does this have upon you? Do you have the humility to give credit where credit is due? Not lip service humility which reserves a place for pride, but true humility of mind and heart which the praise does not even scratch. Praise can be hard to handle, testing our character, showing up problems of which we might not previously have been aware.

If receiving praise is testing of character, receiving lesser praise than someone else can be especially testing! For example, what about the pastor who is very aware that the preaching of a member of his congregation is always so well received? Or what about the person whose gift is recognised, acknowledged and used, but whose work becomes overshadowed by someone else's?

Both of these meanings fit the proverb well, and both remind us that only one thing is of importance, and that is the Lord's commendation (1 Corinthians 4:5).

[Related proverb: 17:3.]

27:22. Obdurate foolishness.

Definition. Typically, a mortar is a steep sided bowl, and a pestle is like a short club with a slightly rounded end, used for pounding and grinding items placed in the mortar. Larger versions have traditionally been used for husking grain to remove the outer covering and then for grinding the grain, while smaller ones are used for grinding spices and the like for food preparation.

Depiction. The picture before us is an amusing one. Imagine a worker pounding away at his grain until all the husks have come off and been blown away – except for one. He keeps pounding, and all the grain is crushed – except for this one piece which contrary to nature resists all attempts to break it down. His natural reaction would be to pick it out and throw it out.

Defiance. No matter how much pummelling a fool receives, it will not remove his folly from him. His folly is inveterate. Others will learn from their mistakes, they will receive correction and be wise. Discipline will not be lost on them; it will prove beneficial. But the fool is something else. See 17:10. He is rather like the drunkard of 23:35. His folly has made him insensitive to correction (12:15), and all he wants to do is to continue in it.

'Foolishness is bound up in the heart of a child; the rod of correction will drive it far from him' (22:15). Children need discipline and instruction and are amenable to it. But we are not looking here at a child. We are not considering a first time offender, but a hardened criminal, one who has make it a lifetime's habit to defy God's laws. Such a person is not responsive to correction, to discipline, to reason, or to any other pressure which may be brought to bear upon him.

Deliverance. Paul reminded Titus that we were all once *foolish*, disobedient, deceived, and so on (Titus 3:3). So how was our folly removed from us? It certainly wasn't beaten out of us. It came about by sovereign, overmastering grace! 'When the kindness and love of God our Saviour toward man appeared ... he saved us...' (Titus 3:4-6).

As Lane says, commenting on this proverb, 'God's judgements are insufficient to bring about repentance and faith – his grace is also necessary.'

[Related proverb: 17:10.]

27:23-27. Good husbandry. The key to this section is v. 24 and can be read in conjunction with 6:6-11 which is a reasoned rebuke to slothfulness. This section is a reasoned encouragement to diligence.

Planning. There was no tension with this proverb when Jesus spoke of not laying up treasures for ourselves on earth and not worrying about tomorrow (Matthew 6:19-21,25-34), for he was not advocating neglect of forward planning and preparation or a careless disregard for what might happen in the future. Due diligence is there through his teaching, and his concern is with priority and attitude, that in all things we should be living for him and in dependence upon him.

Preservation. There is much emphasis these days upon 'renewable resources' because of the consciousness that, the way things are being used, we could be in trouble in the future if and when they run out. There is nothing new about this concept for those who think. In an agricultural society there was never any need for things to run out provided there was proper management. These few verses remind us that resources are limited, even when we think there is an abundance. Wealth is not a reason for taking things easy or neglecting what needs attention.

Perseverance. The diligence enjoined here is depicted as an ongoing, day to day thing. We see here both routine and reward: routine in daily care and attention; reward in fruitfulness and provision. The latter is absolutely dependent upon the former.

Protection. A farmer cannot risk carelessness or complacency. It is important to know the condition of the flocks because they are vulnerable and at risk from predators, hazards and diseases. Regular attention is needed to ensure they are safe and in good condition. The land itself needs care and attention at regular intervals.

Productivity. Also, there is a caution against a self-centred attitude, because this passage speaks not only of satisfying one's own needs (vv. 26-27a) but the needs of those for whom we have responsibility (v. 27b). Because many of the members of the household would have been servants, meeting their needs would be of all-round benefit. Our diligence serves others, and also serves us through our serving them.

Pastoral care. The pastoral situation described here has also rightly been applied to the responsibilities of church leadership, and nowhere is this more poignantly stated than when Paul was taking his leave of the Ephesian elders and in the example he had set them (Acts 20:17-35). See also 1 Peter 5:2-4.

Go through this passage again, clause by clause, considering how the picture applies to the life of the church and, in particular, to your position in it.

28:1. Holy boldness.

Fearful flight. Perhaps there is none so wicked as one who has known the way of obedience and turned from it. Fleeing when no one pursues is a judgement of God against those who despise and disobey him (Leviticus 26:17). That very word which they despise shall be fulfilled against them, and the very things they fear and seek to escape shall overtake them (Deuteronomy 28:22,45; Proverbs 13:21). They live a life looking over their shoulder for fear, and even if no one is there, yet their conscience pursues them relentlessly. Not only shall they flee, they shall also fall (Leviticus 26:36-37).

How sharply this contrasts with Leviticus 26:7-8 and Deuteronomy 28:7.

At the heart of flight is fear, but it is not the fear of God, or, if it is, it is the wrong kind of fear. John says that fear involves torment (1 John 4:18) and that there is no fear in love. John has just spoken there of boldness in the day of judgement (v. 17). It is in that day that some will even call upon the rocks to cover them (Revelation 6:16). They will be that desperate to hide from the wrath of the Lamb, though to no avail.

Fearless footing. Whoever heard of a lion cowering in its lair? The lion stands in its pride, exuding the confidence of its status as the king of beasts; it has no use for fear. Neither do those who know and understand that the Lord has accounted them righteous. If God's people have boldness to enter the Holiest by the blood of Jesus (Hebrews 10:19), if they have confident and free recourse to the throne of grace for their every need (Hebrews 4:16), if they may approach the Father by the Spirit who has been given them (Ephesians 2:18), if in Christ they have boldness and access with confidence through faith in him (Ephesians 3:12), then they have every justifiable reason to be bold as a lion. In themselves they may be weak and despised, but that is of little consequence, for God is for them (Psalms 3:6; 27:1; 112:7-8; Romans 8:31). Biblical history, and the history of the church, more than amply demonstrates the courage and boldness of God's people in standing for their God and Lord, upholding the truth in the face of all kinds of opposition; and whether in this life they have triumphed or suffered, yet they have been gloriously victorious through him who loved them (Romans 8:37).

> *Fear him, you saints, and you will then*
> *Have nothing else to fear;*
> *Make you his service your delight,*
> *Your wants shall be His care.*

Even in the darkest times, 'the people who know their God shall stand firm and take action' (Daniel 11:32, ESV). They will be assured of help and protection from their covenant-keeping God who made and governs all things (Psalm 121).

'God has not given us a spirit of fear, but of power and of love and of a sound mind' (2 Timothy 1:7). How is this statement finding its outworking in your own life?

28:2. Power hungry. Many advisors, or counsellors, can prove to be a blessing and safeguard stability in society (11:14; 15:22), whereas many 'princes' (rulers) are a curse and undermine security.

Setting aside the rule of God. This proverb touches on how these things come about. It is because of 'transgression', which in this case means open departure from the way of the Lord, where his law is cast aside. This was exemplified in the northern kingdom of Israel after the nation was divided. Jeroboam had deliberately led the people into an 'alternative religion', and the subsequent history catalogues power struggles, assassinations and disasters of various kinds as each new ruler attempted to stamp his own style of leadership on the nation. The effect of this was terrible, and the narrative makes clear that it was only through the sheer mercy of God that things were not worse.

When the rule of God is sidelined, the rule of man takes its place, with many clamouring for top positions, because basic human nature is ego-centred. This breeds jealousy, resentment, subversion and related evils as individuals contend for mastery over each other.

Setting up the rule of self. To a lesser extent this problem was seen in the church in Corinth with factions in the church gathering under different names and contending with one another (1 Corinthians 1:11-12). Paul described them as 'carnal' (3:4). There, of course, the problem was not with the leaders concerned, but with the Corinthians' perception of them. They had created many 'princes', and look at the result!

Sometimes, sadly, there can be church leaders who are more interested in personal power than humble service, like Diotrephes in 3 John 9, and when this happens heartache and division follow in the wake. When a church grows tired of sound doctrine, they heap up for themselves teachers ('many princes'), and the consequence is always trouble (2 Timothy 4:3-4).

Submitting to rightful rule. The contrast with 'many princes' is 'a man'– a man of understanding and knowledge. Judah was privileged to have many godly kings in its history, with able men loyal to the leadership providing support rather than contending for power. This was certainly true of David, as can be seen in the catalogue of his 'mighty men' (2 Samuel 23), all of whom were unswervingly loyal to him. Solomon himself (at least in his younger days) exercised such godly and wise leadership that his 'men' and his servants were accounted happy (1 Kings 10:8). There was no question of any wanting to usurp his leadership.

Submitting to Christ's rule. We have the ultimate man of understanding and knowledge in our Lord Jesus Christ. His kingdom and his right in his church will be prolonged into all eternity. Every local expression of this, every local church, will have its life and influence prolonged as long as they serve in willing submission to his rightful and unimpeachable authority. Christ is the head, the 'prince' over his kingdom. He is our Prince of peace (Isaiah 9:6), he is our wisdom (1 Corinthians 1:30). There will never be power struggles in the church while he is accorded his rightful place.

28:3. A poor state of affairs. Human sinfulness is seen at every level of society. There are references to the rich oppressing the poor (for example Exodus 3:7; Ezekiel 45:8; Amos 4:1; Micah 2:2; James 2:6; 5:1-6), exploiting them, taking unfair advantage of their weak and vulnerable position, but at least something comes out of it in terms of productivity, and at least there are meagre returns. Even in Egypt the Israelites had food enough to eat (Numbers 11:5). But here is oppression out of which no good comes, only unmitigated misery.

Receiving forgiveness. An incidental example of this proverb is given in Jesus' parable of the unforgiving servant (Matthew 18:21-35), providing us with an application that we might otherwise not have considered. The servant who was forgiven was undoubtedly poor – immeasurably poorer even than his fellow servants until he was forgiven. Yet he callously abused his master's goodness to him by grabbing a fellow servant by the throat and oppressing him on account of a debt which was paltry in comparison with what had so graciously been cancelled for him.

Recognising forgiveness. We were spiritually bankrupt before God. It is purely by his grace that he has freely pardoned us by his Son bearing the penalty against us (if indeed we are in Christ).

Are we then to oppress our fellows against whom we have some grievance (supposed or real)? Are we, who are the recipients of amazing, undeserved mercy, to be hard-hearted towards others, oppressing them with hatred or unreasonable demands which they cannot meet? What does this achieve except to quench fruitfulness?

Refusing forgiveness. Even among equals there will be those who want to elevate themselves by trampling on others. For some, they will want to maintain a distinction by not allowing old scores to be settled. By refusing to forgive, and even justifying their refusal, they suppose themselves to hold the higher ground, whereas the truth is that they are condemning those better than themselves, causing nothing but pain and hardship, and they are a great hindrance to any kind of productivity.

This proverb addresses the church, as does Jesus' parable, for it is in the church that the wonder of forgiveness is experienced and, sadly, also where the wonder of forgiveness is sometimes so dramatically abused, where believer oppresses believer, leading to want and spiritual famine.

For blessing and fruitfulness, always keep in view what you know you have received rather than what you imagine you are owed.

28:4. Setting a public example – popular and unpopular.

Casting off the law. 'The law' in this proverb is God's law. While to forsake the law is to *be* wicked, the idea before us is more one of a public lead. So, for example, a public figure is praised for his or her boldness in setting a lead in speaking openly in support of some hitherto taboo conduct, thereby making it easier for others to follow. Before, practitioners were afraid to be known as such, but now the shame has been removed by the 'honesty' of some influential person being prepared to come out into the open about it. The removal of the stigma is spoken of as 'a good thing'.

Thus the wicked are praised because of the way their behaviour encourages others of like mind who might otherwise be more cautious. Without law, 'anything goes', and without God's law that 'anything' is wickedness.

Keeping the law. In the second clause 'keeping' the law does not mean mere observance. The distinction may be made with reference to the person who keeps to the speed limit only in the vicinity of a speed camera. That is not keeping the law. That is wanting to get away from it. The word 'keep' means having a proper respect for it with an understanding desire for its maintenance.

The law-keeper, thus understood, is diametrically opposed to the wicked. How does such a one's attitude toward the law affect his or her attitude toward the law-breaker? If you are a Christian then presumably you are a law-keeper, not in the legalistic sense of mere outward observance but in the real sense of valuing and guarding what is precious. So what is your attitude toward the wicked? Do you say, that is their business and is no concern of yours? Do you keep quiet and do and say nothing? If that is the case, you can hardly be said to be a law keeper. The writer of Psalm 119 was indignant (Psalm 119:53), and indignation leads to action. There is plenty of evidence in that psalm that it was because he kept the law that he attracted hostility. In other words, simply by his consistent living he was contending with the wicked. It is impossible in an ungodly society to keep the law without finding oneself in contention with those who disregard it.

Contending for the law. More than that, though, those who keep the law will be active in contending with those who break it. Those who believe passionately in a cause do their utmost to promote it, and certainly do what they can against those who seek to undermine it. Wildlife enthusiasts, for example, will be very active in seeking to safeguard an important habitat against those who want to develop the site for building.

If they will do that, how much more should believers seek to contend with the wicked by doing all they can to uphold the laws God has given. This contention should not take the form of reviling accusation, of course (Jude 9), but persistent and reasoned maintenance of truth against error, and of supporting organisations with influence in particular areas.

Believers should be taking up their position under the banner of God's truth (Psalm 60:4).

28:5. 'The eyes of your understanding being enlightened' (Ephesians 1:18).

Observe the points of comparison in this proverb. In the first place, evil men are contrasted not with righteous men (though they might be), but with those who seek the Lord. Thus one of the principal marks of an evil person is that he or she does not seek the Lord.

The other comparison concerns the level of understanding. The first part mentions justice, and that evil men do not understand it. The second part says that those who seek the Lord do understand. It does not say they understand *it*, or justice, simply that they understand. So although it may be justice which is under consideration, what is being highlighted here is the utter contrast between the two groups. The one is totally in the dark concerning justice; to the other this matter and everything related to it is as clear as daylight.

Romans 3:11 quotes and answers Psalm 14:2-3 and gives the same link between seeking God and understanding. Ephesians 1:18 refers to the eyes of believers' understanding being enlightened, believers who had so been *in* darkness that they are described as having themselves *been* darkness (Ephesians 5:8). In 1 Corinthians 2:14 the apostle talks about the plight of the unbeliever as being completely unable to understand spiritual matters (and the justice of God is a spiritual matter).

The statement of this proverb may seem a bit stark and unrealistic in its contrast. Surely evil men may understand justice insofar as being on the wrong side they may find it catches up with them? They may understand it insofar as they are acquainted with its terms and conditions. They may understand some of its particulars. But does that mean they understand what it is all about, what it really means? Certainly not, or they would immediately forsake their evil ways and seek the Lord. Their view of justice is that it is hard and restrictive, that it imposes penalties, that it is something to be feared. Does that not prove they do not understand it?

To those who seek the Lord, the whole of God's administration becomes clear and meaningful. In particular, his justice is a comfort and delight, liberating and reassuring, for he is just and the justifier of the one who has faith in Jesus (Romans 3:26). This does not mean that we understand it fully in all its particulars or the details of its outworking, but it does mean we understand what it is all about and that it is an expression of the perfection of the character of the God of love. Faith takes the promise of John 3:16 and sees it validated at the cross of Calvary where the justice required by sin was served by Jesus bearing it in the sinner's stead. It sees that the God of justice will not demand what has already been fully satisfied. It sees that his justice has determined and declared eternal life to be the possession of all who have sought him through his Son.

No evil person has even begun to understand that, have they? People often misquote 1 Corinthians 2:9 – 'Eye has not seen...'. The point the apostle is making is that concerning eternal realities and the justice which lies at the heart of them, unbelievers remain totally and completely in the dark. 'But God has revealed them to us,' he says.

What a wonder is this truth!

28:6. Integrity.

The third ingredient. This is another 'Better ... than' proverb similar in style to 15:16,17; 16:8,19; 17:1; 21:9. In each case we would without hesitation say which is the better of the two things being compared, but throw a third into the mix and the flavour is dramatically altered. So here, the preference for riches over poverty is completely overshadowed when integrity and crookedness are introduced into the picture. We are being shown not only how integrity is far more important than wealth, but that it is to be sought and prized as a matter of priority. There is also more than a hint that wealth is no compensation for integrity.

This proverb ought to be stating the obvious. The fact that it needs to be said at all is a sad reflection on human nature.

What do you have? People are often assessed on what they *have* rather than what they *are*. Where are they on the social scale? What kind of house do they live in? Are they making a success of their lives? – a question which is answered in terms of financial prosperity and security and their performance in various areas of life.

To so many people, 'better' means 'better off', so that if they are worse off they feel inferior. There is a vast difference between having this world's riches and being truly rich. Jesus spoke of seeking true riches (Matthew 6:20 – and compare Matthew 19:21), and Peter of the riches of a godly character (1 Peter 3:4-5) and of faith being more precious than gold (1 Peter 1:7).

Whose is it? One principal example of crookedness with riches appears when we consider that all that we are and have has been given by God to be used for his honour and for the benefit of others. It is a mark of perversion (crookedness) to indulge the selfish notion that what I possess is exclusively mine. That is the position of people who say, 'My life is mine to live as I please, and if I want to do this no one has any right to say otherwise.'

How is it being used? This proverb hints at a danger of riches. Wealth often gives the opportunity for independence. It opens the door to do things which are inaccessible to the poor. Unless guided by good principles the temptation to use it in a wrong way is overwhelming. Self-indulgence dominates to the detriment of doing good, and this leads to harmful excesses as the ever-elusive promised satisfaction fails to deliver. That is one of the reasons (to take but one example) why partying and drugs ruin so many lives.

Which route to take? Choices in life are not always as obvious as they seem, and the less discerning can become entangled in the 'strings attached' which they fail to see. Others have compromised on integrity in order to 'get on in life', playing their game by the rules of the world rather than those of the book, advancing themselves at the expense of others, engaging in dubious business deals, giving short measure on quality, keeping in with people of influence by falling in with their lifestyle and attitudes when conscience would dictate otherwise. Riches cannot compensate for lack of integrity.

Keeping it together. 'Integrity' is a good translation here. A person of integrity 'has it all together'. He is not full of inconsistencies and deficiencies. He may be examined without fear of guilt being exposed. He says what he means and means what he says. He has no hidden agenda. Unlike the crooked person, he is not going to fall apart ('dis-*integrate*') when he is probed and tested.

Integrity is a precious possession. It leaves no loose ends and conceals no regrets. It is a basis for forming and maintaining the kind of relationships which crookedness destroys.

A perverse, or crooked person has no settled principles, and therefore has no problem with changing his tune, altering his course, or reneging on his promises. Perhaps even the use of the word 'ways' in the plural emphasises this: when it comes to advancing his own interests, he has 'ways and means'. Crooked ways are the outworking of a crooked heart, and a crooked heart is essentially one which either disregards God and his commands or does no more than render him lip service.

Now, why is it better to have integrity, even if it means being poor, than 'going for it' and compromising on principles? In the light of eternity it is certainly better, for we must all appear before the judgement seat of Christ (2 Corinthians 5:10). However, there is no dichotomy between what is better now and what is better then. Integrity may be better at the judgement, but it is also better now in every way. Those who lack it gain no real satisfaction from their wealth, but only trouble. They have no real peace, for fear lurks in the corners of their lives. Their own deviousness breeds suspicion of others and produces personal insecurity.

Give thought to Acts 24:16; 2 Corinthians 1:12; 4:2; 1 Timothy 3:9; Hebrews 10:22; and the benefits of a clear conscience in each case.

[Related proverbs: 19:1; 28:18.]

28:7. Intelligent law keeping.

Instruction in the law. This is one of a number of proverbs concerned with the father/son relationship (see 10:1; 15:20; 17:21,25; 29:3,15) showing how the conduct of the son reflects upon the father. The saying, 'Like father like son', though not universally true, nevertheless does reflect the fact that many characteristics are not only inherited by children, but are also acquired by them through parental influence. A son who is wayward may be so through no fault of his father, but even so shame (and perhaps blame) will be attached by others to the father. Nevertheless, when a son does 'go off the rails' reasons can often be found for it in a deficiency in parental influence, whether it be over-harsh discipline on the one hand, or neglect of discipline on the other, or failure to instruct, or setting a bad example, or deprivation of love and affection, or maintaining unreasonable expectations, and the like. All these things and others rub off on children in their formative years and play their part in moulding them into the kind of adults they will become. Hence the very great need that the Lord and his Word should be central in the family (which is the father's responsibility) in order to provide the supreme example and pattern which is bound in various respects to be absent from even the best of fathers.

Prohibitions of the law. The law imposes restrictions upon individual freedom. It gets in the way by prohibiting what the individual so often wants to do. We see all around us every day examples of people disregarding laws of the land devised for the common good, often acting as if above the law or as if they knew better. How much more so where the law of God is concerned!

Furthermore, young people often scorn the attitudes and standards of the older generation who are regarded as being out of touch with the times and outmoded in their views. They often regard parents as being out to prevent them from doing the things they enjoy (or think they would enjoy given the opportunity), perhaps charging them with fear or saying it was merely because they could not do those things when they were their age.

Observance of the law. Some people hold dual standards, expecting others to keep the law and criticising them when they don't, yet themselves maintaining only a grudging observance. Here is a son who does not just conform outwardly to the law under parental influence, but who 'keeps' it (see on v. 4). He therefore does not view it in the popular light as a hindrance to enjoyment and satisfaction but desires to uphold it. He is said to be 'discerning'. This means he has thought about it, understood it, seen it for what it is worth, and values it.

Implications in the law. For the Israelite, the law was the law of God in its entirety, headed up in the first of the Ten Commandments as having no god apart from the Lord himself. To keep the law was therefore inseparable from according to the Lord the foremost, supreme place, in life. The law itself, with its provision of sacrifice for sin, showed a person his need of God's grace and pardon, that grace which has now been fully revealed in the cross of Christ.

Obedience to the law. There is much confusion about the place of law for the Christian. However, whoever values it, keeps it and therefore gladly upholds it, is a discerning son of a heavenly Father, understanding what it means, why and for whom it was given, how it applies and what its benefits are. God wants his children to keep his law not only because he says so but also because they themselves want to and that it is given for their good. There should be a conformity of our will to God's will.

Disregard of the law. The contrast is expressed in one of its more glaring forms. Gluttony is a selfish thing, an attempt to derive pleasure through excess of what is proper. It also involves squandering precious resources, taking what is not needed when it might benefit those who do need it. Gluttony extends beyond food and drink into other areas of life. Notice, though, that our attitude to God's Word affects the company we keep. Consider: 'Do not be deceived – evil company corrupts good habits' (1 Corinthians 15:33).

There is a difference between being a *companion* of gluttons and a *friend* to such. The accusation of Matthew 11:19 which Jesus himself testified that others were saying of him failed to make the distinction. They falsely accused him of being a glutton and a drunkard, jumping to completely wrong conclusions because he gave his time to people like that. He gave them his time but he was not one with them. He honoured his Father.

[Related proverbs: 23:19-25.]

28:8. Poor returns? Although it does not specifically say so, this proverb probably has the poor particularly in mind in the first clause. In any case, one who conducts himself along these lines is guilty of a callous hardheartedness which excludes any sensitivity toward his 'victims'.

How it should be. The law specifically forbade those lending to the poor from charging interest (Exodus 22:25; Leviticus 25:35-37). Not only so, it commanded a spirit of generosity to those in need even though there was 'nothing in it' for the lender (Deuteronomy 15:7-11). Furthermore, it made a distinction between who might and might not be charged interest on a loan (Deuteronomy 23:19-20), making clear that within God's family the motive of personal gain was not to be countenanced.

How it often is. The proverb refers not only to charging interest but also to 'extortion' (NKJV). The word used seems to mean going beyond the mere charging of interest to profiteering, which involves taking unfair advantage of debtors. Those in real need may find their grindingly hard existence exacerbated by people who are 'on the make', who use every opportunity to take from them the little they may gain. Sometimes the poor seem to have no choice but to give in to the demands of the grasping lender.

This proverb also covers the case of exploitation of the poor through paying them less for their labour than would be acceptable in other circumstances simply because they have no negotiating power.

Sometimes it seems the ruthless rich have it all their own way and that those they take advantage of have nowhere to turn for help. Yet the law refers to the poor crying out to the Lord, the implication being that the Lord will hear and act (Deuteronomy 15:9). Those who cry out to the Lord have in him a mighty redeemer (23:11). This he demonstrated when he loosed his people from the avaricious grip of Egypt, and although that might seem a very long time ago we have to remember that the Lord does not change.

How it will be. Whereas the extortioner is heaping up wealth for himself, this proverb is suggesting that he will not be allowed to enjoy it because it will be taken from him by someone who has at heart the benefit of those most in need, perhaps even those from whom he has taken without mercy, in which case we have a picture here of the poor being stripped in sorrow and then being supplied in joy.

How does this come about? It comes about because God is at work. He sees all, and he has declared himself to be the one who cares for the poor, the weak, the defenceless, the orphan and the widow. Those in need may cry to him, because of who he is. Things are just the same today as they have always been in this respect. The Lord has not changed.

Just because the Lord is not mentioned in this proverb, it does not mean he is not present. He is very much involved for, as 14:31 indicates, he is reproached by extortioners, and therefore he will act.

We may find this difficult to square against what we see going on in our world. This proverb acknowledges the existence of exploitation and extortion. While this is so often front stage and in our face we have to investigate carefully before we discover what is going on behind the scenes.

[Related proverbs: 14:31; 17:5; 19:17; 22:16.]

28:9. Turning a deaf ear. Suppose you are out coastal walking and you encounter some people following a particular route which you know to be dangerous. You warn them not to go that way. When they seem to treat it lightly you strengthen your warning, only to receive the reply from one of them, 'OK, we heard what you said.' As you watch them carrying on regardless, it is clear they have turned away their ear from your warning. In their ignorance they know better.

Or suppose someone receives a letter in the post informing them that a response is required by law. If they bin it or fail to reply in a timely fashion they may expect a lot of trouble and a penalty. The law will not go away just because they have disregarded it. However much they may wish otherwise, they must know it will catch up with them.

Will we hear God? If it is like this with the laws of men, how much more so is it with the law of God. This proverb talks about hearing the law. When God's Word addresses us we are required to give it our undivided attention as a matter of priority and to respond accordingly.

Contrasting examples. King Jehioakim (Jeremiah 36:20-26), hearing read from the scroll words given by God to Jeremiah, showed his contempt by burning the scroll section by section. He heard the words, but he showed that he had already turned his ear away from hearing what God was saying to him. Though he thought nothing would happen, that did not negate the consequences for his life, as the subsequent history makes clear. How unlike his father Josiah who, when he heard read the rediscovered book of the Law of the Lord, responded immediately in repentance and faith and gave himself wholeheartedly to full obedience (2 Chronicles 34:14–35:19). He received the assurance that the Lord heard him (2 Chronicles 34:27).

Will God hear us? The proverb says of the negligent, '*even* his prayer is an abomination'. True prayer is a response to God speaking to us. It acknowledges God for who he is and expresses dependence upon him. The kind of prayer which is an abomination to God is one which is purely self-centred, wanting something from God while not wanting him. If we turn away from hearing his law, which is equivalent to turning away from him, what right have we to expect that he will respond favourably when we call upon him? It is pure selfishness. We will understand this if we have false friends whose only interest in us is what they can get out of us. They do not really like us, and they would prefer to have nothing to do with us, but unfortunately for them we have things they need or want. Many people treat

God that way. They are not interested in who he is or what he has to say, only in what they think they can get out of him. Read what God says of them in 1:20-33.

But this proverb could also refer to the person who once gave heed to God's Word but no longer does so, to one who once entrusted himself or herself to the lordship of Christ but has subsequently sought to snatch back ownership and control, to one to whom competition from the world's allurements or some other deception has made hearing the law too uncomfortable. Yet there is a way back, through repentance and returning (Isaiah 55:7), to the ear and heart of God, and to blessing where there was barrenness.

So ... are you hearing God's law ... and are you praying?

[Related proverbs: 15:8,9.]

28:10. Examples not to be followed. Jeremiah 50:6 refers to the heart-rending plight of a people who had been led astray by those who should have given them direction in the ways of the Lord.

Dangerous people. Jesus spoke of temptations coming but of the disastrous consequences for those responsible for causing believers to sin (Mark 9:42). In addressing the churches at Pergamos and Thyatira he warned of influential people seducing believers into sexual immorality (surely relevant in our day?) (Revelation 2:14,20). The apostle Paul had strong words for those seeking to draw believers back into legalism, causing them to stray from Christ (Galatians 5:12). On giving his final exhortation to the elders of the church at Ephesus he warned that even from among them would arise those speaking perverse things, drawing disciples after themselves (Acts 20:30). His letters to Timothy and Titus emphasise purity of life and teaching in a world where there is every encouragement to depart from both. He says to Timothy, 'Take heed to yourself and to the doctrine' (1 Timothy 4:16).

Dangerous appeal. This proverb particularly addresses those who have influence over others and applies especially to church leaders. Leaders need to be vigilant lest they be tempted to use their authority for their own advantage rather than solely for the glory of the Lord who has called them. Power can go to the head. Power can be abused. Sinful human nature has unholy biases. Godly leadership must be in accordance with the clear teaching of Scripture and must be completely dependent upon the Holy Spirit for enlightenment. Many sects, as well as churches which have defected from the faith, have gone that way under the leadership of men (and women) who have gone off at a tangent and taken others with them. Like Diotrephes (3 John 9), they have loved pre-eminence instead of according it to Jesus Christ. They have engineered things their way instead of God's way. They have pursued and emphasised their own pet ideas instead of maintaining the clear balance of Scripture, and through their persuasive teaching have drawn others after them.

Then again, this proverb addresses mature believers who are looked up to by others. It is easy for the untaught to reason, 'If it is all right for them to do that, it must be all right.' Therefore a Christian of long standing who has become complacent and allowed sin into his or her life is sending the wrong message to others and may by default be leading others astray.

Diligent application. The 'evil' way spoken of is very broad in its scope, encompassing the small as well as the gross. Like Timothy, we need to take heed to ourselves and our doctrine. Devious teaching or a devious lifestyle (however small the deviation) may have its appeal for our well-being, but no good will come of it. How easy it is to dismiss the 'small' deviation as of no consequence and excuse it! That is a big deception. It requires but a small step in the wrong direction to fall into a pit. History is littered with the corpses of those who have fallen into their own pit. We dare not harbour notions contrary to the Word of God. We must store it up in our hearts and let it mould our lives.

In the light of these observations we might ask: who is blameless, seeing that it is the blameless who will inherit good? Only of God's elect people in Christ can it be said that they are blameless (Romans 8:33). Nevertheless, this side of glory he would have us strive to *be* what we *are* (Romans 6:12-14). Only good awaits those who are in Christ, and what an inheritance it is!

28:11. Discerning scrutiny.

What are you hearing? It is said that money talks, but its speech is often uncouth. The rich have a measure of earthly security, from which vantage point and with an imagined sense of superiority some look down on others. They may be better *off* than others, but that does not mean they are *better* than others. They may have advantages, but that does not mean they are any more able than others. They may have a certain refinement and be more worldly wise than others, but that does not elevate them except perhaps in their own esteem. Historically, the rich have had the upper hand in society, they have called the shots, they have had the influence and the power; but that does not make their position unassailable. The rich are often buffered against scrutiny. Wealth actually confers no right to elitism, though there are many who assume it.

How are you assessing? True wisdom and understanding are not linked to this world's goods. A rich man may have understanding, but so also may a poor man. This proverb points to the fact that a rich person may permit himself to make false assumptions or to entertain false ideas about himself. A poor person does not have that handicap, and if he has intelligence and understanding he can penetrate the armour with which the rich protects himself.

Objective thinking. Just because I have a better camera than you does not make me a better photographer. Just because you have had a better education than I does not make you a more intelligent person. Examples like this demonstrate how false associations can so easily be made. 'Understanding', or 'discernment' here means having the ability to distinguish things which differ, to see the different elements in a situation and to see how they relate to one another.

Enlightened thinking. One of the blessings bestowed upon Christians is that they have been made new (2 Corinthians 5:17). One aspect of this is that they have renewed minds (Romans 12:2). With the Holy Spirit indwelling them, they are enabled to prove, or discern what God's will is. The idea is very similar to what is presented in this proverb in the form of understanding. The eyes of our understanding have been enlightened (Ephesians 1:18), and what refers to spiritual realities also encompasses our conduct on earth. On this earth it is Christians who have real understanding, because they can relate earthly and temporal things to heavenly and eternal ones. Paul talks about God choosing the weak things of the world to put to shame the things which are mighty (1 Corinthians 1:27). It shames the wise, by which he clearly means those who are wise in their own eyes.

Christians need not be intimidated by those who suppose themselves rich, whether in money or education or knowledge or experience or in any other way as if that gives them status. Some who are wise in their own eyes use this as a put down for others. God so often demonstrates the true value of things by taking those of small esteem in the eyes of the world to confound those who think themselves something.

28:12. Psalm 47. Glory or gloom. In this and the two proverbs which follow, though the Lord is not mentioned he is clearly there in the background. He is very much involved without being obtrusive. Thus his people 'see' him and acknowledge him while at the same time the wicked in their blindness deny him.

With this proverb compare 11:10 and 29:2. In this proverb we will look at the points of comparison in the two clauses.

The first parallel. Look at the words held alongside one another in this proverb. First, the righteous and the wicked. The righteous are those who are righteous in God's estimation because by his grace they have been made righteous. They love him, they love his word, they love the truth. By implication they hate falsehood and every evil way. The wicked are those who, having no time for God, are morally corrupt according to his standards. By nature they have antipathy toward righteousness. So the righteous and the wicked are at loggerheads.

The second parallel. The next words held alongside each other are 'rejoice' and 'arise'. The first word may also be translated 'triumph'. Only one thing accounts for the elation of the righteous, and that is when they see the word and work of God prospering. The triumph is not really theirs, but God's, and yet they enter into it with vigour. The contrast is with the wicked gaining the ascendancy. This is never accompanied by joy or elation but rather the opposite, of fear, of uncertainty, and of other dark and ugly things.

The third parallel. The third words paired off are 'glory' and 'hiding'. 'Glory' here refers to something beautiful, something worth setting on display. It is great glory, and so it is surpassingly beautiful, unashamedly displayed. This 'glory' is a display of God's handiwork and of his gracious intervention in the affairs of men, and the result is a prevalence of peace, security, prosperity and of all things good. The wicked may gnash their teeth at it, but they cannot fault it! When they get their way, when they extend their influence, what happens? Men retreat into themselves, they look over their shoulders for fear of some evil pursuing and overtaking them, they shrink from what they fear may happen to them in the future. They may gain some brazen pleasures, but there is no stability, no comfort, nothing of lasting value or virtue, only perhaps a longing after what can never be.

Down to earth realities. We live in a world in which the wicked seem to be on the up and up. The result is that troubles are multiplied. In some places believers very literally go into hiding and cannot come out into the open. But it is not only they who suffer. A curb is put upon freedom, not least freedom of speech in which they are denied the right to declare the right.

Christians need to remember that the whole world lies under the devil's sway (1 John 5:19) and that they are no match for him. It is vitally important to understand the lesson from all the major victories recorded in the Old Testament, that they were gained by God for his people. The imperative for us therefore is to acknowledge him, to wait upon him in total dependence, and then to go forward in faith.

[Related proverbs: 11:10; 28:28; 29:2.]

28:13. Fig leaves.

A universal problem. One of the inescapable features of the human race is that each and every member is a sinner. We all know it, even if we do not all admit it. Whatever our standards, whether high or low, and whatever our criteria for determining it, we are all conscious of wrongdoing. Where we differ is in how we handle this universal problem.

A big cover-up. Sometimes sin is so public that it cannot be hidden. Often, though, it has a clandestine aspect. We do wrong, but we do not want to be found out. The hit-and-run driver finds tell-tale marks on the car on arriving home and goes to great pains to remove them and hopes there were no witnesses to the incident. However, as the weeks pass without further developments, the offender is robbed of any relief because the tell-tale marks on his memory cannot be erased. Many have confessed to crimes long after the event because they could no longer endure the burden of guilt. For others their guilt has ruined their personal lives as they have kept their sins under wraps. Covering sins does not make them go away.

Sins include less dramatic things like lying and pilfering, like backbiting and slander. People try to cover up their sins by all sorts of means, and covering them would include seeking to justify them, or to belittle them. In fact, the one thing the natural man will *not* do is willingly to confess and forsake sin. Man loves sin too much to let it go, and where he is troubled by his sinful actions he does his best to put the lid on them. 'The fewer people know about this the better.'

Humiliating exposure. The problem about sin and guilt is the fear of punishment. We may be amused at the transparency of the child who says, 'It wasn't me', when to adult eyes it clearly was. But are not adults children in the eyes of the all-seeing and all-knowing God? As if anything could be hidden from him! When he called to Adam, 'Where are you?' (Genesis 3:9) it was not because he did not know but that he wanted a confession from the man and his wife. Yet all they did was to pass the buck.

Only one full and effective remedy. Punishment is clearly appropriate for those guilty of sin. A strong sense of humiliation can accompany confession of sin. With God, though, there is a wonderful promise of mercy – on two conditions. The first is *confession of sin* – full and frank confession with no ifs and buts. The second is the *forsaking of sins*. Both are desperately difficult to do. Indeed, they are impossible to do. Yet if God requires it there must be a way. And so there is, because he is the one who gives the ability and provides the motivation.

God's promise of mercy. The trouble is, most people regard God as the enemy. The prophet Jeremiah exhorted king Zedekiah to surrender to Nebuchadnezzar with the promise that if he did so he would live and the city would be spared (Jeremiah 38:17). Notwithstanding the prophet's assurances, the king was so afraid of the consequences of doing so that he forfeited the mercy held out to him. So it is so often with the sinner and God. God promises mercy to the sinner who surrenders all to him. The sinner is so afraid of his loss in so doing that he finds it impossible to take God at his word.

28:14. Happy or fearful? There are two words which are commonly used for fear, and the one most often used for the fear of the Lord denotes the utmost reverence and awe for his majesty and power and consequent submission to him, whereas the one used here means to be afraid in the more conventional sense, as when some frightening circumstances makes one weak at the knees and tremble. It is therefore somewhat unexpected that such a person should be described as *happy*, because we do not usually put happiness and fear together! This word is the one used by the Queen of Sheba when she exclaimed to Solomon, '*Happy* are your men!' (1 Kings 10:8), and the word David uses when he says, '*Blessed* is he whose transgression is forgiven (Psalm 32:1), to describe something incomparably delightful. See also Psalm 2:11-12.

The apostle Paul is just as dramatic when he exhorts servants to obey their masters with 'fear and trembling' (Ephesians 6:5). How much more should such an attitude characterise our conduct before God! However, we should observe that though the name of the Lord is provided in the NIV and ESV translations, this proverb does not actually mention him and, following the apostle's example, we should not limit its scope.

What cause have we for fear and trembling? If we think about our cause before God it should help us think about it in the wider context of our relationship with others. We are to work out our salvation with 'fear and trembling' (Philippians 2:12).

Fear of God. We should tremble before God because of his holiness. Consider Moses (Hebrews 12:21), or Isaiah (Isaiah 6:1-5), or Ezekiel (Ezekiel 1:28; 2:1), or Daniel (Daniel 10:7-11), or the apostle John (Revelation 1:17). Because we are sinners with sinful natures, we should in a healthy sense be afraid of doing wrong in his sight. Our service for God should be characterised by a consciousness of our own inadequacy and our need to depend upon him.

When it comes to our service for others, we should still recognise it is the Lord Christ we are serving (Colossians 3:22-24), and so it should still be done with confidence in him rather than in ourselves.

Fear of self. Have you ever had the experience of being asked to do something daunting, of which you have had no experience, and you have gone into it with a very real fear lest you make a mess of it? Or perhaps it has been an exam, and you don't know what questions you are going to be asked and whether you will be up to answering them. This kind of fear speaks of a lack of self confidence in which you recognise you have limitations, and yet you go on in the hope that you will not disappoint either yourself or others.

Such fear is consistent with true humility. It is the 'lowliness of mind' of Philippians 2:3 which was seen in its perfection in the Lord Jesus in his humanity, who in all things did the will of his Father (John 4:34; 5:30; 6:38) and therefore lived in complete dependence upon him.

By contrast, hardening the heart speaks of a loss of sensitivity either toward God or toward one's fellows. That is what pride does: it starves or strangles proper emotions. But it cannot shut out fear, and what the hard-hearted fear will overtake them: calamity. They have no joy, no real happiness.

This is the time to do a spot check you your own life. Are you happy? Are you tender-hearted? Are you sensitive toward God and then sensitive toward others? Are there any respects in which you are in danger of hardening your heart? What are you going to do about it?

28:15-16. Fearsome predators. Of all the wild animals none were so formidable as the lion or the bear looking for a meal. Here we see them with their victims transfixed and ready to be torn apart for their own satisfaction. Predators will usually target the weak or the defenceless among their prey rather than those able to offer some resistance or be likely to escape. They are after easy pickings.

Power hungry. All this very aptly describes the situation of an oppressive ruler over a poor people. He is not interested in the people other than as a means to satisfy his own cravings and to enhance his own power and prestige. The people live in fear fuelled by a sense of helplessness, unable to break out of their impoverished condition. Throughout history, and certainly today in certain parts of the world, this unhappy state of affairs persists.

Ecclesiastes 10:16-17 refers to the blight of immaturity and covetousness in those who should be wise and generous, and the blessing when they are what they should be. Isaiah 3:4,12,14-15 refers to much the same thing, in this case as a judgement of God upon a sinful people.

Closer to home. While we may either lament the plight of people under such tyranny or be outraged with the injustice of it all, and while we may rightly be concerned about what might and can be done about it, we also ought to recognise that the cause of this kind of thing is not so very far from us. It happens because of the hardness of the human heart and because of its enmity toward God. Verse 16b hits the nail on the head. Covetousness is its root cause, and covetousness combined with opportunity is a deadly combination, resulting in 'unjust' or 'ill-gotten' gain. We see this enacted on the international stage and recoil in horror at what is going on, and yet are in danger of failing to notice its occurrence in the workplace or even in the home. The managing director is a controlling tyrant who holds a knife to the throat of a workforce who have no recourse to alternative employment, in order that he may maintain and feed a luxurious lifestyle. A husband and father keeps his wife and children in fear, forcing them to satisfy his every whim, effectively making them slaves to enable him to indulge his greed.

In the church. Even in churches this ugly trait can manifest itself. Would it be too much to say that many in the church at Corinth were self-centred and grasping which led to ill feeling? Paul found it necessary to address their immaturity by exhorting them not to be children in their understanding (1 Corinthians 14:20). One of the essential qualifications for a church leader is that he should not be covetous (1 Timothy 3:3), for if he is it will invariably lead into his abuse of his position of authority and trust.

Of Judas Iscariot it was said that he was a thief and did not care for the poor (John 12:5-6). His was a position of trust which he abused through covetousness, made worse by his loud protestations on behalf of the poor.

Conclusion. Covetousness needs to be seen for what it is. In those who have little power it may do little damage, but in those who exercise power it can have deadly consequences. The proverb speaks of 'hating' what covetousness leads to. How easy it is to tolerate covetousness and not think it too serious. Jesus said we are to be on our guard against it (Luke 12:15), which means recognising it as an enemy and not letting it get a foothold in our lives, and Paul wrote of it as something which needs to be put to death where it is in evidence in our lives (Colossians 3:5).

Understanding in a ruler will result in care rather than oppression, in sensitivity rather than hardness of heart. The irony is that those who are self-seeking will find their lives cut short, whereas those who have the welfare of their people at heart will find their days prolonged. History has amply substantiated this statement.

28:17. Beyond recall. This proverb is not speaking actively about the violence of committing murder (AV) but about the rebound effect on the one who has committed it. That is, here is a man who, having committed murder, is suffering the torment of oppression and bitterness and burden in his own soul as a result of it. There is a finality about murder. There is no recall from it. No compensation can be offered, no restitution can be made. It is too late for that. God said simply that he would require the life of every murderer (Genesis 9:6) because it was a destruction of one made in his image. This proverb is in keeping with serving the interests of God's justice.

The power of guilt. A man burdened with the guilt of bloodshed is an unhappy man indeed. He is a fugitive without any place of safety to which to flee. He cannot escape his conscience, and he cannot escape the reality of what he has done. Guilt sticks to him like a limpet. Consider Cain's bitter lament (Genesis 4:13-15). There God made it clear that the administration of justice was in his hands, and, where he had decreed, man was not to interfere. He had given a command concerning capital offences, placing responsibility in the hands of properly qualified and authorised men (see also Numbers 35), but reserved the right in certain instances to handle the matter himself, as for example in the case of Cain, and as in the case of David (2 Samuel 12:13).

In destroying the life of another, a murderer has in effect also destroyed his own life. He has no safe haven, and he is to receive no help from others. Others are forbidden from harbouring him or providing for him or supporting him in any way.

The power of grace. Yet when we think of this, should we not also think of the amazing grace of God. Those who murdered his Son (see John 8:40,44; Acts 2:23; 3:15), worthy to suffer the eternal consequences of their wickedness, were nevertheless given opportunity and encouragement to repent and partake of the blessings that death procured.

The deed and the thought. God makes equivalent hatred and the thought of murder with the deed (1 John 3:15, and compare Matthew 5:21-22). Hatred, like murder, eats away at the soul. It gives no rest, it isolates the individual.

This therefore addresses us, even though we are not likely ever to be in the position of having dealings with the kind of murderers depicted here. For, first of all, it should remind us of the value of human life, that man is created in the image of God, for which reason life is to be respected and protected. Then it should warn us of the dire consequences of so despising the life of anyone as to wish them dead. The consequences are subjective because it lights a fire within us which damages us spiritually, emotionally and physically, and objective in that others rightly ostracise us on account of it. Notice how Jesus, in the passage just cited (Matthew 5:21-22) goes on to talk about reconciliation. If someone you know bears intransigent malice toward another, you are to offer no sympathy and give no encouragement on that score. Rather, it is your responsibility to urge that the matter be put right while there is yet time.

28:18. A safe course through life. This proverb is about the walk and the way, about the how and where we go through life.

'Keep to the footpath.' So reads the sign. How do people interpret it? Does it even need interpreting? That depends on their mind set. Some think it is there for a good reason, even though the reason may not be explicitly stated, and so they simply do what it says, maybe without even giving it a second thought or enquiring into the reason. Others may argue that the landowner who has put it there doesn't want people to have the freedom to wander off into his woods and enjoy themselves. Keeping to the marked way is dull, and the sign provides them with an open invitation to leave the path.

His rights and our responsibilities. The landowner who put up the sign was not obliged to give his reasons, or to detail the dangers associated with leaving it. So if God has commanded us to keep to his way (that is, to obey his laws), it is our responsibility to do so without question – and it is equally our responsibility to do so even *with* question! In fact God has given ample reasons for keeping to his way, but the perverse will never be satisfied no matter how many reasons are given. They will still reject his way (singular) in favour of their own ways (plural).

His provision and our protection. The proverb says that those who walk blamelessly (that is, those who respect and seek to obey what God says), will be kept safe, or be delivered. This has two aspects to it. The first is that the way he has prepared is in itself a safe way. It is a path which has been cleared of hazards, and so it is literally a safe path to walk on. The second is that it is the way in which he himself may be found, and when trouble comes from any outside source, he is there to provide deliverance. It is only when we are on the path of obedience that we can reasonably expect help to come from the Lord when we need it. So, whichever way we look at it, his way is both safe and good.

Catastrophe. For those who are perverse, who go wandering off according to their fancy, who despise God's way and look for ways of their own, we are told they will suddenly fall. It does not say they will immediately fall. We sometimes see perverse people apparently prospering. They cock a snook at God and seem to get away with it. The wood is full of dangers, not least the danger of getting hopelessly lost, and suddenly, without warning, one wandering there falls headlong over some hidden obstacle. That is how it is for those who wander through life having disdained God's clearly defined path.

Consider Psalm 37:35-38 which is a kind of testimony on this proverb, and note how it refers to the end of each.

[Related proverb: 10:9.]

28:19. The promise of plenty. Though it is not necessarily captured in the translation, this proverb presents a wry twist upon the notion of having plenty, or of being well supplied.

Two pursuits. He who follows the furrow may expect to have plenty of bread. He who follows frivolity may expect to have plenty of fun. That is what so many seem to think, judging from their pursuit of pleasure. They would not call it frivolity, of course, but that is what it is – essentially it is emptiness, vanity, devoid of substance.

Two rewards. The proverb is blunt in the extreme. Just as the farmer investing his time in productive labour will reap a reward of being well supplied with bread, so the waster investing his time in idle and empty pursuits will reap a reward of being well supplied with emptiness! That translates into poverty in abundance.

Two dimensions. Does it not invite you to consider how you are investing your time? This goes beyond the dimension of the here and now and earthly things, because it is God's Word at which we are looking and everything has an eternal dimension. Proverbs is packed with natural insight and practical advice on daily living in this world, but without the eternal dimension its message is really lost. This is God speaking, and he requires an appropriate response from us – a response which both acknowledges and honours him.

Two illustrations. It is not without significance that two illustrations of sowing and reaping in the New Testament letters are with reference to doing good and giving for the benefit of others over and above the gratification of self. See this in Galatians 6:7-10 and 2 Corinthians 9:6-15. A man reaps what he sows.

Two benefits. This proverb is not advocating all work and no play. All the empty pleasures of those who seek such things not only do not satisfy but they also have a sting in their tail. By contrast those who labour for the Lord often find unexpected pleasures along the way as they do so, as well as having their fill of relaxation and rich fun from time to time. The psalmist said, 'At your right hand are pleasures forevermore' (Psalm 16:11). The Lord's people have many a foretaste of them this side of glory!

[Related proverb: 12:11.]

28:20. True riches. Note carefully the points of comparison and contrast in this proverb. A faithful man is being contrasted with one who is in a hurry to get rich, and abundant blessings for the one are contrasted with punishment for the other.

Going for gold. There is nothing morally wrong with being rich, nor necessarily with coming by riches quickly. What is it about being in haste to make riches that it should be worthy of punishment? In 1 Timothy 6:9-10 Paul writes of those who 'desire' to be rich falling into temptation and a snare and many harmful lusts which plunge them into ruin and destruction. He is not sparing in his description! There is a reason for this. The enticement of riches makes strong appeal to covetousness in the heart of man. Coveting either what belongs to another or what does not belong to us is sinful. The coveting of riches is an expression of the desire to be self-sufficiently independent, to find personal satisfaction from what money can buy. It shifts attention away from dependence upon God, the giver of every good and perfect gift (James 1:17), to reliance on self. Hastening to be rich has its sights set on gold, not on God, and is coveting forbidden fruit. It imagines that to have possessions is to be blessed. But possessions are like dumb idols. They cannot confer blessing. True blessing is conferred by God alone and involves enjoying him and recognising his boundless love in all he bestows.

Value added? There has been no shortage of schemes advertised for making money quickly, most of which involve a minimum of labour, and most of which turn out ultimately to be at someone else's expense. He who hastens to be rich is the person who is on the lookout for himself and is careful not to ask too many questions. He may make his packet, but when the reckoning comes, can it be said that he has actually earned it? He has enriched himself, but has he enriched others? He has taken, but has he contributed in at least equal measure? There will come a time when the accounts will be scrutinised!

Wanting my fair share? In Luke 12:13-21 a demand for fairness (how often do we hear that in politics?) concealed the real issue which was for the man to get his hands on the loot, in response to which Jesus told the parable of the rich fool, culminating in his reply to the man: 'So is he who lays up treasure for himself and is not rich toward God.' He is a fool.

Stocktaking. Consider for a moment what you have. How did you come by it? Was it earned? Was it given? Was it inherited? How much did it cost you? Was it worth it? How you answer these last two questions will depend on your point of view. You could say, 'This item cost £x and it is worth every penny I spent on it.' On the other hand, you might say, 'This item cost me a prolonged strain in my family relationships which I deeply regret.' Or something else you have – perhaps your latest home – was purchased at the sacrifice of the blessings of the Christian fellowship you once enjoyed before you moved there.

These examples illustrate that hastening to be rich has many faces to it. However, each face has its eyes on the riches rather than on God who gives us all things richly to enjoy (1 Timothy 6:17 – and look back at vv. 6-8 there).

Possessions do not equal blessing. How many people reckon wrongly at this point! Would you rather be rich or be blessed? This proverb speaks of those toward whom blessings abound. 'Blessings abound where'er he reigns' wrote Watts in his hymn based on Psalm 72. If Jesus reigns as Lord in every area of our lives, we will abound in blessing.

Giving to receive. A faithful man is not hasty and he is not self-serving. He is one who remains true to his charge, who can be trusted not to desert his post or abandon his calling. If we would know abundant blessing it will be by remaining true to the Lord through thick and thin, unmoved by threat or reward or by any other circumstance or enticement. Faithfulness to the Lord will have its visible manifestation in this world of faithfulness to his people.

We talk about responsibilities in the church, in the family, in the place of work, and so on, and we often think of these in terms of the things we are expected to *do*, whereas it would be better to think in terms of the people to whom we are to render them, for our responsibilities are toward *people*. We ask, not are we faithful in what we do, but are we faithful *to others* in what we do? Most especially, are we faithful *to the Lord* in what we do, doing it for him? As Paul said, it is the Lord Christ we are serving (Colossians 3:24) and he will reward us.

Earthly riches are neither here nor there. They do not even enter into the equation where the Lord's blessing is involved.

28:21. What's in it for me? The transgression, or wrongdoing, in the second clause links directly with the partiality in the first. Showing partiality is, literally, 'discerning faces'. Some vagrants are very good at doing this. By studying the people they see they have a knack of knowing who will be a soft touch and from whom they are most likely to get a free hand-out.

The motive of comfort. Jesus told a parable of an unjust judge (Luke 18:1-6). We may legitimately ask in what respect he was unjust. Why could he not be bothered with this woman? The bottom line is that there was nothing in it for him. It was not worth his while. In the end when he attended to her complaint it was for no better reason than to give himself some peace and quiet.

The motive of gain. 'If I play my cards right there will be something in this for me.' The stakes may be as low as a piece of bread. Big gains, small gains – what does it matter just so long as I get something out of it? Thus in the way I exercise my responsibilities it becomes a matter of political manoeuvring rather than principled management. Partiality takes its cue from faces rather than facts. It filters out what does not suit me and takes action accordingly.

The motive of self-interest. Showing partiality, then, is a manifestation of self-interest which forms the basis of making decisions. Church leaders need to be especially vigilant against succumbing to this temptation. The apostle Paul, having written much to Timothy about how he should conduct affairs in the church, solemnly charged him to do so without prejudice and without partiality (1 Timothy 5:21). Why so, if there were no danger in this area for Timothy and others in his position? In a ministry which involves dealing with people at all levels and in all kinds of situation there is always the temptation to favour one against another for reasons which are not worthy of the name.

It is actually very difficult to be totally impartial because our sinful nature is always wanting to gratify its own desires and can be very unscrupulous in the way it does so.

If you are in a position of leadership over others and if you have decision-making responsibilities, do you gather around yourself those who will rubber-stamp what you want done? That is what Ahab did with his four hundred yes-men (1 Kings 22:6). He excluded Micaiah because he did not like what he said!

The motive of security. It sometimes happens in churches that the leaders are afraid to implement certain policies through fear of upsetting or losing those who provide significantly to the financial support of the church. They are scrutinising faces instead of following principles. It may be they are concerned more for their livelihood than for the welfare of those they are supposed to be serving. It has become a case of 'What will happen to me if…?' Even if it is, 'What will happen to the church if…?', it is still partiality.

'For a piece of bread,' says the proverb. This is not referring to someone who is at the point of starvation. Rather it is saying that something very small in the way of self-gratification can turn out to be a very powerful incentive to showing partiality, and so to transgressing.

This proverb links in with the previous one. Partiality contrasts with faithfulness.

What, then, should be our motive in life and service, and why?

28:22. The pursuit of poverty. In v. 20 the word for haste was a matter of being in a hurry. Here it indicates being agitated or anxious after riches, which implies an unhealthy, consuming preoccupation with such things. By a man with an 'evil eye' is probably intended one who is stingy or miserly, accumulating wealth with a determined but never satisfied anxiety and with the attitude that no one else has any right to benefit from it nor is going to do so.

Miserly misery. In what way shall poverty come upon him? There is a strange irony that the wealthiest of misers have lived out their time in misery and ended their days in a poverty more acute than those who are really poor, just because they were so afraid to lose any of their hoarded resources. So in a sense this person suffers a double poverty. He is so preoccupied with his riches that he does not know, or does not consider, what should be staring him in the face, that he is systematically impoverishing himself, isolating himself from others, growing increasingly suspicious of others because through his twisted sense of values he is no longer able to relate to them as he ought.

Plausible presentation. All this may sound rather extreme, and yet on reflection it is not difficult to see this kind of attitude operating at lesser levels. In materialistic western society great store is set on financial security. But it is an elusive concept. There is always some further insecurity to worry about. Those who with anxious care work hard, making sacrifices to lay up for their old age, or for their children, or against sickness or redundancy, or for some other eventuality, have gone a step beyond prudence. They must be doing their work and therefore cannot be involved in church life, not because they have especial responsibilities at work but because they imagine they need the money. They cannot contribute financially toward some urgent need in the Lord's service; they cannot spare the money because it would be depriving their own children of their support, notwithstanding that there is no imminence whatsoever in their need of support. Is this not just a miserly attitude cloaked in the garb of plausibility?

So what happens? Their own concerns about money, about wealth, about material provision, isolate them from fellowship, from ministry, from blessing among God's people. However much they may gain in a material sense, poverty comes upon them, for their preoccupation with earthly riches progressively deprives them of the true riches as they shrivel spiritually through lack of nourishment.

Without doubt great wisdom is needed in order not only to be able to handle riches well, but also to be able to handle the attitude toward riches well.

What is unique about the Christian attitude toward riches? To answer this consider carefully Matthew 6:25-33; Mark 4:19; Luke 12:15-31; 1 Timothy 6:17.

28:23. Without fear or favour. The scenario before us is that someone has done wrong and needs to be put right. Nothing is said about the nature or the seriousness of the issue. It may involve actions, or words, or attitudes, or associations. But whatever it is, small or large, it is something which needs to be addressed, either for his sake or for someone else's.

Except for the fault-finder like the person in the parable of the speck and the plank (Matthew 7:3-5), it can be hard to confront others, especially friends, when they go wrong. There are many reasons why this might be so, but this proverb speaks in terms of finding *favour*.

As with so many of the proverbs, here we are encouraged to take the long view of the situation. If rebuke is needed, even if you find yourself out of favour in the short term, in the longer term it will turn out better for you to give it than to pretend there is no problem.

Rebuke is right. None of us likes the experience of being put right. It is bad enough when our consciences accuse us of being wrong, let alone our suffering the humiliation of others showing us our faults. If our immediate reaction is to excuse ourselves, or justify ourselves, or leap to our own defence, or for our hackles to rise, we know well enough what might be in for us if we attempt to rebuke others. We suspect it will upset the relationship, and that we will be viewed in a less than favourable light for our audacity, or interference, or whatever it may be called. Be that as it may, it will still turn out better in the end than for the person at the opposite end of the spectrum who seeks to safeguard a relationship by flattery.

Flattery is false. It is a pretence, and its interest is purely selfish. Flattery encourages the person needing rebuke to think well of himself when he should be ashamed. It covers up the true state of affairs and tacitly perpetuates harm rather than promoting good. Failure to give correction when it is needed is tantamount to flattery.

Silence is sinful. Reluctance to give rebuke where it is needed is also selfish. I do not want to do it not because it will hurt the person (that is only an excuse) but because it will hurt *me*.

Rebuke needs to be properly motivated, not like that of Peter who rebuked Jesus when Jesus spoke to him about his death (Matthew 16:22), or the disciples who rebuked those who brought children to Jesus (Matthew 19:13), or those who tried to shut up the blind beggars calling out to Jesus for mercy (Matthew 20:13). In those cases it was based on misconceptions and prejudice. Rebuke is to be based not upon arbitrary considerations but upon God's Word, and while it needs to be properly motivated, whether or not to administer it may not be an option. Leviticus 19:17 is interesting, for it shows that failure to rebuke when necessary is tantamount to hatred. If you love your 'neighbour' (by which is meant any close associate) you will remonstrate with him when you see him going wrong. It is also by implication informing us that we all from time to time are in need of such correction. See Revelation 3:19. He who is not ashamed to call us 'brothers' (Hebrews 2:11) rebukes us in accordance with his law *because he loves us* and desires the very best for us, that we should know comfort and security in his love.

It is worth mentioning at this point that as well as needing to be properly motivated, rebuke also needs to be graciously administered because it should be understood as rendering the person a service.

While this proverb is probably personal rather than public, it is worth noting that one aspect of public ministry is rebuking where necessary (1 Timothy 5:20; 2 Timothy 4:2; Titus 1:13; 2:5).

There is a remarkable example of the outworking of Leviticus 19:17 and this proverb in Luke 23:40. It is astonishing that such a man as a thief worthy of crucifixion should show concern for the eternal welfare of another suffering the same fate, but so it was. He remonstrated with the other and appealed to the Lord, and was shown undeserved favour.

Although rebuke needs to be given from time to time, there are people who will not benefit from it (9:8; 13:1,8). See also 24:25.

[Related proverbs: 27:5,6.]

28:24. Daylight robbery. Paul refers to parents laying up for their children (2 Corinthians 12:14). Good parents invest so much in their offspring: their love, their care, their protection, their nurturing, as well as material provision. They are concerned for their children's welfare.

Abuse. Robbing father or mother is an abuse of privilege and trust, not to mention love. The 'prodigal son' of the parable (Luke 15:11-32) was undoubtedly robbing his father, even though he might have argued, 'It's coming to me in any case, so what difference does it make?' By his demanding, he was depriving his father of giving at the proper time, in the proper manner and for the proper purpose. What good came of it? He destroyed his livelihood, he destroyed his prospects, he destroyed the family bond and broke his father's heart.

Reproach. So it is when we misappropriate what God gives. 'Will a man rob God?' he asks, and answers in the affirmative. 'I have loved you,' he says, and then he declares, 'Yet you have robbed me!' (Malachi 1:2; 3:8). The whole of that book is a catalogue of the people's misappropriation of what God had given interspersed with petulantly reproachful questions on their part. They robbed God because they took for themselves what he had given for the advancement of his purposes (and their blessing) and therefore were destroying the soul of the nation. It was pure greed on their part.

Avarice. There are other, more sinister ways, of robbing parents. Jesus took issue with the Pharisees in such a matter, recorded in Mark 7:9-13. The Pharisees, who loved money as well as praise (Luke 16:14), profited from this practice, as did the giver of the gift who thereby extricated himself from responsibilities toward his parents. And it was all done under a cloak of legitimacy: 'It is no transgression.' But notice how Jesus prefaced his remarks: 'All too well you reject the commandment of God...'.

Neglect. The commandment in question is the fifth. Failure to honour parents is to rob them of what God says is their due. That includes meeting their needs, particularly later in life. Paul has something to say about this in 1 Timothy 5:4,8.

Excuse. This statement, 'It is no transgression,' is a defensive response to something which smells suspect. People can always find ingenious ways to justify what they want to do – or what they do not want to do. Giving to the work of the Lord and honouring one's parents were never in conflict or intended to be viewed as distinct from each other, and are only so taken by those with unworthy motives.

What God withholds from us now is not ours to take by force or to demand from him. Remember that occasion when he gave what his complaining people craved, and sent leanness into their soul (Psalm 106:15). Greed is destructive.

God is laying up for the children of his love. He asks us to honour him with what he has already given, in order that we may enjoy his love and enter into greater blessing (Malachi 3:10).

[Related proverb: 19:26.]

28:25. Do you wish to be successful? Observe the attitudes which are being compared here. The 'proud heart' (AV) is that of one who does not need to trust in the Lord (so he thinks!). But the words in the original probably denote rather a person who is greedy and grasping. So the comparison is really between one who is out for himself to get what he can lay his hands upon by whatever means is available to him, and one who trusts the Lord to provide.

By or for. The comparison is also between what the first one *does* (that is, he 'stirs up strife') and what the second one has done *for* him (that is, he 'will be prospered' – not, as in NIV, 'will prosper', which misses the point).

Do or be done. We are encouraged in our society to be 'go-getters' and not to expect that things will come to us. A strong spirit of competition exists. One climbs the ladder by displacing others. One gains promotion at the expense of others. There are winners and losers. 'Go for it: it's yours. Don't let anyone stand in your way.'

While there may be an inevitable and legitimate side to these statements, in practice one often finds strings are pulled, deals are done under the counter, half truths are told, inconvenient things are hidden from sight. All too often there is a ruthlessness in the way people advance themselves. Their greed 'must have'. The result is strife.

Force. This kind of thing can also happen within the church. Those impatient for recognition or positions of authority can use underhand methods to advance their interest. They think it is up to them. It isn't.

Faith. David probably had several opportunities to grab the throne of Israel before the death of Saul. But he did not. Why not? He trusted in the Lord. The Lord had promised, and David was prospered, because God fulfilled his promise in his way and his time.

The scornful sometimes ask Christians, 'Do you expect your God to hand this to you on a plate?' The Lord has a way of fulfilling his purposes that unbelievers completely fail to recognise. In trusting in the Lord and waiting upon him, the way ahead is opened by him without anyone having to force the door.

The Lord Jesus gave significant teaching on this very matter in Matthew 6:25-34. The Christian's attitude is to be distinctively different from that of those around.

Abraham, impatient to see God's promise of a son and heir fulfilled, took matters into his own hands and the result was strife. He hindered, rather than forwarded, God's purposes. God in his own time fulfilled what he had promised.

The Lord rarely does things according to our time-scale or in the manner we expect. Our times are in his hands (Psalm 31:15). We need to learn that his times are not in our hands! We need ongoing, implicit trust in the Lord, listening for his word, ensuring we understand it, seeking to obey it, and looking to him to lead us. There will never then be any strife caused by us, and he will prosper us in the way he would have us to go (Isaiah 30:21).

28:26. Do you wish to be safe? This is really a companion to the last proverb. If the last one was concerned with success, this one is concerned with safety. People are concerned for promotion and protection, for getting and guarding, for achieving and avoiding.

A stupid attitude. Troubles in life come in many shapes and forms. This proverb says baldly that to trust one's own heart, one's own judgement, to rely upon one's own resources, or to go by one's own feelings is just plain stupid. A person who does so is declared to be a fool. Yet many people go through life with that proud independence which denies the need of outside interference (as they call it!), least of all the involvement of God. 'I can get along quite all right without your help,' they say when offered some kindly advice. Or, 'I can run my own life well enough without the need for God or the prop of religion.'

Dependence. Trusting in one's own heart is a mark of blind pride, or sheer conceit. It fails to acknowledge two things which wisdom does acknowledge. Taking them in reverse order, the first is that no one has a monopoly on understanding. Our own knowledge and ability are very limited in every way, and we need input from others. The second is that no one has full control of circumstances, and we need the protection of someone who does, and that is God alone. Like it or not, God has made us dependent creatures. He has made us to be dependent upon one another, and he has made us to be dependent upon him.

By recognising this and acting upon it we will certainly be kept humble. Peter reminds us that we are to be clothed with humility, and that applies to our relationships with others and our relationship with God (1 Peter 5:5-6). It does not just mean that we esteem others better than ourselves or show concern for others (Philippians 2:3-4). It means we listen to others, we consider what they say, we respect them and acknowledge our need of them. Above all, we listen to God, we consider what he says, we revere him and acknowledge our overriding need of him. In everything we refer to him, and in everything we defer to him.

This proverb talks about being delivered, or being kept safe. These things are not in our hands. It is not about our steering a safe course through life. We do not have the skill, the knowledge, or the ability, to do that. Deliverance from disastrous decisions or actions or situations comes from outside. It comes from the wise counsel someone has given us. It comes from the timely intervention of a friend in whom we have confided. It comes from God who watches over his people for their good, who directs their circumstances.

Think about situations in which you have been too self-reliant. Reflect on why and how they could or should have turned out differently. Apply these principles to your current circumstances.

28:27. Enriching the poor.

Pros and cons – mainly cons. Giving to the poor is an emotive subject. Various arguments are put forward for not doing so, from the suggestion that it is degrading to them to receive free handouts, to the assertion that it merely perpetuates their poverty by discouraging them from working. Or it is argued that in real terms it is actually a waste of money and resources. Giving to the poor is sometimes perceived as someone else's responsibility. Very often, though, the reasons presented are in fact no more than a cover for a reluctance to give, and these reasons are equivalent to hiding the eyes from, or closing them to, the situation, which receives the condemnation of the second clause here.

Look at the comparison in this verse and read this carefully! It compares what one does, and consequently does not have, with what another does not do, and consequently does have.

A concession to our weakness. Why the assertion in the first statement that the giver will not lack? Surely it is for the very reason that there is a natural tendency to think about how much it will cost to give. It is viewed in terms of personal loss. What self-centred creatures we can be at times! A need presents itself, and we are more concerned about whether we can afford to give than to relieve the need, about how it will affect us rather than about how it will benefit others!

Are we worried that we will be the losers by giving to the poor? This statement is not the opinion of men, but carries the authority of the word of God. It is God himself who is telling us this.

'Giving' here is not restricted to providing money. The word is very wide in its application, so put your purses and wallets away for a moment and think also about giving of your time, your expertise, for the benefit of the poor.

The personal touch. The 'poor' are not the unknown and unnamed people elsewhere with whom we have no personal contact. The giving referred to is not an impersonal thing. What is envisaged here is not signing a direct debit mandate for a charitable organisation and letting them get on with the work. It has a personal element, it means being personally and practically involved. There are many poor for whom we do not have responsibility, but for example where we support Christians working in areas of great need which they present to us, mentioning names and circumstances, then we are involved and we do have responsibility. It may cost us to provide help, but so what? We will not lack. Far from it, we will benefit enormously.

Closing our eyes when God wants them open. The negative side is also presented in this proverb. When we withhold our hand from doing good, when we deliberately shut out of our thinking the needs of others, when we are preoccupied only with our own prosperity and material gain, it will prove to be a curse to us. It will as surely turn sour on us as the wanton hoarding of the manna went bad on the Israelites in the wilderness (Exodus 16:20).

Refer back to 19:17 and Jesus' endorsement of these proverbs in Luke 6:38. The blessing of God is attendant upon those generous of heart, whose eyes are fully opened to the good they may do in this world, counting it a privilege rather than an expense.

[Related proverbs: 11:24; 19:17; 22:9.]

28:28. Oppression and liberation.

Hiding in the open. Compare v. 12 and 29:2. Men hiding themselves may be taken literally (as in 1 Samuel 13:6), but it is not necessarily so. In our present day, as has been the case many a time in the world's history, under oppressive regimes people are going about their daily business for whom it would be more than their life is worth to dare to express what is really in their minds. To all intents and purposes they have gone into hiding. They are not free to speak their minds, they are not free to act with any kind of independence. All they can do is to lie low in the hope that better times may arise. Those for whom it is most difficult are believers, because to meet together is so dangerous they have to do so in clandestine fashion, so that the expression of their faith is literally in hiding. See Amos 5:13; 6:10.

Seen and unseen. Back in Elijah's time, when Jezebel was on the rampage, Obadiah took a hundred of the Lord's people into hiding (1 Kings 18:13), and later when Elijah thought he was the only one left, the Lord informed him of seven thousand faithful followers (1 Kings 19:18). This seems to suggest a significant 'underground church' and is a reminder to us that what we see and what is actually there can be two very different things.

Suppression. Even in countries with a Christian heritage, where Christian standards have been abandoned and laws have been introduced which are in conflict with the law of God, there is an increasing tendency for believers to go into hiding. There are certain things they dare not say in public, there are certain things they dare not do openly, there are certain areas of their work life they have to avoid and in which they cannot openly engage because ungodly people, that is, wicked people, are on the lookout to bring them down.

Our world is a battleground between God and Satan. Although the victory is certain, at the present time on this battleground are God's people and Satan's people, namely the righteous and the wicked. The conflict expresses itself in a great variety of ways, but it is always Satan's intention to suppress the truth and, if not to eliminate the righteous, which he cannot do, at least to send them into hiding.

Indestructible. Wickedness is bent on destruction. It always has been and always will be. Not only does it aim to destroy its opposition, but it also destroys its advocates from within. Satan cannot produce, and has no intention of producing, anything good or constructive. On the other hand, those who turn to the Lord, through the righteousness given by the Lord, are on the road to true prosperity and can only increase. Not the most evil or oppressive of regimes can do anything about this, as has been witnessed in China over the last half century and more, and is being witnessed today in some of the most fiercely anti-Christian nations.

Invincible. In practical terms, we who believe in the Lord Jesus Christ need to recognise where the conflict lies, where the power lies, where the victory lies, and pray for the wicked to perish and the righteous to increase as the gospel is proclaimed.

[Related proverbs: 11:10; 28:12; 29:2.]

29:1. Beyond the point of no return. This is a very solemn statement.

What is said and what is not said. 'Often' rebuked indicates patience and perseverance in attempting to produce reform. What it does not say is how often.

What is known and what is not known. 'Sudden' destruction indicates that there is a set but unknown limit to the patience of God.

'Without remedy' indicates that it is too late to make amends.

King Ahab is an example. If you read through 1 Kings 16:29 to 22:40 you will see that he was rebuked many times, probably not least by Micaiah (1 Kings 22:8). He hardened his heart against the word of the Lord time and again. Little did he know that, despite his well laid plans to guarantee his safety, he was about to be cut down on the field of battle, too late for repentance, too late to make his peace with God.

The law of diminishing returns. When one is young and tender, rebuke may be keenly felt. One of the problems about 'hardening the neck' is that the more often it is done the easier it becomes, so that in the end the rebuke hardly registers and just seems like an empty threat. For this reason rebuke is to be treated with the utmost seriousness on the very first occasion it is administered, because to ignore it or sidestep it is to take the first step on a slippery slope to destruction. The more often rebuke is disregarded, the less likely it is to be heeded, and the more imminent is the irreversible destruction.

Two delusions. Some people seem to think they will be given a second chance after death to get right with God. This is merely a big delusion, for they have had many such 'chances' already – so many in fact in the form of rebuke of their ungodliness and their need to turn to the Lord, that they have reached the point of being broken without remedy. Their 'last chance' was truly their last, and by ignoring it they sealed their eternal destiny.

Even more dangerous is the delusion some people are under that they can put off the time when they will seek God. Time and time again they are rebuked for their neglect of the gospel as the call comes to them to repent and turn to the Lord. The Lord convicts them one last time, and one last time they harden their heart, completely unaware that it is the last time, and thereafter the Lord leaves them in their hardness of heart, giving them over to their debased minds (Romans 1:28).

Be sensitive, stay sensitive. We must not make light of this statement where our own lives are concerned. None of us goes through life without rebuke or reproof. The very worst thing we can do is to harden ourselves against it (see 9:7; 15:12; Amos 5:10). We need always to allow it to soften us up, to make and keep us sensitive, responding aright to the justice of the reproof and recognising our need of the Lord. Consider 17:10; 25:12.

[Related proverbs: 1:24-27; 6:15; 24:22; 28:18.]

29:2. Gladness and groaning. Authority (AV, NKJV) may be implied, by comparison with the second clause, but it is not actually stated in the original and could be somewhat misleading. The original speaks of the righteous *increasing*, or *thriving*.

A pervasive influence. We might wish believers to hold positions of authority in the land because of the influence they would be able to exert, and yet we must not overlook the very real influence exercised by God's people wherever they are. It is the righteous, the godly people, who are the real power for good in any society, and people in general greatly benefit from their influence. That is precisely what this proverb is bringing to our attention. Irrespective of who is 'at the top', communities have been transformed when there have been seasons of spiritual revival. When many have been brought to faith, not only have their own families been blessed as a result, but they have been instrumental in doing all manner of good in their neighbourhood and beyond, and the recipients of the blessing they bring have cause to rejoice. All this may take place without any such person being in a position of authority or wielding power in any official sense. It is simply, yet profoundly, God's blessing overflowing to others.

Gladness. So here we have a reminder that the important thing is not status, or office, or power, but practical godliness. It is about being a savour of Christ (2 Corinthians 2:14-16), who went about doing good (Acts 10:38), in a community beset by all manner of troubles and harmful influences. Church growth is all about the spread of the gospel and all the attendant benefits which accompany the word of life and the transformation of lives.

An oppressive imposition. By contrast, look at what happens when a wicked person is in control. We must never lose sight of the true meaning of this word. This is a person who, however plausible, presentable or popular, actively and knowingly pursues an agenda which is contrary to the Word of God. For example, those who deliberately introduce legislation which is at loggerheads with the clear teaching of Scripture are wicked, whatever the reasons they present for so doing. Likewise those who suppress the voice of conscience and the advice of others, riding roughshod over them in order to advance their own ideologies, gathering round themselves a company of 'yes men' to do their bidding, are wicked.

Groaning. One wicked person holding the reins of power can be a source of untold misery. People groan because they are in pain, in this case the pain of oppression, because they long for freedom to enjoy the things which matter in life. Maybe it is to be free from fear or from unreasonable restrictions, to be free to exercise their abilities for the benefit of themselves and others. How many a repressive regime has sought to project the image to the world that all is well with its people, when in fact for so many it has been a life of fear, of censorship, of deprivation, of virtual slavery, with no hope to break free from the stranglehold in which they have been gripped.

Hope. The only real hope for people under such bondage is for the growth of the church, and even today, in the most unlikely of places, God is savingly at work bringing joy and hope to lives which were barren and hopeless.

[Related proverbs: 11:10; 28:12,28.]

29:3. Love and passion.

Some things are incompatible. It might seem obvious, but let it be stated that anyone who loves wisdom will not be found frequenting a brothel.

Who is in mind? Distasteful though it may seem to discuss it, what is a companion of harlots seeking? Is he seeking their benefit? Is he concerned for their welfare? Not at all, he is merely seeking the gratification of his own base desires. His thinking never proceeds beyond himself, and he does not even think about himself properly.

Who benefits? Next, consider the benefits of his actions or the beneficiaries from his actions. The lover of wisdom brings joy to his father. It is presented as a positive action. It is not simply that the father, recognising wisdom in his son, rejoices. That is certainly true. But do not miss that the focus here is on the *son* and what *he* is achieving, and the point being made is that *he* is bringing joy to his father. By loving wisdom (remember its vital connection to the fear of the Lord) the son is doing good to those closest to him.

What is the cost? Now what is the companion of harlots achieving? Who benefits? Does he benefit? To be sure, he may imagine he is having a good time, whereas the reality is that he is destroying himself – physically, psychologically, emotionally, spiritually. Furthermore, for these 'benefits' he pays dearly, and so in addition he is destroying himself financially. Actually the proverb does not state whose wealth is being wasted. It is sufficient to know that his conduct is nothing but wasteful. For his gains he is in every way the loser. Add to that the effect upon his father, and it will be evident that he is positively destroying others along with himself.

In the parable of the lost son (Luke 15:11-31), the father's unspoken and long-term grief over his son's folly becomes apparent in his reaction to his return. Jesus spoke of the son 'wasting his substance with riotous living' (Luke 15:13), later clarified by the older son as 'devouring your livelihood with harlots' (Luke 15:30) – exactly what we find in this proverb.

What is the point? This proverb takes up a case to make a point. If you can see the point in that particular case you should be able to see it in other cases – perhaps cases closer to home for you.

True wisdom *always* looks beyond one's own benefit to the benefit of others, especially to those who are closest. It is not a case of bettering myself at someone else's expense. It may be a case of benefiting others at my own expense, although the reality is that those who do so are never the losers.

What difference are you making? This proverb poses an important question. To whom is your life and conduct making a difference, and what kind of difference is it making? Are you 'adding value' or are you losing it? If you are a Christian you have received so much from your heavenly Father. The wealth he has given you – are you investing it or squandering it? What would an auditor of your accounts say?

[Related proverbs: 6:32; 10:1; 15:20; 27:11.]

29:4. Principle versus pragmatism. This proverb has similarities to v. 14. Although they are connected, v. 14 focuses more upon the security of the *king*, whereas this verse focuses upon the security of the *land*. For 'king' we might with some appropriateness substitute 'government'. We are looking here at those who hold the reins of power. Both clauses are concerned with the same person or persons, and his or their course of action determines the outcome for the land.

Justice is compared with receiving bribes, and the bribes are a means to pervert the course of justice.

The fundamental principle. A king may think in terms of establishing the land by ensuring there is a good army and a sound defence policy, or of exercising an expansionist programme of conquering neighbouring countries, eliminating potential threats or subduing opposition. He may think in terms of forging advantageous trade agreements. He may implement various political changes and push forward new ideologies at home. But whatever he does or does not do, none of these things count for much compared with the overriding requirement of the administration of justice. If the land over which he rules is to be secure, is to be established, is to be made strong, the one thing which must be in evidence is justice, and nothing must be allowed to pervert it. Justice is absolutely fundamental to national security.

An unchanging principle. Furthermore, justice is not a relative concept, where I have my idea of justice and you have yours and both are equally valid. In our day, the concept of justice has largely been replaced by that of rights. People want what they call their rights. It is proving to be a disastrous shift of emphasis. Apart from anything else, it transfers attention from an objective standard to a subjective one. There always has been, and there remains, only one true standard of justice, and that is according to the Word of God. God alone defines what justice means, and it means acting in accordance with his laws. He has set the standard, and he requires us to maintain that standard. It was the responsibility of the king to uphold that standard and to use his powers to maintain it, even though there would be powerful groups who had a different agenda.

Undermining the principle. Bribes can make their appearance in very subtle ways. For example, powerful pressure groups may arise who want to implement changes to the law to suit themselves. They may say that if their demands are met then they will give their wholehearted support, but if not then they will be fierce in their opposition. The king may want very much to get them on his side, but to reason that conceding to their demands is in the national interest and will promote national security is false reasoning. The question to ask is whether their demands are *just*, and the only way to answer this is to have a right standard of justice to begin with.

Instead of asking if the changes they are demanding are just, the king may reason that making concessions to them will strengthen his own position, enhance his popularity and security, and be in the national interest. Nothing could be further from the truth. Such actions will have the opposite effect of overthrowing the land.

What bearing does this proverb have on what is happening in the world today?

[Related proverbs: 16:12; 29:14.]

29:5. Flattery will get you nowhere … or will it?

Flattery is selfish. Flattery is smooth talking, designed to instil a sense of well-being into another person. It is, however, entirely different from speaking well of that person. If I speak well of you, it is because I have your well-being at heart; if I flatter you it is because I have *my* well-being at heart. Flattery is concerned purely with my getting what I want, regardless of the consequences for you. It is essentially selfish. Perhaps I want something out of you that I might not be able to obtain in any other way and so I try to wheedle myself into your favour. Or perhaps I want you to think more highly of me than you might, and so I feign an interest in you and applaud your attitudes and show that I am on your side. Or perhaps it is even to protect myself from possible consequences because if I get on the wrong side of you it could cost me. From whatever angle we view it, though, flattery is purely (and impurely) selfish.

Flattery is deceitful. Flattery may say things which are true or it may say things which are untrue. But even if what is said is true, truth is not the motivator, but deceit. To praise a person's generosity, or kindness, or unselfishness, or whatever it may be, with the intention of softening them up is an example of this.

Flattery is harmful. In self-seeking by flattery one is actually endangering the person who is being flattered. If it praises a person's virtues to the deliberate neglect of what is lacking, it only encourages an artificial sense of well-being. It plays to pride, and pride invariably is followed by a fall (11:2; 16:8; 29:23).

The imagery of the net may suggest the deliberate intention of flattery to bring a person down. The net was carefully concealed, covered over to look like its surroundings, so that an animal venturing unawares into it would suddenly be enmeshed and entangled.

Consider what Satan did to Eve (Genesis 3:1-5). Was this not flattery? His smooth talking suggested, 'You deserve better than this.' She walked right into his net. The consequences were worse than harmful: they were disastrous.

But even when the intention is not for the harm of the one being flattered, and even if the flattery is seemingly innocuous, its potential for harm is still considerable. It encourages the other person to think that all is well when it is not, and so to fall into serious trouble. It is enticing the other person to compromise, it is putting temptation in his or her way. By accepting it or by giving way to it means actually falling into temptation.

Flattery feeds conceit, something to which many are prone. Says the apostle: 'No one should think more highly of himself than he ought, but should think with sober judgement' (Romans 12:3).

Flattery is just another example of the misuse of the tongue. This verse contrasts sharply with what Paul wrote by the Spirit that every man is to speak the truth with his neighbour (Ephesians 4:25).

[Related proverbs: 26:28; 28:23.]

29:6. Something to make a song and dance about. Two people are being compared here, one described as evil, the other as righteous. The subject under consideration is transgression (which is breach of God's perfect law) and what is in view is the situation of each party in relation to it.

Taking the evil person first, here is someone who wants to be free from the fetters the law of God imposes. Take any of the Ten Commandments, and he sees them as an unwelcome imposition upon his enjoyment of life. For example, why should he put God ahead of himself? Or why should he devote time to God? Why should he be bound by outmoded ideas about morality and sex? Why shouldn't he practise a little deceit to get what he wants? What is wrong with coveting things that belong to others? After all, he is just as entitled to these things as they are. Everybody does these things, so why should he not do so?

So much of what the world offers people actually proceeds from the one in whose hands the whole world lies, the devil (1 John 5:19), and he is the father of lies (John 8:44). The freedom promised by disregarding what God commands actually delivers the opposite. Thus those who have deceived others are always guarding their own backs against reprisal. Those who leave God out of their lives to embark on pleasure seeking end up suffering from depression and despair. Those bent on covetousness discover to their dismay that others take from them, while they never get what they want but are always wanting more.

Those who advocate 'free morality' end up in bondage to their own passions and suffer all manner of physical, emotional and psychological ill effects.

Those transgressions in which evil people indulge gain such a hold on them that they find they are unable to break free, and a compulsion holds them in its thrall and brings them into misery. They may look all right on the outside, but know them better and you discover that they are empty and unfulfilled, or anxious or bitter or ridden with guilt. They are certainly not free.

Now for the righteous. Why do they sing and rejoice? For at least two reasons. Firstly, they are *forgiven*. Even the righteous transgress, but there is that constant recourse to forgiveness and cleansing (1 John 1:8-10) which comes with a consciousness of being accepted and loved by God. They have no guilt, because that has been removed by the sacrifice of Jesus Christ upon the cross.

Secondly, they are *freed*. Jesus said, 'If the Son makes you free, you shall be free indeed' (John 8:36). This freedom results in loving those things they once hated and hating those things they once loved and sought after. It involves a complete transformation. So the righteous, as a new creation in Christ (2 Corinthians 5:17), look on God's laws with a new appreciation, with a new respect, with a new love; with a desire to keep them and to honour the one who gave them. They are no longer opposed to the law, or it to them; it no longer has a stranglehold upon them. There is nothing – absolutely nothing – holding them in any kind of bondage, for they are free in Christ, free to love him, free to enjoy him, free to appreciate his world, free to wait upon his word – free to sing and rejoice. Philippians 3:1; 4:4.

29:7. A human rights issue?

Consideration. The righteous 'knows', or 'considers'. The word denotes far more than mere intellectual knowledge or thought without action. (Compare James 2:15-17 where there is knowledge without action.)

By contrast, the wicked do not understand such knowledge. They have no real appreciation of this kind of thing. It is a concept which is completely foreign to them. Or perhaps it is simply that they choose not to understand. Certainly it is no concern of theirs; it is not their problem.

Cause. The poor have a 'cause', they have 'rights', because not only is God their maker (22:2), he has expressed an interest in them. Orphans, widows, aliens, often fell into the category of being poor, and God said that he loved such people and exercised judgement on their behalf (Deuteronomy 10:17-19), especially for those who called upon him in their need (Exodus 22:22-27; Deuteronomy 24:15).

Concern. Taken together, consideration and cause should lead to action. Nothing will be done without consideration, and nothing will be done if the cause is not recognised. God's Word requires us to consider needs, to recognise just causes, and to act.

Instruction. In the Old Testament, the law clearly stipulated that those with limited means should receive care from those able to provide it and that their dignity should be respected (Exodus 23:11; Leviticus 19:10; 23:22; Deuteronomy 15:7-8; 24:19-21).

Example. We can see a good example of meeting the needs of the poor in the collection for the saints in Jerusalem by churches throughout the Roman Empire (1 Corinthians 16:1-3; Romans 15:26-27). The cause arose partly through the persecution of Jewish believers and partly on account of famine. There was an eagerness to help toward meeting the needs (2 Corinthians 8:4; 9:2). Under God, the Gentile church owed its very existence to their Jewish brethren.

Examination. The question we should be asking ourselves is, are we fulfilling our own responsibility in this respect? Do we have open hearts or closed minds? We who have been lifted from the dung heap of life and made to sit in the heavenly places in Christ (1 Samuel 2:8; Ephesians 2:6), we of all people who have received so much should not be closing our eyes, ears and hearts to the needy, but rather we should be on the lookout to see how we can help such people for Christ's sake.

We are not necessarily talking money here. Are we seeking to be instruments of blessing, of doing good, to those who are needy in some way? It might be visiting; it might be raising awareness; it might be organising practical help. Those who are 'poor' (in the widest sense of the word) are often unjustly looked down upon. They need to be treated with the dignity every member of the human race deserves. If they are poor in material terms does not mean they are poor in other ways. They may be rich in other ways, like Ruth. Boaz considered her according to the teaching of the law and ultimately she proved to be of inestimable blessing to him. There is too great a tendency to judge people according to what they have or appear to be, rather than according to what they really are or have to offer – of which we should recognise we truly cannot be the judges.

Let Job have the last word – Job 29:16.

29:8-9. A weapon of mass destruction. No, not nerve gas or the H-bomb or anything like that – the instrument concerned is the tongue. This verse is reminiscent of 11:11. What the 'scoffer', or 'scorner' or 'mocker', is actually doing is inflaming passions with its consequent results. There is an interesting example of this in the riot at Ephesus (Acts 19:23-41). Demetrius and his fellow craftsmen succeeded in setting the city into an uproar, quelled only by the intervention of the city clerk and his judicious words.

Rage. Demetrius exemplifies the scoffer. He had no time for the truth of the gospel which Paul preached in spite of the evidence of its life-transforming power in others. He was more concerned about the threat it posed to his trade, expressed under cover of bringing disgrace to their local goddess. It was pure self-interest.

Rant. This is very much the characteristic of the scoffer. When he finds himself threatened by the truth he then finds a cause by which to defend his self-interest, stirring up others to produce a following. It matters not whether what he says is true or not, only that people should be infected with his passion. So what Demetrius said about Diana (Artemis) was demonstrably untrue, but that did not matter. His rhetoric succeeded in its design to inflame the anger of his fellow craftsmen, which in turn resulted in stirring up latent anti-Christian and anti-Jewish feeling which came very near to resulting in bloodshed.

Reason. Why were they so angry? The official answer was that their goddess was under threat. The real answer was that their livelihoods were under threat. It was not so dissimilar later when Jews at Jerusalem created an excuse for an uproar in order to lay hands on Paul (Acts 21:27-36).

Those whose passion for a cause produces irrational anger and confusion, damage and destruction, are the scoffers of this world. They scorn the truth, they despise reason, they shut out what they do not wish to hear. They wave their banner and mesmerise the gullible, and the result is big trouble.

Restraint. Alas, it is far easier to stir up wrath than to turn it away. Although the city clerk was just as much a pagan as the protagonists of the disturbance, yet he did show wisdom in his handling of the situation. He addressed not the ringleaders or their principal targets but the people at large, most of whom did not even know why they were there!

Resistance. Had the city clerk contended with the principals (who were really foolish people), he would very likely have got nowhere, as v. 9 here indicates. It would have been impossible to make any impression on them. It would not have restored the peace, because the voice of reason would not have prevailed. To try to reason with them once they had raised their insecure banner would only have enraged them further, or they might have scornfully laughed in his face. This is so often how entrenched unbelievers react to the reasoning of the gospel. It makes them angry, or it makes them laugh. Both are ploys of resistance to avoid giving heed to what is being said.

[Related proverb: 11:11.]

29:10. Persecution.

29:10. Persecution. In the second clause, the expression of seeking the 'life' or 'soul' is customarily used in a hostile sense, as for example in 1 Samuel 22:23; 2 Samuel 4:8; 1 Kings 19:10; Psalm 35:4. The rendering of the NIV and ESV are probably more accurate here, with the second clause in parallel rather than in contrast with the first: 'Bloodthirsty men hate one who is blameless and seek the life of the upright' (ESV).

As well as seeking to understand what the proverb is saying we need to ask why we are being told this.

Threat. What gives men a thirst for blood? Apart from the few for whom it is merely a source of sadistic pleasure, in the majority of cases it is because they see a need to eliminate those who represent a threat to their position, their comfort, their views or their objectives. For example, the Pharisees wanted Jesus killed because he was undermining their authority and influence. Back in the time of the kings, Athaliah had a monomania for revenge and power and usurped the rightful heirs to the throne by destroying them (2 Chronicles 22:10).

Rejection. There are none who are perceived to represent a threat to the ungodly like God's people. Right at the beginning, Cain hated his brother and sought his life (Genesis 4:3-8). 1 John 3:12 informs us of the reason for this. What caused this thirst for blood was a pathological jealousy against one who was blameless and upright in his life. Cain saw that God accepted Abel's offering while his own was rejected and he was angered by it. He wanted to be accepted by God on his own terms. In his own mind it was manifestly unfair that Abel should be treated preferentially. Abel's presence continually rankled, and the only way to deal with the problem was to destroy him. He had no real reason to kill his brother, but burning resentment brought him to it.

Fear. Jesus warned his disciples that they could expect similar treatment from certain quarters (Matthew 5:10-12; John 15:18-25). As he said, men hated him without a cause, and it would be a similar story where his faithful followers were concerned. Particularly when the gospel message of repentance and faith is preached and begins to make its mark, it tends to produce fear in determined unbelievers resulting in a deep seated antipathy toward Christians whose lives exemplify the truth they proclaim. We should not be naïve about this and expect that things should be otherwise. Jesus very clearly warned that this would be the case (Matthew 10:34-36).

Out of control? Persecution of believers in this world is possibly more widespread today than it has been at any previous time in history. We should not be offended by its existence as if God were not in control of the situation or had abandoned his people. It was foretold, and it is to be expected, and those who suffer in this way are by no means the losers, for Jesus spoke of their having a great reward in heaven (Matthew 5:12). He also intimated that the gospel would triumph even in the lives of some of these bloodthirsty people, for he would have his people love them, bless them, do them good, and, above all, pray for them (Matthew 5:44).

This verse is not merely informative so that the believer should resignedly acknowledge that this is how things are. By saying that this is happening in this world, a response from us is required. We have seen its effect upon the just and upright one, the Lord Jesus, and how he responded and overcame, and we should not just sit back and let these things happen but fight back with the weapons with which God has supplied us. Which are…?

29:11. When feelings run high. This proverb is about how we handle our feelings (literally, spirit), and although it speaks generally, yet it is especially applicable to the situation where anger is aroused.

No cause? The cause of these feelings is not mentioned here. It is actually not relevant. But surely there are situations, for example of rank injustice or mindless cruelty or gross negligence, which arouse fierce indignation which simply has to be expressed? What is wrong with speaking one's mind in the face of such things, especially if one is on the receiving end?

Passionate. The answer is seen in what passionate anger is: it is anger in which the spirit is aroused, in which heat is generated, in which feelings are very much to the fore. Passionate anger sees its object in isolation and fails to view the whole picture. It is blinkered, it has tunnel vision, and therefore it fails to see things in context. This being the case, it is incapable at this point of reacting properly. In fact, it will react excessively, over the top.

Personal. Furthermore, such anger, whatever justice it pleads, nevertheless tends to be self-centred. It is about how *I* feel, about what *I* think ought to be said or done. It seldom has in mind how to benefit its object, or to understand how and why the anger has been aroused.

Partial. Consider David's conduct in 1 Samuel 25:2-35. He was incensed at the unreasonable and churlish response of Nabal to his request and was giving full vent to his spirit with a view to wiping out Nabal and his family when Abigail wisely intervened and averted disaster. David's rash reaction to injustice without considering the wider implications was foolish. His anger was just, but his response to it was not, as he himself confessed to Abigail.

Another, very different, over-the-top reaction on David's part is seen in 2 Samuel 12:1-12. Once again it was foolish and irrational, and this time rebounded upon himself. He certainly failed to see the full picture in this case!

Precarious. David was by no means a fool and he had a reputation for exercising restraint, yet on these two occasions he did act foolishly in anger. This serves as a warning and an object lesson to those of us whose feelings are liable to be strongly aroused.

Both the fool and the wise man may be aroused to anger and other strong feelings, and in principle there is not necessarily anything wrong in that, but the latter has learnt to keep these feelings in check. This does not mean bottling them up. That will do no good at all. The force of the second clause is that the wise man *conquers* passions by managing them and stilling them, that is, by taking the wildfire out of them. Strong feelings require the restraint of self-control, they need to be objectively analysed, they need to be brought under the influence of balanced reasoning, and the wise person will do this by bringing God's Word to bear on the situation. While the passion burns in the heart, danger exists. Submit it to the Lord, seek from him what the appropriate response should be, and there is the possibility that whatever caused the trouble in the first place can be addressed helpfully.

There are undoubtedly situations within your experience when passions have run high and matters have not been dealt with well. Look back on one in the light of this proverb and give thought to how they could or should have been handled.

29:12. Leading by example. For 'lies' we need to think of falsehood in its broadest sense – lies, untruth, falsehood, misleading statements, deception – the word is quite broad in its coverage.

For 'ruler' we should be thinking of anyone who is in a position of authority, from national leaders to company bosses to pastors and elders over churches.

Deceptions come under a variety of guises and may be received in a variety of ways.

Falsehood – origin and purpose. It comes from someone seeking to influence the leadership to promote his own personal interests. By its very nature it has to be disguised, dressed up to look good and presented with maximum appeal.

Falsehood – manner of reception.

(a) *Believed as truth.* A ruler may receive lies under the impression that they are the truth. When this happens, more often than not it is a reflection upon weakness in the leadership, perhaps a mark of indolence or carelessness in a matter which should be marked by thoroughness and diligent investigation. David was guilty of this when Ziba falsely accused Mephibosheth (2 Samuel 16:1-4; 19:24-30).

(b) *Reluctance to act.* More seriously, a ruler may recognise the falsehood but let things take their course for the sake of peace and quiet, or for security for himself, turning a blind eye to it or treating it as if it were true or acceptable. This is giving in to pressure through being unwilling to face the consequences of maintaining truth. Pilate was guilty of this in condemning Jesus (Matthew 27:24; John 19:12).

(c) *Opportunism.* Even more seriously, a ruler may find it suits him very well to receive and act on falsehood as an opportunity to further his own ends for power, prestige or personal gain. Ahab did this in the case of Naboth's vineyard (2 Kings 21).

Falsehood – consequences. Not uncommonly, falsehood besmirches the character and reputation of others.

The consequence of entertaining falsehood at leadership level is its corrupting influence on those from whom the falsehood originated in the first place. If they can get away with it, then they will inevitably go for more. If they can exploit a weak ruler, or a conceited ruler, for their own benefit, there is no end to which they will not go to make the most of it.

Leading by example cuts both ways, and here we see the unsavoury principle of fallen human nature operating. Ungodly leadership filters down through society through its failure, for whatever reason, to maintain truth and justice.

Those in leadership positions carry responsibilities toward others for which they need wisdom and understanding. They cannot afford to be careless about how they receive what they hear; they dare not allow their own interests to override the maintenance of truth.

29:13. Under the same canopy.

Divergence. This is rather like 22:2. Literally, it says the two 'meet together', but this is probably a figure of speech. In your mind's eye picture a poor man and an oppressor standing side by side. What difference do you observe between them? Everything, you say. One has all the advantages, the other all the disadvantages. One is downtrodden, the other is doing the treading down. One has next to nothing, the other has way more than enough. One is careworn, the other is carefree.

Convergence. The two seem to have so little in common. Now look at them again, this time from some distance, and what do you see? You see two indistinguishable people standing in the light under God's heaven. Here are two people, each of whom has been given his life by God. That is what they have in common.

Whereas in 22:2 we saw the Lord as the creator of both rich and poor, the imagery here presents him as the provider of life for both the poor and the oppressor.

Common provision. Perhaps we are intended to see two things here. The first is God's gracious favour toward the undeserving. If we are Christians we should understand this very well from personal experience. Jesus said that his Father causes the sun to shine upon both the evil and the good, and the rain to fall upon the both the just and the unjust (Matthew 5:45), and we are likewise to have a similar attitude and to do good to all, including those who oppress us, without making distinctions that God himself does not make.

Common responsibility. The second thing to see is the way the two have used the light given them. They stand equal before God in terms of the benefits they have received from him, and yet one has abused those benefits and taken advantage of the other. That is exploitation. Oppression and exploitation go hand in hand.

There was a certain amount of exploitation going on in the church at Corinth, with some taking advantage of others, and Paul asked them, 'What do you have that you did not receive?' (1 Corinthians 4:7). What God has given us is not to be used for oppressing others or one-upmanship over others, but for doing good to others and honouring others.

At its very basic level, God has given us life, intelligence, ability and other endowments, and when we stand alongside one another we should recognise this, that all we are and have has come from God. Whatever our status in the world, he has given us the dignity of our humanity in which we are equal with others.

Common accountability. The implications of this gift of life from God and his gracious favour toward all for the sustaining of life is that all will be answerable to him for their stewardship. He has given us our life, he has enlightened us. How have we responded to that? If we compare ourselves with others at all, it should result in our seeing that in God's book they are equal with us in status and privileges, and it should inculcate in us a respect for them as equals and a wish to conduct ourselves toward them accordingly.

[Related proverbs: 14:31; 22:2.]

29:14. Psalm 9. The sharp end of justice. Favouritism is not to be shown to the poor, nor is he to be deprived of justice (Exodus 23:3,6; Leviticus 19:15). These principles, established so long ago, are timeless in their validity. Justice is to be served faithfully.

In Psalm 72, a messianic psalm, v. 4 refers to the king bringing justice to the poor of the people, and v. 17 says his name shall endure forever. Isaiah 11:4-5 again speaks of this aspect of Messiah's reign.

Comparing this proverb with a similar one at v. 4, that focused on the security of the kingdom whereas this is about the security of the king.

Why be bothered with them? One of the characteristics of the poor is that they have no resources, nothing by which to commend themselves. We might expect the king to be preoccupied with the rich and influential in his kingdom, giving minimal attention to the poor because at the one end they really have nothing to offer him and little by which to benefit his kingdom, while at the other end there is little they can do to harm him. He might see the poor as a drain upon his resources, a burden upon society, or at best a workforce to be exploited.

Serving a cause. This proverb contains a promise the truth of which has been exemplified again and again in history. The poor as well as the rich have rights equally worthy of attention, even though they may seem to be able to give nothing in return. Real justice, however, is not concerned with returns but with truth. A king judging the poor with truth would probably conclude there would be nothing in it for him beyond the satisfaction that he was serving the cause of justice.

Security a consequence. This kind of conduct sends a message throughout his kingdom. In contrast to a ruler who gives heed to falsehood (29:12), here is one who maintains truth for truth's sake. Others will see this. Those of his servants with their own agendas will be frustrated. Those who are faithful will be encouraged. Thus his throne will be strengthened, and he will be the more secure.

Many rulers who have trampled on the needy and disregarded impartial justice have become obsessed about their own personal safety and feared assassination, and in many cases events have shown that their fears were well founded.

Judging the poor with truth is at the sharp end of justice. It is a test of whether or not the king is going to serve justice across the board, of whether his interest is in himself or in truth.

The maintenance of justice without fear or favour is a primary responsibility of those in authority. Here are some references to ponder in this connection: 2 Chronicles 9:8; Psalms 45:6; 61:6-7; 89:4,14,29 etc.; 132:12.

[Related proverbs: 16:12; 29:4.]

29:15. A painful lesson. Partly because of its abuse and partly because of pressure from those who do not understand the true nature of sin, any form of physical punishment of children has of late been viewed in a very negative light. The book of Proverbs, concerned as it is with practical wisdom and in particular with the proper training of the young, views it in a very positive light (13:24; 19:18; 20:30; 22:15; 23:13-14). It indicates this is not just one of a variety of options available depending on the preferences of the parent or the cultural context.

Two forms of correction are mentioned here (rod *and* reproof, not rod *of* correction), the one physical, the other verbal, and the indication is that on occasions both need to be used in conjunction with one another. It is said that they give wisdom, while their neglect results in folly which brings shame to the mother. Correction is the responsibility of the mother just as much as of the father. The neglect of parental discipline reflects upon the parents as well as the children.

A 'laissez faire' attitude to correction is not to be countenanced. Sinners by nature from birth, we become sinners by practice as we grow. Sinful propensities need to be curbed. Correction can be a troublesome and painful business. It can be far easier to bark out a rebuke in an irritated fashion, or even just to let a matter pass because of the trouble associated with doing otherwise. Reproof is not 'giving a telling off'. There is no use in saying to a child, 'Don't you dare say (or do) that again' without giving a reason. The reproof which is to be given means explaining the rights and wrongs of the situation in terms the child can understand. Sometimes, perhaps where danger is involved or a word of correction seems to fail to achieve its intended purpose, something more robust may be needed to reinforce the importance of what is being said and to act as a disincentive to ignoring the correction.

Necessary and beneficial. We have to recognise that the scriptures do give a rightful place to physically painful correction where appropriate, that it is necessary on occasions and also beneficial. In practice it is seldom required, but when it is it should not be shirked. Administered judiciously, with love and concern, with affection and understanding, it is likely that a child will receive it in a proper spirit and will respect and respond to such training. It will put backbone into him and help him in his resolve to face the challenges of the world with strength and determination. On those occasions where this kind of correction is required, to opt for an alternative, such as banishment to a bedroom, or withholding privileges, or imposing sanctions of other kinds, is more likely to lead to brooding bitterness and resentment.

Wisdom? How? The rod and rebuke are administered in order to lead the recipient to the fear of the Lord. Any discipline which lacks this objective falls short. It is not about conformity to an arbitrary standard ('You don't do that because I said so') but about submission to the will of God ('This is what God wants for you'). Correction highlights what is wrong, perhaps seriously wrong, for it addresses a sinful nature. It also highlights the standard which has been breached, namely the Word of God. Furthermore, it is concerned to promote what is best, the child trusting in the Lord for salvation. While it cannot guarantee results, it is nevertheless what the Lord requires, and it does point the child to his need of him.

Carefully consider 2 Timothy 3:16-17.

[Related proverbs: 10:1; 13:24; 17:25; 22:15; 23:13-14; 29:17.]

29:16. Psalm 37. 'The battle is not yours, but God's.'

A one-sided conflict. Look at 28:12,28 and 29:2. Each imply an ongoing conflict in the world between wickedness and righteousness. Looking at it from a human standpoint, the actual conflict is very one-sided, because the wicked hate the righteous without cause and persecute them, an attitude which cannot be reciprocated. No wonder, therefore, that wicked people are often in the ascendancy. This state of affairs has been the subject of concern and complaint by many godly people. See, for example, Job 21:7; Psalms 10:1-6; 73:12; 94:3; Jeremiah 12:1.

Snowball effect. This proverb speaks of the wicked increasing and transgressions increasing, the use of the same word in the original indicating that the two go hand in hand. Yet it conveys something more than this, that it is like the snowball rolling down a hill, gaining in size and gathering momentum as it goes. The righteous often look on this state of affairs with alarm and wonder what will become of it, feeling powerless to do anything about it. And so, in a sense, they are. Time and again through the history of God's people in the Old Testament God demonstrated to them that his, not theirs, were the power and the victory. What did God say to Israel through Moses? 'Stand still, and see the salvation of the Lord' (Exodus 14:13). What did God say to Jehoshaphat and Judah through Jahaziel? 'The battle is not yours, but God's ... Stand still and see the salvation of the Lord' (2 Chronicles 20:15,17). This is the message of the Bible to us repeated over and over again in different ways, and we are to believe it and put our trust implicitly in God.

Watching God work. The reason why the righteous will see the downfall of the wicked is not on account of anything they do, but because of what God does. It is true that they may be instrumental in this insofar as they are obedient to the Lord and proclaim the truth, but in terms of routing the enemy they are really only there watching God work. This was David's confidence in Psalm 37. Psalm 91:8 speaks of the righteous seeing the reward of the wicked. Psalm 92:7-11 refers to the righteous seeing the wicked perish under God's hand, but the godly flourishing.

They cannot win. What we should be reminded about from this proverb is that in this world the wicked *will* repeatedly multiply, and transgressions *will* increase correspondingly. But then, they *will* repeatedly be seen to fall. One way or another, God brings his judgements to bear upon ungodly families, ungodly societies, ungodly regimes, and they fall. The righteous, whom they oppose, whom they persecute, even whom they kill, nevertheless witness their downfall. What has happened time and again in history *will* one day be brought to a final conclusion. Righteousness *will* prevail, and the righteous *will* live to see it, even though they may be slain for their testimony to Jesus (Revelation 6:9-11).

Not seldom, though, do the righteous, even in their own experience, see God at work frustrating the plans and purposes of the wicked, bringing them down unexpectedly, confounding their expectations. Nothing, however, can touch what God has prepared for those who love him. The wicked will fall because God will bring them down. The righteous will never fall because God upholds them.

[Related proverbs: 28:12,28; 29:2.]

29:17. Pains and gains.

Not an option. The literal meaning of the word translated 'discipline', or 'correct', or 'chastise', involves administering blows, but it is used figuratively of verbal correction. It reminds us that the business of giving correction is neither easy nor comfortable for either party. Hard though it is, the parent is *told* to do it, indicating its painful necessity, and is *encouraged* to do it with a promise of its benefits. This verse complements v. 15 and speaks of the rewards of correction.

Painful labour. There are some parents who have experienced long and painful frustration in seeking to train up their children in the fear and admonition of the Lord. It has been exceedingly hard going for them and they have often been overwhelmed with desperation, feeling they were making little or no progress. There have been times of anguish, wishing they did not have to be so severe, longing for more responsiveness and less stubbornness. There have been times even when, however lovingly they have gone about their task, they have wondered if they have been driving their children further away and that their discipline has been having the opposite effect of what they intend.

Yet what causes so much grief in the training period often yields rich fruit later on. It is a fact that the bond between parents and children where the discipline has been long and hard often turns out to be much stronger and enduring, much closer and intimate, than with those for whom everything has been so much easier.

Blessed rest. Two results are stated here. The first is giving rest. The time for rest is when the work has been done. The work of correction is demanding but it does not go on for ever. The proverb does not say, however, that you are to correct your son and then you will get rest. It says *he* will give you rest. *He* will give you the satisfaction that it has all been worthwhile. *He* is then showing you by his life that your task is done and you can now rest in the enjoyment of it, or rather, your enjoyment of *him*. There is in this a deep personal relationship. You have given so much to him in his training, and now he is giving so much back to you in the bond of respect and affection.

Lasting delight. The second result is giving delight to your soul. The two are connected. The original says something along the lines of, 'Yes, indeed, he will give delight to your soul.' More than simply the pleasure of seeing him turn out well, there is the deep delight, the true and full happiness, associated with his following in the ways of the Lord, resulting in real, meaningful fellowship with him. This should be accompanied by a sense of profound thankfulness to God, for it is God who gives the promise; and if it is he who promises, it is he who fulfils.

'My son, do not despise the chastening of the Lord...' (Hebrews 12:6). Is it yielding the peaceable fruit of righteousness in your life (Hebrews 12:11)? Are you giving delight to his soul?

29:18. Restraint and freedom. The word 'vision' or 'revelation' signifies the way God would speak to his prophets and by which they became his mouthpiece, declaring his word to the people.

The word for casting off restraint has connotations of exposure and shame. There is a telling example of this in Exodus 32. When Moses had been gone for over a month in the mountain the people assumed he had perished and they promptly turned back to idolatry and pagan revelry. When Moses at last returned to the camp he saw that they had cast off all restraint (Exodus 32:25), behaving in a shameful manner which was a denial of all that God had done for them hitherto.

Moses was God's mouthpiece, but the people were largely unbelieving and it was only when he was among them that there was a measure of order and right conduct.

This informs us on the problem of sinful human nature. Righteousness is not found naturally. In an ungodly society things will not get better on their own, only worse. This is evident for all to see in a nation which has formerly benefited from a powerful gospel influence. Spiritual decline in the church, where the clear teaching of the Word of God has been replaced by other things, has resulted in a dramatic moral decline in the nation.

God's Word in the mouth of his chosen instruments is essential if lawlessness and perversion of the truth are to be restrained. For unregenerate men and women will only go from bad to worse without this influence. That is how it was in the time of the Judges until Samuel was raised up (1 Samuel 3:1). The imperative in our day is for God to speak.

'But blessed (or happy) is he who keeps the law.' Those who cast off restraint are not really happy. They know nothing of the case. The second clause speaks of an exultant happiness, a secure and unshakable happiness. It is more an exclamation than an explanation.

This clause contrasts with the first. God has revealed himself in the law which he has given. The people of the first clause have no time for the law, for they cast it away. To them, to keep the law is burdensome for it acts as an unwelcome restraint on the way they wish to run their lives. While some might acknowledge that it is good, nevertheless they themselves do not wish to be bound by it. The trouble is, they see 'keeping' the law only in terms of outward observance, following it minimally to the letter, whereas the word here for 'keeping' denotes keeping it in an altogether different sense. It means keeping in the sense in which you would keep the more precious of your belongings. It is the person who values God's Word, for whom his Word is precious and of inestimable worth, who is happy. David could extol the virtues of God's law in Psalm 19:7-11, and say, 'O how I love your law!' in Psalm 119:97.

We need to see the restraint of evil, to be sure, but we need to see more than this. Restraint is restrictive by definition. The natural man does not want it. Like the kings of the earth he wants to break the fettering influence of the Word of God (Psalm 2:3). What is needed is the powerful transformation which only God can bring about whereby the restraint becomes freedom because through regeneration all things have become new. 'If the Son makes you free, you shall be free indeed' (John 8:36).

29:19. Lip service or less. The scenario before us in this proverb is one in which some kind of correction is in order, and what we see is the servant mentally cocking a snook at his master's (or her mistress's) disapproval, with the attitude, 'What are you going to do about it?'

The 'nobody' servant. There are perhaps two extremes to be seen here. At the lower end, there is the servant who is a mere nobody. The position of a servant in a household was an interesting one. Unlike a son, a servant or slave had no ties of blood relationship, no obligations of family honour, no inheritance to look forward to; in short, nothing to motivate him to conform beyond the letter to his master's wishes or instructions. If he resented his servitude it would take more than words to induce his fuller cooperation with his master's demands.

We find some reflection of this in the employee/employer relationship, especially in larger organisations where things are somewhat impersonal. There are people who have a job, but it is all they can get and is not what they want, and so they do their work grudgingly and minimally. Though they understand well enough what is expected of them, they consistently give short measure. Mere words will do nothing to motivate them to a better performance of their duties.

The 'somebody' servant. However, at the upper end, it was not unusual for a servant to gain a position of prominence in a household, and we find notable examples of this in Abraham's servant (Genesis 24), and in Joseph (Genesis 39). Jesus spoke of a servant not being above his master, but it being enough that a servant should be like his master (Matthew 10:24-25), indicating that a servant might have an elevated status. He also told a parable about a master setting a servant over his household and giving him responsibility over all that he possessed (Matthew 24:45-51), something which his hearers would have clearly understood.

Typically, a servant who had worked his way up was in something of a privileged position, having a measure of influence by virtue of his work and experience. Although in one sense he was a dependant, in another his master was dependent upon his service. Therefore a valued servant might well feel himself to be secure and indispensable. This might lead to the temptation to use his position to take liberties, to do things in a way to suit himself but which his master might not approve, under the impression that his master could really do nothing about it. There is the assumption of unassailable importance.

Are you a servant? For those in any kind of service in the world, the exhortation of Ephesians 6:5-8 applies, which goes beyond mere words to a very wonderful promise.

There is an application here to those in the Lord's service. The apostles consistently described themselves and others with leadership roles as *servants* of Christ (Romans 1:1; 2 Timothy 2:24; Hebrews 3:5; James 1:1; 2 Peter 1:1; Jude 1), a position of privilege which was to be exercised honourably. While the majority have so conducted themselves, there have been some who have abused their position, like Diotrephes (3 John 9). Self-examination and 'examining the accounts' are certainly needed from time to time to ensure they are being faithful in their stewardship (1 Corinthians 4:2). Carelessness in this respect may precipitate more severe measures from the Lord.

29:20. An object lesson. The proverb would make perfect sense without the words, 'Do you see?' So why are they there? Is it not because the Lord wants us to open our eyes, to look and consider?

James 3:2 reminds us, 'If anyone does not stumble in word, he is a perfect man, able also to bridle the whole body.' We are all in the same boat. Without due control, our words threaten to capsize us!

Unprocessed effluent. Whether hot tempered or cold hearted, the man we are asked to look at is given to blurting things out, speaking his mind, giving his decided opinion, castigating others, displaying his emotions, or whatever it may be, before properly processing the thoughts which leave his tongue.

We are not being asked to see someone who has on one or two occasions spoken hastily, but a person who is habitually like this. The book of Proverbs consistently depicts the fool as one for whom there is virtually no hope, and so to say there is more hope for a fool than for this person is striking.

Environmentally damaging. We all know what it is to have spoken 'without thinking' and seen the damage it can do. The trouble is, the words cannot be recalled once they have left our lips, and often there is no immediate antidote to the harm they cause.

What we are being asked to do here is to take a good hard look at the sheer folly of unguarded speech. Do you see not only the man but the harm he does? Do you see how this lowers him in the opinion of others? Do you see how unjust are his words? Do you see how this proceeds from a defective character? We are told that even a fool is considered wise when he holds his peace (17:28), but here is a man who has always got something to say for himself – yes, for himself, not for others.

Analysis and treatment. The reason for considering such a man, far from deriding him or making us complacent, is to make us reflect on our own tendencies. Haste in our speech invariably arises from what *we* wish to say rather than what needs to be said, or what should be said, or what will actually do good.

The problem with the fool is that he has no thought for God. The problem with the man hasty in his speech is that he wants to express himself without reference to God. If we are right in saying he does not stop to think, the exhibition he makes of himself only reveals that God is not in his thoughts.

What we should learn from our scrutiny of this man, apart from the damage done by hasty words, is the hopelessness of his position. He has no principle by which to regulate his words. In turn this should cause us to reflect on what principle if any regulates our own words. It is of first importance that the Lord be first in our hearts and therefore first in our thoughts. It is those who walk with him, who habitually are in communion with him, who are noted for their gracious speech. If Moses, the meekest man who walked the earth (apart from the Lord Jesus), could let his guard down under extreme provocation and speak hastily on one occasion (Numbers 20:10-11), how much more do we need to seek to keep close to the Lord and have him in our minds and on our hearts at all times!

[Related proverb: 26:12.]

29:21. Not a bed of roses. A difficulty in understanding the precise meaning of a Hebrew word in the second clause leaves us in some doubt as to the conclusion of this proverb. The best we can say is that it has something to do with the consequences of pampering a servant from childhood, and it is possibly indicating that the servant will become an inheritor along with any sons.

Inappropriate treatment. The idea of pampering a servant is incongruous. It is actually an abuse of his servitude. We observe here someone who is against reason being treated as a favourite and being spared the rigours of his service. A man who does this may have great affection for his servant, but the way he expresses it will not do any good.

In Ecclesiastes 10:5-7 the writer speaks of an evil, an error proceeding from the ruler, in which the status of servant and prince are reversed.

Inappropriate affection. What has led to this pampering? The phrase 'from childhood' may be significant here. Perhaps this was a child born to an existing servant in the household. Perhaps it was a child taken into service. But somehow this child found his way into the master's affection. His master had a soft spot for him and so treated him softly. In many ways the servant degenerated into a servant in name only, gaining privilege without earning it. In fact, in the end he was probably useless as a servant. All it achieved was an undermining of the dignity and usefulness of service.

Untoward consequences. There is a warning here against showing favouritism, and to be on our guard against doing this kind of thing on irrational grounds. Favouritism can have all kinds of untoward consequences, including arousing jealousy in others (consider Jacob's unwise treatment of his son Joseph, Genesis 37:3). It does no good to its object either.

Pampering may have its place in nursing the sick back to health, but the kind of treatment we read of here arises from selfish sentimentality and is contrary to all reason. Pampering has taken the place of proper training and its end result is seen in a weak and useless individual.

Christians are children of God. They have all the privileges of sonship, including a glorious inheritance. God does not pamper them: he nurtures them. They undergo all the rigours of training and instruction and discipline which belong to sons who are going to share the image of Christ. In so doing he gives them dignity and status and worth.

[Related proverbs: 17:2; 19:10; 30:21-22.]

29:22. Fire in the heart. The same two words for anger and fury appear at both 15:18 and 22:24. The words are broadly similar in meaning, and between them they cover all forms of anger from that smouldering in the heart to that raging openly and out of control.

Picture here a smouldering fire out in the open. There is some smoke, beneath which there is a red glow. But that dull red glow is gradually spreading to other inflammable material, and flames begin to appear. Suddenly the fire springs to life and before long it grows into a blazing inferno.

The angry man is like the smouldering fire, spreading his heat to others. The furious man is like the blazing inferno, destructively out of control.

Fire is good only when it is devoted to a specific beneficial use. Even then it is recognised as potentially dangerous and is therefore strictly controlled and well guarded. So it is with anger.

We must recognise that the sinful human heart does not pass the safety standards for the control of anger. It is for this reason that this fire so often spreads and causes damage.

This proverb highlights one of the principal effects of anger and the moral aspect.

Physical consequences of anger. One of the principal effects of anger is strife, which comes about by stirring it up. Actually, it is meddling, a person interfering in a matter where he should be holding his peace or placing it in the hands of the proper authority. For example, the apostle Paul reminds us that governing authorities are appointed by God and that they do not bear the sword in vain. They have the right to exercise wrath against those who practise evil (Romans 13:1,4). A private citizen attempting to do the same thing would be meddling where he should not, rather like Peter drawing his sword and cutting off the ear of the servant of the high priest (John 18:10).

Anger in the human heart is a very dangerous thing. Even if it originates from a sense of injustice, it is often fuelled by frustration, impatience, vanity, fanned by a thirst for power and influence, and a number of other sinful characteristics.

Moral consequences of anger. Just as a fire spreads by setting things under its immediate influence on fire, so anger stirs to life ungodly passions in other people, and the result is strife. Virtually all examples of strife, from the domestic level to the international level, have their origin in the sinful heart of man who has gone about remedying actual or imagined ills in a way which contravenes the principles set down by the Lord.

Like the fire in the censers of Nadab and Abihu this is profane fire not authorised by God (Leviticus 10:1) and calls down his censure. In the heat of their wrath people take it upon themselves to vent their anger in their own way. But it is not God's way. They have overstepped the boundary set by the Lord. They have transgressed. Anger which has run out of control adds one transgression to another to another.

An angry disposition. It may well be that this proverb is particularly aimed at those who have anger issues, because it speaks of an angry man rather than a man's anger. Anger may be lurking beneath the surface and may not even be recognised for what it is. But deep down there is a spirit of discontent, of personal injustice, of resentment or bitterness, and of a wish to do something about it given the opportunity. This is not peace, it is anger. It is a smouldering fire which, unless it is extinguished by submission to the quenching fountain of God's grace, has potential for doing great harm.

[Related proverbs: 15:18; 22:24-25; 26:21.]

29:23. Falling from a height. The proverbs contain many allusions to pride and humility – for example 11:2; 15:33; 16:18; 18:12; 22:4. Pride is that ugly characteristic by which man thinks too well of himself – too well of himself to recognise and acknowledge the worth of others; too well of himself to submit to correction or advice; to well of himself to allow others to be better than he is; too well of himself to lower himself to serving others; too well of himself to bow his heart to the lordship of Christ, to give God first and supreme place in his heart. It is a sad fact that it is pride in man which keeps him from God. While the unbelieving Pharisees were a classic example of this kind of pride (see Matthew 23:12 in its context), the problem is common enough in the world. When we cease to tremble at the word of God (Isaiah 66:2) pride is not far away.

Pride offends pride. It is ironic that pride is often seen in others long before it is recognised in our own heart! When we find it offensive because it offends *us*, it is our own pride rising up in judgement!

Pride is precarious. Why will a man's pride bring him low? It is true that in due course God will bring him down, but the problem is that a man's pride elevates him artificially in his own eyes. It will not stand objective scrutiny. He is riding on a bubble. The bubble has no real substance and will burst with humiliating consequences. Consider Nebuchadnezzar's statement in Daniel 4:30. Did he not have a right to be proud of his achievements? Was his statement not true? There are many people in a similar position, endowed with exceptional abilities who through hard work have obtained fame and honour. Is it not their due? Do they not have a right to stand on their own pedestal? The answer is no. Their endowment, their opportunities, their ability to work and succeed, have all come from God. They owe him everything, and of all people they are the ones who should be acknowledging just how much they are indebted to him. To think that they have achieved what they have solely by dint of their superior ability is the pure imagination of their hearts (Luke 1:51).

Humility is stable. Whatever our position or achievements, we are exhorted to be completely humble. We know how some people dress to be seen, ostentatiously, audaciously, flatteringly, and so on. Their explicit intention is to draw attention to themselves. Christians are to be *clothed* with humility (1 Peter 5:5), drawing attention not to themselves but giving due honour to others and glory to God. To change the image, their feet are upon secure ground and therefore they have no height from which to fall.

Humility is realistic. Humility does not deny one's ability, or status, or gifts, or achievements. It acknowledges them all. But, like the apostle Paul, who asserted that he worked harder than all the other apostles, he ascribed it all to the grace of God working in him (1 Corinthians 15:10).

Humility is honoured. Whereas pride will sooner or later lead to dishonour, a humble spirit will not only *be* honoured, but will *retain* honour. It means taking hold of, or upholding, honour, and not releasing it.

[Related proverbs: 11:2; 15:33; 16:18; 17:9; 18:12; 22:4.]

29:24. Keep your mouth shut … or else! Falling in with thieves was met at 1:10-19, where the heady excitement of the prospect of ill-gotten gains ended with the sobering conclusion that those who join them, unknowingly lie in wait for their own blood and forfeit their own lives.

Even more sobering is the statement of 8:36 that to hate wisdom is to love death.

Though hating life and loving death are things no man in his right mind would do, many by default do just that.

Wider implications. As with so many of the proverbs, we are expected to dig a bit deeper, to think about the principles which are operating behind the particular example set before us.

This proverb ties in with the law at Leviticus 5:1. Placed under oath to testify, this person finds himself in an invidious position on account of his complicity. He dare not speak, but by his silence he perjures himself.

Dangers to guard against. Paul said, 'Do not be unequally yoked together with unbelievers' (2 Corinthians 6:14). Unbelievers often have very different principles from believers, and to throw one's lot in with them on their terms without qualification is asking for trouble.

It sometimes happens that people tell us things in confidence whereby we find ourselves privy to things which are wrong, and yet we are coerced into keeping quiet about them. We should never allow ourselves to be placed in such a position.

Or consider the man in the workplace who is aware of underhand dealings going on, or what is euphemistically described as 'petty theft', to which he shuts his eyes as being 'none of our business'. No doubt he does so for his own peace and to avoid trouble with his workmates. But it is not as simple as that. Suppose it comes out into the open, and the management calls him? If he then keeps quiet and claims no knowledge he commits perjury, with its own condemnation. If he confesses, he is confronted with, 'You knew about it all along? Then why did you not report it?' To this he has no honourable answer. Either way, he is disgraced.

The safe course. Here, then, is a warning against either actively or tacitly becoming party to something which is wrong. On the positive side, it means living such transparently honest lives that no one would dare try draw us in to anything underhand; or, knowing us, would not dare run the risk of open dishonesty in our full view.

This is not a popular line to take. But whoever desires life and loves many days, that he may see good, should keep his tongue from evil, his lips from speaking deceit, departing from evil and doing good (Psalm 34:12).

29:25. Matthew 10:16-31. Vulnerability.
Jesus warned of the offence of the gospel and of dire consequences for those who embraced it and proclaimed it. Yet he said, 'Do not worry' to those who might have every reason for anxiety about how they would defend themselves; and, 'Do not fear them' about those whom, humanly speaking, they had every reason to fear (Matthew 10:19,26,28).

The theory. The question is, who is in control, God or man? The question is, who is more powerful, God or man? We can tick the right boxes, we can give the correct responses, which is fine in theory. But what about in practice? Does what we give mental assent to, work itself out in the cut and thrust of daily life?

The practice. This proverb is about practice. It is not only about the major, life-threatening, or livelihood-threatening, situations, it is also about what we might call the little things of life.

The fear of man takes many forms. The bottom line is that it gets in the way of our honouring the Lord by doing right. We fail to share the gospel with someone when the opportunity presents itself because we are afraid it will adversely affect the relationship, or that it will rebound upon us in an unpleasant way. We fail to confront wrongdoing in others, or contend for what is right, because we fear it will put us out of favour with them, or that they have it in their power to harm us in some way. We compromise ourselves in our conversation with others because it is embarrassing to take a clear-cut line as Christians and to uphold the standard of speech and conduct the Lord expects of us.

Parents might be afraid to speak up for the Word of God and his authority for fear it may rebound adversely upon their children in school.

The self-preservation instinct. There are all manner of ways in which the fear of man may find expression, but they all concern the consequences for *me* or for *mine*. Once we give in to this kind of thinking, we find it all but impossible to extricate ourselves from it. As the proverb says, it brings a *snare*.

There are many examples in Scripture. For example, why did Abraham say Sarah was his sister – twice (Genesis 12:10-20; 20:1-13)? Why did his son Isaac do the same (Genesis 26:6-11)? Why did Zedekiah not take hold of God's promise to him and surrender to Nebuchadnezzar's officials (Jeremiah 38:14-20)? Why did the apostle Peter withdraw from eating with the Gentile believers at Antioch when James and other Jews from Jerusalem joined him (Galatians 2:11-12)?

These examples and others that could be cited (such as Peter denying Jesus, Matthew 26:69-75) warn us about how powerfully we can be tempted with the fear of man at times, and how it can challenge us with respect to our trust in the Lord. How do we know the Lord will keep us safe on such occasions? Let us choose the easy option of the way we can see, not the less certain one of the way we cannot see. And so we deny our faith. The fact that God has promised should be sufficient for us, whatever the circumstances.

In truth, we have no way of knowing whether any of the things we fear will happen. More than likely, they will not. However, even assuming they do, that is no reason to capitulate to the fear of man. Do we believe the Word of God? Do we believe it sufficiently to stake our life and reputation upon it? To put it another way, do we trust in the Lord? In any and every situation in which we are tempted to opt for the 'safe' way of accommodating our speech and conduct to the demands of men and the society in which we live, we should identify the lie. There is only one 'safe' way. That is, to trust in the Lord, which means showing it by speaking and living for him. God says – yes, *God* says – that those who trust in him will be safe. That is, they will be set on high. They will be on the high ground in every sense of the word. They will be above those who oppose them. The ungodly cannot look down on the righteous, they can only look up to them. The righteous are in the position of strength, for they have God on their side (Romans 8:31).

Christians who compromise are rightly despised by unbelievers.

Sometimes we have to learn to reason with ourselves, as David did when under threat (Psalm 56). It will result in the confident assertion of Psalm 118:6-8).

[Related proverb: 30:5.]

29:26. Psalm 146. 'From where does my help come?'

Limitations of willingness. 19:6 was concerned with free handouts. Here, seeking the face of a ruler is probably concerned with more substantial matters. It is common knowledge that some of the promises made by potential leaders on the campaign trail are never fulfilled when they are in power. People have sought their favour and been promised support for their causes, but in the end those causes have lost ground to other more pressing matters or been forgotten or dismissed as inconvenient or of little importance.

Limitations of power. It is because it is the ruler, and the ruler alone, who has the power to make and implement policies, that he will find himself inundated with requests from all quarters. Therein lie a number of problems. The first is that he cannot possibly give attention to all who seek him. He does not have the time. He has to be selective. The second is that he may not want to be bothered with the matters some seek to present for his attention. Irrespective of their merit, it may not suit him or be in his interests to pursue these cases. The third is that it may not actually be possible for him to do what is asked of him. Even a ruler is limited in his powers. In every way man, even at the height of his powers and influence, is very limited. There is so much he cannot, and will not, do.

The God who hears. None of these limitations applies to the Lord. Firstly, were the population of the entire world to petition him simultaneously, that would present no problem to the One who is infinite and without limit in all of his attributes.

The God who acts. Secondly, there is nothing arbitrary about his dealings with men. He is a God of justice. Righteousness and truth are foundational to all his communications with men. No just cause will be dismissed by him, for that would be a denial of who he is. Thirdly, nothing is too hard for the Lord. Nothing in the realm of justice is so complex or so difficult that he should find himself unable to deal with it. God is omnipotent, which means that he is not impotent in the least respect.

Our expectations. When it comes to the rulers of this world, we need to have realistic expectations of them. Like us, they are men; like us they have their faults and weaknesses and limitations. We need to have the psalmist's perspective, expressed in Psalm 146:3-7. God is still on the throne, and he is the one and only true ruler. Rulers among men are only his subordinates, and sadly are often guilty of insubordination.

God's answer. This proverb speaks of justice for man. We might pause to ask what that means. What do we really know about justice? Do we really know and understand about the rights and wrongs of cases? People often confuse real justice with their idea of justice. The cry, 'Give me justice,' is often amplified by self-interest or self-esteem. The proverb does not say that what we want or call justice comes from the Lord, but that justice for man comes from him. It is *his* justice we are looking at here. The claim of Korah, Dathan and Abiram and many others (Numbers 16:1-3) would have met with resounding approval in our day – they had justice on their side! They had a large following of highly respected and influential leaders. Moses was altogether high-handed and unreasonable. But their justice was not God's justice, and his prevailed.

29:27. Incompatible, or, getting in the way.

What marks out an unjust man? How do you know that a person is unjust, or perverse? It is not because they say or do things which upset you, but because they say and do things which are contrary to the Word of God. As observed at v.26, justice is defined by God's standards. Thus what makes an unjust man an 'abomination' to the righteous is not that the righteous perceives an offence against him or what he considers right, but because, as one who loves the Lord and his Word, he sees God's Word being violated by the ungodly. So, for example, when we encounter people who blatantly blaspheme, we are not upset because we don't do it or we don't think it should be done, but because it is an affront to the Lord himself. So an unjust man is an abomination to the righteous because God is offended. It is because God is offended that the righteous is offended, for the righteous is in a right relationship with God and in harmony with his righteousness.

What marks out an upright person? It is someone who loves the Lord. That is true. But how do we know they love the Lord? We know because it shows in their speech and in their conduct. They walk in his ways. Their life is characterised by a heart obedience to his commandments.

Very well. But why should that be an abomination to the wicked? Why can't those who have no time for God just let those who have get on with their lives? The answer is obvious: it is because the righteous get in their way. Regrettably, the NIV omits an important phrase, and thereby a significant emphasis is lost. This proverb is essentially very practical. It refers very specifically to the upright 'in the way'. Even allowing for some ambiguity of meaning, one thing is unmistakable: their way of life is marked by moral rectitude. This encompasses their relationship with others, including the ungodly: and there comes the rub. Upholding what is right necessarily involves speaking out against what is wrong. It means exposing wickedness for what it is. Those with wicked hearts naturally do not like this. Believers understand this because they know what they once were, and still would be but for the grace of God.

Consequences for life. We are reminded here that as long as this earth exists and until the coming great day of reckoning, there will be two parties who will always be at loggerheads. As long as these two parties exist, there is never going to be any true peace in this world. Jesus said, 'I have not come to bring peace, but a sword' (Matthew 10:34). Why? Because his coming into the world and his work upon the cross, and the spread of the gospel through the whole world, have further polarised the opposing factions. This mutual antipathy will exist until at last there is a final separation of the sheep from the goats (Matthew 25:32-33), and only then will there be everlasting peace and bliss among the righteous.

It is on this understanding that Paul wrote that believers should not be unequally yoked with unbelievers (2 Corinthians 6:14-18). It does not work; it cannot work. Those who have tried it have verified it.

Part 5

Proverbs 30:1-33

'The words of Agur'

30:1-3. Humbling observations. The remainder of the Book of Proverbs is different from what has gone before. It is more discursive and thematic, more like chapters 1 to 9, though in a very different style. Although we do not know anything about the authors here, the Holy Spirit inspired their utterances to be placed alongside the wisdom of Solomon in this collection.

The translation of the latter part of the first verse depends on whether we are to understand here the names of people or take them as descriptive terms. The ESV translates thus: 'The words of Agur son of Jakeh. The oracle. The man declares, I am weary, O God; I am weary, O God, and worn out.' This translation certainly fits in very well with what follows.

How much do you know? The words of 'Agur' (or, 'the Gatherer') commence with what might be described as a humiliating confession (1-3). He talks of his stupidity, his lack of wisdom and his deficiency in his knowledge of God. Is this the kind of person from whom we should expect to gain anything of value? Yet in what follows there are remarkable observations and insights. What are we to make of this?

Paul wrote: 'If anyone thinks that he knows anything, he knows nothing yet as he ought to know' (1 Corinthians 8:2). He also wrote: 'If anyone thinks himself to be something, when he is nothing, he deceives himself' (Galatians 6:3). The psalmist declared: 'I was so foolish and ignorant; I was like a beast before you' (Psalm 73:22). After all his anguish and profound reasoning in his mental turmoil to make some sense of what was happening to him, on hearing God's words to him Job confessed: 'Behold, I am vile; what shall I answer you? I lay my hand over my mouth', and, 'I abhor myself, and repent in dust and ashes' (Job 40:4; 42:6).

Have you ever had cause to exclaim, 'How stupid of me not to see it before!'? If so, it was a very just remark!

How strong are you? If Agur is saying he is weary and worn out, it is a declaration of just how weak he is, how limited his strength, how early exhausted from the exercise of his mind. The limitations of his mental faculties and capacity are a problem for him. He reckons it ought not to be so, but it is so. What he knows accuses him of just how much he does not know, and it upbraids him for his deficiencies. Before God, his wisdom is nothing; indeed, his knowledge of God, the Holy One, such as it is, he counts as ignorance.

How far can you see? It is a mark of those who are truly wise that they are the most aware of the serious limitations of their strength, knowledge, understanding and ability. They have glimpsed just how much more is 'out there' which they simply have not begun to comprehend; indeed, that it is just so much that they are able to take in no more than a fraction. Conscious of the knowledge and understanding of God, David is obliged to confess, 'Such knowledge is too wonderful for me; it is high, I cannot attain it' (Psalm 139:6).

How many answers do you have? Here is a man who has learnt one of the fundamental lessons of life. He is much more worth listening to than those who think they have all the answers or who make confident assertions about things clearly beyond their understanding!

30:4. Questions. Throughout what he writes, Agur would have us observe, ask questions, examine the evidence, and draw conclusions. It is a true scientific approach. Here he begins by asking a number of significant questions. He himself gives no answers but lays down a challenge at the end: 'If you know?' The implication is that these are questions to which we ought to know the answers. Sadly, such is the ignorance in the world that, let alone being able to answer these questions, few even get as far as asking them.

The questions before us have something of the flavour of those God asked Job (Job 38:4-11), or those taken up by Isaiah as he portrays the gloriously surpassing power, majesty, wisdom and understanding of almighty God (Isaiah 40:12-14). Jesus himself asserts that he is the one who has ascended to heaven and come down from heaven (John 3:13).

The first question, 'Who has ascended into heaven, or descended?' concerns revelation and communication. In Romans 10:5-9 Paul takes up Deuteronomy 30:12-14, and this has a bearing on this question, the point being that God is not a remote being with no communication between heaven and earth. He is a God who has spoken, personally and intimately, who has a vital interest in the affairs and welfare of men. He is a God who repeatedly revealed himself to his people, for their benefit 'coming down' from heaven to observe and act (for example Genesis 11:7; 18:1,21 – pre-incarnate appearances of God the Son). So many people have their own ignorant, uninformed notions about God. To them God is unknown and, they suppose, unknowable. They never ask this question, they never imagine that God has revealed himself; and so they never seek him, the God of heaven and earth (Genesis 14:19,22; Ezra 5:11; Jeremiah 23:24; Acts 17:24). God who has spoken has revealed himself once for all in his Son (Hebrews 1:1-4).

The second question, 'Who has gathered the wind in his fists? Who has bound the waters in a garment?' is a double one, describing two things which are totally impossible for mere men. As with the first question, to say, 'No one,' would be the wrong answer. If that were the answer there would be no real point in asking the questions. Agur is implying that there *is* someone and is making us think about who this someone is.

The very idea of gathering the wind in our fists is ludicrous, as is binding waters in a garment. The picture, however, is that of stupendous power which controls the elements and directs them. This is the controlling power and authority displayed by Jesus who rebuked the wind and calmed the sea in an instant, which elicited the question from the astonished disciples, 'Who can this be?' (Luke 8:23-25). This verse is not just depicting the creative power of almighty God, but also his controlling, directing and restraining power. Here is an area in which men are utterly helpless, totally at the mercy of elements over which they have no control. Have they no concept of a God who is creator and master of all these things? He is the God who is awesome beyond comprehension who holds all these things in his hands.

These questions require us to look for evidence in order to answer them. The evidence all points in one direction, and one direction only.

The third question, 'Who has established all the ends of the earth?' follows on from the previous one. 'All the ends of the earth' encompasses every last and remotest detail. Here is a God who is infinite in knowledge and power. Everything was made by him and for him (Colossians 1:16; Romans 11:36). We are informed that Father and Son were equally and intimately involved in every aspect of the creation. The whole creation was set in place by him, functioning according to the laws under which he himself has placed it. Everything was not just made by him, it was *established* by him, as a coordinated and fully functioning entity. Yet people in their foolish wisdom assert that it all came about from the destructive and chaotic disorder of a big bang! If they would but look at the evidence, they would be dismissing this notion and asking who has established all the ends of the earth.

The fourth question, 'What is his name, and what is his Son's name, if you know?' These questions culminate in the most remarkable of all, and yet it is a logical conclusion. The answer to all the questions is the God who has revealed himself to men. As Paul said to idolatrous pagans, 'He is not far from each one of us' (Acts 17:27). See from that passage how the apostle directed his hearers to consider the kind of questions Agur is asking here.

We are not to understand 'name' in our modern western sense as a mere title of identification. Rather, we are to think of the God who is who he is, the Being who possesses these glorious attributes.

We have seen how the Son is present in all the answers to these questions. What is remarkable is that Agur at that time should refer to a 'son'. He sees one related to God who is intimately and equally involved in the creative power, authority, control and direction of the affairs of heaven and earth.

If the spiritual wisdom and insight of men a thousand years before Christ came into the world could identify him as a being co-equal with God, how much more should we give due reverence to Jesus as who he is, as Lord, recognising and acknowledging his divine status, his power and dignity, his surpassing glory and majesty, enthroned at his Father's right hand, invested with all authority in heaven and on earth (Hebrews 1:3; Matthew 28:18).

30:5-6. God's essential Word. Having (by asking pertinent questions) focused our attention upon the surpassing greatness of God who created and sustains all things, Agur continues with reference to God's *word*. He is thereby reminding us that God has *spoken*, that it is God's intention to *communicate* with man. Not only does God speak, he protects those who entrust themselves to his care. That is his intention in speaking: it is that we might trust him.

Man without God, for all his boasted independence and ability, is hopelessly and helplessly at sea, completely exposed and vulnerable. He desperately needs the word of God to come to him. It is imperative that he then listens and heeds this word, the only word which has unquestionably been demonstrated to be pure, a tried and tested word. He also desperately needs to entrust himself completely to the God who has spoken in order that he might find safety and security in him.

No lack or superfluity. The writer says, emphatically, that *every* word of God is pure. God has never been guilty of a slip of the tongue, he has never been unclear in his words, he has never deceived or misled by what he has said. Far from it: his words have only and always been true, absolutely right and appropriate, clear and to the point, one hundred percent relevant. None is superfluous, and none is deficient. They are words which demonstrate his care over those who place their trust in him alone. No one who has ever trusted him has found him to be wanting in this department or in any other.

There is a sufficiency about what God has said. Had he needed to say more, he would have done so. We dare not suggest otherwise by adding to what he has said, claiming divine authority for any of our own words, which is something the cults have done with their special extra 'revelations', speaking their own thoughts in the name of God.

No addition or subtraction. God warned against adding to the words of the prophecy given to John on Patmos (Revelation 22:18), for, as always, what God has said is *sufficient*; and he warned against taking from the words of the prophecy (Revelation 22:19), for what God has said is *necessary*: it needs to be heard. This general principle applies to all that God has spoken (Deuteronomy 4:2). *Every* word is pure; every word needs to be heeded (2 Timothy 3:16).

No embellishment or corruption. We are therefore cautioned against embellishing the Word of God with ideas of our own, which includes such things as putting other things on a par with it, such as the teachings of the church, and rules and rituals which have no basis in Scripture. Nor should so-called supernatural experiences or spiritual gifts be added as essential to the Christian life or elevated to a status which places them alongside Scripture.

When it comes to what God has spoken, it is our responsibility to hear him, and to ensure we hear him clearly without the imposition of our own ideas. At many times in the history of the church people have dispensed with or discounted parts of God's Word. But equally, heresies have arisen which have sought to add something to it. By so doing they have in fact taken something away, denying the sufficiency of what God has said, implying that something more from elsewhere is needed for salvation. God alone is our shield and our protector; his word alone is proven and trustworthy.

God's word is authoritative and any who claimed to be speaking with divine authority when he had not sent them were blasphemously doing people the greatest possible disservice. The Lord warned his people about this in Deuteronomy 18:20-22. Jeremiah 20:6 records God's judgement upon Passhur. Jeremiah 28 records God's judgement upon Hananiah. Jeremiah 29:31-32 records God's judgement upon Shemaiah. All these people were speaking falsely in the name of the Lord out of the imagination of their hearts and from him suffered the consequences. In Ezekiel 13 God pronounced judgement upon those who claimed divine authority for what came out of their own hearts.

30:7-9. Two important requests.

Request one. The purity of God's Word does rather reflect upon the deficiency of our own words and those of others. This man has personal integrity at the top of his agenda. Perhaps we should ask ourselves what are our own priorities in life. We ought to be right there with him, because falsehood and lies are the stock-in-trade of the devil. By falsehood and lies he deceived Eve in the garden, and by falsehood and lies he attempted to thwart the accomplishment of redemption as he tempted the Lord Jesus in the wilderness. The virus of deceit has infected every man, woman and child since the fall of Adam, and we have neither a natural resistance to it nor the ability to rid ourselves of it. That is why, like the writer, we need to recognise this and to have the humility to apply to the Lord, why we need to plead with him to take these wretched traits from us. Only by the empowerment of the Holy Spirit can this be accomplished in us.

The reason for it. Why should it be of such concern to us? Fear of being found out? Fear of losing face before others? Fear of things rebounding unpleasantly upon us? But it does not matter if we can get away with it, does it? God forbid that we should ever permit ourselves to think in such a way! Agur is concerned not about himself here, but about dishonouring the name of God – *his* God. God is a God of mercy and truth, and he would have us speak the truth in love (Ephesians 4:15,21,25; 5:9; 6:14). If we have even begun to respond to the Lord's love for us, then purity of speech and conduct and integrity of character should be at the top of our list of 'must haves', and until the day we die we need daily, hourly, minute-by-minute upholding grace. The evidence of this may sometimes be in sore trials and many hardships. So be it, if thereby the dross be removed and we can begin to shine for the Lord.

Request two. But Agur has a second request. God taught the people in the wilderness the lesson of daily dependence upon him for the supply of their material needs as he provided them with manna in the wilderness. He warned the people against being lifted up with the pride and self-sufficiency so often associated with riches (Deuteronomy 6:10-12; 8:11-18).

The reason for it. Agur is aware of his own vulnerability in this area. It is so easy, when everything is going really well, to become casual and careless in our walk with God. We should be praying for daily dependence.

Jesus taught us to pray, 'Give us this day our daily bread' (Matthew 6:11). He also promised to provide (Matthew 6:25-34; 7:7-11). We are not poor if, day by day, we have nothing for tomorrow but sufficient for today.

Agur is a realist as he observes the problems associated with both poverty and riches and as he envisages his own shortcomings in dealing with either. The prospect of either sets the alarm bells ringing in his mind, making him conscious of his continual need of dependence upon the Lord who provides all things good for those who trust him.

Most readers of these words will not be in such straitened circumstances that they are tempted to steal to meet their most immediate needs, but many may have the opposite problem. So ask yourself to what extent you are conscious of your own need of dependence upon God.

These two requests are set in the context of Agur's consciousness of death. This does not imply that he was ill or old, only that he was aware that his life had a terminus point set upon it (Hebrews 9:27), and no doubt that it was to be followed by an accounting. His request contrasts instructively with the attitude of those to whom Isaiah preached who said, 'Let us eat and drink, for tomorrow we die!' (Isaiah 22:13). They were mocking the prophet's warnings, they failed to take death seriously, and all they were concerned about was self-indulgence and 'having a good time', which to them meant disregarding the word of the Lord. This man, however, knew his God, and earnestly desired to live out all his days in a way that honoured him.

30:10. On putting others down. So far Agur's words have largely concerned our relationship with God. The remainder of what he has to say encourages us to look around us and observe life in general, and he starts with an observation of one of the prevalent evils in society in which people think too highly of themselves. That is invariably the cause of maligning others.

The Pharisee in the story Jesus told maligned the tax collector in his 'prayer' to God (Luke 18:10-14). He was exalting himself at the expense of the other man and the only way to do it was to 'put him down'. It is so often the case that self-interest is the predominant factor in maligning others in this way.

Faultfinding. This is not concerned with reporting wrongdoing in others to the appropriate authority, which becomes necessary from time to time. For example, an employee might have to approach his superior if another employee is acting dishonestly at work. What we are presented with here is defamation of character, slander, false and malicious statements, making accusations behind someone's back, the root of which is impure motives. Whatever the 'case' being presented, if face to face confrontation with the 'servant' is deliberately avoided, the issue is undoubtedly wrong.

The power of slander. In this situation the master has the power to act, to discipline or dismiss the servant. A servant who is doing good work and has earned the prospect of promotion may attract opposition from others who are jealous. They may go over his head to the master with all kinds of reasons why he needs to be regarded with caution.

Jealousy can also arise in churches with the result that evil is spoken of another. If not jealousy, it may be blind prejudice. But the outcome is the same, in that servants of the church are run down before others. Their virtues and values are diminished, and their supposed deficiencies and lack of qualification are magnified.

The possibility of retribution. Pride, prejudice, jealousy, are subversive evils which pervert justice and thwart what is right. We might raise an eyebrow at the maligned servant cursing the offender as if this were an over-the-top reaction and unjust in itself. The translation, 'Lest he curse you' is probably more accurate than saying that 'he will curse you'. The writer is indicating is that the slanderer is laying himself open to the possibility of being cursed, and justifiably so, and that the evil is likely to rebound upon his own head.

A curse is mere words. The power of execution lies with another. Proverbs 26:2, which speaks of an undeserved curse not coming to rest, infers the possibility of a *deserved* curse. The slanderer needs to know that those he unjustly demeans and who suffer as a result have recourse to a higher authority who will ensure a proper accounting and see that justice is done, and that the suffering he has caused will rebound upon his own head.

In the scenario presented here, Agur is saying that anyone behaving in this way deserved to suffer accordingly.

Does the believer have occasion to curse anyone for maltreatment? Read Romans 12:14-21 for the answer.

30:11-14. Observe – and be alarmed. The words 'There is ... that', or 'There are ... that' are not in the original, so that our full focus is upon the blatant, unfeeling arrogance involved. To curse one's father and fail to bless one's mother (11) is an inhuman breach of the fifth of the Ten Commandments.

Then there is the claim to be pure, or clean, morally (12). 'In their own eyes' indicates a form of self-assessment according to one's own criteria. 'What I am doing is perfectly all right. Who are you to judge me?' Furthermore, here is hauteur (13), which is disdain of all criticism, being altogether above it. The consequence of this is that they get their teeth into their victims to tear them to pieces (14).

A degenerate society. By writing of 'a generation' (NKJV – the word has a collective aspect to it and conveys more than 'There are those...') Agur is highlighting at least an identifiable group in society displaying these characteristics. Sadly, we are certainly seeing these things in our post-modern society. Respect for parents has probably never been so low. Parental values have been discarded, parental influence and standards scorned as a thing of the past and worthless. Practices, especially in the areas of sex and ethics, clearly contrary to the Word of God, are declared to be acceptable, liberating and to be held as rights, and those who hold them are eager to tear apart those who believe, speak and conduct themselves otherwise.

Nothing new. Things like this went on in periods of the history of the nation of Israel, when God's laws were set aside and other standards were introduced, upheld and promulgated, and not only did God's people suffer greatly but the whole of society came to groan under the burden. There is a natural degeneracy in human nature, an eagerness to substitute the false for the true, the fleshly for the spiritual, the sensual for the sacred. We should not be surprised that this is going on today in our own society.

Replacing what is outdated. Perhaps, though, we are intended to look beyond the rejection and disdain of immediate parents, to the rejection and disdain of national heritage. Standards cherished in the past are thrown off and discarded, to be replaced by what is claimed to be something better but which in reality is merely introducing an official licence for godless self-indulgence.

Casting away restraint. That Agur thousands of years ago could describe the situation so pertinently indicates that human nature has changed not one whit. The problems he observed then are still with us today. Where there is no restraint, the natural man pushes the expression of his sinful desires to its limits.

In the Psalms we can see allusions to the state of affairs of the prevalence of wickedness (12:3; 86:14; 101:5; 119:51,69,78,85; 123:4; 140:5). However, God is able to deal with such situations (see Isaiah 2:12; 13:11; Jeremiah 48:29-30; Malachi 4:1; Luke 1:51; James 4:6).

Our response to these words should certainly be to recoil in horror as we observe what is going on and to fear the potential consequences. At the same time, bearing in mind v. 5, we should earnestly desire, pray for, and work toward the introduction of the cleansing and powerful Word of God into this situation.

30:15-16. Observe – and be moved. If there is a touch of humour at the beginning, it only sets what follows in sharper contrast.

The leech is a bloodsucker having a virtually insatiable capacity. People were often named according to their characteristics, and so it may be intended to be taken here, 'Give' and 'Give' being their names! Their sole desire is for blood, and that is what they unremittingly demand. The more they get, the more they want. They are never satisfied with what they have.

Parasites. Agur is making observations and he wants us to do the same. Observation should lead to reflection, and reflection should lead to some kind of response. There are people we would describe as parasites in our society. They contribute nothing, but take all they can get hold of. Nor are they ever satisfied. If we allow them to attach themselves to us they will go on enriching themselves at our expense unless we do something about it. They will never give anything in return, nor will our giving to them benefit anyone else, directly or indirectly. Bloodsuckers impoverish society. One leech is more than enough. But the leech has *two* daughters. Successful parasites have a habit of multiplying!

In these verses and in those which follow, in each case Agur cites four things – or perhaps five. Saying 'three' and 'four' is a device to indicate that the list is not exhaustive and that we could think of further examples.

Here the examples are at least accompanied with sadness or distress.

The grave. The grave is never satisfied. People go on dying. Every death brings sorrow and pain. It is no use longing for an end to death in this life (note the irony here), because life always culminates in death. It is a formidable reality that each of us must face, though we fear it and recoil from it. But, Paul reminds believers, it is the *last* enemy (1 Corinthians 15:26).

The womb. At the other end of the spectrum we see the plight of the woman who cannot bear children. She is for ever longing to bear a child, but it never happens. There is almost a paradox here that while every child born into this world is destined for death, even so a barren woman cannot be satisfied with her condition.

The earth. Next we are pointed to the earth which continually thirsts for more water. In that climate water was a precious commodity, essential for the growth of crops. While there was often sufficient there was never complete satisfaction where it could be said, 'Enough!' and the land remained thirsty. Then there was the perpetual need for renewal. The image here is one of ongoing dependence and yet at best only partial satisfaction, accompanied by anxious uncertainty about the future.

Fire. The fourth on his list, fire, is utterly destructive. Feed a fire and it will go on for ever. The only way to stop a fire is to deprive it of combustible material. Are we intended to think of destructive evils in our society which can be extinguished only by radical action?

30:17. Observe – and be disgusted. This picks up on v. 11 and is a picture which is particularly unpleasant – and it is intended to be so. Though it is of course not intended to be taken literally, the warning it conveys is equally sobering. The imagery may be drawn from the way some members of the crow family and raptors will attack and first pluck out the eyes of unprotected new-born animals that later, when they die as they inevitably will, they may feed on their carcasses. It is a distressing sight.

The law says: 'Cursed is the one who treats his father or his mother with contempt' (Deuteronomy 27:16). For Israel under the old dispensation anyone who cursed his father or mother was worthy of death (Leviticus 20:9). The law says that parents are to be honoured (Exodus 20:12), even revered (Leviticus 19:3). By adding 'and keep my Sabbaths' in the same sentence in the latter passage, God is indicating that reverence for parents and reverence for himself go very much hand in hand.

What this proverb is saying in effect is: 'As you have done to them, so will it be done to you.' The eye that mocks in this way deserves to be plucked out, just as the tongue which speaks contemptuously against parents deserves to be silenced.

There is a tendency for us to judge what is good and bad according to our own standards. We might disapprove of children who have contempt for their parents and yet recoil in horror at the idea of their having their eyes plucked out. Yet God's command to honour one's parents is one of the fundamental standards of behaviour enshrined in the Ten Commandments. It is every bit as important as any other of the ten, and violating it has horrific consequences, not only in terms of the judgement which may be expected from God, but in society in which the family is the basic unit. When family life falls apart, so society itself crumbles, being eaten away from within.

We read of the Lord Jesus that he was subject, or obedient, to his earthly parents, even though at the age at which he was then he outshone them in wisdom and understanding (Luke 2:47,51). Years later, at a time when he might justifiably be preoccupied with his own suffering, he was still honouring his mother in his care for her as he entrusted her to John's care (John 19:25-27).

30:18-20. Observe – and be awed – or sickened. Some may think on reading these verses that they are concerned with mastery. For example, the eagle is often thought of as master of the skies. However, the phrase 'the way' has more to do with *how* these things happen, and all the examples are concerned with *negotiation* of some kind.

Awesome in the air. The first is the negotiation of the air. The eagle is the most majestic of all birds, effortlessly riding the air currents and master of this element. Just to watch one in the air, surveying or hunting, is awe-inspiring. For all our scientific knowledge we can still watch spellbound by its graceful movements and wonder how it moves with such ease and confidence.

Awesome on the rock. The second is the negotiation of the rock. Watch a serpent, or snake, make its transit across rock. However does it do it? It glides so easily across a surface which would be an insurmountable problem for most other creatures.

Awesome on the seas. The third example is taken not just from nature but from something man has made. Visualise Agur standing high on a hillside overlooking the sea, and there is a ship in sail, hardly more than a speck, surrounded by a vast expanse of water. Yet slowly but surely it is making its way toward its destination, negotiating the medium in which it is found. Once again, we may have a good understanding of the physics of the situation and of navigation, and yet there is something amazing that such a frail vessel should be able to ride the mighty waters.

Awesome in affection. The fourth example is, for want of a better phrase, the negotiation of affection. When we think about all that a man is and what he does, his strength, his labour, his creative skills, his independence and so on – everything we associate with the word 'manly' – yet when he is wooing a young woman another side of him is seen, involving gentleness, sensitivity, and even the weakness of a sense of need. However we analyse it, there remains a profound mystery about the matter of the love between a man and a woman. We may use words like chemistry, or compatibility, but at the end of the day this is something we really cannot get our heads around.

Crude in abuse. After these four 'mysteries' the writer adds a fifth 'way' – the way of an adulteress. Possibly this is an extension of his thoughts about the fourth. An adulteress negotiates her way into the sexual appetite of a man, exploiting his weakness to her own ends, degrading him by subversively exciting in him passions which should have their proper outlet elsewhere. Eating and wiping her mouth is euphemistic for her illicit sexual relationship. Of course the responsibility lay with the man and he allowed himself to be dragged into sin. And that is her excuse. 'It was his choice. He didn't have to do what he did. That is his problem, not mine.'

There are many things in life which we do not understand and which should make us marvel. In all of them we should recognise the greatness of God's creation and man's place in it. It is right that man should stand in awe of it, respect it ... and use it properly.

30:21-23. Observe – and be perplexed. Some things which happen in life seem all too unreasonable, as if they ought not to be allowed to happen. There is an incongruity about them which makes us feel uncomfortable, that this is not the way things are supposed to be working out. Here are some of them.

Power in the wrong hands. First of all, we should not mistake the matter and read the first case as if it were wrong for a servant to rise to power and influence and leadership. There are times in history where this has happened. Joseph started in Egypt as a slave, and eventually he rose to become second only to Pharaoh. By that time, however, he was far from being a servant! The picture here is of someone who really is still a servant holding the reins of power, a position for which he is ill equipped. He may be in that position because no one more suitable was found. We are looking at the wrong man in the job. How often do we see this! We say, 'That person is in the wrong job.' Sometimes we mean that they should be in a much higher position. At other times, however, we mean that they should never have been given that job at all and that their management of their responsibility is woefully deficient. The earth might well tremble when the wrong people hold power in their hands and do not know how to use it!

Insufferable folly. The next example may remind us of the parable of the rich fool (Luke 12:16-21). A fool filled with food only provides further opportunity for his folly. Nabal was a fool, and that was his name (1 Samuel 25). The word denotes not just ignorance or stupidity, but carries with it the notion of moral corruption, of wickedness, of godlessness. How many people there are in the world who are well off, well satisfied, fat cats who preen themselves. There seems an injustice about it. They are doing so well but are actually benefiting no one but themselves. It is a disturbing aspect of society when this kind of thing can go on unchecked. Even for his own sake, a fool ought to suffer for his folly, for then he might even possibly learn some sense! Ecclesiastes 8:14 picks up on this.

A loveless marriage. In the third example we are looking at a woman who is either hated or hateful, having or gaining a husband. Commentators differ on how to take this. At least it should elicit surprise. In general in such cases there is a feeling that something has gone wrong somewhere, that it is almost a denial of what the married state ought to be like.

Exploitation. The fourth example is not indicating a closeness of affection between maidservant and mistress, but rather exploitation of the mistress by her maidservant. The mistress has allowed her maidservant to rule the roost. Domestic management has been turned on its head and the servant has been allowed to become an overbearing tyrant.

What is the common denominator in all these cases? It is in the subject of each: the servant, the fool, the hated woman and the maidservant. It is perhaps in their reaction to the position in which they find themselves. In each case they think of themselves more highly than is appropriate, and hence of others less highly than is appropriate.

30:24-28. Observe – and be instructed. The sage now turns his attention to creatures which are often overlooked or regarded as insignificant. He is showing us that there is something to learn from aspects of their behaviour. There is much we can learn from the natural world if we give our mind to it.

Provision. The ant was referred to at 6:6 as harvesting its food at the appropriate time. Ants may not be strong, but their industry more than makes up for their lack in this department. We may not be strong or significant either, but if we have the wisdom to know when and how to work we shall not lack provision.

Safety. Rock badgers, or rock hyraxes, are small and basically defenceless mammals, and yet their organisation and mastery of the rocky crags where they dwell gives them security. God is described as a rock of salvation, a rock of defence and a rock of refuge for his people (Psalms 31:2; 62:2; 89:26; 94:22). We will flee to him when we understand our weakness and vulnerability; in trusting him we will find protection, safety and security.

Cooperation. Working together, advancing systematically, a swarm of locusts will strip vegetation bare. 'Doing it together' – and that without leadership – is what makes them so formidable. If we want to get something of consequence done we will often not achieve it on our own. We need to learn to work with others, to organise things together, and to go forward together to get the job done.

Overcoming. The 'spider' (NKJV) is probably actually a lizard of some kind (NIV, ESV). If the gecko is in view here, its amazing expertise in climbing surfaces which other creatures cannot negotiate enables it to gain entry to places inaccessible to others. If it uses its skill to 'get to the top' maybe we ought to think about what our God-given skills can achieve.

In all four instances there is an actual or implied 'yet'. In spite of supposed lack of size, or strength, and in the face of supposed deficiency, yet something of real significance is achieved.

Christians may wish they were somebodies when they feel they are nobodies; they may wish they were strong when they are weak; they may wish they had some superior gifts when they have so little to offer. They worry about what they have not got instead of using what they *have* been given; they focus upon what they cannot achieve themselves instead of working with others.

God has made us as we are, and what we are. If we have the wisdom to be diligent with what we have, to *use* what he has given, to add our small contribution in serving with others, to display some tenacity with a God-given objective in view, in dependence upon the empowering of his Spirit, then there may yet be a 'yet' in our lives! 'She seemed to have everything against her and there was nothing special about her. Yet look at how the Lord used her and what was achieved through her!'

30:29-31. Observe – and stand your ground. Agur now looks at some examples of dignified, stately movement. Look at how they walk, and why. Then ask yourself the same questions – that is, how you walk, and why.

Look at them. The lion is not misnamed the king of beasts. Its walk and demeanour show it to be completely fearless. It moves with the elegance and confidence of a top predator.

The next one, literally, 'one whose waist is girded' possibly refers to a strutting rooster (NIV, ESV) rather than a greyhound (AV, NKJV), though we cannot be sure. The cock certainly struts around with the pride of ownership.

The male goat traverses the most formidable of terrain with grace and sure-footed ease. There is nothing clumsy or uncertain about the way it moves.

The final example is that of a king in the midst of his army over which he has charge and full control and in which he has complete confidence.

But what have these things to say to us? They are all in their element; they are masters of their domain. Consequently they are fearless and confident. Our observation of them calls for a measure of admiration and wonder.

Look at you. So, what about you? How do you conduct yourself, you who are made in the image of God?

Paul said, 'If God is for us, who can be against us?' (Romans 8:31). If the creatures or people of these examples have proper cause to be bold and fearless, so do Christians because God is for them. Christians should conduct themselves with a dignity and confidence which befits their status in Christ. For he is King of kings and Lord of lords (Revelation 17:14; 19:16). He is the one who controls the elements, who has all creation at his command (Psalm 96:10) and who is head over all things to the church (Ephesians 1:22). Christians can hold their heads high because they are heirs of all that God has promised them, and they are under the lordship of Jesus Christ who has overcome and who now reigns at his Father's right hand in glory.

Christians are truly humble when they have a proper pride in their Lord Jesus, showing it in this life by fearlessness of others, of threats or of circumstances. By faith in Christ we can resist the devil, though he is like a roaring lion (1 Peter 5:8).

Apostolic example. The apostle Paul, even in chains, conducted himself with dignity, for he knew that God was fully in control of all that was happening to him. He affirmed this in Philippians 1:12-14 and it was his stance in adversity which emboldened others to follow his example. There is no place for a Christian either to cringe or capitulate to opposition or to behave in an undignified manner unworthy of the gospel. We are to walk in a manner worthy of God (1 Thessalonians 2:12). There is every reason to move through this life with quiet, unruffled assurance that we are heirs of God and joint heirs with Christ (Romans 8:17), called into his own kingdom and glory.

30:32-33. The cost of getting one's own way.

Status and stature. The previous verses provide no grounds for self-exaltation. We are to humble ourselves under God's mighty hand and cast all our care upon him (1 Peter 5:6-7). We are very foolish if we begin to think we are anything in ourselves, anything apart from what we are by the grace of God. When the apostle Paul declared that he worked harder than any of the other apostles, he was careful to emphasise that it was all by the grace of God – God's grace toward him, and God's grace with him. There is a difference between exalting oneself and standing tall. The believer has been given status in Christ, and therefore should have stature in his or her way of life.

Repudiation of this folly. One of the results of exalting oneself is that pride leads directly *and inevitably* to sin, and sin is evil. The Scriptures tell us to humble ourselves under the mighty hand of God, that *he* may exalt us at the proper time (1 Peter 5:6; compare Matthew 23:12). They tell us not to think of ourselves more highly than we ought but to think with sober judgement (Romans 12:3). Self-exaltation is sin. It involves devising means by which others will think more highly of us than is our proper due. All too often it so natural to the sinful human heart that it is not identified and acknowledged. Self-exaltation and devising evil are very closely connected. However, when its ugly characteristics are recognised by the offender there is an appropriate response. People clap their hand to their mouth when they realise the enormity of something they have said or done wrong. Although it is too late to recall what has been said or done, it is not too late to prevent further folly.

Thus the writer is indicating that as soon as we become aware of such foolish misconduct we are immediately to put the lid on it, we are not to let it continue.

Result of this folly. We now have illustrated for us what will happen if we fail to desist from proud folly. Go on churning the milk, and butter will inevitably be produced; go on wringing the nose, and it will soon bleed profusely. Go on forcing the anger which accompanies pride, and the result will be strife.

'Churning', 'wringing', 'forcing' (33) (or equivalent words in other translations) are different renderings of the same word aimed at bringing out the full meaning.

Reflection on this folly. Is there anything you are forcing in order to produce what you want? People who want their own way often use force of one kind or another: force of personality, force of words, force to manipulate people and situations to achieve their own ends. The result is pain and trouble. The apostle Paul said, 'The servant of the Lord must not strive.' That is, he must not be involved in foolish, self-centred and ignorant disputes, forcing his own way, but should teach God's Word with humility, gentleness and patience, trusting God to do his own work through his Word (2 Timothy 2:23-26).

Part 6

Proverbs 31:1-9

'The words of King Lemuel'

31:1-9. Power with principles. We have no idea who king Lemuel was, nor does it matter. What does matter is that these are words addressed to a king, or to one about to become a king, and that their teaching applies very well to any in, or aspiring to, positions of authority over others. This would include pastors and teachers and church elders – see 1 Timothy 3:1-7 and how the qualities there tie in with what this passage is saying.

The force of the questions is 'What do you think you are up to?', or, 'What are you contemplating?'

These are the words of a mother to the son she loves, the son she brought into the world and nurtured, the son concerning whom she made vows. To a man in his position there are certain things he should avoid like the plague, and yet they are things which are almost bound to represent powerful temptations to him.

Women. The first is in the area of his sexuality. Many of the kings of those days had many wives and concubines. It was almost expected of them, as a status symbol to mark their power and position. If that was not bad enough, it often led on to open debauchery. These were deceptive pleasures, which destroyed their moral fibre, and then destroyed them.

Wine. The second is in the area of drink. Feasting and banqueting were part of the way of life of kings, with their social engagements and the entertaining of public figures. How easy to indulge like others when the wine ran freely! How easy to get a taste for the liquor and allow it to addle the senses! But the king needed his senses fully with him at all times. Under the influence of alcohol he could and would go astray, and fail to administer justice which was his responsibility.

Self-indulgence destroys sound judgement. Strong drink has a place, to be sure, says Lemuel's mother, to provide some small relief to those in extreme distress (vv. 6-7), but it is certainly not for those in authority who need their wits about them.

Opportunities to abuse what is proper in the areas of sex and alcohol have led to the downfall of many a leader and to the perversion of justice. Powerful temptation in these areas needs to be combated by more powerful principles.

The exhortation of these verses is strong, appealing to a mother's love and vows, to the law and justice, and to the cause of the needy. Only the weak and heartless could shut these out.

Word. The king was never to forget the law, the word of God (v. 5). Indeed, the king was supposed both to write for himself a copy of the law and to read it from day to day throughout his life (Deuteronomy 17:18-20) to the end that he might properly administer justice.

Work. In particular, as appears from vv. 5,8,9, he was to work for the administration of justice, to see that those obtained justice who could so easily be overlooked. It involved initiative on his part. Justice is not a passive thing, meted out to those who apply for it. Those who are to administer it are supposed to be active, with eyes and ears open with a view to rectifying any signs of injustice. The afflicted, those who could not speak for themselves, the poor and needy – these were the people who in all likelihood would not be in a position to seek justice. They could easily be downtrodden. The king was to take the initiative for them, looking out for them and opening his mouth on their behalf.

Does this not remind us of our Lord Jesus, seeking and going after his lost sheep? Power and compassion seldom go hand in hand, but they are seen in our Saviour and are to be emulated by any who have, or aspire to, influence in this world.

Part 7

Proverbs 31:10-31

The virtuous wife

It might appear that these verses are a continuation of the words of Lemuel's mother, perhaps countering what she said in v. 3 with the kind of woman her son should seek as a wife. But because the *Septuagint* separates vv. 1-9 from vv. 10-31 by five chapters it is likely that these verses come from an independent source.

Wisdom personified? Because of their content and their affinity with other parts of the book some have suggested that these verses are allegorising wisdom, as in 1:20-33; 8:1–9:12 where wisdom is personified as a woman. This is the way Gary Brady interprets this section (*Heavenly Wisdom*, page 801: 'It appears to be a recommendation to marry Lady Wisdom'). Undoubtedly this interpretation has strong appeal because wisdom is certainly evident throughout the passage.

If we ask why wisdom should be personified as a woman in the Book of Proverbs, maybe the answer is to be found in the role of woman at creation, that she was created to be an appropriate helper to man, to be his complement in the sense of companionship and function, and that without their union he would not be complete (Genesis 2:18,20,23,24). By analogy that is true of the wisdom we all need to become part of us, with which we need to be united heart and soul.

However, the other passages refer very specifically to wisdom (1:20; 8:1) and then use the personal pronoun 'she' of wisdom; whereas this does not do so but simply refers to a woman, her husband, her children, her household and her conduct – and the whole is applicable to a woman *of wisdom*. Furthermore, v. 30 refers to 'a woman who fears the LORD' being praised, which would hardly fit if the passage were allegorising wisdom.

It is natural, then, to take this closing section at its face value, that it is actually speaking of a woman and, as is evident from the content, a wife, and that it is highlighting some of the many virtues to be recognised in a godly wife who exemplifies the wisdom found in the earlier chapters of the book. If *Proverbs* has focused largely upon the man in his sphere of living, here we find focus upon the woman in the domestic sphere.

The Book of Proverbs, while favourably acknowledging the good wife (12:4; 18:22; 19:14), has made disparaging observations of some women, including the adulteress (2:16) and the prostitute (7:10; 23:27), those who are foolish (9:13-17), those lacking discretion (11:22), those who bring shame (12:4), and the quarrelsome and contentious (21:9,19; 25:24; 27:15). This passage contrasts the situation where those negative qualities are absent, highlighting the positive qualities which are present. (This criticism of women is not at all one-sided, though, because *Proverbs* exposes the faults of men as well as women, and probably more so.)

Furthermore, the book opens with an address to the 'young man' and 'my son' (1:4,8), with the desire that the son might become wise. What he needs to be alongside him as his companion and helper is a wise woman, and this passage points to the kind of qualities to be found in such a woman.

Spelling it out. The twenty-two verses form an acrostic, each verse beginning with a different letter of the Hebrew alphabet, in sequence. This would have helped to make it memorable in the original language. Here is the A to Z of a godly woman!

Peter describes the wife as the weaker vessel (1 Peter 3:7). Though she may be physically weaker, as well as being weaker in the sense of being dependent, that is where it ends. In giving her the honour that is her due, she may prove to be of inestimable value to her husband. Husband and wife are heirs together of the grace of life. There is a *togetherness* about it which, through their complementary roles, leads to mutual comfort and blessing. This is very clear in these verses in Proverbs which show us a woman of strength – strength of character, of industry, of wisdom.

Key qualities. The book of Proverbs closes, then, with something of a eulogy on the virtuous wife. However, it is not 'over-the-top', it is not an example of unattainable perfection. It is not even a model for wives. Rather, it sets out with reference to a few examples the kind of qualities which characterise a wife of whom her husband can justly be proud.

Look carefully and notice just how much there is in these verses which speak of love, security, trust, happiness, well-being, worth, fulfilment, satisfaction. Here is a relationship of a kind which all husbands and wives should desire. Here is a picture of domestic stability, security and strength which demonstrates the fundamental importance of the family unit in society, and a large part of that is attributable to the woman.

How do you relate? Before we proceed to look further at this passage, read through it and look closely at what is there about the relationship between the man and his wife and ask if these things are true of your relationship with your spouse (if you are married) or if you see evidences of these things in the lives of other families around you.

31:10-12. Introducing the lady.

Searching. We do not know who is asking the question. Suffice it to say that the question is asked, and it is an important one. The word translated 'virtuous' (NKJV), 'of noble character' (NIV), 'excellent' (ESV), is wide ranging in its meaning, covering all kinds of excellence.

Recognising. The very first thing to note here is that charm and beauty are not included in this description (see v. 30)! A man may be attracted to a woman on account of her looks, or her deportment, or her vivacity, or some other outward characteristic, but if that is virtually all there is to her he will soon be disappointed. A man on the lookout for a good wife will do well to study the qualities in this description. It should make him ask two questions: first, whether he is worthy of such a companion; second, if he can give to her all that she deserves.

Valuing. How much would you be prepared to pay for such a woman if you could buy her? How much is she worth? Rubies – beautiful and precious stones of very great value, are beyond the reach of most to possess. The value of a 'virtuous' woman is not only above the value of rubies, it is *far* above their value. We are not really on a scale of comparison here. Men – if you look after the things you value, will you not take care of what is of inestimable value?

Trusting. To whom would you be prepared to entrust for safe keeping something in your possession which is very precious and fragile? Knowing it is possible to trust a person and to be let down you would be especially careful in such a case. The kind of trust described in v. 11 is one of complete confidence in one of whom there can be no doubt. This husband has a wife to whom he may entrust his *heart* without any qualms of misgiving. This means his heart is open to her, he holds no secret from her. At the point at which he is most vulnerable, where he would most easily be hurt, he is safe with her. Whatever the circumstances, she is there for him – actively so.

Delighting. Many books feature people searching out great treasure or even stumbling upon it accidentally. Second to romance it fires the imagination. The 'gain' of v. 11 is a word used of 'spoil' or 'plunder', where all manner of good things are there simply for the taking. What more could a man want? The man with such a wife as is described here will have no lack of gain. This is connected with his complete confidence in her. This verse is saying that the man who finds a virtuous wife is in a sense much in the same position insofar as he will find delight in what he gains from her. He will be immeasurably enriched by her. He will not need to look elsewhere to make up any shortfall in what is of value to him.

Blessing. If it is a man's responsibility to provide for his wife and family (which it is), we see what a blessing to him she is throughout her life. 'All the days of her life' shows her faithfulness, that she does not deviate from her purpose. She may be depended upon because to do him good is her purpose in life. She recognises and seeks to fulfil her God-given role as a helper to her husband (Genesis 2:18), as one who by complementarity makes him complete. Her sense of being needed, of being valued, of having something vital to offer, contribute to her delight and sense of fulfilment in her life.

31:13-20. The lady at home. In these verses we see something of the unique gifts God has given to woman, and how therefore she is able to do her husband good.

She is a model of industry in the domestic sphere (vv. 13-15). Her seeking wool and flax would be for clothing and furnishings. Linen is made from flax and linen garments are hard-wearing, absorbent and comfortably cool in hot weather. The word in v. 13 indicates it is her *pleasure* to work with her hands, and this is exemplified in the verses which follow. When it comes to feeding her household, she is not scraping together just anything that comes to hand. The merchant ships went out on a quest for profitable trade, to bring back quality goods, and this wife is likened to them, taking care to put good food on the table which will be appreciated and enjoyed by all.

She is resourceful and shrewd (vv. 16-19). Hers is no nine to five occupation! She is willing to be up before daybreak (v. 15a) and to continue beyond nightfall (v. 18b). What is she doing all this time? She is feeding her immediate and extended household (v. 15), and she is working with the materials she has bought (vv. 13,19) to provide clothing and coverings. More than that, though, we see her exercising initiative, looking ahead, planning for the future for her family, renewing and adding to her resources (v. 16).

She leads by example (v. 15). Notice this reference to her maidservants. They are there, of course, to serve her, but she does not sit back and expect them to do everything or demand that they be up before dawn and work late into the evening at her beck and call. They are part of her household and she treats them with dignity and respect, providing for them from the fruit of her hard work. It is a mark of her appreciation of them that she so treats them.

She has 'get up and go' (vv. 17-19). There is something very positive about her attitude (v. 17). Her taste of success in her labours (v. 18a) energises her to work on when others might stop (v. 18b). So we see her spinning wool (v. 19) in preparation for the next project she has in mind.

She is kind and compassionate (v. 20). This is not a woman who is just wrapped up in her family, for she is involved in the society in which she lives, engaging with the needs which surround her and interacting with others. More than merely responding to begging, she is actively on the lookout to be of help to others in need.

If you are a wife in the home, it is good to stop and think about what you are doing, about what motivates you and what you hope to achieve.

If you are a husband, it is good to stop and think about how you can help and encourage your wife to fulfil her potential, and express appreciation for all that she does.

If you are neither of these, it is good to stop and think about your potential role if applicable, or how you might pray for couples you know to find the kind of fulfilment expressed in this passage.

31:21-27. The lady in society.

She makes provision for hard times (vv. 21-22). The cold of snow is given as an example. Perhaps the references to scarlet and purple conjure up a mental image of rich warmth set against the cold white backdrop. Just as such clothing provides security against the ravages of frost, so the fruit of her industry secures the comfort of her family. It is a matter of prudence with her to have reserves to see them through lean times should they arise. This is in marked contrast to those who live to the limit of their resources without due regard for possible consequences.

She is a credit to her husband (v. 23). In the context, her husband being known 'in the gates' is clearly intended to be a reflection upon *her* character. Whatever his merits, his position of prominence among the elders of the people is largely attributable to his having a worthy wife behind him.

She has skills with which to trade (v. 24). Her abilities extend beyond the family and she uses them to advantage. In so doing others benefit, too.

She acquires a reputation (v. 25). Women are often very particular about their clothing and appearance and – within limits – rightly so! A woman shoddily dressed or dishevelled is no credit to herself or her family. We have just been reading about her clothing in vv. 21-22. However, under the metaphor of v. 25 we now see how she is *really* clothed! She is recognised as a woman of strength of character, of dignity and honour. These are characteristics which will not fade with time or wear out or lose their beauty. No, they are good for all time!

Her speech is edifying (v. 26). What she has to say (unlike the idle gossip for which many women are known) is worth hearing and does good. The expression 'law of kindness' combines two words which we would not normally associate. What it conveys is that kindness is in her nature and that to be kind is a moral precept with her.

She is actively protective (v. 27). By watching over the ways of her household she is looking to their future, thinking about their well-being. She is not content to sit back and take things as they come ('eat the bread of idleness') but is applying her wisdom and her tongue as well as her work to ensure good for their future as far as is in her power.

31:28-31. The last word.

Honour (v. 28). Those closest to her, for whom the lady has toiled and laboured with love, *rise up* and call her blessed. This rising up is something of a public acknowledgement. It is a deliberate act. The real blessing to her is to enjoy her children who have turned out so well as to value the things she values and to have responded in such a way to the love she has poured into their lives over the years.

Praise (v. 29). The last word belongs to the husband, who has unreservedly given her his heart. He acknowledges that there are many women out there who have done well (virtuously, as in v. 10), but none can hold a candle to her.

Love. The word 'love' is nowhere to be found in this passage, and yet love pervades the whole. Here is a woman who is loved, for her husband's heart is hers (v. 11). But to that love she adds value, upon that love she builds, under that love her character has the opportunity to develop and blossom as she is enabled to fulfil her God-given role as a 'help-meet' for him, so that in the end both his life and his love for her are immeasurably richer and fuller as he receives from and responds to this wide ranging, practical expression of her love for him.

The logical conclusion (vv. 30-31). 'Logical' sounds rather cold, but this is far from cold! 'Charm' is really 'favour'. To say that it is deceitful is meaning that someone can be in favour one moment and out of it the next! No one can rely upon being in favour with anyone! Then, as we all know, a woman's beauty (at least, her outward beauty) does not last all that long. What is established upon favour and beauty is bound sooner or later to come crashing down. The wife of noble character is building upon more substantial things than these. Her virtue is identified as having its foundation in the fear of the Lord (v. 30), and likewise its outworking (v. 31). It may be her husband who is in the gates while she is elsewhere attending to her domestic affairs. However, his very presence there, and the kind of man he is through his wife's support, prudence and love, proclaims her merit before all, not to mention the reputation she has gained in other ways. For one who has put so much in, it is only right that she should be rewarded for her efforts. What Paul said about the farmer and his crops (2 Timothy 2:6) surely applies here.

What really constitutes 'the fruit of her hands' (v. 31)? Possibly it could refer in part to the things she has manufactured, but does it not really refer to her receiving back from her children and husband the love and care she has invested in them?

This passage sets before us the unique role a woman has in the home and in society. She is indispensable to her husband, and she is indispensable to those among whom she lives and works. Because of her, and the way she fulfils her role, we see here family life at its best, as it ought to be, strong and secure with dignity and honour, a power for blessing in society. We see a family living contentedly, securely, happily, under the fear of the Lord.

The proverbs, which commenced with a father's instructions to his son (1:8), conclude with the praise of a wife and mother.

Word index

Compiled from chapter 10 onwards, this lists words used in the New King James Version and where they are to be found. If a word appears more than once it indicates different words in the original. Strong's numbers are given in parentheses.

Profits (lit fruit of the hands) (6529/3709)
31:16

Prolong (0748)   28:2,16

Prolong (3254)   10:27

Promptly (7836)   13:24

Prospect (an end) (0319)   24:14,20

Prosper (6743)   28:13

Prosper, to (7919)   17:8

Prospered, to be (1878)   28:25

Prolong (3254)   10:27

Prolong (0748)   28:16

Proud (1343)   15:25; 16:19

Proud (1362)   16:5

Proud (7342)   21:4; 28:25

Proud (2086)   21:24

Proverb (4912)   26:7,9

Provide (–)   27:26

Provide (5414)   31:15

Provoke to anger (5674)   20:2

Prudent (separate mentally) (0995)   16:21;
18:15

Prudent (crafty, subtle) (6175)   12:16,23;
13:16; 14:8,15,18; 22:3; 27:12

Prudent (to make bare) (6191)   15:5

Prudent (circumspect) (7919)   19:14

Pull down (2040)   14:1

Punish, to (6064)   17:26; 21:11; 22:3; 27:12

Punishment (6066)   19:19

Purchase price (4242)   17:16

Pure (clear, clean) (2134)   16:2; 20:11; 21:8

Pure (free from impurity) (2889)   15:26; 30:12

Pure (bright, uncontaminated) (2891)   20:9

Pure (6884)   30:5

Purity (2889/2890)   22:11

Purple (0713)   31:22

Purse, to (7169)   16:30

Pursue (7291)   11:19; 13:21; 19:7; 28:1

Put down, or lower (8213)   25:7

Put out, to (1846)   13:9; 20:20; 24:20

Quarrel (1566)   17:14; 20:3

Quarrel (7379)   26:17

Quick-tempered (soon angry) (7116/0639)
14:17

Quietness (7962)   17:1

Rage (5674)   14:16

Rage, to (7264)   29:9

Rage against (1566)   18:1

Rags (7168)   23:21

Rain (as in a shower) (1653)   25:14,23

Rain (4306)   26:1; 28:3

Rain, latter (4456)   16:15

Rainy (very) (5464)   27:15

Rank (2686)   30:27

Ransom (3724)   13:8; 21:18

Rashly devote (3216)   20:25

Rather than (0408)   17:12

Raven (6158)   30:17

Reach out (7971)   31:20

Reap (7114)   22:8

Rebellion (4805)   17:11

Rebuke (1606)   13:1,8; 17:10

Rebuke (3198)   19:25; 24:25; 25:12; 28:23;
30:6

Rebuke (8433)   13:18; 15:31,32; 27:5; 29:1,15

Receive, to (take, accept, etc) (3947)   10:8;
21:11

Receive, to (admit, take, choose) (6901) 19:20

Receive, to (hedge about, guard, attend to)
(8104)   15:5

Recompense (1576)   12:14

Recompense (7999)   11:31; 20:22

Reconsider (1239)   20:25

Red (0119)   23:31

Redeemer (1350)   23:11

Redness (2448)   23:29

Refining pot (4715)   17:3; 27:21

Scripture reference index

Note: rather than giving page numbers, the references are to the verse(s) of *Proverbs* where they appear in this exposition.

Bibliography

The following have been the principal sources of reference in preparing this exposition:

Bridges, Charles, *A Commentary on Proverbs* (The Banner of Truth Trust, 1968).

Kidner, Derek, *Proverbs* (Tyndale Old Testament Commentaries, Inter-Varsity Press, 1964).

Atkinson, David, *The Message of Proverbs* (Inter-Varsity Press, 1996).

Lane, Eric, *Proverbs* (Christian Focus Publications, 2000).

Brady, Gary, *Heavenly Wisdom* (Evangelical Press, 2003).

Newheiser, Jim, *Opening Up Proverbs* (Day One, 2008).

CHRIST IN CHRISTIAN TRADITION

VOLUME TWO: PART TWO

Christ in Christian Tradition

CHRIST
IN CHRISTIAN
TRADITION

VOLUME TWO

*From the Council of Chalcedon (451)
to Gregory the Great (590–604)*

PART TWO
*The Church of Constantinople
in the sixth century*

ALOYS GRILLMEIER SJ

in collaboration with

THERESIA HAINTHALER

translated by
JOHN CAWTE
&
PAULINE ALLEN

MOWBRAY   WJK

Published in Great Britain by **Mowbray**, A Cassell imprint, Wellington House, 125 Strand, London WC2R 0BB

Published in the United States by **Westminster John Knox Press**, 100 Witherspoon Street, Louisville, Kentucky 40202-1396

German original published as *Jesus der Christus im Glauben der Kirche*, Band 2/2, © Verlag Herder, Freiburg im Breisgau 1989
English translation © Mowbray, a Cassell imprint, 1995

English translation first published 1995

Imprimi potest: Jörg Dantscher SJ
Praep. Prov. Germ. Sup. SJ
Monachii, die 13 Aprilis 1989

British Library Cataloguing-in-Publication Data
A catalogue record for this book is available from the British Library.

ISBN 0-264-67261-5

Library of Congress Cataloging-in-Publication Data
(Revised for volume 2, part 2)
Grillmeier, Aloys, date.
Christ in Christian tradition.
Author statement varies.
Edition statement varies.
Includes bibliographical references and indexes.
Contents: v. 1. From the apostolic age to Chalcedon (451) — v. 2. From the Council of Chalcedon (451) to Gregory the Great (590–604). Pt. 1. Reception and Contradiction. Pt. 2. The Church of Constantinople in the sixth century.
1. Jesus Christ — History of doctrines — Early church, ca. 30–600.
I. Title.
BT198.G743 1975 232'.09 75-13456
ISBN 0-664-21997-7 (v. 2, pt. 2)

The publication of this book has been assisted by a contribution from Inter Nationes, Bonn.

Typeset by Colset Private Ltd, Singapore
Printed and bound in Great Britain by Mackays of Chatham plc

DOMINO FRANCISCO CARDINALI KOENIG
DIALOGI CUM ECCLESIIS ORIENTALIBUS PROMOTORI
ET
INSTITUTIONI 'PRO ORIENTE'
AB IPSO FUNDATAE

With this second part of Volume Two of *Christ in Christian Tradition* the real depiction of post-Chalcedonian christology up to the emergence of Islam begins. Our gaze is directed to the whole *orbis christologicus* in the period from 451 to roughly 620, at first to the *orbis orientalis* and then to the *orbis occidentalis*. We shall endeavour to grasp the unfolding of faith in Jesus Christ for each of the individual partial regions separately according to patriarchates and catholicates, in order to bring into view not only the unity in faith but also the peculiarity of the different Churches. Within the *orbis orientalis* we shall begin with the Patriarchate of Constantinople (Volume Two, Part Two); then there follow the Patriarchates of Jerusalem and Antioch; connected with these is the Armenian and Georgian history of christology for the period indicated. In addition there is the Persian Church ('Nestorians') outside the Byzantine Empire. These will be included together in Volume Two, Part Three. The depiction of the history of the post-Chalcedonian Church of Alexandria, together with Nubia and Ethiopia (Volume Two, Part Four), has already been published in German. Finally, the christology of the *orbis christologicus occidentalis* (between 451 and Gregory the Great (d. 604)) has already been researched to a great extent.

Volume Two, Part Two has been produced with the collaboration of Dr Theresia Hainthaler, who also prepared the manuscript of the German text on a wordprocessor, proof-read and edited it. She participated as well in the research itself, especially in this volume where the end of the Justinianic era was concerned. The Deutsche Forschungsgemeinschaft made this collaboration of Dr Hainthaler possible from 1986 to 1991. Up to 1986 it financed the collaboration of Dr H.-J. Höhn; some sections of the results of his research can be published here. We are very grateful for this support. From 1991 onwards the collaboration of Dr Hainthaler has been financed by the North German Province of the Jesuits, for which we are also extremely grateful. For generous financial support we thank the British Province of the Jesuits, especially Fr Ennis SJ (Province Treasurer), and also Dr Bernhard Duvenbeck, Bad Homburg.

The present English translation of Volume Two, Part Two, which has been checked and authorized by us, was again undertaken by Professor Pauline Allen and John Cawte. This was all the more important as Pauline Allen, in her Byzantine research, covers the same period handled here. Her specialized knowledge enabled her to master the difficult problems of translation and to find the exact expression. John Cawte, a lecturer in philosophy, was equally able to conceptualize the difficult subject-matter and translate in a very careful and precise way. We extend our sincere thanks to them both.

This volume is dedicated, as the German edition has already been, to Cardinal Franz König, retired Archbishop of Vienna, and to Pro Oriente, the foundation established by him; both are promoters of ecumenical dialogue with the Churches of the East.

Frankfurt am Main, 2 February 1993   Aloys Grillmeier SJ
on the Feast of Hypapante (Presentation of the Lord)

CONTENTS

PART ONE
THE ANTI-CHALCEDONIAN POLE
THE CHRISTOLOGY OF PATRIARCH SEVERUS
OF ANTIOCH

PART THREE
THE THEOLOGICAL ACTIONS UNDERTAKEN BY JUSTINIAN I
(518–527 and 527–565)

ABBREVIATIONS

ABAW.PH	*Abhandlungen der Bayerischen Akademie der Wissenschaften*, Munich, Philosophisch-historische Abteilung, NF 1, 1929ff.
ABG	*Archiv für Begriffsgeschichte*, Bonn 1, 1955.
ACO	Acta Conciliorum Oecumenicorum, ed. E. Schwartz, Strasbourg, Leipzig, Berlin; T. IV, vol. 1ff. ed. J. Straub (1971ff.); 2nd series ed. R. Riedinger (1984ff.).
AGWG.PH	*Abhandlungen der Gesellschaft der Wissenschaften zu Göttingen*, Göttingen, Philologisch-historische Klasse NS 1, 1986/87ff.
AHC	*Annuarium Historiae Conciliorum*, Amsterdam 1, 1969ff.
ALW	*Archiv für Liturgiewissenschaft*, Regensburg 1, 1959ff.
AnBoll	*Analecta Bollandiana*, Brussels 1, 1882ff.
AnCl	*Antiquité classique*, Brussels 1, 1932ff.
AnGreg	*Analecta Gregoriana*, Rome 1, 1930ff.
ASS	Acta Sanctorum
Aug	*Augustinianum*, Rome 1, 1961ff.
BBA	Berliner byzantinistische Arbeiten
BHO	Bibliotheca hagiographica orientalis, ed. soc. bollandiani, Brussels 1910.
BHTh	Beiträge zur historischen Theologie, Tübingen 12, 1950ff.
BiblMus	Bibliothèque du Muséon, Louvain 1, 1929ff.
Bibl.SS	Bibliotheca sanctorum, Rome 1961–1969.
BKV²	Bibliothek der Kirchenväter, Kempten 1, 2nd edn 1911ff.
BLE	*Bulletin de Littérature Ecclésiastique*, Toulouse, NS 10, 1899ff.; 20, 1899 (= 3rd series 1)ff.; 30, 1909 (= 4th series 1)ff.
BO	J. S. Assemani, Bibliotheca Orientalis Clementino-Vaticana I–III, Rome 1719–28.
BSAC	*Bulletin de la Société d'Archéologie Copte*, Cairo 1, 1938ff.
Burg	*Burgense*, Burgos 1, 1960ff.
Byz	*Byzantion*, Brussels 1, 1924ff.
ByzF	*Byzantinische Forschungen*, Amsterdam 1, 1966ff.
ByzSlav	*Byzantinoslavica*, Prague 1, 1929ff.
ByzZ	*Byzantinische Zeitschrift*, Leipzig, Munich 1, 1892ff.
BZ	*Biblische Zeitschrift*, Freiburg, Paderborn NS 1, 1957ff.
CA	Collectio Avellana = Epistulae imperatorum pontificum aliorum . . . I and II, ed. O. Guenther, Vienna 1895, 1898 = CSEL 35/1-2.
CAG	Commentaria in Aristotelem graeca, edita consilio et auctoritate Academiae litterarum regiae borussicae.
Cath	*Catholica*, Paderborn 1, 1932ff.
CCG	Corpus Christianorum, series graeca, Turnhout 1, 1977ff.
CCL	Corpus Christianorum, series latina, Turnhout 1, 1953ff.
CCT	A. Grillmeier, *Christ in Christian Tradition*, Vol. 1, London, Oxford 2nd edn 1975; Vol. 2, Part 1, London 1987.
CE	Codex Encyclius
Chalkedon	A. Grillmeier / H. Bacht (eds), *Das Konzil von Chalkedon. Geschichte und Gegenwart*, 3 vols, Würzburg 1951-54, 5th edn 1979 (=unaltered impression of the 4th edition with a new preface).

COD	Conciliorum Oecumenicorum Decreta, ed. Istituto per le scienze religiose, Bologna, curantibus J. Alberigo et al., consultante H. Jedin, Bologna 3rd edn 1973.
CollCist	*Collectanea Cisterciensia*, Seourmont 1, 1939ff.
Conc	*Concilium*, Zürich, Mainz, 1965ff.
CPG	Clavis Patrum Graecorum, vols I–IV, Turnhout 1979ff.
CPL	Clavis Patrum Latinorum . . ., ed. E. Dekkers, Steenbrugge 2nd edn 1961.
CrSt	*Cristianesimo nella storia*. Ricerche storiche esegetiche teologiche, Bologna 1, 1980.
CSCO	Corpus scriptorum christianorum orientalium, Rome 1903ff.
CSEL	Corpus scriptorum ecclesiasticorum latinorum, Vienna 1, 1866ff.
DACL	*Dictionnaire d'Archéologie Chrétienne et de Liturgie*, Paris 1, 1924ff.
DEC	*Decrees of the Ecumenical Councils*, ed. N. P. Tanner, London, Washington 1990.
DHGE	*Dictionnaire d'Histoire et de Géographie Ecclésiastique*, Paris 1, 1912ff.
DOP	*Dumbarton Oaks Papers*, Cambridge, Mass. 1, 1941ff.
DOS	*Dumbarton Oaks Studies*, Cambridge, Mass. 1, 1950ff.
DP	Doctrina Patrum de incarnatione verbi, ed. F. Diekamp, Münster 1907, 2nd edition 1981 ed. E. Chrysos.
DS	H. Denzinger / A. Schönmetzer, Enchiridion symbolorum, definitionum et declarationum de rebus fidei et morum, Barcelona 36th edn 1976.
DSp	*Dictionnaire de spiritualité, ascétique et mystique*, Paris 1, 1932ff.
DTC	*Dictionnaire de Théologie Catholique*, Paris 1903–72.
EKL	Evangelisches Kirchenlexikon, Göttingen, 3rd edn, 1, 1986.
EO	*Echos d'Orient*, Bucharest 1, 1897/98–39, 1940/43.
EphThLov	*Ephemerides Theologicae Lovanienses*, Louvain 1, 1924ff.
EstEcl	*Estudios Eclesiásticos*, Madrid 1, 1922ff.
EvTh	*Evangelische Theologie*, Munich NS 1, 1946/7ff.
FCLDG	Forschungen zur christlichen Literatur- und Dogmengeschichte, Paderborn 1, 1900–18, 1938.
FKGG	Forschungen zur Kirchen- und Geistesgeschichte, Stuttgart 1, 1932ff.
FlorCyr	*Florilegium Cyrillianum*
Frend	W. H. C. Frend, *The Rise of the Monophysite Movement*, Cambridge, 1972.
FRLANT	Forschungen zur Religion und Literatur des Alten und Neuen Testaments, Göttingen 1, 1903ff.
FrThSt	*Freiburger Theologische Studien*, Freiburg, Basel, Vienna 1, 1910ff.
GCS	Die Griechischen Christlichen Schriftsteller der ersten drei Jahrhunderte, Berlin 1, 1897ff.
GOF	Göttinger Orientforschung, Wiesbaden.
GOTR	*Greek Orthodox Theological Review*, Brookline, Mass. 1, 1954ff.
Greg	*Gregorianum*, Rome 1, 1920ff.
Grumel, *Regestes*	*Les Regestes des Actes du Patriarcat de Constantinople* I, I, par V. Grumel, 2nd edn 1932.
HDG	Handbuch der Dogmengeschichte, Freiburg, Basel, Vienna, 1956ff.
HE	*Historia Ecclesiastica*
HeyJ	*Heythrop Journal*, Oxford 1, 1960ff.
HistJb	*Historisches Jahrbuch der Görres-Gesellschaft*, Munich, Freiburg 1, 1880ff.
HThR	*The Harvard Theological Review*, Cambridge, Mass. 1, 1908ff.
HTS	Harvard Theological Studies, Cambridge, Mass. 1, 1916ff.
Irén	*Irénikon*, Amay, Chevetogne 1, 1926ff.
ITS	Innsbrucker Theologische Studien, Innsbruck, Vienna 1, 1978ff.
JAC	*Jahrbuch für Antike und Christentum*, Münster 1, 1958ff.
JEH	*Journal of Ecclesiastical History*, London 1, 1950ff.

JLH	*Jahrbuch für Liturgik und Hymnologie*, Kassel 1, 1955ff.
JLW	*Jahrbuch für Liturgiewissenschaft*, Münster 1, 1921–15, 1941.
JÖB	*Jahrbuch der österreichischen Byzantinistik*, Vienna 1, 1951ff.
JSS	*Journal of Semitic Studies*, Manchester 1, 1956ff.
JTS	*Journal of Theological Studies*, Oxford 1, 1899ff.; NS 1, 1950ff.
JW	Regesta Pontificum Romanorum, ed. P. Jaffé, ed. 2a auspiciis G. Wattenbach curaverunt S. Loewenfeld / F. Kaltenbrunner / P. Ewald, Tomus I, Leipzig 1888.
Kl.Pauly	*Der Kleine Pauly. Lexikon der Antike*, 5 vols (ed. K. Ziegler/W. Sonnleitner), Stuttgart 1964–75.
KlT	Kleine Texte für (theologische und philosophische) Vorlesungen und Übungen, Bonn 1, 1902ff.
KlWbChrOr	*Kleines Wörterbuch des Christlichen Orients* (ed. J. Assfalg / P. Krüger), Wiesbaden 1975.
Lampe, *PGL*	*A Patristic Greek Lexicon. With Addenda and Corrigenda*, ed. G. W. H. Lampe, Oxford 2nd edn 1968.
LexMA	*Lexikon des Mittelalters*, Munich, Zürich 1, 1980ff.
LQF	Liturgiewissenschaftliche Quellen und Forschungen, Münster 1, 1909–32, 1957ff.
LThK	*Lexikon für Theologie und Kirche*, ed. J. Höfer / K. Rahner, Freiburg 2nd edn 1957ff.
Mansi	Sacrorum Conciliorum nova et amplissima Collectio (ed. J. D. Mansi) Florence 1769 (often reprinted).
MémTrav	*Mémoires et travaux*, Lille 1, 1905ff.
MGH	Monumenta Germaniae Historica inde ab a.C. 500 usque ad a. 1500, Hanover, Berlin 1, 1877ff.
MSR	*Mélanges de science religieuse*, Lille 1, 1944ff.
Mus	*Le Muséon*, Louvain 1, 1882ff; p. 34, 1921ff.
NAWG.PH	*Nachrichten der Akademie der Wissenschaften in Göttingen*, Philologisch-historische Klasse.
NHSt	Nag Hammadi Studies, Leiden 1, 1971ff.
NRT	*Nouvelle revue théologique*, Louvain 1, 1869–72, 1940ff.
OCA	Orientalia Christiana Analecta, Rome 101, 1935ff.
OCP	*Orientalia Christiana Periodica*, Rome 1, 1935ff.
OLA	Orientalia Lovaniensia Analecta, Louvain, 1975ff.
OLP	*Orientalia Lovaniensia Periodica*, Louvain 1, 1970ff.
OrChr	*Oriens Christianus*, Rome 1, 1901ff; Wiesbaden 37 (= 4th series 1), 1953ff.
OrSyr	*L'Orient syrien*, Paris 1, 1956 – 12, 1967.
ÖstlChr	*Das östliche Christentum*, Würzburg NS 1, 1947ff.
ParOr	*La Parole de l'Orient*, Kaslik 1, 1970ff.
PatSorb	*Patristica Sorbonensia*, Paris 1, 1957ff.
PG	Patrologiae cursus completus. Series graeca (1–161), accurante J.-P. Migne, Paris 1857–1912.
PL	Patrologiae cursus completus. Series latina (1–221), accurante J.-P. Migne, Paris 1841–64.
PLS	Patrologiae latinae supplementum, Paris 1, 1958–5, 1970.
PO	Patrologia Orientalis, ed. R. Graffin / F. Nau, Paris 1, 1907ff.
POC	*Proche-Orient chrétien*, Jerusalem 1, 1951ff.
PRE	*Realencyklopädie für protestantische Theologie und Kirche* 3rd edn, Leipzig 1, 1896 – 24, 1913.
PS	E. Schwartz, *Publizistische Sammlungen zum Acacianischen Schisma* (Munich, 1934).
PTSt	Patristische Texte und Studien, Berlin 1, 1964ff.

PWK	Paulys Real-Encyclopädie der classischen Altertumswissenschaft. Neue Bearbeitung Bd. 1–6 ed. G. Wissowa, Stuttgart 1894–1909; Bd. 7–35 ed. W. Kroll, Stuttgart 1912–37; Bd. 36ff. ed. K. Mittelhaus/K. Ziegler, Stuttgart, Munich, 1947–72.
RAC	Reallexikon für Antike und Christentum, Stuttgart 1, 1950ff.
RevBén	Revue Bénédictine, Maredsous 1, 1884ff.
RevBibl	Revue Biblique, Paris 1, 1892ff.; NS 1, 1904ff.
RevÉtAug	Revue des études augustiniennes, Paris 1, 1955ff.
RevÉtByz	Revue des études byzantines, Paris 4, 1946ff.
RevHistRel	Revue de l'histoire des religions, Paris 1, 1880ff.
RevSR	Revue des sciences religieuses, Strasbourg, Paris 1, 1921ff.
RevThom	Revue Thomiste, Paris NS 1, 1918ff.
RHE	Revue d'histoire ecclésiastique, Louvain 1, 1900ff.
RivArcCr	Rivista di Archeologia Cristiana, Rome/Vatican City 1, 1924ff.
ROC	Revue de l'Orient chrétien, Paris 1, 1896ff.
RömQ	Römische Quartalschrift für christliche Altertumskunde und für Kirchengeschichte, Freiburg, 1887ff.
RSJB	Recueils de la société Jean Bodin pour l'histoire comparative des institutions, Brussels 1, 1936ff.
RSLR	Rivista di Storia e Letteratura religiosa, Florence 1, 1965ff.
RSPT	Revue des sciences philosophiques et théologiques, Paris 1, 1907ff.
RSR	Recherches de science religieuse, Paris 1, 1910ff.
SBAW	Sitzungsberichte der Bayerischen Akademie der Wissenschaften, Munich, Philosophisch-historische Abteilung.
SC	Sources Chrétiennes, Paris 1, 1944ff.
SL	The Sixth Book of the Select Letters of Severus, ed. E. W. Brooks, Vol. II/1, London, Oxford, 1903.
SpicFrib	Spicilegium Friburgense. Texte zur Geschichte des kirchlichen Lebens, Fribourg 1, 1957ff.
SpicSLov	Spicilegium Sacrum Lovaniense, Louvain 1, 1922ff.
ST	Studi e Testi, Vatican City 1, 1900ff.
StRiOrCr	Studi e ricerche sull'oriente cristiano, Rome 1, 1978ff.
StudEph'Aug'	Studia Ephemeridis 'Augustinianum', Rome 1, 1967ff.
StudPat	Studia Patristica, Berlin 1, 1957ff. (= TU 63ff.).
StudTestAnt	Studia et Testimonia Antiqua, Munich 1, 1966ff.
SubsHag	Subsidia Hagiographica (= suppl. AnBoll), Brussels 1, 1886ff.
SymbOsl	Symbolae Osloenses, Oslo 1, 1922ff.
TD	Textus et Documenta (ser. theol.), Rome 1, 1932ff.
ThéolHist	Théologie historique, Paris 1, 1963ff.
TheolPhil	Theologie und Philosophie, Freiburg 41, 1966ff.
ThLZ	Theologische Literaturzeitung, Leipzig 1, 1876ff.
ThQ	Theologische Quartalschrift, Tübingen, Stuttgart 1, 1819ff.
TR	Theologische Revue, Münster 1, 1902ff.
Trad	Traditio. Studies in Ancient and Medieval History, Thought and Religion, New York 1, 1943ff.
TravMém	Travaux et mémoires, Paris 1, 1965ff.
TRE	Theologische Realenzyklopädie, Berlin 1, 1977ff.
TU	Texte und Untersuchungen zur Geschichte der altchristlichen Literatur, Leipzig 1, 1882ff.
TZ	Theologische Zeitschrift, Basel 1, 1945ff.
VC	Vetera Christianorum, Bari, 1964ff.
VigC	Vigiliae Christianae, Amsterdam 1, 1947ff.
WdF	Wege der Forschung, Darmstadt 1, 1956ff.

WuW	*Wort und Wahrheit*, Vienna 1, 1946ff.
WZ(R)	*Wissenschaftliche Zeitschrift der Universität Rostock*, Rostock 1, 1951ff.
ZDMG	*Zeitschrift der deutschen morgenländischen Gesellschaft*, Leipzig 1, 1847ff.
ZKG	*Zeitschrift für Kirchengeschichte*, Gotha, Stuttgart 1, 1877ff.
ZkTh	*Zeitschrift für katholische Theologie*, Innsbruck, Vienna 1, 1876/7ff.
ZNW	*Zeitschrift für die neutestamentliche Wissenschaft und die Kunde der älteren Kirche*, Berlin 1, 1900ff.
ZPE	*Zeitschrift für Papyrologie und Epigraphik*, Bonn 1, 1967ff.
ZSavSt.K	*Zeitschrift der Savigny-Stiftung für Rechtsgeschichte*, Kanonist. Abteilung, Weimar 1, 1911ff.
ZSem	*Zeitschrift für Semitistik und verwandte Gebiete*, Leipzig 1, 1922–10, 1935.
ZThK	*Zeitschrift für Theologie und Kirche*, Tübingen 1, 1891ff.

INTRODUCTION

In terms of theology and ecclesiastical politics the years between 451 and 604, namely between Chalcedon and the year Pope Gregory the Great died, are dominated by the Fourth Ecumenical Council. They represent the first epoch of its subsequent history, which attains its climax and special form in the era of Justinian. The Council of Chalcedon was definitively acknowledged by the Church of the Latin West; in the East by the Patriarchate of Constantinople, by almost half of the Patriarchate of Antioch and by the majority of the Patriarchate of Jerusalem. In contrast it was recognized by only a minority in Alexandria, to whose sphere of influence the large regions of the Sudan and Ethiopia belonged.

The efforts to maintain or re-establish the unity of the Church on the basis of Chalcedon were all the more futile the more the opponents of the Council could either seize the existing ecclesiastical structures or create new ones. Soon after 431 the Nestorians were driven out of imperial territory. Although Chalcedon seemed to offer the possibility of their reconciliation with the Great Church, this hope was not fulfilled. Thus the Church of Nestorius arose. In Syria, within the imperial territory, the so-called Jacobite (Syrian Orthodox) Church was organized. The activity of the monk Jacob (born c. 490, died 578) was decisive here. His epithet was Burd'ānā, the ragged one or the beggar. In Constantinople in 542/543, at the request of the Ghassanids and with the contrivance of the Empress Theodora, he was ordained as the bishop of Syria. This Church expanded beyond the borders of the Empire into Persian Mesopotamia.

Under Patriarch Paul of Beit Ukkāmē (564–577) there was a temporary convergence with Chalcedon. However, it was precisely at this time that the two lines of patriarchs in Syria came to exist, the Old-Oriental Syrian and the Chalcedonian-Byzantine hierarchies. From 551 there was also a Jacobite see for the Arabs. The anti-Chalcedonian propaganda had also reached Armenia, which had already adopted the *Henoticon* of Zeno with approval. At the Synod of Dvin (506/507 and 552) the Armenian Church had professed Severan christology, rejecting that of Julian of Halicarnassus. Together with the Armenian hierarchy at the Synod of Dvin (506/507), Georgia had accepted the *Henoticon*. About 600, however, the Georgian Catholicos, Cyrius, split with the Armenians and accepted the Council of Chalcedon with a strong leaning towards Byzantium. The heaviest loss for the Chalcedonian imperial Church occurred with the decision of the Patriarch of Alexandria against the Fourth Council. We have already followed the development of this struggle to the year 518. Through his flight to Egypt in 518 Patriarch Severus of Antioch became there an immensely powerful resistance figure and was the symbol of opposition to the Fourth Council. This opposition was so persistent that the anti-Chalcedonian hierarchy could definitively establish itself beside that of the Melkite Patriarch Paul of Tabennisi (538–540), who was loyal to Chalcedon. This anti-Chalcedonian hierarchy considered itself as the only legitimate heir of the Patriarchate. Thus from that time on there were two separate ecclesiastical administrations and even two separate Churches.[1] The condemnation of Patriarch Severus at the Synod of Constantinople in 536 completed this development.

This extrinsic process in church history has already been well investigated and may be presupposed as explained. Thus we are able to concentrate entirely on the depiction of the christological movement itself. Its first clearly defined epoch is the period from 451 to 604, the year Pope Gregory died, especially as far as the Latin West is concerned. But also in the East with these first years of the seventh century there was a noteworthy pause, until the appearance of Muhammad heralded a new era. In this way the first phase of post-Chalcedonian christology received a recognizable unity. Even so, we can also establish a clear *division* between 451 and 604. In the first period which we have already described, the question of the reception or non-reception of the Fourth Council was at the forefront of the discussion. 518 marks a change, and the *Henoticon* era is over. Between 451 and 500, besides the question of the reception, whatever occurred in the factual christological discussion could also be treated without special effort in the context of this exposition. The reader will recall the names of Leo I, Gelasius I or Patriarch Gennadius of Constantinople. The strife about the *Henoticon* in no way intended to place the positive proper statement of the Chalcedonian formula in the forefront. On the contrary. Indeed, it was passed over in silence. In the struggle to develop Chalcedonian christology this could only be a disadvantage. Linguistic and conceptual reflection on the

---

1. C. D. G. Müller, *Geschichte der orientalischen Nationalkirchen* (Göttingen, 1981), 327; cf. J. Maspero, *Histoire des patriarches d'Alexandrie* (Paris, 1923), 135–81.

formula of faith of 451 was condemned to a standstill.

In the last decade of the *Henoticon* era, nevertheless, the foundation for the new had already been laid. However much the battle against the detested Council of 451 inflamed the monk Severus, who from 508 to 511 dwelt in Constantinople for that purpose, now opponents appeared who directly compelled discussion of the language and doctrine of the formula of two natures, bypassing completely the conciliar policies of Emperor Anastasius I. We are fortunate that, in the extant polemical theological work of Severus arising from the altercations with his opponents, the whole spectrum of christological positions is sketched which (more or less — modified or expanded) persists throughout the whole of the sixth century. Three of the victims of his polemic belonged to the Chalcedonian camp, while two adhered to the anti-Chalcedonian one. In this settling of accounts, which tolerated no concessions, Severus himself became the father of the 'Severan' christology which was named after him. 'Severan' means without exception 'Cyrillian'. *Severus Antiochenus — Cyrillus Alexandrinus redivivus!* Yet the copy, when contrasted with the original, will exhibit quite a few highlighted lines and a selective narrowing of the picture of Christ. Thus there is good reason to pursue in a detailed analysis Severus the polemicist in his reckoning with his individual opponents and, in doing this, to determine the content of the opposing positions. Altogether, then, we are dealing with the period between 508 and 528, that is, to the year in which the works of the Patriarch that we want to analyse were translated into Syriac and thus were completed. The predominantly thematic altercation between Chalcedon and Severus lasted, however, at least until 536, the year of the condemnation of the Patriarch and his flight to Egypt, which occurred shortly before this. What follows after 536 can — without great effort, some variations being noted — be placed in the framework which had been created by Severus and his opponents on both the Chalcedonian as well as on the anti-Chalcedonian side. The rest of the Justinianic era had expanded this framework but had not breached it. For even such noteworthy affairs as the Origenists' dispute and the condemnation of the Three Chapters, with the Second Council of Constantinople (553) as the culmination, only promoted that neo-Chalcedonian conciliatory theology which had first become evident in the struggle with Severus.

Even though we are capable of grasping completely the christological development between Chalcedon and the death of Gregory the Great in the way just indicated, nevertheless from this analysis not all of the light and shade in the sixth century picture of Christ in the East and West would be visible. For in the first instance we have been concerned with elevated theology. Even if this speculative conceptual discussion furnishes the main lines of the picture of Christ of such a group, still the particular colour tone has not been captured. One need only think of the difference between the *Christus gloriae* of the East and the *Christus patiens* of the West, as the history of art presents this. To enter into this aspect will not be possible in this work. However, it is precisely in the sixth century that the multiplicity of Byzantine hymns offers a rich substitute for this, as do homilies and the liturgy.

In the period with which we are concerned, the form of the Latin West, emerging from the turmoil of the barbarian invasions, becomes visible to a great extent for the first time. In the East, however, on one side Byzantium and Palestine develop as predominantly Chalcedonian regions, whereas on the other Syria, Armenia and Egypt with the Sudan and Ethiopia develop as Severan churches; finally, in Persia Nestorian theology and the Nestorian Church attain great significance. Everywhere it was the question of how Christ is to be understood that still taxed people's minds. Before the invasion of the Arabs the *Orbis christianus* presented itself in singular wholeness as *Orbis christologicus*, the last vision that history allowed. Hence it appears mandatory not to destroy this vision in our presentation by proceeding according to systematic themes, but rather to allow it to light up during a comprehensive, if arduous, research journey, region by region. Perhaps then the result will be that Christianity was more at one in its faith in Christ than it itself was conscious of in the confusion of the conflict.

First, then, we will wander through the *Orbis christologicus orientalis*, from patriarchate to patriarchate, and finally we shall devote ourselves to the *Orbis christologicus occidentalis* in its entirety.

THE PATRIARCHATE OF CONSTANTINOPLE (500-600)

PRELIMINARY CONSIDERATION

Our purpose is to push forward, from the historical regions of the patriarchates as these had been established definitively in the East in 451, to an understanding of the faith in Christ held by the Old-Oriental/Orthodox Churches, which formed themselves out of these in the sixth century, and of the Nestorian Church, which had been separated since Ephesus. Certainly we would rightly begin in Constantinople.[1] Before its gates, across the Sea of Marmara, lay Chalcedon

---

1. The following works provide comprehensive information about Constantinople as a patriarchate: H.-G. Beck, *Kirche und theologische Literatur*, 60–92; 156–88 (on the hierarchical structure of the Patriarchate); R. Potz, *Patriarch und Synode in Konstantinopel. Das Verfassungsrecht des ökumenischen Patriarchats* = *Kirche und Recht* 10 (Vienna, 1971), 17–21; H.-J. Schulz and P. Wiertz, 'Die Orthodoxe Kirche [Ökumenisches Patriarchat]' in W. Nyssen, H.-J. Schulz and P. Wiertz (eds), *Handbuch der Ostkirchenkunde*, Vol. I (Düsseldorf, 1984), 13–17; J. Darrouzès, *Notitiae episcopatuum ecclesiae Constantinopolitanae. Texte critique, introduction et notes* (Paris, 1981); M. Le Quien, *Oriens christianus in quattuor patriarchatus digestus* I (Paris, 1740; new impression Graz, 1958), 1–350; G. Fedalto, *Hierarchia Ecclesiastica Orientalis*, I. *Patriarchatus constantinopolitanus* (Padua, 1988). On the title 'Ecumenical Patriarch' see H.-G. Beck, *Kirche und theologische Literatur*, 63 with literature; R. Potz, *op. cit.*, 29: this expanded title was first used by John IV Nesteutes (582–595) on the occasion of a synod towards the end of 587. John IV used this occasion to attempt 'to contrast his patriarchal see to the other three sees and to make it an oecumenical one, which in essence was primarily intended to say that he was the imperial Patriarch' (*ibid.*). Thus it was a matter of extending the imperial status of the Patriarch. Originally the development in the East proceeded differently. There were five ecclesiastical administrative units which corresponded to the political organization: Egypt, Oriens, Asia, Thrace and Pontus. For this reason the bishops of Alexandria and Antioch possessed old customary rights to their respective regions. The first Churches of the other three units, namely Ephesus in Asia, Heracleia in Thrace and Caesarea in Pontus, either could not acquire such prerogatives or could acquire them only in a restricted manner. Constantinople appeared alongside them as a sixth unit, with a bishop at the top, 'who in precedence, as second behind the bishop of Old Rome, now comes before the bishops of the other Oriental dioceses' (*ibid.*, 20). On the basis of the old division Constantinople thus had neither a patriarchal territory nor a metropolitan one with suffragans attached to it. In the period before the Council of Chalcedon there emerged 'an institution which would be of great significance for the future of the episcopal see. This is the *Synodos endemousa*, a synod whose composition was not predetermined by the ordinary ecclesiastical constitution ... Corresponding to the name, the bishops, who at the time were sojourning (*endemountes*) in the capital, participated. This synod convened only very seldom; it is an extraordinary element of the ecclesiastical constitution which arose through custom' (*ibid.*, 21). Originally it had little to do with the episcopal throne, but in contrast more to do with the Emperor, who, depending upon the occasion, could for serious reasons summon together the bishops who were residing

itself. If a patriarchate were called upon to confess Chalcedonian faith, then it was the Ecumenical Patriarchate. It preserved it and passed it on to the Greek national Church, which only evolved in the nineteenth century.[2] Immediately after the Fourth Council its main territory and its ecclesiastical future still lay in Asia Minor. The loss of this territory through the advance of the Seljuks and the *halosis* by the Turks in 1453 prepared the end of this Asian-Chalcedonian Church, which into the eleventh century had constituted the centre of the Byzantine Empire. It was in the sixth century with Emperor Justinian that it attained its acme. There is a particular fascination in researching faith in Christ in this era.[3] From the ecclesial viewpoint this large area between Byzantium and Antioch contained all of the great conciliar sites of the Imperial Church from 325 (Nicaea I) to 787 (Nicaea II). Against such a row of historically significant synods and sites, every other patriarchate, Rome included, had to retreat. What a future Greek-speaking Christianity could await — beyond the Patriarchate of Constantinople! Already from 325 the name of Christ was central to this future. It was not for nothing that in Chalke in the atrium of his palace, which was fitted with bronze doors, Emperor Constantine ordered that a statue of Christ be erected.[4] It also signified a programme when Emperor Zeno (474/475; 476–491) characterized the Eastern capital as *mater nostrae pietatis et christianorum orthodoxae religionis omnium*.[5] With this phrase he expressed the self-

right there at the court. It was only natural that the presidency of the synod fall to the bishop of Constantinople. 'With the constant participation of the bishop of Constantinople and because naturally there was a greater proportion of bishops from sees surrounding the capital, the *Synodos endemousa* quickly acquired the character of a synod of the bishop of Constantinople' (*ibid.*, 22). On the basis of this development one can appreciate that the Ecumenical Patriarch had a completely different relationship to the Greek-speaking Church than, for example, his Alexandrian colleague to his region, which on account of its nature and history was so closed.

2. On this see P. Charanis, 'On the Question of the Byzantine Church into a National Greek Church', *Byzantina* 2 (1982), 97–109. The link between the Byzantine 'Rhomaeans' is, according to Charanis, not ethnic continuity, but Greek language and culture and, let us add, also the continuation of Chalcedonian faith. Cf. H.-J. Schulz, 'Die Ausformung der Orthodoxie im byzantinischen Reich', in *Handbuch der Ostkirchenkunde*, Vol. I (Düsseldorf, 1984), 49–132 (with literature).

3. For the period 600–800 see *CCT* III. A help for understanding the Greek Orthodox Church is offered by the work of H.-G. Beck, *Kirche und theologische Literatur*, and subsequently G. Podskalsky, *Griechische Theologie in der Zeit der Türkenherrschaft (1453–1821). Die Orthodoxie im Spannungsfeld der nachreformatorischen Konfessionen des Westens* (Munich, 1988). The unfolding of the orthodox theology of this period is illustrated in the second major part of the work, devoted to the history of theology, using over a hundred authors as examples.

4. See H. Hunger, *Reich der neuen Mitte. Der christliche Geist der byzantinischen Kultur* (Graz, Vienna, Cologne, 1965), 47. This work offers in an outstanding fashion a total picture of that development, which here we want to consider only for the first epoch of the post-Chalcedonian period, with the Justinian era in the centre.

5. *Cod. Iust.* I.2, 16 [a. 477]: Krüger, 14.

awareness of Christian Constantinople. 'As the Jews were the chosen people of God in the Old Covenant, so the Byzantines conducted themselves as the chosen people of God in the New Covenant. That was the incontestable principle of their state constitution and world-view.'[6] The city on the Bosporus was thus not only a city 'protected by God' but also the 'chosen city' of God.[7] Such a claim was calculated not only to surpass the status of the other Eastern Churches, but also to restrict Rome's claim of primacy.

History appears to confirm this trend. Within the period we are concerned with (451–604)[8] there occurred events which signified a change for the Eastern Empire and consequently also for the Patriarchate of Constantinople. The Western Empire ended in 476 with the sack of Rome by Odoacer.[9] The rule of Byzantium was restricted to the Eastern Mediterranean and the East. The significance of the Church of Constantinople, however, increased with this clear shift of the centre of the Empire to the Bosporus. Indeed Justinian I achieved a temporary recapture of Italy, Africa and southern Spain. Of this renewal of the old Roman Empire the invasion of the Lombards into Italy (568) and of the Slavs into the Balkans (c.580) left for Byzantium only the exarchates of Carthage and Ravenna, together with southern Italy and Sicily, and

6. H. Hunger, *op. cit.*, 52–3. Byzantium measures itself not only by Rome, but also by Jerusalem. The *vita* of Daniel the Stylite reports this. When he wanted to move into the Holy Land in order to live there on a pillar, he was referred through the vision of a holy man to 'the second Jerusalem, with the name Constantinople'. Cf. R. A. Markus, *Christianity in the Roman World* (London, 1974), 168–9; H. Delehaye, *Les saints stylites* = SubsHag 14 (Brussels, Paris, 1923), p. XLVI and *S. Danielis stylitae Vita antiquior*, no. 10, 12, 10–16 (Delehaye). We shall encounter the idea of the 'new Jerusalem' with a strange justification in the Ethiopic imperial Church, whose kings are ready to find their point of contact, together with Byzantium, in Jerusalem.

7. H. Hunger, *op. cit.*, 53, who refers to Theodoros Prodromos (twelfth century).

8. The Byzantine era as a whole is divided into the 'early Byzantine' epoch (from the founding of Constantinople to the beginning of the Arabian invasion [634]), the 'middle Byzantine' epoch (634–1071), and the 'late Byzantine' period (1204–1453). Cf. E. Kornemann, *Weltgeschichte des Mittelmeerraumes. Von Philipp II. von Makedonien bis Muhammed*, ed. H. Bengtson (Munich, 1967), 893–947 (III.5: From the Collapse of the Western Empire to the Death of Justinian . . .); 947–75 (III.6: From the Death of Justinian to the Victory of the Arabs . . .); H.-G. Beck, *Das byzantinische Jahrtausend* (Munich, 1978), 29–32: 'Epochs of Byzantine History'; K.-H. Uthemann, art. 'Byzanz', in *EKL*, 610–16.

9. On the significance of this year see the literature in G. Weiss, *Byzanz* = HistZ Sonderhefte 14 (Munich, 1986), section 4.7.2, 39–41. Also H.-G. Beck, *Das byzantinische Jahrtausend* (Munich, 1978), 28–9: 'Recently the reactions of the East to these events have been carefully collated. The impression remains that here, in contrast to the West, one did not believe that an apocalyptic event had to be confirmed. Regret was there, but one would almost like to believe that relief was greater.' Cf. A. Demandt, *Der Fall Roms. Die Auflösung des römischen Reiches im Urteil der Nachwelt* (Munich, 1984).

Thessaloniki in Greece.[10] In order to determine the unique contribution of this Patriarchate to christology, we must first clarify certain presuppositions.

1. The Christianization of the capital and the Asian region

We will take over some of the conclusions from the research on this topic.[11] This research indicates facts which can provide information on the state of Christianization. Such facts are: (a) the necessity of imperial edicts against paganism even well into the sixth century[12] and the completion of processes against pagans in 529, 546 and 562;[13] (b) the closing of the academy of Athens in 529 by Emperor Justinian, which was linked to a general ban on philosophical education and juridical instruction by pagans. Both of these tasks were to be reserved for Christians and state officials. The teachers who had been dismissed in Athens moved at first with Damascius, the head of their academy, to the court of the Persian King, Chosroes I. After the disillusioning failure of this exodus they found acceptance in Byzantium in 532, as the historian

10. See E. Kornemann, *Weltgeschichte des Mittelmeerraumes* (above n. 8), 859–975, also maps X and XI.

11. Cf. J. Geffcken, *Der Ausgang des griechisch-römischen Heidentums* (Heidelberg, 1920), 189–92; W. E. Kaegi, 'The Fifth-Century Twilight of Byzantine Paganism', *Classica et Mediaevalia* 27 (1966), 243–75. In this article, 249, Kaegi comments with regard to the fifth century: 'Theodosius I did not eradicate paganism. Pagans did constitute a substantial minority of the population in the eastern provinces of the Roman Empire. In my estimation, at the beginning of the [fifth] century pagans comprised somewhere between 10 per cent and 30 per cent of the population, while by 500 they appear to have diminished to no more than 1 per cent or 2 per cent and perhaps even less than that.' This can be regarded as the situation in our timespan. However, see the reservations in K. Holl, *Gesammelte Aufsätze zur Kirchengeschichte, II. Der Osten* (Tübingen, 1928), 245–7. Similarly H.-G. Beck, *Geschichte der orthodoxen Kirche im byzantinischen Reich* (Göttingen, 1980), 47–51; idem, *Das byzantinische Jahrtausend*, 260–2, on paganism in Byzantium, where it reads in conclusion: 'The Empire in the sixth century was clearly not yet totally christianized [p. 261] . . . Despite everything, the Christian faith must be reckoned with as being typically the dominating form' (262). Important is the study of G. Dagron, 'Le christianisme dans la ville byzantine', *DOP* 31 (1977), 3–25, with reference to D. Claude, *Die byzantinische Stadt im 6. Jahrhundert* (Munich, 1969). On the following see J. Irmscher, 'Paganismus im Justinianischen Reich', *Klio* 63 (1981), 683–8.

12. Cf. J. Irmscher, *ibid.*, 684–5: decrees from the year 527 (*Cod. Iust.* I.5, 12: Krüger, 53–5). According to Irmscher, paganism lived particularly in the old 'large land-holding senate aristocracy'. In the earlier bans on careers (*Cod. Iust.* I.5, 18: preamble) teachers were also expressly included (*Cod. Iust.* I.11, 10, 2: Krüger, 64).

13. See I. Rochow, 'Die Heidenprozesse unter den Kaisern Tiberios III. Konstantinos und Maurikios' in *BBA* Vol. 47 = *Studien z. 7. Jh. in Byzanz* (Berlin, 1976), 120–30. In the trials of pagans in the years 579–582, the majority involved baptized Christians, particularly from the higher public service class, who had fallen back into paganism and for this reason were condemned to death (*ibid.*, 125).

Agathias reports;[14] (c) the personal politics of Justinian in his work of restoration in Constantinople. Paramount significance was attributed to the jurist Tribonian, then still a pagan, about whom his contemporary, Hesychius Illustrius, wrote: 'This Tribonian was a pagan and godless and the Christian faith was completely alien to him.'[15] Apart from this jurist we encounter John of Cappadocia, a lukewarm Christian, who had been made head of the imperial administration.[16] The jurist John Laurentius Lydus also displayed an ambiguous attitude, for although he was a Christian, he advocated Neoplatonic and teratological ideas.[17] Concerning the personality of Procopius of Caesarea and his Christianity there has also been a lengthy debate without clearly unequivocal solutions being found.[18] To be noted, however, is the fact that besides the relatively small number of men of the type described, Justinian also found collaborators and propagandists in circles that were clearly clerically orientated, among whom in particular was the deacon of Hagia Sophia.[19] Finally, we can also indicate that the Emperor was not satisfied with the state of Christianization which he found at the time when he came to the throne, but demanded further missionary effort. To this task he appointed a significant man, namely John of Ephesus, who indeed was no supporter of Chalcedon, but who in loyalty to the Emperor fulfilled his stipulation to lead the pagans to Chalcedonian faith. According to Michael the Syrian, allegedly 70,000 pagans were converted to Christianity.[20] Later we shall have to discuss the missionary effort in the Sudan.

14. Agathias, *Hist.* 2, 30 and 31: Niebuhr. See J. Irmscher, 'Die geistige Situation der Intelligenz im Zeitalter Justinians', in F. Altheim and R. Stiehl, *Die Araber in der Alten Welt* IV (Berlin, 1967) (334–62), 349–51. The closed academy of Athens and the paganism advocated by it had 'for some time become quite insignificant, so that the Emperor could allow lenience to prevail'. Thus J. Irmscher, *Klio* 63 (1981), 685.

15. *Suidae Lexicon*, s. n. Τριβωνιανός: A. Adler, Vol. 4 (Leipzig, 1935), 588; J. Irmscher, 'Christliches und Heidnisches in der Literatur der justinianischen Zeit', *Revue des Études sud-est européennes* 18 (1980) (85–94), 87.

16. J. Irmscher, *art. cit.*, 88.

17. *Ibid.*, 88–9. According to Irmscher, the view of history of John Laurentius was determined solely by the developments of Roman history. In this pagan and Christian were combined.

18. *Ibid.*, 89–91.

19. On this see R. Frohne, *Agapetus Diaconus. Untersuchungen zu den Quellen und zur Wirkungsgeschichte des ersten byzantinischen Fürstenspiegels* (Diss. Tübingen, 1985). As sources, pagan and Christian works are named, particularly the speeches of Isocrates and the corpus of letters of Isidore of Pelusium. On the significance of this corpus and its compilers for ecclesiastical life in Byzantium at that time, see R. Riedinger, art. 'Akoimeten', in *TRE* 2, 151f.

20. See *CCT* II/1, Ad Fontes, 36–7, with the dates of John's life according to E. Honigmann, in opposition to J. Irmscher, *Klio* 63 (1981), 683–8.

2. The leading forces of theology in Byzantium in the sixth century

As is the case with every capital of a country, so the city on the Golden Horn also required a constant flow of intellectual forces from the province of the Patriarchate and from the whole Empire to be able to satisfy the demands of the Empire and the Imperial Church. A particular impulse for this was not really needed, but rather the flow had to be slowed down and there had to be careful selection. At that time people wandered considerably to and fro in the whole Empire, and the attraction of Constantinople for bishops, priests, monks and ascetics was well known. Naturally this attraction also took hold of lay people, whether Christian or pagan. Let us adduce some of the more famous names: Agathias from Myrina in Asia Minor (536–582), John Laurentius Lydus from Philadelphia, and John of Ephesus; furthermore Anthemius, the co-founder of the new Hagia Sophia after the old had been destroyed in 532 on the occasion of the Nika riot; Paul the Silentiary,[21] and above all Procopius of Caesarea, the historian and adviser to General Belisarius.[22]

Of particular interest to us are the theologians. Only a few names can be adduced if Byzantium is to be either their place of birth or their adopted city. In searching for theologically more significant figures among the patriarchs between 451 and 600 we soon exhaust the list. Only Gennadius (458–471) and Eutychius (552–565; 577–582)[23] appear worth mentioning as the authors of larger works. In the turmoil of the years of the strife concerned with the *Henoticon* under Emperor Anastasius I and then in the Justinianic era, it was difficult for a leader of the Church of the capital to gain status theologically and in terms of ecclesiastical politics. In the power triangle — Pope, Emperor, Patriarch — it was the last who was the quickest to be ground down, as especially the lot of the above-mentioned Eutychius will indicate. The office of safeguarding orthodoxy to which the Patriarch was entitled — this office being especially relevant at the profession of faith by new

---

21. Cf. J. Irmscher, 'Die geistige Situation der Intelligenz im Zeitalter Justinians' in F. Altheim and R. Stiehl, *Die Araber in der Alten Welt* IV, 357–9; P. Friedländer, *Johannes von Gaza und Paulus Silentiarius* (Leipzig, 1912).

22. See B. Rubin, *Prokopios von Kaisareia* (Stuttgart, 1954), also published in *PWK*, Vol. XXIII, 1 (Stuttgart, 1957), 273–599; J. Irmscher, *art. cit.*, 345–9.

23. On Patriarch Gennadius see *CCT* II/1, 166–72; on Patriarch Eutychius see CPG 6937; 6940; Grumel, *Regestes* I², nos. 244–249, 260–263. Somewhat more numerous are the patriarchs whose importance lies in the area of ecclesiastical politics. Their activity was considered in *CCT* II/1 and will also be considered here.

emperors on the occasion of ascending the throne — could only seldom come to expression. For the group of theologians from the class of priests and monks there are also only a few names of significance that can be cited in the fifth and sixth centuries.[24] It will take some effort to assign the leading figure among them, Leontius of Byzantium, to the capital. Even if he was really a Byzantine, as his epithet indicates, the Imperial City on its own, however, did not form him. He found his role in the sixth century only after twice having transferred from there to Palestine and back.[25] The encounters which were formative for him undoubtedly occurred in the Holy Land. His works were composed, it would seem, only in the short period between 543 and 544 in the Imperial City.[26] Despite all of the positive things that we will record, he was not the sole peak of theology before Maximus the Confessor, as some have attempted to represent him. Admittedly we have to accept that in Constantinople itself a great deal of theological work was done. But for this purpose there was no proper academy. Theology could be learned by way of non-academic instruction in individual contacts or in monasteries. In general, in the Ecumenical Patriarchate from the Bosporus to Syria below, there was nothing that corresponded to the schools as these existed in Antioch and Beirut, or then in Gaza and Alexandria, and beyond the borders of the Empire among the East Syrians.[27]

For our period particular significance is attached to monasticism.[28]

24. Apart from Leontius of Byzantium (CPG 6813–6820), CPG III indicates only a few names with the denotation Constantinopolitanus, if we do not take the patriarchs into account; the works of those named, moreover, are hardly of significance for christology.

25. On the tension 'Constantinople–Jerusalem' see G. Dagron, 'Les moines et la ville', TravMém 4 (1970) (229–76), 260–1; idem, DOP 31 (1977), 6.

26. Thus B. E. Daley in the introduction to his Leontius edition.

27. See H. Hunger, Reich der neuen Mitte, 299–369, especially 345–55: The university system. In the curriculum of the university, which according to Hunger can compete with Western teaching in the thirteenth century, there was only one faculty missing — theology. In spite of the significance which in many ways was attached to theology in Byzantium, it was also in later centuries seldom the object of instruction. 'For a theological college there are to be found now as ever no direct witnesses; if a Byzantine speaks of one, he adduces the Syrian city of Nisibis as an example of a theological college' (349), with reference to F. Fuchs, Die höheren Schulen von Konstantinopel im Mittelalter = Byz. Archiv 8 (Leipzig, Berlin, 1926), 5.

28. Cf. H. Bacht, 'Die Rolle des orientalischen Mönchtums in den kirchenpolitischen Auseinandersetzungen um Chalkedon (431–519)', in Chalkedon II, 193–314; D. J. Chitty, The Desert a City (Oxford, 1966), in which, however, monasticism in Constantinople is in the background in comparison with that of Egypt and Palestine; cf. 123–42. See as well H. Hunger, op. cit., 229–98: Monasticism and asceticism as shaping forces. For Constantinople cf. 255–61, 266–85. Those who came from monasticism to the patriarchal throne included Atticus (406–425), Nestorius (428–431), Eutychius (552–565, 577–582), among others; H.-G. Beck, Das byzantinische Jahrtausend, 207–31, where on 214–22 critical statements are also made about Eastern monasticism; idem, Geschichte der orthodoxen Kirche im byzantinischen Reich (Göttingen, 1980), 43–7.

Since the middle of the fifth century the monastery of the Sleepless Monks of Eirenaion, which was situated opposite Sosthenion in the middle Bosporus, had become a significant spiritual and intellectual centre.[29] When the patrician Studios planned the foundation of a new monastery, he turned to the Sleepless Monks and requested monks and a religious rule. The monastery of Marcellus thus received the rôle of being a mother house for Eastern monasticism, as then the monastery of Studion itself would be for further foundations after the ninth century.[30] The monastery of the Sleepless Monks must have stood out for this purpose precisely because it had created a monastic tradition that was specific to Constantinople. To this tradition belonged the 'active apostolate' as well as the 'rebellious agitation' that was prepared to fight for 'orthodoxy' above all.[31] According to G. Dagron, these monks had conceived from a particular understanding of Christendom that Constantinople had a unique calling, as the great city of Eastern Christianity and as the new centre of the Empire.[32] They gazed into the future. To what extent the fact that they belonged to certain social classes also played a rôle in this is difficult to prove. In any case, in contrast to them the episcopal hierarchy had committed itself to a political organization which preceded the foundation of Constantinople and which in great part corresponded to the division of the Empire and of

29. On the Sleepless Monks see G. Dagron, 'La Vie ancienne de saint Marcel l'Acémète', *AnBoll* 86 (1968), 271–321, with further literature; *idem*, 'Les moines et la ville', *TravMém* 4 (1970), 229–79, where the topic is the pre-Chalcedonian monasticism in Constantinople; R. Riedinger, art. 'Akoimeten' in *TRE* 2, 148–53. Riedinger notes at the beginning that the name *akoimetoi* (sleepless) was first given to the monks when they settled in Eirenaion, the third settlement overall (around 430–440). G. Dagron, 'Les moines et la ville', *TravMém* 4 (1970), 253, n. 125, says that round the middle of the fifth century there were about 10,000 to 15,000 monks in the neighbourhood of Constantinople, and he comments on their organization.

30. Cf. G. Dagron, 'La Vie ancienne de saint Marcel l'Acémète', *AnBoll* 86 (1968), 274; *idem*, 'Les moines et la ville', *TravMém* 4 (1970), 254, where he emphasizes that from the end of the fourth century onwards Constantinople attracted and integrated monks from the provinces, from Syria, Egypt and Armenia. He says that the foundation of the Sleepless Monks was from the very beginning 'cosmopolitan and polyglot' in its organization. Only in Constantinople of the sixth century was there a blossoming of national monasteries: *ibid.*, 255, with reference to R. Janin, 'Les monastères nationaux et provinciaux à Byzance', *EO* 32 (1933), 429–38; *idem*, *Les Églises et les Monastères des grandes centres Byzantins* (Paris, 1975).

31. Cf. G. Dagron, 'Les moines et la ville', *TravMém* 4 (1970), 257, where the tense relationship between the hagiographical and sociological consideration of monasticism is set out for Constantinople. For Constantinople in general the following holds: 'révolution urbaine et révolution chrétienne sont concomitantes'. Thus *idem*, 'Le christianisme dans la ville byzantine', *DOP* 31 (1977) (3–25), 15.

32. G. Dagron, 'Les moines et la ville', *TravMém* 4 (1970), 276; cf. P. Charanis, 'The Monk as An Element of the Byzantine Society', *DOP* 25 (1971), 61–84; D. Savramis, *Zur Soziologie des byzantinischen Mönchtums* (Leiden, Cologne, 1962).

the dioceses by Diocletian; because of this it limped behind the real development of the East. The consequence shows itself in two ways. Institutionally, it was not until fifty years after the first tentative appearance of the idea (at the Council of 381), viz. at the Council of 451, that Constantinople's primacy of honour after Old Rome could announce itself with the Emperor's help on the political level. Psychologically, this would mean for men like Chrysostom and Gregory Nazianzen, even when they occupied the patriarch's chair, that they were and remained 'provincials', while the monks, as soon as they arrived from the provinces, became absolute representatives of the population of Constantinople.[33]

The Sleepless Monks had only a short heyday. It lasted from their foundation by Abbot Marcellus (448–before 484) to their condemnation as Nestorians by Pope John II on 25 March 534. They were decided Chalcedonians, as were the monks of the Studion monastery that was founded with their help, and were well known because of their outstanding library, which also contained the *acta* of the Council of Chalcedon.[34] This could be used by Facundus of Hermiane in the years 546–548 and the Roman deacon Rusticus in 565. According to admittedly contested suggestions, there are traces pointing to the monastery of the Sleepless Monks which are linked with forgeries, historically pregnant, that were produced there and belong to our sources.[35] In spite of everything, the monastery of the Sleepless Monks was no substitute for a theological academy.

The circus parties (the demes) are a final, if not unimportant, factor in the ecclesiastical and political life of Constantinople. It is not our task to explain the relationship of the circus parties to the religious groupings in the post-Chalcedonian period. The proper business of the demes was the organization of races in the racecourse. In Constantinople in 602

---

33. G. Dagron, 'Les moines et la ville', *TravMém* 4 (1970), 276. Besides Constantinople, the west coast of Asia Minor possessed great monastic centres. For the post-Justinianic era see F. Winkelmann, 'Kirche und Gesellschaft in Byzanz vom Ende des 6. bis zum Beginn des 8. Jahrhunderts', *Klio* 59 (1977), 477–89.

34. On the library of the Sleepless Monks see E. Schwartz, *PS*, 206: 'It was their [the Sleepless Monks'] belligerence, averse to compromise, which drove them to procure and gather copies of all the documents that were important for ecclesiastical politics, so that their library became nothing short of an arsenal for propaganda, the most important weapon for which at that time was the publication of documents.'

35. R. Riedinger, art. 'Akoimeten' in *TRE* 2, 148–53, connects this library with the author of the Ps. Dionysian writings, whom he would like to consider as Peter the Fuller, and also the authors of the forged letters to Peter the Fuller and the compilers of the Erotapokriseis of Ps. Caesarius and of the letters of Isidore of Pelusium, and the revisers of the homilies of Ps. Macarius/Simeon.

there were 1,500 registered members in the Greens, and 900 in the Blues, which permits one to make a judgement about the Justinianic era also. The most recent research denies any delimitation of the demes according to particular city areas or certain classes of the population and their religious point of view, for example in the sense that the Blues would belong to the upper class and advocate Chalcedonian orthodoxy, while the Greens belonged to the middle and lower classes and were orientated in an anti-Chalcedonian direction. Originally, it is suggested, the demes were 'fan clubs'. Their engagement and action in religious, social and political demonstrations are said to be determined by the fact that in the Byzantine milieu there was little freedom of speech, yet the demes were suited in outstanding fashion to serve as a mouthpiece for public concerns according to the circumstances. Although they may have had their significance, both in terms of ecclesiastical politics and as a means of propaganda, theology as such was neither enriched nor changed through their intervention.[36]

3. The Empire and the ideology of the Imperial Church

From the beginning of the Constantinian Empire the history of theology and especially of christology had to take into account its entwinement with the idea of the Imperial Church.[37] The reign of Emperor Justinian I signified a climax that had not previously been attained.[38] However, this ruler, the theologian among the emperors, in comparison with his predecessors and their interventions, introduces not only power and authority to carry through a particular ecclesiastical political course of action in questions of faith, as in particular the *Henoticon* of Emperor Zeno and the *Henoticon* politics of his successor Anastasius have shown us, but also contributions to content and attempts at solutions. In doing this he consciously employs the Constantinian idea of unity of faith, and welfare of the Empire. This idea now foundered definitively. The separa-

36. See G. Weiss, *op. cit.* (n. 9), no. 11.28, 267–8, with a short history of research. As the major works of opposing interpretation, the following are named: J. Jarry, *Hérésies et factions dans l'empire byzantin du IVe au VIIe siècle* (Cairo, 1968) and Alan Cameron, 'Demes and Factions', *ByzZ* 67 (1974), 74–91; *idem*, *Circus Factions. Blues and Greens at Rome and Byzantium* (Oxford, 1976). There is a brief overview by P. Schreiner, art. 'Demen', in *LexMA* III, 686, who takes the side of Alan Cameron. G. Weiss occupies a middle position.

37. See *JdChr* I³, 388–403; *CCT* I², 250–64 (Emperor Constantine); *JdChr* II/1, 231–8; *CCT* II/1, 204–10 (individual bishops in the *CE*).

38. This comes to expression in the 'mirror for princes' of Agapetus Diaconus, *Capitula admonitoria* (CPG 6900): PG 86, 1164–85, especially chs 21, 37, 45–46, 51, 61–63. Cf. R. Frohne, *op. cit.* (n. 19), 125, 133, 137, 139, 145 (German translation), with summary 151–8.

tion could no longer be healed with previously applied methods and previously employed motives; the unity of the Imperial Church could no longer be saved. For the first time Christendom prepared not only to suffer fairly small splits, but to be divided into rather large institutionalized entities. Was this necessary because of the cause, i.e. the content of the formulas of faith that were pitted against each other? Is it possible that in the first stage of this separation a basis of unity could still have been found that provided a fundamental *koinonia* of faith for centuries?

In spite of this failure, the Justinianic era is permeated with its own unique brilliance, which also gives style and luminosity to the picture of Christ. What is the source of this Byzantine *splendor mysterii*, which is expressed so impressively in the liturgy, hymns and in painting that it is utterly impossible for us to capture it in the framework of this depiction? Is this picture of Christ Byzantinized, i.e. falsified with inauthentic elements, to such an extent that it must once again be freed from these with every effort? 'Byzantine' stands for a particular understanding of the mystery of Christ which must be tested with regard to its universal validity.[39]

39. On the following: E. Kornemann, *Weltgeschichte des Mittelmeerraumes*, 927-30; H. Hunger, *Reich der neuen Mitte*, 61-107 (II: The Byzantine Emperorship as the Imitation of God); H.-G. Beck, *Das byzantinische Jahrtausend*, 78-86 (II.8: The Ideology of Dominion); 87-108 (III: Political Orthodoxy); *idem*, 'Senat und Volk von Konstantinopel. Probleme der byzantinischen Verfassungsgeschichte' in H. Hunger (ed.), *Das byzantinische Herrscherbild* = WdF 341 (Darmstadt, 1975), 353-78.

PART ONE

THE ANTI-CHALCEDONIAN POLE
THE CHRISTOLOGY OF PATRIARCH SEVERUS
OF ANTIOCH

Even though the discussion concerning the Council of Chalcedon and its dogma about Christ had begun immediately on the ending of the Council, it reached its culmination, however, only with the emergence and activity of the monk Severus, Patriarch of Antioch (512–518). His epoch-making intervention was a reaction to the attempt by supporters of Chalcedon to snatch back the theological initiative in the Greek-speaking region, after it had progressively slipped from them during the struggle about the *Henoticon*. The rebound was so powerful that the Chalcedonians were once again quickly put on the defensive. The out-ward course of this event, which occurred principally in the reign of Emperor Anastasius, is already familiar to us. We shall now turn to the theological discussion proper, its course and its results, first during the time between the Council of Chalcedon (451) and the death of Gregory the Great (604). Chalcedonians and anti-Chalcedonians will have the floor in like manner. But first we will concentrate on the christology of the leader of the opponents of the Council, the monk and patriarch Severus. It represents the anti-Chalcedonian pole at its strongest. He became the challenger for the entire sixth century, which christologically would attain its highpoint in the Second Council of Constantinople (553). Although the works of the Patriarch are extant mainly only in Syriac translation, with him we still remain in the Hellenistic-Byzantine region. The extent to which his theology penetrated the concrete form of the Old-Oriental Churches will be depicted in detail for each of them. On the whole Severus was the disputatious *polemicist*, but also the enthusiastic, sometime fanatical *herald*, and finally the *theologian* and *synthesizer* of the anti-Chalcedonian picture of Christ.

CHAPTER ONE

THE DISPUTATIOUS POLEMICIST

SECTION ONE

SEVERUS AND HIS ADVERSARIES

With his becoming a member of the monastery of Peter the Iberian, Severus had inherited the opposition to Chalcedon.[1] Still, special impulses were needed for this opposed position to become differentiated thematically and to assume a propagandist character. Quickly, however, in addition to the controversy with the supporters of the Fourth Council, there resulted a repeated disputation with friends in the same party, which indeed, in the case of Julian of Halicarnassus, led to a deep division. Although Severus had to fight against opposed fronts, still all the individual phases and themes of the discussion had a consistent point of reference, namely Cyril of Alexandria and his *mia-physis* christology. The Alexandrian is for Severus simply 'the king of the explication of dogmas' (*rex explicationis dogmatum*).[2] His pupil will do nothing else than think through logically the formulations of the model, and if necessary also intensify them. All partners in the dialogue will be measured by how they stand towards this great teacher. Among the Fathers there is for Severus no higher authority than Cyril. Even Athanasius or the Cappadocians recede before the Alexandrian.

---

1. On the life and conduct of *Severus of Antioch* see Lebon, *Chalkedon* I, 426f., n. 4; Frend (1972), 201–8; W. A. Wigram, *The Separation of the Monophysites* (London, 1923), 57–60; R. C. Chesnut, *Three Monophysite Christologies* (Oxford, 1976), 4–5. We have three biographies of Severus, those of: (1) Athanasius of Antioch; (2) John of Beth Aphthonia; (3) Zacharias Rhetor; further there is A. Vööbus, 'Découverte d'un memra de Giwargi, évêque des arabes, sur Sévère d'Antioche', *Mus* 84 (1971), 433–6; *idem*, 'Discovery of New Important Memre of Giwargi, the Bishop of the Arabs', *JSS* 18 (1973), 235–7. On the influence of *Peter the Iberian* on Severus see Brooks, *SL* II, sect. V, 11, 328: '. . . the highest assurance and a fixed mind, when our holy father Peter the bishop from Iberia was offering and performing the rational sacrifice', is a model for Severus in his stance against Chalcedon and all heretics.

2. See Severus Ant., *C. imp. Gram.*, Or. III. 2, cap. 22: CSCO 102, p. 4,20–3.

§ 1. The discussion with the supporters of Chalcedon and the reasons for it

Though naturally dynamic, the monk Severus still needed external stimuli to intervene in the theological debate. We will now present three of these, which originated from the Chalcedonian side.

I. THE *FLORILEGIUM CYRILLIANUM* AND THE *PHILALETHES* OF SEVERUS

The first inducement for Severus to take up his pen came from an (Egyptian) monastic cell or scholar's study: one or several supporters of Chalcedon, well and truly familiar with the works of Cyril, were not of the opinion that the great opponent of Nestorius also had to be considered rightfully as the enemy of the two-natures doctrine. Comprehensive extracts from his writings were intended to prove that he could also have accepted the Chalcedonian formula, because for Cyril too the two natures remained unmingled after the union. In this way he was to be reclaimed and vindicated as a witness to Chalcedon.[3] This claim severely nettled Severus. The florilegium, which in all probability was compiled about 482 in Alexandria, came into the hands of Severus in Constantinople during the years 508–511, after it had travelled via Rome in the luggage of John Talaia.[4] His response was the *Philalethes*, the friend of truth, which he composed while still in the Imperial City.[5]

---

3. See Hespel, *Le Florilège Cyrillien*.
4. *Ibid.*, 29–33. On John Talaia see C. Pietri, 'D'Alexandrie à Rome: Jean Talaia, émule d'Athanase au Vᵉ siècle', in ΑΛΕΞΑΝΔΡΙΝΑ = *Mélanges Claude Mondésert* (Paris, 1987), 277–95.
5. See R. Hespel, *Sévère d'Antioche, Le Philalèthe*: CSCO 133 (T), 134 (V) (Louvain, 1952); foreword to the Syriac edition, I–VII, where the structure of the work and its manuscript tradition are explained. Hespel had first of all to clarify the relationship of the *Cod. Vat. syr.* 139 to the text of the Cyrillian florilegium (=*FlorCyr*). J. Lebon had assumed that this codex (and with it also *Cod. Marc. gr. Venet.* 165), which had previously been regarded as an authentic witness of the *FlorCyr*, had nothing to do either with this collection or with its refutation, the *Philalethes* of Severus. According to Lebon, *Cod. Vat. syr.* 139 was a Syriac translation of a writing directed against the *Philalethes*, this writing being in the form of a Cyrillian florilegium. In it John of Caesarea is said to have fixed the interpretation of Cyril in the *Philalethes*. After this writing there followed then (according to Lebon, who could not examine *Cod. Vat. syr.* 139 itself) the '*Apologia* for the *Philalethes*', composed by Severus. In *Cod. Marc. gr. Venet.* 165, Lebon saw the original text of the florilegium, compiled by John of Caesarea, to refute the *Philalethes*. Cf. Lebon, 130–3. Draguet, *Julien d'Halicarnasse*, was the first to be successful in clarifying the relationships and the historical course of events. Cf. Hespel, *Le Florilège Cyrillien*, 48–51. According to this interpretation *Cod. Vat. syr.* 139 contains the whole text of the *Philalethes*, composed between 508 and 511, and of the anonymous Chalcedonian *FlorCyr*. *Cod. Vat. gr.* 140 contains the '*Apologia* for the *Philalethes*' of Severus, in which there are important citations from the

This name stands for Cyril, and the text counts as a masterpiece of anti-Chalcedonian christology. Severus had the opportunity to explain his relationship to Cyril's christology. According to him the 244 chapters of the work of the Chalcedonians were gathered from Cyril's writings with the intention 'of showing that the teacher of orthodox faith had thought and expressed the same things as those who wish after the inexplicable unification to divide our one and only Lord and God Jesus Christ into two natures'.[6] The monk challenged the right of the Chalcedonian compiler(s) of the florilegium to lay claim to Cyril because in his opinion he was an unambiguous witness for the contrary.[7] It was the purpose of the *Philalethes* to demonstrate this.

The intention of both works, the florilegium and its refutation, is to make out of Cyril a 'dyophysite' as well as a 'monophysite', whereby a differently accentuated understanding of Christ — be it in the sense of the *dyo physeis* or the *mia physis* — can be illustrated. The historical development of Cyril was in fact so ambivalent that his works could become a common arsenal for contrary christologies depending upon what one sought in them. Anti-Arian and anti-Apollinarian in the beginning, anti-Nestorian after 429 — Cyril's works guaranteed a twofold leitmotif, not only for the compiler of the florilegium and the *Philalethes* but also for the whole christological development between 510 and 604.

II. THE EMERGENCE OF THE MONK NEPHALIUS AND HIS FIGHT AGAINST SEVERUS

That Severus came to Constantinople in 508 with a large entourage of monks resulted from the aggressive activities of Nephalius, who had been born in Nubia and was a monk in Egypt.[8] Initially he was a radical

---

FlorCyr. In *Cod. Marc. gr. Venet.* 165 Draguet found the original Greek text of the *FlorCyr* up to no. 231 (230). As also in the *Cod. Vat. syr.* 139, before the florilegium proper there is found here the definition of Chalcedon, as well as the parallel placing of conciliar forms and texts of Cyril, and finally the 230 excerpts from Cyril. For nos. 231–244 of the *FlorCyr*, *Cod. Vat. syr.* 139 is the sole witness. Cf. Hespel, *Le Florilège Cyrillien*, 208–216. See Zacharias Rhetor, *Vita Severi*: PO 2, pp. 105,18–106,7.

6. See Sévère d'Antioche, *La polémique antijulianiste III, L'apologie du Philalèthe*, tr. R. Hespel = CSCO 318 (T), 319 (V) (Louvain, 1971), p. 12,34–37.

7. *Op. cit.*, *Apologia* to no. 52 of the *FlorCyr*: CSCO 319 (V), p. 29,8–9: '... I have proceeded along the line of the teachings and texts of blessed Cyril'. More strongly: *op. cit.*, Severus' introduction: CSCO 319, pp. 1,31–2,1: 'If you had believed the writings of *Philalethes* [=Cyril], similarly you would have believed in me; and if I name myself, I speak of the wise Cyril and of the other holy Fathers whose teachings are cited in the *Philalethes*.'

8. See Lebon, 118–75; C. Moeller, *Chalkedon* I, 670–1. For further literature, see below.

supporter of the anti-Chalcedonian movement and an intransigent extremist, as the opponent of the more moderate *Henoticon* politics of Peter Mongus of Alexandria (482–490). He became just as passionate in his defence of the Fourth Council, which came to expression in an *apologia* of the Synod; this is lost as such but its sequence of ideas is discernible in its refutation by Severus.[9] He transferred from Egypt to Palestine and harassed the monastery of Severus near Majuma so severely that Severus, as mentioned, had to take flight and seek protection (508–512) from Emperor Anastasius I. But the Chalcedonian convert, who was the first to attempt thematically to combine the language of dyophysite christology with that of the monophysites in a dialectical synthesis, also followed him there. The name coined for this attempted synthesis is 'neo-Chalcedonianism'.[10] It will be a particular task to track down this *nouvelle théologie* in its representatives and variations.

III. THE *APOLOGIA FOR THE SYNOD OF CHALCEDON* OF JOHN THE GRAMMARIAN

With this work we encounter one of the leading figures of the initiative mentioned above, for he was the first to try to present a relatively structured system for it.[11] The vehement response of Severus to this work, which is also lost, was published in 519 only after his deposition as Patriarch of Antioch (512–518): *contra impium grammaticum*! To some extent from this response the *apologia* can be reconstructed.[12]

In its first part the dyophysite teaching is expounded and the critique of the opponents of the Council of 451 presented (nos. 1–28). A first section of this offers an analysis of general concepts (nos. 4–8) and a second the Grammarian's critique of the 'monophysite' theses (nos. 9–28). In the second part we find a historical and theological presentation of Cyril's relationships to the Orientals (nos. 29–49). However, the end of chapter 37 and chapters 38–57 of the second book of Severus' refutation are lost, and with them a number of texts between nos. 29 and 30

---

9. Cf. Severus Ant., *Orationes ad Neph. ii* (CPG 7022): J. Lebon, *Severi Antiocheni orationes ad Nephalium, eiusdem ac Sergii Grammatici epistulae mutuae* (Louvain, 1949) = CSCO 119 (T), pp. 1–69; 120 (V), pp. 1–50. John of Beth Aphthonia says that Severus destroyed this *Apologia* like a spider's web, this occurring around 519. Cf. PO 2, 232. Cf. Evagrius, *HE* III, 33: Bidez-Parmentier, p. 132,4–15.

10. On the significance of Severus (and Philoxenus of Mabbog) for the emergence of neo-Chalcedonianism during their sojourn in Constantinople see C. Moeller, *Chalkedon* I, 669.

11. See CPG 6855; M. Richard, CCG 1, 6–46; Lebon, *C. imp. Gram.*: CSCO 111, 93.101 (T), 112, 94.102 (V) (Louvain, ²1952); Greek excerpts in Richard, CCG 1, 49–58; on this A. de Halleux, 'Le "synode néochalcédonien" d'Alexandrette (ca 515) et l' "Apologie pour Chalcédoine de Jean le Grammairien". A propos d'une édition récente', *RHE* 72 (1977), 593–600; C. Moeller, *Chalkedon* I, 672–4.

12. See the overview in Richard, CCG 1, 2–5.

(particularly about Theodoret). In the third part John offers a critique of the first treatise of Severus: *Ad Nephalium*. In the fourth part there is a florilegium (nos. 70–118), attached to which there would certainly have been a theological summing-up.

John the Grammarian wanted to find a *via media* between the teaching of Chalcedon and its opponent Severus, with Cyril in the background. But it was Severus who won the initial battle. With his assaults on the Grammarian he could make him look so ridiculous that he was utterly discredited among the learned and not so learned.[13] However, the neo-Chalcedonian intent did not disappear; but that would take us beyond the person of Severus.

With these paragraphs we have presented only the major anti-Chalcedonian works of Severus. The polemic against Chalcedon naturally found expression also in the famous cathedral homilies and his letters, which deserve not to be passed over.

§2. The controversies of Patriarch Severus within his own party

The anti-Chalcedonian movement, whose undisputed leader Severus had risen to be because of his activities (see *CCT* II/1, Part Two, Ch. Four) and his writings, was severely affected externally by the change of 518, and internally by misunderstandings between friends and the splits that resulted from these.

I. THE QUARREL WITH JULIAN, BISHOP OF HALICARNASSUS

This struggle was carried on under the theme of the 'uncorrupted-ness of the body of Christ' and was already becoming apparent in Constantinople in 510. But in 520 its stage became Egypt after both Severus and Julian fled there from Justin I. Only in 527 was peace restored. The thesis of Julian was that the body of Christ, even before the resurrection, was 'uncorrupted' and 'incorruptible'. Was this a new Eutyches? In any case this was what Severus suspected and objected to.

---

13. Cf. Severus Ant., *Letter to the Deacon Misael, in 537*: Brooks, *SL* II, 198; John of Beth Aphthonia, *Vita Sev.*: PO 2, 249–50. Anastasius of Sinai had falsely ascribed this success to the *Philalethes*. On account of its authority this new work replaced the entire Scriptures and the Fathers among the supporters of Severus and James of Baradai. Cf. *Hodegos* IV 1: CCG 8, p. 98,90–106. Cf. on this Hespel, *Le Florilège Cyrillien*, 43–4.

The discussion was opened by the *Tomus* of Julian.[14] At first there was an exchange of letters between the two bishops.[15] Then Julian expanded the second edition of his *tomus* with *additiones*.[16] Finally, in order to add strength to his *tomus*, he composed an *apologia*[17] and a sort of treatise: 'Against the blasphemies of Severus'.[18] Severus found the debate so important that he responded to each of these writings.[19] Particularly significant is the title *Censura tomi Iuliani*, thus a critique of the *tomus*; the third letter to Julian is a précis of this (CPG 7027 and 7026); then there followed a *Refutation of the theses of Julian* (CPG 7028), an argument about the *additiones* (CPG 7029) and about the *apologia* of Julian (CPG 7030). In the *Apologia for the Philalethes* Severus defended himself against the suggestion that he had advocated 'Julianist' ideas in this work, which he had already composed in Constantinople (CPG 7031).[20]

Severus did not succeed in convincing Julian. The opposition became increasingly fierce and led finally to a break between the two, and with this to a split in the anti-Chalcedonian movement. In a second series of strongly polemical writings Julian continued the battle, after the *Censura tomi Iuliani* in particular had nettled him intensely. Against this writing he composed a large work of ten *logoi* in which against the florilegium of Severus he placed another, compiled of biblical and patristic texts, and defended the terminology of his tome. From this Severus produced four fragments in his *Apologia for the Philalethes*. With this writing just mentioned the series of works by Severus against Julian comes to an end. They occurred before 528, because in that year the Syriac translation of Paul of Callinicum was published in Edessa. There is no indication that this controversy was continued beyond that date.

II. THE CONTROVERSY WITH SERGIUS THE GRAMMARIAN

In this controversy, as in the discussion between Severus and Julian, once again the *mia-physis* christology becomes apparent as the source

14. See Severus Ant., *Censura tomi Iuliani* (CPG 7027). On the course of the controversy, with writings and counter-writings, see R. Hespel, *Sévère d'Antioche. La polémique antijulianiste I* = CSCO 244 (Louvain, 1964), I–II; *idem, op. cit.* IIA = CSCO 295 (Louvain, 1968), I–III; *idem, op. cit.* III = CSCO 318 (Louvain, 1971), pp. V–IX. The major work is that of Draguet; *idem*, art. 'Julien d'Halicarnasse', in DTC 8b (1925), 1931–40.

15. Severus Ant., *Epistulae tres ad Iulianum* (CPG 7026): R. Hespel, CSCO 244 (T); 245 (V): Ep. I, pp. 6–7; Ep. II, pp. 9–14; Ep. III, pp. 163–214.

16. Cf. Severus Ant., *Contra additiones Iuliani*: R. Hespel, *op. cit.* IIA = CSCO 295 (T), 296 (V) (both Louvain, 1968).

17. Cf. Severus Ant., *Adversus apologiam Iuliani*: R. Hespel, *op. cit.* IIB = CSCO 301 (T), 302 (V) (both Louvain, 1969).

18. Hespel, CSCO 244, I.

19. See CPG 7026–31.

20. Lebon, 128, believed that this *apologia* could be considered to be an anti-Chalcedonian work. See Hespel, *Sévère d'Antioche. La polémique antijulianiste III*: CSCO 318 (T), VII–VIII; 319 (V) (both Louvain, 1971).

of misunderstandings among its supporters.[21] Sergius seems to have arrived at his errors, sharply attacked by Severus, by taking over Apollinarian errors, which for their part assume the Aristotelian doctrine of mixture.

Thus Severus fought not exclusively against Chalcedon and its supporters, but also against particular opinions and groups which had developed in his own movement. This process continued until 557 in the *tritheist controversy*,[22] with regard to which Severus could no longer take up a position. But here once again it would have been evident, as in the polemics against Julian and Sergius, (1) what a burden the *miaphysis* ideology, resting on the Apollinarian forgeries, constituted for the Old-Oriental Alexandrian tradition; (2) that Severus also was not successful in undoing this bundle, indeed that he was incapable of doing this, undoubtedly because in no way was he even prepared to think through the possibilities of the way indicated by Chalcedon in its choice of terminology. Consequently he cut himself off from the possibility of presenting the problem differently, namely by showing where and how in Christ the unity, and where and how the distinction of God and human being, should be placed. It would however be false because of this to speak simply of the failure of his christology. With the Alexandrian tradition he inherited a rich treasure of christological ideas which he utilized in his own way. We will have to examine whether this led to a deepening and clarification or to a constriction and one-sided solidification of christological thought.

21. The writings of Sergius Gram.: CPG 7102–5; on these see Lebon, 163–72, 538–51; I. R. Torrance, *Christology after Chalcedon. Severus of Antioch and Sergius the Monophysite* (Norwich, 1988).

22. See A. Van Roey, 'La controverse trithéite jusqu'à l'excommunication de Conon et d'Eugène (557–569)', OLP 16 (1985), 141–65.

SECTION TWO

THE CHRISTOLOGICAL RESULT OF THE POLEMICS OF PATRIARCH SEVERUS

Under the pressure of the controversy between Chalcedon and Alexandria the relationship of Cyril to Chalcedon necessarily became the theme of christology after 451: how did the principal formula of the Fourth Council relate to the teaching of the *mia physis* of the Word incarnate? Chalcedon had to lead to a *rélecture* of the great Church Father, or — according to the other side — Cyril would lead to a correction or abolition of the Council.

§1. The discussion with the Chalcedonian opponents and the Severan response

I. THE INTENT AND THE SIGNIFICANCE OF THE *FLORILEGIUM CYRILLIANUM* (*FlorCyr*)

The compiler based himself on the Fourth Council. He intended to read Cyril along the line of the Council's principal formula, and this in two stages. In the first, the definition is divided into individual statements over against which references from Cyril are placed as parallels (nos. 1–10). In this way the character of novelty or heresy was to be taken from the principal formula of Chalcedon. In the second, much more lavish process the compiler proceeded thematically and presented the two most controversial themes of Chalcedon as the foci for his selection: (a) the distinguishing of the two natures and (b) the theopaschite statement (God has suffered) and its correct interpretation.[23] In this process it was presupposed that it was precisely Chalcedon with its teaching of the two natures which offers the possibility of confessing the divinity of the Logos (here concretely, God Word) as incapable of suffering and free from suffering and immortal, and of expressing in contrast the suffering and mortality of the human nature (here concretely, of the temple). Is this formulation felicitous? It is strongly reminiscent

23. See Hespel, *Le Florilège Cyrillien*, p. 111,17–21 (title): 'Various excerpts (*chreseis*) from Cyril, Archbishop of Alexandria, in which it is shown that the distinction of the two natures and the impassibility and immortality of God-Logos, (on the other side) the passibility and mortality of the temple are proclaimed by him.'

of the way in which the Antiochenes warded off Apollinarian 'theo-paschitism' and thus riled Cyril; this indeed with the phrase 'the temple'! Certainly this does not mean that the excerptor is Chalcedonian in the sense of retreating to Antiochene christology. He had before his eyes the whole controversy after Ephesus with its documents, and retained its style.

On the first stage
(R. Hespel, Le Florilège Cyrillien, 103–11)

In this the Chalcedonian definition in its individual phrases is compared with Cyrillian statements. Accordingly the expressions of the two natures (no. 4) in the one hypostasis (no. 7) had to stand in the centre. Basil of Seleucia, with whose part in this formula we are already familiar,[24] would here certainly have cast a wider net. Here would have been the great opportunity to analyse the intent of Chalcedon with its distinction between *hypostasis* and *physis* and to demonstrate the unity with Cyril despite the new step in terminology. This was no longer to be achieved with texts which in fact speak of two natures, but rather by showing that Cyril could combine the *mia-physis* formula with these. It is precisely this point, then, that Severus fastened on to. As useful and as justified as the first series of texts might be, without an accompanying hermeneutic it was not convincing.

On the second stage
(*ibid.*, 111–216)

In this process, as we said, the themes are confined to the two offensive points ('two natures' — the communication of properties), and the attempt was made with a multiplicity of references to prove the agreement of Chalcedon with Cyril. For us it is not so important to re-enact this process and thus once again to present an interpretation of Cyril, seeing that we have already attempted this in the framework of our depiction of the pre-Chalcedonian period. Our focus is on the reaction of Severus of Antioch and *his* relationship to Cyril, from which indeed the Cyrillianism of the Old-Oriental Churches is derived. Nevertheless the Cyrillian florilegium has value for us because of its Chalcedonian-motivated selection from his works. Here it is appropriate to ask some critical questions and to make a few remarks.

(1) It is not difficult to cite many places in Cyril in which the distinction between the two natures (τῶν δύο φύσεων τὸ διάφορον) is expressed. Equally the Patriarch let there be no doubt that this distinction remains preserved too in the uniting of the two natures. For this reason the conclusion would also be clear that the Logos made flesh in the incarnation 'has two natures' or 'is in two natures'. Cyril had some passages that almost lead to this assumption and that could make Severus nervous.[25] But an explicit statement about this is not found.

(2) It is one thing to establish the *real* presence of unmingled godhead and unchanged

---

24. See *JdChr* I³, 755–9; *CCT* II/1, 230–2, with notes 122–7.

25. Cf. *JdChr* I³, 679–86, 755–9; *CCT* I², 478–83. Worthy of serious attention are the remarks of M. Simonetti, 'Alcune osservazioni sul monofisismo di Cirillo di Alessandria', *Aug* 22 (1982), 493–511; in n. 26 on 500f., Simonetti refers to Cyril Alex., *De recta fide ad reginas or. 2*: ACO I, 1, 5, p. 36; PG 76, 1360C: τῆς ἐνωθείσης αὐτῷ φύσεως, δῆλον δέ, ὅτι τῆς ἀνθρωπίνης. This writing is excerpted in the *FlorCyr* in nos 165–75. The passage cited by Simonetti, however, is not to be found there. Simonetti also refers to Cyril's *De Incarnatione Unigeniti* (CPG 5227), which is a transliteration of the *De recta fide* into the form of a dialogue. Simonetti establishes this text later as *De recta fide* (against G. M. de Durand, SC 97). See as well PG 76, 1192A, 1197B, 1169C (Simonetti, 500).

humanity, but another to apply to this the *formal* predication of 'twoness'.[26] Even if Cyril perhaps in the course of time may have found his way to this point, Severus fundamentally refused to go that way.

(3) The obstacle was the *mia-physis* formula, which was indispensable for christology and traditionally maintained. It demanded that Cyril see the two natures unconditionally in the state of union *(henosis)* and acknowledge that the twoness was present only in the abstract consideration *(theoria)* and as *ratione prius* (never real). The compiler of the florilegium thought that he had done enough when he cited places which expressed a *real* differentiation of God and human being in Christ,[27] but had not yet advanced to the *formal* statement of a twoness after the union. Severus could fasten on here. He always avoided the logical deduction of the Chalcedonian 'in two natures'.

(4) The salient point would have been to show from the formula of Chalcedon that Cyril (and Severus) sought the unity and the differentiation on one and the same ontological level, that is on the level of nature, which of necessity had to lead to a contradiction. He would have had to explain that the unity 'in the hypostasis or the prosopon' represented a *real* union which excluded the dreaded twoness of the 'person', yet maintained the *real* duality of the natures.

(5) For this purpose he would also have had to examine critically, in terms of their cogency, the images and comparisons which Cyril adduced for the unmingled unity in Christ, the body–soul analogy and the images of the 'burning thornbush' and the 'glowing coal'. These attempts would also have to be placed within the history of philosophy. But that would place excessive demands on the excerptor, and admittedly too would have meant his renouncing a telling argument against the Alexandrians.

(6) As much as the Alexandrian monophysite terminology contained irreconcilable elements and aspects dangerous for understanding Christ, the Cyrillian florilegium signified nothing more

---

26. N. A. Zabolotsky, 'The Christology of Severus of Antioch', *Ekklesiastikos Pharos* 58 (1976) (357–86), 373, articulates this distinction well: 'According to Severus, one can count only things that have their originality; to count means to consider an essence as "hypostasis", or as the highest expression of a peculiarity — "person" *(πρόσωπον)*. Thus, the aversion for a cipher, for a duplicity, reflected in the formula "one incarnate nature" contains the formal side of the ideas of Severus and of other opponents of the Chalcedonian Council. But in a material sense, essentially, Chalcedon's adversaries did not and could not refute the duplicity in the one Person of the Lord.' Severus had no misgiving about allowing numeration in the theology of the Trinity. Cf. *Ep. ad Iohannem presb. et archim.*: PO 12, 215: 'The Holy Trinity is capable of numeration in respect of hypostases; but in that it is one and of the same essence, it stands outside number.' Cf. *Hom.* 125: PO 29, 239. He could refer to Basil, *Ep. 214 ad Terentium*, no. 4: Y. Courtonne, *S. Basile, Lettres*, vol. 2 (Paris, 1957), 205: ἀριθμείτωσαν. On the problem see R. Arnou, 'Unité numérique et unité de nature chez les Pères, après le Concile de Nicée', *Greg* 15 (1934), 242–54. In the spirit of Severus, Patriarch Paul the Black of Antioch (564–577), in his synodal letter to Patriarch Theodosius of Alexandria (535–566) (CPG 7203), still chided the Chalcedonians on account of their love for duality which they had inherited from Leo I. His Tome 'split the one Christ through the duality of the natures after the union. He allocated to each (nature) forms, predicates, activities and general qualities corresponding to this number *(aequales eis numero)* . . . It is characteristic of them to divide through intellectual vision, because in a subtle self-deception of the intellect they see two, from which the inexpressible unity is constituted. They should not remain in this intellectual hallucination, but accept the true union and reject the *number* of the natures, because the *number* is expression for a host of subjects, but not for the nature of the things.' Cf. CSCO 103, pp. 226,23–26; 227,33–38.

27. See Cyril Alex., *Ep. 45 ad Succensum I*: PG 77, 232CD = ACO I. 1, 6a, p. 153,16–20; cf. Severus Ant., *Philal.* nos 38–41: CSCO 134, 21–2; no. 39: *ibid.*, p. 22,1–8. In addition there are works from the pre-Ephesian works of Cyril, the *Thesaurus* and *C. Synousiastas*, where he had to speak differently against the Arians and radical Apollinarians than he would later have to do against Nestorius. See below.

than a stimulus for reflection for the opponents, a certain justification of the Chalcedonian position, but still not a compelling argument. For this reason Severus, starting with his presuppositions, could draw contrary conclusions from the same Cyrillian material. We want to depict in broad strokes how in his critique of the florilegium the Patriarch justified and also sharpened his Cyrillian understanding of Christ.

II. THE CYRILLIAN CHRISTOLOGY OF THE *PHILALETHES* OF SEVERUS

A florilegium is necessarily selective, not only on account of its compass, but also simply because of its purpose. It was not difficult to find sufficient texts of Cyril which express the 'unmingled distinction' in Christ. Through the accumulation of these the impression could be given that Cyril was very close to the two-natures teaching, if indeed he could not be regarded as its defender. Severus sought to destroy this suspicion entirely. This is the negative side of his refutation of the florilegium. The positive side is that he for his part highlighted many of the facets of Cyril's understanding of Christ, and consequently placed Cyril as the unconditional representative of the *mia-physis* christology.[28] Thus from the same timber a different Christ could be carved. It is strange that no attempt was made to find common ground with an opponent and to emphasize this.

1. 'Sacrilegious plunderer of the inspired words of Cyril'

Many an author can object to a critic: 'You do not cite me completely. Had you taken my words in context, then you would have come to another judgement.' This was the constant complaint of Severus, applied to the method of selection employed by the excerptor. In a general way he raised it at the very beginning of his critique of the thematic part of the collection.[29] He also gives a good reason for saying that the author of the florilegium can almost always be found guilty of using

28. Thus in his critique of the *FlorCyr* nos 37–40, where the two natures seem to be proximate, Severus comes elegantly to the 'one nature of the incarnate Word'. Cf. *Philal.*, nos 37–40: CSCO 134, 210–12.

29. Cf. Severus Ant., *Philal.*: CSCO 134, 150–3. Also in the '*Apologia* for the *Philalethes*', he criticizes the *FlorCyr* fiercely: CSCO 319, 12,37–13,10: he maintains that it is a compilation, made by several authors, but put in circulation as if it is by one person; the suspect John Talaia brought it to Rome; an extreme supporter of Nestorius, John, treasurer in the days of Patriarch Macedonius (496–511), then gave it to the patrician, Appion, with the intention that it serve as an instrument in an action against Severus, who at that time was in Constantinople (508–511).

the scissors too quickly: Cyril always combines two trains of thought when he speaks of the two natures. The question that must be asked is: is it a matter of the time before the union (which exists only in *theoria*), or is it the time after the union when one may no longer speak of a duality? Besides establishing the integrity of divinity and humanity in the one Emmanuel, Cyril also considered the event of the union and incorporated it in the end-result. And there Christ is no longer two, but *one physis*, *one hypostasis*. The excerptor, delighted at having discovered statements in Cyril about the material integrity of the two natures, leaves aside the remarks about the event of the union and believes in this way to have found a confession of Cyril to the two natures. This would have been correct only if the Patriarch had confessed to a duality also *after* the union, which for him, however, means the same as a twoness of persons. The confession to twoness in Christ was made dependent on two conditions: (1) it must be seen *in fieri*, which is why Cyril always says, 'the two natures from which (ἐξ ὧν) Christ becomes one', which (2) has the same meaning as the demand to accept the twoness only in the *theoria*. Thus Severus' constant critique of the excerptor's Chalcedonian technique of cutting concerns not simply the length of excerpts but relates to a substantial abridgement of Cyril's line of thought.[30] If one takes the whole process as a unity, then the twoness (intellectually conceived) before the union is no longer present after the union. This is shown by a response of Severus to no. 4 of the first part of the florilegium:

> In fact whoever assigns to God the Word a one and only incarnated hypostasis and a one and only person also attributes to him a one and only nature of the incarnated God the Logos. For that which with whatever two (elements) as a starting-point has been gathered together

---

30. In the eyes of Severus, the author of the *FlorCyr* revealed himself in his Nestorian colours in no. 10: Hespel, p. 115,7-14, by omitting in the text an important ὁ αὐτός which was intended by Cyril to place a special accent on the unity in Christ. On this see *JdChr* I[3], 705f.; *CCT* I[2], 500. Severus noticed the omission immediately: *Philal.* on no. 10, *Apologia*: 'N'oubliant pas, une nouvelle fois, de pratiquer un vol sacrilège sur les textes, il a supprimé ici aussi le mot qui exclut la séparation en deux, comme suit: "Parfait qu'il est selon la divinité et parfait qu'il est, 'le même', selon l'humanité". Ainsi donc, après avoir retranché "le même", il pense, dans sa sottise, que chacune des natures est parfaite dans l'isolement de sa subsistance . . .' Cf. CSCO 134 (V), p. 176,23-29. Since the *FlorCyr* does not contain any commentary, one cannot decide with complete certainty whether the omission was intentional or a mistake. The former can perhaps be accepted because of the fact that the excerptor was of the opinion that the *mia physis* of the anti-Chalcedonians was in point of fact understood as a mixed nature. This emerges from his title which stresses that he wants to prove from Cyril 'the distinction of the natures' (cf. Hespel, *Le Florilège Cyrillien*, p. 111,18-19). With the 'one and the same' omitted, the text certainly spoke more strongly in its dyophysite sense which, however, on that account also proved itself heretical in the eyes of Severus.

has on the one hand ceased to be 'two', but remains (on the other hand) 'one' after being put together: even if he, without giving up anything, lets appear the elements out of which he is constituted [cf. the 'recognized in two natures' of the definition of Chalcedon], because they have been united without mingling, so he remains still in a definite way 'one', and it is impossible that in the future he is 'two', this being because of the inseparable character of the union.[31]

From all this one must recognize that (if) the union brought about the ending of the duality and separation of the two natures, still it did not wipe out the difference of the natures from which Christ is one.[32]

Whether Severus criticizes the Cyrillian florilegium for its procedure or its theological cogency, or whether he develops his christology positively in his own explications (*apologia*), he constantly aims at a rehabilitation of Cyril. We could really be satisfied with this. Nevertheless it is useful to consider the Cyrillian picture of Christ somewhat more closely, along the heightened lines of Severus, so that the preconditions can be created for us to understand better the discussion with Severus within Byzantine theology.

2. On the christology of the *Philalethes* of Severus

The Cyrillian florilegium is characterized by the intention to prove the permanent difference of the two natures in Christ from Cyril himself, in order to be able to lay claim to this undisputed authority for Chalcedon. Severus seeks to escape this danger by opposing a dynamic consideration of Christ to the static one of the Chalcedonians. The material duality of divinity and humanity in Christ ought to be only the *transitory* phase of the consideration, this being removed by the vision of the unified unity. Only here may the viewing intellect find rest. This intention serves the emphasis of the formula rejected by Chalcedon: 'from two natures one (person)'! The execution of this line of thought belongs, according to Severus, to the correct statement about Christ, because otherwise this statement would stop at the *material* duality of God and human being and would necessitate the acceptance of a *permanent formal* duality. The constant hammering of this necessity makes the christology of Severus even more heavily weighted towards 'unity' than that of his master Cyril. Severus pursues his preoccupation in two ways: (a) explanation through analogies; and (b) language and depiction that are directly conceptual.

31. Severus Ant., *Philal.* (part 1), no. 4: CSCO 134 (V), p. 139,9–18. *Ibid.* (part 2), no. 42, *Apologia*: CSCO 134, p. 213.

32. *Ibid.* (part 1), no. 4: CSCO 134 (V), p. 140,4–7; in a similar way already in no. 2: *ibid.*, pp. 135,28–136,2; as well on no. 14: *ibid.*, pp. 184,34–185,4. The 'duality' destroys the unity if one speaks of it after the uniting of the natures.

(a) Analogies for the unity in Jesus Christ

(i) The body–soul comparison

The body–soul analogy in its application within christology has attracted special attention particularly in recent times.[33] Although utilized in christology since Eusebius of Emesa, through Cyril and Severus it gains a not innocuous intensification because it is enlisted in the proof of the *mia-physis* formula.[34] Likewise both teachers confess the acceptance of a soul in Christ — in constantly repeated rejection of Apollinarius. As an example we can take the *apologia* of Severus to no. 42 of the Cyrillian florilegium, which he substantiates with two further texts from his master, doing this because the excerptor used the scissors too soon. We will concentrate upon these texts,[35] present them first, and then let the *apologia* of Severus follow.

> We are composed of body and soul, and we see two natures (*kyana*), the one that of the body, the other that of the soul; but the human being is one from the two due to the union. And the fact that he is composed out of two natures does not permit us to conclude that he who is one is two men, but rather one single man, as I have said, on account of the composition from body and soul.[36]

> And the man that we are may serve us as an example. For with regard to him we comprehend two natures, one that of the soul and the other that of the body. However, although in subtle reflection we distinguish or in the imagination of the mind perceive a distinction, we still do not juxtapose the natures and do not allow in them the power of the separation to exhaust itself entirely, but we understand that they belong to a single unique being in such a way that from then on the two are no longer two, but through the two a single living being has been formed.[37]

33. See K.-H. Uthemann, 'Das anthropologische Modell der Hypostatischen Union. Ein Beitrag zu den philosophischen Voraussetzungen und zur innerchalkedonischen Transformation eines Paradigmas', *Kleronomia* 14 (1982), 215–312; F. Gahbauer, *Das anthropologische Modell. Ein Beitrag zur Christologie der frühen Kirche bis Chalkedon* = ÖstlChr 35 (Würzburg, 1984), 348–419. K.-H. Uthemann, *Anastasii Sinaitae Viae Dux* = CCG 8 (Turnhout, Louvain 1981), 273–5; 277–8. On Severus, *ibid.*, 277,55–66. Many ideas are furnished by R. A. Norris, 'Christological models in Cyril of Alexandria', in TU 116 (1975), 255–68; P. Stockmeier, 'Das anthropologische Modell der Spätantike und die Formel von Chalkedon', *AHC* 8 (1976), 40–52; *idem*, 'Die Entfaltung der Christologie und ihr Einfluß auf die Anthropologie der Spätantike', in H. P. Balmer et al. (eds), *Im Gespräch der Mensch* (Düsseldorf, 1981), 248–55.
34. See F. Gahbauer, *op. cit.*, 32–55 (Eusebius of Emesa); 348–419 (Cyril of Alexandria).
35. Severus Ant., *Philal.*, no. 42: CSCO 134 (V), 213f.
36. *Op. cit.*, p. 214,6–12 = Cyril Alex., *Ep. 45 ad Succensum I*: PG 77, 233A.
37. *Ibid.*, p. 214,14–23 = Cyril Alex., *Ep. 46 ad Succensum II*: PG 77, 245A. Some other passages on this: *Ep. ad Valent. ep. Icon. 4*: ACO I 1,3, p. 92,15–21: 'As consequently the human being is one from body and soul, he [Christ] too is confessed in faith as one Son and Lord. For it is assumed that there is *one physis and systasis* of the human being, even if it is thought of (as coming from) different and differently formed natures. For, as one generally concedes, the body possesses another nature than the soul, but its specific nature contributes to completing the *hypostasis* of the one human being. The difference of the things named remains hidden neither

Although in these texts Cyril himself did not employ the *mia-physis* formula, but spoke only of the one Christ, Son and Lord, the Word become flesh, Severus comes expressly to this formula and as a result intensifies the text of Cyril.

> For it is only because we examine in precise reflection the elements of which Emmanuel is constituted that we say that there are two natures that have been unified; by entertaining in our mind the idea of union we conclude that the *one single nature of the Word incarnate* has been formed. For the hypostatic union means these two things: that there has been a union of two or more realities to become one and the same thing, and that this from this time on no longer breaks up into them [the elements] which have naturally united, for they have united to become a single being. For in fact these elements which have naturally united no longer subsist in the isolation of their own subsistence, but are obviously in a *single nature and a single hypostasis*; they allow only the starting-point to appear from which the single being is constituted, because they have been united without mingling and thus escape division into two or more.[38]

Were we to take these texts together, then Cyril and Severus appear to see in the application of the body–soul comparison to 'Emmanuel' (= unity from God and human being) univocity and not an analogy. Anyway, in both cases the same result is arrived at: a substantial unity, a ἕνωσις φυσική, which at the same time remains an 'unmingled unity', a ἕνωσις ἀσύγχυτος.[39] But there are important texts in the same *Philalethes* in which this unity in both cases is still not placed on the same level. It is Cyril himself who in the *Scholia on the Incarnation of the Only-begotten*[40] differentiates more strongly. The question is to what extent Severus accepted this.

Cyril maintains that the 'business of the union' is enacted in various ways. Firstly he mentions the moral agreement, for example in the friendly reconciliation of people who were separated from each other in feeling and thought. Then there is unity in the natural domain between elements which are different from each other but are joined through (a) juxtaposition

in thought nor in knowledge. Their matching or coming together with inseparable character completes a living thing, the human being.' Cf. F. Gahbauer, *op. cit.*, 355; 358–60: Cyril uses the expression σύστασις for the unity of body and soul, as Plato previously, *Epinomis* 981A, whereby ensues 'one form and one living being'. Gahbauer refers to Athenagoras, *De resurr. cadaverum* 15, and Methodius, *De resurr.* 34 (here once again in connection with Plato, *loc. cit.*). σύνθεσις can also take the place of σύστασις.

38. Severus Ant., *Philal.*, no. 42, *Apologia*: CSCO 134 (V), p. 213,15–31.

39. On the early history of this terminology see H. Dörrie, *Porphyrios' 'Symmikta Zetemata'* = Monograph. z. klass. Altertumswissensch. 20 (Munich, 1959), 166–225; L. Abramowski, 'ΣΥΝΑΦΕΙΑ und ΑΣΥΓΧΥΤΟΣ ΕΝΩΣΙΣ als Bezeichnung für trinitarische und christologische Einheit', in *eadem, Drei christologische Untersuchungen* (Berlin, New York, 1981), 63–109.

40. Cyril Alex., *Scholia de incarn. Unig.* (CPG 5225): PG 75, 1376C–1377B = ACO I. 5, 1, pp. 220,13–221,6 = Hespel, *Le Florilège Cyrillien*, no. 99, pp. 153f. On this see M. Richard, 'Le pape saint Léon le Grand et les "Scholia de incarnatione Unigeniti" de saint Cyrille d'Alexandrie', *RSR* 40 (1951/52), 116–28 = *Op. Min.* II, no. 53.

(παράθεσις), (b) mixing (μίξις), and (c) blending (κρᾶσις). *Parathesis* remains a purely external union which Cyril identifies with the *synapheia* of Nestorius.[41] It exists, for example, in the purely moral bond between Peter and John. Admittedly, *per se* the becoming one of the Logos of God and our nature transcends human conceptualization. It does not conform to any of the mentioned processes of joining; rather it is inexpressible and beyond the knowledge of all created being. Even the union of body and soul in us ourselves transcends our intellect. If we have to work with comparisons in order, with the help of lower realities, in some way to bring utterly subtle things close to our conceptualization, then Cyril believed that he was able to have recourse to this *unity of body and soul*, although even it remained utterly inadequate. Nevertheless this comparison does express some aspects: 'For the soul appropriates everything that belongs to the body, although in its own nature it is saved both from the passions which are natural (to the body) as well as those that come from without. The body in fact is driven by natural desires and the soul feels these with it on account of the unity with it, without of course itself participating with it in any way in these' (pp. 261, 31–262, 1). The soul certainly feels pain with its tormented body because it is its body, 'but it itself in its own nature need endure nothing of that which affects it [the body]' (*ibid.*, p. 262, 5–7).

There is still more to say concerning *the unity of Emmanuel*. He has a soul that is united to him; this has consciousness of the suffering of the body so that it bows docile before God, although it itself is spared the blows. The soul is thus united to the body and yet distanced from it. This holds even more of the divine Logos *vis-à-vis* his human nature. He has full power over the weaknesses of the body and can suspend these. But he makes them his own because it is precisely his body which suffers.

Cyril is thus conscious of the analogy which prevails between the unity of body and soul in human beings and between godhead and ensouled body in Emmanuel. In the *apologia* to no. 99 of the *FlorCyr* Severus does not examine this critique of the body–soul comparison in Cyril. He emphasizes only the one point which his master also holds on to: as the unity of body and soul is a substantial unity, so also is the unity of Emmanuel a 'hypostatic unity', not simply a moral relationship, such as that of friendship, of pleasure, of agreement in will, of equality in status and power — as Nestorius proposes! But, according to Cyril and Severus, in what does the 'substantiality' of this unity subsist? In terms of effect both cases are the same in that there is a single concrete existence which Cyril and Severus characterize as a single *physis*, *hypostasis*. Is this same result, however, also arrived at in both cases in the same way? Is the way in which union happens the same in 'Emmanuel' as in human beings? Cyril allows us a certain insight into his understanding through the introduction of the concept ἴδιος (ἰδία σάρξ, ἴδιον σῶμα), thus of the relationship of ownership which prevails between their components in Emmanuel and in human beings. The body, and consequently also all the affections of the body, the Logos makes his own in the strong

41. In the Syriac translation of the *FlorCyr* in the *Philalethes* the latter two Greek expressions are rendered as follows (CSCO 133, p. 320,3): *mixis*: ḥultono, *krasis*: mawzogo. Cf. I. R. Torrance, *op. cit.*, 249, Appendix C.

sense of the word (ἰδιοποιεῖν), as is stated at the end of no. 99 of the *FlorCyr* (CSCO 134, p. 262, 14–15). We shall quote a few other passages from Cyril.[42]

> That is why we say that the body was the possession of the Logos, not of any other man separate from him who was conceived as Christ and Son. As one says, however, that the body of each individual belongs to his person, so one must also think about Christ.[43]

> For when Christ says: 'I will raise him up', he has the capability of raising up those who have fallen asleep, not only wrapped in his own flesh but being in unity with his own flesh does the God-Logos in him say 'I', and this perfectly justifiably. For Christ is not cut into a duality, nor ought anyone think that the body of the Once-born is foreign to him as also, so far as I know, no one would claim that the body is foreign to our soul.[44]

> And as well one must also consider that. The divinity is one thing and our human nature is also something different, at least according to the mode which is in the natures, but in the union which occurs according to true unity there is a single Christ from both, as we have frequently said. But if the *hypostases*, as you [Nestorius] say, are separated and thought of as existing each for itself, how then could the unity amount to one person, if one does not presuppose that the one belongs to the other, as one also thinks of the soul of the human being as the possession of its body, although it possesses a nature different from this? For certainly there is no doubt that body and soul are not the same.[45]

Cyril is thus prepared even in the discussion with Nestorius to concede certain limitations in the interpretation of the body–soul analogy and its application to Christ as the connection of God and human being. One should not be led astray by expressions like 'physical union'. One has to attempt to determine more closely his notions of that. We can approach that only gradually. Let us return to the concept of possession or the relationship of ownership which prevails between body and soul in human beings and between divinity and humanity in Christ. Cyril can make the latter understandable more easily than the relationship of possession between body and soul. For he can call upon the creative power of the Logos to explain his appropriation of the body. What is created is the possession of the one creating, the creator.

Already in the *Thesaurus*, an early writing, Cyril comes to speak of this, and in his disputation with the Arians and their interpretation of Prov 8,22: 'Yahweh created me when his purpose first unfolded, before the oldest of his works' (PG 75, 253C–292A). Here we can presuppose the history of the interpretation of this verse (see *CCT* I², Index for Prov 8,22). While the Arians refer the being created to the Pre-existent, it is interpreted by the Nicenes as referring to the humanity of Christ: 'He is begotten by the Father before the ages, as he says; but he is created as human, as he became flesh for our sakes, as the evangelist says' (PG 75, 280C).

42. Cf. F. Gahbauer, *Das anthropologische Modell*, 348–54.
43. Cyril Alex., *Apolog. c. Orient.* 96: ACO I. 5, p. 137,24–28; F. Gahbauer, *op. cit.*, 349.
44. Cyril Alex., *In Ioannem lib. X., cap. II*: Pusey, *In D. Io. Ev. II*, p. 543,20–7; F. Gahbauer, *op. cit.*, 348f.
45. Cyril Alex., *C. Nestor.* III 6: ACO I. 1, 6, p. 73,1–8; F. Gahbauer, *op. cit.*, 353.

From this being created arises immediately the relationship of possession between the Logos and the humanity united to him. Cyril establishes this connection explicitly: 'He [the Logos] states of himself that he is created, on the basis of the creation of the body, although he is by reason of his nature uncreated. Because the flesh belongs indeed to him and not to another, he can call that his own whatever happens to this (flesh) [namely being created]' (PG 75, 281C).

One should not pass over such argumentation too quickly. The reference to the creator–creature relationship for divinity and humanity in Christ relates christology to the biblical teaching of creation (as is particularly clear right at the beginning of his comments on Prov 8,22 [PG 75, 280BC]). Only the creative power of God and the Logos can realize anything like the incarnation. Consequently also the depth of relationship of possession between humanity and divinity of Christ is of a completely different proportion from that in the body–soul relationship of the human being. In Christ it is a question of the appropriation of a created nature by the uncreated Logos. Precisely because of this infinite distance the FlorCyr (no. 203) cites our passage from Cyril's Thesaurus to demonstrate the continuation of the two natures even after the union. Severus examines this. But while the excerptor emphasizes from this the distinction of the two natures, Severus in his apologia on this places the accent on the unity in the difference.

> We call the same one created and mortal according to the flesh, uncreated and immortal according to the godhead. In fact it is the characteristic of the flesh on account of its nature to die and to be created. We do not deprive the Logos, however, of these things, this being because of the union, wherefore we can say of him that he had been created and died, while on account of his nature he is uncreated and immortal.[46]

The special feature of this God–human unity was already strongly underscored by Severus in the introduction to the Philalethes: the flesh had not been created in the first place for itself independent of the union with the Logos, but 'it had been constituted for him without ever being separated from him; in its being constituted and in its becoming reality the created flesh had already been united to the Word who was before the ages and uncreated, up to the point that we distinguish from him, only through a (mental) trick, the human things and speak of the two natures of the single Christ'.[47]

Whether consciously or unconsciously, in this way an Augustinian idea is taken up which excludes any temporal distinction between creation and assumption of the humanity by the Word.[48] The assumption of the human nature of Christ happened in the act and at the time of its creation. With this reference to the henosis as the creative act, the foundation for the relationship of ownership has been given without there necessarily having to be an ontological doctrine of henosis submitted as well. In this way the act of union is grasped at the same time as personal event, and thus removed from the domain of material-physical mixing. Thus the integration into the doctrine of creation signifies a correction to the application of the Greek teaching of mixture to the union of God and human being in Christ.

Such a creative activity, as it is seen at work in the explication of the 'appropriation' of the human nature by the Logos, naturally cannot be accepted where it is a question of the relationship of ownership between soul and body. The former is not the creator of the material part of the human being. If the soul possesses this as its own, then this occurs

---

46. See Severus Ant., Philal. on FlorCyr, no. 203, Apologia: CSCO 134 (V), p. 283,25–31.
47. Idem, Philal. on the two-natures formula: CSCO 134 (V), p. 108,8–14; JdChr I³, 771; not in CCT I².
48. More information in A. Grillmeier, loc. cit. (n. 47).

because it has been given to the soul by the transcendent creator. For Cyril and for all *Christian* advocates of the body–soul analogy this is a self-evident presupposition.[49] It is for this reason too that the difference in the relationship of ownership is not analysed in the two *analogata*. There is also no reflection on the fact that in both cases the 'possession' is very different. Thus it was used only to establish that Logos-body and soul-body form a substantial unity. The body–soul unity can be for that reason a help to understanding the unity of God and a human being in Christ. It should, however, have been necessary to clarify to what extent this analogy held up in general.

(ii) Burning thornbush (Ex 3,2–3) and glowing coal (Is 6,6–7)

These images too are already familiar to us. Their employment transcends party boundaries.[50] While the second image emphasizes only the reciprocal penetration, that is, the becoming one, the first stresses as well the unmingledness in becoming one, or rather the imperishability: the thornbush is not consumed. Thus we have an 'unmingled unity', represented, however, in physical processes. With this we return to the Stoic *krasis*. Nevertheless the materialism of the Stoics has to be excluded. The Neoplatonists emphasized this in their taking over of physical images to explain the 'unmingled unity' of body and soul. Two things may not be taken over: (1) a *synchysis*, understood as the erasure of previous characteristics; (2) the συμφθαρῆναι, which means the doctrine of the mutual spoiling or erasure of soul and body as such.[51] What is still reminiscent of the Stoic teaching of *krasis* in the comparisons mentioned was, however, still very different from it and led well beyond Stoic materialism, independent 'of all notions of space, place, materiality'.[52] In Christ it is still a matter of *perichoresis*, the unmingled penetrating/permeating of the 'incorporeal Logos' in the spiritual-bodily human nature.

---

49. This is treated under the theme of the pre-existence of souls. See C. Dratsellas, *The Problem of pre-existence of souls in St. Cyril of Alexandria*, offprint from ΠΟΝΗΜΑ ΕΥΓΝΩΜΟΝ = FS B. M. Vellas (Athens, 1968), where there is an overview of the various positions adopted by the Fathers with regard to the pre-existence of souls, from Origen to its clarification in the Origenists' strife under Emperor Justinian; especially, however, with regard to Cyril's teaching. On the theory of the pre-existence of souls in Origen (especially in *De princip.* [CPG 1482]: H. Crouzel/M. Simonetti, SC 252 [Paris, 1978]), cf. H. Crouzel, *Théologie de l'image de Dieu chez Origène* (Paris, 1955), 130–3: L'anthropologie d'Origène.

50. See *JdChr* I[3], 722–6; *CCT* I[2], 515–19.

51. Explained in more detail in H. Dörrie, *Porphyrios' 'Symmikta Zetemata'* (Munich, 1959), 173.

52. L. Abramowski, *art. cit.* (above n. 39), 70, n. 30.

Because, however, physical processes had been chosen or could have been chosen at all as the starting-point of the comparison, so now also 'direct language' must be assigned a rôle in the interpretation of the incarnation, just as in their body–soul teaching among the Neoplatonists. Here we come to the terminology of mixing. We shall enquire briefly about the position of Severus, as interpreter of Cyril, in the use of such language.

(b) Direct, conceptually demarcated language

The linguistic problem is centred on the concept of 'unmingled unity' (ἀσύγχυτος ἕνωσις) in its application to christology. With this term the result of the union is indicated. But if one wants to know what conception of oneness is associated with this, then one must specify the act of union and investigate its terminology, and here the verbs of 'mixing' play a special rôle.

The philosophers have already played out the problem and distinguished various levels of *henosis* according to the assumed types of mixing. The lowest level is the παράθεσις, the *iuxtapositio*, the simple one beside the other in external contact. Then follow μίξις (Hespel: *combinaison*, combination) and κρᾶσις (Hespel: *mélange*, blending).[53] *Parathesis* exists in a collection of individual things of the same type (a heap of grain) from which the individual grain can easily be taken out. *Mixis* is realized when qualities thought to be corporeal permeate the bodies to be united. Examples of this are fire in iron and light in the air. The Stoic Chrysippus applied this *mixis* concept to the relationship of soul and body. *Krasis* is mingling with partial weakening of the original qualities. An example is the pouring together of fluids which, for instance, produce perfume. A separation is only possible with special means. *Synchysis* is the most intense degree of union. From two material elements there results a third with completely new qualities. Examples are medicines. This is a step towards 'distinguishing in the sense of modern chemistry compounds from mixtures'.[54] A separation into the component parts is no longer possible.

In the *Scholia de incarnatione unigeniti* Cyril takes up this terminology; *FlorCyr* no. 99 reproduces an extensive extract from this.[55]

---

53. Cf. H. Dörrie, *op. cit.*, 25–7; L. Abramowski, *art. cit.*, 79f.

54. Cf. H. Dörrie, *op. cit.*, 26f.

55. *FlorCyr*, no. 99: from Cyril Alex., *Scholia de incarn. Unig. cap. VIII*: PG 75, 1376C–1377B; ACO I, 5, 1a, pp. 220,13–221,6. Severus Ant., *Philal*. no. 99: CSCO 134, 261f.

After he has spoken of the union on the inter-human moral level, he proceeds to the connection of things in nature and names the three grades just mentioned: *parathesis, mixis, krasis*. Then he immediately excludes the possibility that one of these three grades could be applied to the God-human unity in Christ. In this way Cyril in the *Scholia* allows only the general term *henosis* to apply. For the application to anthropology and christology he demands that there be both an 'unmingled' as well as a 'substantial' unity. Cyril has become very circumspect with regard to comparisons. He no longer finds in the creaturely domain any appropriate and adequate model for the union.[56] Consequently the Patriarch rejects in this writing, certainly composed after the Union of 433, all the terms apart from *henosis* to characterize the substantial and unmingled unity demanded for christology — *mixis, krasis*, but also *synapheia*. The last can express only a moral connection.[57] For the divine-human unity in Christ does not result from the 'assumption' of a human being already previously existing (*homo assumptus!*). It is to be understood rather as a process of becoming which proceeds from the Logos as Logos, the subject in his 'own nature' — as John 1,14 demands.[58]

In this way the Patriarch disclaims all philosophical *henosis* terminology as this corresponds to the character of the letter composed only after the Nestorian struggle, and sent to Rome in Greek and Latin.[59] Hence we must assume that in the question of the applicability of philosophical terminology to christology Cyril has become more moderate. Remarkably, however, the *FlorCyr* exploited also older writings of the Patriarch, which were composed before the Nestorian controversy, and made them useful for its purpose of supporting the two-natures doctrine of Chalcedon. For in these there also appears a greater emphasis on philosophy and its conceptual language, also with regard to terms which Cyril in the struggle with Nestorius would reject. What is particularly important for the excerptor is this: as a consequence the reality of the two natures is so nonchalantly emphasized that Severus is clearly in a predicament. It concerns two quite large series of excerpts from the *Thesaurus* written about 412 and from the writing against the *Synousiasts*, a radical group of Apollinarians. In the *Thesaurus* Cyril argues with the

---

56. *FlorCyr*, no. 99: Hespel, *Le Florilège Cyrillien*, p. 153,10–12: . . . ἀπόρρητος δὲ παντελῶς καὶ οὐδενί που τάχα τῶν ὄντων διεγνωσμένος πλὴν ὅτι δὴ μόνῳ τῷ πάντα εἰδότι.

57. Cf. Cyril Alex., *Scholia de incarn. Unig. cap. XIII*: PG 75, 1385A: 'Also we investigate and wish to learn what it means then to be incarnate and that God's Word has become a human being; we see that it does not mean assuming a human being as in a uniting in the equality of dignity or of authority, or only in an homonymous sonship; rather, according to us, it is a question of becoming human, yet admittedly so that no alteration or transformation occurs . . .' This text is not included in the *FlorCyr*. Cf. the text of nos 103–4: Hespel, *op. cit.*, 156f.

58. Cf. on this especially *Scholia, cap. XXV*: PG 75, 1396B–1399B, where the necessary demarcations for this becoming are made, particularly 1397B. On this text see M. Richard, *Le pape saint Léon le Grand et les Scholia de incarnatione Unigeniti de saint Cyrille d'Alexandrie*, in *Op. Min.* II, no. 53 (116–28), 118. Severus comments on this text in *C. imp. Gram.* III 35: Lebon, CSCO 102 (V), 154f.

59. M. Richard, *art. cit.*, 121–8.

Arians,[60] thus defending the unity of the Logos with the Father on the basis of the one nature; in the other writing he has to emphasize the completeness of the humanity in Christ. In all passages the discussion is dependent on 1 Timothy 2,5 — 'the mediator between God and humankind'. Against the Arians, in the foreground stands the 'union' with the Father; against the Synousiasts,[61] it is the unity with us humans. Hence it is certainly a question of the terminology of union, not, however, immediately with regard to the one Christ, but rather to his twofold unity with God and with us. It is clear that in this way too the 'one' Christ himself comes into focus, as Severus, basing himself on the concept of mediator, rightly says:

> For because He is mediator between God and humankind, and out of two natures, namely godhead and manhood, He is one Emmanuel, thus He has reconciled to the Father who is in heaven human nature, that is, the whole race of human beings. (Severus Ant., Or. 1 ad Nephal.: CSCO 120 (V), p. 35,18–21)

(1) *Thesaurus*, ass. XV
FlorCyr, no. 205: Hespel, 197; PG 75, 284B

If the Logos of God, according to you, you discoverer of all godlessness, is a creature (κτίσμα), how are we through union with him (συναφθέντες αὐτῷ) joined to God (κολλώμεθα, lit. stuck on) and (thus) divinized? How is Christ mediator between God and humankind? He adheres to us (ἅπτεται ἡμῶν) as a human being. But if he is a creature and not God, how can he adhere (ἅψεται) to God? What manner of adhering is there in him? Things that are different according to their essence (ἀνόμοια κατὰ τὴν οὐσίαν) must not adhere to each other in a physical way (οὐκ ἂν ἀλλήλοις φυσικῶς συναφθείη ποτέ).

(2) *C. Synousiastas*
FlorCyr, no. 80: Hespel, 143,25–144,10; Pusey, 482–483,18

[cit. 1 Tim 2,5–6]: As the same he mediates at once God and humankind by reconciling us to the God and Father through himself and in himself; and he joins (συνείρων, conserere, adds) into a unity (εἰς ἕνωσιν) that which on account of its nature in unmeasurable distance (διαφορά) was brought to otherness (πρὸς ἑτερότητα). In Christ it runs together to an unmingled and inseparable unity (συνδεδραμηκότα πρὸς ἕνωσιν ἀσύγχυτόν τε καὶ ἀδιάσπαστον). In godhead he adheres namely to the Father (σύνηπται ... θεϊκῶς), but he also adheres to us as a human being (συνήφθη δὲ καὶ ἡμῖν ἀνθρωπίνως). But if his flesh is really damnable (i.e. it must be thrown off him), as he [the Synousiast] says, he is wholly distant from mediating between us and his Father.

(3) *Thesaurus*, ass. XXXII
FlorCyr, no. 228: Hespel, 206–207; PG 75, 504AC
[cit. 1 Tim 2,5]: If Jesus the Christ ..., mediator between God and humankind, does not physically (φύσει) and essentially (οὐσιωδῶς) be together with God and human beings, but

---

60. Cf. J. Liébaert, *La doctrine christologique de saint Cyrille d'Alexandrie avant la querelle nestorienne* (Lille, 1951); cf. *JdChr* I³, 605–9; *CCT* I², 414–17. See chs 22–24 and 28 of the *Thesaurus*.

61. Severus Ant., *Or. 1 ad Nephalium*: CSCO 120 (V), p. 4,25–27: Synousiasts are 'people who have mingled the flesh of the Lord with the divinity and foolishly said it was transformed into the substance of God'.

only joins (συνάπτων) in friendship that which is far from reciprocal communion (κοινωνίας), namely humanity and divinity, how can Paul call him *one*? (. . . Moses and Jeremiah and the prophets were also mediators). How was the *one* Christ mediator, if there were not something foreign (τί ξένον) in him? But he is one as Paul says in accordance with the truth; indeed foreign (ξένος) and unlike the others . . . Hence as that which lies in the middle between two in fact touches both with its own extremes and holds what is separated together in unity (τοῖς ἰδίοις ἄκροις ἐφάπτεται, συνέχον εἰς ἑνότητα τὰ διῃρημένα), and Christ is the mediator between God and human beings, so it is clear that he is by nature united (ἅπτεται φυσικῶς) to God as God, but to human beings as a human being. He is namely our peace (Eph 2,14) and binds human nature on account of his likeness to us into unity and communion with the divine being.

The three texts are closely related to each other, and this from various viewpoints. (1) They all begin from the mediator text of 1 Timothy. (2) The primary intention of the three texts is not to interpret the unity of Christ in himself, thus not with the question of how Christ is one in himself; rather the theme is unity with the Father and union with us, because both are endangered by contrary heresies. If one professes the Arian denial of the godhead of Christ, our union with God is destroyed because our mediator would be united with God only in the manner of a creature, that is, he thus remains estranged and distant from God. If one follows the Synousiasts, there is no true union with us because they do not take seriously the reality of the body of Christ. Strangely there is no reference to the fact that the Apollinarians, the ancestors of the Synousiasts, maintained that Christ had no soul and thus surrendered as well a communion in essence between Christ and us. But if in contrast one professes the true divinity and true humanity of Christ, whose substantial unity is here presupposed and not drawn into focus, then the nature of Christ as mediator, according to 1 Timothy 2, is fulfilled in its entire breadth and in its significance for salvation. (3) The three texts belong to a physical doctrine of redemption which is grounded completely ontologically. The being of Christ decides our communion with God. The surrender of Christ in his human freedom does not enter the picture.

On the basis of this formulation of the question the three texts are most opportune in many respects for the excerptor of the *FlorCyr*.

(1) The distinction of the natures in Christ is strongly emphasized; this is particularly the case in text 2, no. 80. The distance between divinity and humanity in Christ, their *diaphora*, is immeasurable. If the incarnation is taken seriously, then it leads to otherness (ἑτερότης)![62]

62. On this concept see W. Beierwaltes, 'Andersheit. Grundriß einer neuplatonischen Begriffsgeschichte', *ABG* 16 (1972), 166–97; *idem*, *Proklos, Grundzüge seiner Metaphysik* (Frankfurt, ²1979), 310–13 with n. 33. Here 'otherness' is brought into connection with

Cyril speaks outrightly of a movement which takes place between two poles, from the godhead to the true and whole human being. He calls them ἄκρα, the furthest points, extremes that stand opposite each other as contraries, and hence as foreign (ξένον) (cf. texts 2 and 3), indeed as 'separate' (text 3). One can hardly depict the *diaphora*, the difference of the natures, more strongly. The redemptive act of Christ now resides in the fact that these poles are brought together; this happened precisely in the person of the mediator. Here the three texts agree in a new regard, namely (2) in the choice of the terms with which the becoming one is signified. First, it is still to be noted that Cyril is arguing here soteriologically and not christologically: the two poles which are now to be joined in the mediator are God and humanity, the total humanity. The event of union, insofar as it had taken place in Christ himself, moves to the background; but it is necessarily presupposed and implied. This is now described with a complex of words which for the later Cyril would be nothing short of questionable, namely with verbs of the stem ἄπτω, συνάπτω, ἐφάπτω — to stick, to adhere, to fasten. In addition there are some synonyms such as 'to stick on', 'to join', 'to hold together' (cf. texts 1 and 3). That leads of course to the 'physical *koinonia*' of realities which are properly 'according to their essence unlike', thus indeed are not *homoousia* (cf. text 1). There is no doubt that now the true unity of God and humanity is established. In Cyril's sense this is the case only because in employing the *synapheia* terminology his starting-point is an older tradition. This concept is in fact in an old tradition a synonym for *henosis*, or rather συνάφεια is recognized as τρόπος ἑνώσεως or the way to unmingled unity, ἀσύγχυτος ἕνωσις. The most important witnesses for this are found in the Latin West. Namely Tertullian and Novatian describe the 'unmingled unity' unhesitatingly with the words *coniungere*, *cohaerere*; this happens in both trinitarian doctrine and in christology.[63] Also in Ambrose there appears 'a trace of the equation συνάπτω-ἑνόω'.[64] The Antiochenes are thus not the discoverers of the christological *synapheia* terminology, but rather its

---

middle-being and the *mediator* Christ. See also *idem, Denken des Einen. Studien zur neuplatonischen Philosophie and ihrer Wirkungsgeschichte* (Frankfurt, 1985). For the history of the subsequent influence of this philosophy Beierwaltes mentions Ps. Dionysius and John Scotus Eriugena. See *idem, Proklos*, Index. We shall discuss later the significance of Cyril for Ps. Dionysius expressly. Of interest is the combination in Proclus of the two words so important for Cyril, ἑτερότης and συνάπτειν: *Theologia Platonica* IV 28: Saffrey-Westerink (Paris, 1981), 81,8.

63. See L. Abramowski, *art. cit.* (above n. 39), 80–93.
64. *Ibid.*, 89; Ambros., *De fide ad Grat.* I 9: CSEL 78, 61.

defenders. With it, however, they intend more than a purely accidental or moral unity.

Thus one could undisputedly denote an 'unmingled unity' (ἀσύγχυτος ἕνωσις) in Christ or also in the Trinity as *synapheia*. For this one does not at all need auxiliary notions as these were tied to the words for 'mixture' (μίξις, κρᾶσις); they could even be excluded because one was so sure of the expressiveness of *synapheia* in relationship to the *henosis* of God and humanity in Christ (thus Tertullian, Basil, Ambrose, and in their way also the Antiochenes, and even Nestorius). An extended version of 'unmingled unity', however, could also incorporate *mixis* and *krasis* (Augustine, Novatian).[65] Cyril was admittedly more and more allergic to the use of 'mixture words'[66] although he conceded: 'Some Fathers have also employed nouns of mixing (τῆς κράσεως ὄνομα).'[67] But as Cyril excluded the vocabulary of mixture, so he also finally decided against the *synapheia* group and returned to the term *henosis*.[68]

The reaction of Severus of Antioch

It is immediately striking that the Patriarch does not comment on any of the excerpts nos. 80, 205, 228 of the *FlorCyr*. He passes over all of the excerpts from the text *Contra Synousiastas*, which comprise nos. 76–90 in

---

65. L. Abramowski, *art. cit.*, 93f. Severus too refers to a few Fathers with such a terminology of mixing: for example, to Ps. Julian (Apollinarian forgery!), to Cyril with a passage that proves little. Cf. *Or. 1 ad Nephalium*: CSCO 120 (V), pp. 44,34–45,10. More interesting is his reference to Greg. Naz., *Ep. ad Cledonium I*: PG 37, 184BC, where Gregory applies the terminology of mixing to the combination of spiritual, incorporeal and inseparable natures either with each other or with corporeal natures, within which the incarnation can be understood. Severus cites this passage in the *Or. 1 ad Nephalium*: CSCO 120 (V), p. 27,2-19, and praises Gregory greatly on account of it: 'See how lucidly he shows how the incorporeal is united unmingled and unseparated to the body, and yet suffers no mixing (*confusio*) which occurs in the case of mixing together with transformation: that is the property, namely, of fluid bodies that flow together and are mingled with an influence each on the other (*ex mutua implicatione*) and lose their own nature.'
66. Cf. Cyril Alex., according to the *FlorCyr*, nos 12, 35 and 99.
67. Cyril Alex., *Adv. Nestor. I*: PG 76, 33B, quoted by Severus Ant., *Ep. 2 ad Sergium*: CSCO 120 (V), pp. 84,20–85,15; cf. pp. 61,35–62,2. According to Severus the Fathers used such expressions, 'because they wanted to express the highest degree of unity of things uniting'. Cf. also Severus Ant., *Ep. ad Oecumen.*: PO 12, 179f. He censured the misuse of such terminology in the altercation with Sergius (see below).
68. Cyril Alex., *Scholia, cap. XIII*: PG 75, 1385A; particularly clear in *Apol. c. Theodoret. pro XII cap., anath. X*: PG 76, 445B: the Antiochenes would only confess the *henosis* for the purpose of deception; in reality, however, they would proclaim an external *synapheia* of relationship, as this is common among human beings. In spite of the *henosis*, as Cyril professes it, the difference (*diaphora*) of the natures, however, remains preserved (*Scholia, loc. cit.*: PG 75, 1385BC). In order to bring the strict unity in Christ to expression, Cyril has recourse to the schema of becoming which speaks of the 'economic' assumption of flesh and blood (1385A). On this model see R. A. Norris, 'Christological Models in Cyril of Alexandria', in *TU* 116 (1975) (255–68), 259ff.

the florilegium.[69] He dismisses the texts from the *Thesaurus* less radically. But even then he has nothing to say with regard to no. 205.[70] He appears embarrassed that the older Cyril delivered such weapons to the Chalcedonians by stressing so much the difference, the otherness, the strangeness of divinity and humanity, also in reference to the one Christ, and on the other hand by depicting the 'unity' with the vocabulary of *synapheia* which was so dubious. Furthermore, there is not a single reference to the *mia physis*, although — most annoying with regard to the Chalcedonians — it is conceded that the *synapheia* can effect a physical union, and hence there is nothing missing in the 'unmingled unity'.

Through the *FlorCyr* Severus had stumbled upon the fact that christological language had a greater breadth than he was happy with in the battle against Chalcedon. He reacted resolutely to the embarrassing declarations of Cyril's excerptors with the demand for a purification of language which should thrust into the background and exclude from further use all words and formulas of earlier Fathers, but especially Cyril himself, which could speak for the acceptance of a 'duality' in Christ. We observe this reaction of Severus both in the discussion of the *FlorCyr* and as well as with his next opponent, who will challenge him still more strongly than a purposeful selection from Cyril, namely the presbyter and grammarian, John of Caesarea. On top of that came the short controversy with the amateur theologian Sergius, where again it became necessary to eliminate the linguistic terminological stumbling-blocks from the inheritance of Cyril. In this case, from the compilers' point of view they were on the opposite side of the street. It was not a question, that is to say, of liquidating the final remains of the christology of separation, but of misunderstandings which resulted from the use of the words 'mixture' and 'mixing' and synonyms. Hence it will be possible to describe Severus' work of purifying language in its final completeness only after unfolding the further controversies.

---

69. Cf. Severus Ant., *Philal.*, on nos 76–90: CSCO 134 (V), 250f. His comment: 'Dans les chapitres qui suivent celui-ci [sc., no. 75] jusqu'au quatre-vingt-dixième, l'adversaire a perdu de vue qu'il frappait dans l'air et luttait en vain.'

70. See Severus Ant., *Philal.*, where there is a hiatus between no. 204 and no. 221; cf. R. Hespel, CSCO 134 (V), 285. Also with regard to John of Caesarea, Severus is annoyed by his adducing evidence of the fact that Fathers have used the word *synapheia*. Cf. Richard, *Iohannis Caesariensis ... Opera* = CCG 1, p. 24,526–532.

III. SEVERUS OF ANTIOCH AND THE THEOLOGY OF MEDIATION
OF NEO-CHALCEDONIANISM

The Cyrillian florilegium signified a new highly organized attempt to construct a bridge between Chalcedon and Alexandria, this occurring simply through the confrontation of purposefully selected texts from Cyril with the definition of 451, in particular with the two-natures formula. The excerpts were intended to speak for themselves and to be intrinsically effective. They presuppose a benevolent reader which Severus, however, was not prepared to be. He did not even get involved in attempts where such texts were subjected to the necessary analysis and interpretation. The two names Nephalius and John the Grammarian show us this. Unfortunately their works are preserved only in extracts for which, for the great part, we are indebted to the critic Severus.

1. Nephalius: from monophysite to supporter of Chalcedon

Nephalius[71] seemed to live for conflict and opposition: at first the opponent of his Patriarch Peter Mongus in Alexandria, he found a new adversary in Palestine, where he emigrated after not having been accepted by the clergy of Egypt. But just as quickly this zealot created a disturbance in the friendly atmosphere of this patriarchate. No doubt with the agreement of Patriarch Elias (494–516),[72] he began where the strongest fortress of the opponents of Chalcedon was, with the successors of the great Peter the Iberian and the monasteries around Majuma near Gaza. He secured for himself the support of the clergy of the individual towns.[73] The debate began certainly on the intellectual level in public discussions which were intended to serve the defence of Chalcedon. This may have led to the written version of a speech on the two natures in Christ which

---

71. See the literature mentioned above, n. 8; in addition, S. Helmer, *Der Neuchalkedonismus. Geschichte, Berechtigung und Bedeutung eines dogmengeschichtlichen Begriffes* (Diss. Bonn, 1962); P. T. R. Gray, *The Defense of Chalcedon in the East (451–553)* = Studies in the History of Christian Thought XX (Leiden, 1979) 105–11; *idem*, 'Neo-Chalcedonianism and the Tradition from Patristic to Byzantine Theology', *ByzF* 8 (1982), 61–70; L. Perrone, *La chiesa di Palestina* (1980), 148–151; A. Grillmeier, 'Das östliche und westliche Christusbild', *TheolPhil* 59 (1984), 84–96 (on P. T. R. Gray). The ideas of Nephalius can be derived with some effort from Severus Ant., *Or. 1 et 2 ad Nephalium*, edited and translated by Lebon in CSCO 119 (T), 1–69; 120 (V), 1–50; in addition Zacharias Rh., *Vita Severi*: PO 2, 102–4; John of Beth Aphthonia (BHO 1061; CPG 7527), PO 2, 231–3.

72. Cf. E. Schwartz, *Kyrillos von Skythopolis* = TU 49,2 (Leipzig, 1939), 377f.: Elias is said to have betrayed the spirit of union of Martyrius.

73. Zacharias Rh., *Vita Severi*: PO 2, 103,9–13.

was circulated. This *apologia* and the violent course of action of this new supporter of Chalcedon against the monks around Majuma challenged the leading figure among them, Severus, to respond. We possess — sadly, not completely — his two addresses to Nephalius.[74]

The new apologist of the 'two natures' was not blind to certain, as he expressed it, apologetically determined strong statements of the Council. The Fathers of 451, in accordance with the manner of combating heretics, here used 'somewhat large words' (*mele abyāṭā*)[75] to tear out by the roots the docetism of Eutyches and to plant pure doctrine in its place. As a former radical Cyrillian, Nephalius also no doubt felt that with regard to Chalcedon the idea of the unity in Christ *vis-à-vis* the distinction of the two natures, intended to stress the truth of the incarnation, should have been more strongly safeguarded. The objection that the Council favoured Nestorius suggested itself to him. But despite this public criticism Nephalius placed himself entirely in the service of the Council, and this in two ways: (a) through the florilegium which substantiated the formula of Chalcedon with patristic authorities;[76] and (b) through an expansion of this formula with a few additions intended to support it. Both were a contribution to the spirit of the tradition, to a continuation of the new interpretation of Chalcedon.

(a) We can pass over the individual *patristic passages*. For Severus it was settled that a patristic proof for 'two natures' could not be provided. Of course he conceded that the reality of divinity and humanity in Christ, the latter expressed through the *incarnata* of the *una natura* formula, continues to remain unmingled. Thus the 'two natures' are also in Cyril within easy reach, as the large *FlorCyr* indeed wanted to prove to us. But here Severus remained the staunch traditionalist: the great master Cyril had never formally applied 'two' to Christ, and this was the gospel for his pupil.[77] His altercation with John the Grammarian

74. The title used by Severus reads not 'against' but 'to' Nephalius, which he himself comments on towards the end of Or. 1: 'That, however, is written by us to Christians for the purpose of defence, not as an attack (*antilogia*)': CSCO 120, p. 7,18–19.

75. Cf. Severus Ant., *Or. 1 ad Neph.*: CSCO 119, p. 3,24; 120, p. 3,10–19. According to Lebon, 121, the Greek expression was perhaps παχυμερής.

76. The entire dossier of Fathers can no longer be ascertained. From the *Or. 2* of Severus we know that the following were adduced by Nephalius as authorities: Gregory Nazianzen (CSCO 120, 31–32); Proclus of Constantinople (*ibid.*, 33, 14ff.); John Chrysostom (*ibid.*, 34–35) and previously Cyril of Alexandria (*ibid.*, 15,31–33; 22,25–23,12; a further passage from Cyril is cited in n. 77). Severus replies as well with patristic authorities (35–36) and then adds a longer florilegium (36–42).

77. Severus Ant., *Or. 2 ad Neph.*: CSCO 120, p. 21,1–5: Cyril says in *Ep. 40* to Acacius of Melitene: 'It is absolutely certain that there is only one nature of the Son; we know, however, that it has become flesh and a human being' (PG 77, 192D–193A). But: 'What would he have

will make this even more clear to us than the addresses to Nephalius, as Leontius of Jerusalem will point out to us (PG 86, 1845A). The patristic *rélecture* of Chalcedon has also become a linguistic, terminological issue. The proposals of Nephalius are not revolutionary, but they are still worth noting.

(b) *Two concessions to Cyril*: One concerns the expression 'united natures'. Nephalius wanted to bring close together once again the two formulas which were contested at Chalcedon and seem to be in opposition to each other, viz. 'out of two natures' and 'in two natures'; this was to occur through speaking of the 'united natures' (φύσεις ἐνωθεῖσαι). 'In two united natures' should signify as much as 'out of two one' (ἐκ δύο εἷς). We can recognize these trains of thought from Severus' refutation.[78] He argues not unskilfully with the acts of Chalcedon. There the Fathers had rejected the first suggested proposal for a *horos*, a proposal composed by Patriarch Anatolius of Constantinople, precisely because it contained the formula 'out of two natures'. At the forefront of this action were the two Roman legates of Pope Leo I who had threatened their departure should the 'out of two' continue to be retained. In its place the new *horos* with its profession of 'in two natures' was then composed and accepted.[79] Thus — so argued Severus — even now the 'out of two natures' cannot be made to coincide with 'in two natures', even if the state of being united is expressly emphasized.

> See how they [the Fathers of Chalcedon] characterize the formula 'out of two' as heretical but define as orthodox the formula 'two united [natures]', whereby they have prepared the ground for Christ's being called two natures after the union.[80]

had to have said, if Christ were to be in two natures? "There are two natures of the Son: he has indeed become flesh and a human being".' Only with this formal affirmation of the duality would Severus have allowed himself to be convinced.

78. Cf. the following passages: *Or. 2 ad Neph.*: CSCO 120, p. 9,16–18: 'It is not the same to say that Christ is "out of two [natures]" and "in two [natures]" after the union, even if the expression is added: "united natures". The Synod itself testifies to that.' *Ibid.*, p. 13,27–30: 'The crafty hearer will, however, respond immediately: "See, Cyril forbids the separation of the natures after the union; I [Nephalius] call them then also united (*illas unitas dico*)" '; *ibid.*, p. 22,25–28: with reference to Cyril Alex., *Ep. 45 ad Succensum I*, Nephalius says: 'Why should we not thus say: Christ is *in* two *united* natures?'; *ibid.*, p. 23,13–14: (Severus:) 'Do not come to me again and say to me: "We too do not separate them [the natures], but call them united".'

79. See ACO II 1,2, p. 128, no. 34; p. 129,30–130,3. Cf. *JdChr* I[3], 753–4; *CCT* I[2], 543–4; *Chalkedon* I, 396–8.

80. Severus Ant., *Or. 2 ad Neph.*: CSCO 120, p. 9,27–30. It is said that with the 'out of two' the following were also rejected by the Fathers: 'one through *synthesis*' and above all the 'one nature of the incarnate Word'. Were the Fathers of Chalcedon to have acknowledged the two formulas as really having the same meaning, they would not have condemned Dioscorus, but would have had to have characterized as a wrangler the one who conducted an unnecessary fight against equally valid expressions (*ibid.*, pp. 9,30–10,3).

Thus for Severus not even 'in two united natures' is sufficient to achieve in efficacy his preferred 'out of two'.[81] From the texts of Nephalius, which are more intimated than literally cited, it is impossible to decide whether with his suggestion he wanted to make the 'out of two natures' superfluous or to recommend the simultaneous use of both formulas, which would correct each other. For Severus even this could not be considered, as his concluding words on this topic signify.

'If you consider all this so you will cease to say: the two natures and the two forms are one Christ after you have professed the union.' That that does not suffice is apparent with Theodoret and Andrew of Samosata, who also speak of the union of natures and yet split up the mystery of the *oikonomia*.[82] Hence according to Severus even the 'two united natures' cannot compete with the expressiveness of the *mia-physis* formula.[83] It sounds like the judgement after a judicial process when he says: 'Should we thus declare as innocent those [i.e. the 'Antiochenes' Theodoret and Andrew of Samosata and naturally Chalcedon] because they call the union undivided (*individuam*) and (characterize) it at the same time as highest and indissoluble and eternal, or should we not turn our face away from them (as from the convicted) who speak of two natures also after the union and contradict their own utterances and sway towards both sides?'[84]

The first attempt of Nephalius to mediate thus found no favour. How does it stand with the second, if this as such were really made by Nephalius? It is a question of the formula 'hypostatic union' (ἕνωσις ὑποστατική). This formula was just as offensive to the Antiochenes as the one of 'physical union' (ἕνωσις φυσική) which for Cyril was equivalent. For 'physical' signified for them as much as 'necessary by nature', while the incarnation after all is purely 'from grace'. *Unio hypostatica* was also unacceptable to them. If this expression, however, finally still found its way into post-Chalcedonian language and especially into scholastic theology, then an intrinsic change in interpretation had to have occurred. Ought we to attribute the initiative for this certainly not insignificant step of introducing a new linguistic ruling to Nephalius, as has been assumed?[85] For this purpose may we call upon the following text in Severus?

---

81. Similarly in *Or. 2 ad Neph.*: CSCO 120, p. 35,22–7 as a summary of a patristic argument, which Severus characterizes as manipulated: 'This is thus the sum of your authorities. While you ruin them and explain them according to your whim, and deceive the simple by mentioning the natures out of which the one Christ is, you say insidiously: "If two natures are brought together and united, we must say that this one Christ is recognized as being two natures".'
82. Severus Ant., *Or. 2 ad Neph.*: CSCO 120, p. 45,28–34.
83. *Ibid.*, p. 46,10–12. Cf. also p. 49,21–34.
84. *Ibid.*, p. 47,6–10.
85. See R. Helmer, *op. cit.* (n. 71), 158.

But you can say that the Chalcedonian Synod meant the *hypostatic union*. It says namely in its definition that 'the one and same Christ . . . is known in two natures; yet *on account of the union* the distinction of the natures is not annulled; rather the characteristic of each of the two natures was preserved [Lebon translates literally: *uniuscuiusque ex duabus naturis*], which, however, came together in one person and hypostasis'.[86]

It could be that Nephalius introduced *unio hypostatica* into the discussion. One has the impression, however, that it is Severus who wants to impute something to his opponent so that he can then divest him of the right to speak of a 'hypostatic union' — or so that he can bring him to accept along with it the *mia-physis* formula. For he says to his partner: 'Whoever namely talks of one *hypostasis* must also necessarily speak of the one nature.'[87] If Nephalius does not take this step, then his 'two united natures' will also not result in a 'hypostatic union'. One sees that if theologians embark on a compromise with the language of the *mia-physis* christology, then the day is not too far away when the simultaneous corrective use of both the one-nature formula and the two-natures formula can be recommended. There is no evidence that Nephalius had already taken this step; it is also not probable. For Severus certainly would have immediately taken issue with this attempt, which in his eyes was futile.

It is surprising that Severus also had to defend himself against the accusation of theopaschi(ti)sm, which attributes suffering to the godhead of Christ as such. The opponents of the *mia-physis* formula took care to raise this issue. As a former 'monophysite', Nephalius, in contrast to Severus, would have become considerably more cautious. For the latter also does not attempt to explain how the impassible God in the flesh, remaining impassible, can really suffer. He defends himself, however, against the suggestion that God suffers in the godhead by calling upon his usual witnesses.[88] He certainly did not wish to follow the manner of interpretation indicated by Leo of Rome, nor did he want to allow the question 'which nature was hanged on the cross'.[89] Without the solution of this difficulty, however, Severus could not really repudiate the reproach of theopaschi(ti)sm. We shall meet this problem again. The extent to which Severus knew himself to be obligated to the ecclesial kerygmatic tradition is indicated by a beautiful text from his first address to Nephalius, with which we shall end.[90]

---

86. Severus Ant., *Or. 2 ad Neph.*: CSCO 120, pp. 12,29–13,1.

87. *Ibid.*, p. 13,1–5, where Severus ends with the words: '*Qui enim unam hypostasim dicit, necessario et unam naturam dicet.*'

88. *Ibid.*, p. 42,4–13.

89. *Ibid.*, p. 44,8–16; p. 36,19–24 (with reference to Pope Leo: PL 54, 775).

90. Severus Ant., *Or. 1*: CSCO 120, pp. 6,28–7,17.

If anyone says that the flesh of the Lord descended from heaven or passed through the Virgin as through a channel, and describes it not rather as from her in accordance with the law of conception, even if formed without man, he is condemned. Neither the conception nor the birth from Mary, nor the dealings with human beings, nor cross, tomb, resurrection from the dead, ascension into heaven happen according to appearance, but all according to truth: for we needed real healing, because we had really sinned. Thus we await in truth the coming Christ in exactly the body in which he bore the suffering of the cross which brought salvation; thus namely will he be seen by those who have pierced him (Jn 19,37). We hold in our mind not the so-called theopaschism — far be it — but we say that the Lord of glory, as stands written, suffered in the flesh (cf. 1 Pet 4,1; 1 Cor 2,8). Although it is namely proper to the body to suffer, so the impassible Word was united to one capable of suffering; and because the body is proper to him, thus too the suffering is stated of him. But according to our faith the incarnation of the Lord is neither without soul nor without spirit, rather ensouled, endowed with spirit and understanding. We impose the ban on the appearance doctrine (*phantasia*) of Eutyches and Valentinus and the ungodliness of the Manichaeans and the foolishness of Apollinarius and the dreadful division of the *oikonomia* by Nestorius.

2. John of Caesarea, presbyter and grammarian

The next opponent with whom Severus of Antioch took up the fight was the presbyter and grammarian John of Caesarea, with his *Apologia for the Council of Chalcedon*.[91] Whether this amateur theologian, as Severus regarded him, had anything to do with the author of the Cyrillian florilegium or with Nephalius or not, he ought to be regarded as the real promoter of the attempt to mediate between Cyril, the theological authority dominating everything, and Chalcedon with its

91. Cf. CPG 6855–62. Richard, *Iohannis Caesariensis ... Opera* = CCG 1; in this are: 1. *Apologia concilii Chalcedonensis*, a) Lat.: pp. 6–46; cf. J. Lebon, *Severi Antiocheni liber contra impium Grammaticum* = CSCO 111, 93.101 (T); 112, 94.102 (V Lat.); b) *Excerpta graeca*: Richard, *op. cit.*, 49–58; C. Moeller, 'Trois fragments grecs de l'Apologie de Jean le Grammairien pour le concile de Chalcédoine', *RHE* 46 (1951), 683–8. The effort that Severus had made in composing the work against the Grammarian he describes in the letter to the Presbyter and Archimandrite, Elisha, from the years 519–521(?): PO 12, no. XXXIV, 272ff. 2. *Capitula XVII contra Mono-physitas*: Richard, *op. cit*, 61–6. On this, K.-H. Uthemann, 'Rezension zu M. Richard, CCG 1', in *ByzZ* 73 (1980), 70–2. Of the *XVII Capitula* Uthemann denies that nos XII–XVII belong to John the Grammarian, because in them the concept of *enhypostasis* which is important for John is missing. On the person of the Grammarian: according to C. Moeller, 'Un représentant de la christologie néochalcédonienne au début du sixième siècle en Orient', *RHE* 40 (1944/45) (73–140), 103, n. 1 and according to Richard, CCG 1, p. VI, n. 12, with Caesarea the city of the same name in Cappadocia and not in Palestine is meant. However, this is uncertain, as is shown by A. de Halleux, 'Le "synode néochalcédonien" d'Alexandrette (ca 515) et l' "Apologie pour Chalcédoine" de Jean le Grammairien', *RHE* 72 (1977), 593–600. He shakes the major argument of C. Moeller. Studies: Moeller, *Chalkedon I* (637–720), 672–4; S. Helmer, *op. cit.* (n. 71), 160–76; P. T. R. Gray, *op. cit.* (n. 71); L. Perrone, *op. cit.* (n. 71) 249–60 among others; P. Allen, 'Neo-Chalcedonism and the Patriarchs of the Late Sixth Century', *Byz* 50 (1980), 5–17; A. Grillmeier, 'Das östliche und das westliche Christusbild. Zu einer Studie über den Neuchalcedonismus' (=P. T. R. Gray), *TheolPhil* 59 (1984), 84–96.

fresh start. More clearly than with his two predecessors, there are two methodological levels that can be discerned in his writings, on the basis of which reconciliation could be brought about: (1) work on the 'concept' and (2) diplomacy in the use of formulas. How does Severus react to this?

(a) Work on the concept

At last it is recognizable that the effort to clarify contested concepts had begun, something that would already have been timely with the Council of 451. The chances of success for the new initiative were not very great. Most of all Severus was responsible for that. The monk received the suggestions of the Grammarian coolly, and remarked that a Homeric philologist and crammer would do better to keep his finger out of theological affairs.[92] He was particularly angered over the Grammarian's doubt about the authenticity of certain texts.[93] This is a reference to the *Symbol* of Gregory the Wonderworker, which the Grammarian declared to be inauthentic because in it *homoousios* occurs, a word which had been unknown before Nicaea (325). Severus cites the contested verse.[94] One would now have expected that the much more pressing problem of the Apollinarian forgeries in general would also have come up for discussion, something that would have suggested itself with the name of Gregory the Wonderworker and its misuse perpetrated by the Apollinarians. Nevertheless it will become apparent why the Grammarian himself could hardly have had an interest in pointing out the inauthenticity of texts with the *mia-physis* formula. In the excerpts which have been passed on by Severus there is also no reference to this.

92. Cf. Severus Ant., *C. imp. Gram., Or.* I 9: CSCO 112, p. 37,14–15: Et forsitan putas te ad iuvenculos, qui apud te instituuntur, loqui; *Or.* II 12: CSCO 112, p. 89,11–18: Quomodo enim haec non sint lacrymis digna: quod (scilicet) ii, qui in explicanda pueris ira apud Homerum (cantata) omnem aetatem triverint, minimeque forsan feliciter rem gesserint, cum ineruditionis pallio, illotis pedibus, ut dicitur, irruant in divina [sc. in theology] eaque perperam explicent. After that Severus criticizes the method of the Grammarian, using the texts of the Master, i.e. Cyril, partly through abbreviating and partly through adding. On the rôle of a 'grammarian' in Greek *paideia* and his significance for Christian exegesis and theology, see C. Schäublin, *Untersuchungen zur Methode und Herkunft der antiochenischen Exegese* = Theophaneia 23 (Cologne, Bonn, 1974), 34.

93. Cf. Severus Ant., *C. imp. Gram., Or.* II 9: CSCO 112, p. 78,26–33.

94. Cf. Greg. Nyss., *De vita Gregorii Thaumaturgi* (CPG 3184): PG 46, 912D–913A. Cf. on this L. Abramowski, 'Das Bekenntnis des Gregor Thaumaturgus bei Gregor von Nyssa und das Problem seiner Echtheit', *ZKG* 62 (1973), 145–66. There is a short account of her arguments against the authenticity of the symbol known to us today in J. M. Rist, *Platonism and its Christian Heritage* (London, 1985), no. XII: Basil's 'Neoplatonism': Its Background and Nature, reprinted from P. J. Fedwick (ed.), *Basil of Caesarea: Christian, Humanist, Ascetic* (Toronto, 1981) (137–220), 209–10.

His critique relates to other weaknesses of the opponent's argumentation and its foundations.

(i) A surprise attack by the Grammarian: the distinction between physis *and* ousia

For Chalcedon, as for Severus, the controversy about concepts revolved around the word *physis* and its meaning. In order to prove the legitimacy of the 'two *physeis*' of Chalcedon, John called in, not at all clumsily, the concept *ousia*. By precise definition he attempted to contrast it with the concept *hypostasis* and to give to it its own function in establishing the two-natures formula. In fact Severus was in no slight quandary. For the Grammarian, Basil of Caesarea had already performed important preliminary work, admittedly not in any way complete; this is in the context of the discussion about the trinitarian formula of the three hypostases in the one divine *ousia*. This historical recourse did not greatly please Severus. He denied that the Grammarian had understood correctly the principal document, viz. letter 214 to Terentius.[95] The following passage is the one in question.

> On the one hand each of us participates in the general way of being of the essence, on the other hand each is 'this' or 'that' through the peculiarities each possesses. [Then follows the application to the divine trinity.] Hence the essence is also common there as, for example, the goodness of the godhead or whatever else can still be thought. The hypostasis, however, is discernible in the particularity of fatherhood, sonship or in the power to sanctify.[96]

95. Cf. John Gram., *Apol.* 14: Richard, CCG 1, I 1, pp. 8,72–9,110.

96. Basil. Caes., *Ep. 214,4 ad Terentium*: Courtonne, *II*, p. 205; PG 32, 789A4–15: Περὶ δὲ τοῦ ὅτι ὑπόστασις καὶ οὐσία οὐ ταυτόν ἐστι . . . ἐκεῖνο ἐροῦμεν, ὅτι ὃν ἔχει λόγον τὸ κοινὸν πρὸς τὸ ἴδιον, τοῦτον ἔχει ἡ οὐσία πρὸς τὴν ὑπόστασιν. Ἕκαστος γὰρ ἡμῶν καὶ τῷ κοινῷ τῆς οὐσίας λόγῳ τοῦ εἶναι μετέχει καὶ τοῖς περὶ αὐτὸν ἰδιώμασιν ὁ δεῖνά ἐστι καὶ ὁ δεῖνα . . . On this see A. de Halleux, ' "Hypostase" et "Personne" dans la formation du dogme trinitaire (ca 375–381)', *RHE* 79 (1984), 313–69, 625–70; on Basil: 318–30. Basil wants to protect the comes, Terentius, from the forgeries of the old-Nicenes of Antioch (Paulinus), for whom *ousia* and *hypostasis* are synonymous and who consequently speak only of the one *hypostasis* of the godhead and the three *prosopa*. For the acceptance and further development of this linguistic rule see Gregory of Nyssa: CPG 3196 = *Ad Petrum fratrem de differentia essentiae et hypostaseos* (Ps. Basil, *Ep.* 38); CPG 3138 = *Ad Graecos ex communibus notionibus*; CPG 3139 = *Ad Ablabium quod non sint tres dei*. On the topic itself see C. Stead, 'Ontology and Terminology in Gregory of Nyssa', in *idem, Substance and Illusion in the Christian Fathers* (London, 1985), IX, reprint from H. Dörrie et al. (eds), *Gregor von Nyssa und die Philosophie* (Leiden, 1976), 107–27 with a report of the discussion. For the Latin linguistic usage it is to be noted that from Tertullian the first category of Aristotle, *ousia*, was translated by *substantia* and not *essentia*, which etymologically would have been more appropriate. The reason for this presumably lay in the fact that the Latins considered *essentia* as the bearer of the accidents, which could find no application to God. Marius Victorinus certainly refers to this in *Adv. Arium* I, 31: A. Locher, *Marii Victorini Afri Opera Theologica* (Leipzig, 1976), p. 65,16–19: *sed dicunt scripturae lumen esse deum, spiritum esse. haec autem substantiam [οὐσίαν] significant non enim accidens.* Cf. no. 30, p. 64,1–15.

The presbyter of Caesarea now applies this distinction to the Chalcedonian christological formula. In so doing he does not deny the concept of *physis* in favour of the concept of *ousia*, but pushes it into the background.[97] Behind this is the following line of thought: together with Severus, the Grammarian is prepared to accept the formula 'from two natures' (ἐκ δύο φύσεων). For this involves a graded process of thought which he can perform: at first glance the 'two natures' are still considered in the state of not-being-unified, whereby it is presupposed that here it is only a matter of an abstract *theoria*. For the humanity of Christ ought never to be assumed as real outside the *henosis*. This first *actio* is sufficient, however, to enable precisely this reality so to come into sight that it can also be recognized as persisting in the state of being united with the godhead. In this way the Grammarian intends to create the possibility of speaking of a duality in Christ. For this, however, the concept of *ousia* was more appropriate than the concept of *physis*, at least with Severus in view. For *physis* means for Severus 'that which is there from birth', thus the hereditary being or essence which is the bearer of all life acts. In Christ this is the God-nature. It is so much his own that even the substantially united humanity cannot receive the name of a *physis*. For this reason too there cannot be a duality of *physeis*.

It is different with the word *ousia*, especially if Basil's analysis of concrete being, as present in the letter to Terentius, is assumed. For it offers the possibility, which Severus had given up, of grasping conceptually and characterizing the unmingled humanity in Christ also in the state of being united, without allowing it to come to the feared teaching of the two hypostases. If Jesus is both true God as well as true human

97. Severus Ant., *C. imp. Gram., Or.* II 17: CSCO 112, p. 118,7–14, notes the intent of the Grammarian to shift from the concept of *physis* to the concept of *ousia*: 'The duality of the natures (*physis*) which cuts the one Christ into two you make into essences (*ousia, substantia*) understood in the universal sense, and you say that they [the essences of godhead and humanity] understood in the universal sense are united according to the hypostasis or — to use your word — hypostatically. Thus explain to us how these essences, I mean in so far as they express what is common (*koinon*) with the godhead and the humanity, are able to be united to each other and to be placed together hypostatically, so that they form one hypostasis.' Admittedly the line of thought of the Grammarian is twisted in this account. What he wanted to take only on the logical level, Severus transfers to the ontological. See the whole of no. 14 in Richard, CCG 1, 8–9. The same difficulty in understanding the Grammarian's line of thought — and this is once again on account of the lack of distinction between abstract essence and concrete nature — Severus shows in *C. imp. Gram., Or.* II. 22: CSCO 112, pp. 146,33–147,2: 'Thus we have clearly pointed out how with our way of speaking of "out of two natures" we do not understand that the natures themselves are in the universal sense essences which comprehend many hypostases, whereby in your foolish godlessness it would result in the sacred Trinity being incarnate in the whole of humanity and the whole human race . . .' The whole of ch. 22 speaks in this sense.

being, understanding which proceeds by way of abstraction ought rightfully to discover in him on the one hand the God-essence and on the other the human-being-essence. One ought also to speak of two *ousiai* to the extent that the *ousia* only becomes *hypostasis* through the *idiomata* added to it. If Severus wanted to forbid the application of this conceptual word to the humanity of Christ, he would run the danger of denying its reality. Because with *ousia* only the general (be it of divinity or humanity) is denoted, thus the *koinon* without the *idiomata*, so the assumption of two hypostases or persons is excluded. Severus can even use the formula 'from two natures (*physeis*)' with good conscience only because by *physis* he can understand *ousia*.[98] The usage introduced by the Fathers of maintaining in Christ a twofold *homoousion* — with the Father namely on the basis of the one godhead, with us on the basis of the common humanity — leads to the same result. A twofold *homoousion* means two *ousiai*.[99]

---

98. Cf. John Gram., *Apol.* 19: Richard, CCG 1, I 1, p. 10,128–130: *Quomodo autem Christum etiam 'ex duabus naturis' dicemus, si 'naturarum' nomen loco 'substantiarum' [ousiai] ab illis non intelligatur?*

99. It is precisely this reference to the twofold *consubstantialis* that Severus finds annoying. For this reason he cites and rebuts it often, not, however, without interpreting the text in a way which is dangerous for the Grammarian. It is found for the first time in the *Apologia*, frag. 19: Richard, CCG 1, p. 10,137–139: *Quomodo autem Christum et Patri consubstantialem et nobis consubstantialem statuunt et duos quidem consubstantiales confiteri non cessant, duas autem substantias negant?* (How can they [the Fathers] characterize Christ as consubstantial with the Father and consubstantial with us and not cease to confess two consubstantialities [masculine] and to deny two *ousiai*?) Cf. Severus Ant., *C. imp. Gram.* II. 21: CSCO 112, p. 140,8–11. The text returns in II. 29: pp. 177,6–9; 178,22–25. Fortunately we have a Greek text, independent of Severus, passed on through the DP and the fragments transmitted there, fragments falsely ascribed to Eulogius of Alexandria (CPG 6972). A comparison of the Syriac-Latin version with the Greek makes utterly clear — what neither J. Lebon nor M. Richard noticed — that Severus in the three words 'et **duos quidem consubstantiales**' used the masculine while the Greek text is composed with the neuter: Πῶς δὲ καὶ ὁμοούσιον τῷ πατρὶ καὶ ἡμῖν ὁμοούσιον τὸν Χριστὸν μετὰ τὴν ἕνωσιν ὑποτίθενται καὶ οὐ ναρκῶσι δύο μὲν ὁμοούσια ὁμολογοῦντες, ἀρνούμενοι δὲ τὰς δύο οὐσίας (Richard, CCG 1, p. 51,77–79), where instead of ἀρνούμενοι it mistakenly reads ἀρνούμεναι. Cf. DP, p. 71,13–15. In this way Severus ascribes to the Grammarian a profession of two *hypostases* or persons in Christ, i.e. he makes him a Nestorian. A. Van Roey kindly brought to my attention the fact that the Syriac text of *C. imp. Gram.* II. 21 and 29: CSCO 112, pp. 140,10; 177,8; 178,24 has a masculine expression which is such that it can also be rendered in the neuter. One could thus translate: *duos quidem consubstantiales* or: *duo quidem consubstantialia*. A. Van Roey refers to the Syriac translation of Cyril Alex., *Ep. 46 ad Succensum II*, in *C. imp. Gram.* I. 7, CSCO 112, p. 72,4–5, where in Greek there is the neuter *homoousia*, which is rendered in the Syriac by the masculine. The Greek text, now known, of our section demands the neuter, however: *dyo homoousia = duo quidem consubstantialia*. But by these means Severus could not have gained the respect of the Grammarian. In fact what it amounts to is that the Grammarian said *homoousia* (neuter) for which Severus placed in Greek *homoousioi* (masculine), and hence accused his opponent of Nestorianism. There is no doubt that John consciously chose the neuter form, because indeed he cites the expression of Gregory Nazianzen: In Emmanuel there is indeed an *aliud et aliud*, but not an *alius et alius* (ἄλλο καὶ

The presbyter John now attempts to illustrate this conceptual analysis with examples taken from various areas.

(1) From the Greek teaching about the elements: the four elements represent four 'differentiated essences' (διάφοροι οὐσίαι). They can, however, combine in an 'inseparable union' (ἀδιαίρετος ἕνωσις) to become 'one hypostasis', thus wood, stone and so on. This example from nature, however, has the disadvantage that in the one *hypostasis* there was a κρᾶσις, a mixing, even a σύγχυσις, a blending.[100] For this reason it is better to draw examples from another domain, namely

(2) From anthropology:

> In each of us the *ousia* of the soul is other than the *ousia* of the body; at the same time, however, the two *ousiai* in coming together to a single thing (καθέκαστον) form one *prosopon*, for example, that of John or of Paul or that of another, and yet remain two.[101]

Nevertheless John confesses that even the body–soul analogy has its limits in its application to Christ:

> . . . Thus there occurred in Christ the uniting of the two *ousiai* to become one *hypostasis*, one *prosopon*, when this is shown only dimly through examples. The *oikonomia* in Christ, however, runs away from every type of uniting [taken from the earthly domain] and outstrips all human understanding.[102]

The Grammarian attempts to secure this preference of his for the *ousia* concept in two directions. With his choice of words and concepts he moves simultaneously on two levels, namely on that of the abstract (*ousia*) and on that of the concrete (*hypostasis*). If he places the concept of *ousia* at the forefront he can come under the suspicion that the

---

ἄλλο, οὐκ ἄλλος καὶ ἄλλος) (cf. Greg. Naz., *Ep.* 101, 4: PG 37, 180A16–B3; in Richard, CCG 1, no. V, p. 57,241–242). Moreover the text reads in fragment 21 of the *Apologia*, in Richard, p. 11,160–163: 'Thus where the Fathers place "*physis*" in the singular without adding "[the *physis*] of the God-Logos", they describe the *ousia* and say that there are two natures in Christ; they recognize him [Christ] namely according to the "one thing and another" and as "consubstantial with the Father and with us".' One can hardly avoid the conclusion that Severus undertook the alteration described consciously in order to place his opponent in the wrong. Just as the Chalcedonian formula of two natures, so too according to Severus the formula of two *ousiai* leads to Nestorianism which, particularly in chs 27, 30 and 32 of Book II (CSCO 112, 168–170, 180–183 and 191–196), he explains with repeated arguments. '*Scito ergo quod dicendo duas substantias* [= two *ousiai*], *duas quoque hypostases dicis, etiamsi latere velis*' runs the concluding word of Severus on this problem (cf. II. 33, p. 209,23–24), which had concerned him particularly in chs 23–28. Here he is not completely sincere. As we shall see later, in the altercation with Julian of Halicarnassus and Sergius he could very well employ exactly this argument of the Grammarian concerning the two *ousiai*.

100. Cf. John Gram., *Apol.* IV. 2: Richard, CCG 1, I 2, p. 53,136–140.

101. *Ibid.*, pp. 53,141–54,145.

102. *Ibid.*, p. 54,156–160, especially 157–158: τῶν δύο οὐσιῶν γέγονεν ἕνωσις εἰς μίαν ὑπόστασιν καὶ ἓν πρόσωπον.

humanity of Christ is not an objective reality, but a mental construction, hence appearance. For this reason he stresses too the real existent content of the *ousia*. But in this way he brings it closer to the *hypostasis* concept and courts the danger of introducing with 'Nestorius' two hypostases. In a rather long fragment of his *apologia* which is transmitted in the DP in Greek under the name of Eulogius of Alexandria, he tries to escape this dilemma. He clarifies how he understands the reality of the *ousia*, particularly as far as the humanity of Christ is concerned. But in the same fragment he also takes pains to show that being real on its own does not yet make the humanity of Christ into a *hypostasis*, that is, into a second person. To this end he emphasizes, with reference to Cyril of Alexandria and Athanasius, the closeness of the *hypostasis* concept to 'reality', 'existence', and so on. Thus he gives to it a meaning through which what is common to *ousia* and *hypostasis* is brought into relief and what is special, which differentiates both, is bracketed. The important section is cited in translation because it is at the same time important for a new concept which the Grammarian here introduces into the discussion, namely that of the *enhypostaton*.[103]

(4) One should know that for the holy Fathers *hypostasis* is used in the place of *ousia*, as Cyril also assumes. In the third Anathema he says, namely: 'If in the one Christ anyone separates the hypostases after the union ...'. *Hypostasis* signifies here what exists (ὑφεστηκός); for the 'Godbearer' who constantly fought against the blasphemies of Nestorius would not have named two hypostases in the one Christ if he had not used them in the place of *ousiai*.

(5) [John wanted to derive the same result from Athanasius, *Ep. ad Afros*, PG 26, 1036B 5–9, with reference to Jer 9,9; hence he reasons:] The *hypostasis* is *ousia* and has no other meaning than that of the being itself which Jeremiah calls *hyparxis* in saying: 'And they heard not the voice of the *hyparxis*' [LXX]. [According to the Masoretic text it is a question of people in devastated Jerusalem no longer hearing the voice of the herds. They had been robbed indeed with the whole 'possession' of the people, of its *substantia*.] The *hypostasis* and the *ousia* thus mean *hyparxis*, existence; it *is* namely and *exists*.

(6) If now anyone characterizes according to this meaning the *ousiai* as real (ἐνυποστάτους), that is, as existent, then one too would not deny that. For the *hypostasis* differentiates itself from the *ousia* not according to being, but through being general (τῷ ... μὲν κοινῶς εἶναι) with which I mean the *ousia*; in contrast the *hypostasis* is the being one's own (ἰδικῶς) when it has with the general also its own. Thus we do not characterize our *ousia* in Christ in the sense of being real (ἐνυπόστατον) as a *hypostasis* which exists for itself in its characteristics and is a *prosopon*, but insofar as it exists and is. Sometimes namely *hypostasis* signifies (reveals) that which *ousia* is, as has been shown namely when it has been stripped of the characteristic *idiomata* and of what becomes visible in the *prosopon*.

The argumentation of the Grammarian admittedly is not convincing. In the third Anathema, Cyril speaks only conditionally of two *hypostases*,

---

103. John Gram., *Apol*. IV. 4–6: Richard, CCG 1, I. 2, pp. 55,189–56,211. On this Severus Ant., *C. imp. Gram.*, Or. II. 24: CSCO 112, pp. 150–156.

namely for the case that one sees them bound to each other only in a moral way and thus in the sense of Nestorius in Cyril's interpretation. Only in a christology of separation, not for Cyril himself, are there two *hypostases*. Hence John cannot prove from the third Anathema that Cyril intended to speak of two *hypostases* or *ousiai*. Even his recourse to Athanasius and his synonymous use of *ousia* and *hypostasis* is of no use. For the Alexandrian is an old-Nicene and cannot at all perform that upon which the Grammarian builds his entire argumentation, namely Basil's distinction of *ousia* and *hypostasis* as general in contrast to special. Thus if John intends to construct being real or existence as the bridge between the concepts of *ousia* and *hypostasis*, he confuses two conceptual systems, the Athanasian (old-Nicene) and the Basilian (neo-Nicene). In any case his historical examples for the legitimacy of speech about two *ousiai* fade away. Despite this, however, his whole attempt of calling upon the concept of *ousia* to justify the Chalcedonian formula of two natures is not worthless. For in the reality of the one Christ the abstract essence of humanity and divinity must be determinable even for Severus, if there is to be any sense at all in speaking of an unmingled unity.

Severus does not enter, however, into this really legitimate reflection of the Grammarian. He is not prepared to accept the latter's distinction of *ousia* and *hypostasis*, but rather attempts to tie him in knots and to characterize his depiction of the incarnation as absurd. But this does not happen without distorting the words of the opponent. He finds two weak passages in John's remarks:

(1) '*Tota humanitatis substantia in illo* [= *in Christo*]': As in the Son the whole essence (*ousia*, *substantia*) of the godhead is, so in Christ, in the Son become human, is also the 'whole human essence'. In this way the Grammarian wants expressly to give a rebuff to Apollinarius, who teaches that the Son assumed only a part of this humanity, namely flesh without a spiritual soul. The Son 'assumed (rather) the whole human essence which is flesh animated by a rational spiritual soul: because these are generally completely present in each and every human being, they are rightly called essence. For among themselves the individually constituted human beings are separated not through the essence, but through the peculiarities they have, height, colour, and in general terms, through the peculiarities of personal features'.[104]

(2) The distinction of *ousia* and *hypostasis* as the 'general' in contrast to the special through the 'individual' features.

Now Severus consciously interprets the Grammarian differently from the way in which the latter understands himself. For when the latter emphasizes the assumption of the 'whole essence of the human being', he means by that the *integra essentia hominis* in contrast to the assumption

---

104. John Gram., *Apol.* I. 4: Richard, CCG 1, I. 1, p. 9,100–110. Cf. *ibid.*, no. 57, p. 23,510–512; no. 65, p. 27,623–624; *JdChr* I², 484 (Apollinarius).

of a partial substance. It is a question of the *natura completa*, of the complete human nature. Severus, however, interprets this assumption of the *tota natura* as the assumption of the *natura universalis*, of the universal essence of humanity. He argues against John in the following way:

> God's Word himself participated fully in that which belongs commonly to the *ousia*, because it is united to one single body endowed with a rational soul, but not to the whole *ousia* and to all flesh endowed with a rational (soul). But your utterances lead you to this, for you say: 'He assumed, however, the whole *ousia* which consists of flesh endowed with an intelligent and rational soul'.[105]

Severus was striving to evade the attempt of the Grammarian to postulate that one had to accept two essences in Christ. For this reason he sought to make out that the stressing of the *ousia* by his opponent was a false tack. If, according to John, the Son of God assumes the 'universal essence of the human being', he takes up the whole human race into the hypostatic union. Every single human being is then, on account of his assumed *ousia*, a real Son of God. This reproach certainly does not touch the real thought of the Grammarian, who rightly establishes in Jesus of Nazareth the universal humanity as he finds it elsewhere in every individual human being. The censure of Severus would then also fall, for example, on the incarnation doctrine of Gregory of Nyssa, to whom, in point of fact, renowned historians of doctrine have attributed this teaching of the assumption of the whole human race.[106] If the presbyter of Caesarea, however, wants to defend himself against the interpretation of his teaching by Severus, he must point out that the humanity of Jesus is individually formed as is that of each and every human being. Then on account of his Cappadocian teaching on *ousia* and *hypostasis* only with difficulty can he avoid the necessity of

---

105. Severus Ant., *C. imp. Gram.*, Or. II. 17: CSCO 112, p. 128,22–28. Cf. the letters XV (PO 12, 210–221), XVI (211), II (186ff.): the *henosis* was not a *henosis* of the *humanitas i.s. generico* (*'nāšūthā*) with the Godhead.

106. Cf. R. Seeberg, *Lehrbuch der Dogmengeschichte II* (Erlangen, Leipzig, ³1923), p. 201, n. 1. Seeberg names W. Herrmann (1875), A. Ritschl and A. von Harnack, *Dogmengeschichte II*⁴, 166: The Logos is said not to have assumed a human individuum, but the species humanity. In opposition was F. Loofs, *PRE VII*³, 152; definitive rebuttal by K. Holl, *Amphilochius von Ikonium in seinem Verhältnis zu den drei großen Kappadociern* (1904), 222ff. Seeberg says with regard to this, *op. cit.*: 'It is the old relationship of the first of humanity to the race which directed Gregory's thoughts, not a Platonic idea. Moreover, the very thought that in Christ all are physically divinized would exclude the effort of individuals for salvation, which is so strongly stressed.' Fundamentally, it must be said of the inadequacies of the conceptual language introduced in this context that not all the consequences which occurred in the course of reflection and discussion on it were really recognized or wanted by the Fathers. For this reason all the attempts to master the mystery of the incarnation or trinity conceptually must always be measured by the kerygmatic statements of faith of the individual Fathers or of the Church at their time.

accepting in the human being Jesus a second *hypostasis* beside the 'Son of God'. For the *ousia* cannot be realized as universal essence, but only as individualized, concrete *physis*, that is, as *prosopon*. Thus he comes to hear from Severus: 'There is no *prosopon*-less *physis*.'[107] With this comment the Grammarian is challenged to present a theory of incarnation which represents a *via media* between the alleged assumption of the whole of humanity and a doctrine of two *hypostases*. Will he be able to achieve this with his Cappadocian assumptions? He attempts the solution by way of a concept which had already been introduced before him, but which receives from him a new application.

(ii) The concept of enhypostaton

In order to reply to the objections of Severus, the Grammarian coins the formula of the 'two natures enhypostatically united'.[108] Let us first take up only the word *enhypostatos*.

John the Grammarian did not himself introduce this concept into theological discourse.[109] It found particular importance in the theological discussions about the Trinity in the fourth century, as Jerome and Epiphanius testify.[110] In the question of the trinitarian formula the monk of Bethlehem stood on the side of the old-Nicene Paulinus of Antioch, and hence against Meletius. The Meletians demanded from him confession of the three hypostases in the one godhead, a formula which was for him a neologism,[111] but aroused in him in particular the suspicion of Arianism. For this reason he asked his opponents, the Meletians, for an explanation of this formula, which was interpreted by them as

---

107. Cf. John Gram., *op. cit.* IV. 2: CCG 1, I. 2, p. 53,121–122: καί φασιν, οὐκ ἔστι φύσις ἀπρόσωπος.

108. *Ibid.*, p. 53,118–120: Ἡμῶν γὰρ ἐνυποστάτως ἡνωμένας δύο φύσεις λεγόντων ἐθελοκωφοῦσι καὶ περιξύοντες τῆς ὁμολογίας ἡμῶν τὸ ἐνυποστάτως ἡνωμένας, προβλήματι κέχρηνται . . .

109. According to Lampe, *PGL*, 485b, ἐνυπόστατος is found in the sense of 'real', 'actual', 'existent' as early as Iren., Frag. 19 (PG 7, 1240C), as well as Origen, Didymus, Ps. Athanasius, etc.

110. On Jerome see A. de Halleux, ' "Hypostase" et "Personne" ' (above n. 96), 331–41; on Epiphanius cf. *Panarion, haer.* 72,11: Holl III, 265–266. In question is a profession of faith which the Marcellan community of Ancyra addressed to the Egyptian bishops banished to Diocaesarea. In this in continuation of Marcellan teaching the community professed the 'three *prosopa* of the holy Trinity which are unlimited, *real*, one in essence, equally eternal and perfect' (τρία πρόσωπα ἀπερίγραφα καὶ ἐνυπόστατα καὶ ὁμοούσια . . .) (p. 266,4–5). Cf. W. Gericke, *Marcell von Ancyra* (Halle, 1940), 23, where besides other inaccuracies, *enhypostaton* is taken not in the sense of 'real', but in the sense of the inexistence, i.e. the perichoresis of the three divine persons.

111. Jerome, *Ep.* 15,3: Hilberg, CSEL 54 (Vienna, 1910), 64: *trium* ὑποστάσεων . . . *novellum a me, homine Romano, nomen exigitur.*

tres personae subsistentes or, in Greek, τρία πρόσωπα ὑφεστῶτα. Jerome says for this: τρία ἐνυπόστατα.[112] Here this expression means nothing other than 'real', 'existent'.

Marius Victorinus too refers in the same direction; in his 'theological works'[113] it is true that he does not have *enhypostaton*, but employs rather often for it the cognate term ἐνούσιος.[114] As for John the Grammarian and his conceptual reflections, the Chalcedonian definition was the starting-point, so for the comments of Marius Victorinus it was the *homoousios* of Nicaea. Thus for him the noun οὐσία together with the abstractions, adjectives and verbs associated with it come into his world of vision. Thereby the Latin *substantia* corresponds to the Greek οὐσία.[115] Hypostasis and ousia are synonymous.[116] In this regard he could be characterized as an old-Nicene, although for the difference of Father, Son and Spirit in the one God he accepts the formula: *una substantia* (οὐσία), *tres subsistentiae*.[117] The *substantia* (οὐσία) is the being of the divinity itself (*id ipsum, quod est esse*); this being, however, subsists in a threefold way, as God Father, as Logos and as Holy Spirit. Father and Son (and Spirit) have the same hypostasis or — as the Latins say — the same substance (οὐσία); for this reason they are only one God, but as *esse formatum* they are threefold (*tres subsistentiae*).

112. Jerome, *loc. cit.*, who transmits the demand of the Meletians of Antioch, clothed in an anathema: *si quis tres hypostases ut tria ἐνυπόστατα, hoc est ut tres subsistentes personas, non confitetur, anathema sit* (65). For the Meletians the formula of the 'three subsistent *prosopa*' was not sufficient to be able to exclude Sabellianism definitively. Cf. Basil Caes., *Ep. 236 ad Amphil.* no. 6; Courtonne III, 54; PG 32, 884C: 'Those who say that *ousia* and *hypostasis* are the same thing see themselves forced to confess only different *prosopa*, and while they avoid speaking of three *hypostases* they find themselves inevitably caught in the web of Sabellius.' Jerome himself suspected the Meletians of Arianism, i.e. the division of the one godhead into three separate substances. Cf. *Ep.* 15,3 and 4, cited in A. de Halleux, *art. cit.* (above n. 96), 336, n. 4.

113. Cf. A. Locher, *Marii Victorini Opera theologica* (Leipzig, 1976) with indices.

114. To be compared are: ὑπερούσιος, *supra substantiale*, quintessential; ἀνούσιος, *sine substantia* (p. 100,17). Cf. *Adv. Arium* II. 1: Locher, pp. 100,16–101,19. Many call the *hyperousios* also *anousios*. Cf. also Locher, p. 7,15–16; p. 18,18: *anousios = insubstantiale* (for God) (negative theology). Ἐνούσιος, what has being and substance, which he also translates by *insubstantiatum* (p. 59,6–7 *bis*).

115. On the whole topic cf. H. Dörrie, Ὑπόστασις. *Wort- und Bedeutungsgeschichte =* NAWG.PH 1955, no. 3, 74–84; admittedly *ousia* is mentioned only occasionally.

116. Cf. Marius Vict., *Adv. Arium* II. 6: Locher, 106–7. Starting from the parable of the prodigal son and the designation of the estate of the father as *hypostasis* (*substantia*), he speaks of the transmission of the divine *hypostasis* or *ousia* from the Father to the Son. He can establish the *homoousios* between Father and Son from both words.

117. Marius Vict., *Adv. Arium* II. 4: Locher, pp. 105,24–106,2: Here he distinguishes *ousia = substantia =* that which is grasped purely under the aspect of ὄν, being. There is, however, an ὄν *formatum*, in which the form is to be distinguished from that which is formed by it. One calls the formed being *hypostasis* or in Latin *subsistentia*: *iam enim formatum esse subsistentia est* (p. 105,26–27).

Perhaps from Marius Victorinus and his concept of ἐνούσιος something can also be gained for understanding ἐνυπόστατος, even if this is not found in his writings. The first of these words is found five times in the *opera theologica*.[118]

Enousios: It is to be translated as: in being, in essence, in reality, in substance. Because God 'is', God is *enousios*.[119] In Latin one would certainly have to say for this: *insubstantiatus*, as *Adv. Arium* I 26 shows: 'If everything is one, namely in the substance [that is, in a chain of being which stretches from God, Jesus, Spirit, over the *nous*, the soul, the angels to the corporeal], so are nevertheless God and the Son not only an *insubstantiatum*, but a *consubstantiatum*. *Insubstantiata* are namely all beings (ὄντα) in Jesus, that is, in the Logos, as it says: "All things are created in him" (cf. Col 1,16). Ὁμοούσια [*consubstantialia*], however, these are not.'[120] All things have their ground of being and their 'being in the essence' in the divine Logos as their exemplary and efficient cause. For this reason they participate in his essence, but nevertheless are not one in essence, *homoousia*!

Substantia–subsistentia: Existing 'in essence', however, are always individual beings. They are effected through the fact that the 'form' (*forma*) comes to the universal essence: *quod est esse principale cum forma subsistentia dicitur*.[121] A 'subsistence' is for Marius Victorinus the final and highest realization of being. Even in God being is realized as *ousia*, substance and even more as subsistence.[122] The concepts of οὐσία and ὑπόστασις are for him still synonymous, so much so that he can deduce the *homoousion* for Father and Son from the fact that they have the same *hypostasis*.[123] From this it follows that Marius could also have formed or understood the concept of *enhypostaton*. But then it would also have no other meaning than that of *enousion*, namely 'in being, to be in reality'.

The significance of enhypostaton in John the Grammarian

The word *enhypostaton* appears in only a few places.[124] We shall ask first of all about the general, fundamental meaning of the word, and then about its application to christology.

(1) Fundamental meaning: it is existence, reality, in the sense of ὕπαρξις. This emerges from the struggle of the Grammarian for his 'formula of two *ousiai*'. For what concerns the reality, *ousia* is equivalent

---

118. Cf. the index in Locher with reference to the *Op. theol.*, pp. 100,17; 101,5.8.21.23.

119. Marius Vict., *Adv. Arium* II. 1: Locher, pp. 100,17; 101,5.8.21.23.

120. *Idem, Adv. Arium* I. 26: Locher, p. 59,5–8.

121. *Idem, Adv. Arium* II. 4–6: Locher, pp. 104–7, esp. p. 105,30.

122. In the formed being Marius distinguishes *existentia, substantia, subsistentia. quod enim ὄν est, et existit et subsistit et subiectum est* (p. 105,15–16).

123. *Idem, Adv. Arium* II. 6: Locher, p. 107,3–10: *ergo lectum est de deo vel* ὑπόστασις *vel* οὐσία, *hoc autem et de Christo intelligitur. dictum est:* **ego in patre et pater in me** (cf. Jn 14,10). *quod quidem ideo bis dictum, quia in patre esse potuit filius, non tamen et in filio pater, sed ut plenitudo atque idem unum in singulis esset. si autem eadem* ὑπόστασις, ὁμοούσιον *ergo. eadem autem; nam* **Christus deus de deo et lumen de lumine**. *ergo* ὁμοούσιον. *id autem si ex aeterno et semper, necessario simul; ergo vere* ὁμοούσιον.

124. Cf. the index in Richard, CCG 1, p. 153: I, 96, 108, 182, 201, 206, 256; II, 109; also adverbially, I, 118, 120, 133; II, 25, 66, 122, 123.

to *hypostasis*.[125] The distinction lies not in more or less reality, but only in the mode of existing: the *ousia* exists as the universal in the individuals, while the *hypostasis* signifies the final, concrete individual substance.[126] It is clear that thus the *enhypostaton* is present most definitely in the *hypostasis*. This means: to be real as *hypostasis*.[127] The prefix *en* does not refer to another being in which this *hypostasis* would inexist, but rather to the proper reality of this concrete *enhypostaton*.

(2) *Enhypostaton* in the christology of John the Grammarian: ought one to use the predicate *enhypostatos* also of the human nature of Christ? John attempts to limit the application, this again confirming the meaning just arrived at.

> Consequently we do not say that our *ousia* is enhypostatically in Christ as a *hypostasis* which is characterized *per se* and is a *prosopon* (οἷον ὑπόστασιν καθ'ἑαυτὴν χαρακτηριστικὴν καὶ πρόσωπον οὖσαν), but insofar as it has existence and is (ἀλλὰ καθὸ ὑφέστηκέ τε καὶ ἔστιν). For sometimes the *hypostasis* reveals what pertains to the *ousia* as is shown when it is deprived of the characteristic *idiomata* and all of those things which are seen in the *prosopon*.[128]

On this account John the Grammarian is cautious in his application of the predicate *enhypostatos* to the humanity of Christ, because he does not want to represent it as an independent *hypostasis*; this would have inevitably brought upon him from Severus the reproach of Nestorianism. Yet he wants to retain this concept for the human being of Christ, and indeed in its fundamental meaning 'to be real, actual', certainly not in the sense that it is *ousia*, and indeed not as *hypostasis*. At this point it would have been best for him to have introduced the word *enousios*. For the human nature of Christ, his *ousia*, does not have those characteristic features from which it would constitute a purely human *hypostasis*, a 'mere human' in the sense of Paul of Samosata or Photinus. For then, *vis-à-vis* the Logos, it would be an *allos*, an other. Thus we recognize that the prefix *en* is not yet pointing the way to a subject that lies outside the human *ousia* of Christ, but rather into this very *ousia*, into the reality that is proper to it as such.

---

125. Johannes Gram., *Apol.* IV. 5: Richard, CCG 1, I. 2, p. 55,199–200: ἡ γὰρ ὑπόστασις καὶ ἡ οὐσία ὕπαρξίς ἐστιν. ἔστι γὰρ καὶ ὑπάρχει. The *ousia* is an objective reality, even if it is only discovered by the abstracting intellect as universal in individual things.

126. Cf. *ibid.*, IV. 6, p. 55,202–5: 'The *hypostasis* is differentiated from the *ousia* not by being "what is" [the *quid esse*], but through the universal being, I mean the *ousia*, while the *hypostasis* exists individualized (ἀλλὰ τῷ τὴν μὲν κοινῶς εἶναι, φημὶ δὴ τὴν οὐσίαν, τὴν δὲ ὑπόστασιν ἰδικῶς, ὅταν μετὰ τῶν καθόλου καὶ ἰδικόν τι ἔχοι).'

127. *Ibid.*, p. 55,205–7: ... ἐνυπόστατον ..., οἷον ὑπόστασιν καθ'ἑαυτὴν χαρακτηριστικὴν καὶ πρόσωπον οὖσαν.

128. *Ibid.*, pp. 55,205–56,211.

John the Grammarian, however, cannot escape the axiom with which Severus confronts him: there is no *prosopon*-less *ousia*! Hence he must show that the unmingled *ousia* of Christ nevertheless finally becomes the *hypostasis* or also that it participates in the reality of the *hypostasis* and does this through the *idiomata* peculiar to the Logos. This participation is mediated to the human *ousia* of Christ by way of the 'enhypostatic union' or of the *synthesis*.[129] With this a new formula has been coined which differs from the Cyrillian 'hypostatic union' through the prefix *en*. With this formula have we already arrived at the concept of *enhypostasis* which so quickly attracted the attention of historians of doctrine and has been interpreted in the sense of insubsistence of the human nature of Christ in the *hypostasis* of the Logos? In answering this question one must note that the Grammarian understands this 'enhypostatic *henosis*' in the framework of the Basilian teaching of *ousia* and *hypostasis*. It is a question of the human essence of Christ which, according to the *koinon*, the general, does not differ at all from the essence of other human beings, but which can have its specialness only in the manner that it does not stand beside the Logos as an *allos*, as an other. Hence it can become hypostasized through the communication of the *idiomata* of the Logos as Logos. Through this communication it participates in the *hypostasis*-being of the Son, in his *idiomata*, and attains the degree of a hypostatic actualization. In this connection John the Grammarian appears to look only at these *idiomata* which are due to the human nature of Christ from the Logos. He does not ask about the purely human qualities such as size, colour, appearance, which nevertheless cannot be denied to the individuality of this human being, Jesus of Nazareth. This emerges from a fragment of his *apologia* preserved in Greek.

> To him [i.e. Christ as Logos-subject] belongs according to his nature the divine; to him and not to another also the human on account of the enhypostatic union (διὰ τὴν ἐνυπόστατον ἕνωσιν). For not in another but in him exists this his own flesh (ἀλλ' ἐν αὐτῷ ἡ ἰδικὴ αὐτοῦ ὑπέστη σάρξ) . . . Indeed it [the flesh] has the general (τὸ κοινόν) of the human *ousia*, namely flesh animated by a spiritual soul; but only in the God-Logos did it have the specialness (τὰ ἰδικά), that means not to be the flesh of another. How is it [the flesh] now a *hypostasis* because it does not exist at all for itself?[130]

The *idika*, which could thus make the human *ousia* in Christ an individual, ultimate subject existing for itself, come to it solely from the pre-existent divine Logos-subject who is constituted as *hypostasis* in God.

---

129. *Ibid.*, IV. 2, p. 53,132–133: οὐσιῶν . . . τῶν ἐν συνθέσει καὶ ἐνυποστάτως ἡνωμένων.
130. *Ibid.*, IV. 3, p. 55,181–188.

In this way, going speculatively beyond Chalcedon, that notion is emphasized which sees the 'one *hypostasis*' already pre-existent in the (concrete) Logos-subject and does not consider it only as the result of the *henosis*. We have established that the beginnings of this are to be found quite soon after Chalcedon.[131] Now it is clear that the 'one *hypostasis*' is also firmly established really and ontologically in the Logos, and not only according to the kerygmatic schema of a christology from above.

In this passage, what does the expression 'enhypostatic union' mean? Ought we to interpret it from the final words of the text just cited, which state of the flesh of Christ that it does not 'exist for itself'? Ought we here to interpret the word 'enhypostatic' on the basis of its prefix as an 'insubsisting', in distinction to the meaning first established: real, actual? From our text this much is clear: the human *ousia* of Christ has, in addition to the content of its essence, only this one *proprium*: to be the flesh of the Logos alone and of no other. The bond which links the human nature of Christ to the Logos as subject is not yet formally seen in the 'insubsistence', the existing in, but in a relationship of possession. This restriction imposes itself if one examines how John thinks of the 'becoming united enhypostatically' in its execution. He understands by it hardly anything other than what Cyril wants to express with the concept of 'appropriation' (*ἰδιοποιεῖν*). One has to interpret the following text in this sense.

(In contrast to the eternal, uncreated, impassible divine nature of the Logos, his flesh is temporal, created and subject to suffering:) But if it is *his own* flesh, so it is clear that also everything due to the flesh belongs to him; for everything is taken over as his possession (*οἰκειοποιεῖται*), even if his divine nature itself has not been subjected to this (suffering).[132]

Yet the whole of the Grammarian's remarks lead beyond Cyril when (1) a conceptual distinction is made between *ousia* and *hypostasis* and when (2) the concept of *hypostasis* is explained as 'existing for itself'. This 'existing for itself', however, does not yet mean more than 'to exist completely individualized'; thus the Grammarian penetrates only as far as grasping the individuality. The Grammarian seems (3) consciously not to speak of the 'physical or essential union' (*ἕνωσις φυσική, οὐσιώδης*)

131. See *JdChr* II/I, 189–96; 263–4; *CCT* II/1, 166–72; 233–5.
132. John Gram., *Apol.* VI: Richard, CCG 1, p. 57,259–261 and 267–272. Cyril of Alexandria usually supports the meaning of *enhypostatos* mentioned above, when in the *Thesaurus de Trin.* VIII (PG 75,101C9–104A9) he opposes the *enhypostata* to things such as, for example, knowledge, wisdom, will, which 'exist in certain beings as angels and human beings'. Because the Son of God in contrast 'is enhypostatic' (*ἐνυπόστατος ὤν*), he will thus be in no way similar to the anhypostatic will.

as Cyril does, but of the 'enhypostatic union'. In Cyril, the Apollinarian nature-*synthesis* still resounds when he emphasizes the 'substantial' and not only 'accidental' unity of God and a human being. Christ is a 'really-one concrete subject out of two natures'. This danger of still thinking in the manner of the nature synthesis is now clearly excluded precisely through the distinction of *hypostasis* and *ousia* (*physis*). For the unmingled human *ousia* of Christ participates in the being of *hypostasis* solely through being possessed by the Logos and the communication of his special features. The idea of *hypostasis* as the ultimate, incommunicable subject in contrast to 'essence' or 'nature' has now already come into view. Nevertheless one should not let oneself be misled by the word *enhypostatos* into seeing already a formal expression of the function of the 'insubsistence' of the humanity of Christ in the Logos-*hypostasis*. 'Insubsistence' can only be found in it to the extent that the human nature of Christ is inseparably taken under the *hypostasis* of the Logos through the communication of the divine *idiomata*, and is individualized through the *idiomata* that are proper to the Logos.

(b) A compromise for peace

The significance of John of Caesarea in the history of theology lies not so much in the domain of conceptual analysis as in his use of christological formulas. He was the first promoter of the idea of reconciling Chalcedonians and Cyrillians/Severans through playing with antithetical formulas. In a special way the appellation 'neo-Chalcedonian' applies to him, should this term continue to be used by researchers. We shall have to return to this. Cyril of Alexandria now also receives a new chance from the side of the supporters of Chalcedon. If the compilers of the large *Florilegium Cyrillianum* had attempted to point out how close the Patriarch was to the two-natures formula, so now the Grammarian, even more decidedly than Nephalius, adds the *mia-physis* formula and its terminological compass to Chalcedonian language, ostensibly to represent the mystery of Christ in a fully valid way. From the fragments which have been preserved by Severus we can develop a reasonably complete conception of this attempt.

(i) Cyril as an example of tolerance and of the willingness to compromise

In the behaviour of Cyril at the Union of 433 John also sees a model for clearing away the differences about Chalcedon. This is a legitimate thought. He depicts the situation in this way.[133]

---

133. Severus Ant., *C. imp. Gram.*, *Or.* III 1, 12: CSCO 94, p. 153,1–31; John Gram., *Apol.* 37: Richard, CCG 1, I. 1, pp. 17,333–18,362.

(1) The Orientals (that is, the Antiochenes in the party of John of Antioch) proclaimed two natures in Christ and refused to assent to the formula of the 'one incarnate nature', because for them this smelled of heresy.

(2) Through this action Cyril's patience was severely tested, because he had made himself the patron of this formula and had justified it, as he declared in his second letter to Succensus. He said: (a) the Orientals lived in darkness, not because of their positive confession, but because of their refusal to allow as a valid statement the formula of the one incarnate nature. (b) He himself has understood this formula in orthodox fashion. It means nothing other than: 'There exists one Son, one nature of the Word, but who has become flesh.' (c) As far as the issue at stake was concerned, the Orientals could also have taught this, although they showed no appreciation for the formula itself.[134] Thus Cyril himself saw here a fundamental consensus.

From this analysis of the situation in 433 the Grammarian now judges the possibilities of an agreement between the Chalcedonians and the Severans. (1) Cyril does not reject the statement of the two natures; he demands, however, (2) from his Antiochene partners the confession of 'the one incarnate nature of the Logos'.[135] The Orientals in fact could have allowed themselves to be 'illuminated' to the extent that they were ready to accept in the same way the two-natures formula together with the one-nature formula and to profess them in orthodox fashion. The ones remaining in the darkness are the Severans, who before as well as after wanted only the *mia-physis* formula to be regarded as valid.[136] They still would not recognize that both dispositions are present in Cyril and also that the two-natures formula was not rejected by him. At the same time the Grammarian knows that Cyril does not take over for himself the two-natures formula as such[137] (the Alexandrian, however, did not demand from the Antiochenes the recognition of the *mia physis*).

134. Severus Ant., *loc. cit.*: CSCO 94, p. 153,10–26; John Gram., *loc. cit.*: CCG 1, pp. 17,342–18,358.

135. Severus Ant., *loc. cit.*: CSCO 94, p. 153,27–31; John Gram., *loc. cit.*: CCG 1, p. 18,358–362: *Itaque non reicit assertionem duarum naturarum, sed confessionem unius* **naturae** *incarnatae, carne praedita anima rationali postulat. Vos autem adhuc et nunc tenebris offundimini, dum Orientales illuminati sunt et utramque formulam aeque et recte confitentur.*

136. See the texts cited above.

137. This appears in the cautious words of John the Grammarian, *Apol.* 40: Richard, CCG 1, pp. 18,382–19,387 (CSCO 94, p. 154,12–18): *Quapropter beatus Cyrillus et eos, qui duas naturas de Emmanuele dicunt, recipiebat, cum haereses Apollinarii fugeret, rursusque assertionem unius naturae Dei Verbi incarnatae profitebatur propter sectionem Nestorii. Cum enim utrumque proclamatur, rectae sententiae indicium habetur; cum vero una confessio reicitur, mala suspicio haereseos oritur.*

The position of Cyril, despite some slight eisegesis, is to some extent correctly rendered. It is false, however, to claim that the Orientals would have professed both formulas. The intention of the presbyter reveals itself clearly: to bring the historical positions of 433 so closely together so that Severus too could give up his rigid either–or position without losing face. The suggestion of excluding both Apollinarius and Nestorius through employing both formulas simultaneously seemed to be so plausible to the Grammarian and so easily realizable that he was severely disappointed at the categorical negative of the Severans.

(ii) The reaction of Severus and his supporters
The resistance to the Grammarian's idea of peace sprang up immediately and was fierce. Fragment 39 of John's *apologia* manifests this.

> They [i.e. the Severans] will say, however: 'You use this expression [i.e. the *mia-physis* formula] in a malevolent way!' Ah! This impudence of opponents! If we were to speak only of two natures and not also proclaim that other confession: namely, one is the incarnate nature of the Word, then your accusation would have a base. But what legitimate charge against us still remains for them? Who will not rather rebuke rightfully the ones who utter their anathema against those who characterize the two natures as hypostatically united?[138]

Severus feels that the Grammarian interpreted the Union of 433 according to his own desires and had formed for himself a straightforward judgement. He gave John of Caesarea the following to think about.[139] The letter of the Orientals to Cyril[140] did not contain the *mia-physis* formula at all. Cyril remedied the confession of the Orientals, which according to his notions was insufficient, by adding the formula 'out of two' (*ex duobus*).[141] The Grammarian's attempt to employ the two contested formulas simultaneously was for him a futile enterprise. For whoever remains with the 'duality' of Chalcedon and wants to combine the *mia-physis* formula with it maintains contradictions, namely: 'to become united and not to become united are the same'.[142] Already in the second speech against the Grammarian, Severus had rejected the attempt to achieve the 'remedy' of Chalcedon by equating the *mia-physis* formula with the new creation 'two united natures' (*duae naturae*

---

138. Severus Ant., *C. imp. Gram., Or.* III 1, 19: CSCO 94, p. 222,6–14; John Gram., *Apol.* 39: Richard, CCG 1, p. 18,374–381. Partial citations of this text are found in *Or.* II 12: CSCO 112, p. 89,27–31; *Or.* III 1, 12: CSCO 94, p. 154,9–12; *Or.* III 1, 13: *ibid.*, p. 165,10–13.

139. See Severus Ant., *C. imp. Gram., Or.* III. 1, 12: CSCO 94, pp. 154,19–156,13.

140. See John Ant., *Ep. ad Cyril Alex.*: PG 77, 169–173.

141. Severus Ant., *C. imp. Gram., Or.* III. 1,12: CSCO 94, pp. 155,27–156,1 = Cyril Alex., *Ep.* 39: PG 77, 180B4.

142. Severus Ant., *C. imp. Gram., Or.* III. 1, 12: CSCO 94, p. 156,13: *idemque dicunt esse uniri et non uniri.*

unitae).[143] In the same way the equation of 'two united natures' and 'one composed nature' was dismissed.[144] To substantiate his refusal Severus referred to 'Athanasius', whose name, however, conceals Apollinarius.[145] Fundamentally he could not permit such an equation because the cursed 'two' is contained in one of the formulas.[146] For this reason the equation of 'out of two natures' and 'in two natures' can never be successful. Only in the first of the two formulas is the duality really overcome. Thus one can place as many verbal brackets around the two natures as one likes, as, for example, two 'united' or two 'undivided' natures: the gulf remains unbridgeable: 'Namely that one is equal to two belongs to the impossible.'[147] Thus whoever prepares this salad of formulas can only have the poisonous duality in mind.[148]

It is still too early to reflect on the expression 'neo-Chalcedonian'. Yet one can see clearly that for the Grammarian it is a question of 'interpreting' for the confessors of the *mia-physis* formula and the supporters of the old-Alexandrian tradition, *vis-à-vis* the two-natures formula of Chalcedon, by taking over Cyrillian elements. As a Homeric philologist, the Grammarian would have been so practised in the analysis of concepts and language that he would have realized that an equation can never be arrived at through exact conceptual analysis: the one incarnate nature of the Logos = one *hypostasis* in two natures. He strove rather for a 'functional' balance of the two formulas to ward off the antithetical threat to the one doctrine of the incarnation of God in Christ, through

143. Cf. Severus Ant., *C. imp. Gram.*, *Or.* II. 10: CSCO 112, pp. 80–3, esp. pp. 81,23–82,11.
144. *Ibid.*, p. 81,23–26.
145. Severus Ant., *C. imp. Gram.*, *Or.* II. 10: CSCO 112, pp. 80,33–81,13 = Apollinar., *Ad Iouianum*: PG 28,25; Lietzmann, 250–251. See CPG 3665. On the citations of Athanasius in Severus see C. Lash, 'Saint Athanase dans les écrits de Sévère d'Antioche', in *Politique et théologie chez Athanase d'Alexandrie. Actes du colloque de Chantilly 23–25 sept. 1973*, ed. C. Kannengiesser = *ThéolHist* 27 (Paris, 1974), 377–94.
146. Severus Ant., *C. imp. Gram.*, *Or.* II. 10: CSCO 112, p. 81,19–22: *Etenim dualitas solvit unionem atque omni ex necessitate natura humana in id redigitur, ut non adoretur, cum dualitatis sectione separatur a Deo Verbo adorando.* For this reason 'Athanasius' said absolutely: *non duas naturas unum Filium.* If the Grammarian were to be correct, then it would have to read: *Non duas naturas separatas unum Filium, sed duas naturas individuas et unitas* (ibid., p. 81,34–36).
147. Severus Ant., *C. imp. Gram.*, *Or.* II. 12: CSCO 112, p. 92,1: *Etenim idem esse unum et duo, ex impossibilibus est* . . . How much Severus was annoyed by the placing on a par of 'two undivided united natures' and the *mia-physis* formula is shown by the parallel passages in Richard, CCG 1, p. 15,275–278 in the apparatus to no. 31. Cf. CSCO 94, pp. 115, 116, 121, 185–6. In the *Or.* II. 12: CSCO 112, p. 89, 26–27 he calls the Grammarian *novus reconciliator et mediator oppositorum verborum.*
148. Whoever admits 'two' for any gap at all smuggles it into everything, so that there are 'two hypostases, two sons, two lords, two Christs'; cf. Severus Ant., *C. imp. Gram.*, *Or.* II. 13: CSCO 112, p. 94,28–30.

Apollinarianism on the one side and through Nestorianism on the other. Henceforward no Nestorian should be able to call upon Chalcedon on hearing the statement: even the Chalcedonians profess the 'one nature of the incarnate Word'. And no Apollinarians, no Eutychians or Manichaeans should be able to maintain their errors when they hear: 'in two natures, undivided and unmingled'. In the tension of such a dialectic the entire truth of the incarnation lights up. As long as one stays on the level of the kerygma or of christological proclamation, this dialectical use of formulas may render some service. But if one enters upon the analysis of concepts, the contradictions cannot fail to appear. Chalcedon had applied to christology the distinction between *hypostasis* and *physis* which had been accepted by Cyril for the theology of the Trinity. Severus remained with the linguistic usage of Cyril. Through taking on board the *mia-physis* terminology the Grammarian sought to combine the old-Nicene equation of *physis-hypostasis* with the neo-Nicene/ Chalcedonian distinction of the two concepts.[149] Gregory Nazianzen would certainly have shaken his head. In the eyes of Severus there was only one thing that helped against the subtle Homeric philologist from Caesarea: a thoroughgoing purification of christological language, which would make impossible all reference to ambiguous formulas of the Fathers in the fourth and fifth centuries. The monk of Majuma took as the standard for this selection the Cyril of the anti-Nestorian letters after 429, while the 'earlier' Cyril was pushed into the background. For

149. For Severus and his usage of 'hypostasis' and 'essence' (*ousia*) in trinitarian teaching cf. *Hom*. 125: PO 29, p. 239: 'Father, Son and Holy Spirit are three different *hypostases*, not mingled with each other, in one unique essence (*ousia*) . . . We say that essence and *hypostasis* are concepts which indicate the existence of existing things. The essence [derived from εἶναι, to be] brings to notice that the subject exists, and the *hypostasis* that it subsists . . . (234). The essence indicates a commonality; the *hypostasis* a particularity (236) . . . With regard to the Trinity the essence is the godhead, for the Father is God, the Son is God and the Holy Spirit is God; none of them is more God than the other on account of the identity and equality of the honour of the essence (*ousia*). With regard to the *hypostasis*, that of the Father, that of the Son and of the Holy Spirit is in each case another' (239). It is to be noted that here Severus distinguishes between *hypostasis* and *ousia*. The concept *physis* is not considered in this passage. A Greek fragment helps us further; in it *physis* is enlisted for trinitarian teaching and is taken to be synonymous with *ousia*, which, however, is not possible for the incarnation, the order of the *oikonomia*. In the *Solutio argumentorum Severi* (CPG 6815) Leontius of Byzantium brings the following objection: 'It is to be agreed that in theology *hypostasis* and *ousia* or *physis* are not the same; in the *oikonomia*, however, they are identical. If namely the novelty of the *mysterium* signifies a novelty also for the natures, so this will be true too, according to the divine Gregory, I believe, for the terms. Hence, according to him, to each of the two concepts the content (*Logos*) and the definition of the other apply' (PG 86, 1921B). That is, through the mystery of the incarnation the concepts of *hypostasis* and nature have received a new meaning and a new definition. Cf. Severus Ant., *Ep. 3 ad Joh. ducem*: Diekamp, DP, pp. 309,15–310,12, in which he also refers to Ps. Dionysius. We shall return to the problem in Leontius of Byzantium. Cf. Lebon, 239–58.

the history of christology and its methodology this process is of some significance. Can orthodoxy only be attained by being constricted, and depth only by an impoverishment of language? We are already acquainted with this problem from the post-apostolic period.

(c) The Severan purification of christological language.
The custodian of faith

How consciously Severus approached the business of supervising language is evident from his basic comments on his self-imposed task. He discovered in himself the feeling of a 'vigilant and sensible custody'[150] which he had discovered before in his great models Cyril and Athanasius. Both teachers, each in the situation of his time, acted 'in the manner of a doctor' at the appearance of 'epidemics'.[151] The 'widespread disease' in Cyril's time was the new teaching of Nestorius.[152] The 'two natures' of Chalcedon showed its rapid spread. The attempts of Nephalius and John the Grammarian to discover this formula already in the earlier Fathers and to legitimate it with their authority would indeed have represented an epidemic as a healthy development (bona valetudo). In the case of infection abstinence and strict dietary rules had to be prescribed. However, the same medicinal treatment was not always suitable. In one case the drinking of water could be recommended; in another case, however, it could be extremely deleterious. This was to be transferred to the application of the christological language of Cyril and other Fathers, insofar as they had allowed themselves to speak of 'two natures'. What was once good did not always have to be so![153] Thus for Severus the therapy was unambiguous: the sole medicine against Chalcedon was the consistent erasure of the two-natures terminology in its entire range from theological vocabulary. Only in this way was the Nestorian 'disease of separation'[154] to be eradicated effectively. The Florilegium Cyrillianum, Nephalius and the Grammarian had made the immediate object of this therapy ready to hand for Severus, because they had gathered together everything in the Fathers that could be adduced in favour of the two-natures formula of Chalcedon. For this the monk coined the collective

---

150. Severus Ant., C. imp. Gram., Or. III. 2, 22: CSCO 102, p. 1,7–21.
151. Ibid., p. 1,20–21: sanctus Cyrillus medici more, attento morbo, prohibitionem ipsum morbum impugnantem statuit.
152. Ibid., p. 2,27–28: morbo vaniloquiorum Nestorii in ecclesiis grassante. Or, p. 2,33–34: exitiali morbo aliquam civitatem invadente . . .
153. Ibid., pp. 2,20–3,5.
154. Ibid., p. 1,15: divisionis morbus.

expression 'coarser language' (*lingua crassior*),[155] which once could have been good but now had to be replaced by more refined expressions. The conservative Severus, who was very quickly ready with the argument from tradition, particularly when Cyril was up for discussion, thus allowed himself to correct individual Fathers and regarded this procedure as legitimate.[156] The purification of language that had been demanded now touched the description of the incarnation of the Logos either in the process (*in fieri*) or in the final state (*in facto esse*).

(i) Linguistic correction for the incarnation in fieri

Even the way and means used to describe the process of hypostatic unity were decisive with regard to whether the 'effect' is rightly grasped. Hence all expressions that showed only an accidental, adoptionist unity in Christ had to be excluded. Such an expression would exist if the starting-point of the event of union was so represented that a duality was firmly present beforehand. According to Severus such a conception was necessarily connected with the verb 'to assume' (ἀναλαμβάνειν, προσλαμβάνειν, Lat.: *assumere*). Even worse was the use of συνάπτειν, with the substantive συνάφεια in the meaning of 'to join', 'to connect', 'connection'. Indeed Severus, with the Apollinarian writing Ps. Julius, *De unione*,[157] knew of the fact that *synapheia* also guaranteed a substantial unity. It denoted in the result a firmly established unity (συμπλοκή, ἑνότης). Indeed, even unsuspected witnesses such as the great Cappadocians, Basil and Gregory Nazianzen, were said to have used the *synapheia* terminology.[158] But they also added '(established) according to the *hypostasis*' in order to be successful in bringing to expression the hypostatic or substantial unity (ἕνωσις ὑποστατική, κατ'οὐσίαν) and not a purely moral unity in Christ.[159] To his regret Severus had to concede that Cyril too had spoken of *synapheia*, as we have already established, but always with a meaning completely different from

---

155. *Ibid.*, ch. 27: CSCO 102, pp. 49,35–50, 3: (*Patres*) . . . *saepe crassius locuti (sunt) de incarnatione Domini, quia de illa tunc nulla prorsus quaestio movebatur. Crassius autem eos locutos esse dico quoad unam alteramve vocem* . . .

156. Cf. Severus Ant., *C. imp. Gram.*, Or. III. 2, 22: CSCO 102, 1–7, esp. pp. 1,18–2,19 and 7,8–22; cf. also John Gram., *Apol.* 56: Richard, CCG 1, 22.

157. Ps. Julius, *De unione* 4–5: Lietzmann, pp. 186,20–187,8.

158. Cf. Basil, *Ep. 210 ad primores Neocaes.* 5: PG 32,776B8; Greg. Naz., *Ep. 101 ad Cledon. I*: PG 37, 180B: κατ'οὐσίαν συνῆφθαί τε καὶ συνάπτεσθαι . . .

159. Severus Ant., *C. imp. Gram.*, Or. III. 2, 23: CSCO 102, pp. 11,22–12,11.

Nestorius, who had made this word the shibboleth of his separation.[160]
It was for this reason indeed that the great master abandoned this loaded
term as a christological one — an example which he, Severus himself,
follows.[161]

(ii) Insufficient designations of the incarnation in facto esse

(1) Christus duplex

Talk of a 'doubling' in Christ was startling for Severus. It was only a
variation on the cursed 'two'! In settling accounts with the 'godless
Grammarian' it was precisely this irritating *duplex* that came up for
discussion. Various Fathers had used it.[162] With it they wanted to protest both against the denial of the divinity of the Logos by the Arians
as well as against the suppression of Christ's soul by the Apollinarians.
Both had an interest in accepting in Christ only *'one physis'*: the Arians,
so that from the Logos' becoming one with created flesh they could
assign the result in its totality to the created ordo;[163] the Apollinarians,
so that they could ascribe the overcoming of sin to an 'invisible *nous'*

160. *Ibid.*, ch. 25: CSCO 102, 37, with a citation from Cyril Alex., *De s. Trin., Dial. VI*:
PG 75,1032D: *Ceterum ante concursum ad carnem* (πρὸ τῆς πρὸς σάρκα συνδρομῆς) *et adhaesionem secundum unionem* (καὶ τῆς καθ'ἕνωσιν συναφείας) *Dominum fuisse Filium nullo negotio
videbimus*. But on this Severus says: *nec quisquam dicet sanctum Cyrillum adhaesionem hic nominare
sicut Nestorius illam nominavit: eandem enim tum concursum ad carnem, tum unionem vocavit*. Thus
Cyril used the concepts *syndrome* and *henosis* synonymously.

161. Severus Ant., *C. imp. Gram.*, Or. III. 2, ch. 23: CSCO 102, pp. 12,21–13,9 with
reference to Cyril Alex., *Ep. 17 ad Nestorium*: PL 77, 112BC; ch. 23: CSCO 102, pp. 12,35–13,3
with reference to Cyril Alex., *Quod unus sit Christus*: PG 75, 1285 (*synapheia* has occasionally
been used by us and handed on by the holy Fathers; nevertheless it is to be abandoned); ch. 23:
CSCO 102, p. 13,10–12; ch. 25, p. 37,4–7, where Cyril (PG 77, 112) is cited: *Imo nomen adhaesionis* **(synapheia)** *repudiamus ut impar ad unionem significandam*. With regard to this Severus says,
ibid.: *omnibus viribus hanc reprobationem sectamur, et nomen adhaesionis apud nos in suspicionem cadit*.

162. On *Christus duplex* and its use by individual Fathers: (a) Greg. Naz., *Or. de Epiphan.*:
PG 36, 328: '[Christ] is sent [not as God], but as a human being. He is indeed twofold'; cited
by Severus Ant., *Or. 2 ad Neph.*: CSCO 120, pp. 31,27–32,2; *C. imp. Gram.*, Or. III. 2, ch. 23:
CSCO 102, p. 14,31–32; repeated in ch. 37: p. 171,27–34. Gregory also applies this *duplex* to
the unity of body and soul: cf. CSCO 102, pp. 15,18–17,4; similarly John Chrysostom. Severus
has to object that someone had made nonsense of the passage in Gregory. Cf. John the Grammarian, *Apol.* 105: Richard, CCG 1, 42 with reference to Leo M. (b) The Grammarian had
discovered a particularly vexing passage in Gelasius of Caesarea: In Christ it is said *duplicia omnia*
(διπλᾶ πάντα) *et vera omnia, et perfecta omnia*, cited in CSCO 102, p. 174,13–14; Richard, CCG
1, no. 106, p. 42,1047–1048. Cf. F. Diekamp, *Analecta Patristica* = OCA 117 (Rome, 1938),
45 (Greek and German).

163. Cf. the question of the Arians in Athan. Alex., *C. Arian*. III. 27: PG 26, 381A: 'If he
[the Logos] was true God from God, how could he become a human being ... How do you
[the Nicenes] dare to say the Logos partakes of the essence of the Father, since he has indeed
a body so that he bears and suffers this?'

and not to a fallible human principle of decision-making.[164] In order to hinder the Arian as well as the Apollinarian *mia physis* or the diminution, be it of the divinity or humanity of Christ, the Fathers began again — as early as the period of the docetist *gnosis* — to speak of 'perfect God' and 'perfect human being' in Christ and to bring the 'duality' of Christ into view. Against the Arians the distinction of the 'times' in the incarnation, namely the time before and the time after the incarnation, also served this purpose. Although this was still a historical schema of distinction (the one God-Logos as pre-existent and then incarnate), the Greek Fathers tended to make it an ontological one (Christ, perfect in divinity, perfect in humanity). This second schema, promoted by the Cappadocians and the Antiochenes, Theodore of Mopsuestia and Theodoret, had the intrinsic tendency to be understood paratactically and to concentrate the 'duality' in Christ statically. According to Severus, Nestorius and Chalcedon were the disastrous end-result of this: *Christus duplex*, i.e. Christ, two natures, two hypostases!

The Grammarian's conjuring up again of these evil spirits of division and separation, disguised under the names of holy Fathers, was extremely irksome to Severus. Hence he fell decisively in line with the anti-Nestorian Cyril and rejected the whole attempt to speak of the *Christus duplex*.

> After its rejection by Saint Cyril we refuse once and for all to call Christ 'twofold', as he (Cyril) also rejected the word 'adhere' (*adhaesio*; Greek: συνάφεια), although it was employed (*dictum*) well by the Fathers. It counts indeed in maintaining the force of Nestorius' illusion (*opinio*, *doxa*).[165]

So Severus brought attention back from the ontological static schema of acknowledged Fathers to the historical schema of the distinction of the 'two times' in the economy of salvation: there was only *one physis* in Christ which endured a process which the Scriptures depict in a 'double narrative'. The 'objective' distinction was entirely transposed into the 'subjective' report of the two times in the holy Scriptures.[166] The temporal succession of pre-existent Logos and his *status incarnatorius*

---

164. See the examples in *JdChr* I³, 486, nn. 19–21; *CCT* I², 333, nn. 19–21.

165. Severus Ant., *C. imp. Gram.*, Or. III. 2, ch. 23: CSCO 102, p. 17,10–14: . . . *recusamus duplicem dicere Christum.*

166. Cf. Severus Ant., *C. imp. Gram.*, Or. III. 2, ch. 38: CSCO 102, p. 174,20–1: *Dixit enim Athanasius duplicem esse divinarum Scripturarum narrationem: illum nimirum semper deum esse, illumque postea propter nos immutabiliter factum esse hominem.* Just before this Severus has a citation from Athanasius, *C. Arian.* III. 29: PG 26, 385AB, in which the hermeneutical principle for the distinction of the 'two times' is clearly developed. Cf. in general Athan. Alex., *C. Arian.* III. 28–29, 43, 55: PG 26, 381C–388A, 413AB, 437B. The whole of ch. 38 of the Or. III. 2 is important for this: CSCO 102, 173–178. Severus rebukes the Chalcedonians for laying claim imper-

ought not to be condensed to 'two natures' or to a 'doubling', any more than the distinction of the Fathers between a divine and a human act and speech in Christ. Indeed Severus too could not manage without making an ontological distinction. For his 'out of two one' or the 'out of two natures' were founded on an admittedly theoretical, but still ontological view of the one Christ 'before the union'. Because the unity remained, however, an unmingled one, the 'godless Grammarian' could indeed come to the idea of perpetuating this theoretical view by demanding the formula of the two (abstract) *ousiai* (essences) in Christ. Here Severus believed he had to call a halt: at no price ought there to be talk of a 'duality' as long as the consideration was concerned with the constitution of Christ himself and stayed within the incarnate Word. In his works there could be a 'two' only *extra Christum*.

(2) Christ the 'assumed human being'

For Severus the often-employed formula *homo assumptus*, the 'assumed human being', was on a par with *Christus duplex* in its effect. It too was protected by respected Fathers, such as Gregory Nazianzen[167] and even Cyril himself.[168] It was alleged to have been misused by Diodore of Tarsus, Theodore of Mopsuestia and Nestorius in the sense of a unity that was only according to behaviour.[169] Severus maintained that for this reason Cyril did not employ this term strictly speaking, but expunged it absolutely from christological vocabulary. Cyril was said to have been certainly aware that it appeared in several Fathers,[170] but he

missibly to texts in which there is talk of a *duplicitas*, even if there is expressed by this only the distinction of the times and only the difference on the level of divine and human speech and action, thus not on the level of the natures. In other words, Severus says it is an illegitimate *metabasis eis allo genos*, when the Chalcedonians make of this distinction of the times a static-ontological doubling, namely a *naturarum vel hypostasium duplicitas, ut in duo unam ex duobus hypostasim atque naturam, sc. naturam et hypostasim Dei Verbi incarnatam dissecarent* (p. 176,15–18). Severus had already treated this theme in *C. imp. Gram., Or.* III. 1, ch. 7: CSCO 94, 73–96. We shall cite from this only p. 89,17–23: *Aliud enim est scire quidnam Unigenito Verbo nudo nondum-que incarnato et quidnam inhumanato loqui conveniat, et aliud illud dividere, cum hypostatice unitum est carni rationaliter animatae, duplicitate naturarum, atque singulis naturis sermones aptare dicendo esse unius quidem naturae tale quid, alterius autem aliud quid loqui.* Leo I of Rome in particular is meant by this.

167. Greg. Naz., *Ep. 101 ad Cledon.* I: PG 37, 177B (against Apollinarius), adduced by Severus Ant., *C. imp. Gram., Or.* III. 2: CSCO 102, p. 8,11–14. The two words προσληφθῆναι and ἀναληφθῆναι are synonymous for him.

168. Cf. Severus Ant., *C. imp. Gram., Or.* III. 2: CSCO 102, pp. 8,26–9,2.

169. *Ibid.*, p. 8,29–30: σχετικῶς κατὰ σχέσιν τῆς γνώμης.

170. *Ibid.*, p. 9,26–33: the '*Antiochene* usage' is said, however, not to be found among the Fathers. In *this* sense Cyril said: *Hominem assumptum esse a Deo non videtur sanctis Patribus.* He did not say this, according to Severus, in the Jewish sense of the letter of the law, but only with regard to the 'mind of the Fathers' (*mentem doctorum cognoscens*).

was convinced that in them it had not had an 'Antiochene' interpretation. Indeed this Antiochene interpretation of the formula he never approved of. According to Severus one could rightfully maintain that Cyril rejected this improper form of speech 'without distinction'.[171] However, the Grammarian could produce a citation from Cyril's *Thesaurus* which is very much like the Antiochene Nestorian language.[172] The human nature of Christ is compared namely with the *poderes*, the garment of the high priest, which the Logos had to put on in the incarnation.[173] Disagreeable in this citation from Cyril was also the fact that the concrete *homo* was used for denoting the humanity of Christ and as the equivalent of this stood indeed the image of the *temple*. 'Assumed human being' sounded all too much like an already present, already existing human being, who only subsequently to his coming-into-existence had been assumed into the unity of the *hypostasis* of the Logos. Creation and assumption of the humanity of Christ, however, coincided for Severus as much as they did for Augustine, who had found an excellent expression for this.[174]

(3) Anthropos theophoros, homo deifer

This suspicious expression was apparently protected by the authority of Gelasius of Caesarea (CPG 3520), who was highly esteemed by Severus.[175] In reality this fragment belongs to Eustathius of Antioch, who had fallen badly into disrepute. This emerges from a florilegium of Pope Gelasius I.[176] Because Cyril had already forbidden this word 'God-bearing',[177] Severus had an easier match here.

---

171. *Ibid.*, p. 9,33–35: *quapropter indiscriminatim, ut dixi, abnegavit formulam, ut aditum praecluderet impiorum sententiae, qua hominem secundum relationem (kata schesin) Deo Verbo coniungunt.* On Cyril's christological use of language see, however, *JdChr* I³, 609, n. 12.

172. Cyril Alex., *Thesaurus*, ass. 21: PG 65, 361D1–15; in John Gram., *Apol.* 60: Richard, CCG 1, 26: *Eodem autem modo etiam de Christo. Etenim, erat quidem Verbum in principio, multo autem postea tempore factus est pro nobis pontifex, veluti poderem quendam, id est, hominem ex Maria, sive templum assumens.*

173. Cf. Lampe, *PGL*, s.v. ποδήρης.

174. Augustine, *C. serm. Arian.* 8: PL 42, 688: *nec sic assumptus est ut prius post assumeretur, sed ut ipsa assumptione crearetur;* that is, the creation of the humanity of Christ and its union with the Word absolutely coincide. Cf. *JdChr* I³, 771, n. 6.

175. Cf. Severus Ant., *C. imp. Gram.*, Or. III. 2, ch. 23: CSCO 102, pp. 17,23–18,20.

176. See *Collectio Berolinensis, testimon.* 7: Schwartz, *PS*, p. 96,25–27: *Homo autem deum ferens.* This corresponds to the text in CSCO 102, p. 17,23–25: . . . *Itaque ille vir deifer.* Cf. F. Diekamp, *Analecta Patristica* = OCA 117 (Rome, 1938), p. 47, fragm. X. With Severus, Diekamp ascribes it to Gelasius of Caesarea and moreover translates inaccurately: 'jener *gottbekleidete* Mann' — 'that man *clothed with God*'.

177. Severus Ant., CSCO 102, p. 17,25ff.: *de universali prohibitione sapientis Cyrilli, qui decrevit nullo modo Christum hominem deiferum nominatum iri* (cf. Cyril Alex., PG 77, 120D). *Deifer* was rejected just as much as *Christus duplex, ibid.*, p. 18,7–20.

(4) Anthropos kyriakos

Severus was less irritated by this formula.[178] He was, however, mistrustful, as the *FlorCyr* wanted to interpret it in favour of the two-natures formula of Chalcedon.[179] The rejection would certainly have been much stronger if he had not falsely accepted[180] that Athanasius himself had used this expression, in any case differently from Andrew of Samosata, in whose writings it was also to be found.[181] This fierce critic of Cyril had taken offence at his remark: 'After the union the natures in Christ are not to be separated.' He found the addition 'after the union' superfluous and misleading. For it insinuates the notion of two phases in the one event of the incarnation: at first there were two realities which were brought together. But one ought not to represent the *anthropos kyriakos* (the human being, who is Lord, who is in glory) in this way. For from the moment of coming into existence he was united to the divine essence.[182] Naturally Cyril too did not think other-

---

178. The passages of Severus with *anthropos kyriakos* are collected by J. Lebon, 'S. Athanase a-t-il employé l'expression ὁ κυριακὸς ἄνθρωπος?', *RHE* 31 (1935) (307–29), 316–29. The following passages are important: Severus Ant., *C. imp. Gram., Or.* III. 1, ch. 17: CSCO 94, pp. 210,23–211,15; *Or.* III. 2, ch. 23: CSCO 102, p. 10,13–18 (on Athanasius); as well *C. imp. Gram., Or.* III. 1, ch. 14: CSCO 94, p. 176,1–16 (against Andrew of Samosata), and ch. 15: CSCO 94, 177–181. On the topic cf. A. Grillmeier, ' Ὁ κυριακὸς ἄνθρωπος: Eine Studie zu einer christologischen Bezeichnung der Väterzeit', *Trad* 33 (1977), 1–63. On Severus see 2, n. 6.

179. See Hespel, *Le Florilège Cyrillien*, no. 193, 192. The *FlorCyr* produces a citation from Cyril, *Or. 2 ad Theodorum*: Pusey 512,2–13; PG 76, 1449A (Latin) in which Cyril refers to Greg. Naz., *Ep. 101 ad Cledon.* I: PG 37, 177BC. In this the Apollinarians are attacked who hold the *anthropos kyriakos*, 'as they say', to be a human being without a soul. By this it is not said that Gregory had appropriated this expression. *Cod. Sin. graec.* 1690 (13th c.) has the reading *kyrion* for *kyriakon*, even if it is certainly incorrect. To the annoyance of Severus the *FlorCyr* makes capital out of this text for Chalcedon: Cyril is said to have professed the 'perfect *homo assumptus*' which would signify as much as two natures.

180. Severus Ant., *C. imp. Gram., Or.* III. 1, ch. 17: CSCO 94, pp. 210,22–211,15, esp. p. 210,26–30: *Dividere autem in duo hunc unum et dicere a Deo Verbo Christum, qui ex Maria et homo dominicus est, assumptum esse, alienum quidem est ab Athanasio, pertinet autem ad eos, qui duos Christos et Filios cogitant . . .* Severus refers to the *synapheia* teaching of Nestorius; then he interprets the alleged passage of Athanasius through a citation from the Letter to Epictetus, PG 26, 1053BC, cited in *C. imp. Gram., loc. cit.,* p. 211,2–15. The extent to which *kyriakos anthropos* is found in Athanasian and pseudo-Athanasian writings is treated in A. Grillmeier, *art. cit.* (above n. 178), 33–8.

181. The text of Andrew of Samosata is in Severus Ant., *C. imp. Gram., Or.* III. 1, ch. 14: CSCO 94, pp. 175,32–176,20.

182. Andrew of Samosata, in Severus, *loc. cit.,* p. 176,5–13: *Stultissimum et absurdissimum est artificium! Primo quidem hoc ipsum quod 'post unionem' dicitur, ratione caret. Etenim, non concipitur homo dominicus ante unionem divinam, nec unquam ipsi defuit illa beata natura, nam 'Sapientia aedificabit sibi domum (Prov 9,1)', et profecto non removetur inhabitans a templo. Proinde ineptum et stultum est dicere 'post unionem', quasi prius constitutus fuisset homo, postea vero effecta fuisset aliqua coniunctio.* Thus Andrew here advocates a christology 'from above' which allows in the incarnation the creation of the humanity of Christ to coincide with the *henosis*; cf. the expression of Augustine (above n. 174). Cf. Severus Ant., *loc. cit.,* ch. 15: CSCO 94, 177–179; *JdChr* I³, 771, n. 6.

wise. Only in theory, in thought, does he distinguish these two times in the one Christ, whom he describes as 'the one nature of the Son as the one who has become a human being and flesh'.[183] Ultimately even Severus reduces everything to the schema of an exclusive *christology from above* into which neither the 'God-bearing' human being nor the 'human being in the Lord's dignity' fits.[184]

§2. From the discussion among the anti-Chalcedonians

As early as the first decade after Chalcedon splits appeared among the opponents of the Fourth Council themselves. Timothy Aelurus, the first Patriarch of anti-Chalcedonian Egypt, had had his bitter experiences, which still need to be described in detail. Although at that time there were fanatics who aroused concern, Severus had to deal not only with theologically untrained extremists, who had not yet died out even in his time, but with theologians like Julian of Halicarnassus or with educated grammarians like the otherwise unknown Sergius. Common to both was the fact that they intensified the *mia-physis* christology of Cyril and his greatest spiritual disciple, and hence too, in the eyes of the leader of the anti-Chalcedonians, endangered it. Such altercations are significant for us because they allow a deeper insight into the picture of Christ of the adherent of the *mia physis*.

I. JULIAN OF HALICARNASSUS AND HIS INTERPRETATION OF THE EARTHLY EXISTENCE OF JESUS CHRIST

Around 510 Julian, the Bishop of Halicarnassus, encountered the renowned monk Severus in Constantinople. In 511 he placed himself on the side of Severus in the conflict with Patriarch Macedonius of Constantinople (496–511).[185] At the end of the patriarchate of Severus in

183. Severus Ant., *loc. cit.*, p. 179,9-11 cites Cyril Alex., PG 77, 192: *Verum, post unionem, tanquam sublata iam in duas sectione, unam credimus esse naturam Filii, tanquam unius, verum inhumanati et incarnati.* Cyril is said to have coined the formula, condemned by Andrew (*Desine dividere naturas post unionem*), only against Nestorius (and Theodore of Mopsuestia), and then in the schema of the distinction of the 'two times' (*ex temporali comparatione*).

184. In all probability the reaction of Severus to the expression *kyriakos anthropos* would have been more harsh, if he had been aware of the *Commentarius brevis (in Psalmos)* of Hesychius of Jerusalem (CPG 6553); ed. V. Jagič, *Supplementum Psalterii Bononiensis. Incerti auctoris explanatio graeca* (Vienna, 1917). Hesychius has numerous witnesses with the expression *kyriakos anthropos*, some with an explicit Antiochene stamp.

185. Cf. the Chalcedonian Theod. Lect., *HE*, fr. 484: Hansen, p. 138,6-8: Among the opponents of Macedonius 'were Julian, the bishop of Halicarnassus in Caria, the monk Severus, who became attackers (*polemioi*) of the faith (i.e. of Chalcedon), but also of themselves'.

Antioch (518) both were again to be found as fugitives in Egypt. Julian, who sojourned in the vicinity of Alexandria in the monastery Henaton, soon gave offence through a *Speech about the confession of faith*, although he was fundamentally on the anti-Chalcedonian side.[186] Severus heard of this and was particularly irritated by Julian's claim that his teaching could also be substantiated in the *Philalethes*, the showpiece of the Patriarch's polemic.[187] Just how much its author was affected by this is apparent by his reactions in several writings against Julian,[188] but particularly in the *Apologia for the Philalethes*.[189] This claim must also make us curious, because with it the question is raised of the origins of Julian's teaching and, in particular, its relationship to the Alexandrian-Cyrillian-Severan tradition. But first we must concentrate on this teaching itself, and in doing this we shall touch upon an old point of controversy about which we will have to take a position. For the voluminous work of Julian, which was attacked both from the Chalcedonian as well as the anti-Chalcedonian side, has disappeared except for 154 fragments, unless fresh discoveries are made.[190] The misinterpretation of his views — this is the judgement we have to pass today after intensive research — is to be located in the increasingly fierce polemic of his fellow bishop, Severus. From his *Critique of the Tomus* onwards Severus let it be known that

---

186. Cf. Michael Syr., *Chron.* IX. 27: Chabot II, 225: '. . . and he held a speech against the dyophysites. But he did not compose it in a clean and unobjectionable way.'

187. On the cause of the dispute see Liberatus, *Brev.* 19: ACO II, 5, p. 134,4–22; Severus ibn al-Muqaffaʿ, *History of the Patriarchs*: PO 1, 453–455.

188. Severus Ant., *C. Addit. Iul.*: CSCO 296; *Adv. Apol. Iul.*: CSCO 302.

189. Cf. Severus Ant., *Apol. Philal.*: CSCO 319, p. 1,15–19: 'Ils ont osé dire que le livre de mon humilité *Le Philalèthe* est en accord avec les fables de l'hérésie phantasiaste de Julien et confirme son opinion abominable et immonde, faisant (là) des déclarations relevant de celles que le vent emporte et de l'incrédulité des Juifs.'

190. See Draguet, *Julien d'Halicarnasse*, 45*–78*; R. Hespel, *Sévère d'Antioche, La polémique anti-julianiste I*: CSCO 244 (Louvain, 1964), I–III. Julian's works which need to be mentioned are: (1) *Letters*: Three letters of Julian to Severus and his replies are preserved in Syriac; ed. R. Hespel: CSCO 244 (T), 245 (V), 6–7, 8–9, 159–162; Fragments 1–5: Draguet, *Julien d'Halicarnasse*, pp. 45*–46*. (2) *Tomus* of Julian through which the discussion was started; in Draguet, *Julien d'Halicarnasse*, Fragm. 6–49, 46*–56*; nos. 42–49, 54*–56*, are characterized as *Propositiones haereticae*: R. Hespel, CSCO 245, 215–234. (3) *Additiones Iuliani* to his *Tomus*, incorporated into the second edition; they are the reply of Julian to the 'Critique of the Tomus' by Severus. Fragm. 50–56: Draguet, *op. cit.*, 56*–58*. (4) *Apologia* for the *Tomus*; Fragm. 57–74: Draguet, *Julien d'Halicarnasse*, 58*–62*; Julian replies to the charges of Manichaeism and Eutychianism. (5) A type of treatise: *Contra blasphemias Severi*: a work which is divided into ten *logoi*; in these Julian discusses the arguments of the 'Critique of the Tomus' of Severus and probably produced a patristic counter-florilegium to the witnesses adduced by Severus; Fragm. 75–129: Draguet, *Julien d'Halicarnasse*, 62*–73* (to strengthen the theses of the *Tomus*). (6) A *Disputatio contra Achillem et Victorem nestorianos*; Fragm. 130–131: Draguet, *Julien d'Halicarnasse*, 73*. (7) Fragments 132–154: Draguet, *Julien d'Halicarnasse*, 73*–78* cannot be attributed to any particular work. On the fragments preserved in Greek, see Hespel, Avant-propos to CSCO 295, III. See CPG 7125–7127.

he saw Julian with his teaching of *aphtharsia*, that is, with his view of the uncorruptedness of the body of Christ, in the nets of Eutyches and Manes.[191] Even if here the banned Patriarch was still somewhat reserved in his judgement, his supporters, like the Chalcedonians too, allowed nothing good in the Bishop of Halicarnassus. Everywhere he was taken to be a docetist, that is, as supporting the teaching that Christ's body was a semblance, or a Eutychian, who denied the oneness in essence with us and taught the transformation of the human nature of Jesus into the godhead. Suffering, death, and resurrection are thus void; God's whole economy of salvation disintegrates into nothing. Julian entered the catalogue of heretics of the various parties in the list of the chief heretics.[192] Severus acquired his negative impression of his opponent also in discussions with Julianists who took umbrage at his teaching that Christ had a flesh that was the same as ours in essence (*homoousios*). From this he concluded that the disciples of Julian would profess 'a kind of uncreated flesh' or even (in addition) that the uncreated Logos condensed (*condensé*) himself in the incarnation to flesh 'as water solidifies to ice'.[193]

Let us remain first of all within the controversy between the two bishops, so that we can arrive at a judgement for ourselves about the teaching of Julian from the rejoinders of Severus and the citations and judgements offered in these.

191. Severus Ant., *Crit. Tom.*: CSCO 245, pp. 125,31–126,12. By falsely interpreting miracles, especially the virgin conception of Christ, Julian is claimed to have denied the passible and mortal quality of the body of Christ and the authenticity of the passion. Thus he fell into the nets of the Eutychians and godless Manichaeans. In contrast Julian accused Severus of having accepted human suffering and death in Christ and thus having reduced him to simply a human being in the manner of Paul of Samosata, Photinus and Nestorius.

192. On the catalogue of heretics see *JdChr* II/1, 90–4.

193. Cf. Severus Ant., *C. Addit. Iul.*, ch. 24: CSCO 296, pp. 63,7–64,2. From the Patriarch's profession of 'Christ's flesh being consubstantial to us' the Julianists derisively concluded that he was a 'worshipper of a creature'; they meant that Severus by this profession confessed two persons in Christ. For his part from this he deduced the doctrines of the Julianists sketched above. The reproach that he was a worshipper of a creaturely flesh he countered with a depiction of the relationship between created flesh and uncreated Logos, with recourse to Athanasius, *Ep. ad Adelph.*: PG 26, 1073D–1076A. From this it follows that one ought to worship the flesh of Christ without being the worshipper of a creature. Cf. CSCO 296, p. 64,3–23. He derives the legitimacy of worshipping the flesh of Christ from the *mia-physis* formula. The Julianists discussed here appear to be the radical representatives of this teaching; they behave towards their master like the extremists with whom Timothy Aelurus did battle during his exile. Cf. CSCO 296, pp. 65,7–66,21. How Severus had recourse to Timothy Aelurus and Dioscorus is witnessed by his work *Adv. Apol. Iul.*, ch. 19: CSCO 302, p. 251,1–9; ch. 20: p. 254,12ff.; ch. 22, p. 259.

1. Cyrillian-Severan points of departure for Julian

Julian had claimed to have come to his conception of the total uncor-
ruptedness (*aphtharsia*) of the body of Christ through the *Philalethes* of
Severus. The irritated Patriarch reports this in his *apologia* for this work.
It is worth the effort to follow the trail.

(a) The 'glowing coal' (Is 6,6–7) and two different interpretations by Severus[194]

Cyril of Alexandria had already interpreted this image in reference to
the incarnation. In no. 101 of the *FlorCyr*, Cyril's text from the
Scholia[195] is adduced by the compiler as proof for the two-natures
teaching. We shall begin with this.[196]

> Now we say that the coal represents for us the symbol and the image of the incarnate Logos
> ... One can see in the coal, as in an image, the Logos who has proceeded from the Father
> and has been united to the humanity; but he has not ceased to be that which he was; rather
> he has transformed into his *doxa* and power (εἰς τὴν ἑαυτοῦ δόξαν τε καὶ ἐνέργειαν)
> what had been assumed, i.e. united to him. Just as the fire informs the wood and expands
> itself in it as it takes possession of it, without at all causing the wood to cease being wood,
> rather allowing it to blend into the appearance and power of the fire, as this [viz. the fire]
> effects in it [viz. the wood] what is proper to the former and thus appears to be completely
> one with it, so, also, represent to yourself the things with Christ! For God has ..., in an
> ineffable way united with humanity, retained what this was but also retained what he was;
> once truly united, it [the humanity] is one with him. For he has made his own what is
> its [humanity's] and now pours out into it the power of his own nature (ἐμποιήσας δὲ καὶ
> αὐτὸς αὐτῇ τῆς ἰδίας φύσεως τὴν ἐνέργειαν).

The collector of the *FlorCyr* had naturally only looked at the emphasis
of the two elements being unmingled, and wanted to conclude from that
the preservation of two natures in Christ.[197] Cyril, like Severus after
him, was primarily interested in stressing the unity. Nettled by the claim
of the *FlorCyr*, Severus had endeavoured to outline particularly clearly

---

194. Severus Ant., *Apol. Philal.*, ch. 101: CSCO 319, 32–72; as well, *idem*, *Philal.*, rebuttal
of no. 101 of the *FlorCyr*: CSCO 134, 265–267. We need to note that R. Hespel, CSCO 319,
34, n. 2, indicates that in CSCO 134, p. 267,24 there is an abbreviation of the text of the
Philalethes. To be added to this is CSCO 319, pp. 33,34–34,10.

195. Hespel, *Le Florilège Cyrillien*, no. 101, 154–155 from Cyril Alex., *Scholia* (CPG 5225):
PG 75, 1377D–1380D = ACO I 5, 1: p. 221,17–31. This is also adduced by Severus in *Ep. ad
Oecum. com.*: PO 12, 180–181.

196. Cyril Alex., *Scholia*, following Hespel, *Le Florilège Cyrillien*, 154f.

197. In Ex 3,1–5 (the burning bush) the Fathers found a parallel to Is 6,6. This passage was
interpreted, according to interest, as referring to the unity in Christ (the interpenetration of
fire and bush) or to the difference of godhead and humanity (the bush is not consumed). Thus
Cyril as well as Nestorius was able to use this analogy. Cf. *JdChr* I[3], 723–4; *CCT* I[2], 516–17.

the direction adopted by Cyril to emphasize the unity in Christ. This was directed against Chalcedon.[198]

(i) Anti-Chalcedonian interpretation of Cyril's text by Severus
Before the confrontation with Julian, Severus was always concerned with stressing the unity in Christ. So against the *FlorCyr* he had to extract from Cyril's interpretation everything that spoke in this sense. In so doing he formulated the following somewhat carelessly in his *apologia* to no. 101 of this florilegium.[199]

> In fact when the God-Logos in his august union with the humanity . . . allowed this to change, even transformed this, not indeed into his own nature — for this remained what it was — but into his glory (*doxa*) and into his own power (*energeia*), how then can you refer to the teaching of the Synod of Chalcedon and the Tome of Leo . . ., which have distributed [the *operationes*, the activity of the *energeia*] to the Logos and the human being in Christ?

Notwithstanding all the lack of mingling in Christ, Severus sees his unity guaranteed by the fact that there is a continuous influencing control from the side of the godhead on the humanity which is proper to him. Its effect is the transformation of the united humanity into the *doxa* of the Logos and a flowing over of the divine *energeia* to the human powers in Jesus. Julian could be particularly happy with the following statements.

> For in many cases it is apparent that the Logos did not permit the flesh to move according to the law of the nature of flesh [reference to Jesus walking on the water or the miraculous course of events on the occasion of his death on Calvary, at the resurrection and in the appearances before his disciples] . . . How does (all this) belong to the flesh if it was not endowed with the power (*energeia*) of the Logos, an entitlement of the godhead, if it was not to be regarded as one with him, corresponding to the holy word of the holy Cyril? . . . This all the more so as this (flesh) was indeed material and touchable with the hand, thus did not cease to be flesh, whereby it *stood above corruptibility* . . .[200]

In his *apologia* to no. 101 of the *FlorCyr* the Patriarch had gone beyond Cyril's *Scholia* and also added a passage from his *Apologeticus contra Theodoretum pro XII capitibus*. It expounded in a particular way the notion which Cyril formed of the tension between the states of the humanity of Christ, depending upon whether this came under the influence of divine activation or used its normal human power. In this Cyril, so to say, pardons the Incarnate One for shedding tears in a human way and

198. Cf. Severus Ant., *Philal.* on no. 101: CSCO 134, pp. 266–267, to which is to be added CSCO 319, pp. 33,34–34,10.

199. CSCO 134, pp. 266,28–267,1; in part almost word for word in *Ep. ad Oecum. com.*: PO 12, p. 184,4–7.

200. *Ibid.*, p. 267,11–24.

for having experienced the conditions of fear. All this indeed was only 'corresponding to the economy of salvation (*oikonomia*) by his [the Logos'] sometimes allowing the flesh to suffer what was proper to it (ἐφιεὶς τῇ σαρκὶ καὶ πάσχειν ἔσθ'ὅτε τὰ ἴδια) in order to make us more magnanimous'.[201] In the *Apologia for the Philalethes* Severus adds the following to the words of Cyril just cited.[202]

> If he thus allowed the flesh sometimes to endure that which is proper to it, so it is evident that he [the Logos] did not leave it unreservedly the properties which are proper to it, depending on the opportunities and the laws which the ungodly determined.

In contrast to the excerptors who were interested in the distinction of the two natures, Severus had emphasized in the appearance of Christ the predominance of the divine nature and the instrumentality of the human potencies dependent on it. At the same time it seemed to him that the pre-eminent means of binding divinity and humanity was the precedence given to the divine power (*energeia*). The predominance represented for him the normal state in the divine-human appearance of Christ. The more the humanity of Christ appeared as vibrating with divine powers, the more the substantial unity in Christ was shown.

Julian now transferred this conception of the primacy of the divine power in Christ also to the static persisting qualities of the body of Christ and placed accents that corresponded to this. The one Christ, the new human being, had to be distinguished through incorruptibility (*aphtharsia*) in the place of the universal human corruptedness (*phtharsia*), through impassibility (*apatheia*) in the place of the universal subjection to suffering, and through immortality (*athanasia*) in the place of unavoidable mortality. Julian adopted the main passage for this emphasis on certain features in the picture of Christ from the *apologia* of Severus, that is, from his comments on no. 101 of the *FlorCyr* as he produced them in the *Philalethes*. From these he gathered that even before the resurrection the body of Christ was spared corruptedness (*phtharsia*). We learn of this from the later writing of Severus, *Apologia for the Philalethes*. The Patriarch saw that Julian had held on to his words about the transformation (*transformatio*) of the bodiliness of Christ into the *doxa* and *energeia* of the Logos. With strong agreement Julian had also accepted the words of his friend about the 'infusion of everything that was proper to the Logos into the humanity of Christ'. Hence he could believe that he had

---

201. It is a question of PG 76, 441BC = ACO I, 1, 6a, 18–24. This passage also appears again in the *CA* of Leontius of Byzantium, PG 86, 1329C.

202. Severus Ant., *Apol. Philal.*, ch. 101: CSCO 319, p. 34,7–10.

Severus himself as a confederate in the claim: the body of Christ is uncorrupted, not subject to suffering, and immortal from the very moment of the union of divinity and humanity.[203]

(ii) Anti-Julianist interpretation of the 'coal–fire' analogy

Severus recognized now that not only the words of Cyril but also his own were capable of excessive interpretation. The fire that was beginning had to be extinguished immediately. The first measure was violent abuse of the opponent. Then the Patriarch showed that Cyril, in interpreting the unity in Christ according to the model already familiar to us (divinity : humanity = soul : body), also explained the analogy of the glowing coal.[204] He also now conceived more carefully his own interpretation of the image of 'fire–coal' applied to the incarnation.[205] He maintained that Cyril did not say that the flesh of Christ had been wholly transformed into superiority to suffering and immortality, also that he did not say that into the body of Christ flowed the wholly transcendent *doxa* which is proper to the godhead alone (Jn 17,5).

Julian was thus involved in constructing a picture of Christ which, according to the conviction of the Patriarch, brought with it the danger of detracting from the earthly reality of Christ. This had to be prevented under any circumstance. The predicament for Severus consisted in so developing the earthly reality of the body of Christ that Julian could not come up with the reproach of Nestorianism. For the apportioning of the 'physical qualities' into purely divine and purely human and their appropriation to 'divinity' and 'humanity', was, according to the general conviction of the anti-Chalcedonians, *per se* Nestorianism and the teaching of the detested Tome of Leo. In order to solve the difficult problem Severus now sought to tread a middle path: strong emphasis on the 'one power' which flows from the Logos into the humanity, and a careful delimitation of the divinization or divine properties in the humanity of Christ. For this purpose Severus first of all entrenched himself behind a row of citations from Chrysostom.[206] From these he then drew his conclusions.

---

203. Severus Ant., *ibid.*, p. 34,12–20: 'The phantasiasts, however, . . . [to whom Julian also belongs] . . ., were of the opinion that it is sufficient to say the following: If the Logos of God really transformed the assumed body [we mean the body which he united to himself] into his own *doxa* and *energeia* and infused into it everything which is his, then this (body) would be elevated above suffering and be immortal from the first moment of the union.'

204. Cf. Cyril Alex., *Scholia*: PG 75, 1377BD = ACO I, 5, 1a, p. 221,6–16 (Latin: *ibid.*, p. 189,11–20); CSCO 319, pp. 34,35–35,14.

205. Severus Ant., *Apol. Philal.*, ch. 101: CSCO 319, p. 35,15ff.

206. *Ibid.*, pp. 36,1–40,3. Severus says of Julian, p. 41,3–4: 'C'est sans modération et sans compétance qu'ils comprennent tout.'

(1) In the pre-Easter phase of his earthly existence the Logos infused into the hypostatically united flesh the *energeia*, the power and activity, that befits him as God, and the *doxa*, but this only to the degree that it has been apparent to us during his earthly life. According to Severus, Julian had accepted that the earthly Jesus already had that *doxa* which is to be bestowed on us after the resurrection at the end of the ages.[207]

(2) According to Severus, Julian did not distinguish between the *functional* overflowing into the humanity of Christ of the *energeia*, proper to God, which always remains available, and the *physical qualitative* changes in the humanity of Christ as perduring, indeed from the beginning of the united human existence of Jesus. He was said to deduce the latter invalidly from the phrase of Cyril, which Severus had adopted, of the *transformation* of the humanity of Christ into the perfect glory. Hence he lacked the gift of distinguishing. What is valid with regard to the *energeia* does not apply to the persisting qualities, such as, in particular, the *aphtharsia*.[208] There is no doubt that the Logos could have elevated his flesh above suffering. At his disposal stood the divine *energeia* as the ever-flowing power of *transformatio*. For our sake, however, he wanted his humanity to fit into the limits which are proper to us in order too to be able to conquer Satan definitively.[209] The transfiguration of Christ on Tabor is said to be an example on the part of the Logos of self-limitation in the communication of the divine power.[210]

(3) With this distinction of *functional energeia* and *static qualities* Severus wanted to achieve two things. *Firstly*, with the special position of the 'one *energeia*' in Christ as the real divine power proper to God which is always at the disposal of the united body he secured for himself a way of repudiating the charge of Nestorianism. A Ps. Julius citation, thus an Apollinarian text, which he put before Julian, came to his aid here. 'And there is not found, not even a single separation of the Logos and his flesh in the sacred Scriptures, but he is one nature, one *hypostasis*, one *prosopon*, one *activity* (*energeia*, power), completely God, completely a human being, just the same one.'[211] Thus here he could show a maximum of the influencing control of the Logos on his humanity and its absolute enmeshment in the *mia physis*, before which any reproach of Nestorianism was condemned to silence. *Secondly* this *energeia* remains functionally communicable; thus it can be stronger or weaker, and hence allow room for the earthly life of Jesus.

(4) Because Julian did not see this distinction and placed the persisting static qualities on the same level as the *one energeia*, he could not do justice to the earthly life of Jesus. It is false to claim for the incorruptibility of the body of Christ, the *aphtharsia*, the maximum from the conception and the beginning of the incarnation. Thus he had extracted too much from the allegory of the glowing coal.

207. *Ibid.*, p. 40,9–23.

208. *Ibid.*, p. 41,10–13: 'Ils [the Julianists] déclarent en effet que si, de concert avec le Dieu Verbe, le corps que celui-ci s'est uni a été enrichi de la même activité convenant à Dieu (que la sienne), on dira certes aussi que l'incorruptibilité est une activité propre au corps!' Then follows ll. 20–21: 'Etre incorruptible en effet est une charactéristique [thus a quality, a state], et non pas une activité du corps.'

209. *Ibid.*, p. 40,20–35. Thus a concession to the theory of the devil's rights (une victime conforme à la loi et à la justice sur la mort).

210. *Ibid.*, pp. 50,13–51,10: Severus seeks to make clear in the event of the transfiguration on Tabor how he understands the difference between his and Julian's interpretation of Mt 17, 1ff. According to Julian the real divine glory, as it corresponds to the end state, shows itself. According to Severus it was not the *doxa* which belongs solely to the invisible, incomprehensible divine essence that appeared in Christ, but a *doxa* which can belong to a 'corporeal', provisional, imperfect appearance. Thus Severus attempts to conform to the picture of Jesus' appearance, as this is presented in the gospels.

211. See Lietzmann, I, pp. 198,14–199,2: CSCO 319, p. 53,33–36. In this strong text the unity in Christ is seen on two levels, one static and one dynamic. In the firmly established form of the one incarnate God-Logos, the one *energeia* proceeds more or less continually from above to below.

(5) Quite skilfully Julian had brought into play the attribute of holiness and the worthiness of the humanity of Christ for adoration — also an anti-Nestorian theme. He did acknowledge that here in the attribute of holiness, and the consequent worthiness of the flesh for adoration, there was no place for any restriction, any *temperatio*. For here it is simply a question of the dignity proper to God as God: Christ is holy and worthy of adoration also as a human being according to the degree of the divine property. But if worthy of adoration, he is then also impassible, incorruptible and immortal! For the Scriptures forbid us to adore what is mortal, transitory and corruptible.[212] Thus with the 'holiness' Julian discovered a static attribute which is also to be awarded to the humanity of Christ in its divine measure, and this from the beginning to the end! Severus did not have an easy task in rebutting this argument and maintaining his postulated special position of the *energeia*. He took refuge in his *mia-physis* formula and warned that one ought not to apportion the *adoratio Christi* to two. For there is only 'one simple adoration without division into two natures'![213] In this way Severus left the problem unsolved.

(b) The wood of the Ark of the Covenant and the aphtharsia of Christ in the works of Julian

For his teaching on *aphtharsia* Julian referred, to the anger of Severus, to a Marian homily of the latter during his patriarchate in Antioch.[214] The theme was the explication of the ark of the covenant (κιβωτός) as the mystery of the incarnation of the Logos from Mary. According to Exodus 25,11 and 33,1–2 the holy ark consisted of imputrescible acacia wood, and, furthermore, was covered inside and out with gold. This image inspired the speaker to comments which Julian too could have formulated to the letter.[215]

Does not Christ offer himself to us thus [like the ark]? He is one from two, from the godhead as from gold that shines in bright splendour, and from humanity which is *removed from corruptedness* as imputrescible wood on account of the conception of the God-Logos in purity, without seed, worked by the Holy Spirit and the Virgin Mary . . . In fact the word: 'Inside and out the wood was plated with gold' means that (Ex 25,11). Notice here how appropriate the symbol is: as that imputrescible wood is indeed from natural wood and of the same type (*genos*) and of the same essence (*ousia*) as all other timbers which decay attacks and destroys, with the one exception that this is imputrescible [that is, not subject to decay]; so too was the flesh of Christ, endowed with a rational, spiritual soul, of the same type (*genos*), of the same nature (*physis*) and the same essence (*ousia*) as ours; it had, however, one advantage: it was free and far from the corruptedness of sin. For it was conceived of the Holy Spirit by the Virgin; and it was united to the Logos, to him who has committed no sin and in whose mouth there was no deceit (1 Pet 2,22). Moreover, as the wood of the ark stood above decay and was free of it but could still be cut up and burned, so indeed the whole

212. Cf. Severus Ant., *Apol. Philal.*, ch. 101: CSCO 319, p. 61,20ff.
213. *Ibid.*, p. 62,1–9.
214. Severus Ant., *Hom.* 67 on the BVM: PO 8, 349–67.
215. *Ibid.*, pp. 357,4–359,3. The allegory of the twofold gilding of the Ark of the Covenant is found in Ps. Irenaeus, *Fragm.* 8, which belongs, however, to Hippolytus, namely to *In I Reg., quae de Helcana et Samuele* (CPG 1881 [2]: here further details). Now more comprehensively in B. E. Daley, *Leontii Byzantii Opera*, in the florilegium to *CNE* 14, where the Greek text is presented.

pure body of Christ had no share in sin and the corruptedness resulting from it, but could nevertheless suffer mishandling, blows, injury, death and all suffering of this sort. And when he came into the tomb and descended into the underworld, he had still not yet experienced the corruptedness which is present there, and this because of his resurrection from the dead [cit. Acts 2,31]. Thus it follows that the body of Christ has shown itself in everything as incorruptible, because he was in no way subjected to the debasement that comes from sin; certainly he was susceptible to the corruption (*phtharsia*) which is tied to death and burial but has excluded it without being seized by it, on account of its union with the Logos. For the latter is by his very nature incorruptible, impassible and immortal.

The Bishop of Halicarnassus could regard these words of the Patriarch with good reason as a summary of his own thoughts on the *aphtharsia* of Christ: in them the humanity of Christ was characterized literally as being absolutely 'removed from corruptedness'; its conception in Mary was elevated above all concupiscence. Particularly to be noted is the fact that Severus specified that debasement was excluded which 'comes from sin'! In this regard the humanity of Christ was doubly protected: through connection with the 'sinless Logos' and the virginal conception. This being the case, incorruptedness, insofar as it is connected to freedom from sin, had to distinguish the reality of Christ from its very beginning. No one could on this account reproach the Patriarch with teaching that Christ's body was an illusion. For, as he himself explained the analogy, the acacia wood tied together two qualities. It was not from the outset subjected to decay, but it could be cut up and burnt. This was intended to say: true suffering and death could strike the 'incorruptible' body of Christ. By doing this did Severus not accord *aphtharsia* a special place? It does not fit in with 'impassible, elevated above suffering' (ἀπαθής) and 'immortal' (ἀθάνατος). Accordingly, had Severus not prepared all the impulses for the Julianist conception of the thoroughgoing uncorruptedness of the body of Christ and also to a large extent supplied the linguistic formulation? An *aphtharsia* in principle was manifestly united with a factual corruptedness, in so far as it was a question of the suffering and death of Christ. Expressly excluded was admittedly the putrefaction in the grave, through reference to Acts 2,31. The reference to the unity of the human flesh of Christ with the immortal Logos finally closed that crack through which corruptibility in Christ could force an entry. For this Logos is 'incorruptible, impassible, immortal'!

Severus also then conceded in the second mention of Homily 67 that in *Philalethes* he explained without distinction that the body of Christ is incorruptible; even in the homily itself he did not differentiate sufficiently.[216] Hence he now considered it his task to purify his

---

216. Severus Ant., *Apol. Philal.*; CSCO 319, pp. 112,28–113,25.

terminology and to distinguish in the application of the words 'incorrupt'–'corrupt':

(1) Christ is simply and absolutely 'incorruptible' when the word means 'without sin';

(2) Christ is 'corruptible' in 'suffering without blame' ($\pi\acute{a}\theta\eta$ $\mathring{a}\delta\iota\acute{a}\beta\lambda\eta\tau a$): suffering hunger, thirst, tiredness, blows, cross, death;

(3) absolute incorruptibility and factual uncorruptedness coincide in Christ only with the resurrection.[217]

Julian could really be content with Severus' formulation: 'Indeed, in so far as uncorruptedness is identical with the absence of sin, we all confess alike that it also existed in the body from the very beginning of its union with the Logos.'[218] In these words was expressed the closest agreement between the two bishops.[219] Nevertheless, the gulf between them both was opened up and was no longer to be closed, from either side: through exaggerated formulations by Julian which were open to misunderstanding and not covered by traditions, and through the vulgarization, the selective denunciation and finally the declaration of such statements as heretical by Severus.

2. The Apollinarian work *Kata meros pistis* as Julian's source

In chapter 101 of the *Apologia for the Philalethes* Severus reported that in refuting Julian he referred to the *Kata meros pistis*, a writing of Apollinarius which he, however, ascribed to Gregory the Wonderworker.[220] Here we can observe in an utterly special way that the Apollinarian understanding, only partly corrected, flowed into the discussion of both bishops. We present the text in a somewhat extended citation.[221]

[The ecclesial confession and world-saving faith in the incarnation of the Logos who has communicated himself to the human flesh which he assumed from Mary; he remained in his sameness and underwent no change or alteration in his godhead; he was united to the flesh

217. *Ibid.*, pp. 113,20–114,12, where at the end it reads: 'Partout en effet c'est en ayant en vue l'issue et l'achèvement de la résurrection même que j'ai nommé l'impassibilité et l'immortalité.'

218. Severus Ant., *Apol. Philal.*: CSCO 319, p. 92,21–28; or pp. 76,33–77,5, and *passim*; particularly, however, *Ep. III ad Iul.*: CSCO 245, pp. 174,17–175,3. The citation above: p. 174,24–26.

219. Cf. *Crit. Tom.*: CSCO 245, pp. 174,16–175,24; 180,31–181,28 (here Severus defines his use of concepts). Here too the Patriarch takes up the means for purifying language.

220. Severus Ant., *Apol. Philal.*, ch. 101: CSCO 319, pp. 63,5–72,9.

221. Apollinar. Laod., *Kata meros pistis* 2–3: Lietzmann, p. 168,11–21.

according to humankind (καθ'ὁμοίωσιν ἀνθρωπίνην) so that he united the flesh to the godhead (*loc. cit.* ll. 5–10).] The divinity abolished the passibility of the flesh by the fulfilment of the mystery. After the destruction of death follows uninterrupted impassibility and immutable immortality, and the original human beauty is restored through the power of the godhead. It is bestowed on all human beings through the appropriation of faith. But if some now harm the holy faith and either assign to the godhead human qualities (development, suffering or an increase in *doxa*) or separate from the godhead the body which grew and suffered, as if the suffering body existed for itself, thus these are outside the ecclesial confession of the Church.

So much for the *Kata meros pistis*. Julian had reproached Severus with having abbreviated the confession of faith which both ascribed to Gregory the Wonderworker.[222] A certain ground for this suspicion lay in the fundamental hermeneutical approach of the *Philalethes*. In this rejoinder to the *FlorCyr* its author criticized the confession of the 'Wonderworker' with the intention of protecting the citation of Cyril in *FlorCyr* no. 101 (*Scholia*) (PG 75, 1377D–1380D) against a dyophysite interpretation. This emphasis on unity now induced Julian to the exuberance that expresses itself in Fragment 102, which stands in close relationship to the quotations in the *Philalethes*.[223]

> The Logos of God communicated himself to a human flesh and in the humanity has entered into a connection according to humankind. With regard to this he [the 'Wonder-worker'] spoke (analogically) of the meeting of soul and body and characterized (their) union as inseparable. After the completion of the mystery proclaimed by the law and the prophets — the fulfilment of the law is indeed Christ, the godhead abolished the subjection of the flesh to suffering (παθητικόν); from that time on it was impossible both to characterize the *pathetikon* as accompanying a flesh which belongs to the Impassible and also (to accept) that it dominates with force the realm of nature. For the union of the flesh with the Logos is fulfilment of the mystery.[224]

The text is very difficult. It can only be explained on the basis of its entwinement with the Apollinarian confession and other witnesses of the fourth century which Julian took over to a large degree, but also once again corrects. He employed, in fact, all the key concepts of the *Kata meros pistis* § 2, especially the expressions *pathetikos* and *apatheia*, and furthermore the doctrine of the significance of the incarnation of the Logos of God for the restoration of the original state of humankind. Still there is an important distinction to be noted here. While the Apollinarian text also includes the death of Christ and also founds the restoration of the paradisal *apatheia* and immortality on it, Julian passed over the death on the cross and placed the incarnation in the forefront. Severus stressed this

222. Severus Ant., *Apol. Philal.*, ch. 101: CSCO 319, p. 64,5–7.
223. Julian Hal., in Severus Ant., *Apol. Philal.* on ch. 101: CSCO 319, p. 64,24–33.
224. *Ibid.*; Greek in Draguet, *Julien d'Halicarnasse*, 68*–69* (no. 102).

dissonance between the *Kata meros pistis* and Julian, and in the context presented a notable critique both of the *Kata meros pistis* and also of two texts of Athanasius. The theological position of both the Patriarch and his opponent can be determined more precisely from this. It is a question of the incarnation and the cross in the salvific work of Christ, but also of the recognition of the soul of Christ in the *Kata meros pistis* and in Athanasius. Severus concluded from this: even the greatest authorities must be subjected to a critique on particular points. Julian too was referred to the gift of discernment. Because he did not employ it, his deductions from his 'authorities' were not valid.[225]

Notable critique of authorities by Severus

(1) The position of Christ's death: Severus says with reference to the *Kata meros pistis* and his own teaching: '. . . the completion of the coming [of Christ] and of the *oikonomia* is according to the flesh, the crucifixion, the death, the resurrection and the bodily ascension into heaven' (*Apol. Phil.*, ch. 101: CSCO 319, p. 65,10–12). The Patriarch rightfully makes reference to the *Kata meros pistis* (Lietzmann, p. 168,11–12). In this he felt himself one with the 'Wonderworker'.

(2) The confession of the soul of Christ: Severus here openly criticizes his witness and concedes that in the *Kata meros pistis* nothing is said about the fact that 'the flesh which the God-Logos united to himself was animated by a spiritual soul' (CSCO 319, p. 70, 9–11). Such a reproach was not easy for him. Openly he stresses that in other teachers too one ought not to accept everything without reservation. Even in the holy Scriptures, the prophets and the evangelists one must in certain details watch critically and gauge them on the totality (*ibid.*, p. 70, 12–18).

Even Athanasius is here put under the magnifying glass. Although there are some lacunae in the Syriac manuscripts of the *Apologia for the Philalethes*, it is still clear from the context that Severus places in opposition to each other two texts or writings from the great Athanasius and must emphasize a serious difference: the Letter to the philosopher Maximus[226] and the Tome to the Antiochenes.[227] The Letter to Maximus is openly criticized, even indeed rejected 'because

225. On the following see Severus Ant., *Apol. Philal.* on ch. 101: CSCO 319, pp. 70,9–71,26. Previously Julian was reproached because he was said to have neither experience nor education in the divine and patristic teachings (p. 69,5–6). On the following see G. Bardy, 'Sévère d'Antioche et la critique des textes patristiques', in *Mémorial Louis Petit* = Archives de l'Orient Chrétien I (Bucharest, 1948), 15–31; M. Richard, 'Les florilèges du Ve et du VIe siècle', in *Chalkedon I*, 721–48, esp. pp. 733–6; *JdChr* II/1, 75–7; *CCT* II/1, 66–7.

226. Athan. Alex., *Ep. ad Maximum* (CPG 2100): PG 26, 1085–1089. Syriac: R. W. Thomson, *Athanasiana Syriaca II*: CSCO 272 (T), 37–41; CSCO 278 (V), 31–34. On this see M. Tetz, 'Zur Edition der dogmatischen Schriften des Athanasius von Alexandrien', *ZKG* 67 (1955/6) (1–28), 18–19. In a recent investigation C. Kannengiesser, 'L'énigme de la lettre au Philosophe Maxime d'Athanase d'Alexandrie', in ΑΛΕΞΑΝΔΡΙΝΑ = *Mélanges P. Claude Mondésert* (Paris, 1987), 261–76, proves that this letter did not originate from Athanasius himself, but represents a forgery which is composed in connection with *Oratio III c. Arianos*, nos. 26–58, considered by Kannengiesser to be spurious. In particular *Ep. ad Max.* 3–4 are related to this part. See the translation in Kannengiesser, 263–5.

227. Athan. Alex., *Tomus ad Antioch.*, no. 7: PG 26, 796A–809B. From this Severus cites only no. 7: 804B9–14; on the Syriac text see R. W. Thomson: CSCO 272 (T), 35; CSCO 273

in it there is no mention of the fact that the flesh [of Christ] is animated by a human soul, although God has become a perfect human being [with body and soul] and not only [flesh?]'. Factually this letter does not speak of the soul of Christ. Severus does not take his refuge, for instance, in denying the authenticity of the letter. He concedes this,[228] but immediately sets against it another letter, the Tome to the Antiochenes (§ 7), which according to the opinion of Severus, speaks of the soul of Christ, although it cannot be proved according to the contemporary position of research.[229]

What the Patriarch wants to prove with this reference to Athanasius is this: as he conducts himself critically with regard to his authority, so too Julian must allow caution to prevail with regard to his witnesses. As Athanasius corrected himself with reference to the teaching of the soul of Christ, so too 'Gregory the Wonderworker'. Indeed, what his confession in the *Kata meros pistis* does not contain is supplied by his confession of faith composed later: 'Whoever explains the body of Christ as (body) without soul (ἄψυχον) and without spiritual soul (without *nous*, ἀνόητον) and does not confess it as perfect in everything and as one and the same, let him be anathema.'[230] This reference does not aim at moving Julian to acknowledge the soul of Christ, but at his teaching of *aphtharsia*. He does not have the right to refer for this to Cyril of Alexandria and the 'Wonderworker', nor any longer to their interpretation through Severus in *Philalethes* (to FlorCyr no. 101 with the *apologia*). Just as Athanasius and the 'Wonderworker' had corrected themselves concerning the teaching of the soul of Christ, so now Severus himself wants to retract these incautious statements in the *Philalethes* concerning the time of Christ's *aphtharsia*.

This *aphtharsia* of Christ according to the teaching of Julian must now be interpreted as Severus presents it, and then as it was *per se* historically.

(V), 28–9. R. Hespel, CSCO 319, p. 70,24–29 with n. 9 did not discern the origin of this text. If he had done so it would have been easier for him to recognize also the author of the *Ep. ad Maxim.*, because Severus ascribes both texts to the same author. This indication is also missing in C. Lash, 'Saint Athanase dans les écrits de Sévère d'Antioche', *ThéolHist* 27 (Paris, 1974), 387.

228. Cf. Severus Ant., *Apol. Philal.*, ch. 101: CSCO 319, p. 70,15–29.

229. In the more recent research the indications that the observation of Severus has a sound foundation are increasing: even the genuine Athanasius does not have any doctrine of the soul of Christ. Also the predicament in which C. Stead still found himself seems to be eliminated. Cf. C. Stead, 'The Scriptures and the Soul of Christ in Athanasius', *VigC* 36 (1982), 233–50. *In Ps 15,9c–10* is said to remain the sole clear and allegedly decisive text for the teaching of Christ's soul in Athanasius: καὶ ποία τις ἦν ἡ ἐλπὶς τῆς σαρκὸς αὐτοῦ ἢ ὅτι ἀναλήψεται τὴν ἀποτεθεῖσαν ψυχήν; cf. G. M. Vian, *Testi inediti del Commento ai Salmi di Atanasio* = StudEph'Aug' 14 (Rome, 1978), 21, no. 13. But M.-J. Rondeau, *Les commentaires patristiques du Psautier (IIIᵉ–Vᵉ siècles)* = OCA 220 (Rome, 1985), 214, n. 593, now shows that the authenticity of the *Expositiones in Pss* is to be doubted; she refers to G. Dorival, 'Athanase ou pseudo-Athanase?', *RSLR* 16 (1980), 80–9. With this falls the last witness which can be adduced for the teaching by Athanasius of a soul in Christ. Cf. *JdChr* I², 460–79. On the *Tomus ad Antiochenos, ibid.*, 472–7.

230. The 'Confession of Gregory the Wonderworker' is found in Greg. Nyss., *De vita Gregor. Thaum.* (CPG 3184); cf. Hahn, *Bibliothek der Symbole*, p. 283,20–21 (XI). L. Abramowski is against the authenticity of this symbol, 'Das Bekenntnis des Gregor Thaumaturgus bei Gregor von Nyssa und das Problem seiner Echtheit', *ZKG* 87 (1976), 145–66; on this see M. Simonetti, 'Una nuova ipotesi su Gregorio il Taumaturgo', *RSLR* 24 (1988), 17–41.

3. The teaching on *aphtharsia* of Julian of Halicarnassus as judged by Severus of Antioch

Just as the reciprocal misunderstandings between Chalcedonians and anti-Chalcedonians had proved to be almost insuperable, so a similar process of misinterpretation repeated itself within the anti-Chalcedonian party itself.

(a) Polarization between Julian and Severus

We have previously seen that Julian believed that he had only developed the formulations of Severus himself and the teaching of trustworthy, commonly esteemed witnesses of the past. His critic, however, found that this had led to the betrayal of the mystery of the incarnation in the sense of Manes, Eutyches and the old docetists. This was the first response of the Patriarch to Julian's claim that in the *Philalethes* he (Severus) made concessions to Nestorianism on account of accepting that before the resurrection the body of Christ was subject to corruptibility. For whoever characterizes the body of the Lord as 'corruptible' considers it as not really united to the godhead.[231] Whoever, like Severus, apportions corruptibility and incorruptibility to humanity and divinity respectively introduces the teaching of two natures and two powers (*energeiai*).[232] No other remark could infuriate the Patriarch so much as the charge of Nestorianism. His fury over this increased when he observed that Julian's notion quickly found many supporters. Lesser minds were said to have made extracts from this 'sinister book' (the *Tome*) of Julian and in this way carried out propaganda. The whole body of the Church was thus in danger.[233] Hence action had to be taken quickly and energetically. Correspondingly the reaction was extremely hard.[234] The result could only be that Julian's opinions were gravely distorted. For this reason it is worthwhile tracking down the 'genuine' Julian.

A theological border-crosser

In poorly marked countrysides it is easy to cross borders. This is the situation of both bishops. A plus or a minus point in 'orthodoxy' was

---

231. Cf. Severus Ant., *Apol. Philal.* on ch. 101: CSCO 319, pp. 66,27–67,2; Julian Hal., *Fragm.* 150: Draguet, 77*.

232. Severus Ant., *Adv. Apol. Iul.*, ch. 19: CSCO 302, pp. 245,30–250,32. Cf. *Fragm.* 147: Draguet, 76*.

233. Severus Ant., *Apol. Philal.* on ch. 101: CSCO 319, p. 71,13–26.

234. There are three writings of Severus to be mentioned here: 1. *Contra Addit. Iul.* (CSCO 296); 2. *Adv. Apol. Iul.* (CSCO 302); 3. *Apol. Philal.* (CSCO 319).

easily possible there where the decisive point for the unity or the distinction in Christ remained blurred. Both theologians were fighting for an adequate depiction and grounding of the unity in Christ; both professed the *mia-physis* formula; both saw in the Council of Chalcedon the triumph of Nestorianism. Before the quarrel between them broke out, they saw the unity in Christ under the strong influence of the Apollinarian tradition, in the 'one power' (*energeia*) which, deriving from the Logos, moved the humanity of Christ more or less in everything; common to them too was the acceptance of the fact that the *henosis* of divinity and humanity must express itself also in the qualities, the condition of human being, particularly in bodiliness. If the first were the inheritance of the *mia-physis* teaching of Apollinarius, also mediated by Cyril, then the latter was introduced into the discussion particularly by Gregory of Nyssa. The teaching about the properties was used in a sense that it safeguarded the *one hypostasis* in Christ, whatever the difference of qualities of divinity and humanity might be. However, where was the border here? The more the divinization of the humanity was stressed, the more the unity seemed to be strengthened — indeed with endangerment to the peculiarity of the humanity of Christ. The stronger, however, the unmingledness of the properties was put in relief, all the more one appeared to approach the two-natures teaching of Chalcedon and thus a christology of separation, especially if these *idiomata* were expressed with words derived from the roots φύειν, φύσις. Here lay the problem of Julian of Halicarnassus. A quotation of Cyril in Severus delivered to him the weapons for an attack on the Patriarch.[235]

'Even if we say that in regard to the special quality the flesh is of another nature (ἑτεροφυής) than the Logos begotten of the Father, it is still his, however, through the inseparable union . . .'

The question suggested itself: How can Severus still maintain the *mia-physis* formula and thus the true unity in Christ, if he admits a 'natural otherness' in Christ? Still more sharply runs a section of the second letter of Cyril to Succensus in which the body–soul analogy is evaluated:[236]

'These elements [that is, body and soul] are different in their kind (ἑτεροειδῆ) and are not the same as each other in essence (ὁμοούσια); admittedly, once united they form the one nature of the human being . . .' (Then follows the application to the *mia physis* in Christ.)

For Julian this meant: if divinity and humanity in Christ suggest or express after the union also a difference of kind or of nature, then two

235. Cyril Alex., *Ad Diodor.*, Syriac in P. E. Pusey, *S.N.P. Cyrilli . . . in D. Ioannis evangelium III* (Oxford, 1872), pp. 500,6–501,4; Severus Ant., *Adv. Apol. Iul.*, ch. 19: CSCO 302, pp. 248,27–249,3.

236. Cyril Alex., *Ep. 46 ad Succensum II*: PG 77, 241BC; cited in Severus Ant., *Adv. Apol. Iul.*, ch. 30: CSCO 302, p. 275,5–10.

natures and thus two persons are acknowledged. Hence he had to demand: as Cyril/Severus apply the 'out of two one' to the *physis* of Christ and thus induce the *mia physis*, so the same must hold too for the properties. Thus if the union brings about the one *physis* then that must be extended to the physical qualities (to the ποιότητες κατὰ φύσιν). As there ought not to be any otherness of the natures, so also the 'qualitative otherness' (the ἑτεροφυής) must be excluded. Hence the unity of Christ is grounded not only in *one physis* or in the *one energeia* which proceeds from the one *physis*, but also becomes apparent in the qualitative-physical consequences for the united human nature of Christ. The adaptation of the qualities of the humanity of Christ to those of the godhead continues to remain, as in Gregory of Nyssa, the indispensable means for understanding the one Christ. In contrast to Gregory this assumption is intensified in Julian through the Apollinarian *mia physis*! This was expressed in his seventh anathema which Severus has passed down to us.[237]

> If anyone divides up the one nature of the human being into what is unbodily and what is in the flesh and says: this (the flesh) is corruptible according to nature, even if it has not sinned, the soul in contrast escapes the condemnation to death; (whoever calls upon this analogy) in order to represent the Lord as '*naturally corrupted*' according to the flesh and as '*incorrupt*' according to the spirit (i.e. the godhead), introduces by this means a duality of the Christs, the natures, *the properties*, and the sons: the one is (son) by nature, the other only in the applied sense. (Whoever teaches in this way) let him be anathema, because he struggles against the incarnate Lord who said of himself he was born of the Father and possesses everything the Father possesses (cf. Jn 10,36; 17,10). He goes beyond the divine Scriptures.

Hence there arose for Julian the necessity of presenting a new teaching of the relationship of divine and human properties in Christ. He does this in regard to both form and content.

(i) Determination of norms for the relationship of the properties
Julian expressed in a dialectical way what he demanded for the reciprocal relationship of divine and human qualities in so far as they are revealed in the Incarnate One: there ought to be between them only a 'difference as non-difference' thus only a διαφορὰ ἀδιάφορος.[238]

---

237. Julian Hal., *Anathema septimum*, in Draguet, *Fragm*. 71, 62*; Severus Ant., *Adv. Apol. Iul*., ch. 30: CSCO 302, p. 274,13–23.

238. Severus Ant., *Adv. Apol. Iul*., ch. 19: CSCO 302, p. 247,6–10. Cf. ch. 21: p. 257,28–34; *Fragm*. 148 in Draguet, 76*: προσηγόρευσα τὸ διάφορον ἀδιάφορον. For this formula there are two Syriac versions: (a) 'J'ai appelé indifférent la différence'; (b) 'J'ai appelé non-différence la différence.' The first version would mean: 'The difference in Christ is indeed real, but can be overlooked'; the second in contrast would mean: 'There is no difference at all.' According

In your foolishness you have written: with regard to Christ we want to say that the *difference*
is *non-difference*. You have an inebriated mind and you mingle divinity and humanity out
of which the one Christ exists, the one person, the one *hypostasis*, and the one incarnate
nature of the Logos himself.

One will have to concede that this is a bold formulation which can
leave the door wide open for misunderstandings. Admittedly Julian
wanted to speak only of the properties in Christ; Severus, however,
immediately interpreted this with regard to the relationship of divinity
and humanity in Christ as such. The distinction between both he saw
repudiated in the new formula, and indeed not only in the concrete
reality, but also in the *theoria*, that is, in the abstract consideration of
both essences 'from which' the one *physis* arises through the *henosis*.
What the Bishop of Halicarnassus really meant, he endeavoured to make
clear in an analogous relationship.[239]

See what I mean with *diaphora adiaphoros*, the 'non-different difference': 'difference' —
somewhat different are seeing, hearing, smelling, tasting and touching. 'Non-different' —
because in all human beings are found each of the members and each of the parts; but what
is formed from them is one and is brought together as one *energeia*, one *physis* activated by
an unseparated soul.

Applied to Christ, the analogy is intended to mean that the unity from
divinity and humanity is for Julian so much in the foreground that the
difference between both takes second place. The bishop here no doubt
had in mind the Apollinarian writing *Letter to Dionysius*.[240]

If, however, they do not acknowledge the one according to the union, so they are able as
well to divide out the one into many and to name many natures [in him] as indeed the body
is multiform from bones, nerves, sinews, flesh and skin, nails and hair, blood and spirit:
all of these are different from each other, but it is only one *physis*, so that also the true godhead
is one with the body and not divided into two natures.

As this analogy illustrates, Julian wanted to say nothing other than what
Severus also meant with his 'one nature from two'. Admittedly through
its formal character the new formula looked oversubtle and seductive.

to Draguet, *Julien d'Halicarnasse*, 166–7, the first version is wrong and poorly attested. Julian
himself had coined the formula: τὸ διάφορον ἀδιάφορον. It is intended dialectically and
expresses the fact that the Nestorian division is to be followed up to its last detail, even in Severus.

239. Julian Hal., *Fragm.* 148: Draguet, 76*; cited in Severus Ant., *Adv. Apol. Iul.*, ch. 21:
CSCO 302, p. 257,28–34. On this R. Draguet, *Julien d'Halicarnasse*, 166–8. Julian characterizes
the variety of the senses as the *diaphoron*; but there remains *adiaphoron*, because all individual
senses are integrated into the one acting subject.

240. Lietzmann, pp. 257,19–258,4. Cf. R. Draguet, *Julien d'Halicarnasse*, 168–9. By this
analogy the Apollinarian author wanted to show that from the specific distinction between
humanity and divinity in Christ one ought not to deduce a distinction of the natures. According
to Draguet this was also the intention of Julian in *Fragm.* 148.

In an overly harsh way Severus pointed this out and sought for himself a support which he carefully avoided naming. It concerns the introduction of the *ousia* concept by John the Grammarian of Caesarea to ground the formula 'in two natures'. In his *Speech against the ungodly Grammarian* Severus attempted to wrest from him the miracle weapon of the distinction of *ousia* and *physis*. As it now turns out the Patriarch had already recognized its effectiveness and thus he could now direct it against Julian. Two texts witness to this.

> Thus when you call the difference a non-difference, corresponding to the intention of this foolishness, Christ is to be equal in essence to us according to the divinity and in contrast equal in essence to the Father according to the humanity; on the other hand, in your view they constantly pass over into each other and transform themselves, the one into the other! The flesh would pass over into the essence (*ousia!*) of the Logos himself, and on the other side the Word would transform himself into the essence (*ousia!*) of the flesh itself, so that we can amuse ourselves with your 'non-different difference'.[241]
>
> Thus as the natural state makes the one essence of Father and Son visible — the godhead of both is one and the same — so too the natural property shows the essence (*ousia*) of the only-begotten Word as different from the humanity which he has united hypostatically to himself and *from them* (*ex quibus*) is named one and the same Emmanuel. And you have dared to call indeed this so well-founded and established difference a non-difference. In an unsuitable manner you have applied the description of the 'non-different difference' to the mingling of divinity and humanity ... And this difference shows itself precisely in the fact that the godhead of the only-begotten Logos and the humanity which he united to himself substantially are not the same essence (*ousia*); the one is not the essence of the other; admittedly, after both are united in an inexpressible way they constitute *one* hypostasis and *one* nature (*physis*), that of the Logos himself, but as incarnate. But you bring the non-different difference already into the discussion for the elements *from which* the unity (the one, the united) (results) and you fling yourself into the mire of the mingling.[242]

Thus Severus deduced from the incriminating expression 'non-different difference' that Julian no longer distinguished between divinity and humanity in Christ according to the *theoria*. Even before the intellectual operation of the *ex quibus* the difference between the two *ousiai* is abandoned. Thus this formula itself became superfluous for Julian. For Severus he would profess real monophysitism. Hence what the Patriarch did not want to admit in his controversy with the Grammarian of Caesarea was now tacitly accepted: in spite of the one *physis* in Christ one has in *theoria* to distinguish the two *ousiai*, the two abstract essences.[243] Because Julian, too, allegedly sacrificed this distinction in

241. Cf. Severus Ant., *Adv. Apol. Iul.*, ch. 19: CSCO 302, p. 247,10–18.
242. *Ibid.*, ch. 21: pp. 256,27–257,21.
243. According to Severus Ant., *Adv. Apol. Iul.*, ch. 22: CSCO 302, p. 260,1–17, Julian also adduced Theodotus of Ancyra for his 'non-different difference', as if the latter had also denied the intellectual distinction of divinity and humanity in Christ. Severus declares, however, that Theodotus wanted to make the misuse of this intellectual distinction impossible only for the

his ingenious formula, the last possibility of avoiding the *synchysis*, the mingling, in his christology, was surrended. In this manner of reasoning Julian has certainly been done an injustice. In no way did he claim that the two *ousiai*, divinity and humanity, are the same in Christ; he sought their identity not on the abstract level, but on the level of the concrete, there where also, according to Severus, the unity is realized: in the one *physis*. His paradigm, which we have already quoted, of the differences of the senses and their identity in the one human being, signified this. Admittedly the analogy was not correctly carried through; it was not even in general convincing. He simply spoke according to the Apollinarian *Epistula ad Dionysium* (cf. n. 240 above). Julian remained, like this letter, at the level of considering the concrete *physis*, while Severus lets the distinction be based on the abstract *ousia*, the unity on the concrete *physis*. The Grammarian of Caesarea was able to have the last laugh.

(ii) The teaching of the properties of Christ's body in terms of content
What does Julian's teaching about the *idiomata* of Christ's body contain? The bishop offers us no systematic enumeration of all the properties which are particular to the flesh of Christ.

Phthora *and* aphtharsia *as christological themes in Julian*
In the centre of the discussion between the two bishops stood the question of the uncorruptedness, or the incorruptibility, the *aphtharsia* of Christ's body before Easter, or vice versa, of its corruptedness, or corruptibility, *phthora*. This problem was critical for the Chalcedonians as well as for the anti-Chalcedonians. The restoration of the *aphtharsia* of humankind as motive for the incarnation and as fruit of Christ's death had already fascinated Athanasius. But for him it was clear that only in

---

Nestorians. He claims that the right understanding and correct application of this distinction was had only by the defenders of the *mia-physis* formula by their confessing 'that this one being is not divided "through the thought and consideration of the intellect" '. This is true even 'if they show that the difference of the quality (*poiotes*) and the unlikeness of the essence (*ousia*) remain present in reciprocal relationship for the elements which come together in the inexpressible union' (CSCO 302, pp. 260,18–261,1 with a citation from Theodot. Ancyr., *Hom. 1 in die nativ.*: PG 77, 1361C). He says that among the advocates of the two-natures teaching, in contrast, even stressing the 'purely intellectual distinction' (*ibid.*, p. 260,14–15) does not lead to the avoidance of a separation into 'two'. For Severus it is a question of taking away from the bishop of Halicarnassus every argument from the Fathers for his 'non-different difference' (CSCO 302, pp. 261,4–262,2). Thus here once again he also concedes the difference of the two essences (*ousiai*) in Christ. This is also the case in his letter to the Presbyter and Archimandrite Elisha from the years 519–521(?) in PO 12, no. XXXIV, 273–4 with reference to Theodotus of Ancyra.

the resurrection did Christ enjoy the *aphtharsia* of the body.[244] Cyril of Alexandria taught nothing different.[245] This teaching only became the key theme of a christological controversy through Julian. What did he understand by it?

(1) *Phthora* without reference to sin: in general Julian could describe as corruptedness any change, even in a healthy substance. As an example of this is the removal of the rib from the side of the sleeping Adam; here there is only a διαφθορά or a *phthora* of a lesser degree which was rather an 'alteration' (ἀλλοίωσις) than an injury of Adam's 'perfect nature'. Even a diminution (ἐλάττωσις), or indeed even an illness (νόσος) can be included in the concept on the sole condition that there is no reference to sin (ἁμαρτία).[246] No doubt Julian took over the word *diaphthora* from Psalm 16,10 (LXX 15,10) by way of Acts 2,31, not without interpreting it in his own way. *Diaphthora* was for him the lowest degree of *phthora* and its activity. If Christ was already freed from this lowest level, then *a fortiori* he was freed from every more intensive form.[247]

Julian starts with the compound words *diaphthora* and *kataphthora* (= *phthora* + *dia* or *kata*) in order to indicate the different level of the activity of *phthora* in nature and in human beings. *Diaphthora* is the passage to *phthora* proper. Julian speaks in this way in Fragment 8 where he refers to profane authors. In contrast *phthora* is already used of stronger power of activity (Frag. 51). According to R. Draguet, M. Jugie, in his article 'Gaianite (controverse)' in DTC 6, col. 1003, wrongfully claims that Julian understands by *diaphthora* the complete decomposition of the body. He presupposes a false reading, following Mai, *Spicil. Rom.* X, p. I, 192. Cf. Draguet, *Julien d'Halicarnasse*, 104, n. 7. — The highest level of *phthora* is *kataphthora*.

(2) *Phthora* with reference to sin (*hamartia*): it is especially in the christological context that Julian speaks of this connection. If one assumes this content for *phthora* and claims that the body of Christ is corrupt (corruptible), this would amount to saying that Christ is under sin.[248] This is to be unconditionally rejected (cf. Heb 4,15, together with 2,15).

244. On the prior history of the teaching of incorruptibility (*aphtharsia*) cf. Y. de Andia, *Homo vivens. Incorruptibilité et divinisation de l'homme selon Irénée de Lyon* = Etudes Augustiniennes (Paris, 1986); cf. Athan. Alex., *De incarn.* 7,5: PG 25, 109A. It was the task of the God-Logos to lead what was corrupted again to incorruptibility; cf. *Ep. ad Serap.* 2,1: PG 26, 609A. In Christ *aphtharsia* occurred first with the resurrection: Athan. Alex., *De incarn.* 20,2: PG 25, 132A.

245. Severus Ant., *Adv. Apol. Iul.*, ch. 6: CSCO 302, pp. 177,25–178,15. It is fundamentally contested whether Julian can have recourse to Cyril for his ideas.

246. Cf. Draguet, *Julien d'Halicarnasse*, 100–7.

247. Cf. *ibid.*, 104. Severus Ant., *Crit. Tom.*: CSCO 245, pp. 45,32–48,6.

248. Cf. Draguet, *Julien d'Halicarnasse*, 134–5.

Consequently the whole earthly life, the pre-Easter Jesus too, is completely free from corruption that otherwise defiles all human beings.[249]

(iii) Terminological clarification

When Julian uses the group of words *phthartos, aphthartos, phtharsia, aphtharsia*, he means not so much a potential disposition for an actual property, but already the actual state. Hence they are not to be translated as: corruptible, corruptibility, incorruptible, incorruptibility, but as: corrupted, corruptedness, uncorrupt, uncorruptedness. This holds both for the moral order (concupiscence, sin-holiness) and also for the physical domain (sickness, death, putrefaction in the grave).[250] While in the normal linguistic usage of the Fathers it was natural to consider, for example, *aphtharsia* and *pathos* as mutually exclusive, contrary poles (of purely physical nature), in Julian's writings *aphtharsia* and *pathos* (death included) go together, because he includes a completely new way of looking at things in his consideration. No human-earthly experience, such as hunger, grief, sickness and even death, is subsumed under his concept of *phtharsia*, in so far as all of these experiences have been endured in freedom and authority and not out of unavoidable necessity. For him *phtharsia* is present with the necessity, coming with sin, of the acceptance of these by fallen human beings. Now if Christ is characterized by Julian as *aphthartos*, then this means that he is not subjected to any such necessity, coming from sin, of suffering physical or psychic states, especially death. Rather he is free and has full control over the conditions of his humanity.

Phthartos thus means the one who is subjected to corruptedness by natural necessity and indeed because he is in sin and conceived out of concupiscence. Such a *phtharsia* is not in Christ.

The *aphtharsia* of Christ also includes the morally neutral passions which are 'without blame', that is, the πάθη ἀδιάβλητα. On account of these Christ cannot be called *phthartos*.

That Julian supports that terminology follows from some texts handed down by Severus:

> (1) In your speech against those who characterize Christ as impassible in the flesh you have written and formulated as absolute decree: in no way ought one to call suffering corruptedness (*corruptio*), because together with the holy Scriptures also the profane sages themselves would support you.[251]
>
> (2) He [Julian] in fact has thoughtlessly written in accordance with the notions of his mind that passions (*pathe*) are not to be termed corruptedness (*phthora*) apart from those which come from evil, thus the perverse ones [i.e., the πάθη διάβλητα]; to the others, however, which are not against virtue, but are without blame (ἀδιάβλητα), such as hunger, thirst and wounds which frequently afflict us [and indeed as necessarily accepted passions], one

---

249. See Julian Hal., *Fragm.* 17: Draguet, 49*: [Severus] 'For you have written: "If the word of Cyril, who dwells among the saints, is valid: After the resurrection our Lord had further (*loipon*) an incorruptible body, then they accept that before the resurrection he was corruptible; and they should also say that he was in sin".' Cf. Cyril Alex., *Ep. ad Succensum* I: PG 77, 236B. Here also belongs the seventh anathema of Julian already cited above (Draguet, *Fragm.* 71, 62*).

250. Cf. Draguet, *Julien d'Halicarnasse*, 106, with reference to G. Krüger, art. 'Julian v. H.', in *PRE* IX, 607.

251. Severus Ant., *Crit. Tom.*: CSCO 245, p. 133,11–16. In this way Severus transmits the following words of Julian: 'Where [in the scriptures] the passions are not characterized as corruptedness, as they are also not among the profane sages.' Cf. Draguet, *op. cit.*, 49*, *Fragm.* 18.

ought in no way to give the name *phthora* [in Christ]. And he appears to have supported this in his entire incriminated work.[252]

This terminology is to be noted if one is not to do Julian an injustice. Because in his writings the concept of *phthora* means only that corruptedness which is necessarily imposed upon human beings as a consequence of sin, it must be excluded from Christ. This form of the concept *phthora* — with its positive side, *aphtharsia* — has the advantage that the christological teaching about the proprieties or properties is raised above a purely physical teaching of divinization, through reference to the freedom with which the Logos disposes of his human nature. That with this conception, however, the right positioning of 'freedom' in Christ has not been given, must still be discussed in particular. With this insufficiency Julian admittedly does not stand alone. Here Severus is in the same predicament, and with him most of the Fathers. With this topic we touch on the lacuna in the christological anthropology at that period, as we shall encounter it time and time again. Nevertheless, through his teaching of *phtharsia–aphtharsia* we are with Julian in the domain of this anthropology and, in connection with it, referred to that of the teaching about the original state (protology). Thus we come to the wider ordering of Julian's conceptions of corruptedness or incorruptedness.

(iv) The anthropological-protological framework of Julian's teaching on aphtharsia

Julian's critique of Severus was certainly motivated by an anti-Nestorian attitude, on the basis of which he had discovered gaps in the interpretation of Christ's unity even in the most decided opponent of Chalcedon: whoever so divides up the physical properties in Christ, as Severus does, divides Christ himself into two natures, no differently from Leo and Chalcedon. Really Julian could have been satisfied with a linguistic correction of Cyril and Severus, for example, with regard to ceasing to describe the divine and human properties as 'different by nature' (ἑτεροφυής) or as other by essence (ἑτεροούσιος, i.e., of another essence!). But a purely terminological abstinence did not satisfy him. For this reason he presented a positive teaching about the properties which

---

252. Severus Ant., *C. Addit. Iul.*, chs 13–23: CSCO 296, p. 25,23–30. Julian is said to have gathered 'witnesses' for his 'abominable opinion' only through citations from Scripture and the Fathers which are incomplete and torn from the context (*ibid.*, pp. 25,30–26,2). Julian had referred particularly to Basil, *Ep. ad Sozopolitanos*: PG 32, 972B, where the distinction is made between 'physical passions' (πάθη φυσικά) and 'passions from wickedness' (πάθη ἀπὸ κακίας). Julian excludes the 'physical passions' from the designation *phthora*. He declines to designate these passions in Christ and only in Christ as *phthora*. Christ is not subjected to them by necessity.

was conceived in the historical framework of the economy of salvation, particularly with regard to the original state of humankind, original sin, and the restoration of the original condition through Christ.

According to Julian, the human body created by God was not subject to corruptedness before the fall. In the original condition this had no place in the nature, in the *physis* of the human being. Only after the fall was it in the nature, but it was still not φυσικῶς, i.e., corresponding to nature. It has come to it from outside, and it is opposed to nature, παρὰ φύσιν. Under *phthora* must thus be understood an alteration of what existed in human beings corresponding to their nature (κατὰ φύσιν). 'On account of sin the corruptedness has come over us after the transgression; our nature is earthly and on account of Adam's transgression is wholly subject to corruption' (Frag. 44 and 100). Expressions of this kind are frequent in Julian. They confirm a fact which is principal in his eyes: the introduction of a new order into creation, that is, a new *oikonomia*, as against nature. On the basis of this new order Julian judges what has occurred with human beings.

In sinning Adam harmed not only himself. The nature which Adam should have transmitted to his sons is now touched by this corruptedness, so that the individual will be wholly penetrated, body and soul (Frag. 124). The *phthora* swamps the whole course of the human race and of individual lives. It dominates conception (Frag. 23, 24, 41) and death (Frag. 7,12 for both); it holds sway over human beings for the whole time which stretches from the beginning to the end of their existence (Frag. 11, 12); it only ends in the grave (Frag. 115, 126). To be noted in particular is that Julian does not characterize the body before sin and without sin as 'corrupted', even according to its natural constitution. There must first be an alteration 'according to nature' for human beings to be subjected to *phtharsia*. But when Julian speaks here of *physis*, this word has a twofold use in the framework of his protology:

(1) he speaks of *physis* in human beings before sin;
(2) and of *physis* in human beings after sin.

These divergent ways of looking at things remove an apparent contradiction in Julian's statements about *phthora*. On one occasion he can emphasize that corruptedness, suffering and death do *not* correspond to nature: this holds for nature in the original state, before sin. But then on another occasion he can characterize *phthora* as 'natural'. This holds for the state of *physis* after sin.

This 'naturalness' in the second sense acquires even a special intensity: it means not only that the suffering and death of human beings correspond to their constitution after the fall, but that they have intrinsically the character of 'necessity'. Because Adam's sin sullied human nature, so to say as *peccatum naturae*,[253] the punishment falls on the nature and strikes everyone who shares in it by virtue of descent from Adam. This means the decision to be subjected to corruptedness and death, or not to be subjected, is taken from the descendants of Adam.

Christ the new Adam and the corruptedness of human beings

How does Julian bring the facts of the life and dying of the earthly Jesus into the compass of his terminology? What is φυσικός, physical, in

---

253. On *peccatum naturae* see Draguet, *Julien d'Halicarnasse*, 124–7. M. Jugie, *Julien d'Halicarnasse et Sévère d'Antioche. La doctrine du péché originel chez les Pères Grecs*, Extrait des 'Echos d'Orient' (Paris, 1925), in particular polemicized against this expression. With regard to the terminology of Patriarch Severus: for him *phthartos*, corruptible, is to be understood as materially, substantially corrupted. It is interchangeable with *pathetos*, passible, subjected to suffering; *thnetos*, mortal, subjected to death. Whoever is subjected to corruption is also a possible subject for suffering and death.

him? How do ἄφθαρτος, uncorrupted, and yet also παθητός and θνητός, passible and mortal, go together? Julian avoids the absolute and unrestricted statement: Christ has suffered φυσικῶς. He permits this statement only when there is added: ἑκουσίως, from free decision, or better: in freedom and authority. Thus he confesses that Christ truly, and in this sense also physically, suffered, but in complete disposition over himself, over his humanity, and was in no way subjected to a natural necessity of suffering and death. In this sense he also states the *aphtharsia*, the uncorruptedness, of Christ's body.[254] This interpretation of the suffering and dying of Christ he combines with the word παθητικόν and its use. Let us leave it at first untranslated. He expresses himself on this topic in the context of the question, to what extent Christ's body is the same as ours in essence (*homoousios*). Severus had accused him of denying this. In reply he says:[255]

> We, we use the expression 'the same as us in essence' (ὁμοούσιος ἡμῖν) not, for instance, on account of the fact that (he had suffered) like any normal passible being [i.e., necessarily subject to suffering] (κατὰ τὸ παθητικόν), but on account of the fact that he is of the same nature (φύσις) [as us].

Julian means that he restricts the concept of *homoousios* to the *ousia*, the essence of Christ, but he does not relate it to what is meant by *pathetikon*. This word does not denote *passibilitas*, passibility, as such. Were this meaning connected with it, the result would be a denial of Christ's passibility and the reality of his suffering — which Severus indeed presupposes. *Pathetikon* denotes only a special circumstance in suffering or the kind of suffering, as this belongs namely only to the παθητικὸς φθαρτός, the sufferer in Adamitic corruptedness. This circumstance is nothing other than the *necessity* with which the corrupted human being is subjected to suffering and death. It is the calamity of suffering and death! This post-Adamitic 'dereliction' is so important for Julian that on account of its absence in Christ the predicate 'corrupted', *phthartos*, also can no longer be applied to him. If our suffering and dying is *necessarily* present with the possession of the Adamitic nature, then this does not hold for Christ, even though in fact he took upon himself suffering and death. For this reason he is continuously *aphthartos*, uncorrupted, from the incarnation, or from the very first moment of his earthly existence.

---

254. Cf. *Fragm.* 133: Draguet, 74*. If Christ had been subjected to suffering and death out of necessity, he would have brought us no redemption.

255. Severus Ant., *C. Addit. Iul.*, ch. 26: CSCO 296, p. 69,18–21. The text is found often, at times in differing lengths: ch. 26, p. 68,8–15; ch. 29, p. 81,25–28; ch. 31, p. 89,4–7; ch. 36, p. 111,20–23; ch. 40, pp. 128,35–129,1.

(v) The free decision to suffer and to die

This Julianist conception of Christ's power to have at his disposal the destiny of his assumed body must still be presented in more detail, in its origin and range. Here once again Julian had recourse to the fourth century, to its christology 'from above', to its teaching of divinization, and above all to the idea that the humanity of Christ in the course of its earthly existence was at the constant disposition of the Logos. Gregory of Nyssa had sketched this picture of Christ to establish the unity in the Incarnate One, despite all distinction of God and human being.[256] Although Christ as a human being keeps his true human *ousia*, this is not simply the case, however, with his earthly characteristics and properties. Divine *idiomata*, such as wisdom, power, holiness and then, what Julian provides with a special accent, superiority to suffering, take the place in Christ of human limitation. They tie the human *ousia* so definitely to the Logos-subject that the *hypostasis* is one.[257] Gregory himself now gives a pointer which particularly approaches the notions of Julian. In the fourth speech on the beatitudes, we read:[258]

> He [Christ], who has shared everything with us, sin excluded (cf. Heb 4,15; 2,15) and had in common with us the same emotions (affects, παθήματα), did not consider hunger as sin, nor did he refuse to experience the suffering associated with it; rather he accepted the drive of nature to desire nourishment. After he had fasted for forty days he hungered (cf. Mt 4,2); he gave then the [bodily] nature the opportunity to do its own thing when he wanted.

That the Logos must first create the *kairos* for the assumed human nature in order for it to be able to show and to exercise the properties and functions properly its own, is the suggestion that Julian takes over from Gregory of Nyssa. In this there really exists no great difference between himself and Severus. The Patriarch certainly considers corruptibility, mortality and continuous passibility as physical qualities in Christ. In him they signify no relation to sin and are accordingly 'blameless passions' (πάθη ἀδιάβλητα) which do not detract from the honour of God. Nevertheless Severus also supports the idea of the 'divine permission to suffer' which the Logos gives to his human nature.[259]

256. Cf. *JdChr* I³, 539–47; *CCT* I², 370–7.
257. Cf. *ibid.*, esp. 546; 376f. respectively.
258. Greg. Nyss., *De beatit. or.* IV (CPG 3161): PG 44, 1237A: ἔδωκε γὰρ ὅτε ἐβούλετο τῇ φύσει καιρὸν τὰ ἑαυτῆς ἐνεργῆσαι. Cf. Greg. Nyss., *Ad Theoph. adv. Apoll.*: Jaeger-Mueller, III/1, 128; PG 45, 1277B.
259. Cf. Severus Ant., *C. Addit. Iul.*, ch. 26: CSCO 296, p. 68,20–22, where he says of the Logos: 'and he suffered like us with the exception of any sin, and (this), without it escaping their [i.e. he refers to the teachers of the Church] notice that he voluntarily took this upon himself *by allowing* the flesh to behave according to the laws of its nature . . .' But Severus

Without detracting from its honour, the godhead thus surrenders the assumed humanity to *phtharsia*, to corruptedness.

Julian admittedly fixes this dependence of the human-natural functions in Christ on the Logos so strongly that *for that very reason* the predicate *aphtharsia* is due to the earthly Jesus uninterruptedly right from his birth to his death.[260] In this way he has departed from the linguistic usage that had been common before him. He demands for the allocation of the predicate *phthartos* a negative omen which all human beings have, Christ alone excepted: namely the παθητικόν, the subjection to suffering caused by sin, although otherwise none of the natural qualities is changed. Whatever is capable of material dissolution also remains dissolvable in Christ; what is mortal remains mortal and in fact dies. But because all this happens from the free disposition of the Logos-*physis*, the *aphtharsia* is guaranteed in Christ without restriction.[261]

Severus too in his way has connected two things: actual physical sufferings and the voluntary nature of their acceptance by the Logos. An unambiguous text will make this clear to us. In it he speaks of emulating the passible Jesus as the way to life.[262]

concludes: on account of the word 'voluntarily' the Fathers did not deny the fact that Christ suffered in the same way as we do (*ibid.*, ll. 23-4). In the important letter to the Comes Oecumenius about the 'qualities and activities' Severus quotes similar-sounding words of Cyril, which E. W. Brooks could not verify: 'For, though it is said that he hungered and thirsted, and slept and grew weary after a journey, and wept and feared, these things did not happen to him just as they do to us in accordance with compulsory ordinances of nature; but he himself voluntarily permitted his flesh to walk according to the laws of nature, for he sometimes allowed it even to undergo its own passions.' See PO 12, 184-185.

260. Cf. Julian Hal., *Fragm.* 16: Draguet, 49* from Severus Ant., *Crit. Tom.*: CSCO 245, p. 37,18-20: [Julian]: 'How should one not believe that the uncorruptedness continuously affected the passible body of our Lord, even where he voluntarily suffered for others?'

261. Completely in the spirit of Patriarch Severus, Paul of Antioch in his synodal letter to Theodore of Alexandria in 575 again establishes this. Cf. CSCO 103, pp. 228,36-230,25. He develops an extensive phenomenology of the earthly Jesus in order to refute the heresy of Julian, who he claims was in the succession of Marcion, Valentinus, even of Manes and Eutyches, and accepted 'that Christ really bore none of the passions, but that the mystery of Christ was a deception' (p. 229,29-30). Paul of Antioch says against Julian: 'He has not assumed a passionless and naturally immortal body, as according to your babble Adam had before the transgression' (p. 229,32-34). Paul emphasizes explicitly that the status of the *phtharsia* coincides with passibility and mortality: '*Itaque, quia natura passibile et mortale, et in hoc sensu tantum etiam corruptibile, corpus animatum et sanctissimum assumpsit Verbum Deus ...*' (p. 230,7-9). One can, however, demonstrate that Julian himself did not approach the teaching of Eutyches. He did not deny the consubstantiality of Christ with us. Zacharias Rhetor ascribes this error to John the Rhetorician, about whom we have no further information. Cf. *HE* III, 10: Brooks I, CSCO 87, p. 112,20-29, where also the proximity to Apollinarius is presented.

262. Severus Ant., *Adv. Apol. Iul.*, ch. 6: CSCO 302, p. 175,9-18. In addition Severus cites a passage from John Chrysostom, *Hom.* 67: PG 59, 462, in which this voluntariness is also stressed. He could also have named the Latin Hilary of Poitiers. Cf. *JdChr* I³, 584-8; *CCT* I², 396-400.

For this purpose he [Christ] accepted *natural* and *necessary* passions; in doing this he revealed in contrast to this *necessity* the *voluntary* character [of this acceptance of passions] as fruit of an entirely divine munificence. Precisely at the height of this *necessity* (Hespel: *au sein de ces nécessités*) the *divine-voluntary* character manifested itself; for he ordered, as God, who he was, that the natural needs come into effect in his body. Thus it was every time, if he wanted it to be so, and not otherwise, that the passions (πάθη) of sleep, of hunger and of fear or of any other blameless emotion, of which the Gospel speaks, made themselves known (in him).

The teaching of the dependence of Christ's humanity on the Logos for the actualization of the 'blameless passions' persisted among the Severans, admittedly with the same restrictions that Severus himself had made. The long synodal letter of the Severan Patriarch, Paul of Antioch (564–577), to Theodore of Alexandria from the year 575 illustrates this. With regard to Julian of Halicarnassus the pre-Easter and post-Easter Christ is presented in the following way.[263]

Previously [before the resurrection] he took, as necessity occasioned him, food as we do too; however, with the difference: he himself allowed his body, when he wanted it, to experience the natural blameless passions (πάθη); he was Lord of this nature itself. Now [after the resurrection] exclusively, to establish the resurrection he showed the marks of the wounds and gave other signs for this. They were namely not to believe that he appeared to them in a body other than in that which he had taken from Mary and hypostatically united to himself, admittedly now elevated into the state of incorruptibility.

(b) A concluding consideration of the dispute between Severus and Julian
When Severus reproached his opponent Julian with the statement that he professed Manes and Eutyches, this is apologetic exaggeration and against historical truth. The analysis of the conceptual language of the bishop has shown us that the difference between him and Severus was in the first place terminological. What Julian understood by the *aphtharsia*, the uncorruptedness, of the body of Christ did not mean the abolition of the human reality of Christ, but rather a prerogative of Jesus, the new Adam. Because he is elevated above sin and stands above the punishment of corruption of the post-Adamitic human race, he is not subjected to its unavoidable necessity, but by the free decision of the divine Logos in him has taken upon himself body, suffering and death. On this basis both bishops could have met. Severus, however, steered the interpretation of his opponent's christology on to a false track. The majority of the theologians at that time followed him.[264] But not a few of the supporters of the bishop of Halicarnassus also pointed in the wrong

---

263. Paulus Ant., *Ep. synod. ad Theodor. patr. Alex.*: CSCO 103, p. 230,17–25.
264. See Draguet, *Julien d'Halicarnasse*, ch. VII: La doctrine de Julien et la tradition, 216–56. The post-Severan altercation with Julian is here presented at the appropriate place.

direction, so that the reproaches raised against him could more and more appear to be justified. We will observe attentively the traces of this *Julianism* in the different ecclesiastical regions. This development certainly finds some early signs in Julian himself. We will attempt to record here these one-sided elements in order to reach by this means a concluding judgement about his picture of Christ.

(i) A constructional error in the system

The decision of Julian with regard to terminology signified a trend towards a christology of divinization. Even to characterize the earthly, pre-Easter Jesus as 'uncorrupted' was highly misleading for all those who followed the customary ecclesiastical use of language. The notion of a transfiguration of Christ's body as a permanent state was bound to occur to each of them, even though Julian was not of this opinion. But the misunderstanding lay deeper. It affected all anti-Chalcedonian theologians, more or less. For in refusing to distinguish conceptually between *physis* (nature) and *hypostasis* (hypostasis, person, subject), they remained on the level of pre-Chalcedonian unclarity which was the root of all misunderstandings: they attempted to construct a theory of the unity in Christ from the concept of nature and on the level of nature. This means that they sought to arrive at the substantiality of the connection of divinity and humanity by way of a natural adaptation, by way of the divinization of the human in Christ. Chalcedon chose to go the new way — to construct the unity in Christ from the analysis of the *subject*, but on the basis of the distinction between the concepts of *nature* and *ousia*. The old-Orientals wanted to demarcate unity and difference with the same intensity, but both on the level of *physis*, of nature (*in natura et secundum naturam*). In this way there resulted an uncertain oscillation regarding the demarcation of the extent of the influence which must devolve upon the humanity of Christ from the Logos as the *mia physis* in order to ensure the unity. We have stressed the rôle of the *mia energeia* in the picture of Christ presented by the supporters of the *mia-physis* formula. In addition to this came the trend to show the *one* image of Christ, the incarnate Logos, through a christological *doctrine of properties*. We have seen how Julian here believed it necessary to close certain dangerous gaps in Severus' picture of Christ; we have also seen why the Patriarch wanted to divert his opponent from the doctrine of properties and to refer to the emphasis on the one *energeia*.

It follows from this that the misunderstanding between the two bishops derived from the unsolved dilemma of the *mia-physis* christology.[265] If the two of them sought both unity as well as difference in Christ on the level of nature, then it could only be a question of a reciprocal shifting of boundary stones, here to add more to the revelation of the *doxa*, there a reservation to lessen the divinization — both needed divinizing properties and constant influence from above. This failure in construction is more clearly obvious in Julian than in Severus. Some texts and citations which we still want to adduce show this, as also does the value which Julian gave to the virgin birth of Christ from Mary.

Fragment 63: 'The flesh [of Christ] did not first of all exist (for itself), but at the same time that it came to exist the nature of the Logos subsisted in it through the union with the Logos, and for that reason it transcends the physical laws.'[266]

A quotation: Julian cites with assent the statement of an otherwise unknown Alexandrian rhetorician called John, a contemporary of Peter the Iberian: 'Everything of Christ proceeds in a manner which transcends our nature.'[267]

To illustrate this statement Julian refers in the first place to the virginal conception in Mary.[268] It is a conception without *mixis* and thus without concupiscence (cf. Frag. 48 together with Frag. 7, 11, 24). The whole earthly life of Jesus, however, is seen in a certain state of exception which extends to everything (Frag. 12), even to suffering and death (Frag. 126, 127), and even to the grave. In all this Christ certainly remains a true human being (ἄνθρωπος ἀληθής), but not a normal human being (ἄνθρωπος κοινός). For he is not subjected to the normal conditions of human existence. That does not mean that Julian personally came close to the teaching of Eutyches, viz. that Christ's body is not the same as ours in essence (*homoousios*), but only Mary's is. Zacharias Rhetor ascribes this error to John the Rhetorician just mentioned.[269] Nevertheless the door to dangerous speculations was opened, as the later developments will show. Julian himself had seen Christ's exception in the fact that he, who in no way stood in relationship to sin, could freely determine whether his bodiliness should be exposed to earthly needs and passions and death or not. It was for all that an uncorruptedness anchored in the spiritual. The temptation was great to see the qualities of the bodily itself also altered in Christ and even in Mary, as an Ethiopic text will show us later. Dualistic influences which devalued the bodily and the sexual had been active since the time of Marcion and Manes, and were very highly explosive for christology. A misleading terminology in the teaching of *aphtharsia* could easily put one on the wrong path.

(ii) The understanding of the virginal birth of Jesus

Severus expressed the suspicion that from false motives Julian, with Eutyches and Manes, stressed too strongly birth from the Virgin and,

265. Even if, following Lebon and others, we glean from the *mia-physis* christology of the anti-Chalcedonians of Severan stamp the universal ecclesial understanding of the incarnation of God in Christ, it is still an odd formula with its historical baggage, which has time and again been a source of false interpretations that on each occasion have provoked controversies. Julian of Halicarnassus and Sergius (see below) are proofs of this.

266. Cf. Draguet, *Julien d'Halicarnasse*, 60*.

267. *Ibid.*, 68*, *Fragm.* 100; cf. Zacharias Rh., *HE* III, 10: Brooks I, CSCO 87, 112-113.

268. Effects of Julian's or the Julianists' christology on mariology will be noted in the course of the presentation.

269. Zacharias Rh., *HE* III, 10 (above n. 267).

in general, unjustifiably accorded priority to the event of Christ's birth over his death on the cross. Severus maintained that in this way Julian wanted to deny the passible mortal character of Christ's body, for which purpose he also called upon the evangelical reports of the miracles of Jesus.[270] The Patriarch assumed that Julian attributed a preternatural quality to the flesh of Christ on account of the birth from the Virgin, like the type of body which Adam had before the fall. But in fact, according to the Patriarch, the birth from the Virgin and the Holy Spirit did not abolish the consubstantiality of Christ's body with us, nor the possibility of taking on oneself the 'blameless passions'. Moreover, it ought not to be understood as a condemnation of marriage and of marital intercourse between husband and wife. It is rather a reference to our baptism out of water and the Holy Spirit which brings us new birth and the pledge of resurrection. The incarnation of Christ has brought us this.[271] According to Julian, stated Severus, marriage and sexual intercourse are a corruptedness, *phtharsia*, on account of which he demanded a different type of birth and a spiritualizing of Christ's flesh. Hence the body of Christ has a 'superior condition' (*condition supérieure*) because it was conceived by Mary alone without seed, analogous to the body of Adam, which is from earth and not from seed. In contrast Severus gave to Christ's body and hence also to ours this 'condition supérieure' only with the resurrection.[272]

In Julian a further theme led to the same goal: he placed the beginning of Christ's *aphtharsia* already in his birth. For this reason the birth from the Virgin received the character of a creative new beginning, of a new ἀρχή.[273]

> He [Christ] himself has introduced for nature a new beginning through a restoration of the elements with regard to their original condition; for this reason he has not demanded the help of the husband for the conception, because the activity of the Holy Spirit has surpassed them.

Julian is said to reach this false explanation from an erroneous interpretation of Cyril's *Ad reginas* (PG 76, 1372BC; ACO I, 1, 5a, pp. 40,37–41,6). He cites just Rom 8,29 (Jesus the first born among many brothers) too much instead of referring also to Col 1,18 (first born among the dead). If Christ were to have had all this already through his birth, his death and resurrection would have been superfluous. Again Severus says: birth from the Virgin is the anticipation of our birth from the Spirit (Jn 3,6); the resurrection of Christ, however, is the way to our definitive restoration in immortality and impassibility. Cyril is said to have already established

---

270. Severus Ant., *Crit. Tom.*: CSCO 245, pp. 125,31–126,1.
271. *Ibid.*, pp. 128,22–129,11.
272. *Ibid.*, p. 151,15–29.
273. Severus Ant., *Adv. Apol. Iul.*, ch. 9: CSCO 302, p. 192,6–9.

this theological balance between Christmas and Easter.[274] We see that already here the problem of a choice between a theology of the incarnation and a theology of the cross comes into view.

Thus according to Severus the evangelical report of the virginal conception of Jesus in Mary ought not to become the reason for denying the passible and mortal character of Christ's body.[275] This conception of Christ does not abolish his consubstantiality with us, a thought that one could perhaps accept for Julian, if one looks at his definition of *homoousios*. It concerns only the *ousia*, not the *pathetikon*! With some justice it can be argued that the birth from the Virgin is also conceived by Julian as an 'exception' to the *homoousios*, without his denying the reality of the body of Christ by this claim. No doubt because of the vehemence with which Julian stressed this 'exception', Severus inferred bad intentions.[276]

He states it is false to decree: 'If the birth from the Virgin and the resurrection, if the beginning and the end (of the life of Jesus) have taken place according to the new considerations (Hespel: *convenances nouvelles*) and exceeding the universal character of our nature, so it is obviously

274. Cyril Alex., *De recta fide ad Theodos. imp.*: PG 76, 1185AB and other passages. Cf. Severus Ant., *Adv. Apol. Iul.*, ch. 9: CSCO 302, pp. 192,10–195,19. In this context we find the first citation from Ps. Dionys. Ar., *De div. nom.* II 9: PG 3, 648B; P. Scazzoso, *Dionigi Areopagita, Tutte le opere* (Milan, 1981), 278, with Severus Ant., *Adv. Apol. Iul.*, ch. 25: CSCO 302, p. 267,6–19. Severus cites the text in order to emphasize that this mystagogue also teaches that Christ 'has become a human being in one substance and in the manner of a human being', even if we do not know the manner by which Christ was formed in the womb of the Virgin.

275. Cf. Severus Ant., *Crit. Tom.*: CSCO 245, pp. 125,31–126,1.

276. *Ibid.*, pp. 70,7–12; 66,26–35. Severus also repeats his stern judgement of Julian in his letter to the Oriental monks (*c.* 520–525), in PO 12, no. XXXV, 275–291, esp. 286–287: '. . . they do not consent to confess that the true flesh of God and the Word . . . suffers like us and is susceptible of innocent passions, but say that he suffered in semblance, and that the flesh was impassible and immortal at the time of the voluntary and saving cross; and besides other impossible things the wretched men foolishly speak of false passions, and in false words they name phantasy incorruptibility, and deny the true incorruptibility, and they fail to notice the wisdom of the dispensation, whereby the impassible God united to himself those of our passions which do not fall under the description of sin, wishing in it to taste our death voluntarily, destroy its dominion over us, and by means of the resurrection to set us free in incorruptibility, that is in impassibility and immortality, and raise us to our first state in which also we were created.' An unreal form of suffering and death would have made the incarnation unnecessary. For the divine passionlessness and immortality the Logos already had by reason of his divinity (*ibid.*, 287). In the same letter Severus complains about Julian's intolerant procedure as well as his hectic propaganda activity (*ibid.*, 289–290). After Julian's death Severus warned several Syrian bishops to be vigilant with regard to the spreading of Julian's teachings in the East. Cf. E. Brooks, *SL* II, V, *Ep.* 14 to the bishops John, Philoxenus and Thomas, 349–50. On the further altercation of the Severans with the Julianists, see *JdChr* II/1, 76–7; *CCT* II/1, 67 (Severan florilegia against the Julianists); also CPG 7127 with reference to further research by R. Draguet on Syriac unedited sources against Julian: 1. 'Une pastorale anti-julianiste des environs de l'année 530', *Mus* 40 (1927), 59–89; 2. 'Pièces de polémique antijulianiste', *Mus* 44 (1931), 254–317; 54 (1941), 59–89; *idem, Julien d'Halicarnasse*, 81–8.

necessary to exclude from the sameness with the universal character of our nature also the other aspects [thus in particular the *phtharsia*].'

It is not yet the time to speak about the movement which Julian of Halicarnassus inspired with his ideas. It was of significance to contrast the historical Julian against Julianism, which will present itself more and more in the course of this description as an exuberant outgrowth from an original idea that could have been checked. First we must stay with the basis in order to bring into view the peculiarity of the christological disposition of the *mia-physis* teaching from the confrontation of its leading figures among themselves. The comparison between the powerful Patriarch of Antioch and a theological novice, however, also serves this purpose.

II. THE ESSENCE AND BEING OF CHRIST CONCEPTUALIZED: THE AMATEUR THEOLOGIAN, SERGIUS THE GRAMMARIAN

In spite of all the subtle polemic in the depiction of the christology of Severus we have still remained predominantly in the domain of theologizing governed by the mystery of faith. With the correspondence between Severus and Sergius the 'concept' receives a special position. Christ is to be found a place in Aristotle's doctrine of categories.

1. A problem shared with Julian of Halicarnassus

Although we cannot ascertain whether Sergius had personal contact with Julian or the Julianists, the question raised by the non-theologian, Sergius, touched that of Bishop Julian and his supporters. Once again the drive to secure completely the unity of Christ holds first place. There arises once more a suspicion of the acceptance of different properties, divine and human respectively, in the one Christ — a doubt which Severus also could not eliminate in Julian: there is a threat of a division into two natures and two *hypostases*, if in the properties of Christ a 'difference of nature' is accepted. Once again in the background we recognize the fundamental structure of the *mia-physis* teaching as the source of excessive demands on the interpretation of the person of Jesus Christ. In the solution of the question raised a partial agreement is also evident. Yet the whole of the correspondence between Sergius and Severus remains rather in the domain of personal guidance than in that of a propagandist publicity campaign. The public is not yet addressed by the Patriarch, although he reckons with the possibility that his addressee seeks an audience.

Sergius, called the 'Grammarian', is a loner. He gives the impression of a philosopher and private scholar who has ventured into the area of theology, but has got entangled in his own linguistic and conceptual net. For all that, he is ready to learn. His admiration is for the Patriarch Severus, to whom he turns with his difficulties. But hardly had the correspondence begun to develop, when the Patriarch was forced to flee into the desert. After the third letter of the Grammarian the fugitive seemed to be convinced of the suspicious character of his addressee's concepts, and the correspondence ended up in discord, although as a whole it was conducted moderately. The origins of Sergius and the course of his life are unknown to us.[277] From the correspondence it emerges that even after the change of 518 he could have remained in the *dioecesis oriens* and was keen to come to the aid of his oppressed brothers in faith.[278]

Before 518 Sergius had contacted the famous Patriarch of Antioch. In doing so he expressed his dogmatic opinions on christology to the great master, after having previously contacted converts who had made their way from the 'error' of Chalcedon to the truth. Severus immediately recognized the 'amateur' in the theological attempts sent to him, and warned him of ill-advised activity. In the first letter of reply Sergius indeed received praise for his keenness and progress with reference to 1 Timothy 4,15. Nevertheless the meaningful warning followed.[279]

> But avoid writing doctrinal teachings and do not easily approach this, for such things belong, as you know, to those who are much instructed and have meditated diligently on the scriptures inspired by God, and have grown rich on the toils of the things of the same Spirit, the tested former teachers of mysteries in the holy Church, and not to those recently instructed in the knowledge of the divine teachings.

Moreover, in dealings with the converts Sergius should adhere only to the Symbol of Nicaea and not present his own texts to them as a text of faith. Sergius himself had given occasion for the instruction by two things: he had expressed his dissatisfaction with the overly mild manner of the Patriarch and his clergy in proceeding with the return of Chalcedonians to 'orthodoxy', and moreover he had dared to interpret

277. On the following see Lebon, *Chalkedon* I (425–580), 429, n. 14; 445, 474–6, 495, 520f., 537f., 548–54. Frend, 206, n. 2; 209; I. R. Torrance, *op. cit.*, esp. 6–7.

278. Sergius Gram., *Ep. III ad Sever. Ant.*: CSCO 120, p. 119,9–10; I. R. Torrance, *op. cit.*, 6, rightfully concludes that Sergius was not a bishop. Sergius appears, however, on account of the banishment of the anti-Chalcedonian bishops to have felt that in his letters he was giving expression to the opinion of the forsaken Churches. Severus thought nothing of this apostolate and advised his correspondent at the end of the controversy, in the future 'to run on his own'. See *Ep. III ad Serg.*: CSCO 120, pp. 134,32–135,2.

279. Severus Ant., *Ep. I ad Serg. Gram.*: CSCO 120, p. 70,9–14.

the *regula fidei* on his own authority. In doing this he had coined as *kephalaion* the sentence: 'We do not speak of two natures or properties (*dilit'*) after the inexpressible union [in Christ].'[280] Through the mediation of Bishop Antoninus of Aleppo, the Grammarian had presented his suggestion of a formula to a gathering of bishops, which is not determined more closely.[281] It remained the main theme of the discussion between Severus and Sergius up to the third piece of reciprocal correspondence, which occurred certainly in the period after 518. For the Patriarch wrote in his reply:[282]

> Therefore show (me) when, in the six years (512–518) I spoke in the Church of the Antiochenes and wrote many letters, at any time I once said Emmanuel is *one ousia*, and of *one* signification (*šawdo'o*, γνώρισμα) and of *one* property (*dilit'*; ἰδιότης).

2. The zealot of the unity in Christ

From the first letter Sergius claimed to acknowledge in Christ only one 'undivided property', and that on the basis of the 'one *physis*'.[283] It is the *proprietas Christi*, the *one* particularity proper only to Christ, which he has in mind as the closest bond of unity. It is not surpassed in expressive power by any purely 'human quality'. Walking on water and leaving the grave unhindered witness to this.[284] The whole economy of salvation tends towards this omega point, the one *Christus proprium* which is as proper to the Incarnate One as the *risibile*, the ability to laugh, which is simply the *proprium* of the human being. This sign of recognition (*gnorisma*) is revealed and realized in the virgin birth, through the sufferings and death of the Incarnate One to his ascension and his sitting at the right hand of God.[285] It is the sign of Emmanuel (cf. Is 7,14). In an almost Augustinian manner Sergius sketches this illumination of his after meditating on the visions of Daniel (Dan 7,8). He now knows that he has been ushered into the 'darkness of these divine things'.[286]

280. Sergius Gram., *Ep. I ad Sever. Ant.*: CSCO 120, pp. 51,19–52,4.

281. Lebon, 168, had proposed the Synod of Tyre, allegedly in 514. Cf. I. R. Torrance, *op. cit.*, 7. On this see, however, *JdChr* II/1, 321f.; *CCT* II/1, 284f. (following A. de Halleux).

282. Severus Ant., *Ep. III ad Serg. Gram.*: CSCO 120, p. 132,10–14; Syriac: CSCO 119, p. 172,21–23; also in Athanasius and Cyril he cannot find such a sentence: CSCO 120, p. 125,4–7. On the date of *Ep. III* after 518 see *ibid.*, p. 135,1.8: Severus speaks of the fact that his enemies follow his tracks in the desert; p. 136,2–3: Patriarch Dioscorus II of Alexandria (d. 14 October 517) is mentioned as already dead.

283. Sergius Gram., *Ep. I ad Sever. Ant.*: CSCO 120, p. 52,26 and pp. 52,32–53,1: . . . *unam ex duabus Dei incarnati proprietatem admittamus.*

284. *Ibid.*, p. 53,2–6.

285. *Ibid.*, p. 53,7–16.

286. Sergius Gram., *Ep. II ad Sever. Ant.*: CSCO 120, p. 72,3–19.

Sergius, however, in his newly attained peace felt disturbed on two sides. First came the old comrades of his earlier ignorance (they are difficult to determine) who alleged much 'against the properties', and indeed with reference to a writing of Severus; then the Chalcedonians replied, likewise surrounding themselves with excerpts from Severus and spreading the teaching of the properties which were to be distinguished, but in the sense of Sergius were 'separated'.[287] Then, when the response of the Patriarch to the first letter was received, Sergius' confusion was complete. It contained the call to tread the *via media* between the two parties and to hear witnesses which Severus produced. Among these was Cyril's statement which for him was utterly unintelligible: '[The word "union" (*henosis*)] implies no confusing and no mixing of the natures with each other.'[288] It was precisely on this word of 'mixing' that Sergius had fastened to avoid any division in Christ. This word *mixis*, *krasis*, was all the more important to him because he wanted to deny, just as energetically as Severus, the total *con*-fusion, the *synchysis*:[289]

287. *Ibid.*, pp. 72,20–73,2.

288. Cited in Severus Ant., *Ep. I ad Serg. Gram.*: CSCO 120, p. 57,3–12, esp. 9–10; cf. p. 73,14–15. Cyril Alex., *Adv. Nest. II*: PG 76, 85AB: the mystery of Christ knows the distinction (*diaphora*), but not the separation (*dihairesis*): οὐ συγχέων [τὰς φύσεις] ἤ ἀνακιρνῶν τὰς φύσεις (CSCO 120, p. 73,14–15).

289. Sergius Gram., *Ep. II ad Sever. Ant.*: CSCO 120, p. 73,15–18. Besides the discussion with John the Grammarian and Sergius the Grammarian, Severus had yet a third opportunity to take a position on the terminology and theory of the *unio hypostatica*. In the long letter 25 to the people of Emesa (PO 12, 222–248) he had an argument with a member of the community of Emesa who had fallen victim to a misunderstanding of a statement of Cyril, which reads: 'For, because the Word who is from God the Father took flesh and came forth as a human being like us, he would not for this reason be also termed a double thing. For he is one, and not without flesh, who in his own nature is without flesh and blood' (*Adv. Nestor.* II 6: Pusey VI, 112; PO 12, 225). From the sentence: 'In his own nature he [the Logos] is without flesh and blood' the Christian of Emesa had concluded that the *henosis* of the Logos with the flesh has an end and he would be again in his pure divinity (PO 12, 225–227). This could remind one of Marcellus of Ancyra, but it stems rather from an overblown Cyrillianism. This error gave Severus (presumably between 512 and 518) the occasion to sketch his own doctrine of the *unio hypostatica* with broad strokes. This time it was not so much a separation as a mixing that he had to avert. Consequently the concepts mixing and mingling were rejected and the incarnation was characterized as the 'synthesis out of two elements', corresponding to the name of the incarnate 'Emmanuel': 'but even so he preserved the absence of mixture (*hultanā*) in the divine essence and did not change the essence of the Godhead into the nature of flesh' (228). Severus speaks of the fact that 'from the unmixed union of the incarnation, and the composition out of two elements, the godhead and the manhood, Emmanuel should be made up, who in one *hypostasis* is ineffably composite; not simple, but composite' (229–230). This is elucidated using the body–soul analogy (230). The terminology of mixing is excluded once again (233): the Logos is indeed in his own (pre-existent) nature without flesh and blood. Even the incarnation signifies no 'mixing of the flesh with the essence of the godhead'; he retains the divinity 'sublime and pure and unmixed in the characteristics of its own incorporeal character'; even in the hypostatic union he leaves the humanity as it was in its own *characteristica* (233). Severus here really comes close to the *idiomata* teaching of Leo the Great, admittedly with the difference that he will not concede an *agere secundum propriam formam* for the humanity in Christ.

Now, I acknowledge that once the divine union is mentioned, confusion (τὰ τῆς συγχύσεως) is set aside, (but here) the union is not thought of in a faulty way when the natures are unmixed in a divine and inexpressible mingling (contemperatio) and in a hypostasis.

But what could Severus understand by 'mingling'? Only tentatively did he attempt to determine the content of this concept.

(1) Negatively. He is not satisfied with the information that in the mia-physis formula the added word 'incarnate' implies the reference to another nature, and thus a confusion is excluded. This statement is nothing other than the secret recognition of two natures or the denial of the hypostatic unity. With this explanation of the mia-physis formula one arrives at a unity 'by decree'.[290]

(2) Positively. On his side he makes the claim:

Thus, I learn that the combination of two or more simple things into one [thing; Cyril would say ἕν πρᾶγμα] belongs to the principle of composition, in which what is complete is also a part. And (yet) afterwards [i.e. when the combination has taken place] the (constituent) parts are not from then on adjudged according to the principle of duality, since once and for all one ousia and one quality (msud'oṭa, gnorisma) has come into being.[291]

If the becoming one ought to be characterized as a 'mixing' (hlṭ), then it seems for the Grammarian that Gregory Nazianzen indicated a growing together, a συμφυΐα, as the correct mean between an external juxtaposition (parathesis) and the confusion (synchysis). The result is then one 'image' (yuqna = εἰκών) and one hypostasis.[292]

But because Severus with Cyril and his *Scholia de incarnatione Unigeniti* wanted to allow as valid finally only the expression *henosis* in the place of the terms for mixing (*krasis, mixis*), Sergius saw himself placed before an insoluble *aporia*. Through this restriction both theologians took from him the possibility of finding the right word for the act of union in Christ.[293] The sole escape for him was offered by the acceptance of a *synthesis* of the 'parts', not only to form one *physis*, but also one *ousia* and one 'property'.[294]

Therefore as I keep silent wise Cyril again urges on (my) thoughts, who speaks best by means of your priestly tongue, but it is not yet understood by me, who am of small account. But I read the law to you as well: 'He [Christ] is composed so as to become one in the middle, of human properties, and those which are above man.' The Father seems to say that the Incarnate Word was one in every respect, *I mean both nature and property*, when he mingled

290. Cf. Sergius Gram., *Ep. II ad Sever. Ant.*: CSCO 120, pp. 73,20–74,6. J. Lebon translates the Syriac *hdyut'dlut sym'* of CSCO 119, p. 100,2-3 as *unio ad suppositum*, which would produce an interesting, forward-looking formula. However, the Greek text ἕνωσις κατὰ θέσιν is certainly to be assumed. What is being rejected is nothing other than the Nestorian 'adoption as Son'. The Syriac stem *sym'* is found in the Syriac expression for υἱοθεσία, i.e. positing assumption as Son (*sīmutho bnayo'*). Cf. C. Brockelmann, *Lexicon Syriacum* (1928), 470b.

291. Cf. Sergius Gram., *Ep. II ad Sever. Ant.*: CSCO 120, p. 74,10–15, repeated almost word for word in *Ep. III ad Sever. Ant.*: CSCO 120, pp. 114,27–115,2.

292. Sergius Gram., *Ep. II ad Sever. Ant.*: CSCO 120, p. 73,21–30, with reference to PG 37, 181. The presentation of the appearance of Christ hinted at here is strongly reminiscent of texts in Theodoret. Cf. *Ep. 146*: PG 83, 1393B, cited in *JdChr* I³, 699.

293. See above, pp. 72–4.

294. Sergius Gram., *Ep. II ad Sever. Ant.*: CSCO 120, pp. 75,27–76,3. Torrance, 168f.

the natures along with the properties. But (I say) this as a suggestion rather than a decree, for in what opinion should I be headstrong?

The adduced sentence of Cyril[295] was written in an anti-Nestorian exuberance and signified an intensification of the confusion rather than a clarification. Because of this Sergius was induced to seek salvation in a philosophical solution.

3. Incarnation as event in the realm of being

It signified an intensification of Cyril's sentence just cited when Sergius advanced from confessing one *physis* to accepting one *ousia*, one essence. With the formula of the one *physis* he still remained in the domain of the *ens concretum*, which is Christ. The concrete being of the Incarnate One admits along with full ontological unity a 'composition' in which the components, divinity and humanity, have entered without change. The 'one nature composed out of two natures' was a formula born out of a historical view, from the view of the economy of salvation; this view was philosophically neutral and assigned to the result, the one Christ, no particular place in Aristotle's table of categories. Sergius, however, took this new step by claiming the '*henosis* of the *ousia*, according to the essence'. This means nothing other than the following: in his eyes through the mystery of the incarnation there is created a new essence, a new *abstract ousia* of absolute singularity, which Sergius called *Christ* and which he determined more closely philosophically by further explanation.[296]

I remember that in my lines there is (the formula that *Christ*) is 'from two natures', and all the propriety of the inhomination of the Word is a mystery.

His speculative understanding of this unity 'Christ' emerges first from the application of the body–soul analogy, that is, the composition of the human being from body and soul to the 'incarnate Logos'. The past participle 'incarnate' ought not to be understood as a simple adjective, like for example 'black', applied to the one concrete human being. Rather

295. Cyril Alex., *De recta fide ad Theodos. imp.* 40: PG 76, 1193BC: 'It is thus dangerous to dare to dissect [in Jesus Christ]. One is namely the Lord Jesus Christ and through him the Father has created all things. He was the creator as God and life-giving as life; through the human and superhuman properties (*idiomata*) he has become a certain in-between (ἀνθρωπίνοις τε αὖ καὶ τοῖς ὑπὲρ ἄνθρωπον ἰδιώμασιν εἰς ἕν τι τὸ μεταξὺ συγκείμενος). He is the mediator between God and human beings, according to the scriptures (1 Tim 2,5); according to nature he exists as God, even when he is not without flesh; he is truly a human being, but not purely a human being like us; he remained what he was and became, nevertheless, flesh.'

296. Sergius Gram., *Ep. II ad Sever. Ant.*: CSCO 120, p. 75,15-17.

it must be considered as a part of the essence. Just as the human being is not defined as the synthesis of rationality and blackness (*nigritudo*), but as a 'rational animal' or as a synthesis of *animal* and *ratio*,[297] so too Christ as unity of essence is realized from divinity and humanity (with body and soul). He is a new *ousia* and in this way also fulfils the rôle of an intermediate being, as Cyril had suggested. Certainly 'unity' is present most clearly in simple beings. But a composition can also lead to perfect unity when it has as its result *one* new *ousia*. According to Sergius, Cyril was also of this opinion.[298] What Sergius here suggests as a solution is nothing other than the application of Aristotle's doctrine of categories to Christ. Apollinarius, who had already preceded him in this direction, also appears here as a witness. We cite this text which is characteristic of Sergius.[299]

The words φύσις and οὐσία mean the same as far as we are concerned, the one being derived from πεφυκέναι and the other from εἶναι and you, O Theologian, agree with me (on this). For you have said somewhere in (your) letter, 'Where composition and natural coming-together of *ousiai* or of natures is constituted.' [Severus must concede this.[300]] Therefore, if we teach 'from two natures [*physeis*], one nature [*physis*] of the Word incarnate', how do we sin against the mystery, if, by means of words with the same meaning, we fulfil the same doctrine, (in saying) that from two *ousiai* there is one *ousia* of the Word incarnate? But this 'incarnate' I have omitted, in as much as it is frequently declared, but I do not dissolve the composition because of this ... I urge you, O Father, to endure for a little my presumption with regard to the precision of the philosophers; even if they are outside our fold, we shall greatly clarify the explanation. Among these philosophers, Aristotle, who is called νοῦς, said these words somewhere ...: 'But *ousia* is, if one will speak with an example, such as man, horse.'[301] But it is not the case that he does not acknowledge the composition of the living creature because of this. For everything which is simple is understood, rather than falling under the senses. Therefore how do I defraud the truth, when I call the incarnate Word '*ousia*', and understand this (*ousia*) (to be) incarnate?

With the incarnation of the Word a new species has thus entered into

---

297. Ibid., p. 75,21–26 (on the analogy 'human being'): 'For "being rational" (*logikon*) completes an *ousia* that it should be one; thus (a man is) a rational mortal living thing (*animal rationabile*), and if someone should remove that "being rational", he destroys the subject in every respect' (i.e. the essence 'human being' is no longer present).

298. Sergius Gram., *Ep. III ad Sever. Ant.*: CSCO 120, p. 116,19–25 with reference to Cyril Alex., *Ep. ad Succensum II*: PG 77, 241B 12–15 (the composed human being is introduced as an example). In *ibid.*, p. 116,14–19 Basil is also adduced as a witness for this teaching.

299. Sergius Gram., *Ep. III ad Sever. Ant.*: CSCO 120, pp. 115,12–116,2.

300. Sever. Ant., *Ep. II ad Serg. Gram.*: CSCO 120, p. 103,12–17: 'But we have one care (*zelus*), namely that we should establish and demonstrate plainly that where a composition and natural coming together of *ousiai* or natures is constituted, as in the case of a constitution of a man like us, it is superfluous and quite senseless to say that the living creature is composed from those things which appear in the *ousiai*.'

301. Aristotle, *Categ.* 4, 1b,27: CSCO 120, p. 115, n. 4.

the hierarchy of beings. The '*ousia* Christ' is so much one and so particular that for Sergius the formula 'the one incarnate nature of the
Logos' can be abbreviated. The *one ousia* of Christ already says everything. It has, however, the advantage that the unity in Christ is now
expressed more precisely. There is not only a 'pre-existent *physis*' of
which in time the 'incarnate' is stated. In the sense of Sergius this formula
is the description of a historical event rather than a definition. This can
now simply run: the one *ousia* Christ. It encompasses the Logos and the
humanity of Christ with body and soul. Although combined,
categorically it is still completely one and unique, and for that reason
there must correspond to it also its own properties or characteristics
which otherwise are not realizable. In the place of the invisible, intangible Logos now comes the newness: visible, tangible Logos, because the
incorporeal godhead is now the bodily and incarnated.[302] Through the
union of ensouled flesh with the Logos, Christ's consubstantiality with
us is not harmed, but as the flesh composed with the godhead it receives
'a precedence over our flesh', which Sergius explains in more detail in
his doctrine of properties.[303]

> Likewise I acknowledge on the one hand that the ensouled flesh which is united to the Word
> — for I fear to say 'mixed'! — is human and of our nature, but on the other hand insofar
> as it is composed to (be one with) God, it exists (with) those special (properties) in comparison
> to our flesh. For it did not accept sin (as a result) of transgression; it was not obliged to
> hunger and thirst and sleep, but to be occupied with the Word to which it was united,
> which willed to suffer these things for the sake of the confirmation of the inhomination.

This interpretation of the person of Christ has to be considered in
more detail.

(1) *The united essences*: (a) The two *ousiai* are the true godhead and true
humanity of Christ. In the synthesis they are also not abolished either,
even if in a certain way they adapt to each other, at least as far as the
humanity is concerned. Sergius also cannot be accused of genuine real-
monophysitism. (b) These two essences are each a totality. Here Sergius
consciously contrasts himself to the Apollinarians, who hold their synthesis as possible only because of the fact that the Logos is united to
a flesh without a soul, thus to a partial reality. One of their fundamental
propositions states: 'two perfect things cannot become one'.[304] (c) But
Sergius also pays a tribute to this principle by allowing for the establishment of the true unity in Christ that the two perfect essences in Christ

302. Sergius Gram., *Ep. III ad Sever. Ant.*: CSCO 120, pp. 116,33–117,3.
303. *Ibid.*, pp. 117,29–118,2.
304. Cf. Ps. Athanas., *De trin. dial.* 4: PG 28, 1253B; Ps. Athanas., *C. Apollin.* 1,2: PG 26,
1096B.

have the *function* of being partial realities, although they retain their ontological totality.[305] Also in his writings, in spite of repeated emphasis of the reality of Christ's soul, there is still no discernible special activity ascribed to it. He will certainly ascribe to the Logos, as the principle of the nature, the mental decision of suffering, not just to the one Logos-subject as such *ratione communicationis idiomatum*. (d) Obviously the two essences do not confront each other as equals. The *ousia* of God is indeed 'above *ousia*', a phrase which is reminiscent of Ps. Dionysius.[306]

(2) *The act of the synthesis*: At first Sergius did not want to do without the concept of mixing (*mixis, hlṭ*).[307] Indeed we have seen how he speaks with Gregory Nazianzen of a *symphyia*, a growing together.[308] Later under the influence of Patriarch Severus he dispensed with this terminology of mixing, or he explained it in the sense of *synthesis*,[309] a concept which then becomes the leading one.[310] One comes closest to Sergius' notion of the goal if one applies the Aristotelian relationship of matter and form to the unity of God and human being in Christ. Form and matter, like body and soul, communicate reciprocally as parts of the

---

305. Cf. Sergius Gram., *Ep. II ad Sever. Ant.*: CSCO 120, p. 74,10–15: the 'synthesis' in Christ is according to Sergius a combination of two or more simple elements in which what is 'complete' also becomes a 'part' of the whole so that the parts are no longer adjudged according to the principle of duality (*iam partes secundum dualitatis rationem non discernuntur*). For from them 'one *ousia* and (one) quality has come into being'.

306. Cf. Sergius Gram., *Ep. III ad Sever. Ant.*: CSCO 120, p. 118,21–22: 'But accurate speech determines that we should speak of God as being above *ousia*.' ll. 33–34: 'For God is in truth above *ousia* and property (*dilit'*).'

307. Cf. the text cited above from *Ep. II ad Sever. Ant.*: CSCO 120, 74 (above n. 305) which reads further: 'Therefore unless the natures, from which Christ is, were mixed inconfusedly, how shall I say that those things which thus remained unmixed with each other were hypostatically united? How shall I retain the principle of composition, when the natures are retained just as they were? For it is impossible for me to conceive of a union of things mutually unmixed, as they (the Chalcedonians) say, and necessarily thereby Christ would have to be thought of [lit., as we should have to think of] as two natures.'

308. Sergius Gram., *Ep. II ad Sever. Ant.*: CSCO 120, p. 73,23. Lebon translates *symphyia* by *congermanitas*, relationship.

309. Cf. I. R. Torrance, *op. cit.*, 44: 'Indeed, we have seen, that in this *Third Letter* Sergius speaks of κρᾶσις, μίξις and σύνθεσις as if they were almost equivalent.' Cf. CSCO 120, p. 113,24–30.

310. The main text for *synthesis* is in *Ep. III ad Sever. Ant.*: CSCO 120, pp. 114,25–115,2: '. . . I shall give first a definition of composition. For as I deal with the mystery, I have not yet used (defined) terms, although I have spoken in this way. But I have learned that the principle of composition is like this: (namely) the coming together (*congregatio*) from two or more simples (*simplicia*), which have come to some one thing, in which also what is complete (*teleion*) (in itself) is a part, (and) afterwards the parts are not investigated with regard to the principle of duality, since once and for all there has come into being one *ousia* or quality.' Cf. the almost identical text in *Ep. II ad Sever. Ant.*: p. 74,10–15. I. R. Torrance, *op. cit.*, 43; text from *Ep. III*: ibid., 207; text from *Ep. II*: ibid., 167.

essence and thus produce an *essential synthesis*,[311] which as a third reality
rises above the two 'parts': 'from two essences one essence' runs the main
formula of Sergius to the vexation of Severus.[312] This is thus the new
'essence of Christ', as Apollinarius too had it in mind — with the
intended denial of Christ's soul. The 'middle' has now been found in
the form of 'middle being'.[313]

(3) *The 'result' of the synthesis*: Jesus Christ is thus not only to be
expressed as a unique event of the history of salvation, but also as an
event in the realm of being. Within the category of *ousia* the *arbor
Porphyriana* received a new branch: in addition to *ens materiale, vivum,
sensitivum, rationale*, the highest level of which is the human being, there
is now in the eyes of Sergius the *animal rationale [divinum]*, namely Christ.
If Sergius had not produced the old misgivings against the term
'God-human being', it would, thought of as one *ousia*, best express his
idea. In fact the concept 'theandric' which Ps. Dionysius had coined is
already close to it (see below). Sergius, however, did not recognize that
in his natural synthesis (*synthesis in natura et secundum naturam*) the divine
transcendence of the Logos had to accept a severe violation. The Logos
becomes a *part* of the creature, not greatly different from what the Arians
and Apollinarians thought. A divine-creaturely natural being fitted into
Aristotelian categories: that is the result of the synthesis of Christ as
Sergius understood it. Worse than a mingling of partial substances as
physical realities is this ontological synthesis of divinity and humanity
in one *ousia*! Instead of physical parts which, when only accidentally
altered, produce a new reality, the act of the Sergian synthesis makes
from the divinity and humanity of Christ two essential parts, *partes essentiales*, which give themselves away into a totality of the new essence,
and in this unity are essentially dependent on each other. The monophysitism of Sergius is hence not a physical one, but a metaphysical
monophysitism.

311. Cf. the expression *'synthesis* in the human way' in Apollinarius. See *JdChr* I[3], 483: *CCT*
I[2], 331.
312. Cf. Sergius Gram., *Ep. III ad Sever. Ant.*: CSCO 120, pp. 115,12–116,5.
313. Remember his example of the mule: 'Middle beings (μεσότητες) occur when different
properties (ἰδιότητες) come together into one, as in the mule the property of the ass and of
the horse; no middle being, however, has both extremes as wholes in it, but only as parts. A
middle being from God and a human being is, however, in Christ; he is thus not a whole human
being [something that Sergius would not say], but a mixing of God and human being.' See
Lietzmann, 234, § 113.

4. One being — one property — one *doxa*

To the new *ousia* of Christ there must correspond a new property, a special feature in the qualitative representation. The starting-point for this claim is Cyril's sentence already cited: 'Because the incarnate Word has thus also mixed the properties with the natures, he is in every respect one, I mean one nature and one property.'[314] However, with this mixed quality a whole bundle of distinctions is meant which are evident in the concrete form of the Incarnate One. Sergius subsumes them under the concept *doxa*.[315] To them belong birth from the Virgin, the taking of nourishment in pure freedom from instinctiveness, sinlessness, invisible wandering among the Jews without being seen (cf. Jn 10,40–42), wandering on the sea (Jn 6,16–21), resurrection, ascension, sitting at the right hand of the Father, and the second coming. Hence under this *doxa* Sergius does not understand static qualities, but a series of extraordinary events as they are covered in the main by the evangelical reports. The exception to this is the absolute bodily absence of needs which is reminiscent of notions in the writings of Clement of Alexandria[316] and which we will soon encounter in an intensified way. Sergius is concerned to show the individual manifestations as the expressions of the unity of Christ, so to say as the 'one new theandric efficacy' in the sense of Ps. Dionysius.[317]

> You see how some natures receive their [properties] and activities not cut apart or separately recognized, but the divinity and humanity of the Word who was incarnate appear together. Let them show me what was done after the incarnation (which) was purely human. And I will not say a tear, for that came divinely, for he was immediately summoning Lazarus whom he pitied, and, though he was putrifying, the dead man became alive and made haste to run. They speak of sweat and perplexity in relation to the passion? But these things also (happened) divinely, and surpass our reasonings, so that by means of human passions he might lead men [to] impassibility (*apatheia*). But what will they say about (his) death? Will he await this utterly human thing, which takes possession of the body? We are persuaded: thus God is he who preserved even the properties of the divinity, and suffered humanly. For because

---

314. See above n. 295 (with PG 76, 1193BC); now as well Sergius Gram., *Ep. II ad Sever. Ant.*: CSCO 120, pp. 75,32–76,2. Cf. the judgement of I. R. Torrance, *op. cit.*, 48: 'Sergius' Christ, instead of being one person in two natures, with two sets of properties, will be a new compound with his own emergent properties.' He states that one can understand in this way the statement: 'The product of the composition is "one quality" as well as "one *ousia*" ' with reference to *Ep. III ad Sever. Ant.*: CSCO 119, p. 150,23–24; CSCO 120, p. 115,1–2; cf. previously *Ep. II*: CSCO 119, p. 100,15–16; CSCO 120, p. 74,14–15.

315. Sergius Gram., *Ep. III ad Sever. Ant.*: CSCO 120, p. 118,4–6. The *caro crassa* is made through the *synthesis* or *henosis* with the divinity *prorsus gloriosa*.

316. Cf. *JdChr* I³, 263–5; *CCT* I², 136–7.

317. Sergius Gram., *Apolog.*: CSCO 120, pp. 140,25–141,5.

of this he also became a complete human being that he might bear our weakness (cf. Is 53,3), and giving (his) back on our behalf to scourging (Is 50,6), he conferred honour upon the wound which the ancient [serpent] set against our soul.

Under the one quality or *proprium* of the one Christ Sergius thus understood the whole undivided image of Jesus which results from seeing together all the mysteries of the life of Jesus. Experiences of futility, hunger, suffering and death are not overlooked, but from time to time brought into relief and placed in the light of the radiation of the godhead. From this description it emerges that Sergius' picture of the concrete Christ coincides with that of Severus. Rightly the student stresses: 'I have these things, which I learned from the Father [Severus].'[318] But what makes difficulties for the teacher is the abstract terminology with which this concrete undivided picture of Christ is explained by Sergius. The Patriarch is alarmed by the expression of the 'one (abstract) *ousia*' and the 'one property' which is supposed to correspond to this one *ousia*.[319] The Grammarian Sergius offers his own theory for this concrete consideration of the picture.[320]

> For a quality [šawdo'o, γνώρισμα] does not exist without an *ousia*, nor should we recognize *ousiai* without signs. Therefore when I said that two *ousiai* were composed, along with them I was also uniting the signs.

Sergius regards it as necessary to establish the 'incarnate Logos' in the

318. *Ibid.*, p. 141,6. Then to prove this student relationship to Severus there follows a florilegium from the letters of the Patriarch to him, with fifteen texts (pp. 141,8–142,27).

319. Severus equates the concept of *ousia* with the other concept of 'physical quality' (φυσικὴ ποιότης). He places a very strong emphasis on the fact that in the hypostatic union 'the particularity of the natures in Christ remained without confusion, and particularity implies difference in natural quality' (I. R. Torrance, *op. cit.*, 33). If Sergius on the other hand spoke of the fact that in Christ there is only one *ousia* and only one quality, then Torrance claims that this would have meant for Severus that the flesh of Christ had become consubstantial with the Word through losing its intrinsic difference from it. In Sergius too the one *ousia* of Christ is intrinsically different, just as in the one essence of a human being body and soul remain different. His mistake lay in applying the body–soul comparison to Christ *univocally*, not *analogically*. Thus divinity and humanity in Christ become *one ousia* to which then a proper Christ-characteristic must correspond in the area of the qualities. Cf. I. R. Torrance, *loc. cit.*: 'We have already tried to show that Sergius' emphasis upon the "one propriety" is his way of expressing that Christ as presented by the Biblical facts, does not fit any previous propriety, but is utterly new, different and unique. "There is one propriety of Christ, in which no-one from those who are invisible or visible shares" [Sergius, *Ep. I*: CSCO 119, p. 72,23–24; CSCO 120, p. 53,12–13]. To understand Sergius, we must give due weight to his attempt to express this radical newness and difference of the figure of Christ.' Cf. as well Sergius Gram., *Ep. III ad Sever. Ant.*: CSCO 120, p. 113,27–30: 'For I understand the supreme union of God to flesh endowed with a soul, and without confusion maiming the meaning, for (the flesh) has not changed to that which is eternal.'

320. Sergius Gram., *Ep. III ad Sever. Ant.*: CSCO 119, p. 155,4–9; CSCO 120, p. 118,18–21. On *suud'* cf. I. R. Torrance, *op. cit.*, 29–30.

realm of essences in order also to close the gaps which in his opinion Severus had allowed in christology through his rejection of the one *ousia* and the one property. In this way he falls into the Aristotelianism of Apollinarius. Luckily for him he still remains on an isolated academic height. One recognizes that he must not be so negatively judged on the basis of his concrete picture of Christ as on his abstract theory. He is as it were a desk heretic who goes wrong more in terminology than in fact. However, such one-sided placements of accent are not innocuous. For finally the concrete picture of Christ is also constricted. For the sake of his theory of unity Sergius must stress the revelation of the divine so much that the earthly Jesus threatens to be concealed. For if in Jesus with the human-all-too-human the divine is not also immediately manifest, he already sees the smoke of the Nestorian separation begin to rise. Is it still possible here for the *kenosis* of Jesus to come into play? Even if it is not denied, it is nevertheless constantly hidden by the *doxa*.

This is the price Sergius had to pay for refusing the doctrine of properties accepted by the Council of Chalcedon. He touches on it, even if only negatively. For with the concept of *gnorisma* (the mark, *šawdo'o*) which he introduces, he takes up the definition of 451 in which we read: 'one and the same Christ ... unmingled in two natures, unchanged, undivided and without division known (γνωριζόμενος)'. If here it is emphasized that Christ is recognizable in two natures, despite Christ's undivided form of divinity and humanity, Sergius places the accent elsewhere. There is only *one* nature, indeed only *one ousia* recognizable, although there is a gradation: first the tears, then the miracle of waking from the dead; thus first the expression of the human and then that of the divine. A text of his *apologia*, his last writing, sums this up very clearly.[321]

Therefore what did the Father of the Church (Severus) say as a result of these unholy (statements)? Did he, like those who were quoted before [the Chalcedonians], set up two

---

321. Sergius Gram., *Apolog.*: CSCO 120, p. 139,3–15. In the lines that follow he lists again separately the properties of the Logos and those of the flesh: the *Logos* — invisible, untouchable, high above every passion; the *ensouled body* — hunger, thirst, suffering. Indeed Sergius can say in a completely Chalcedonian way: 'Therefore (even) as he remained the Word — thus preserving to himself the properties of divinity — yet preserving the integrity of the flesh, (so) too he receives these (properties) of our flesh.' Then, however, he disassociates himself from Chalcedon and stresses before Severus: 'You see how the definition has preserved for him [the Logos] immutability, (holding) him at the same time God and body. Of him who displays the particularity of the body in a godly manner, we do not say that the natures exist and each one (of) them is seen out of its own properties and activities (as indeed Chalcedon says with Leo I), but we hold that the Word himself became flesh, and (*he* and not the *flesh*) displayed these (properties) of the flesh' (*Apolog.*: Torrance, 231–2, cf. CSCO 120, p. 139,16–34).

natures, understanding these in Christ after the union, and attributing an (individuating) particularity to each of them? Not at all, but in speaking in agreement with the Fathers, he attributes these properties of our flesh to the Word who was incarnate [who is to be conceived as one *ousia*]. Therefore these people [supporters of Chalcedon] say that the *temple* of the Word was seen, hungered, thirsted, suffered, rose; but the Father (Severus) along with Cyril proclaims Emmanuel, or rather along with Isaiah (7,14), *Emmanuel* who was born from a woman, and along with John (cf. 1 Jn 1,1ff.) cries out in a loud voice that (the Word) was seen and touched, and clearly established that he hungered and thirsted, and that he was fastened to a cross, and having endured death for three days, he proclaims that he bestows life on human beings.

Under the title of his doctrine of properties Sergius really expounds nothing other than the usual communication of *idiomata*. He offers here the common ecclesial manner of speech which attributes to the one Logos-subject both the divine as well as the human. And yet this *one* subject is so conceived that it can, as a *natural unity* of divinity and humanity, bear both series of *idiomata*. In this sense he interprets the name Emmanuel as a unity of divine and human nature. In the continuation of the text of the *apologia* just cited this unity is then once again represented as a third which comprises both part-natures. There emerges the characterization of this unity as 'composed nature' which can bear the double series of *idiomata* undivided.[322]

And let no one think the definition is foolish, introducing a peculiarity and nature (existing) independently: for the principle of things which are composed joins some two or more, but completes one nature of the living creature: it allows the peculiarity of each one of them to appear, but yet not divided but recognizable together, as we are able to find out in the case of the nature of human beings. To be cut is the property of a body, but to perceive a blow is of an animated body: but it does not receive cutting in some (one) nature, but show perception in another, but there appears in one and the same composite nature both cutting of the body and perception of the soul. A (person) rejoices, and by means of a laugh makes known the cheerfulness of the soul: and is grieved, and a tear has announced distress.

Thus also in the case of the one composite nature of Christ, we will see the Word is born, but from a virgin mother: it is not the case that in one nature it happened to him that he should be born, but in another he effected what is strange, as Leo raved, saying, 'The Word performs that which is of the Word, but the body completes that which is of the body,' but (there is) one nature which is born, and in a miracle effected being born; hungered, thirsted, not compelled, but willingly; walked, but the sea was able to be walked on by (his) feet; and at the end he died, not that he had awaited the necessity of death,

---

322. Sergius Gram., *Apolog.*: CSCO 120, p. 140,1–24. Once again the composite 'nature' of the *animal rationale* is presented as an illustration and transferred univocally to Christ. Just as the human being is a composite nature, so too is Christ. He is the *una natura composita*. While Severus, however, starts only from the concrete nature, the *mia physis*, Sergius dares to speak also of a new abstract essence, the *mia ousia synthetos*, which Christ is. As the composite *ousia* it gives rise to the divine–human series of *idiomata*: the virgin birth in place of a normal birth; the series of passions, but proceeding by divine permission; wandering, but free from the law of gravity; acceptance of death, but without physical necessity.

but when it was right he dissolved death (*solvit mortem*), for 'I have the power to lay down my life and to take it up again' (Jn 10,18), and he taught the truth of (these) words by means of the resurrection.

In this way the life of Jesus occurred: not two cleanly distinguished series of happenings of which one can be attributed to the God-nature and the other to the human-nature. Rather the *one physis*, understood as the *one ousia*, produces the *one* series of events (*mia energeia*) which, however, in every single event allows the double aspect, corresponding to the composite *ousia*, to become evident. We recognize clearly that the Grammarian proposes nothing other than Severus' christology of the one *physis*, the one *energeia*, without defending a real monophysitism. The formula of the *one ousia* and of the *one property* has in its abstract form a clearly heretical character and was capable of dangerous misunderstanding. But as Sergius, however, dissolves his abstract formula in the concrete analysis of the one *physis*, he proposes nothing other than what Severus does too.

With regard to Sergius' overdrawn christology there are still some particular deficiencies to be stressed; these concern only Sergius himself.

(1) Sergius has taken over the fundamental Apollinarian error of explaining the unity in Christ by way of a synthesis of natures. Even his express avowal of a spiritual soul in Christ does not eliminate it. Through his error, however, he puts up with a crucial violation of the divine transcendence. He makes the godhead a part of the essence in a synthesis from creator and creature. On the basis of this understanding the Arians had abandoned the divinity of the Logos and had made him a creature, this in the framework of a christological Logos-*sarx* theory.[323]

(2) Through the teaching of the one combined quality which he demands for his picture of Christ, he cannot succeed in making the earthly Jesus manifest in his unmingled humanity. At every stage he must also point out in the words and deeds of Jesus the manifestation of the divine, if he is not to make himself guilty, according to his presuppositions, of the Chalcedonian–Nestorian division. The unrenounceable mystery of the *kenosis* and abandonment of Christ can no longer be proclaimed in its entire depth. An unadulterated *theologia crucis* is no longer possible. It is completely veiled by the *theologia gloriae*.

(3) On account of the abstract *mia-ousia* teaching and its extension to the qualities or *idiomata* of Christ's one essence, one can rightfully

---

323. On this see *JdChr* I³, 383, with reference to Athan. Alex., *C. Arian.* III 27: PG 26, 381A; *CCT* I², 247.

reproach Sergius with an exaggerated static christology in which soteriology comes off badly.[324] Yet it would not be correct to deny the soteriological aspect altogether. Just as he interprets the one quality of Christ which he claims, he understands by it ordinarily the so-called mysteries of the life of Jesus, that is, events which as such are conceived by him as salvific acts of God. In individual texts they are related expressly to 'our salvation'. The preponderance of the static is predetermined by the way he poses the question.

Severus of Antioch and his 'synthesis' concept

Here is the place to examine the use of the words *synthesis, synthetos* as alternatives to *henosis* in the writings of Severus and members of his party.[325] In the sixth century, in Greek as well as in Latin theology, they will gain an unexpectedly great significance. The Patriarch did not bring about a new creation but only carried on an old tradition[326] and marked out boundaries for the understanding of it. History will admittedly show that he could not close the gate. The argument with the Grammarian Sergius was the occasion that evoked a more intense consideration of the term *synthesis*.

Sergius had devised a 'mixing without mingling' and related this to the natures of Christ. With reference to Cyril, Severus rejected this expression and put in its place the word *synthesis*.[327] He maintained that Cyril thus does not speak of a mixing, but of a composition, and this in harmony with Gregory Nazianzen, who used this expression *synthesis* and not 'mixing' to explain the union of the Logos with a flesh endowed with reason.[328] Already here *synthesis* is a synonym of *henosis* and not of

---

324. I. R. Torrance, *op. cit.*, in particular reproaches Sergius for overlooking soteriology. He stresses, however, that in his *Apologia* Sergius refers to it more. Cf. CSCO 120, p. 139,14–15: the listing of the mysteries of the life of Jesus, which he emphasizes together with Cyril and Severus, he concludes with: *vitam hominibus largitum esse praedicat. Ibid.*, p. 140,22: the death of Christ means the overcoming of death in general (*solvere mortem*). *Ibid.*, pp. 140,25–141,5: this section shows the soteriological objective of the passion of Christ well. But according to Sergius this goal is attained only through the unity in Christ, insofar as it leads to one *ousia* and to one divine-human quality, which one could characterize with the words of Ps. Dionysius as μία θεανδρικὴ ἐνέργεια. It is perhaps worthwhile to note this relationship.

325. See Lebon, 292–7, 319–26; *idem, Chalkedon* I, 474–6, 486–91.

326. On the previous history of *synthesis, synthetos* see *JdChr* I[3], Index.

327. Severus Ant., *Ep. II ad Serg.*: Lebon, CSCO 120, 80 with reference to Cyril Alex., *Ep. II ad Succensum*: PG 77, 241BC and dialogue *Quod unus sit Christus*: PG 75, 1285C; Durand, SC 97, 362; *De trinit. ad Herm. dial. 1*: PG 75, 692. Severus, however, refers to Apollinarius (Athanasius for him).

328. Greg. Naz. according to Severus Ant., *Ep. II ad Serg.*: Lebon, CSCO 120, 84–86.

mixis, so that hence in effect a third entity in the manner of mixing is excluded. Severus saw such a mixing in the one *ousia* and one property of Christ proposed by Sergius. As a parallel expression for *henosis*, however, *synthesis* must fulfil certain conditions: excluded from the very outset was a *parathesis* because it effects only an extrinsic unity. But if, too, there must not occur any mixing, then the only possibility remaining is to find on a new level a new status of substantial unity without the transformation of the components. This level is that of 'existence'; divinity and humanity in Christ 'exist only in the status of the *synthesis*' (ἐν συνθέσει ὑφεστώτων). The opposite would be 'self-existence as monads' (ἐν μονάσιν ἰδιοσυστάτοις).[329] With decisiveness Severus thus removed the concept of *synthesis* from the order of essences into that of existence. It becomes a parallel expression to '*henosis* according to the *hypostasis*' which is always to be regarded as *henosis* 'from two' in the mental distinction. Hence it comes then to the strong formula 'one composed nature' (μία φύσις σύνθετος), which is gladly used by the anti-Chalcedonians. In this way the formulas '*henosis* according to the *synthesis*' and '*henosis* according to the *hypostasis*' have the same meaning. Consequently 'the one composed nature' becomes the characterization of the end result of that process which Severus sees expressed in his favourite formula: 'the one incarnate nature'.

In spite of this, as J. Lebon stresses, this formula is found only seldom in the monophysite christological writers. Severus is the sole witness for *mia physis (kai hypostasis) synthetos*.[330] Some reasons can be adduced for this.

(1) The first witness for the formula is found to be the Arian, Lucius of Alexandria (Patriarch 373–378);[331] (2) Severus must have been hampered by the fact that Cyril of Alexandria appeared not to know this formula;[332] (3) the linguistic usage of Apollinarius must have created a suspicious impression: φύσις σύνθετος is the same as φύσις σύγκρατος.[333] The expression was thus encumbered as much by its Arian-Apollinarian past as by its new misuse by Sergius the Grammarian.

329. Leontius of Jerusalem, *C. Mon.*: PG 86, 1848A provides this text for Severus. Lebon, *Chalkedon* I, 476, n. 59, wrongly has 'Léonce de Byzance'.

330. Lebon, 319, with reference to Severus Ant., *Ep. ad Ioann. ducem* (CPG 7071 [31]), Frag. in DP, Ch. 41, XXIV–XXV: Diekamp, 309–10, a passage which will concern us again later (Ps. Dionysius).

331. Text in DP, Ch. 9, XV: Diekamp, 65; English translation in *CCT* I², 245. Lucius defends the *Logos-Sarx* unity without the soul of Christ.

332. See, however, Cyril Alex., *Ep. 46 ad Succensum* II: PG 77, 241BC.

333. Cf. Apollin., *De unione* 5: Lietzmann, 187; *Anacephalaeosis*, n. 21: Lietzmann, 244; *Ep. 1 ad Dionys.*, n. 9: Lietzmann, 260: the placing side by side of *henosis, synodos, synthesis* (σύνθεσις ἀνθρωποειδής = Christ).

In addition there was the fact that the Chalcedonians wanted to make capital out of the word *synthesis* for the 'two natures', as will become clear.

Insofar as Severus accepted it, it was the same as saying a composed *physis* or a composed *hypostasis*. Both were synonymous with 'one nature of the incarnate Word'. For *synthesis* was for him not so much a static ontological end result, as rather the characterization of the historical process of the assumption of the flesh by the Logos according to the *hypostasis*. To this characterization *physis, hypostasis, synthetos* Severus gave a twofold point: it banned from Christ both any division or duality as well as any mingling. Many variants on the fundamental formula appeared: 'the one composed *physis* (*hypostasis*) of the Logos' became 'Logos *synthetos*',[334] by which naturally the composition with the body is meant. Thus one ought not to introduce any 'composition' in the essence, the *ousia*, of the divine Logos himself. '*Synthesis*' always refers to the historical *henosis* with the flesh.

334. Cf. Lebon, 321, n. 2.

CHAPTER TWO

THE PREACHER

By H.-J. Höhn

As the list of his great theological works previously presented shows us, Severus was in the first instance a sharp polemicist. Through his call to the patriarchal see of Antioch he received the chance to participate in the fight against Chalcedon also as a preacher. That he availed himself of this is shown by the series of his 125 cathedral homilies which he delivered during his Antiochene patriarchate.[335] Indeed here too he cannot deny his polemical streak, as for him it is not possible to separate cleanly between the theologian and the pastor, between abstract christology that works with concepts and concrete preaching explaining the life of Jesus. To the stylistic means of his preaching belong both the traditional wealth of formulas, predominantly of Cyrillian stamp, and also the elevated ways of theological scholarly argumentation, that is, scriptural exegesis and patristic interpretation, as well as philosophical, rhetorical dialectic. Nevertheless, speculative analysis seems not to have been his forte.[336] His letters clearly show a predilection for canon law.

I. CLASSIFICATION AND FUNDAMENTAL THEOLOGICAL STATEMENT OF THE HOMILIES

According to their content and character the cathedral homilies can be subsumed into four groups:[337] (1) sermons on the major feasts of the

---

335. For a general introduction to this corpus, as well as for information on the history of the text and its tradition, see M. Brière, *Les Homélies cathédrales de Sévère d'Antioche. Introduction générale à toutes les homélies*, PO 29, 7–72. Cf. on this F. Graffin, 'La catéchèse de Sévère d'Antioche', *OrSyr* 5 (1960), 47–54; *idem*, 'Jacques d'Edesse réviseur des homélies de Sévère d'Antioche d'après le ms. Syriaque Br. M. Add. 12159', in *Symposium Syriacum* = OCA 205 (Rome, 1978), 243–55; C. J. A. Lash, 'The Scriptural Citations in the *Homiliae cathedrales* of Severus of Antioch and the Textual Criticism of the Greek Old Testament', in *StudPat* 12 (1975), 321–7.

336. Cf. on this Lebon, *Chalkedon* I, 425–580, especially 451–576.

337. Cf. A. Baumstark, 'Das Kirchenjahr in Antiocheia zwischen 512 und 518', *RömQ* 11 (1897), 31–66, especially 36ff. Baumstark's judgement of the literary and rhetorical quality of the first three groups is not very flattering: 'The pieces of the first group bear throughout the stamp of epideictic eloquence of orators. The strength of these . . . declamations lies in a spirited

liturgical year; (2) sermons on martyrs and saints; (3) exegetical homilies on the pericope for the Sunday; and (4) occasional sermons, in part doctrinal and in part exhortatory. Because the homilies are arranged in a strictly chronological order, they enable us to gain an insight into the course of the Antiochene liturgical year, an insight which is not insignificant for an appreciation of religious life at that time.[338] If the homilies of the four groups are taken together, they permit an approximate picture of ecclesiastical and social relationships.[339] For a reconstruction of Severan christology, those speeches which follow the Antiochene calendar of feasts and treat 'dogmatic' questions must be given most attention. Here Severus traverses the New Testament year after year, as it were in the perspective of a 'theology of the mysteries of the life of Jesus',[340] in order to produce evidence for and to illustrate his anti-Chalcedonian interpretation of the revelation of divinity and humanity, or the relationship of both, in Jesus Christ. In doing this he was less concerned with a reflection on the mysteries as happenings than with the soteriological and spiritual significance of these events. In the *baptismal catecheses* which were held each year on the Wednesday of Holy Week, he gladly settled accounts with real or supposed adherents of Nestorius, Eutyches, Apollinarius, Manes and others and thereby found the opportunity to offer condensed 'monophysite' dogmatics.

Common to these homilies is a 'christology from above', which in the history of theology shows the greatest proximity to the conception of Cyril of Alexandria, as one would naturally expect.

pathos of language, rather than in a strictly logical line of thought . . . there is never a concluding review, a comprehensive formulation of results gained' (36–7). While a part of the sermons on saints stays 'in the manner of the rhetoric of the sophistic school with an enraptured panegyric of the ones being honoured, this occurring, however, often in generalities, another part gives a sketch of the life or . . . an account of the *passio*'. Now and then 'moral admonitions are urged and at the end, if saints possess their own church in Antioch, the speaker frequently has still to express some pious begging for some pressing needs of the same' (37). Also in the third group the peculiarity of the sophistic *epideiktikos* is 'still quite frequently to be noticed and to no small extent impairs a sound interpretation of Scripture' (38). Of most interest to Baumstark are the speeches of the fourth group, which are tied to various occasions, because there Severus appears in his immediate relationship to the community and cultivates a direct form of preaching.

338. Cf. on this A. Baumstark, *art. cit.*, and *RömQ* 13 (1899), 305–23; *idem*, 'Der antiochenische Festkalender des frühen sechsten Jahrhunderts', *JLW* 5 (1925) (123–35), 132–5.

339. Cf. on this, for example, F. Graffin, 'La vie à Antioche d'après les homélies de Sévère. Invectives contre les courses de chevaux, le théatre et les jeux olympiques', in G. Wiessner (ed.), *Erkenntnisse und Meinungen* II = GOF *Syriaca* 17 (Wiesbaden, 1978), 115–30. On the somewhat unsettled religious situation in Antioch during the patriarchate of Severus, see G. Downey, *A History of Antioch in Syria from Seleucus to the Arab Conquest* (Princeton, 1961), 507–13.

340. On the development of this *topos* since the patristic period see A. Grillmeier, 'Mit ihm und in ihm. Das Mysterium und die Mysterien Christi', in *idem*, *Mit ihm und in ihm*, 716–35 (literature).

The Logos is true, immutable God and Son of the Father, who also through the incarnation does not lose or weaken his divinity. Indeed to the earthly Jesus was given a soul endowed with reason — he is a complete human being and 'is like us in all things but sin' (Heb 4,15) — yet it does not appear to be a theological factor of the salvific efficacy of Christ. For it is the constant effort of Severus to conceive of Christ as the Logos 'who has become flesh for the sake of our salvation', this to the degree that there consistently arises the notion of a 'hegemony of the Logos', through which every restriction or lessening of the divinity of the Incarnate One is intended to be warded off. Where the Patriarch has recourse to the *mia-physis* formula, he understands it as it were as the conceptual re-enactment of the event of the incarnation. The gaze is always directed towards the Logos, first in considering his pre-existence, and then his incarnation, passion and ascension, so that everything appears as the history of the *one* divine nature of the Logos. For this reason the incarnation is for the Patriarch nothing less than the historical combination of the purely divine mode of existence and of the truly human reality in this one Logos who is one *physis*, one *hypostasis* and one person, but indeed as incarnate.[341]

If in the following Severus himself is very frequently given the floor, the intention behind this is to characterize his theology by his own methods and not to qualify it from the outset from the point of view of 'orthodoxy'. First of all it will be a question of working out the claim to validity and the aspect of truth of a *mia-physis* christology, that is, of disclosing those reasons from which Severus deduces the justification for rejecting the two-natures formula of the Council of Chalcedon. Only after these reasons have been reconstructed and understood is it possible to proceed to evaluate them. In view of the composition of the cathedral homilies, a twofold approach for such a reconstruction offers itself. In a first stage we ought to examine the repertoire of figures of speech, metaphors, examples, polemical passing shots, etc., which Severus utilizes to elucidate his catechetical message. In a second stage it is particularly a matter of examining those key passages which characterize Severus as a 'dogmatician'. Certain overlappings and repetitions in this process are consciously accepted, because a concentric circling of a theological position can develop a considerably greater degree of vividness than a strictly linear progression of thought.

341. In nearly every homily are to be found formulas of confession in the *mia-physis* language: 'Jesus Christ is one from two, from the divinity and from the humanity, which possess their respective *integritas* according to the particular form of the essence (*notio*). The same is truly God and truly a human being and he is known in one *hypostasis*. One is the person, one the incarnate nature of the Logos . . .; although he is from the same essence as we are, yet elevated above sin and alteration, we do not affirm, nevertheless, that he has relinquished being of the same essence as God the Father' (Hom 61: PO 8, 264). Cf. similarly: Hom 20: PO 37, 60; Hom 21: PO 37, 78–80; Hom 33: PO 36, 428; Hom 42: PO 36, 48; Hom 58: PO 8, 216–218; Hom 70: PO 12, 36–38; Hom 80: PO 20, 330; Hom 93: PO 25, 45–46; Hom 94: PO 25, 54–55; Hom 109: PO 25, 771; Hom 115: PO 26, 313–314; Hom 125: PO 29, 240.

II. 'MYSTERIES OF THE LIFE OF JESUS' ACCORDING
TO A KERYGMA OF THE *MIA PHYSIS*

Severus' entire theology, the exposition of the mysteries of the life of Jesus as well as the discussion of individual christological questions, is a variation of the one fundamental insight into the unity of the subject in Jesus Christ, which is the Logos; he 'has' become flesh without his having been transformed into flesh (cf. Hom 23: PO 37, 117–126). In this way 'subject' is not contrasted with 'nature', but is understood concretely as the *hypostasis* of the Son in his God nature. Correspondingly, the beginning of the earthly existence of the God-human being, Jesus Christ, is depicted entirely in the style of a 'descending christology', in which nevertheless the anthropological, soteriological element is throughout rightfully acknowledged. Thus the proclamation through Gabriel of the birth of Jesus (Lk 1,26–38) reveals not simply 'that God the Logos, who is without beginning and eternal, in an inexpressible way, without change and mixing, dwells in the virgin womb and assumes flesh' (Hom 2: PO 38, 278); it unveils as well the salvific character of this event (*ibid.*, 280):

> The Lord assumed flesh from the womb of the Virgin of our substance and . . . blessed the origin of our race. If he had not gone through all of these phases, sin excepted, if he had not assumed flesh in the womb, if he had not been formed during the period of nine months and if he had not been born, he would not have taken away the curse which was issued against Eve.

Although Severus constantly emphasizes that the Logos has assumed flesh which was animated by a soul endowed with reason and understanding, he just as often draws attention to the fact that this event is due entirely to divine initiative. The Logos who is consubstantial with the Father has 'not received this flesh from the seed of man, but from the Holy Spirit, who apart from every desire worked this conception in a creative and divine manner' (Hom 101: PO 22, 267).

The confession 'born from Mary the Virgin' possesses for this reason a correspondingly high value.[342] Occasionally, objections presented and philologically supported criticism are vehemently rejected (Hom 83: PO 20, 412–413):

---

342. Cf., for example, Hom 7: PO 38, 316; Hom 10: PO 38, 360; Hom 14: PO 38, 408–410; Hom 36: PO 36, 468–470; Hom 83: PO 20, 412–413; Hom 101: PO 22, 267. On this see also J.-M. Sauget, 'Une découverte inespérée: L'homélie 2 de Sévère d'Antioche sur l'Annonciation de la Theotokos', in R. H. Fischer (ed.), *A Tribute to Arthur Vööbus. Studies in Early Christian Literature and its Environment, Primarily in the Syrian East* (Chicago, 1977), 55–62; E. Porcher, 'Un discours sur la sainte vierge par Sévère d'Antioche', *ROC* 20 (1917), 416–23.

But the unbelieving Jews, who distort what is right and in so doing turn against the Holy Spirit, say that some of them who have interpreted the holy books translate: 'See, a young girl will conceive' and not 'See, a virgin will conceive.' A young girl is a woman who is married and has known her husband. But the divine books throughout also give to a virgin the appellation of a young girl. Correspondingly it says in the Book of Deuteronomy (Dt 22,27) about the rape of a small maiden in a remote spot: 'the betrothed maiden uttered a cry, but there was no one who could protect her'. Then it is certain that that person who cried there was a virgin, before he raped her.

Like the virginal conception, the remaining circumstances of the *birth of Jesus* are also proof of the divine *oikonomia*, sign of God's mercy and expression of his love towards the world. It is precisely the ordinariness of his coming which is the most expressive image for the unreservedness and unsurpassability of the incarnation of the Logos.

Like a king who wants to sojourn in a small town, which is unknown and utterly in no position to support his sojourn, who often makes himself small and suppresses the size of the proud appearance or of the pomp which surrounds him, in order to be able to be accepted by this town; consequently he cannot come as a king and deny in a general way who he is, so too the Son and Logos of the Father, the inconceivable and infinite, wanted to come into the world under a human form . . . (Hom 63: PO 8, 296)

With all his stressing of the historicity of the salvific event, Severus insists again and again, however, that the notion of an alteration of the divine nature or of its mixing with the human nature ought not to creep into the picture of the incarnation. Naturally it holds that Jesus Christ 'is one without division and without mingling of the two natures, namely of divinity and humanity' (Hom 14: PO 38, 410). This fundamental formula of his christology should not be missing in preaching either, any more than the *mia-physis* formula itself.

For it is impossible that the uncreated and immutable nature should change into a creature or that something from what is created should be transformed and pass over into the uncreated being. Rather he remained what he was and has united himself hypostatically with a body which possesses a rational soul in such a way that *out of two natures*, out of the uncreated divinity and the created humanity, he has appeared to us as a single Christ, a single Lord, and a single person (*prosopon*), a single *hypostasis*, a single incarnate nature of the Logos. (Hom 38: PO 8, 216–217)

According to Severus there is no New Testament witness that can be adduced for dividing up Christ into two natures after the union. Each episode of his earthly life substantiates the opposite: from the outset the Magi, who learned of the birth of Jesus through the observation of the stars, testify to the fact that he is 'God and king in one' (cf. Hom 36: PO 36, 466). The question of *how* the unity of the natures is to be thought of more closely Severus can answer only negatively. Excluded first of all will be any version of adoptionism, according to which the Logos 'appropriated' a child already existing in the womb of the Virgin. 'If it had been so, the Logos himself did not assume flesh and become a human being, but he made a person (*prosopon*) his own, and consequently after the union of this kind one must count two natures, two *hypostases* and two persons' (Hom 38: PO 8, 222). The incarnation of the Logos cannot be thought of as a happening in the manner like, for example, the transformation of the staff of Moses into a snake or the light in Egypt into darkness. That would be an alteration, as this occurs in corporeal things which are subjected to quantity and quality (Hom 42: PO 36, 50).

Here too the body–soul analogy is too feeble to explain the mystery, and leads finally into a 'negative theology', which, through waiving an explanation of the *mysterium*, expresses more than comparisons that are rash.

> . . . we know that the soul is united to the body by nature without our being able to say how and in what way, for this surpasses our power of understanding. Thus we also know in reference to the Emmanuel that the Logos participated in blood and flesh as we do by nature and at the same time in a supernatural way. If one wants to say 'how', this surpasses every word and every thought. (Hom 58: PO 8, 219)[343]

A certain aid for understanding in the form of metaphors, which Severus expands explicitly in his polemical works, is found also in his sermons: the reciprocal permeation of wood and fire in the glowing coal[344] or the picture of the burning bush (Ex 3,2–4).[345] With the already known explication of the motif of the Ark of the Covenant (*kibōtos*) with its imputrescible, but still mutable and burnable wood (see above, p. 87, n. 215), a symbol is introduced for the sinlessness of Jesus, and thus a core problem is addressed which is encountered in all further remarks on the mysteries of the life of Jesus. It concerns the question, how the union of the human nature with the Logos affects

---

343. Cf. Hom 44: PO 36, 96–98: 'We say that the human being, ours, which is composed from a soul and a body and which is in a single *hypostasis*, is a mortal, rational animal; still on the one side it is mortal through the body, on the other side rational through the soul; nevertheless it is still the whole animal which is called mortal and which as whole is characterized as rational; and the elements from which it is composed in a natural way are not mingled and it is not at all divided into two. It is also this way with the Emmanuel, because he is one from two natures, and one single *hypostasis* and one single incarnate nature of the Logos, without in any way the elements having to be mingled, from which the inexpressible unity comes to pass, and also, while one remains, without furnishing access to the duality from which the division arises. For he, who is really one, will never be two; and if he proceeds to become two, he has necessarily ceased to be one.'

344. Cf. Hom 48: PO 35, 316–317; Hom 90: PO 23, 153–154.

345. Cf. Hom 109: PO 25, 752–755.

the human.[346] The line of Severus' fundamental response is that the hypostatic union in no way signifies a lessening of the corporeal. The weakening of its reality would only apparently be of advantage to a more unambiguous stressing of the divinity of Jesus, and would obstruct rather than free us to perceive how unreserved the incarnation of the Logos is. Indeed the dramatic event concerning the *flight* of the holy family to Egypt demonstrates to Severus the necessity of adhering to the physical reality and relevance of the body of Jesus for the sake of the historicity of the incarnation.

> For it would have been necessary that — as in the case of an hallucination — he be invisible, in order to deceive the sight of those who saw him and to escape the hands of Herod, if he has appeared to us really only in imagination and he has given himself a heavenly or aetherial body and not that which is like ours. But this impure and ungodly opinion has been driven away and widely rebuffed by the angel who turned to sleeping Joseph (Mt 2,13.20). (Hom 8: PO 38, 332)

Jesus' stance with regard to Jewish law substantiates just as much the concreteness of the self-surrender of the Logos to the world; Jesus 'submits to *circumcision* which is assigned to him, he offers a pair of turtle doves and two small doves; he fulfils everything that stands in the law' (Hom 10: PO 38, 356). Even more emphatically formulated is the removal of the 'phantasmagoria' of Arius, Eutyches, and the Manichaeans in the sermon on the *baptism* of Jesus.[347]

> If [Jesus Christ] is not one from two without mingling, that is, from divinity and humanity, and thus a single *hypostasis* of the incarnate God-Logos, he would not have said: 'You are' (cf. Mk 1,11), but: 'That one who is in you is my Son.' For if the humanity by nature was so separated from the divinity, the consequence would have been that it also like us needed adoption . . . But what he was by nature, we will be by grace. (Hom 38: PO 36, 490)

Such figures of argument are able to be applied against Chalcedon and the Nestorians because they are accused of the same error, namely assuming the continuation of the duality of natures after the inseparable union of divinity and humanity. 'If this were correct, [God's voice at the descent of the Holy Spirit after the baptism] would have said: "In this there is my Son!" and not: "This is my Son!"'. But because he said

---

346. Cf. Hom 67: PO 8, 358–359.

347. The Antiochene calendar of feasts assigns the homilies 10, 38, 62, 85, 103 and 117 to the feast of the Epiphany of the Lord: 'The name of the feast was *ta phota*, its character completely that of a baptismal feast. The old significance of a birth feast of Christ seems to have been forgotten' (A. Baumstark, 'Das Kirchenjahr in Antiocheia', 54). Cf. on this too J. Mateos, 'Théologie du baptême dans le formulaire du Sévère d'Antioche', in *Symposium Syriacum* = OCA 197 (Rome, 1974), 135–61; B. Botte, 'Le baptême dans l'Église syrienne', *OrSyr* 1 (1956) (137–55), 148–55.

expressly: "This one there is my Son!" (cf. Mt 3,17), he has shown that the one who is seen, because he has become flesh, is also, as the same according to nature, the invisible Logos and the true Son of the Father' (Hom 10: PO 38, 362).[348] In this way it is clear that only the stressing of the immediacy of the historical event takes seriously the incarnation of the one divine nature without encroaching on its divinity. For Severus, every speculation that the earthly Jesus only *became* the Son of God through the baptism in the Jordan is erroneous.

> For the word 'he is' (cf. Mt 3,17) shows the truth and identity according to essence in order to ward off the hideousness of Arius, who says: 'There was a time when the Son was not.' In fact he is eternal, just as the voice testifies, as it called in the name of the Father: 'This one there is my Son!' For on the one hand it refers to creatures who come into existence in time, so that one says: 'He was' and 'he will be'; but on the other hand God is eternal, he was limited neither in the past nor will be in the future. But at all times he is present and he is without end, eternally the same and without any alteration. (Hom 10: PO 38, 362)

According to Severus two elements constitute the theological significance of the baptism in the Jordan. Firstly, it is a question of the revelation of the Trinity of God, that is, of the disclosure of a knowledge of the unity in essence and hypostatic difference of Father, Son and Spirit.[349] 'Just as the Father is in the Son and the Son is in the Father, so also is the Holy Spirit in the Father and in the Son on account of the unity of essence' (Hom 85: PO 23, 36). Severus thus finds in the salvific economic Trinity the revelation of the immanent Trinity. Secondly, the soteriological dimension of the baptism in the Jordan consists in the fact that Jesus on that occasion brought about the forgiveness of sins and 'opens heaven which since Adam was closed, and through this he shows that baptism has the power to clear the way to

---

348. Cf. also Hom 66: PO 8, 342: 'But if that one, who was baptized in the Jordan in our place and in accordance with the *oikonomia*, was not the Logos himself who assumed flesh, but if it is the human being, separated and distinct from the Logos — according to the teaching of those, who think like Nestorius and accept two natures after the union — then the Holy Spirit would have to descend upon the water like on us and to sound the voice which came from the person of the Father. According to your opinion the water was divested of the Father and of the Spirit, because the voice was to be perceived only after the coming out (of the water). It is in fact after the coming out (of the water) that the descent of the Spirit in the form of a dove occurred. It is completely certain, however, that the Logos, who assumed flesh — for he is one and indivisible — when he stepped into the waters of the Jordan, possessed in himself the Father and the Spirit, because they have the same essence, and, after he climbed from the water, received the Spirit for us and was to hear for us this word: "You are my Son", so that through him we are named children, because on account of sin we had become opponents and enemies.'

349. Cf. Hom 10: PO 38, 358–362; Hom 32: PO 36, 488; Hom 85: PO 23, 35–36; Hom 117: PO 26, 350–351. See as well the letter of Severus to John Romanus: PO 12, no. XXIV, 219–222.

heaven' (Hom 10: PO 38, 358) and 'to shatter the power of the depraver' (*ibid.*, 356). Correspondingly there is the fact that Jesus himself did not need the 'purification'; through the water of the Jordan sins were not forgiven him, but he, who was without sin, hallowed the water in advance for us.

> How would he have needed that, because he was born through the will of God for us to wisdom, justice and the forgiveness of sins? Then for us he received under the form of a dove the coming of the Holy Spirit whom he from nature already possessed, because he is of the same essence. And not only when he plunged under the water did he draw the witness of the Father who declared him as his Son and the descent of the Holy Spirit on him, so that no one should think that he, like us, attained sonship through baptism; for he possessed it in virtue of his essence, as too the Father and the Holy Spirit did. When he descended into the water for our sake and not for himself, he made baptism perfect. (Hom 66: PO 8, 341)

We realize that Severus will succeed as little as Cyril in making the humanity of Christ the vessel of messianic gifts of the Spirit. The fear of giving the Arians an argument against the divinity of the Son, by the Son being made the 'recipient of the Spirit', dominated him in this, just as the intention, *vis-à-vis* the Nestorians, not to allow this humanity to appear as independent subject or as person, by being the targeted receptacle of the reception of the Spirit. The Spirit is, so to say, channelled through Jesus of Nazareth to the totality of humankind to be redeemed. In Cyril these problems were treated under the theme 'anointing'.

For Severus the same hermeneutic is to be applied also to the *fasting* of Jesus and his *temptation*. When it says that he was led by the Spirit into the desert (cf. Mt 4,1) in order to be tempted by the devil, this does not mean any kind of necessity to which he was bound to subject himself (on his own account). Both are the expression of his voluntary humiliation: it happened representatively for human beings and as a model of a victorious fight against the devil.[350] 'How would the temptation have been necessary for him who has borne the sins of the world ... if he had not made my temptation his own, in order to bend the inflexible depraver for me?' (Hom 15: PO 38, 424). To the devil himself the divinity of Jesus has remained completely hidden, but for Severus it manifests itself in the fact that Jesus knows in advance his instructions and his plans.[351] The revelation of his messianity is to be arranged

---

350. Severus' interpretation of Jesus' forsakenness (Mt 27,46) and dread (Mt 26,38–39) also takes this direction: Jesus has assumed this human imperfection in order to free us from it. He is said to have had it in his power to be completely free of it. In such interpretations the anti-Arianism of the fourth century was still active, being carried over into the fifth century through Cyril. Cf. Hom 59: PO 8, 237–242.

351. Cf. Hom 15: PO 38, 424–426; Hom 66: PO 8, 345–349; Hom 105: PO 25, 647–649.

solely in accordance with the divine *oikonomia*; it determines also the time of his public appearance and work.[352]

We see in the interpretation of Jesus' baptism and temptation that Severus does not know how to make the messianic pardoning of the humanity of Christ apparent to his hearers — for fear of giving the Arians and the Nestorians material to underpin their denial of the divinity of Christ or the true unity in Christ.

With all this the framework is already established with which the deeds of Jesus, above all his miracles, are to be interpreted: 'The same, who without alteration has become truly a human being, was also by nature God. We deem the miracles not as repression or destruction of the flesh, but also the human-finite measure and the voluntary poverty not as denial or abolition of his divinity' (Hom 83: PO 20, 405). Severus seeks in his explanation of Matthew 14,22–33 to demonstrate into what *aporiai* the interpretation of the miracles which, like the *Tomus Leonis* and the Council of Chalcedon, underpins the two-natures formula, becomes entangled.

> Let us distinguish for each of the natures what is characteristic of it, and let us call characteristic what each does! In the same way as the Word, who can be neither touched nor seen, was seen and touched, so is the same who heals, walks over the lake. Do we now say that it is his characteristic work that he walked on the water? They give us this as an answer, those who after the union introduce two natures, that this is the divine nature. But how would this be the characteristic of the divinity to walk on corporeal feet, and not that of the human nature? And how is it not foreign to a human being to walk over the surface of the water? Hence it is time for you to seek a third nature to which you can ascribe an action of this kind. (Hom 4: PO 38, 302)

Not two persons, not a third mixed nature explain the miracles of Christ, but — this Severus intends to impart to his hearers — only the 'one incarnate nature of the Logos'! But can the *mia physis* give this without contradiction? Can it guarantee the immutability of God?

Apparently Severus' fundamental axiom of the immutability of the incarnate nature of the God-Logos was not so evident for his listeners that further critical enquiry and counter-questioning were absent. So he had to offer a considerable amount of theological rhetoric to rebut the conjecture that the event of the *transfiguration*, should it not have happened purely in the imagination of the apostles, proves an alteration with regard to the person of Jesus. Severus saves himself here with

---

352. Cf. Hom 119: PO 26 on the question, why it was only at the wedding feast of Cana that the time of his official ministry began: of necessity the Jews would have been even more in doubt about him; hatred and unbelief would certainly have been the effect of an *earlier* miracle, because 'it was not the time, appropriate for the human being, to effect such things' (421).

reference to the fact that Jesus could be no other than the one who he was:

> Is it, thus, that the fact that he allowed to shine forth his own countenance in a radiance which is worthy of God, like the sun, and that his clothes glistened from the brilliance of the light, lets recognize, or shows, any alteration in being, so that he has ceased to be a human being, which he in truth wanted to become without alteration, disregarding the fact that he remained God? Or is it above all so, which is really true, that namely he was the same who ignited a small spark of his personal sublimity for revelation, disregarding the fact that he wanted to confirm the thought of the disciples, insofar as that was possible? (Hom 42: PO 36, 52–54)[353]

The gradual revelation of the messiahship of Jesus, taking place in accordance with the *oikonomia*, is also the principal theme of the interpretation of the *entry of Jesus into Jerusalem*, which is in part strongly allegorized.

> When our Lord and God Jesus Christ came to the point, because he surrendered himself voluntarily to the salvific cross to fulfil in that the whole *oikonomia*, in order to take upon himself for us every contempt and ignominy and to debase himself even to death ... he arranged it in such a way that his entry into the Jerusalem of God was worthy and happened in a symbolic way, since he announced to us through this his second glorious advent. (Hom 20: PO 37, 46)

Severus' depiction of the *passion* and *crucifixion* comprises a fundamental discussion with the basic contemporary christological positions, in the centre of which stood the problem of the suffering of Jesus. The style and content of his argumentation are shaped by his endeavour on the one side to entangle the two-natures formula in contradictions, and on the other side to show that in his understanding of the hypostatic union such problems do not even arise.

> Perhaps some of those, who after the inexpressible union divide our single Lord and God Jesus Christ into the duality of natures, will ask themselves ...: 'Who is it that cries out on the cross: My God, my God, why have you forsaken me (Mt 27,46 par)?' For us it is the God-Logos, who without alteration has become flesh, who has cried that out, who has voluntarily become poor for us and who, insofar as he has become a human being, has called his God Father. For he was nailed on the cross, insofar as that body was nailed on it with which he is united in a hypostatic manner. For he has remained impassible, insofar as he is God, but he is not a stranger to suffering: the body which has suffered belongs to him and to no one else; hence it occurs rightfully if one believes that the suffering indeed belongs to him. You, however, when you say that there is a difficulty here, in your stupidity take away from his flesh that which is united with it. (Hom 22: PO 37, 88)

Severus attempts to avoid a logical contradiction and the heresy of

---

353. Cf. similarly Hom 60: PO 8, 249: 'In his countenance he shone like the sun of the divine glory and in his clothes, in which he was dressed, he became white like light. For he himself was the sun of justice.' On the understanding of the transfiguration, as Severus has presented it in his altercation with Julian of Halicarnassus, see above n. 210.

theopaschism (that is, that the God-Logos suffered in his divinity) by being able to express under two different aspects two different, mutually exclusive characteristics of Jesus Christ: with regard to his divinity he remained impassible; with regard to the flesh he suffered (cf. Hom 109: PO 25, 767–768).

> If Peter ... had not known the incarnate Logos, who also suffered for us, as the single Christ, he would not have said of him in his letter (1 Pet 4,1): 'Christ suffered for us in the flesh', but he would have spoken of the two *christoi* ... If he had not known that the same, insofar as he is God, is impassible, but, insofar as he is a human being, is passible, he would not have added 'in the flesh'. For this unity of the God-Logos with his flesh is sublime and inseparable. It draws this special character to itself, that is, the addition of the *differentia specifica*: in the flesh. (Hom 22: PO 37, 88)

Severus considers as correspondingly erroneous the question, posed according to the manner of the Sophists, which of the two natures was nailed to the cross or whether the side which was pierced by the soldier's lance belonged to humanity or divinity.

> For if that one, who was by nature without body, became embodied on account of the *oikonomia* for our sakes — without alteration — this body is altogether his and the side of the body is in every way completely his. (*ibid.*, 100)

Here Severus could have reached agreement with the Chalcedonians. These only put more precisely that it is the one divine *hypostasis*, that is, the one divine subject, which suffered not in the nature of the divinity, but only in the nature of the humanity.

A similar problem is raised by the question, to what extent the *death of Jesus* is to be conceived as a separation of body and soul, if the hypostatic union is to be understood as an insoluble union of the Logos with his body animated by a rational soul. There had been an interpretation which had assumed that the death of Jesus meant a separation of the Logos from his body.[354] At the time of Severus the position could be regarded as already obsolete. Skirting around ontological considerations, he sees in the death of Jesus predominantly the dimension of the vicarious effecting of salvation. With his last words on the cross (especially Lk 23,46: 'Father, into your hands I commend my spirit'), Jesus wanted 'to sanctify the departure of our soul; for us, when we depart this life, he gives over into the hands of the heavenly Father our spirit, which shall no longer be caught in the clutches of death and in the fetters of sin' (*ibid.*, 104). What death means in general, and specifically for Jesus, remains in such a perspective largely unconsidered.

---

354. On the theologoumenon of the separation of the Logos in death, see A. Grillmeier, 'Der Gottessohn im Totenreich', in *idem, Mit ihm und in ihm* (²1978) (75–174), 108–142.

On the one hand the soul is separated from the body by the will of him who governs all things, and on the other hand the God-Logos — for he is the one who governs them — unites each of the elements in a hypostatic manner in such an unsurpassable unity ... On the basis of this union he destroys — with respect to the body — corruption and gives life back to those who are in the grave ... With respect to his soul ... the God-Logos, because he unites hypostatically to himself a soul, does not leave the body empty nor robbed of the unity which is proper to it.[355]

On occasions, however, Severus places the death of Jesus in a final large framework, when he refers to the fact that the cross of Jesus mediated to us the knowledge of the Trinity.[356]

As with Christ's death on the cross, a similar way of thinking is applied to the interpretation of the *descensus ad inferos*.

For he has descended into the lower regions of the earth not with the divinity alone, ... but in an inexpressible way united with the soul which the good shepherd surrendered for his sheep (cf. Jn 10,11). He appeared to the souls confined there to free those over whom death reigned. (Hom 49: PO 35, 350)

Hades or Sheol has for Severus only a meaning for the time before Christ. With the descent of the Son of God into the netherworld the end of Sheol has come, because he freed the souls bound in it.[357] An epoch in the history of salvation has come to a close.

The real fulfilment of the ages, however, is guaranteed through the *resurrection, ascension* or *exaltation of Christ*. With the ascent, the descent of Emmanuel reached its final meaning. Severus has here once again an explicit christological interest, that is, one that concerns the being of Christ. If the Logos before the incarnation was 'single and not composite, incorporeal, and after the incarnation one from two' (Hom 24: PO 37, 136), then the mysteries of the completion of the life of Jesus in no way signify an alteration of his divinity as such, but only their definitive revelation in the event of the incarnation.

Thus he who has ascended into heaven is no other than he who descended from there ... And if he also descended without flesh and has ascended with the flesh, this is so precisely for this reason that he is one and the same, it is also he and no other who has ascended.

355. Hom 22: PO 37, 105. On the history of the development of these notions that are connected with the *descensus Christi*, see the article just cited.

356. See the letter of Severus to John Romanus: PO 12, no. XXIV, 220–222. Through the sign of the cross we show 'that it is through the cross that we have obtained knowledge in the Trinity ...' (221). Cf. also Hom 24: PO 37, 134–144; Hom 71: PO 12, 52–70.

357. Cf. W. de Vries, 'Die Eschatologie des Severus von Antiochien', OCP 23 (1957) (354–80), 361–2; Severus does not speak of the fact that the liberated souls have entered immediately with Christ into heaven; but he often emphasizes that Christ 'has ascended to heaven, while he bore all of us in himself, because he had become flesh in our condition' (Hom 71: PO 12, 66; Hom 90: PO 23, 158; Hymn 105 on the feast of the ascension: PO 6, 143–144).

[But if one assumes on the contrary the Chalcedonian formula of one *hypostasis* in two natures, then he who has ascended is other than the one who descended] (Hom 47: PO 35, 313)[358]

Here Severus takes into account the *history of salvation* schema to interpret the event of descent and ascent. The means for this is the early Christian *typology*. For this endeavour we shall select a summary representative passage concerning Joseph-Jesus.

Joseph was sold by his brothers, so too Christ by Judas. He was thrown into a pit and he rose up out of it, as Jesus was laid in the grave and rose. He was robbed of his colourful robe, as too our Saviour of his seamless woven garment. He descended towards Egypt, as also did the Emmanuel into this world. He was thrown into gaol, he allowed the cup-bearer and servant of the Pharaoh, who was locked up there, to come out, he ruled in Egypt, as our Saviour too appeared in the regions of Sheol, . . . who with the flesh has returned to heaven — he who fills the universe in an incorporeal and unrestricted way. (Hom 80: PO 20, 327)

In the course of our study, time and again we had the opportunity to refer to the significance of the *return of Christ* and his function as *judge of the world*. Severus is no exception to this. As a homilist he is inclined to stress the severity of the *judgement* of God (Hom 80: PO 20, 334). All creatures, all beings with a rational, freely responsible intellectuality, are gathered before the judgement seat of Christ at the end of the ages. With regard to this Severus shares the views of his time.[359] The image of the Son of Man coming again in glory as judge is also a favourite theme of his.[360] In his writings the protology is combined with eschatology when he compares the condition in paradise with that after the judgement. The re-establishment of the paradisal condition of imputrescibility and immortality does not satisfy him as the fruit of Christ's work of salvation. After the judgement humanity does not return again into paradise; rather, on the basis of the incarnation Christ introduces us in a new fashion into the kingdom of heaven.[361]

---

358. Cf. also Hom 24: PO 37, 134–144; Hom 71: PO 12, 52–70.

359. Cf. W. de Vries, *art. cit.*, 367–74. A detailed depiction of the last judgement is found in Homily 73 on the holy martyr Barlaha: PO 12, 90–96.

360. Severus Ant., *Hymnus* 87: PO 6, 127–128. The return of the Son of Man constitutes the main content of letter 71 to the deaconess Anastasia: PO 14, 107–117.

361. Severus Ant., *Ep.* 96 to Solon, Bishop of Isauria: PO 14, 183: 'That Christ by means of his Incarnation raised or raises us to these primitive conditions is certain. But this must be understood as far as concerns incorruption and the abolition of death . . . That Emmanuel invites us to prizes and crowns that surpass the primitive state, making our right actions means of support for further assistance, and that he does not raise us to Paradise again, but introduces us in a new fashion into the kingdom of Heaven, is manifest and is never a matter of doubt, not even to those who are very perverse.' In the context Severus refers to Gregory Nazianzen, Gregory of Nyssa and Chrysostom.

III. THE CREDO OF THE CATECHUMENS — THE
ANTI-CHALCEDONIAN CATECHESIS

On several occasions Severus found the opportunity to present programmatically and systematically his fundamental christological position in an elevated proclamation. Besides his address after his elevation as Patriarch of Antioch[362] and the sermons occasioned by visiting some surrounding places (Hom 53–61), it is particularly the annual homilies for the catechumens which provide information about the style of argumentation and manner of thinking characteristic of Severus in his catechesis (Hom 21, 42, 70, 90, 109, 123).

The construction and content of individual baptismal catechetical homilies exhibit the same structural elements each time.[363] The broadly constructed introduction begins with the report of a biblical account of a theophany (e.g. of Ex 19,16–19: Hom 21; Ex 3,10–13: Hom 109). To it is related the content and claim of every further catechetical instruction, in which, supported by scripture and tradition, it is a question of nothing other than the bringing to mind of God's self-manifestation. After this there comes a brief *explanation of the credo* with its fundamental trinitarian and christological statements, nevertheless not following a precisely determined version of the *Nicaenum* and/or the *Constantinopolitanum*. The sketch of salvation-history, as the baptismal creed offers a model of this, also forms the thematic guide for the major part of the homily-catechesis, which has as its focus a reflection on the incarnation of the Logos. To this belongs each time as well a succinct theology of the mysteries of the life of Jesus, which is full of polemical sideswipes at the Arians, Manichaeans, Apollinarians (who anonymously could still smuggle in so much of their christological language), Eutychians, Nestorians and Chalcedonians. The homily ends with an incidental description and theological *interpretation of the rite of baptism*.

Severus formulates his theological preoccupation in a particularly trenchant way in three *anathemas* which he uttered against the exponents of the most important dogmatic counter-positions (Hom 109: PO 25, 770–771).

(1) If anyone says that the Word of God brought the flesh from heaven or that it is from another matter or that it has transformed itself into flesh, or that it has thickened or hardened itself, like ice from water, or that it has assumed a form, like the impression of a seal [in soft wax], or that it appears like a phantom or ghost or dream image, and if he does not confess that the Son of God, who was without flesh and blood before the ages, has assumed flesh which is of the same essence as we are, from the Holy Spirit and the holy mother of God, the Virgin Mary, in a hypostatic union . . ., let him be far from the grace of the true and divine incarnation.

(2) If anyone has imagined the flesh of our Lord without soul and reason and in this way has caused the perfection of the incarnation to disintegrate, may he inherit the lot of the foolish and senseless virgins, so that the door of the marriage chamber remains closed before his nose and the hope of a future life is taken from him.

(3) If anyone does not confess that the Word of God, who became flesh and a human being without alteration — although he names him as sole Son, sole Lord, sole Christ, sole person, sole *hypostasis*, sole incarnate nature of the Word — but not that he [the Word] is impassible, insofar as he is God and that he, in accordance with the holy books, suffered

362. Hom 1; see *JdChr* II/1, 318–19; *CCT* II/1, 281–2.
363. On the following cf. J. Gribomont, 'La catéchèse de Sévère d'Antioche et le *Credo*', *ParOr* 6/7 (1975/76), 125–58; F. Graffin, *art. cit.* (n. 335), 47–54.

in the flesh, and if anyone says the flesh was altered or mingled with the divine being, let him be anathema and delivered over to terrible and unending sufferings.

Key passages of Severan christology are found also in remarks about the correct understanding of the *hypostatic union*. Severus assimilates the union of divine and human natures to the moment that the Logos dwelt in the Virgin and thus the body animated by a rational soul too began to exist. The arguments which had once been formed against early Christian adoptionism and Nestorianism were now applied to supporters of the two-natures teaching.

> Show us one instant in which, while they exist, the body, or better still the human nature with which he united himself, did not partake of the Logos, and I must say that there are two natures! But because they exist in an inseparable manner, I do not have the courage to destroy through duality the hypostatic union, which cannot be ripped asunder.
>
> It must also be explained why we, when we speak of two natures, add with regard to them: 'which in their particular aspect (*notion particulière*) are intact'. [Severus shows this with the body–soul comparison.] The spiritual soul is as soul something intact and perfect. For the soul receives the body not as a complement to its existence. For it exists also as separated from this in its separatedness (*isolément*) through itself . . . Nevertheless the soul, which is whole in its singularity and whole under its regard, proceeds to be a part of the human being when it is united to the body. Equally the body as body is something whole, which according to the definition of the body and under its particular aspect (*notion particulière*) lacks nothing. Nevertheless it is in the totality of the living being only part.
>
> Hence we say also with regard to the Emmanuel that in this way the union took place, that is, from the divinity and from the humanity which under this particular aspect are entire. For these elements, which in the union have the function (*taxis*) to be parts, in order to form a single *hypostasis*, do not lose the integrity proper to them, because they are joined together without mingling and diminution. (Hom 70: PO 12, 38–40)

The Antiochenes, earlier so sensitive to the denouncing of their teachers and heretics, must now hear from the pulpit of their own cathedral that men like Theodoret and Nestorius do not accept a real hypostatic union, but only a unity of love, 'which is founded on a connection of mercy and love . . . it comprises not the birth of God who has become flesh, but rather excludes the birth and denies it and does not assent to the fact that the Virgin became the mother of God (*theotokos*)' (Hom 58: PO 8, 224). From the pulpit Severus certainly attributes to the Council of Chalcedon the intention of meaning one person with its 'one *hypostasis* in two natures'. All the same, he did not succeed in discovering in it the true dogma of the incarnation.

> But if there is in reality one single *hypostasis*, there will also be one single incarnate nature of the God-Logos. Or, if there are two natures, there will also necessarily be two *hypostases* and two persons and the Trinity will be devised as a quaternity. But, so say these godless ones, we hold on to two natures and a single person (*prosopon*) and unite these two natures through the appellation as Christ, Son and Lord, and through the power [hence only through a moral bond] . . . We say . . . that this distinction is insidious and deceitful and has for its goal to let us assent to what is not, and vice versa to declare as false what is real. (*ibid.*, 225)

Directed to the Chalcedonians (= the 'Nestorians') once again is a similar reflection on the trinitarian implications and complications which Severus, together with other opponents of the Council, finds in the two-natures formula.

> If there is not one nature and one single incarnate *hypostasis* of the God-Logos, it is utterly necessary that consequently we add falsely to the Trinity a fourth person. For the duality establishes each nature in itself, separate and for itself, and if once the human nature is distinct from the Logos [which for Severus means separate], one necessarily has to ascribe to it a proper person. And when it is time, the heavenly throne will reject that one which is foreign, and not only because he is foreign, but more still because he is a supernumerary; for how is that one not a supernumerary who makes a quaternity from the Trinity and introduces into heaven and allows to live there a human being who was made God, and who simultaneously regards him as uncreated and a creature worthy of worship and suddenly creates and assembles a new God, as the pagans are accustomed to fabricate and to name such falsely as gods, who seek them among human beings and allow them to ascend to heaven? (Hom 47: PO 35, 311–313)

Severus thus expresses to his listeners his whole polemic against Chalcedon, and this in such a way that it is no doubt also too exacting for an adult catechism. He says to them that in the dogma of Chalcedon there is a contradiction between the claim that each of the two natures maintains its properties and that at the same time there is only one *hypostasis* and one *prosopon*. He demands that his hearers understand what *hypostasis* is (namely one *ousia*, to which a fullness of concrete features and properties is added, so that as a result there is a concrete, individual entity, whose *prosopon* these characteristics form). Could the normal hearers understand the fact that from this background the two-natures formula of Chalcedon had really to be rejected, because it is claimed that it teaches two *hypostases* and destroys the unity of Christ? In fact the whole Severan christology is contained in such homilies, and one would dearly like to know to what extent they were understood by the hearers. In conclusion we shall give two suggestive examples illustrating this.

The one activity of the incarnate God-Logos

> Therefore godless are those, who with regard to Christ teach two natures which act; for it is necessary that each nature has an action which is proper to it and different, that is, an acting movement/motion. If we confess Christ as one from two . . ., and as one person, one *hypostasis* and one single incarnate nature of the Logos, consequently it will be one who acts and one movement which bears him in action, although the *works* are different, that is, the completely performed deeds which come from the action. For some fit God, others the human being; but they are performed by one and the same, by God who without alteration has become flesh and a human being. And this is not surprising, (but) similar to the works of a human being, of which some are intellectual, the others visible and corporeal . . . It is, however, a single human being, composed of a body and a soul, who

does this and that, and there is only one single working movement. Hence, when Christ is concerned, we recognize a change of words. Some suit God, others the human being . . . But on this account we do not say that there they belong to that nature and here to this nature. For they were expressed undistinguished of the one and the same Christ.

But some conduct themselves in an ungodly way, at the same time they suffer from a final ignorance with regard to the alteration [change] of deeds and words; they have set up two that act and speak, when very significantly they have named the persons 'natures' and have concealed two sons and two Christs under the lion's skin. (Hom 109: PO 25, 758–760)

One nature, one *hypostasis*, one Christ, one *energeia*, one activity — duality only in the effects, lying outside Christ, on the one action! We shall return to this text.

Ousia — physis — hypostasis

Only in one homily did Severus explain what was to be understood more precisely by 'essence' and *hypostasis*, and this more explicitly in a trinitarian context.

'We say that essence and *hypostasis* are concepts which indicate the existence of existing things. "Essence" (*ousia*) discloses that the subject (is and) exists and *hypostasis* says that it subsists' (Hom 125: PO 29, 235). With regard to the Trinity, the essence is the godhead: Father, Son and Spirit are God without diminution or gradation. With regard to the *hypostases*, in each case a particularity is expressed of the godness of the Father, Son and Spirit. Thus for the Father the non-begotten applies (*agenetos* in the twofold meaning of 'unbecome' and 'unbegotten'); at the same time, however, the begetting is in reference to the Son; for the Son the being begotten of the Father, independently of time, and for the Spirit the proceeding from the Father. 'The particularities (*propriétés*) remain fixed and unalterable; they characterize without mingling each of the *hypostases* and do not divide the common essence.' (*ibid.*, 239)

In the trinitarian terminology Severus thus distinguishes clearly between *ousia* (*physis*) and *hypostasis*, and the formula 'three *hypostases* in the one *ousia* (*physis*)' creates no difficulties for him (*ibid.*). A corresponding translation to christology was denied to him on account of the *mia-physis* formula, also, however, on account of the imperfect determination, taken over from the Cappadocians, of the relationship of *ousia*, *physis* and *hypostasis* (see below).

The Trishagion

That the distinction of the *hypostases* does not cancel the commonality of the essence, Severus shows in relation to the question, to what extent the Trishagion may be directed to the Son and/or to the whole Trinity.

This statement of praise is made of the only (Son) of God, of the Word, who for us assumed flesh and became human. That the Father too is by nature God, mighty and immortal and so too the Holy Spirit equally, is certain for everyone. But in opposing the stupidity of the pagans and the incredulity of the Jews, for whom a crucified one is a folly and a scandal (cf. 1 Cor 1,23), we say: Holy are you, God, you who without change became a human being for us and remained God; holy are you, Mighty, you who in weakness have shown the superiority of power (cf. 1 Cor 1,25); holy are you, Immortal, you who have been crucified for us, you who bore in the flesh the death that came through the cross, and you who have shown that you are immortal, even as you were in death. On account of the unbelievers it is very fitting that we say that this statement of praise is directed to the Son. The Father and the Holy Spirit have never been in humanity, neither in weakness nor in death. But the only Son, the Word of God, who became flesh, voluntarily took this on himself. And when he was in adversity, he showed in a brilliant way that he was impassible, powerful and immortal God. For this reason we present to him threefold praise and allow it to ascend to him: 'You are holy', in order to show that he is no other outside the Trinity, who like one of the creatures was enriched through partaking of their holiness, because he is by nature holy as God, above all he is one of the three *hypostases* through whom the others are able to be sanctified, and because the praise of the Son is praise of the Father and of the Holy Spirit. Because their essence is one, the praise is also one, and whoever praises one of the three *hypostases* has in no way separated from it the doxology of the two others; for the doxology of the Son contains the doxology of the Father and of the Holy Spirit.[364]

From many of these homilies polemic leaps out at us. If we may expect something of the faithful of a metropolis like Antioch, one can still ask whether the comments on theological concepts were really understood and led to religious deepening. Nevertheless, we ought not to isolate this preaching from the liturgy and the poetic hymns of the Patriarch (CPG 7072–7078).[365]

---

364. Severus Ant., Hom 125: PO 29, 245. On this see V.-S. Janeras, 'Les byzantins et le trisagion christologique' in *Miscellanea liturgica ... Lercaro II* (Rome, 1967), 469–99, especially 470–7.

365. On the number of hymns that are ascribed to Severus see E. W. Brooks in PO 14, 209 (indexes to PO 6 and 7).

CHAPTER THREE

SEVERUS THE DOGMATICIAN AND HIS PICTURE
OF CHRIST

Neither opportunity nor aptitude drove the Patriarch of Antioch to recapitulate and present his theological opinions systematically. A certain effort is needed to gather his christology and his dogmatics together from his various writings and to give them a structure. As is already discernible from the foregoing presentation, christology is central to Severus. This theological centre is again dominated by the idea of the unity in Christ, which, in endless repetitions and with growing concentration, both linguistically and intellectually, permeates his writing and speech. Nevertheless there are numerous clues to enable one to represent Severus as theologian, responsible bishop, as organizer and spiritual monk, in any case as unsubdued advocate of his convictions — a task which is still to be done. We shall give here only a few incomplete indications to round off our presentation.

It could appear that Severus was led to intervene in the post-Chalcedonian skirmishes only through provocations, but through the power of his polemic he himself became the provocateur and leading theologian of his time. But in everything he remained the traditionalist and became more and more so. His model is Cyril of Alexandria, whom he copied very often, simplified and intensified in certain aspects, but never really transcended. His contribution to the solution of the christological problem that was affecting everybody remained for that reason confined to the horizon which was proposed by Cyril.

The same is true of his trinitarian teaching. With Cyril, Severus belongs in the tradition of Meletius of Antioch and the Cappadocians with their principal formula of three *hypostases* in the one essence. This separates him from the linguistic and conceptual usage of Athanasius, who is indeed also the great Father for him, but did not attain the significance of Cyril. Pneumatology stays, as we shall still see on occasions, in the framework of the 'king of dogmas', and for that reason Severus does not come to a satisfactory evaluation of the messianic endowment with the Spirit. The anti-Arian perspective of the fourth century still remains decisive. It is in the altercation with Julian of Halicarnassus that he cast out widest in terms of dogmatic speculation. Relatively explicitly, he spoke about his understanding of the original condition and the consequences of the fall of the first parents. From this there emerges a sound approach to the valuing of human beings and their freedom. He rejects the *peccatum naturae*, which forms the negative background for the *aphtharsia* teaching of Julian. Although a committed monk, he defends the holiness of marriage and the dignity of woman against dualistic, Manichaean criticism of the human body.[366] This is also linked up with his position in christology, and this in a twofold regard. (1) The positive valuing of the bodiliness of Jesus separates him definitively from docetism and from all monophysite tendencies, even in the form of Julianism. (2) It is precisely the rejection

---

366. See the fine section on the mariological proof of the dignity of woman in Hom 83: PO 20, 419–420.

of the Julianist *aphtharsia* teaching that prompts him to a clear profession of a theology of the cross. Even if we share Draguet's position that Severus misunderstood Julian, Julian of Halicarnassus was also really open to misunderstanding. His *doxa* christology misled numerous supporters into the renewed reception of older gnostic, docetist evaluations of the bodiliness of Christ. In contrast, with his christological realism, his theology of the cross and his whole attitude towards human life, Severus can also offer a healthier christology. With the apologetically conditioned concentration on the christological problematic of unity, the picture of Christ even in Severus has a slant which offers little help in constructing a modern christology with a stronger appreciation of the uncurtailed humanity of Christ. In what follows we shall pay particular attention to this. All too strongly Severus remains tied to the tradition which in the Apollinarian forgeries secured for itself a wide-ranging influence, to which Cyril too paid his tribute. Apollinarius remains even longer present in the Church. Without a doubt Severus already contributes to the monoenergist, monothelite crisis of the seventh century. Only in this discussion will it be seen how important the Chalcedonian picture of Christ is for the future of christology. Admittedly here a contemporary of the Patriarch intervened as a new important figure: Ps. Dionysius the Areopagite.

Unfortunately we must pass over here what the relationship between christology, sacramental theology and ecclesiology meant for Severus, and also what he has to say about soteriology. We refer to these themes as they have been dealt with already by research into Severus.[367] A complete depiction of this religious, realistic churchman should quickly become the preoccupation of ecumenical research.

In conclusion we shall attempt a synopsis of the typical characteristics of the dogmatic picture of Christ from the apologetical-polemical works, the homilies and letters of the Patriarch, as we have already analysed them.[368]

---

367. Cf. W. de Vries, *Sakramententheologie bei den syrischen Monophysiten* = OCA 125 (Rome, 1940); *idem*, *Der Kirchenbegriff der von Rom getrennten Syrer* = OCA 145 (Rome, 1955) with numerous illustrations; *idem*, 'La conception de l'Eglise chez les Syriens séparés de Rome', *OrSyr* 2 (1957), 11-124; H. Engberding, 'Die Kirche als Braut in der ostsyrischen Liturgie', *OCP* 3 (1937), 5-48; W. de Vries, *art. cit.*, 116, emphasizes the significance of the concept of *koinonia* (šawtofūto) for the West Syrians in the context of the fight concerning Chalcedon: 'La *communio* est un lien sacramento-juridique qui enlace les membres de la véritable Eglise du Christ, à l'exclusion de tous autres. L'autorité ecclésiastique est juge de l'appartenance à cette *communio*, dont le signe concluant est la célébration eucharistique.'

368. For the following the reader is referred to J. C. L. Gieseler, *Commentationis, qua Monophysitarum veterum variae de Christi persona opiniones inprimis ex ipsorum effatis recens editis illustrantur, Particula I et II* (Göttingen, 1835 and 1838) (still without cognisance of the Oriental sources); Lebon; *idem*, *Chalkedon* I, 425-580; G. Bardy, art. 'Sévère d'Antioche', *DTC* 14 (1941), 1988-2000; Frend; R. C. Chesnut, *Three Monophysite Christologies: Severus of Antioch, Philoxenus of Mabbug and Jacob of Sarug* (Oxford, 1976), 9-56; N. A. Zabolotsky, 'The Christology of Severus of Antioch', *Ekklesiastikos Pharos* 58 (1976), 357-86; V. C. Samuel, 'One Incarnate Nature of God the Word', *GOTR* 10 (1964/65), 37-53; *idem*, 'The Christology of Severus of Antioch', *Abba Salama* 4 (1973), 126-90; *idem*, 'Further Studies in the Christology of Severus of Antioch', *Ekklesiastikos Pharos* 58 (1976), 270-301; M. Simonetti, 'Alcune osservazioni sul monofisismo di Cirillo di Alessandria', *Aug* 22 (1982), 493-511; summary presentations of Old-Oriental theology: M. Gordillo, *Compendium Theologiae Orientalis* (Rome, ²1939); M. Jugie, *Theologia dogmatica Nestorianorum et Monophysitarum* (Paris, 1935) (= *idem*, *Theologia dogmatica christianorum orientalium ab ecclesia catholica dissidentium*, Vol. V).

I. THE RÔLE OF THE PATRIARCH SEVERUS IN THE
CHALCEDONIAN–POST-CHALCEDONIAN PROCESS
OF UNDERSTANDING THE MYSTERY OF CHRIST

Let us once again recall briefly what is to be differentiated here. There is a catechetical, homiletic transmission of faith which can and must refrain from more exacting concepts and formulas, but nevertheless can proclaim the mystery of Christ according to the spirit of the scriptures. It precedes the *théologie savante*, which has its own requirements and opportunities, particularly also its special perils. We have attempted to depict the share of the Patriarch in proclamation which bears the Church's life of faith. In doing this we have established how quickly he was diverted into the language and problematic of reflective theology. This is a consequence of the time when Severus entered into the post-Chalcedonian discussion; it was the time of deciding about the validity of the Council of Chalcedon with its two-natures teaching which he detested. A skirmish about formulas was imminent. Though they may have become hollow phrases once again, as earlier in the fourth century, according to the depiction of Gregory of Nyssa,[369] Severus was vastly removed from this. For him it was a question of the preservation or destruction of received faith in the one Jesus Christ, true God and true human being. But our question is: did the theologian on the patriarchal throne make a genuine, lasting contribution to formulating the christological problem more clearly, to analysing the differences between the parties and to inaugurating a reconciliation?

A missed opportunity to clarify the problem

Vis-à-vis this complex task, as we have just outlined it, Severus, to the detriment of the matter, certainly did not solve the first part of the question, a delimitation of the problem that could lead further: how in the 'composed Christ' is the unity and the difference to be established and formulated? Chalcedon had indicated a way through its distinction between *physis* and *hypostasis*. But because Severus did not want to take over this linguistic rule, and because he maintained the close bond between the two concepts, the two-natures formula was hence for him the recognition of two *hypostases*. Even if the Fathers of Chalcedon committed a sin of omission by not making explicitly clear that they wanted to clarify the christological problem by distinguishing between

---

369. Greg. Nyss., *Or. de deitate Filii et spiritus sancti* (CPG 3192): PG 46, 557BC.

subject and nature, in fact this path of reaching a solution had already been trodden. They sought the unity in Christ on the level of the *subject* or of the *bearer* of the true divinity and humanity; the difference, however, on the level of this twofold *manner of being*. They distinguished, in the language of Gilbert of Porretaine, between the question about the *quis* (who?), and the question about the *quid* (what?). The unity of the *quis*, of the bearing subject, should be expressed by *hypostasis*, the distinction of the borne by *physis*. Centuries before, Origen had already hinted at this methodology for seeking unity and distinction on different levels in connection with the trinitarian problem.

Opposed to the modalist, Sabellius, Origen established for trinitarian theology the clear distinction of the persons in God, especially for Father and Son. The writing *Disputatio cum Heraclide* (CPG 1481: SC 67), only discovered again in this century, reports the fact that in this distinction the teaching of two gods was suspected by the faithful. To solve these difficulties Origen demands 'that the object must be carefully handled and that it is necessary to show under what relation they are two and under what aspect these two are a single God. For the Scriptures have taught us (to see) in many cases where two things form a unity' (SC 67, ch. 2,29–32, p. 58).

It is also a question of the same thing in christology, where Severus spoke of the unmingled unity (the *henosis asynchytos*). It is thus a question of unity in duality, and of duality in the unity. The result of the assumption of human being by the God-Logos could not be a *unum simplex*, as the Logos as divine spirit was. It had thus to be shown how Christ is one and how at the same time he is different. This way of putting the question was blocked for Severus by the exclusivity of the *mia-physis* formula. It meant for him a restriction in the use of *physis*, which was employed extensively by him as synonymous with *hypostasis*. The synonymy barred for the Patriarch the approach to the new way which Chalcedon points out: to denote in Christ the level of the *one subject*, of the one *quis*, by *hypostasis*, and the level of the what being, of the *quid*, in contrast by *physis*, and to locate the difference there. This methodological, linguistic deficit, however, also became one of content. For the concept *physis* (*kyana*) with its etymology could become the key to valuing the human being of Christ. Severus, however, could not tolerate conceding to the humanity of Christ with this designation an active principle of operation. Precisely in this natural ability to be the source of human acts, he sensed already the independence from the ultimate bearing subject. With this serious decision of a linguistic kind, the prospect for the analysis and evaluation of the human activity of Christ was severely restricted or entirely blocked. In his dread of a second subject in Christ the Patriarch rejected even the expression: Christ 'suffered in the nature of humanity'. Although this formula had been employed well by orthodox Fathers, he still stressed that Cyril finally forbade its use. In the fight against the *morbus divisionis* no chink was to be left open for Nestorian-Chalcedonian misuse. In the synthesis, which is called Christ, there is no necessity, however, for *physis*, even when expressed of the one entire human being, to become the second *principium quod* alongside the Logos-subject. From a philosophical and terminological point of view Severus could not demonstrate any contradiction, if the solution emerged, that one and the same ultimate subject subsists in two complete principles of operation. The Fathers of Chalcedon could justifiably gather this from the Cyrillian formula: one and the same is perfect in the divinity and perfect in the humanity. If that which was divine could be characterized as 'nature', so too could that which was entirely human. By refusing to the human being of Jesus the characterization 'nature', Severus closed himself off from the recognition that the humanity of Christ had to have original knowledge, willing in spontaneity and freedom, ultimately consciousness. It is just this that Leo I could express better with his 'each of the two natures or forms is active', even if he did not succeed in making evident the unity of the bearer with the same clarity.

We see that here it was a question of the whole picture of Christ, which beyond the concepts and formulas enabled one to see the inner vivacity of him, who according to the faith of the Church is both perfect God as well as a perfect human being. Concepts and formulas could here open the wider perspective, but also block it.

II. THE SEVERAN PICTURE OF CHRIST AS AN ALTERNATIVE TO CHALCEDON

In Severus was concentrated the end of a long development which had already shown itself embryonically at the beginning of the fourth century in Alexandria. It unfolded one-sidedly and heretically in Apollinarianism, and experienced in Cyril of Alexandria an essential restraint, without being freed, however, from all one-sidedness. This will now be shown briefly in the christological, dogmatic synthesis of the Patriarch.

1. The fundamental orientation: a christology from above

According to Severus, the mystery of Christ can fundamentally only be approached starting from the God-Logos, in the sense of John 1,14. The descent of the Only-begotten of God into the world through the incarnation is so exclusively conceived from above that access to the person of

Christ from the 'earthly Jesus' is subject to grave suspicion from the very start. A christology 'from below', as we find it present towards the end of the fourth century as a reaction to Apollinarianism in the East, and which we demand today as a indispensable complement to the examination 'from above', is not considered at all. Even the constantly repeated confession of the reality of a human soul and spirituality of Christ does not change this. A more penetrating examination of the human psychic life of Christ and of all the changes in the humanity of Christ was under the suspicion of a probation doctrine and of an adoptionism, for which stand the names of Paul of Samosata and Nestorius, as well as Leo.

2. A christology aimed at 'unity'

Just as clearly as the interpretation of the person of Christ begins from above, so just as exclusively was it aimed at securing the unity; the distinction of God and human being was demarcated and circumscribed with extreme caution. In the eyes of Severus the 'duality' was the real danger for orthodoxy. This securing of unity was executed in a twofold way: first in the attunement of the entire theological statement by a fundamental formula, then in the particular view of the life-activity in the one Christ, as God and a human being.

(a) Mia physis: *the fundamental formula with its variants*
Through the Patriarch Severus the *mia-physis* formula, which infiltrated Alexandrian theology from unknown Apollinarian sources and was to some extent adapted by Cyril, attained universal dominance in the Old-Oriental christology.[370] For Severus it maintained an absolute character. According to his opinion, without it the mystery of the incarnation could no longer be expressed adequately, insofar as it is possible at all.

---

370. It is undoubtedly with reference to this formula that the name 'Monophysites' was formed in the seventh century, analogous to the earlier 'Dyophysites', both being used as opprobrious names. Cf. E. Schwartz, PS, 171, n. 1: 'The characterization of the entire opposition against Chalcedon as "monophysite" is modern and is tolerable at the most in the history of the dogma, but not in the history of the facts, in which it is not a matter of a conceptual formula but of the historical realities.' Chalcedonian orthodoxy had still other names for the anti-Chalcedonians: 'Dioscorans', 'Severans', διακρινόμενοι, that is, those who separate. Frend, XIII, translates *diakrinomenoi* as 'hesitants', that is, 'those who "had reservations" about accepting its [Chalcedon's] definition'. Here it is best if we speak of the post-Chalcedonian supporters of the *mia-physis* formula or the *mia-physis* christology. On the formula see especially Lebon, *Chalkedon* I, 478–91.

Only through it were Chalcedon and Leo I overcome.[371] In distinction to Apollinarius, the confession of the human (spiritual) soul, and thus of the complete spiritual-corporeal reality of Christ, had a firm place with the opponents of the Fourth Council, as well as with its supporters. Complete consensus ruled in this regard. For this reason, despite the dependency on Apollinarian sources and their tendencies, one may apply the appellation of a Logos–sarx christology neither to Cyril nor to Severus, as long as by that only the confession of divinity and humanity in Christ is aimed at. Accordingly, where possible, we shall avoid the term 'monophysitism'.[372] The sarkic reality of Christ as such was just as clearly expressed by Severus as by the Chalcedonians. The Patriarch gave expression to this in rejecting Eutyches, Valentinus and Manes, and in his passionate, overly severe battle against Julian of Halicarnassus and the scholasticus Sergius, and as well in the interpretation of the individual mysteries of the life of Jesus, which had gladly been made the starting-point for their speculations by gnostics and docetists.

An emphatic formula like 'the one nature of the incarnate Word', however, created around itself so to say a climate of interpretation and expression, which it produced time and again in its employment, despite corrections effected subsequently. To be noted is the fact that Cyril did not correct the wording of the formula itself. Only additional explanations protect it from real heretical interpretations. How could one know that with some of the early defenders of this naked formula old conceptions did not resonate? Even in the fundamentally orthodox usage a one-sided basic formula could still have its significant consequences for the understanding of Christ as a whole. We shall seek to discover some illustrations of this in Severus himself.

---

371. Severus Ant., *C. imp. Gram., Or.* III, ch. 8: CSCO 94, 114–115: Severus challenges the Grammarian to show how Chalcedon and Leo's *Tomus* I could have squared with the following confession of Cyril: 'We confess that in unity: one Christ, one and the same Son, one incarnate nature of the Son . . . If they [Chalcedon and Leo] say nothing of this and do not confess the one incarnate nature — whoever does not say that feigns in vain to claim that he confesses one and the same as Lord and Son and Christ — how are you then not full of stupidity, not to say foolhardiness . . .?'

372. The representatives of the Orthodox Old-Oriental Church defend themselves rightly against this designation. Still on that account this term is not superfluous, given that there is still a real monophysitism, either *de facto* or at least as an intellectual possibility.

(i) The rejection of the denotation physis *(nature) for the humanity of Christ*

Only the Logos obtains from Severus the denotation 'nature' in the full meaning of the word *physis*. It ought not be given to the humanity of Christ. On this point Severus proceeds beyond Cyril.

With a certain right the grammarian, John of Caesarea, had referred to the possibility of establishing the two-natures language in Cyril, at least by way of allusion.

(1) He recalls the word of Cyril: '. . . if he [Christ] had not put on the *nature* of the poor', as Severus reports (*C. imp. Gram., Or.* III, ch. 35).

(2) Even more important to him was the formula in Cyril, 'Christ suffered according to the nature of humanity' (τῇ φύσει τῆς ἀνθρωπότητος παθεῖν). It had become a problem for the Patriarch of Alexandria, as *Ep. 46 ad Succensum* II, 4 (PG 77, 244–245) (after 433) shows.[373] He was confronted with the question: if, to ward off theopaschism, one says Christ suffered only according to the flesh, then one makes the suffering of Christ irrational and involuntary. But if one says he suffered with a rational soul, and thus also voluntarily, then this means as much as if one said: *Christ suffered in the nature of the humanity.* If that is the case, then one must concede that after the union there are two natures in Christ. *Vis-à-vis* Succensus, Cyril dodges the issue by having recourse to 1 Pet 4,1: 'because Christ suffered *in the flesh* . . .' and recommends this formula, although the other one too, which says that Christ suffered in the nature of the humanity, does not harm the Logos of the mystery, 'even if it were applied malevolently by some' (245B). For the human nature is nothing other than the flesh which is animated by a rational soul. It is thus 'overzealous' when some formulate: 'he suffered in the nature of the humanity as though it [this nature] wanted to separate from the divinity and to give to it a reality outside (the divinity), so that two were known and not a single one, who of course became flesh and a human being, the Logos from God the Father' (245BC).

Apparently the suspicion that Cyril ascribed suffering to the godhead as such, and thus supported 'theopaschism', also agitated Pope Sixtus (432–440) in Rome, because the Alexandrian defended himself against this in *Ep.* 53 to Pope Sixtus. The letter is extant in only two fragments. In the first text Cyril says (according to Leontius of Jerusalem, PG 86, 1832A): 'I will never be guilty of thinking anything foreign to the truth or of having called the divine nature of the Logos passible' (PG 77, 285C). The second fragment, transmitted only incompletely (*ibid.*, 285C–288A), is rendered by Richard as: 'I regard the nature of God as impassible and immutable and inalterable, even if according to the human nature [certainly to be expanded] as passible, and Christ as one in both and out of both.'[374]

According to Severus Ant. (*C. imp. Gram., Or.* III, ch. 19: CSCO 94, pp. 219,32–220,30), he will acknowledge this formula with Cyril (*Christus natura humanitatis passus*), but only on condition that the unity in Christ is expressed in an absolutely certain way, 'one from two, and in one person and *hypostasis* and one nature, namely the incarnate nature of the Logos'. Nevertheless it would be better to say: 'he himself [Christ] suffered *in the flesh*. For what is

---

373. Severus Ant., *C. imp. Gram., Or.* III 2, ch. 35: CSCO 102, p. 149,15–24. John Chrysostom too had been adduced by the Grammarian, because he had said the *nature* of the human being in the exaltation of Christ attained to the throne of God: *C. imp. Gram., Or.* III 2, ch. 36: CSCO 102, 166–167. Severus, however, interprets all these passages not with regard to the individual humanity of Christ, but with regard to the assumption of the human race as such.

374. Cf. Richard, 'Le pape saint Léon le Grand et les Scholia de incarnatione Unigeniti de saint Cyrille d'Alexandrie', in *Op. Min.* II, no. 53, 127f. In a florilegium of Ps. John Maron this fragment is found refurbished in a dyophysite sense: cf. Richard, *ibid.*, 127, with reference to F. Nau, *ROC* 4 (1899) (188–226), 198 and 211.

the nature of humanity other than flesh animated by a rational soul?' (thus p. 221,26–35). Hence Severus only repeats and intensifies Cyril. In *C. imp. Gram., Or.* III. 2, ch. 22: CSCO 102, p. 7,14–18, Severus regrets having admitted in addresses to Nephalius in an effusive figure of speech that the earlier teachers had spoken of 'two natures after the inexpressible union'. But he says that the wise Cyril finally forbade this to ward off the sickness of the Nestorian duality. On the 'two natures in the Fathers' see the *Or. II ad Nephal.*: CSCO 120, pp. 26,4–35,21. From the passages adduced there the Chalcedonians have, according to Severus, built the 'fortress of their authorities', which he, Severus, will raze (p. 35,22).

Thus Cyril of Alexandria certainly came close in some passages to John the Grammarian, even if the formal commitment to the expression 'two natures' is never found.[375] With all his awareness of these concessions Severus was cautious and no longer followed his master here. The disinclination to give the denotation *physis*, nature, to the humanity of Christ was motivated by the fear that the human being of Christ could be considered as equally eternal and equally original as the divine being. Christ, however, was not a human being 'originally', that is, by nature, but only οἰκονομικῶς, according to the plan of salvation and the free decision of God's will.

What does the *mia-physis* formula mean, then, if the conceptual word may be applied only to the Logos in his divinity? Cyril and Severus answer this question clearly. For the former let us recall *Ep.* 40 to Acacius of Melitene, where it reads: 'Understandably the *physis* of the Logos is a single one; we know indeed that it has become flesh and a human being.'[376] The human being of Christ, with body and soul, is thus characterized by the addition 'become flesh'. Severus also explicitly affirms this in the *apologia* to no. 51 of the *FlorCyr*.

By our saying 'become flesh' we signify the essence of the humanity [N.B. Severus explicitly names this the *ousia* and not the *physis*], admittedly not in a separate subsistence, but in unity with the Logos, so that no one can imagine speaking on this basis of two natures after the union.[377]

According to Severus the 'Fathers' had already given this interpretation, by which he means nothing other than the pseudonyms of the Apollinarian forgers.

---

375. See above n. 25 with reference to Cyril Alex., *De recta fide ad reginas*. On this see Severus Ant., *C. imp. Gram., Or.* III, ch. 9: CSCO 94, p. 127,18–19; Greek in PG 86, 1845B; M. Simonetti, *art. cit.*, 500, n. 26. Accordingly Lebon would have needed to formulate his comments for Cyril in *Chalkedon* I, 482, n. 74 more cautiously, where he says: 'La *physis* du Christ est aussi toujours sa divinité.' Cf., however, 499, n. 124. According to Severus one can speak of two natures in Christ only intellectually, or in the mental image of the spirit, in thought, but never as realities. Cf. J. Lebon, *Chalkedon* I, 499–509.

376. Cyril Alex., *Ep. 40 ad Acac. Melit.*: PG 77, 193B. This letter, even if not the passage above, is cited in Severus Ant., *Ep. ad Eleusin.*: PO 12, 204.

377. Severus Ant., *Philal.*, ch. 51: CSCO 134, p. 221,14–18.

Because they in fact have said 'incarnate', they have indicated that the flesh did not cease to be flesh and that it is not constituted in isolation, separate from the union with the Logos. For this reason the nature (*physis*) of the Logos is rightfully described as unique.[378]

If with Cyril, Timothy Aelurus and Severus the *mia-physis* formula is explained in this sense, then it would be unfair immediately to deduce from it 'monophysitism', as a confession of a mixed nature, as the Chalcedonians, with few exceptions, were accustomed to do. For the reality (*pragma*), of which the one is first expressed, is this one *physis* of the eternal Logos, which also remains the one immutable, even when, according to the plan and decision of the *oikonomia* of God, the human reality as historical-earthly mode of existence appeared. If the *mia-physis* is explained in this way, then there is expressed in it not an ontological, but a factual, historical view. The divine Logos in his pre-existent nature is considered according to the schema of the 'two ages', which the Nicenes set up against the Arians, in order to attribute the statements about Christ's lowliness in the gospels not to the eternal Logos as such, but only to the condition of the incarnation. Admittedly this schema of the 'two ages' is only valid if the Logos, whose eternal existence is expressed in one and incarnation in the other, is strictly one and the same. It would be precisely the determination of this ontological unity in the historical schema that would matter. Cyril, however, believed that with the reference to the sequence of the two conditions he had eliminated every doubt with regard to the reality of the human existence of the Logos.[379] Severus follows him in this.[380] However, how is the unity of both understood?

If one thinks namely of the real intention that Apollinarius and his students pursued with this formula, the explanations of both Patriarchs appear as *benigna interpretatio*. For Apollinarius wanted to construct a unity of nature between Logos and body without soul in Christ, this according to the body–soul comparison applied univocally to the

378. *Idem, Philal.*, on the two-natures formula: CSCO 134, p. 113,16–20. Similarly in *C. imp. Gram. Or.* III, ch. 36: CSCO 102, p. 166,20–22: 'If we were to pass over this term [incarnate] in silence, your abuse [that is, the rebuke that we would be teaching a diminution of the humanity of Christ] would be in order; but because it has necessarily been added, where is there then a kind of diminution or subtraction?' Severus knows about the letters of Isidore of Pelusium, who had created such difficulties for the *mia-physis* formula. Cf. *ibid.*, ch. 39: CSCO 102, p. 183; Richard, CCG 1, nos. 111, 115, 116. The monk Eustathius, *Ep. de duabus naturis*: PG 86, 917B, claims that Severus took over the use of *physis* for the pre-existent divinity of Christ from Timothy Aelurus (*Aeluri vestigiis insecutus*).

379. Cf. Lebon, *Chalkedon* I, 481f.

380. On the passages named in n. 378 see the *Philalethes*: CSCO 134, p. 133,10–11: 'Car il suffit, pour signifier parfaitement le fait qu'il est devenu homme, de dire qu'il s'est incarné.'

Incarnate One. The whole was in his opinion a 'synthesis of the type that occurs in human beings'. From a soteriological interest he had made the Logos the physical soul of the *sarx*, in order to establish on this basis the impeccability of the Saviour, but also to explain by means of it the miraculous healings of Christ, as well as finally the efficacy of the sacraments. Integrity, consistency and vividness of the picture of Christ were assured in equal strength. The reality of the Logos was to be seen physically in the life and work of the *sarx* of Christ. Even the word *mia* received its force of expression from this consistency.

Without regard for the emotive value of such a picture of Christ, the Fathers of Constantinople in 381 undid this Apollinarian structure and confessed the total reality of the humanity of Christ. Not considering the Apollinarian groups, this became the confession of all christological parties, the Alexandrian as well as the Antiochene. The old tradition (Tertullian and Origen) was confirmed anew. Everything was ready for the development between 381 and 451 to result in the confession of one *hypostasis* in two natures of Christ. If the forgeries of the Apollinarians had not been successful, the Chalcedonian solution would certainly have determined more and more the East's picture of Christ. The *mia-physis* christology, however, continued to exist in concurrence with the Chalcedonian theology of two natures. What connected both was the confession of the entire humanity of Christ.[381] But one can recognize clearly in Severus, with Cyril in the background, what a restricted formula signified for the idea of Christ, even if the confession to the one Christ, perfect in divinity, perfect also in humanity, was common ground. The *mia physis* became the exclusive leitmotiv of his preaching and reflection.

In his endeavour to pursue it up to the rescinding of Chalcedon, a twofold tendency revealed itself in his understanding of Christ. (1) As much as Severus interpreted his major formula only on the basis of the 'two ages', there was still in its wording the constant compulsion to think of the unity of divinity and humanity in Christ according to a type of nature unity. The body–soul comparison works in the same direction: both elements unite to form a new nature, so to say a *tertium quid*. The word *mia* in the mouth of Severus is certainly more than the sequential succession: the one Logos — incarnate. The *mia physis* remained not just the starting-point, but became the result of the

381. See above nn. 226–30.

union.[382] The 'one *physis*' was the united divinity and humanity. We saw that Sergius Scholasticus drew the consequences from such notions, as Julian of Halicarnassus did too in his way. The *proton pseudos* of the Apollinarian nature synthesis demanded also the inclination to accept a natural symbiosis between divinity and humanity in Christ. We shall be able to substantiate this assumption immediately. But before that we still have to discuss another of Severus' efforts. (2) He notes naturally that there was not a natural *tertium quid* in Christ. The confession of the complete human nature of Christ no longer allowed the ontologically understood nature unity of Apollinarius. Hence he devised a new formula which signified a correction, even if he did not want to concede this: 'the one *composite* and incarnate nature'.[383] The word *synthesis* is chosen by Severus on the basis of the knowledge that in the 'Emmanuel' or 'Christ' it is not a matter of a simple nature (*natura simplex*), as this is present in the divine Logos. *Synthesis* is intended to bring into view the distinction in the unity. Nevertheless here once again a correction must be included immediately, because the Apollinarians used this concept to denote Christ as a 'nature unity' or as a 'human-being-type synthesis', that is, as a whole in which the Logos fills the physical function of the animating principle *vis-à-vis* the *sarx*. In a similar way Sergius the Grammarian wanted to consider the divinity and humanity in Christ as part essences, which through *synthesis* would form a new *ousia*.[384] In

---

382. On this problem see V. C. Samuel, 'The Christology of Severus of Antioch', *Abba Salama* 4 (1973) (126–90), 158–62, 161: 'The phrase "one nature", then, is not to be used with reference to Christ without the word "incarnate". Therefore, the "one" in the phrase is not a simple one, or the "one single", as John Meyendorff renders it [J. M. Meyendorff, *Christ in Eastern Thought*, 17]; it is the one which includes the fulness of Godhead and manhood. Jesus Christ is not "single-natured", but He is one "composite" nature.' Samuel refers to *C. imp. Gram., Or.* I, ch. 7: CSCO 94, p. 92,14–20: 'When the only-begotten Logos of God is compared with himself according to the temporal distinction, he is divested and at the same time not divested; he is basically one and the same person and *hypostasis*, first indeed simple and incorporeal, but then composite and incarnate; one could thus be of the opinion that a distinction between two is made, as can be demonstrated clearly from the words of Cyril.'

383. On these designations of the 'one composite and incarnate nature', see Lebon, *Chalkedon* I, 483–91. A *synthesis* comes to expression in the following formulas: (a) '*physis* of the incarnate Word'; (b) '*physis* of Christ'; (c) '*physis* of the Emmanuel', and above all in (d) '*mia physis synthetos*' and in σύνθετος πρὸς τὴν σάρκα. J. S. Assemani (2,25ff.) and J. A. Dorner (2,165) consider the expression μία φύσις διττή-διπλῆ as equivalent to these. But this expression is first found in the later anti-Chalcedonian authors. For Severus it would still be unacceptable, because in Christ every duality must be excluded. At best it is *in theoria* that there can be talk of this. Cf. *Ep. II ad Sergium*: CSCO 120, p. 88,3–4.

384. Cf. above on Sergius Gram., pp. 116–20. On this point see Severus Ant., *C. imp. Gram., Or.* II, ch. 17: CSCO 112, p. 115,24–27: 'It was thus not the union of essences (οὐσιῶν) that occurred, but [the union] of the one *hypostasis* of the God-Logos with a singular flesh, which is endowed with soul and spirit and stems from the Virgin and *theotokos*.' Cf. p. 116,4–7, where

spite of such misuse Severus wanted to hold on to this conceptual word, although with it he actually conceded that in a certain regard a duality in Christ would have to be acknowledged. He believed that he could save himself by once again calling upon his 'from two' from which just *one* has become, in which two abstract essences (*ousiai*), but not two concrete natures (*physeis*), can be distinguished only through a 'most subtle operation of the intellect' (*subtilissima pro posse intelligentia*).[385] For concretely the result of this *synthesis* is just this, 'that from both one nature and *hypostasis* is formed and subsists (as such)' (*loc. cit.*). Hence this *synthesis* means nothing other than what the favourite word of Cyril and Severus, *henosis*, says.[386] Of course Severus in no way saw through the speculative difficulties of the *mia physis synthetos* of his, so that here the Chalcedonian theologians, in particular Maximus Confessor, could begin to defend the necessity of the Chalcedonian distinction of the two natures. We shall follow this discussion as it develops.[387]

(ii) Subsidiary formulas

The principal formula was accompanied by several variants which also stemmed from Cyrillian tradition.

'From two natures (hypostases).' The Patriarch of Antioch gladly recalls the refusal of the Fathers of Chalcedon to approve the 'from two natures' of the first draft of the formula of faith. In its place was put, he says, the 'in two natures', the *tessera* of Nestorianism.[388] The *ek dyo* represented for him the simplest way to avoid the detested duality in Christ and still retain the possibility of distinguishing divinity and humanity in the *theoria*.

---

the peculiarity of this *synthesis*, as a uniting of the concrete nature of the God-Logos with a particular flesh, is once again emphasized.

385. Honestly admitting to being anxious, in *C. imp. Gram., Or.* III, ch. 16: CSCO 94, p. 195,7-17, Severus attempts to describe the *synthesis* in such a way that the Chalcedonians would not be given the slightest chance to deduce a duality from it. He will not accept the suggestion of John the Grammarian, which is that Christ is to be characterized as 'two united natures' (*duae naturae unitae*) (*op. cit.*, ch. 8: CSCO 94, p. 110,11-13). Only *unum ex duobus*, never an explicit expression of abiding 'duality', is acceptable to him.

386. Cf. Severus Ant., *C. imp. Gram., Or.* II, ch. 17: CSCO 112, pp. 115,17-116,24, especially p. 115,23-24; *ibid.*, p. 116,4-7; *idem, Philal.*, no. 112, Frag. A: CSCO 134, p. 268: (There is a *unio hypostatica* in Christ, because he is constituted) 'à partir de deux ... en une unique personne et en unique nature et hypostase du Verbe incarnée. Car c'est cela l'union hypostatique.'

387. See the subtle explanations of J.-M. Garrigues, 'La personne composée du Christ d'après saint Maxime le Confesseur', *RevThom* 74 (1974), 181-204, especially II/1, 189-96: La critique de la 'nature composée' sévérienne.

388. See Lebon, *Chalkedon* I, 510-34.

'*From two things (realities)*, ἐκ δύο πραγμάτων.' This formula sounds
very thingish. In this way the reality of divinity and humanity is intended
to be expressed in the face of any weakening; but equally too only the
intellectual distinction of both.[389]

'*From two natures one nature (or one incarnate hypostasis)*.'[390] This
formula can be understood as a variant of the schema of the 'two ages'.

'*From two (ἐκ δύο)*.' This is the final simplification to which Severus
gladly resorts to give expression to his aversion to any duality.

> Everything really depends on the formula 'from two'; from them both the hypostatic union
> is effected as well as (the fact) that there is only one incarnate nature of the Logos, and also
> this, that one ought understand those two (realities) from which the union happens, as
> distinct and of a different kind only in thought, and that one ought no longer speak of two
> after thinking of the one.[391]

'From two' thus becomes the shibboleth of anti-Chalcedonian
christology, and its rejection was for Severus the *proton pseudos* of
Chalcedon. For in this way it renounced the possibility of hindering the
division of Christ into two.[392] Because the 'from two' moves towards
the 'one nature', it comes to be on a par with the *mia-physis* formula
in general.[393]

There is no need to provide any further proof that the stressing or
securing of the unity in Christ was the hub of Severan dogmatics. Every
controversy about a grasping of the difference or duality in the person
of Christ he replied to with an examination of the entire linguistic area
of traditional incarnation teaching to see whether the act of uniting or
the unity itself was sufficiently expressed, or whether gaps were allowed
through which the division would infiltrate. If, with this concentration

389. Cf. Cyril Alex., *Apol. c. Theodoret.*: ACO I. 1, 6, p. 162,1-2; PG 75, 245AB, cited in
JdChr I³, 683, n. 29.

390. Cf. Severus Ant., *Philal.*: CSCO 134, 105-130 (introduction), where first of all the two-
natures formula is criticized. The refutation begins on 130ff., where the variants are then offered.
Cf. *C. imp. Gram.*, Or. II, ch. 6: CSCO 112, 66-69; *C. imp. Gram.*, Or. III, ch. 9: CSCO 94,
115-134.

391. Severus Ant., *C. imp. Gram.*, Or. III, ch. 10: CSCO 94, p. 141,20-25.

392. *Ibid.*, p. 157,11-18: the formula 'one Christ from two' by itself hinders any cutting up.
If one rejects it, then there follows the duality of the Sons and the Christs. The Patriarch's
reproach of Chalcedon revolves around the exclusion of the 'from two' in favour of the 'in two'.
Cf. *ibid.*, ch. 18, p. 214,23-33; p. 218,5-11, where Severus says that the *ex duabus naturis* is *destruc-
tivum . . . dualitatis.*

393. Severus Ant., *C. imp. Gram.*, Or. III, ch. 12: CSCO 94, p. 158,29-34: '. . . this "from
two" is proper to the hypostatic union; the end (*terminus*), however, of this union is the one
incarnate nature of the God-Logos'. Similarly in *Philal.*, ch. 62: CSCO 134, p. 231,27-30,
Severus relentlessly combines two expressions: a single Christ from two natures and the confession of the one incarnate nature of the God-Logos.

on unity, the Patriarch gave to the picture of Christ its centre and filled it with such illuminating power that the faith was immediately appealed to, he still did not offer any new help to theological understanding that went beyond Cyril. To clarify the crucial point, in what regard Christ is one and in what regard two, he contributed nothing new. Only faintly illuminating is the knowledge that the being one of a nature, of a *physis*, with its bearer, the subject, is something other than a *unio in natura et secundum naturam*. The body–soul paradigm, which was acknowledged by him as the most expressive analogy, broke down precisely in this respect: the coming together of soul and body as two incomplete nature parts to form one nature meant as well the coming into existence of a new abstract essence (*ousia*). Although Severus commented that the error of Sergius the Grammarian lay in the fact that he saw as present in Christ not only *one* concrete *physis*, but also *one* abstract new *ousia*, he did not arrive at the idea of investigating his speculative start for christology. His foundation for the unity of divinity and humanity in Christ remained trapped every time in the region of the relationship of nature to nature. This will show itself in our next stage of presenting his dogmatics.

(b) The mia energeia

Jesus Christ is for Severus not a mere ontic, static unity from two natures, but a constant *symbiosis* of divinity and humanity, in which priority is granted to the divine principle. The altercation with Julian of Halicarnassus showed that he saw the *henosis* in Christ established in two ways: (1) in an exchange of properties and (2) in the unity of the *energeia*, that is, of the dependence of the human activity in Christ on the divinity in the whole area of willing and knowing. When he saw that Julian transgressed the right limits with his *aphtharsia* teaching, he attempted to push the idea of the divinization of the humanity of Christ into the background, and for this purpose to found the *henosis* in the first place on the basis of the one activity, the *mia energeia*. In this the peculiarity of the Severan picture of Christ becomes clear in an utterly special way, and indeed as a counterpoint to Leo I's *agit enim utraque forma*.

> If he [Leo] in spirit were to hold and confess the hypostatic union, he could not say that each of the two natures keeps its propriety (*proprietatem*) without detraction, but he would say, like Cyril, that the Logos now and then permitted the flesh to suffer what is proper to it and to operate according to the laws of its nature. Thus the Logos would bear that as its own which is of the flesh, and still not relinquish what he has according to his essence (*ousia*), also not the superiority to suffering and his highest nobility.[394]

394. Severus Ant., *C. imp. Gram.*, Or. III, ch. 29: CSCO 102, p. 79,18–25.

Hypostatic union signifies for Severus first and foremost a clear Logos-hegemony in Christ. The subordinate part is the *sarx* of Christ: 'It is evident that it has not retained its propriety without diminution' (*evidens est eam [carnem] non tenuisse sine defectu suam proprietatem*). At the same time this diminution of what is proper to it is an enrichment through the divinity. Severus refers to the transfiguration or the miraculous pouring forth 'of the source of life, of the blood and water of forgiveness after the piercing of the divine side' of Jesus (CSCO 102, p. 79,4–9). The origin of such an understanding of the functions of the inner God–human life of Jesus was as old as the Apollinarians' teaching of the *one energeia*, of the one *operatio* in Christ, which could have its seat and its source only in the *dynamis* of the Logos.[395]

How Severus understands the life activity in Christ is stated by him quite clearly in Homily 109, cited above: as long as the person of Jesus Christ itself is considered, no duality ought to be expressed. There is a 'two' only in the effect of Christ's activity, never in himself, be it in relation to the natures, the powers of knowing and willing, and whatever else is within Christ. Against the attacks of Theodoret on his anathemas, Cyril had conceded that there is to be observed in Christ a certain doubling (*duplicitas*), namely in regard to the words (*voces*) and the activities (*actiones*). For if Christ is also one and the same, he still shows different ways of producing words and deeds: some are effected in a divine way, the others in a human way. Despite this distinction of his master, Severus stresses that it is indeed only one and the same speaking and acting, and then formulates incisively: 'There is only one single activity (*energeia*), only one single operative motion (*motus operativus*), as there is also only one single speaking of the incarnate Logos, be it that the actions and the words have been different.'[396]

There emerges from these words a conception of the God–human action and speech of Christ, in which everything is deduced from the divine Logos as nature principle. Every activity flows from above, even if the human principle of activity is engaged. How Severus understands the inner functioning of the one *energeia* of Christ he makes clear *vis-à-vis* the 'godless Grammarian' regarding the healing of the leper:

While the incarnate God spoke with human tongue and said with human and clear voice to the leper: 'I will, be clean' (Mt 8,3), he showed through the effect that the voice, in

395. Cf. on this *JdChr* I³, 489; *CCT* I², 335–6.

396. Cf. Severus Ant., *C. imp. Gram.*, Or. III, ch. 38: CSCO 102, p. 175,6–7. Leo's Tome figures as the counter-image to this (*ibid.*, pp. 175–6).

keeping with the mixing (*mixtio*) worthy of God, has gone forth from the incarnate God; for the healing of the leper went together with the heard word.[397]

The miracle-working of Christ thus provides the model for how the 'one *energeia*' is to be understood. The activity starts from the divinity as the real source; it mixes itself with the human voice (or as well with the touch of Jesus' hand) and produces the miraculous effect in the sick person. The human voice is only the vehicle of the divine flow of will; for without a doubt Severus ascribes the 'I will' to the volition of the divinity. The human will of Christ clearly does not need to be active. Severus takes up the explanation of the miracle from Cyril, who, along the lines of a statement from Gregory of Nyssa in his Catechetical Oration,[398] already excluded the 'caricature' which Leo of Rome[399] in his Tome is said to have given of the activity of Jesus.

When he cleansed the leper, he did not offer (only) a speech and also did not say: 'My Father may will and you will be healed.' Rather he combined the healing with his own movement of will (*nutus*), as he who had in himself the paternal authority and the glory of the majesty of the Father. After he had expressed his decision (*nutus*) from his good will, he added the touch with his hand and granted it results. Thus we should learn that the holy workplace of the purification [of the leper] is also his holy body and is gathered with divine willing with best results for our sanctification.[400]

To clarify the notion of the process of healing, it is to be noted that Cyril (and with him Severus) attributes everything explicitly to the divine willing (βούλησις, act of will) of the Logos. There is no talk of Christ's human act of will. The touch with the hand is only the instrument through which the power of the divinity, which is bestowed on the holy body, acts on the sick person. This single *energeia* as activity, which is effective in this miracle, is now explained by Severus according to the body–soul analogy. He explains this most clearly in his first letter to the grammarian, Sergius, which we want to examine in more

397. *Ibid.*, ch. 32: CSCO 102, p. 94,27–32.

398. Severus Ant., *C. imp. Gram.*, Or. III, ch. 32: CSCO 102, p. 94,27–33, with reference to a text of Gregory of Nyssa (PG 45, 80), which the Grammarian wanted to utilize in order to deduce from it the two-natures teaching, along the lines of Leo's *agit enim utraque forma*. Against this Severus writes: 'The teacher did not say that the human nature spoke, the divine nature, however, acted, but that with the divine was mixed the voice that was produced in a human way.'

399. Severus cites three passages from Leo's Tome (p. 95,15–25).

400. Cyril Alex., *Comm. in Mt* (CPG 5206), a text which Lebon could not verify, but which is to be found in an abbreviated form in E. Schwartz, *Codex Vat. gr. 1431* (Munich, 1927), p. 42,3–7: CSCO 102, p. 96,21–29.

detail. Following Ps. Basil, *Contra Eunomium* IV,[401] he distinguishes in the human activity the agent (ἐνεργήσας), the action (ἐνέργεια) which in itself has no reality (is not ἐνυπόστατος), and the effect (ἐνεργηθέν).[402] Although in the human being, which is composed of body and soul, the genuinely human body–soul activity in effect produces two different types of work, intellectual and sensible-corporeal, there is nevertheless only one process of activity (*motus operativus, id est impetus ipsius voluntatis unus*),[403] because the human being itself is a nature unity. It is always, for example, Peter (cf. Mt 14,28f.) who posits and executes the act of the will, although the walking on the water is a matter for the body. This co-ordination of a nature unity from spirit and body the Patriarch sees to be present also in the Emmanuel.

> One can see the same in the case of Emmanuel. For there is one who acts (ἐνεργήσας), that is the Word of God incarnate; and there is one active movement which is activity (ἐνέργεια), but the things which are done (ἐνεργηθέντα) are diverse, that is, (the things) accomplished by activity ... And it is not the case that, because these things which were done were of different kinds, we say that conceptually there were two natures which were effecting those things, for as we have said, a single God the Word incarnate performed both of them.[404]

Hence the Logos is always conceived by Severus as *agens*, as ἐνεργήσας, always involved in the works mentioned. He is not only the final, bearing subject, to which according to the law of the communication of *idiomata* even purely human acts are ascribed, while the ability (*facultas*), which releases them from itself, would be the human nature. According to Severus, in every activity of the Emmanuel, that is, the incarnate Logos, the divinity participates as *facultas*, as nature principle, and not only as final, bearing subject. To prove this thesis the Patriarch goes through the various *opera mixta* which Christ effected as God–human actor,[405] and then concludes:

> therefore that action is of the incarnate Word, to whom belongs at the same time divine character and humanity indivisibly.[406]

---

401. On the disputed authorship of this book see CPG 2837; *JdChr* I³, 529–35 with n. 2; *CCT* I², 361–7. We refer to Severus Ant., *Ep. I ad Sergium*: CSCO 120, 53–70; R. Chesnut, *Three Monophysite Christologies*, 30–4.

402. Cf. Ps. Basil, *C. Eunom.* IV. 1: PG 29, 689C.

403. Severus Ant., *Ep. I ad Sergium*: CSCO 120, p. 60,29–33: 'And the man who acts (in both cases) is *one*, consisting of soul and body, and the activity is *one*, for the active movement is *one*, which is the impetus of volition, but the things which are done (*opera*) are diverse, for one is intellectual but the other is sensible and bodily.'

404. Severus Ant., *Ep. I ad Sergium*: CSCO 120, pp. 60,33–61,9.

405. *Ibid.*, 61–62.

406. *Ibid.*, p. 62,5–7.

Against this are contrasted the two activities of Leo, who in the eyes of Severus accepted with the two acting nature principles also two bearing subjects, that is, two persons.[407] The hypostatic union demands for the entire work of Christ that the Logos participate in the activity of Christ not only as the possessor or bearer of the human nature, but also as divine nature principle, even if in varying degree. In Christ every impulse to act comes from the Logos-power, as in every activity of the human being the soul is always involved. The model of interpretation of the soul–body action of the human being holds true in the strict sense, and not only analogically, for the Emmanuel.[408] Ps. Julius, who is cited explicitly against Sergius, is here the godfather.[409] The *mia physis* is here indeed the immediate consequence of the vital Logos–*sarx* unity, which is Christ. But how does Severus picture the same formula in conjunction with his clear confession of the soul of Christ? How is the intellectual spontaneity of the intellectuality of Christ incorporated into his interpretation of the activity of the Incarnate One? The Patriarch indeed stresses that the Logos uses his body not as a lifeless, inanimate instrument.[410]

In fact Severus finds it difficult to recognize and appreciate the genuine activity of the human willing of Christ[411] and to reconcile it with the *mia-physis* formula. In order to show his conception completely we must present a long text which Severus wrote against John the Grammarian. 'He [John] had heard that the teacher [= Ps. Athanasius] speaks of two wills,[412] of one (will) of fear, the human, which has its cause from the flesh, and the other, divine, prepared to suffer.'[413] The foolish

---

407. *Ibid.*, p. 62,13–21.

408. Cf. *ibid.*, p. 63,12–28.

409. *Ibid.*, p. 64,9–11 = Ps. Julius, *De fide et incarn.* 6: Lietzmann, p. 199,16–17. The summary of Severus, *loc. cit.*, p. 64,11–19.

410. *Ibid.*, p. 62,18–21. He says that only if Leo I with his *agit enim utraque forma* was right would the humanity of Christ be moved by a foreign force lying outside of it.

411. R. Chesnut, *Three Monophysite Christologies*, 34, cites the following sentence from *Ep. I ad Sergium*: CSCO 120, p. 62,22–29 for such an explicit consideration of the soul of Christ: *Apparet enim* **propria virtute** *usus tamquam Deus inhumanatus, et per voces Deo dignas hoc confirmat* ..., and translates: 'It appears that he used *the strength of his soul* as God incarnate.' The *propria virtute*, which Severus means, is not, however, the human soul of Christ, but the power of the Logos. For only if this is the case is his proof against Leo's interpretation of the stilling of the storm at sea conclusive, which is allowed to be worked by the human voice as Severus assumes. Chesnut, however, refers on pp. 25–9 to the two major passages which speak of the relationship between the divine and human 'wills' in Christ: *Hom.* 83: PO 20, 415–417 and *C. imp. Gram.*, *Or.* III, ch. 33: CSCO 102, 132–133.

412. See PG 26, 1021,25–32. It is not, however, a writing of Athanasius, but Marcellus of Ancyra, *De incarnatione et c. Arianos* (CPG 2806). Cf. M. Tetz, 'Zur Theologie des Markell von Ankyra', *ZKG* 75 (1964), 217–70; *JdChr* I³, 426–9; *CCT* I², 284–7.

413. Severus Ant., *C. imp. Gram.*, *Or.* III. 2, ch. 33: CSCO 102, p. 132,27–30.

THE DOGMATICIAN AND HIS PICTURE OF CHRIST

Grammarian is said to believe on account of this that the Emmanuel is divided into two. What then?

The body–soul analogy and the willing of Christ

(*C. imp. Gram., Or.* III. 2, ch. 33: CSCO 102, pp. 132,31-133,7): Do we not see in the human being, as we are, who is one nature and *hypostasis* from body and soul, how he can now spontaneously demand nourishment . . ., but then also can reflect on that and despise the material food, and in its place surrender himself to heavenly thoughts in desiring likeness to God? Thus there are two wills in the human being; one wills what is of the flesh, the other what is of the soul which is created according to the image of God. Should we for this reason divide the human being and consider it as two natures and *hypostases*? By doing this we would make fools of ourselves.

Application to Christ

(CSCO 102, p. 133,7-21): Even less is Christ divided into two natures. He is indeed one from two, from divinity and humanity, one person and *hypostasis*, the one nature of the Logos, become flesh and perfect human being. For this reason he also displays two wills in salvific suffering, the one which requests, the other which is prepared, the one human, the other divine. As he voluntarily took upon himself death in the flesh, which was able to take over suffering and dissolved the domination of death by killing it through immortality — which the resurrection had shown clearly to all — so in the flesh, whose fruit he could take over — it was indeed rationally animated — he voluntarily took upon himself the *passio* of fear and weakness and uttered words of request, in order through the divine courage to destroy the power of that fear and to give courage to the whole of humanity, for he became after the first Adam the second beginning of our race.

[In the text further on we then learn that 'the two wills ought not to be assigned to two natures', this once again starting from the text of Ps. Athanasius or Marcellus of Ancyra]:

(CSCO 102, pp. 133,34-134,21): The teacher of divine dogmas has characterized very well the request (of Christ) to avert suffering as 'will'; in this way he shows that it occurs *for us* against the inclination and will to have fear and trembling in the face of danger, but Christ took this over voluntarily. Thus there was really a will (as intention) present, no involuntary suffering. He [Ps. Athanasius] immediately showed that he acknowledges the one Christ from two and does not divide up into two wills what belongs to one and the same, namely the incarnate God, by adding this after the passage cited: [Athanasius] 'He suffers from weakness, but he lives from the power of God' (2 Cor 13,4). The power of God is, however, the Son who suffered from weakness, that is from union with the flesh (συμπλοκή), as a human being he prayed to be freed from suffering; he lives, however, through his [the Son's] power (PG 26, 1024).

The Word of God was thus united to the flesh, which was endowed with a rational soul and was not divided after the union through the doubling of the natures. For that word 'union' (συμπλοκή) . . . denotes *one* being existing from two in unmingledness, a formula which expresses essential union, but is rejected by the Council of Chalcedon. Thus one and the same prayed as a human being to avoid suffering . . . and as God said: the spirit is willing, and voluntarily proceeded to suffer. Hence let us apportion neither the wills nor the words (*voces*) to two natures and forms.

What Severus wants to see excluded is the view of Leo I of an *actio* or *operatio* proper to both forms and natures, each with its own spontaneity and freedom. There is certainly a human soul in Christ with knowledge and will, but there is only one *agens* and for this reason also only one *actio* and *operatio*, which proceeds from the spontaneity and freedom of the one *agens*, namely the Logos. This singularity lies established in the hypostatic union, through which the rational animated *sarx* is subjected to the Logos as *organon*.[414] Severus explicitly reduces the explanation of the whole *energeia* to this Athanasian concept.

> (CSCO 102, p. 135,2–10): The incarnate Word has done and said this, for it is united hypo-statically to the body and through adhering together (συμφυΐα) it had this as an organ[415] for the deeds, as the soul too, which is peculiar to each one of us, has chosen its own body as organ; the Logos does not act through an extrinsically (united) God-bearing human being, as the ravings of Nestorius would have, nor in the way in which an artisan uses a tool and thus completes the work and (not) like the way a cithara player strikes the cithara.

From these remarks one must certainly conclude that Severus cannot regard in the activity of the 'incarnate Logos' his human will as the spontaneous or even autonomous source of acts. All intellectual *energeia* starts from the Logos principle, even if the intellectual abilities in this process were to be regarded as co-moved or really are so. That this is the Patriarch's understanding of the will as ability and willing as action is certainly shown with particular clarity from Homily 83, where he interprets Is 7,15: 'He [the Emmanuel] will eat butter and honey until the time in which he understands how to reject evil and to choose good.' For Severus it is the problem of the freedom, of the free decision, in the incarnate Logos that is spoken about here. What is the principle performing the free choice? On the basis of the verse from Isaiah the explanation is easy for him.[416]

> With respect to him [the new Adam] the prophet Isaiah says: 'Before he knows or chooses evil, he will choose good' (7,15). For before the child recognizes good or evil, he spurns evil in order to choose good. None of us, who is tested as a child, already has knowledge of good and evil. Only with the advance of time, it [the child] begins to distinguish them. But because the Emmanuel is by nature also God and goodness itself, although he has become a child according to the *oikonomia*, he did not await the time of the distinction; on the contrary. From the time of swaddling clothes, before he came to an age of distinguishing between good and evil, on the one side he spurned evil and did not listen to it, and on the other he chose good. These words 'he spurned' and 'he did not listen' and the other 'he chose' show us that the Logos of God has united himself not only to the flesh, but also

---

414. Cf. Severus Ant., *C. imp. Gram.*, Or. III, ch. 33: CSCO 102, p. 136,17–20; *Ep. I ad Sergium*: CSCO 120, p. 62,8–21.

415. The teaching of the *organon* is found particularly in Athan. Alex., *Or. III c. Arian.* (CPG 2093): PG 26, 376. Athanasius wants to accept the reality of the divine and human activities in Christ, but stresses: *Proprium enim utriusque agnoscentes et utrumque ab uno peragi considerantes atque intelligentes, recte credimus, nec umquam errabimus* (cited in Severus: CSCO 102, p. 135,20–22).

416. Severus Ant., *Hom. 83*: PO 20, pp. 415,15–416,15.

to the soul, which is endowed with will and understanding, in order to allow *our* souls, which are inclined towards evil, to lean towards choosing good and turning away from evil. For God as God does not need to choose good; but because *for our sakes* he assumed flesh and a spiritual soul, he took over for *us* this redress (*redressement*).

This homily certainly shows more clearly than the controversy with the Grammarian that the principle of free decision for the human activities also of the Incarnate One is precisely this Logos in his divinity. For he already makes a choice, because the human spiritual organ is not yet capable of action or choice. Hence if the Patriarch transfers the freedom to decide and the actual decision to the Logos as such, then in the interpretation of the freedom and sinlessness of Christ he has not essentially passed beyond Apollinarius. There is no doubt that he explicitly accepts an intellectual soul in Christ. But he does not venture to make this soul the principle of choosing which functions by itself. In the view of Severus this would make the human being Jesus appear as a second person alongside the Logos. In Emmanuel the decision for good occurs through a self-movement of the human spiritual principle, but simply with the hypostatic union of the naturally good Logos with the spiritual soul. In the soul the choice for good has already been made with the *henosis*. *We* are the place of human decisions. For the union of our soul with the Logos in the incarnation is now the model for *us*, who must decide in the battle against evil only from case to case. This evasiveness by referring to *us* in the interpretation of the graced endowment of the human spirit of Jesus is typical of Severus. With the hypostatic union the humanity of Christ has everything which is necessary to fulfil the messianic task, as the interpretation of the descent of the Holy Spirit on Jesus at his baptism has already shown us. Everything which appears to flow as gifts in the human nature of Jesus does not need to stop there, in order to take its place there; it only flows through, because from the very start it is only present for our sake.[417] This interpretation of the endowment of Christ's spirit is the inheritance of the anti-Arian teachers of the fourth century. Their fear that the Logos of God may be made, for example at his baptism, into a receptive principle, and thus into a creature, is then combined in Cyril and Severus with the anti-Nestorian dread that the humanity of Christ might be made into an autonomously active principle of salvation, and thus into a *hypostasis* of its own alongside the Logos. In spite of the repeated emphasis of the reality of body and soul in Christ, its spiritual-bodily share in the realization of salvation remains undervalued. The hegemony

417. Cf. *ibid.*, pp. 416,15–417,17.

of the Logos, which was essential for the system of Apollinarius, who
explicitly denied a human soul in Christ, is also still so narrowly conceived by Cyril that no spontaneously original function in the
divine–human action of Christ is added to the corporeal and spiritual
powers of Christ's humanity. Severus is the drawer of the same picture
of Christ in even stronger lines. Between Cyril and him, however, stands
the mystical figure of Ps. Dionysius.

The Ps. Dionysian vision

It is surprising, especially in this context, to encounter the christologically most important citation from the mysterious author of the
Ps. Dionysian writings. It is taken from the fourth letter to Gaius and
introduced by Severus into a letter to the strategos John, which is
transmitted only in fragments. There emerges in it a formula, which will
take its great place in history only in the seventh century, but the
essential content of which can be found already in Cyril. We shall present
first the major Severan text and then place the formulations of Cyril
beside those of Ps. Dionysius. It is clear that a coherent line of transmission is recognizable.

> Severus Ant., *Ep. 3 ad Johannem ducem* (CPG 7071,31: DP, 309,XXIV): As we have already
> developed in full breadth in other writings, we understood and understand the statement
> of the utterly wise Dionysius the Areopagite, who says: 'Since God has become a human
> being, he performed among us a new divine–human activity', of the one composite (activity)
> (μίαν ἐνοήσαμεν σύνθετον καὶ νοοῦμεν); it cannot be interpreted other than as a
> rejection of every duality; and we confess the incarnate God, who operated in this new
> manner [this divine–human activity], as the one divine–human nature and *hypostasis* and also
> as the one incarnate nature of the God-Logos (καὶ τὸν ἀνδρωθέντα θεὸν τὸν ταύτην
> καινοπρεπῶς πεπολιτευμένον μίαν ὁμολογοῦμεν φύσιν τε καὶ ὑπόστασιν θεανδρικήν,
> ὥσπερ καὶ τὴν μίαν φύσιν τοῦ θεοῦ λόγου σεσαρκωμένην).

Here is found the magic word of the new divine–human activity
(καινὴ θεανδρικὴ ἐνέργεια), which Severus characterizes as 'one', even if
'composite', and considers as a logical interpretation of the *mia-physis* formula. It has been too little noted that Ps. Dionysius took up the notions
and terminology of Cyril, with which in his commentary on John
he interprets the healing of the daughter of Jairus (Mk 5,35–37;
Lk 7,49–56), and which he uses to explain the effects of the eucharistic
body of Christ, as he finds them in John 6.[418]
After Severus in his discussion of the *aphtharsia* teaching of Julian of

---

418. Cf. Cyril Alex., *In Ioann. IV*, ch. II,VI, 54–59: PG 73, 576C–596C; *S.P.N. Cyrilli ...
Alexandrini in D. Ioannis evangelium ...* ed. P. E. Pusey, I, 528–547. The detailed analysis of this
will follow in CCT II/3.

Halicarnassus had moved from substantiating the *mia physis* by having recourse to the exchange of *idiomata*, or the divinization of the humanity of Christ, to doing it by having recourse to the unity and singularity of the *energeia*, he had to place particular demands on the *operatio*. Because the *henosis* is insoluble and uninterrupted, its preservation necessitates a constant flow of *energeia* or a constantly active and invariable hegemony of the Logos. There cannot be any more or less. But Severus distinguished various strengths in the controlling influence of the Logos on his humanity. The highest degree is present in the miraculous healings. But what is the case in the everyday life of the Incarnate One? We have seen that Severus, in the tradition of Gregory of Nyssa and Cyril of Alexandria, could not properly imagine such an everyday life. The hypostatic union signified for the humanity of Christ the constant claim to participation in the divine life. For this reason on each occasion it also needed permission on the side of the godhead to hunger and suffer, even to die. Such a release of the flesh for the 'blameless passions', however, was due really to a restraining of that power, on which the hypostatic union was built. In warding off the teachings of Julian, Severus trapped himself here in an insoluble dilemma. The *henosis* of Christ was not sought on the right level. This is shown also in a new way.

(c) Knowledge and growth of Jesus

From tradition Severus had taken over the teaching that 'the Logos of God, elevated over all creatures and perfect in everything' has remained in the incarnation without alteration. This creates difficulties for him in explaining the growth of Christ (cf. Lk 2,40). He is for Severus

> A single Christ without division or partition, in one person, one *hypostasis* and one single nature of the Logos become flesh, without one being able to say that, due to (qualifying in) virtue, he would have become perfect ... In fact how should he have become perfect, who is himself in essence justice, wisdom and holiness; rather he mediates to every created and rational nature participation in all these perfections, and is the source of all good things and distributor of virtue.[419]

The Patriarch also finds it difficult to acknowledge theologically the scriptural words about the *kenosis* and the growth of Jesus in their full compass.

> 'Is it not truly stupid [for Christ himself] to speak of humiliation and also of advance or of becoming perfect in virtue ...?' Is not everything only a fitting into our measure for our salvation![420] What has to be warded off is the Antiochene probation theory, according to which

---

419. Severus Ant., *Crit. tom.*: CSCO 245, p. 74,8–17. The growth of Jesus is ascribed to the *sarx*; Christ's suffering is possible because he is also consubstantial with us.

420. *Ibid.*, pp. 74,36–75,5.

Christ is said to have earned for himself the fullness of sonship through moral behaviour
and the acquisition of virtue.[421] What increases in the earthly Jesus is only the 'progressive
revelation of wisdom' in accordance with the law of the *oikonomia*.[422] The nature of the Logos
is always perfect and wisdom itself.[423] In all 'growth' in Christ it is only a question of *our*
becoming perfect, for which he is the absolutely valid example.

Because Julian of Halicarnassus had recourse for his ideas, which
are familiar to us, to the *Philalethes* of the Patriarch, particularly to
chapter 44, the latter in his *apologia* for his work had to speak about
the problem of Christ's growth, be it in knowledge, be it in the perfection of body and soul. Athanasius, in the struggle with the Arians,
had already had his difficulties with this problem.[424] His solution
turned out to be so convoluted, because he did not introduce any human
soul in Christ as the bearer, for example, of the ignorance of the day
of judgement, but had to ward off the ignorance from the Logos as
Logos (Mk 13,32). Although Cyril of Alexandria accepted a soul in
Christ, neither the *Thesaurus* nor the *Dialogue* lets one ascertain that he
acknowledged in Christ a human knowledge or a development of human
understanding.[425] In the discussion with Theodoret and Antiochene
christology in general, the fear of accepting a humanly limited knowledge in Christ increased, as Severus shows in his *Apologia for Philalethes*,
chapter 44. The question about Christ's knowledge is solved for him
by the fact that 'Christ himself is by nature the wisdom and justice of
God the Father (1 Cor 1,30), through whom everything, which is at
all capable of wisdom, has become wise . . .' An imperfection in Christ,
however, can be accepted only by those who isolate the human being
in him from the God-Logos, so that they then declare 'through deeds
he became perfect, he who proceeded from Mary and from David and
has become perfect in virtue'. For this reason they must also accept that
this human being is capable of sin and error and is weighed down

421. *Ibid.*, 76ff.: to speak of a becoming perfect in Christ would be to concede a sinful lack
in him, as Cyril had already stressed against Theodoret (PG 76, 444D–445A); see also Severus
Ant., *Apol. Philal.*, ch. 44: CSCO 319, p. 22,4–23, with the comments of Hespel.

422. Severus Ant., *Crit. tom.*: CSCO 245, p. 76,18–20.

423. For Severus Ant., *ibid.*, pp. 92,17–93,24, Christ is sinless from infancy according to
Is 7,15–16 (LXX), a position which the theology of the Church in general took over, even if
it has attempted to establish it in different ways. Beyond the question of impeccability, Severus
promoted his particular conception of interpreting Lk 2,40. Jesus has no need of development,
because 'he is not subjected to any passion which comes from evil and sin, and he is exclusively
good as God' (p. 93,13–15). The moral decision is transferred entirely into the divine will of
the Logos. Cf. R. Chesnut, *Three Monophysite Christologies*, 28.

424. Cf. *JdChr* I³, 467–8; *CCT* I², 314–15.

425. *JdChr* I³, 605–9 with reference to J. Liébaert; *CCT* I², 414–17.

through concupiscence.[426] Here, admittedly, Severus draws a border against Julian: he distinguishes between the weaknesses, which go together with sin and are therefore 'blameworthy', and the others, like thirst, hunger, tiredness, fear, which are 'blameless'. Only the former are not reconcilable with the reality of Christ, the others he took over freely in condescension. Thus he, the God-Logos, in the flesh which he united hypostatically to himself and which in a natural way is capable of suffering and dying, can take over 'natural and blameless passions, death as well, and thus die for us'.[427]

---

426. Cf. Severus Ant., *Apol. Philal.*, ch. 44: CSCO 319, pp. 22,4–23,4.

427. *Ibid.*, p. 23,5–24. We should like to note what R. Chesnut, *op. cit.*, 29, says: 'Sometimes Severus talks as though there was only one decision on the part of God to submit to the laws of nature; at other times, he talks as though there was a new decision to make every time, whether to grow hungry or sleepy or anxious. Either way, as far as Severus is concerned, by an act of *will* God *voluntarily* submitted himself to the laws of human nature or necessity and took upon himself a rational, willing human hypostasis. And this act of *God's* will is what is of significance to Severus, and not the human will.' It would be worthwhile making clear that, because the moral decisions appear to proceed completely from the Logos as Logos, Severus does not need any responsible human decision in the human will of Christ. This is co-moved by the Logos. For this reason Severus has not fully transcended Apollinarius' *'nous* which is not capable of defeat'.

CONCLUDING REFLECTION

THE PANORAMA OF CHALCEDONIAN AND
NON-CHALCEDONIAN CHRISTOLOGIES

With the one person Severus and his imposing, diverse work, a row of
fundamental christological positions emerged, which allow an insight
into the state of christology around 520 and a prospect of further
development. The discussion about Chalcedon had finally come to the
problem itself, to the question about the mutual relationship to each
other of different traditions and ways of speaking. What is the situation
at the end of the discussion between Severus and his opponents?

(1) After the *Henoticon* politics of Emperors Zeno and Anastasius had
created insecurity in the Church, the Chalcedonian suggestion to solve
the christological question was taken notice of afresh, that is, through
the Cyrillian florilegium. It was intended that this suggestion be brought
closer to the Alexandrian side too, by demonstrating its agreement with
the greatest pre-Chalcedonian authority, Cyril of Alexandria. The
Patriarch himself was so to say to be won for Chalcedon by searching
out in his entire work the beginnings of the two-natures language. His
mia-physis formula and the sharpness of his anathemas were carefully
bracketed and suppressed. It was intended that both parties could in good
conscience agree on a two-natures christology. For this suggestion the
name 'strict Chalcedonianism' has already been established. This expression is justified, because the language of the Fourth Council was to
prevail as the sole norm.

(2) Through Severus of Antioch the linguistic and conceptual counterpoint to the two-natures teaching of 451 was now contrasted as sharply
as possible. The *mia-physis* christology stood in unambiguous unity before
the eyes of the Greek world in a work which surpassed everything contemporary. If Cyril had undergone a development and betrayed a certain
bilingualism, then the 'new Cyril' decidedly intervened and carried out
a purification of language, which represented now the pure type of
mia-physis christology, as a closed christology from above with the
emphasis on the *henosis*, but also with the clear confession of the reality
and earthly existence of the humanity of Christ. The troublesome thing
was that there were still glimpses of Apollinarius. The well-intended

interpretation of the *mia physis* through Cyril could not wipe out its inherent virulence.

(3) The history of ideas displays enough examples of the fact that such contrary positions call for mediation in language and conception. Instead of such one-sided purification of language in the sense of the two natures, or respectively in the direction of the one nature, a synthesis of language was intended to create peace. This was the intention of the monk Nephalius, and of the grammarian John of Caesarea. Instead of reciprocally purified conceptual language and the barriers to understanding created by this, it was intended that each time the language of the other partner would be learned and practised together, perhaps from the realization that neither of the two systems by itself can express the whole truth and avert all misunderstandings of faith in Christ. In this strategy the *mia-physis* language received the task of banning the nightmare 'Nestorius', and the *dyo-physeis* terminology the task of banning the phantasma of Valentinus, Manes and Eutyches. Because both tendencies represented a continuing threat, henceforward the equally legitimate use of both systems of language should be explained as necessary, and recognized as the condition for 'orthodoxy'. In a similar way one could also demand the combination of a christology from above with one from below. If it is a matter here of first attempts, so it should be our task to pursue further the development of this theological peace initiative.

(4) If in so-called 'neo-Chalcedonianism' a middle was sought from both extremes, which at the same time was intended to lessen the dangers of the positions on both sides, then such dangers have also in fact become evident. On the Severan side one speaks in an exaggerated formulation of the 'aphthartodocetism' of Julian of Halicarnassus and of the 'real monophysitism' of the amateur theologian Sergius. On the Chalcedonian side we need to examine what is to be understood by the 'Nestorianism' of the East Syrians. Of late there has also been an attempt to discover among the Chalcedonians so-called 'Antiochenes', who are said after 451 to have combined with the formula of 451 the pre-Chalcedonian, Antiochene christology of separation.

PART TWO

RETROSPECTIVE THEOLOGICAL CONSIDERATION OF CHALCEDON

The challenge to the supporters of Chalcedon through the Cyrillian-Severan *mia-physis* christology did not come to a stop with the accession of Emperor Justin I (518–527) to the throne and with his restoration politics. Neither imperial edicts nor ecclesiastical feasts celebrating Chalcedon could dispense with truly theological discussion. In 518 the formula of Chalcedon, despite a broad reception in the Greek- and Latin-speaking areas, was still a long way from an explanation that could substantiate it. There was still need for a great deal of work on the concepts and the supposition concerning them, that is, that they could be applied to the total conceptual form of the 'hypostatic union'. But, above all, the act of union itself had hardly come into perspective, despite the repeated examination of ancient philosophical *henosis* terms. If a radical splitting of the Church were to be definitively prevented, then there had to be an agreement between the parties at variance on a generally acceptable formula, or, what was really desirable, on a clarified understanding of the *horos* adopted by the Fourth Council. As we have established with Severus' opponents, Nephalius and John the Grammarian, in contrast to the compilers of the *FlorCyr* there was just as much a readiness to compromise on the Chalcedonian side as on the Severan. We have observed the beginnings of the so-called neo-Chalcedonian synthesis. Yet it was not based on clarified concepts, but simply on the intention to affirm, through the simultaneous use of contrary formulas, the common element of truth present in them and to exclude the extremes which dissolve the dogma of the incarnation, christologies of mingling and separation. Could the attempt to reach this goal also succeed by way of a profound examination and new determination of the disputed concepts and their assignation within the Chalcedonian formula? In the entirety of a continuous theology and politics of Chalcedon this had to be a real preoccupation of the Church after 518. We shall now proceed to study the groups of theologians and documents that sought to resolve difficulties in this way. First of all we shall consider their crown witness.

CHAPTER ONE

LEONTIUS OF BYZANTIUM, THE CROWN WITNESS OF CHALCEDONIAN CHRISTOLOGY

SECTION ONE

THE PERSON AND WORK OF LEONTIUS

It is only now that researchers are in a position to reach agreement with regard to essentials about the person and literary corpus of the bearer of this name. After the epoch-making work of F. Loofs, which was published over a hundred years ago,[1] research was guided in the wrong direction. Erroneous judgements regarding his identity were possible for various reasons, but especially because the patristic sources had possessed a whole catalogue of people bearing the name Leontius.[2] Until recently there was no attempt to produce a critical edition of the authentic works which were or should be ascribed to one and the same Leontius. This important goal is now close to completion.[3] The necessary foundation

---

1. F. Loofs, *Leontius von Byzanz und die gleichnamigen Schriftsteller der griechischen Kirche* = TU III, 1–2 (Leipzig, 1887); *idem*, art., 'Leontius von Byzanz', in *PRE* 11 (Leipzig, ³1902), 394–8.

2. See the indexes for ACO IV 3, 2, 2 (Berlin, 1982), 286–289; R. Schieffer offers twenty-eight cases where a Leontius has been ascertained, without clearly separating the bearers of the name. Our Leontius of Byzantium is named in nos. 20 and 22, which are to be referred to the same bearer. Cf. the enumeration of twenty Leontii in F. Loofs, *op. cit.*, 226–7. For our Leontius see nos. 13, 14, 16.

3. See B. E. Daley, *Leontius of Byzantium: A Critical Edition of his Works, with Prolegomena* (Diss. Oxford, 1978). Cf. *JdChr* II/1, 66–8. Daley provides a comprehensive report on the history of the text and the transmission of the Corpus Leontianum. He gathers the biographical and literary-historical data which concern the author, and in this way creates new foundations for interpreting the history of dogma and theology. An exhaustive bibliography offers the underpinnings for understanding the research on the life and work of Leontius. Because the work has not yet appeared in print, we shall still cite according to PG 86, while making use of the newly edited text. The following texts are ascribed to Leontius of Byzantium (CPG 6813–6820), for which we shall use the attached abbreviations:

Contra Nestorianos et Eutychianos (λόγος α') (CNE): PG 86, 1273A–1309;
Epilyseis (*Solutiones Argumentorum Severi*) (Epil): PG 86, 1916C–1945;
Epaporemata (*Triginta Capita contra Severum*) (Epap): PG 86, 1901B–1916B;
Contra Aphthartodocetas (λόγος β') (CA): PG 86, 1316D–1356C;
Deprehensio et Triumphus super Nestorianos (λόγος γ') (DTN): PG 86, 1357B–1385B;
Adversus Fraudes Apollinaristarum (AFA): PG 86, 1948A–1972A; for judging this writing now see A. Tuilier, 'Remarques sur les fraudes des Apollinaristes et des Monophysites', in J. Dummer

for a new presentation and evaluation of his theology has been created. Here admittedly we are limiting ourselves to the central content: the theoretical and concrete christology of the author, who has been determined to be Leontius of Byzantium.

From the works themselves there is little to be ascertained about his person. He is characterized as 'monk', 'ascetic', 'hermit', or as 'Abba Leontius'.[4] As a young man, in his own depiction, he was the adherent of a group of Chalcedonians, who had chosen Diodore of Tarsus and Theodore of Mopsuestia as their models and masters.[5] Through a special 'grace from above', however, he was freed from the teeth of these lions to a life of 'virtue' and, driven by a yearning for this, to become a pilgrim.[6] On the insistence of friends, but also from love of the 'right thing', the convert decided as well to define his position in several books, even though he says he could show neither the necessary secular educational background ($\xi\xi\omega\ \pi\alpha\iota\delta\epsilon\iota\alpha$) nor the ability ($\xi\xi\iota\varsigma$) for this.[7] Following the experiences of the authors of the FlorCyr, of John of Caesarea, of Bishop Julian of Halicarnassus and the novice theologian Sergius Grammaticus, there would also be a risk that the monk from Palestine would rile the old lion, Severus, through his attacks. Yet one ought also to accept that the chances of achieving a box-office success with polemical writings of the earlier type against Leontius were very much reduced around 535/536. In 531 the new defender of Chalcedon had already begun to hold disputations with the 'monophysites' in the

---

(ed.), *Texte und Textkritik* = *TU* 133 (Berlin, 1987), 581–90. Together with S. Rees, 'The Literary Activity of Leontius of Byzantium', *JTS* 19 (1968) (229–42), 240–2; D. Stiernon, art., 'Léonce de Byzance', in *DSp* 9 (1976) (651–60), 655; Tuilier takes the work *AFA* as belonging to the questionable, or non-authentic works;

Fragmenta Incerta (with Appendix III, *Excerpta Leontina*): PG 86, 2004C–2009C.

4. Cf. B. E. Daley, *op. cit.*, 1 (Title). As far as the four titles are concerned, according to Daley they could be used alternately for individual desert monks, in particular for those who lived as semi-hermits in a lavra. On this see below re Palestine. Apart from the works of Leontius, Daley refers to Sophronius of Jerusalem, in Photius, *Bibl. cod.* 231: Henry V, 66; PG 103, 1092A5–6; as well to Patriarch Germanus of Constantinople, *De haer. et syn.* (CPG 8020): PG 98, 72A1–2.

5. See the following particulars in Leontius, *DTN*: (a) PG 86, 1357C: Leontius characterizes himself as 'member of a *thiasos*'; (b) PG 86, 1360D–1361A: this consists of 'Chalcedonians', who, however, only seem to be such; (c) PG 86, 1360D, 1364A, 1377D; for they are supporters of Diodore and Theodore of Mopsuestia.

6. Leontius Byz., *DTN*: PG 86, 1360AB.

7. Leontius Byz., Prologue to the collection of his works: PG 86, 1268B–1269A; *DTN*: PG 86, 1360B. According to B. E. Daley, *ed. cit.*, introduction, II, Leontius is, however, 'clearly a man of considerable dialectical training, with extraordinary sharpness of mind and strong theological passions'.

basilica of Constantinople.[8] He had soon made a name for himself, for in 532 he was already taken notice of to such an extent that he could participate, at least in a subordinate rôle, in the dialogue which was held in Constantinople between the supporters and opponents of Chalcedon.[9] To be sure, at the time of this meeting Severus was not yet in the capital. This was the case only in 534–536, and then on the initiative of Empress Theodora.[10]

Whether in this period Leontius saw or spoke with the deposed Patriarch himself is not reported. As the *apocrisiarius* of the monks of Palestine, he took part in the Home Synod of Constantinople, which lasted from 2 May to 4 June 536. The 'monophysite' patriarch at that time, Anthimus, was anathematized; Severus, together with Peter of Apamea, was condemned anew. For the first three sessions the 'monk Leontius' is listed among the representatives of the Palestinian monasteries and as signatory of three petitions from the Oriental monks. The three documents were addressed to the Emperor, Patriarch Menas and the Synod itself, and to Pope Agapetus. In the corresponding synodal list 'Leontius, monk and abbot and *apocrisiarius* of the whole desert' is named.[11] In the petitions, in contrast, the form of address is expanded,[12] without anything new being said. Nevertheless it is assumed that the *apocrisarius* of the monks was instructed about the activity of Severus during his sojourn in the palace of Empress Theodora. Every piece of information must have been welcome to him. Leontius could still read the Severan writings in the original Greek version. One does not have the impression, however, that he concentrated in a special way on the person or the individual works of the Patriarch, just as he

8. Cf. Cyril Scyth., *Vita Sabae* 72: Schwartz, p. 176,7–15.

9. Cf. ACO IV, 2, p. 170,5–6. R. Schieffer, ACO IV, 3, 2, 2, p. 288(b) separates the Leontius named here as no. 20 (*monachus Hierosolymitanus*) from no. 22.

10. Cf. Evagrius Schol., *HE* IV 10–11: Bidez-Parmentier, 160–161; Severus was not immediately ready to follow this call, as Evagrius reports referring to a letter of the fleeing Patriarch. Cf. Zacharias Rh. cont., *HE* IX 15: ET Hamilton-Brooks, 253. (a) Arrival of Severus: *HE* IX 15: ET Hamilton-Brooks, 253; IX 16: ET Hamilton-Brooks, 261; IX 19: ET Hamilton-Brooks, 265; (b) sojourn in Constantinople at the time when Pope Agapetus I was present: IX 19: ET Hamilton-Brooks, 267; (c) in March 536 the expulsion of Severus and Anthimus from the city by Emperor Justinian I at the instigation of the Pope, who died, however, on 22 April 536. See novel 42: *Corpus iuris civilis*, Vol. III, *Novellae*, ed. Schoell-Kroll (Berlin, 1895), 263–9. Empress Theodora helped Patriarch Severus flee to Egypt. Cf. John of Eph., PO 2, 302. See E. Honigmann, *Evêques et Evêchés*, 153–4; on the whole matter, *ibid.*, 152–4; E. Stein, *Histoire du Bas-Empire* II, 382, 386–7; P. Allen, *Evagrius Scholasticus*, 182–5.

11. ACO III, 130, *subscriptio* 76; 158, *subscriptio* 76; 165, *subscriptio* 80; 174 (without *hegoumenos*), *subscriptio* 82.

12. ACO III, p. 37,1–2: *subscriptio* 74 (to Emperor Justinian); p. 50, *subscriptio* 117; p. 145, *subscriptio* 73.

also did not directly attack the person of Julian of Halicarnassus. In both cases he aimed more at the 'group', the 'Headless Ones', the 'Aphthartodocetists' than at their leading theologians. Whether reference was made to them historically has to be demonstrated in each individual case.

One thing is certain: after 518, or rather after 527, Leontius of Byzantium accepted the challenge that was addressed to the Chalcedonians by Severan-Julianist christology. With more or less new proofs he attempts to demonstrate that the *mia physis* is untenable. Expressed positively, by doing this he draws the basic lines of a Chalcedonian picture of Christ. It was obviously difficult for him to paint into this picture the attractive power which the Christ of the Severan *mia physis* or of the Julianist *aphtharsia* radiated. Severus and Julian continued to exercise influence in the Constantinople of Justinian I and Theodora, even after they had been definitively banished and condemned. The old Emperor himself is the best proof of this. Although Nestorianism appears to stand in the forefront as the opposed thesis, if we may extrapolate from the writing *CNE*, nevertheless an analysis of the work shows that the schema 'Nestorian-Eutychian' is artificial. Both the attached florilegium as well as the further development of the dispute in the two following works (*Epil* and *Epap*) enable us to recognize that the real opponents of Leontius are the Severans.

We shall now attempt to determine the rôle of the monk Leontius of Byzantium in a twofold regard which stems from his works: firstly, he is the speculative theologian, and this above all in *CNE*, *Epil* and *Epap*; then he offers something like an outline of a picture of Christ, which can provide information for modern problems. This is particularly the case in the writing *CA*.

SECTION TWO

THE CHRISTOLOGY OF LEONTIUS OF BYZANTIUM
HIS CONTRIBUTION TO SOLVING THE
CHALCEDONIAN PROBLEM

I. A SHORT REPORT ON RESEARCH

In research since the study of F. Loofs,[13] the monk Leontius of Byzantium has in many cases been overrated, this in part being caused by the fact that Loofs had accepted untenable biographical and literary historical presuppositions. In the subsequent controversy, however, judgements that were too negative were also made about the author, whose identity is difficult to determine.

1. Literary-historical identifications

F. Loofs identified the theological writer Leontius with three other bearers of this name from the sixth century, namely with

(a) the Scythian (Gothic) monk Leontius, the active participant in the so-called theopaschite controversy (CPL 653 a); this was the major error. Loofs won numerous supporters for this thesis: V. Ermoni, J. P. Junglas (*LThK* [1]VI, 511–12), O. Bardenhewer (V, 9–10), B. Altaner, *Patrologie* (1938, 330), who then himself definitively excluded it: 'Der griechische Theologe Leontius und Leontius der skythische Mönch', *ThQ* 127 (1947), 147–65. As early as 1914, however, E. Schwartz, ACO IV 2, p. XII, took a critical stance;

(b) Leontius of Jerusalem, author of *Contra Monophysitas* (CPG 6917) and *Contra Nestorianos* (CPG 6918). Here Loofs was followed by W. Rügamer, *Leontius von Byzanz, ein Polemiker aus der Zeit Justinians* (Diss. Würzburg, 1894) and S. Rees, 'The Life and Personality of Leontius of Byzantium', *JTS* 41 (1940), 263–80; also too in his later article, 'The Literary Activities of Leontius of Byzantium', *JTS* 19 (1968), 229–42. In opposition, M. Richard, 'Léonce de Jérusalem et Léonce de Byzance', *MSR* 1 (1944), 35–88 = *Op. Min.* III, no. 59. After Richard and against him, the Romanian deacon Ilie Fracea, in his dissertation submitted in Athens, Ὁ Λεόντιος Βυζάντιος. Βίος καὶ Συγγράμματα (Κριτικὴ Θεώρηση) (Athens, 1984), once again advocated identifying the two, Leontius of Byzantium and Leontius of Jerusalem. According to Fracea there was only one Leontius, who came from Constantinople, became a monk in Palestine and defended orthodox christology against Nestorius and monophysites. Fracea gave a detailed overview of the genuine works which he ascribed to Leontius of Byzantium (pp. 164–246). A. de Halleux provided an analysis of the dissertation in his review, *RHE* 81 (1986), 139–43. Our position will be given in later remarks.

(c) Leontius Scholasticus (Ps. Leontius) (CPG 6823), the author of *De sectis*. According to Loofs, *De sectis* is nothing other than an adaptation of a lost treatise of Leontius of Byzantium. Against Loofs, J. P. Junglas, *Leontius von Byzanz. Studien zu seinen Schriften, Quellen und Anschauungen* = FCLDG 3 (Paderborn, 1908); S. Rees, 'The *De Sectis*: A Treatise Attributed to Leontius of Byzantium', *JTS* 40 (1939), 346–60; M. Richard, 'Le traité "De Sectis" et Léonce

---

13. F. Loofs, *op. cit.* (above, n. 1).

de Byzance', *RHE* 35 (1939), 695–723 = *Op. Min.* II, no. 55; J. Speigl, 'Der Autor der Schrift "De Sectis" über die Konzilien und die Religionspolitik Justinians', *AHC* 2 (1970), 207–30.

2. Biographical identifications

Here we presuppose with B. E. Daley that Leontius, the author of the *Corpus Leontianum* (*CNE, Epil, Epap, CA, DTN*), is identical with Leontius, the participant in the *Collatio cum Severianis* in 532 in Constantinople, as well as with the theologian and monk of the Constantinopolitan Home Synod in 536 and with the Leontius of the *Vita Sabae* of Cyril of Scythopolis.

Cf. B. E. Daley, *Leontius of Byzantium*, Introduction; *idem*, 'The Origenism of Leontius of Byzantium', *JTS* 27 (1976), 333–69, where Daley argues against D. B. Evans, *Leontius of Byzantium: An Origenist Christology* = DOS 13 (Washington DC, 1970) and S. Otto, *Person und Subsistenz. Die philosophische Anthropologie des Leontios von Byzanz. Ein Beitrag zur spätantiken Geistesgeschichte* (Munich, 1968). L. Perrone, 'Il "Dialogo contro gli aftartodoceti" di Leonzio di Bisanzio e Severo di Antiochia', *CrSt* 1 (1980), 411–42, makes worthwhile observations.

3. On the method

In what follows we shall start from a turning-point, which can be observed in the writings of Leontius and which is contingent on his method of adapting to the opponent with whom he is dealing in his works. We shall establish that in the three writings *CNE*, *Epil* and *Epap*, *ratio theologica* and dialectic predominate, whereas in *CA* it is the biblical consideration, concerned with the economy of salvation, and the sketching of a picture of Christ in accordance with Chalcedonian principles.

II. THE CHRISTOLOGY OF LEONTIUS OF BYZANTIUM

From the observations outlined above two tasks emerge for us: (1) an analysis of the Chalcedonian, anti-Severan language, which Leontius uses for concepts and in formulas, and his contribution to solving the Chalcedonian question; (2) his total picture of the God–human reality and of the soteriological mission of Jesus in the anti-Julianist polemic of Leontius.

1. The Chalcedonian, anti-Severan language of Leontius

The powerfulness of the challenge which Severus issued to the Chalcedonian-Byzantine theologians expressed itself in particular demands for Justin's restoration after 518. With the fundamental negation of the *mia-physis* christology of Severan stamp and a return to the 'one *hypostasis* in two natures' on the side of Imperial Church politics, there awaited anew for theology the task of showing how in Christ 'the one and the same, perfect in divinity and perfect in humanity', the unity in the *hypostasis* and the duality in the natures, was to be understood and established. Did Leontius of Byzantium display a consciousness of the problem which corresponded to this situation? In his case what was the relationship between the existing biblical, ecclesial kerygma of the 'Logos who became flesh' and the reflex entry into the christological question?

(a) The 'subject of the incarnation'

For Cyril and Severus the determination of the subject of the incarnation was already given with John 1,14; the Logos is present in the flesh. A remnant of Antiochene schooling seems in contrast to have remained in Leontius. As B. E. Daley concedes, in a series of texts the monk begins his theological analysis not with the eternal Logos and the history of his works among human beings, but with the divine fait accompli 'Jesus Christ', who is for him both God as well as human being.[14] How would he respond to the question: who is the real personal 'you' in Jesus of Nazareth, whom you confess as God and human being? It is as if Leontius answered: the hypostasis, the concrete person 'Jesus Christ' is neither simply divine nor simply human, although his Christ exists and acts wholly as God and wholly as human being; to be human and divine is the business of the natures and not of the person or hypostasis. In fact Leontius never identifies explicitly and by virtue of logical allocation the 'one hypostasis' with the Logos as Logos.[15] His denotations for Jesus of Nazareth are normally Christos, Soter, Kyrios.[16] To this subject denoted as Kyrios he also assigns the human attributes, actions and experiences. Is the Christ-subject also for this reason understood 'ontologically' as a tertium quid, as the correspondent of the Patriarch Severus, Sergius Scholasticus, in his way had understood this in all its strictness? The constancy of the characterization just described seems to point positively in this direction.[17]

---

14. Cf. B. E. Daley, 'The Christology of Leontius of Byzantium: Personalism or Dialectics', in Papers from the Ninth Conference on Patristic Studies 1983, Oxford, England = Patristic Monograph Series, The Philadelphia Patristic Foundation (typescript).

15. Idem, art. cit.

16. Cf. L. Perrone, 'Il "Dialogo contro gli aftartodoceti" di Leonzio di Bisanzio e Severo di Antiochia', CrSt 1 (1980), 430–1, with reference to B. E. Daley, 'The Origenism of Leontius of Byzantium', JTS 27 (1976) (333–69), 359, n. 4. On Kyrios see especially CA: PG 86, 1325C4; 1337A8; 1341C7; 1345C8–11; 1349A1f.; 1352B11; soma of the kyrios: 1345D12; 1348B8.C2.

17. Cf. B. E. Daley, art. cit., 360: Leontius 'is careful to present his Christ "symmetrically". He is careful to attribute the human soul and flesh, as well as the human actions and experiences of the Incarnate Word, to "Christ" or the "Lord" rather than to "a person of the blessed Trinity"; he avoids the other dramatic assertions of Christ's divinity popular with his Neo-Chalcedonian contemporaries, like the celebrated "theopaschite formula" . . . He does not deny the correctness of such statements, when properly understood." (For this Daley refers in n. 1 to Epil: PG 86, 1944C2–4. Cf. also DTN 42: PG 86, 1380C1–5).

From these textual findings grave conclusions were drawn for judging Leontius' understanding of Christ.

(1) For Leontius Jesus Christ is a *tertium quid* in the order of essences.[18] Such an interpretation represents a great imposition on the theologically and dialectically trained Leontius. He would be put on a par with the theologically quite unsure Sergius, the opponent of Severus. 'Christ', as the new third entity, would be a new 'essence' from the infinite divinity and created humanity, as Sergius, who was just mentioned, had this in mind. The consequence would be a real theopaschism with its violation of the divine transcendence, as this would occur with a 'nature synthesis'. On the basis of his Antiochene past Leontius had without doubt a keen eye for the inviolability of the divinity, which did not allow any physical synthesis in the manner of Apollinarianism. Certainly one can and must accept that Leontius had not yet transposed the *formal* realization of the 'one *hypostasis*' into the *hypostasis* of the Logos as such. Such a step needed time. The lack of this formal identification does not mean, however, that the monk was not conscious of the completeness and self-containedness of the Logos as such, which excluded every combination in a 'third'. That the theory of a *novum tertium quid* is not admissible is shown by the unambiguous statements about the Logos, who in the one Christ takes the rôle of the subject of the incarnation and the dominant position in the whole structure of the Incarnate One, as it is *actually* described.[19]

(2) Still more incriminatory is the interpretation which would like to

18. Thus according to P. T. R. Gray, *The Defense of Chalcedon in the East (451–553)* (Leiden, 1979), 101. In the meantime Gray has moved away from this interpretation.

19. These passages are cited following L. Perrone, 'Il "Dialogo contro gli aftartodoceti" di Leonzio di Bisanzio e Severo di Antiochia', *CrSt* 1 (1980), 430 n. 55: (a) *CA*: PG 86, 1324D.1325B: the 'assuming' subject is indeed characterized as *Kyrios*, to whom the whole human reality of Christ is contrasted as 'assumed'. (b) PG 86, 1329C: the 'Logos' is introduced as the subject which gives permission for suffering (τοῦ Λόγου ἐφιέντος τὸ παθεῖν). Then twice in 1329CD there is talk of the '*henosis* with the Logos' which does not even effect the *aphtharsia* of the body, but only the substantial *henosis*, through which the heretical doctrine of two persons is excluded. (c) To the actuation of the will of the assuming Logos is ascribed the ability to suffer, or respectively *apatheia*. The Logos is the dominating principle: PG 86, 1332AB. (d) Through the Holy Spirit the Logos exercises a creative efficacy with regard to his own 'temple', that is, his humanity: PG 86, 1352D8–1353A3; esp. 1353A: The Logos surrounds himself with a temple created through the power of the Holy Spirit (ἑαυτὸν περιπλάσας). A notion of a *tertium quid* can in no way be connected with the following section (PG 86, 1353A4–B3). The same is true with regard to the opinion that Leontius supports the adoration of the humanity of Christ. He does not speak of a 'special' adoration of this humanity. His gaze is directed to the adoration of the one *hypostasis* in Christ. In contrast the Nestorians proclaim anthropolatry, because they accept two *hypostases* in Christ (*CNE* I: PG 86, 1273C; *DTN*: PG 86, 1380D.1385CD). See V. Grumel, art. 'Léonce de Byzance', in *DTC* 9, 418–19.

make Leontius an Evagrian Origenist.[20] Here too Christ is seen as a
'new third', even if the components are different. Allegedly this Christ
would be a synthesis from the pre-existent *nous*, conceived in Evagrian
terms, which, itself a created essence, combines with the human *sarx*
to become a *nous*-Christ. To refute this interpretation one can refer to
a sentence in the *CNE*. In this sentence Leontius distinguished clearly
between the Logos as such and the same Logos in the state of the
incarnation: 'the Logos is not the complete Christ; he is this only when
the human is united to him, even though he has his completeness as
God'.[21] There is no *nous* slotted in between. Quite the opposite: we
find repeated with particular regularity the formula 'union according to
the essence' or 'according to the *hypostasis*', the meaning of which must
be evaluated in detail. In no case ought these two formulas be called
upon to interpret the *henosis* in Christ according to the manner of a
tertium quid.

(b) Distinction of hypostasis and physis

If the Chalcedonian restoration were to succeed there had to be an
advance in clarifying the key concepts that were causing division. These
themselves, however, were embedded in more comprehensive linguistic
structures, the bases of which were different ways of grasping the
mystery of Christ. If the 'monophysite' said: 'the one nature of the
incarnate Word', the content of the concept *physis* was to be revealed
by the historical point of view. First it was the Logos that was viewed,
his *physis* or *hypostasis*; about it was stated that it has become flesh. In
this way the concept is defined in its meaning; only that can be termed

---

20. D. B. Evans, *Leontius of Byzantium: An Origenist Christology* = *DOS* 13 (Washington
D.C., 1970). What is worthwhile in this book should not at all be overlooked, especially the
textual and historical observations with regard to Leontius. Nevertheless the thesis about the
Origenism of Leontius is unacceptable. The following take issue with this thesis:
A. de Halleux, in his reviews in *RHE* 66 (1971), 977–85; *Mus* 84 (1971), 553–60; B. E. Daley,
'The Origenism of Leontius of Byzantium', *JTS* 27 (1976), 333–69; A. Le Boulluec, 'Con-
troverses au sujet de la doctrine d'Origène sur l'âme du Christ', in L. Lies (ed.), *Origeniana Quarta*
(Innsbruck, 1987) (223–37), 232–3. Endorsing the opinion of D. B. Evans are: J. Meyendorff,
Christ in Eastern Christian Thought (Washington D.C., 1969), 43–9; *idem, Byzantine Theology:
Historical Trends and Doctrinal Themes* (New York, 1974), 35f.; also P. T. R. Gray, *The Defense
of Chalcedon*, 101f.: 'It is impossible not to see in this Origenistic notion of the νοῦς-Christ
the only conceivable explanation for Leontius' *tertium quid*.' The following accept the thesis of
Origenism for Leontius without discussion: W. H. C. Frend, *The Rise of the Monophysite Movement* (Cambridge, 1972), 278f.; C. von Schönborn, *Sophrone de Jérusalem: Vie monastique et confession dogmatique* = *ThéolHist* 20 (Paris, 1972), 48f. For a refutation see B. E. Daley, *art. cit.* and
L. Perrone, *art. cit.*, 429–30.

21. Leontius Byz., *CNE* 2: PG 86, 1281CD.

the nature of the Logos which is proper to him intrinsically, that which with him has proceeded from the Father (φύσις from φύειν). From this point of view the *physis* of Christ can only be one. To characterize the humanity of Christ too by *physis* would be equivalent to a contradiction. Hence the humanity of Christ could be acknowledged as whole and real, which must be conceded for the whole Cyrillian-Severan tradition. However, it ought not receive the title *physis*, because it has not arisen from the divinity by way of a *phyein*, but through God's special salvific disposal.

The Antiochenes and the Chalcedonians referred, however, to the birth of the human being, Jesus, from Mary, which also demanded the denotation of *physis* for the humanity. Which then was the one *hypostasis* in Christ? After three quarters of a century of dispute it was now in Leontius' court to seek an answer. Severus had always taken the *concrete physis* or *hypostasis* of Christ as his starting-point. He had become indignant when John the Grammarian set in opposition to this concrete view of the one *physis* the abstract one of two essences (*ousiai*). Leontius took up this trail and approached the christological problem on the basis of Aristotle's teaching about categories.[22]

We shall start with two texts in which Leontius is concerned with the clarification of the fundamental Chalcedonian concepts, with *CNE* I: PG 86, 1280 and with *Epilysis*: PG 86, 1945A.

(1) Nature and hypostasis *according to* CNE *I: PG 86, 1280A*
'Nature is (however) not *hypostasis*, because the [following] proposition is not reversible: a *hypostasis* is also nature; but nature is not *hypostasis*.' After establishing this, Leontius indicates the following determinations:

(a) for nature (*physis, ousia*)
1. Nature has the predicate 'to be' (τοῦ εἶναι λόγου)
2. Nature has the meaning of εἶδος (species, genus)

(b) for *hypostasis*
1. *Hypostasis* has in addition the predicate 'to be for itself' (καθ'ἑαυτὸ εἶναι)
2. *Hypostasis* reveals 'this one or that one', i.e. the individual in the species

---

22. On this fundamental stance see J. P. Junglas, *Leontius von Byzanz* (Paderborn, 1908), ch. 3, The philosophy of Leontius of Byzantium, 66–92; V. Grumel, art. 'Léonce de Byzance', in *DTC* 9 (1926), 405–8 (*ousia, physis, eidos*). According to Leontius the word *physis* has a twofold sense: (a) the essence or the constitutive elements of a substance; (b) on account of the multiplicity of the individuals in one nature *physis* denotes the universal in relation to the individuals and receives the denotation of *eidos* (*species*, kind). Thus we have two meanings: the physical and the logical. *Ousia*: (a) That which is common to all substances; this is the 'second *ousia*'; as such it denotes the existence of a thing, and not the what or how of a thing. (b) The particular nature of a being, thus the 'first *ousia*'. The latter is the most common usage in Leontius; *ousia* is synonymous with *physis* (cf. PG 86, 1273A, 1280A, 1309AB). *Ousia* gains a special significance, because it is a being, which is worthy of existing in itself and not in another.

3. Nature shows the peculiarity of the general reality (καθολικοῦ πράγματος χαρακτῆρα δηλοῖ)

3. *Hypostasis* contrasts being singular to the universal (τοῦ κοινοῦ τὸ ἴδιον ἀποδιαστέλλεται)

After this delimitation there follows a response to the question: where in the realm of being can there be talk of *physis* or *hypostasis*?

In summary it must be said that one speaks principally of *one physis* (*mia physis*) with regard to things that have the same essence (*homoousia*) and things which have the same being (the same *logos* of being). The concept *hypostasis* denotes those which are the same according to nature, but are numerically different, or things which are composed of different natures, but possess one community of being in contemporaneous *perichoresis*. I mean that they participate in being, not by reason of the fact that they extend the reciprocal essences (this is the case with regard to essences and their corresponding predicates — these are called properties —) but insofar as the nature and essence of each one is not considered in itself, but together with the others that are combined or assimilated with it. One sees this happen in various things, not least with body and soul, whose *hypostasis* is common, but [each of] whose natures is its own and their reason (*logos*) is different.

From this text it emerges that (1) 'nature' and *hypostasis* are not synonymous, and (2) the particular meanings of each are not gathered and contrasted with great care. When Leontius, for example, says that the first special feature for *physis* is the predicate 'to be', we have a more accurate statement in Severus of Antioch with his combining this predicate not with *physis* but with *ousia*, which belongs etymologically to *einai*. It is important which examples are adduced for the application of both concepts. The advocates for the *mia-physis* formula receive a pre-established meaning for both, which they weaken with the intention of making them unusable by their opponents. One can also speak of *mia physis*, if things having the same essence are considered. Granted this holds only on the logical level, Leontius overplays the use of this formula on the physical level. But it is to be noted in particular that Leontius sees the formula of the one *hypostasis* in two natures as not in the least present in the case of the human being, who, despite two *physeis*, namely body and soul, is nevertheless *one hypostasis*. We shall come to speak about this 'anthropology' in its own right. It is of the greatest significance for the monk.

(2) Nature and hypostasis according to Epil: PG 86, 1945AD

It is well to notice this: *hypostasis* does not mean simply and principally the perfect (τὸ τέλειον), but that which exists for itself (τὸ καθ'ἑαυτὸν ὑπάρχον), and in the second place it means the perfect.

Nature (φύσις) in contrast does not at all mean that which exists for itself (τὸ . . . καθ'αὐτὸ οὐδαμῶς ὑπάρχον δηλοῖ), but the perfect . . .

We should know this: what the natures denote, the essence presents; what the *hypostasis* denotes has the *ratio* of accidents, be they separable, or be they inseparable. The characteristics of simple things are simple, which are combined with the [things] that are composed and combined. As this is the case with human beings, so also in their definition: it characterizes their essence (*ousia*) as living, rational, mortal, receptive of contrary statements. The concrete concept of their essence entails that. *Hypostasis*, however, is characterized by form, colour, size, time, place, parents, rearing, instruction and what goes with that. Everything taken together cannot be true of anyone else; rather all of that belongs to one determinate (τοῦ τινος) human being.

And in the *idiomata* of the nature there share above all those which belong to the same essence; and in the *idiomata* of the *hypostasis* those also share whose *logos* (*ratio*) is different, if they have been assumed into the unity and community of being (συμφυΐα).

This is the case with the Emmanuel: he is namely one *hypostasis* of divinity and humanity; accordingly the hypostatic predicates are common to both; he is not, however, one *physis*, and thus he does not have the *idiomata*, as they would belong to the one *physis*.

If everything is also stated of him as of one, this is not, however, according to the same respect (οὐ κατὰ τὸ αὐτό), and not as of *one physis*. As one and the same is visible and invisible, mortal and immortal, tangible and intangible, this is still not according to the same respect, nor according to the same *logos* (*ratio*).

Because he is thus one and the same, everything is stated as of one, and precisely on account of the one *hypostasis* and (one) *prosopon*. But because the whole is not predicated according to the same respect, but according to one or other [reality] (κατ'ἄλλο καὶ ἄλλο),[23] hence the whole is also not expressed of a single and simple *physis*, but of different and composed natures, which in the union also preserve their natural property (φυσικὴν ἑαυτῶν ἰδιότητα).

Thus Leontius of Byzantium was intensively occupied with contrasting nature and *hypostasis* linguistically and conceptually in order to be able to justify the Chalcedonian way. Without further ado we recognize that, together with the theologians of the end of the fifth century, he is dependent on the Cappadocian theology of the Trinity, but also on the language of the philosophers. On the one side are the expressions *physis* and *ousia*, on the other the denotations *prosopon, hypostasis, atomon, hypokeimenon*, as Leontius summarizes in *CNE* I (PG 86, 1305). With these last expressions he enriches the language of the Cappadocians, using the philosophers, particularly Porphyry.[24]

For the theology of the Trinity Severus had condescended with Basil to enlist the distinction of *koinon* and *idion*, in order to distinguish nature and *hypostasis*. But he refused, as we have seen, to take this step too

23. Cf. Gregory Naz., *Ep. 101 ad Cled.* I: PG 37, 180AB; *JdChr* I³, 538–9.

24. M. Richard, 'Léonce et Pamphile', *RSPT* 27 (1938) (27–52), 31–2; *Op. Min.* III, no. 58, draws attention to this. He adduces a text from Porphyry, *Isagoge* = *Aristotelis Opera*, ed. Acad. Reg. Boruss. t. IV, p. 2b, l. 47: 'One calls this *atoma* [inseparable, primal unities], because each of them consists of properties, the collection of which does not fit any other, which is part of a kind.' The words of *Epilysis* just cited refer to this (PG 86, 1945BC), in particular: 'Colour ... denote the *hypostasis* ...' On this point Richard stresses that the description of the *hypostasis* by the Cappadocians was already quite close to this determination of *atomon*.

far for the order of the *oikonomia*, against both the Chalcedonians, like John the Grammarian, and the friends of his party, like Sergius Scholasticus. The 'headless one' of Leontius' *Epil*, who really speaks for Severus, still adopts the same standpoint and for that reason attacks Leontius' definition of *hypostasis*. He also continues to acknowledge it only for the *theologia*, not for the *oikonomia*. The 'novelty of the mysterium' is said to demand a *logos* and *horos* proper to it.[25] In contrast Leontius rightfully stresses that these same words (namely *hypostasis* and *ousia*) had to retain the same definition for both areas, even if the application of these concepts is to be regarded analogically (PG 86, 1921CD), and the transcendence of these mysteries is always naturally presupposed (PG 86, 1924AB). He also supports the distinction between *hypostasis* and *physis*, while the 'headless one' would like to retain their synonymous usage (PG 86, 1924C–1925B).

Yet here Leontius lands in grave difficulties: the *ratio* of the *hypostasis* coincides with that of the *individuum*.[26] In *CNE* he is not yet conscious of this. Not even once does he ask himself whether or not the human nature of Christ is individualized through the *idia*. Only in the *Epil* does he face up to the criticism of his opponents, which had increased in the meantime, and against his will allow himself to tackle this question. He has to admit that the human nature of Christ is individual. But nevertheless it is not a *hypostasis*, at least not in relation to the Logos.[27] Must this dilemma not become a stimulus that could not be ignored, to reflect on the concept of *hypostasis* from an utterly new perspective?

(c) Discoverer of the formal *ratio* of subsistence?

After Loofs it had been assumed that Leontius of Byzantium, or rather the one taken to be this Leontius, had aimed at a double breakthrough, namely: (1) the discovery of a twofold concept of *hypostasis* and (2) the isolation of the particular function of 'insubsisting' in the interpretation of the appearance of ἐνυπόστατον, which was translated by 'that which insubsists'. A large perspective appeared to open up. Both elements were

---

25. Cf. Leontius Byz., *Epil* 3: PG 86, 1921B–1925A. The 'Headless One' refers in contrast to Gregory of Nyssa, and intends by that his *Refutatio Confessionis Eunomii* III 3: PG 86, 1921B; Gregory Nyss., *loc. cit.*: Jaeger II, p. 131,19–22 = PG 45, 468B13–C3, or 705D11–708A2 (according to the apparatus of B. E. Daley's edition).

26. Cf. Leontius Byz., *Epil*: PG 86, 1928B9–11: '[The *hypostasis*] is separated [distinguished] from what is common (*koinon*) through what is proper (*idion*)'; 1928C8–9: 'that, which is determined by what is its own, characterizes the *hypostasis* of each thing'; *CNE*: PG 86, 1277D: 'The *hypostasis* denotes [delimits] the *prosopon* through characteristic traits.'

27. Cf. M. Richard, 'Léonce de Jérusalem et Léonce de Byzance', *MSR* 1 (1944) (35–88) = *Op. Min.* III, no. 59, 26–7, with reference to *Epil*: PG 86, 1917A-C.

gathered from an important text of *CNE*, which for that reason deserves attentive consideration.[28]

> Hypostasis, gentlemen, and the enhypostatized (ἐνυπόστατον) are not one and the same thing. For *hypostasis* refers to the *individuum*, but hypostatic to the essence; and *hypostasis* defines the person (*prosopon*) by means of the particular characteristics; the enhypostatized (ἐνυπόστατον) means, however, that it is not an *accident* − *it has its being in another and is not perceived in itself*; of this kind are all qualities, both those that are called properties of the essence as well as those which are added to the essence; none of the latter is *ousia* [i.e. an existing thing], but is always perceived in combination with the essence, like colour in the body and knowing in the soul.

The confusion about this section has to be cleared away by correctly interpreting a concept that was evaluated too rashly. It is a question of the famous ἐνυπόστατον, which without closer inspection has been interpreted as the high philosophical expression 'insubsistence'. Correct punctuation too can offer a decisive contribution in eliminating this error. This concerns the sentence at the beginning of our long text: '... enhypostatized (ἐνυπόστατον) means, however, that it is not an accident − it has its being in another and is not perceived in itself; of this kind are all qualities ...' We have to note two points here: (1) the expression *enhypostaton*; and (2) the inserted clause which needs to be attributed correctly.

(1) We have already encountered the expression *enhypostaton* in John of Caesarea. There we referred to its previous history which led us back to the fourth century. But even up to the time of John of Caesarea, who was a contemporary of Leontius of Byzantium, it had the same meaning as in the fourth century. A philological observation would have been necessary to prevent an over-interpretation of the prefix *en* in *enhypostatos*: 'Now the words ἐνυπόστατος and ἐνούσιος seem to me quite clearly to be examples of those Greek adjectival formations in which the prefix ἐν- is joined to a substantive to signify the possession of some thing or quality, as opposed to an *alpha privative*, which would signify its absence.'[29] It was precisely in this regard that Loofs missed

---

28. Leontius Byz., *CNE* 1: PG 86, 1277C14–1280B.

29. Cf. B. E. Daley, 'The Christology of Leontius of Byzantium' (above, n. 14) refers to the words ἔμφωνος–ἄφωνος; ἔνυλος–ἄνυλος; ἔντιμος–ἄτιμος, and comments: ''Ενυπόστατος, in such a reading, would simply mean "hypostatic", having a concrete existence, as opposed to "anhypostatic", or purely abstract.' As evidence Daley adduces John Philoponus, the contemporary of Leontius, who in spite of great theological differences retained a strikingly similar vocabulary. In his *Comm. in Physica* II 1: *CAG* XVI, p. 205,19 he defines the ἐνυπόστατα πράγματα as 'things which possess a nature (τὰ φύσιν ἔχοντα)'. Opposed to them are things which owe their existence only to theory (μόνῃ τῇ ἐπινοίᾳ) (*ibid.*, I 1, p. 4,19).

the mark.[30] He furnished the prefix *en* with its own dynamic, which expressed a direction through which two independent substances are brought together in an existential relationship. Thus he said, for example, that body and soul in the thought of Leontius were two different, independent essences or substances, which were *enhypostasized* in one concrete human being. Or fire and water too were said to be two different natures which were enhypostasized in one burning torch. Loofs commented that in the examples mentioned there was not an order set up between the enhypostasized, assumed, and the assuming part, the *hypostasis*.[31] Leontius, it is claimed, did not say which of the two natures, which were combined through the *enhypostasis*, assumed the other. For all that, Loofs presupposed that the term *enhypostatos* referred an essence away from itself to another, instead of allowing it to be in itself, as the prefix *en* expresses, according to B. E. Daley. But for the fact that precisely at the time of Leontius the old meaning of *enhypostatos* as 'in its own reality' still held, we have clear evidence from his immediate surroundings, namely from the Eirenaion monastery, the centre of the Sleepless Monks. There the fictitious letters to Peter the Fuller were fabricated; these will concern us in more detail. Here we shall extract from them only their witness to the meaning of *enhypostasis*.

In the ninth letter of the later collection, the second letter of Pope Felix to Peter the Fuller, the word appeared three times and its meaning always admitted of clear determination.[32] In all the falsified letters to Peter the Fuller it was a question of the so-called Trishagion controversy (or concretely, about the formula 'Holy God, Holy Mighty, Holy Immortal God' and its extension through the addition 'who has been

---

30. B. E. Daley, *art. cit.*, renders the cited text of Leontius according to the understanding of Loofs as follows: '*Hypostasis*, gentlemen, and the enhypostasized are not the same . . . For the *hypostasis* signifies the individual, but the enhypostasized the essence; and the *hypostasis* marks off the person with its characteristic traits, while the enhypostasized signifies that that is not an accident which has its being in another and is not perceived in itself.' Cf. F. Loofs, *Leontius von Byzanz* (above, n. 1), 67–8.

31. F. Loofs, *op. cit.*, 67–8: 'Which of the two parts of the composed is the ἐνυπόστατον, which assumes into its *hypostasis* also the φύσις of the other, the author does not say here' (in PG 86, 1304BC).

32. *Collectio Sabbaitica* VIII, *Ep. Felicis altera*: ACO III, pp. 19–23. The occasion for composing a part of the Letters to Peter the Fuller was present in the years 511–512, when the Oriental monks who came to Constantinople with Severus sang the Trishagion, which in Constantinople was referred to the Trinity, with the addition: 'who has been crucified for us'. On the monastery of the Sleepless Monks as the place of the forgery, see E. Schwartz, *PS*, 292–293. The letter above belongs to an extension of the original collection and is connected by Schwartz (*op. cit.*, 300) with the conflict in 519. In any case we are now very close to Leontius of Byzantium.

crucified for us', as will be presented in more detail in Chapter Two, III. 2, pp. 254–9). The Antiochenes at the time of Peter understood this formula as applying to the incarnate Logos, who suffered the crucifixion in the assumed flesh. In Constantinople, however, this same formula was related to the immanent Trinity and, in contrast to the Antiochenes, the conclusion was drawn that it was the divinity of the Logos that was crucified; this was regarded as blasphemy and interpreted as Arian-Apollinarian 'theopaschism'. In this context the forger of the ninth letter of the *Collectio Sabbaitica* formulated three statements with regard to the divinity of the Logos, which he wanted to defend with the expression *enhypostatos*. Initially we shall not translate this expression, but insert it in a transliteration of the Greek.

(1) When it stands written that the Logos became flesh (Jn 1,14) and that the Logos was God (Jn 1,1c), then the Logos is not invented as another God beside the Father [meaning as Logos of lessened divinity, which would be capable of suffering]. The Logos is not denoted simply [i.e. as Logos in any sense whatever], but as *Logos enhypostatos* and God the Son, so that we recognize from our lowliness [i.e. from the consideration of the *logos* which dwells in us as human beings] the sameness of the essence of the Father and of the Logos and of the Holy Spirit (λόγος γὰρ οὐχ ἁπλῶς, ἀλλὰ λόγος ἐνυπόστατος καὶ θεὸς ὁ υἱὸς εἴρηται).[33]

(2) Hence, because the Only-begotten of God could not suffer in his own [divine] essence, the created and ensouled body of the Logos suffers, which this very *Logos enhypostatos* of God united to himself from the womb of the holy Virgin without marital intercourse, in order to emerge from woman (πάσχει τὸ γεγονὸς ἴδιον τοῦ λόγου ἔμψυχον σῶμα, ὅπερ αὐτὸς ὁ τοῦ θεοῦ ἐνυπόστατος λόγος ... ἐνώσας ἑαυτῷ προῆλθεν ἐκ γυναικός).[34]

(3) The *enhypostatos Logos* of the Father and God entered through hearing, and mystically brought about the pregnancy of the holy Virgin (ὁ γὰρ τοῦ πατρὸς ἐνυπόστατος καὶ θεὸς λόγος).[35]

In the three passages adduced there is talk of the God-immanent Trinity, in which, in contrast to Arius, a full reality of the divine *hypostasis* is attributed to the Logos. In this there is no talk of the reciprocal relationship of the divine *hypostases* or even of an insubsistence. It is a question only of the same *hypostasis* reality for the Logos, as this is possessed by the Father and the Holy Spirit. *Enhypostasis* thus means: to have 'reality as *hypostasis*', and indeed divine reality.

(2) The idea of translating the expression *enhypostaton* by 'insubsisting' was also suggested by the false attribution of the phrase: 'this has its being in another ...' It was referred to the word *enhypostaton*, instead of to συμβεβηκός, which means accident and of which it is correctly

stated: 'it has its being in another'.[36] It is precisely that which Leontius, however, will not accept as correct for *enhypostaton*. That which is denoted as such has its own reality — a statement which only becomes understandable when the origin of Leontius' teaching about body and soul is considered. This problem is temporarily deferred.

A further text for 'enhypostasy'

For his interpretation of 'enhypostasy' Loofs also referred to a seductive formulation in *Epil*, which must be discussed.[37]

> That some say, however, that the humanity of Christ had not been formed in advance [of the union] and had not pre-existed and had not been assumed as complete (τελεία), but that it exists in the Logos (ὑποστῆναι ἐν τῷ Λόγῳ) and hence one *hypostasis* is formed from both, has indeed something true in it, but in part also not. We will also concede that it did not exist in advance [of the union] or had been formed in advance; but on that account we will not concede that this is the reason for the forming of one *hypostasis* from both, as if this could not occur in another way and it is not possible for God to unite himself [to become one *hypostasis*] with a perfect human being. What kind of union then would make excessive demands on God? It is not the time of the union, nor the place, nor the incomplete state of the body which made the one Christ, but the *manner of the union* (ὁ τρόπος τῆς ἑνώσεως) made the one Christ. Not because it [the union] would have been impossible [if the humanity of Christ had already existed in advance of it], but because it was not fitting that the humanity of Christ should have existed as a simple humanity with divinity, we reject the [idea of] creation in advance . . .

Loofs had regarded the words 'existing in the Logos' as a phrase, which would have been common to Leontius as well as to his opponents, and he had judged it as a statement parallel to his interpretation of *enhypostaton*. Loofs claimed that Leontius understood this 'insubsisting' as nothing other than a *praedicatio* of a normally independent nature or substance of another.[38] In doing this he claimed that Leontius had recourse to Aristotle's distinction between a 'first' and a 'second' *ousia* or substance. The 'second substances', as abstract, could be stated of the 'first substances' (i.e. of concrete individuals). For Christ the special case

---

36. Cf. H. Stickelberger, 'Substanz und Akzidens bei Leontius von Byzanz', *TZ* 36 (1980), 155.

37. Leontius Byz., *Epil* 8: PG 86, 1944C1-D3.

38. F. Loofs, *op. cit.*, 68: 'In fact the ἐνυπόστατον εἶναι in compositions is a predicative being of otherwise independent φύσεις or οὐσίαι.' With regard to content this interpretation is very much open to dispute. For in it the enhypostasy, as Loofs understands it, would be made out to be an equation: the divinity of Christ is the humanity of Christ, which is to be strictly rejected. Loofs saddles Leontius with an offence against the fundamental rules of the *communicatio idiomatum*, namely that it is not *abstracta de abstractis* (divinity : humanity), but *concreta de concretis* (God : human being), which are to be predicated. In Loofs' understanding, enhypostasy, already falsely interpreted in itself, would in addition be transferred to the *ordo praedicatorum*, the ideal order.

would only consist in the fact that of the 'first substance', i.e. the Logos or Son of God in the Trinity, it is not the 'divinity' which is stated as 'second substance', but the 'humanity', thus a 'second *ousia*' of a completely different kind. Loofs maintained that as one can predicate several accidents of one and the same *individuum*, so too can one predicate several 'second *ousiai*', although they are more than accidents. In no case would the *hypostasis* be doubled by this.[39] One can hardly interpret Leontius worse than Loofs did.

But only if we have excluded this false interpretation of Leontius' word which we have just discussed can we ask about its particular meaning. A particular relationship is assumed to exist between the humanity of Christ and the Logos, a relationship which one can characterize as having its existence or subsistence in the Logos. Thus one can certainly discover here the idea of insubsistence, which leads to the unity of the *hypostasis* in Christ. Yet to see in this a new concept of *hypostasis* or a new idea, not grasped previously, of insubsistence would be to go too far. This 'insubsisting' comes about namely in no other way than that of the communication of the divine *idiomata* to the humanity of Christ, through which this Christ becomes 'one and the same Logos and Son of God in the flesh'. How this communication is realized Leontius explains when he reflects on the relationship of the two natures.

(d) The major objective of Leontius: the justification of the formula of the 'two natures'

The interest of Leontius is not directed in the first instance to establishing the *mia hypostasis*, but the *dyo physeis*. Here two problems confront him which he attempts to resolve with regard to the 'headless one' in the *Epilysis*. (1) What does the number two mean; how must it be understood, without immediately dividing the numbered realities by its application? (2) How is the 'manner of union' to be grasped, so that the two natures in Christ do not become two *hypostases*? We shall discuss the first question briefly. The second deserves a longer investigation.

Leontius knows from Severus how much the proponents of the *mia physis* are horrified by the *dyas*, the duality. We know the significance of the monads teaching for the Arians.[40] The *dyas*, one could say, is for both *malignantis naturae*, i.e. intrinsically evil and intolerable for

---

39. We shall pass over the further conclusion of Loofs, *op. cit.*, 72, that Leontius with this theory falls in line with the Cyrillian tradition. It is refuted by the comments that follow.
40. See *JdChr* I[3], 360–6.

christology.[41] The orthodox, i.e. Leontius, for this reason wants to neutralize the essence of the number: 'The nature of the number considered in itself neither joins them together, nor separates them; it also has no underlying realities.'[42] Whether in counting I speak of unity or I divide depends on the counted realities. We can speak, for example, of five metres of wood and mean by that a single *undivided* piece of wood, which is measured using a particular scale. We can think, however, of one trunk sawn into five individual pieces. Similarly we can speak of ten bushels of corn and can ignore whether the one heap of corn is in fact divided according to ten separated containers or not.

Thus for the Trinity and for the *oikonomia* there is also a different, respective application of a number which is in itself neutral. When we confess three *hypostases* in the one essence of the godhead, we do not divide up the one indivisible essence into three quanta, because by that difference and division would be expressed of it, as the Arians would have it. But it is different in the *oikonomia*, where the *hypostasis* of the Logos is united with the humanity. However, here too the number two does not imply a division, but only a difference. 'Above' and 'below' are two contrary denotations. But they could be realized in one and the same subject, which occupies now this position and then that.

> Thus it is also with the *oikonomia*. If we speak of two *physeis*, then we reveal their difference (τὸ ἑτεροειδές), not their separation (τὸ κεχωρισμένον). We banish from them, even if they are not without reality (ἀνυπόστατοι), the number (counting) of the *hypostases*, as on the other side we confess there the number of the essences (*ousiai*) . . .[43]

Admittedly Leontius observes that, in this juxtaposition, the use of human concepts fails, and everything should end in silence. Not only the application of *hypostasis* or *ousia* signifies the risk of a *kainotomia*, but every denotation, every name and every word does the same.[44]

Thus from the form of the major christological concepts, Leontius believes he has justified the possibility of applying number, whether it

---

41. Cf. *ibid.*, 364 on the significance of the *dyas* in the Platonists. The Headless One says in Leontius Byz., *Epil* 2: PG 86, 1920A: 'Every number is a how many (*poson*), the *monas* alone is without how many (*aposon*). Thus if the without how many (*aposon*) and with it being inseparable (*atomon*) is proper to the monad then it is proper to duality and every number to express the how many (*poson*) and with it the separation.'

42. Leontius Byz., *Epil* 2: PG 86, 1920A. Cf. Leont. Schol., *De sectis*, VII, III–IV: PG 86, 1241–1244 and Ch. 29 of the DP: Diekamp, 216–221 on the theme: the duality expressed of Christ is not that of number, but that of the nature.

43. Leontius Byz., *Epil* 2: PG 86, 1921A.

44. *Ibid.*, 3: PG 86, 1924AB.

be one or two. What is the relationship of duality to unity in Christ?
How does Leontius finally establish the unity?

2. The interpretation of the 'unity' in Christ

From the text cited above it has become clear that with his concept of
hypostasis the monk has not advanced beyond the Cappadocian version.
The formal *ratio* of the *hypostasis* coincides with that of the *individuum*.
The idea of 'subsistence' in its differentiation from the idea of
'individuality' is not yet directly in question. But it receives a new chance
indirectly, insofar as in Leontius, as in no one else before him, the problem of the 'manner of the union'[45] is emphasized. With this statement
of the problem a new access is opened to his christology, not only for
us but also for history.

The conceptual language which Leontius uses for the problem of
the union is now strongly tied to the body–soul analogy, or to the
unity of body and soul, as an analogy for the christological *henosis*. For
this we are referred surprisingly to neo-Platonic philosophy, as it is
represented in the *Symmikta Zetemata* of Porphyry and then in Nemesius,
the bishop of Emesa.[46] The whole complex of the transmission of this
idea reveals to us the christology of Leontius in a singular way. We find
the path which Greek philosophy had trodden in interpreting human

---

45. Cf. on this J. P. Junglas, *Leontius von Byzanz* (Paderborn, 1908), 88–92. As the main text
Junglas names *Epil*: PG 86, 1925C (see also *CNE* I, Obj. 7: 1297C–1308A). He says that the
following are to be regarded precisely as a commentary on the *Epil* text: Maximus Conf., *Op.
theol. pol.* 18: *Union. def.* (CPG 7697, 18): PG 91, 213A–216A; John Damasc., *Fragm. de unione*
(CPG 8087, 8): PG 95, 232–233. Junglas, however, overestimates their similarity to those of
Leontius. Both later authors in their enumeration of the various types of *henosis* indicate indeed
an extensive agreement with Leontius, but differentiate themselves from him in taking the
terminology and definition further in the decisive term ἕνωσις οὐσιώδης, substantial union.
Junglas reads into Leontius the latter understanding.

46. On Porphyry see H. Dörrie, *Porphyrios' 'Symmikta Zetemata' = Zetemata* H. 20 (Munich,
1959) (here cited as *Zetemata*). On Nemesius: Nemesius Em., *De natura hominis* (CPG 3550):
PG 40, 504–817; Ch. 3 (PG 40, 592–608) is edited by R. Arnou, 'De "Platonismo" Patrum',
in *TD* 21 (Rome, 1935), 50–58 (Greek and Latin); G. Verbeke and J. R. Moncho, *Némésius
d'Emèse De Natura Hominis. Traduction de Burgundio de Pise. Ed. crit. avec une introduction sur
l'anthropologie de Némésius* (Leiden, 1975); H. R. Drobner, *Person-Exegese und Christologie bei
Augustinus = Philosophia Patrum* 8 (Leiden, 1986), 221–5. On Priscian see R. Helm, art. 'Pris-
cianus', in *PWK* 22 (1954), 2328–46. On the Christianity of Priscian, *ibid.*, 2330. His work:
Solutiones ad Cosroem regem I: ed. Dübner, pp. 558,13–560,98; *Suppl.* CAG I,2, pp. 50,25–52,22;
many texts in H. Dörrie, *op. cit.* On the relationship of Leontius to Nemesius-Porphyry see A.
Grillmeier, 'Die anthropologisch-christologische Sprache des Leontius von Byzanz und ihre
Beziehung zu den Symmikta Zetemata des Neuplatonikers Porphyrius', in H. Eisenberger (ed.),
FS Hadwig Hörner (Heidelberg, 1990), 61–72.

beings on a higher level in the christology of Nemesius, and, probably through cribbing from him, in Leontius of Byzantium. This is true for comprehending the realities in question: namely body and soul in the human being, and divinity and humanity in Christ. After these realities (πράγματα) were determined, and then contrasted and delimited reciprocally, all the more pressing was the question about the *henosis*, the union of these essences which were comprehended this way or that. Behind the anthropological question stood the whole problem of multiplicity and unity in the world, of matter and spirit. Christology offered a tremendously broad framework to extend these cosmological-anthropological perspectives into new dimensions. Nemesius had seized this possibility. In his own singular way Leontius follows Nemesius along this path, both in choice of language and also in the speculative presentation of the christological problem. Does he progress further than his model?

(a) The depiction of the body–soul analogy

If one approaches Leontius subsequent to Severus of Antioch, one is struck by a distinction in the way in which divinity and humanity in Christ are characterized. As one who confesses the *mia-physis* formula, the Patriarch thinks and speaks almost only in the terminology of *physis*. The concept of *ousia* has little chance with Severus, because in his eyes it was misused by John the Grammarian and Sergius Scholasticus, as has already been shown. For this reason he avoids the use of *ousia* as far as possible. It is completely the opposite with Leontius of Byzantium. *Ousia* is strongly to the fore, to depict indeed the body–soul teaching and christology. Still, *vis-à-vis* Severus, one must not overlook the fact that Leontius starts from *ousia* in the meaning of 'single essence' (οὐσία πρώτη),[47] the Patriarch in contrast from the abstract essence, the δεύτερα οὐσία, as this had been brought into play by John the Grammarian and Sergius Scholasticus. This difference in the use of the *ousia* concept is conditioned both by the monk's manner of logical argumentation as well as by his sources.

In their enquiry about the soul, the middle Platonists asked in the first place about its *ousia*, its essence. The teaching about the uniting of both was not yet their problem. Plotinus too had not yet concerned himself with it. The innovator for this problematic was Porphyry, precisely in his *Symmikta Zetemata*.[48] For the Fathers who wanted to take over the

---

47. Leontius expresses the *deutera ousia* by the word *eidos*.
48. See H. Dörrie, *Zetemata*.

body–soul analogy for christology, it was of necessity important to start from a form that was appropriate for this purpose. Not everything that the Greeks offered was useful. According to an old Greek notion the soul, in being tied to the body, loses its full freedom and thus forfeits its true existence.[49] An ephemeral soul could not be an image for the imperishable, eternal Logos. Porphyry, who was the enemy of Christians, a fact which Nemesius does not forget to mention,[50] had done some preliminary work for christology. What he had to offer we experience through the mediation of the bishop of Emesa.

(i) The soul as οὐσία, indeed as οὐσία ἀσώματος, αὐτοκίνητος, οὐσιώδης

Greek philosophy here uses strong expressions to denote the substantial reality of the soul. It is especially the predicate 'incorporeal' which is regarded as the highest statement about the divine. It is the expression which emphasizes most perfectly the 'effectively transcendent'.[51] Only the 'incorporeal essences' are also 'perfect *hypostases*' (τέλειαι ὑποστάσεις): thus the soul and the *nous*. They have *energeia*, power and activity.

The objective of the Platonists here was to substantiate the immortality of the soul, something that could not be achieved with the Stoic teaching of mixing. The Peripatetics also failed here. They made the soul into a principle of form, into the entelechy of the body, which ceases with this. In this way Aristotle defended himself against a dualistic teaching about body and soul. Nemesius does not consider this, when he is incorrectly of the opinion that Aristotle denied the substantial character of the soul in his teaching about entelechy.[52] With Plotinus and Porphyry, however, something new came into the interpretation of the relationship of body and soul. Both emphasize 'with all dialectical means the transcendence of the soul', which immediately spawned a new question: how can it dwell in and unite itself with the body, which stands in fundamental opposition to it?[53] But let us remain for the moment with the depiction of the soul's level of being and the corresponding denotations. Here we shall establish a striking relationship between Porphyry, Nemesius and Leontius.

(1) Porphyry: cf. H. Dörrie, *Zetemata*, 179–187: on the incorporeality of the soul; 187–198: the soul as ΝΟΗΤΗ ΟΥΣΙΑ. In addition 20, 44 (*incorporales essentiae*). On the self-movement of the soul: 20, 60, 123, 124, 188, 193–5. On the substantiality of the soul (*ousia*): 9, 10, 43, 112, 169. Porphyry defends the incorporeality of the soul against the Stoics; the substantiality of the soul against the Peripatetic.

(2) Nemesius of Emesa, *De natura hominis* (CPG 3550):
All of the three denotations mentioned are taken over.[54] The core sentence reads: the soul 'incorporeal and essentially in itself': ἀσώματος οὖσα καὶ οὐσιώδης καθ'ἑαυτήν: PG 40, 592A12–13.

49. *Ibid.*, 198.
50. Nemesius Em., *De nat. hom.*, ch. 3: PG 40, 601B–604A.
51. H. Dörrie, *Zetemata*, 186.
52. Thus G. Verbeke/J. R. Moncho, in the Introduction sur l'anthropologie de Némésius (above n. 46), XLIV, n. 47.
53. Cf. H. Dörrie, *Zetemata*, 14.
54. On Nemesius see F. R. Gahbauer, *Das anthropologische Modell. Ein Beitrag zur Christologie der frühen Kirche bis Chalkedon* = ÖstlChr 35 (Würzburg, 1984), 24–6; JdChr I³, 574–6.

(3) Leontius of Byzantium:
in general on the concept of *ousia*: PG 86, 1277D–1280B, 1309AB;
the soul of the human being as οὐσία: *CNE* I: PG 86, 1280B, 1281B;
the soul of the human being as ἀσώματος: *ibid.*, 1281B;
the soul of the human being as αὐτοκίνητος: *ibid.*;
the soul of the human being as ἀθάνατος, ἀνώλεθρος: *ibid.*;
the soul of the human being as οὐσιώδης: *ibid.*, 1296C–1297A.

(ii) The formula of the 'own being' of the soul

(1) Porphyry coins as the strongest expression for this: 'the soul exists for itself'; it can take on a state in which it is completely for itself (ἡ ψυχὴ καθ'ἑαυτὴν γενομένη).[55] 'It is its own reality, and not simply reality in and in respect to another for the duration of its existence', by which the qualities are meant. Only for the reason that the soul exists 'in and for itself' ought it be reckoned among the 'whole and perfect *hypostases*' (Porph., *sent.* 30; 15, 12 M.).[56] This 'for itself' (καθ'ἑαυτό) says in addition to that: the soul has a state in which it is 'in relationship' to the body (σχέσει).[57] The contrary to that is, however, this καθ'ἑαυτὴν εἶναι, i.e. to be for itself in the sense of 'not being related'. The soul has this state in the hereafter or in a dream.

(2) Nemesius takes over verbatim from Porphyry this formula of the 'own being' of the soul, and with him takes the stand 'that the soul can separate itself from the body at will'.[58] For christology the expression 'in relationship' (*en schesei*) will have to be noted, just as much as the 'to be for itself'.

(3) Leontius of Byzantium: his heavily discussed formula εἶναι, ὑπάρχειν καθ'ἑαυτό must certainly be seen against the background of Porphyry. For Leontius it is a question of stressing the substantiality of a being in contrast to the accident, 'which has being in another and is not considered in itself'.[59] But on that point one has to ask what Leontius has to say about *schesis*.

(b) The range of the body–soul analogy

In no Chalcedonian author of the sixth century whom we have previously discussed can we observe such a comprehensive recourse to anthropology as a model for christology as we can in Leontius.[60] The

55. See H. Dörrie, *Zetemata*, 198–225.

56. Cf. *ibid.*, 220; also 178.

57. See the important parallels between Nemesius and Porphyry in H. Dörrie, *ibid.*, 70; in addition 88: 'Porphyry was the first to contrast the related existence of the soul . . . to the relationless existence of the soul, turned in on itself. The soul itself is not doubled; it has, however, a double life in not being related and in relationship . . .' Considered in itself, the soul has dwelling in itself the *energeia*. Derived from that it has the *schesis*, through which the soul as an incorporeal being is tied to the body not through localized presence, but through relatedness. Could such a notion be taken over?

58. Nemesius Em., *De nat. hom.*, ch. 3: PG 40, 597A; R. Arnou, *TD* 21, 53.

59. Leontius Byz., *CNE*: PG 86, 1277D5–6, a clause which refers to *symbebekos*, the accident, and not to *enhypostaton*.

60. Leontius Byz., *CNE*: PG 86, 1289C: τὸ παράδειγμα τοῦ ἀνθρώπου, cf. *ibid.*, 1304B. Cf. J. P. Junglas, *op. cit.*, 79–85; V. Grumel, art. 'Léonce de Byzance', in *DTC* 9, 404–5; M. Richard, 'Le traité "De sectis" et Léonce de Byzance', *RHE* 35 (1939) (695–723), 707–9; *idem*, 'Léonce de Jérusalem et Léonce de Byzance', *MSR* 1 (1944), 35–88 = *Op. Min.* III, no. 59. In all these works the relationship to Nemesius-Porphyry is not yet noted.

immediate occasion is the debate with the Nestorians and Eutychians, which had still not been concluded. The unity and differentiation of body and soul in the human being presented itself as the closest and most expressive illustration for the Chalcedonian formula of the unity of the *hypostasis* in two natures. But it holds true of the relationship of body and soul that 'the *hypostasis* is common, the nature is proper and according to definition different'.[61] The opponents of Leontius criticized this comparison and its power of proof. They found the first difference between the paradigm and Christ in the fact that the Logos is already perfect before the human being, which also has its completeness. In contrast the human being is composed of 'incomplete parts'. The Aristotelians could say, 'from incomplete natures' (*naturae incompletae*). In Christ, on the other hand, it is different: 'He has perfect parts, if one can speak of parts at all.'[62] In response Leontius stresses that the establishment of this fact by his opponents serves only to prove that there are two separate *hypostases* in Christ. He means here the Nestorians. In contrast the Eutychians in an ignorant manner would misuse and alienate this paradigm, in order to discover in it the 'prototype of the *synchysis* and its exact image', the *mia physis*.[63]

But lack of understanding and misuse should not stop one from making full use of an old tradition which had left its traces in the writings of the theologians. Admittedly, and the monk concedes that the anthropological model fits Christ only imperfectly, the 'dissimilarity' is not to be overlooked.[64] For this reason from the outset Leontius will delimit the exploitation of the comparison to one central point: 'We shall use the example to explain that the Logos in his essence itself (*ousia*) is united to our body and is never seen without it.'[65] Thus in relation to both elements of the comparison he works out this conclusion, which is important for him: in the union of an invisible and visible, of an immortal and mortal element, as these occur in 'human beings' and in Christ, their properties remain intact. That which before the union is invisible or visible remains so also after the uniting, which is emphasized particularly for the visible, mortal part against the 'Monophysites'. Hence Leontius can proceed in this way to prepare this paradigm for Chalcedonian christology.

61. Leontius Byz., *CNE*: PG 86, 1280B9–10: κοινὴ μὲν ἡ ὑπόστασις, ἰδία δὲ ἡ φύσις, καὶ ὁ λόγος διάφορος.
62. *Ibid.*: PG 86, 1280C.
63. *Ibid.*
64. Cf. *ibid.*: PG 86, 1280D.
65. *Ibid.*: PG 86, 1281A1–2: αὐτῇ τῇ οὐσίᾳ τὸν Λόγον ἡνῶσθαι τῷ ἐξ ἡμῶν σώματι.

(c) The manner of the union (ὁ τρόπος τῆς ἐνώσεως)

We do not need to present in their entirety once again the various types of union which had been taken over from ancient philosophy and discussed by the Fathers.[66] Leontius presupposes in particular four central forms of mixing.

(1) *Parathesis (compositio)*: a form of union, as in a heap of corn or sand, or in a gathering of human beings (army, choir);

(2) *Mixis (mixtio)*: bodily conceived qualities permeate a body. Example: iron glowing with fire, air filled with light;

(3) κρᾶσις *(mixtura)*: mingling of fluids (water–wine), but in such a way that the elements preserve their original qualities, although in combining they clearly weaken each other;

(4) σύγχυσις *(concretio, confusio)*: the union is all-encompassing. In the new body there arise new properties. One can no longer split the result up into its original parts. Thus from the Stoic point of view, body and soul are understood materially as ἡνωμένον ζῷον. The previous qualities cease to exist in the common transitoriness of their combined parts.

For the body–soul unity Porphyry decided to eliminate two things from the Stoic *henosis*: (a) the *synchysis* as the extinguishing of the previous qualities; (b) the idea of common perishability (συμφθαρῆναι). That resulted in his formula of 'unmingled union' (ἀσύγχυτος ἔνωσις),[67] which was avidly accepted by the Fathers. It held good for the Chalcedonians as well as for the non-Chalcedonians. (c) In this process the incorporeality of the soul is particularly to be emphasized. Porphyry developed the conditions for the 'manner of union' of body and soul in the important *zetema* 'on the union of soul and body'.[68] The line of thought of this investigation can be elicited from the third chapter of *De natura hominis* of Nemesius of Emesa.[69]

What connections between Porphyry/Nemesius and Leontius can be discovered?

(i) The very wording used to state the problem, namely the formula of the 'manner of union' (τρόπος τῆς ἐνώσεως), is striking. In Leontius it receives indeed a special accent.[70] In Nemesius it is found in a context which clearly refers back to Porphyry. In Porphyry the 'how of the union of soul and body' plays a major rôle, as emerges from the reproduction of his *zetema* in Nemesius.[71] The Neoplatonist speaks of the *eidos*

66. See above, pp. 40–1 (on Severus of Antioch).

67. Cf. H. Dörrie, *Zetemata*, 173–174.

68. *Ibid.*, 12–103.

69. Cf. *ibid.*, 12–99.

70. Cf. Leontius Byz, (a) *DTN*, ch. 42 (Daley's numbering): PG 86, 1380BC. Leontius emphasizes: οὐ περὶ λέξεών ἐστιν ἡμῖν τὸ ἀμφισβητούμενον, ἀλλὰ περὶ τοῦ τρόπου τοῦ ὅλου κατὰ Χριστὸν μυστηρίου . . . ὁ τρόπος δηλαδὴ τῆς ἐνώσεως, οὐσιωδῶς, ἀλλ'οὐ σχετικῶς γεγονώς . . .; (b) *CNE*, Obj. 7: PG 86, 1297C: Ἐπειδὴ ὁ πᾶς κεκίνηται πόλεμος, τοῦ τρόπου τῆς ἐνώσεως. This is the subject of his Zetesis; (c) *Epil*: PG 86, 1940C: τρόπος τῆς ἐνώσεως; particularly clear is the position of themes in *Epil*: PG 86, 1944C: οὔτε γὰρ ὁ χρόνος τῆς ἐνώσεως, ἢ ὁ τόπος, ἢ τὸ ἀτελὲς τοῦ σώματος, ἀλλ'αὐτὸς ὁ τῆς ἐνώσεως τρόπος τὸν ἕνα Χριστὸν πεποίηκεν . . .

71. On this see the overview in H. Dörrie, *Zetemata*, 36–37 and the analysis of the individual passages, 37–99. As early as his second chapter Nemesius asks about the 'how of the union' (39).

of the *henosis*, which Priscian translates as *forma adunationis*.[72] Plotinus had already formulated the thought that 'the way of mingling has to be investigated'.[73]

(ii) The concrete interpretation of the unity: the major objective of Leontius is to demonstrate the union in Christ as 'essential' (οὐσιώδης) (PG 86, 1925C9) or as 'union according to the essence' (ἕνωσις κατ' οὐσίαν) (PG 86, 1301C9). In contrast to a simply accidental, or a moral or a graced combination, as this prevails between Christians and God (PG 86, 1301AC), there has to be accepted in Christ this essential, substantial combination. 'The truth of the unity according to the essence is to be extolled with loud voice; one has to philosophize about it, as corresponds to the truth' (PG 86, 1301C9–11).

How does Leontius explain this 'essential unity'? We shall present a text from *CNE*:[74]

> In order that the distinction be clear to us between the union of things, which are united according to the essence, but which, however, are not changed, and the union of such things, whose nature it is to be changed in the union, in order that we thus know what is the form of the first and the result of the second kind, we want to make the following distinction (*dihairesis*): All things are one with each other through universal, common predicates (ταῖς καθ'ὅλου κοινότησι) [the universals]; they are distinguished from one another by specific differences (ταῖς εἰδοποιοῖς διαφοραῖς); through the union one does not mingle that which is different, nor separate what is united through the distinctions. Rather, to speak paradoxically in the tradition of the Fathers, they are united in distinction and distinguished in being united.
>
> There are two groups of unions and distinctions: many things are united in kind (*eidos*) and distinguished in the *hypostases*; others are different in kind (*eidos*), but united in the *hypostases*; and for these things which are united according to kind, but distinguished in the *hypostases* [or, distinguished according to kind, in contrast united in the *hypostases*],[75] the one group has a simple kind of union and distinction, the other a composite manner;[76] the individual explanation for this does not pertain to the present investigation; it also goes beyond the knowledge and understanding of most people.

---

72. *Ibid.*, 40.

73. Plotinus, *Enneadis* I 1[53] 4,10. Citation in H. Dörrie, *op. cit.*, 45: ζητητέον δὲ τὸν τρόπον τῆς μίξεως.

74. Leontius Byz., *CNE*: PG 86, 1301C15–1304A14. B. E. Daley offers an alternative English translation of this text in *JTS* 27 (1976), 344.

75. This expanded variant is added by B. E. Daley in his new edition: ⟨ἤγουν τῶν διηγημένων μὲν τοῖς εἴδεσι, ἡνωμένων δὲ ταῖς ὑποστάσεσι⟩ (to 1304A).

76. By a 'simple union' (ἁπλῆ ἕνωσις) Leontius means the combination of simple parts which are not composed. The body of the human being is of this kind, because it is composed of four elements. The 'composed union' (ἕνωσις σύνθετος) is one from already composed things, and this happens in two ways: (a) by way of mingling (*synchysis*) (PG 86, 1304D): an example of this is the blending of earth and water; (b) by way of preserving the unified parts (without *synchysis*): examples of this are a wick and flame; wood and fire; air and water; body and soul; Logos and body–soul. Thus the unity in Christ is for Leontius a *henosis* of composite parts.

We must rather speak of things which stand in relationship to each other through composition (σύνθεσις) or combination (συμπλοκή), or mixture (κρᾶσις) or union (ἕνωσις), or whatever else one may call essential relationships of things with different *eidos*; thereby we leave it to those who squabble about terms (*onomatomachoi*) to decide which term is more expressive or more suitable. We are bent on knowing and have little time for choice of words.

What Leontius is aiming at is briefly stated: 'the result must be a genuine, substantial unity from unmingled singular features of divinity and humanity'.[77] The name for the result is not so important, whether *prosopon*, or *hypostasis*, or *atomon* or *hypokeimenon* (subject). In any case one needs to reject the 'Nestorian' solution of a unity, which would be founded only on the like worth or authority of divinity and humanity in Christ, or on a relatedness which implies separation (σχέσις διαιρετική). By these means *koinonia* and the exchange of predicates (the communication of *idiomata*) cannot be established. On the positive side the unity in Christ belongs in the area of a 'composite union' (σύνθετος ἕνωσις) and is defined as 'the essential relationship of natures which are of a different kind' (οὐσιώδης σχέσις τῶν ἑτεροειδῶν) (PG 86, 1304A8); that is, realities of a different kind can relate to each other in a substantial relationship, which results in a *hypostasis*.

In view of the expectations which had been entertained since Loofs with regard to the Byzantine theologian, the result of this arduous deduction is disappointing. That the union in Christ is 'substantial' (οὐσιώδης), a fact which is expressed equally by the formulas 'union according to the essence, according to the *hypostasis*' (ἕνωσις κατ' οὐσίαν, καθ'ὑπόστασιν), is not peculiar to him, but, with the exception of the Nestorians, belongs to the permanent stock of theology. If once again, however, Leontius stresses the substantiality of the *henosis* so strongly, then that is best explained by his unnamed source, namely Nemesius of Emesa. The latter's opponents were the Eunomians, who transferred to the area of christology anthropological notions about the unity of body and soul, which Porphyry fought against.[78] They taught namely that the God-Logos is not united to the body according to his *ousia*, but on the basis of the potencies (δυνάμεις), be they of the divinity, or of the humanity of Christ. In this opinion they would have been followers of Aristotle, who saw body and soul united only on the basis of these potencies.[79] It is against this that the 'union according to the *ousia*' must be insisted upon.

77. Leontius Byz., CNE: PG 86, 1305C: ἐν μέν τι τούτων εἶναι τὸ ἀποτέλεσμα τῆς τε θεότητος καὶ τῆς ἀνθρωπότητος ἀσύγχυτος ἰδιότης.

78. Cf. Nemesius Em., *De nat. hom.*, ch. 3: PG 40, 605A; Arnou, *TD* 21, 57.

79. See H. Dörrie, *Zetemata*, 19; 101–102; 113, n. 3; 115; 142, n. 1.

What is striking in Leontius, however, is the special accent which he places on this understanding of the 'manner of the union'. According to him this teaching belongs to the principles, to the ἀρχαί, which are fundamental for orthodoxy.[80] In an unusually strong way the monk uses expressions from the semantic field around *ousia*.[81] From this we can obtain a certain insight into the state of his speculation about the

80. Cf. Leontius Byz., *DTN* 42 (Daley's numbering): PG 86, 1380B9–13. Nevertheless these first principles should not be understood as purely philosophical principles in Aristotle's sense, but the fundamental truths of christology, as Leontius immediately amplifies in this connection (1380C): 'But what are these principles? They are namely the manner of union, which is effected according to the essence and not according to the *schesis*.' As an example Leontius then adduces the anthropological analogy, this time, however, in the language that he finds in the controversy with Paul of Samosata at the Synod of Antioch in 268: 'namely that the Logos is in the complete humanity, that which in us is the inner human being, as it is composed according to the Apostle . . .' Leontius does not render the position of the opponents of Paul correctly. He smuggles into their teaching on the humanity of Christ the confession of a complete humanity (that is, with soul and body), while the unity in Christ was understood, however, as a strict Logos–*sarx* bond. Cf. Leont. Byz.: PG 86, 1380BC with the details in *JdChr* I³, 296–9. One should not read into this reference to the 'first principles' a self-surrender of the *fides* to the philosophical *ratio* with its methods, as is suggested by K.-H. Uthemann, 'Syllogistik im Dienst der Orthodoxie. Zwei unedierte Texte byzantischer Kontroverstheologie des 6. Jahrhunderts', *JÖB* 30 (1981), 103–12, especially 106. Quite the contrary. The words adduced by Leontius (PG 86, 1380BC) are strongly reminiscent of Theodotus of Ancyra, *Expositio symboli Nicaeni* (CPG 6124): PG 77, 1313–1348, especially 1325BC, in which the teaching of the principles is developed. Certainly Theodotus presupposes the teaching of the *principia circa quae sunt scientiae* of Aristotle (*Anal. post.* A 32.88b 27ff.), thus the teaching of the fundamental concepts of the individual sciences from which these have to proceed, in contradistinction to the *principia ex quibus demonstratur*, that is, the first universal principles of thought. But the application is to be noted. What Theodotus means is this: 'The *fides Nicaena* ought not be interrogated by reason, for it is the "principle" of faith . . . People who deviate in thinking from this formula of faith [Nicaea] are consequently not Christians, regardless of the fact that they may otherwise have something pertinent to say about the faith. For no one outside the Church demands from the "principle" of the respective science that it be deduced, rather one takes over the "principle" from one's teacher in the faith, without producing any reflection opposed to it. And truly the "principle" of the faith in the Only-begotten is [should be] this reflection of the Fathers.' The statements on Theodotus are taken from H.-J. Sieben, *Die Konzilsidee der Alten Kirche* (Paderborn, Munich, Vienna, Zürich, 1979), 232–5; 234 the translation of Theodotus, *Exp. symb. Nic.* 8: PG 77, 1325C. On the influence of the Aristotelian teaching on principles see already, however, Basil, *In hexaemeron* I, 5–6: PG 29, 13A–17A.

81. See in particular *DTN*, ch. 42 (Daley's numbering): PG 86, 1380BC, where as determinations of the union, there follow one after the other: οὐσιωδῶς, οὐ σχετικῶς, κατ'οὐσίαν καὶ οὐσιώδης ἕνωσις combined with τήν τε μίαν ὑπόστασιν τῶν δύο φύσεων. In addition CNE: τῇ οὐσίᾳ τὸν Λόγον ἡνῶσθαι (1281A); ἀνθρώπου φύσει συνάπτεσθαι οὐσιωδῶς (1285B); finally the formula in CNE is very strong: ἄῤῥητος γὰρ ὄντως ἐστὶ καὶ ἀνεννόητος μόνη ἡ κατ'οὐσίαν τε καὶ οὐσιώδης καὶ ἐνυπόστατος ἕνωσις (1300A). The contrasting picture is clearly recognizable in the sentence of the Eunomians which is adduced, and which Nemesius renders as follows: 'In some, especially in the Eunomians, it is said that the God-Logos is united to the body not according to the *ousia*, but according to the potencies (*dynameis*); it is not the substances (*ousiai*) that are united and mingled, but the potencies (*dynameis*) of the body are united to the divine potencies; the potencies of the body, and indeed of the organic (body) are, so to

unity in Christ. The unity comes about from 'essence' to 'essence', without mediation of the spiritual or corporeal potencies, as these would be proper to the divinity and humanity respectively (thus not through knowledge, will or senses), but through the *koinonia* of the substances. Leontius' thoughts on this subject had once again been stated by Nemesius before him:[82]

> The purely incorporeal nature permeates everything unhindered, but it itself experiences a permeation from no side. It is united precisely for the reason that it permeates; but because it itself experiences no permeation, it remains without mixing or mingling.

The substances (*ousiai*), in our case the divinity and humanity of Christ, communicate themselves reciprocally without mediation; this happens by way of a permeation (*penetratio*), which occurs, however, only from the side of the Logos with regard to corporeal nature, not vice versa. In this argument Nemesius uses the word χωρεῖν, which is well known from the Stoics, and παρουσία,[83] which has a strong meaning. The notion which here underlies the body–soul unity implies that the spiritual soul penetrates the whole body unhindered, without being bound to one bodily place or to a partial region. While the soul receives nothing from the body, through its *parousia* it changes the

---

say, the senses according to Aristotle. With them, so they claim, the divine potencies blend. But no one, this is my opinion, will concede to them that the senses are corporeal potencies . . . Thus it is better, as has already been said, to maintain that the unmingled union of the substances (οὐσιῶν) happens corresponding to the proper nature of the incorporeal' (Nemesius Em., *De nat. hom.*, ch. 3: PG 40, 605AB; R. Arnou, *TD* 21, 57–8). The strong use of *ousia* is mediated through Porphyry, who stands here in the tradition of Aristotle. Cf. J. H. Waszink, art. 'Aristoteles (1/9)', in *RAC* I, 657: 'In the third century AD, Porphyry, who in logic was completely on the side of the Peripatetic, through his *Eisagoge* made Aristotelianism accessible to wider circles, and thus also for the Christians.' But it is true of Aristotle, in contrast to Plato, that he acquired the concept of *ousia* anew. 'To this goal-conscious orientation of all philosophizing to the concept of *ousia* is to be ascribed the fact that Aristotle's doctrinal system had achieved a monumental closedness — a closedness that allowed it to become a model for millennia.' Thus H. Dörrie, art. 'Aristoteles', in *Kl.Pauly* 1 (581–91), 590. Nemesius, and following him Leontius, wanted to express two things by using this language and conceptualization, both the reality in Christ of the divinity and humanity which were to be united, as well as the reality of union and the unity itself. For this reason the phrase from the *CNE* (PG 86, 1300A) just cited (*enhypostatos* stated of the *henosis*) has to be translated as 'substantial and real union'.

82. Nemesius Em., *De nat. hom.*, ch. 3: PG 40, 605B–608A.

83. On this see H. Dörrie, *Zetemata*, 70–71; 72–73: 'The mere presence (and this too should not be thought of spatially) effects already that union which is not mingling.' This is the opinion of Porphyry. From the *Symmikta Zetemata* Nemesius cites precisely this text (PG 40, 604A) and then comments that Porphyry spoke here of soul and body, but what was said is true in its purest form of the union of Logos and humanity in Christ (604B). Leontius speaks also of the dwelling of the soul in the body, but uses for this not the word *parousia*, but διαγωγή, sojourn, dwelling.

body into its own *energeia*.[84] Porphyry further determines the body-soul relationship by the expression 'as in a relationship' (ὡς ἐν σχέσει). The soul is also tied from the side of the body by a *schesis* or a desire (τῇ πρός τι ῥοπῇ). But in the soul there are two states that must be distinguished, one free from relation, in which it preserves 'its own being' (καθ'ἑαυτὴν εἶναι), but also the state of related existence. It carries on, one could say, a double life, in being non-related and in relationship. In this way Porphyry expresses the tension which exists in the 'unmingled *henosis*' of body and soul. Leontius of Byzantium too retains the unity of body and soul in the same strong tension, and this with regard to the Chalcedonian teaching of two natures. In this context Richard speaks of an abuse (*abus*) of the anthropological analogy, which Leontius pushed to its limits, especially in the first book of *CNE*. The formula of the 'one *hypostasis*' in 'two natures' holds in the same way of the human being as a unity of body and soul, and of Christ, as the one *hypostasis* in divinity and humanity.[85] Most enlightening for his understanding of the relationship of body and soul as an analogy for christology is a section of *Epilysis*. Here he stresses first that divinity and humanity in Christ are not combined in a 'natural unity' (φυσικῶς), and explains this by means of his anthropology:[86]

> I am far from conceding that the God-Logos has his union with our nature on the basis of the definition of his nature; rather I do not at all accept this way of speaking [which says] that the human soul by nature (φυσικῶς) enters into relationship with its body without divine power [i.e. without divine decision of power].

Thus in *CNE* too Leontius could define the soul without a reference to the body: 'What does the soul lack to have its own and independent life, in order to have an incorporeal and self-moving substance?'[87] Without further ado we recognize Nemesius, and behind him Porphyry. In this way Leontius certainly gained leeway for underlining the transcendence of the Logos and his freedom with regard to the incarnation, as well as the duality of natures in Christ. He loosened the

84. See the texts in H. Dörrie, *Zetemata*, 83–84. Nemesius Em., *De nat. hom.*, ch. 3: PG 40, 600A; Arnou, *TD* 21, 54: the soul belongs to the νοητά, the *intelligibilia*, and shares their properties.

85. Cf. Leontius Byz., *CNE*: PG 86, 1281B–1284A, a particularly important section.

86. *Idem*, *Epil*: PG 86, 1940B; to be noted is the improvement of the text by M. Richard, 'Léonce de Jérusalem et Léonce de Byzance', in *Op. Min.* III, no. 59, p. 19, n. 68.

87. Leontius Byz., *CNE*: PG 86, 1281B. According to Leontius there are two *complete* substances in human beings. *De sectis* teaches the opposite to this. How there can still be one nature in human beings, Leontius explains in a very convoluted way. Cf. *CNE*: 1289B–1293A. Cf. M. Richard, 'Le traité "De sectis" et Léonce de Byzance', in *Op. Min.* II, no. 55, 708–709.

body–soul unity in order to refute the *mia physis* and to have a conclusive analogy for the two natures. But this was achieved at the cost of anthropology. For this reason he had to seek a counter-balance in stressing the *henosis*. We shall see how other authors of the sixth century, Leontius of Jerusalem and the author of *De sectis*, turned away from this solution.

Leontius knows well that with the taking over of the word σχέσις, which is rendered by relationship, relation, and in Latin too by *habitudo*, a loaded expression is introduced. However, he also certainly recognizes that, for christology, it cannot simply be avoided, but it has to be delimited by more detailed determinations. Hence on the one side he can demand for the 'manner of union', as we have seen, that it must be 'substantial' (οὐσιωδῶς) and ought not only be 'relationship' (σχετικῶς) (*DTN*, ch. 42: PG 86, 1380B; cf. *Epil*: PG 86, 1925C). Precisely if mingling (*synchysis*) may not occur and the *henosis* has to be realized as 'unmingled' (*asynchytos*), one has of necessity to accept a 'relationship' between divinity and humanity, as between body and soul in the neo-Platonic view. Leontius now avails himself of composite expressions: for the unity in Christ it is sufficient to have a 'substantial relationship' (οὐσιώδης σχέσις) (*CNE*: PG 86, 1304A10–11); to be excluded in contrast is a 'dividing relationship' (σχέσις διαιρετική), as this has been ascribed to the Nestorians (*CNE*: PG 86, 1305C) The latter is realized only according to the dignity, by the assumed human being receiving the same honour as the Logos. This entails a contradiction, because in the one, or rather, in the combining (συνάπτειν) of the divinity and the human being Jesus, it is immediately once again divided, through the acceptance of two *hypostases*. It is worth noting how modestly Leontius summarizes the results of his investigation into the union in Christ:

> Thus it remains after our investigation of the expression 'essential union' (ἐκ τῆς ἐξετάσεως τοῦ λόγου τῆς κατ'οὐσίαν ἐνώσεως), that we understand the special features (ἰδιότητα), both of the divinity as well as of the humanity, without mingling, according to the examples adduced above. We have compiled only a weak picture of the truth which transcends everything, [a picture], however, that shows that there is *one* single end-result from it (ἀποτέλεσμα), whether we call it *prosopon*, or *hypostasis*, or indivisible (ἄτομον), or subject (ὑποκείμενον) or whatever else you please. About this I shall not argue.
>
> But those who, through dignity or authority [of the Logos with regard to the human being Jesus] or another separating relationship in the combining, at the same time separate (ἢ τινι τοιαύτῃ σχέσει διαιρετικῇ διὰ τοῦ συνάπτειν χωρίζοντας), our disputation has already refuted and has found them guilty of separating the natures by [the acceptance of two] *hypostases* and of not accepting an exchange of statements [between the natures] (καὶ μηδεμίαν κοινωνίαν ἢ ἀντίδοσιν ἐχούσας ἢ ἀντιδιδούσας).[88]

88. Leontius Byz., *CNE*: PG 86, 1305CD.

With these words Leontius himself testifies that even he did not aim at a breakthrough in the question of the distinction of *hypostasis* and *physis*.

III. LEONTIUS OF BYZANTIUM AND THE CHALCEDONIAN PICTURE OF CHRIST

We shall certainly have to disclaim seeing in Leontius of Byzantium the forerunner of a new speculative epoch in christology, as he has been represented from F. Loofs down to S. Otto. The analysis of his conceptual language and formulas no longer allows him to be seen as a great innovator. To discover in his christology the turn from concept to axiomatic theory is difficult to justify. However, it would be erroneous to consider the significance of Leontius for Chalcedonian christology only under these restrictions. We shall attempt something different. We want to push forward beyond his dry conceptual language and his syllogisms to his total theological conception of Jesus Christ, with which he attempted to parry the seductive misinterpretations of the earthly appearance of Jesus. Here he performed worthwhile service for christological development, doing this on the basis of his fundamental, sober Chalcedonian attitude. The whole compass of the problems, however, is not yet grasped by Leontius. He is still not a systematic theologian in the later sense. As the development in the next decades of the sixth century will show, three themes belong together if one reflects on the significance of the union of divinity and humanity in Christ for the properties of the humanity of Jesus: *incorruptibility (uncorruptedness)* of the body, participation in the *omniscience* of God, and relationship of being created and *being uncreated* in Christ. The 'holiness' of the body of Christ also belongs here, but only occasionally is it a theme. For Leontius the incorruptibility (uncorruptedness) of the body of Christ comes to the fore, as the writing 'Against the Aphthartodocetists' shows.[89] What christological tendencies are visible here?

89. For an overview see J. Pelikan, *The Christian Tradition* 1 (Chicago-London, 1971), 266–77, especially 271–4. First of all we shall devote ourselves to the main question of the *aphtharsia*, as this is treated by Leontius: Leont. Byz., *Dialogus contra aphthartodocetas* (CPG 6813) (*CA*): PG 86, 1316D–1356C. On this see V. Grumel, 'La sotériologie de Léonce de Byzance', *EO* 40 (1937), 385–97; *idem*, art. 'Léonce de Byzance', in *DTC* 9 (1926), 400–26, especially 422–3. L. Perrone, 'Il "Dialogo contro gli aftartodoceti" di Leonzio di Bisanzio e Severo di Antiochia', *CrSt* 1 (1980), 411–42, produces a report on research on this dialogue and new contributions to the interpretation of the *genus litterarium*.

1. The 'Aphthartodocetists' ('Aphthartics')
of Leontius of Byzantium

We encounter the denotation 'Aphthartodocetists' for the first time in
the writings of John the Grammarian around 515.[90] Whom is Leontius
attacking in his writing *Contra Aphthartodocetas (CA)*?[91] According to
Draguet it must be held that the concept of *aphtharton* in *CA* implies
being 'by nature incapable of suffering and dying'. Julian of Halicarnassus
is different again. By this term he understands that Christ was excepted
from the *peccatum naturae* and its consequences, as these affect all human
beings. 'Uncorrupted' means for Julian's Christ '*not* to be subjected *by
necessity* to the corruptedness that stems from sin'. Certainly Jesus could
suffer and die, not from unavoidable fate, but in the free disposition of
the Logos, which decided about the whole life of Jesus. Initially Draguet
had accepted that the 'Aphthartodocetists' of Leontius' writing *CA* had
supported the teaching of Julian in the interpretation of Severus.[92] At
first he did not want to accept that Leontius was dependent on the
Patriarch in any way, but then found himself ready to make certain
corrections to his opinion. Another interpretation was represented by
Richard, who supported a dependence in the direction indicated:[93]
corresponding to the elements offered by the Patriarch to interpret Julian,
he claimed that the monk interpreted his Chalcedonian opponent too,
and in so doing had consciously distorted his teaching. Leontius, he
maintained, had wanted in this way to strike his anti-Origenist opponent, namely the neo-Chalcedonian Ephraem of Antioch, who has still
to be treated in our work.[94] The assumptions of Richard, however, do
not stand up to examination.

In order to achieve a clear result, according to L. Perrone what is
needed is a methical reflection which has to consider the following:
(1) *CA* first of all has to be considered in itself; (2) the reactions

90. John Gram., *Adv. aphthartodocetas*: M. Richard, CCG 1, 68–78. Docetism is ascribed
incorrectly to the opponents of Leontius, but an *aphtharsia* teaching correctly. For this reason
we choose the following expression to characterize this group — aphthartics.

91. See F. Loofs, 'Die "Ketzerei" Justinians', in *Harnack-Ehrung. Beitr. z. Kirchengeschichte*
(Leipzig, 1921), 232–48; J. P. Junglas, *Leontius von Byzanz* (Paderborn, 1908), § 12, 100–5; R.
Draguet, *Julien d'Halicarnasse* (Louvain, 1924), 176–8; L. Perrone, *art. cit.*

92. R. Draguet, *op. cit.*, 107–8; 202, n. 4; 208–9; 212, n. 2.

93. M. Richard, 'Léonce de Jérusalem et Léonce de Byzance', *MSR* 1 (1944), 35–88 = *Op.
Min.* III, no. 59.

94. M. Richard, 'Léonce de Byzance était-il origéniste?' *RevÉtByz* 5 (1947) (31–66), 36ff.;
Op. Min. II, no. 57. According to Richard the *CA* bypasses in a twofold way the real picture
of the aphthartics: (1) through an unreliable depiction of the doctrines discussed; (2) through
deficient proofs of the existence of those supporting them. Cf. L. Perrone, *art. cit.*, 415, n. 10.

of Severus and Leontius to the aphthartodocetist teaching have to be compared.[95] As a result of this reflection the first facts that have been established, macroscopically as it were, are: In *CA* the argument from scripture and the tradition of the Fathers, which are in the background in the other writings, dominate.[96] Speculative argumentation, *ratio theologica*, is applied less rigorously and formally than in *CNE*, *Epil* and *Epap*, without, however, being excluded. For the method of Leontius, seen as a whole even in *CA*, remains a rational one, an impression which is intensified if one compares with it the method of Severus of Antioch. By 'picture of Christ' we mean the concrete presentation which Leontius makes of the 'earthly Jesus' in opposition to the interpretation of the 'Aphthartodocetists'. Here for the first time the fundamental Chalcedonian lines are applied to the form of the earthly Jesus, with discussion about what in this life was normality and what was extraordinary. Is it a 'Byzantine picture of Christ', as we are accustomed to see it? In any case the posing of the question will prove to be useful, also with regard to the significance of Leontius for piety.[97]

2. Jesus Christ in his *aphtharsia*

The central point of *CA* is the interpretation and justification of the *aphtharsia* or uncorruptedness of Christ in the form in which it exercises its fascination, according to the communication of Leontius, upon the supporters of Chalcedon.[98] This combination of Chalcedonian two-natures teaching and the acceptance of a thorough-going *aphtharsia* of Christ is the strange thing about the dialogue partners of Leontius. This is an important difference from the Julianists with whom Severus had to deal. Together with the two natures they also profess the

95. L. Perrone, *art. cit.*, 416. Here the author investigates the dialogical character of *CA*, which he states is a real dialogue pursued with representatives of the Chalcedonian-aphthartic synthesis. For this reason he reduces the danger of presenting a purely fictitious opponent too one-sidedly and with distortions (422). Perrone refers to M. Hoffmann, *Der Dialog bei den christlichen Schriftstellern der ersten vier Jahrhunderte = TU* 96 (Berlin, 1966); B. R. Voss, *Der Dialog in der frühchristlichen Literatur = Studia et Testimonia Antiqua* 9 (Munich, 1970); *JdChr* II/1, 89.

96. *Idem, op. cit.*, 66. To be noted is the fact that among the twenty-seven testimonials in the *CA* florilegium is to be found one testimony to Ps. Dionysius Ar., *De div. nom.* (no. 1). See L. Perrone, *art. cit.*, 437–8.

97. For this reason we are prevented from accepting the assumption of S. Otto, *Person und Subsistenz* (Munich, 1968), who finds axiomatics in Leontius in a special way. There may well be some indications of it.

98. Leontius Byz., *CA*: PG 86, 1317CD: led astray by the attraction of the word *aphtharsia* 'some of us' have gone over to the teaching of Severus and Julian of Halicarnassus and have thus surrendered the whole mysterium of the incarnation.

Tomus Leonis.[99] Correctly they apportion the *apatheia*, the freedom from suffering, to the Logos as Logos, while they ascribe suffering to the human nature and also advocate the so-called communication of *idiomata*: of the one Incarnate One they state both the divine superiority to suffering as well as the human capacity to suffer, depending on whether 'one and the same' is considered in his divinity or in his humanity (PG 86, 1320AB). That is orthodox teaching. Inconsistently there was in Constantinople a group of Chalcedonians who had obstinately sworn to ascribe to the earthly Jesus freedom from suffering and corruptibility in general, and indeed as a perduring physical quality (PG 86, 1320B).

Leontius recognized the harm which the ecclesial understanding of the incarnation of Christ would suffer because of this. It would be turned around and practically annihilated. What does this new teaching imply? How was it justified?

As Chalcedonians, the dialogue partners of Leontius strongly profess positions which one would expect from Julianists who stand on the platform of the *mia-physis* teaching. The beginnings of the exaggerations of the Chalcedonians lay in the particular understanding of the *henosis*, an expression of which Leontius is very fond. The union in Christ here receives not only the function of combining the two natures, but also of altering them. Here an old conception of the antique teaching of mixing crept in, which holds that a substantial joining demands also a certain alteration of the parts that unite. Now it was clear to all the Fathers that the unity in Christ must have its significance for the humanity of Christ, despite the demand for an 'unmingled *henosis*'. The union of God and a human being is indeed a joining of 'infinite' and 'finite'. The more serious, the more 'essential', the more 'substantial' it had to be taken, the more the tension increased. Could the state of the *kenosis* still be taken seriously? Even to speak of that was also difficult for the Aphthartodocetists of Constantinople, as we encounter them in *CA*. Philippians 2,5–11 appears to play hardly any rôle.

Those enthusiastic about the *aphtharsia* of Christ demand that the effect of the *henosis* commence immediately with the coming into existence of Christ, whereby it is difficult to denote the precise moment. The Logos has certainly assumed from Mary in the womb something corruptible (φθαρτόν); but he changed it immediately into *aphtharsia* (εὐθέως

---

99. Thus they acknowledge Leo's incriminating formula 'each of the two forms acts' (*agit enim utraque forma*).

αὐτὸ πρὸς ἀφθαρσίαν μετεκεράσατο).[100] Thus the central point of the teaching of Julian of Halicarnassus is taken up, but in a modified, intensified form. Julian himself did not accept any effective, qualitative alteration of the humanity of Christ, but he saw this only as not subjected to the *necessity* of corruptedness. In freedom the Logos could resign his body to suffering or preserve it from this. The perduring capacity to suffer as such he did not see interfered with by this. The Aphthartodocetists of *CA* demand more: the *aphtharsia* begins immediately with the assumption of humanity, and tied to it is the *apatheia*, as the actual state of Jesus. Now a particular intervention of the Logos is needed, not to hold suffering at a distance, but first to admit it at all. The 'miracle' in the life of Jesus and the 'natural' (the λόγος φύσεως) change places.[101] Indeed these strange Chalcedonians are convinced of the reality of the human nature and its real capacity to suffer. They are not docetists who accept a fictitious body or fictitious suffering. The name 'Aphtharto-Docetists' is artificial as a heresiological construct and ought not be applied to the Chalcedonian risk group at Constantinople.

It is worthwhile going into this strange aberration in more detail. This particular state of Christ's human nature occurs firstly on the basis of the union and is not required for it, if one looks at its nature and takes it in its nature (κατὰ φύσιν). 'The body is not free from suffering and uncorrupted according to nature, but by power of the union with the God-Logos.'[102] For this reason the 'essential, substantial combination' of the humanity of Christ with the divinity becomes not only an unfulfilled claim to uncorruptedness during life on earth, but leads to an actual change: 'How was it then possible that that which was united to the uncorrupted Logos did not shed the corrupted nature?'[103] Leontius finds the whole process rather complicated: first of all the body of Christ is supposed capable of suffering from the side of the mother (PG 86, 1328D), but then immediately to be uncorrupted (1329AB). Leontius summarizes the consequences that this leads to in his judgement: thus if the Logos did not want, nothing of natural

100. Leontius Byz., *CA*: PG 86, 1329B5-6.

101. *Ibid.*, PG 86, 1321B11-12: νόμῳ θαύματος, ἀλλ'οὐ λόγῳ φύσεως. Cf. *ibid.*, 1329C: 'Christ has indeed suffered, but not out of necessity' (ἀνάγκη φύσεως, ἀλλὰ λόγῳ οἰκονομίας τοῦ Λόγου ἐφιέντος τὸ παθεῖν). Here there is certainly allusion to a phrase of Cyril of Alexandria, which had already played a rôle in Severus of Antioch (cf. above, pp. 104-5, n. 259 with reference to PO 12, 184-185).

102. Leontius Byz., *CA*: PG 86, 1325B.

103. *Ibid.*, PG 86, 1329A2-3; 1329A1 refers to a more far-reaching act: τὸ προσληφθὲν εἰς ἀφθαρσίαν μετεσκευάζετο (what was assumed was transformed into uncorruptedness).

symptoms would be bestowed on the flesh (1332A). The picture of
Christ is developed and presented as in a negative: impassibility and
immortality in Christ are the 'natural' state and rejoice in the stability
and unchangeableness of natural laws, insofar as a particular intervention
does not happen. The actual suffering in the body of Christ happens
because of a miracle (θαύματος λόγῳ).[104]

It is important to recognize how much is at stake in this for the picture
of Christ and the whole religious relationship of Christians to the life
of Christ. On the whole there was a threat of a devaluation of the
incarnation itself. The descending Christ, as it were, ought no longer
to touch the ground, but rather he must immediately be 'released'
from it. Where was there still a place for kenosis and the cross? Was
Philippians 2,5–11 completely forgotten? What possibility was still there
for an imitatio Christi, the crucified? From the intensity of the reaction
of Leontius to this false stressing and ordering of the aphtharsia of Christ
we recognize that he must have feared quite considerable damage for the
ecclesial picture of Christ. Hence it is of significance to grasp this reaction
in its peculiarity and to appreciate it. Perhaps it is on the success or
lack of success of this critique that the real significance of Leontius
is to be decided more clearly, rather than on his work on concepts
and formulas.

3. Leontius' critique of the aphtharsia teaching and his own contrasting picture

(a) Fundamental objections and their evaluation

Not all of Leontius' counter-arguments are convincing. His claim that,
if Jesus had been impassible from the beginning, he would not have
freely relinquished this privilege (PG 86, 1329CD), sounds rather weak.
Against this speak the Pauline passages of the kenosis (Phil 2,5–11) and
of the voluntary poverty of Christ (2 Cor 8,9). For Leontius himself
it is significant that he frees himself to some extent from the
theologumenon that dupes his dialogue partners, namely from the idea
of suffering 'when the Logos permits'. Indeed, he too accepts an
intervention of the divine Logos in questions of Christ's suffering, but
he has an essentially better formulation of it. Moreover, it needed no
'exemption'. Only in one particular respect should it be necessary. For
'the Logos allowed a nature, which naturally could suffer, to do without

---

104. Thus the aphthartic in *CA*: PG 86, 1333D.

sin (ἀναμαρτήτως) that which corresponded to its nature'.[105] In this way a good theological element is introduced into christology, the idea of a graced guarantee of the sinlessness of the human will of Christ. Such a graced help signifies no alteration to the human capabilities of Christ. Nevertheless for Leontius it remains the case that, in order to make the human nature of Christ passible, there is no need for permission from the Logos.[106] This important recognition entails a correction of the christology of Gregory of Nyssa and other Fathers of the fourth and fifth centuries,[107] in whose writings, because of their understanding of the unity in Christ, it had to be 'natural' for him not to suffer. Certainly Leontius too sees the transforming will of the Logos at work in the life of Jesus, not for the purpose of permitting suffering, but on the contrary, when it occurs, of allowing the definitive, eschatological freedom from suffering to shine through in the transfiguration. For the flesh of Christ 'had impassibility not with the union, but from the will of the one uniting, who disposed of it to his advantage (οἰκονομοῦντος) according to the occasion'.[108] Whether this reversal is sufficiently established is to be tested in the context of the fourth fundamental proposition just cited.

> On the contrary it is thus: when the flesh bears the sufferings that are natural to it, the Logos with many others sends it control over the passions (τὴν κατὰ παθῶν ἐπικράτειαν). For the 'physical bond' (συμφυΐα) of the Logos with the flesh is inseparable and absolutely insoluble. To be free from suffering was not possible for the body in every respect. For it had this freedom from suffering (τὸ ἀπαθές) not from the union as such, but from the will of the one united (Logos), who disposed of this according to the moment and the need. If this is not the case, one must concede one thing of both: either the nature did not suffer at all, provided that it had become free from suffering through the union, or, if it has suffered, it has completely fallen out of the union.[109]

Here Leontius makes clear some important features of the Chalcedonian picture of Christ. (1) The *henosis* with the Logos means for the human nature of Christ no qualitative change, apart from the fact that

---

105. *Ibid.*, 1332A.

106. *Ibid.*: 'It was not the case that the flesh was superior to suffering (ἀνωτέρα κατὰ φύσιν παθῶν οὖσα) and only became passible through the Logos.' The aphthartic summarizes the position of Leontius on this question concisely: 'Christ is passible, and this on the basis of his bodily nature (*physis*), and not from the will of the divinity' (PG 86, 1340A5–6).

107. On Gregory of Nyssa see *JdChr* I³, 546. See above, p. 104, n. 258 (on Severus of Antioch).

108. Leontius Byz., *CA*: PG 86, 1332AB.

109. *Ibid.*, 1332A–B6.

it belongs to the Logos, and is to be held as holy, the same as he is.[110] Leontius thus leaves the Chalcedonian 'unmingled' completely intact. The *henosis* is referred back to its true function. The Aphthartologues had accepted an ontological nexus between *henosis* and *apatheia* of such a kind that Leontius could confront them with the following: if Christ actually suffers, then for this period the *henosis* must cease. (2) In the picture of Christ subjection to suffering is the natural and perduring base; for the period of the earthly life superiority to suffering is the seldom-granted exception. (3) But because in Christ too the *sarx* is naturally weak, it needs the graced help of the Logos for his humanity, so that it receives the moral power to master suffering (*epikrateia*) sinlessly. This is good theology which, however, has an odour of Nestorianism to the other side.

For Leontius' discussion partner sees the redemptive character of Christ's suffering endangered. If the interpretation of Leontius is correct, his opponent is of the opinion that then Christ would suffer only for himself and not for us. (Christ would indeed be nothing more than simply a human being: so one could extend this line of thought.) Hence the monk must enter in greater detail into the peculiarity of Christ's redemptive suffering: the Logos retains the highest power of disposition over his own body, even if this is subjected to the universal human necessity of suffering — an assumption that cannot occur in the system of Julian of Halicarnassus — and this certainly also has an effect on Leontius' discussion partner. Thus the Logos could prevent suffering if he wanted; in relation to suffering he is hence only a *removens prohibens*, not the one who through his disposal has first to enable suffering

---

110. Cf. *ibid.*, 1353AB: Leontius distinguishes two sources of the sanctification of Christ's humanity: (1) the power of the Holy Spirit, which became effective at the virginal conception of Christ; (2) the union of the Logos with our nature. He ascribes to it (a) freedom from sin; (b) the entire holiness which is given with the flesh's being seized by the union and thus is proper to the Logos. This holiness does not rest on a simple influence on the flesh (*energeia*), but on the 'substantial, essential union with the Logos'. *Vis-à-vis* the aphthartic, Leontius can acknowledge this holiness without on that account immediately demanding a physical alteration in the *sarx* of Christ in the sense of the *aphtharsia*. Here, however, it is a matter of the 'ontological holiness', not of moral perfection in Christ. On the first question cf. fragments 43 and 48 in Julian of Halicarnassus; R. Draguet, *Julien d'Halicarnasse* (Louvain, 1924), 150 and 55–6; on ontological and moral holiness cf. D. Stiernon, Art. 'Léonce de Byzance', *DSp* 9 (1976) (651–60), 658–9 with reference to PG 86, 1353A ('L'impeccabilité et la totale sainteté' du Christ), to 1324CD, 1373B and 1332D. Leontius argues with Theodore of Mopsuestia and finds fault with his teaching of the ignorance and subjection to the 'passions' which have necessarily to be assumed, in order for progress and the acquisition of virtue in Christ to be accepted.

(cf. Jn 18,6; Mt 26,53). The Logos, however, will not prevent it.[111] For the redemptive power of this suffering rests precisely on the fact that the suffering is indeed naturally conditioned, and it is mastered without sin.[112]

Here the monk offers a presentation, seldom found among the Greeks, of the relationship between nature and supernature in human action.

(b) Christ's impassibility in the tension between nature and supernature

(i) Fundamental considerations

For the first time in Greek theology the distinction between 'nature and supernature' is articulated explicitly and then applied to the *apatheia* of Christ. Occasioning this determination of language was the reversal by the Aphthartologues of 'rule' and 'exception' in relation to the passibility or superiority to suffering in the life of Jesus. In their sense *apatheia* would be 'natural' also for the (united) humanity of Christ, being able to suffer 'supernatural'. Against this stands the thesis of Leontius: if the power to master (*epikrateia*) suffering is also supernatural (*hyper physin*), then it still does not annul the natural faculties (τὰ φυσικά); rather it develops these potencies and enables them to do their own work and to receive help which lies beyond this.[113]

> The supernatural does not annul the natural, but only leads it higher and urges it on to be able to do that too and to receive the power for what is beyond ... Consider for me the flesh of the Lord in its natural powers after the supernatural and marvellous union. The supernatural does not have any place there where the nature does not have what is natural. The miracle is annulled if that which is above nature [namely the *henosis* in Christ], changes the nature; and ambition (*philotimia*), which violates truth, becomes hybris.

In a felicitous formulation there is found here the Greek version of the Latin scholastic axiom: *gratia supponit, non tollit naturam*. Grace presupposes nature, it does not annul it. Leontius has discovered this insight in the Chalcedonian terms 'unmingled' and 'undivided'. Once again the dialogue partner, enthused by the *aphtharsia*, places the opposite picture there, although he appears to assent in principle to the remarks of Leontius about 'natural–supernatural', exemplified in the figure of Jesus. Still he remains without insight and states that what are to be characterized as miracles are the sufferings; that Christ, the Logos in the

---

111. In *CA* (PG 86, 1332C) Leontius refers to Athanas., *De incarn.* 21, 7: SC 199, p. 344,42–44; PG 25, 133C4–7; *ibid.*, 44, 8: SC 199, p. 428,53–56; PG 25, 176C1–5 (B. E. Daley, *Opera*, apparatus for these passages).

112. Leontius Byz., *CA*: PG 86, 1332A.

113. *Ibid.*, 1333B2–5; 1333CD.

flesh, is impassible and immortal corresponds to the indissoluble natural laws.[114] Leontius feels himself challenged by this thesis to show in the concrete life of Jesus his abstractly formulated rules about the relationship between nature and supernature.

(ii) Nature and supernature in the concrete life of Jesus
With a few strokes Leontius sketches the normal day-to-day life of Jesus, the Son of God. It took thirty years before the time of working miracles was allowed to begin.[115] Even in the public life of Jesus, miraculous signs remain the exception. The divinity of the Kyrios revealed itself only in a long process:[116]

> All this [i.e. the life of Jesus] took place from the hour of his birth to his ascending the cross and the three days in the tomb in this sequence and in natural order (τάξει φυσικῇ). To reveal his divinity, which was not yet explained to the multitude, he worked in the whole course of the time (πρὸς τὴν ὅλην ἀκολουθίαν) miracles with his body only rarely, to reveal his own divinity, as stated, not to annul the truth of his body. [According to Leontius no miracle is directed to a bodily change to the body of Jesus for its own sake. He recalls indeed facts which appear to be opposed to this, like the event of the transfiguration, the walking on the sea, the forty days' fast, the virgin birth (1336C).] All this he did to reveal the treasures of the divinity, not to annul or to change the assumed humanity.

Clearly Leontius is concerned to preserve the true humanity and to exclude every docetist vaporization.[117]

> As the Kyrios of all things has communicated his own to the flesh without moving out of himself (he remained immoveable in himself and retained the firm natural place [in transcendence]), so too his humanity remained in its natural constitution; it had the physical dispositions and functions (*energeias*) of the body, also did not relinquish the universal, blameless passions, possessed rather substantially (οὐσιωδῶς) the pattern (ὅρος) of the perfection proper to us [human beings], but shared in the goods of the Logos, indeed it possessed the Logos as the source of all goods and thus allowed, on account of the Logos, to flow out of itself everything which the Logos had.

We can grant Leontius that, in contrast to the intensive tendencies of the Aphthartics of Constantinople to sublimate, he brought his Christ once again back to earth. He has clearly called to mind the *homoousios*

---

114. *Ibid.*, 1333D.

115. Leontius alludes briefly to the 'childish miracles' of the apocryphal infancy narratives (PG 86, 1336A). On this cf. E. Hennecke/W. Schneemelcher, *Ntl. Apokryphen* I, 290–9; A. Orbe, *Cristología Gnóstica* I (Madrid, 1976), 448–88.

116. Leontius Byz., *CA*: PG 86, 1336BC. In this text there is a fundamental difference from Leontius of Jerusalem, who in his picture of Christ apportions a diametrically opposite position to the miraculous, as we still have to depict. This ought to be a decisive reason against identifying both Leontii, as I. Fracea does (above, p. 185).

117. *Ibid.*, 1336D–1337A.

of Jesus with us, and in this way has also created the foundation for our imitation of Christ.[118] It rests on the true relationship both to the humanity as well as to the divinity of Christ. For between us and Jesus there is a true kinship (*syngeneia*), further a similarity of suffering (*homoiopatheia*), which bring us into relationship with the humanity of Jesus. The relationship to the divinity of Christ, however, mediated through his being human, makes the imitation of God (*theomimesia*) possible for us.[119]

(iii) A test question for Leontius: the human will in Christ

In the discussion about the annulment of the state of impassibility of Christ's *sarx*, a state supposed by the Aphthartics to be 'natural', the question arises: who is the bearer of this act of the will, or the organ for bringing it about? Leontius has the impression that the opponents allow the *sarx* as such to participate in this. He takes this observation, true or false, as the occasion for refuting from a new side the notion of a thoroughgoing *aphtharsia* of Christ's body.[120]

> To believe, however, that a flesh which is naturally superior to suffering and immortal, has voluntarily permitted what was not due to it, means first not to know that willing and not-willing are proper not to the flesh, but to the soul, in which the capability of free will and the inclination to tend towards both sides [i.e. freedom of choice] are found. Secondly you make it [the flesh] guilty, because it has willed that which is against the nature (παρὰ φύσιν) of the willer [the flesh] and has chosen that which was not natural. This is the outermost border of the sin.
>
> This too is not to be passed over unnoticed: there are three causes (*aitiai*) from which every act proceeds: one comes from the natural potency; the second from the corruption of a natural *habitus*; the third appears as an ascent and an advance to something better: of them the first is the natural act, the second is against nature, the third is above nature and is so called.
>
> The act, which is against nature and is an aberration of natural attitudes and potencies, harms the essence (*ousia*) itself and its natural activities; the natural act, however, proceeds from an unimpeded cause, and this corresponding to nature; the supernatural act, however, leads up and raises and strengthens for what is better, for what, by remaining in its natural powers, it would not have been able to accomplish.
>
> Now what is above nature does not suppress what is natural, but rather leads it further and also gives it impulses to be able to do what is natural and gives the power for what transcends.

The Aphthartics feared that, by accepting a flesh in Christ that was

---

118. *Ibid.*, 1336D and 1337AB. On the problem of the *imitatio Christi* also see 1348D–1349D. It is only made possible for us through the truth of the weaker nature in Christ, which in its passibility furnishes the basis for approximation on our side.

119. See V. Grumel, 'La sotériologie de Léonce de Byzance', *EO* 36 (1936), 385–97, especially 391–2 (PG 86, 1349A).

120. Leontius Byz., *CA*: PG 86, 1332D6–1333B5.

intrinsically passible and corruptible, suffering and death would not be able to have any significance for salvation at all. They were of the opinion that only a flesh that was elevated above suffering could be meritorious,[121] by choosing suffering by its own decision. Leontius now shows that the Aphthartologue is completely confused in his idea of the *sarx* and does not bring the correct anthropological presuppositions at all for solving the problem. Willing and not-willing, he stresses, are not acts of the flesh, but of the rational, free soul, which can decide on the basis of knowing two sides. By drawing attention away from the *sarx* to the spiritual will of Christ, Leontius would like to bring the problem of the bodily *aphtharsia* for soteriology in perspective and to represent the solution of the opponent as inappropriate from the very beginning. Redemption does not depend on whether Christ goes into suffering with an uncorrupted or corruptible body, but primarily on the decision of the human will. Admittedly, according to Leontius one must start with the *sarx*, which after the supernatural and marvellous *henosis* with the Logos also remains in its naturalness, corresponding to the laws which hold for it.[122] Insofar as it itself is intended to participate in supernatural properties (namely the *aphtharsia*), then this also presupposes that the nature remains in its naturalness.[123] These reflections make no impression on the Aphthartologue. He maintains his fundamental thesis: passibility is bestowed on the body of Christ by way of miracle; uncorruptedness and immortality, however, are the normal state, resulting from the *henosis*, a state which shares the immutability of the indissoluble laws of nature.[124]

In this context, however, the incorporation of the human will of Christ and its freedom into the question of the acceptance of suffering is more important for us than the 'normalization' of the concrete human existence. Here Leontius really touches on something self-evident, but which apparently was not so easy to discover. One must go back as far as Gregory of Nyssa to discover a similar emphasis on the will of Christ. Admittedly the Cappadocian does not address the situations of suffering in the life of Christ, but the opposite, the 'exception', the working of miracles by Jesus. Because the text is of great significance for the development of the Greek picture of Christ, we shall cite it fully and place it

121. *Ibid.*, 1332B.
122. *Ibid.*, 1333CD.
123. *Ibid.*, 1333D6–7: οὐδὲ γὰρ τὰ ὑπὲρ φύσιν ἔχει χώραν, μὴ τῆς φύσεως ἐχούσης κατὰ φύσιν.
124. *Ibid.*, 1333D.

in the framework of a prehistory for the text of Leontius cited above, indeed as well for the representation of the monoenergist controversy. It was certainly quite an unreasonable imposition on Gregory's audience in the paschal vigil to receive such difficult theological reflections.[125]

> When the Holy Spirit descended on the Virgin and the power of the Most High overshadowed her, in order to allow the new human being to come into existence in her ... at that time, Wisdom built herself her house and through the overshadowing of the power, as it were like through the imprint of a seal the material (*plasma*) was stamped from within, at that time the divine power mixed with both parts, out of which the human nature consists, both with the soul, I mean, as also with the body, by mixing with each of the two parts in him in corresponding ways. Then after these two had become mortal through disobedience (because death of the soul was the alienation from real life, the death of the body, however, decay and dissolution), death must be driven out of these two by the mingling of life. Because the divinity was mingled with each of the two parts of the human being in the corresponding manner, were the signs of recognition (*gnorismata*) the paramount nature [namely of the divinity] evident through both [soul and body].
>
> For the body refers to the divinity [dwelling] in it by effecting healing through its touch; the soul, however, proves the divine power by that powerful will; for as the sense of touch is proper to the body, so is the movement of choice (ἡ κατὰ προαίρεσιν κίνησις) proper to the soul.
>
> There the leper approaches, already emaciated and wasted in body. How on the Lord's part does the healing happen for this person? The soul (*psyche*) posits the act of the will and the body touches and through both (together) suffering vanishes; the leprosy left him, it reads, on the spot (cf. Mt 8,3). On another occasion he did not want to dismiss starving the many thousands crowding around him in the desert; so he broke the bread with his hands.
>
> You see, how through both [through act of the will and touch] the divinity which dwells in both (συμπαρομαρτέω, συμπαρέπομαι) is known publicly, both through the deed of the body, as also through the act of the will of the soul (τῷ τε ἐνεργοῦντι σώματι καὶ τῇ ὁρμῇ τοῦ ἐν τῇ ψυχῇ γινομένου θελήματος).

Gregory of Nyssa here strikes the same chord as Theodore of Mopsuestia, who likewise saw the true justification of salvation endangered by the Apollinarian-Arian denial of the soul.[126] Unfortunately these realizations were again blocked in Cyril of Alexandria, as his explanation of the raising of the daughter of Jairus and the youth from Nain shows. The soul of Christ is not mentioned. The path is already laid which will lead to a new controversy that no longer has any room left for the soteriological activity of Christ's soul: monoenergism and monothelitism. In his commentary on John, Cyril intends to explain the efficacy of the bread of life (that is, the eucharist), promised and finally given by Christ. For him the foundation for this

125. Gregor. Nyss., *De trid. spat.*: *Op.* IX (E. Gebhardt), 291–292.
126. On this cf. *JdChr* I³, 619–22.

is the *energeia*, as this comes into play in the events where Christ raises people from the dead.[127]

> On this account, we find, the redeemer is active in raising the dead, not only through the word alone, nor even through simple divine orders, but he calls up the holy flesh as it were as a co-worker, in order to prove that it can bestow life [in the eucharist] and has become as it were one with it.
>
> When he raised the daughter of the ruler of the synagogue: 'Little girl, get up', he took her hand, as it is written (Mk 5,35–37 par.): with his order that effects everything (παντουργῷ προστάγματι) he made her alive as God; he also made her alive, however, through contact with his holy flesh, and consequently showed the one activity that has grown together from both (μίαν τε καὶ συγγενῆ δι'ἀμφοῖν ἐπιδείκνυσι τὴν ἐνέργειαν) ... [Then there follows the explanation of the raising at Nain (Lk 7,13–17) and finally the summation:] he wants to raise the dead not only by word, but, in order to prove that his body bestows life, ... he touches the dead and through it [his body] gives life into those already putrifying.

It must strike one that now the soul of Christ, as one cause participating in the raising, is missing. Logos and *sarx* are contrasted directly. But they once again combine in their activity into 'a single kind of activity' of nothing less than growing mutuality. Without doubt the fourth letter of Ps. Dionysius the Areopagite[128] refers to this passage of Cyril, when his formula speaks of the 'simply new theandric *energeia*', which Christ executes among us. Before we are able to go into this important letter in detail, let us only refer to the fact that in the explanation of the activity of Jesus Christ in the miracles we see two lines present from the fourth to the sixth century: the Cyrillian-Areopagite, which is unreservedly affirmed by Severus, and the line of Gregory of Nyssa, which is undoubtedly again accepted by Leontius of Byzantium. The level of reflection attained by Leontius is even higher than that of Gregory, because he has discussion partners who stand on the ground of Chalcedon and thus really affirm the dialectic of 'unmingled and undivided'. Leontius is not content with formally stressing this tension, but he understands that the concrete life of Jesus in its normality has to be placed there as the real accomplishment of the economy of salvation. Jesus, as a true human being, stands there with his intellectuality and power of will, but this in the full power of his divinity, and thus mediates the effects of redemption. The Aphthartics have fallen prey to an unhealthy supra-naturalism — a word that we can derive from the linguistic formulation of Leontius himself. He shows even Jesus the human being as a finite spiritual power needing the help of God's grace,

---

127. Cyril Alex., *In Ioann. Ev.* IV: PG 73, 577C3–D8; P. E. Pusey, *S.P.N. Cyrilli ... in D. Ioannis ev.*, Vol. 1, p. 530,8–26.
128. Ps. Dionys. Ar., *Ep. IV ad Gaium* (CPG 6607): PG 3, 1072. See *JdChr* II/3.

which, however, stands at his disposal by virtue of his dignity as Son, but still does not annul the 'nature' in him.

The Chalcedonian defender of thoroughgoing *aphtharsia*, driven into a corner, now seeks refuge in protology, that is, in referring to the original condition of Adam in Paradise, with whom he compares Christ.

(c) Passibility and mortality of Christ in the light of protology

The *aphtharsia* of Christ seemed to suggest itself on the basis of the horizon of a larger history of salvation. Jesus was regarded by Paul as the new Adam (cf. 1 Cor 15,20–22; Col 1,18; Rom 5,12–18; Gen 3,17–19).

> But how could he be called this, if he had not borne the body of the one first created [= Adam]? But this first created one was incorruptible, before he sinned. Hence too the body of the Lord is uncorrupted. For he was always without sin.

The *aphtharsia*, which in these words is presupposed for Adam and Christ, is different from the one which Julian of Halicarnassus had accepted. 'To be uncorrupted' means here 'to be by nature incapable of corruption and mortality',[129] or, expressed positively, to be uncorrupted by reason of a 'reconstruction' of a normal human nature into something superhuman, and this on the basis of the *henosis* with the Logos.[130] According to Julian, let us recall, Christ's individual human nature was from the very beginning in general human terms normal, insofar as the physical qualities were concerned. The 'exception', which made Christ 'uncorrupted', was the freedom from that necessity to be delivered over to suffering and death, which burdened the sons of Adam because of the *peccatum naturae*. To be passible and mortal was possible for Jesus without a miracle; the fact that both were apportioned to him did not bear the character of a curse on Adam, because the new Adam could choose with regard to his destiny in freedom. But Leontius' discussion partner was not satisfied with this version of *aphtharsia*. Jesus had also to be physically impassible. For had he assumed a passible, mortal nature, he would have had enough to do to save himself and to defeat death. We, however, would have been left in the cold.[131]

Because protology, as the teaching about the original condition of

---

129. On the sinlessness of Christ see PG 86, 1348B. R. Draguet, *Julien d'Halicarnasse* (Louvain, 1924), 177, places great value on the contrasting of Julian to the aphthartic in the *CA* of Leontius; pp. 173–4 against J. C. L. Gieseler and R. Seeberg. Also to be noted is the controversy between Draguet (*op. cit.*, 201–4) and M. Jugie, art. 'Gaianite (Controverse)', in *DTC* 6 (1915), 1002–23.

130. Cf. Leontius Byz., *CA*: PG 86, 1325A; 1328D–1329B.

131. *Ibid.*, 1332B.

human beings, was brought into play, one might expect that Leontius would not only develop his christology in detail, but also his teaching about the original condition. However, he does not want to take a position with regard to the original quality of Adam's body, although he indicates that he does not consider the doctrine of Adam's paradisal *aptharsia* convincing.[132] Obviously he does not wish to open up too much territory to his opponent in an initial skirmish. Besides, he distinguishes two things, *aphtharsia* and *athanasia*. All admit that Adam died. According to Leontius it is more difficult to decide about his uncorruptedness with regard to sin. He requests, however, that one weigh the fact that Christ in coming chose the form of his body not only with regard to Adam, but also with regard to us. Why should Christ have made his choice only with regard to the one and his (Adam's) uncorrupted body, and not rather with regard to the corruptedness of the many? If Christ actually assumed a corruptible body with regard to the many, then, according to Leontius, everything speaks for the fact that Adam too is to be subsumed under that. Hence he can ask: 'For what reason should the body of the first created have been incorruptible? He did not have immortality in his constitution [which is proved through the fact of his death: 1348B], much less so incorruptibility. For it would have been different had he not used the wood [the tree] of life. The transgression did away with his chance of actually enjoying it, as the Fathers say.'[133] Still Leontius does not want to make any final decision about Adam's original state. The problem being considered regarding the corruptedness of Christ's body must also be solved without it. It is a question of the redemption of humankind as this actually happens from the fall of Adam. Thus at the conclusion of *CA* the problem is once again referred back to the context of *henosis* and *aphtharsia*.

(d) Christ's uncorruptedness — conception through the Spirit — henosis
On the basis of his *henosis* concept the Aphthartic maintains an immediate exceptional situation for the humanity of Christ, beginning with the incarnation, while for the Christians it is a gift 'in hope' (cf. Rom 8,18–30). This claim challenges Leontius to a concluding exposition.[134] In the thesis of his opponent he finds a denial of the historicity of the order of the incarnation: 'Thus from the very beginning of the

132. *Ibid.*, 1348D.
133. *Ibid.*, 1348C.
134. *Ibid.*, 1349D–1353C.

mystery we have the whole mystery already. Hence the rest of the *oikonomia* was superfluous.'[135] 'Further detours' (*periodoi*) would not be necessary. The *henosis* concept is overloaded. Leontius attempts to free it from this excessive demand. To some extent he is successful with his distinction between the historical process for forming the body of Christ, the λόγος τῆς οὐσιώσεως τοῦ σώματος, and the event of the union as such, which he renders by his favourite phrase, the 'manner of union', the τρόπος τῆς ἐνώσεως.[136]

> The former occurred by virtue of the presence and indwelling of the Spirit by way of creative formation (δημιουργικῶς διαπλάττειν), the latter not by reason of the activity of the Logos (οὐκ ἐκ τῆς τοῦ Λόγου ἐνεργείας), but by virtue of the perfect and essential union (ὁλικὴ καὶ οὐσιώδης ἔνωσις).

The two acts, which affect the earthly existence of Jesus, are delineated in more detail with regard to their peculiarity and attribution. Each has its own bearer, each its particular object. The becoming of the body, its *ousiosis*, is set in motion by the creative activity (δημιουργικὴ ἐνέργεια) of the *Holy Spirit*, who bestows fertility on the Virgin, who for her part contributes the *hyle*, the matter. The share of the Logos is determined in this way: he inhabits immediately, with the beginning of his formation, the temple founded by the Holy Spirit (κατ' αὐτὴν τὴν πρώτην ἐνοικεῖ διάπλασιν). This happening is not characterized as 'activity' (*energeia*), which immediately reminds us of Nemesius, but as essential, total self-communication (ἀλλ' ἐκ τῆς πρὸς αὐτὸν ὁλικῆς καὶ οὐσιώδους ἐνώσεως). With the beginning of the work of the Holy Spirit, the *henosis* also commences. It occurs already in the womb, in the 'workplace' of the formation of the human nature of the Logos. The Logos is, as it were, in the centre of a construction site. Through the activity of the Spirit there occurs around him the construction of his earthly abode, which he will not enter from the outside, but has united to himself from within (συναφθείς), to the adornment of our nature.[137] Because the body of Christ was formed slowly, step by step, one can recognize that the *henosis* as such does not entail the

---

135. *Ibid.*, 1352C1–3.

136. *Ibid.*, 1352CD.

137. *Ibid.*, 1352D–1353A. In the terminology and images used in this text (temple, indwelling, the term *synapheia*) the Antiochene material attracts attention. Here one will be reminded of Proclus of Constantinople, who is perhaps immediately meant by Leontius in the words: 'one among us has very elegantly said . . .' Proclus has the image of the 'workshop of the *henosis* of the natures' (in the womb of the Virgin). Cf. PG 65, 681A11; ACO I 1, 1, p. 103,13; Severus Ant., *Or. 2 ad Neph.*: CSCO 120, p. 33,16, where the phrase of Proclus is cited.

demand to accept a perfect state of bodiliness,[138] but remains open for accepting our body in its condition, as it existed after the fall of Adam.[139]

> The Lord united to himself according to the *hypostasis* such a flesh with which the condemned (Adam) appeared clothed after the fall; we are all, however, from his mass.

According to Leontius the activity of the Holy Spirit in the virginal conception of Christ does not effect an uncorrupted body, so to say, *ab ovo*, but one which could in principle accept suffering and corruptibility, without having to be moved into a situation of exception (= miracle) by the Logos. That is a worthwhile piece of knowledge, which we will find quite lacking in a later Ethiopic text. Leontius only demands a supernatural intervention for preservation from corruption (*phtharsia*) in the powerful deed of the resurrection. In contrast the *henosis*, the union or assumption of the humanity through the Logos, effects (a) the sinlessness of Christ, (b) the perfect holiness, (c) the unity of Sonship.[140]

> The singularity [peculiarity] of the body cannot be known from the union with the Logos, but from the power of the Holy Spirit, who forms the body itself without the original organs (procreative organs) of nature; the union of the Logos with our nature, however, has effected freedom from sin, the entire holiness and complete union and blending (*henosin kai anakrasin*) with the whole assuming (Logos), the unity of sonship in being and in appellation and the whole appearance of the condition of the Son (καὶ ὅλης τῆς υἱικῆς ἰδιότητος τοὺς χαρακτῆρας φανοτάτους ἐπιφαίνεσθαι). For this reason the gracing is inseparable, because indeed the union is inseparable (ὧν ἀναφαίρετος ἡ μακαριότης, ἐπειδὴ καὶ ἡ ἕνωσις ἀδιαίρετος).[141] Thus we recognize that the constitution and peculiarity of the body have proceeded from the activity of the Holy Spirit; the union, however, does not derive from the pure activity of the Logos, but from the substantial union with the Logos himself.

138. Leontius Byz., *CA*: PG 86, 1353A. It is expressed differently in Leontius Jer., *CN* IV 9: PG 86, 1669BC.

139. Leontius Byz., *CA*: PG 86, 1348D.

140. *Ibid.*, 1353A3–B3.

141. M. Jugie, 'La béatitude et la science parfaite de l'âme de Jésus viateur d'après Léonce de Byzance', *RSPT* 10 (1921), 548–59; *idem*, 'Quaedam testimonia byzantinorum de glorificatione humanitatis Christi a primo instanti conceptionis', *Angelicum* 9 (1932), 469–71, wanted to discover in these words the doctrine of the beatific vision in the earthly Jesus. In opposition to this V. Grumel, 'Le surnaturel dans l'humanité du Christ viateur, d'après Léonce de Byzance', in *Mélanges Mandonnet* II (Paris, 1930) (15–22), 21–2; *idem*, 'La sotériologie de Léonce de Byzance', *EO* 36 (1937) (385–97), 394, especially n. 3: the part of the sentence which reads ὧν ἀναφαίρετος ἡ μακαριότης, ἐπειδὴ καὶ ἡ ἕνωσις ἀδιαίρετος is only a *genetivus epexegeticus*. For with regard to content *makariotes* denotes the *bona* which the *henosis* signifies for Christ. It encompasses, namely, freedom from sin, permeating holiness, complete union with the Logos, and the title of Son. Similarly, P. Galtier, 'L'enseignement des Pères sur la Vision béatifique dans le Christ', *RSR* 15 (1925), 54–62.

THE EXPANDED CIRCLE OF STRICT-CHALCEDONIAN THEOLOGIANS OF THE TYPE OF LEONTIUS OF BYZANTIUM

The witnesses of strict-Chalcedonian christology of the kind expressed by Leontius of Byzantium are small in number and of varying theological significance. The first to be mentioned is a metropolitan of Ephesus, an episcopal see which otherwise was orientated towards Alexandria.

I. HYPATIUS, ARCHBISHOP OF EPHESUS (531–c.538)

1. Biographical notes

According to his public appearances Hypatius must rank as one of the outstanding bishops of the Imperial Church in the first half of the sixth century.[1] Emperor Justinian had become aware of him and on several occasions called on him to carry out important commissions. These concerned the Chalcedonian politics of the Emperor. The first occasion for this occurred in April 531. When the great Abba Sabas, as the delegate of the bishops of Palestine, was approaching Constantinople, Hypatius, together with Papas Eusebius and under the leadership of Patriarch Epiphanius of Constantinople (520–535),[2] had to journey to meet him and escort him into the Imperial City.[3] Considerably more important was his being summoned to participate in the so-called *Collatio cum Severianis*, which was held in 532 in the capital. This must be regarded as the major theological event in the life of the Metropolitan of Ephesus.[4] The third imperial commission led to Rome, where Hypatius, together with Demetrius, the bishop of Philippi, had to travel as Justinian's envoys to Pope John II. If in the doctrinal dialogue of 532

---

1. See F. Diekamp, *Analecta Patristica* = OCA 117 (Rome, 1938), 109–53: VII. Hypatius von Ephesus; J. Gouillard, 'Hypatius d'Éphèse ou Du Pseudo-Denys à Théodore Studite', *RevÉtByz* 19 (1961), 63–75; Y.-M. Duval, *Le livre de Jonas dans la littérature chrétienne grecque et latine. Sources et influence du Commentaire sur Jonas de saint Jérôme* (Paris, 1973), 657–62.
2. See Grumel, *Regestes* I², nos. 217–227.
3. Cf. Cyril Scyth., *Vita Sabae*, no. 71: E. Schwartz, *Kyrillos von Skythopolis* (Leipzig, 1939), p. 173,12–19; F. Diekamp, *Die origenistischen Streitigkeiten im sechsten Jahrhundert* (Münster, 1899), 14–15; *idem, Hypatius von Ephesus* = OCA 117, 109.
4. See F. Diekamp, *Hypatius von Ephesus* = OCA 117, 110–111; 112–115.

it was a question of winning the Severans for Chalcedon, then for the delegation to Rome it was a question of a current issue that was prompted by the controversial formula: 'one of the Trinity, Jesus of Nazareth, the son of the Virgin Mary, was crucified'. By denying this sentence several Sleepless Monks caused unrest. Their condemnation by the Pope was the goal which the two bishops had to reach in Rome.[5] The last transmitted report on Hypatius that bears a date concerns his participation in the *Synodos Endemousa* of Constantinople under Patriarch Menas (536–552).[6] It took place from 2 May to 4 June 536 and was concerned with the deposition of the Severan-minded Patriarch Anthimus,[7] which with the agreement of the Emperor had already been declared by Pope Agapetus in February or the beginning of March 536. Hypatius cast his vote in the fourth session.[8] In the final session there followed the anathema on Severus of Antioch, Peter of Apamea and Zooras. Hypatius probably spoke in the name of all the synodal participants.[9] For he signed the *acta* immediately after Patriarch Menas and before the Latins present, that is, those who had accompanied Pope Agapetus, who had died in Constantinople in the previous April.[10] A final testimony to the episcopal activity of Hypatius comes from the year 537 or 538.[11] The date of his death is unknown.

2. Hypatius of Ephesus as a christological author

From the few remains of his theological works only fragments of *catenae* can be investigated with regard to christology.[12] Apart from the reference to the legendary death of Arius and its extraordinary

5. *Ibid.*, 111. Cf. Justinian emp., *Ep. ad Iohannem II papam* (CPG 6874).

6. Grumel, *Regestes* I², nos. 232–43.

7. On Patriarch Anthimus, who, as bishop of Trebizond, and without having a successor there, uncanonically occupied the see of Constantinople, see E. Schwartz, *Kyrillos von Skythopolis*, 396–8. Anthimus had been ordained as an orthodox confessor of the four synods (ACO III, p. 31,21); he had also accepted the *Tomus* of Leo; both only 'for appearance sake'. Moreover he had promised the Emperor to do everything which the encumbent of the Apostolic See prescribed. But the Patriarch belonged to the protégés of Theodora, even in his 'Chalcedonian period'. Schwartz, *op. cit.*, 398, n. 3, conjectures that in the winter of 535/536 Anthimus was gained by Severus for the Aposchists (Severans). Through the mediation of Theodora the two met, as John of Beth Aphthonia reports. See PO 2, 254. Pope Agapetus was well informed about Anthimus from various sides and dismissed him as an uncanonically appointed usurper, without investigating his stance on Chalcedon. Schwartz, *op. cit.*, 397, nn. 1 and 6.

8. ACO III, 178–9, no. 126.

9. Cf. F. Diekamp, *Hypatius*, OCA 117, 115; ACO III, p. 182, no. 131,2.

10. Cf. ACO III, 182, no. 131,6–12.

11. See F. Diekamp, *op. cit.*, 115, 117.

12. *Ibid.*, 115–153, especially 129–153.

remembrance in the streets of Constantinople in the commentary on Zachariah (VIII),[13] no reference is found to events in the history of doctrine. Even the allegorical interpretation of prophetical texts in the Old Testament as referring to Christ, though they are relatively numerous, does not go beyond the customary exegesis of the Fathers. Thus as the main source for the christology of Hypatius there remain the discussions at the doctrinal dialogue in 532. There exist extensive reports about these from both parties, the Chalcedonians and Severans. The fact that we have a double report of these discussions has only become clear quite recently. Because of this recent research theological evaluation of the event now has a secure foundation.

(a) The sources[14]

(i) On the Chalcedonian side

Bishop Innocent of Maronia gives an extensive report of the doctrinal dialogue of 532 (in the following = I), in the form of a letter to the presbyter, Thomas of Thessaloniki, which is now extant only in Latin:[15] 'It [the report] goes so much beyond a private letter that the addressee could be regarded as a literary fiction. To a large extent it fulfils the requirements of minutes, and in some passages expands to become a historico-theological investigation of the questions raised. Instructional comments and a pedagogical art of evening out the argumentation and, as it were, drumming it in by repetition, certainly originate from the compiler of the minutes. Soon after the dialogue, the report did such sterling service for an episcopal delegation of the Emperor to the Pope in Rome that one is tempted to ask whether at least some parts of the report were written specifically for this purpose.'[16] In these sentences we have an apposite description of the peculiarity of the Chalcedonian report.

(ii) On the Severan side

Credit for discovering new documents and of giving order to the whole of the material is due to S. P. Brock.

13. *Ibid.*, 146; also A. Grillmeier, *Mit ihm und in ihm* (Freiburg, Basel, Vienna, [2]1978), 237–8, n. 31.

14. On the new state of the sources see (1) S. Brock, 'The conversations with the Syrian Orthodox under Justinian (532)', *OCP* 47 (1981), 87–121; (2) J. Speigl, 'Das Religionsgespräch mit den severianischen Bischöfen in Konstantinopel im Jahre 532', *AHC* 16 (1984), 264–85; *JdChr* II/1, 370–5.

15. Innocent Maron., *Ep. ad Thomam presb. Thessalonicensem de collatione cum Severianis habita* (CPG 6846): ACO IV, 2, 169–184. A writing of Innocent on the theopaschite formula (CPG 6847) will be referred to further below. On the rôle of Patriarch Epiphanius of Constantinople in the convocation (531) and conduct (532) of the doctrinal dialogue, see Grumel, *Regestes* I[2], no. 222a with literature.

16. See J. Speigl, *art. cit.*, 265, who stresses the character of the 'court minutes', but also accepts that the text was written on the basis of a real experience by a participant who was filled with admiration for the proceedings.

(1) The *Plerophoria* on the faith of the Severan bishops summoned by Emperor Justinian, which they presented to the Emperor.[17] These function as a certain check for the other sources still to be mentioned, and at the same time they expand them.

(2) A Syriac report (S) 'from what the orthodox [= Severan] bishops said in the presence of the Emperor, when they were summoned by him to make an *apologia* concerning the true faith and to suggest a way by which the Churches might be (re)united'.[18] The Emperor and the Syrian bishops appear here as the real partners. The discussion between the two groups of bishops is mentioned only briefly. Important is the list of bishops who participated in the *collatio* (S 8).

(3) A new Syrian text (Harvard syr 22)(= H), discovered and edited with an English translation by S. P. Brock.[19] The report begins with the second meeting of the Syrian bishops with the Emperor. It breaks off with the depiction of the combined audience with the Emperor on the third day of the dialogue. Both reports, S and H, are closely related. Probably S depends on H, because in parts literal correspondence can be established.[20] In H we have detailed information about the *collatio* from the Severan point of view, concerning the events of the two days of dialogue and the combined audience with the Emperor on the third day. The editor, S. P. Brock, attributes his find with great probability to Abbot John of Beth Aphthonia, who is mentioned in the church history of Zacharias Rhetor (cont.) as accompanying the Syrian bishops and reporting on the doctrinal dialogue.[21]

(b) The character of the collatio

The two main sources, I and H, show that the 'confessionalization' of both parties, Chalcedonians and anti-Chalcedonians, is already well advanced, although both still know that they are tied to the Imperial Church.[22] Interesting too is the model for selecting the participants in the dialogue. Let us first take the group around Hypatius: from the European part of the Empire (Thrace) come John of Bizya (Europa province) and Innocent of Maronia (Rhodope province); from Macedonia (Macedonia prima) comes Demetrius of Philippi; Asia Minor is represented by Anthimus of Trebizond and Stephen of Seleucia in Isauria. The Greek motherland does not

---

17. Preserved in Zacharias Rhetor cont., *HE* IX, 15: CSCO 84 (T), 115–123; 88 (V), 79–84. Here characterized by J. Speigl, *art. cit.*, 265–6, as G (Glaubenserklärung: exposition of faith).

18. Edited by F. Nau with a French translation: PO 13 (1919), 192–196. S. Brock, *art. cit.*, 113–17, proposes far-reaching corrections to Nau, and he himself produces a new English translation (he regrets that this text was previously overlooked in research); 117–18: analysis of the double list of names.

19. See S. Brock, *art. cit.*, 92–113. HarvSyr22 is damaged at the beginning. Cf. J. Speigl, *art. cit.*, 266–7.

20. Cf. J. Speigl, *art. cit.*, 266, n. 17.

21. On John of Beth Aphthonia see CPG 7484–5; Zacharias Rhetor cont., *HE* IX, 15: Brooks CSCO 84 (T), 115–123; CSCO 88 (V), 79–84; Hamilton-Brooks, 246–53; corrected translation in Frend, 362–4.

22. Cf. F. Winkelmann, *Die östlichen Kirchen in der Epoche der christologischen Auseinandersetzungen (5. bis 7. Jahrhundert) = Kirchengeschichte in Einzeldarstellungen* I/6 (Berlin, 1980), 133: 'It is also to be borne in mind that even until the end of the sixth century the anti-Chalcedonians did not develop a contrary political-theological conception, but stood on the ground of the Byzantine Emperor–Church relationship, as long as there existed the hope that monophysitism could have been the major ideological foundation.' *Ibid.*, 102, reference to the imperial conviction of the banned Severan bishops in the petition which they addressed to Justinian after the suppression of the Nika riot (532), according to Zacharias Rhetor cont., *HE* IX, 15 and Michael Syr., *Chron.* IX, 22. Emperor Justinian nevertheless regards the Severans as 'separated from the Church'. Cf. I 4: ACO IV, 2, p. 169,18: *pro his qui cum Severo episcopo ab ecclesia desciverunt.* Both sides, however, considered themselves as 'orthodox'.

provide a participant. Nevertheless one can speak of a 'good spread' in the origin of the members of the commission: 'Trebizond in the extreme East of Cappadocian Pontus, Seleucia in South-East Cilicia of Asia Minor and Ephesus, located in the middle of Western Asia Minor, are three points, geometrically so well chosen, that one could hang on them in a balanced way the entire weight of the Asia Minor countryside.'[23] All those summoned come from the Patriarchate of Constantinople, with the exception of the bishops of Seleucia (Patriarchate of Antioch) and Philippi, which is already to be reckoned as belonging to the Roman sphere of influence. On the Syrian side the following certainly take part in the *collatio*: Sergius of Cyrrhus, Thomas of Germanicia, Philoxenus of Doliche, Peter of Theodosiopolis (Rēš'ainā), John of Constantina or Tella, and Nonnus of Circesium.[24] Both parties have a small number of clerics and monks with them. Among the Chalcedonians Leontius of Byzantium stands out; among the Severans on the other side Abbot John of Beth Aphthonia is prominent, who according to Zacharias Rhetor cont. (*HE* IX 15) 'had accompanied the bishops to Constantinople, composed a report, and for that reason may have been the author of the Syriac minutes'.[25]

(c) The goal of the doctrinal dialogue

Patricius Strategius, who was to report to the Emperor on the development of the discussions and occupied a place of honour in the assembly, explained to the Severan participants that the Emperor had summoned them not 'in imperial authority, but in paternal and priestly concern (*compunctione*)', so that they could present to the Chalcedonians their uncertainties, to which the bishops would have to respond.[26] According to the Emperor's intention Chalcedon was *in possessione*. No compromise was to be sought. No resolutions were to be prepared. Thus it was not a matter of a synod, but of a panel to provide theological information. On the one side were the leading supporters of the Council, which in the eyes of the Emperor was not contestable, and on the other representatives of the Severan-Alexandrian opposition, among whom it was assumed there were inhibiting difficulties which were, however, capable of being resolved. The *collatio* of 532 was thus thought of as a doctrinal dialogue on the theological level, with the aim of clarifying the Severan uncertainties and of restoring ecclesial unity.[27]

(d) The course of the doctrinal dialogue

We may suppose that there were problems enough, such as: What do you Chalcedonians understand by *hypostasis* when you contrast *physis* with it? How do you envisage the realization of the *henosis* in Christ, when he is understood as strictly 'one', and yet exhibits two realities, two natures? How do you get around Nestorianism? We would thus have to expect from the Severan side a whole catalogue of questions that would be handled point by point. This group would have been in a position to determine the course of the dialogue simply on their own basis, according to purely pertinent aspects. Above all, accusations should not take the place of enquiries. We can thus expect that in the minutes of the Severans (H) this excellent intention of the Emperor would manifest itself in the first place and that question after question would be presented. But there is great disappointment. From H we learn that Hypatius was the first to

23. J. Speigl, *art. cit.*, 269.
24. Cf. I 6: ACO IV, 2, pp. 169,26–170,1; J. Speigl, *art. cit.*, 271–2, where the disparities between the lists of participants are discussed.
25. *Ibid.*, 272; S. Brock, *art. cit.*, 118.
26. Thus in I 8: ACO IV, 2, 170.
27. J. Speigl, *art. cit.*, 273, who chooses the expression 'religious dialogue'. Because it is not a question of a difference in religion, but of differences in faith, we prefer to speak of a 'doctrinal dialogue'.

speak, and that he produced 'his usual old inanities' (H 4, p. 94).[28] According to I 9 (ACO IV, 2, p. 170) the Orientals began the dialogue. Their speaker was perhaps Sergius of Cyrrhus, the old episcopal city of Theodoret.[29] He refers to the *plerophoria* presented to the Emperor, into which the Syrians had woven their uncertainties and everything that had become a scandal for them (in Chalcedon) (H 2; I 9). Therefore the *collatio* could have taken the path desired by the Emperor, if Hypatius were to concede that his party had read this text. In fact the Bishop of Ephesus makes reference to this document. From it he immediately singles out the fundamental view of the Severans, that is, the continuous condemnation of the Council of Chalcedon expressed in it. Instead of enquiry, there is thus accusation! What the Chalcedonians reproached the Severans with is what the Severans criticized with regard to the imperial representatives: they would produce accusations against orthodox Fathers in order to forestall an examination of 'their own wicked beliefs' (H 4).

First Day: The problem of Eutyches

According to H 4, Hypatius attempted to put the Syrians in the wrong with the statement that in the *plerophoria* they attacked Chalcedon, which was, however, directed against Eutyches. Apropos of this he had the catchcry, rather the question: What do you Syrians think of Eutyches (I 10: ACO IV, 2, 170)? They bluntly anathematized the Archimandrite (H 5; cf. I 10). Yet there awaited the next question: How can you then describe Patriarch Dioscorus as orthodox (according to I 11: ACO IV, 2, 170), even though in 449 at Ephesus with the bishops he declared the heretic Eutyches to be orthodox, but condemned Patriarch Flavian and the Bishop of Dorylaum as heretics? The Syriac report (H 4-9) confirms that the theme Eutyches-Dioscorus formed the main object of the first day's discussion. Agreement prevailed between both parties with regard to the condemnation of Eutyches, for whom, in fact, not one of the great leaders of the anti-Chalcedonians even interceded. It was otherwise with Dioscorus, who had presided at the imperial Council of Ephesus II (449), at whose instigation Eutyches had been rehabilitated (cf. I 11-14: ACO II, 4, pp. 170,34-171,5). The Syrians were angered by this point (H 4), because the attack was then concentrated on Dioscorus, after the scandal about Eutyches had been removed. Nevertheless, it was with satisfaction that they established that Hypatius had also condemned the Alexandrian Patriarch not on account of his teaching, but on account of his indiscretions in treating questions of faith.[30] The Chalcedonians, however, sought to incriminate Dioscorus especially, because they wanted to take away from the Syrians the reason for doubting and calling into question the legitimacy and necessity of a new council after the Imperial Council of 449.[31] As a common result for the first day Innocent of Maronia wanted to record the conviction on both sides that Chalcedon had been legally summoned and was to be received, in so far as Eutyches had been condemned and the 'general council' of Dioscorus had been thus corrected.[32] By establishing this, however, Hypatius aimed not only at a general

28. We follow the text H in S. Brock, giving the numbers and pages; and text I according to ACO IV, 2.

29. Thus the conjecture of J. Speigl, *art. cit.*, 273, n. 59, with reference to E. Honigmann, *Evêques et Evêchés*, 68-70, which is to be supplemented by the introduction in S (PO 13, 192; Brock, 113). In S Sergius is named first among the participants in the *collatio*.

30. Thus H 9: S. Brock, *art. cit.*, 96.94.117; S 8: PO 13, 196; cf. *JdChr* I³, 734-7; *CCT* II/1, 46-7.

31. What is striking is that in I, 17: ACO IV, 2, 171, Ephesus II (449) is described as *concilium universale*. On this see H. J. Sieben, *Die Konzilsidee der Alten Kirche* (Paderborn, Munich, Vienna, Zürich, 1979), 247-50.

32. Cf. I 18: ACO IV, 2, p. 171,23-5. On the question whether the 'injustices and blindnesses of that general council' (= Ephesus II) have to be corrected by another universal council, the *contradicentes* answer: 'In every regard it had to happen this way.' To which Hypatius says: 'Thus

affirmation of the Fourth Council, but concretely at the recognition of its two-natures teaching. But the Syrians would have nothing to do with this. The main reason for the dissent thus did not come to the fore on the first day. The intermediate solution of a partial recognition of Chalcedon, insofar as it was ratified at all by the Syrians and was not simply present in the Chalcedonian reporting of the dialogue, did not accomplish very much. 'For this reason the question that now remained was what this Council had done incorrectly so that further talk and response about it could be conceded to them [the Syrians].'[33]

Second Day: A mistake made by the Council of Chalcedon?

With the question about possible mistakes made by the Fourth Council the discussion could once again have been steered along the lines determined by the Emperor. The Syrians once again had the chance to begin with their doubts and reservations with regard to Chalcedon. For they began anew by referring to their *plerophoria*, which was even read out. Subsequently, however, they did not take up the question about the 'mistakes' of the Council, but directed attention to their own document: 'Say if you have anything you find fault with in this statement (*plerophoria*).'[34] This text, however, contained a sharp rejection of Leo's Tome and the definition of Chalcedon. The whole Council was thus in error, and the concession made on the first day to a partial recognition of the Fourth Council we may suppose was once again rescinded. Nevertheless once again the Chalcedonians took up the question raised the previous day, namely, what else was wrong with the Council?[35] The Syrians replied: the reacceptance of Bishop Ibas of Edessa in spite of his controversial letter to the Persian Mari, and of Theodoret of Cyrrhus.[36]

It is here that the lines of the discussion diverged: with these two names the Syrians steered towards the painful theme of the later dispute about the three names, the so-called Three Chapters (Ibas, Theodore of Mopsuestia, Theodoret), while, according to the report of Innocent of Maronia, Bishop Hypatius brought the dialogue first to the two-natures teaching. In their reports each of the two parties claimed victory for itself.[37] For the moment we shall postpone the discussion about the two names and consider only the dispute about the two natures, so that we can form a judgement about the state of christology according to the conception of Hypatius, regardless of how the dialogue may have proceeded historically.

According to I 21 (ACO IV, 2, p. 171,40ff.) the two-natures formula was from the very start the theme of the second day's discussion. After a brief recapitulation of the first day and after having established agreement about whether the Fourth Council had been summoned legally (I 19–21), Hypatius introduced the formula, with the question to the Severans: 'What do you reproach the Council with as a transgression, so that we can give an account of it?' The Severans

Chalcedon is a lawfully summoned council, so that those things which a universal council lacked, or, as you say, saw less (correctly), could be corrected by a universal council.' The Severans say to this: 'It was indeed summoned well and of necessity, if only it had also found a proper conclusion.' The two-natures teaching indeed ruined everything. To this partial acknowledgement of Chalcedon on the part of the Severans in I corresponds the cautious formulation in H 9: Brock 96, where without criticism the Chalcedonians can say 'that the synod of Chalcedon had met very usefully on the matter of Eutyches'.

33. See J. Speigl, *art. cit.*, 276, with reference to I 21 (171, 39f.); similarly H 13: Brock, 98.
34. Cf. H 12: Brock, 96.
35. Cf. H 13: Brock, 98. The question appears to be unjustified because of the restriction already mentioned, which is recorded in I 21: ACO IV, 2, p. 171,38–9: Chalcedon indeed began lawfully, but did not find a proper conclusion: . . . *si et iustum finem suscepisset*!
36. H 14: Brock, 98.
37. On the conflict over Ibas and Theodoret see H 18: Brock, 100 and I 78: ACO IV, 2, p. 182,21–22: *in his ergo dictis, contradicentes* (= the Syrians): *De his quidem persuasum est nobis*. On the conflict over the two natures see J. Speigl, *art. cit.*, 277.

answered: 'Above all, the novelty of the two natures. While Cyril and his predecessors had proclaimed "out of two natures one incarnate nature of the Word of God after the union", they [the Fathers of 451] claimed the novelty of "in two natures".'[38] We shall treat each of the two reports separately.

(i) The two-natures theme according to I

The provocative word 'novelty' induced Hypatius to clarify its scope. 'Novelty' could have (1) a positive sense, insofar as something which was not previously present, now, however, causes surprise as being new in content. But in this term (2) there could also lurk a rejection of true tradition, and thus it could also denote something harmful. The Syrians were now supposed to say in what sense they understood Chalcedon as a 'novelty'. They replied audaciously: 'In both respects.' In doing this they appealed to the tradition of the *mia-physis* formula, as they said it was to be found everywhere: in the Church of Alexandria (Cyril, Athanasius), in the Church of Rome (Popes Felix and Julius), in Asia Minor (Gregory the Wonderworker, Dionysius the Areopagite): 'All of them have determined (*decernentibus*) as binding one nature of the God-Logos after the union; but all of these [the Fathers of Chalcedon] have disregarded this and have presumed to proclaim two natures after the union.'[39] Thus they were the innovators, and innovators in the negative sense. The legitimate tradition was on the side of the Severans. Hypatius, however, called this tradition into question by skilfully tossing the word 'forgery' into the debate.

The so-called Apollinarian forgeries

In this way a long overdue theme was taken up publicly, namely the question of the legitimacy of the *mia-physis* formula as a *tessera* of orthodoxy. Through Cyril's authority it was able to develop its effectiveness between 428/429 and 532, thus over more than a century, without the critical question about its origin being persistently raised. The doubts of Bishop Hypatius certainly did not conform to the line of dialogue determined beforehand by Emperor Justinian, but they were, however, in order. With good reason we recall here Hypatius' theological adviser, Leontius of Byzantium, and his work *Against the deceits of the Apollinarians*.[40] Admittedly we

38. Cf. I 21: ACO IV, 2, 171: *Ante omnia duarum naturarum novitatem.*

39. Cf. I 22: ACO IV, 2, p. 172,2-7. M. Richard, 'Léonce de Jérusalem et Léonce de Byzance', *MSR* 1 (1944)(1-54), 51-53 = *Op. Min.* III, no. 59, [51]-[53], gives a brief analysis of the 'Fathers' named by the Severans and their texts. By 'Athanasius' we should understand Ps. Athanasius, *Quod unus sit Christus*: Lietzmann, *Apollinaris von Laodicea*, 296. On 'Felix' see Lietzmann, *op. cit.*, 318, frag. 186; on 'Julius' cf. Innocent Maron., *De Collat.* §25: ACO IV, 2, 173; on 'Gregory the Wonderworker' see Apollin., *He kata meros pistis*: ACO, *ibid.* On Ps. Dionys. Ar., *De divin. nominibus* I 4: Zacharias Rhetor cont., *HE* IX, 15: Brooks, CSCO 88, 82; PG 3, 592. M. Richard, *op. cit.*, [49]-[51], refers to the fact that in many passages this extract from the Severan florilegium coincides with the florilegium which Leontius of Jerusalem refutes in *C. Monophysitas*: PG 86, 1853A-1876C. His description fits exactly the *Professio fidei* which the Severans presented to Emperor Justinian: *De Coll.* §9: ACO IV, 2, 170. This *professio* only exists in an extract in Zacharias Rhetor cont., *HE* IX, 15: Brooks, CSCO 88, 83; M. Richard, *op. cit.*, [51]. This should also be regarded as an indication that Leontius of Jerusalem wrote in Constantinople.

40. See PG 86, 1948A-1976A; B. E. Daley, *Leontii Monachi Byzantini Opera*, no. 6 (= *AFA*); as an introduction, *ibid.*, LV-LVIII. Daley defends the plausible position that *AFA* was composed as a dossier for Bishop Hypatius and his dialogue partners of 532. The work is not a theological treatise, but a collection of materials from the works of Apollinarius and two of his students. The introduction (PG 86, 1948AB), a section in the middle of the text (*ibid.*,

should not expect from this collection in itself much for the outcome of the dialogue of 532, or for the subsequent attitude of the Severans. In their report H there was no direct or express comment on the proof of Hypatius, that the authorities adduced by the Orientals in favour of the 'out of two natures one' and the *mia-physis* formula were forgeries, a claim which must have certainly startled the Severans.[41] They would have nothing directly to do with it.[42] What is interesting, however, is the self-protective remark of the Severans in H 19 (Brock, 102), which follows the report about the reading out of the letter to Mari of Bishop Ibas of Edessa. After this the Chalcedonians were said to have been left speechless: 'In reply, the opposing bishops could find neither defence, nor (evidence of) *forgery*' (my italics). Because the authenticity of Ibas' letter was never disputed, this reference nevertheless bears witness to the fact that the Severans were made to feel insecure, this effect being achieved by the word 'forgeries'. One could now ask to what extent the work of Leontius of Byzantium (*AFA*) played a rôle in the dialogue of 532. Hypatius himself may have had difficulties with it, for the writing leaves it to the reader 'to undertake the work of comparison [between the texts manufactured under orthodox names and the works of Apollinarius and his school] and to draw the necessary conclusions . . . Not once does he draw attention to the fact that in nos. 6 and 7 the letter of Julius to Dionysius, in nos. 15 and 16 the writing *de unione*, in nos. 39 and 40 the *Kata meros pistis* of Gregory the Wonderworker are cited directly as the property of Apollinarius.'[43] Nevertheless with the reference of the Bishop of Ephesus to the falsified transmission of the *mia-physis* formula an impetus was given for further theological argumentation by the Chalcedonians, as the decades and centuries after 532 were to show.

What is striking is the fact that earlier doubts about the authenticity of the *mia-physis* texts had passed into oblivion.[44] After 532, however, remarks on this theme

1969AB) and some comments at the end (*ibid.*, 1973C–1976A) may be considered as Leontius' own contribution. The verifications for the citations from the various writings are recorded by Daley in the apparatus, and in one case there is also the comment: *fragmentum hic primo inventum*, that is, that Leontius is the first witness for this text.

41. Cf. I 22: ACO IV, 2, p. 172,3–7: besides Cyril they name Athanasius, Felix and Julius of Rome, Gregory the Wonderworker and Dionysius the Areopagite as *unam naturam dei verbi decernentibus post unitionem*, cf. S. P. Brock, *art. cit.*, 119 (I 22–8 has no corresponding passage in H).

42. H. Lietzmann, *Apollinaris von Laodicea*, 124, rightly comments that the Severans made no effort to defend the authenticity of the witnesses questioned by the Chalcedonians. For it would certainly have been their business to give thought to the legitimacy of the *mia-physis* tradition. However, in the meantime Cyril, the 'king of the dogmas' (Severus), and Severus himself had 'interpreted' and sanctioned this formula, and thus enabled its reception.

43. *Ibid.*, 106. Lietzmann has even more reservations with regard to Leontius' gathering of materials.

44. We call the following considerations briefly to mind: (1) It can be established that this is first recognized in the Roman uncials, as Leontius of Jerusalem, *C. monophys.* (CPG 6917), PG 86, 1865B, knows: of Pope Julius there is 'nothing to be found in the books of the archives' (instead of ἀρχαίων in this passage it should read ἀρχείων). A. Tuilier, 'Remarques sur les fraudes des Apollinaristes et des Monophysites', in J. Dummer, *TU* 133 (Berlin, 1987), 583, however, asks one to consider the fact that the archives of the Roman Church were destroyed under Diocletian and were only gradually restored under Damasus. (2) Roughly at the same time as the first declaration of the alleged Julian citations in Rome through the documentation of Eutyches, there appeared in Rome the writing of an anonymous person who responds to an enquiry posed to him in this regard in the writing *Quid contrarium catholice fidei senserit Eutychis*. He repeatedly emphasizes the fact that the letter of Julius, tendered as proof, is a forgery. Cf. ACO II, 4, 145–151; especially pp. 146,39–147,2; 149,22–23.35. (3) Emperor Marcian, *Letter to the monks of Alexandria from 452*: ACO II, 5, p. 3,30–32; Greek: ACO II, 1, 3, p. 130,14–16. The anonymous author just cited (2) may have written before Emperor Marcian. (4) *Letter of the Palestinian monks to Alcison*, composed in 515, in Evagrius, *HE* III, 31: Bidez-Parmentier,

increase.[45] Four different writings are involved: (1) Emperor Justinian, *C. monophysitas*,[46] who uses the same source as the following (later) works: (2) *Doctrina Patrum*,[47] (3) Leontius of Jerusalem, *C. monophysitas*[48] and (4) the writing *De sectis*.[49] In addition to these authors Bishop John of Scythopolis deserves special attention.[50] In the question about the authenticity of the Julius letter, Leontius of Jerusalem deals with the special explanatory work of John of Scythopolis:

> Moreover John, the bishop of Scythopolis, who occupied himself hard and long with the earlier writings of Apollinarius, has found this authority [that is, the alleged Julius text] in these writings with exactly the same words. That this [letter of Julius] belongs to Apollinarius, he [John] states clearly, illustrating this by adducing several pages from this [Apollinarian] book. He [Ps. Julius] says that the body of the Lord was deprived of a human soul and [human] life, which Julius in fact never said. It reads [in Ps. Julius]: the body received its life from the divine holiness, not from the faculty of a human soul.[51]

In the 530s there was thus present (among Chalcedonians) a broad consciousness of the Apollinarian forgeries,[52] which had become the major court of appeal against Chalcedon. As the Syriac document H shows, the Severans did not allow themselves to be impressed by this.

A discussion about the two natures

Let us return to the two-natures question. According to the I report, the second day's discussion was not at first about Ibas of Edessa and Theodoret of Cyrrhus, but dealt immediately with the two natures.[53] The opposition between 'one nature' and 'two natures' had been brought

p. 129,11–14: 'They have also forged many speeches (*logoi*) of Fathers, and through headings have ascribed many texts of Apollinarius to Athanasius and Gregory [the Wonderworker] and Julius . . .' Cf. P. Allen, *Evagrius Scholasticus. The Church Historian* (Louvain, 1981), 147–9. This reference is used as a framework for reporting a forgery of a 'document about the faith' by the supporters of Dioscorus, which Patriarch Elias of Jerusalem (494–518) had sent to Emperor Anastasius. Evagrius stresses the effectiveness of these forgeries.

45. See H. Lietzmann, *Apollinaris von Laodicea*, 108–28.

46. Justinian Imp., *C. monophys.*: E. Schwartz, *Drei dogmatische Schriften Justinians* = *ABAW.PH* 18 (Munich, 1939), pp. 21,6–22; 19,9–10; 18,16–19,7.

47. *DP*, ch. 9, X–XI: Apollinarian forgeries: Diekamp, 62–63, with more details on 374, where the parallels to Justinian are mentioned.

48. Leontius Jer., *C. monophys.*: PG 86, 1865B13–C3.

49. Leontius Schol. (Ps. Leontius), *De sectis* (CPG 6823): PG 86, 1253C–1256D.

50. H. Lietzmann, *op. cit.*, 117, indeed refers to John of Scythopolis, but does not go any further into his knowledge of the Apollinarian forgeries. On John of Scythopolis see F. Loofs, *Leontius von Byzanz und die gleichnamigen Schriftsteller seiner Zeit* = *TU* 3,1–2 (Leipzig, 1887), 269–72; S. Helmer, *Der Neuchalkedonismus* (Bonn, 1962), 176–81; L. Perrone, *La chiesa di Palestina* (Brescia, 1980), 240–9; B. Flusin, *Miracle et histoire dans l'oeuvre de Cyrille de Scythopolis* (Paris, 1983), 17–29: 'B. Le milieu culturel et théologique: Jean de Scythopolis'; B. R. Suchla, *Die Überlieferung des Prologs des Johannes von Skythopolis zum griechischen Corpus Dionysiacum Areopagiticum* = *NAWG.PH* 1984, 4 (Göttingen, 1984), 177–88; eadem, *Eine Redaktion des griechischen Corpus Dionysiacum Areopagiticum im Umkreis des Johannes von Skythopolis, des Verfassers von Prolog und Scholien. Ein dritter Beitrag zur Überlieferungsgeschichte des CD* = *NAWG.PH* 1985, 4 (Göttingen, 1985), 179–94.

51. Leontius Jer., *C. monophys.*: PG 86, 1865BC.

52. A. Tuilier, *art. cit.*, gives suggestions worth considering for how the Apollinarian forgeries are to be explained.

53. See above n. 37.

to mind by the Chalcedonians' attempt to justify the reacceptance of bishops Ibas and Theodoret, condemned in 449, by referring to the letters of Cyril. The letters alluded to are those of the Patriarch which had been decisive for the Union of 433.[54] It is said that in these Cyril had acknowledged the manner of speaking of 'two natures'. We are already acquainted with this theme from the controversy between the compilers of the Cyrillian florilegium and Severus. As Severus had categorically rejected such an acknowledgement, so too the Severan bishops of 532 referred to Cyril's writings containing the *mia-physis* formula[55] and denied the existence of the two-natures formula. In contrast the Chalcedonians explained that for their part they were ready to submit patristic evidence for this.[56] But matters did not come to a head, for on the evening of the second day there was insufficient time, and on the third day an unexpected change in the programme was made.[57] The Emperor invited the parties to a combined audience.[58]

The discussion about the two-natures formula in Innocent, however, occupied more space and was allocated to the second day. This discrepancy can no doubt be explained by the fact that the 'impressive argumentation of Hypatius for the two-natures teaching' (I 39–63: ACO IV, 2, 176–180) did not represent a genuine report of minutes, but was to be understood as 'documentation, which could be collected from the records and preparation of Hypatius for this discussion. Thus the first impression would be confirmed that the report of Innocent, in rendering the content of the dialogues, strongly served the interests of documenting its own standpoint, and did not confine itself to reproducing the course of the dialogue by way of minutes.'[59] This does not prevent us from making clear the christological position of the Chalcedonians at the doctrinal dialogue.

The christological problem in Hypatius of Ephesus according to the representation of Innocent

Once the history of the *mia-physis* formula appeared dubious against the background of the Apollinarian forgeries, the way was clear for the positive discussion of the formulas and concepts introduced at Chalcedon.

Hypatius called to mind clearly the historical task of the Fourth Council: the teaching of the two natures had been formulated in order to exclude the falsification of faith through the teaching of one *physis* introduced by the Arians and Apollinarians. The Arians and

---

54. On the Union of 433 see *JdChr* I[3], 703–7; see the important article of M. Simonetti, 'Alcune osservazioni sul monofisismo di Cirillo di Alessandria', *Aug* 22 (1982), 493–511; on 504 Simonetti gathers all of the Cyrillian passages together, where Cyril 'non esita a parlare di due nature di Cristo, pur sottolineando energicamente la loro unità'. As we have seen, Severus wants to deny this absolutely.

55. Cf. H, nos. 29–30: Brock, 106. The Severans name Cyril Alex., *Ep. 44 ad Eulog.*: ACO I, 1,4, 35–37; *Ep. 40 ad Acacium Melit.*: ACO I, 1, 4, 20–31. On the appearance of the *mia-physis* formula in Cyril in chronological order, see *JdChr* I[2], 674, n. 2.

56. Cf. H 31.32: Brock, 106–7.

57. See J. Speigl, *art. cit.*, 277: 'According to the Syriac minutes H, the patristic argument of the imperial party for the two-natures teaching on the second day would no longer have had a chance.'

58. Cf. I 79: ACO IV, 2, p. 182,23–28.

59. Thus J. Speigl, *art. cit.*, 278. The concluding comment in I 78: ACO IV, 2, p. 182,21–22, does not contradict this: *in his ergo dictis, contradicentes: 'De his quidem persuasum est nobis'*. This declaration of agreement by the Severans can hardly be accepted as authentic. It is a redactional addition in I; cf. the result in H.

Apollinarians were at one in that they both denied the divine nature of the Logos either explicitly, or implicitly by wanting to represent the Logos as 'created' or as 'passible'.[60] But if Christ were true God and true human being, then the talk of two natures, which were united, however, in the one *hypostasis* and in the one *prosopon*, suggested itself. What did Hypatius have to say positively with regard to the main Chalcedonian concepts? In the bishop's first statement the confusion in the usage of concepts was clearly evident, in that in the same sentence the terminology of Ephesus and Chalcedon, of Nestorius and Cyril, was mentioned. This happened in connection with the question why Chalcedon, in contrast to the Council of Ephesus (431), had not accepted the third letter of Cyril to Nestorius. Hypatius did not deny the reservation of the Fathers, but attempted to explain it in a convoluted argument from the difficult conceptual language of the appended anathemas, in particular the third in the list.[61]

> If the Council of Chalcedon accepted and confirmed all the formulas and definitions of faith of the Council held at Ephesus against Nestorius, what reason did it have to reject this letter? They [the Fathers of Chalcedon] wanted to define one person and one ⟨hypostasis⟩ (*subsistentiam*) against the blasphemies of Nestorius, which divide the two natures into two persons and two *hypostases* (*subsistentias*). But this letter introduced a mention of the two *hypostases*. This is why they properly deferred naming it [the letter] so as not to come into opposition either to it or to themselves, but rather it proposed another letter of his, which was praised because of its agreement with the symbol of the Council of Nicaea [CPG 5304], and that [letter] which was written to the Orientals [CPG 5339].

As we see, there appear here the main Chalcedonian concepts: *natura* (*physis*), *persona* (*prosopon*), *subsistentia* (*hypostasis*). From his interpretation of *subsistentia* (*hypostasis*) Hypatius at first attempts to demonstrate that the Fathers of Chalcedon would have come into opposition to Cyril's letter containing the anathemas, were they to have adduced it, for the reason that this letter speaks of two *hypostases* in Christ, whereas they themselves would speak only of one. Hence it can only be the third anathema which is meant, but in an interpretation not intended by Cyril.

---

60. I 23: ACO IV, 2, p. 172,13–17: *neque enim Arrius aliquando vel Apollinarius duas naturas confessi sunt, sed unam naturam dei verbi incarnatam ipsi magis noviter protulerunt, ut creatam et passibilem ipsam divinam verbi naturam introducerent. adversus quos duas substantias atque naturas omnes sancti patres decreverunt.* Hypatius passes over the fact that with Nicaea the Apollinarians fundamentally retained the divinity of the Logos, but the passibility of the Logos necessarily follows from their conception of the *mia physis*. To the assumption of a real *passio* of the Logos as Logos, however, was tied implicitly the denial of the divinity of Christ, a conclusion which indeed the Arians drew, but Apollinarius himself did not.

61. I 28: ACO IV, 2, p. 173,21–9. It is to be noted that the Fathers of Ephesus already treat Cyril's anathemata letter differently from his second letter to Nestorius. Cf. *JdChr* I[3], 688–9; ACO I, 1, 2, pp. 26,19–20,26.

The anathema reads:

> If anyone divides the *hypostases* in the one Christ after the union, joining them only in a
> connection according to dignity, or authority, or power, and not rather in a coming together
> according to the physical unity, let him be anathema.[62]

John the Grammarian had already drawn attention to this '*hypostases*
text', and had shrewdly endeavoured to make use of it for himself.[63]
No one, says John, can be seriously of the opinion that Cyril sees in
the one Christ two *hypostases* already existing prior to the union, but
which are now 'united *hypostases*', retaining their station as such also in
the union. What he reproduces in his anathema is the opinion of
Nestorius, in the way in which the Alexandrian understands it. The third
anathema can also be paraphrased as follows: 'If anyone accepts two
hypostases after the union, let him be anathema. And anyone who does
not confess the "physical union" accepts two *hypostases*.' The reservation
of Chalcedon *vis-à-vis* the anathemas letter was certainly not conditioned
by the terminological vagueness of the third anathema, but by the entire
tendency of these twelve chapters, which seemed to the Fathers not to
exclude Apollinarianism, and above all Eutychianism, sufficiently clearly.
In the teaching of the 'physical union' (*henosis kata physin*) which Cyril
demanded, they suspected the Apollinarian nature-synthesis of divinity
and humanity in Christ.

After almost one hundred years, this would have been the opportunity
to focus on the real terminological problem of Chalcedon and its
'novelty', that is, to clarify the distinction between *hypostasis* (*subsistentia*)
and nature (*physis, natura*), and correspondingly to elucidate what
differentiates the 'union according to *hypostasis*' from a 'union according
to nature' (*henosis kath'hypostasin* — *henosis kata physin*). In fact this discussion tentatively touches the problem. For the Severans reply to Bishop
Hypatius: 'In the letter of the twelve chapters he [Cyril] takes the two
hypostases for two natures.'[64] Thus they perceive a different use of concepts: in his interpretation of the third anathema Hypatius takes the
word *subsistentia* (*hypostasis*) for 'subject'; the Severans render the
Cyrillian 'two *hypostases*' by 'two natures', and believe in this way that
they find in Cyril's words a condemnation of the two natures of
Chalcedon. In contrast Hypatius has recourse to the conceptual history
of the fourth century, and would like to transfer the distinction between

62. Cyril Alex., *Ep. 17 ad Nestor.*: COD, p. 59 III; DEC, p. 59 III; p. *59 3.

63. See above, pp. 58–61.

64. Cf. I 29: ACO IV, 2, p. 173,29–30: *In epistola XII capitulorum duas subsistentias pro duabus
naturis dicit.*

hypostasis and *physis*, introduced into trinitarian theology, to the *oikonomia* as well, that is, to the doctrine of the incarnation,[65] and on that basis to arrive at a clarification of the third anathema. If the Severans on the other hand want to remain with the old synonymous usage of *physis* and *hypostasis*, then they will experience difficulty with its application to trinitarian teaching. For if they attempt to protest to the Chalcedonians that Cyril with his condemnation of 'two *hypostases*' has already condemned the 'two natures' — presupposing that *physis* is synonymous with *hypostasis* — then they themselves have to accept in the Trinity three separate *hypostases*, different according to nature. Hypatius passes over in silence the fact that Cyril, Severus and the Severans have given up the synonymous use of these concepts in the *theologia*, and with the Cappadocians distinguish in the 'one nature' of the godhead 'three *hypostases*', but in the *oikonomia* still take *physis* and *hypostasis* as synonymous. That is certainly inconsistent, but a historical reality. Hypatius (Innocent of Maronia) should have been aware of this. He could justifiably have emphasized such a terminological perversity, without attributing false teachings to the opponent.

Hence, if we follow I, once again formula is opposed to formula. The clarification of the concept has not begun at all. The continuation of the text also illustrates this.[66]

[The *contradicentes* = Severans say] And the letters of Cyril which were specifically adduced at the Council of Chalcedon, namely the one written to Nestorius [CPG 5304] as well as the one to the Orientals [CPG 5339], contain the 'from two natures' ⟨and not the 'in two natures'. The Bishop [Hypatius]: Do you accept then a difference between 'from two natures' and⟩ 'in two natures'? The *contradicentes* [Severans] said: Yes, to the highest degree. The Bishop [Hypatius] said: What do you mean? The opponents: To say 'from two natures' means according to Cyril and the holy Fathers the one incarnate nature of the Logos; 'in two natures' means two persons and two *hypostases*.

---

65. *Ibid.*, 29–31: 173,30–174,13: Hypatius first of all refers to the earlier synonymous use of *substantia* (*ousia*), *natura* (*physis*) and *subsistentia* (*hypostasis*), which had been traditional for trinitarian theology. Then he depicts the misunderstanding which occurred between the East (with the formula: in the Trinity there is one *hypostasis* = one nature) and the West (in the Trinity there are three persons in one nature). He says that the East has seen Sabellianism in the Western formula, and the West has reproached the Orientals with an Arian division of the one godhead into three unequal *hypostases* (*subsistentias*). Through the linguistic knowledge of the holy Athanasius, however, the reconciliation between East and West was achieved. Hypatius is thus of the opinion that Athanasius did away with the synonymous use of *physis* and *hypostasis*; but here he has in mind a pseudo-Athanasian writing. The real Athanasius was an old-Nicene. Cf. his *Ep. ad Afros eppos* 4: PG 26, 1036B: 'The *hypostasis* is the *ousia* and means nothing other than this very thing which is.'

66. I 32–33: ACO IV, 2, 174. The text placed in brackets ⟨ ⟩ is E. Schwartz's addition.

This was the customary Severan argumentation. The dialogue was thus completely stalled. Hypatius could only argue along these lines: your 'from two natures' does not provide any further help either. For if for you 'nature' is the same as *hypostasis*, then your formula 'from two natures' presupposes two existing *hypostases* which have been united. Then this brings one down again on the side of Nestorius. The Bishop of Ephesus notes that no decision will be arrived at on this level and would like to play down the opposition between the formulas. For this purpose he has recourse to the Flavian Synod of 448 where there had still been a certain unity. The rôle of Bishop Basil of Seleucia is also recalled.[67] At this assembly, which Hypatius says took a clear position against Eutyches, both the formula 'out of two natures' (Flavian) as well as the other 'in two natures' were to be heard, without bringing with them the accusation of heresy. Indeed, in his rescript to Emperor Theodosius II, Patriarch Flavian did not once reject the *mia-physis* formula.[68] Nevertheless at Ephesus (449) he was condemned by Patriarch Dioscorus. Hypatius concluded from this that the oscillation between both sides had to be abandoned. For Chalcedon also recognized that nothing so approached the Eutychians, as opponents of the 'two natures', as 'this Manichaean confession of one nature', which signifies mingling and docetism.[69] Thus he stated that the Fourth Council posed *vis-à-vis* Flavian an 'explanatory formula' (*explanativam potius vocem*), 'which confesses one person and one *hypostasis*'. By this means Flavian's correct faith was acknowledged and his statements confirmed.[70] Hypatius thus believes that through his mediating position he has demonstrated to the Severans that the formula of faith of 451 was the wise, indeed the sole way out of the crisis regarding Eutyches.

This attempt by Hypatius to solicit understanding ought to be acknowledged. It consists in nothing other than re-enacting the decision of Chalcedon, concerning both its major formula and its relationship to Cyril. In contrast to John the Grammarian, the Bishop of Ephesus and his companions do not demand that both formulas need to be used to

---

67. I 33: ACO IV, 2, p. 174,24–30. Cf. *JdChr* I³, 733–4, 757–8; II/1, 241–3.

68. As a proof this rescript is cited verbatim in I 34: ACO IV, 2, 174–175. The main sentence of Flavian reads: *et unam quidem dei verbi naturam, incarnatam tamen, dicere non negamus, quia ex utrisque unus idemque dominus noster Iesus Christus est* (p. 175,14–16). Schwartz remarks that Rusticus offers a different translation (cf. ACO II, 5, 116–117); Grumel, *Regestes* I², no. 105; *Chalkedon* I, 196 and 398–401.

69. I 35: ACO IV, 2, p. 175,27–29: *nihil ita recreat eos qui cum Eutychen adversantur orthodoxae duarum naturarum confessioni, nisi confusa et conmixta et imaginaria vel Manichaica unius naturae confessio.*

70. I 35: ACO IV, 2, p. 175,29–31.

express the faith correctly, namely the Chalcedonian two-natures formula against Eutyches and the Alexandrian one-nature formula against Nestorius. 'One *hypostasis* in two natures': this definition, by its distinction between, and not the synonymous use of, the major concepts, fulfils both apologetic tasks. By the reference to the *fraudes Apollinistarum*, the Apollinarian forgeries, the authenticity of which the Severans did not attempt to uphold, the Chalcedonian decision could moreover also be spared the reproach of 'novelty'. The critical stance with regard to the letters of Cyril was also Chalcedonian, which again was nothing other than the re-enactment of the procedure of the Fathers of Ephesus. Cyril has a determining part in the definition of 451 through the two letters acknowledged by the Synod, the second letter to Nestorius approved at Ephesus and the *Laetentur* letter of 433. He is also called as a witness to the two-natures language, but not as a promoter of the one-nature formula.[71] Hypatius with his group stands firmly on the ground of Chalcedon, sadly also in the sense that he does not try to analyse and define his main concepts and to demonstrate how effective they can be in dealing with the problems at hand.

(ii) The two-natures theme according to H

While according to I the two-natures teaching forms the major theme of the second day, H places this discussion only at the end of the same day. Each of the two parties refers for its position to Cyril as the main authority. The Chalcedonians rely above all on the letter which Cyril

---

71. I 36: ACO IV, 2, p. 175,33–38: 'We accept [from Cyril] what agrees with his synodal letters [that is, ratified by Ephesus and Chalcedon respectively]; what, however, is not in agreement we neither condemn nor do we follow it as ecclesiastical law. As synodal letters we consider, as was said above, the letters which have been accepted and confirmed by the holy councils [Ephesus and Chalcedon], that is, the one to Nestorius [CPG 5304: *Garriunt multi*] as well as the one written to the Orientals [CPG 5339: *Laetentur Caeli*].' There follow extracts from these two letters together with the formula of union (176, nos. 39 and 41). In contrast to these synodally recognized letters, all the other letters, written more secretly (*secreto*) or in friendship, which are particularly exposed to forgery, must be passed over (I 43: ACO IV, 2, p. 177,10–15). With regard to this compromise the Severans insist on the evaluation of the whole of Cyril, particularly the letter to Eulogius and the second letter to Succensus, and begin immediately to read from them. The letters in question are CPG 5344 and 5346. According to H 30 they also demand the reading out of the letter to Acacius of Melitene (CPG 5340), a demand which because of lack of time, however, cannot be granted. Thus the Cyril of the *mia physis* is produced by the Severans; in contrast it is the Cyril who also allows the two-natures formula to be valid, who is produced by Hypatius (especially in I 45–63: ACO IV, 2, pp. 177,25–180,3). That Hypatius could rightly appeal to this follows from M. Simonetti, 'Alcune osservazioni sul monofisismo di Cirillo di Alessandria', *Aug* 22 (1982), 493–511, especially 510–11, n. 50, where he refers to Cyril's writing *Quod unus sit Christus*.

wrote in connection with the Union of 433,[72] which to some extent is justified historically. But with equal right the anti-Chalcedonians can distil the Cyril of the *mia-physis* formula.[73] In this regard the main documents are the letter to Eulogius,[74] which is read out, and the letter to Acacius of Melitene,[75] which because of the lateness of the hour could no longer be read out. Moreover the imperial auditor emphasizes that its contents are equivalent to those of the letter to Eulogius.[76] The Chalcedonians want to place in opposition to these documents a dossier from the Fathers in favour of the two-natures language.[77] The Syrians encourage them in this project, because they, like Severus, are certain of the fact that the attempt would not succeed.[78]

The dialogue then takes an unexpected turn. Both parties are invited to an audience with the Emperor, the Chalcedonians being the first. After some time the Syrians are also summoned. Immediately they have the suspicion that behind their backs their dialogue partners have urged breaking-off the dialogue altogether, because of their embarrassment at not being able to produce the patristic proof which they had announced. The main reason for this premature ending, however, is no doubt the Emperor's realization, gained from information he had received about the course of the dialogue, that his goal could not be achieved, namely to lead the Severans back to unity with the 'imperial confession'. This concluding audience is thus equivalent to an admission that the Emperor's initiative has failed. Only one bishop, Philoxenus of Doliche, changes from the Severan to the Chalcedonian side.[79] Nevertheless the dialogue has an effect on later history, as the Syrian report (S) enables one to discover. To begin with, the Emperor succeeded in having the Syrians formulate, with all assurances, the conditions under which they

---

72. Cyril Alex., *Ep. 39 ad Iohann. Ant. de pace* (CPG 5339): ACO I, 1, 4, 15–20; II, 1, 1, 107–111; PG 77, 173–181 (*Laetentur* letter).

73. Cf. H 29–30: Brock, 106.

74. Cyril Alex., *Ep. 44 ad Eulog.* (CPG 5344): ACO I, 1, 4, p. 35,14; 36,11–12; PG 77, 225B.D.

75. *Idem, Ep. 40 ad Acac. Melit.* with several attestations of the *mia-physis* formula: ACO I, 1, 4, p. 26,8–9, 21–22; PG 77, 182D–193AB; cf. *JdChr* I[3], 674, n. 2.

76. H 30: Brock, 106. Once again cf. M. Simonetti, *art. cit.*

77. H 31: Brock, 106; I 79: ACO IV, 2, p. 182,23–25.

78. Cf. H 34: Brock, 108. The Syrians confirm that for the third day the Chalcedonians did not have their promised testimonies of the holy Fathers prepared, and the former comment: 'indeed they could not have done so'.

79. Cf. E. Honigmann, *Evêques et évêchés*, 72–3; ACO IV, 2, pp. 169,27; 184,2; J. Speigl, *art. cit.*, 271. How Emperor Justinian further attempted indirectly to achieve his purpose with the Severans and failed is depicted by J. Speigl, *art. cit.*, 280–2. Nothing new for christology results from this.

would agree to the restoration of the unity of the Church.[80] Still they give to their agreement a particular meaning. They do not speak of conditions which the Severan side would have to fulfil in order to come to unity, but rather of the conditions for the Chalcedonian side. For according to their conviction it was the Chalcedonian side that was marked with the sign of schism:[81]

> We do not think that those who have specifically withdrawn themselves from communion with the opposite party will be united, unless they anathematize those who speak of two natures after the inexplicable union, as well as the Tome of Leo, and what took place at Chalcedon in opposition to the orthodox faith.

That is an unambiguous renunciation of the Council. For the moment nevertheless the Syrians do not demand any condemnation of particular names (Ibas and Theodoret). But the Roman demands, that particular *libelli* be signed (by which no doubt the *formula Hormisdae* is meant), should cease. Here there follows a special proposal which the Emperor himself made for union and which already points to the next phase of the discussion, as the text S reveals.

(1) The Severans should anathematize Diodore, Theodore, Theodoret, Ibas, Nestorius and Eutyches.
(2) They could accept the twelve anathemas of Cyril and anathematize those against whom they were written.
(3) They might confess the one nature of the incarnate Word, but they should refrain from anathematizing the supporters of the two natures; instead they should express their condemnation of those confessing Nestorian views (under whom naturally each Severan also subsumed the Chalcedonians).
(4) The slogan 'the two united and inseparable natures' should be accepted by both sides as a formula of reconciliation.[82]
(5) Finally they should partially recognize Chalcedon by condemning Eutyches; however, they do not need to accept the actual formula of faith of 451. They should cease to anathematize the *Tomus* of Leo; the *libelli Romani* should not be suspended.[83]

The Emperor's endeavour was in vain. The report S comments in conclusion in no. 7: 'These things failed to persuade the orthodox bishops.' Thus if we consider the Emperor's active steps to achieve unity, in this concentrated form over three days, they have to be regarded as a failure

---

80. In doing so they stress the private character of their step; cf. S 3: Brock, 115: 'The orthodox bishops say: "The canon does not allow five insignificant bishops, bishops moreover of small towns, to provide any common (statement) on the faith by themselves".'

81. S 5: Brock, 116.

82. S. Brock, *art. cit.*, 116, n. 92, adding by way of explanation: 'I.e. the Syrian Orthodox should distinguish between the ordinary upholders of Chalcedon and those who did so as a convenient front to hide their genuinely Nestorian position.'

83. Cf. S 7: Brock, 116–17.

as such. As far as the procedure was concerned, it did not produce the planned exchange of doubt and solution. Instead of question and answer, there were only attack and accusation. If we were to take Justinian's strategy, as it has just been presented, and contrast it with the main theses of Hypatius, then in the place of the strict-Chalcedonian position of the imperial representative the Emperor's new attitude is already apparent. We still have to address this topic.

II. HERACLIANUS OF CHALCEDON

To the circle of Chalcedonian bishops and theologians from the Patriarchate of Constantinople there also belonged Heraclianus, who from 537(?) to 553 was the bishop and metropolitan of Chalcedon.[84] Between 520 and 535 we find him as a priest of the Great Church in Constantinople and *synkellos* of Patriarch Epiphanius (520–535).[85] In 520, together with Bishop John of Claudiopolis in Isauria and the deacon Constantine, he was sent to Rome, arriving on 30 November 520,[86] in order, after the change of 518, to seal the peace between Byzantium and Rome in the name of the Patriarch and his synod. This delegation was also intended by Emperor Justin (and Justinian) to petition for the ratification of the trinitarian theopaschite formula by the Pope.[87] This formula stated that Jesus Christ, the Son of the Virgin, who suffered in the flesh, is rightly confessed as 'one of the Trinity', or as 'person in and from the Trinity'. In 532 Heraclianus, still as a priest and theologian, was a participant in the doctrinal dialogue which we have just described.[88] In 535 he was sent to Rome a second time, in order to present a letter of Emperor Justinian to the King of the Goths,

---

84. See CPG 6800–6801; E. Honigmann, *Heraclianus of Chalcedon (537 A.D.?), Soterichus of Caesarea in Cappadocia and Achillius = ST* 173 (Vatican City, 1953), no. XXII, 205–216.

85. Cf. ACO IV, 2, 170; R. Schieffer, ACO IV, 3, 2, 1, p. 215, who emphasizes the distinguished position of Heraclianus. Cf. E. Honigmann, *op. cit.*, 213 on Heraclianus: 'Eminent ecclesiastical leaders like Heraclianus were certainly not at the time a common occurrence in the Byzantine Church . . .'

86. Cf. Epiphanius, *Relatio ad Hormisdam*: CA, *ep.* 233, no. 7 and *ep.* 234, no. 10, pp. 709, 713 for mention of Heraclianus. Between the Pope in Rome and the Patriarch in Constantinople there is complete agreement. Emperor Justin (Justinian) likewise sends a letter: CA, *ep.* 235. In no. 2 see the names of the delegates.

87. Justin (Justinian) imp., *Ep. ad Hormisd.* (from 9.9.520): CA, *ep.* 235, no. 3: CSEL 35, 2, p. 715: *nobis etenim videtur, quoniam filius dei vivi dominus noster Iesus Christus ex virgine Maria natus, quem praedicat summus apostolorum carne passum, recte dicitur unus in trinitate cum patre spirituque sancto regnare, maiestatisque eius personam in trinitate et ex trinitate non infideliter credimus.*

88. Cf. ACO IV, 2, 170.

Theodahat.[89] Certainly from 537, as a bishop and metropolitan, he led the Church of Chalcedon, to which he had been appointed by Bishop Soterichus of Caesarea in Cappadocia in his capacity as exarch of the dioceses of Pontus.[90] According to Patriarch Photius, Heraclianus was a model of orthodoxy.[91] To what extent his influence also had an effect on Patriarch Ephraem of Amida in the see of Antioch and on his fellow *peritus* at the doctrinal dialogue of 532, Leontius of Byzantium, as is occasionally assumed,[92] is difficult to determine. In any case he was a notable supporter of strict-Chalcedonian christology, with an Antiochene tint, for Photius mentions that Heraclianus considers the suspect Diodore of Tarsus as one of the 'Fathers'. He seems to have consistently maintained this position.

It was different with his consecrator, Bishop Soterichus, who was just mentioned,[93] who had been nominated metropolitan of Caesarea by Patriarch Macedonius of Constantinople (496–511) and on that occasion had professed Chalcedon, but then changed to the anti-Chalcedonian side. At the time of the Synod of Sidon (511) he was an acknowledged personality among the opponents of the Fourth Council.[94] Naturally he was also then the target of condemnations, thus by Patriarch John of Jerusalem, the saints Sabas and Theodosius, and by Hypatius, whose anathema he attracted together with Nestorius, Eutyches, Severus and all anti-Chalcedonians.[95] After the change of 518, however, Soterichus went to Constantinople in order to come to an understanding with the

89. See Cassiod., *Var.* X 25: PL 69, 814C; see also CA, *ep.* 88: CSEL 35, 1, p. 333,24.

90. Cf. E. Honigmann, *op. cit.*, 213.

91. Photius, *Bibl. cod.* 85: PG 103, 288A–289A; R. Henry, II, 9–10.

92. This is adduced as a possibility by J. Lebon, 'Ephraem d'Amid, patriarche d'Antioche (526–544)', in *Mélanges C. Moeller* I (Louvain, Paris, 1914), 213. Lebon refers to J. P. Junglas, *Leontius von Byzanz* (Paderborn, 1907), 56ff.

93. Cf. E. Honigmann, *op. cit.*, 208–13.

94. *Ibid.*, 208. Soterichus, however, should not be regarded as the one who suggested the Synod of Sidon, or even as the one who presided. In a letter from 510 Severus, who at that time was still in Constantinople, communicated to him that Macedonius was plotting a revolt (*stasis*) in order to hinder the addition of 'crucified for our sake' to the liturgical Trishagion. Cf. Evagrius, *HE* III, 44: Bidez-Parmentier, 146,8; cf. G. Garitte, 'Fragments coptes d'une lettre de Sévère d'Antioche à Sotérichos de Césarée (CPG 7071, 13)', *Mus* 65 (1952), 185–98. Coptic text and Latin translation, *ibid.*, 190–8. According to Severus, the chanting of the expanded Trishagion was directed against the supporters of Chalcedon *qui res Nestorii [im]pii [sen]tiunt* (192). To be noted is the fact that according to Severus Ant., *Ep. ad Dioscorum II Al.*, written in 516–517: SL IV, 3, p. 291 [258], and *idem, Ep. ad Hippocr.*: PO 12, 317, the bishops of Cappadocia I and II were in favour of a union with Dioscorus II and Severus.

95. Winter 516/517, according to Cyril Scyth., *Vita Sab.*, ch. 56: Schwartz, pp. 151,24–152,2; Theophan., *Chron.*: de Boor, 158–159.

new patriarch, John II the Cappadocian (518–520).[96] In fact he then accepted Chalcedon, as Cyrus, the bishop of Tyana, also did.[97] Nevertheless Soterichus did not immediately have the confidence of Pope Hormisdas, who wanted to have him deposed. Emperor Justin I, however, defended the bishop.[98] When Soterichus died, his successor in 537 was Theodore Askidas, a name which will claim our attention in the next phase of christology.

In spite of the lacunae in the evidence, one can discern that Heraclianus made some attempts to execute what the doctrinal dialogue of 532 was intended to effect, namely a clarification of the concepts and formulas separating the parties. The *Doctrina Patrum* (*DP*) quotes from a letter to Soterichus long or short excerpts arranged under various *topoi*, but which concern the Chalcedonian concepts and formulas, and in general the problem of how one ought to speak of unity and duality in Christ. As these fragments show, their content corresponds to the state of christology between 510 and 537.

1. Accents in the use of concepts

In Heraclianus too the *ousia* concept comes clearly to the fore, that concept which gained its significance from John the Grammarian and Leontius of Byzantium on the Chalcedonian side, and from Sergius Scholasticus on the anti-Chalcedonian front. In the sixth chapter the *DP* intends to show that *physis* and *hypostasis* are not the same, but that on the other hand *ousia* and *physis* are the same, just as *hypostasis* and *prosopon*. In order to show this, a fragment from the letter of Heraclianus to Soterichus is adduced. With regard to content it does not advance beyond the distinction of *ousia* and *hypostasis* established by Basil. It is not legitimate when the bishop calls upon the Council of Nicaea as an authority for the distinction between the two concepts, for there indeed *ousia* and *hypostasis* were used synonymously.[99] He himself contrasts

96. Severus Ant., *Ep. ad Eleus. ep. Sasimae*: SL VI, 1: Brooks II, 361–362. The outcome of the matter was at first still uncertain for Severus.

97. Severus Ant., *Ep. ad Proclum et Euseb.* (Cappadocia II), whom he cautions against defecting, SL V, 13: Brooks II, 344: 'It was already a fact: "Cyrus has lapsed: Soteric has fallen." Will the enemies of truth also be able to laugh and say: Proclus and Eusebona were thrown into the same ditch?' The *DP* contains a fragment from Cyrus of Tyana in ch. 41, XXXVf.: Diekamp, 313 (against Chalcedon).

98. Justin emp., *Ep. ad Hormisd.*, from 7.6.520 = *Ep.* 111 in Thiel, 914–916; CA, *ep.* 193: CSEL 35, 2, p. 650.

99. Cf. COD, 5; DEC, 5; *5; Heraclian. ep., in *DP*, ch. 6, XVIII: Diekamp, p. 43, 9–15.

physis and *hypostasis*. It is also on this basis that a fragment of the *DP*, which is taken from the same letter, is to be judged.[100]

> Your Holiness knows that the Fathers of the Council of Chalcedon say that the coming together (συνδρομή) of divinity and humanity happened in one *hypostasis*, which means the same as confessing frankly the union according to the *hypostasis*.

One must not extrapolate from this formula a typically neo-Chalcedonian oscillation, even if it was selected with an eye to Cyril.

2. Anthropology and christology

Of no particular significance is the discussion about the question whether there are not three natures in Christ. For if the humanity of Christ consists of body and soul, it already contains in itself two natures. Heraclianus does not respond directly to this question.[101] His texts, however, can still be adduced for this purpose, for in these he makes suggestions about the philosophical denotation of compound things, and thus of human beings as well. Heraclianus is of the opinion that not all subdivisions — whether in scholastic language we call these essential parts or integral parts (*partes essentiales* or *partes integrantes*) — need to be stated together in the total denotation of a being. Thus one can consider 'humanity' as one nature and 'divinity' as the other in Christ.[102]

These few samples show that in his letter to Soterichus, from which no doubt all of the fragments of the *DP* belonging to him are taken,[103] Heraclianus moves in the area of philosophical-theological reflection on the mystery of faith of Chalcedon, and on that basis deals with the anti-Chalcedonian Soterichus. The loss of the letter in its entirety is to be regretted.

---

100. Heraclian. ep., *Ep. ad Soterich.* (Frag.): *DP*, ch. 21, VII: Diekamp, 134.

101. In contrast this is done by the fragment from the *defensiones* of Eulogius Alex. (CPG 6972): *DP*, ch. 29, XIII: Diekamp, 209–210.

102. Cf. *DP*, ch. 29, XI and XII: Diekamp, 207–208. The same consideration is developed in ch. 30, I, in connection with the question about number in the denotation of composite things.

103. Cf. the comments in CPG 6800. In the *Opusc. theol. polem.* Maximus Confessor cites a short fragment from Heraclianus' writing *Against the Manichaeans* (CPG 6801: PG 91, 125CD), which, however, is so short that its christological statement is difficult to determine. Cf. Photius, *Bibl. cod.* 85: PG 103, 288f.; R. Henry II, 9–10.

III. THE SLEEPLESS MONKS OF THE MONASTERY OF EIRENAION AND THE FABRICATED CORRESPONDENCE WITH PETER THE FULLER

The Sleepless Monks of Eirenaion must be considered the most important centre of strict-Chalcedonian christology in the region of Constantinople. They were not directly subject to the Ecumenical Patriarch, but to the titular metropolitan of Chalcedon.[104] From the pontificate of Pope Felix (483–492) to the year 534, their monastery was a factor of the highest importance in the struggle concerning Chalcedon. For this purpose there was established in its library an extensive collection of documents which became 'frankly an arsenal for propaganda'.[105] The effort of the monks, both in theology and in ecclesiastical politics, was so strong that they themselves could demand from Emperor Anastasius over the head of the Patriarch of Constantinople a pro-Chalcedonian political line, although a breach with the Patriarch of Alexandria was imminent. This opposition to the Emperor who promoted the *Henoticon* brought them more closely together with the Pope in Rome,[106] whether as informants, or whether also as critics of Roman behaviour. More than their activities in ecclesiastical politics, it is the christological views of the monks themselves which interest us here. We have an unusual source for these, namely a whole collection of supposed letters, which were said to have been addressed from all over the world to Patriarch Peter the Fuller (Gnapheus), who at the time of their composition was already dead. Before Peter became Patriarch he had been a monk of the Eirenaion monastery and had become a priest there. Accused of Eutychianism, he had to leave the monastery, but through the favour of the Emperor Zeno he was soon ordained as bishop and made the Patriarch of Antioch (471). Driven out of Antioch after some seven to nine months, he returned to his former monastery (471–476). Then once again he succeeded in occupying the see of Antioch for a short time. Deposed again, he was able to retreat to Euchaita (Helenopontus) (477–485), but from there he was able to

---

104. Cf. E. Schwartz, *PS*, 204–205; R. Riedinger, art., 'Akoimeten', in *TRE* 2, 148–53; *JdChr* II/1², 295–6, n. 82. The heyday of this monastery lasted from about 448 (under abbot Marcellus, who died before 484) to the condemnation of the Sleepless Monks as 'Nestorians' by Pope John II on 25 March 534. On the lead-up to this see in addition E. Wölfle, 'Der Abt Hypatios von Ruphinianai und der Akoimete Alexander', *ByzZ* 79 (1986), 302–9; *idem*, *Hypatios. Leben und Bedeutung des Abtes von Rufiniane* = Europ. Hochschulschriften XXIII/288 (Frankfurt, Bern, New York, Paris, 1986).

105. E. Schwartz, *PS*, 204–206. The most important weapon is the publication of documents (206).

106. Cf. *JdChr* II/1, 296, 303–4.

take over the Antiochene Patriarchate for a third time (485–488). While attempting to bring the autocephalous Cypriots under his jurisdiction (488), he died.

The personal ties between Peter the Fuller and the Sleepless Monks on the one side and the christological tensions on the other offered a historical background for the production in the Eirenaion of fictitious documents, in the form of letters, which were intended to fight against a christological liturgical formula supported by him. What christology there is in these is to be attributed to the Chalcedonian monks of the Eirenaion monastery. In order to understand their statement we must first of all briefly present the history of the collection itself and the subsequent conflict concerning the so-called Trishagion, which provided the occasion for it.

1. The forged correspondence with Peter the Fuller

According to E. Schwartz, monks in or around Constantinople invented the following situation:[107]

> Peter the Fuller, who in general is considered the legitimate patriarch of Antioch, demands in a letter addressed to Acacius of Constantinople [472–489] that the phrase ὁ σταυρωθεὶς δι' ἡμᾶς [crucified for our sake] be added to the Trishagion. At the instigation of the Roman bishop Felix [III (483–492)] and Acacius of Constantinople, who had been needled by the former, many bishops declared this claim to be heretical, and several times remonstrated with Peter about his novelty; Pope Felix himself warned him twice. Because all this had no effect, and in further letters he still demanded the addition, he was excommunicated by Felix in the last letter of the Vatican collection;[108] it seems as if the same judgement is to be reckoned as being passed by Acacius too. There is no need to argue especially that all this is fiction. How unconcerned the compiler of the letters is about history is betrayed by his grotesque chronology of Photinus and Paul of Samosata; the ignorance was even for that time too gross, and in the exemplar of the collection of letters used by the Latin translator the blunder was, as far as possible, corrected.

Three versions of this collection of letters exist. An original core, composed by a single author, was very quickly, or perhaps immediately after the composition, extended by newly added letters.[109] We shall now

107. E. Schwartz, *PS*, 292. On the whole matter see pp. 287–300 and the *praefatio* to ACO III, pp. XI–XIIII.

108. Cf. Ps. Felix, *Ep. ad Petr. Ant.*: CA, *ep.* 71, nos. 3–5: CSEL 35, 1, pp. 164–6.

109. Three recensions of this collection of letters exist: (a) *Coll. Vaticana*, the oldest with seven letters; provisional edition by E. Schwartz, in *PS*, 125–150; new corrected edition in ACO III, 217–231; (b) a Latin translation with eight letters, preserved in the CA, ed. Günther, CSEL 35, and in the *Collectio Berolinensis*, nos. 51–58; (c) the third and latest edition of ten letters (Greek), inserted into the *Coll. Sabbaitica*: ACO III, 6–25. The *Coll. Vat.* is very close to the Latin translation, but is, however, not identical with it, because there are differences in the extent and in the arrangement. It stems from one of the Palestinian Sabas monasteries and was put together

enquire into the occasion for this forgery, the conflict over the so-called Trishagion hymn, and its significance in the history of doctrine.

2. *Lex orandi* — *lex credendi:* the conflict concerning the Trishagion hymn[110]

(a) The historical findings

There are several forms of the hymn that need to be distinguished. One must start from its core, the biblical Trishagion according to Isaiah 6,3. We encounter this biblical acclamation at the Council of Chalcedon, but it is extended with three predicates and tied to a request. In the first session, 8 October 451, we hear an acclamation of the Oriental bishops, with which they greet the deposition of Patriarch Dioscorus: 'Long years to the Senate! Holy God, holy mighty, holy immortal, have mercy on us' (ἅγιος ὁ Θεός, ἅγιος ἰσχυρός, ἅγιος ἀθάνατος, ἐλέησον ἡμᾶς).[111] Attempts to determine the origin and theological understanding of the Trishagion formula for the pre-Chalcedonian period produce only a blurred picture. For the North African/Italian area G. Kretschmar has established 'that the seraphim hymn, the thrice holy from Isaiah 6,3, was related to God, Father, Son and Holy Spirit, and that this interpretation came from the East, to all appearances from Alexandria, even before the *Sanctus* appeared in the liturgy'.[112] Its use in the fifth century can be dated. A. Baumstark seeks the roots of the Trishagion in the contact between Christian and synagogal worship towards the end of the second century.[113] Fitting this assumption would be the indication of the

between 542 and 544 (Schwartz, *PS*, 288). On the inauthenticity of the collections, see *ibid.*, 291–292. The intention of the latest edition is most evident in the letters VIII–X: ACO III, 18–25. These letters were taken up into the *Coll. Sabb.* at the time when the controversies against Maxentius and his companions broke out in Constantinople on account of the formula 'one of the Trinity suffered'. The mixing that thus occurred of the polemic against this formula with the expanded Trishagion produced a contradiction, of which the redactors were not aware and which contributed to increase the confusion. This will be described below.

110. The Thrice Holy to be discussed here first of all, which is to be distinguished from the *Sanctus* of the eucharistic prayer, found its entry as *Aius* into the Gallic liturgy. In the Latin liturgy it can still be found in the Office of Good Friday and in the *preces feriales* of Prime. On this cf. J. M. Hanssens, *Institutiones Liturgicae de ritibus orientalibus*, Vol. III (Rome, 1932), 108–51. The material for the following section was prepared by H.-J. Höhn.

111. Cf. ACO II, 1, 1, no. 1071, p. 195.

112. See G. Kretschmar, *Studien zur frühchristlichen Trinitätstheologie* = *BHTh* 21 (Tübingen, 1956), 141. Cf. also *idem*, 'Neue Arbeiten zur Geschichte des Ostergottesdienstes II: Die Einführung des Sanctus in die lateinische Meßliturgie', *JLH* 7 (1962), 79–86.

113. A. Baumstark, 'Trishagion und Qeduscha', *JLW* 3 (1923), 18–32; on the origin of the Trishagion cf. in this context also H. Engberding, 'Zum formgeschichtlichen Verständnis des ἅγιος ὁ Θεὸς ... ἐλέησον ἡμᾶς', *JLW* 10 (1930), 168–74; N. Walker, 'The Origin of the "Thrice Holy" ', *NTS* 5 (1958/9), 132–3.

monk Jobius (sixth century) in his treatise *De verbo incarnato* that, with reference to Psalm 42,3 (τὸν Θεὸν τὸν ἰσχυρὸν τὸν ζῶντα), a Jewish convert related the Trishagion to God in opposition to the pagan gods.[114] Nevertheless from the history of late Jewish liturgy and the development of Christian liturgy, there are many reasons which make it unlikely that the Trishagion was directly taken over from Jewish worship.[115] Genuinely Christian impulses can probably be claimed for Revelation 3,7; 4,8; 6,10, where a conceivable starting-point for a christological interpretation of the hymn could also be assumed.[116] Of only slight historical value are the apologetically tinted, legendary reports in our collection of Peter the Fuller's letters: the formula, nevertheless without the addition, is said to have been included in the liturgy at the time of Bishop Proclus (434–446).[117] We encounter this legend too in the *Liber Heraclidis*,[118] and there it is associated with an earthquake, understood as a proof of divine power, which would continue until the Trishagion found its place in the Byzantine liturgy.[119] This passage, which has to be regarded as a later interpolation, is indeed not acquainted with the ominous addition, but it is certainly acquainted with some phrases referring to the reproach of theopaschitism, which alludes to the controversies between 451 and 470.

The unsatisfying historical findings thus permit only a few sure assumptions about the appearance of the Trishagion. Apparently it arrived in the capital Constantinople from the diocese of Oriens. Its use at the Council of Chalcedon may have gained for it the reputation of a formula that could be used in theological struggles, or those concerning ecclesiastical politics, which in any case was justified beyond measure

114. Jobius mon., *De Verbo incarnato commentarius* (CPG 6984): Photius, *Bibl. Cod.* 222: PG 103, 772A; R. Henry, III, 180.

115. Cf. C. W. Dugmore, *The Influence of the Synagogue upon the Divine Office* (Oxford, 1944), 107ff.

116. Cf. A. Gerhards, 'Le phénomène du Sanctus adressé au Christ. Son origine, sa signification et sa persistance dans les Anaphores de l'église d'Orient', in A. M. Triacca/A. Pistoia (eds.), *Le Christ dans la liturgie* (Rome, 1981), 65–83, especially 68–9 (literature).

117. See the testimony in the texts of the Fuller letters in Schwartz, *PS*, pp. 242; 133,10ff.; 138,19ff.; 142,4ff.; 143,5ff.; 147,3ff.; Jobius in Photius, *Bibl. Cod.* 222: PG 103, 772BC; R. Henry, III, 181; Theophanes: de Boor, 93. With this legend the originality of the Trishagion formula was intended to be secured for Constantinople against Antioch. This occurs in a particularly explicit way in the latest recension, in the second letter of Pope Felix to Peter: ACO III, 19–23.

118. Cf. F. Nau, *Le livre d'Héraclide de Damas* (Paris, 1910), 317–23; L. Abramowski, *Untersuchungen zum 'Liber Heraclidis' des Nestorius* = CSCO 224, Subs. 22 (Louvain, 1963) 130–2.

119. On the historical bases for this legend see B. Croke, 'Two Early Byzantine Earthquakes and their Liturgical Commemoration', *Byz* 51 (1981), 122–47.

through conflicts on account of the contrary interpetations of the hymn. While at Constantinople the Trishagion was referred solely to the Trinity, in Antioch, which was considered the centre of 'monophysitism', it received a christological explanation.[120] As Severus' supporters who emerged in Constantinople around 510 maintained, the much-discussed insertion 'who was crucified for us' was common there from the time of Patriarch Eustathius. It seemed to them that the addition was suited to showing the unity of the acting subject in the incarnate Logos against any dyophysite position. The fact that the implications for trinitarian theology of such a manner of speaking were not reflected upon is understandable on the one hand, because of this specific christological interest; on the other hand the christological relation in the Trishagion hymn itself is not expressed. Hence in terms of trinitarian theology the whole hymn becomes a shock for the Chalcedonians, which one is accustomed to characterize by the name 'theopaschitism': for can one of the Trinity (taken as such) suffer, without the suffering being ascribed to the divinity?

(b) On the conflict concerning the addition 'who was crucified for us'
When in 471 the opposition to the formula of Chalcedon came to power with Peter the Fuller in Antioch, the expansion of the Trishagion, which had been known there for a long time, was introduced into the official liturgy.[121] Patriarch Calandion (479–484), who was of strict-Chalcedonian persuasion, had attempted to give a 'moderate' christological interpretation by placing before it the vocative Χριστὲ βασιλεῦ. With the return of Peter the Fuller to the See (485–488) this second addition was removed.

The conflict about the Trishagion flared up anew, when in 510 the Palestinian and Antiochene monks who were residing in Constantinople

---

120. Cf. the communication of Ephraem of Antioch (526–545) to Zenobius in Photius, *Bibl. Cod.* 228: PG 103, 957BC; R. Henry, IV, 115: '. . . that the Orientals (= Syrians) have a predilection for this hymn in the celebration of our Lord Jesus Christ and that under these circumstances they commit no error when they add "you who have been crucified for us". But the people in Byzantium and in the West relate it . . . to the consubstantial Trinity. For this reason they do not allow one to add "you who . . .", so that the idea of suffering is not carried into the Trinity. In numerous provinces in Europe the words, "Holy Trinity, have mercy on us" are added in the place of the "you who . . ." This addition makes clearer the intention of the orthodox, who cherish a preference for the Trinity with the invocation "holy, God, holy, strong, holy, immortal", in order to eliminate the "you who . . ." by an exact and fitting formula.'

121. The following description is guided by E. Schwartz, *PS*, 243–248, 259–260, 292–293; V.-S. Janeras, 'Les byzantins et le trisagion christologique', in *Miscellanea Liturgica* . . ., FS Lercaro, Vol. 2 (Rome, Tournai, New York, 1967), 469–99, especially 470–5.

sang the addition 'who was crucified for us'. This stirred up the local monks, because they suspected monophysite propaganda behind it. That was the time in which the letters addressed to Peter the Fuller could have been composed in the monastery of the Sleepless Monks. Their concern was clear: the expanded Trishagion formula should be discredited by demonstrating that it was an old heresy invented by Peter the Fuller.

In the forged letters he is charged theologically with having applied a statement, which pertains to only *one* divine *hypostasis*, to all *hypostases* of the Trinity. In this way the absurd notion arose that the Holy Spirit was crucified. But it is only permissible to transfer general statements from one *hypostasis* to another. Thus Father, Son and Spirit are each holy and God, but do not form three gods, because they are distinguished from each other solely by their *hypostases* and their *properties*. That is the tradition from Basil onwards.

For the actual course of the conflict there were, however, other events that were decisive. The Constantinopolitan monks called upon their Patriarch Macedonius in this question as the defender of orthodoxy and at the same time called Emperor Anastasius a 'Manichaean', through disillusionment at his procrastination in this affair. This began the process which ended with the downfall of the Patriarch, as we have already described.[122] On 7 August 511 he was led out of the city and confined in Euchaita. The events of 512 were even more dramatic. Marinus of Apamea, a friend of Severus of Antioch, attempted to convince the Emperor that the disputed Trishagion clause did not violate orthodox trinitarian doctrine, and at the Sunday mass on 4 November 512 made a renewed attempt at securing for the expanded Trishagion formula a firm place in the Byzantine liturgy. This initiative once again provoked a vehement protest, accompanied by riots in the streets of the capital which were not even to be checked by a *commonitorium* of Patriarch Timothy (511–518), which was intended to make the addition compulsory for all churches in the imperial city. There were tumultuous scenes at a procession, held to commemorate surviving a rain of ashes (an earthquake?) which had afflicted the region in 473. The houses of Marinus and Pompey, the Emperor's nephew, were set alight, statues and pictures of the Emperor were destroyed. Areobindus, the husband of Anicia Juliana (daughter of the West Roman Emperor), was proclaimed rival Emperor. The revolution seemed to be perfect. It was only with the utmost effort that the aged Anastasius succeeded in getting a hearing before the raging crowd and bringing it to its senses. Finally his authority prevailed. Heavy penalties were imposed upon the agitators.

122. Cf. *JdChr* II/1, 301–15.

The *chronique scandaleuse* of the Trishagion provisionally ended in Constantinople only in 518, not because a consensus was reached, but because the political constellation had completely changed. On the Feast of Chalcedon the Trishagion was also given back its pure form, freed from the theopaschite addition, in the Byzantine liturgy.[123]

The movement against the Trishagion addition also spread to its centre of origin, to Antioch, through the deposition of Patriarch Severus of Antioch. In the same year that the institution of the Feast of Chalcedon had been demanded, he had to surrender his see. The last of his 125 cathedral homilies, which is devoted entirely to the Trishagion, can be appraised as the comprehensive attempt against the objections of the Chalcedonians to demonstrate that this hymn with its addition was orthodox.[124]

Severus seeks the basis for his argument first in those fundamental theological propositions which were shared by his opponents, before he proceeds to explicate his specific application of these fundamental propositions. We are aware that he employs a different conceptual language for the theology of the Trinity from that for the *oikonomia*.

> Father, Son and Holy Spirit are three distinct *hypostases* and are not confused in one single essence . . . With regard to the Trinity the essence is the godhead, for the Father is God, the Son is God, the Holy Spirit is God; none of them is more God than the other on account of the identity and equality of honour of the essence. With regard to the *hypostasis*, other is that of the Father, other is that of the Son, and other that of the Holy Spirit. (PO 29, 237-239)

Then Severus develops the peculiarities of the three *hypostases*, of the unbegottenness of the Father, the begottenness of the Son and the procession of the Spirit. On the peculiarity of the Son he also comments that, without alteration of his nature or its mingling with the human nature, to it belongs the fact of having become a human being by having assumed from Mary a body endowed with a rational soul. Here the Patriarch begins with his interpretation of the Trishagion additions, which is rendered in short propositions. We shall note in particular the clarification of the so-called theopaschite addition 'you who were crucified for us', for the expansion of the acclamation by the addition of 'holy God, holy mighty, holy immortal God' created fewer problems. It is only a matter of deciding whether it should be understood in a trinitarian or a christological way.

Severus, however, interprets everything christologically. Thus he has

123. *Ibid.*, 360-3.
124. Severus Ant., *Hom.* 125: PO 29, 232-252.

no great difficulty in explaining the theopaschite addition. (Cf. the quotation above, pp. 146–7 with n. 364.)

It was particularly the Nestorian misunderstanding of this addition that had to be warded off. Whoever namely was of the opinion that the Trishagion could be dissected and that the 'You are holy, God' could be allocated to the Father, the 'You are holy, mighty' to the Son, and the 'You are holy, immortal' to the Holy Spirit, had to mean, according to Severus' deductions, that the addition 'You who were crucified for us' was addressed to a fourth person (cf. PO 29, 247). Against the reproach that with the expanded Trishagion a formula was introduced which could not be supported by apostolic tradition, Severus asked that it be borne in mind that many another custom which could not call immediately upon apostolic tradition did not cease for that reason to be orthodox. He conceded, however, that the Trishagion in Antioch had not yet been sung long enough, and the Alexandrians, Libyans and Egyptians did not address this praise to Jesus Christ.

In fact the 'Holy, holy, holy Lord of hosts' said by the seraphim is reported to us by the prophet Isaiah . . . But the 'Holy God, holy mighty, holy immortal' was added much later. If then we have accepted the addition in this phrase as pious, and confess him as true God who was crucified, we do not call the confession of our faith 'new', for it is added to this praise for a good reason, because it combats the Jewish folly of Nestorius . . . It is in our city that it began, where too the name of the Christians began; but it has already reached the Churches of Asia and now makes its way to all the Churches. (249)

3. The teaching of the forged correspondence with Peter the Fuller

(a) In Trishagio crucem? — *on the understanding of the Trishagion*
While at Antioch the Trishagion was referred exclusively to the Kyrios Jesus and thus the theopaschite addition was not a scandal, as Severus has just shown us, in Constantinople it was applied to the Trinity and thus was bound to become a problem. The addition 'You who have been crucified for us' was then no longer acceptable, because it appeared to be formulated about the triune God as such.[125] Let us present some major passages on the theme from this correspondence, from the oldest collection which refers the Trishagion to the immanent Trinity. As an example let us cite the first letter of Pope Felix.[126]

125. In *Ep. Flaccini* (Latin only), CA, *ep.* 77: CSEL 35, 1, p. 212, no. 19, Flaccinus asks: *unde igitur hoc dogmatizare 'in trisagio crucem'? num ex patribus?*
126. Ps. Felix, *Ep. ad Petr. Full.*: ACO III, 231, no. 7; CA, *ep.* 71, no. 7: CSEL 35, 1, p. 166, no. 7.

What is more abominable than this, that with you the Father and the Holy Spirit remain without honour and are belittled by the seraphim, because they are said not to confess the Trinity when they call holy, holy, holy, but solely the person of the Son?

Reference to the Trinity is demanded in all the Fuller letters, but in such a way that the theopaschite addition has to be omitted.[127] The legend already mentioned (p. 255) of a special revelation made to a child at the time of Patriarch Proclus, was intended to underscore the originality of the Trishagion interpretation in favour of the Church of Constantinople against Antioch.[128] It is in opposition to this that Peter the Fuller is said to have allowed the heresy to be proclaimed 'that one of the Trinity died, who is the God-Logos himself'.[129] The reference of the Trishagion to the Trinity is emphasized particularly strongly, also terminologically, in this second letter of Pope Felix. If namely the theopaschite addition 'one of the uncreated Trinity has been crucified' is ascribed to the Son, then he is declared mortal according to his divinity. This would mean, however, the denial of the Nicene *homoousios* and the dissolution of the one unseparated Trinity. For the first time it is thus subjected to number, because the middle is wrenched out. Father and Spirit are now separated from each other.[130] Peter the Fuller is unmasked as a heretic.

(b) The christological position of the correspondence with Peter the Fuller
There is not much to be expected with regard to christological content, considering the severe judgement about the education of the forgers which E. Schwartz passes from a philological standpoint.[131] Just as they do not grasp the structure of the Antiochene statement of the Trishagion, that is, its application to Christ, they leave us even more in the lurch when it is a question of elucidating the two-natures language. Let us illustrate this by the letter of Quintian, the alleged bishop of Asculanum.[132]

127. Anteonus, *Ep. ad Petr. Full.*: ACO III, 217, no. 2; CA, *ep.* 74: CSEL 35, 1, p. 188, no. 2.
128. See above, n. 117.
129. Ps. Felix, *Ep. II ad Petr. Full.*: ACO III, p. 23,9–10.
130. *Ibid.*, p. 21,4–6.
131. Cf. E. Schwartz, *PS*, 292–300, especially 294. He criticizes in detail the 'curious Greek of the letters which (is) characterized only insufficiently by the predicate "Latinizing" '. The explanation for this Schwartz finds in the fact that 'the compiler or the compilers of the letters had learned literary Greek not on the basis of Greek as a mother tongue, but as a foreign language; of the two imperial languages, Latin was the more familiar to them. They had to write Greek because they wanted to defend the Greek liturgy, and their opponents, the Palestinian and Antiochene monks, understood only Greek' (296).
132. Quintian., *Ep. ad Petr. Full.*: CA, *ep.* 72: CSEL 35, 1, pp. 170–82; here according to the Greek text ACO III, 227–229 (older version).

Peter the Fuller perverts the *evangelium Christi* 'not by the fact that he proclaims one Son from two natures and in two natures, our Lord Jesus Christ, and him as crucified for us, but by the fact that out of a perverse desire for novelty he goes so far as to speak . . . of the strong, immortal God as the crucified one nature of the Trinity'.[133] And not only that. 'You speak also of the one nature of the God-Logos and of the flesh. If there is only one nature of the God-Logos and the Father, then there is, so to say, only one nature of the Father, the body and the Logos.'[134]

Here then the forger lets it be known that he ascribes to Peter the Fuller the formula 'from two natures before the union of the God-Logos with the flesh'. But he says that this formula is impossible, because he who is from Mary according to the flesh did not pre-exist.[135] In this case Peter should explain how he interprets the Trinity in its one divinity, if the incarnate Son has only one nature and not two. In constantly new phrases the forger lists the numerous evil consequences of Peter's false assumption,[136] a process which presents as well many proofs for the necessity of the two-natures teaching. Above all it is stated that an orthodox explanation of the impassibility of the *Logos* would demand a two-natures teaching. Instead of 'God who suffered according to the flesh' (*deus passus carne*), he proposes saying: 'Christ suffered according to the flesh' (*Christus passus carne*).[137] Then there follow twelve anathemas against Peter the Fuller, which, particularly the eighth, express the strict-Chalcedonian teaching; these are also intended to hit at Nestorius.[138]

> And if anyone speaks of two persons or *hypostases*, and not rather of two natures which have come together in one person or *hypostasis*, let him be anathema.

The most detailed presentation of the two-natures teaching is found

---

133. *Ibid.*, ACO III, p. 227,22–26.

134. *Ibid.*, p. 227,27–28.

135. *Ibid.*, p. 228,3–4.

136. *Ibid.*, 228–229, nos. 5–11. Peter makes himself guilty of many heresies, those of Valentinus, Marcion, Eutyches and Sabellius. He is reproached with a detailed list of heresies in the letter of Justicinus of Sicily, which also belongs to the oldest collection, although it is missing in the *Coll. Vat.* Cf. ACO III, 12–13: Manes, Valentinus, Eutyches, Paul of Samosata, Nestorius, Arius.

137. *Ibid.*, p. 228,30–37 (nos. 9–10). See the anathema II, 229, no. 12. This could easily be interpreted as Nestorianism, because Nestorius himself has recourse to this terminology.

138. *Ibid.*, 229, no. 13. In the seventh anathema the writer rejects the abstract denotation θεανθρωπία as a formula for the incarnate Christ, because he fears a mixed essence in it. He demands in its place 'God and human being', thus the concrete denotation. The Latin text cannot express very well what is meant. Cf. CA, *ep.* 72: CSEL 35, 1, p. 178,22–23 (VIIII): *Si quis deum hominem et non magis deum et hominem dicit, damnetur.* On the whole matter see A. Grillmeier, art., 'Gottmensch III', in *RAC* 12 (1982), 316–17.

in the letter of Flaccinus, which is transmitted only in Latin.[139] We shall confine ourselves to the section in which Christ himself addresses Peter the Fuller in direct speech.[140] In this there is expressed a strong christology of distinction, which in some formulas is reminiscent of the old Antiochenes and Pope Leo. Christ says:[141]

> What belongs to my created flesh you should not tie to me and should not assign createdness, being made, suffering or death [to me] as one of the Trinity.[142] Nothing beyond what was, is and will be [namely the divinity] should you introduce into it [the Trinity], but you should also not deprive the divinity of my flesh (through the *mia-physis* formula). For I am by nature his Word. I gave to it [the flesh] what is mine, not through the transferral of what is mine by nature, but according to grace; and that [the flesh] has not transferred what is its by nature, but by grace I wanted through it to become [incarnate], as if being clothed with an ensouled human being. Because I am by nature the Son of God, I also confess myself as the natural son of man ... The property of each of the natures is intact in me.[143] Whoever does not preserve these [natures] and maintains that I had only one nature, maintains that the incarnate God is no longer God, not uncreated, no longer free from suffering, but passible; they render me completely bereft of everything which is mine.

Illuminating as these forged letters to Peter the Fuller may be for characterizing the theological situation in the dispute about the Trishagion in Constantinople, they provide little for the substance of christology at that time. They produce no support at all for the Chalcedonian party. In many regards they betray a very simple christology, when, for example, they interpret the *descensus Christi* (in a literal interpretation of Job 40,25) in the following way: the divinity of Christ hid itself as a hook in the soul of his holy body, in which he descended into Hades, in order to conquer it.[144]

IV. THE MONK EUSTATHIUS AND HIS PLEA FOR THE TWO NATURES

We are not leaving the environment in which we have moved up until now when we add the short letter of the monk Eustathius to Timothy

---

139. Flaccin., *Ep. ad Petr. Full.*: CA, *ep.* 77: CSEL 35, 1, pp. 206–12.

140. *Ibid.*, nos. 11–19: pp. 209–12.

141. *Ibid.*, nos. 12–14: pp. 209,14–210,11.

142. By this he means 'not according to the divine nature'.

143. *Ibid.*, no. 13: p. 210,6–7: *salva enim in me utriusque naturae proprietas.* Cf. Leo M., *Tom. ad Flav.*: TD 9, V. 54–55, p. 24: *Salva igitur proprietate utriusque naturae, et in unam coeunte personam.*

144. Cf. Acacius, *Ep. ad Petr. Full.*: ACO III, p. 18,34–36. The emphasis on Christ's descent into Hades as a descent according to the 'soul' is found in the works of Eustathius, who is about to be discussed. Cf. n. 170.

about the two natures.[145] Its significance is based (1) on a relatively detailed and frequent citing of the writings of Patriarch Severus,[146] (2) on its affinity with the christology of Leontius of Byzantium and thus (3) on its testimony for a strict-Chalcedonian teaching.[147] It seems indeed that Eustathius is inclined to combine the formula rejected at Chalcedon 'from two natures' with that of 'in two natures'. However, he does not make that a condition for a correct confession of faith.[148]

1. The situating of the letter of Eustathius chronologically

There seem to be some co-ordinates for establishing the date of the letter. The doctrinal dialogue of 532 suggests itself as the *terminus post quem*. The report about this by Innocent of Maronia speaks of the relationship of Patriarch Dioscorus to Eutyches and the consequences this has for the latter's deposition at the Council of Chalcedon. The letter of Eustathius quite clearly approaches some of the points in the discussion of 532, which would presuppose that the doctrinal dialogue was concluded. A comparison of the sources also yields the same result. A particular *topos* is the alleged 'repentance of Eutyches'.[149] By referring to this the

145. Eustath. mon., *Ep. de duabus nat.* (CPG 6810): PG 86, 901–942 according to A. Mai, *Nov. coll. II* (1833); here the new edition by P. Allen could be used, for which the editor is thanked. We shall cite it according to the chapter division and the line numbers in the new edition (CCG 19, Turnhout, Louvain, 1989).

146. These numerous citations were made use of by F. Loofs, *Leontius von Byzanz* (Leipzig, 1887), 54–9; by J. P. Junglas, *Leontius von Byzanz* (Paderborn, 1908), 105–19; J. Lebon, *Le monophysisme sévérien* (Louvain, 1909), 307–8; 350, n. 1; 373–5; P. Allen, 'Greek Citations from Severus of Antioch in Eustathius Monachus', *OLP* 12 (1981), 261–4.

147. A brief assessment is found in C. Moeller, 'Le chalcédonisme et le néo-chalcédonisme', in *Chalkedon* I, 684–5, n. 137; as well by M. Richard, 'Les florilèges diphysites', *ibid.*, 743–4 with a brief classification of the patristic citations of Eustathius: (1) a small group of texts from texts which are common to almost all the diphysite authors of the sixth century; (2) a few from the texts attacked by the anti-Chalcedonians (Leo's *Tomus*, formula of Chalcedon); (3) a florilegium of anti-Chalcedonian texts which is related to that of Justinian; (4) extracts from the works of Severus himself.

148. Cf. the lines 1004–1006 (Allen) = PG 86, 941: Εἰ οὖν σύνθετός ἐστιν ὁ Χριστός, οὐ μόνον ἐκ δύο συνενήνεκται φύσεων, ἀλλὰ καὶ ἔχει ταύτας ἐν ἑαυτῷ; that is, 'from two natures' rightly understood already means 'in two natures', for Christ still has them in himself.

149. Cf. Eustath. mon., *Ep. de duab. nat.*, no. 46, ll. 865–867; PG 86, 936B with *Coll. c. Sev. hab.*: ACO IV, 2, nos. 10–14, pp. 170,27–171,4. The *Coll.* lists the following assertions: (1) Eutyches is also regarded by the Severan side as a heretic; (2) Dioscorus, however, rehabilitated him (449) after his condemnation by Flavian (448), and in contrast condemned Flavian; Dioscorus could do this, because Eutyches had perhaps shown repentance (nos. 12 and 13). Eustathius: (1) Severus condemns Eutyches, but recognizes Dioscorus (ll. 861–864: 936AB); (2) the assumption that Eutyches had presented Patriarch Dioscorus with an improved *Libellus* and thus shown repentance (no. 46, ll. 864–873: 936B) (*eum lapsus poenitebat*) is false. Leont. Jer., *C. monoph.*: PG 86, 1884D–1885D; here as well the repentance of Eutyches is mentioned.

Severans want to justify Patriarch Dioscorus and his reception of the Archimandrite. Until now we know of this only from Innocent of Maronia.[150] From a comparison of the different reports it follows with some degree of certainty that Eustathius wrote after 532. From further observations, however, we can still narrow somewhat the *spatium utile* for the composition of the letter, even if we do not want to go as far as E. Schwartz, who wants to place the letter after the death of Emperor Justinian.[151] Worth noting is the manner in which Eustathius uses the Greek *Corpus Severianum*. He still has it at his disposal, because he can make original excerpts from 'various treatises'.[152] On this account, however, the letter does not have to be placed earlier than 536, that is, before the year in which Emperor Justinian ordered the Severan writings to be burned.[153] This judgement was certainly not carried out immediately and everywhere. There is also no need to conclude from the language of the work that Severus was still alive at the time of the composition of the writing, when the present tense is used in reference to the Patriarch.

> And he condemns those who speak of two natures after the *unio*. If after the union the two [natures] have become one, how does he himself consider the two natures so many years after the union in Christ? How can he deny once again what he considers and writes and says?[154]

If one interprets the prior indication of time 'almost six hundred years after the *henosis*'[155] somewhat liberally, then a possible date for the composition of the letter is in the middle or the second half of the sixth century.

150. As Eustathius introduces the *mia-physis* formula as an invention of the heretics and in particular of the Apollinarians, he seems to allude to the discussion of the Apollinarian forgeries at the doctrinal dialogue. Cf. ed. Allen, no. 8, ll. 92–96: PG 86, 905CD.

151. Cf. E. Schwartz, *Drei dogmatische Schriften Justinians* (Munich, 1939), 113–114. In contrast P. Allen, *op. cit.*, 398–403, introduction with n. 55.

152. Cf. Eustath. mon., *Ep. de duab. nat.*, no. 25, ll. 463–464: PG 86, 920C; P. Allen, *art. cit.*, 262.

153. Justinian emp., *Constitutio Sacra c. Anthimum, Severum, Petrum et Zoaram*: PG 86, 1095D–1104B; on Severus: 1097C–1100D: ... *Quare universis interdicimus aliquid de libris ipsius possidere ... nec dicta et scripta Severi maneant penes aliquem Christianum, sed sint profana et aliena ab Ecclesia catholica, igneque comburantur a possidentibus, nisi qui ipsa habent, velint periculum pati* (1099C). All calligraphers and stenographers who manufacture these books are threatened with amputation of the hand (*ibid.*).

154. Eustath. mon., *Ep. de duab. nat.*, no. 24, ll. 453–456; PG 86, 920C.

155. *Ibid.*, no. 24, ll. 450–452: PG 86, 920B: καὶ ταῦτα ὁ μετὰ ἑξακόσια σχεδὸν ἔτη τῆς ἐνώσεως δύο φύσεις ὁμολογῶν σκοπεῖν ἐν τῷ Χριστῷ.

2. On the classification of the theological content of the letter

There are some indications of the affinity of this writing with the documents of strict-Chalcedonian orientation between 532 and the beginning of the 540s. The clearest is the relationship to Leontius of Byzantium and his milieu, a fact which can be demonstrated in the conceptual language of Eustathius.

(a) Eustathius finds in Severus a Cyrillian passage which explains the process of the God–human union by means of the body–soul analogy. In body and soul we recognize in the case of human beings 'two natures', one is the soul, the other the body. Nevertheless both come together into 'one': 'Thus the two are no longer two, but from both one living being is perfected.'[156] This also follows for Christ: he is 'one living being'. In this Severus follows the master, and as an interpreter of Cyril is certainly correct. Eustathius, however, finds this a misinterpretation, and says: 'The distorters of right things should hear it. The teacher [Cyril] did not say that from both one nature is perfected (ἀποτελεῖσθαι), but one living being (ζῷον) which is the same as saying that one person (prosopon) is perfected.'[157] From this word ἀποτελεῖσθαι Eustathius is stimulated to speak of the 'end-result' (ἀποτέλεσμα) in the 'union from two', which he says is, nevertheless, not the 'one nature', but the 'one prosopon'.[158] This is 'what is aimed at' (telos).

In this terminology Eustathius is clearly in line with Leontius of Byzantium, as his *CNE* indicates.[159]

> Thus it remains after our investigation of the expression 'essential union' (τοῦ λόγου τῆς κατ'οὐσίαν ἑνώσεως), that we understand the special features, both of the divinity and the humanity, without mingling, according to the examples [analogies] adduced above. We have compiled only a weak picture of the truth which transcends everything, a picture, however, that shows that there is one single end-result [product] from it (ἓν μέν τι τούτων εἶναι τὸ ἀποτέλεσμα), whether we call it a *prosopon*, or a *hypostasis* or an *individuum* (*atomon*) or subject (*hypokeimenon*) or whatever else you please. About this I shall not argue.

This terminologically rich text finds its further counterpart in Eustathius, where we should not forget Cyril and Severus in the background.[160]

> We say that Christ is from two natures, just as the one body is from many members and parts, but not from two persons as well. Heaven forbid! Because the humanity of Christ never existed for itself (ἰδιουποστάτως), no proper *prosopon* will be attributed to what does not exist for itself, as Severus assumes: [Severus:] 'If we characterize Christ as out of two natures, then we also say he is two natures and in two natures, by our holding onto the words "unmingled" and "undiminished".' If indeed the two natures form the one *prosopon* (ἀποτελεστικαί εἰσι τοῦ ἑνὸς προσώπου αἱ φύσεις), insofar as there is talk about 'from two', why then not also the end-result [end-product] (τὸ ἀποτέλεσμα)? That is what we

156. *Ibid.*, no. 53, ll. 976–978; it is a question of Cyril Alex., *Ep. 2 ad Succensum* (CPG 5346): PG 77, 245AB. The conclusion reads: ὥστε τὰ δύο μηκέτι μὲν εἶναι δύο, δι'ἀμφοῖν δὲ ἓν ἀποτελεῖσθαι ζῷον.

157. *Ibid.*, no. 53, ll. 978–981; PG 86, 940BC.

158. *Ibid.*, no. 50, ll. 943–947; PG 86, 937D: 'For this reason the Fathers have beautifully said that Christ is two natures, that he consists of them, brings them together, and thus is both. This composition is a *prosopon*, not insofar as it is composed, but insofar as it is the end-result (*apotelesma*).' The one *prosopon* is what is really aimed at in the process of union (*telos*).

159. Cf. above, p. 211, n. 88, Leontius Byz., *CNE*: PG 86, 1305C.

160. Eustath. mon., *Ep. de duab. nat.*, no. 14, ll. 220–31; PG 86, 912AB.

mean by the end-result [end-product] itself, which is composed from them (τὰ ἐξ ὧν συνέστη αὐτὸ τὸ ἀποτέλεσμα).

We can hardly accept the alleged sentence of Severus as genuine. It is the 'interpretation' of Eustathius which he reads into the 'from two natures' of the Patriarch. But stimulated by the Cyrillian-Severan terminology, Eustathius moves in a striking way in the language of Leontius, as we see from the text just cited.

(b) *Enhypostatos*: a still more significant affinity between Leontius and Eustathius, beyond that of *apotelesma*, is *enhypostatos*. The latter employs it three times in order to denote by it the reality of something, be it of the two natures, be it of the union from both.[161]

(c) *Synthesis, synthetos*: in Leontius these concepts surface in connection with the theory of the union in Christ, in association with other words which he examines for their applicability to his purpose.[162] Eustathius stresses the concept *synthetos* particularly strongly in order to express the two-natures teaching as duality in unity.[163]

> This is the expression *synthetos*: it signifies the coming together of two things; whoever reads *synthetos* thinks of two things from which that composition is made, which it also has in itself; and they remain these (two) as long as what is composed is really a composition. If, then, Christ is composed, he comes not only from two natures [as from one preceded and now disappeared], but he retains them in himself, as one who consists of them, and he is them both, so that he is not as another in other things. The principle of the *synthetos* thus remains preserved.

In fact this linguistic field around *synthetos* fits in very well with the Chalcedonian two-natures teaching, and the concept will retain its significance in Greek theology. It is thus no surprise when Severus does not like it and rejects it.[164]

Finally we can also refer to a similarity *in negativis*: Leontius and Eustathius alike have no love for the concept *hypostasis*. To characterize the unity they prefer *prosopon*, and in this regard Leontius displays a somewhat richer language than his colleague. One could certainly extend the comparison between them even further. The agreement between the two monks is sufficiently clear, but this still provides no hint with regard to chronology. Both stand in the same defence against Severus, fit into the milieu of Constantinople and defend a purely Chalcedonian christology, as will now be briefly demonstrated for Eustathius.

3. Eustathius as defender of strict-Chalcedonian language

As in Leontius, so too in Eustathius the two-natures theme is to the fore. Unfortunately Eustathius also fails to see the problem of the distinction of the main Chalcedonian concepts *hypostasis* and *physis*. His view is confined to the possibility of proving that in Christ, despite the

161. Eustath. mon., *Ep. de duab. nat.*, no. 9, ll. 123–125; PG 86, 908B. In no. 13, ll. 210–211; 909D *enhypostatos* stands as a counter-concept to φαντασιώδης and οὐσιώδης and means once again real, actual; in no. 15, l. 248 (912C) *enhypostatos* stands opposed to *anhypostatos*, or as 'being' to 'non-being'; in no. 18, l. 336 (916B) Eustathius says of the *mia physis* of Severus that he understands it as 'substantial' and 'real' (οὐσιώδη καὶ ἐνυπόστατον). Thus with his linguistic usage Eustathius fits into the environment of Leontius of Byzantium and the compilers of the letters of Peter the Fuller.

162. See Leont. Byz., *CNE*: PG 86, 1301–1304.

163. Eustath. mon., *Ep. de duab. nat.*, no. 54, ll. 1000–1008; PG 86, 940D–941A.

164. See above, pp. 159–60.

'essential *henosis*', a duality has to be accepted. His dialogue partner is Severus.

(a) The Severan mia-physis formula in the interpretation of Eustathius

The monk knows that Severus is a follower of Cyril when he refers the denotation of the 'one *physis*' to the pre-existent Logos. He shows sympathy for this, but is surprised at the fact that then this denotation is also applied to the result of the union, although the 'ensouled flesh' is now included as well. Logically there has still 'to be seen in the *synthesis*(!) two existing [real] natures, and not one single nature'.[165] After the Logos in the union assumed everything from the human being, soul, body, flesh, his human being cannot have lost this one thing, namely to be called 'nature'.[166] This argument is not bad, but pays too little attention to the fact that Severus does not give to the 'one *physis* of the divinity' a general meaning, but one that is proper to God alone, in the sense, for example, of 'God's own proper nature'. There cannot be a second. Nevertheless Severus would then have to add: 'no second nature of the same kind'. Eustathius too will not speak of such a second nature of the same kind. He certainly knows that the same concept can be applied on different levels, that is, used analogically. The human nature of Christ does not have the 'station' of the God nature, but it must still be denoted as nature. He says that Severus must be able to think along these lines too.[167]

> But we stress this: as in the assumption of the humanity all is preserved and named, and on account of the union the particular denotations are not shed, so too the nature is called 'nature', and on account of the *synthesis* is neither contracted [namely to denote the one nature] nor does it disappear because of the synthesis. Each of the two natures remains, not only what each is by nature, but also has the denotation for the nature. You are also of that opinion, Severus, when you treat each of the two natures by itself (*ἰδίως*); or you decline to call them, when taken together, 'two natures', so that you do not afflict the docetists in every regard (that is, from false consideration for the docetists).

(b) Does Severus really speak of two natures?

Eustathius is cautious when he wants to ascribe to Severus the statement of two natures. He limits it to the case where Severus speaks of the two natures disjunctively, that is, each by itself, not conjunctively, or considered together.[168] He admits that the Patriarch never speaks of two

---

165. Eustath. mon., *Ep. de duab. nat.*, no. 19, ll. 356-357; PG 86, 916C: καὶ ἐν τῇ συνθέσει ὑφισταμένας φύσεις ὁρᾶν, οὐχὶ μίαν μόνον φύσιν.
166. *Ibid.*, no. 19, ll. 357-361; PG 86, 916CD.
167. *Ibid.*, ll. 363-370; PG 86, 916D.
168. Cf. *ibid.*, no. 9, ll. 108-123; PG 86, 908AB.

natures when he considers them in the state of being united. Hence he can only put forward the logical demand that to be consistent, Severus must accept two natures and denote them as such, also in the state of being united (ἐν συνθέσει). In order to escape this necessity, the Patriarch has recourse to the old anti-Arian schema of the distinction of the two times.[169] He is of the opinion that by recourse to the different states of the one *physis* he can avoid the real distinction into two *physeis*. And in the concrete how does this distinction of the 'times' or of the 'states' of the divine Logos appear? Eustathius says that we are not confronted simply with differences of time, but with realities. This is said in a text which is also terminologically interesting, which in a special way allows the 'nature-schema' of Eustathius to be recognized, but taken together with the 'distinction of the times'. Each time which is to be distinguished in Christ corresponds also to a nature, so that four times and four natures are contrasted with each other. Christ is first of all considered in the time before the incarnation, then in the time of the incarnation. This makes two natures. But the Only-begotten died in the nature of flesh. He descended as 'soul', to the 'souls', which resulted in a third nature. Finally he awakened his body and ascended with it above all the heavens before the countenance of God, which referred to a fourth nature.[170]

---

169. *Ibid.*, no. 20, ll. 373–399; PG 86, 917AB. He is said on this account to be guilty of a contradiction, because he 'denotes the one nature as two natures' (l. 381; 917A8–9). Severus himself, however, testifies that the Fathers before him have accepted two natures in Christ (no. 6, ll. 49–61; 904D–905A). Eustathius refers honestly to a writing of Severus, *Expositio fidei*, which according to K.-H. Uthemann, *Anastasii Sin. Viae Dux* = CCG 8, 442, seems to be an excerpt from the *Or. I ad Nephalium*. In this Severus defends himself against misusing the name of Cyril, because a development occurred in the latter through apologetic necessity.

170. *Ibid.*, no. 22, ll. 430–434; PG 86, 920A: Καὶ διατοῦτο οὐ μόνον ἐρωτήσωμεν τίς φύσις ἀσάρκου θεοῦ καὶ τίς σεσαρκωμένου, ἀλλὰ καὶ τίς φύσις ἐμψύχου μόνον θεοῦ — ἄσαρκος γὰρ ἐπεδήμησεν τοῖς ἐν ᾅδου — καὶ τίς φύσις θεοῦ, σεσαρκωμένου μέν, σαρκὶ δὲ ἀφθάρτῳ καὶ ἀθανάτῳ. The different applications of the *physis* concept are not unproblematical. Insofar as it is a matter of the 'divinity' and 'humanity' of Christ, the application is covered by Chalcedon. But if now the soul, descended into Hades and united with the divinity (the ensouled God), and then 'the exalted Christ' are placed beside them as a third and a fourth *physis*, the content of the *physis* concept changes. The discussion with Severus is not made any easier by this. Yet here Eustathius is witness to a rare terminology, and that attests his wide reading in patristic literature. He speaks of the 'ensouled God, descending into Hades only in the soul' (ἔμψυχος μόνον θεός). In no. 23 Eustathius repeats these questions of no. 22 in a modified form (no. 23, ll. 442–445; PG 86, 920B). The distinction is the same. The formulation of the 'soul being God, descended into Hades' stands at the end of a long development in the *descensus* theology. That Eustathius knows it places him in a far-reaching tradition. On this see A. Grillmeier, 'Der Gottessohn im Totenreich', in *idem, Mit ihm und in ihm* (Freiburg, Basel, Vienna, ²1978), 159–71.

For this reason we ask not only what is the nature of God without the flesh and what is the nature of the Incarnate One, but also what is the nature of the God who is only soul, for he dwelt without flesh in Hades; (we ask) as well what is the nature of God, who indeed became flesh, but is now in incorruptible and immortal flesh.

Eustathius knows that such a dividing up is a horror for Severus. For the question 'which nature in Christ?' already means a dissolution of the unity, exactly what Severus objected to in the detestable Leo I of Rome and his *Tomus* (no. 24). But what does the witness of Severus signify for Eustathius? What Severus does not want to concede is found in particular Fathers before Cyril.[171] Thus the monk feels certain of his ground. Admittedly the two-natures schema of Chalcedon is now presented in a way which makes it even harder for Severus to acknowledge in his opponents the will to retain the unity in Christ. This follows too from the further problematic of Eustathius.

(c) One or two activities in Christ?

Over and above the two natures Eustathius defends with Leo I also the two activities, the divine and the human, in Christ, in the framework of a critique of a Christmas sermon of the Patriarch, within which the walking of Jesus on the lake is said to be interpreted 'in a monophysite way'.[172] In contrast to this the monk undertakes to interpret this miracle in the sense of Leo I's *Tomus* to Flavian.[173]

> Although he [Severus] distinguishes the nature of the flesh from the nature of the divinity, he still condemns those who confess two natures, but most of all himself. For he acknowledges two natures in Christ, indeed as subsisting and remaining. But then he brings

---

171. Eustath. mon., *Ep. de duab. nat.*, no. 7, ll. 71–73; PG 86, 905B: 'It is sufficient for us that Severus testifies that the manner of speaking of the two natures is found in the holy Fathers, and in many Fathers, not only in one or two.' Eustathius stresses too that if we began already with the corrections made to the two-natures teaching of the Fathers which they produced before the heretics, then the manner of speaking of the *mia physis* 'must also be relinquished, since it has been invented by the heretics' (no. 8, ll. 82–104; 905CD). The monk complains about the authoritarian procedure of Severus who 'distinguishes (the natures) as two when he wishes and again joins them together into one, as if he had the authority to speak and to act' (no. 9, ll. 126–127; 908B). Eustathius can rightly refer to certain inconsistencies in Severus. Against the Grammarian, for example, Severus stresses that divinity and humanity retain their undiminished reality in the synthesis. Why then does he not accept two natures? (Cf. no. 15, ll. 252–266; 912D–913A). Or if Severus takes the words *ousia* and *physis* synonymously, why does he then censure Sergius Scholasticus, when the latter modifies the *mia-physis* formula into a *mia-ousia* formula? Cf. *ibid.*, no. 10, ll. 162–165; 909A.

172. Ibid., nos. 29–30, ll. 559–587; PG 86, 924C–925A. Severus will admit only an 'undivided activity': ll. 570–571; 924D3. *Ibid.*, nos. 30–36, ll. 588–741; PG 86, 925A–932A. Eustathius thus confesses Pope Leo I's *agit enim utraque forma quod proprium est*, which is rejected by Severus.

173. *Ibid.*, no. 42, ll. 803–813; PG 86, 933AB.

them together, I know not how, into one ... If there was only one nature in Christ, then it is superfluous to stress 'insofar as God' and 'insofar as a human being', or 'the nature of the flesh' or 'the nature of the divinity', or 'to him who was born to suffer' and 'to him who was born not to suffer'. For that refers precisely to the two natures.

As in Leontius of Byzantium, so too in Eustathius the theological emphasis is on the duality of the natures. In contrast to this the interpretation of the unity of the *hypostasis* recedes. Nor even does the term *hypostasis* emerge. For this reason the monk fails to advance beyond Leontius or John the Grammarian. Yet in comparison with the latter there is a clearer line with regard to the evaluation of the *mia-physis* terminology and of the neo-Chalcedonian compromises in general. For Eustathius the confession of the two natures unambiguously excludes the formula of the one nature in such a way that the idea of the simultaneous use of both formulas can no longer exist.[174]

If the two natures are really two, they cannot be called one. But that there are two natures in Christ, Severus not only stated, but also wrote.

Thus Eustathius is to be reckoned among the supporters of a strict-Chalcedonian language. He also clearly makes reference to the text of the definition of 451 and renders it in his own words. He understands well that the principal terms of Chalcedon and in particular its 'in two natures' can be derived from Cyril himself.[175]

What is the difference between saying 'Christ is in two natures' and what Severus, the double-headed fox, says, corresponding with the blessed Cyril: 'perfect in the divinity and perfect in the humanity', and it is impossible for 'two' not to appear in 'two', yet not in the persons. For in Christ there are not two persons.

If Eustathius is not an outstanding theologian, still through his own study of the sources he creates for himself a clear conviction of the expressive power of the Chalcedonian formula, from which, though, he omits the concept of *hypostasis*.

---

174. *Ibid.*, no. 54, ll. 991–994; PG 86, 940CD. Eustathius knows that Cyril used the *mia-physis* formula to ward off the erroneous teaching of Nestorius. Cf. no. 55, ll. 1018–1019; PG 86, 941AB. For the right understanding of this formula in Cyril, he refers to his letter to Eulogius (CPG 5344; PG 77, 224–228) and his *Prosphoneticus* to the Alexandrians (CPG 5265).
175. *Ibid.*, no. 52, ll. 970–975; PG 86, 940B.

CHAPTER THREE

LEONTIUS OF JERUSALEM AND HIS PICTURE OF CHRIST

We encounter a new type of Chalcedonian christology in the works of an author who is characterized as Leontius of Jerusalem, but whose identity is difficult to determine.[1]

SECTION ONE

ON THE PERSON AND WORK OF LEONTIUS OF JERUSALEM

F. Loofs had identified the two Leontii, the one from Byzantium and the one from Jerusalem,[2] as one and the same person. The writings ascribed to the latter, *Against the Monophysites (Contra monophysitas)* (CPG 6917) and *Against the Nestorians (Contra Nestorianos)* (CPG 6918), he considered as adaptations of a lost original of Leontius of Byzantium.[3] The two works named only attracted notice and a new

---

1. Cf. the colophon in PG 86, 1769/70: Τοῦ πανσόφου μοναχοῦ Κῦρ Λεοντίου Ἱεροσολυμίτου.

2. The new edition of the works of the latter is being prepared by P. T. R. Gray.

3. F. Loofs, *Leontius von Byzanz und die gleichnamigen Schriftsteller der griechischen Kirche* = TU 3, 1–2 (Leipzig, 1887). On the identity of Leontius of Byzantium and Leontius of Jerusalem see 183–94. This thesis is taken over by W. Rügamer, *Leontius von Byzanz. Ein Polemiker aus dem Zeitalter Justinians* (Diss. Würzburg, 1894), 33–43; thus Rügamer is against equating Leontius of Byzantium with the Scythian monk Leontius, and Leontius of Byzantium with the 'Origenist Leontius' of the *Vita Sabae*. Nevertheless Rügamer will not accept the statement on 194–7, that the *Contra Monophysitas* is the later adaptation of a part of the 'scholia of Leontius', which as well is said to be the basis for *De sectis*. Furthermore he rejects Loofs' hypothesis about the adaptation of the *Contra Nestorianos* (41–3). In other respects too he repeatedly distances himself from Loofs. Thus Rügamer uses the two works named in his presentation of the christology of Leontius of Byzantium. A different opinion is found in J. P. Junglas, *Leontius von Byzanz* = FCLDG VII 3 (Paderborn, 1908) and V. Grumel, art., 'Léonce de Byzance', in *DTC* 9, 400–26. But since CPG 6917 and 6918 were regarded by most authors in Loofs' way of thinking as *opera dubia* or *spuria*, for the most part they remained unconsidered for the history of doctrine. D. Stiernon, art. 'Léonce de Byzance', in *DSp* 9 (1976) (col. 651–60), says in col. 655: 'Le Contra Nestorianos ... et ... le Contra Monophysitas ... sont attribués par les mss au "moine très sage ... Léonce le hiérosolymite", en qui il convient de voir un Léonce distinct

assessment through the research of M. Richard,[4] who conceded Leontius of Jerusalem a significant place in the history of doctrine in the sixth century. Two works have to be distinguished: one against the Monophysites, and the other against the Nestorians.[5] *CM* falls really into two distinct *opuscula*. (a) 63 *capitula* or *aporiai* (PG 86, 1769–1804): Leontius demands from the Monophysites answers to this series of objections, similar to the *capitula XXX* of Leontius of Byzantium. The argumentation is consistently speculative, but a few patristic authorities are adduced.[6] (b) *Testimonia sanctorum* (PG 86, 1804–1900A9). The conclusion (1900A9–1901A2) is not authentic. As Richard remarks, Leontius does not really produce a florilegium, but rather an exposition in the genre of 'questions and answers' (*erotapokriseis*).[7] With F. Loofs and M. Richard, one should probably accept that the *aporiai* represent the continuation of an extensive work, which expounded the arguments of the Severans and refuted them, but which is no longer extant. The *aporiai* and the *testimonia sanctorum* are to be considered as two appendices, as it were, to this work.

CN originally comprised eight books, of which, however, we possess only seven, with chapters of varying number and length.[8] The

---

du nôtre' (= Leontius of Byzantium). The assigning of these writings to Leontius of Byzantium is still defended by J. H. I. Watt, 'The Authenticity of the Writings Ascribed to Leontius of Byzantium. A New Approach by Means of Statistics', in *StudPat* 7 = *TU* 92 (1966), 321–36; S. Rees, 'The Literary Activity of Leontius of Byzantium', *JTS* 19 (1968), 229–42; I. Fracea, Ὁ Λεόντιος Βυζάντιος. Βίος καὶ Συγγράμματα (Κριτικὴ Θεώρηση) (Athens, 1984), 217–46.

4. M. Richard, 'Léonce de Jérusalem et Léonce de Byzance', *MSR* 1 (1944), 35–88 = *Op. Min.* III, no. 59; *idem*, 'Les florilèges diphysites', in *Chalkedon* I, 740–2; see *CCT* II/1, p. 60. For M. Richard, *Op. Min.* III, no. 59, pp. 81–8, 'Leontius of Jerusalem' is the *apocrisiarius* of the Palestinian monks, the participant in the doctrinal dialogue of 532 and in the Synod of Constantinople in 536, who is closely connected with the court of Justinian. On this see above, pp. 181–4.

5. See the literary-historical explanation in M. Richard, *Op. Min.* III, no. 59, pp. 37–9, on the *Contra Monophysitas* (*CM*) (CPG 6917); and pp. 39–43 on the *Contra Nestorianos* (*CN*) (CPG 6918). The new suggestion by M. Breydy for dating the *CM* (after 641) and on the Leontius question in general, which he makes in his recent edition, *Jean Maron. Exposé de la foi*, CSCO 497–498 (1989), and presents in other articles, cannot be discussed here.

6. *Aporia* 12: Gregory of Nyssa; *Aporia* 18: Gregory Nazianzen; *Aporiai* 21 and 44: Cyril of Alexandria.

7. Here we have to distinguish: (i) a more speculative presentation (1804D–1817B); (ii) a patristic section with a dyophysite florilegium (1817C–1849C) and a critical investigation (1849C–1876C) where in particular it is a question of the Apollinarian forgeries; (iii) a historical section with refutation of monophysite objections against the Council of Chalcedon. On the *CM* see P. T. R. Gray, 'An Anonymous Severian Monophysite of the Mid-Sixth Century', *Patristic and Byzantine Review* 1 (1982) 117–26. From the *CM* Gray gathers texts of a Severan who cannot be identified.

8. An overview indicates the christological themes:
1. The *synthesis* of the natures of Christ: 52 chs.

peculiarity of *CN*, in terms of the history of literature, was shown decisively by the discovery that Leontius of Jerusalem 'not only gives the Nestorian views or, as is customary in polemical writing, caricatures them, but that he *cites* them, that there are thus Nestorian texts preserved for us in *Adversus Nestorianos*. Through their sheer quantity these texts represent a considerable increase in the pool of resources for the history of Antiochene theology.'[9] The 'Nestorianism' which Leontius of Jerusalem had in mind was in various regards just as undervalued as his own writing.[10] In the study just cited L. Abramowski has recorded all the Nestorian citations and has compiled a complete list (pp. 51-5). The 'Nestorian' who speaks in these 'supports the view that two natures are two *hypostases*, and two *hypostases* two *prosopa*, the unity is presented in the one *prosopon*'.[11] But from this new insight into the textual situation one should not conclude that the complete citations already reproduce the complete text of the Nestorian writing, for only seven books of the *CN* are extant. 'As far as the Nestorian is concerned, the loss of the eighth book of Leontius is a real misfortune ..., because it is only in the eighth book that Leontius wanted to refute the Nestorian's formulations for the *unity* of the person of Christ, which in his opinion were inadequate.'[12] Because we can recognize from the citations of

2. The one *hypostasis* of Christ: 49 chs.
3. Against the two-sons teaching: 14 chs.
4. Mary *theotokos*: 49 chs.
5. The divinity of Christ (in divine nature): 33 chs.
6. Against the expression: 'God-bearing human being' *theophoros anthropos*: 10 chs.
7. The formula *unus de Trinitate passus est*: 11 chs.

9. L. Abramowski, 'Ein nestorianischer Traktat bei Leontius von Jerusalem', in *III. Symposium Syriacum 1980* = *OCA* 221 (Rome, 1983) (43-55), 43-4, where the conclusion reads: 'With the exception of I 52, the last chapter of the first book, where no citation appears, every chapter begins with a citation' (44).

10. Thus M. Richard himself, *art. cit.*, 68 (even in 1944) wrote: 'D'abord on aurait grand tort de chercher dans les questions du *Contra Nestorianos* la doctrine réelle de théologiens nestoriens byzantins dont nous ignorons jusqu'aux noms. L'exposé que nous présente Léonce de Jérusalem est tout théorique et artificiel.' This judgement is repeated in part verbatim by C. Moeller in *Chalkedon* I (1951), 687. Two other authors found in the opposing citations in *CN* II, 13 (PG 86, 560BC-1516D) some belonging to Leontius of Byzantium. Thus D. B. Evans, *Leontius of Byzantium. An Origenist Christology* (Washington, 1970), 139; he is followed by P. T. R. Gray, *The Defense of Chalcedon in the East (451-553)* (Leiden, 1979), 128-31. The basis for this lies in an unclarified concept of *enhypostatos*.

11. L. Abramowski, *art. cit.*, 45. Abramowski emphasizes the clear Greek of these texts, which is in very marked contrast to that of Leontius of Jerusalem himself, to his disadvantage. She says that unfortunately the Latin translation in PG 86 'frequently succumbs to the obscurity of Leontius' Greek', and that on some occasions in the translation Nestorian citation and counter-argument are joined without distinction.

12. *Ibid.*, 45-6.

the opponent that he is attacking an earlier writing of Leontius, our knowledge of literary history is thus also expanded.

'There were three writings:

(a)   a writing of Leontius of Jerusalem, which is no longer extant,
(b)   the Nestorian's attack on this writing, which is partly preserved in the excerpts of Leontius,
(c)   Leontius' writing in defence, which is also no longer complete.'[13]

Classification both chronologically and in the history of ideas

The corpus of Leontius of Jerusalem must have been composed in the years between 536(538) and 543/544, thus in the period after the condemnation of Severus at the Synod of Constantinople (536) and his death (538), and before the outbreak of the Three Chapters dispute.[14] M. Richard speaks of the time between 525 and 550 as 'une des périodes les plus brillantes de la théologie byzantine'.[15] He groups Leontius of Jerusalem with Leontius of Byzantium and Theodore of Raithu.[16] Leontius thus belongs to the class of educated monks who with their ascetical-theological training also acquired secular knowledge. In contrast to Leontius of Byzantium, who is more orientated to psychology, his namesake takes his analogies for christology more from physics of an Alexandrian stamp.[17] M. Richard speaks in defence of moving Leontius of Jerusalem's literary activity to Constantinople, but in doing so he gives him the rôle which is attributed here to his namesake.[18] In the course of our investigations we shall produce various indications of the fact that the author of CN and CM also wrote in Byzantium, without wanting

13. *Ibid.*, 46. Here, with the help of the Nestorian citations, certain christological themes for the lost writing of Leontius are reconstructed.

14. Thus M. Richard, *art. cit.*, 62–3; L. Abramowski, *art. cit.*, 43 with reference to A. Basdekis, *Die Christologie des Leontius von Jerusalem. Seine Logoslehre* (Diss. Münster, 1974), XVII and 12, n. 30, where further suggestions for dating are discussed (S. Helmer, C. Moeller, F. Loofs).

15. M. Richard, *art. cit.*, 62–3.

16. *Ibid.*, 63.

17. *Ibid.*, 70 with reference to *CN* I, 17: PG 86, 1464–1465 in comparison with Leontius of Byzantium, *CNE* I, 2: 1280D.

18. *Ibid.*, 81–8. P. T. R. Gray situates the author in Jerusalem on the basis of the MSS tradition. S. Helmer, *Der Neuchalkedonismus* (Bonn, 1962) (202–15), 207 (with note) refers to the frequent anonymous use of the writings of the Areopagite in the writings of Leontius. This is 'only understandable for Constantinople, where in 532 the court bishop Hypatius had rejected the Areopagite writings as inauthentic, but not for Palestine, where at the same time John of Scythopolis was already composing his *scholia* on the writings of Ps. Dionysius'.

to claim them as strict proofs. Some comments in Leontius of Byzantium seem to refer to his namesake. If this can be demonstrated, then conclusions could be drawn for the chronology,[19] but these are not essential for judging the two authors.

19. This is true especially for Leontius of Byzantium *vis-à-vis* Leontius of Jerusalem. We shall return to this.

SECTION TWO

THE CHRISTOLOGY OF LEONTIUS OF JERUSALEM

In comparison with Leontius of Byzantium, Leontius of Jerusalem appears as the sharper thinker and the more felicitous innovator of language. The novelty that he introduces consists in (1) a sharper version of the one subject in Christ and with this the concept of *hypostasis* and (2) the theory of the *henosis* of the two natures in Christ in the one *hypostasis*, a theory which is expanded terminologically and strengthened speculatively. We shall attempt to capture both in the fullest way possible, and in conclusion to work towards his new picture of Christ.

I. ANALYSIS
THE LINGUISTIC AND CONCEPTUAL TOOLS

1. A new consciousness of the problem

(a) Distinctions

The first advance of Leontius of Jerusalem consists in the fact that he consciously distinguished between a nature union (*unio in natura et secundum naturam*) and a *hypostasis* union (*unio in hypostasi et secundum hypostasim*). In contrast to the Apollinarian nature synthesis of the fourth century and the lack of clarity of the Cyrillian-Severan *mia-physis* formula, with this distinction there is for the first time the theoretical differentiation of union according to the *hypostasis* and the nature synthesis. In it there is a clear dismissal of Apollinarianism and every form of monophysitism.[20] More difficult, however, is the differentiation from the Nestorian and his teaching of two *hypostases*. But for the Nestorian too the correct distinction concerning both the Logos and the human being in Christ is found: in the incarnation 'the Logos does not assume an additional *hypostasis* in order now to attain the perfection of the *hypostasis*; he possesses only *the* (*hypostasis*) which he also had after

---

20. Leontius Jer., *CN* VII, 3: PG 86, 1765C: 'The flesh is not proper to the *physis* of the Logos; at the end of the ages it would be truly proper to his *hypostasis*.' Leontius, however, can take over the Cyrillian formula of the ἕνωσις φυσική, be it with certain difficulties. Cf. *CN* I, 50: PG 86, 1512CD; *CM*: PG 86, 1844B, a formula which Leontius of Byzantium rejects: *Epil*: PG 86, 1940AB.

the addition of the *nature* which he did not have'.[21] Whether Leontius pursues christology 'from above' or 'from below', it is completely clear that the one subject in Christ is seen as the *hypostasis* of the Logos. The human being in Christ 'does not possess like us his own proper human *hypostasis* which separates him from every similar or dissimilar nature, but the common and indivisible *hypostasis* of the Logos, both for his own [human] as well as for the [divine nature] which is over him'.[22] The problem which we had to clarify in the case of his namesake (of Byzantium), namely, whether he considered the subject in Christ as a *tertium quid*, does not even arise for Leontius of Jerusalem.

(b) The determination of the subject in Christ

We recall that the definition of Chalcedon did not attempt any speculative explanation of where in the one Christ the one *hypostasis* is realized, and under the assumptions at that time could not have aspired to this. The formal 'concept' of the *hypostasis* was not yet located in the one Logos-subject. The one Christ was presented as a complex totality, seen from the end-point of the incarnation and its result, in the unmingledness of the two natures and of the properties of each, which, however, have come together in one person and in one *hypostasis*.[23] The Fathers knew that the whole event of union had as its starting-point the perfect Logos and Son in the pre-existence. Nevertheless the concept of the 'one *hypostasis*' was not applied to this, but to the final form of him who had assumed flesh and in the 'one *hypostasis*' let the two natures be recognized. From this view of the one concrete *hypostasis* in the end-result (*apotelesma*, as Leontius of Byzantium said) the theologians laboriously attempted to change to the predicative placing of the 'one *hypostasis*' in the pre-existent Logos, in order to determine from there how the humanity of Christ is to be integrated into this pre-existent uniqueness. Thus where precisely is the one *hypostasis* realized? What does *hypostasis* mean when it is already there in the pre-existent Logos and nevertheless has to integrate into itself a second complete existence, which is also *physis* (nature) or *ousia* (essence), even if in historic finitude?

21. Leontius Jer., *CN* VII, 4: PG 86, 1768aA.
22. Leontius Jer., *CN* V, 29: PG 86, 1749BC. Cf. *CN* II, 48: PG 86, 1601A: In Christ there is only one ego, which Leontius explains in connection with Jn 2,19 ('Destroy this temple . . .'): 'This one and the same *prosopon*, which is signified by the pronoun "I", comprises the destroyed body, the soul which speaks through the body, and the God who resurrects what was destroyed.' The additive view of the 'ego' is not a counter-instance to what was said above, as will immediately become clear.
23. See the definition in *CCT* I², 544.

Why is it also not a *hypostasis*? In view of the Logos in God, how must I grasp and define *hypostasis*, if a contradiction is not to emerge from a consideration of the Incarnate One? What happens when the complete human nature is taken up into the one *hypostasis*?

These questions afflicted both Leontii in the same way. They were formulated anew in the work of the Nestorian whom Leontius of Jerusalem opposed in his *CN*. Until then the greatest handicap was the Basilian metaphysics of *hypostasis* and its transferral from trinitarian teaching to that of the incarnation: *hypostasis* is the *ousia* with the *idiomata*, or the *koinon* together with the *idion*.[24] We know that the Cyrillian-Severan tradition escaped this problem by wanting to use the Basilian teaching about *hypostasis* only for the *theologia*, not for the *oikonomia*. That amounted to an ostrich policy. The Chalcedonians received the more difficult inheritance by taking over the Cappadocian terminology and the combination of the theologies of the Trinity and of the incarnation, introduced by Gregory Nazianzen: in the *theologia*, one nature and three *hypostases*, and in the *oikonomia*, one *hypostasis* (from the Trinity) in two natures. A valid answer had been given neither to the Severans nor to the Nestorians when they asked: Why is the humanity of Christ also not *hypostasis*, if it is complete *physis* and also has its *idiomata*? Or is the humanity of Christ not an *individuum concretum*, not something distinct from the universality of the essence? Leontius of Byzantium did not face this question unambiguously. How did the other Leontius react to these questions?

First objection: the prosopon of Christ

We shall start with some attempts by the Nestorian to demonstrate two *hypostases* or *prosopa* in the Incarnate One by proposing a '*prosopon* of the nature', which is a ἕν not on the basis of the union, but 'by nature', namely the *prosopon* of the God-Logos. The other ἕν, the Christ-*prosopon*, whose unity and uniqueness are due to the *henosis*, is contrasted to this.[25]

Leontius investigates this terminology, and he too sees in Christ the one natural *prosopon* on the basis of the one *physis* of the Logos. This one *prosopon* does not change, rather it remains the same in the state of assuming humanity. With 'Christ' a second *prosopon* is not added. *Prosopa* are not united, but the *natures* are united into the *prosopon*. Thus there remains the one *prosopon*, which the pre-existent Logos has, which at

24. *Ibid.*, 367–73.
25. Leontius Jer., *CN* II, 34: PG 86, 1592B.

the same time is also the one *prosopon* of Christ, that is, of the Logos united with the humanity.[26] There is thus complete identity of the *prosopon*, of the person, of the subject before and after the incarnation. The pre-existent *hypostasis* of the Logos himself is the subject of the incarnation who assumes a human nature, which neither is nor has its own *prosopon*.[27] In this way there arises not merely a relationship of possession, as when one person acquires another. The Logos did not acquire (ἐκτήσατο)[28] a *sarx*, but he became flesh — a distinction which is familiar to us from the fourth century. We shall encounter it anew in the Syrian region. Because the one *hypostasis* has entered into this entitative relationship with the *prosopon*-less *sarx*, it can bear both series of 'physical names', that is, the predicates of both divine and human natures. While this Logos presented himself before (πάλαι) only in the one *prosopon* of 'one nature', he is now a two-natures *prosopon*.[29] This access to being is proper to the creative power of God alone.[30]

> If God alone is the cause of nature and *hypostasis*, what prevents him from putting one nature into another? Is not everything really possible for him?

The examples which then follow from the *physis* of animals and plants are admittedly not suitable for illustrating the specific peculiarity of the God–human union, which has been stated in a new linguistic way. Leontius finds there the taking over of natures into other *hypostases*, for example, by way of assimilating nourishment, or the transformation of *hypostases* into other natures, as in the case of the caterpillar–butterfly.[31] He would be better off speaking of nature synthesis or nature transformation. Fortunately he does not insist on a strict application of these analogies from nature to christology. The 'one *hypostasis*' of the Incarnate One is the unchanged *hypostasis* of the Logos, which assumes 'a nature without a *prosopon*' through a creative action which pertains to God alone, an action which first allows the 'assumption' of the flesh to be characterized as a 'becoming'. The one Logos in the flesh is a hypostatic entitative unity in two natures.

---

26. *Ibid.*, PG 86, 1592C: ἕν ἐστι τὸ πρόσωπον Χριστοῦ, ὅ ἐστιν ἐκ μιᾶς φύσεως ἕν πρόσωπον τοῦ Λόγου.

27. Leontius Jer., *CN* II, 35: PG 86, 1593B: καὶ ἄνθρωπος ἄρα γέγονεν τῇ τῆς φύσεως τῆς ἀνθρωπίνης προσλήψει, εἰ καὶ ἀπροσώπῳ ἡ αὐτὴ ὑπόστασις τοῦ Λόγου.

28. Leontius probably meant by this that the Logos did not appropriate to himself an already existing human nature.

29. Leontius Jer., *CN* II, 35: PG 86, 1593C: Christ is ἕν πρόσωπον μονοφυές before the incarnation, and διφυές after the incarnation.

30. *Ibid.*

31. *Ibid.*, 1593D.

Second objection: the Basilian concept of hypostasis

The decisive point has not yet appeared clearly. Leontius of Byzantium (see above, pp. 181–229) did not get beyond explaining the one fact that the humanity of Christ also has its human *idiomata* and thus must be a *hypostasis*. How does Leontius of Jerusalem proceed? The Nestorian formulates this difficulty.

> If the Logos has become a human being, he is in fact a particular human being [that is, recognizable as an *individuum*] (τίς ἄνθρωπος). It is only in this way that he can be a human being at all! But if he is a particular (individual) human being, he is a *hypostasis*. Hence there are two *hypostases* in Christ, or the *hypostasis* of the Logos ceases (to be).[32]

The response of Leontius of Jerusalem runs as follows:

> But from the first moment of its existence this particular (individual) human being Christ is divine according to the *hypostasis*. This means the same as the statement: according to his *hypostasis* God became a human being through the union of a human *ousia* with the divine *ousia*.[33]

The question remains: does Leontius of Jerusalem admit that the humanity of Christ is one individual being, thus one concrete *ousia* with *idiomata*? Does this humanity in its individuality also remain in the state of being united?

What is new is the fact that Leontius of Jerusalem is not closed to this insight. In contrast to Basil and his followers, he allows particularity to be ascribed to the human nature of Christ. He says expressly: 'We say that the Logos has taken over an individual nature into his own *hypostasis*.'[34] Can two individualized natures with their *idiomata* be united in *one hypostasis*? If they can, then several problems result from this. (1) How does Leontius of Jerusalem grasp the concept of *hypostasis*? (2) How does he understand the taking up of the human nature of Christ into the one *hypostasis*? In reality the response to the second question will resolve the first question.

(c) A new concept of hypostasis*?*

In the first chapter of *CN* II, Leontius of Jerusalem presents a whole series of meanings for the word *hypostasis*,[35] which in fact are so far

---

32. Leontius Jer., *CN* II, 43: PG 86, 1597AB.

33. *Ibid.*, 1597B.

34. *Idem*, *CN* I, 20: PG 86, 1485C: οὕτω φαμὲν τὸν Λόγον ἐκ τῆς ἡμετέρας φύσεως εἰς τὴν ἰδίαν ὑπόστασιν προσλαβέσθαι φύσιν ἰδικήν τινα. The opposite would be the assumption of the 'universal human nature' as such or the assumption of the total nature of human beings, which Severus accused John the Grammarian of Caesarea of doing.

35. Cf. Leontius Jer., *CN* II, 1: PG 86, 1528D–1532A.

removed from our problematic that we can pass over them. The first relevant conception for us is the following:

> We speak of *hypostasis* when, because different individual natures (φύσεων διαφόρων ἰδικῶν), with their *idiomata* (ἰδιωμάτων) with them come together, but not *prosopa*, as one or at once, because of the union there comes into existence (σύστασις) a single atom.[36]

The conception of *hypostasis* that follows this should precede it.

> We speak of *hypostasis* in a generally acknowledged sense not when different natures (φύσεων) come together, but when several partial idioms (μόνων ἰδιωμάτων μερικῶν πλειόνων) (come together), forming one general *idioma* (ἓν ἰδίωμα καθολικόν) from all, in one subject (ὑποκειμένῳ ἑνί), or in one single nature.[37]

Finally then he writes:

> Whether in a single, or composite, or individual or common (nature), like the divine nature or in one nature (φύσις) only, or in several united, provided they are totally in existence, this state or composition of partial *idiomata*, or of a common *idioma*, as thought of in a subject, is called *hypostasis*.[38]

One will understand this tailor-made definition of *hypostasis*, if one keeps in mind the application of the concept: the individual cases which Leontius means are the divine nature (which is simple, but also general, because it is in Father, Son and Spirit), the human nature, which is composed, or Christ with his two united natures. But it is not these different ways of considering separated or united natures that constitute the *hypostasis*, but only the coming together of several individual *idiomata* in a simple or composite nature, insofar as there is present a subject with irrevocable individualization, a τόδε τι, thus an utterly determined, unrepeatable subject. It finally reads: 'each *hypostasis* is separated in its own monad'.[39] Hence the last thing that Leontius can say is: 'Individualization and separation of inseparable essences into an individual number as far as the *prosopon* is concerned.'[40] Being a *hypostasis* means being the final monad:

---

36. *Ibid.*: PG 86, 1529C4–8. Cf. A. Basdekis, *Die Christologie des Leontius von Jerusalem. Seine Logoslehre* (Diss. Münster, 1974), 17.

37. Leontius Jer.: PG 86, 1529C8–12.

38. *Ibid.*, 1529C12–D4.

39. *Ibid.*, CN II, 5: PG 86, 1544A10–11: πᾶσα ὑπόστασις ἐν τῇ μονάδι ἑαυτῆς διακρίνει.

40. *Idem*, CN II, 1: PG 86, 1529D9–11: τόδε τι καθ'ἑαυτὴν ἀπότασίς τις οὖσα καὶ διορισμὸς τῶν ἀδιορίστων οὐσιῶν εἰς τὸν κατὰ πρόσωπον ἀριθμὸν ἑκάστου. Cf. A. Basdekis, *op. cit.*, 17–18.

It is rather the *idion* of the *hypostasis*, that it both discerns by their own (nature) the atoms from others which qua nature are the same, and assigns individuality to each of them.[41]

This concept of person can only prove its worth in its applicability to christology when the way in which Leontius represents the 'union according to the *hypostasis*' is investigated. He clearly feels the narrowness of the Basilian concept of *hypostasis*. It is only a step that separates him from breaking through this. The combination of *hypostasis* and *idiom*, which he still maintains, prevents him from taking this step. But it still seems that something new opens up.

2. New language for the *henosis*

There is now an increase in neologisms which are intended to encompass the event of the '*henosis* according to the *hypostasis*' and which are aimed at the *hypostasis* as such, although it is a question of the unification of natures.

(a) συνυποστάναι (from συνυφίστημι) = to subsist together: 'In his own one *hypostasis* subsist together the human and the divine natures of the Logos.'[42]

(b) ἐνυποστάναι (second aorist of ἐνυφίστημι) = to subsist in. Christ's *sarx*, as a passible nature, has its subsistence in the impassible Logos.[43] Faith in the mystery of Christ demands from us the following confession:

> The Logos has clothed his eternal *hypostasis*, which existed before the human nature, and the fleshless nature which existed before the ages in the last ages with flesh, and hypostatically inserted the human nature into his own *hypostasis* and not into that of a simple human being.[44]

In this way the verbs ὑφίστημι and ὑποστάναι with the prefix ἐν become the technical expression for 'to cause to subsist in', and in the second aorist for 'to subsist in'. Here the history of a great christological concept begins. Related word-formations now multiply.

(c) προσωποποιεῖν = 'to personalize', 'to make the person', to take

---

41. Ibid., 1532C10–12: ὑποστάσεως γὰρ μᾶλλον ἴδιον, ὃ καὶ τῶν ὁμοίων κατὰ φύσιν διακρίνειν τὰ ἄτομα ἰδίᾳ ἀπ'ἀλλήλων, καὶ καθ'αὑτὰ δεικνύειν ἑκάστου.

42. Idem, CN VII, 2: PG 86, 1761AB; not to be confused with this is the expansion of ἐνυπόστατος = real, actual, to συνενυπόστατος, as it is present in CN V, 30: PG 86, 1749D1–D5. On ἐνυπόστατος see below.

43. Idem, CN VII, 6: PG 86, 1768C: ἡ πρόσθεσις τῆς σαρκὸς αὐτῷ προσείληπται, ἐνυποστᾶσα τῷ ἀπαθεῖ αὐτῷ ἡ παθητὴ (σάρξ). The assumed flesh is taken up into the *hypostasis* of the Logos and thus has its *hypostasis* in it.

44. Idem, CN V, 28: PG 86, 1748D: αὐτῇ τῇ ἰδίᾳ ὑποστάσει ... τὴν ἀνθρωπείαν φύσιν ἐνυπέστησεν.

into the unity of the person or to bestow personality.[45] As the unity of the *hypostasis* is synonymous with the unity of the *prosopon*, the formation of this word is easily understandable christologically.

(d) The *henosis* as *synthesis* — *Christos synthetos*. *Synthesis* is one of the oldest words in the history of the interpretation of the unity in Christ, as Origen showed us. Sergius Scholasticus, to the anger of Patriarch Severus, takes pleasure in this.[46] With Leontius of Jerusalem (and then Justinian), christology really becomes a 'confession of the *synthesis* of the natures'.[47] The opposite of *synthesis* is the pure *parathesis*.[48]

(e) Expanded descriptions. On the basis of this clarified understanding of the taking of Christ's human nature under the *hypostasis* of the Logos, there occurred further formulations of an understandable kind: 'to transfer one nature into another *hypostasis*' which only God, as the creator of nature and *hypostasis*, can do.[49] Or: 'We may say that the humanity of the Saviour does not have a subsistence of its own (ἐν ἰδιαζούσῃ ὑποστάσει), but from the very beginning subsisted in the *hypostasis* of the Logos.'[50] In any case the idea of the insubsistence of the aprosopic human nature in the *hypostasis* of the Logos is contrasted with any *henosis* 'in the nature and corresponding to the nature'.

(f) Verbal adjectives with the root (ὑφ)ίστημι (στατός). The word-formations which have as their starting-point the verbal adjective from ἵστημι, στατός together with various prepositions are extraordinarily rich, for example, ἐνυπόστατος, ἀνυπόστατος, συνυπόστατος; or composites too, like ἰδιουπόστατος, ἑτερουπόστατος. As we already know, we have to be particularly careful in interpreting these terms. They can lead to rash conclusions. The Nestorian takes advantage of this state of affairs.[51] For him it is a question of proving two *hypostases* in the one Christ: on the one hand Christ is consubstantial (*homoousios*) with the Father, on the other hand also with King David. The twofold *homoousios*

45. *Idem, CN* V, 25: PG 86, 1748A: τῇ γὰρ ἰδίᾳ ὑποστάσει αὐτὴν [= σάρκα] ἀνειληφώς, ἐπροσωποποίησεν: by the Logos taking up the flesh into his own *hypostasis*, he hypostatized and personalized it. Cf. A. Basdekis, *op. cit.*, 24–5. The verb named above means as much as ἡ εἰς πρόσωπον ἕνωσις (*CN* III, 8: PG 86, 1636A).

46. On Sergius Scholasticus see above, pp. 118–20.

47. Leontius Jer., *CN* I, Prooemium: PG 86, 1401A: ὁμολογία τῆς τῶν φύσεων συνθέσεως. Besides the substantive there is also the verb συντίθεσθαι. His fondness for playing with *synthetos* and other words finds expression particularly in *CN* IV, 3: PG 86, 1657A. The concept σύστασις or the verb συστάναι is related to the term *synthesis*: *CN* IV, 3: PG 86, 1657C: ἐκ Λόγου γὰρ ἀιδίου καὶ σαρκὸς ὑποχρόνου, ὁ Δεσπότης ἡμῶν Χριστὸς ὅλος συνέστηκε.

48. *Idem, CN* I, 1: PG 86, 1409B.

49. *Idem, CN* II, 35: PG 86, 1593C: μετατιθέναι φύσιν τινὰ εἰς ἑτέραν ὑπόστασιν.

50. *Idem, CN* II, 14: PG 86, 1568A.

51. Cf. *idem, CN* II, 5: PG 86, 1540AB.

is balanced as on scales: as the Logos has his own *hypostasis* (*ἰδικὴν ὑπόστασιν*) *vis-à-vis* the Father, so as a human being he must also have one *vis-à-vis* David. It is impossible, he says, that the human being Jesus is without his own *hypostasis vis-à-vis* King David, 'for the non-hypostatic cannot properly be consubstantial with the enhypostatic [= which David is]'.[52] Once again we encounter the tempting antithesis *enhypostatos-anhypostatos*. What is placed in opposition here does not yet lead beyond the previously known interpretation of the two adjectives. It is a question of the simple realization that what is 'anhypostatic', that is, that which does not have any reality, cannot be consubstantial with the 'enhypostatic', that is, the real. This is confirmed a little later in *CN* II, 10, with a slight variation of the same objection.

If the Orthodox (Leontius) accepts 'that the human being Jesus subsists, that is, exists, but does not have or is not a *hypostasis*, how is a contradiction not taught, if one says that the existent is anhypostatic, that is, does not have reality'?[53] For the Nestorian himself the solution is clear; to have an entire human nature is the same as having an existing, real nature, not an anhypostatic one, but also the same as having a hypostatic nature which subsists in itself. If the Chalcedonians refuse to denote the human nature of Christ as a *hypostasis*, then this means for the Nestorian that as nature it is unreal, an *anhypostaton*. Leontius of Jerusalem counters as follows:

> We do not want to show the *anthropos kyriakos* as anhypostatic — not at all — but also not as idiohypostatic [with its own *hypostasis*], that is, as separated from the Logos. For who doubts the fact that it is not the same thing to call something anhypostatic and idiohypostatic?[54]

In other words, when we grant reality to the human nature of Christ, we do not immediately make it a nature subsisting in itself, or a *hypostasis*, as the Nestorian understands it. If the human nature of Christ is thus not an 'own *hypostasis*' (*idiohypostatos*), as the Nestorian intends, it is still not anhypostatic, which Leontius of Jerusalem now explicitly interprets as 'not being at all'.[55] But we shall wait in vain for the famous *enhypostatos*, with the alleged meaning of 'subsisting in', to be inserted between the extremes 'own *hypostasis*' and 'not-hypostatic' as the solution. There had been the same opportunity for this word in *CN* II,

---

52. *Idem*, CN II, 5: PG 86, 1540A9–10: τὸ γὰρ ἀνυπόστατον τῷ ἐνυποστάτῳ ὁμοούσιόν ποτε οὐχ ἂν λεχθείη.
53. *Idem*, CN II, 10: PG 86, 1556A1–3.
54. *Ibid.*, 1556A4–8.
55. *Ibid.*, 1556A10: ὅλως μὴ εἶναι.

5 (PG 86, 1540AB). To the equation by the Nestorian of 'twofold *homoousios* in Christ = twofold *hypostasis*', Leontius places in opposition the other equation 'twofold *homoousios* = two natures'. These 'two natures' are for the Nestorian admittedly a *sophisma*.[56] For a solution Leontius certainly grasps the word *enhypostatos*, but without changing its meaning (real). There too it forms the counter-term to *anhypostatos* = unreal, not existing, and thus must also be translated as real, existing. This conclusion is confirmed by the fact that *enhypostatos* is stated of the Father as the first *hypostasis* of the Trinity.[57] In short, *enhypostatos* means here once again 'real', and it is related only to Christ's two natures. Thus it follows that the acknowledgement of divinity and humanity in Christ as *enhypostata* does not mean that they are *idiohypostata*, that is, that each constitutes its own proper *hypostasis*. For Leontius of Jerusalem, Christ is only *one hypostasis* in the real two natures. He excludes two characterizations for the humanity of Christ: ἰδιουπόστατος and ἑτερουπόστατος.[58] In *CN* II, 13 there seems to be a last chance for the interpretation of *enhypostatos* as 'subsisting in' (another *hypostasis*).[59]

The two natures, we say, subsist in one and the same *hypostasis*,[60] admittedly not as if one of the two could be in it *anhypostatically*, but rather that *both can subsist in the one common hypostasis, and each of the two* (natures) *in one and the same hypostasis, whereby each* (of the two natures) *is enhypostatic.* For in order to be something, it is necessary that this same thing is also wholly on its own. If the natures have being, they must also subsist (= exist) and be *enhypostatic*. But because they are not independent of each other, since admittedly a union has occurred between them, it is not necessary that each of the two exists on its own (ἰδίᾳ ὑφεστηκέναι). Thus it is clear that the two *enhypostata* (= the two natures) must not be *heterohypostata* (= *hypostasis* beside *hypostasis*), but are thought as being in one and the same *hypostasis*.[61]

There is no doubt that in this text there is talk of subsistence, even of

---

56. *Idem*, *CN* II, 5: PG 86, 1540B.

57. *Ibid.*, PG 86, 1540D2: τῷ Πατρὶ τῷ ἐνυποστάτῳ ὁμοούσιος. Neither for the Nestorian nor for Leontius of Jerusalem is the Father 'insubsisting' in another *hypostasis*. It is only a question of his reality in the divine nature, through which he is consubstantial with the Son.

58. *Ibid.*, PG 86, 1540C8 and D9: the humanity of Christ is not 'its own *hypostasis*' nor 'another *hypostasis*'.

59. *Idem*, *CN* II, 13: PG 86, 1561B8–C9.

60. *Ibid.*, PG 86, 1561B8–9: τὰς γὰρ δύο φύσεις ἐν μιᾷ καὶ τῇ αὐτῇ ὑποστάσει λέγομεν ὑφίστασθαι.

61. *Ibid.*, PG 86, 1561C7–9: Δῆλον οὖν ὅτι οὐχ ἑτερουπόστατον εἶναι, ἀλλ' ἐν μιᾷ καὶ τῇ αὐτῇ ὑποστάσει νοεῖσθαι ἀμφοῖν αὐτῶν τὸ ἐνυπόστατον δεῖ. Shortly before: the two natures have a common *hypostasis*. And in one and the same *hypostasis* is each an *enhypostaton*, that is, has its own reality (1561B10–13). In the background is still the statement from *CN* II, 5: PG 86, 1544A10–11: 'Each *hypostasis* is separate in its own monad' (πᾶσα ὑπόστασις ἐν τῇ μονάδι ἑαυτῆς διακρίνει).

subsistence in, as one can perceive from the italicized lines. The word *enhypostaton* also seems to be included in this. But if one looks more closely, it still retains its old meaning of 'real' or 'existing'; it still stands in opposition to *anhypostatos*, meaning 'unreal'. For the objection of the Nestorian still hangs in the air: if the human nature of Christ is not a *hypostasis* on its own account and in itself, it is anhypostatic, that is, without existence. When in contrast Leontius of Jerusalem sees two *enhypostata* in the one *hypostasis* of the Logos, he characterizes them both as real.[62]

We have established that the adjective *enhypostaton* also in Leontius of Jerusalem retains its old meaning: real, having reality. Even an expanded neologism, which Leontius attempts with συν-εν-υπόστατος, does not proceed beyond this.[63] It is a question of clarifying the significations flesh, human being, divinity in the one Christ. It is in this context that the expression appears: in Christ the 'divinity' is *syn-en-hypostatos* with 'flesh' and 'human being', which the Latin translation inappropriately renders as *consubstantialis*, because elsewhere it still stands for *homoousios*. What no doubt is meant is that the divinity in Christ is as co-real as the human nature.

(g) Some further word formations: Leontius of Jerusalem's pleasure in new expressions was unrestrained. We shall mention only a few neologisms which by themselves are easy to understand:

(i) with ὑφίστημι, στατός: δισυπόστατος = dyhypostatic (*CN* II, 5: PG 86, 1544B); ἑτερουπόστατος = having another *hypostasis* (1540D).

(ii) with φύσις in *CN* II, 35: PG 86, 1593C:

(1) μονοφυής = in one nature; διφυής = in two natures. As pre-existent Logos Christ has a μονοφυὲς πρόσωπον (*prosopon* in one nature), after the incarnation a διφυὲς πρόσωπον (*prosopon* in two natures); the human *physis* in him is ἀπρόσωπος (without *prosopon*).

(2) Before the union the *sarx* of Christ did not exist, but it became nature in being co-nature with the supernature (that is, the Logos), as in *CN* I, 14: PG 86, 1457C (φύσις καὶ συμφύησις τῷ ὑπερφυεῖ). Here this is an imitation of Ps. Dionysius.

(3) The characterization of the confessors of the *mia-physis* formula as μιξοφυσῖται, mixers of natures, sounds derisive.[64]

---

62. Thus above the translation must be 'whereby each [of the two natures] is real' [instead of 'enhypostatic'].

63. Leontius Jer., *CN* V, 30: PG 86, 1749D1–5.

64. *Idem, CM*: PG 86, 1841B; 1889B; *CN* I, 49: PG 86, 1512A2.

II. SYNTHESIS

If this heading is given to indicate the theme of the second section, it is merely a signpost to mark the central points and goal of Leontius of Jerusalem's efforts; it is not our intention to say that he developed a systematic christology. In the first place he is a speculative theologian, who more energetically than his predecessors and contemporaries tackles the task posed by Chalcedon, which until then had not been completely resolved. This is the task of showing the *henosis* in Christ as the *synthesis in hypostasi et secundum hypostasim*, thus as a unity which leaves the two natures in their intactness, connecting them, however, entitatively, without this resulting in a new nature. It is still a question of justifying the Chalcedonian formula in its pre-philosophical, but very successful form: Jesus Christ, one and the same, perfect in divinity, the same perfect also in humanity. We can also say that he has still to come to terms with the question of how the custom of the earlier Church can be justified, viz. the custom of expressing the mystery of the incarnation of the Son of God in the rules of the so-called *communicatio idiomatum*, of the communication of properties, or of the *praedicatio idiomatum*, the attribution of divine and human predicates to one and the same subject. The problem of Nestorius is still very acute, as Leontius gathers from the writing to which he attempts to respond in his *Contra Nestorianos* (*CN*).

What is new is that he makes a decided attempt to arrive at an ontology of the Chalcedonian formula of the one *hypostasis* and the one *prosopon*, by having recourse to the concepts introduced by the Cappadocians, Basil and Gregory of Nyssa, and to some extent by carrying further initiatives that we were able to discern among the Chalcedonians and neo-Chalcedonians after 451. If we now hear of an ontology of the Chalcedonian formula, we should not switch off from the very start and presuppose the uselessness of such an attempt. The task of the historian must be to join in the tentative exploration of the Fathers in an almost impassable area, that of the speculative justification of Chalcedon, and to follow step by step their efforts to understand the faith. We shall see that Leontius of Jerusalem discovered a good clue. We may also believe that he understood his task as a believing theologian, indeed as a Chalcedonian theologian. This is revealed by an outline of his main christological thesis, which he himself describes as the *Canon of Orthodoxy*.[65] We shall place it at the beginning.[66]

---

65. *Idem*, *CN* II, 14: PG 86, 1568C9.
66. For the whole text see *ibid.*, 1568A8–C10.

1. The interpretation of the unity in Christ

The Canon of Orthodoxy

We know of one *hypostasis* which is also common to both (natures), which pre-existed the *ousia* of the human being, being previously proper (*idikē*) to the Word in the common *ousia* of the divinity. It created the nature (*physin*) of the *kyriakos anthropos*[67] for itself, and embraced it (*συνάψασα*) and took it together with its own nature (*physis*). At the same time it began to be a *hypostasis* of the nature of the flesh and to be from its own (*ἐξ ἰδικῆς*) [and simple *hypostasis*] the common [*hypostasis*] and was constituted as multifaceted.

For the *hypostasis* of the Logos now is not distinguished (*διακρίνεται*) as it previously was by a single *idioma* in the birth from both the Father and (through the difference of the *hypostasis*) the Spirit, but also from being from more natures and abounding in natural and personal *idiomata*. [There follows a rejection of the reproach that in this way a fourth person is added to the Trinity.] But if the *hypostasis* was added to the flesh before it assumed it, which no one would assert in an orthodox manner,[68] how, after the assumption, that is after it remains in both assumed and assuming, can it remain in it and a distinction of each be preserved from the other, which constitutes the *hypostasis*?

Therefore it is necessary to understand correctly that the nature of the Logos is common with the Father and the Spirit, but the *hypostasis* is individual (*ἰδική*) with regard both to the Father and the Spirit and to all human beings not born from the holy Virgin, and it is common only with the flesh taken by the Word from the *theotokos*. And again it is necessary to understand correctly that this flesh from the holy *theotokos* has a commonality with ours with respect to nature, and is common to all who come from Adam, but with respect to the *hypostasis* it is individual (*ἰδική*) with regard to us and the Father and the Spirit, being common only with the Word. This canon of orthodoxy is transmitted to us by the theologians.

This is the way the Chalcedonian confession[69] appears, after the theologians have become conscious of the task of distinguishing more sharply between *physis* and *hypostasis*, and of locating in the Logos-subject the concept of *hypostasis* which has now been worked out. Worthy of notice is the fact that Leontius of Jerusalem achieved the clarification of his Chalcedonian language in discussion above all with the Nestorians, while Leontius of Byzantium went through a similar process in discussions with the Severans. For this reason each of them places the accent in a different place: Leontius of Jerusalem extends the understanding of the one *hypostasis*, while Leontius of Byzantium builds up the two-

---

67. On the signification of the incarnate Logos as *kyriakos anthropos* in Leontius of Jerusalem see A. Grillmeier, ' 'Ο *κυριακὸς ἄνθρωπος*. Eine Studie zu einer christologischen Bezeichnung der Väterzeit', *Trad* 33 (1977) (1–63), 47–51.

68. Here one could think of a polemic against Leontius of Byzantium, who thought that it was possible that an already existing human being could be taken up into the *prosopon*-unity of the Logos, although he himself was not prepared to hold this. Cf. above Leontius of Byz., *Epil* 8: PG 86, 1944CD.

69. Although Leontius of Jerusalem interprets the Chalcedonian formula, he does not mention the Council.

natures teaching. The real advance which appears to have been achieved consists in the fact that the concept of *enhypostasis* or insubsistence has emerged formally and is used to explain the unity of the subject in Christ, in the duality of the natures. But how does the Logos-subject realize his hypostatic function *vis-à-vis* the human nature of Christ? Does Leontius of Jerusalem have a useful explanation of this? This topic must first be approached on the basis of his concept of *hypostasis*.

(a) The ontology of the enhypostasis

The Basilian concept of *hypostasis* is still operative in Leontius of Jerusalem. *Hypostasis* is the *ousia*, the essence, individualized by *idiomata*. The weakness of this approach is that its model is construed too physically. The concept of *hypostasis* is derived from things in nature, from the *ens physicum concretum*, and is intended to fit the anorganic and the organic, the material and the spiritual nature in the same way. But for this reason the concept is overtaxed. Thus when we investigate the way in which the unity of the *hypostasis* occurs, this is also purely physical. We shall study this in *CN* II, 7, where the intention is to exclude the unity in Christ occurring in the Nestorian manner as *henosis* of two existing *hypostases*.[70]

> On the contrary, becoming and subsisting coincide [in the case of the human nature of Christ]; we acknowledge, however, that it is not in a *hypostasis* proper to itself alone, that is, that of a simple human being, but in the *hypostasis* of the Logos which pre-exists it. In it the Logos also grasped the particularities and *idiomata* of the human nature; in the coming together of two natures he showed *one prosopon*, both from the two natures as well as through the piling up of the characteristics of each of the two essences, and thus proved himself to be the One from the holy Trinity.

To solve the Nestorian difficulty Leontius of Jerusalem attempts to proceed, so it seems, along the same path that Cyril, Severus and all the supporters of the formula 'from two natures' took: only in *theoria* or 'in thought' are the two natures to be accepted before the union; really, *de facto* there exists for them in Christ only the 'one incarnate nature'.[71] Leontius of Jerusalem as well seems to proceed in this way: before the union and without it the humanity of Christ too would be, in *theoria*, in its *idiomata*, thus a *hypostasis*. But it is allowed no time to be a *hypostasis* for itself.[72] That this is behind his reflections follows from the continuation of the text of *CN* II, 7.[73]

70. Leontius Jer., *CN* II, 7: PG 86, 1552D.

71. Cf. *idem*, *CM* 58: PG 86, 1801AB: ἐν ἐπινοίᾳ.

72. Cf. *idem*, *CN* II, 14: PG 86, 1568B: the human nature was never outside the *hypostasis* of the Logos.

73. *Idem*, *CN* II, 7: PG 86, 1552D–1553A.

He [Christ] is in reality only one single, non-human *hypostasis*. For he has the divine nature with its (divine) *idiomata*. But he is not only in the divine *idiomata*. In addition to the divine he is overrich in particularities, which are gathered to him through the assumption of the new (second) nature.

Before the human *idiomata* of the human nature of Christ could impart hypostatic character, they were already appropriated to the divine subject.[74] To what audacious conclusions Leontius sees himself obliged by this fundamental assumption will be indicated later. First of all against many a malicious suspicion he has to secure this idea of his of the taking over of the human characteristics into the Logos-subject. For the following doubts arise:

(1) According to this idea, is not *hypostasis* still united with *hypostasis*, so that the result is two *hypostases*? The theme raised in *CN* I, 20[75] is still present. In response Leontius says that there is only *one hypostasis* active, the divine. It does not experience any composition with another finished *hypostasis*, but only an enrichment of its divine *idiomata* by the *idiomata* of the human nature. Christ is thus not a synthesis of two *hypostases*.[76]

(2) Does there not occur a synthesis according to nature, if the human *physis* is united to the godhead? Reply: Christ is not a synthesis of the two natures which become one *physis*. Rather what happens is only something in the *idiomata* of the *hypostasis* of the Logos: they are in fact to some extent 'more composed' than before the incarnation, without the *hypostasis* as such being changed.[77]

(3) In *CN* I, 42 there is a similar reply to the objection of the Nestorians, which says that in Chalcedonian teaching the nature of God receives an increase (προσθήκη). The reply of Leontius is: 'Not the nature, but the *hypostasis* of the Logos experiences an increase.' But also *hypostasis* does not come to *hypostasis*; rather it is only *idiomata*, that is, 'elements of the *hypostasis*' (στοιχεῖα ὑποστάσεως) which are united

---

74. Cf. *idem*, *CN* II, 21: PG 86, 1581CD: 'the flesh has never subsisted without God (μὴ ἀθεεί) and for itself in purely its own nature'.

75. PG 86, 1485C6–7.

76. PG 86, 1485D.

77. Leontius says this in *CN* I, 20: PG 86, 1485D4–7: 'The natures were not composed in mixing; there is also no composite *hypostasis*, because it is not from *hypostases*; rather the *idioma* of the *hypostasis* of the Logos becomes more composite (ἀλλὰ συνθετώτερον ἰδίωμα τῆς τοῦ Λόγου γέγονεν τῆς ὑποστάσεως; the Migne text incorrectly has ἀλλ'ἀσυνθετώτερον, which makes no sense). After the incarnation the simple *idiomata* in it [the *hypostasis*] are increased. This, however, effects no change, either in the nature or in the *hypostasis* of the Logos.'

with the simple *idiomata* of the *hypostasis* of the Logos.[78] Thus the happening of the incarnation is positioned exclusively in the region of the *idiom*. *Hypostasis* and *nature* remain without any increase. Leontius thus attempts to steer between Scylla and Charybdis: either one new (third) nature, or two *hypostases*. The saving factor is the new synthesis in the *idiom* of the Logos-*hypostasis*, which is now made clear in an analogy, namely 'the iron becomes fire'[79] when it is put into glowing coals.[80]

Not every synthesis necessarily produces a new nature or *hypostasis*. The iron, placed in coals and glowing right through with fire, shows neither a foreign nature nor a new *hypostasis*. The *hypostasis* of the iron and that of the fiery coals are related in the same way. In the *hypostasis* of the iron, the nature of the fire, which considered in itself is anhypostatic,[81] is united to the nature of the iron, by its coming together with the nature (of the iron) in one *hypostasis*.[82]

While the natures are not mixed, only one *hypostasis* is formed: 'in the glowing metal ($\mu\acute{\upsilon}\delta\rho\sigma\varsigma$) one cannot recognize two *hypostases*', he writes in *CN* II, 12.[83] The same is true of Christ: in him there occurred a synthesis, in which what was previously uncombined was fitted into the one *hypostasis* of one of the two, which at the same time became the *hypostasis* of those that were combined.[84] The whole richness of the divine nature was thus bestowed on ours, a fact which presents a soteriological reference of Leontius that has still to be noted. He presents a type of doctrine of physical redemption. We shall see how his understanding of the *henosis* works itself out in his concrete picture of Christ.

If in Leontius of Jerusalem we pay attention to the orientation which is predominant in the previous remarks, our gaze is always directed away from the *sarx* of Christ towards the *hypostasis* of the Logos. This is conditioned by the effort of the Nestorian, through stressing the *idiomata*

78. Leontius Jer., *CN* I, 41–42: PG 86, 1501AC. The Nestorians want to concede only that God can unite himself with the created nature only according to the will and not according to the nature. Against this Leontius argues that it is possible for God equally to unite himself with the creature according to the will as well as according to the nature. Here Leontius uses the expression: $\phi\upsilon\sigma\iota\kappa\grave{\eta}$ $\H{\epsilon}\nu\omega\sigma\iota\varsigma$ (1501C).

79. *Idem, CN* I, 49: PG 86, 1512A6: $\pi\upsilon\rho\omega\theta\epsilon\grave{\iota}\varsigma$ $\acute{o}$ $\sigma\acute{\iota}\delta\eta\rho\sigma\varsigma$.

80. *Ibid.*, 1512AB.

81. *Ibid.*, 1512B1–2: $\phi\acute{\upsilon}\sigma\iota\varsigma$ $\pi\upsilon\rho\grave{o}\varsigma$ $\grave{\alpha}\nu\upsilon\pi\acute{o}\sigma\tau\alpha\tau\sigma\varsigma$ $\kappa\alpha\theta'\alpha\grave{\upsilon}\tau\grave{\eta}\nu$ $\sigma\grave{\upsilon}\sigma\alpha$, that is, the fire as such is not substantial, is not a nature existing in itself, but only a property which needs another nature as base. On this philosophy of nature see John Philoponus, *De opif. mundi*, II 10–11: Reichardt (Leipzig, 1897), 76–7.

82. *Idem, CN* I, 49: PG 86, 1512B2–3: $\sigma\upsilon\nu\epsilon\tau\acute{\epsilon}\theta\eta$ $\tau\^{\eta}$ $\phi\acute{\upsilon}\sigma\epsilon\iota$ $\tau\sigma\^{\upsilon}$ $\sigma\iota\delta\acute{\eta}\rho\sigma\upsilon$, $\sigma\upsilon\nu\upsilon\pi\acute{o}\sigma\tau\alpha\tau\sigma\varsigma$ $\alpha\grave{\upsilon}\tau\^{\eta}$ $\gamma\epsilon\nu\sigma\mu\acute{\epsilon}\nu\eta$.

83. *Idem, CN* II, 12: PG 86, 1557C.

84. *Idem, CN* I, 49: PG 86, 1512B: $\kappa\alpha\tau\grave{\alpha}$ $\mu\acute{\iota}\alpha\nu$ $\tau\grave{\eta}\nu$ $\theta\alpha\tau\acute{\epsilon}\rho\sigma\upsilon$ $\tau\^{\omega}\nu$ $\sigma\upsilon\gamma\kappa\epsilon\iota\mu\acute{\epsilon}\nu\omega\nu$ $\upsilon\pi\acute{o}\sigma\tau\alpha\sigma\iota\nu$.

of the flesh, to demonstrate that this too is a *hypostasis*. Leontius must then allow himself to wonder whether nothing 'idiomatic' at all happens to the *sarx* in the *henosis*.[85] His response is as follows:

> To the person who looks more exactly, it is clear that all the *idiomata* of the flesh of the Lord are held together by a total idiom[86] which encompasses all his *idiomata*. This is the following: the flesh has never subsisted without God (μὴ ἀθεεί) and for itself in simply its own nature.[87]

The being-united to the *hypostasis* of the Logos is now the comprehensive idiom of Christ's *sarx*. Thus Leontius first of all continues to leave the accent completely on the Logos-*hypostasis* and to bind the flesh to it. This happens because he considers the principal idiom of the united flesh to be precisely this, tied to the Logos-subject according to subsistence. This is the all-encompassing and dominant 'idiom' of this flesh, by which it becomes a 'this' (ἤδε). Everything which otherwise is visible and 'idiomatic' in the *idiomata* 'of this humanity in divine *hypostasis*' is the expression of this *enhypostasis*,[88] and is thus considered on the basis of the divinity.

> Whatever *idiomata* appear in him individually which are other than in all (other) human beings, these are fitting for God, such as the sinless birth, his entire infallible life, his perfectly good disposition, his extraordinary power to work miracles, his knowledge surpassing wisdom, his perfect and supernatural virtue[89] . . . If the divine works do not ever appear without the divine nature, the *idiomata* [which show themselves in this concrete human nature] must be proper to the entire *hypostasis*.[90]

Here the fundamental tendency separating Leontius of Jerusalem from his namesake Leontius of Byzantium becomes obvious: the revelation of the *divine* Logos-*idiomata* in the humanity of Christ has a comprehensive significance. It may not leave any gaps, because otherwise there is the danger of a duality of *hypostases*. Because he transposes this divinization into the region of the *idiomata* in contrast to the *ousia*, he believes that he escapes both the reproach of the 'two-persons teaching' as well as that of a mixing of the natures. He does not want a synthesis according to

---

85. Cf. *idem*, *CN* II, 21: PG 86, 1581C–1584A.
86. *Ibid.*, 1581C13–14: ἐνὶ καθολικωτέρῳ αἰτίῳ αὐτῶν πάντων ἰδιώματι.
87. *Ibid.*, 1581CD.
88. *Ibid.* Can there still be talk of a φύσις ἰδική which Leontius, however, wants to admit?
89. ἡ παντέλειος καὶ ὑπερφυὴς ἀρετή (PG 86, 1581D), which is the language of Ps. Dionysius.
90. *Ibid.*, 1581D.

the nature, as the 'mixophysites' teach. The *ousiai* remain untouched.[91] Only the *idiomata* of the divine *hypostasis* communicate themselves. We shall see how this fundamental idea of the communication of properties has an effect on his picture of Christ. Can he at all really exclude the objection of the Nestorians, which reads: If the earthly properties are visible in Jesus, does an earthly *hypostasis* result? What, for example, is the form and figure of the body of Christ?

Leontius can hardly avoid the reproach of presenting purely hairsplitting excuses, in order to escape both Nestorianism as well as monophysitism. But what he analyses and evaluates is nothing other than what is common to both parties, the Nestorians as well as the Chalcedonians: the Cappadocian concept of *hypostasis*. This proves insufficient for taking the Chalcedonian distinction between *hypostasis* and *physis* further towards an acceptable theory of *henosis*. Leontius of Jerusalem also entangles himself in difficulties regarding the theology of the Trinity. He makes the incarnation into an idiom in the *hypostasis* of the Logos in such a way that this is now also invoked for the relative distinction of the second *hypostasis* of the Trinity from the Father and the Spirit. Before the incarnation the characteristics of the pre-existent Logos *vis-à-vis* Father and Spirit in the Trinity are the following: being begotten by the Father, himself not being a begetter, not being the principle of origin of the Spirit, himself not proceeding in the manner of the Spirit.[92] After the incarnation there is added to the *idiomata* of the Logos, 'to be incarnate'. This is now an *idioma hypostatikon* of the Logos, 'which adds to the *prosopon* of the same a differentiating and original (*autogenomenon*) property, by which he is distinguished from the Father and the Spirit, who are one and the same as him in nature'.[93] Through this addition of a new property to the simple *idiomata* of the Logos no 'counting' is introduced into his *hypostasis*.[94]

91. This still remains the case for Leontius of Jerusalem, when he characterizes the becoming of the human nature of Jesus in Mary as *ousiosis*, the uniting of this human nature with the Logos, however, as *synousiosis*. Cf. *CN* IV, 17: PG 86, 1684B. He speaks in the same passage of the *synthetos Christos*. Cf. the similar language of Leontius of Byzantium, *CNE*: PG 86, 1352C11–12.

92. Leontius Jer., *CN* II, 24: PG 86, 1585C. In *CN* I, 20: PG 86, 1485B the Logos is still ascribed a function in the proceeding of the Spirit. He is διαπορθμευτής of the Holy Spirit, which recalls the old formula that the Spirit proceeds from the Father through the Son.

93. *Idem*, *CN* I, 28: PG 86, 1493D.

94. *Idem*, *CN* II, 24: PG 86, 1585D2–3.

(b) The union in Christ as synthesis

In the interpretation of the *henosis* Leontius of Jerusalem assigns a particular function to the word *synthesis*.[95] One may suspect that he saw himself induced to do this not only by external reasons. Rather it seemed to him that from the very nature of the matter this concept was especially suited for making his idea of the 'manifold *hypostasis*'[96] which was 'common' to the Logos and the flesh possible and to sustain it. For had he wanted to seek only a particularly expressive word to establish the unity, perhaps another choice would have suggested itself; one can think, for example, of Cyril or Severus. Or he could simply have stayed with the word *henosis*. It is interesting that in the word *synthesis* he finds the word *henosis* is made more precise.[97]

> For the *henosis*, which is not also *synthesis*, must be considered either as local juxtaposition (κατὰ παράθεσιν τοπικήν) (for example, a stone set in a gold ring, or two neighbouring countries like Judea and Samaria[98]) or as [connection] by virtue of a moral relationship[99] or as physical (family) relationship (for example, parents–children; individual living things of the same kind; archetype–image).[100]

Thus according to Leontius of Jerusalem, *synthesis* expresses an entitative unity, that is, 'the *synthesis* of the divine and the human natures'.[101] At the same time the compositum *synthesis* enables the two natures to be brought into play.

In the foreword to the *CN* Leontius describes the theme of his work.[102] He develops this on the basis of eight reproaches of the Nestorian against the Chalcedonian formula of the one *hypostasis* in two natures. The first reproach states summarily, 'that we do not think correctly about the *synthesis* of the divine and the human natures'.[103]

---

95. Cf. also P. T. R. Gray, 'Leontius of Jerusalem's Case of a "Synthetic" Union in Christ', *StudPat* 18,1 (Kalamazoo, Michigan, 1985), 151–4.

96. Leontius Jer., *CN* II, 14: PG 86, 1568A: ὑπ. κοινὴ – ποικιλωτέρα.

97. *Idem*, *CN* III, 8: PG 86, 1632D–1633A.

98. One has seen in this example a reference to the original homeland or also the actual sojourn of Leontius in Palestine; a migration to Constantinople is not excluded by this.

99. κατὰ προαιρετικὴν σχέσιν. What is meant is the Nestorian 'connection through relation' among human beings or of human beings to God.

100. In these examples it is a matter of separate persons or things.

101. Leontius Jer., *CN* I *prooem.*: PG 86, 1400A.

102. *Ibid.*: PG 86, 1400A–1401A.

103. To this alleged false understanding of *synthesis* belong in the mind of the Nestorian furthermore (2) the unity of the two natures in the *hypostasis*; (3) the uniqueness of the sonship; (4) the title *theotokos*; (5) the lack of the teaching of the *psilos anthropos*; (6) the lack of the title *theophoros anthropos*; (7) the formula 'one of the Trinity suffered'; (8) in general the acceptance of the *henosis kath'hypostasin*.

On this account Leontius puts forward particular demands for the use of this word.[104]

(1) Negatively: it is not permissible to speak

(a) of a 'composite nature' (*physis synthetos*),[105] because in this mixing would be expressed. We recall how unwilling Severus was, *vis-à-vis* the suggestion of Sergius Scholasticus, to confess an *ousia synthetos* in Christ;[106]

(b) of a '*synthesis* of the *hypostases*',[107] which would be Nestorianism;

(c) of a 'composite *hypostasis*' (*hypostasis synthetos*);[108] for Christ is 'not from *hypostases*'.

(2) Positively: only *one* formulation is allowed: 'the natures experience a composition according to the *hypostasis*'.[109] This occurs, however, by reason of the fact that the idiom of the *hypostasis* of the Logos experiences a composition through the incarnation and the assumption of the human nature.[110] Once again it is then stressed that, through this shifting of the event of *synthesis* into the *idiomata*, the *physis* and the *hypostasis* itself are excepted from *synthesis* and change.[111]

Leontius of Jerusalem has thus carefully delimited the use of the term *synthesis*. This must be noted for the later history of the term in the era of Justinian.[112]

(c) Hellenistic and biblical interpretation of the incarnation

The efforts of Leontius of Jerusalem to defend the 'one *hypostasis* of Christ in two natures', which we have just presented, should not be dismissed as due to Hellenism. Against the *mia-physis* tradition Chalcedon and even Nestorianism had something important to defend: the completeness of the human nature, of the human being of Christ. The more one confessed it, the more the difficulty increased in interpreting and showing the true unity in the *hypostasis*. The objections of the Nestorian in the *CN* meant a serious discussion of the Chalcedonian solution, a discussion which went the whole way. Was it at all possible, by way of Greek ontology, to find an explanation for the ecclesial faith in the

---

104. Leontius Jer., *CN* I, 20: PG 86, 1485AD.
105. *Ibid.*, 1485D3–4.
106. Cf. above, pp. 116–20.
107. 1485C8.
108. 1485D5.
109. 1485D2–3: κατὰ τὴν ὑπόστασιν οὖν ταῖς φύσεσιν ἡ σύνθεσις.
110. 1485D: συνθετώτερον ἰδίωμα τῆς τοῦ Λογου γέγονεν ὑποστάσεως.
111. 1485D9–10.
112. Cf. M. Richard, 'Léonce et Pamphile', in *Op. Min.* III, no. 58, p. 38.

incarnation, an explanation that may still be cautious, but could still to some extent be reassuring? Was it not shown to be impossible from the very beginning, if Christ, the God–human being, was represented as a *synthesis* from the infinite–finite? The Nestorian places the problem in this perspective.[113]

What is united with another becomes this either as whole with a whole or as part with a part, or as part with a whole. To speak otherwise of union is impossible. Now in the case of the infinite one can speak neither of a whole nor of a part. Hence the God-Logos, because infinite, is not united with the human being from us;[114] if he is united, he is composite and finite, which is godless.

Leontius gets involved in this great theme,[115] being conscious of the fact that it is an 'enormous' question. The sole escape open to him is to refer to God's creative power with regard to being, which alone can make such a *synthesis* possible.

. . . Could not God, who had devised all that exists and all their compositions (συνθέσεις) and had made them exist and to be what they were (εἶναί τε αὐτά, καὶ τοιῶσδε εἶναι), produce and devise for himself a newer and closer composition than those known to us, intending on behalf of what exists to join himself to one of those existing, and to make known to them a hitherto unknown manner [of union]?[116]

In this way Leontius achieves a formulation which goes beyond Greek ontology and places faith in the incarnation in a quite immense perspective. Indeed the monk reverses the objection of the Nestorian and says that the immensity of the infinite only becomes evident when it engages in finitude.[117]

Otherwise there is nothing so big for the infinite if it is not contained by the finite [reference to the heavenly bodies]. But if unhindered in its entirety and in its infinity, it can go (χωρῆσαι) into the smaller object which is circumscribed by it, while being in no way cramped (στενοχωρούμενος), this happens really because of a natural power enclosing the infinite with no constraint at all nor circumscribing [its ability] to effect what it wants.

With these words one is reminded of the inscription on the tomb of Ignatius of Loyola quoted by Hölderlin: *Non coerceri maximo, contineri tamen a minimo divinum est.*[118]

113. Cf. Leontius Jer., *CN* I, 1: PG 86, 1401B; cf. I, 48: PG 86, 1505D–1512A; from 1509B application of the question to Christ.
114. This formulation returns again in I, 1: PG 86, 1413A7–8: Οὐκ ἄρα συνετέθη ὁ Θεὸς Λόγος τῷ ἐξ ἡμῶν ἀνθρώπῳ.
115. In the chapter just mentioned, *CN* I, 48.
116. *Ibid.*, I, 1: PG 86, 1413AB.
117. *Ibid.*: PG 86, 1412AB.
118. Cf. H. Rahner, 'Die Grabschrift des Loyola', in *idem, Ignatius von Loyola als Mensch und Theologe* (Freiburg, Basel, Vienna, 1964) (422–40), 424.

In support of his opinion Leontius cites Colossians 2,9: 'For in him alone dwells the whole fulness of the godhead bodily.' By the choice of the expression 'enter into' (χωρεῖν),[119] he nevertheless has recourse to the interpretation of the *henosis* by the *perichoresis* of divinity and humanity, which he has already transcended by his idea of insubsistence. This, however, is not rescinded. More significant is the discovery that, in order to explain the possibility of a *synthesis* of finite and infinite, as it is realized in the Incarnate One, 'the Christian faith and the Hebrew teaching'[120] from their foundations and in their main features must be brought into play. In this way the biblical-Christian concept of God and Christian anthropology are appealed to. They flow together to form what we can call Leontius of Jerusalem's picture of Christ.

2. Leontius of Jerusalem's picture of Christ

From the clear insight into the nature of the *henosis* in Christ as a union in the Logos-subject and according to the subject, in contrast to a nature synthesis (*unio in natura et secundum naturam*), one may expect that Leontius of Jerusalem knows how to preserve the unmingling of the natures in sketching his picture of Christ. To some extent he is also successful where he allows himself to be guided by biblical christology. If Philippians 2,5–11 does not appear often in his writings, nevertheless, together with other passages,[121] it plays a significantly powerful rôle to allow the *kenosis* in the total interpretation of the life and person of Jesus to show to advantage. In view of the fact that he is examining the writing of the Nestorian, we shall also appreciate that the divinity of Christ will be strongly accented. Thus, for instance, *CN* V, 1 offers a good example of a fairly balanced picture of Christ. Jesus of Nazareth has not ascended in steps to being God, as Leontius renders the teaching of the Nestorian; he is from the very beginning in the womb of the Virgin the hypostatic unity of Logos and *sarx*.

At the same time, however, it was the will of the Logos himself, in the full living through of the flesh even to his physical size, to be poor (with us) ... Not through robbery or injustice, but in justice and in living through a pure life, after the death of the flesh the

119. PG 86, 1412A15. The *perichoresis* is the manner of the insubsistence.
120. See the important conclusion of *CN* I, 1: PG 86, 1413BC. To be noted in particular are the two expressions σύνθεσις τῶν ὄντων and τὰ πάντα σύνθετα.
121. It is a question of Phil 2,5–11; 1 Cor 2,8 in tension with Mt 16,16; Mk 1,1; Jn 17,5; 12,28. In *CN* V, 23: PG 86, 1745B the Nestorian and Chalcedonian interpretations of Phil 2,5–11 are placed in opposition to each other; the Nestorians perceive in it the two *hypostases* of Christ; Leontius deduces from it the Chalcedonian teaching of the one Logos in two natures.

Logos, who created everything in the word, wanted to raise humanity united with him as the first-born of spiritual immortality and eternal honour and beatitude.[122]

On account of the hypostatic unity the revelation of the divinity always has to proceed at once with the proof of genuine humanity. The whole life of Jesus is thus revelation of his two natures: birth,[123] death,[124] and resurrection.[125] Leontius of Jerusalem resists the temptation to which, according to Leontius of Byzantium, the Chalcedonian aphthartics succumbed,[126] viz. to deduce from the substantial union the immediate uncorruptedness and superiority to suffering of the body of Christ. Both remain reserved for the state of elevation.[127] Jesus proclaims and reveals himself in a twofold regard, as glorified and as stripped of glory. The divinization of the humanity of Christ is only perfect with the resurrection.[128] It confers the *aphtharsia* and the elevation to rule the universe (κόσμου κατακράτησις).[129]

In spite of this fundamental distance from the contemporary Chalcedonian aphthartics, and despite his preserving the human historical reality of Jesus, Leontius of Jerusalem does not embrace that sober picture of Christ which his namesake from Byzantium drew.[130] Rather in his sketching of the figure of Christ he gives such a significant rôle to miracles and the miraculous that in certain features he comes close to the aphthartic supranaturalism which we have depicted. Thus for his picture of Christ he simply puts forward the fundamental proposition: 'in no regard is there (in Christ) anything of him or about him which can be thought of as stripped of the divinity'.[131] Does the *kenosis* never

122. Leontius Jer., *CN* V, 1: PG 86, 1724C.

123. *Idem*, *CN* II, 21: PG 86, 1581D.

124. *Idem*, *CM* 33: PG 86, 1789AB.

125. *Idem*, *CM* 39: PG 86, 1792D–1793A. *CN* V, 2: PG 86, 1725B. In particular 1725C shows the combination of divinity and humanity, of suffering and glorification.

126. See above, pp. 213–17.

127. Leontius Jer., *CN* V, 1: PG 86, 1724C: ἑαυτὸν ὁ ἔνδοξος ἅμα καὶ ἄδοξον ἀνακηρύττων; cf. Jn 12,16; 13,31.

128. *Idem*, *CN* IV, 37: PG 86, 1712A: 'The Logos is God according to nature, the flesh, however, (is not God according to nature, but) is divinized in its nature of flesh after the resurrection to the fullest extent (εἰς τὸ παντελές).'

129. Cf. *idem*, *CN* V, 1: PG 86, 1724D. Here too it is emphasized that the truth of the flesh is not annulled, but is only transferred into a higher state. On the other hand the incarnation signifies no change of the divinity. In the whole history of Jesus the two natures remain preserved.

130. Cf. Leontius Byz., *CA*: PG 86, 1336BC; *CNE*: PG 86, 1352C–1353A.

131. Leontius Jer., *CN* IV, 37: PG 86, 1712A: οὐδὲ κατὰ λόγον τινά, τὶ τῶν αὐτοῦ ἢ περὶ αὐτῶν γυμνὸν κατανοῆσαι θεότητος. Latin: *nihil . . . vacuum divinitate.* It is not too bold to invoke precisely such ideas in order to explain the *Christus gloriae* of the Justinian era.

reach so deeply into the history of Christ that the divinity could be fully hidden? Clearly Leontius of Jerusalem here is reluctant to concede this. The reason for this is easily determined. It lies in his not carrying through consistently his own new concept of insubsistence, and in the continuing effect of the Basilian-Cappadocian teaching about the *idiomata*. In the *concrete* interpretation of the unity of the *hypostasis* in Christ, Leontius does not maintain his own *theories*, which could have shown the way out of all difficulties: (1) to distinguish clearly the union in the subject or in the *hypostasis* from the synthesis according to the nature; (2) to respect the execution of the union in the 'insubsisting', as an existential event or act, this execution being rightly appropriated to the creative power of God. On the basis of these theories it would have been possible to secure the balancing of *kenosis* and *doxa* in the one Christ, the incarnate Logos. The incorporation of the Basilian concept of *hypostasis* with its teaching about the *idiomata* was the reason that the new insights of Leontius of Jerusalem were not sufficiently effective. This needs some further clarification.

As the concretizing and individualizing elements in the building up of the individual being, the *idiomata* belong to the domain of 'condition'.[132] If it is now one's intention to explain the insubsistence of the human nature in the *hypostasis* of the Logos by means of the *idiomata*, then one is forced to remain in the area of the nature synthesis (*unio in natura et secundum naturam*). If one wants to show the inseparability of God and human being in Christ, or, expressed positively, to show the substantiality of this unity against the attacks of the Severans and Nestorians with the help of the teaching about the *idiomata*, it is difficult to accord to the *kenosis* the soteriological place which is so important to it in the interpretation of Christ. In fact Leontius of Jerusalem is now endeavouring to show the uninterrupted *henosis* of the natures in Christ on the basis of being able to realize constantly the divine *idiomata* in him. This explains why he is one of the strongest defenders among the Fathers of the divinization of the humanity of Christ. On this basis his being assigned to the ranks of neo-Chalcedonians would also have to be considered; admittedly this classification has still to be tested to see if it is justified.[133]

We now want to observe the monk at work sketching his picture of Christ. He begins with two particular facts in the person of Jesus

---

132. In contrast to the 'common quality' (κοινὴ ποιότης), which constitutes the type, the species, in question here is the ἰδία ποιότης, the particularization as an individual.

133. On this see the excursus below: On the concept 'neo-Chalcedonianism', pp. 429–34.

which signify a felicitous starting-point: the sinlessness of Christ and the creative power of the Logos. The first provides the special opportunity of starting from the spiritual-moral *idiomata*, thus of becoming freed from the 'physical object' as the starting-point for the teaching on *hypostasis*. Being a person and being 'spirit' belong together. Will Leontius of Jerusalem notice this? The second steers us away once again from a pure teaching about properties to the area of the existential.

(a) Christ is God, because sinless

In Leontius of Jerusalem the sinlessness of Christ, already mentioned in the confession of Chalcedon, is ascribed a particular relationship to the divinity of Christ.[134] For him it is the most original and proper feature for recognizing the divinity of Christ,[135] because it is realized in the whole Christ, God and human being, and not only in the divinity. Like the Council of Chalcedon, orthodox faith too confesses that Christ has become like us in all things, sin alone excepted (cf. Heb 2,17–18; 4,15; Jn 8,46). Thus here it is not a question of sinlessness and righteousness, insofar as they are realized in the divine essence, but in a finite, and by nature fallible, human being, thus lived out in human freedom. Both Leontii come to speak expressly, each in his own way, about the theme of freedom in the framework of christology. Would not accepting a human freedom in Christ, however, mean standing before the abyss of Nestorianism and its probation teaching? Would not the sinlessness of Christ have to be anchored in his divinity, not only as postulate, as the demand of the divine holiness on his own human freedom, but physically? Apollinarius had built his soteriology on the fact that in Christ the sole physical principle of decision was the 'undefeatable *nous*'.[136] Where do the free decisions in Christ occur? Does Leontius of Jerusalem have an unambiguous answer? Perhaps it is to be found in the following text.[137]

> If therefore, as we admit, both sin and justice come from our (human) condition and from our free will in accordance with our nature, the sinlessness or justice of our Lord Jesus Christ is testified to by the Holy Spirit; and you must admit that this (*pneuma*) is his free will (*autexousion*), by which he is justified, just as we are from our free will (*autexousion*). But if we know that what is the free will (*autexousion*) and principle (*aition*)

134. Leontius Jer., *CN* I, 19: PG 86, 1484C–1485A.

135. *Idem*, *CN* IV, 37: PG 86, 1705C: τὸ ἰδικώτατον Θεοῦ γνωριστήριον ... ὅπερ ἐστὶ τὸ ἀναμάρτητον. In *CN* II, 21: PG 86, 1581D Leontius describes somewhat more broadly what is 'befitting God' in Jesus' conduct of life, cf. Acts 10,38 (see above, p. 292).

136. Cf. *JdChr* I³, 486, n. 21.

137. Leontius Jer., *CN* I, 19: PG 86, 1484D.

of justice in our nature, is in Christ's nature the Holy Spirit, who is truly true God, how could you not quite clearly, if unwillingly, admit that the divine nature in Christ is from the Holy Spirit?

The decision seems to have been taken already. Leontius of Jerusalem speaks of the divine Pneuma as Christ's principle of freedom. The Pneuma is his *autexousion*. But what does he mean by this Pneuma? What is the situation with Christ's human principle of freedom? Is it already excluded or sacrificed by this reference to the pneumatic *exousion*? The continuation of *CN* I, 19 seems to offer a way out.[138]

> What the leading spiritual principle (ὁ ἡγεμονικὸς λόγος) effects only partially (μερικῶς) in us, the divine Word effected (κατώρθωσεν) totally (παντελῶς) in Christ, in addition to [or together with] our leading principle, as it exists in him and in others. Therefore [the Logos] himself and no other is the cause of his own justice, either because he is co-existent with the Holy Spirit [i.e. as the second *hypostasis* of the Trinity], or he is said to be Holy Spirit[139] from the nature, not from the *hypostasis*.

According to this difficult text how does the inner constitution of Christ, who proves himself in sinlessness, appear? Leontius does not make it as easy for himself as Apollinarius, who can establish the sinlessness in the divine Logos, insofar as this is the sole spiritual principle of the *sarx*. He also does not argue like Severus, who knows only *one* *energeia* in Christ, although he also accepts a spiritual soul in Christ. The sinlessness, however, is guaranteed in the sole hegemony and energy which proceeds from the Logos and controls everything. Severus does not ask about a human-intellectual decision. Does Leontius venture to allow Christ's human freedom to participate actively in the sinlessness, that is, in the moral decision? It seems that one can in fact understand him in this way. He certainly accepts a co-operation between Logos (or respectively Pneuma) and human *hegemonikon*. This can be deduced from the unusual manner of expression used to signify the effect of the Logos or of the Pneuma as 'additional to our *hegemonikon*'.[140] By 'our *hegemonikon*' there can and must be understood our genuine, human principle of will, insofar as it is in Christ. Against the background of the Cyrillian-Severan hegemony of the Logos, this discovery cannot be too highly estimated. Logos-Pneuma and human will act as one in Christ. Admittedly the expression 'Logos-Pneuma' has still to be further

138. Leontius Jer., *CN* I, 19: PG 86, 1485A.

139. The word *pneuma* was used either personally for the third *hypostasis* or essentially for the divine nature. Whether one or the other, the Logos co-works with his humanity.

140. Cf. *CN* I, 19: PG 86, 1485A3–6, especially: πρὸς τῷ ἡμετέρῳ (ἡγεμονικῷ λόγῳ); the preposition πρός with the dative means additionally, besides, apart from, in addition.

deciphered. Behind this Leontius sees nothing other than the divine principle of grace which the human will of Christ also needs to achieve sinlessness. Leontius recognizes that Christ is only a model when his human freedom is brought into play. But in this exercise of freedom Jesus, as a finite human being open to temptation, needs the divine help of grace, all the more so as Leontius of Jerusalem considers the sinlessness of Jesus to be the real proof of the super-humanity of Jesus, that is, his divinity. This sinlessness is guaranteed in Christ by the fact that to his human *autexousion* is hypostatically united the divine principle of grace, namely the Logos or Pneuma of God. That this chain of thought could play a rôle in Leontius of Jerusalem is clear from an objection of the Nestorians, which Leontius himself cites:[141]

> If, as the sinless companion (κοινωνόν) of its constitution (*hyparxis*), the flesh has the Logos who is by nature omnipotent, how can one call the flesh itself sinless? What kind of victory is that over evil, where such an unconquerable helper is received? To him, and not to the flesh, is due all the praise.

This difficulty could only be resolved if the human being Jesus were to participate in the moral decision in his human will. In the response which Leontius gives to this objection the possibility remains entirely open for the insertion of a spiritual principle in the humanity of Christ. Nevertheless the argumentation here takes a different tack, for first of all the monk draws attention to the fact that it is not a question of the flesh, but of 'our nature' insofar as it is threatened by Satan through sin and death. This threat is so much the greater as the evil one 'dwells (in us) in some way personally (καθ'ὑπόστασιν)', as is clear in the possessed. By the Logos himself being united (hypostatically) with our nature, its 'guard' himself dwells in it and makes 'the flesh sinless'. 'And the sinners, who are consubstantial with this [the flesh of Christ], he already here honours with the sinless spiritual essence, but only there admittedly in full perfection.'[142]

141. Leontius Jer., *CN* I, 47: PG 86, 1505AB.

142. *Ibid.*, PG 86, 1505D. P. T. R. Gray, 'Leontius of Jerusalem's Case for "Synthetic" Union in Christ', *StudPat* 18,1 (1985), 151–4, has displayed these soteriological approaches well in connection with three texts from Leontius of Jerusalem, *CN* I (chs. 6, 18 and 47), from the interpretation of the 'one person and *hypostasis*' of Christ as *synthesis*. This hypostatic/synthetic union has three effects. (1) Because the flesh of Christ receives subsistence in God, the rest of humankind shares in the inalienable, immortal being with the Word (ch. 6: PG 86, 1425C). (2) The (universal) human nature is divinized by virtue of this 'essential *synthesis*' in Christ (ch. 18: PG 86, 1468C). This process is executed in two steps: on the basis of the *creatio* there takes place the *recreatio* as a participation in the divine nature which goes beyond being in the image of God; the 'essential *synthesis*' becomes 'divinization' (*ektheiosis*). (3) Only the *unio/synthesis* with the divine nature can clearly overcome the 'hypostatic union' with Satan indicated above, which threatens human beings (ch. 47: PG 86, 1505CD).

We see that the sinlessness of Christ is discussed here from a soterio-logical point of view. He presupposes that it is a question of our entire corporeal-spiritual nature. This has come into the power of Satan to such an extent that it is as if there is a hypostatic union with him. In Christ the same entire human nature is 'possessed' by the Logos, and Satan no longer has any access: in us, admittedly, in this life it is not yet so definitive as in the person of Christ himself. For us only eternity will guarantee definitive sinlessness.

In this soteriological argumentation we should assume that both for the human being as such as well as for the humanity of Christ, the sinlessness of the spiritual human being is involved, which is realized in the first analysis as a spiritual decision. As Satan is active in the will of the human being, so now in Christ, as the archetype of the Christian, the divine Logos or Pneuma principle is active. Here Leontius of Jerusalem can interchange Pneuma and Logos by having recourse to the old patristic manner of speaking, by which the nature of God is called Pneuma. Although Leontius knows that Pneuma usually signifies the third person of the Trinity, the divinity of Christ is also the divine essential Pneuma.

Here then follows the question, how far Leontius of Jerusalem draws upon pneumatology to explain the sinlessness of Christ. For the explana-tion of the *impeccabilitas Christi* cannot be seen solely from the *ontological* constitution of Christ. The question must be asked: how does the Logos become *active* in the human will of Christ? It is the problem of the Spirit's bestowing of grace on the humanity of Christ, that is, of the Messiah. This christological pneumatology has its own history. Cyril of Alexandria was not successful in allocating a sufficient function to the Spirit in the interpretation of the baptism of Christ.[143] Dread of the Arian position hindered him from doing this. Because the divine Logos is present in Christ by nature, Cyril's Christ does not need the grace of the Spirit for himself. He receives it only for us.[144] For the humanity of Christ, Leontius of Jerusalem now distinguishes clearly between the *henosis* with the Logos, and being graced or anointed with the Spirit.[145]

Jesus himself had become the Kyrios on account of the divine Logos, and Christ through the anointing of the Spirit; God has made this Jesus, whom the Jews crucified, Lord through the Logos and Christ through the Spirit (cf. Acts 10,38; Rom 1,4).

143. Cf. *Qērellos* III, 32,2–35,4: B. M. Weischer (Wiesbaden, 1977), 73–79. Similarly in Severus; see above, pp. 136–8.

144. When in Leontius Jer., *CN* V, 19: PG 86, 1741B the Nestorian speaks of the teaching of the 'Egyptian', which says that Jesus receives the power to be effective not first through the Spirit, but has it by virtue of the Logos in him, Cyril of Alexandria may very well be meant.

145. Leontius Jer., *CN* V, 18: PG 86, 1741A.

In the twofold lining of the Ark of the Covenant with gold, within and without, the twofold gracing of Christ is also symbolized.[146] Leontius ascribes the inner lining (the *endosis*) to the Logos, and the outer (*perithesis*) to the Pneuma. Thus the latter concerns the messianic work of Christ. Here is the field of probation (cf. Acts 2,22). In the first instance, however, Jesus does not receive the finite gifts of the Spirit, but the uncreated Pneuma itself.[147] But from there it is only a short step to recognizing that there are in Christ also transitory and finite gifts of the Spirit. It was not difficult to discern that the human will of Christ, finite as it was, solely by being hypostatically united with the Logos did not already have the equipment of the Spirit which he needed for his task as messiah and redeemer. We have already seen that, more clearly than others, Leontius contrasted the peculiarity of the hypostatic *henosis* in Christ with a union according to the nature. But with Gregory of Nyssa he knows that the *henosis* must reveal itself in 'moral characteristics'.[148] The problem of the sinlessness and impeccability of Christ is thus brought by Leontius towards a deeper solution, but it is still not yet completely clarified. It is precisely for this reason that he has overtaxed the *anhamarteton* as proof of the union according to the *hypostasis*. Had he expounded more clearly the fact that the human impeccability of Christ can only be realized by pneumatic inspirations and the strengthening of Christ's spirit and will,[149] he would also have recognized that through grace God could bestow at will sinlessness or even impeccability on every human being.[150]

(b) Christ and the creative power of God

As the other 'real characteristic of God', which is discernible in Christ, Leontius of Jerusalem names the creative power.[151] One and the same power, which at the beginning formed the human being, is in a particular way evident in and through Christ and has become effective: *in*

---

146. On this allegory see above, pp. 87-9.

147. *Ibid.*, *CN* V, 19: PG 86, 1741B.

148. Cf. Gregory of Nyssa, *Ep.* 38 in Basil: PG 32, 328C: τὰ τοῦ ἤθους γνωρίσματα; on this Leontius Jer., *CN* II, 21: PG 86, 1581CD.

149. Whereby the hypostatic union with the Logos is only the title and, so to say, the unsurpassable proof of justification for this; it must first be transposed into actual help.

150. The Nestorians could have given him a nod in this direction with reference to Theodore of Mopsuestia. Cf. *JdChr* I³, 615-19.

151. Leontius Jer., *CN* I, 19: PG 86, 1480A10-11: τὸ ἰδίως Θεοῦ χαρακτηριστικόν, τὸ δημιουργικὸν λέγω. Here a relationship between Leontius Jer. and Justinian can be shown (on the edict of 551 see below).

Christ, because, as the *Canon of Orthodoxy* stresses, in his divine *hypostasis* he 'has himself created the nature of the *kyriakos anthropos*';[152] *through* Christ, because the demiurgic activity of the Logos is not only based on the beginning of his earthly existence, but, as the active power of working miracles, remains present throughout his whole life on earth even to his resurrection and exaltation. The evaluation of miracles in the christology of Leontius of Jerusalem can be discerned at a glance in his assessment of the twofold birth of Christ, which has the pronounced tone of a confession of faith, similar to his *Canon of Orthodoxy*.[153]

> Nothing else is so eternally, indistinguishably, perfectly, unchangeably, indivisibly, completely and unmovedly begotten, as he [the God-Logos] in his first birth. But also nothing besides his second birth is thus without seed, uncorruptedly [i.e. without violating the virginity], supernaturally begotten and conceived of the Holy Spirit, and without time (ἀχρόνως) perfected, formed, and provided with organs, and in everything perfected as a result of the substantial Logos in the chaste womb of the immaculate one[154] to be temple and tabernacle of the Logos, when the human flesh which was perfected from her alone and united instantly (ἐν ἀκαρεῖ, in a moment)[155] with him [the Logos].

The interpretation of the second birth stresses the creative happening both for the mother as well as for the son. Thus, as Christ is conceived and born, this does not belong to the 'natural property of the house' (that is, the mother), but to the 'natural property' of the divine Logos, who as God entered this house *clausa porta*, without being confined, and left it in the true reality of flesh, without harming the mother. In this

152. Cf. *idem, CN* II, 14: PG 86, 1568A.

153. Idem, *CN* IV, 9: PG 86, 1669B–1672A: Leontius refers to the teaching of the holy Fathers for this one orthodox confession, which has a christological part (1669B1–C9) and a mariological part: the virginity of Mary at conception and birth (1669C10–1672A); the latter part is understood, however, as testimony to the divinity of Christ.

154. In *CM* 23: PG 86, 1784D Leontius Jer. speaks of Mary as the holy place (ἅγιον χωρίον), in which the union of the natures of Christ happened from the very beginning. This is reminiscent of the special mariological-christological terminology in Constantinople, especially in Proclus. Cf. *JdChr* I³, 727–30; E. Lucchesi, 'L'ORATIO I "De laudibus S. Mariae" de Proclus de Constantinople. Version syriaque inédite', in *Mémorial André-Jean Festugière* (Geneva, 1984), 187–98.

155. By this expression Leontius Jer. wants to say that in the incarnation of Christ the creation of the body and the reception of it into the one *hypostasis* of the Logos coincide. Cf. Augustine, *C. sermon. Arian.* 8,2. PL 42, 688; cited in *JdChr* I³, 771, n. 6. With a play on words Leontius Jer. describes the dogmatic peculiarity of the incarnation in *CN* IV, 17: PG 86, 1684B: the nature of the Logos has experienced in Mary not the beginning of existence (*ousiosis*), but only the beginning of co-existence (*synousiosis*) (with the *sarx*); the *flesh*, however, received the beginning both of *ousiosis* and also of *synousiosis*. In the coincidence of conception and reception into the hypostatic unity there also results the uniqueness of the sonship in Christ. On this theme see *CN* III, 1ff., especially III, 7: PG 86, 1621C–1624C; III, 8: 1629A8ff. Our status as adoptive children is distinguished from this: 1629CD.

way the divinity of the Logos shows itself, and his superiority to
suffering[156] and the power of his Pneuma (that is, his divinity).

Leontius is interested in assessing the Chalcedonian possibility that,
in the one picture of Christ as he appears, the two natures are recognizable at every moment in their *gnorismata*, in their *characteristica* and
proper features. In the defence against Nestorianism the expression of
the divinity of Christ demands particular attention. In the pattern of his
picture of Christ the signal lights of the divine are so closely positioned
that no gap remains for the shadows of the teaching of the two *hypostases*
to continue. Because the equation — God's most proper characteristic =
creative power = miracle — now holds good, the tendency increases to
refer back to miracle in order to secure the divinity of Christ on all sides.
Thus in one fundamental statement we read: '[Christ] shows in the
miraculous occurrences [at the resurrection] that he himself is the
creator and preparer of the fleshly and pneumatic nature ... through
the fact that he can work miracles at all times.'[157] Birth from the
Virgin, healing of the person born blind, resurrection from the dead:
these are the signs in which the divine creative power of Christ shines
out most clearly; for this reason they are a demonstration of his divine
nature, which must seize the whole life and being of Jesus, especially
after the exaltation.[158]

> Because the God-Logos is in him according to nature, and the flesh [of Christ] has become
> entirely divinized after the resurrection, we have no reason, either under a partial aspect or
> under any other regard, to think anything in him or about him as divested of the divinity
> (γυμνὸν ... θεότητος). To that also, which is not divine by nature, is given the name which
> is above all names and that Jesus, whom the Jews crucified, has become Lord and God
> (Phil 2,11; 1 Cor 2,8).

156. Cf. the Nestorian objection in *CN* IV, 9: PG 86, 1665D–1668A, which wants to deduce
theopaschism from the orthodox confession of one *hypostasis*.

157. Leontius Jer., *CN* I, 19: PG 86, 1480C (and the whole section A–C): θαυματουργεῖν
ἀεὶ δυνάμενος.

158. *Idem*, *CN* IV, 37: PG 86, 1712AB. Cf. *CN* IV, 17: PG 86, 1684C: 'If no miracle beyond
the physical power gives testimony for it [the peculiarity of the birth], then he who was born
in accordance with natural powers is not known as God.' Because it is the Logos who forms
the body of Christ, he also gives to it the power 'to come out and emerge in a spiritual way'.
Virginity *in* the birth thus belongs to the divine sign and to the proclamation of faith. Cf. *CN*
IV, 9: PG 86, 1669C–1672A. While the Nestorians want to ascribe the virginal birth to the
Holy Spirit and his unique overshadowing (cf. Lk 1,35), Leontius sees in it a reference to the
constant bond of the *sarx* with the Logos. Our Lord namely is conceived of the Spirit and Mary,
as two causes which are of 'different essence' (*heteroousioi*). Thus in Christ the divine *pneuma*-
essence is united with the flesh. Cf. *CN* I, 19: PG 86, 1477AB with reference to 2 Cor 3,17.
This miraculous birth of Jesus is, however, the archetype of our rebirth from faith, baptism
(*CN* II, 20: PG 86, 1581B) and incorporation into the Church (*CN* I, 18: PG 86, 1468BC).

(c) The miraculous in Leontius of Jerusalem's picture of Christ

Through a comparison of Leontius of Jerusalem's presentation of Christ with that of other Chalcedonians of his time it should be possible to determine more precisely his position on the question of the 'miraculous' in the figure of Jesus. We shall compare him with Leontius of Byzantium and the aphthartic refuted by him. In the background we should also keep in sight Severus of Antioch, the decided opponent of Chalcedon, and Julian of Halicarnassus and his large group of followers. Like a kaleidoscope, these names present the varying colour tones and lines in the picture of Christ sketched by them. The position of the miraculous in Jesus, the incarnate Logos, was an acute theme in the piety and theology of Constantinople in the first half of the era of Justinian.

(i) On the one side we have the extreme position of the Chalcedonian aphthartics.[159] Because the hypostatic union transfers the human nature of Christ into divine dignity, everything human must be judged from this point. Corruptibility, passibility, mortality do not correspond to the 'normal condition' which befits this humanity united to God. For this reason the divine Logos must give his permission, if his body is to be allowed to have this *pathē*, and in general the ordinariness (the normality) of the life of a human being. What from a Chalcedonian viewpoint is perfectly normal for the Incarnate One, his *kenosis*, becomes the exception. The exaltation, which according to Philippians 2,5–11 is present only at the end of Jesus' life, begins already with his conception. The gilding of christology is perfect. One has only to think out the consequences for piety with its human experiences of the everyday. 'Like to us in all things' becomes a thought that is no longer comprehensible. The 'unmingled' of Chalcedon is bypassed, even if the two natures are acknowledged. Only if one assumes that the Logos must give permission is Christ's human nature preserved from having prescribed for it, as it were necessarily and unrestrictedly, the condition of *apatheia* and *aphtharsia* from the very first moment of the *henosis*. That is so un-Chalcedonian, even more than the christology of Severus of Antioch. The fundamental error consists in having regarded the substantial *henosis* in Christ as a 'nature-unity', in spite of the confession of the two natures.

(ii) Against this aphthartic theologian, Leontius of Byzantium exhibited an emphatically more sober picture of Christ. The miraculous in the life of Jesus is the exception. Of all the theologians of his time he has drawn the fundamental Chalcedonian lines in his interpretation

---

159. See above, pp. 213–17; especially Leontius Byz., *CNE*: PG 86, 1333D–1337B.

of the earthly life of Jesus most clearly.[160] According to the judgement of his own contemporaries, however, they lead to the Nestorian picture of Christ. The sparseness of the miraculous in the life of Jesus must in fact have proved unattractive for certain circles of the population and for the ascetics. We can deduce this from the great success which the Julianists achieved at the time in the whole of the East, even compared with Severus of Antioch.[161] Emperor Justinian is indeed the most convincing illustration of this. His theological act ends with an aphthartic experiment.

(iii) The position of Leontius of Jerusalem. Between the exuberance of the Chalcedonian aphthartics at Constantinople and the realism of Leontius of Byzantium, the namesake of the latter takes a middle position which is not easy to determine. With his fundamental dogmatic clarity we can assume from the beginning that he does not fancy the aphthartics mentioned. But that there are certain elements in common cannot be denied. (1) For the interpretation of the picture of Christ Leontius too places great stress on the hypostatic union, the *henosis* or *synthesis*. Thus he wants to present it as the ultimate basis for explaining the miraculous mysteries in the life of Christ, especially the virgin birth, the sinlessness and in particular the resurrection. Impassibility, incorruptibility are indeed present only with the resurrection; they are, however, not the result of an accidental power active in Christ, but the expression of the hypostatic *henosis*.[162] Christ as God raises himself and by this shows himself as God. (2) Despite this stressing of the substantial union in Christ, which Leontius of Jerusalem has in common with the Chalcedonian aphthartics, he does not get involved in their supranaturalness. But is he for that reason already pursuing the realistic line of his namesake? His writing *Against the Nestorians* shows another picture. He develops a doctrine of *theiosis* or divinization, which still moves him very close in feeling to the Chalcedonian aphthartics. The 'divinization' determines the picture of Christ.

The discussion with the Nestorians, whose texts Leontius renders so

---

160. Cf. above, pp. 217–22.

161. This will be shown later in this work when we depict the development in Syria and Egypt. Cf. *JdChr* II/4, 45–7.

162. Cf. Leontius Jer., *CN* I, 19: PG 86, 1473CD. Leontius is replying to the objection of the Nestorians: 'If we ascribe *apatheia* and *aphtharsia* to the *synthesis*, we deceive ourselves. The *kyriakos anthropos* has that according to the witness [of scripture] from the resurrection.' By this they mean that an act of power by God on the human being Jesus is a sufficient basis for *aphtharsia* and *apatheia*. One cannot see in it a proof of the unity of *hypostasis* in Christ. Leontius cannot give a satisfactory answer to this.

fully in the *CN*, points in the same direction. It is precisely their objections which force him to many an exuberance in emphasizing the *henosis*
and its repercussions on the humanity of Christ. We have recognized,
however, that nothing is responsible for these embarrassments other than
his taking over of the Basilian teaching about *idiomata*, which in practice
the Nestorians too employ, only more consistently than Leontius. With
this Basilian concept of *hypostasis* he offers the Nestorians an open flank.
Rescue for him would lie in rejecting this interpretation and in having
recourse to his own discoveries with regard to the *henosis*. The idea of
insubsistence, as Leontius envisages it, is of such a kind that it is not
related to the Cappadocian conception of *hypostasis* and to the over-
emphasis on the *theiosis* which results from this. What is needed is
the new interpretation of the concept of subsistence or of the *hypostasis*
as such. Leontius' clear distinction between a nature-synthesis and a
hypostasis-synthesis also moves in this direction. The rôle of the act of
creation in the coming into being of the union in Christ also fits in well
with the existential approach of his idea of insubsisting. Were one to
remove the Basilian-Cappadocian remnants from the *henosis* teaching of
Leontius of Jerusalem, the way would be clear for a more profound
Chalcedonian teaching about *hypostasis* and for the understanding of the
'hypostatic union'. Leontius of Jerusalem would then be in a position
to give to his namesake better conceptual tools to defend his genuine
christological realism without suspicion of Nestorianism. Each Leontius
would supplement the other. The richer donor would certainly be
Leontius of Jerusalem. He could also rescue the aphthartic of Constantinople from his embarrassments: there is a true substantial unity in
Christ, in the unity of the subsistence, of the subject, of the *hypostasis*,
which allows the natures of God and human being their peculiarity, and
which above all creates room for the *kenosis* according to the scriptures.
The hypostatic *henosis* does not need to be and should not be made the
real cause of the divinization. Soteriology then has its proper foundation.
Although all of this is correct and Leontius may be regarded as the best
christological author of his time, we detect nonetheless a certain
exuberance which must be explained and curtailed.

(d) The *divinized* kyriakos anthropos

Leontius of Jerusalem is a witness for the christological term *kyriakos*
anthropos, although in him its original derivation from Philippians 2,11
(the exaltation of the human being Jesus into the glory of the *Kyrios*)

is already obscured.[163] Nevertheless in his writings it is still a title given to Christ, which in a special way can give expression to the divine *doxa* of the *Kyrios*, because Leontius combines with it a conception of the *henosis* as *synthesis*. We shall illustrate this, using the important chapter 18 of *CN* I.[164]

The Nestorians ask about the recipient of the favour of the incarnation, if one understands it, as Leontius does, as a *synthesis* of the God-Logos 'with the human being taken from us'. Who benefits from the *henosis* — the Logos himself, or the human being with whom he unites himself, or both, or neither the one nor the other, or rather we, or God? The response states that it is we, the redeemed. What is given to us, however, has become clear in Christ, the first-born, head of redeemed humanity.

> Only through the greatest benevolence on the part of [the divine nature] to us did its incarnation occur. As a result, through unity with God, to the *kyriakos anthropos* accrued the wealth of the divinization, to him as first-fruits of the human mass [or dough] and the first-born of many brothers and head of the body of the Church, being first and receiving first and without intermediary, because of its [i.e., the divine nature's] union and unification with him in the *hypostasis*, into his own nature.
>
> To the rest of the mass [dough] of humanity and the rest of the brothers from the seed of Abraham, and the body of the Church, pass in a secondary manner and by participation and with an intermediary the effects of the natural union with him, the first *kyriakos anthropos* benefited from us. [This happens] from the union with him who is from the same mass [or dough], even if he is the first-fruits, and as an only-begotten brother, even if he is first born, and from his body, even if as the head he mediates for us, being one mediator between God and human beings, the human being Christ Jesus our Lord.[165]

In this text we have an almost enthusiastic christology of the divinization, which is derived from a forced understanding of *henosis* and *synthesis*. Leontius almost forgets his fundamental propositions about the distinction between a nature-synthesis and a *hypostasis*-synthesis.[166] The sluice gates are opened for the flowing of the divine wealth over into the humanity of Christ (the *aparchē* for us) by the recognition of the fact that the human being has now become the 'proper nature' of the God-Logos. According to Leontius of Jerusalem, God and human being are so closely drawn together that the flowing over of the gifts of the divinity is a matter of course. He must be asked whether he does not see his splendid insights into the peculiarity of the *henosis* in the

---

163. Cf. above n. 67.

164. Leontius Jer., *CN* I, 18: PG 86, 1465C–1472A.

165. *Ibid.*: PG 86, 1468B10–C15.

166. He speaks of the *henosis kath'hypostasin* as a συναΝακρατικὴ ἔνωσις with the human nature to be ἰδικὴ φύσις αὐτοῦ (PG 86, 1468C).

hypostasis — in contradistinction to the *synthesis* in the nature[167] — endangered or even abandoned. By his good start Leontius so guarantees a substantial unity in Christ that the manifestation of the divine in Christ can be distinguished from it. Christ is and remains the one incarnate Son of God just as much in the *kenosis* as in the *theiosis*. For Leontius of Jerusalem, however, there belongs to the one whole picture of Christ the assumption of his entire human nature, with body and soul and what the *oikonomia* of God put at Christ's disposal for his supernatural equipment and credentials.[168]

> But it is confessed that, in assuming our nature (τὰ φυσικὰ ἡμῶν), the Lord was not deprived of what is above our nature (ὑπὲρ φύσιν ἡμετέραν). Much shows this: his conception without semen which is different from the way we come into being, and his virginal birth, as well as his fasting for forty days without feeling hunger, and such like. Therefore in Christ we believe that this was arranged (in a way that) transcends our nature, so that even as his flesh existed, it was also ensouled, and the flesh of the divine Logos was ensouled with a rational and thinking soul.

A further comment on distinguishing the two Leontii

At the conclusion of the analysis of the works of the two Leontii (of Byzantium and Jerusalem), it would seem to be certain that we have in fact to assume that there are two authors. Their identification, attempted of late by Ilie Fracea,[169] cannot be upheld. Reference must be made in particular (1) to the new language of Leontius of Jerusalem in the interpretation of the insubsistence of the humanity of Christ in the *hypostasis* of the Logos; (2) to the rich utilization of the term *synthesis*, in the place of *henosis* or together with *henosis*, in Leontius of Jerusalem; (3) to the strong emphasis on miracles and the miraculous as evidence

---

167. What 'union in the nature and according to the nature' means in contrast to 'union in the *hypostasis* and according to the *hypostasis*' is expressed by Severan texts in the *CM* of Leontius Jer. We shall cite a major text from the collection, which P. T. R. Gray has studied in his article, 'An Anonymous Severian Monophysite of the Mid-Sixth Century', *Patristic and Byzantine Review* 1 (1982) (117-26): Frag. 12 (120) of 'Julius of Rome', (Apollinarian forgery): 'It is confessed in Him [= Christ] that the created is in union with the uncreated, and the uncreated is in commixture [!] with the created, one nature having brought together a partial activity out of each part, and the Word bringing things to completion in the whole, with the divine completeness — the very thing that comes about in the common man out of two *incomplete* (!) parts, which make up one nature, and are signified by one name' (Leontius Jer., *CM*: PG 86, 1865B16-20 = Apoll., *De unione* 5: Lietzmann, 250-1). See the commentary of Gray, *art. cit.*, 120-2. He emphasizes particularly that in the interpretation of the body–soul analogy Ps. Julius denotes the united natures as 'incomplete parts'. Ps. Julius applies this to Christ. Indeed the divinity is complete, but it must augment the human *sarx* as 'soul', and thus becomes part of the whole. In this view there is a profound violation of the divine transcendence of the Logos.

168. Leontius Jer., *CN* II, 20: PG 86, 1580D–1581A.

169. See above, n. 3.

of the divinity of Christ in Leontius of Jerusalem (*CN* IV, 37: PG 86, 1712A) in contrast to the explicit stressing of the rarity of miracles in the life of Jesus in Leontius of Byzantium (*CA*: PG 86, 1336BC; *CNE*: PG 86, 1352C–1353A).

PART THREE

THE THEOLOGICAL ACTIONS UNDERTAKEN BY JUSTINIAN I (518–527 AND 527–565)

With the beginning of the Chalcedonian restoration under Emperor Justin I (518–527), his nephew, Petrus Sabbatius, who was called Justinian,[1] appeared in the group of actors on the stage of ecclesiastical politics and theology.[2] From 525 onwards he was accompanied by his consort, Theodora, who influenced him increasingly.[3] The theological actions of Justinian began as early as 519 and were to continue during the whole of his joint regency (until 527) and his sole reign (until 565). We can highlight the tenor of these reasonably clearly by some key phrases.

(1) The movement in favour of the theopaschite addition: 'One of the Trinity was crucified' (with variants); (2) the attempt to win over the

1. This name was given to him at his adoption by Justin. On the early history of Justinian see A. A. Vasiliev, *Justin the First. An Introduction to the Epoch of Justinian the Great* (Cambridge, Mass., 1950), 92–6. When Justin ascended the throne (518), Justinian was already thirty-six years old. The son of a farming family in Illyricum, at the age of twenty-five he had been brought by his uncle to Constantinople (somewhere around 507), and received a comprehensive education, also in Greek, this being considered as preparation for a military career. On Justinian see (1) the sources: L. Bréhier, in Fliche-Martin, *Histoire de l'Eglise* 4, 437, n. 1; CPG 6865–6893. The texts have been made easily accessible by Mario Amelotti and Livia Migliardi Zingale, *Scritti teologici ed ecclesiastici di Giustiniano = Florentina Studiorum Universitas. Legum Iustiniani Imperatoris Vocabularium*. Subsidia III (Milan, 1977); in the following abbreviated as Amelotti-Migliardi Zingale, *Scritti teologici*. On research see: (1) in general: R. Bonini, *Introduzione allo studio dell'età giustinianea* (Bologna, ³1979), 123–8: Nota bibliographica; see as well the detailed bibliography of O. Kresten in H. Hunger (ed.), *Das byzantinische Herrscherbild* = WdF 341 (Darmstadt, 1975), 415–48; see further the current bibliography in *ByzZ*. (2) special studies: A. Hohlweg, 'Justinian', in *Die Großen der Weltgeschichte*, Vol. II (Zürich, 1972), 748–77 with bibliography 776–7; P. T. R. Gray, art., 'Justinian', in *TRE* 17 (1988), 478–86.

2. After the assassination of Vitalian (520), Justinian became Consul in 521. In 525 he became Caesar, on 1 (or 4) April 527 he became co-regent with Justin, and, after his death, Emperor (1 August 527), cf. A. A. Vasiliev, *op. cit.*, 96, n. 73; A. Hohlweg, *art. cit.*, 750.

3. Cf. A. Hohlweg, *art. cit.*, 750–2; W. Schubart, *Justinian und Theodora* (Munich, 1943), especially 48–58; R. Browning, *Justinian and Theodora* (London, 1971), 64–9 with the spiteful section from Procopius' *Secret History* (9, 10–22) and a critique of it. See in addition Averil Cameron, *Procopius and the Sixth Century* (London, 1985), 67–83 (Procopius and Theodora). As the official concubine of a certain Hecobolus, the governor of Pentapolis, Theodora dwelt in North Africa and, when dismissed by him, on her return journey to Constantinople came into contact in Alexandria with the leading anti-Chalcedonians, like Patriarch Timothy IV (III) and Severus of Antioch. Here she experienced a kind of religious conversion and renounced her former way of life. With this event Theodora's future path in theological questions was established. In 525 she married Justinian; during the Nika riot in 532 she saved his crown. On this cf. J. A. S. Evans, 'The "Nika" Rebellion and the Empress Theodora', *Byz* 54 (1984), 380–2.

Severans (532); the condemnation of Severus of Antioch, Patriarch Anthimus (536) and the fight against them (542/543); (3) a doctrinal decree of 542/543 against the Origenists, within which the anathema against the 'monophysites' is also repeated; (4) the action against the Three Chapters (544–553); (5) the final stage: Justinian's aphthartic text (on the uncorruptibility of the body of Christ).[4] Because the documents that pertain to these actions stand in clear contrast to each other, the Emperor himself has already offered us the principle for arranging the material, which we have only to follow.[5] It may be assumed that Justinian had come into contact with theologians and theological questions even before the change of 518, but this cannot be documented concretely.[6] If he was already in the capital in 507 and was also stimulated to study by an interest in theology, then one may wonder how it happened that he did not succumb to the influence of the generally admired Severus of Antioch, who was then present in the city. Was the *Henoticon* of Zeno not a temptation for him? Not taking into account the fact that he was destined for a military career, it is probable that the strict-Chalcedonian stance of his uncle Justin and of the powerful Vitalian[7] account for such reserve. One may also think of the influence of the Sleepless Monks, as will immediately become clear.

---

4. On these activities as a whole see M. Amelotti, 'Giustiniano tra teologia e diritto', in G. G. Archi (ed.), *L'imperatore Giustiniano. Storia e mito* (Milan, 1978), 133–60; also printed in *Scritti teologici*, VII–XXIX; we cite according to this edition. E. Schwartz, 'Zur Kirchenpolitik Justinians', in *idem, Zur Geschichte der alten Kirche und ihres Rechts = Ges. Schriften* IV (Berlin, 1960), 276–320; M. Simonetti, 'La politica religiosa di Giustiniano', in G. G. Archi (ed.), *Il mondo dell'diritto nell'epoca giustinianea. Caratteri e problematiche* (Ravenna, 1985), 91–111; G. Prinzing, 'Das Bild Justinians I. in der Überlieferung der Byzantiner vom 7. bis 15. Jahrhundert', in *Fontes Minores* VII, ed. D. Simon, 1–99. For further literature on the activities individually see below; in general: J. Meyendorff, *Byzantine Theology – Historical Trends and Doctrinal Themes* (New York, 1974); M. V. Anastos, 'Justinian's Despotic Control over the Church as Illustrated by his Edicts on the Theopaschite Formula and his Letter to Pope John II in 533', in *Mélanges G. Ostrogorsky* II, 1–11 = *idem, Studies in Byzantine Intellectual History* (London, 1979), no. IV.

5. Cf. Amelotti-Migliardi Zingale, *Scritti teologici*, XI with reflections on the systematization of Justinian's themes and writings. Amelotti stresses that the coincidence of clearly divided problem areas and chronological succession is typical of Justinian: 'Si accorda perfettamente con la nostra immagine di Giustiniano il vederlo isolare i problemi e affrontarli via via, quando nel suo convincimento politico o nel sopraggiungere degli eventi la loro soluzione s'impone.'

6. When A. A. Vasiliev, *Justin the First*, p. 135, comments: 'Justinian . . . had an excellent theological education', then that is a conclusion drawn from the later period after 527. It should be noted that Constantinople did not possess a theological school. In the Emperor's first theological action one can still discern considerable uncertainty in theological questions.

7. On the 'Chalcedonian' aura of Vitalian, whose personality at first clearly outshone that of Justinian, see the reports about the acclamations of the people, which after the change of 518 were accorded him in Tyre and Palestine, *ibid.*, 149–58.

'ONE OF THE TRINITY WAS CRUCIFIED'

Justinian entered the theological arena quite soon after Justin had seized power, first of all only as the diplomatically active letter-writer who acted for or against the real players. Such were the Scythian or Gothic monks[8] who appeared in Constantinople at the end of 518 and had chosen as a formula of propaganda a sentence which theologically was really harmless: 'one of the Trinity was crucified'. How the recently re-established unity of the Church could quickly be endangered because of this is shown in the various letters of Justinian, together with numerous other documents, which are related to two chronologically separate phases of this one action. This event had a prehistory. A brief review of that will make it easier for us to understand the conflict about the phrase 'one of the Trinity was crucified'.

I. THE PREHISTORY TO 518/519

1. Origin

For methodological reasons it is advisable to distinguish the formula *unus ex trinitate incarnatus est* from the formulas in which suffering (*passus*), death (*mortuus*) or crucifixion (*crucifixus*) is stated of the subject *unus ex (de) trinitate*. We find the formula *unus ex trinitate incarnatus* for the first time in Proclus, the Patriarch of Constantinople (434–446), in the following passages:

(a) Proclus, *Tomus ad Armenios* (CPG 5897) 21: ACO IV, 2, p. 192,7: τὸν ἕνα τριάδος, σεσαρκῶσθαι; Latin: p. 202,25: *unum ex trinitate incarnatum*.

(b) Proclus, *Ep. uniformis ad singulos Occidentis eppos* (CPG 5915) 7: ACO IV, 2, p. 66,16–17: *unum ex trinitate ... deum verbum factum hominem.* (On the authenticity cf. Diekamp, *ThR* 16 (1917), 357f.)

---

8. On the Scythian monks see the *bibliographia selecta* in F. Glorie, *Maxentii aliorumque Scytharum monachorum necnon Ioannis Tomitanae urbis episcopi Opuscula* = CCL 85A (Turnhout, 1978), XVII–XXII; older literature in V. Schurr, *Die Trinitätslehre des Boethius im Lichte der 'skythischen Kontroversen'* = FCLDG 18, 1 (Paderborn, 1935) (in what follows abbreviated as V. Schurr, *Trinitätslehre*), 141–2, n. 137 (sources and bibliography); on the earlier history: J. Zeiller, *Les origines chrétiennes dans les provinces danubiennes de l'Empire Romain* (Paris, 1918) (no presentation of the controversy after 519).

A further instance would be a passage in the so-called *Tomus secundus ad Armenios* in Innocent of Maronia, ACO IV, 2, p. 72,38–39. Schwartz, however, considers this second *Tomus* to be inauthentic (*Konzilstudien*, 43–4).

For the real theopaschite formula too, the *unus ex trinitate crucifixus* or *passus*, Proclus was called upon not only by Severus, but also by Innocent of Maronia and Facundus of Hermiane. This attribution to Proclus, nevertheless, has been decisively contested by M. Richard.[9]

(c) John Maxentius, *Libellus fidei*, X, 17–19 (ed. Glorie, CCL 85A) produces three citations from a work which 'Proclus, the bishop of this city, . . . (wrote) to the Armenians'; in these we find the formulations *unus ex trinitate est, qui crucifixus est* (p. 16,215), *unus est de trinitate, qui passus est* (p. 17,239) and *unus ergo de trinitate est crucifixus* (p. 17,245). However, the three sections from which John Maxentius cites are not present in the *Tomus ad Armenios*.

Innocent of Maronia also transmits these three sections under the name Proclus: ACO IV, p. 73,1–11 (first section), 13–27 (the next two sections follow, concurring in meaning with the *Libellus fidei*, pp. 16,229–17,248; as his source he gives *ex libro III de fide* or *ex sermone de fide*.

(d) Proclus, *Ep. IV ad Ioannem Antiochenum* (CPG 5901): DP, p. 48 IV (Greek) (under the name of Cyril of Alexandria; another manuscript ascribes the fragment to Basil (writing to John of Antioch), yet another to Bishop Pamphilus of Abydos; the latter is familiar as the writer of a (forged) letter to Peter (the Fuller): ACO III, 9–10, where the subject is the Trishagion): ἕνα τῆς τριάδος κατὰ σάρκα ἐσταυρῶσθαι;

in Severus of Antioch, *C. imp. Gram.* III, 41: CSCO 102, 247 (according to Severus it is a fragment from Proclus, *Ep. ad Ioh. Ant.*, with the *incipit: ut videtur, insignis poetae instar*): *unum ex trinitate carne crucifixum confitemur*;

Latin: Facund. Herm., *Pro def.* I, 1, 9: CCL 90A, pp. 5,61–6,66; PG 65, 876C–877A; Liberatus, *Brev.* 10: ACO II, 5, p. 111,16–20.

2. Spread

(a) The Eutychian monk Dorotheus produces the formula at the fourth session of the Council of Chalcedon (17 October 451): ACO II, 1, 2, p. 120,16–20,23f.

(b) Peter the Iberian (453–488) is taught about it in a vision. Cf. John Rufus, *Plerophoriae* (from 515), ch. 37 = PO 8, 86–87.

(c) Emperor Zeno, *Henoticon* (§ 7): 'One of the Trinity . . . became incarnate', see *CCT* II/1,

---

9. M. Richard, 'Proclus de Constantinople et le théopaschisme', *RHE* 38 (1942), 303–31 = *Op. Min.* II, no. 52, esp. 323–31. Richard maintains that a formula like this in a letter to John of Antioch would never have met with approval in Antioch in 438, and on the other hand would have been cited by Cyril and his supporters with great pleasure. But there is no echo of either of these responses at all. Theodoret too in the *Eranistes* is unaware of the formula. According to Richard, however, if fragment (d) is not authentic, then neither is fragment (c), since both seem to be from the same hand (according to Schwartz, *Konzilstudien*, p. 28, n. 3 and p. 47). Richard considers it historically illegitimate to deduce from the formula *unus ex trinitate incarnatus est* to the other formula *unus de trinitate passus est*, because not everybody would have regarded such a logical operation as permissible. Richard's reasoning is confirmed by the interpolations at the end of the second *apologia* of Nestorius (in the *Liber Heraclidis*); the interpolations were written after the death of Theodosius II and report violent disputes about theopaschitism in Constantinople, but the formula *unus ex trinitate* . . . does not appear. (We are grateful to Prof. L. Abramowski, to whom we owe this observation.)

253. From here it was taken over into the *libellus* of the Alexandrian *apocrisiarii* which these handed over to the papal delegation of 497 in Constantinople: CA, *ep.* 102, no. 11: CSEL 35, 472; in Rome this *libellus* was translated by Dionysius Exiguus into Latin: CA, *ep.* 102: CSEL 35, 473.

(d) Emperor Anastasius I: Confession of faith, in Zacharias Rhetor cont., *HE* VII, 8: Brooks, CSCO 88, p. 30,16–27; Hamilton-Brooks, 173: '. . . I confess that one of the *persons* [*hypostases*] of the Trinity, God the Word, . . . became incarnate . . . was crucified . . .' In his *suggestio* to Pope Hormisdas of 29 June 519, the deacon Dioscorus comments that Emperor Anastasius has prescribed the *unus de trinitate crucifixus* for the Catholics. On the condemnation of those who refuse to confess 'one of the Trinity was crucified' at a *Synodus Endemousa* in Constantinople (according to Victor of Tunnuna in 499; more correctly in 507), summoned at the instigation of Philoxenus of Mabbog under Emperor Anastasius, see *CCT* II/1, 270–1. Because the whole Antiochene and Leonine tradition, as this had passed into the Chalcedonian formula, was rejected at the Synod, one understands why the *unus de trinitate crucifixus* was regarded with such suspicion in the West. Cf. H. de Noris, 'Dissertatio I. in historiam controversiae de Uno ex Trinitate passo', in *idem, Historia Pelagiana et Dissertatio de Synodo V. Oecumenica* (edition: Padua, 1708 – appendix 105–136; a further dissertation on the Scythian monks, *ibid.*, 137–156, esp. 108). See also V. Grumel, 'L'auteur et la date de composition du tropaire 'Ο Μονογενής', EO 22 (1923) (398–418), 404–10.

(e) Philoxenus of Mabbog (d. 523), *Dissertationes decem de uno e sancta trinitate incorporato et passo* (*Mēmrē contre Ḥabib*): PO 15, 443–542 (Latin); PO 38, 479–633; PO 39, 549–753 (French); PO 40, 203–351 (French).

(f) Severus of Antioch, *C. imp. Gram.* III, ch. 29; cf. John of Beth Aphth., *Vita Severi*: PO 2, 236–237: at the instigation of Severus an imperial delegation was sent to Patriarch Macedonius to ask him where he stood with regard to the sentence *unus de trinitate incarnatus*. The Patriarch of Constantinople rejected the formula. Severus saw in it the touchstone of 'true faith'.

(g) The forged letters to Peter the Fuller; see above, pp. 259–60; V. Schurr, *Trinitätslehre*, 147, n. 151, compiles the texts from these letters, insofar as they contain our formula, which is to be distinguished from the expanded Trishagion of Peter the Fuller. We may assume that the formula 'one of the Trinity became flesh, (or) was crucified' was readily seized as the shibboleth of orthodoxy in the fight against any Nestorianism, before it became the battle-cry against Chalcedon through the *Henoticon* and the Severans. It was well-known in the monasteries of St Euthymius and St Sabas near Jerusalem, especially through the *Tomus* to the Armenians, from whom numerous monks had come to Sabas.[10] It was precisely among these monastic Fathers that Proclus' formula became the instrument for warding off Nestorianism as well as Eutychianism.[11]

The propaganda for this formula quickly encompassed further circles in the Near East. As early as 520 Catholic clerics and monks from Jerusalem, Antioch and Syria Secunda submitted to Emperor Justin a confession of faith, in which the *unus ex sancta et unius essentiae trinitate* was

10. Euthymius himself came from Melitene, the metropolis of Armenia II, and as presbyter there had exercised supervision over the monks before he came to Jerusalem in 405. E. Schwartz, *Kyrillos von Skythopolis* (Leipzig, 1939), 358.

11. Cf. V. Schurr, *Trinitätslehre*, 145. In the *Vita Euthymii* no. 26, Cyril of Scythopolis comments that the Saint confessed against Nestorius and Eutyches that 'the God-Logos, the one from the holy and consubstantial Trinity, became flesh' (Schwartz, p. 40,14–15). Sabas himself confessed the formula of Proclus, but not the expanded Trishagion of Peter the Fuller (*Vita Sabae*, no. 32: Schwartz, pp. 117,25–118,20), and was distressed about the Nestorian monks who 'venerate Christ, the one from the holy and consubstantial Trinity, but not as our true God' (*Vita Sabae*, no. 38: Schwartz, p. 127,21–24). On the confession of Abbot Abraham shortly before 500 see V. Schurr, *Trinitätslehre*, 145–6, n. 144.

recommended as the right interpretation of Chalcedonian faith.[12] On the basis of the tradition, originally Constantinopolitan, which was not yet burdened with the Severan controversy, the Scythian monks too will have gained their understanding of the trinitarian theopaschite formula. For them it was the *via media* between Nestorius and Eutyches and did not raise the claim of being a formula of union between the larger blocks, the supporters and opponents of Chalcedon, or the Nestorians and the Severans.[13]

Justinian's first action, while still Justin I's co-regent, concerned the theme 'one of the Trinity who was crucified'.

II. JUSTINIAN AND HIS ACTIONS IN THE CONFLICT OVER THE FORMULA *UNUS EX TRINITATE CRUCIFIXUS*

1. The appearance of the Scythian monks in Constantinople

The Scythian monks,[14] who signified the first theological challenge for Justinian, came from the region south of the mouth of the Danube, which had Tomi as its capital. They lived in tension with their bishop Paternus, and in contrast had close ties with their compatriot Vitalian, particularly through their confrater, the monk Leontius, who was a relative of the army commander. Perhaps they came with their protector into the imperial city when Justin, after seizing power, summoned him and made him *magister militum*. The *dramatis personae* found themselves together: Justin, Justinian, Vitalian, the monks, as well as the legates of Pope Hormisdas, who, perhaps at the direct suggestion of Vitalian,

---

12. See CA, *ep.* 232a: pp. 705,6–706,16. The Emperor passed on this confession with his recommendation to Pope Hormisdas (9 September 520: CA, *ep.* 232, pp. 701–3).

13. On this problem see V. Schurr, *Trinitätslehre*, 148–51. Schurr rightly places the Scythians in that tradition of orthodox circles of the Orient, in which the formula of Proclus 'was spread as the core-word and password of orthodoxy and existed as their property, before the supporters of the *Henoticon* and the Severans used it for propaganda' (149). Schurr considers the theopaschite conflict as the 'advance of the theology of the Palestinian lavras into the West' (see below on Euthymius and Sabas) 'and its breakthrough to victory under Justinian'. See 229 with reference back to 142–67.

14. See B. Altaner, 'Der griechische Theologe Leontius und Leontius der skythische Mönch. Eine prosopographische Untersuchung', *ThQ* 127 (1947), 147–65; *idem*, 'Zum Schrifttum der "skythischen" (gotischen) Mönche', *HistJb* 72 (1953), 568–81; F. Glorie, CCL 85A (Turnhout, 1978) VIII–XVI: *Documenta et Testimonia*; XXIII–XLI: *Prolegomena*. They are monks from the triangle between the mouth of the Danube and the Black Sea, the old land of the Scythians, into which the Goths had penetrated so that a mixed culture resulted. See 'From the Land of the Scythians', *The Metropolitan Museum of Art Bulletin* XXXII 5 (1975) (on the acculturation process between the Goths and the Scythians). Cf. H. Wolfram, *Geschichte der Goten. Von den Anfängen bis zur Mitte des sechsten Jahrhunderts. Entwurf einer historischen Ethnographie* (Munich, 1980), especially 40–136 (Migration to the Black Sea . . .; constitution and culture of the Goths on the Danube and the Black Sea); 448–60: ethnography. See the literature, particularly on 5–13. J. A. McGuckin, 'The "Theopaschite Confession" (Text and Historical Context): a Study in the Cyrilline Re-interpretation of Chalcedon', *JEH* 35 (1984), 239–55.

had been sent to Constantinople (before 25 March 519) to restore the unity of the Church. The hour was thus favourable for the Scythian monks.

We discern a particular intention or a programme in their appearance: they wanted to protect the Council of Chalcedon, probably in the face of Severan opponents, against the reproach of Nestorianism[15] by producing a greater synthesis between the Cyril of the *mia-physis* formula and the unification christology of Proclus. Serving them for this purpose were: (1) a more differentiated assessment of the Cyrillian *mia-physis* formula and of the acknowledgement of its corrective function *vis-à-vis* a one-sided use of the two-natures formula; (2) the simultaneous use of the two formulas 'from two natures' and 'in two natures'; (3) the insistence on the confession of Mary as the 'true and real *theotokos*', directed above all against the Sleepless Monks, as we shall see; (4) the use of precisely this formula *Christus unus ex trinitate incarnatus et passus*; and (5) the manner of speaking of the *Christos synthetos* or *Christus compositus*.[16]

They wasted no time in accusing the Constantinopolitan deacon Victor of heresy before the legates and in handing over to them a *libellus*.[17] The Roman delegation, consisting of the bishops Germanus and John, the deacons Felix and Dioscorus, an Alexandrian who lived in Rome, and the presbyter Blandus, refused to accept the Scythian

15. That the Scythians were of the opinion that the Council of Chalcedon was not sufficient against Nestorius and for this reason needed to be expanded, was reported by the deacon Dioscorus in his *suggestio* to Pope Hormisdas of 15 October 519: CA, *ep.* 224, no. 7: CSEL 35, 686: 'May Your Beatitude [Hormisdas] know that these Scythians say that all who accept the Synod of Chalcedon are Nestorians, and say "the Synod is not sufficient against Nestorius", and one ought to accept the Synod as they themselves have expounded (it).'

16. With V. Schurr, *Trinitätslehre*, 149, n. 155, for this programme we have to refer to (1) the *suggestio* of Dioscorus (CA, *ep.* 224, no. 3: p. 685), where the concerns of the monks are given: *habuerunt intentionem de uno de trinitate crucifixo et de Christo composito et de aliis capitulis*; (2) the *Capitula* of John Maxentius: no. 1 (simultaneous use of formulas); no. 2 (*Maria dei genetrix*); no. 4 (*unus de trinitate*); no. 9 (*Christus compositus*); see CCL 85A, 29–30; (3) John Maxentius, *Libell. fid.* XI, 22: CCL 85A, p. 18,277–279; here Maxentius stresses the connection between the confession of *dei genetrix* and the formula *unus de trinitate* . . .; (4) John Maxentius, *Dialog. c. Nestorian.*: Book I deals particularly with Mary, the mother of God; Book II develops especially (a) the *unus de trinitate* and (b) *Christus compositus*; (5) the letter of the monks to the African bishops, part I (with the themes named).

17. See the information in F. Glorie, CCL 85A, XXIV, who assigns this meeting and the handing over of the *libellus* to the period between 25 March and 29 June 519. Cf. CA, *ep.* 228. The *libellus* was also presented to the Patriarch of Constantinople. See *Libell. fid.*: CCL 85A, 5–25. According to CA, *ep.* 224, the deacon Victor confessed strict-Chalcedonian teaching. Cf. CCL 85A, XXV.

memorandum.[18] Vitalian took the part of the Scythian party from the very beginning and excluded the papal legates from further discussion; to this discussion, however, he invited the Patriarch of Constantinople and the deacon Victor, and probably also the monks.[19] Thus, at least according to external conduct, the strict-Chalcedonian Vitalian became the supporter of the theopaschite-trinitarian formula of the monks, who now decided, probably on his advice, to send a delegation to Rome (the summer of 519), in order to gain Pope Hormisdas for their cause.[20]

2. The Scythian appeal to Rome and the stance of Justinian

(a) The appeal to the Pope

Where did Justinian stand? When Pope Hormisdas demanded from his legates a report of success,[21] Vitalian and Justinian seized the opportunity to report to Rome about the monks, concerning whom the papal legates themselves made some very critical remarks.[22] No doubt influenced by the negative attitude of the papal legates, in the heat of the moment Justinian wrote a letter, in which the names of the monks are mentioned[23] and clearly warned against. The Pope should 'receive' them appropriately and 'send them far away'. Their empty prattle (vaniloquia) introduced novelties into the Church, which were contained neither in the four Councils nor in the letters of Leo. They should be given 'a corresponding penance and be dismissed'. Such 'restless people' (inquieti homines) should not be allowed to disturb the unity and peace

---

18. John Maxentius, Libell. fid., tit.: CCL 85A, 5.

19. Cf. Suggestio Dioscori ad Hormisdam: CA, ep. 224, nos. 6–7. Dioscorus knows nothing about the result of the discussion.

20. Cf. F. Glorie, in CCL 85A, XXVI, n. 27. To the group of travellers belonged the monks John, Leontius, Achilles and Mauritius. Cf. CA, ep. 187 and 191. In Rome they met their compatriot, Dionysius Exiguus, who to support the Scythian cause translated several writings from Greek into Latin, namely Cyril Alex., Ep. 45 and 46 ad Succensum (cf. ACO I, 5, 295–302); his epistula synodica to Nestorius and Proclus' Tomus ad Armenios; on the further translations into Latin see B. Altaner, art. cit., ThQ 127 (1947), 150, n. 13.

21. Hormisdas pp., CA, ep. 219: 680–681; CA, ep. 220 and 221: 681, 681–682. The legates write on 29 June 519: CA, ep. 217: 677–679.

22. CA, ep. 217, nos. 5–12: 677–679.

23. Justinian, Ep. ad Hormisd. (CPG 6867) of 29 June 519: CA, ep. 187, 644–645; Amelotti-Migliardi Zingale, Scritti teologici, no. 3, p. 8.

which had been newly regained (after the Acacian schism).[24] What Vitalian wrote is not preserved; however, he probably spoke for the monks, as is clear from the letter of the papal legates of 29 June 519. The monks reportedly attempted to win Vitalian over for their new plans, which would have been all the easier, for, as was stated, a relative of the powerful man was among them.[25] What is significant now is that Justinian evidently had second thoughts about his first letter, and, a few days after sending his letter of 29 June 519, forwarded an 'express letter',[26] which was intended to reach the Pope more quickly than his first. In this second letter new notes were sounded. The Pope was supposed to answer the questions of the 'pious monks' as quickly as possible and send them back to Constantinople with this decision 'before our delegate [with the letter of 29 June] arrives before Your Holiness'. Otherwise there was imminent danger to the unity of the Church. From this letter onwards Justinian favoured the Scythian monks. On 15 October 519 a new letter was sent to Rome, in which Justin's co-regent once again urged that the questions be answered quickly and the trinitarian-theopaschite formula be accepted.[27] On 19 January 520 his pressure on the Pope increased. Together with Emperor Justin and Patriarch John he reported to Rome that from various provinces of the East intercessions had arrived, speaking of certain *capitula* about the inseparable Trinity, which one could not turn one's back on.[28] Indeed the letter of Justinian has been lost; from the response of the Pope to him, however, we know that the topic was nothing other than the

24. In his letter to Hormisdas of 29 June 519 (CA, *ep.* 216; F. Glorie, CCL 85A, XXVI–XXVII) the papal deacon Dioscorus also condemns the monks in strident tones. When these claim that Chalcedon is not sufficient against Nestorius and they demand new discussion, this reveals a criticism of the Fourth Council, the characteristic motive for which fits into what today is described as the neo-Chalcedonian approach. In opposition to this Dioscorus persistently sets his strict-Chalcedonianism. Chalcedon is said to be devalued by this; apart from the Council itself, the letters of Leo, and the letters of the bishops in the CE, the Council needs no further addition, because this would destroy what had already been achieved.

25. Cf. CA, *ep.* 217, no. 11, p. 679: *propter istas novas intentiones Vitaliano magnifico viro subripuerunt et talia vindicare.*

26. Justinian, Letter from the beginning of July 519 (CPG 6869): CA, *ep.* 191, 648–649; Amelotti-Migliardi Zingale, *Scritti teologici*, no. 4, p. 9. See the Pope's reply of 2 September 519 (= CA, *ep.* 189), in which he passes over in silence Justinian's inconsistency.

27. Justinian, *Ep. ad Hormisd.* (CPG 6868): CA, *ep.* 188, 645–646, of 15 October 519; Amelotti-Migliardi Zingale, no. 5, p. 10. The letter arrived in Rome on 17 November 519. On the same day the deacon Dioscorus wrote once again against the monks: CA, *ep.* 224, 685–687.

28. Justinian emp., *Ep. ad Hormisd.*: CA, *ep.* 181, 636–637; John Const., *Relatio ad Hormisd.*: CA, *ep.* 183, 638–639.

formula *unus ex trinitate passus est*.[29] On 9 July 520 Justinian once again supported the Oriental petitions with Pope Hormisdas[30] and this time he himself defended the formula of the monks, in part with words from St Augustine, even if in a modified form.[31] The concept of *persona* was inserted into it. In this way he removed the fear of the Latins that through the trinitarian-theopaschite formula the divine nature as such was being made the *organon* of suffering. Justinian considered the question to be so urgent that on 9 September 520 he sent a new letter to the Pope, which Bishop John, the presbyter Heraclianus and the deacon Constantine were to deliver.[32] He requested anew a complete answer (*integrum responsum*) which left nothing further in doubt. To reassure the Pope he once again slipped in his *persona* formula. 'One of the Trinity' is interpreted as *persona in trinitate et ex trinitate*.[33] With this expression a bridge could also be built to the deacon Dioscorus. Against this attempt, however, Maxentius, the real rabble-rouser in the whole theopaschite affair, made a decided stand. For him only the pure formula 'one of the Trinity suffered' was tolerable. He reproached the deacon with only wanting to introduce Nestorianism once again into the Church by this formula 'Christ — one person of the Trinity'.[34] That this accusation was aimed at the Roman deacon becomes quite clear from

29. Hormisd. pp., *Ep.* 112 = CA, *ep.* 206 from the end of March 520. Cf. F. Glorie in CCL 85A, XXXIV, n. 68, with reference to the *libellus* of John Maxentius, IX 14; XI 20: Glorie, pp. 14,190-191; 17,253-255.

30. Justinian, *Ep. ad Hormisd.* (CPG 6870), of 9 July 520: CA, *ep.* 196, p. 656,5-27; Amelotti-Migliardi Zingale, *Scritti teologici*, no. 6, pp. 11-12.

31. Cf. F. Glorie in CCL 85A, XXXIV-XXXV. He states that the formula *unus ex trinitate* can be understood with Augustine as *aliqua ex trinitate persona*.

32. Justinian, *Ep. ad Hormisd.* (CPG 6873) of 9 September 520: CA, *ep.* 235, 715; Amelotti-Migliardi Zingale, *Scritti teologici*, no. 8, p. 14.

33. *Ibid.*, CA, *ep.* 235, p. 715,22-25; Amelotti-Migliardi Zingale, *loc. cit.*, p. 14,14-16: *recte dicitur unus in trinitate cum patre spirituque sancto regnare, maiestatisque eius personam in trinitate et ex trinitate non infideliter credimus*.

34. John Maxentius, *Dialog. c. Nestorian.* II, XXI: CCL 85A, 105-106. Maxentius introduces as the position of the 'Nestorian': *non, unum ex trinitate, sed, unam personam Christum ex trinitate, melius arbitror confiteri*. Maxentius says that it is the Catholic definition to confess: *deum verbum, dominum nostrum Iesum Christum, cum propria carne, unum fateri ex trinitate, licet non sit secundum carnem de substantia trinitatis* (vv. 1016-1020). By this is meant Dioscorus. But even the deposed patriarch of Alexandria, Theodosius (535-566), a decided Severan, introduces the term *hypostasis* in order to interpret correctly the *unus ex trinitate* against 'Sabellians'; cf. (1) his *Tractatus theologici ratio et scopus* (CPG 7136): CSCO 103 (V), p. 25,5-9: *Et inde ausi sunt et ille dicere: essentiam Trinitatis incorporatam esse per unam ex hypostasibus; et idem praedicant de natura divina. Ibid.*, 26 (on his work, ch. VI): ... *circa inhumanationem unius e Trinitate sancta, Verbi Dei, discimus hypostasim ipsius Verbi tantum incorporatam esse*. To it corresponds (2) the statements in the *Oratio theologica* (CPG 7137), ch. VI: CSCO 103 (V), pp. 51,32-53,30. Reference is made in this to the word *hypostasis* in Ps. Dionysius Areop., *De div. nom.* I 4; the incarnation is said to take place *per*

the 'reply' of Maxentius to Hormisdas' letter[35] to the African bishop, Possessor, who from 517 was residing in Constantinople. In this reply we read:[36]

> Here it is the right place for us to show how and why the heretics, of whom Dioscorus is one, proclaim Christ as *one person* of the Trinity, but do not condescend to confess *Christ* as *one* from the Trinity. They assent that Christ has the *prosopon* of the God-Logos, but is not himself the God-Logos . . . In this wily way they indeed admit that Christ is a *person* of the Trinity; however, in no way do they want to confess him as *one* of the Trinity.

In his criticism of Hormisdas' letter, Maxentius reduces the *persona* concept of the deacon Dioscorus to the meaning which it had received in the controversy between Cyril and Nestorius in the years 429–431. *Prosopon* is seen as the *prosopon* of the appearance of the divine in Jesus, who is then conceived as a simple human being; thus it is seen as the expression of a purely accidental unity between the God-Logos and the human being Jesus of Nazareth, which Maxentius too still interprets as a behavioural unity and as the indwelling of the Word in the human being Jesus.[37] Thus Maxentius connects this extreme Nestorian understanding of the unity in Christ with the *persona* formula of Dioscorus. This must be regarded as pure polemic.

(b) Intervention of the senate and people of Rome

So far neither the letters from the imperial court nor the journey of the Scythian monks to Rome had been able to move Pope Hormisdas to a decision about the trinitarian-theopaschite formula. The four monks from the East tried yet other ways to achieve their goals. They turned

---

unam ex suis hypostasibus (ibid., p. 52,10–11). (3) The signature to his *Epistula canonica* (CPG 7138): CSCO 103, 59. (4) His synodal letter to Paul of Antioch (CPG 7142): CSCO 103 (V), p. 84,13–21.

35. *Epist. quae dicitur esse Papae Hormisdae ad Possessorem* . . .: CCL 85A, 115–121 (of 13 August 520); on this see F. Glorie, *ibid.*, XXXVI: the bishop Possessor had been consulted about Faustus of Riez and his theology of grace. He himself now requests from the Pope enlightenment on this question (CA, *ep.* 230, of 18 July 520). In his reply (CA, *ep.* 231, of 13 August 520: CCL 85A, 115–121) Hormisdas speaks of the Scythian monks who have just departed from Rome for Constantinople and he reprimands their *superbia et tumultus* in the sharpest possible words (especially nos. 6–10). Maxentius wanted to defend the Scythian monks against this letter, which he declared was forged, and compiled a long response: *Responsio adversus epistulam*: CCL 85A, 123–153. On Dioscorus see no. XXVI, 134–135.

36. John Maxentius, *Resp. adv. epist. Hormisd.* I, 8 (XXVI): CCL 85A, pp. 134,348–135,368. Maxentius wants to allow the word *persona* only if it is understood as *naturalis personae vocabulum*. But then he claims it is sufficient to say: *Christus unus ex trinitate*. See no. XXVII, vv. 368–380.

37. *Ibid.*: CCL 85A, p. 135,359–365, 381–388. Christ would not be one *iuxta compositionem* (from God the Word and the human nature), but *iuxta alterius in altero habitationem* . . . *sive secundum gratiam, duarum personarum socialem unitionem unam personam Christum intellegunt*.

to the senate and the people.[38] The senator Faustus, a supporter of the strict-Chalcedonian tradition, now commissioned the presbyter Trifolius to examine the teaching of the Fathers to see whether the 'one of the Trinity has been crucified' was found among the Fathers. We have the result of his investigation:[39] he lumped together the theopaschism of the Scythians with that of the Arians and Apollinarians. According to Trifolius the Scythian formula was not to be found in the four Councils, for in this formula, which is foreign to tradition, suffering was expressed of the divinity, whereas the flesh was said to remain free of suffering. For this reason, he said, the Council of Chalcedon condemned this formula when it was presented by the monks Dorotheus and Carosus.[40] Trifolius claimed that the reference by the monks to the *Tomus ad Armenios* of Patriarch Proclus was invalid, because the theopaschite formula was certainly introduced as a forgery,[41] just as similar things were done with the letters of the Fathers Athanasius, Cyril and Leo. 'If anything is found in the words of the holy Fathers which does not agree with the holy letters or the definition of the Council of Chalcedon, then evidently we are dealing with a forgery of the heretics.'[42]

(c) A side-stage

The Scythian monks thus found no understanding for their request in Rome, and for that reason they turned in writing to African bishops, who had been banished by the Vandals to Sardinia.[43] Their spiritual leader was Fulgentius of Ruspe. This *epistula* was delivered to the exiles by the deacon John. To a great extent it is a revision of that *libellus fidei* which the Scythians had wanted in vain to present to the papal legates

---

38. Cf. F. Glorie, *Prolegomena* in CCL 85A, XXXIII. The time of this action cannot be determined precisely.

39. Trifol. presb., *Ep. ad beat. Faustum senat. c. Ioannem Scytham monachum*: ed. F. Glorie, CCL 85, 137–139; also in Schwartz, *PS*, pp. 115–117. On the authenticity, see *ibid.*, 300. On the person of Faustus and his hostile attitude to Byzantium, see *ibid.*, 231, 274.

40. Cf. on this H. Bacht, 'Die Rolle des orientalischen Mönchtums . . .', in *Chalkedon* II, 237–42. Trifolius refers to Chalcedon, *actio* IV, no. 108: Greek — ACO II, 1, 2, p. 120,23–24; Latin (Rusticus) — ACO II, 3, 2, p. 127,15–16. Trifolius cites the confession of Carosus and Dorotheus as condemned by the Council (CCL 85, p. 139,67–70): *confitentes salvatorem nostrum Iesum Christum, qui descendit . . . crucifixus,* **unum** *de trinitate esse passum* (according to the translation Φ^i). The Greek *acta* and the translation of Rusticus (see above) omit the *unum*. Rusticus' text reads: *credimus illum passum trinitatis esse*.

41. In fact the formula *unus de trinitate passus est* cannot be established in the authentic works of Proclus; cf. above, p. 318 with note 9.

42. Trifol. presb., *Ep. ad b. Faustum sen.*, no. 8: CCL 85, p. 140,94–97.

43. Cf. on this V. Schurr, *Trinitätslehre*, 159–60.

in Constantinople in 519.[44] In none of the imperial or Roman documents with which we have previously dealt is there any sign that the explosive nature of the *libellus fidei*, or of the 'Letter to the bishops', was discerned. It was solely the formula 'one of the Trinity' that caused a sensation. To Roman ears another text must really have been more objectionable, although it begins in a completely Chalcedonian manner.

> According to the tradition of the holy Fathers, we confess our Lord Jesus Christ in two united and unconfused natures, that is of the divinity and of the humanity, in one person or *hypostasis*. We do not agree with those who proclaim one incarnate nature of God the Word and shun the faith of the venerable Council of Chalcedon, nor do we accept those who deceitfully proclaim two natures, but in no way confess the one incarnate nature of God the Word, thinking that it is contrary to the confession of the two natures, as if the one incarnate nature of God the Word signifies anything other than the two natures ineffably united.[45]

This statement, already quite clear in itself, can be expanded by means of the writings of the monks and bishops of the Black Sea region, so that a total picture of a Latin christology results, which could become for Justinian the model and content of his future policy. Even in the West it was able to make an impression and provide a stimulus. For this total picture we must have recourse once again to the year 512.

3. Latin neo-Chalcedonian christology in the Black Sea region between 512 and 533

After Severus' opponent John the Grammarian,[46] in the texts of the Scythians just named (*libellus fidei* and their letter to the African bishops) we encounter again the willingness to consider both confessions in expressing right faith: the *mia physis* against Nestorius, the *dyo physeis* against Eutyches and his lot. Nevertheless it is justifiable to ask whether this consideration also includes the simultaneous use of both formulas so strongly stressed by M. Richard, which is his condition for allocating the name 'neo-Chalcedonianism'.[47] What is important is his observation that the definition of Chalcedon is already a synthesis with Cyril's

---

44. Scyth. mon., *Ep. ad Eppos*: CCL 85A, 157–172. F. Glorie notes in the apparatus the variants from the *libellus fidei* (CCL 85A, 5–25).

45. *Ibid.*, (II), 3: CCL 85A, pp. 158,33–159,43, to be compared with *Libellus fidei* VIII, 13: p. 13,161–168, and with John Maxentius, *Capit.* 1: p. 29,4–6. As proof then follows Cyril Alex., *Ep. 46 ad Succensum*, 3 in the translation of Dionysius Exiguus, 4 (see the apparatus on [II], 3). See the English translation of the letter by J. A. McGuckin, *JEH* 35 (1984), 247–55.

46. See above, p. 69, n. 138.

47. M. Richard, 'Le Néo-chalcédonisme', *MSR* 3 (1946), 156–61 = *Op. Min.* II, no. 56.

formulaic language, even if Richard does not exhaust all the possibilities of this discovery.[48] The extent to which the Scythians wanted to invoke the *mia-physis* formula to interpret Chalcedon, however, still needs to be examined. In fact they came to speak of the confrontation of the two conceptual systems twice. What motive lay behind this?

(a) The Scythian monks and neo-Chalcedonianism

Their *libellus* submitted to the papal legates, as well as the letter to the bishops, shows plainly that the Scythian monks are conscious that their synthesis is unfamiliar to Chalcedonians; they know that the one-nature formula is considered to be incompatible with the two-natures formula.[49] For its fresh judgement on the *una natura* the letter to the Africans refers, as shown, to Cyril of Alexandria and his interpretation of the formula, the *libellus fidei* refers in contrast to its recognition by Patriarch Flavian,[50] who also confesses the 'from two natures' rejected by Chalcedon. The monks do not attempt a conceptual analysis in order to be able to produce the equation of 'two natures' and *una dei verbi natura incarnata* (the one nature of the incarnate God-Logos). In this context they also do not get involved in the synonymous usage of *hypostasis* and *physis* present in Cyril, but rather resort to hermeneutics. Through the juxtaposition of formulas that sound contradictory, they call for reflection on the orthodoxy of the other side. The motive which animates them is very commendable; it is already active shortly before their appearance in the 'Letter of the Orientals', which had been addressed in 512 to Pope Symmachus,[51] at the time when the pressure of Emperor Anastasius and his *Henoticon* policy was most noticeable to the supporters of Chalcedon.[52] This letter was a cry for help to Pope Symmachus from Scythia and Thrace, the European provinces in the North-East of the Byzantine Empire. It stemmed from Chalcedonian-orthodox bishops, who abandoned no aspect of Chalcedon, but who, for the sake of their dioceses, did not want to break with the Acacians

---

48. As the analysis of the *horos* of Chalcedon by A. de Halleux has shown us. See *JdChr* I³, 755–62, especially 758, 761–2.

49. Cf. *Libell. fid.* VIII, 13: CCL 85A, p. 13,164–166: *nec illam sententiam, quam quasi contrariam quidam synodo aestimant, id est, unam naturam dei verbi incarnatam, avertimur.* Similarly Scyth. mon., *Ep. ad Eppos* (II), 3: p. 159,40–41: *aestimantes hoc* [= the one-nature formula] *duarum naturarum contrarium.* The *quidam* nevertheless weakens considerably the state of judging the *una natura*.

50. *Libell. fid.* VIII, 13: p. 14, 172–176.

51. Ep. Orient., *Inter epp. Symmachi ppae*: Thiel I, 709–717; see *CCT* II/1, p. 309, n. 255.

52. Cf. V. Schurr, *Trinitätslehre*, 108–27.

(supporters of the *Henoticon*).[53] We find ourselves in the period between 512 and 518. What dogmatic position is present in the letter of the Orientals? The authors confess the Council of Chalcedon and its two-natures teaching, the *Tomus* of Leo; for this reason they are persecuted by the supporters of the *mia physis*; many of them have been sent into exile.[54] They even admit that 'their Father' Acacius has failed.[55] He is no longer living; were they now, however, to break communion with his supporters, they would be driven out and their dioceses would be deserted. The Pope is requested not to condemn them, but rather to take them into communion with him.[56] Admittedly the Romans must have begun to wonder at the following suggestion for mediation: the Oriental bishops do not want to join in the schism of Acacius, but want to reject the formula of the Alexandrians 'from two natures one nature after the union'. But as a *via media* they propose '*from two natures and in two natures*'. The Fathers are said to have spoken already in this way.[57]

Thus it is intended that a simultaneous usage of formulas be allowed, which had been excluded at Chalcedon.[58] The *Epistula Orientalium* thus really confines itself to a 'minor point', the famous *ex duabus* and *in duabus*.

It would certainly have needed some rethinking, both historically and

---

53. *Ibid.*, 122. Schurr adduces the following considerations for determining the senders: (1) they call Acacius their father, thus they belong to the ecclesiastical territory of Constantinople (unlike the bishops of Illyria, Dardania and Dacia, who belong to the Roman patriarchate); (2) they confess Chalcedon (nos. 3, 4, 9, 10 in Thiel) and the primacy of the Pope over the whole Church. Schurr, 122–4, proves that *epistula* 13 of Pope Symmachus of 8 October 512 (Thiel, pp. 717–22) is the response to this theologically and pastorally distinguished letter from the East.

54. Cf. Ep. Oriental., nos. 3 and 5: Thiel, 711, 712–713.

55. *Ibid.*, nos. 2, 3, 6: Thiel, 710–711, 711, 713.

56. *Ibid.*, nos. 5–8: Thiel, 712–714.

57. *Ibid.*, conclusion of no. 9 and the beginning of no. 10: Thiel, 715–716; on 716 they sketch their position: *sic et nunc illis*, 'ex duabus *quidem* naturis' *dicentibus*, 'in duabus' *autem non confitentibus, nos* 'ex duabus' *et* 'in duabus' *pariter dicimus. Ex duabus enim dicentes, ex quibus subsistit unitas, in duabus autem, in quibus visus est et palpatus est et assumptus post passionem et resurrectionem, confitemur, et in quibus veniet iudicaturus vivos et mortuos.*

58. Cf. JdChr I[3], 753–4. We recall that for the Roman legates at Chalcedon the equations held true: 'from two natures' = Dioscorus = monophysitism; 'in two natures' = Leo = orthodoxy. For this reason they did not accept the proposal of Patriarch Anatolius for a christological definition. It is on the basis of this memory that the response of Pope Symmachus is to be judged. Cf. on this *CCT* II/1, 309–10. The Pope does not deal with the suggestion of the Orientals, but rather warns of the great errors to which the three patriarchal cities of the East (Constantinople, Antioch and Alexandria) had succumbed, namely Nestorianism, the *nefanda ludibria* of Peter the Fuller, and Eutychianism. Cf. Symmach., *Ep. 13 ad Oriental.*, no. 2: Thiel, 718–719: a severe, gloomy picture of the dogmatic offence of the East!

speculatively, for the Orientals' proposal for mediation to be accepted. But in Rome there was no prospect of this.

Do we find this synthesis 'from two natures — in two natures' also among the Scythian monks? Can one discern a connection with the letter of the Orientals of 512? Lest the intentions behind the letter of 512 and those behind the actions of 519 be confused, we would like to highlight the difference immediately. In their letter of 512, the Orientals sought to mediate between the moderate supporters of Acacius and of the Acacian schism and Rome. The union of 518 was still not realized, but a union was striven for. The Scythians, in contrast, had not joined in the Acacian schism[59] and they assumed the union that had been realized in the meantime. They wanted to mediate 'dogmatically', not between Chalcedonians and Severans, but among the Chalcedonians themselves. If this important difference is not taken into account, the Scythians with their proposals of mediation, however, were completely in line with the *Epistula Orientalium*. They came from the same dogmatic tradition as the authors of the letter of 512, but took it further by incorporating the *mia-physis* formula in the discussion and putting it in creative tension with the two-natures formula. Thus we return to the letter of the monks to the African bishops, more precisely to the passage already cited about the two versions of christological language.[60]

In this passage the Scythian monks do not demand explicitly that the main contrary statements be confessed simultaneously or alternately; they ask only that in interpreting one's own confession the other also be considered. Whoever confesses 'one nature of the incarnate Word' should not interpret this as a rejection of Chalcedon, and whoever says the 'two natures' should do this honourably in such a way that they remain open for the discovery that the *mia-physis* formula too is compatible with Chalcedon, if one interprets it like Cyril of Alexandria. For this purpose there also follows a quite lengthy citation from the second letter to Successus.[61] Accordingly the monks no doubt see the seemingly contradictory formulas as mutually corrective, but they do not demand an actual alternate use of these formulas. Through calling to mind the *mia-physis* formula as interpreted by Cyril they want to show how the *unus ex trinitate crucifixus* can be understood in an orthodox way. Given this openness, it is the monks' opinion that each party is well able to stand

---

59. See John Maxentius, *Resp. adv. ep. Hormisd.* I, 8 (XXXIII): CCL 85A, p. 137,450–454: *Monachi autem, quos inique laceras, in tantum ab hoc crimine alieni sunt, ut numquam per dei gratiam catholica communione discesserint.*

60. Cf. above p. 327 and n. 45.

61. Scyth. mon., *Ep. ad Eppos* (II), 3: CCL 85A, p. 159,45–53.

by its formula, be it the two-natures formula or the one-nature formula, on condition that the latter is understood in the sense of the second letter to Succensus. They themselves stand by their pure-Chalcedonian two-natures formula, especially in the polemic against the Headless Ones (Severans),[62] to whom they ascribe the false use of the *una natura*. Through calling to mind the *mia-physis* formula and its Cyrillian interpretation they want to show that the *unus ex trinitate crucifixus* can be correctly understood. For the monks there is, as it were, a parallelism between the two formulas:

una natura Dei Verbi	incarnata
= unus ex trinitate	incarnatus (crucifixus)

If the one can be correctly interpreted with Cyril,[63] then so too can the other. The goal of the whole endeavour is not so much to introduce an equally justified use of the two systems of formulas, as rather to validate the Chalcedonian system of language in the sense of the unity of Christ. To be noted is the fact that in this way the monks remain in the Constantinopolitan-Palestinian tradition, as it had been created even before Chalcedon by Proclus. In exactly the same way as it suits the Scythians to insist on a christology of union, the strict-Chalcedonians (Dioscorus and the Sleepless Monks) seek to exclude any danger of theopaschism,[64] by reference to Ephesus and

---

62. Cf. John Maxentius, *Resp. c. Aceph.* II, 2: CCL 85A, p. 44,13–14: 'Without any doubt there are two natures in Christ'; *ibid.*, VI, 11: pp. 46,106–47,122. The various witnesses for the two natures are noted by F. Glorie in the *Index nominum et verborum selectorum*, *s.v. deitas, divinitas, humanitas, natura*. We highlight: *Prof. brev. cath. fid.* 6: pp. 35,43–36,48; *Resp. c. Aceph.* I, 1: p. 43,6: it is regarded as a foolish confession to set up 'one nature after the union in Christ'; cf. *ibid.*, II, 4: p. 44,27: 'two natures after the union', for which the Chalcedonians gladly refer to Cyril, where, however, this formula is not found.

63. According to John Maxentius, *Resp. c. Aceph.* VI, 11: CCL 85A, pp. 46,109–47,122, the *mia-physis* formula immediately expresses the two natures: *At si voluerint dicere, verbum incarnatum sive unam naturam dei verbi incarnatam, eo ipso quo hoc dicunt, duas procul dubio dicere convincuntur in Christo naturas, duarumque, non unius, nomina naturarum* . . . In this connection Maxentius uses the body–soul analogy in order to explain by means of it the possibility of speaking both of one as well as of two natures: everybody is convinced that the human nature exists *from* two, or better *in* two natures, body and soul. Thus he claims one could also say 'incarnate soul', or as well 'the one nature of the incarnate soul'. Just as two natures are acknowledged here, this is also true for the incarnate Word.

64. See the positions of the 'Nestorian' in John Maxentius, *Dial. c. Nestor.* II, XII: CCL 85A, p. 92,568–569: *Incarnatus quidem deus est, passus autem deus non est, sed caro dei*; *ibid.*, II, XIII: p. 93,586–588: *Deus quidem passus non est, quia deum passibilem praedicare, sacrilegum est; sed deus sui corporis fecit proprias passiones*; II, XIV: p. 94,639: *Carnem dei dixi passam, non autem dei verbi.* The Formula *unus ex trinitate* is suspicious to the 'Nestorian'. He says it endangers the *homoousios* of Nicaea, and that this would be better safeguarded by *unus in trinitate*; cf. II, XIX: p. 101,874ff. The whole altercation becomes a battle of words, as the 'Nestorian' highlights (II, XXIII: p. 107,

Chalcedon.[65] Dioscorus too is a traditionalist and refuses to go beyond the wording of the two synods, just as on the other side Maxentius does not want the *unus ex trinitate* to be watered down, especially not through the insertion of the word *persona*. According to Maxentius, however, the deacon Dioscorus has made himself guilty of this 'heresy'. Dioscorus says namely: 'One *person* from the Trinity, but not one from the Trinity.'[66] Then he is said in this way to reinterpret the unity of person in Christ in the Nestorian sense: 'they state that "Christ" has the *persona* of the God-Logos, but that Christ is not himself the God-Logos'.[67] The whole bundle of alleged Nestorian ideas about the incarnation is tied to this use of the word *persona* in Dioscorus: the teaching of two persons, of two sons, of the indwelling, of the purely social, i.e. moral unity (*socialis unio*) of human beings.[68] In spite of all contrary protestations the dialogue partner, Dioscorus, is consequently a heretic in the eyes of the Catholicus Maxentius.[69] We observe here that this dispute broke out among the Chalcedonians. Maxentius did not know that the word *persona* in his favourite formula was introduced not only by Dioscorus, but also by Justinian,[70] and above all by Fulgentius in his letter of reply to the Scythian monks. In this letter the word 'person' signifying Christ is strongly accentuated and it is incorporated into a christology which is also acceptable to the Scythians.[71]

The fact that the insertion of the word *persona* into the Scythian

1069–1073): *Neque trinitatem, neque ex⟨tra trinitatem, neque unum ex⟩ trinitate, deum verbum confiteor: sed filium dei deum pro nostra salute ex femina secundum carnem natum passumque confiteor; tuis autem nolo uti sermonibus: nec eum unum ex trinitate confiteor.* Then he says in conclusion: . . . *aliud est, rebus congruere, et verbis tantummodo dissonare* (II, XXII: p. 108,1090–1091). He also concedes that the *unus ex trinitate est Christus* can be proved from the writings of the Fathers, but he still does not want to accept it for himself (II, XXV: p. 110,1166–1168).

65. Cf. *ibid.*, II, XXV: p. 109,1130–1148.

66. John Maxentius, *Resp. adv. ep. Hormisd.* I, 8: CCL 85A, p. 134,343–344, especially pp. 134,348–135,354.

67. *Ibid.*, p. 135,352–354.

68. *Ibid.*, p. 135,352ff., 359ff.; the two-sons teaching, however, is expressly rejected by the 'Nestorian'. *Dial. c. Nestorian.* II, IX: p. 87,408–410; he confesses Christ, the one Son, in two united natures.

69. John Maxentius, *Dial. c. Nestorian.* II, XXV, p. 110,1175.

70. Cf. Justinian, *Ep. ad Hormisd.* (CPG 6870) of 9 July 520: CA, *ep.* 196, nos. 6–7, p. 656: to say simply *unus ex trinitate* without adding the name of Christ could be ambiguous: *sine Christi namque persona nec credi trinitas religiose potest nec adorari fideliter* (with reference to Augustine).

71. Fulgent. Rusp., *Ep.* 17, ch. 3, no. 6: PL 65, 455CD = CCL 91A, p. 568,180–183. *Unus est igitur Christus dei filius in natura divinitatis et carnis, in quo singularitas personalis non confundit humanam divinamque naturam, et inconfusa unitio naturarum non facit geminam inesse personam.* Instead of *unus (ex trinitate)* Fulgentius usually prefers to say *Deus unigenitus.* Cf. also *ibid.*, ch. 5, no. 10: PL 65, 457BC; CCL 91A, 570.

formula was unjustifiably rejected did not mean, however, that the term was simply banished from the christology of John Maxentius. On the contrary, in his efforts to secure and deepen the interpretation of the unity in Christ, he made a contribution to its conceptual clarification that is not to be despised.

(b) The positive contribution of the Scythians to post-Chalcedonian christology

(i) Nature–person: abstract and concrete

In contrast to the period which saw the sharp altercation between Cyril and Nestorius, in the first decade of Justin's restoration many advances in christological language can be established. It is well known what confusion had arisen because of the fact that the difference between the concrete and abstract naming of Christ's divinity and humanity (*divinitas–humanitas* vis-à-vis the concrete terms *deus–homo*) was carefully distinguished only on rare occasions. What Nestorius in fact wanted to exclude unconditionally was the statement that the 'divinity' suffered. He expressed this, however, in concrete terms: the God in Christ did not suffer, the human being Christ suffered. The conflict was sparked off by this. The Scythian monks knew very well how to distinguish in this regard, and their language is more flexible than that of their contemporary Roman partners like the priest Trifolius. The naming of the aspect under which Christ is to be considered as God and human being is strongly emphasized: according to the humanity — according to the divinity.[72] These distinctions have already become a matter of course.

(ii) The concepts of person and nature

More significant than this, however, is the attempt to distinguish more clearly between the concepts of person and nature. The problem is recognized.[73] Together with *persona* there often appears the word *subsistentia*, the rendering of the Greek *hypostasis*, while *substantia* means the

---

72. Cf. John Maxentius, *Prof. brev. cath. fid.* 4: pp. 34,27–35,36; *secundum humanitatem — secundum divinitatem*. The concrete and the abstract significations are combined well: *hunc eundem hominem esse figuram substantiae sive imaginem patris . . . non tamen secundum humanitatem, sed secundum divinitatem* (p. 35,33–36). Admittedly Maxentius does not grasp the real sense of the biblical statement behind this. According to Col 1,15, Christ the human being is the image of the invisible God; cf. Heb 1,3, where the humanity of Jesus is also included.

73. See F. Glorie, *Index nominum*, CCL 85A, p. 362: *persona, personalis; subsistentia: s.v. Christus*, 325–330; *trinitas*: 375–376.

same as *natura*.[74] What meanings do the monks attach to the individual words?

Persona and *subsistentia* have the same meaning.[75] Maxentius, however, speaks of a misuse of the words:

> In an ungodly way certain people believe that the Synod [Chalcedon] attributes (the word) *persona* (*prosopon*) to the human being, but the *subsistence* to God the Word;[76] not that they do not know that for the Synod subsistence (*hypostasis*) and person are the same, but so that they may not appear openly to introduce two subsistences or two persons, they [the 'Nestorians'] use this utterly bad argument.[77]

The background to this reproach is the refusal of the papal deacon Dioscorus and the Sleepless Monks to acknowledge the formula 'one of the Trinity was crucified'. Instead they want to say 'one person of the Trinity, but not one of the Trinity'.[78] The reason for this change is said to be the secret Nestorianism of this expansion, as we have already depicted above. What positive meaning, however, does Maxentius attach to *persona* and *subsistentia*, if he wants to acknowledge one and the same significance? In the *Dialogue against the Nestorians* he explains his concept of person and his insistence on the one person in Christ in the following way.[79]

> I believe (namely) that God the Word is not united to a human being who already remains in his own subsistence (*in propria manenti subsistentia*) nor to a flesh already [before the union] formed and animated, through which the person of any human being at all is understood to come about; but the subsistence (*hypostasis*) or person of the Word of God assumed a human nature, which never subsisted as common nature besides God the Word, but rather having originated from him and being assumed by him it has become properly *his* (*ipsius*) nature; it remains not in its own (subsistence) but in that by which it has been assumed, that is, in the subsistence or person of God the Word; and for that reason there are not two subsistences, but there is only one subsistence or person of the two natures — namely of the Word and of the flesh.

Up to this time this is certainly the clearest Latin explanation and interpretation of the 'one subsistence or person in divine and human natures' or already of the doctrine of 'insubsistence'.

---

74. Cf. *ibid.*, 372: *s.v. substantia*.

75. Cf. John Maxentius, *Capitula* I: CCL 85A, p. 29,4–5: *duas (naturas) unitas in una subsistentia atque persona* ...; *idem, Prof. brev. cath. fid.* 1: in the Trinity there are *tres tamen subsistentiae sive personae* (*ibid.*, p. 33,4–5).

76. What is meant is the doubling of *hypostasis* and *persona* in the definition of Chalcedon (v. 21 of the definition; see *CCT* I², p. 544): 'Concurring into one Person (*prosopon*) and one *hypostasis*.'

77. John Maxentius, *Libell. fid.* IX, 14: CCL 85A, p. 14,177–182. That is, the Nestorians attribute the *subsistentia* to the Logos, whose *persona*, however, is the human being Jesus.

78. *Idem, Resp. adv. ep. Hormisd.* I, 8: CCL 85A, p. 134,343–344.

79. *Idem, Dial. c. Nestorian.* I, XI: CCL 85A, p. 67,445–455.

The interpretation of being a person is enriched by an important element which advances beyond the *hypostasis* of the *idiomata* of the Cappadocians, namely the definition of a person as 'remaining in itself or in its subsistence' (*manere in seipso* or *manere in sua subsistentia*). Here person is considered as the final 'being for itself or in itself', which is bestowed on the concrete nature of Christ by the Logos. In this way it is possible to leave the human nature its full individuality and still to relate it as a finite existence to the one Logos-subject, without a duality of persons resulting. This 'remaining in itself' we shall encounter again soon in the important deacon Rusticus. It can be assumed that he learned it by watching the Scythians.[80] Unfortunately these new approaches were not yet recognized by their own inventors. Through these approaches alone the equating of *individuum* and person could have been overcome. Shortly after the previous passage, however, Maxentius again fell back into the old position.[81]

Nature is distinguished from person, because person signifies an individual thing [!] in a nature. Nature is known to signify the common matter out of which many persons are able to subsist. On this account each person indeed contains at the same time a nature, but not every nature embraces a person in the same way ...

'Person' is thus once again equated with the *individuum* of a universal nature. This is indeed 'really' correct, but the very fact that the human nature of Christ is an individual nature for Maxentius and still does not have its own subsistence means that he must be questioned further about what the formal *ratio* of being a person is. He does not get as far as this question. Moreover for Maxentius it is the same whether it is a rational or non-rational nature. 'Person' can be signified as a thing! Boethius, his contemporary, here takes a decisive step forward, as we shall see.[82] Admittedly the Scythians emphasize vigorously that in the incarnation the Word assumed a complete human being with a spiritual soul and a body.[83] The problem of how the concept of person is related to rationality did not occur to them. Nevertheless certain approaches to

---

80. Cf. Rustic., *C. acephal.*: PL 67, 1239B; A. Grillmeier, 'Vorbereitung des Mittelalters', in *Chalkedon* II, 821.

81. John Maxentius, *Dial. c. Nestorian.* I, XIV: CCL 85A, p. 69,523–528.

82. Cf. V. Schurr, *Trinitätslehre*, 14–74.

83. On Christ's soul see John Maxentius, *Prof. brev. cath. fid.* 2: CCL 85A, p. 34,12–13; Scyth. mon., *Disput. XII capit.* B': pp. 201,150–155; 204,241–242; *Refut. Nest. dict.* I: p. 215,27–33, 33–36: *Ita et illa ineffabilis divina filii dei maiestas in sua persona et substantia una est, cum assumpta anima sua compote mentis suae sive rationis, et solido ac perfecto corpore suo.*

this in classical antiquity had been made, which would be evaluated for christology and trinitarian theology by their contemporary, Boethius.[84]

(iii) The interpretation of the union in Christ as compositio

With remarkable frequency the concept of *synthesis* (*compositio*, composition) used to interpret the union in Christ also begins to establish itself in Chalcedonian christology of the sixth century. As a matter of course it emerges in Latin translation among the Scythian monks. It is, however, taken from the sources which were previously authoritative for them. A clue leads once again to Palestine, to the monastic supporters of the 'one of the Trinity was crucified', namely to the monastic leader Euthymius. Opponents of the Council of Chalcedon and supporters of Theodosius, who had usurped the patriarchal see of Jerusalem, came to Euthymius to make him give up Chalcedon and the two-natures teaching. He gave a historically interesting reply: the teaching of the Council about the one Christ in two natures agrees with that of Cyril of Alexandria. 'When we hear this Synod say that Christ is in two natures, we do not believe that it brings a separation or cutting up into the one *composite hypostasis of Christ*, but recognize that it signifies the distinction of the natures, according to the words of Cyril of Alexandria who is among the saints: "not as if the distinction of the natures was annulled by the union".'[85] According to this statement the expression 'Christ's composite *hypostasis*' would have been used by the Chalcedonians themselves immediately after 451.[86] The other source for this was probably sufficient for the Scythian monks, namely the (alleged?) *acta* of the Synod of Antioch (268) against Paul of Samosata, which the deacon Petronius cites in two long fragments in the 'Letter to the

---

84. Cf. V. Schurr, *Trinitätslehre*, 66–7, especially n. 122; listed here are: (1) Cicero, *De officiis, lib. I, cap.* 28, § 97. (2) The grammarian Diomedes (second half of the fourth century), *Artis grammaticae libri III*: H. Keil, *Grammatici Latini I* (Leipzig, 1857), p. 334,19–23: *Persona est substantia rationalis.* V. Schurr, 67 (with S. Schlossmann), considers, however, that in the case of Diomedes it could be a later gloss. Gregory Naz., *Or.* 33: PG 36, 236A speaks of rationality in the area of the divine *hypostasis*. Cf. Gregory Nyss. = Ps. Basil, *Ep.* 38: PG 32, 326C: inclusion of the moral characteristics of individuation in the realization of the *hypostasis*.

85. Cyril Scyth., *Vita Euth.*, no. 27: Schwartz, *Kyrillos von Skythopolis*, pp. 43,25–44,4; cf. Cyril Alex., in ACO I, 1, 1, p. 27,2–3.

86. The *Vita Euthymii* was written only after 554. Cf. E. Schwartz, *Kyrillos von Skythopolis*, 413–14. The suspicion arises that the *hypostasis synthetos* of Euthymius is a formulation of Cyril of Scythopolis.

(African) bishops'. The authenticity is disputed. M. Richard[87] considers them to be Apollinarian forgeries from the fifth or the sixth century. There is as well a second Apollinarian source, namely the Ps. Athanasian writing *Quod unus sit Christus*.[88] In the text of Malchion, who was an opponent of Paul of Samosata, Christ is composed from single elements, the Logos and the human body; he is an indivisible figure which subsists in unity. The execution of the *compositio* demands two real substances, Logos and *sarx*, while Paul is said to be happy with an accidental *participatio* of the human being Jesus in the divine wisdom or to accept only a loose indwelling. 'Entitative unity from two realities': this result the Scythians also found in Malchion's concept of *compositio*;[89] what did not strike them is that in this the soul of Christ has no place and that a nature-synthesis occurs between Logos and *sarx* (*unio in natura et secundum naturam*). The important thing for them is the rejection of Nestorianism. In the writing *One is Christ*, *unitas et compositio* have the same function, that is, to be one and composite as the counter-terms to dwelling in and purely operating in (*inhabitatio, inoperatio*). They lead here too to the 'one *substantia Christi*' in opposition to the 'two subsistences and two persons' of the Apollinarian opponents.[90] Entitative 'composition from two realities' was for the Scythians the main christological formula.[91] They directed it equally against the Nestorians and the Headless Ones, that is, the confessors of the *mia physis*.[92] It

---

87. On Malchion and Paul of Samosata, cf. CPG 1706 and 1707. In favour of the authenticity see H. de Riedmatten, *Les actes du procès de Paul de Samosate* = *Paradosis* 6 (Fribourg, 1952), 148–50 (S, 25); against the authenticity see M. Richard, 'Malchion et Paul de Samosate. Le témoignage d'Eusèbe de Césarée', *EphThLov* 35 (1959), 325–38 = *Op. Min.* II, no. 25. See the texts in CCL 85A, pp. 160,89–161,118.

88. CPG 3737: H. Lietzmann, *Apollinaris von Laodicea*, pp. 295,21–296,9; here CCL 85A, p. 161,105–118.

89. Scyth. mon., *Ep. ad Eppos* (III), 6: CCL 85A, p. 160,81–83: *Hinc etiam a sanctis patribus adunatione ex divinitate et humanitate Christus dominus noster compositus praedicatur.*

90. Cf. *ibid.* (III), 6: CCL 85A, p. 161,115–118.

91. Cf. John Maxentius, *Capitula c. Nestorian.* 9: CCL 85A, p. 30,34–35: *Si quis non confitetur compositum Christum post incarnationem, anathema sit.* According to the *Dial. c. Nestorian.* II, II: p. 78,71–72, the 'Nestorian' refuses to describe Christ as *compositus* because he considers it to be impossible to unite an infinite (*incircumscripta*) and a finite (*circumscripta*) nature. With a view to this the catholicus refers to the human *compositum* (body–soul) as the analogy acknowledged by the Fathers for the divine–human unity (*ibid.*, p. 80,173–177). The 'Nestorian' counters with the statement that a *compositio* presupposes 'parts', and asks whether we can describe God as 'part' of Christ. The catholicus responds: 'The God-Logos is not smaller than Christ, because he himself is Christ [in the flesh]' (*ibid.*, p. 81,193–194).

92. Cf. John Maxentius, *Resp. c. Aceph.* II, 3: against the supporters of the *una natura* Maxentius defends an *adunatio, quae compositionem facit, refugiat simplicitatem, susceptionemque procul dubio a filio dei humanae naturae significet*; the result is then the two natures, *ex quibus et in quibus subsistit una et singularis Christi persona* (CCL 85A, p. 44,21–26).

became the main term of unity in Christ which in all its conditions is so precisely defined, as elsewhere for instance, is the expression *henosis*: the composition occurs at the very moment of conception.[93] It is a creative act, as the resurrection of Christ is too. The whole Trinity participates in it, even if it is only the flesh, the human nature of Christ, that is the object of this creating (and resurrecting). Insofar as Christ is one of the Trinity, one can also say that he 'together with the Father and the Holy Spirit creates and resurrects himself according to the flesh'.[94] Only the acceptance of a *compositio* is protection against ascribing suffering to the simple and impassible godhead itself,[95] or on the other side (in the case of the Nestorian separation) of making suffering a purely human thing that has no significance for our salvation. In short, in the expression *compositio* the Scythians, with numerous theologians of their time, saw a concept which excluded equally two false interpretations of the incarnation, the Nestorian separation and the Eutychian mixing, and which at the same time interpreted positively the unity of Christ as 'essential' (*essentialis*). It was in this way that Maxentius explained his christological *tessera*, the 'one of the Trinity was crucified'.

III. THE DECISION ON THE THEOPASCHITE QUESTION UNDER POPE JOHN II (533–535)

All the efforts of Emperor Justin and his nephew Justinian, of the patriarchs of Constantinople and of the Scythian monks themselves could not achieve in Rome an acknowledgement of the formula 'one of the Trinity has been crucified'. On 9 September 520 Justinian had written his last attested letter on this question to Pope Hormisdas (CPG 6873). But the topic in no way left him in peace. After he had become the sole monarch (527), from various actions we recognize his resolve to restore the religious unity of the Empire. From that time the confession of the theopaschite formula was not omitted from any document related to christology. The influence of Empress Theodora — in this Chalcedonian–anti-Chalcedonian mixed marriage — is from now on to be taken into consideration.[96]

---

93. John Maxentius, *Dial. c. Nestorian.* II, II: pp. 81,216–82,226. A *compositio* only after the birth would be an 'indwelling'.

94. *Ibid.* II, XVIII: CCL 85A, p. 100,844–850. Cf. *idem, Breviss. adunat. ratio* 2: p. 40,10–14. In this way a Nestorian doctrine of indwelling is excluded from the outset. The union in Christ is *naturalis, non socialis: ibid.* 3, p. 40,16–17.

95. *Ibid.* II, II: p. 81,195–219.

96. Victor of Tunnuna, *Chronicon a.* 529: *MGH auct. ant.* XI/2, ed. Mommsen, 197, reports that the Empress demanded the theopaschite formula unconditionally.

The *Codex Iustinianus* I,1,5 contains a confession of faith which is perhaps to be dated 527.[97] In it the *unus ex trinitate* is expressly mentioned.[98] In 532, at the conclusion of the doctrinal dialogue with the Severans, which we have already treated, we encounter our formula once again. According to the report of Innocent of Maronia, it was through it that the accusation was brought against the Chalcedonians before the Emperor, to the effect that they would deny 'that God suffered in the flesh or that he [Christ] was one of the Trinity and that the miracles and the sufferings did not belong to the one and the same person'.[99] At the special audience which the Patriarch of Constantinople, Epiphanius, and archbishop Hypatius had requested in order to deal with the accusations of the Syrians on account of the *unus ex trinitate*, the Emperor asked: 'Do you not confess that both the suffering as well as the miracles belong to the same person of our Lord Jesus Christ, and that he is the God who suffered in the flesh and that he is one of the Trinity?' Hypatius made an explicit *confessio*, in which a positive response was given to all the points raised by the Emperor.[100] Justinian could be satisfied and feel that he was in a position to extend his initiative in favour of the disputed formula to the whole Empire, and above all to be able to make a new approach for it in Rome. On 15 March 533 the Emperor issued in edict form a confession of faith which was addressed to the citizens of Constantinople, but also to the important cities from Trebizond to Jerusalem and Alexandria.[101] Into a text which is compiled in a completely trinitarian, creed-like manner is consciously inserted: 'one of the Trinity, the God-Logos, became flesh'[102] and the denial of the following statement is condemned: 'our Lord Jesus Christ, the Son of God and our God, who became flesh and a human being and was fixed to the cross, is one of the consubstantial Trinity'.[103] The second letter, of 26

97. Justinian, *Cum recta intemerataque fides: Cod. Iust.* I, 1, 5, ed. Krüger, 6–7; on the dating see *ibid.*, p. 7, n. 2 with reference to *ibid.*, I, 1, 6, no. 3: *quod iam pridem in primordiis nostri imperii cunctis patefecimus.* By this is probably meant the beginning of the sole reign.

98. *Ibid.*, I, 1, 5, no. 2: Krüger, 6b.

99. ACO IV, 2, no. 82: p. 183.

100. ACO IV, 2, nos. 83–6: p. 183. Hypatius in no. 85: *similiter et unum esse ex trinitate secundum divinam naturam tam credentes quam confitentes, secundum carnem vero unum ex nobis placuisse ei credimus fieri.* The formula is cleverly composed and raises no problem for a Chalcedonian. See J. Speigl, 'Das Religionsgespräch mit den severianischen Bischöfen in Konstantinopel im Jahre 532', *AHC* 16 (1984), 280–1.

101. Justinian, *Cum salvatorem et dominum: Cod. Iust.* I, 1, 6: Krüger, 7a–8a; Amelotti-Migliardi Zingale, *Scritti teologici*, 32–35 (Greek and Latin according to the *Chronicon Paschale*, ed. Dindorf [Bonn, 1832], 630–633).

102. *Ibid.*: Amelotti-Migliardi Zingale, p. 35,5–6; *Cod. Iust.* I, 1, 6, no. 6: Krüger, 7b.

103. *Ibid.*: Amelotti-Migliardi Zingale, p. 35,14–15; *Cod. Iust.* I, 1, 6, no. 7: Krüger, 8a.

March 533, was sent to Patriarch Epiphanius.[104] Without doubt the main intention was once again to preserve ecclesiastical unity. As Justinian lets the Patriarch know, it was finally determined by the Pope and Patriarch of Old Rome, who received a similar letter. All the themes and formulas of the theopaschite action that are now sufficiently familiar to us return once again.[105] What is striking in all these documents is that neither the formula of the Severans nor that of the Chalcedonians (one nature — two natures) is adduced. It is only in the letter to Patriarch Epiphanius that the four General Councils are mentioned.[106]

In June 533 Emperor Justinian sent the bishops Demetrius and Hypatius (cf. above, p. 230) to Rome to Pope John II (533–535) with a letter of 6 June 533.[107] Justinian's request was now to recognize the Scythian monks and to condemn the Sleepless Monks; this signified precisely the reverse of the request which he had expressed in his first letter to Pope Hormisdas at the end of June 519. As Pope John communicated, the Sleepless Monk, Cyrus, appeared in Rome with some companions who wanted to proceed against the Scythians, but who for this reason were themselves found guilty of heresy. Because they were unwilling to follow the apostolic admonitions of the Pope, they were excluded from the catholic Church until they repented of their error and signed a regular confession. Then, however, the ecclesial community would again be open to them, which would also induce the Emperor to grant forgiveness.[108] The point at issue is most clearly expressed in the letter of John II to the senators of Constantinople.[109] The three questions that required a decision were still those that had been presented in 519:

(1) whether Christ may be called 'one of the Trinity', that is, 'as one holy person of the three persons of the holy Trinity';
(2) whether Christ suffered as God in the flesh who, according to divinity, however, is free from suffering;
(3) whether really and in the true sense Mary may be named the mother of God and mother of the God-Logos who became flesh from her.

---

104. Justinian, *Epiphanio . . . archiep. et oecumenico patriarchae: Cod. Iust.* I, 1, 7: Krüger, 8a–10b.
105. *Ibid.*, nos. 4, 5, 6: Krüger, 8b–9a.
106. *Ibid.*, nos. 11–21: Krüger, 9b–10b.
107. *Cod. Iust.* I, 1, 8, no. 24: Krüger, 11b; CA, *ep.* 84 (also in *ep.* 91, nos. 8–22).
108. John II, *Ep. ad Iustinian. aug.*, of 25 March 534: CA, *ep.* 84, nos. 25–28: CSEL 35, 326–327; Amelotti-Migliardi Zingale, *Scritti teologici*, 20–21.
109. *Idem, Ep. ad Senatores*: ACO IV, 2, 206–210. The christological part is summarized in DS 401–2; cf. F. Glorie, in CCL 85A, XXXVIII.

All three questions were now answered positively. The Pope gave a clear, short summary of the faith of the Roman Church on the basis of the *Tomus* and the letters of Pope Leo and of the four councils: *sicut Roma hactenus suscepit et veneratur ecclesia*.[110] So simply ended the fourteen-year dispute which from the very beginning of Justin's reform led to a crisis within the Chalcedonian party not without its dangers, as Emperor Justinian emphasized many times in his letters. The hymn, which according to Theophanes was sung in the Church of Constantinople in 535/536 by order of Justinian, can be regarded almost as a conclusion to this altercation.[111]

> Only-begotten Son and Logos of God, immortal by nature.
> For the sake of our salvation you took it upon yourself
> To become flesh from the holy mother of God
> and ever-virgin Mary.
> Without change become a human being and crucified
> Christ God, through death treading death with the feet,
> One of the holy Trinity
> jointly glorified with the Father and the Holy Spirit.
> Save us!

The hymn could be sung by both Severans and Chalcedonians. It was completely orthodox. This was not yet the last word on the first theological action of Justinian. At the Council of 553 with canon 10 of the anathemas against the Three Chapters, the capstone, as it were, was put on a building which was to be dedicated to the *unus e Trinitate crucifixus*:

> If anyone does not confess that our Lord Jesus Christ, *who was crucified in the flesh*,[112] is true God and Lord of glory [cf. 1 Cor 2,8] and one of the holy Trinity, let him be anathema.[113]

In this form every sting was taken from the canon. Nevertheless the conflict did not end without losses for the Church of Constantinople.

---

110. John II, *Ep. ad Senatores*, no. 29: ACO IV, 2, p. 210,5–6.

111. See V. Grumel, 'L'auteur et la date de composition du tropaire 'O Μονογενής', EO 22 (1923), 398–418. Cf. CPG 6891. Grumel considers it probable (but only that) that Justinian himself is the author of the hymn, or at least the person who inspired it. In any case the hymn is unknown both in Constantinople and in the Empire before 519. Between 531 and 539 it was adopted into two liturgies. The text is found on 400–1. Grumel sees it closely related to the monophysite patriarch Anthimus; indeed, he is of the opinion that Justinian himself became a monophysite (418). This must be examined more closely in what follows.

112. So too Cyril of Alexandria's twelfth anathema: CED (Greek, 61; English, 61*).

113. *Constantinop. II., Actio VIII, can. X*: ACO IV, 1, 218 (Latin); *ibid.*, 242 (Greek). See also the fourth anathema in Justinian's letter to the monks: Schwartz, *Drei dogmatische Schriften Justinians*, p. 42,32–36.

The most severely affected were the Sleepless Monks, who were now condemned as Nestorians.[114]

> The Sleepless Ones (*Aquimitos*), however, who call themselves monks, the Roman Church also condemns, because they have publicly appeared as Nestorians; on their account I do not neglect to admonish you with pastoral care, for the sake of the canon which does not permit a Christian to speak or to have fellowship with excommunicated people; you should avoid all simple dialogue with them and consider nothing as common between you and them. I do this, therefore, that I may not be found guilty of silence, if I were in no way to have brought this to your notice, most Christian son.

With this condemnation the heyday of the Sleepless Monks came to 'a sudden end'.[115] Their services in establishing the validity of Chalcedon during the Acacian schism[116] were apparently quickly forgotten.[117] However, we can decide for ourselves whether this condemnation was correct, on the basis of the third redaction of the forged letters to Peter the Fuller, which had their origin in the monastery of the Sleepless Monks. In letters VIII–X they had already taken a position with regard to the contentious theme of the Scythian monks. As the *unus ex Trinitate crucifixus est* was explained there, there was no trace at all of Nestorianism.

> The enhypostatic God-Logos of the Father, by entering through the ear, effected in a mystical way the pregnancy of the blessed Virgin. Insofar as he is the consubstantial only-begotten Son of the Father and one of the undivided Trinity, uncreated and invisible, he also remains free of suffering and immortal. Thus what is uncreated and immortal does not combine [mix] with creation and does not support talk of the polytheism, when you say one of the Trinity dies. Insofar as he was born of woman, was of the same race, of the same stock, of the same nature as us but without sin, he took suffering upon himself.[118]

The Sleepless Monk thus ascribed to Peter the Fuller genuine theopaschism (on account of the *unus ex tribus*) and in addition, on account of his confession of the Trishagion in its expanded, theopaschite form, condemned him as a supporter of Paul of Samosata, Photinus, Artemos,

---

114. John II, *Ep. ad Senatores*, no. 30: ACO IV, 2, p. 210,9–15.

115. R. Riedinger, art. 'Akoimeten', in *TRE* 2, 148.

116. Cf. H. Bacht, 'Die Rolle des orientalischen Mönchtums . . . ', in *Chalkedon* II, no. VI: 266–91.

117. R. Riedinger, *art. cit.*, 148, says that the Sleepless Monks were already condemned as Messalians in the years 426–427 and driven across the Bosporus. Important nuances to this, however, are produced by E. Wölfle in his accurate study 'Der Abt Hypatius von Rufinianai und der Akoimete Alexander', *ByzZ* 79 (1986), 302–9. In the years 546–548 Facundus of Hermiane and in 565 the Roman deacon Rusticus visited the monastery of the Sleepless Monks, in order to take advantage of their library in the conflict about the Three Chapters.

118. Ps. Felix, *Ep. II*: *Coll. Sabb. ep. VIIII*: ACO III, p. 21,29–35.

the two-sons teaching and Manichaeism.[119] At the end he explains in a completely unobjectionable way the Church's faith in the incarnation, which he said, however, Peter the Fuller denied.[120]

Just as the Sleepless Monks for their part falsely accused the Scythian monks of theopaschism,[121] so now after fourteen years of conflict they themselves had to accept being condemned unjustly as Nestorians. It is to be regretted that after the resolution of the Acacian schism a new conflict had broken out among the Chalcedonians themselves, which ended with the condemnation of the unwavering defenders of the Council in the difficult years of the *Henoticon* dispute.

119. *Loc. cit.*, p. 22,9–14.
120. See especially *loc. cit.*, p. 23,4–10.
121. We find this once again expressed forcefully in the letter just cited: ACO III, p. 24,21–37, where the *unus ex trinitate* is linked to the Trishagion.

CHAPTER TWO

THE STRUGGLE FOR THE SEVERANS AND ITS THEOLOGICAL OUTCOME

A second group of actions launched by the Emperor after the assumption of office by Justin and Justinian's sole rule concerned the anti-Chalcedonian party, of which Severus of Antioch had become the leader. These actions oscillated between offers of reconciliation and condemnations, between favour and persecution. This changing of attitude was held together on the one hand by the Eusebian-Constantinian motive of equating unity of faith and the welfare of the Empire,[122] and on the other hand by Justinian's consideration for his wife Theodora and her outspoken stance in favour of Severus. However, our main objective is not the depiction of changing ecclesiastical politics, but the development of Justinian's christology.

I. JUSTINIAN'S INDIVIDUAL ACTIONS IN DEALING WITH THE ANTI-CHALCEDONIANS (SEVERANS)

1. Measures for persecution[123]

In the early part of 519 the banishment of anti-Chalcedonian bishops began, and at first continued until 522. Vitalian attempted to take his revenge on Severus in particular, who had ridiculed him publicly in his thirty-fourth cathedral homily after the failure of a revolt in 513 at

---

122. Cf. the *novella* 132: ed. Schoell-Kroll 665: 'The first and the greatest good of all human beings, we believe, is the right confession of the true and pure faith of the Christians, so that in every respect it is strengthened and all the holy priests of the world are bound together in unity and proclaim unanimously the pure faith of the Christians.' As well the motto which Procopius in his *Secret History*, ch. 13, ascribes to Justinian, the effort namely 'to lead all together into one unified faith in Christ' (ἐς μίαν γὰρ ἀμφὶ τῷ Χριστῷ δόξαν ⟨συναγαγεῖν⟩ ἅπαντας ἐν σπουδῇ ἔχων): Haury-Wirth III, p. 85,14–16; O. Veh I, 116–17. It was for no other reason that in the conflict about the Three Chapters on 28 May 547 Justinian delivered to Pope Vigilius, who was staying in Constantinople, two letters of Emperor Constantine to ponder, in order to move him to condemn these Three Chapters. Cf. the Latin translation in ACO IV, 2, 101–104.

123. E. Honigmann, *Évêques et évêchés monophysites*, 142–54, places as the heading for the conclusion of his investigation: L'extinction de la hiérarchie sévérienne (518–538). According to a list that was probably compiled at Constantinople, apart from Severus 52 other bishops lost their sees. The severity of the action against the Oriental monks is movingly depicted in the *Chronicle* of Michael the Syrian. Cf. IX, 14 and 15: Chabot II, 170–8; IX, 19: 185–9.

Antioch.[124] The Chalcedonian bishops too joined in the persecution of their opponents. A notorious case was the successor of Severus of Antioch, Paul the Jew (519–521), who received this epithet from his opponents. At a synod he wanted to commit the Syrian bishops to accept Chalcedon. He could only hold out, however, until 1 May 521.[125] A fierce persecutor of the opponents of Chalcedon was the former *Comes Orientis*, Ephraem of Amida, who was Patriarch of Antioch from 526 to 545. In particular the victims of his measures were the bishops who had hidden themselves in the border regions of his patriarchate. In the winter of 536/537 he visited the most important centres of resistance.[126] Nevertheless, as early as 527, after Justinian's assumption of power, numerous bishops were able to return from exile.

2. The doctrinal dialogue of 532 in Constantinople

The pre-conditions for this *Collatio cum Severianis*[127] were created to a great extent by Theodora, albeit with intentions that went further than those of her husband. On account of the harsh suppression of the opponents of Chalcedon in Antioch, many of them attempted to come to the capital in order to regain their lost positions with the help of the Empress. Even in the summer of 531, Justinian had recalled from exile whole groups (*tagmata*) of monks[128] and had stopped the laws of persecution being executed.[129] Thus those six bishops who are already

---

124. Severus Ant., *Hom.* 34: PO 36, 430–7 (Syriac and French). Severus also composed a hymn for the victory of Emperor Anastasius: PO 7, 710–11.

125. E. Honigmann, *op. cit.*, 148, n. 5.

126. Cf. Michael Syr., *Chron.* IX, 16: Chabot II, 181b; Zacharias Rh. cont., *HE* X, 1: Brooks, CSCO 88, 118–19; ET Hamilton-Brooks, 297–300; J. Lebon, 'Ephrem d'Amid', in *Mélanges ... C. Moeller (1863–1913)* I (Louvain/Paris, 1914), 197–214; E. Honigmann, *op. cit.*, 149. In addition see below (on Antioch).

127. See above, pp. 232–48.

128. Zacharias Rh. cont., *HE* VIII, 5: Brooks, CSCO 88, p. 56,29–33; ET Hamilton-Brooks, 212. Cf. E. Schwartz, 'Zur Kirchenpolitik Justinians', in *Ges. Schriften* IV, 282; sources: *idem*, *Kyrillos von Skythopolis*, 389, n. 1.

129. Cf. E. Schwartz, *Kyrillos von Skythopolis*, 392; Michael Syr., *Chron.* IX, 21: Chabot II, 192b: 'Justinianus ... ordonna que la persécution cessât, et que les persécutés revinssent à leurs demeures. Beaucoup revinrent, à l'exception des évêques qui ne rentrèrent pas dans leurs sièges; cependant les péchés l'empêchèrent. L'empereur se préoccupait de la paix des églises; cependant les péchés l'empêchèrent. L'impératrice fidèle, Theodora, se préoccupait encore davantage de la paix des églises et persuadait à l'empereur d'y travailler.' Michael then describes how the Empress accommodated more than 500 of the wanted clergy (especially monks) in a large court of the palace of Hormisdas. Severus, Theodosius and Anthimus and many wanted bishops she accommodated for years in her palace. In contrast to the Emperor's tolerance, which Michael the Syrian depicted positively above, is the negative

known to us as participants in the *Collatio* of 532 also received the invitation to come to Constantinople. From the desert, however, they first demanded imperial assurances of their freedom. When these were given, they were prepared to come into the Imperial City. During the time of their sojourn in Constantinople (531/532) there occurred, however, the notorious Nika riot (January 532), which could almost have cost Justinian his life and crown, had it not been for the perseverance of Theodora and her intervention to save him and his rule.[130] In a devastated city and after the severe political upheavals of the winter of 532, there was not much hope for the doctrinal dialogue. What Justinian was striving for at that time is expressed in the edict of 15 March 533. It contains a profession of faith which does not contradict Chalcedonian orthodoxy, but which could appear acceptable also to the Severans.[131] For in it everything is omitted which could provoke them, above all the two-natures formula and the mention of Chalcedon. In contrast the theopaschite formula is acknowledged.[132] The policy of the *Henoticon* seemed to have returned. The Emperor was seriously concerned to restore the unity of the Church through peace and not through persecution.[133]

3. The crisis of the Chalcedonian restoration in the East in the years 535/536

With Emperor Justinian's new religious policy, the Severans recognized the chance to permeate the capital more and more with their influence, and on that basis to make a fresh attempt to abolish Chalcedon. In

judgement in the *Secret History* of Procopius of Caesarea, chs. 15 and 16 (Haury-Wirth III, 94–104; Veh I, 128–42). Procopius deplores nothing more persistently than intolerance and imperial involvement in matters of faith. Cf. Averil Cameron, *Procopius and the Sixth Century* (London, 1985), 119–20, especially with reference to the *Secret History*, 13,4–5; 18,30,34; 19,11 (with commentary in O. Veh I, 299–300; 305–7).

130. See Procopius Caes., *Persian Wars* I, 24: Haury-Wirth I, 123–34; O. Veh III, 174–88, with commentary 480–2; Procopius experienced the Nika riot personally (Veh, 439). Theodora's address in O. Veh III, 182–4, is 'without a doubt historical' (*ibid.*, 481). According to Procopius, in the putting down of the riot by Belisarius and Mundus more than thirty thousand people of the citizen body died. See R. Browning, *Justinian and Theodora* (above n. 3), 109–12; J. A. S. Evans, 'The "Nika" Rebellion and the Empress Theodora', *Byz* 54 (1984), 380–2.

131. Justinian imp., *Ep. ad Constantinop.* (CPG 9313): *Cod. Iust.* I, 1, 6: Krüger, 7–8.

132. *Ibid.*, no. 7: Krüger, 8a. In the letter to Patriarch Epiphanius of 26 March 533 (CPG 9314): *Cod. Iust.*, I, 1, 7: Krüger, 8–10 and in the letter to Pope John II, of 6 June 533 [CPG 9315]: CA, *ep.* 84 [= CPG 6874], the four synods were explicitly mentioned and acknowledged as binding. Cf. CA, *ep.* 84, nos. 17 and 18: CSEL 35, 324.

133. Cf. E. Schwartz, 'Zur Kirchenpolitik Justinians', in *Ges. Schriften* IV (276–320), 283.

November 533 they took advantage of the panic that occurred among the population because of the earthquake, to organize a demonstration by the people against the Fourth Synod.[134] There soon appeared significant opportunities to take drastic measures.

(a) Empress Theodora and the filling of vacant patriarchal thrones

After the failure of the doctrinal dialogue of 532 a new initiative to unite the religious parties was introduced: the patriarchal leaders of the anti-Chalcedonian opposition, Severus of Antioch (in exile in Egypt) and Timothy IV (III) of Alexandria were to be invited to the capital in the years 534/535 for direct negotiations. Unexpected obstacles arose, however, which Empress Theodora knew how to turn skilfully to her advantage. On 7 February 535, Patriarch Timothy IV (III) died. The Empress made sure that a decided opponent of the Fourth Council, the deacon Theodosius, could ascend the throne of St Mark. Alexandria, however, was divided and dominated by the Julianist party. In spite of the support of the imperial officials, the new Severan patriarch was driven out as early as 10 February 535 by the Julianist Gaianas. But he too could only hold out for 103 days, when Theodosius was once again appointed, even if for only a short time.[135] At Constantinople the Chalcedonian patriarch, Epiphanius, died (5 June 535). Theodora was successful in bringing to the patriarchal throne of the capital a man who had her trust, Anthimus, previously the bishop of Trebizond. In 532 he had taken part in the doctrinal dialogue of Constantinople while still on the Chalcedonian side.[136] What was important was that in the winter of 534/535 Severus had come to Constantinople and had been accommodated in the imperial palace.[137] He quickly succeeded in bringing the new patriarch over to his side. Thus, under the protection of Theodora, an influential trio (consisting of Severus, Timothy or after his death his successor, Theodosius, and Anthimus) could be constituted, whose goals were expressed in an extensive correspondence. These consisted of nothing other than the abolition of the Chalcedonian restoration of 518/519 and

134. *Chron. Pasch.* 629 BC: the praying crowd called to Christ: 'Take and burn the decree composed by the bishops of the Synod of Chalcedon.' Cf. E. Stein, *Histoire du Bas-Empire* II, 380.

135. Cf. J. Maspero, *Histoire des Patriarches d'Alexandrie* (1923), 110–17 on Gaianas; 117–19 on Theodosius.

136. Cf. ACO IV, 2, p. 169, 11; J. Speigl, 'Das Religionsgespräch mit den severianischen Bischöfen im Jahr 532', *AHC* 16 (1984), 261–85.

137. Cf. John Beth Aphth., *Vita Sev.*: PO 2, 252–3; John Eph., PO 2, 302; Zacharias Rh. cont., *HE* IX, 19: Brooks, CSCO 88, 93; ET Hamilton-Brooks, 265. Theodora is here named as the instigator of this summons; cf. Brooks, p. 93,5–7; ET Hamilton-Brooks, 265; see in addition IX, 20: Brooks, p. 95,31; ET Hamilton-Brooks, 270.

the return to the positions under Emperor Anastasius, with certain more radical aspects included, which the dead Emperor would not have permitted. In his letters to Severus[138] and Theodosius,[139] Patriarch Anthimus offered nothing other than to restore communion on the basis of the first three councils of 325, 381 and 431 and of the *Henoticon* of Emperor Zeno, the latter being interpreted as a condemnation of Chalcedon and the *Tomus* of Leo I. In his letter of reply Severus spoke of his willingness for an already 'realized conjunction' between Anthimus and himself.[140] He intended to relay this to Patriarch Theodosius. Anthimus asserted to Theodosius as well that the same should be accepted as the basis of communion: the first three synods, Zeno's *Henoticon* (likewise interpreted as a condemnation of Chalcedon and Leo I) and Cyril's twelve anathemas.[141] Theodosius himself in his reply to Anthimus accepted these conditions completely.[142] In a letter to Severus he had already stated that he was fully in agreement with the teaching of Anthimus.[143] Because Emperor Justinian himself was now exposed to the immediate influence of the highly admired Severus — according to Zacharias Rhetor, the Emperor received the exile 'in a friendly manner'[144] — the Chalcedonian reform of 518/519 seemed to hang by only a thin thread. The two most important patriarchal sees of the East were already occupied by the opponents of the Fourth Council. In Jerusalem there appeared to be some uncertainty, as is clear from the letter of Pope Agapetus I to Peter of Jerusalem.[145] Patriarch Ephraem of Antioch was the last support for Chalcedon among the Eastern patriarchates. If

138. Anthimus, *Ep. ad Sever. Ant.* (CPG 7087): in Zacharias Rh. cont., *HE* IX, 21: Brooks, CSCO 88, 96–100; ET Hamilton-Brooks, 271–6; in addition IX, 22: Severus to Anthimus: Brooks, 100–5; ET Hamilton-Brooks, 276–81; IX, 23: Severus to Theodosius: Brooks, 105–7; ET Hamilton-Brooks, 281–3.

139. Anthimus, *Ep. ad Theodos.* (CPG 7088): Zacharias Rh. cont., *HE* IX, 25: Brooks, 111–13; ET Hamilton-Brooks, 287–90; the reply of Theodosius: IX, 26: Brooks, 114–17; ET Hamilton-Brooks, 291–5; *idem, Ep. synodica ad Severum* (CPG 7134): CSCO 103 (V), p. 2,30–33 (*Henoticon*).

140. Zacharias Rh. cont., *HE* IX, 22: Brooks, p. 105,13–14; ET Hamilton-Brooks, 280. Cf. John Beth Aphth., *Vita Sev.*: PO 2, 253–6. That Anthimus wished to restore the unity of the Church on this basis is also shown by his letter to Jacob Baradai, bishop of Edessa (CPG 7085), in F. Nau, 'Littérature canonique syriaque inédite', *ROC* 14 (1909), 123–4, particularly at the end where Theodoret and Ibas of Edessa are then named as opponents.

141. Cf. Zacharias Rh. cont., *HE* IX, 25: Brooks, CSCO 88, p. 112,15–25; ET Hamilton-Brooks, 289.

142. Cf. *ibid.*, IX, 26: Brooks, CSCO 88, 114–15; ET Hamilton-Brooks, 293.

143. Cf. *ibid.*, IX, 24: Brooks, CSCO 88, 108–9; ET Hamilton-Brooks, 285.

144. *Ibid.*, IX, 19: Brooks, CSCO 88, p. 93,4–5; ET Hamilton-Brooks, 265; in addition IX, 15: Brooks, p. 84,25–28; ET Hamilton-Brooks, 252–3.

145. Agapet., *Ep. ad Petrum* (CPG 9325 [9319]): ACO III, 152–3.

Theodora and Justinian had shared the same intention, it is possible that Peter would have succumbed to the influence of Severus, and Ephraem too would have lost his see.

(b) The Chalcedonian reaction

The supporters of Chalcedon in Constantinople were alarmed. The archimandrite and monks there, strengthened by a delegation of monks from Syria II and from the desert near Jerusalem (Sabas' monasteries), dared to make an attack on Anthimus, Severus, Peter, the former metropolitan of Apamea,[146] and the fanatical monk Zooras, a Syrian from Sophanone and a former stylite, who had settled in the exclusive residential area Sykai, performed baptisms and liturgies and brought numerous supporters to the anti-Chalcedonian party.[147] The monks demanded from Anthimus an unambiguous profession of Chalcedon, the acknowledgement of the Tomus of Leo I and the condemnation of Patriarch Dioscorus, who was deposed at Chalcedon. Anthimus, however, refused to meet this demand.[148] Consequently the monks sent a delegation to Pope Agapetus I in Rome, who on 13 May 535 had become the successor of Pope John II.[149] Patriarch Ephraem too, however, turned to Rome through the doctor Sergius of Rēšʿainā, who was intended to deliver a letter to Pope Agapetus I[150] in order to move him to intervene in Constantinople. A journey by the Pope to the East at just this time, however, was also being pushed by Theodahat,[151] the king of the Goths, who hoped in this way to achieve the cessation of Justinian's military operations in Dalmatia and Sicily. In December 532 Pope Agapetus departed for Constantinople, where he arrived in March

146. Peter of Apamea had in any case come to Constantinople. Cf. E. Schwartz, *Kyrillos von Skythopolis*, 392–3; cf. R. Schieffer, *Indices*, ACO IV, 3, 2, 2, pp. 385b–386a.

147. Cf. R. Schieffer, *op. cit.*, 508a.

148. See the *Relatio monachorum*, CPG 9325 (2), delivered at the Council of Constantinople on 2 May 536, ACO III, 134–6, especially no. 62: pp. 134,27–135,6.

149. *Ibid.*, p. 135,9,23, the monks mention their *libellus* to Pope Agapetus. Whether this, however, was presented to the Pope at Rome or only in Constantinople is not clear. The *relatio* itself was composed after the death of Agapetus I (p. 136,6–7).

150. Cf. Zacharias Rh. cont., *HE* IX, 19: Brooks, CSCO 88, 93–4; ET Hamilton-Brooks, 266–7. Pope John II had died on 8 May 535.

151. On the Goths under (King) Theodahat and the intentions of the latter regarding the papal journey of Agapetus I, cf. Procopius, *Gothic Wars* I, 3,6–11: Veh II, 22–23,40–47,46–93, with commentary 1014–16, especially, however, 1017–21. Theodahat negotiated secretly with Justinian's delegation, the bishops Hypatius and Demetrius, for the purpose of yielding Tuscany to Justinian in return for the conferral of the dignity of senator on the Goth and his transferral to Byzantium. On Agapetus I see Veh's commentary, 1017. Theodahat was assassinated in 536.

536.[152] In a short time his presence changed the situation. Anthimus was deposed as patriarch and only acknowledged as bishop of Trebizond; but it was intended that he should reclaim his see only after he had proven his Chalcedonian orthodoxy. His successor on the patriarchal throne was the priest Menas,[153] whom the Pope himself ordained as bishop on 13 March 536. The new patriarch as well as Justinian signed confessions of faith which contained the well-known formula of Hormisdas, admittedly expanded by additions (in § 3), in which was contained the Chalcedonian doctrine of the two natures in the one person of Christ.[154] Agapetus I even sent a letter to Patriarch Peter of Jerusalem.[155] In this he expressed his surprise that Peter did not bring to the notice of the Pope in Rome the uncanonical appointment of Anthimus. With a feeling of satisfaction he commented moreover that since the days of Peter the Apostle it was the first time that an Eastern bishop has been ordained by the bishop of Rome.[156] In its significance the harmony between Agapetus I and Emperor Justinian certainly compared with that between Emperor Justin and Pope Hormisdas, insofar as now the imminent restoration of the *Henoticon* policy was excluded, and Constantinople was definitively won for the Chalcedonian restoration. The monks of the capital contributed to the extension of what had been won, and presented Pope Agapetus I with an indictment against Anthimus.[157] They demanded that decisive action be taken against Severus, Peter of Apamea, Zooras and people of like mind[158] and that the writings of Severus should be burned. A similar document was

152. Cf. Zacharias Rh. cont., *HE* IX, 19: Brooks, CSCO 88, 94; ET Hamilton-Brooks, 267. See E. Stein, *Histoire du Bas-Empire* II, 342–5 (on Theodahat).

153. Patriarch Menas (13 March 536 — 24 August 552); Grumel, *Regestes* I², nos. 232–43; CPG 6923–34.

154. Menas Const., *Libellus fidei* (CPG 6923), of 13 March 536: Grumel, *Regestes* I², no. 232; CA, *ep.* 90; *Libellus . . . Iustiniani* (16 March 536): CA, *ep.* 89 (CPG 6876 with 6874–5). *Vis-à-vis* the Hormisdas formula of 519 the texts are expanded by the naming of the four synods, as well as the dogmatic letters of Leo I; in the mention of the Council of 381 (§ 2) the canon about the elevation of the See of Constantinople is omitted. Also the theopaschite formula, approved by John II, does not appear here. Nevertheless Pope Agapetus I in CA, *ep.* 82 and 91, of 18 March 536, confirms Justinian's confession of faith (CA, *ep.* 91, nos. 8–22 of 6 June 533), in which this formula is contained (in no. 14).

155. JW 897; CPG 9325 (5) = [9319]: ACO III, 152–3; PL 66, 47–50; read out at the synod of 536.

156. ACO III, p. 153,16–21.

157. *Libellus monachorum ad Agapetum*, CPG 9325 (3): ACO III, pp. 136–47. In this they describe the activity which the 'Aposchists' had developed in the imperial city by baptisms and liturgies. In particular they want to achieve the complete exclusion of Anthimus, also as far as the Church of Trebizond is concerned (p. 140,34).

158. ACO III, p. 141,15–28.

presented to Pope Agapetus by the Oriental bishops, their *apocrisiarii* and clerics,[159] in which it was demanded that action be taken against Severus, Zooras, Isaac the Persian and against Anthimus. Thus everything pushed for a synodal purification of the denounced evils, in other words a council which could have taken place in Constantinople under the presidency of Pope Agapetus. But then Agapetus fell ill, and died on 22 April 536.[160]

4. The Synod of Constantinople 536 and its christological outcome

(a) The task and course of the Synod

After the unexpected death of Pope Agapetus I, Emperor Justinian probably felt himself obliged, as it were, to execute his will and to complete the measures introduced against Anthimus and those of like mind.[161] Hence he ordered Patriarch Menas to summon all of the bishops present in Constantinople to a *synodos endemousa*. It was intended that further participants should be those bishops whom Pope Agapetus had already sent to the Imperial City in 535, furthermore the deacons and *apocrisiarii* of the patriarchs of Antioch and Jerusalem, as well as the metropolitans of Cappadocia I, Galatia I and Achaia. 'The convocation by the Emperor and the presence of the representatives of the Apostolic See elevated the synod far above the level of an ἐνδημοῦσα almost to the status of an ecumenical synod.'[162] What was also called for was to make people realize in an impressive way that the Chalcedonian restoration was already endangered and that it had undiminished validity. This was the real significance of the synod; it was not to give doctrinal clarifications to the christological problem. Had it taken place with Agapetus

159. ACO III, 147–52 = CPG 9325 (4).

160. E. Caspar, *Geschichte des Papsttums* II (1933), 226, n. 3, ventures to suspect that possibly Theodora eliminated the 'troublesome man' by force, although he cannot establish a suspicion of this kind in contemporary sources. See, however, the monstrous general comment of Procopius in the *Secret History*, ch. 13: O. Veh, 119. See the *Vita Agapeti* in the *Liber pontificalis*, ed. Duchesne, 287 and E. Caspar's critique, 226.

161. Cf. E. Schwartz, 'Zur Kirchenpolitik Justinians', in *Ges. Schriften* 4, 287–8.

162. *Ibid.*, 288. Schwartz also remarks that the *acta* were sent around to absent metropolitans and bishops for their signature (with evidence in n. 1).

presiding, this task would have been expressed in a unique manner.[163]

The Synod had five 'actions' (on 2, 6, 10, 21 May and 4 June 536). At the conclusion of the session on 6 August 536 a constitution against Anthimus, Severus, Peter and Zooras was decreed by Emperor Justinian (CPG 6877). The person of the deposed Anthimus was the central point. In an elaborate process the deposed patriarch was summoned before the Synod. Three delegations, each consisting of seven bishops, priests and deacons, were despatched to find and summon him. They found him neither in the palace of Hormisdas nor in the other houses and monasteries where he could have been presumed to have been, nor in his villa, where, however, two of his friends, Stephen and Longinus, were staying. Then delegations reported each time on their return about the futile search. In fact Anthimus was staying, probably under the protection of Empress Theodora without Justinian's knowledge, in a room of their palace. Even after the intervention of Agapetus, the Empress in no way abandoned her endeavour to bring to power once again the three deposed patriarchs, Anthimus, Severus and Theodosius.[164] In any case Theodora wanted to spare her protégé, Anthimus, interrogation and condemnation in praesentia by the Synod. This she also achieved; the damnatio in absentia, however, was not to be prevented.

On account of the fact that the accused could not be found, and new deadlines had to be set repeatedly for his appearance before the Synod, the greater part of the five sessions (actiones) consisted in the reading out and hearing of the reports of the lack of success by the delegations.[165]

---

163. On the Synod of Constantinople 536 see CPG 9313–29; Grumel, Regestes I², nos. 233–8; Hefele-Leclercq, Histoire des Conciles II/2, 1142–55: Concile à Constantinople et à Jérusalem en 536. E. Schwartz, art. cit., 287–90; A. de Halleux, 'Trois synodes impériaux du VIᵉ s. dans une chronique syriaque inédite', in R. H. Fischer (ed.), A Tribute to Arthur Vööbus (Chicago, 1977), 295–307; on the Synod of 536: 296–300. On the Synod of Jerusalem, of 19 September 536, see CPG 9331. On Anthimus see E. Honigmann, 'Anthimus of Trebizond, Patriarch of Constantinople (June 535 – March 536)', in idem, Patristic Studies = ST 173 (Rome, 1953), 185–93.

164. Liberatus, Brev. 20: ACO II, 5, p. 136,19–24, reports on their attempt to win Pope Agapetus' deacon Vigilius for the abolition of Chalcedon and on the deacon's willingness. On the question of the authenticity of this report see E. Honigmann, art. cit., 189.

165. Actio I of 2 May 536: first delegation for the search: ACO III, no. 72, 153–4; corresponding report on the lack of success in actio II, of 6 May: ACO III, nos. 79–85, 159–60. Second delegation: no. 86, 160–1. Corresponding report on the lack of success in actio III, of 10 May 536, nos. 109–18, 174–6. Third delegation with a deadline of six (in all ten) days: ibid., no. 119, 176–7, appointed at the third session, but dated from the 15 May 536, added to the acta of the fourth session of 21 May 536, with the corresponding report on the lack of success: ACO III, no. 121, 177.

(b) Judgement and christological result of the Synod

(i) Conclusion of the fourth actio

After the last report of lack of success in all searches on 21 May 536 the fourth session was closed with a final questioning of the members of the Synod on the *causa* Anthimus, and a *memoriale* of the monks of Jerusalem, which concerned Zooras in particular. Patriarch Menas asked first the Italian, then the Greek bishops for their *sententia*.

The Romans were brief and stated in Latin that they would adopt the judgement of deposition, which Pope Agapetus delivered before his death.[166] In the name of the Greek bishops Hypatius, the metropolitan of Ephesus, took the floor and formulated the charge against Anthimus:[167]

Anthimus has made himself guilty of many transgressions:

(1) In uncanonical manner he seized the patriarchal see of Constantinople and endeavoured to secure the agreement of the clergy and people.

(2) Secretly, however, he subscribed to the teaching of Eutyches, although he still made a profession of the four synods and also pretended to accept Leo's *Tomus*.[168] This was, however, to deceive the Emperor, the apostolic see of Rome and the patriarchs.[169] But Pope Agapetus I discovered that he denied ecclesial dogmas, in particular the teaching of the two natures which the Synod of Chalcedon defined against Eutyches.[170] Thus he is a supporter of Dioscorus and Eutyches.

(3) Because he has evaded the canonical process and has missed the acceptable moment for repentance, he must now be separated, as an unsuitable member, from the body of the holy Churches, deposed as bishop of Trebizond and, according to the judgement of the holy Pope [Agapetus], be declared to have forfeited every holy office and authority (ἀξίας καὶ ἐνεργείας).

With the whole Synod, Patriarch Menas endorsed this charge and the corresponding judgement, which was confirmed by acclamations of the bishops and the monks and with the shout to anathematize Peter of Apamea, Zooras and Severus as well. In this way the ground was laid for the fifth *actio*. Monks of Jerusalem wanted to achieve a further resolution by the Synod, namely a decree to destroy the Eutychian monasteries, in particular those of Zooras.[171] Patriarch Menas recognized the explosive nature of this demand and stressed that in accordance with the

---

166. ACO III, no. 124, 178.

167. *Ibid.*, no. 126, 178–80.

168. *Ibid.*, pp. 178,31–179,8.

169. *Ibid.*, p. 179,11–14.

170. *Ibid.*, p. 179,25.

171. *Ibid.*, no. 129, p. 181,20–32; the dens of the heretics should be smoked out. For what purpose then, it is asked, does Peter of Apamea need a monastery? Only to be able to have all the heretics there! Severus, Peter and Zooras, this 'trio the Trinity anathematizes' (p. 181,28–9).

canons such decisions had to be presented to the Emperor and the Apostolic See for examination and ratification.[172]

(ii) The fifth actio of 4 June 536 and its significance for the reform of 519

The significance of the Synod of 536 consisted in the fact that the crisis threatening Justin's Chalcedonian reform of 518/519 was removed and the patriarchate of Constantinople was kept for Chalcedonian faith. This result was achieved in a twofold way: (1) through the condemnation of the leaders of the reaction and their definitive deposition; (2) through a new confession of the four synods and of Leo's *Tomus*. With an abundance of documents the Synod secured this result, which was then ratified by an imperial constitution. Unfortunately the theological discussion of 536 was of less value here than at the doctrinal dialogue of 532. It was in the first three documents that all the charges against the three or four opponents of Chalcedon were collected, which were not free of exaggerations and distortions.[173] The four accused were unjustly placed in a retinue of the heresies of Eutyches, Nestorius and Manes, to which Patriarch Dioscorus was also said to have belonged, although the fact that he distanced himself from the archimandrite was on record. Severe accusations were made particularly against Severus, his past life, his association with magic and demons, his hypocritical behaviour in the *Henoticon* question and his disruption of the peace of the Alexandrian Church. His writings had to be committed to the fire, as were formerly the books of Manes and Nestorius.[174] All were accused of paraliturgical celebrations of the eucharist and baptism,[175] and of showing contempt for the Apostolic See of Rome.[176] From the declarations of the various groups at the Synod there emerges the positive result that there is the newly attained unity of Constantinople, Antioch and Jerusalem on the one hand, and on the other with the Apostolic See of Rome, indeed with the 'entire holy, catholic and apostolic Church',[177] through the explicit confession of Chalcedon and Leo's Tome. This found expression

172. *Ibid.*, no. 130, 181–2.
173. See the *libellus* of the bishops of Syria Secunda to the Emperor: *ibid.*, 30–2; the *libellus* of the monks to the same addressee: *ibid.*, 32–8; the *libellus* of the monks to Patriarch Menas: *ibid.*, 38–52.
174. See the analysis of the documents in Hefele-Leclercq II, 1150–2.
175. Cf. ACO III, p. 111,25.
176. *Ibid.*, p. 112,25ff.
177. Cf. the *libellus* of the monks to the Synod: *ibid.*, pp. 43,37–44,15.

in the individual *sententiae* of the Synod[178] and in Justinian's constitution.[179] Through this Synod Justinian himself was freed from his wavering and uncertainty, particularly through the intervention of Pope Agapetus I, which he especially highlighted.[180] At the Synod itself no further attempt was made to stress what was common in the faith in Jesus Christ. The 'formation of a confession' had been firmly cemented.

At the Council of Constantinople (680/681), too, Anthimus was not forgotten as a heretic. He was cited there on the basis of some fragments from his *logos*[181] to Emperor Justinian, as confessing one *physis*, and correspondingly one will and one *energeia*, as well as one *sophia* and one knowledge (see below).

II. IMPERIAL DOGMATIC DECREES ON SEVERAN CHRISTOLOGY

Emperor Justinian seized the opportunity of the division of the miaphysite Church of Alexandria into the supporters of Patriarch Theodosius (535/536) and those of Gaianas to restore the Chalcedonian hierarchy there. At the suggestion of the Roman deacon Pelagius, a monk, Paul, from the Tabennesi monastery[182] was ordained as patriarch (538). Violent actions, bad example in the conduct of his life (accumulation of riches), an (unproven) reproach of his being involved in disposing of a scheming deacon led to his deposition on the order of Justinian. His case was handled by a special commission appointed by the Emperor

---

178. See *ibid.*, 110–19; p. 110,20–21.

179. CPG 9329 with [9330] = 6877: *Constitutio Iustiniani imp. c. Anthimum, Severum, Petrum et Zooram* (of 6 August 536): ACO III, 119–23; *Nov.* 42: Schoell-Kroll, 263–9.

180. ACO III, p. 120,6–25; *Nov.* 42: Schoell-Kroll, p. 264,43–55.

181. See Anthimus, *Sermo ad Iustinianum* (CPG 7086): Mansi XI: *Concil. Constantinop.* III (680/1): a) *actio* X, col. 440–1; *actio* XI: col. 516–17. The citations are part of a *logos* which in Latin is translated on one occasion by *liber*, and on another occasion by *sermo*; Mansi XI, col. 441 speaks moreover of *logos protos*; in col. 517 the same text is described as *logos prosphonetikos*, which can mean that it was presented to the Emperor or addressed to him (Latin: *sermo acclamatorius*). In the *acta* of the Synod of 536 no reaction to this is found. No one still accused Anthimus of a concrete heresy, which would certainly have been the case if this *sermo* had been well known. Could it have been composed after his deposition (536) and addressed to the Emperor? Then it would hardly have been preserved in the patriarchal library; it was, however, contained in a *liber chartaceus* which in 680/681 was taken out to examine the fragments. Because at the Council of 680/681 these fragments were cited in the context of the monoenergist question, just as Justinian's letter to Zoilus (CPG 6879), we shall consider it together with this letter (see below).

182. Cf. E. Stein, *Histoire du Bas-Empire* II, 389–92. Pelagius, as deacon of the Roman church, belonged to the delegation which Pope Agapetus I sent to Emperor Justinian on 15 October 535. Even after Pope Agapetus' death he remained as the Roman *apocrisiarius* in Constantinople.

at Gaza in Palestine, to which the patriarchs Ephraem of Antioch, Peter of Jerusalem, Archbishop Hypatius of Ephesus and the papal *apocrisiarius* Pelagius belonged' (the beginning of 540).[183] After the city of Alexandria and several monasteries seemed to have been won for the Chalcedonian confession under the combined pressure of this patriarch Paul and the imperial officials, Emperor Justinian seized the opportunity to explain the faith by some dogmatic writings: (1) to the new patriarch Zoilus (540–551), who had been elected at Gaza; and (2) to the 'converted' Alexandrian monks. In a reasonably conclusive manner he wanted to settle accounts with Severus of Antioch and his supporters.[184] This combination of disciplinary action and dogmatic instruction which we discern in the case of Alexandria corresponds completely to Justinian's consciousness of a twofold responsibility, on the one hand for the *honestas sacerdotum*, that is, the lifestyle of the bishops, and on the other for the 'true dogmas of God'. This is the way he expressed it in the introduction to *novella VI*, addressed on 7 April 535 to Patriarch Epiphanius of Constantinople.[185] In the writings which were sent out of 'solicitude for the dogmas' to the patriarch and monks of Alexandria (CPG 6879 and 6878), we find Justinian's most detailed discussion of Severan christology. Let us look at these documents more closely and attempt to determine their place in the theological development of the sixth century. We shall no doubt be able to moderate E. Schwartz's harsh judgement of Justinian as 'the imperial dilettante' (in theological matters).[186]

---

183. Cf. Liberatus, *Brev.* 23: ACO II, 5, 138–140; Procopius Caes., *Secret History* 27, 3–22: Haury-Wirth III, 166–9; O. Veh I, 229–31; Zacharias Rh. cont., *HE* X, 1: Brooks, CSCO 88, 119–120; ET Hamilton-Brooks, 297–8. John of Nikiu, *Chron.*, ch. 92, 1–10: trans. Charles, 145–6; J. Maspero, *Histoire des patriarches d'Alexandrie*, 144–51; in addition see E. Stein, *op. cit.*, 391–2, n. 1. See too R. Aubert, art. 'Gaza (Concile de)', in *DHGE* 20 (1984), 176–7.

184. See Amelotti-Migliardi Zingale, *Scritti teologici*: III. Scritti relativi ai monofisiti, to which are accounted: (a) the troparion Ὁ μονογενὴς υἱός (CPG 6891), *ibid.*, 43–4; (b) the constitution against Anthimus, Severus, Peter and Zooras, with which we have already dealt (CPG 6877), *ibid.*, 45–55; (c) the dogmatic letter to Zoilus (CPG 6879), *ibid.*, 57–63; (d) the letters to the Alexandrian monks (CPG 6878), for which reference is made to E. Schwartz, *Drei dogmatische Schriften Justinians* (Munich, 1939), 5–43; Latin translation in *Subsidia* II, 5–79, according to the Greek text of E. Schwartz. PG 86, 1104–46. See R. Haacke, 'Die kaiserliche Politik in den Auseinandersetzungen um Chalkedon', in *Chalkedon* II, 155–63.

185. Justinian imp., *Nov.* 6, *praef.*: Schoell-Kroll, 35–6: *Nos igitur, maximam habemus sollicitudinem circa vera dei dogmata et circa sacerdotum honestatem.* Cf. M. Simonetti, 'La politica religiosa di Giustiniano', in G. G. Archi (ed.), *Il mondo del diritto nell'epoca giustinianea. Caratteri e problematiche* (Ravenna, 1985) (91–111), 93–4; G. Pilati, *Chiesa e Stato nei primi quindici secoli* (Rome, Paris, Tournai, New York, 1961), 59–73.

186. Cf. E. Schwartz, *Drei dogmatische Schriften Justinians* = *ABAW.PH* 18 (Munich, 1939), 114.

1. The dogmatic letter to the Alexandrian monks

This letter gives a good overview of the state of Justinian's christology in 540, before the outbreak of the Three Chapters dispute. The Emperor has appropriated well the Chalcedonian view of the incarnation and reproduced it in a manner which did not yet show the preferences that were otherwise regarded as marks of his christology, the *unus ex trinitate* excepted. It was indeed because of the latter that he began here too with an explanation of trinitarian faith.[187]

(a) On the mia-physis formula

The disputed formula quickly appears (no. 5, p. 8,25–26). Because the addressees were previously supporters of the one-nature formula, the Emperor lays the main stress on the explanation of the two-natures teaching (nos. 6–21) and on combating the *mia physis* and its tradition. The only terminological concession which distinguishes him from the Chalcedonian definition is the addition of the formula 'from two natures' to the synodal 'in two natures' (nos. 8–9, p. 9). In order to make it easier for the monks to give up the *mia-physis* formula, for which they could refer to Cyril, the Emperor strives particularly to highlight Cyril's relationship to the two-natures language. In this way he takes over the intention of the Cyrillian florilegium, which we have already presented in detail.[188] It is important for him that Cyril himself interprets the monophysite formula in the sense of the two natures (nos. 15–17, p. 10): the words 'one nature' refer to the *Logos asarkos* before the incarnation; the Father (Cyril), however, did not stop there, but added: 'which became flesh, so that he represents to us through this incarnate [nature] the other, that is, the human nature' (no. 16, p. 10,26–27). Severus could not deny that Cyril used the two-natures language. He wanted, nevertheless, to limit this phrase strictly, and to represent it as occasioned by special circumstances. Justinian would like to demonstrate, however, that this was the constant practice of the 'Father' acknowledged on all sides.

> From all that has been said [cf. Cyril's texts in nos. 156–66], it is proved that Cyril, who dwells among the saints, before, in and after the condemnation of Nestorius did not cease to proclaim constantly the profession of the two natures. (no. 167, pp. 35–6)[189]

187. We shall follow the edition of Schwartz, *ibid.*, 7–43, and his division according to nos. 1–200, and cite the page and line of this edition.

188. See above, pp. 22–3.

189. Cf. M. Simonetti, 'Alcune osservazioni sul monofisismo di Cirillo d'Alessandria', *Aug* 22 (1982), 493–511.

Justinian knows that Severus rejects the entire two-natures tradition: 'To speak of two natures is full of every condemnation, even if it is used by several holy Fathers in an unobjectionable manner' (no. 151, p. 31).[190]

(b) Mia physis synthetos

Not only is the classical *mia-physis* formula repudiated, but also especially the Apollinarian manner of speaking of the 'one composite nature' (nos. 57–68). In this context we need to note what Justinian has to say about the use of the body–soul paradigm (cf. nos. 27–56, pp. 12–16). On account of its use by Apollinarius it is considered by him with suspicion, especially because of the teaching of the *synthesis* associated with it and its application to Christ. The main text for this is the Apollinarian 'Treatise on the Incarnation', ch. 13 (nos. 60–61, pp. 16–17), with the description of Christ as a 'single living being' from Logos and *sarx*, for 'the flesh is, as flesh of God, one living being with him, composed to (form) one nature' (no. 61, p. 17,7–8). What Justinian particularly takes exception to is the fact that this synthesis teaching is found in an alleged letter of Pope Julius and in a letter of Athanasius to Jovian (nos. 71–72, p. 18). To prove these texts to be forgeries, the Emperor proceeds in a way similar to that of Leontius of Byzantium (in *AFA*):[191] he compares them with authentic texts of Apollinarius (nos. 74–76, pp. 18–19). In the first text he finds the offensive formula of 'the one essence from God and human being', which is 'one' because there has been 'a composition of God with the human body' (no. 74, pp. 18–19). This way of speaking teaches nothing other than a mixing (*synkrasis*) of divinity and humanity in Christ (no. 76, p. 19). Even Polemon, the student of Apollinarius, is said to have recognized that the *synthesis* teaching was wrong, and that the *mia-physis* formula was also affected by this (nos. 65 and 66, p. 17). 'From what has been said it is clear that those who take the one incarnate nature of the God-Logos as composite follow the error of Apollinarius. In contrast Cyril, who dwells among the saints, did not speak of the one incarnate nature of the Logos other than meaning two natures, which is why he adds: we speak of two natures' (no. 67, p. 17). Cyril thus rejects the manner of speaking of the 'composite nature, as of the one *physis* from flesh and divinity' (no. 67, p. 17,33–35, with further evidence from Cyril against the expression *synthesis*: nos. 68 and

---

190. This text of Severus is cited by Eustathius monk, *Ep. ad Timotheum Schol.* (CPG 6810): PG 86, 904D, now ed. Allen, no. 6, ll. 52–54; the citation is from Severus' *Ekthesis pisteos*.

191. See above, pp. 237–8, n. 40. Justinian mentions that he exposed the forgery through investigations in the papal archives (no. 86, p. 21).

69, pp. 17–18). Justinian thus attacks the expressions *synthesis–synthetos* by clearly emphasizing their misuse by Apollinarius, which consists in the fact that Christ, God and human being, is considered as a 'nature-unity'. Insofar as the *mia-physis* formula is derived from this understanding, it is to be strictly rejected, just as much as the expression (*mia*) *physis synthetos*. Only the denotation *Christos synthetos* may be allowed, similar to the *mia-physis* formula in Cyril's understanding (cf. nos. 70 and 69, p. 18). Here we can confirm that the Emperor, more than any of the theologians of his time, recognizes the distinction between Christ conceived in an Apollinarian way (= a nature-synthesis in the strict sense) and the Cyrillian understanding of the 'one nature', which should not be interpreted as a profession of 'one *ousia*' (no. 70, p. 18).

For Justinian there exists a community of like mind in the use of the *mia-physis* formula between Manes, Apollinarius, the Headless Ones, and, closer at hand, Timothy Aelurus, Dioscorus of Alexandria and Severus (cf. nos. 89, 93, 94–107). Timothy Aelurus is especially dangerous because he denies Christ's human nature the 'signification as *physis*' (*logos physeos*), which exposes him as a docetist (no. 107). Detailed counter-arguments from scripture and the Fathers are intended to prove this (cf. nos. 108–149). The Emperor states that Severus is wrong when he claims that he cannot discover the formula of the two natures in the Fathers (nos. 151–153); Cyril is indeed a clear witness for it throughout his entire work (nos. 153–168, pp. 32–6).

(c) Conceptual clarifications

The fact that Emperor Justinian adapted well to the state of teaching about the incarnation in 540 in Constantinople emerges from his clear observations (1) on the Chalcedonian usage of christological concepts (nos. 168–186, pp. 36–9), (2) on 'number' in trinitarian and incarnational teaching (nos. 187–191, pp. 39–41), and (3) on the *Trishagion* (nos. 192–198, pp. 41–2). Nevertheless he does not contribute anything of his own which goes beyond what had been achieved by the leading authors of the sixth century (John the Grammarian, then Hypatius, Leontius of Byzantium and Leontius of Jerusalem).[192] He is also dependent on them in judging the historical development, as his interpretation of Cyril shows. This is true at least until 540.

---

192. On the assessment of his florilegia see M. Richard, cited in *CCT* II/1, 62.

(i) Decision for the Chalcedonian two-natures language

From the clear rejection of Severus and his interpretation of the history of concepts there follows for Justinian a firm choice in favour of Chalcedonian language (nos. 168–169, p. 36), which is supported by a new proof from the Fathers. Although the Severans must concede the twofold reality[193] in Christ, divinity and humanity, and that the 'kerygma of the Fathers'[194] speaks clearly of the two natures, they would still refuse to draw from that the linguistic and conceptual consequences. Furthermore *physis*, *ousia*, *morphē* remain for them synonymous with *hypostasis* and *prosopon*, which is said to be the pretext for the errors of all heretics (no. 169, p. 36,28–30). Corresponding to his comments to Patriarch Zoilus, after a brief florilegium[195] the Emperor now suggests a purification of language:

'We have said this to prove that *ousia* and *physis* and *morphē* state the same, but that *ousia* and *hypostasis* are not the same, as the heretics say in their error, and that it is allowed to learn from the *theologia* about the holy Trinity.' This is aimed at the refusal of Severus to apply the Basilian language used of the Trinity also to the *oikonomia*, to the incarnation (no. 175, p. 37). Justinian says that Cyril himself left the way free for this (nos. 176–178, pp. 37–8) and distinguishes in his *Dialogues on the Trinity* (CPG 5216; PG 75, 697) between *ousia* (the *koinon*) and the *hypostasis* (*kath'hekaston*) (no. 178, p. 37).[196] From other Fathers the Emperor then deduces that *prosopon* and *hypostasis* are also used synonymously.[197] In any case, in this manner he settles his own way of speaking, even if he does not give a complete picture of the history of the terms.

(ii) The number 'two' in christology

For the claim that Cyril rejected the formula *mia physis*, the Emperor relies on Cyril's writing *That Christ is one*[198] (no. 185, p. 39). In this, to be sure, the argument is directly against the (alleged) statement of Apollinarius (or rather of some extremists of his party), that the body of Christ is 'consubstantial' with his divinity. Cyril denies this energetically, as well as the Apollinarian justification of it, that is, that it is only in this way that one can conceive that Christ is a single son. He actually reverses the argument of his opponents and says: if there is not another and another (*heteron* and *heteron*) in Christ, how can one

---

193. No. 168, p. 36,26: τῶν κατ'ἀλήθειαν πραγμάτων.

194. *Ibid.*, p. 36,24.

195. The Ps. Athanasian writing *C. Apoll.* II 1, John Chrysostom, Basil, Cyril (*Thesaurus*): nos. 170–174, pp. 36–7.

196. Justinian, however, remains silent about the fact that the passage adduced from Cyril says nothing about adopting this distinction for the teaching about the incarnation.

197. Nos. 178–180, pp. 38–9, with citation from Gregory Nazianzen and Gregory of Nyssa, directed against Apollinarius: nos. 181–183, p. 39.

198. Cyril Alex., *Quod unus sit Christus*: PG 75, 1289BC; Durand, *SC* 97, p. 370,24–30 with n. 1, pp. 370f.

then speak of union, *henosis*, at all? 'In any case not if it is a question of something which is already one numerically; only in the case of two or more things does one speak of union' (no. 185, p. 39). Thus from this text Justinian assumes that Cyril rejected the *mia physis*. To that he adds a reflection on the number two, which was a horror for Severus. The Emperor alludes to him when he speaks of heretics who refuse to apply the number to the united realities (God and human being) in Christ (no. 187, pp. 39–40). He says what a contradiction it is that they still confess that Christ is perfect God and perfect human being. When they refuse to apply the number two to this, they deny the twofold *teleion*. Justinian states that that leads directly to Apollinarius,[199] against whom he is fighting with all his resolve (nos. 189 [with Gregory of Nyssa]–191, pp. 40–1). It is worth noting how he formulates it: 'From what has been said it is clear that where a union results from various realities, the number of what are united is discerned in every respect' (no. 192, p. 41). Because Severus does not consider that, the Emperor says, he applies the Trishagion, which holds for the Trinity, solely to the Son, who then, however, cannot participate in the *doxa* of the Father and the Spirit. This is how Arius and Nestorius talk. Hence Justinian makes himself the defender of the Constantinopolitan understanding of the Trishagion, or the advocate of the number three for the Trinity and of the number two for christology. In doing this he does not ascend to speculative heights, as Leontius of Jerusalem had done. His solution, destined for the monks, can, as it were, provide insight with the use of a calculator.

In eleven anathemas Justinian then summarizes his trinitarian teaching (no. 199, A. 1–3) and his teaching on the incarnation (A. 4–11). What he contributes to the purification of language is the pure adoption of the strict-Chalcedonian tradition. We find no trace of neo-Chalcedonian tendencies. At the end (no. 200, p. 43) there follows the confession of the four synods in a way that could not be expressed more clearly.

2. The dogmatic letter to Patriarch Zoilus of Alexandria (539/540)

Emperor Justinian is certainly more radically seized by the theological tension of the Chalcedonian–Severan altercation about the understanding of Christ in the sixth century than any simple dilettante could succeed in being. The excerpt from his letter to Patriarch Zoilus, which is

---

199. Lietzmann, Frag. 81, cit. no. 188, p. 40.

transmitted in the *acta* of the Council of Constantinople in 680/681,[200]
shows this. Though the question handled there is about one or two
activities in Christ, this letter to Zoilus, at least in terms of content,
is related to further texts which deal with one or two *energeiai* with
regard to Christ's knowledge. With this question a new theme is
broached in the sixth century.

Excursus: *On the question of Christ's knowledge in the sixth century*
In the first place this concerns fragments from a *logos* of the deposed
Patriarch Anthimus, which were cited in *actiones* X and XI at the Third
Council of Constantinople. A further document which has only now
become accessible illustrates this background with special clarity, namely
the large fragments from the *Tomus* of the deposed Alexandrian patriarch
Theodosius (end of 537) to Empress Theodora, which were previously
unpublished.[201] These excerpts are part of a chapter of B. L. Add.
14532 with the title: 'On the teaching of the *Agnoetai*: by Theodosius,
Constantine and Anthimus.'[202]

(a) *The initiative of the deacon Themistius (c. 536–540)*
With the exile of Patriarch Theodosius to Derkos near Constantinople
a discussion that was originally Alexandrian moved to Constantinople.
Apparently the deposed Patriarch Anthimus was also active in it. We
shall present first the texts of Anthimus and Theodosius and analyse their
interpretation of Christ's ignorance. It is easier to proceed from
Anthimus to Theodosius than vice versa, for the latter introduces impor-

---

200. Justinian emp., *Ep. dogmatica ad Zoilum* (CPG 6865): Amelotti-Migliardi Zingale, *Scritti teologici*, 57–63; PG 86, 1145–50.

201. Theodosius Alex., *Tomus ad Theodoram Augustam* (CPG 7133; previously only known from the short Greek citations in Mansi X, 1121B, 1121C; XI, 273,445; F. Diekamp, *DP*, 314, XLII). The new Syriac texts offer in addition other important fragments; they are presented provisionally by A. Van Roey, 'Théodose d'Alexandrie dans les manuscrits syriaques de la British Library', in J. Quaegebeur (ed.), *Studia Paulo Naster oblata, II Orientalia Antiqua = OLA* 13 (Louvain, 1982), 287–99; on the *Tomus ad Theodoram Aug.* see 289–90, no. 4: B. L. Add. 12154, fol. 141V–151R . . . De saint Théodose . . . (fol. 148R,7–148V,25 also in Add. 14541); 298, no. 15: the *Tomus ad Theodoram* was written only after 536 (when Theodosius moved to Constantinople). One may assume that it was already in existence when Justinian wrote his letter to Zoilus. Theodosius was in exile first of all in Derkos, but soon (in 538) in the capital with numerous other anti-Chalcedonians, probably in Theodora's palace. See the evidence in E. Stein, *Histoire du Bas-Empire* II, 385, n. 2. Prof. A. Van Roey kindly placed at my disposal his Latin translation of the fragments, as well as a Latin translation of large parts of B. L. Add. 12155 and a further text from Add. 14532, which will be evaluated here. See now Van Roey-Allen, *OLA* 56, pp. 42–56.

202. A. Van Roey, *art. cit.*, 293: in this the three bishops named take a position on the teaching of Themistius.

tant differentiations which are lacking in the radicalism of Anthimus.

The dispute about the knowledge or ignorance of Christ began in Alexandria with the deacon Themistius, a supporter of Severus and an opponent of Julian of Halicarnassus.[203] Of his own free will or under pressure he came to Constantinople, where a break occurred between the deposed patriarch and the deacon regarding the question of Christ's knowledge.[204] The discussion dragged on into the time of the Chalcedonian Patriarch Eulogius of Alexandria (581–608), who informed Pope Gregory I (d. 604) of it. The main arena for this discussion was thus Constantinople, particularly through the activity of the deposed patriarchs Theodosius and Anthimus, and in addition of the bishop Constantine and the monk Theodore. It is probably to Constantinople that still another witness of the conflict points, namely Ps. Caesarius in his *Erotapokriseis*, which we are able to quote in its new edition.[205] As a Severan and an opponent of Julian of Halicarnassus, Themistius probably only drew the conclusions from Severus' christological anthropology: as the body of Christ was subjected to mortality and corruption, so too was Christ's human spirit finite and, in relation to knowledge, subject to human limits, as for instance John 11,34 and Mark 13,32 showed.

In the minds of the Fathers these texts were dubious, because the Arians had already used them to deduce an argument against the divinity of the Logos. The Nicenes solved the difficulty by ascribing Christ's ignorance to the humanity of Jesus.[206] In this way embarrassing

---

203. Cf. E. Amann, art. 'Thémistius', in *DTC* 15, 219–22. See CPG 7285–92. According to Liberatus, *Brev.* 19: ACO II, 5, p. 134,18-22, he was already a deacon under Patriarch Timothy IV (III) (517–535); it is said that Timothy was the first to whom he presented his ideas on Christ's ignorance of certain things. According to Leontius Schol., *De sectis* (CPG 6823), V, IV-VI: PG 86, 1232, this doctrinal conflict flared up under Patriarch Theodosius (535–566), but only after his translation to Constantinople.

204. Liberatus, *Brev.* 19: ACO II, 5, p. 134,18–22, speaks of the origin of the dispute: Themistius says to Patriarch Timothy IV (III): *si corpus Christi corruptibile est, debemus eum dicere et aliqua ignorasse, sicut ait de Lazaro* (Jn 11,34), *hoc Timotheus negavit dicendum. a cuius communione Themistius desciscens schisma fecit, et ab ipso dicti sunt in Aegypto Themistiani.* Cf. Timothy presb., *De iis qui ad ecclesiam accedunt* (CPG 7016): PG 86, 41B, no. 2: *Agnoitae*; also Sophronius of Jer., *Ep. synod.*: PG 87/3, 3192Cff. On Themistius see as well T. Hermann, 'Monophysitica', *ZNW* 32 (1933), 287–93; Photius, *Bibl. cod.* 108: Henry I, 14; PG 103, 381; cf. E. Schulte, *Die Entwicklung der Lehre vom menschlichen Wissen Christi bis zum Beginne der Scholastik* = FCLDG 12, 2 (Paderborn, 1914), 121–4.

205. See R. Riedinger, *Pseudo-Kaisarios. Die Erotapokriseis* = GCS (Berlin, 1989). I am grateful to the editor for letting me have the galley proofs and his comprehensive *index verborum*.

206. See the witnesses in A. Vacant, art. 'Agnoètes', in *DTC* 1, 589–93; J. Marić, *De Agnoetarum doctrina. Argumentum patristicum pro omniscientia Christi hominis relativa* (Zagreb, 1914). In the appendix 113–20, Marić offers the patristic witnesses to the *Agnoetai* known up to his time.

situations arose only for those Fathers who considered 'ignorance' as 'blameworthy *pathos*' and saw Christ's sinlessness as endangered by it. 'Ignorance' (*agnoia*) was already seen by the ancient Greeks in relation to moral evil, indeed as the font and reason for false moral decisions. Thus with regard to Christ, if ignorance were to be conceded in him, his 'sinlessness' would be undermined.[207]

Let us examine briefly this theme 'ignorance and propensity for sin (*peccabilitas*)' in connection with the *Agnoetai* dispute begun by Themistius. With regard to this we have in B. L. Add. 12155 excerpts from a treatise by the monk Theodore, which was called the *Confutatio brevis* (Ἔλεγχος ὡς ἐν συντόμῳ)[208] and was subdivided into various (perhaps three) tractates (*mīmrē*).[209]

(b) The monk Theodore and his controversy with Themistius

The kernel of the response of the monk Theodore to the individual *audaciae* (according to Van Roey-Allen perhaps ἐπιχειρήματα) consists in his warning to distinguish various degrees of ignorance and corresponding to this various degrees of culpability. In the second *audacia* Themistius had stated the following:

> If every ignorance is culpable and subject to blame and the charge of sin, then each of us should investigate in how many matters and things he finds himself in ignorance, and whether anyone can endure the just judgement of God, after he had found himself to be in ignorance in all these things.[210]

Theodore begins his critique with two issues: (1) Can Themistius at all judge the extent and the peculiarity of his ignorant mistakes? (2) The

---

207. Cf. Leontius Byz., *CNE* III, 32: PG 86, 1373B. The reproach against the Nestorian runs: 'With the darkness of ignorance you cover him [Christ], if he knows nothing, for he is united to the Logos only according to dignity. How can you see him, however, filled with ignorance and not also with sin? Sin stems from ignorance as the river from the source . . . You call him ignorant to such an extent that he did not even once know the tempter who tempted him.' For the other stance see below Leontius Schol., *De sectis*, X, III: PG 86, 1264AB.

208. Theodore monk, *Confutatio brevis* (CPG 7295): the detailed information on sources and references is as follows. A. Van Roey was kind enough to translate lengthy sections of this and to add notes: see now Van Roey-Allen, *Monophysite Texts of the Sixth Century* = OLA 56, pp. 92-102. (Here Theodore names a further title of Themistius, which is not cited in CPG 7285-92, namely an *Apologia pro Theophobio*); see also OLA 56, p. 93. This text is as no. 388 (Theodore's *Confutatio brevis*, with the anathemas of the 'dyophysite synod', that is, of Justinian's edict against the Origenists; see E. Schwartz, ACO III, 213-14; IV, 1, 248, n.) in the long florilegium of B. L. Add. 12155. Cf. W. Wright, *Catalogue* II, 921-55; see CPG 7295, *Nota*, with reference to T. Hermann, art. 'Monophysitica', *ZNW* 32 (1933), 287-93.

209. Cf. Photius, *Bibl. Cod.* 108: PG 103, 381; Henry II, 78-9.

210. See Van Roey-Allen, OLA 56, p. 92,7-11.

concept of 'sin' needs to be differentiated. Themistius always assumes that 'sin' is what deserves *supplicium* (death penalty) and (severe) penalty. It is a severe, actual sin. But 'sin' can also mean that in ignorance one can be 'capable' of sin and thus too deserving of disapprobation (*improbatio*) and blame (*increpatio*). In this sense the teachers said that every ignorance is subject to blame and also to sin. For this extended concept of 'sin' Theodore refers to John Chrysostom.[211] Hence Themistius is said to suffer from a lack of understanding and an inability to distinguish.

Theodore, however, does not want to allow even this potential sinfulness on the basis of ignorance for Christ as a human being. He is 'incapable of evil, that is incapable of sin (*impeccabilis*), as we all confess' (*OLA* 56, p. 93,52–53). For the angels (seraphim) and for many creatures in general it is true that there is a certain lack of wisdom and an *inclinatio ad peccatum*. Theodore cites a certain text of Cyril, which cannot be verified, as well as Basil, *De spiritu sancto*: PG 32, 137B; SC 17bis, 382; but above all he refers to his father Severus, *Contra Felicissimum* (CPG 7032). This text shows that Severus simply refers omniscience and thus absolute sinlessness back to the hypostatic union of the Logos with a body endowed with a rational soul.[212] With regard to the question of Christ's ignorance Theodore clearly distinguishes between 'factual sinlessness' (*impeccantia*) and 'absolute incapability of sinning' (*impeccabilitas*) on account of the hypostatic unity (*OLA* 50, p. 95,102–111). With Cyril, Theodore knows of the fact that Christ *naturaliter ignorat in sua humanitate, sed cognoscit accipiendo*, for he became like us in all things (Heb 2,17). Finally, the 'Father' Theodosius is cited as already being dead.[213] Theodore (*OLA* 56, p. 98,199–215) thus also concedes an *ignorantia* in Christ with reference to Athanasius, *Ep. II ad Serapionem* (PG 26, 621–624), because from it one can conclude:

211. John Chrys., *In illud: Vidi dominum* (CPG 4417), hom. 3: PG 56, 115, where ψόγος (*improbatio, increpatio*) and τιμωρία (*supplicium*) are distinguished.

212. Van Roey-Allen, *OLA* 56, p. 94,91–94: *Corpus sanctum et sine peccato inde ab ipso utero, animatum et rationale, sibi univit Verbum hypostatice et non indigebat dono ut fiat divinior sapientia et gratia. Qui enim sine peccato est non caret sapientia; qui autem caret sapientia etiam peccato subiectus est.* There follow further *testimonia* from Severus, which certainly contain nothing other than the teaching of Cyril of Alexandria, whom he also cites further: the human being Christ is filled with the wisdom and omniscience of the Logos.

213. *Ibid.*, pp. 97,191–98,198: *Ratio substantiae nostrae naturae, ait* [Theodosius], *non possidet ex seipsa intelligentiam rerum futurarum. Et si propter hoc solum scandalisatur aliquis in Christo, dicit sapiens Cyrillus, simul cum hoc et alia reprehenduntur. In hoc. In quonam? In eo quod non ex seipsa humanitas Domini Nostri Christi profert cognitionem rerum magis divinarum et propterea dicitur ignorare.* Van Roey-Allen comment that this text cannot come from Theodosius' *Oratio theologica*, because here there is no trace of the Agnoetic dispute, but it comes perhaps from the *Tomus ad Theodoram*.

See, (Athanasius) calls ignorance (the fact) that (human beings) have (their) knowledge only by receiving and acquiring, and not from themselves. (*OLA* 56, p. 98,219–221)

He concludes:

This valiant one [Themistius] does not know, as usual, that it is not the same to know or not to know, and to have knowledge by receiving or by nature; hence he declares the statements (of Cyril) to be contradictory. (*OLA* 56, p. 102,360–363)

Thus with Cyril and Severus, the Severans have an integrated solution to the Agnoetic question: the humanity of Christ is indeed by nature subjected to ignorance (without sin), but through the hypostatic union there is omniscience and with it impeccability. A 'created grace of Christ', which is granted to his humanity by the Holy Spirit, they do not invoke. It is only Theodore who knows the problem 'ignorance and sin'.

(c) Anthimus and his interpretation of Christ's knowledge

A first fragment contains typical monophysite and monoenergist theses.[214]

We confess the one incarnate nature of the God-Logos, which together with its own flesh is to be adored in worship, in this one incarnate nature of the God-Logos; we do not permit talk of an ignorance of the divinity or (of an ignorance) of his rational and intellectual soul by which that is animated which is assumed from us, is consubstantial with us, a passible body which is united to the God-Logos according to the *hypostasis*. If there is only one *hypostasis*, one nature of the incarnate God-Logos, then without doubt there is also only one will, one activity, one wisdom and one knowledge for both.

The intention of the text is perfectly clear: the vision of the one *physis* and *energeia*, which is already familiar to us, is now extended to the 'one wisdom and one knowledge'. The divine and human knowledge in Christ are equated with regard to scope. Neither in the one nor in the other is there ignorance or not-knowing. In practice this means that there is only *one* knowledge, the divine, which also fills the human spirit of Christ.

The *acta* of the Council of 680/681 produce from the same *logos* of Anthimus a very interesting patristic justification, namely from Cyril's commentary on John, with the depiction and interpretation of the raising of the daughter of Jairus.[215] Christ raised the dead not only by word and command; he also put his flesh into action in doing this. Through

---

214. Anthimus, *Sermo ad Iustinian.* (CPG 7086): Mansi XI, col. 440E–441A.

215. Cyril Alex., *In Ioannis Evangel.* IV: PG 73, 577C3–15. This text is cited twice: Mansi XI, col. 441–442, 517–518.

speech and touch together occurs a single coherent activity: 'vivifying as God through a command effecting everything; he also enlivens, however, by the touch of his hand and shows by this the one activity grown together from both (μίαν τε καὶ συγγενῆ δι'ἀμφοῖν ἐπιδείκνυσι τὴν ἐνέργειαν)'.[216] Anthimus adds his own reflections to this.

> Because we also know that the property of the divine intellectual activity consists in the knowledge of all things, we are taught that there is only one and the same divine activity; how should we also not confess that there is in the one Christ only one and the same knowledge of all things (as we have already said) according to his divinity and according to his humanity?[217]

We shall add yet another fragment from this *logos* to Emperor Justinian, which is contained in B. L. Add. 14532.[218]

> Because we follow the prophetic speech we in no way attribute ignorance to the one Son, our Lord Jesus Christ (composite and indivisible). For to say that the God-Logos, insofar as he is God-Logos, does not know the last day and the (last) hour (cf. Mt 24,36 and Mk 13,32), is full of Arian, or rather Judaic impiety. (To say that he does not know it) in his humanity makes a division of the one Lord into two persons, two Sons, two Christs, two natures and two *hypostaseis*, and into their separate activities and properties and a complete (division). Saint Gregory Nazianzen also taught this in his second speech on the Son, saying: 'Is it not clear for all that he [Christ] as God knows [the day], but says as a human being that he does not know, if one separates the visible from the intelligible.'[219] See how this wise teacher explained the word of the gospel, saying: 'if one separates the visible from the intelligible', and taught us that we can attribute ignorance to him [Christ] when we make use of a division in *theoria* about the one composite Christ and ask about the content of the substance of his animated flesh.
>
> And [Anthimus] a little later: 'For us there is one *hypostasis* and one incarnate nature of the God-Logos, as there is also without doubt only one will. We know too only one activity, and one wisdom, and there is (only) for both one knowledge. Therefore whoever says that he knew as God, but as a human being he did not know, separates in an unconscionable

---

216. It will be seen how important this passage became for Ps. Dionysius the Areopagite and for the *mia-energeia* teaching in general.

217. Mansi XI, col. 441/442C.

218. See Van Roey-Allen, *OLA* 56, p. 65. I am most grateful for being able to use the Latin translation in advance of its publication.

219. Gregory Naz., *Or.* 30 (CPG 3010) (= *Or. theol.* IV), 15: PG 36, 124B; Gallay-Jourjon, *SC* 250, p. 258,14–16; Barbel, 200–1. This same passage from Gregory Nazianzen is also dealt with by Constantine, the bishop of Laodicea, in a *logos prosphonetikos* before Empress Theodora, cf. CPG 7107–10, together with p. 574; but the *logos* just named is not noted. Referring to it Constantine explains to the Empress that in the one Christ one should only distinguish in thought between the knowing divinity and the ignorant humanity. Considered in itself and by itself (its essence) the humanity is said not to have any knowledge of the last day or any divine powers, but certainly has everything in the state of union. Only in *theoria* can one speak of 'asking', 'receiving', 'being anointed with the Holy Spirit', 'having become Lord and Christ' (*quasi tantum naturam carnis animatae in se et separatim considerans*). I have to thank Prof. A. Van Roey for the Latin translation of these fragments from B. L. Add. 14532, fol. 177Vb, of which only the main thoughts can be communicated here. See now Van Roey-Allen, *OLA* 56, pp. 70–1.

way the one indivisible Son into two natures, two *hypostaseis*, just like the impious Theodoret. We believe, however, with God's grace, as we have already said: his divine, rational and intellectual soul, consubstantial with our souls obtained, after its union with God the Word, an existence together with his body, consubstantial with our bodies; immediately with its union to that (body) it had all of his divine activity, wisdom, and omniscience, so that every single knowing is the same for both the God-Logos and the rational and intellectual soul.'

Anthimus thus presents a picture of Christ conceived totally from above. As the order and sole power to raise the dead proceeds from the Logos, mediated by the simultaneous corporal contact, so too the one knowledge, the divine omniscience, comes from the Logos into Christ's humanity.[220] The idea of the 'one activity' (*mia energeia*) is consistently applied to the region of knowledge.

(d) The one activity in Christ and the question of Christ's knowledge in Patriarch Theodosius

In his treatise on Christ's knowledge to Empress Theodora, only just recently researched and edited, Patriarch Theodosius of Alexandria (535–566), who was summoned to Constantinople and deposed by Justinian, produces a much more differentiated interpretation of Christ's knowledge than Anthimus could offer. In it we can see the oldest and most significant treatment of the question in the East. It was certainly composed between 536 and 540.[221] The solution of the question was conditioned by specific options: (1) on the classification of ignorance either under the 'blameless' or the 'not blameless' affections (πάθη διαβλητά, ἀδιάβλητα); (2) on the assumption or non-assumption of an autonomy of Christ's human knowledge, whether occurring autogenically in the human nature or on the presupposition of a 'single activity' (*mia energeia*) from above, which allowed the human knowing in Christ no spontaneity and independence. The Apollinarian nature-unity (Christ = *synthesis in natura et secundum naturam*) now had a concrete effect on the partial region of the *one energeia*, namely knowledge. Whoever followed the line: one nature, one will, one activity, would have to proceed consistently to the μία γνῶσις, the one knowledge. The

---

220. Severus too accepts only the one universal knowledge and the substantial, divine wisdom in Christ; if there is talk of an increase in wisdom and grace (Lk 2,40), then that is only an advance in the 'revelation' of his divinity (*congruenter ostendens divinitatem suam, non autem tanquam adauctam habens sapientiam et gratiam et ex non plenitudine ad plenitudinem deveniens. Quid enim plenius esset quam substantialis Sapientia, ex qua omnis rationalis creatura sapiens efficitur?* Cf. Severus Ant., C. *imp. Gram.* III, 31: CSCO 102 [V], p. 87,3–7).

221. *Tomus ad Theodoram augustam* (CPG 7133), introduction, edition and Latin translation prepared by Van Roey-Allen, *OLA* 56, pp. 16–56.

Chalcedonian-Leonine two natures, two activities demanded in contrast two powers of knowing and two manners of knowing. With their teaching the Chalcedonians were put on the defensive. Theodosius attacked the initiative so vigorously that from the Chalcedonian side only a tentative, partial reply resulted. We will find it in Justinian's letter to Patriarch Zoilus.

The Tomus of Patriarch Theodosius to Empress Theodora

The starting-point of Theodosius' Tomus to Theodora[222] is the truth of Christ's human nature, which is consubstantial with us. As has been customary since Cyril, it is emphasized by the theologians of the mia physis in an almost stereotypical manner that this nature has a rational soul which experiences all the natural, blameless affections (passions), the πάθη ἀδιάβλητα: hunger, thirst, sleep, tiredness, piercing of the body, pains, wounds, death, sadness, anguish and the like. These experiences occur only in the flesh which the Logos allows to undergo suffering willingly from time to time. As the human soul according to its nature is distinguished from the flesh, but still on account of the union considers in 'sympathy' the flesh's experience of pain as happening to itself, so too it is the case with the Logos as far as the experiences of suffering of his humanity are concerned.

In the case of the 'Emmanuel' one must admittedly distinguish three types of this appropriation (appropriatio):

(1) the first manner: the assumption, with the permission of the Logos, of the natural, blameless, true passions which happen to the ensouled flesh;

(2) the second manner: the assumption of our poverty (need, indigentia), as this corresponds to the natural, essential limitedness of human nature; it enables the Emmanuel to request, to receive, to be made holy, to be anointed with the Holy Spirit, to become Lord and Christ, to receive the name above all names, also 'not to know the future'.

Nevertheless the needy soul of Christ receives the divine riches from the very moment of the union, although they would not come to it on the basis of its essence (secundum rationem essentialem et naturalem carnis).

(3) Christ also appropriates our rebellion against God, offence, sin — indeed not real — but because as head of the whole body of the Church he has taken on himself everything that is ours: our sin, our forsakenness.

---

222. We follow the Latin translation of Van Roey-Allen for CPG 7133, OLA 56, pp. 42–56: Wright II, 982–3.

Christ becomes a sinner not by his own decision, but indeed by his becoming a member of sinful humanity.

Theodosius sees in this *second manner* of appropriation the decisive solution to the question. He underpins his interpretation with six Cyrillian citations from works that precede or follow the Council of Ephesus. It is based on the unmingled unity of infinite divinity and of finite, burdened humanity.[223] If one surveys these passages, it turns out that Cyril was ready to concede a genuine appropriation of ignorance in Christ. But then he decided to consider this natural need as only one *de iure*, not as one *de facto*, as real. Fundamentally Christ's human nature was in need of knowledge as a natural necessity. In reality, however, this lack was always already filled, as Cyril states in his commentary on Matthew (on the passage, Mt 24,36: 'no one knows the day or the hour').

> He says that he does not know, not as God; admittedly he was not only the God-Logos, but became and was a human being who does not know the future according to his nature and the measure of humanity, but often receives this from *God's* revelation.[224]

Here Cyril speaks first of all of the possibility that human ignorance in general can be dispelled by divine revelation. All the more has Christ a right to this. This right is given with the *henosis*.

This is also the opinion of Patriarch Theodosius in his assessment of the long fragment from Cyril. Christ appropriated the imperfections of our nature, which it has by reason of the constitution of its essence, and also ignorance of the future. As Logos, however, he has this knowledge and an omniscience (*et omnium [rerum] scientiam habet*). Does the divine knowledge thus simply abolish creaturely ignorance? Can one no longer truly say that Christ also assumed ignorance? For Theodosius it would be an abolition of the economy of salvation to deny the genuine appropriation of the whole complex of imperfections and deficiencies in Christ. But the Patriarch does not advance beyond a *de iure* appropria-

---

223. Cyril Alex., (a) *De sancta trinitate dial.* (CPG 5216) VI: PG 75, 1008D: received sanctification of Christ's humanity; (b) *Quod unus sit Christus* (CPG 5228): PG 75, 1277C; Durand, *SC* 97, 348–9: Christ receives the anointing; (c) *ibid.*: PG 75, 1320C = *SC* 97, 430–1; (d) Isaiah commentary (CPG 5203) on Is 11,2: PG 70, 313BC: Christ as a human being receives the gifts of the spirit of wisdom, not for himself, but for us; (e) *Scholia de incarn. unigen.* (CPG 5225), c. 5: PG 75, 1374BC; ACO I, 5, p. 187,1–10: the Word which is perfect in everything has appropriated human need (*indigentia*); (f) *Comm. in Mt* (CPG 5206): PG 72, 444–5: ignorance of the day of judgement: Cyril concedes that Christ perhaps also appropriated this, which in a natural way he had in his human nature (or must have been able to have had).

224. *OLA* 56, p. 49,254–257; PG 72, 444.

tion.[225] By virtue of this 'ignorance *de iure*' the Emmanuel could say that he does not know the day of judgement, although he knew it by virtue of his divine knowledge.[226]

> Because he, however, was not purely a simple human being like us — although a human being like us, he remained what he was, God — so we do not say that he — not even in his humanity — was robbed of these things: for his animated flesh received through its union with the Logos all divine holiness, efficacy (*efficacitatem*) and also wisdom and omniscience.[227]

Theodosius thus decides for Cyril's solution, that in Christ there existed only an ignorance of his humanity *de iure*:

> The 'Father' (Cyril) shows clearly that the Emmanuel did not have ignorance in reality, not even according to his humanity; only through appropriation did he hide himself in accordance with the economy of salvation . . .[228]

That Cyril in reality does not recognize an ignorant Emmanuel, he states more certainly than any other, when he says in the second book of his *Thesaurus*:

> Christ acts in accordance with the economy of salvation (οἰκονομεῖ), when he says that he does not know the hour, although in reality he does.[229]

From scripture and the Fathers Theodosius wants to prove that Christ, according to all three types of appropriation (here we are highlighting only the second), appropriated our being and lot. In this way he believes he has mastered the question of Christ's humiliation in all its aspects, particularly in relation to the honourable and dishonourable passions and the passions that are worthy or unworthy of God (sins): Christ suffers natural things, because he is in essence a human being; he suffers need, as this pertains to nature; from the outside he also appropriates our sin, by becoming the head of a sinful body (thus not from inside through his own sin).

For the problem of Christ's knowledge Theodosius takes over a method used by the Cyrillians/Severans to solve the question of one nature or two natures. As the Severans want to distinguish the two natures only in *theoria*, so too the assumption of human ignorance is only

---

225. Cf. *ibid.*, p. 50,311-313: *Quemadmodum enim conveniebat naturae humanae et eius rationi substantiali et rationali, in inopia omnium illorum erat etiam Emmanuel.*

226. *Ibid.*, p. 50,313-314: *Ideoque non mentiebatur quando ut homo humiliabat seipsum in ignorantiam futurorum.*

227. *Ibid.*, pp. 50,314-51,319.

228. *Ibid.*

229. Cyril Alex., *Thesaurus* (CPG 5215): PG 75, 377D.

in *theoria*, even if according to a clear entitlement: Christ, viewed in the state of separation, has in his humanity true not-knowing. In the status of the union Theodosius, with reference to the Fathers, does not allow real ignorance. As the separation of divinity and humanity in Christ exists only in *theoria*, so too does the assumption of ignorance. For this reason the Fathers too concede no real ignorance:

> ... Agree therefore with the holy Fathers that the rational soul (of Christ) ... through the union [with the Word] at the same time received his holiness, divine power, wisdom and omniscience.[230]

Theodosius gains a special argument for Christ's omniscience as a human being by classifying knowing among the *activitates*, that is, the *energeiai*. Then, however, it is true for him that in Christ there is only one *physis*, one *hypostasis*, one activity, that is, the fundamental Severan thesis for the one Christ. His concluding judgement shows that he is just reproducing Severus:

> With regard to the activity — for knowledge is an activity and not less the foreknowledge of the future — the holy Fathers have handed on to us that there is only this one (*energeia*), namely the divine, in the composite Christ. It is not in accordance with tradition to say that he [Christ] acts in the one and does not act in the other [N.B. against Leo], knows (in the one and) does not know in the other. For we must confess either (1) that there is both in his humanity and in his divinity a knowledge [proper to each] — which is foolish and ungodly, or (2) that there is only one *divine* knowledge — which is true, correct and has been said by the holy Fathers about the Emmanuel. For this reason no ignorance at all remains in him.[231]

Christ's knowledge thus has a special position. It is classified as 'activity', as *energeia*, and is distinguished from the πάθη, the passions. In the domain of the *energeia* there is for Theodosius not *in alio et in alio* in Christ.[232] Everything is concentrated in the Logos and proceeds from him. Although Theodosius speaks only of Christ's knowledge, the willing of Christ also belongs naturally to the one *energeia*. To the 'one knowledge' there corresponds necessarily the 'one *thelesis*'.[233] There is

---

230. *OLA* 56, p. 54,447–451. Theodosius attempts to collect all opposing statements from individual Fathers. A text from Gregory Naz., *Or. II de Filio*: PG 36 124A, which he quotes, cannot be substantiated here.

231. *OLA* 56, p. 55,479–487.

232. *Ibid.*, pp. 55,497–56,503: *Relate autem ad activitatem divinam nequaquam (possumus dicere 'in alio et in alio'). Non enim idem sapiens est et non sapiens, potens et impotens, bonus et non bonus, vita et non vita, gratia et non gratia, veritas et non veritas — dicit enim de eo, ut dixi: 'Plenus gratia et veritate'* (Jn 1,14) *— nisi quis haec omnia dicere vult de eo ratione differenti humanitatis sicut enim de nobis, separatim considerans ea ex quibus compositus est Christus.*

233. Which is intimated by talk of *potens* = omnipotent.

no room for human freedom, for that would once again be Nestorian separation.

Theodosius applies to the domain of the *energeia* precisely Cyril's and Severus' linguistic rules with regard to *physis*: as one can speak of two natures before the union in *theoria*, and after the union, however, only of one, so too this holds true with regard to Christ's knowledge.[234] It is only in *theoria* that I may speak simultaneously of Christ's omniscience and ignorance, as long as I consider the natures in themselves.

> But when you still say, after thinking of the union, that God the Logos knows the future, but that the rational, intellectual soul which is consubstantial with us and united to him does not perceive it, how do they escape the danger of division and separation? How do they avoid saying that there are two sons and two natures?[235]

The one divine light of omniscience and God's infinite knowledge thus flows into Christ's human soul with the *henosis*, and allows no shadows of the human limitations of knowledge to return to it. This consideration from above is so determined that the human spiritual faculties are not even considered as the organs for executing the divine omniscience. To speak as well of one will in Christ (namely the divine) suggests itself. If this were the case, however, the principle of Christ's redemptive obedience as a human being would be radically placed in jeopardy, even though Theodosius still stresses so often that Christ has a rational soul. All of its possible functions are performed by the Logos. It is for this reason that in 540 monoenergism, as it will be discussed in the seventh century, is already present in all its rigour and is defended expressly.[236] There is no longer talk of the involvement of the human *intellectual faculties*.

According to Theodosius the *actiones* or *activitates* have to be distinguished from the *passiones naturales*. Here he is forced to bring into play the divine and the human natures, each in its own way.

---

234. When for the question of the distinction of a twofold manner of knowing in Christ Theodosius refers to the well-known 'mental or theoretical distinction' in Cyril, he probably has in mind the *Ep. ad Succensum* II: *Ep.* 46, PG 77, 245A. This purely mental distinction in Cyril, however, concerns only the 'two natures', not the two ways of knowing. The application to Christ's knowledge does not occur here.

235. OLA 56, p. 56,515–519.

236. In the fragmentary text of the *Tomus ad Theodoram* one cannot discern whether Christ's human faculty of knowing is still used as *organon* and 'co-moved'. This obscurity continues to exist in all the Severan authors with the exception of John Philoponus of Alexandria (see *JdChr* II/4, 129–31 (T. Hainthaler)).

But in relation to the natural passions (*passiones naturales*) it is permissible to speak of 'in one — in the other'; one and the same is mortal in the humanity and immortal in the divinity; the same is passible in the humanity and impassible in the divinity.[237]

To these *passiones*, which are conceivable only in Christ's humanity as an executive organ, belong hunger, growth, loathing. The divinity is free of these. That means an extraordinarily great deal for the picture of Christ and the interpretation of his redemptive action. In this picture Theodosius cannot grant to Christ's human, intellectual faculties an active rôle, but only a passive, purely instrumental one. All *energeia* and *dynamis* in Christ are from the divine side of Jesus and flow from above down below. In this way the 'unmingled and undivided' of christology in general, even of the non-Chalcedonian type, is endangered and glossed over. In this picture of Christ the divine activity is almost as powerful as in Apollinarianism, even if the human soul is always stressed.

(e) Ps. Caesarius, Erotapokriseis *and the idea of Christ's knowledge*
It is only now that the preconditions have been established for questioning a contemporary of the patriarchs Theodosius and Anthimus about his idea of Christ's knowledge. This is Ps. Caesarius and his *Erotapokriseis*, which, according to its editor and researcher, R. Riedinger, is to be dated shortly before 550.[238] In order to guarantee a higher authority for the work, the compiler, whose mother tongue was not Greek, put it under the name of Gregory Nazianzen's brother, Caesarius (d. 368/369). Of course, the consequence of this was that in particular the authors of the third and fourth century had to be exploited for questions of the sixth century, were the forgery not to be detected immediately.

One of those topical questions from the sixth century which had to be embedded in the older forms of presentation was the problem of

---

237. *OLA* 56, p. 55,493–495.

238. *Pseudo-Kaisarios. Die Erotapokriseis. Erstmals vollständig herausgegeben von R. Riedinger* (Berlin, 1989). For an induction into this work we refer the reader to the introduction, pp. VII–XI, and in addition to the bibliography, XII–XIV. As the most important preliminary study, see *idem, Pseudo-Kaisarios. Überlieferungsgeschichte und Verfasserfrage* (Munich, 1969). The *Erotapokriseis* of Ps. Caesarius are significant because 'they paraphrase extant and lost writings of the Fathers from Clement of Alexandria (around 190) to Proclus of Constantinople (435–436). Thus they enable one to check the original transmission of these texts, and in other cases even to reconstruct lost writings ... The *Erotapokriseis* ... were composed with great probability by a protégé of Empress Theodora (died 548), who could use the rich library of the Sleepless Monks for his paraphrases': R. Riedinger, art. 'Akoimeten', in *TRE* 2, 151–2. How Ps. Caesarius stands with regard to Theodora will no doubt have to be stated more precisely (see below).

Christ's knowledge, which occurs in our context. We can already sur-
mise that here the Arians and their opponents had to emerge as the major
combatants, although it is patent that it is the Agnoetic dispute of the
sixth century which is under discussion. This does not exclude the fact
that the fundamental trinitarian dogma is still stressed strongly. But this
occurs in such a way that one can recognize that the first and second
phases of the Arian conflict are over, and that there exists agreement
about the eternity and truth of Christ's divine sonship, the *homoousios*,
and about the main trinitarian formula of one *physis* and three *hypostases*
(= *prosopa*).[239] There also exists agreement about the fact that the
incarnation which is ascribed to the Logos means no increase or change
to the Trinity (Q. 12). This Trishagion (Q. 13) too does not signify a
problem for the unity of the godhead; because it is sung in the singular
(*hagios* . . .) and not in the plural (*hagioi*) by the angels, it does not express
any polytheism.[240]

The knowledge of Christ

With Question 15 the theme of Christ's knowledge is introduced.[241]
The ignorance of the day and hour of the consummation (Mt 24,36) is
indeed one of the major themes since the discussion with the Arians.
The point of the question is not clearly seen at the beginning: in
Question and Answer 15 everything is related to the inner-divine relation
of Father, Son and Spirit, and the community of *gnosis* is stressed (with
reference to Jn 17,10, that is, the whole community of goods between
Father and Son, which is understood in the trinitarian sense)
(Q. 15,12–15).

Q. 16 poses the insistent question, however, that if everything is common between Father and
Son, even knowledge, then does the commonality also encompass knowledge of the Father's
will? 'Caesarius' is evasive in the counter-question: what is greater — 'day' or 'hour', or the
'Father'? The answer is self-evident and the conclusion unambiguous: whoever knows the greater
cannot be subjected to ignorance with regard to the lesser (Q. 17). Ps. Caesarius thus does not
distinguish between the inner-divine knowledge of Father and Son, and the knowledge of the
Father (or of the day of judgement) by Jesus as a human being.

The Question–Answer 18 on the solution of the well-known difficulty

---

239. This is particularly expressed in Questions 10–13: ed. Riedinger, 17–18.

240. Ps. Caesarius also fights against Sabellianism (Q. 10) and emphasizes the persons very
strongly by the statement that there are three *prosopa* and three *hypostaseis*, linking both terms
in an emphatic manner: *hypostasis enprosopos* and *prosopon enhypostaton*. The word *enhypostatos* is
frequent in Ps. Caesarius, but always has the old meaning of real, actual. See the index in
Riedinger with nine occurrences.

241. *Erotap.* 15: Riedinger, 20.

'the Father is greater than I' (Jn 14,28) also remains in the intra-trinitarian domain. The Father differs from the Son only by being the Father. Everything else is included in the unity of essence. The incorporation of Christ's humanity does not occur.

In reply to Question 20, once again the 'ignorance of the day of judgement' is broached in order to fulfil a promise made earlier to give a more detailed explanation.[242] Once more at the beginning only the intra-trinitarian equality of Father and Son is solidly introduced as an argument against the Son's ignorance of the day of judgement, but then with John 1,14 the Incarnate One is described as incarnate Logos and as speaker of the words of Matthew 24,36.[243] In the whole section the divinity and the equality with God of the Incarnate One is stressed so strongly that only one conclusion remains possible: the ignorance of the day of judgement is conceived as a statement about Christ that is meant 'economically' or 'intellectually' (allegorically) (ὅπερ οἰκονομικῶς καὶ νοητῶς φησιν).[244] In reality, in the Son as Logos there is the same knowledge as in the Father.

The following sentence seems to offer hope for a more adequate solution that does justice to the incarnation: 'there are *two* knowledges; we are taught namely by the scriptures about a twofold knowledge, one according to the *energeia* [activity], the other according to seeing'.[245] However, it is only after a digression that one discovers that by this is meant the reciprocal knowledge before and after sexual union and even this union itself;[246] this is illustrated by Adam and Eve and other biblical persons. The application to Christ is intended to follow from a distinction which has only the number two in common with the biblical example: the Son knows the day and the hour very well, because he indicates their omens and terrors, and through his description of the characteristics he manifests his divine knowledge; but he does not want to answer the corresponding question in more detail, but by stressing

---

242. *Erotap.* 20: Riedinger, pp. 22,1–24,70, where Epiphanius, *Ancoratus*: Holl, pp. 27,14–30,23, is paraphrased. Cf. R. Riedinger, *Pseudo-Kaisarios* (1969), 285–6.

243. In Ps. Caesarius it is striking that the term βροτός for a human being (see Riedinger, *index verborum*), and in addition the birth from Mary is depicted as θεανδρικὴ προέλευσις Q. 20,23). We shall later discuss his relation to Ps. Dionysius the Areopagite.

244. *Erotap.* 20: Riedinger, p. 22,25–26.

245. *Erotap.* 20: Riedinger, p. 23,32–33: δύο δὲ γνώσεις, διττὴν καὶ εἴδησιν ὑπὸ τῆς θείας γραφῆς παιδευόμεθα, τὴν μὲν κατ' ἐνέργειαν, τὴν δὲ κατ' ὄψιν. Here Ps. Caesarius transcribes the *Ancoratus* of Epiphanius: Epiphanius, *Ancor.* 20, 1–10: Holl, 28–9.

246. *Erotap.* 20: Riedinger, pp. 23,48–24,62. Here Epiphanius, *Ancor.*: Holl, p. 29,4–8,13–19, is paraphrased.

his ignorance wants to exhort the believers to prepare for this hour.[247] Any ignorance, be it only that of a day or of an hour, is categorically denied for the creator of the aeons, in whom are all the treasures of knowledge (Col 2,3).

Nevertheless there is in God a distinction in the knowledge between Father and Son which corresponds to the twofold knowledge previously developed: an, as it were, theoretical knowledge of God about the judgement (which the Son also has) and the corresponding *praxis*, that is, the carrying out of the judgement. This 'practical knowledge of the judgement' is thus also for the Son of Man not yet reality; it will become so on the day when he comes again.[248] To this extent there is still an 'experience' which is yet to come.

Refutation of the Agnoetai

Perhaps for the first time in the sixth century we encounter the term *Agnoetai* in Question 30 to Ps. Caesarius.

> Sufficiently instructed about our previous questions, we request still further the statements (*phonas*) of the *Agnoetai* to be refuted; they say namely that the Redeemer does not know the tomb of Lazarus, also does not know about the woman with the flow of blood who seizes the hem (of his garment), and that he was not at all perfect God, for he made advances and increased in wisdom and age as the Gospel says (Lk 2,52; 2,40).[249]

One does not need to be surprised by the emergence of the name *Agnoetai*, for shortly after 536 there occurred in Constantinople the break between Patriarch Theodosius and Themistius, and the formation of a group ('sect') around the deacon began quickly. That it soon received the name *Agnoetai* is only natural and could have been arrived at in the monastery of the Sleepless Monks, where we supposedly find the compiler of the *Erotapokriseis* at work in these years. What Ps. Caesarius offers as an answer,[250] however, reveals no contact with the type of approach which Theodosius and Anthimus attempted to the problem of Christ's knowledge.[251] With regard to the examples of Jesus' ignorance adduced in Question 30, he takes refuge in their classification under 'economical speech', that is, it belongs to the free incarnational adaptation of Jesus to our manner of limitation. Thus in Matthew 16,13 or

247. Here the model is Isidore of Pelus., *Ep.* I, 117.
248. *Erotap.* 21: Riedinger, p. 24,1–14. Cf. Epiphanius, *Ancor.*: Holl, p. 30,1–5,14–15.
249. *Erotap.* 30: Riedinger, p. 30,1–5.
250. *Erotap.* 30: Riedinger, 31–2.
251. This could be an indication that Ps. Caesarius did not belong to the inner circle of Theodora's protégés and is not to be reckoned as a real Severan. He is not initiated into Theodora's 'secrets'.

Luke 2,52.40 no demonstration of real *agnoia* is produced (p. 31,10); rather the equality of the Son with the Father is proven by the scriptures (Jn 11,34). God's questions to the fallen Adam and to Cain (where is your brother Abel?) and the questions of Jesus in Bethany are not an objection to the knowledge of God and of Jesus. These cases do not attest to an *agnoia*, but only an *oikonomia* of God and of Jesus in intercourse with human beings,[252] that is, the tailoring of God's knowledge to our capacity to understand.

How Ps. Caesarius conceives the communication of the fullness of God's knowledge to the human spirit, he does not say. Nevertheless he belongs to the theologians who grant to Christ's soul a function of its own, and explicitly reject the substitution of the human spirit by the 'Logos', understood in an Arian or Apollinarian way.[253] Christ's human soul is necessary as the receptacle of the psychic and psychosomatic sorrowful experiences, which the Arians only all too happily wish to ascribe to the Logos principle as such, in order to show it as created.[254] In fact, in Questions and Answers 23–29 Ps. Caesarius lists numerous psychosomatic activities of Christ which are intended to underpin the reply to the Arians: hunger and thirst, spiritual anguish, bodily sweating caused by anxiety, growth and development. But the compiler is immediately at pains to exclude particularly 'unholy wickedness', the opposite of sinlessness (p. 29,7), and *agnoia*, ignorance (p. 31,10), and to explain the help of the angel after the temptation in the desert (p. 30) and the consolation after the anxiety on the Mount of Olives (p. 29) as not being real need. The taking over of all these passions is explained explicitly as the assumption of ἀδιάβλητα πάθη, as morally unquestionable weaknesses (Q. -A. 24, p. 27), in order to refute the Manichaeans. Hence we also observe from Ps. Caesarius' statements that the Agnoetic question was acute in Constantinople between 536 and 550. Nevertheless his manner of approaching the problem, fearful as he is of yielding too much to the 'humanity', is still different from that of Theodosius and Anthimus. He does not speak of the *mia energeia*, the one flow of activity, which is present in the picture the two deposed patriarchs had of Christ. For this reason we cannot regard Ps. Caesarius simply as a Severan. In him we encounter none of the main formulas of Severus or Theodosius, neither the *mia physis* nor the *mia energeia*.

---

252. *Erotap.* 31: Riedinger, p. 33,5, in general p. 33,4–23.
253. Cf. especially the Questions 25–29: Riedinger, 27–30.
254. Cf. *Erotap.* 28: Riedinger, 28 with reference to Epiphanius, *Ancor.*: Holl, p. 45,14–26.

He is rather a 'late-Henoticist', who avoids both the *mia-physis* formula as well as the *dyo-physeis* formula.[255]

How seductive Theodosius' view was will be evident at the end of the sixth century in the theology of Eulogius of Alexandria (581–608). This patriarch seems to be immediately dependent on the *Tomus* of Theodosius to Theodora. We shall refer to this briefly.

(f) Christ's ignorance in Patriarch Eulogius of Alexandria (580–607)

Although Eulogius is a Chalcedonian, albeit with a neo-Chalcedonian tint,[256] he takes over extensively the teaching and arguments of Theodosius.[257] In an important argument the two theologians are alike: like Theodosius, Eulogius of Alexandria too takes refuge in the purely intellectual consideration of the different states of Christ's human nature, of the real *status unionis* in contrast to the only mental *status separationis*.[258]

> Whoever ascribes ignorance either to his divinity or to his humanity will never escape the crime of certain recklessness. If, as the blessed Cyril teaches, we separate fact from fact in subtle thoughts (*ennoiai*) or in the imagination of the spirit according to the art of *theoria*, then we see the characteristics of each of the two natures, as they are in themselves ... The sign that is proper to the simple and pure humanity is ignorance. In this regard ignorance can be ascribed to Christ's humanity, considered as simple and pure human nature.

When Eulogius refers here to Cyril, without adducing evidence,[259] he has probably copied Theodosius, who indeed with reference to Cyril speaks of Christ's two knowledges 'in thought', but probably means by this only a passage from the second letter to Succensus about the 'mental distinction' of the two 'natures'. The writings of Theodosius were

---

255. Typical in this regard is the *apokrisis* to Question 35: Riedinger, p. 35,24–26: 'on account of the indivisible and inseparable union of the Logos and the flesh and of the *one hypostasis*, which should not be taken apart by any reflection or thought'. Severus would not have neglected to mention as well here the *mia physis* and the *mia energeia*. There seems to be a greater affinity to Ps. Dionysius the Areopagite, as the frequent expression *theandrikos* will show us.

256. Cf. E. Schulte, *op. cit.*, 124–7; C. Moeller, 'Chalcédonisme et néo-chalcédonisme', in *Chalkedon* I, 690–3; S. Helmer, *Der Neuchalkedonismus* (Bonn, 1962), 236–43. See *JdChr* II/4, 66–72 (T. Hainthaler).

257. On his works see CPG 6971–9. We are basing ourselves on Photius, *Bibl. cod.* 230: PG 103, 1080D–1084D; Henry V, 57–60.

258. Photius, *Bibl. cod.* 230: PG 103, 1084B. On Cyril's distinction 'in thought' (ἐν ἐννοίαις) see *Ep. ad Succens.* I: PG 77, 232D–233A; *Ep.* II: PG 77, 245A. See above n. 234.

259. Which E. Schulte, *op. cit.*, 125, also establishes; see *ibid.* on the reference to Gregory Nazianzen, who is also mentioned by Theodosius.

certainly familiar to him, because they were highly esteemed in Alexandria, as Patriarchs Theodore and Damian testify.[260]

Theodosius and Eulogius of Alexandria show us how in the evaluation of ignorance in Christ and its rejection Chalcedonians and non-Chalcedonians can meet.[261] Nevertheless the profound difference in the justification cannot be overlooked. Theodosius argues above all on the basis of the idea of the *one energeia* or from a decided rejection of the two activities in the sense of Leo I. Eulogius, however, is a determined defender of Leo's *Tomus*.[262] If Eulogius nevertheless accepts Christ's omniscience, even with regard to human knowledge, it is because he ascribes an immediate significance to the *henosis* as such, thereby abandoning the *mia-energeia* teaching.

> Christ's humanity too, which has been united to the inaccessible and essential wisdom in one *hypostasis*, cannot be in ignorance about anything either of the present or of the future . . . [cit. Jn 16,15: everything that the Father has is mine], if they do not want in their temerity to ascribe ignorance to the Father himself.[263]

Gregory the Great takes over the teaching of his friend Eulogius, when in 600 an enquiry came from the deacon Anatolius,[264] and confirms

---

260. Damian Alex., *Epistula synodica ad Iacobum Baradaeum* (CPG 7240): Michael Syr., ed. Chabot II, 333; Theodore Alex., *Epistula synodica ad Paulum Antiochenum* (CPG 7236), Chabot, CSCO 103 (V), p. 211,17–22.

261. Eulogius probably also takes over from Theodosius the third mode of appropriation described above, which is present in the incarnation: Christ, as 'head' of the imperfect humanity, appropriates its sin and curse: cf. Theodosius, above, p. 370, with Photius, *Bibl. cod.* 230: PG 103, 1082BC: *Figurate dicitur illum pro nobis peccatum et maledictum factum esse; neque enim fuit quidquam horum. Sed veluti sibi caput vindicat ea quae sunt reliqui corporis, ita Christus ea quae corporis sunt sibi assignat.* Thus we see how Eulogius too strives to distinguish various ways of appropriating the imperfections. Cf. the comments on Theodosius' second mode with PG 103, 1082C: *Secundum rei veritatem . . .*

262. Photius, *Bibl. cod.* 225: PG 103, 940B–949D; Henry IV, 99–108; cf. *cod.* 226: PG 103, 949D–953A; Henry IV, 108–11, comments which are directed particularly against Theodosius.

263. Eulogius, *C. Agnoitas*: Photius, *Bibl. cod.* 230: PG 103, 1081A; Henry V, 57–8. One can discern here the Patriarch's affinity with the Chalcedonian aphthartics, whom Leontius of Byzantium combated. They claim the *aphtharsia* (incorruptibility) for Christ's body before the resurrection purely on the basis of the *henosis*. F. Diekamp, *Analecta Patristica* = OCA 117, 154–60, produces a long fragment from a treatise of archbishop Stephen of Hierapolis against the *Agnoetai* (CPG 7005). The major part of the writing is lost. The bishop's position is summarized at the end as follows: 'No one should ascribe ignorance to Christ's divinity in the Arian manner or to his humanity in the way of Paul [of Samosata] or of Nestorius. As one and the same according to the person and *hypostasis* he has the clear knowledge of this day and of this hour (cf. Mt 24,36; Mk 13,32) and of his holy Father and the life-giving Spirit, with whom he blesses, sanctifies and enlightens every human being who comes into this world . . . (cf. Jn 1,9).' Cf. the following citation from Gregory the Great.

264. Gregory M., *Registrum epistularum* (CPL 1714), X, 21 (to Eulogius, from August 600): Norberg, CCL 140A, pp. 852,20–855,111.

that it stands in agreement with the Latin Fathers, especially with Augustine. Many scriptural passages refer in their statement to Christ's humanity.[265]

But the Only-begotten, who became a human being for our sake, knew in the nature of the humanity the day and the hour of judgement, not on the basis of the human nature, but 'because God became a human being, he knows the day and the hour of judgement by virtue of his divinity'.[266]

Nevertheless, 'whoever is not a Nestorian can in no way be an *Agnoetes*'.[267] For how can one who confesses the incarnate wisdom of God himself say that there is something which the wisdom of God does not know, or that the Word of God created something which he did not know (Jn 1,1)? For the rest Gregory refers to examples in the Old Testament, where there is talk in a human way of God's not knowing (Abraham, Gen 22,12; Adam, Gen 3,9; Cain, Gen 4,9–10).

(g) The attitude of De sectis

De sectis describes the *Agnoetai* as Theodosians.[268] Themistius is not referred to here. It is said that the only thing which separates the *Agnoetai* from the Theodosians is the view of the knowledge of Christ's humanity. After the presentation of a dialogue between the two[269] the author of *De sectis* formulates his own position.

Firstly it is said that one should not investigate this question meticulously. Secondly the synod [= Chalcedon?] composed no teaching about this. Thirdly all the Fathers were of the opinion that Christ did not know,[270] which follows from the fact that he was like us in all things. Moreover the scriptures also report Christ's learning (Lk 2,52), which implies a not-knowing.[271]

---

265. In Mk 13,32 (neither the Son nor the angels knows the day and the hour) it is the Son of Man that is meant, not the Son who is consubstantial with the Father; cf. *ibid.*, p. 853,38–42.

266. *Ibid.*, pp. 853,53–854,58.

267. *Ibid.*, p. 854,76–77.

268. Leontius Schol., *De sectis*, X, III: PG 86, 1261D. Cf. *ibid.*, V, VI: PG 86, 1232D.

269. According to which the *Agnoetai* say: 'Because Christ is like us in all things (κατὰ πάντα ... ἔοικεν ἡμῖν), he did not know.' As a scriptural proof for this ignorance they cite the well-known passages: Mk 13,32; Jn 11,34. The Theodosians say in contrast: Christ said that kat'oikono-mian, so that the disciples would stop asking questions. After the resurrection he no longer said that the Son does not know it.

270. An apposite statement, which is to be understood against the background of the anti-Arian discussion.

271. Leontius Schol., *De sectis*, X, III: PG 86, 1264AB: 'We say, however, that one must not investigate this so precisely. For the synod also did not presumptuously compose any teaching about this. One must only know that many of the Fathers, nearly all, apparently say that he did not know. For if it is said that he is like us in all things and we do not know, it is evident that he too did not know. And the scripture too says that he increased in age and wisdom. Clearly he learned, therefore he did not know.'

It is remarkable that here, after Eulogius, the *Agnoetai* are in fact soberly and clearly justified (the reasoning produced by the *Agnoetai* is almost verbatim the same as *De sectis* gives for the opinion of the Fathers), and Christ's ignorance is declared to be in conformity with the Fathers and the scriptures. *De sectis*, however, also abstains from a speculative proof.

Evaluation

The question about Christ's human knowledge, resulting from the tension between the Severan and the Julianist interpretation of Christ's earthly corporeality, engaged the theologians during several decades of the sixth century. During this time the Severan party was in command. From the very beginning the way in which the question was posed was unsatisfactory and correspondingly so too were the solutions. The Chalcedonian *asynchytos* was almost forgotten in this discussion. Only tentatively does the idea emerge that Christ's human spirit needs the 'revelation' in grace and the communication of divine knowledge, even if the title for this grants him a special position, namely as 'Son' to have every right to the entire 'estate' of the Father. Nevertheless with this claim the receiving vessel remains finite. Here too a place for the *kenosis* must remain secured.

Justinian's letter to Zoilus

To judge from the lemma with which Justinian's letter is cited at the Council of Constantinople (680/681), it is probably the reply to a letter of Patriarch Zoilus. Unfortunately it is known and preserved only in this fragment. The interest of the Council concerned, however, the teaching of the two activities in Christ. It is precisely to this theme that the selected text is geared. It proclaims unreservedly Leo I's teaching of Christ's twofold manner of action, corresponding to the *utraque forma*. In this way Justinian's letter sketches in fact a completely different picture of Christ from that of Theodosius, who was writing at the same time and also in Constantinople.[272] Justinian's document does not give the impression that he already knows about the Patriarch's *Tomus* to Theodora. Nevertheless the Emperor evidently assumes that there were discussions about the *mia energeia* also in Alexandria.

The Emperor establishes his thesis of the twofold activity in Christ

---

272. We follow the text in Amelotti-Migliardi Zingale, *Scritti teologici*, 58–61; Greek in Mansi XI, 429–32; Latin according to J. Merlin, *Concilia generalia* II (Paris, 1524), here: 59–61; another Latin translation according to Hardouin III: *ibid.*, 62–3; cf. Mansi XI, 819–20.

straightforwardly from Cyril, in the same way that Theodosius establishes his conception. The first citation is from Cyril's *Thesaurus*,[273] in which is emphasized the natural distinction between divine and creaturely action, without direct reference to the divine–human activity of Christ. A second Cyrillian text from the *Treatise on right faith* to Emperor Theodosius leads closer to the *mono–dyo-energetic* problem, indeed even to the psychology of Christ. The significance of this text lies in the emphasis on the human, intellectual-psychological activity.[274]

> The whole Word which is from God was united to the entire human nature, as it is in us. For he has not left unconsidered the better in us, the soul, and not only devoted the efforts of his coming to the flesh. For he has used both his own flesh as instrument (*organon*) for the works of the flesh and for the natural weaknesses which have nothing to do with sin, and also the soul (to experience) the human, blameless infirmities. Indeed after a long walk he hungered and he endured fear, sadness, dread of death, and death on the cross. No one forced him to do this; of his own accord he surrendered his own life for us, in order to reign over the living and the dead; the flesh as ransom for the flesh of all, truly a worthy gift; the soul for the souls of all as ransom (*antilytron*) for all . . .

We have here one of the few places in which there is also talk of the spiritual soul as an *organon*. Nevertheless we are still far removed from the problem of Christ's knowledge, as Theodosius treated it. Still it is of significance that Justinian clearly presents by way of summary the teaching of Christ's twofold manner of action, once again with Cyril.

> It is human passion to die; divine activity to become living again; he shows what is discernible from each: that which he is with us and at the same time that which he is beyond us as God.[275]

A clear confession of Chalcedonian teaching follows as conclusion:

> You see how the venerable Father [Cyril] has passed on the [teaching of the] activities of the two natures in the one *hypostasis* or the one person of Christ, our God.[276]

Summary

On the basis of the reputation which Justinian enjoys in the more recent writing on the history of doctrine, the impression made by the imperial documents which we have just analysed is surprising: they contain a pure, strict-Chalcedonian christology, a christology orientated on Leo I. Evidently the Emperor drew hope from the 'conversions' which he

273. Cyril Alex., *Thesaurus* (CPG 5215), ass. 32: PG 75, 453BC; ACO II, 5, p. 147,27–29.
274. Cyril Alex., *Or. ad Theodos. imp. de recta fide* (CPG 5218), 21: PG 76, 1164AB; ACO I, 1, 1, p. 55,14–24.
275. *Ibid.*, 43: PG 76, 1200A; ACO I, 1, 1, p. 72,3–5.
276. Amelotti-Migliardi Zingale, *Scritti teologici*, p. 60, 13–14.

believed he could ascertain in Alexandria to be able to restore unity of faith along this line. His real goal, which he hoped to achieve in his efforts to win the Severans between 532 and 536 and in the two letters addressed to Alexandria, was always the unity of teaching, the true guarantee of the welfare of his reign. On the basis of this intention, in which his whole consciousness of responsibility peaked, is the conclusion of his dogmatic constitution of 536 to be understood, which is considered to be one of the most powerful texts of Byzantine influence on Christian teaching. The unity of faith should be restored by command.

Commanded unity

We forbid, however, all who attempt to rend asunder the catholic Church of God
    whether it be according to the teaching of the heretical Nestorius,
    or according to the tradition of the senseless Eutyches,
    or according to the blasphemy of Severus,
    who thought similar things to them,
    or their followers
to bring sedition into the holy churches and to say anything about the faith. Rather we ordain all these [named] to remain silent, not to summon gatherings around them, to receive no proselytes (accedentes), and not to dare to baptize unlawfully (parabaptizare), or to defile holy communion and to give it to others (of like mind) or to expand the forbidden teachings. Whoever does this either here in this imperial city or in another lays himself open to all danger [penalty]. We also forbid everybody to receive these [named] . . . [277]

---

277. Justinian emp., *Constitutio contra Anthimum, Severum, Petrum et Zooram*: Amelotti-Migliardi Zingale, *Scritti teologici* II, p. 52,23–32 (Greek); p. 53,21–29 (Latin).

CHAPTER THREE

THE TWOFOLD CONDEMNATION OF THE ORIGENISTS

I. EMPEROR JUSTINIAN'S DECREE AGAINST THE ORIGENISTS FROM THE YEAR 543

While the theopaschite formula 'one of the Trinity was crucified' was still being fought about and the struggle to win over or to defend the Severans was in progress, in Palestine a new chance was presenting itself for imperial intervention in theological controversies. These controversies have passed into history under the name 'Origenist disputes of the sixth century'.[278] At first Constantinople remained untouched by these, but then became the place where the decisive battles were fought. This is thus a fresh instance of the removal of doctrinal discussions from the province or the other patriarchates into the capital and into the Emperor's palace.

Let us recall (1) the prehistory (cf. Scythian and Palestinian monks) of the theopaschite question and its conclusion in the imperial city with the participation of the Pope; (2) the negotiations with the Alexandrian and Syrian Severans in the years 532–536 and their condemnation at the Synod of 536, and the subsequent imperial documents; (3) the transfer of the discussion about Christ's knowledge or ignorance from Alexandria (cf. Themistius) to Byzantium as the result of the removal of Patriarch Theodosius to Derkos near Constantinople at imperial decree. The most important document on this issue, which has only just been made accessible by A. Van Roey, was written under the protection of Empress Theodora.[279] Also in all its phases the prehistory of the Origenist controversies under Justinian had taken place away from Constantinople.[280] Only with the so-called 'Synod of the Oak of 403' in the second Origenist dispute (cf. Patriarch Theophilus of Alexandria) were St John Chrysostom and Constantinople drawn very painfully into the affair.[281] During his sojourn in the capital the Alexandrian Patriarch wrote a letter against the Origenists (*hoi ta Origenous phronountes*) in order to justify his action against the four 'Tall Brothers' and their defender, John Chrysostom. Nine fragments

278. Cf. F. Diekamp, *Die origenistischen Streitigkeiten im sechsten Jahrhundert und das fünfte allgemeine Concil* (Münster, 1899), §§ 4–6, 32–66; L. Duchesne, *L'Église au VIᵉ siècle* (Paris, 1925), 156–218; E. Schwartz, 'Zur Kirchenpolitik Justinians' (1940), in *Gesammelte Schriften* IV, 276–320; E. Stein, *Histoire du Bas-Empire* II, 392–5, 654–83; A. Guillaumont, *Les 'Kephalaia Gnostica' d'Évagre le Pontique et l'histoire de l'origénisme chez les Grecs et chez les Syriens* = PatSorb 5 (Paris, 1962), 124–70.

279. See Theodos. Alex., *Tomus ad Theodoram aug.* (CPG 7133): A. Van Roey-P. Allen, *Monophysite Texts of the Sixth Century* = OLA 56, pp. 42–56.

280. See the overview in H. Crouzel, art. 'Origenes', in *LThK* 7 (1962), IV: Origenist. Streitigkeiten, col. 1233–5. On the first Origenist dispute (Methodius of Olympus, Peter I of Alexandria, Eustathius of Antioch), see J. F. Dechow, 'Origen's "Heresy": From Eustathius to Epiphanius', in *Origeniana Quarta* (Innsbruck, 1987), 405–9.

281. Cf. A. Biglmair, art. 'Eichensynode', in *LThK* 3 (1959), 722.

from that letter are preserved in an anti-Origenist florilegium of the second quarter of the sixth century.[282] The eighth fragment is devoted to the idea of the spherical form of the resurrected body, which we still have to discuss. However, even after the activities of Patriarch Theophilus there were still Origenists in Egypt, as the Egyptian *chora* in the middle of the fifth century will show us. From the struggle there with Gnostic, Manichaean and Origenist circles of monks and clerics which took place away from Alexandria, we can only assume that no news of this reached the imperial city,[283] although imperial officials on the Nile were involved in it.

The decisive impulse to involve the imperial authority in the Origenist turmoil came from Palestine — a century after the cessation of the battles in the Upper Egyptian countryside, which had presumably remained hidden from the imperial court.

Emperor Justinian was drawn into the Origenist affair and made the main player by two groups: from the Origenist side as well as from the anti-Origenist side.

1. Origenists in Constantinople

As we have already shown, the theme 'Origenism' became acute with the appearance of the monk father Sabas in the capital in the years 530–532. The *Vita Sabae* reports that the monk father discovered that among his companions Leontius of Byzantium was an Origenist, and as a result of this separated himself from him and left him behind in Constantinople.[284] We do not need to return to the discussion about the peculiarity of Leontius' Origenism.[285] A. Le Boulluec speaks of an 'origénisme politique', a formula which on the one hand places Leontius among the pro-Origenist actors, but on the other does not make him a real representative of Origenist theses and doctrines. According to E. Schwartz, Leontius (after the separation from the archimandrite Sabas) quickly arranged 'to act as the *apocrisiarius* of the monks in Jerusalem and the ἔρημος at the court'.[286] His presence in Constantinople and his

282. It is found in the *Cod. Athous Vatopedinus* 236 (12th century). The fragments of Theophilus are edited by M. Richard, 'Nouveaux Fragments de Théophile d'Alexandrie', in *NAWG.PH* 1975, 57–65 = *Op. Min.* II, no. 39; the fragments 3–11, pp. 61–5.

283. Cf. A. Grillmeier, 'La "Peste d'Origène". Soucis du patriarche d'Alexandrie dus à l'apparition d'origénistes en Haute Égypte (444–451)', in ΑΛΕΞΑΝΔΡΙΝΑ, *Mél. C. Mondésert* (Paris, 1987), 221–37.

284. Cyril Scyth., *Vita Sabae* 73,74: Schwartz, pp. 176,10–20; 179,8–10; Festugière III/2, pp. 105,10–20; 109,9–11.

285. See above, pp. 188–9. The discussion concerns principally the thesis of D. B. Evans, *Leontius of Byzantium. An Origenist Christology*.

286. See the information in E. Schwartz, *Kyrillos von Skythopolis* (1939), 388–92. 'Whoever had bestowed on him [Leontius] the function of an *apocrisiarius* or τοποτηρητής cannot be deduced from the passages cited; there hardly remains any conjecture left other than that the Emperor himself did it' (390–1).

participation in the doctrinal dialogue (532) and in the Synod (536) are already familiar to us. But he is not the leading Palestinian Origenist in the imperial city. Among the eighteen monks who participated in the Synod of 536 were the two real leaders of the movement, who also remained there after the Synod, namely Domitian, *higumenos* of the monastery of Martyrius, and the deacon Theodore Askidas from the New Lavra. In Constantinople itself these two monks, with the support of Leontius, gained in Papas Eusebius (d. 543), the presbyter and cimeliarch of the main church of the imperial city,[287] an influential agent at court, who in 537 successfully recommended them as archbishops of the important metropolitan sees in Ancyra (Domitian) and Caesarea in Cappadocia (Theodore Askidas). Both hardly took care of their episcopal cities, but rather intrigued assiduously with the Emperor on behalf of the Origenists in Palestine.[288] They were able, however, to conceal their own dogmatic standpoint from the ruler.

2. The anti-Origenists and the involvement of the Emperor in the new theological dispute

Given this tactical position, how could the Emperor have taken action *against* Origenism? Would the Emperor have been willing to allow himself to be diverted from his plan for reconciliation based on christology?[289] Here we need to note the following. (1) As will emerge, in the new dispute as far as the *subject-matter* is concerned, there is ultimately one decisive theme, the question of the salvation of Christians and its solution based on the correct understanding of the person of Christ. (2) Also from the *tactical* point of view the Origenist dispute did not signify a diversion from the christological theme; it became rather a prelude to Justinian's final and decisive christological action, namely the Three Chapters dispute and its crowning conclusion, the Council of 553. This is linked particularly to the name of Theodore Askidas.

We are approaching a new phase in the struggle about Chalcedon in

---

287. Cf. *ibid.*, 263, Register s. n.; F. Diekamp, *Die origenistischen Streitigkeiten*, 37.

288. Cyril Scyth., *Vita Sabae* 83: Schwartz, pp. 188,24–189,9; Festugière III/2, 119.

289. On the following see F. Carcione, 'La politica religiosa di Giustiniano nella fase iniziale della "seconda controversia Origenista" (536–543). Un nuovo fallimentare tentativo d'integrazione tra monofisismo e calcedonianesimo alla vigilia della controversia sui Tre Capitoli', *StRiOrCr* 8 (1985), 3–18, in discussion with R. Devreesse (who maintained that this dispute occurred accidentally) and L. Perrone, *op. cit.*, 203–4 (una reazione al predominio eccessivo esercitato per lungo tempo dal problema cristologico).

which, however, the goal should not be lost sight of: to win the Severans back to the unity in faith of the Empire. Theodore Askidas steered the Emperor's enthusiasm for theological action towards the possibility of winning the opponents of Chalcedon for the detested Council by a new interpretation of it, but at the same time he distracted the Emperor from the Origenists. The game the Emperor became involved in was not without its danger. He was ready to concede to the leaders of the Origenists a mediating rôle in the christological dispute,[290] for which they were highly unsuited. That does not mean, however, that there was a 'Chalcedonian Origenism' or that Leontius of Byzantium can be shown to be its main actor.[291]

The immediate prehistory of the Origenist turmoil occurred on Syrian and Palestinian ground, particularly in the monasteries around Jerusalem (and Gaza), as will be shown.[292] It was only through leading anti-Origenists from the Holy Land that Constantinople became the stage of the final battle in the question concerning Origenism. For the course of events there are two reports with differing depictions of what happened: (a) the report of the deacon Liberatus and (b) the report of Cyril of Scythopolis.

(a) The report of the deacon Liberatus[293]

The main rôle is played by the Roman deacon and papal *apocrisiarius*, Pelagius. He appeared in Gaza, where on the instructions of the Emperor he had participated in the investigation of the affair of the Alexandrian patriarch, Paul.[294] On the journey there he met anti-Origenist monks in Jerusalem. These monks brought to the *apocrisiarius* in Gaza a *libellus* (indictment) with extracts from the writings of Origen, and offered to travel with the deacon to Constantinople in order to obtain the condemnation of Origen and the quoted propositions. This initiative was carried out. Pelagius made himself the advocate for the matter with the Emperor. Probably through envy of the powerful favourite, Theodore Askidas, Patriarch Menas (536–552) joined him and supported the petition to Justinian to condemn Origen and the *capita* which had been submitted. The Emperor accepted the idea readily (*facillime*) and immediately ordered the twofold damnation which had been suggested.[295] On imperial orders it was signed by the patriarchs Menas, Zoilus of Alexandria, Ephraem of Antioch and Peter of Jerusalem, and finally by Pope Vigilius in Rome.

---

290. D. B. Evans, *Leontius of Byzantium. An Origenist Christology* (Washington D.C., 1970), 131, succeeded in showing this.

291. See above n. 285; F. Carcione, *art. cit.*, 7; for a critique of D. B. Evans see the detailed reviews of A. de Halleux in *RHE* 66 (1971), 977–85; *Mus* 84 (1971), 553–60.

292. See in *JdChr* II/3 (on Palestine). The Origenism which was certainly also continuing to have an effect in Egypt does not seem to have been considered by the Emperor.

293. Liberatus, *Brev.* 23: ACO II, 5, 138–40; F. Diekamp, *Die origenistischen Streitigkeiten*, pp. 39,26–40,14.

294. See above, p. 356.

295. Liberatus, *Brev.*: ACO II, 5, p. 140,7–8: *iubente eo dictata est in Origenem et illa capitula anathematis damnatio.*

(b) The report of Cyril of Scythopolis[296]

This report contains the following details.

After the Synod of Gaza, Papas Eusebius made his way to Jerusalem. Allegedly he still knew nothing of the Origenist heresy, and thus must first have been won over by Leontius of Byzantium and persuaded to intercede with the Emperor on behalf of the forty monks who had been expelled from the Great Lavra. He compelled the abbot Gelasius either to take the forty expelled monks back again, or to banish as well four decided opponents of the Origenists from the Lavra. The abbot and his anti-Origenist subordinates chose the second alternative and discharged Stephen and Timothy, opponents of the Origenists, and four other monks. However, this turned out to the Origenists' disadvantage. Those who were expelled won over Patriarch Ephraem of Antioch for their cause and showed him the already well-known work of Antipater of Bostra (CPG 6687). At a synod the Patriarch anathematized the Origenist teaching. This had severe repercussions on the Origenists of the New Lavra in Palestine and their leader Nonnus. They forced the Patriarch of Jerusalem, Peter (524–552), to strike Ephraem's name from the diptychs, which again produced great agitation in Jerusalem and the non-Origenist monastic groupings. Patriarch Peter proceeded diplomatically: he asked Sophronius, the abbot of the Theodosius monastery, and Gelasius, the abbot of the Great Lavra, to come to him and requested from them the text of an indictment (libellus) against the Origenists, with the petition not to proceed with the disputed striking of Ephraem's name from the Jerusalem diptychs. The libellus was quickly composed and handed over to the Patriarch. Together with a report of his own about the novelties of the Origenists, the Patriarch sent the list of charges to Emperor Justinian. The result was the imperial edict of 543.

The two reports (of Liberatus and of Cyril of Scythopolis) are different in many points and raise particular questions regarding the course of events:

(1) Liberatus: immediate return of Pelagius to Constantinople after the Synod of Gaza, accompanied by a delegation of monks and the calling in of the Emperor.

(2) Cyril: between Gaza and the journey of the monks there are various events: Papas Eusebius visits Jerusalem; six monks are discharged from the Lavra; they repair to Antioch where a synod is held; the ecclesiastical communion between Antioch and Jerusalem is broken.

But now, however, because we have to place (with A. Jülicher and E. Stein)[297] the Synod of Gaza at the beginning of 540, there is sufficient time for the events in Palestine and Antioch reported by Cyril. Thus the attempt by F. Diekamp[298] to establish a chronology is unnecessary.

3. The imperial decree[299] of 543

It was not complicated for the initiative of the Palestinian anti-Origenists to acquire a hearing before Emperor Justinian, through the offices of the deacon and apocrisiarius Pelagius, not least because of the preparatory

296. Cyril Scyth., Vita Sabae 85: Schwartz, 191–2; Festugière, III/2, 121–2.

297. E. Stein, Histoire du Bas-Empire II, 391–4.

298. F. Diekamp, Die origenistischen Streitigkeiten, 41–6 recommended the report of Cyril of Scythopolis as the starting-point, and in improving the old dating by A. v. Gutschmid established the following: the Synod of Gaza at Easter 542, the Synod of Antioch for the summer of 542, the breaking-off of communion between Jerusalem and Antioch as well as the dispatch of the anti-Origenist writs to Constantinople in late autumn 542, Justinian's edict in January 543.

299. Justinian emp., Edictum c. Origenem (CPG 6880): ACO III, 189–214; Amelotti-Migliardi Zingale, Scritti teologici, 68–118 (Greek); 69–119 (Latin); this edition forms the basis for our comments.

work done in Palestine.[300] According to F. Diekamp, the enthusiasm of
the monks led to one of the 'most important documents of Justinian's
religious politics', which was 'at the same time a faithful expression
of the views and convictions dominant among the anti-Origenists'.[301]
Nevertheless we should not expect too much from this document. The
reproaches raised against 'Origen' are already hackneyed and allow little
to be detected immediately of the more profound religious significance
of the controversy, either among the Origenists or among the anti-
Origenists. Only a more intense study of the background could lead to
one's sensing the depth and the seriousness of the internal discussion
of 'Origen' in the monastic circles around Jerusalem and Gaza. This is
true at least for the edict of 543, which remains caught almost completely
in the tumultuous Origenist debate before and after 400. Admittedly
names like Stephen Bar Sudaili from Syria, who emerged in Palestine
in 540, or like Evagrius and his 'Origenism' which came into view
in 533, or the crossing of Origenism, Gnosticism, Marcionism and
Manichaeism in Upper Egypt in the middle of the fifth century, are
smoke signals witnessing to a smoldering subterranean fire, which
threatened the ascetical world of the Near East for almost two centuries.
We shall attempt first of all to gather from the imperial edict the
themes of the accusations raised against the Origenists and to establish
their content. Our real task consists in demarcating the peculiarity of
the Origenism condemned in the decree of 543 within the history
of doctrine.

(a) On interpretation or method

(i) In making a judgement about the reports on the Origenists, the
heresiological principles of the polemicists concerned must be noted
(Methodius of Olympus, Jerome, Epiphanius, Theophilus of Alexandria
for the fourth and fifth centuries; Emperor Justinian and the reports of
the monks for the sixth century).[302]

300. This does not mean that Justinian simply took over the *libellus* of the monks.

301. F. Diekamp, *op. cit.*, 46.

302. On the problem of heretics in Justinian, one must distinguish between the heresies
condemned in the *Codex Iustinianus* and the imperial theological sources. In comparison to the
latter, the former bear witness to a less assured theological judgement, because no theologians
participated in the formulation of the *Cod. Iust.* Cf. on the *Cod. Iust.*: A. Berger, 'La concezione
di eretico nelle fonti giustinianee', in *Atti della Acc. Naz. dei Lincei 352* (Rome, 1955), 353–68.
Berger treats the difference of the catalogue of heretics in the *Cod. Theod.* in comparison to the
Cod. Iust. He established that in the *Cod. Iust.* the concept of heretic was defined independently
of the Church for the domain of imperial law, for use by state authorities (365). The 'definitions'
of 'heretics in general' and the individual heresies in the *Cod. Iust.* are, according to Berger, so

(ii) The attempt must be made to distinguish between 'Origenian', that is, what belongs to the historical Origen, and 'Origenist', that is, the extension and further interpretation of approaches offered by the historical Origen.[303]

More and more, however, it is being recognized that the 'Origenist' problem cannot be explained on the basis of purely patristic sources or official imperial documents pertaining to ecclesiastical matters, but must also be researched from the viewpoint of the history of religions. These investigations are extraordinarily demanding. We shall attempt to close to some extent the gaps that exist by giving references to the corresponding areas of research.[304]

(b) Justinian's picture of the Origenist heresy

At the beginning of the decree of 543 Origen is seen as being in absolute opposition to God. As is also customary with other heretics, he has mixed with correct teaching some of his otherwise godless writings. But this is not his property, but the possession of the holy Church of God.[305] The Emperor places the *dogmata* of Origen beside the 'pagan [Platonic], Arian and Manichaean errors'.[306] Such general classifications

different that one can hardly understand 'come gli organi esecutivi dello Stato potessero liberarsi dall'imbarazzo creato da un tale stato di cose' (356). With Biondi, Berger stresses the necessity of the collaboration of law-givers and theologians — a collaboration which more or less existed for the imperial edicts.

303. On judging the 'heresy' of Origen see H.-J. Vogt, 'Warum wurde Origenes zum Häretiker erklärt?', in *Origeniana Quarta* (Innsbruck, 1987), 78–99, with Seminar I: texts for the main paper (Vogt) 100–11; with Seminar II (J. F. Dechow): 'The Heresy Charges Against Origen', *ibid.*, 112–22. Important material for clarifying the problem 'Origen — Origenists' is found in A. Le Boulluec, 'Controverses au sujet de la doctrine d'Origène sur l'âme du Christ', *ibid.*, 223–37, with further literature; M. Harl, 'La préexistence des âmes dans l'oeuvre d'Origène', *ibid.*, 238–58; U. Bianchi, 'Origen's Treatment of the Soul and the Debate over Metensomatosis', *ibid.*, 270–81; H. Crouzel, 'L'Apocatastase chez Origène', *ibid.*, 282–90; G. Dorival, 'Origène et la résurrection de la chair', *ibid.*, 291–321. These are the important investigations into the major charges raised by Justinian against 'Origen'.

304. We refer first of all to G. Widengren, 'Researches in Syrian Mysticism. Mystical Experiences and Spiritual Exercises', *Numen* 8 (1961), 161–98; J. W. Sedlar, *India and the Greek World. A Study in the Transmission of Culture* (Totowa, New Jersey, 1980); H. Waldmann, 'Ansätze zur Integration östlichen Gedankengutes bei Origenes (Mazdaismus, Zurvanismus)', in *Origeniana Quarta* (Innsbruck, 1987), 459–64. There are further references in *JdChr* II/3 (on Syria).

305. Justinian emp., *Ed. c. Origen.*: Amelotti-Migliardi Zingale, *Scritti teologici*, p. 73,1–3. In the continuation of the text the 'pagan [Platonic]', the Manichaean and Arian elements in Origen are stressed in the sharpest possible words.

306. *Ibid.*, 68–9: *Origenem eiusque dogmata, paganorum et Arianorum et Manichaeorum erroribus affinia asserere.*

can be greatly misused heresiologically. Certainly there can be in them many a valid reference, but to prove them is extraordinarily difficult.[307]

The particular errors of 'Origen'

(i) Errors in the theologia

The Emperor begins with Origen's 'blasphemies' against the holy and consubstantial Trinity. He is said to teach a strict subordinationism in the Trinity; the Son cannot see the Father, and the Holy Spirit cannot see the Son; indeed Son and Spirit are creatures. The divine power is limited; all genera and species are equally eternal with God.[308] What the Alexandrian is reproached with here is to be found in Athanasius under the title 'blasphemies of Arius', precisely the denial of the homoousios, in addition to the claim that the Father is invisible to the Son.[309] As a charge against Origen the trinitarian errors are noted in Jerome's letter to Avitus.[310]

(ii) Errors in the doctrines of creation and salvation (oikonomia)

(1) The pre-existence of souls and their fall

The longest part of the imperial edict is devoted to the explanation and refutation of the Origenist teaching of the pre-temporal creation of all human souls, of their fall, and also of the teaching of reincarnation.[311] To this is also joined a brief reference to the plurality of worlds which God created before ours and will create after ours.[312] Shenute will show us what a large rôle this latter idea played among the monks in Upper

---

307. G. S. Gasparro, 'Il problema delle citazioni del Peri Archon nella Lettera a Mena di Giustiniano', in *Origeniana Quarta* (Innsbruck, 1987), 54–76, provides a first-rate aid for interpreting Justinian's decree. In general the four volumes of the *Origeniana* (1975, 1980, 1985, 1987) published to date contribute a great deal to our topic.

308. Justinian emp., *Ed. c. Origen.*: Amelotti-Migliardi Zingale, *Scritti teologici*, p. 71,1–17. The sole source from the fourth century for this statement of God's limited power is Theophilus of Alexandria's Easter Letter from 402 (Jerome, *Ep.* 98,17,18; *Ep.* 124,2). Cf. G. S. Gasparro, *art. cit.*, 61–3, with n. 79 and 80.

309. Cf. *JdChr* I³, 372–3.

310. Jerome, *Ep.* 124 *ad Avitum*, 2: CSEL 56, pp. 97,6–98,6; J. Labourt, *Saint Jérôme Lettres* (Paris, 1961), VII, pp. 96–7: Christ as Son is not generated, but created; the invisibility of the Father for the Son; cf. Görgemanns-Karpp, *Origenes Vier Bücher von den Prinzipien*, 89, n. 9, on the various texts in Rufinus, Jerome and Epiphanius, *Haer.* 64,8; cf. G. S. Gasparro, *art. cit.*, 63–5; these charges of Jerome are here correlated with fragments I and IV–VIII of Justinian's florilegium from the *PA*. Cf. Amelotti-Migliardi Zingale, *Scritti teologici*, 107, 109–111.

311. Justinian emp., *Ed. c. Origen.*: Amelotti-Migliardi Zingale, *op. cit.*, pp. 71,16–97,12.

312. *Ibid.*, p. 71,21–26.

Egypt at his time.[313] The Emperor has only a brief comment on this:

> We regard these (blasphemies) forbidden for all Christians; we have patent proofs for this ungodliness and consider it superfluous to deem it worthy of refutation.[314]

As a side-issue we also bracket the teaching of the ensoulment of the celestial bodies, the sun, the moon and the stars.[315] In contrast the teaching of the creation of human souls in their pre-existence, of their fall and of their enclosure in bodies is treated in detail. Originally the souls were created as pure intelligences (*noes, mentes*) and as powers (*dynameis, virtutes*) and destined for the vision of God. Through surfeit (*koros*) of or revulsion to this vision they turned to wickedness, and grew cold (*psychos*, cold) in the love of God, and for that reason received the name *psychai* (actually 'those grown cold') and as a punishment were banished into bodies.[316] According to Justinian this is based on a false interpretation of the creation of human beings in the image and likeness of God (Gen 1,26). Origen can relate that scriptural text only to the creation of the body, because the souls were already regarded as pre-existent. Regarding the pre-existent souls, their orders (*taxis*), their activity before the fall, their faculty of memory concerning the earlier condition, the possibility of sin being committed before they are included in a body, the significance of staying in the body, Justinian poses similar questions to those which the archimandrite Shenute posed a good century before in his instruction to the monks and clergy of Upper Egypt.[317] Emperor Justinian traces the teaching of the pre-existence of souls and their fall back to Manes.

> For he [Origen] was educated in the mythologies of the Hellenes and was interested in spreading them; he pretended to explain the divine scriptures, but in this manner mixed his own pernicious teaching in the documents of the holy scriptures; he introduced the pagan

---

313. In *JdChr* II/4, 193-7, we go into this teaching in more detail.

314. Justinian emp., *Ed. c. Origen.*: p. 71,24-26.

315. *Ibid.*, p. 97,13-16; on this G. S. Gasparro, *art. cit.* 65-6, with reference to the fragments XXI and XXII from the *PA*, which are found in Jerome, *Ep.* 124,4,9: CSEL 56, 99-100, 107-111. Here (66) too is the evidence for the spread this idea in the polemic against Origen (to which Pamphilus, Theophilus of Alexandria, Epiphanius and Jerome testify). But perhaps the above reproaches will be clarified again on the basis of the text of Shenute against the Origenists, as we still have to point out (in Vol. II/4); see T. Orlandi (ed.), *Shenute, Contra Origenistas. Testo copto con introduzione e traduzione* (Rome, 1985), §§ 0385-7.

316. *Ibid.*, pp. 73,11-75,1.

317. Cf. *ibid.*, pp. 75,10-26; 79,15-29 to be compared with Shenute, *Contra Origenistas*: ed. T. Orlandi, especially §§ 0333-0344, 0357. Because Shenute's instruction places these problems in a broader context and treats them in a more original way than Justinian, we shall discuss them in detail in the context of Shenute's fight against the Origenists and Gnostics (*JdChr* II/4, 193-213).

and Manichaean error and the Arian madness, so that he could give to them what the holy scriptures could not understand precisely. (p. 73,4–8)[318]

It is significant that the Emperor joins to the criticism of Origen's protology and anthropology an explanation of the Church's teaching on human beings and lets this flow into a brief christological and soteriological interpretation of history.[319]

But if the souls pre-existed and, according to Origen's myths, were in another order (*taxei*), why then did God form only Adam? For instance at the same time had only Adam's soul sinned and therefore only one body was formed by God? If there were other souls before that, it would have been necessary at the same time to make other bodies to receive these souls. How could a sinful soul, according to their theses (*logous*), be sent for punishment into a body and nevertheless be placed by God in the garden of desire? For if it were exiled into the body to undergo punishment, then it would not have been transferred into that paradise, but to a place of punishment.

But God so loved human beings, whom he created after all creatures, that God in his goodness after the transgression of the command given to them and the consequent expulsion from paradise (when the human race increased and the volume of sin became full, because the thoughts of human beings were inclined in wicked desire towards evil) did not abandon his image, but rather, according to the revelation of the scriptures, in various ways reproached and cultivated it. As we after a severe illness require greater care, the only-begotten Logos of God, the one, that is, one person of the holy Trinity, on account of his fondness for human beings became a human being; but in doing that he remained God. His divine essence was not changed into the human, nor the human into the divine; he is discernible in each of the two natures, unmingled and undivided ... Although human nature from the beginning was divested of paradise on account of disobedience ... the only-begotten Son of God inseparably united our nature according to the *hypostasis* in the womb of the holy and glorious *theotokos* and perpetual virgin Mary and thus bestowed on us a great grace and gave us the kingdom of heaven.

The question that interests us in particular, whether Justinian also deals with Origen's teaching of the pre-existent soul of Christ, is touched upon only briefly. Apparently for the Emperor it is already refuted by his general anthropology.[320] However, he comments briefly:

But because Origen added as well to the other blasphemies that the soul of the Lord was pre-existent and the God-Logos was united to it before he came from the virgin; St Athanasius himself thus removed this madness in his letter to Epictetus when he says: 'Rightly they

---

318. On the idea of *koros* see M. Harl, 'Recherches sur l'origénisme d'Origène: la "satiété (κόρος) de la contemplation comme motif de la chute des âmes', in F. L. Cross (ed.), StudPat 8 (Berlin, 1966), 373–405. This motif is found in the PA as elsewhere in the polemic of the fourth century. Cf. G. S. Gasparro, art. cit., 61; Justinian emp., Ed. c. Origen.: p. 73,13–15 and anathema I, ibid., 117. We refer here again to Shenute, Contra Origenistas: ed. T. Orlandi, esp. §§ 0333ss., 27ff. On the doctrine of the relationship of body and soul among the Manichaeans see J. W. Sedlar, India and the Greek World (Totowa, New Jersey, 1980), 214–19.

319. Justinian emp., Ed. c. Origen.: pp. 79,22–81,12 (Latin). Cf. the brief repeated summary, p. 83,4–14.

320. Ibid., pp. 87,30–89,6.

will all condemn themselves who believe that there was before Mary the flesh (born) from her, and that the God-Logos had before it [the flesh] a human soul and before the advent [in the incarnation] was always in it.'[321]

This brevity is also explained by the fact that in the submission presented by the Palestinians to Justinian the typically Evagrian intensification of the Origenist teaching on the pre-existence of Christ's soul was not yet a target.[322]

(2) The Origenists and the migration of souls

To the teaching on the pre-existence of souls is connected the other on the migration of souls. Justinian's edict contains as fragment XV the following text from *PA*.

If [on the contrary] the soul descends from the good and leans towards wickedness and embraces this more and more, then if it does not change its ways it becomes brutish through irrationality and animalistic through malice. [And shortly after that:] and it chooses to become an animal and to assume, may I say, a life in water and perhaps (τάχα!) it slips (ἐνδύεται) into the body of this or that irrational animal to the extent that the advancing fall into wickedness deserves.[323]

This text contains many difficult problems which have been discussed many times.[324] Within the framework of a history of christology we see it as our task to give a brief bibliographical report on the history of the problem and to refer here already to the fact that Shenute's instruction against the Origenists in Upper Egypt must now be taken as a text for comparison.

321. Cf. Athanas. Alex., *Ep. ad Epict.* (CPG 2095), 8: PG 26, 1064A14–B2; G. Ludwig, *Epistula ad Epictetum* (Jena, 1911), p. 13,7–10. Cf. R. W. Thomson, *Athanasiana Syriaca Part I*: CSCO 258 (V), p. 61,18–21: 'So when one understands the meaning of this saying, he rightly condemns those who thought that what was taken from Mary existed before her, and that the Word had a human soul before her and was always in her before his coming.' On the Syriac translation see R. Y. Ebied/L. R. Wickham, 'A Note on the Syriac Version of Athanasius' *Ad Epictetum* in MS. B. M. Add. 14557', *JTS* 23 (1972), 144–54 (in debate with J. Lebon, 'Altération doctrinale de la Lettre à Épictète de saint Athanase', *RHE* 31 [1935], 713–61).

322. On the teaching about Christ's soul see A. Le Boulluec, 'Controverses au sujet de la doctrine d'Origène sur l'âme du Christ', in *Origeniana Quarta*, 223–37. In n. 1, p. 233, the author refers to further studies: J. L. Papagno, 'Flp 2,6–11 en la cristología y soteriología de Origenes', *Burg* 17 (1976), 395–429; M.-J. Pierre, 'L'âme dans l'anthropologie d'Origène', *POC* 34 (1984), 21–65; R. Williams, 'Origen on the Soul of Jesus', in R. Hanson/H. Crouzel (ed.), *Origeniana Tertia* (Rome, 1985), 131–7.

323. Justinian emp., *Ed. c. Origen.*: 112–13 (Greek/Latin). Cf. Origen, *De principiis* (CPG 1482) I, 8, 4: Görgemanns-Karpp, *Origenes Vier Bücher von den Prinzipien*, 262–5.

324. G. Dorival, 'Origène a-t-il enseigné la transmigration des âmes dans les corps d'animaux? (A propos de P Arch I, 8, 4)', in H. Crouzel/A. Quacquarelli (ed.), *Origeniana Secunda* (Rome, 1980), 11–32, gives an excellent treatment of this question.

Metempsychosis teaching in Origen?

The accusation that Origen taught the migration of souls existed as early as the beginning of the fourth century.[325] The point at issue is in particular the text and interpretation of *PA* I,8,4. Is the translation of Rufinus a faithful rendition of Origen's thought? Various solutions are offered.

First thesis: In *PA* I,8,4 Origen either explicitly dismissed metempsychosis or at least rejected it with regard to the migration of souls into the bodies of animals. Rufinus renders *PA* I,8,4 faithfully.[326]

Second thesis: The abbreviated translation of Rufinus falsifies Origen's thought:

(a) with reference to Justinian: Origen considers metempsychosis as a hypothesis, which Justinian attests with his *tacha* (perhaps). To this extent there is not a total falsification in Rufinus, but certainly a partial one through the erroneous attribution of scriptural arguments, which belong to Origen, to other authors (*quidam*).[327]

(b) with reference to Jerome:

(i) *Ep.* 124,4: CSEL 56, p. 100,19–24: summary of *PA* I,8,4;

(ii) *Ep.* 124,14: *ibid.*, p. 116,6–17: citation of a text from *PA* IV,4,8. In *PA* I,8,4 Rufinus completely falsifies Origen's thought: Origen is said to have presented the migration of souls into the bodies of animals as certain teaching. Justinian's fragment is to be interpreted wholly on the basis of metempsychosis. There are still further witnesses who render the true thought of Origen.[328] Thus it would be possible to reconstruct Origen's text approximately.[329]

According to G. Dorival, however, it is impossible to reconstruct Origen's original text *PA* I,8,4.[330] The only thing which can be accepted after evaluating all of the sources[331] is that, at the time when Origen wrote his *PA*, Alexandrian Christians accepted the banishment of souls into the bodies of animals. Origen himself in his late works, the writings against Celsus (249), criticized in harsh words the metempsychosis into the bodies of animals and rejected it as Platonic and Pythagorean teaching.[332] Now, however, in the development of his teaching between his first work *PA*, which is transmitted as a

---

325. Pamphilus, *Apol. Orig.* 5: PG 17, 579. In this question the migration of souls from human body to human body (also from man to woman) has to be distinguished from the migration of souls from human bodies to animal bodies.

326. Thus with variants: M. J. Denis, H. Crouzel, W. Theiler, M. Simonetti. The fragments in Jerome and Justinian create difficulties.

327. Thus F. H. Kettler, *Der ursprüngliche Sinn der Dogmatik des Origenes* (Berlin, 1966), 14–21.

328. Namely Gregory Nyssa, *Dial. de anima et resurr.* (CPG 3149): PG 46, 112–113; in Görgemanns-Karpp, *op. cit.*, 282–3; and *De opif. hom.* (CPG 3154), 28: PG 44, 229–232; in Görgemanns-Karpp, *op. cit.*, 280–3.

329. Thus P. Koetschau, according to G. Dorival, *art. cit.*, 16–17 with n. 23. G. Dorival suspects that F. H. Kettler also inclines towards this viewpoint.

330. G. Dorival, *art. cit.*, 17–19. The attempt of Görgemanns-Karpp is also not recognized.

331. In G. Dorival, *art. cit.*, 23–8.

332. Origen, *C. Cels.* III, 75; IV, 17; IV, 83; V, 49; VIII, 30; cited in G. Dorival, *art. cit.*, 29.

whole, and his last work, *Contra Celsum*, the Alexandrian shows 'une remarquable stabilité de la pensée'.[333] Thus with this fundamental position there is scarcely a chance for the teaching of the banishment of human souls into the bodies of animals.[334]

Because Justinian indeed sees Origen's teaching in connection with pagan philosophy on the one hand and with Manichaeism on the other, we need to refer to the state of research.

After some oscillation among Platonists of the second century, for instance Albinos and perhaps also Plotinus, on questions of the banishment of souls into the bodies of animals,[335] later Platonists took an increasingly clearer stance against it. In Porphyry it is completely excluded, as the teaching about souls in his *Symmikta Zetemata* shows in particular.[336]

(3) A special eschatological opinion: the spherical form of the resurrected body

It is a question of the 'rather singular idea of the spherical bodies of the resurrected' (*nozione assai singolare dei corpi sferici dei resuscitati*),[337] which is attributed to Origen himself.[338] This teaching is not found in the works of the Alexandrian which are known to us. It appears to be the result of speculations which started from the concept of 'form', *eidos*, and confused it with that of 'appearance', 'figure', *schema*, 'in the banal sense of the visible, physical body'.[339] This 'interpretation' (lecture) of

---

333. G. Dorival, *art. cit.*, 4.2, 30. The only development which occurred for Origen between Alexandria and Caesarea in Palestine was 'une évolution de la situation concrète d'Origène' (31). In Alexandria popular circles held the doctrine of the migration of souls into the bodies of animals; in Caesarea it was taught at the most in philosophical or heretical circles.

334. Cf. also W. A. Bienert, 'Die älteste Apologie für Origenes?', in *Origeniana Quarta* (Innsbruck, 1987), 123–7.

335. Cf. H. Dörrie, 'Kontroversen um die Seelenwanderung im kaiserzeitlichen Platonismus', *Hermes* 85 (1957), 414–35 = idem, *Platonica Minora* (Munich, 1976), 420–40.

336. Cf. H. Dörrie, *Porphyrios' 'Symmikta Zetemata', Zetemata* 20 (Munich, 1959) and above, pp. 200–12 (on Leontius of Byzantium); G. Dorival, 'La transmigration des âmes', in *Origeniana Secunda* (Rome, 1980), 31: 'A l'époque d'Origène, la doctrine de la transmigration dans les corps d'animaux n'a plus bonne presse dans les milieux philosophiques qui ont tout particulièrement contribué à former Origène.' Interesting, wide-ranging perspectives in the history of religion and philosophy are certainly opened up by J. W. Sedlar, *India and the Greek World* (Totowa, New Jersey, 1980), 22–32: V. Soul-Wandering. He concludes (p. 32): 'Clearly the Greeks themselves were puzzled as to where the metempsychosis-idea came from: they agreed only that it was an idea somehow alien to their own mainline tradition . . .'

337. G. S. Gasparro, *art. cit.*, 61.

338. Justinian emp., *Ed. c. Origen.*: p. 99,7–35 and in anathema V, p. 117.

339. See G. Dorival, 'Origène et la résurrection de la chair', in *Origeniana Quarta*, 291–321; esp. III., 315–19. On 315–16 Dorival has important documentation for this, namely fragment 8 from the letter of Patriarch Theophilus of Alexandria against the Origenists (anno 403), which M. Richard discovered: 'Nouveaux fragments de Théophile d'Alexandrie', *Op. Min.* II, no. 39, pp. 63–4. The entry in CPG 2612 has to be expanded. Cf. G. S. Gasparro, *art. cit.*, 61 with nn. 70–73; 74–75 with reference to G. Dorival, H. Crouzel and A.-J. Festugière; the last mentioned wanted to trace the teaching of the spherical form of the resurrected body back to a gross error

Origen by the Origenists is said to be favoured by two elements: (i) by his reduction in the resurrected of the typical composition of the human body (there are no members, no face, no entrails, etc.); (ii) by the fact that Origen's teaching of the 'corporeal form' was difficult to understand, and, in addition, from the time of Methodius, Origenists and anti-Origenists had associated with *eidos* the notion of the external form, of the physical appearance.

Now an external form is necessarily defined by geometrical data in space. Moreover, the sphere is the most perfect form in text-book Platonism, as is also the form of the corporeal vehicle of the soul after death; on the other side, the resurrected are compared (but not put on a par) with the resplendent celestial bodies which are spherical (*PA* III,6,4). It is not surprising, consequently, if the notion of a resurrected, spherical body is elaborated by people with reference to Origen, or rather by people who want to deepen his teaching and to draw out all the implications, everything that was not said.[340]

Theophilus seeks to refute the notion of the spherical form of resurrected bodies by referring to the appearances of the resurrected Christ:

Christ, risen from the dead, appeared to his disciples not in the form of a sphere.[341]

Others refer to the transfigured body of Christ and ascribe to it the normal human form.[342] It is Antipater of Bostra who deals most thoroughly with the mysteries of the life of Jesus in order to refute by that means the Origenist teaching on the resurrected body.[343] In this context we do not need to go into more detail about Origen's general teaching on the resurrected body.[344]

---

of the Origenist and anti-Origenist monks of the sixth century (in *RSPT* 43 [1959], 81–6). This, however, is definitively refuted by fragment 8 (just discussed) from the letter of Theophilus of 403, and in addition by the polemic of Antipater of Bostra, who wrote in 460 (G. Dorival).

340. Thus G. Dorival, *art. cit*, 319.

341. Cf. M. Richard, 'Nouveaux fragments de Théophile d'Alexandrie', *Op. Min.* II, no. 39, p. 64,7–8; Christ's resurrected body is already the guarantee for our own resurrected form (p. 64,14–15).

342. Thus Jerome, *Contra Ioannem Hieros.* 29: PL 23, 398A, without making reference to Origen.

343. Antipater Bostr., *Contradict. in Euseb.* (CPG 6687) , ch. 15, in John Dam., *Sacra parallela*: PG 96, 496CD with reference to Phil 3,20; 1 Cor 15,43–44; on the transfiguration (Mt 17,2ff.): 497AB. On the appearances of the resurrected Jesus: 489D; 497B; Christ's return which is already intimated by the transfiguration (497B; Lk 9,27).

344. On this see G. Dorival, 'Origène et la résurrection de la chair', in *Origeniana Quarta*, 291–321; cf. H. Crouzel, in *BLE* 81 (1980), 175–200, 241–66.

(4) The teaching of the universal restoration (apokatastasis pantōn)

As Origen's last aberration Justinian names the teaching of the universal restoration.[345] In this is completed the διαδοχὴ τῆς πλάνης (*erroris successio*) which is associated with the name of the Alexandrian. With this there is a whole complex of partial statements which have to be presented briefly. We shall start with the edict of 543.

> For the legacy of his [Origen's] error steals into the souls of the weaker ones and brings it about that they follow him in the sins which he committed from the very beginning. Because Origen's following has not yet received enough of the ungodliness of the pre-existence of souls and his other blasphemous prattle about the holy Trinity, under the influence of his perverse words that add this as well to their own error: the punishment of all godless human beings and even of the demons will have an end; both the godless human beings and the demons will be restored to their pristine order (ἀποκατασταθήσονται . . . εἰς τὴν προτέραν αὐτῶν τάξιν).[346]

This is said to contravene Christ's words (Mt 25,46.34.41). For morally weak human beings it is claimed that such an outlook has a demoralizing effect. If, moreover, the *supplicium* of the damned will have an end, this means as well, Justinian says, that the promise of eternal life for the righteous becomes empty. 'Eternal' must have the same meaning in both cases (p. 101,22–23). Why is there then an economy of salvation in Christ at all, with incarnation, crucifixion, death, tomb and resurrection of Christ? Why is there a *martyrium*, if devils and the godless have the same final state as the saints?[347]

The edict of 543 against Origen was intended to be given through Patriarch Menas to all bishops and monasteries in Constantinople. It was sent to all the patriarchs of the Imperial Church, also to Pope Vigilius. All Christians were intended to get to know it. In the future no bishop is to be ordained without renouncing all earlier heretics and finally those condemned under Justinian, beginning with Sabellius and up to Theodosius of Alexandria (with Peter of Apamea and Severus), but especially Origen, in whom pagan unbelief and Arian error are united.[348]

---

345. Cf. H. Crouzel, 'L'Apocatastase chez Origène', in *Origeniana Quarta*, 282–90.

346. Justinian emp., *Ed. c. Origen.*, p. 100,4–10 (Greek); p. 101,4–10 (Latin).

347. In Amelotti-Migliardi Zingale, *Scritti teologici*, p. 101,25–27; *loc. cit.*, pp. 100,38–104,18 (Greek); 101,34–105,17 (Latin) this is refuted with testimonies from Gregory Nazianzen (PG 35, 437,945), Basil (PG 31, 1264–1265,444), John Chrysostom (PG 47, 313; 61, 75) and a list of scriptural citations.

348. Twenty-four texts from *Peri Archon* are adduced as proof: Amelotti-Migliardi Zingale, *Scritti teologici*, 106–16 (Greek); 107–17 (Latin).

Nine Anathemas,[349] which summarize the main theses of the decree, form the conclusion of the imperial edict.

1. The pre-existence of the souls of human beings as spirits and holy powers, their surfeit (*koros*)[350] of the vision of God and their growing cold in love; their banishment into bodies as punishment.
2. The pre-existence of Christ's soul, its union with the Logos before the birth from the Virgin.
3. Formation of Christ's body in the womb of the Virgin before its union with the Logos and the soul. Leontius of Byzantium too had concerned himself with this problem in a cautious way.[351]
4. Likening of the Logos on his descent with all the powers of the various levels of being.
5. The spherical form of resurrected bodies. According to A. Guillaumont, *op. cit.*, 143, this notion is not yet present in the Origenism of the fourth century. However, the new state of the sources after a discovery by M. Richard (1975) is presented by G. Dorival, *Origeniana Quarta* (Innsbruck, 1987), 315–19 (see 3. above).
6. The animation of the celestial bodies and the water above the firmament.
7. Christ's crucifixion for the demons in the other world.
8. Restriction of God's creative power and the eternity of the world.
9. Temporal limiting of the damnation of demons and human beings (their *apokatastasis*).

What once for Epiphanius was the main issue in the Origenist errors and was still criticized by Theophilus of Alexandria, the subordination of the Son to the Father, is no longer mentioned, and for this reason too the reproach is not renewed that it was the cause of the error of Arianism.

(c) The assessment of Justinian's decree

The peculiarity of Justinian's decree against Origen finally becomes clear in a special way through G. S. Gasparro's literary-historical analysis of the florilegium from the *Peri Archon* appended at the end of the decree. With this its place too in the history of the struggle against Origenism is defined. Of the twenty-four citations from the *PA* in Justinian, nine correspond to the letter of Jerome to Avitus (Fr. I, XII, XIII, XV, XVI, XIX, XXIII, V, XX).

The compiler of the extracts follows the order of Jerome's text for Fr. XII–XXIII, with two transpositions. There is also a series of correspondences in individual themes between Justinian and Jerome in such number and in their ordering that one can hardly speak of an accident.

349. See the nine propositions: *ibid.*, 116–19 (Greek and Latin); German in F. Diekamp, *Die origenistischen Streitigkeiten*, 49–50. Diekamp enumerated ten anathemas. The last is a personal condemnation of Origen, which is related to the previous nine. There is a French translation, also with ten anathemas, in A. Guillaumont, *Les 'Kephalaia Gnostica' d'Évagre le Pontique* (Paris, 1962), 140–1.

350. On the word and idea of *koros*, surfeit, see the decree of 543: Amelotti-Migliardi Zingale, pp. 72,15 and 116,14. However, see above n. 318.

351. Cf. Leontius Byz., *Epil* 8: PG 86, 1944C1–D3. See the text above, p. 197. In the theoretical reflection to some extent he approaches the 'Origenist' reflection rejected in anathema III.

According to G. S. Gasparro, one can thus not assert that Justinian obtained his information about Origen exclusively from the florilegium in *PA* (attached to his decree). For in the decree there are subjects which are not documented in the florilegium. But taken together the decree and the florilegium reproduce an anti-Origenist schema, which in the course of the first Origenist crisis of the fourth and fifth centuries provided the basis for the three main opponents of Origen: Epiphanius, Theophilus of Alexandria and Jerome. The connecting thread for the presentation of the main theses of Origen is *epistula* 124 of Jerome, both for the compiler of the florilegium and also for the author of the decree itself. However, G. S. Gasparro does not want to claim that the letter of Jerome was the exclusive basis for the compilation of the florilegium. The compiler, however, finally made his own choice regarding the principal theme of Jerome and into this incorporated other subjects of the anti-Origenism of the fourth century. The author of the imperial letter used substantially the material contained in the florilegium, but in addition drew upon the remaining anti-Origenist repertoire that was handed on. To an extent that cannot be verified the florilegium could reflect the *capitula* which, according to Liberatus, the anti-Origenist monks had with them to bring about the condemnation of the Origenists by the Emperor through the mediation of the *apocrisiarius* Pelagius. The christological and religious problematic of the whole discussion about the decree of 543 against Origen thus hardly leads beyond that of the turn of the fifth century. Nevertheless it is possible that the faith and asceticism of a great part of the Palestinian monks were seriously endangered — in a manner that is not expressed at all in the imperial document. For this reason as well the crisis was in no way overcome.

4. A contemporary witness for the Origenist question of 543

It is worth noting that in his *Erotapokriseis* Ps. Caesarius also comes to speak of Origen's teaching on the pre-existence of souls, Christ's soul included. In connection with the teaching on the fall of Satan, he singles out from the Origenist errors this one thesis and rebuts it in detail.[352] In question 168 he formulates the Origenist teaching on souls as follows:

> What do you think of the leather clothes which Adam and Eve put on after their expulsion (*ekptosin*)? For we have heard from someone who expressed it well: human beings existed as rational spirits and rational, incorporeal living things. After sinning in disobedience against

352. See Ps. Caesarius, *Erotapokriseis*, 167–75: ed. Riedinger (Berlin, 1989), 145–53. That there is not yet any reference to the state of the Origenism question of 553 should also be adduced as an argument for the composition of the *Erotapokriseis* shortly after 543.

God the *nous* was abstracted and cooled, and for this reason was called soul because the warmth of the *nous* became cold and could no longer remain with the higher ones (*anō*) and stay with them in service, but has put on this body which scripture calls leather clothing; intended as a penalty for the sinner and as a gaol for punishment.[353]

This teaching of the pre-temporal fall is decidedly rejected, in the main with arguments that had been given in Epiphanius. Here we must forgo an analysis of the sources. The counter-argument insists particularly on the reference to holy and righteous people like Abel, Job, up to the patriarchs and Anna, whose life cannot be understood, it is said, as punishment in the prison of the body (cf. Qs. 168–170). Ps. Caesarius concludes here with the call:

> Remove, O Christ, those who swindle the pre-existence of souls, so that we do not succumb to the risk of calling your soul too a cooled *nous*. (p. 148,23–24)

II. THE NEW CONDEMNATION OF THE ORIGENISTS IN CONNECTION WITH THE SECOND COUNCIL OF CONSTANTINOPLE (553)

1. The sources

(a) See CPG 6886: *Epistula Iustiniani ad Synodum (Constantinopolitanum 553)*: Amelotti-Migliardi Zingale, *Scritti teologici*, 122–5; CPG 9352: *Canones XV contra Origenem*: ed. J. Straub, ACO IV, 1, 248–9 (Appendix).

(b) F. Diekamp, *Die origenistischen Streitigkeiten im VI. Jahrhundert und das fünfte allgemeine Concil* (Münster, 1899); Text: 90–7. A. Guillaumont, *Les 'Kephalaia Gnostica' d'Evagre le Pontique et l'histoire de l'origénisme chez les Grecs et les Syriens* = PatSorb 5 (Paris, 1962), 143–70; M. Richard, 'Le traité de Georges Hiéromoine sur les hérésies', *REB* 28 (1970), 242–8 = *Op. Min.* III, no. 62; the main section is cited in J. Straub, *Praefatio*, ACO IV, 1, (XXVI–XXIX) XXVIII; F. Carcione, 'La politica religiosa di Giustiniano nella fase conclusiva della seconda controversia origenista (543–553). Gli intrecci con la controversia sui Tre Capitoli', *StRiOrCr* 9 (1986), 131–47.

2. The history of research

F. Diekamp, *op. cit.*, 82–120, proved that the documents CPG 6886 and 9352 are related to the Fifth Council; on 120–4 he referred to the fact that in earlier authors there had been a confusion of the synods of 543 and 553. In his analysis of the text, 90–7, he was able to show that the letter of Justinian which was referred to and the fifteen anathemas belong together. Neither offers Origen's teaching, but that of the Origenist

---

353. *Ibid.*, Q. 168, p. 146,1–7. Here Ps. Caesarius is dependent on Epiphanius, *Ancor.* 62–63: Holl, 74–6.

monks in Palestine.[354] Particular elements used to prove this relationship were highlighted by J. Straub in ACO IV, 1, XXVI–XXIX. Any
doubts about it were finally removed by M. Richard, who in 1961
discovered in the National Museum at Ohrid the complete treatise on
heresies by the monk and presbyter George, composed in the first half
of the seventh century. Of the sixteen chapters of the work, chapter 9
is devoted to the Origenists: 'About the Origenists, in which too
Evagrius and Didymus [will be discussed].'[355] Chapter 9 concludes in
§ 16 once again with reference to the Council of Constantinople, in the
anathemas of which it is said one can recognize the entire godlessness,
inhumanity and falsity of the Origenists.[356]

Thus there can be no doubt that the Council of 553 dealt with
Origenism, or with Origen, Evagrius and Didymus. A similar confirmation was finally found in Syriac.[357]

3. The chronology

Because the condemnation of the Origenists clearly belongs to the
Council of 553, but cannot be placed after the opening of it on 5 May
553, an interim solution has to be sought.[358] It consists in the fact that
Emperor Justinian instructed the bishops[359] to deal with the question of

354. Cf. A. Guillaumont, Les 'Kephalaia Gnostica' d'Évagre le Pontique, 148–9, where the
conclusions of Diekamp are confirmed; cf. Justinian emp., Ep. ad Synod.: Amelotti-Migliardi
Zingale, Scritti teologici, p. 123,5–6: cum ergo compertum habeamus esse Hierosolymis quosdam nimirum
monachos qui Pythagorae, Platonis Origenisque Adamantii impios errores sectentur ac doceant . . .

355. George mon., De haeresibus ad Epiphanium (CPG 7820), 9: M. Richard, Op. Min. III,
no. 62, pp. 257–62. The §§ 1–3, pp. 257f. concern Origen, but end, however, (in § 3)
with the information: 'In recent times the Fifth Synod gathered at Constantinople anathematized
this one [Origen], together with Evagrius and Didymus who were of like mind.' In § 4 in contrast the anathemas I–IV and the corresponding passages in Justinian's letter are largely rendered
verbatim. Cf. Richard, 258, with F. Diekamp, op. cit., 90–2.

356. George mon., De haeresibus, 9: Richard, p. 262,7–9.

357. A. de Halleux, 'Trois synodes impériaux du VI⁶ s. dans une chronique syriaque inédite',
in R. H. Fisher (ed.), A Tribute to A. Vööbus (Chicago, 1977), 295–307. On Constantinople
II: 300–2. A. de Halleux stresses (301): 'Tout en demeurant, de la sorte, discrètement
antisévérienne, la présentation du synode de 553 porte essentiellement sur l'origénisme,
qui fut effectivement condamné par les pères déjà rassemblés à Constantinople, en quinze
anathématismes répondant à une lettre de Justinien.' The names of Didymus, Origen and
Evagrius (and perhaps of Theodore Askidas) are not in the right order here; in any case at least
two of them are badly 'corrupted' (défigurés) by a copyist.

358. Cf. F. Diekamp, Die origenistischen Streitigkeiten, 129–38.

359. Ibid., 133: 'In August [552] and in the following months participants arrived in Constantinople; the opening of the synod, however, was delayed for a long time, because the Pope
[Vigilius] refused to participate in a gathering in which the Oriental bishops formed the overwhelming majority.'

the Origenists, which, contrary to his expectation, had not been settled by his decree of 543. These bishops had already arrived months before the opening of the Council which was intended to be devoted to the question of the Three Chapters. This 'synodal act' took place on the level of a *synodus endemousa* and was not considered by the Emperor himself as a session of an ecumenical council.[360] Nevertheless the commission with regard to the Origenists was clear:

> Read through the submitted *ekthesis* carefully and condemn and anathematize at the end each of its individual chapters, together with the ungodly Origen also all who think and feel the same. (pp. 124,25–27; 125,25–27)

4. The anti-Origenist canons of 553 in English translation[361]

I. If anyone accepts the mythical pre-existence of souls and the monstrous restoration that follows from this (*apokatastasis*), let him be anathema.

II. If anyone says that the origin of all rational beings was incorporeal and immaterial intelligences (*noes*) without any number or names, so that they formed a *henade* on account of the sameness of essence (*ousia*), of power (*dynamis*) and of activity (*energeia*) and on account of their union (*henosis*) with the God-Logos and knowledge (*gnosis*); that they became sated with (*koron labein*) the divine vision and turned to what was worse, each corresponding to its inclination (*rhope*) to it, and assumed lighter or denser bodies and were labelled with names with respect to the fact that the difference of names exists, like bodies and powers too, from above; and that for this reason some became the cherubim, others seraphim, and again others principalities, powers, dominations, thrones, angels and all the other heavenly orders which exist and were so named, let him be anathema.

III. If anyone says that the sun, the moon and the stars are themselves part of the same *henade* of rational beings and that what they are happened through a turn to what was worse, let him be anathema.

IV. If anyone says that the rational beings (*logika*) became cold in divine love and were bound to more dense bodies of our kind and were named human beings, and that those who had attained the acme of evil were bound to cold and dark bodies and are called the demons and spirits of evil, let him be anathema.

V. If anyone says that from the condition (*katastasis*) of the angels and archangels will be the condition of the soul, from that of the soul the demonic and the human, from the human, however, once again there would be angels and demons, and that every order (*tagma*) of the heavenly powers has arisen either entirely from those lower or from those higher or from higher and lower, let him be anathema.

VI. If anyone says that the genus of demons has a twofold manner of appearance, composed from human souls and from higher spirits which have fallen into this state; that, however, one (single) *nous* from the whole *henade* of rational beings remained unmoved with respect to the vision and the divine love, which, having become Christ and the king of all spiritual beings, leads the entire corporeal nature, the heavens, the earth and what is in between; and that the

---

360. F. Diekamp, *ibid.*, 135 emphasizes that the letter to the bishops concerning the Origenists does not even once contain the term 'synod', although it is addressed to a gathering of bishops, as the conclusion of the letter shows. Cf. Amelotti-Migliardi Zingale, *Scritti teologici*, p. 124,24 (Greek); 125,24–25: *sanctissimi patres, ut in unum collecti*.

361. ACO IV, 1, 248–9. See the Greek text and a German translation in Görgemanns-Karpp, *Origenes*, 824–30 (text); 825–31 (translation).

cosmos really has in itself elements that are older than it, dryness, moisture, warmth and cold and the idea according to which it was formed and through which it came to be; thus that the all-holy, consubstantial Trinity did not create the world and this had come about in this way, but that the *nous*, as they say, as the demiurge existing before the world, gave created being, let him be anathema.

VII. If anyone says that Christ [= *nous*] is said to exist in the form of God and before all the ages was united to the God-Logos and at the end of the ages emptied itself into what is human and showed mercy, as they say, on those who in multiform ways had fallen out of the *henade* and, with the intention of leading them up, came to all and assumed the form of the various bodies and acquired their names, by becoming all things to all (cf. 1 Cor 9,22), to the angels an angel, to the powers a power, and to the other orders and types of rational beings he was changed to each in the appropriate manner and thus participated in us similarly in flesh and blood (cf. Heb 2,14) and became for human beings a human being, and whoever does not confess that the God-Logos emptied himself and became a human being, let him be anathema.

VIII. If anyone does not say that the God-Logos, consubstantial with the Father and the Holy Spirit, is the one who became flesh and a human being, thus that the one from the Trinity is the Christ in the real and not only in a figurative sense, on account of the *nous*, as they say, which emptied itself because it was united to the God-Logos himself and thus was properly named Christ; whoever for this reason names that [*nous*] Christ and this [Christ] God on account of the other, let him be anathema.

IX. If anyone says that it was not the Logos of God who descended into Hades in the flesh, endowed with a spiritual and rational soul, and as the same once again ascended into heaven, but what is called by them the *nous*, which they impiously characterize as the real Christ, having become such through knowledge of the monads, let him be anathema.

X. If anyone says that the Lord's resurrected body is an ethereal and spherical body, that the other resurrected bodies too will be like this, that moreover the Lord will shed his own body first and in a similar way the nature of all the bodies will return to nothing, let him be anathema.

XI. If anyone says that the coming judgement means the annihilation of all bodies, and at the end of the fable immaterial nature stays and in the future nothing of matter will continue to exist, but only the pure *nous*, let him be anathema.

XII. If anyone says that the heavenly powers too and all human beings and even the devils and the spirits of evil will be united unchanged to the divine Logos, like the *nous* itself, which is called Christ by them, which was in the form of God and emptied itself, as they say, and that the sovereignty of Christ will have an end, let him be anathema.

XIII. If anyone says that neither Christ nor one of the rational beings will exhibit a difference in any way at all, neither according to essence, nor knowledge, nor power over everything nor efficacy, but that all will be at the right hand of God, like their so-called Christ, and also will participate in their concocted pre-existence, let him be anathema.

XIV. If anyone says that all rational beings will form a *henas* through *hypostases* [persons] and numbers being annulled with the bodies, and that the end of the worlds and the laying aside of bodies and the abolition of names follow the knowledge relating to the rational beings, and that there will be sameness of knowledge as of *hypostases* and that in the fabricated *apokatastasis* there will be only pure intelligences [*noes*], as they exist in their foolishly invented pre-existence, let him be anathema.

XV. If anyone says that the change (ἀγωγή) of the intelligences is the same as their earlier change when they had not yet descended or fallen, that their beginning is the same as their end and their end the measure of their beginning, let him be anathema.

5. The origin of the Origenist propositions condemned in 553

Through the research of A. Guillaumont the real source of an important part of the teachings condemned in the fifteen anathemas of 553 has been discovered, especially for the propositions 6–9 and 12–13: it is Evagrius' *Kephalaia Gnostica* in their original form as they are preserved in only one of the two Syriac translations.[362] By combining this information with the results of earlier research it is now possible to clarify to some extent the development of the anti-Origenist decisions between 543 and 553. The following documents have to be compared:[363]

(1) The anathemas of 543 which have already been cited.
(2) Theodore of Scythopolis, *Libellus de erroribus Origenianis* (CPG 6993): PG 86, 232–6.[364] The author abjures his Origenist past. His formulations represent a mediation between Justinian's anathemas of 543 and 553.
(3) The propositions condemned in 553 at the instigation of Emperor Justinian, for which two things had to be clarified: their relationship to the anathemas of 543 and their position with reference to the Council of 553.
(4) The list of the Origenist errors in the *Vita Cyriaci* of Cyril of Scythopolis (written after the Council of Constantinople): it is a witness which is independent of the fifteen anathemas.[365]

We shall briefly characterize the differences between the four lists of errors.

(i) The list of Theodore of Scythopolis (PG 86, 232B–236B)

Nine of Theodore's *Kephalaia* correspond almost verbatim with the nine anathemas of the edict of 543. The following, however, are new:

no. 4 (233C): Christ's reign will have an end.

no. 11 (236A): 'We shall be equal to . . . our redeemer Christ, our God; and the God-Logos must be united to us, as he has been united to the flesh received from . . . Mary, according to the substance and the *hypostasis*.'

no. 12 (236B): Bodies, Christ's body too, are destined for dissolution.

---

362. See A. and C. Guillaumont, 'Le texte véritable des "Gnostica" d'Évagre le Pontique', *RevHistRel* 142 (1952), 156–205. The first communication of this was given at the Third International Conference on Patristic Studies, Oxford 1959; *StudPat* 3 = *TU* 78 (Berlin, 1961), 219–26; idem, *Les 'Kephalaia Gnostica' d'Évagre le Pontique* (Paris, 1962), esp. 151–70; idem, *Les six centuries des 'Kephalaia Gnostica' d'Évagre le Pontique* = *PO* 28, 5–264 with a new edition of the until then well-known (ed. W. Frankenberg, 1912) Syriac translation (S_1, pp. 16–256) and a first edition of the Syriac translation S_2 (version intégrale, 17–257) following the unique MS B. L. Add. 17167 from the Surian monastery. See *PO* 28, Introduction, 5–14.

363. This comparison is carried out by A. Guillaumont, *Kephalaia Gnostica*, 140–51, with n. 91. See 140–1: the anathemas of 543; 144–6: the anathemas from 553; 151, n. 91: the *libellus* of Theodore of Scythopolis (PG 86, 232B–236B); 150–1: the list of the *Vita Cyriaci*.

364. On this see F. Diekamp, *Die origenistischen Streitigkeiten*, 125–9; A. Guillaumont, *Les 'Kephalaia Gnostica' d'Évagre le Pontique* (Paris, 1962), 151, n. 91; J. Irmscher, 'Teodoro Scitopolitano. De vita et scriptis', *Aug* 26 (1986), 185–90.

365. This survey of the Origenism question, which was composed after 553, will be dealt with in our presentation of the Origenist disturbances in Palestine (Vol. II/3).

According to A. Guillaumont, the new elements, which the Palestinian Origenists added to the traditional Origenism condemned by the edict of 543, seem reasonably clear. We are on the way from the first to the second edict.

(ii) The two edicts of 543 and 553

If we look from 553 back to 543, we find the following covered in the first edict:

(1) the teaching of the pre-existence of souls (I); the incorporeal *noes* and their fall (II);
(2) the teaching of their exile into the body (IV);
(3) stars as fallen, rational beings (III);
(4) spherical form of resurrected bodies (X);
(5) *apokatastasis* which includes demons (XII and XV).

The differences:

(a) What is lacking in the later edict:
Vis-à-vis the edict of 543, that of 553 has nothing corresponding to its anathema VII (Christ's crucifixion for the demons in the coming world) and anathema VIII (limitation of divine power; eternity of the world); the body is no longer conceived as the place of punishment (I).
(b) What is added by the later edict:
In comparison to that of 543 the edict of 553 develops the theory of the body significantly more intensely. It is connected with a doctrine of the 'names' which, like the bodies, differentiate the fallen beings from each other (II and IV). The theory of the coherent transition from one order of rational beings to another is also new (V).

Two things in particular are important.

(a) The radical understanding of the *apokatastasis*; it encompasses not only the reintegration of the demons, as in 543, but beyond that the annihilation of bodies (X and XI), names and every difference among the substances. This is postulated on account of the very clearly formulated principle: the beginning is identical with the end (XV). The pristine *henade* will be completely restored (XIII and XIV).

(b) It is precisely 'this concept of a *henade*, that all intelligences form together in their pre-existence and their condition of "nakedness" which will be completely restored again at the end, which is entirely lacking in the anathemas of 543 and represents a fundamental element of the conciliar text of 553'.[366]

366. A. Guillaumont, *Les 'Kephalaia Gnostica'*, 147.

6. The theological and ascetical significance of the condemnation of Origenism in 553

The condemnation of Origenism in 553 did not have the world-wide echo which the Three Chapters dispute would create. The discussion was fought out successfully in particular with the formerly affected monks, and within this group especially the monks of Palestine. Even there it affected predominantly, according to the principles of Evagrianist asceticism, only a class, indeed an exotic group of monks, who after a hard *praktikē* were trained for the *theoria*, and after this preparation confessed the extreme Evagrianist christology.[367] Nevertheless it is fitting to note the explosive nature of this position. It was only in the sixth century that it had its effect, as the canons of 553 and later our statements on the patriarchate of Jerusalem will show.

(a) The subject of the incarnation. The most important change to the form of the traditional economy of salvation concerned the determination of the subject of the incarnation. It was no longer the Logos, the second *hypostasis* of the Trinity, but Christ's pre-existent soul, which first received its typically Evagrianist mark only in the *Kephalaia Gnostica*. It becomes the pre-existent *nous* 'which is united to the knowledge of the unity' (*Keph. Gnost.* I, 77). Because the 'anointing' exists in this union through the knowledge, this *nous* (= soul) is already called 'Christ', before the incarnation (*Keph. Gnost.* IV, 18,21). It itself does not belong to the Trinity; it is the 'tree of life', which is planted at the fountain of living water, the Trinity, and saturates itself from it (*Keph. Gnost.* V, 69). Thus this *nous*, with which the Logos is connected but not identical, comes into the flesh.[368] It is the mediator between Logos and *sarx*.

(b) This *nous*-Christ is the demiurge or mediator of creation. The Trinity itself is the creator only of spiritual beings (*logikoi*); for the creation of the corporeal nature or the world it is served by the 'Christ', that is, the *nous* which is united by vision to the Logos (*Keph. Gnost.* IV, 58).

(c) All decisive works of the economy of salvation or of the redemption, from birth to the descent into Hades, are ascribed to this *nous*-

---

367. For this christology see *JdChr* I³, 561–8 with further literature.

368. See A. Guillaumont, *op. cit.*, 153, n. 98; *JdChr* I³, 565–8; A. Grillmeier, 'Markos Eremita und der Origenismus', in *TU* 125 (Berlin, 1981), 269–72: on the christology of Evagrius (with texts from the commentary on Pss 131,7; 44,8; 104,15; 118,3); cf. *Keph. Gnost.* S₂ VI 14: *PO* 28, 223.

Christ. The death of the Incarnate One as such has no significance. An assumption of the flesh into heaven, as is already the case with the resurrection of the body, is irrelevant for salvation. For 'the extended, material body is incapable of knowledge' and there is connection with God only through knowledge (cf. *Keph. Gnost.* IV, 80).

(d) From this conception of 'Christ' it follows that all rational beings can ascend above natural contemplation to the 'essential *gnosis*' and can thus become *Christoi*. This idea is the Evagrianist foundation for the doctrine of the *Isochristoi*, which the Palestinian Origenists around Nonnus and Theodore Askidas defended. Evagrius himself had expressed the same goal with the less pretentious Pauline title 'co-heirs of Christ' (Rom 8,17) (*Keph. Gnost.* III, 72 and IV, 8). Endowed with this 'essential knowledge', every *nous* now has in the same way Christ's prerogatives, to be called 'God', to exercise the functions of the demiurge and to create new worlds (*Keph. Gnost.* V, 81).[369]

(e) Now the multiplicity which was present with the corporeal world is overcome and all rational beings, Christ's *nous* included, have become the perfect *henade* (Anathema XIV).[370] With the annihilation of the corporeal, separate existences (*hypostases*) and number are annulled. At the end existence and knowledge are identical. According to A. and C. Guillaumont[371] there are in Evagrius elements of Platonism and Neoplatonism, Stoicism, Gnosticism and Hellenistic Judaism, but these have also been further developed independently. Without a doubt this process was continued among the Origenists of the fifth and sixth centuries, in whom there are many aspects reminiscent of Proclus, especially in the interpretation of the transition from one to many and the doctrine of the *henades*.[372] Not without reason does Abba Cyriacus ask, as Cyril of Scythopolis reports, about the 'hell' which spat out these Origenist thoughts; they are not from God, 'it is Pythagoras, Plato, Origen, Evagrius, Didymus from whom they have borrowed these abominable

---

369. *PO* 28, 211: 'Lorsque le *nous* recevra la science essentielle, alors il sera appelé aussi Dieu, parce qu'il pourra fonder aussi des mondes variés.' There is no talk of this idea in the fifteen anathemas, but it certainly figures in the catalogue of Abba Cyriacus: cf. Cyril Scyth., *Vita Cyriaci* XII: Schwartz, p. 230,9–10; Festugière, *Les moines d'Orient* III/3, 47 (XII): 'ils disent, que dans l'apocatastase, nous serons les égaux du Christ'.

370. There it reads: πάντων τῶν λογικῶν ἑνὸς μία ἔσται. Cf. Görgemanns-Karpp, *Origenes*, 830.

371. A. and C. Guillaumont, art. 'Evagrius Ponticus', in *RAC* 6 (1966) (1088–1107), 1104–5; idem, art. 'Évagre le Pontique', in *DSp* 4 (1961), 1731–44.

372. On this development see W. Beierwaltes, *Denken des Einen. Studien zur neuplatonischen Philosophie und ihrer Wirkungsgeschichte* (Frankfurt, 1985), esp. the chapters 'Henosis' (123–54); 'Entfaltung der Einheit. Zur Differenz plotinischen und proklischen Denkens' (155–92).

and blasphemous teachings'.[373] The true path of the monk to perfection is the 'humble way of Christ', not these frivolous speculations, but brotherly love, hospitality, virginity, help for the poor, psalmody, long vigils, tears of remorse, fasting, prayer, meditation on death.

373. Cyril Scyth., *Vita Cyriaci* XIII: Schwartz, 230; Festugière, *Moines d'Orient* III/3, 47.

CHAPTER FOUR

THE THREE CHAPTERS DISPUTE (544–553)

The so-called Three Chapters dispute became the most significant and at the same time the most contentious theological action of Emperor Justinian.[374]

SECTION ONE

PREHISTORY

The action involving the three names did not occur by accident. It had a prehistory which strongly agitated the East as early as the fifth century, a prehistory with several clearly definable initiatives arising from different motives. On the surface it was fundamentally a matter of condemning the three names: Theodore of Mopsuestia, Theodoret of

---

374. For details about the Three Chapters dispute see E. Caspar, *Geschichte des Papsttums. Von den Anfängen bis zur Höhe der Weltherrschaft*, Vol. 2 (Tübingen, 1933), 243–86; C. J. Hefele/H. Leclercq, *Histoire des conciles d'après les documents originaux*, Vol. 3 (Paris, 1909), 1–156; E. Schwartz, 'Zur Kirchenpolitik Justinians', in *idem*, *Gesammelte Schriften* IV (Berlin, 1960), 276–328; W. Pewesin, 'Imperium, Ecclesia universalis, Rom. Der Kampf der afrikanischen Kirche um die Mitte des 6. Jahrhunderts', in *Geistige Grundlagen römischer Kirchenpolitik = FKGG* 11 (Stuttgart, 1937); E. Amann, art. 'Trois-Chapitres', in *DTC* 15, 1868–1924; H.-M. Diepen, *Les trois chapitres au concile de Chalcédoine. Une étude de la christologie de l'anatolie ancienne* (Oosterhout, 1953); R. Haacke, 'Die kaiserliche Politik in den Auseinandersetzungen um Chalkedon (451–553), in *Chalkedon* II, 164–77; A. Grillmeier, 'Vorbereitung des Mittelalters', in *ibid.*, 806–34; E. K. Chrysos, *The Ecclesiastical Policy of Justinian in the Dispute concerning the Three Chapters and the Fifth Ecumenical Council* (Thessaloniki, 1969) (modern Greek); on this see G. Weiss, *ByzZ* 64 (1971), 373–5; W. de Vries, 'The Three Chapters Controversy', in *WuW* Suppl. 2 (1974), 73–82; F. Carcione, 'La politica religiosa di Giustiniano nella fase conclusiva della seconda controversia origenista (543–553). Gli intrecci con la controversia sui Tre Capitoli', *StRiOrCr* 9 (1986), 131–47; R. Schieffer, 'Zur Beurteilung des norditalischen Dreikapitel-Schismas. Eine überlieferungsgeschichtliche Studie', *ZKG* 87 (1976), 167–201; *idem*, 'Das V. Ökumenische Konzil in kanonistischer Überlieferung', *ZSavSt.K* 90 (1973), 1–34; A. C. Outler, ' "The Three Chapters". A Comment on the Survival of Antiochene Christology', in R. H. Fisher (ed.), *A Tribute to Arthur Vööbus* (Chicago, 1977), 357–64; J. Speigl, 'Der Autor der Schrift De Sectis über die Konzilien und die Religionspolitik Justinians', *AHC* 2 (1970), 207–30; *idem*, art. 'Dreikapitelstreit', in *LexMA* 3 (1986), 1381–2; P. T. R. Gray, art. 'Justinian, Kaiser (ca. 483–565)', in *TRE* 17, 478–86.

Cyrus and Ibas of Edessa. Their number could be added to by names like Diodore of Tarsus and other teachers from the Antiochene school. The expression 'Three Chapters'[375] should be taken first of all in this broad sense.

I. INITIATIVES BETWEEN 432 AND 449[376] WITH SEVERAL CENTRES OF ACTION

1. The centre of Edessa

The prehistory began with the fight of Bishop Rabbula of Edessa against Theodore of Mopsuestia (d. 428) and his supporters in Edessa before the peace of 433.[377] The driving motive was the complete exclusion of Nestorianism. Andrew of Samosata informs us about this in a letter to Alexander of Hierapolis;[378] his source was probably Ibas of Edessa, who reported that Theodore of Mopsuestia had been anathematized by Rabbula, and not only Theodore but all who read his writings, possessed his codices and did not bring them to be burned. Rabbula was a confessor of the *mia physis*.[379] He also began his campaign against the 'school of the Persians' in Edessa, which was completely aligned with the teaching

---

375. F. Carcione, *art. cit.*, 135, n. 17: 'The expression "chapter" is nothing other than the . . . translation of the Latin "*capitulum*", which corresponds in its turn to the Greek κεφάλαιον. In ecclesiastical Greek this expression was synonymous with anathema, and it was in this sense that Justinian and his contemporaries used it in the case being considered. With his edict [of 543] the Emperor wanted to pronounce three anathemas, each corresponding to a condemnation of the writings of the three accused respectively, whereby the one directed against Theodore of Mopsuestia also included his person. Soon, however, the name for Justinian's politico-ecclesiastical action was used to designate the object of this action. "Three Chapters" then denoted no longer the three anathemas formulated by the Emperor, but the accused themselves; hence condemnation of the Three Chapters signified acceptance of the Justinianic condemnation, while defence of the Three Chapters signified its rejection.'

376. Cf. M. Richard, 'Acace de Mélitène, Proclus de Constantinople et la Grande Arménie', in *Op. Min.* II, no. 50. The main source is the Armenian 'Book of Letters': J. Ismireantz (Tiflis, 1901); M. Tallon, *Livre des Lettres* (Beirut, 1955); L. Frivold, *The Incarnation. A Study of the Doctrine of the Incarnation in the Armenian Church in the 5th and 6th Centuries according to the Book of Letters* (Oslo, Bergen, Tromsø, 1981).

377. There is a detailed presentation in G. G. Blum, *Rabbula von Edessa. Der Christ, der Bischof, der Theologe* = CSCO 300, Subs. 34 (Louvain, 1969), 165–95; L. Abramowski, 'Der Streit um Diodor und Theodor zwischen den beiden ephesinischen Konzilien', *ZKG* 67 (1955/6), 252–87.

378. Andrew Sam., *Ep. ad Alex. Hierap.* (CPG 6374) from the beginning of 432: ACO I, 4, 2, 86–7; cf. G. G. Blum, *op. cit.*, 165, nn. 1 and 2. Andrew also puts John of Antioch in the picture about it. Cf. L. Abramowski, *art. cit.*, 254.

379. ACO I, 4, 2, p. 86,34–35.

of Theodore.[380] It was there that his scriptural commentaries were translated into Syriac (by Qioras, Ibas, Cumas and Probus). According to Simeon of Beth Aršam,[381] Ibas had received the 'Nestorian teaching' of Theodoret of Cyrus and had passed it on to the 'school of the Persians' (the presbyter Elīša' bar Qūzbāyē). The Antiochene school thus had a great power-base in Edessa. Rabbula believed that in the interests of a true christology he had to close the school and expel its teachers and students from the city, which probably happened as early as 431.[382] Hence already in the first phase of the conflict we have the three names — Theodore of Mopsuestia, Theodoret and Ibas of Edessa — on whom the Three Chapters dispute will concentrate.

2. The centres of Alexandria and Constantinople

After the death of Rabbula (dated to 8 August 436) the agitation against Theodore was taken up anew by the archimandrite Basil, the deacon of Patriarch Proclus.[383] The Patriarch of Constantinople had already previously been drawn into the conflict by a synod of the Armenians and two of their presbyters. On their own initiative they came with critical *libelli* and a volume of excerpts from Theodore, 'presumably compiled in Edessa or Melitene',[384] to Patriarch Proclus in Constantinople in order to ask his judgement on Theodore.[385] The result was the famous *Tomus ad Armenios* (435). Theodore's name was suppressed in order not to provoke any alarm among the strict supporters of Nestorius and in the circles of John of Antioch.[386] The deacon Basil, clearly not satisfied with Proclus' 'diplomatic solution of the Armenian affair' (L. Abramowski), came to Cyril richly equipped with documents (the *libelli* of the Armenians, the *Tomus* of Proclus and his own writings) to move him to an open attack on Theodore. The initiative, however,

---

380. On the history of this school see G. G. Blum, *op. cit.*, 169–74, esp. 174, n. 36; C. Schäublin, *Untersuchungen zu Methode und Herkunft der Antiochenischen Exegese* = *Theophaneia* 23 (Cologne, Bonn, 1974), 11–15.

381. Cf. Assemani, *BO* I, 203–204. 350; for more information on Simeon see *JdChr* II/4, 311–30.

382. G. G. Blum, *op. cit.*, 174, n. 36. Ibas' exile lasted to the death of Rabbula (436). On the discussion about the year of Rabbula's death see 7–8, n. 16.

383. On this see G. G. Blum, *op. cit.*, 190–1 with n. 37; Innocent Maron. (CPG 6847): ACO IV, 2, p. 68,23–37.

384. See L. Abramowski, *art. cit.*, 254.

385. See Liberatus, *Brev.* 10: ACO II, 5, pp. 110,19–29; 110,31–111,6, with verbatim excerpts from Innocent Maron.: ACO IV, 2, p. 68,6–14.14–25.

386. On the prehistory and history of Proclus' *Tomus* see *JdChr* I[3], 729–30, esp. n. 9; see a correction of my comments in L. Abramowski, *art. cit.*, 266, n. 44a.

foundered.[387] With his entire original dossier, enlarged by a further *libellus*,[388] the deacon then sought to win Proclus for the fight against Theodore; this was not successful. A third *libellus* from the deacon was forwarded to Emperor Theodosius II with the same purpose; once again this was in vain.

Another action against Theodore was initiated in 435 by the Antiochene deacon and archimandrite Maximus before the Emperor and Proclus.

> Instead of direct measures Proclus now sent the *Tomus ad Armenios* to Antioch with an accompanying letter, in which the Orientals were called upon to subscribe, and he included excerpts transmitted from Armenia . . . The forwarding of the *Tomus* and the accompanying written material provided the occasion for John to summon a synod in Antioch . . . This synod decided to subscribe the *Tomus*, but the appended excerpts were not condemned, because they were recognized to be the property of Theodore.[389]

3. The centre of Jerusalem

In 438, while on a journey to Jerusalem, Cyril of Alexandria met a high court official, who presented him with a comprehensive indictment with many signatures, in which it was reported that the Oriental indeed rejected Nestorius, but in his place now honoured Theodore. In a letter[390] Cyril communicated that he had written to Antioch that one should suppress the 'impious dogmas' of Theodore in the Church. He said that after his return to Alexandria the deacon and archimandrite Maximus had come to him, depicting in the blackest colours the situation in Antioch, and had requested Cyril to intervene in the fight with an explanation of the symbol of Nicaea, misinterpreted by the supporters of Theodore; Cyril stated that he had done this. This *tomus*, Cyril said, had gone to the Emperor through Maximus in a 'splendid parchment volume'. In addition he had written three books against Diodore and Theodore.[391] Cyril's appeal to Antioch and the reactions there, however, threatened to imperil the work of the union of 433. Upon the

---

387. ACO IV, 2, p. 68,25–28; on this see L. Abramowski, *art. cit.*, 255.

388. ACO IV, 2, p. 68,28–30; according to Tillemont's proof and the reference of Abramowski (255), this second *libellus*, whose author is concealed by the title, is preserved in the *acta* of the Council of 553: see *actio* V, no. 14: ACO IV, 1, pp. 83,5–85,5.

389. L. Abramowski, *art. cit.*, 255–6.

390. Cyril Alex., *Ep. 70 ad Lamp.* (CPG 5370): PG 77, 341AC; read out in *actio* V of 553: ACO IV, 1, 86, no. 18.

391. Cf. Cyril Alex., *Ep. 69 ad Acac. Melit.* (CPG 5369): PG 77, 337–40, cited in *actio* V of 553 (ACO IV, 1, 107–8, no. 72). Theodore's seductive 'Nestorianism' (*ante litteram*) is stressed here in sharp words: *sicut doctor vult, sic sapit grex* (p. 108,13–14).

Antiochenes explaining that they would rather be burnt than condemn the two church teachers, Diodore and Theodore,[392] Cyril made a volte-face and advocated restraint in order to avoid a schism. Proclus too wrote a letter to the deacon Maximus[393] to move him towards moderation (he exhorted him as follows: *nihil ad confusionem vel tumultum Ecclesiarum pacem habentium agi*). As with Cyril (*Ep.* 72), so too with Proclus,[394] it was recalled that the condemnation of the dead was not admissible. Even Emperor Theodosius II had considered this subject, which had been brought to him in writing by Proclus or by John of Antioch and his synod of 438.[395] Accordingly it did not come to an imperial condemnation of Theodore of Mopsuestia. The attempts which we have depicted foundered because of the diplomatic ability of John of Antioch (d. 441/442) and of the vigilance of Pulcheria.[396] The lively correspondence of these years between the two synods of Ephesus was not forgotten in 553, as the various documents which were read out at the Fifth Council have shown us.

4. The theatre of Armenia

Although Rabbula had accepted the peace accord of 433 between Cyril of Alexandria and the moderate Antiochenes, he continued the fight against Theodore of Mopsuestia and carried it into Armenia (probably from as early as 432), because translations of the works of Theodore into Armenian had been delivered there through the 'school of the Persians'. His associate in this action was Acacius of Melitene, who warned the Armenian Patriarch Sahak about Theodore of Mopsuestia and above all about Nestorius.[397] Here we shall pass over developments in Armenia, because these will be dealt with in their own right in the appropriate context.

---

392. Cf. Cyril Alex., *Ep. 72 ad Proclum* (CPG 5372): PG 77, 344–5; read out in *actio* V of 553: ACO IV, 1, 109–10, nos. 77,78.

393. Proclus, *Ep. 11 ad Maxim.* (CPG 5908): in Facundus of Hermiane, *Pro def. tr. cap. VIII* II, 5–7: CCL 90A, 232–3.

394. *Ibid.*, p. 232,51–52; cf. p. 234,97–102.

395. Cf. Theodos. emp., *Ad synod. Ant.: Coll. Cas.* no. 310: ACO I, 4, 241; Facund. Herm., *Pro def. tr. cap. VIII* III, 5: CCL 90A, p. 235,41–46; Liberatus, *Brev.* 10: ACO II, 5, p. 112,20–25.

396. See E. Schwartz, *Codex Vaticanus gr. 1431 = ABAW.PH* 32, 6 (Munich, 1927), 91–3; Facund. Herm., *Pro def. tr. cap. II* II, 9–15: CCL 90A, 46–7 is important.

397. Cf. Acacius Melit., *Ep. ad S. Sahak* (CPG 5794); Latin in Richard, *Op. Min. II*, no. 50, 394–6; French in M. Tallon, *Livre des Lettres* (Beirut, 1955), 29–33; on this, G. G. Blum, *op. cit.*, 182–95; L. Abramowski, *art. cit.*, 254.

5. Further development

With the death of Rabbula, in Edessa itself his opponent Ibas occupied the episcopal see,[398] as a result of which the 'school of the Persians' could once again revive, but not without severe internal conflicts in this Church.[399]

As bishop of Edessa, Ibas had strong opponents, especially among the monks, and in particular the monk Barṣaumā[400] from the monastery Basmul, who died probably in 457/458. The opposition agitated against him in Antioch, Alexandria and Constantinople, and accused him before Emperor Theodosius II of heresy and the misappropriation of ecclesiastical property. A commission established by the Emperor, consisting of the bishops Photius of Tyre, Eustathius of Beirut and Uranius of Himeria, investigated the reproaches in the early part of 449 at Beirut and Tyre. These inquiries, however, ended with an acquittal for Ibas (CPG 8902 [3]).

An exhibit in the Three Chapters dispute would be a letter of Ibas to Mari[401] which had been written in 433 after the establishment of peace between Cyril and the Orientals. In this the author depicted the discord which had arisen in the Oriental Church after the Council of Ephesus (431).[402] The writing provoked the fiercest opposition in the followers of Rabbula in Edessa (to 449).

In Edessa it ended up in a new hearing under the Comes Theodosius, at which Ibas' letter to Mari and the accusations from Beirut were read out.[403]

Statements of Ibas were circulated with the intention of making him

---

398. See L. Hallier, *Untersuchungen über die Edessenische Chronik mit dem syrischen Text und einer Übersetzung* = *TU* 9, 1 (Leipzig, 1892), 110, no. LIX etc.; G. G. Blum, *op. cit.*, 196, n. 1.

399. See. G. G. Blum, *op. cit.*, 196–207.

400. See A. Vööbus, *History of Asceticism in the Syrian Orient II* = CSCO 197, Subs. 17 (Louvain, 1960), 196–208. According to a letter of Emperor Theodosius II (ACO II, 1, no. 48, p. 71) to Barsauma of 14 May 449, he is cognizant of the fact that in the Anatolian cities there are several bishops with 'Nestorian impiety'.

401. On the person of Mari see M. van Esbroeck, 'Who is Mari, the addressee of Ibas' letter?', *JTS* 38 (1987), 129–35. On the basis of the discovery of a letter from 452, written in Arabic, van Esbroeck can prove as fairly certain that the Persian Mari came to know Ibas in the school of Edessa, that later he became a Sleepless Monk in the Eirenaion, and finally was archimandrite in a monastery in the vicinity of the Eirenaion. This position is contrary to that of G. G. Blum, *op. cit.*, 166–7.

402. Ibas Edess., *Ep. ad Marim Persam* (CPG 6500–1): Greek translation: ACO II, 1, 3, pp. 32–4 (391–3); Latin translation: (a) ACO II, 3, 3, pp. 39–43 (478–82) (*versio antiqua*); (b) ACO IV, 1, 138–40 (from the *acta* of Constantinople II [553]); (c) CCL 90A (Facundus of Hermiane) 170–3.

403. See CPG 9013; the christologically suspect propositions are found in G. G. Blum, *op. cit.*, 199–202.

appear to be a 'Nestorian'.[404] The altercation reached its climax at the synod summoned in Ephesus in 449 by Emperor Theodosius II.

The Council was occasioned in part by the unrest in Edessa about Ibas. In the imperial document summoning it a prior decision against him had been pronounced.[405] The proceedings and hearings of Beirut and Edessa were discussed again at Ephesus and the letter to the Persian Mari was read out.[406]

Ibas was then deposed as bishop and excluded from the ecclesial community.[407] Together with him Theodoret of Cyrus, Domnus of Antioch (CPG 8938 [6] and [7]) and Irenaeus of Tyre were divested of episcopal office and banished from the Church (22 August 449).

The basis for the Three Chapters dispute in the sixth century, however, was laid at the Council of Chalcedon through the revocation of the condemnation of 449 and the rehabilitation of Theodoret of Cyrus (26 October 451) and Ibas of Edessa (26 and 27 October).[408]

II. A PROPOSAL OF EMPEROR JUSTINIAN IN 532

At the end of the doctrinal dialogue of 532 Justinian had proposed a compromise,[409] viz., accepting Chalcedon to safeguard correct understanding. He pronounced, however, a condemnation of Diodore of Tarsus, Theodore of Mopsuestia, Theodoret of Cyrus and Ibas of Edessa, but also of Nestorius on the one side and of Eutyches on the other, which was intended to mollify the Chalcedonians.[410] This proposal did not

404. The reproaches against Ibas contained the misunderstandings which prior to Ephesus (431) were customary in the struggle about the correct linguistic usage regarding the *communicatio idiomatum* between Alexandrians and Antiochenes. See *JdChr* I³, 731-7 (the trial of Eutyches and the Synod of Ephesus II [449]).

405. Cf. J. Flemming, *Akten der ephesinischen Synode vom 449, syrisch mit G. Hoffmanns deutscher Übersetzung und seinen Anmerkungen herausgegeben* = AGWG.PH 15, 1 (Berlin, 1917); the Emperor's decree concerning Ibas: 5-7; F. Haase, *Altchristliche Kirchengeschichte nach orientalischen Quellen* (Leipzig, 1925), 293ff.

406. See J. Flemming, *op. cit.*, 14-21 (*Relatio de Iba prima*); 20-33 (*Relatio de Iba secunda*) according to CPG 8938 (1) e and f; the reading out of the letter to Mari: *ibid.*, (1) g; Flemming, 32-55.

407. See CPG 8938 (1) h; J. Flemming, *op. cit.*, 54-69. Cf. G. G. Blum, *op. cit.*, 200-1.

408. See A. Schönmetzer, 'Zeittafel', nos. 121-124, in *Chalkedon* II, 951. We should note that the text of the letter of Ibas was not commented on at Chalcedon itself. Cf. ACO II, 1, 3, 32-3.

409. See above, p. 247. In this context we also recall Leontius of Byzantium's disowning of Theodore of Mopsuestia: PG 86, 1360D. Cf. E. Schwartz, 'Zur Kirchenpolitik Justinians', in *Ges. Schriften* IV, 300, n. 2.

410. See S. P. Brock, 'The conversations with the Syrian Orthodox under Justinian (532)', OCP 47 (1981), 116-17.

spring from his hostility towards the Antiochenes, nor from a particular interest in the condemnation, but was driven by the determination to bring about the union of post-Chalcedonian parties which were denouncing each other. Even though this proposal was not accepted, it still showed the Emperor's theological uncertainty, and the ease with which he was prepared to relinquish the strict-Chalcedonian position in favour of a compromise, without demanding that the Severans accept the substance of the Chalcedonian definition. What he demanded after the Syrians' statement was precious little:[411]

> 'They should accept the synod at Chalcedon as far as the expulsion of Eutyches was concerned, but they need not accept the definition of the faith made there . . .' The Severans close their report with the meaningful statement: 'These things failed to persuade the orthodox.'

In order to restore the unity of faith, the Emperor was prepared to sacrifice a great deal — but without success.

411. *Ibid.*, with the revised translation of B. L. Add. 12155, translated by F. Nau in *PO* 13, 192–6.

SECTION TWO

COURSE AND RESULT

The central action against the Three Chapters was the Fifth Ecumenical Council, the Second Council of Constantinople from 5 May to 2 June 553. The occasion, the course and the subsequent history of this Synod were bound to stir up the entire Imperial Church in East and West. In point of fact it was a question of the Emperor's aim, through a new interpretation of Chalcedon, to win over the Severans and still to save the Eusebian and Constantinian ideal of imperial unity. However, there were parties at work in Constantinople who knew how to make Justinian's undertaking a massive game of intrigue for their own purposes.[412]

I. 'REVENGE FOR ORIGEN'

In spite of the condemnation of Origenism in 543, Theodore Askidas had been able to remain doggedly in his position at court in order to continue working for his party or sect. After his opponent, the papal *apocrisiarius* Pelagius, had left the field by returning to Rome, he could bring his influence to bear on the Emperor unchallenged.

Theodore had subscribed the Emperor's first decree against the Origenists, probably also from the conviction that the real Origenism had not yet been fatally hit. Still he must have been aware that further information and petitions from Palestine against his supporters and their real 'heresy' would reach the Emperor.[413] For this reason he devised the

---

412. Liberatus, *Brev.* 24: ACO II, 4, pp. 140,13–141,11, reports in detail about the rôle of Theodore Askidas, bishop of Caesarea in Cappadocia (ACO IV, 3, 2, 2, p. 457a). In a writing of 14 August 551 (E. Schwartz, *Vigiliusbriefe* = SBAW 1940, 2 (Munich, 1940), 10–15), Pope Vigilius complained agitatedly against the doings of Theodore Askidas: for instance, p. 9,27 (*auctor totius scandali*); p. 15,20 (*novus error Theodori*). In this writing Vigilius declared Theodore deposed as bishop (p. 14,14–20), but this had no effect. Theodore Askidas was witness to the oath that Pope Vigilius swore before Justinian on 15 August 550 (ACO IV, 1, no. 11, 198–9), condemning the Three Chapters; Theodore's stance against Ibas at the Council of 553: ACO IV, 1, no. 9, pp. 143,14–146,32; his condemnation of the Three Chapters: ACO IV, 1, p. 222 (8). Cf. E. Schwartz, 'Zur Kirchenpolitik Justinians', 50–71.

413. Facundus of Hermiane, *Pro def. tr. cap.* I, II, 3–4: CCL 90A, 8–9, considers in detail the intentions of the Origenist Domitian, bishop of Ancyra, and his accomplices (like Theodore Askidas). He speaks of the *furor* of these crypto-Origenists about the condemnation of 543, and of their endeavour to bring the Church into a state of confusion. As testimony to this he adduces

plan to use all means to direct the Emperor's eagerness for theological decisions away from Origenism, towards a target which in the Church of Constantinople could always claim immediate interest,[414] namely the continuation of the fight against Nestorius by using the names of Theodore of Mopsuestia, Theodoret of Cyrus and Ibas of Edessa. The attack on Theodore of Mopsuestia was all the more striking as he had already been forgotten within the borders of the Imperial Church.[415] As the great authority, he continued to have an effect on the Nestorians who had emigrated to Persia. On that account Chalcedon could not really be suspected of concealing Nestorianism under the name of Theodore of Mopsuestia. The dangerous nature of this name had its effect indirectly, namely through Theodoret and Ibas. Both had been deposed by the Synod of Ephesus II (449), and in contrast had once again been restored to office by Chalcedon and admitted to the Synod. The misdemeanour of Theodoret consisted in having composed several writings against Cyril or the Council of Ephesus.[416] More than Theodoret's name, however, that of Ibas was sullied by the letter to Mari already referred to. In order to demonstrate that this letter was heretical, the person and work of Theodore of Mopsuestia had to be anathematized, for Ibas' letter contained an unambiguous *laudatio* of the bishop, who had died in peace with the Church.[417] What were fatal were the characterization of Theodore as 'teacher of the Church' and the highlighting of his ongoing effectiveness in distant Persia. From there a secret weapon against Chalcedon could also be forged.

Theodore Askidas, however, knew the situation too well to attack

Domitian's *libellus* to Pope Vigilius (CPG 6990), in which the bishop confessed *deo extorquente*: *quod eius complices Origeniani, cum viderent non se posse proprium dogma defendere, neque sibi quidquam spei de conflictu restare,* **ad ultionem** *eorum quae contra Origenem gesta sunt, haec Ecclesiae scandala commoverunt.* In contrast to this G. Every, 'Was Vigilius a Victim or an Ally of Justinian?', *HeyJ* 20 (1979), 257–66, is inclined to consider that the Origenists were not the instigators of the Three Chapters dispute (264).

414. On the Byzantines' passion for orthodoxy see B. Lourdas, 'Intellectuals, Scholars and Bureaucrats in the Byzantine Society', *Kleronomia* 2 (1970), 272–92.

415. Facundus Herm., *C. Mocian.*, 63: CCL 90A, p. 415,536–538; PL 67, 866C: *nunc in praeiudicium magnae synodi Chalcedonensis resuscitatur eius quaestio ante centum et viginti annos finita et oblivioni iam tradita.*

416. Theodoret Cyr., *Impugnatio XII anathematismorum Cyrilli* (CPG 6214); *Libri V contra Cyrillum et concilium Ephesinum (Pentalogus)* (CPG 6215); *Pro Diodoro et Theodoro* (CPG 6220); see *JdChr* I³, 692–700.

417. Ibas Edess., *Ep. ad Marim Persam*, here according to Facundus Herm., *Pro def. tr. cap.* VI, III, 11: CCL 90A, p. 171,74–78 (among those pursued by Rabbula were also teachers who were already dead): *quorum unus est beatus Theodorus, praeco veritatis et doctor Ecclesiae, qui non solum in sua vita colaphizavit haereticos per veritatem suae fidei, sed et post mortem spiritalia arma in libris propriis ecclesiae filiis dereliquit.*

Chalcedon directly and openly. Neither the Emperor nor the people of Constantinople nor the supporters of the Council in the Great Church in general could have collaborated in this. Hence Theodore invented the thesis that Ibas' letter had not been written by him at all; he successfully convinced the Emperor of this. In this way the restoration of Ibas by Chalcedon could also not be blamed on the Council, and the Emperor was free to anathematize the heretical composition of unknown origin, without riling the Chalcedonians. Thus to all appearances the condemnation of the Three Chapters served only to win back the Miaphysites. Nevertheless, Justinian denied later to the East Illyrian bishops, whose opposition was expressed in a synodal writing, that the condemnation of the 'Three Chapters' should be understood as a concession to the Severans.[418] He emphasized that in the first place he reacted in this way on account of the intrinsic godlessness of the Three Chapters themselves, and on account of the danger that they would serve as camouflage for genuine Nestorianism, which in this way, with the suppression of the name of Nestorius, would infiltrate the Church.[419]

II. THE INDIVIDUAL DECREES OF THE EMPEROR IN THE QUESTION OF THE THREE CHAPTERS BEFORE THE FIFTH ECUMENICAL COUNCIL

1. *In damnationem trium capitulorum* (CPG 6881)

In a first treatise Emperor Justinian accepted the plan thought out by Theodore Askidas, and pronounced the threefold anathema:

(a) against the person of Theodore of Mopsuestia together with his works;

(b) against the anonymous letter to the Persian Mari and anyone who claimed that the author was Ibas of Edessa;

(c) against Theodoret's writings against Cyril.[420]

---

418. Justinian emp., *Ep. c. tria capitula* (549/550) (CPG 6882): Schwartz, *Drei dogm. Schriften* (1939), pp. 47,26–48,5; PG 86, 1043CD; see especially the sentence: he says he uttered the threefold condemnation, 'so that the will of those is fulfilled who would have separated themselves from the catholic Church'.

419. *Ibid.*: Schwartz, *op. cit.*, p. 47,30–33; PG 86, 1043D.

420. Justinian emp., *In damnationem trium capitulorum* (CPG 6881), from the year 544/545, is only extant in excerpts: in E. Schwartz, 'Zur Kirchenpolitik Justinians', in *Ges. Schriften* IV, Appendix, 321–8, with additions to W. Pewesin, *Imperium, Ecclesia universalis, Rom* (Stuttgart, 1937), 150–8, with an evaluation of Facundus Herm., *Pro defensione trium capitulorum libri XII* (CPL 866): CCL 90A, 3–398; Amelotti-Migliardi Zingale, *Scritti teologici*, 129–35 (on the basis of the edition in CCL 90A) with nineteen certain fragments and an uncertain one from

This first treatise did not attain great significance, was not included in a contemporary collection, and has been lost in its entirety. More informative will be the citations which first appear in the totality of Facundus' *defensio*.

2. Justinian's letter against the Three Chapters (CPG 6882)[421]

This letter is probably addressed to the episcopal participants of an Illyrian synod[422] who had refused to subscribe the edict of 543/544. Justinian's reply is a good introduction to the manner in which he had accepted the ideas of Theodore Askidas. Two main areas illustrate the Emperor's argumentation: (a) he is determined factually to incriminate the Three Chapters; and (b) he energetically wards off the objection that the action against the Three Chapters is directed against Chalcedon.

(a) The incrimination of the Three Chapters

The Emperor reacts in a quite agitated way to the Illyrian writing[423] and shows that he is convinced of the heresy of the Three Chapters (PG 86, 1045A). Whoever defends them would openly contradict the Synod of Chalcedon, deceive the simple and deliver the Christian people to schism (PG 86, 1045AB). It would be particularly misleading to characterize Cyril as an Apollinarian (*ibid.*, C), as the letter of Ibas also claimed (PG 86, 1047A, 1049C). The Emperor says that whoever defends this letter makes himself guilty of the two-persons teaching, like Theodore of Mopsuestia and Nestorius (PG 86, 1051BC).

It is typical of Justinian to adduce the *Unus ex sanctae Trinitatis personis* to ward off this teaching of two persons (PG 86, 1053D). We should note that the letter of Ibas is condemned because he is said to reproach Cyril on account of the *mia-physis* formula, but falsely interprets it as mixing divinity and humanity (PG 86, 1055A). Cyril, Justinian main-

Facundus. B. E. Daley, 'The Origenism of Leontius of Byzantium', *JTS* 27 (1976) (333–69), 334, sees in Justinian's first edict against the Three Chapters still 'a part of his [Leontius'] legacy', although Leontius died shortly before its publication. See below on the Council of 553.

421. E. Schwartz, *Drei dogmatische Schriften Justinians = ABAW.PH* 18 (Munich, 1939), 47–69; Amelotti-Migliardi Zingale, *Scritti teologici, Subsidia* II, 81–121 (= the Greek text of Schwartz), with a Latin translation; PG 86, 1041–95; PL 69, 275–327; a German translation (of Schwartz, 47) by H.-G. Beck, *Byzantinisches Lesebuch* (Munich, 1982), 223–4.

422. Cf. Victor Tunnun., *Chron.* (549): Mommsen, in *MGH, auct. ant.* XI/2, p. 202,6: an Illyrian synod wrote to Emperor Justinian.

423. Cf. the introduction to CPG 6882: Schwartz, p. 47,11–17; PG 86, 1043B; several times he labels the bishops as men without education (*agrestes, agroikoi*). See H.-G. Beck, *op. cit.*, 223–4.

tains, meant nothing other than that 'in Christ there is one *hypostasis* or person of the divinity and humanity' (PG 86, 1055B).[424]

In all Three Chapters Justinian finds the teaching of two persons. It is in this sense that he interprets Theodore's formula: 'two natures, one power of God, one person'.[425] The letter of Ibas repeats this teaching.[426] It is not necessary to follow any further in its Justinianic version this historical interpretation of the Antiochene teaching, which was directed above all to warding off Apollinarianism.[427] The Emperor makes no effort to incorporate the historical situation of the Antiochene christology into his judgement of it. This would also have contradicted the interests of Theodore Askidas, who indeed aimed at the condemnation of the three *capita*. Thus the rift between the Antiochenes and the Alexandrians, in spite of all the Emperor's attempts to secure union, was reopened. The union of 433, which Ibas had expressly confessed, was invalidated.

What was new, however, and insinuated by Theodore Askidas, was the Emperor's often repeated claim that Ibas had not at all composed the letter to Mari ascribed to him. It was stated that it had been foisted upon him.[428] The Emperor incorporated this assumption too into his interpretation of the Chalcedonian rehabilitation of Ibas.

Justinian attempts to prove the anonymity of the letter of Ibas: Ibas swore that after 433 he had not written anything against Cyril (cf. Schwartz, *op. cit.*, no. 63, p. 64,29–33). The letter to Mari, however, was written after 433. Hence Ibas is not implicated in the authorship (p. 64,34–35). The Synod condemned the contents of the letter, which it also vainly demanded from Ibas. For this reason he was deposed (p. 65,2–5).

In contrast we should note that in sessions X and XI of the Council of Chalcedon[429] on 26 and 27 October 451, the reports of Tyre (CPG 8903) and of Beirut (CPG 8902) and the *relatio*

424. In this context, in opposition to Cyril and Severus, however, Justinian distinguishes clearly between the concepts *physis* and *hypostasis* (PG 86, 1055B11–14). He also tries to find this distinction already in Cyril (*ibid.*, CD). He says that in contrast Theodore of Mopsuestia took the term 'nature' for 'person', and in this way came to his teaching of two persons (1073AB).

425. Cf. Schwartz, *Drei dogm. Schriften*, no. 49, p. 59,23–25; no. 51, p. 60.

426. Cf. ACO IV, 1, no. 3, p. 138,27–28: *duae naturae, una virtus, una persona, quod est unus filius dominus Iesus Christus*. With regard to this Justinian says that the result is the teaching of two persons: Schwartz, *op. cit.*, no. 49, p. 59,34–35; PG 86, 1071C. Cf. Schwartz, no. 61, p. 63,32–35.

427. See *JdChr* I³, 610–34, 692–707.

428. Schwartz, *op. cit.*, p. 48,14: 'the so-called letter of Ibas'; p. 52,28–29; cf. PG 86, 1045C, 1055D; see especially, however, Schwartz, no. 63, pp. 64,22–65,22; PG 86, 1081D–1085A.

429. See A. Schönmetzer, 'Zeittafel', in *Chalkedon* II, 951, nos. 122, 124; CPG 9011, 9013; the numbering of the *actiones* in Φᶜ reads IX and X; ACO II, 1, 3, pp. 11–16, 16–42. The Latin translation: II, 3, 3, pp. 15–20, 20–52.

of the clergy of Edessa were read out (CPG 9013[2]), but also the incriminated letter of Ibas,[430] without any doubt being expressed about its authenticity.

The fabrication of the inauthenticity of the letter of Ibas is devoid of any foundation.

(b) The condemnation of the Three Chapters — no renunciation of Chalcedon

Justinian then replied to the Illyrians' claim that through the condemnation of the letter of Ibas 'the definition of Chalcedon will suffer damage' (PG 86, 1079C). How did the Emperor attempt to rebut this objection, which he took very seriously?[431]

(i) In order to dispel any doubt about his fidelity to Chalcedon from the very beginning, Justinian expressly confessed that Chalcedon was orthodox and that the ecumenical councils numbered four.

> This was established by the definitions of the holy Synod of Chalcedon; the Synod expressed no novelty against the faith. Rather all over and in everything it followed the confession of faith which the Lord gave through his holy apostles and which the holy apostles proclaimed, the 318 holy Fathers handed on to God's Church and the 150 Fathers ratified by the dogmatic explanation about the divinity of the Holy Spirit. This faith too is followed by the holy Fathers who gathered at the earlier Council of Ephesus. The holy Council of Chalcedon, however, anathematized those who handed on another symbol or another explanation of faith beyond that presented by the 318 Fathers.[432]

(ii) The person of Ibas and his reinstatement in office are not an incrimination of Chalcedon, because at first the Council was summoned without Ibas, and the bishop manifested a new attitude towards the Fourth Council. He distanced himself from the letter to Mari[433] and by doing so released, as it were, this letter for condemnation without Chalcedon being incriminated by this.[434]

> Admittedly this letter from beginning to end oozes impiety (asebeia) and hybris vis-à-vis Cyril.[435]

How can one defend Chalcedon better than by teaching the opposite of the so-called letter of Ibas and of Theodore's letters? Against their

---

430. Ibas Edess., *Ep. ad Marim Persam*: Greek: ACO II, 1, 3, pp. 32,9–34,27; Latin: ACO II, 3, 3, pp. 39,26–43,2; ACO IV, 1, pp. 138,6–140,23.

431. Cf. Justinian emp., *Ep. c. tria capit.*: Schwartz, 63–6; PG 86, 1079D–1087A.

432. *Ibid.*: Schwartz, p. 64,4–11; PG 86, 1081BC. The conciliar decision excluding any further formula of faith (going beyond that of 325), which had been taken at Ephesus (431) (cf. *DEC* 65, *65) and which had been raised repeatedly by the traditionalists against Chalcedon, was also in fact formulated by the Council of 451. This was also intended to acquit the Council of Chalcedon. Cf. ACO II, 1, 2, p. 130 (326), 4–11.

433. Schwartz, *op. cit.*, p. 65,18–22; PG 86, 1083D–1085A.

434. Cf. Schwartz, *op. cit.*, p. 64,29–36; PG 86, 1083AB.

435. Schwartz, *op. cit.*, p. 65,35–36; PG 86, 1085C.

teaching of two persons 'the Synod maintains the hypostatic union (*kath'hypostasin henosin*) of the two natures and proclaims one person (*prosopon*) or rather the one *hypostasis* of Christ, of the only-begotten Son of God'.[436] In everything the Synod of Chalcedon follows the First Council of Ephesus, honours Cyril with the titles 'Father' and 'Teacher', and confirms that synodal letter to which are appended the twelve chapters (anathemas).[437]

(iii) Chalcedon, however, is also not implicated by the alleged letter of Ibas, because the parts of the *acta* which contain it do not belong to the authentic *acta* of Chalcedon as these were preserved in Rome, in the Patriarchate and imperial palace of Constantinople.[438] The proscribed letter is in contradiction to the definition of Chalcedon and does not belong to it. Hence its condemnation cannot implicate the Fourth Council.

In his conclusion the Emperor once again makes the 'rustic' bishops of Illyrium aware of their backwardness. He criticizes their *ekthesis pisteos* (of 549). They should either study the Fathers or be silent. Justinian also rejects the presumption of prescribing how the Emperor should respond to the Egyptian Patriarch Zoilus. The bishops should now be quite clear, for Justinian writes that whoever defends Theodore of Mopsuestia and his writings, the alleged letter of Ibas and Theodoret's writings which were directed against right faith, should be reckoned among the heretics, and is excluded from the catholic Church whose head is Christ, the only-begotten Son of God.[439]

3. Emperor Justinian's edict of 551 (CPG 6885)

With the decision of Empress Theodora to carry through the condemnation of the three *capita* by bringing Pope Vigilius from Rome to Constantinople (22 November 545) the Three Chapters dispute entered its really tragic phase, which was severely damaging for the Church in

436. Schwartz, *op. cit.*, p. 63,34–35; PG 86, 1081A5–8. Cf. *JdChr* I³, 758–9.

437. What is meant is Cyril's third letter to Nestorius (CPG 5317). At Ephesus, however, no vote was taken on this letter. It was only read out and included in the *acta*: ACO I, 1, 2, pp. 36,19–20,26. At Chalcedon as well, corresponding to the union of 433, one could not have recourse to Cyril's third letter to Nestorius and his anathemas. Thus at Chalcedon there was no ratification of the twelve anathemas. On the symbol of Ps. Theodore of Mopsuestia which was condemned at Ephesus (431) (ACO I, 1, 7, pp. 97,26–100,4), and subsequently at Chalcedon, see CPG 3871.

438. Schwartz, *op. cit.*, p. 66,13–23 (no. 65); PG 86, 1087AB.

439. On the whole subject cf. Schwartz, *op. cit.*, nos. 80–81, p. 69; PG 86, 1093C–1095B.

East and West.[440] The Pope arrived in Constantinople only on 25 January 547. On the way to the East he had sojourned in Sicily until the summer of 546 and had received there numerous petitions of the Sardinian and African bishops, urging him not to condemn the Three Chapters. The Roman clergy had also expressed this warning at his departure.[441] On his arrival in the Imperial City the Pope excommunicated Patriarch Menas and deposed him. The excommunication applied to all the other signatories of the condemnation of 544/545 (CPG 6881).[442] However, on 29 June 547, at the request of Empress Theodora,[443] the Pope and the Patriarch were reconciled. In the middle of June 547 Vigilius secretly condemned the Three Chapters in two identically worded letters to the Emperor and the Empress (CPG [9336]), letters which Justinian later had read out at the Council of 553 (*Actio* VII).[444] The so-called *Iudicatum* of the Pope, a document of 11 April 548 (CPG [9337]),[445] in which he communicated to Patriarch Menas his condemnation of the Three Chapters, admittedly while still adhering to Chalcedon,[446] was intended to play a special rôle. Yet the West, especially Africa, saw in this *Iudicatum* a renunciation of Chalcedon. The opposition to it was so fierce that Vigilius had to request the Emperor to return the document to him to be annulled.[447] The freedom of action which the Pope had hoped for and which he thought he had

440. See R. Haacke, 'Die kaiserliche Politik in den Auseinandersetzungen um Chalkedon (451–553)', in *Chalkedon* II, 95–177, especially 166–74. Cf. E. Schwartz, 'Zur Kirchenpolitik Justinians', 308.

441. Facundus Herm., *Pro def. tr. cap.* IV, III, 5: CCL 90A, 122.

442. His *apocrisiarius* Stephen had separated himself from communion with Patriarch Menas immediately after his acceptance of the decree: Facundus Herm., *op. cit.*, IV, III, 4: CCL 90A, 122. In nos. 4–7 the African depicts how the West joined forces against this Three Chapters affair.

443. Cf. Theophanes, *Chron.* A. M. 6039: de Boor, p. 225,25–28. According to E. Schwartz, 'Zur Kirchenpolitik Justinians', *Ges. Schriften* IV, 309, n. 3, the Empress did not have any 'strong interest in the dispute'. She died on 28 June 548.

444. Cf. ACO IV, 1, 187–8; cf. CPL 1694. Numerous Western bishops, worked on by Theodore Askidas, also subscribed.

445. *Iudicatum Vigilii ppae* (frag.): CA, *ep.* 83: CSEL 35/1, 316–17, ACO IV, 1, pp. 11,21–12,6.

446. Vigilius later spread it about that he had been forced to produce the *iudicatum* and that he had been insufficiently informed. On the Western reaction to this *iudicatum* see E. Schwartz, 'Zur Kirchenpolitik Justinians', *Ges. Schriften* IV, 310–13. The Pope's fiercest opponent was the deacon Rusticus, who revealed how the *iudicatum* came about. Probably even before 550 Vigilius was formally excommunicated by an African synod because of his condemnation of the Three Chapters. A defence of these Three Chapters was brought before the Emperor: Victor Tunnun.: Mommsen, p. 202,12; Facundus Herm., *C. Mocianum*: CCL 90A, 401–12, nos. 2, 24, 48, 50.

447. Cf. Vigilius, *Constitut.*: CA, *ep.* 83, no. 297: CSEL 35, 315; E. Amann, art. 'Trois-Chapitres', in *DTC* 15, 1895–6.

regained, he surrendered definitively, however, on 15 August 550, by having to swear before Justinian, Theodore Askidas and the *patricius* Cethegus on the four gospels and the nails of the cross that he would work towards the condemnation of the Three Chapters in the sense of the Emperor and that he would inform him of all the actions of the opposing party.[448] In the meantime the Emperor attempted to improve his argumentation against Theodore of Mopsuestia and his posthumous condemnation. From one of the synods summoned at Mopsuestia (17 July 550) he hoped to learn when the dead bishop had been struck from the diptychs there.[449] In this way he hoped to show that the *damnatio post mortem* had already been practised.

The Emperor attempted to use his previous method of attaining a goal by means of edicts on a final occasion by his *confessio fidei* of June 551.[450] It is the last great document in the Three Chapters dispute before the Council of 553. From it we can ascertain two facts: one about the state of Justinian's christology before the Council of 553, the other about the then current basis for condemning the Three Chapters. One is closely related to the other.

The Eusebian-Constantinian ideal of unity as a motive for a comprehensive *homologia* is proclaimed in the document from the first line. The explanation of the trinitarian doctrine presents no special problem (Schwartz, p. 72,13–28; PG 86, 993D–995B). The christological remarks dominate the *confessio* (Schwartz, 72–90; PG 86, 995–1013); then there follow thirteen *Kephalaia* (*capita*) which will be of particular interest to us.

In our last discussion of a truly christological document, the dogmatic letter to Zoilus (CPG 6879), we were able to establish that Justinian still embraced strict-Chalcedonian christology. Now our attention is

---

448. *Vigilii iuramentum* (CPG [9342]): ACO IV, 1, 198–9. Cf. Vigilius, *Ep. ad univ. populum* (5 February 552) (CPG [9346]): Schwartz, *Vigiliusbriefe*, pp. 4,26–5,1.

449. CPG 9340; ACO IV, 1, 115–30. In one letter to Justinian and in another to Vigilius it was ironically reported that in the list of former bishops no Theodore was to be found, but there was certainly a Cyril. It was also claimed, however, that a Cyril had never been bishop of Mopsuestia. Thus it was alleged that the name of Cyril was put into the diptychs in the place of the heretic Theodore. Cf. ACO IV, 1, 129–30, no. 65.

450. Justinian emp., *Confessio fidei* (CPG 6885): E. Schwartz, *Drei dogmat. Schriften Justinians* = *ABAW.PH* 18 (Munich, 1939), 72–111; this text with its *versio lat. antiqua* in Amelotti–Migliardi Zingale, *Scritti teologici*, *Subsidia* II, 129–69. Cf. R. Schieffer, 'Zur lateinischen Überlieferung von Kaiser Justinians Ὁμολογία τῆς ὀρθῆς πίστεως (*Edictum de recta fide*)', *Kleronomia* 3 (1971), 285–301; *idem*, 'Nochmals zur Überlieferung von Justinians Ὁ. τ. ὀ. π. (*Edict. de recta fide*)', *Kleronomia* 4 (1972), 267–84. Our citations here follow Schwartz and PG 86, 993–1035.

directed to the formulas and concepts which he utilizes in the new document.

(a) The distinction between hypostasis *and* physis *also in the* oikonomia
In a way different from Severus, Justinian takes over the distinction between *hypostasis* and *physis* (*ousia*) from the trinitarian formula to use it also for the *oikonomia*, that is, for christology in the framework of the Chalcedonian teaching of the one *hypostasis* in two natures, the *mia physis* being rejected.[451] In the Trinity there is one nature (*physis* or *ousia*) and three *hypostases* (Latin: *subsistentiae*). Arius alone confesses three natures in God.[452] From the three *hypostases* in the Trinity only one entered into composition with the flesh.[453] Because there are not three natures (*physeis*) in the Trinity, so too no one can say that 'one of the three natures is composed with the flesh', which once again is directed against the *mia physis*.[454] Justinian defines the *termini* of the *synthesis* well: it happened not from nature to nature, but from divine subject (*hypostasis*) to created nature. For this reason too the Emperor does not like the so-called body–soul analogy for explaining the *synthesis* in Christ, for this expresses a synthesis of nature to nature. He knows of its appearance in the Fathers; he says that they used it to illustrate the 'unity' in Christ.[455] But there was also a misuse on the other side, namely representing the unity in Christ as a nature unity and in this sense speaking of *mia physis*.[456]

Thus in Justinian the trinitarian and incarnational terminology are brought into harmony. The distinction between the two types of union: (1) 'of nature to nature' (Apollinarians, monophysites) and (2) 'of subject to nature' is well understood and maintained (cf. Schwartz, p. 86,30–33; PG 86, 1009D–1011A).

The Emperor finds the distinction between the concepts *hypostasis* (*prosopon, subsistentia*) and 'nature' (*physis*) or 'essence' (*ousia, substantia*) already present in the Fathers:

---

451. Schwartz, p. 80,15–17; PG 86, 1003AB. Here it is presupposed that this formula is understood in the sense of a mingling.

452. Schwartz, p. 86,28–29; PG 86, 1009D. This is a distortion of the Arian teaching.

453. Schwartz, p. 86,25–26; PG 86, 1009D.

454. Schwartz, p. 86,27–28; PG 86, 1009D.

455. Schwartz, p. 82,8–14; PG 86, 1005AB.

456. *Ibid.*, Schwartz, p. 83,12–14: *isti autem hominis exemplo utuntur, ut unam naturam sive substantiam (ousian) deitatis et humanitatis Christi introducerent, quod demonstravimus alienum esse pietatis.*

For all the Fathers in harmony teach us that 'nature' (*physis*) or 'essence' (*ousia*) or 'form' (*morphē*) is one thing, but *hypostasis* (Latin: *subsistentia*) or 'person' (*prosopon*) is something else, and 'nature' or 'essence' or 'form' signifies what is common (*koinon*), *hypostasis* or 'person', however, what is particular (*idikon*).[457]

(b) The unhistorical basis for condemning the Three Chapters

Although in the decree on correct faith we find the fundamental Chalcedonian formula of one *hypostasis* in two natures and a clear rejection of the *mia-physis* formula, nevertheless the terminology is refined beyond Chalcedon in the sense of a cautious new interpretation. On the basis of the usage of concepts which had grown in the course of the sixth century, Justinian judges the teaching of the Three Chapters from the fifth century, hence from a period in which the Antiochenes attempted to ward off the crass Apollinarian understanding of the unity in Christ by emphasizing the totality of Christ's humanity. Their suspicion that they were dealing with Apollinarianism gave rise to their rejection of formulas like 'from two natures one', 'one nature of the incarnate Word', 'union according to the *hypostasis* and *physis*', which were to be found in the Cyril of the anti-Nestorian period. These especially offended them. From the viewpoint of the sixth century, however, what was lacking in the Antiochene response of Diodore of Tarsus up to Theodoret was more sharply presented than it could have been in 431, given the historical state of affairs. The fact that the Antiochenes themselves had made advances in the direction of a more profound understanding of the unity in Christ was suppressed in the polemics. This comes to expression particularly clearly in the thirteen *Kephalaia* (*capitula*) or anathemas of the decree.[458] Because these were taken over by the Council of 553 in a somewhat altered form and were expanded and focused, they should be evaluated in this context. We shall assess them here only in order to form a judgement about whether there is already something typically 'neo-Chalcedonian' in Justinian himself with his decree about correct faith.

Excursus: On the concept 'neo-Chalcedonianism'[459]

J. Lebon created this expression in imitation of the terms old-Nicenism and neo-Nicenism, which had become customary for the history of doc-

---

457. Schwartz, p. 86,18–21; PG 86, 1009C.
458. Schwartz, pp. 90,16–94,34; PG 86, 1013C–1019B.
459. Cf. C. Moeller, 'Le chalcédonisme et le néo-chalcédonisme', in *Chalkedon* I[5], 648. On the history of the problem (with a bibliography) see A. Grillmeier, 'Der Neu-Chalkedonismus', in *idem, Mit ihm und in ihm* (Freiburg, Basel, Vienna, [2]1978), 371–85; S. Helmer, *Der Neuchalke-*

trine of the fourth century between 325 and 381.[460] This terminology
was intended to establish and typify a change in conceptual usage and
in the understanding of the trinitarian dogma, as this had taken place
between the Council of Nicaea and the First Council of Constantinople.
If the old-Nicenes employed the concepts *hypostasis* and *physis* (*ousia*)
synonymously, the neo-Nicenes distinguished both words, so that they
could speak of three *hypostases* and one *physis* (*ousia*) in the Trinity.[461]
In particular this was the work of Basil and Gregory Nazianzen.[462] The
latter took over this distinction of concepts from the doctrine of
the Trinity (*theologia*) into the doctrine of the incarnation as well, the
oikonomia. While Cyril of Alexandria followed this linguistic convention
for the *theologia*, for the *oikonomia* he held fast to the old synonymous
use of *hypostasis* and *physis*, which continued to be the old-Alexandrian
tradition. This, then, had particular repercussions in his adoption of the
fundamental christological formula of the Apollinarians on the basis of
the so-called 'Apollinarian forgeries': 'the one *hypostasis* [nature] of the
incarnate Logos'. With this formula Cyril fought above all against
Nestorius, and in general against the Antiochene christology of Diodore,
Theodore of Mopsuestia and Theodoret. They confessed 'two natures'
in Christ, which was now interpreted, in old-Alexandrian terms on the
basis of the synonomy of *physis* and *hypostasis*, as the teaching of two
persons or two *hypostases*.

The dissolution of the synonymous use of *hypostasis* and *physis* —
already presaged in the Constantinopolitan tradition (Proclus of
Constantinople[463]) — did not bring the hoped for peace at Chalcedon,
but division. Old-Alexandrian-Cyrillian and Chalcedonian formulas were
opposed in an irreconcilable manner.

Apart from the Imperial Church's attempt at reconciliation, as
expressed in the *Henoticon* of Emperor Zeno,[464] individual theologians

---

donismus (Bonn, 1962); S. Takayanagi, 'Neo-Chalcedonianism: Its Significance in the History
of Christology', *Katorikku Kenkyu 'Catholic Studies'* 47 (1985), 99–143 (Japanese), xi–xiii (English
summary).

460. Cf. J. Lebon, *Le monophysisme sévérien* (Louvain, 1909), 522, also 119–23, 155–63, 507.
He posits two characteristics for this: a particular group of Chalcedonian theologians had recourse
to Cyril of Alexandria to validate the Council; these theologians were to some extent the first
scholastics, who built up a scientific teaching about the incarnation with the help of philosophy.

461. Cf. A. de Halleux, '"Hypostase" et "Personne" dans la formation du dogme trinitaire
(ca 375–381)', *RHE* 79 (1984), 313–69, 625–70.

462. *JdChr* I³, 538–9.

463. See *JdChr* I³, 727–30.

464. On this see *CCT* II/1.

now made proposals aimed at mediation, which were situated on the level of linguistic formulas. On the basis of such observations J. Lebon spoke of 'neo-Chalcedonianism'.

Two opponents of Severus of Antioch, the monk of Majuma, namely the monk Nephalius, and the grammarian John of Caesarea, believed that they could restore unity by proposing a simultaneous usage of both the Alexandrian *mia-physis* formula and the Chalcedonian *dyo-physeis* formula — one to ward off Nestorianism, the other to exclude Eutychianism.[465]

When in his well-known article on Nephalius[466] J. Lebon's student C. Moeller took up this suggestion and expanded it, a misunderstanding arose; as neo-Chalcedonianism Moeller characterized a 'dialectical theology' which, he said, worked with two traditions and attempted to bring them together by means of a rational explanation.[467] Were one to follow these tracks laid down by Lebon and Moeller, however, one could include in fact under the term 'neo-Chalcedonianism' a fair share of the literature immediately preceding Chalcedon. For this reason the year 433, with the union between Cyril and the Antiochenes, had really anticipated the neo-Chalcedonian synthesis (*néo-chalcédonisme avant la lettre*).

Here M. Richard intervened, simply by means of a few pages.[468] He stressed rightly that Cyril from the very beginning belonged to the christology worked out at Chalcedon.[469] He established, however, a firm boundary: neo-Chalcedonianism is distinguished from strict Chalcedonianism by the fact that it uses both major christological formulas (*mia physis* and *dyo physeis*) 'as the essential condition of a correct presentation of faith'. This is the way in which C. Moeller, subsequent to M. Richard, formulated it.[470] In this way a useful definition was found.

In the course of this investigation we have sought witnesses of this neo-Chalcedonianism dialectic. In Constantinople[471] they formed only a small group, insofar as we look strictly at the antithesis of the two basic christological formulas: Nephalius (after 507), John the Grammarian from Caesarea, who could be refuted by Severus, however, only when the latter was in exile

---

465. See C. Moeller, 'Le chalcédonisme et le néo-chalcédonisme', in *Chalkedon* I[5], 637–720, esp. 670–1 (Nephalius); 672–6 (John the Grammarian).

466. C. Moeller, 'Nephalius d'Alexandrie', *RHE* (1944/5), 73–140.

467. *Ibid.*, 117.

468. M. Richard, 'Le Néo-chalcédonisme', *MSR* 3 (1946), 156–61 = *Op. Min.* II, no. 56; further studies in A. Grillmeier, 'Der Neu-Chalkedonismus', in *idem*, *Mit ihm und in ihm* (Freiburg, Basel, Vienna, [2]1978), 371, n. 1 (b).

469. T. Šagi-Bunić and A. de Halleux have significantly deepened this knowledge: see *CCT* I.

470. C. Moeller, in *Chalkedon* I, 666f.

471. Here we also include Nephalius and John the Grammarian insofar as the altercation between them and Severus was certainly already in progress when the latter was residing in the Imperial City (508–511). Nephalius was the reason for this journey.

(519). It was above all the Scythian monks under their leader John Maxentius who saw to it that there was a longer-lasting and more vehement discussion about neo-Chalcedonianism in the Imperial City.[472] Later in the Palestinian region we shall encounter Theodore of Raithu. For this whole group the antithesis of one and two natures stood at the centre of their conception. That ecclesiastical orthodoxy could bother at all about the *mia-physis* formula resulted from its 'baptism' by Cyril of Alexandria.

C. Moeller also adduced Leontius of Jerusalem as a representative of the necessity of using both formulas to express right faith.[473] But here we have to differentiate. We have three texts in which Leontius does not demand the 'alternating usage', but only allows it after a 'consideration of goods' or after a discernment of spirits. For one should not parrot everything that the heretics say.

First text: 'Discernment of spirits'[474]

Not so, my pious ones, not so, but let us consider what matters (*ta diapheronta*) (cf. Rom 2,8; Phil 1,10), we who have exercised our senses in distinguishing good and evil. We test everything and retain the good (1 Thess 5,21).

Thus for the sake of truth — to the gallows with all who say with a heretical intention: 'one incarnate nature of the God-Logos'. But all who speak of a duality of the undivided, united natures in an impious understanding are also to be detested. In contrast, however, all who speak of the one incarnate nature of the God-Logos, but as of one other nature, namely that of the flesh to which the nature of the Logos is united according to the *hypostasis*, are to be accepted; and all who confess the duality of the inseparably united natures of Christ, not insofar as they are seen as *ousia*, but in relation to the *hypostasis* itself of the natures, that is, to prove the one person (*prosopon*) of both, by respectfully deeming each of the two confessions as the same.

Second text: 'From two' and 'in two'[475]

Because we proclaim in common that the Lord is *from* two natures and at the same time *in* two natures, we are prepared to curse the Synod, every being (*pasan physin*), even an angel himself who descended from heaven, if he did not want to confess the same (cf. Gal 1,8). Why do they not agree to confessing the same with us, by saying with us 'from two' together with the 'in two'? Why do they not condemn Severus and Dioscorus and their like-minded supporters? Because Flavian of blessed memory says in his confession of faith: 'the one nature of the God-Logos, nevertheless become flesh and a human being . . . from both', we too do not hesitate to confess that our one Lord Jesus Christ is from both, because the holy Synod [of Constantinople 448] also says this full of respect; why, after all this, should the Synod not agree?

472. See above, pp. 327–38; cf. S. Helmer, *Der Neuchalkedonismus* (Bonn, 1962), 117–27.
473. C. Moeller, 'Le chalcédonisme et le néo-chalcédonisme', in *Chalkedon* I[5], 686: 'Il [Léonce de Jérusalem] admet les deux formules comme nécessaires à la foi.'
474. Leontius Jer., *CM, Testimonia SS.*: PG 86, 1812CD.
475. *Idem, CM*: PG 86, 1844BC.

Third text: 'Necessity of hermeneutics'

(After Leontius has reproached the false use of 'undivided' by the Nestorians and praised the corrected use by Cyril,[476] he examines the *mia-physis* formula in Cyril):

> We can also interpret that other expression 'the one incarnate nature of the God-Logos' with Arius, as if the Son would have had no immutable nature; or with Apollinarius, as if the Logos himself had taken the place of the ensouled *nous* and animated the non-rational flesh; or with Eutyches, as if the Logos himself was changed into flesh.
>
> Thus if we do not test carefully the thoughts of those confessing, we shall never understand correctly this or that expression. The Father [Cyril] says that one should not accept heretics, because they err against the [right] understanding of the union of the natures, even if their expressions sound good. For they call the natures undivided not according to the *hypostasis*, but according to the relationship.[477]

In none of the three important texts from the *CM* does Leontius of Jerusalem demand the alternating confession of the two antithetical formulas: 'one *hypostasis* in two natures' — 'the one incarnate nature of the God-Logos'. He simply establishes that in the Cyrillian one-nature formula and in the other christological expressions there is the possibility of a false and a correct understanding, a discovery which theologians of the sixth century elsewhere, for instance in Africa, make. The right interpretation is to be acknowledged; the false one is to be rejected. For this reason Cyril and Flavian of Constantinople are the two authorities.

Hence Leontius of Jerusalem cannot be reckoned among the neo-Chalcedonians in Richard's sense, who demand simultaneous speech in two different conceptual systems. At the most his juxtaposition of 'from two natures' and 'in two natures' approaches this demand. For this juxtaposition, however, he has recourse to Flavian's Synod of 448.[478]

Leontius of Jerusalem, however, is distinguished from the strict Chalcedonians of the type of Leontius of Byzantium[479] by the emphasis he places upon the union and by his teaching of divinization, and in this

---

476. *Idem, CM*: PG 86, 1853AB.

477. *Idem, CM*: PG 86, 1853BC.

478. In these texts we already have important elements which we shall encounter in Justinian's edict, *Keph.* 9, and in the Council of 553. We should interpret this as an indication that Leontius of Jerusalem was read (and lived?) in Constantinople and probably wrote from the context of the questions being asked there.

479. These are at a great distance from Cyril. Thus for instance Leontius of Byzantium, in stressing Christ's human will and freedom, stands in opposition to Cyril (above, pp. 222–6). Strict-Chalcedonians, like Hypatius, recognize Cyril as an authority only to a limited degree; cf. the noteworthy text, ACO IV, 2, p. 175,33–38: 'We accept [from Cyril] what is in agreement with his synodal letters [i.e. those ratified by Ephesus or Chalcedon]; what does not agree with these we do not condemn, but we also do not observe it as ecclesiastical law. As we said above, we consider as synodal letters those letters which were accepted and ratified by the holy Councils [Ephesus and Chalcedon], namely the one to Nestorius as well as the one to the Orientals.'

he comes close to Cyril. Nevertheless he lays the foundation for his christology on the basis of the Cappadocian teaching about *idiomata*, *not* through recourse to Cyril.[480]

We now want to characterize as 'neo-Chalcedonians in the extreme or integral sense'[481] those theologians who demand for the correct presentation of faith in Jesus Christ, the incarnate Son of God, the simultaneous use of two systems of formulas: the *mia-physis* formula against Nestorianism, understood as the teaching of two *hypostases*; the two-natures formula against Eutyches, as representing a christology of mingling. They want to remain Chalcedonians, but overlook the incompatibility of the two conceptual systems. 'Moderate neo-Chalcedonianism' we shall call that christological position which remains on the basis of Chalcedon (with the distinction of *physis* and *hypostasis* and the formula of the one *hypostasis* in two natures), but seeks to *supplement* the language of Chalcedon by the additional incorporation of Cyrillian terms and formulas, especially from the twelve anathemas, without demanding, however, the simultaneous use of the *mia-physis* formula or allowing it (this occurring, at the most, under definite conditions).

With respect to his theology of union and his tendency towards divinization Leontius of Jerusalem can be reckoned among the moderate neo-Chalcedonians, insofar as some of his theological emphases indicate a convergence towards Cyril which goes beyond the Cyrillianism of Chalcedon.

(c) Neo-Chalcedonian terminology?

(i) The decree of 551 does not demand the simultaneous use of the *mia-physis* formula and the two-natures language, and thus is not an instance of extreme neo-Chalcedonianism. For *Keph.* 9 cannot be interpreted in this sense.[482] The Emperor indeed admits that the *mia-physis* formula can be correctly understood, namely in the sense of the twofold consubstantiality of the one Christ with the Father according to the divinity, and with us according to the humanity; but according to Justinian there is also a fundamentally false understanding of this formula in the sense

---

480. Leontius of Jerusalem differs from him in important points. Leontius of Jerusalem makes a clear distinction between a nature union and a hypostatic union (above, p. 276). For him *synthesis* is the central point, not *henosis* (above, pp. 294–5). Instead of Cyril's hegemony of the Logos, Leontius of Jerusalem clearly recognizes the endowment of Christ's humanity with grace by the Spirit (above, pp. 300–4).

481. Instead of 'neo-Chalcedonianism' one could also speak of 'neo-Cyrillianism'.

482. Schwartz, 92; PG 86, 1015D.

of Apollinarius and Eutyches, which is anathematized. From this viewpoint Justinian cannot bring himself to allow the *mia-physis* formula the function of a necessary corrective to the Chalcedonian formula.

(ii) Nevertheless we can discover in the decree of 551 traces of a moderate neo-Chalcedonianism, in the sense of supplementing the strict-Chalcedonian terminology with elements of the language determined by Cyril's twelve anathemas.

(1) 'Distinguishing according to the *theoria*' (*Keph.* 8)

If anyone confesses number [=duality] of the natures in our one Lord Jesus Christ, that is, in the incarnate Logos, and thereby takes their [the natures'] distinction (*diaphora*), from which he is composed, as not only according to the *theoria*, in which it [the distinction] is not annulled on account of the union, but uses the number for division (*dihairesis*), let him be anathema.

'Distinction according to vision or *theoria*' is a typically Cyrillian point of view,[483] with which the Alexandrian attempts to reconcile the 'unmingled' with the 'undivided' of the two natures. He contrasts a difference of God and the human being in Christ, which *secundum rationem* always remains, with the real being one of both in the one Christ. The presence of a simple distinction according to 'vision' guarantees as well the 'unmingled' of both natures, and also their real 'undivided'. The introduction of this concept of *theoria* thus signifies no change to the Chalcedonian two-natures teaching, but only an intensified protection against its misinterpretation.

(2) 'From two natures' — 'in two natures'. This synthesis, rejected at Chalcedon, as everybody knows, is now undisputed (Schwartz, 74,14–16 with 16–17; PG 86, 997A). Justinian has no dread of Chalcedon's two natures nor of the number 'two' (see below).

(3) 'The one composite Christ.'[484] After the appearance of the Scythian monks in Constantinople the word 'composition' (*synthesis, synthetos; compositio, compositus*) played an increasing rôle. Now it becomes the key word in Justinian's christology.

'From two natures, that is, from divinity and humanity, one composite Christ' (Schwartz, 74,14–16). 'Because we speak of composition, we must also confess both that there are parts in the whole and that the whole is known in its parts' (Schwartz, 74,20–21; PG 86, 997A); 'Division or separation we do not introduce into his one *hypostasis* (Latin: *uni eius subsistentiae*); we indicate, however, the distinction of the natures from which he is composed . . . because each of the two natures is in him' (Schwartz, 74,18–20; PG 86, 997A); whoever refuses to speak of the number of the natures in Christ attempts to introduce mingling (Schwartz, 86,11–13; PG 86, 1009B).

483. Cf. Cyril Alex., *Ep. 46 ad Succens.* II: PG 77, 245A.
484. See also below (5).

Such language would have been an abomination for Severus.

(4) 'Union according to the *hypostasis*.' 'Each of the two natures remains in the definition and reason of its own nature; for the union happened according to the *hypostasis*' (Schwartz, 74,22–24; PG 86, 997AB). This 'hypostatic union' is justified on the basis of Philippians 2,6–7 (Schwartz, 74,29–30; PG 86, 997B). What does union according to the *hypostasis* mean?

It says 'that the God-Logos, that is, the one *hypostasis* from the three *hypostases* of the godhead in [this] its own *hypostasis* . . . created (*edēmiourgēsen*) for himself from her [i.e. from Mary] a flesh animated with a spiritual and rational soul, which is [his] human nature' (Schwartz, 74,24–27; PG 86, 997B).

A little later Justinian repeats this statement almost verbatim, expanding it, however, with an interesting explanation: 'which means that the God-Logos is united to the human *nature* and not to the *hypostasis* or *person* of another' (Schwartz, 86,30–33; PG 86, 1009D–1011A).

To some extent the two texts reveal to us how Justinian envisages the 'hypostatic union', not in a conceptual, ontological analysis, but as a concrete happening: the union coincides with the act of creating Christ's human nature. Other Fathers already saw it this way.[485] But two things should be noted. (i) Justinian says *plasmavit sibi* (*edēmiourgēsen heautoi*), that is, the divine *hypostasis* creates this spiritually ensouled human nature for himself, for the purpose of being *hypostasis* for it and to exist humanly in it as divine *hypostasis*. Fundamentally this is a good *concrete* explanation of the insubsistence or *enhypostasis* of Christ's human nature in the hypostatic Logos.[486] (ii) The Emperor does not think of considering *formally* the *ratio* of the *hypostasis* or subsistence in order to determine the 'hypostatic union'. He remains on the level of existence.

(5) *Unus de sancta Trinitate* (Schwartz, 72,33; PG 86, 995C). This formula is *not* Cyrillian, but a pre-Chalcedonian element (Proclus) and belongs to the Emperor's linguistic repertoire from the time of his first theological action. For him it is the expression of the unity of Christ in the real divine subject, the person of the Word. The 'incarnate Word' is the bearer of suffering (Schwartz, 74).

After the incarnation he is also one of the Trinity, the only-begotten Son of God, our Lord Jesus Christ, *composed* from *both* natures. We confess Christ as composite, however, in the tradition of the teaching of the holy Fathers. (Schwartz, 76,29–32; PG 86, 999BC)

485. Cf. the passages in *JdChr* I[3], 771–2, n. 6.
486. Cf. the highlighting of this text in P. T. R. Gray, *The Defense of Chalcedon in the East (451–553)* (Leiden, 1979), 157.

(d) Evaluation

Vis-à-vis the historical text of the definition of 451 some innovations can be established which do not change Justinian's fundamental Chalcedonianism, but rather on the whole refine a further interpretation already introduced.

(i) First of all the term 'one *hypostasis*' is no longer applied, as at Chalcedon, to the outcome, the end-result (*apotelesma*; cf. Leontius of Byzantium), but to the pre-existent Logos, for whom alone it is correct.

(ii) The assumed human nature participates in a *hypostasis* only by inexisting in the *hypostasis* of the Logos.

(iii) This happens by means of a creative action of the Logos, centred on the Logos, who creatively makes (*demiourgein*) *for himself* permanently the human being, for it remains inseparably 'his nature'.

(iv) Justinian terms the unifying action as *henosis*, but most often as *synthesis*. The two expressions are fundamentally of equal value; however, *synthesis* appears to have the advantage of excluding a *synchysis*, a mingling. We should note too that Justinian uses the formula 'the one composite *hypostasis* of the Logos', but he does not allow the other, 'the one composite nature' (*mia physis synthetos*).[487]

> If some say, however, that one must speak of Christ as of a composite *hypostasis* then also of a composite nature (*mia physis synthetos*), then we shall show that this is foreign to piety.[488]

For in this formula *physis* would be employed absolutely, without the addition of *idiomata*, so that *physis* is purely conceptual, indeterminate and thus 'anhypostatic'. There can be no synthesis at all with such an absolute. The union or synthesis certainly occurs between the Logos-subject and a concrete *physis*. Through its creation for the Logos-subject the *physis* receives, however, its *hypostasis*, its *subsistentia*, its *personalitas* in the Logos himself; in him too the beginning of its existence is based.[489]

(v) Finally Justinian's formula of incarnation immediately before the Council of 553 has several variations.

(1) 'We speak of the union of two natures and of the one *hypostasis*' (Schwartz, p. 86,30; PG 86, 1009D).

(2) 'The Logos of God is also as one become flesh, one *hypostasis*, recognized, however,

487. Schwartz, pp. 86,36–88,1; PG 86, 1011A.
488. Schwartz, p. 86,21–23; PG 86, 1009CD.
489. Schwartz, p. 88,10–12; PG 86, 1011B.

in each of the two natures, namely in the divine [nature], in which he exists [according to Phil 2,6], and in the human [according to Phil 2,7]' (Schwartz, p. 86,33–36; PG 86, 1011A).

(3) The result is:

'Before the incarnation there were not two natures of the Lord, nor after the incarnation was there one from the two,[490] even if they are recognized as in one *hypostasis*' (Schwartz, p. 88,24–26; PG 86, 1011D).

In the decree of 551 Justinian thus certainly handed on the Constantinopolitan christology of his time not merely as a 'dilettante', but with a commendable understanding of the problems of incarnational theology. We find no flirting with the Severan or Theodosian *mia-physis* teaching. There can also be no talk of a pronounced neo-Chalcedonianism, for example in the sense of John the Grammarian. Although *hypostasis* (*prosopon*) is clearly contrasted to *physis* and *ousia*, there is still no attempt to gain a definition of *hypostasis* which goes beyond the 'individualized' *physis* or *ousia*. Sadly we miss the endeavour to judge the Antiochene/anti-Apollinarian christology of the fourth and fifth centuries fairly, even though the Emperor clearly saw through the falseness of the Apollinarian teaching.

In Justinian we find for the first time the sketch of a complete interpretation of Christ's person and its union of divine and human nature in the one divine *hypostasis* of the Logos. This sketch reproduces fundamentally the Chalcedonian formula of the one *hypostasis* in two natures, but for its stronger interpretation in the sense of *henosis* it draws upon a series of Cyrillian elements. From time to time it is evident that in important points Leontius of Jerusalem can be considered as a model for this.

With this consideration we have already anticipated the synthesis of the Fifth Ecumenical Council.

III. THE FIFTH ECUMENICAL COUNCIL OF CONSTANTINOPLE (553) AND ITS CHRISTOLOGICAL STATEMENT

The Second Council of Constantinople took place in eight *actiones* from 5 May to 2 June 553. It was summoned by Justinian himself. The Emperor did not participate in it *in persona*, just as Pope Vigilius did not either, but he had a decisive influence on the discussions and the decisions about the Three Chapters.[491] The framework within which

490. This is equivalent to a rejection of 'one nature from two natures'.
491. Cf. J. Straub, *Praefatio* to ACO IV, 1, XXXII–XXXIV.

the Synod, which was composed principally of bishops from the East Roman Empire,[492] was intended to proceed was determined by the *forma* that the Emperor ordered to be read out before it began.[493]

1. The task of the Council according to Justinian

In this *forma* the Emperor unmistakably called to mind the Eusebian-Constantinian principle of unity as the basis of his *rei publicae gubernatio*.

> We have made it the starting-point and foundation of our rule to unite the separated bishops of the holy Churches of God from the East to the West, and to end all conflict which was instigated against the holy Synod of Chalcedon by the supporters of the impious men, Eutyches and Nestorius.[494]

Chalcedon's agreement with the three previous synods is the foundation of the Emperor's understanding of a council. Clearly the dread of Nestorianism stands as a leitmotiv in the foreground. According to Justinian, however, it is now the new tactic of the opponents of the Council not to revive Nestorianism directly, but to smuggle it into the Church by a detour through Theodore of Mopsuestia, the teacher of Nestorius, as well as through Theodoret's writings against Ephesus and Cyril, and finally through the letter allegedly written by Ibas to the Persian Mari.[495] True (Chalcedonian) faith can only be defended by excluding

---

492. See E. Chrysos, *Die Bischofslisten des V. Ökumenischen Konzils (553)* = *Antiquitas*, R. 1, Vol. 14 (Bonn, 1966). The total number of participating bishops was 168: *op. cit.*, 44–51; the dogmatic canons of the Council were subscribed by 166 bishops. All (Eastern) patriarchs presided in common, with the newly nominated Patriarch of Jerusalem, Eustochius, being represented by three bishops (ACO IV, 1, 221, nos. 4–6). From imperial Egypt only ten bishops participated under the Chalcedonian Patriarch Apollinarius. Pope Vigilius did not belong to the Council and was considered at least by the Emperor as a defendant. Cf. E. Chrysos, *op. cit.*, 53: ACO IV, 1, pp. 200,38–201,2 (=*actio* VII, no. 14; the Pope did not receive a title). There were 94 (?) participants from the Patriarchate of Constantinople (Chrysos, *op. cit.*, 80–109), 41 from Antioch (*ibid.*, 113–25), and five from Jerusalem (or four according to L. Perrone, *La chiesa di Palestina* [Brescia, 1980], 218–19; ACO IV, 1, 3–4, nos. IV–VI, XX). There were as well the synodal members from East Illyricum: one from Dacia (but four were present in Constantinople), eight from Macedonia (Chrysos, *op. cit.*, 128–38). Finally the lists of bishops from 553 name nine bishops from Africa (as representatives of three of the six provinces). Because no bishop participated from the anti-Chalcedonian Churches which were in the process of becoming organized (Syria) or were already organized (Egypt), the plan to win over these Churches by condemning the Three Chapters had in essence already foundered.

493. See ACO IV, 1, 8–14 (CPG 6887).

494. *Ibid.*, no. 7, p. 10,13–17. Cf. F. Carcione, 'Vigilio nelle controversie cristologiche del suo tempo', *StRiOrCr* 10 (1987), 37–51. The Emperor stresses his rôle as the custodian of orthodoxy, cf. *ibid.*, 49–50.

495. ACO IV, 1, no. 8, pp. 10,24–11,3.

these 'impious Three Chapters' (*impia tria capitula*). Pope Vigilius too 'not only once or twice, but often anathematized these impious Three Chapters, both in writing and orally'.[496] On 7 January 553 Vigilius tied his own hands by agreeing in reply to a letter of Patriarch Eutychius (CPG 9355[2]) to an ecumenical council held under his presidency, with all his rights being preserved.[497] Finally, however, because his conditions were not fulfilled, he refused to participate in the Council which the Emperor ordered to be opened on 5 May 553 under the presidency of Patriarch Eutychius (in union with the other patriarchs or their representatives). In his *Constitutum* (I) of 14 May 553, inspired (and redacted) by the deacon Pelagius,[498] the Pope delivered his judgement on the Three Chapters. In this the Pope condemned in 60 chapters various errors which were taken anonymously from the works of Theodore of Mopsuestia (CPG 3858[b]). He explained his assent to Ephesus (I) and Chalcedon, his agreement with Proclus and Cyril and his rejection of Theodore's heretical teachings. The latter's name, however, should not be stated and no judgement should be passed on one who was dead.[499]

Then there followed anonymously five errors which are attributed to Theodoret.[500] If one wanted to condemn Nestorian errors under the name 'Theodoret', then Chalcedon itself would be affected. Finally Vigilius claimed that the letter of Ibas was orthodox and had been accepted by the Fathers of Chalcedon: *orthodoxa est Ibae episcopi a patribus pronuntiata dictatio*.[501] The efforts of the Pope were in vain. When he

---

496. *Ibid.*, no. 10, p. 11,11–15. Justinian then adduces parts of the so-called *iudicatum* of Pope Vigilius of 11 April 548 (CPL 1694 [9337]) with this threefold condemnation. On the text see CA, *ep.* 83, nos. 299–302, pp. 315–17; ACO IV, 1, pp. 11,21–12,6.

497. *Ep. Vigilii ppae ad Eutychium* (CPG 9355 [3]): ACO IV, 1, 16–18; 236–8 (Greek). The conditions which Vigilius set were the following: participation of the Latins and the holding of the synod in Sicily or Italy, which the Emperor did not accept.

498. *Vigilii Constitutum* (I) (CPL 1694): CA, *ep.* 83, 230–320; JW 935. See ACO IV, 1, XXIX on the three texts of Vigilius which belong together: *Constitutum* I; *Ep. II ad Eutychium* (8 December 553): ACO IV, 1, 245–7; the so-called *Constitutum* II of 23 February 554: ACO IV, 2, 138–68.

499. Cf. CA, *ep.* 83: CSEL 35/1, 237–93.

500. Cf. *ibid.*, 293–6.

501. Cf. *ibid.*, nos. 236–79, pp. 296–309; for the cited sentence see p. 305,26–27. With the assertion that Ibas' letter had been accepted as orthodox by the Fathers of Chalcedon, Vigilius erred with the whole of the Western Church. Cf. ACO II, 1, 3, 32–4; R. Haacke, in *Chalkedon* II, 165, n. 90; E. Zettl, *Die Bestätigung des V. Ökumenischen Konzils durch Papst Vigilius* (Bonn, 1974), 12–13. Cf. CPG 6500–1 on the letter of Ibas; G. G. Blum, *Rabbula von Edessa . . .*, CSCO 300 (Louvain, 1969), 196–203.

tried to present his *Constitutum* to the Emperor on 25 May 553, the latter did not accept it.[502]

In the Church of the East before 553 these three persons named were judged critically, but without the demand that they or their writings be anathematized, as Leontius of Byzantium showed us.[503] According to his *Constitutum* I the Pope, together with the Western bishops, defended the Three Chapters, in contrast to his *iudicatum* of 11 April 548, in which he had condemned them.[504] For the Fathers of the Council of 553 Pope Vigilius had excluded himself from the ecclesial community, because he had confessed the heresies of Nestorius and Theodore of Mopsuestia. His name should be struck from the diptychs.[505] With reference to the earlier contrary statements of the Pope, in *actio* VIII of the Council on 2 June 553, the bishops then condemned the Three Chapters.[506] Pope Vigilius and the Council thus stood in open opposition which signified an extremely severe crisis for the relationship of East and West and simply for the Imperial Church. Was this the last word of the Pope to the Council and on the question of the Three Chapters?

Until recently there was uncertainty about whether Vigilius finally ratified the Fifth Council or not. We are concerned in particular with two documents: (1) the letter *Scandala*, that is, *Epistula* II of Pope Vigilius to Eutychius of 8 December 553, and (2) the letter *Aetius* of 23 February 554, or the so-called *Constitutum* II.[507]

---

502. It is for this reason, it seems, that his text was never published. Cf. E. Zettl, *op. cit.*, 13.

503. Cf. Leontius Byz., *DTN*; on this see *JdChr* II/1, 66–7; there is talk, however, of Theodore's 'blasphemies' (cf. PG 86, 1384B). The Chalcedonians in the East and West were disinclined to anathematize the three names, especially because the first to do this, and with increasing ferocity after 532, were the anti-Chalcedonians *in praeiudicium synodi Chalcedonensis*, as Facundus of Hermiane said: *Pro def. tr. cap.* IV, IV, 23: CCL 90A, p. 127,172.

504. On the motives for this change see E. Zettl, *op. cit.*, 13: 'There remains hardly any other solution than to accept that Vigilius now reached the convictions of the Latins that the condemnation was not possible without prejudice to the Council of Chalcedon.'

505. *Conc. Const. II, actio VII* (from 26 May 553): ACO IV, 1, 201–2 (CPG 6888). In this Justinian describes the Pope's individual stages and establishes: *praeterea ipse semetipsum alienum catholicae ecclesiae fecit defendens praedictorum capitulorum impietatem, separans autem semet a vestra communione. his igitur ab eo factis alienum christianis iudicavimus nomen ipsius sacris diptychis non recitari, ne eo modo inveniamur Nestorii et Theodori impietati communicantes* (p. 202,5–9). Nevertheless Justinian does not want to know anything about abandoning unity with the Holy See as such, initiated either by himself or by the Council Fathers (202,11–12). In practice he distinguishes between 'sedem' and 'sedentem'.

506. See the *Sententia Synodica*: ACO IV, 1, 208–15 (Latin); 239–40 (Greek).

507. The *Constitutum* II (CPG [9365]; CPL 1696) (ACO IV, 2, 138–68) was discovered by E. Baluze in *Cod. Paris. Lat.* 1682; cf. E. Zettl, *op. cit.*, 17–19. The introduction and the signature at the end are missing. The letter *Scandala* (CPG [9364]; CPL 1694) (ACO IV, 1, 245–247) is now attested to by three MSS: *Cod. paris. gr.* 1115, fol. 36v–38v; Arundel 529, fol. 87r–91r and Athous Iviron 381, fol. 314r–316r; cf. J. Straub, *Praefatio*, ACO IV, 1, XXV.

Doubts about the authenticity[508] of the so-called *Constitutum* II (*Aetius*) persisted undeservedly for a long time. *De facto* they were dismissed in the dissertation of E. Zettl CSSR, *Die Bestätigung des V. Ökumenischen Konzils durch Papst Vigilius. Untersuchungen über die Echtheit der Briefe Scandala und Aetius* (JK. 936,937), which was written in 1929 under the supervision of C. Silva-Tarouca, but was not published. The author was successful in proving clearly that the two letters of Vigilius are authentic. This important study was first given a correct evaluation by J. Straub in the course of the edition of the *acta* of the Fifth Ecumenical Council.[509] The relationship between Pope Vigilius and the Fifth Ecumenical Council is now explained and clearly presented by J. Straub in the *praefatio* to ACO IV, 1, XXIX–XXXII.

Particularly important is proof of the agreement between the letters *Scandala* and *Aetius* (*Constitutum* II) on the one hand, and of both with the *acta* of the Council on the other.

> On 2 June the Council had ended with the definition of the *sententia synodica* and the canons (*anathemata*); the letter [*Scandala*] was subsequently added to the *acta*, which were concluded with the subscriptions. The Pope, who himself stayed away from the Council, was not included among the signatories; rather he made known his assent to the condemnation of the Three Chapters in the form of an *epistula decretalis*, a *constitutum*. Not once did he refer to the decision of the Council, but took over verbatim nonetheless the formulations of the *sententia synodica* which appeared to him decisive, and especially Canons XII and XIIII, in order in this way to proclaim his agreement with the Council, while preserving the 'Petrine doctrine'.[510]

In each of the three MSS in which the letter *Scandala* is transmitted it is remarked that this letter of 8 December 553 was addressed to Eutychius and to the Council.[511] Thus in an official writing,[512] that is, with full papal authority, Vigilius condemned the Three Chapters. Justinian had attained his goal, but between himself and the Pope the primacy of papal (teaching) authority remained unclarified.[513]

---

508. It was decidedly denied (together with the authenticity of *Scandala*) by C. Silva-Tarouca, *Fontes Historiae Ecclesiasticae medii aevi in usum scholarum* I (Rome, 1930), 52, with n. 2; furthermore it was called into doubt by E. Amann, art. 'Trois-Chapitres', in *DTC* 15 (1950), 1868–1924, esp. 1923; by C. Moeller, in *Chalkedon* I[5], 687–90; *idem*, 'Le cinquième concile oecuménique et le magistère ordinaire au VIe siècle', *RSPT* 35 (1951), 413–23; I. Ortiz de Urbina, 'Quali sententia "Tria Capitula" a sede romana damnata sunt?', *OCP* 33 (1967), 184–209, still denied its authenticity.

509. Cf. J. Straub, 'Die Verurteilung der Drei Kapitel durch Vigilius (*Vigilii Epistula II ad Eutychium*)', *Kleronomia* 2 (1970), 347–75; *idem*, Foreword to E. Zettl, *op. cit.*, on its publication by the author himself in *Antiquitas*, R. 1, Vol. 20 (Bonn, 1974), V–IX.

510. J. Straub, *Praefatio*, ACO IV, 1, XXX.

511. *Ibid.*

512. Greek: διατυπώσει τοῦ παρόντος ἡμῶν γράμματος (ACO IV, 1, p. 247,28). Hence E. Caspar, *Geschichte des Papsttums* II (Tübingen, 1933), 282, speaks unjustly of a 'private retraction' (of the *Constitutum* of 14 May 553). Cf. also *Aetius* of 23 February 554: *praesentis nostri plenissimi constituti auctoritas* (ACO IV, 2, p. 168,12).

513. Cf. J. Straub, *Praefatio*, ACO IV, 1, XXXII, who also comments that it remains questionable whether *Constitutum* II (=*Aetius*) was appended subsequently to the *acta* of the Council.

2. The christological statement of the Council

Preliminary comment

From the course of the Three Chapters dispute as a whole and of the Second Council of Constantinople in particular we have in fact a twofold question to answer: (1) What did the Council, with all of the documents pertaining to it, condemn?; (2) What positive statement did it contribute to the history of the Church's christology?

On the one hand the first question needs very complicated investigations, but on the other it can receive a relatively simple response. The Three Chapters dispute, like the earlier Arian–anti-Arian conflict in the fourth century, called for an almost incalculable documentation, in the concrete instance here innumerable extracts from the works of Theodore of Mopsuestia, Theodoret of Cyrus and Ibas of Edessa's letter to Mari, made by friend and foe of the Three Chapters. One will immediately recognize that, in spite of the important research work that has already been carried out, the critical examination and judgement of these documents still demands an extraordinarily great expenditure of time and energy. One point attracts attention in a special way: does the material produced by opponents and defenders offer a reliable basis to answer the question whether the Three Chapters were rightly or falsely condemned? The question is important, for it concerns the authority of an ecclesiastical assembly assumed to be ecumenical. In the first instance it concerns patristic scholars,[514] ecclesiastical historians and researchers

---

514. See the important research of M. Richard, 'La tradition des fragments du traité Περὶ τῆς ἐνανθρωπήσεως de Théodore de Mopsueste', *Mus* 56 (1943), 55–75 = *Op. Min.* II, no. 41. CPG and CPL now offer an excellent listing of the sources of the textual material cited and discussed in the whole dispute about the Three Chapters, and for the Three Chapters under the names:

I. CPG: (1) Theodore of Mopsuestia: CPG 3827–73. We should note in no. 3856 *De Incarnatione* that one must distinguish between a *traditio genuina* and a *traditio alterata*, which already indicates the whole problem. Does this distinction stand the test? In a work discovered posthumously on the fragments of Theodore in Lagarde, the well-known Orientalist R. Köbert (d. 1987) made critical comments on the Syriac texts in Lagarde, pp. 104,27–105,24 and Sachau, pp. 70,2–71,9 and their mutual relationship. It is still not published, but it is being prepared for publication by L. Abramowski.

(2) Theodoret of Cyrus: CPG 6200–78, esp. no. 6214 (*Impugnatio XII anathematismorum Cyrilli*) with reference to ACO IV, 3, 1; no. 6215 (*Libri V c. Cyrill. et concil. Ephes. [Pentalogus]*); no. 6216 (*De theol. s. trin. et de oeconomia*); no. 6220 (*Pro Diodoro et Theodoro*); in addition nos. 6226–30 (*Ex serm. Chal. c. Cyrill. habito*) and 6240, among many more.

(3) Ibas of Edessa: CPG 6500–1.

(4) To be added are:

    (a) CPG 9332–66 (*Concilium Constantinop.* II: 553)

    (b) R. Schieffer, *Index Generalis Tomorum I–IIII, Index prosopographicus, sub nom. Ibas*, ACO IV,

into the history of councils. The adequate working through of this question would completely transcend the framework of this study, above all of this volume. Consequently we must choose the simpler way and establish only the end-result of this condemnation: namely a renewed condemnation after 122 years (since Ephesus [431]) of Nestorianism and of its main theses: of the teaching of two *hypostases* or persons; of the denial of the *theotokos* title to Mary; of the teaching of two sons and of other teachings, this time only with the difference that with these teachings three particular names were incriminated. These were Theodore of Mopsuestia, not only with the condemnation of his works, but also of his person *post mortem*; Theodoret of Cyrus, on account of his special individual works; and Ibas of Edessa or an anonymous letter with Nestorian teachings 'allegedly' circulating under his name. On account of the last two names the Council of Chalcedon was also drawn into the dispute. It was finally a question of whether the Council could be completely cleared of the suspicion of encouraging Nestorianism, which now called for positively defined terminology in the *sententia synodica* and in the canons of the Fifth Ecumenical Council. In these the positive dogmatic outcome of the Council was expressed, and it is to this that we now wish to turn.

(a) Analysis: Chalcedonian christology in the dogmatic interpretation of the Council of 553

In the eighth *actio* of the Council on 2 June 553 the assembly was closed with the *Sententia Synodica* and the approbation of fourteen canons.[515]

(i) The Sententia Synodica

To our disappointment, in the twenty-eight paragraphs there was hardly one positive dogmatic explanation, as for instance the *horos* that Chalcedon offers; rather that 'Nestorianism' which was said to threaten

---

3, 2, 1, 227–9; Theodorus Mops.: *ibid.*, *fasc.* 2, 460–2; Theodoret: *ibid.*, 452–4.

II. CPL: 1694–7 (Vigilius); 1698–1703 (Pelagius I); 866–8 (Facundus of Hermiane).

III. Facundus, Bishop of Hermiane, *Pro defensione trium capitulorum l. XII* = CCL 90A (Turnhout, 1974), 1–398.

On Facundus of Hermiane see L. Abramowski, 'Reste von Theodorets Apologie für Diodor und Theodor bei Facundus', in *StudPat* 1 = *TU* 63 (Berlin, 1957), 61–9.

On Pelagius: *Pelagii Diaconi ecclesiae Romanae 'In Defensione trium capitulorum'*, ed. R. Devreesse = *ST* 57 (Vatican City, 1932); R. Devreesse, *Essai sur Théodore de Mopsueste* = *ST* 141 (Vatican City, 1948), 243–58; on this see L. Abramowski, 'Die Zitate in der Schrift "In Defensione Trium Capitulorum" des römischen Diakons Pelagius', *VigC* 10 (1956), 160–93.

515. See CPG 9362; *Sententia Synodica*: ACO IV, 1, pp. 208,1–215,7 (Latin); Greek (*ex parte*): *ibid.*, 239–40. On the canons see below.

to penetrate the Church secretly through the writings and teachings of the three bishops, Theodore of Mopsuestia, Theodoret of Cyrus and Ibas of Edessa, was warded off in a more negative manner. From a council of the early Church we should not expect any historico-critical investigation of suspect texts. No modern hermeneutic was applied to them. What was pondered were in particular the 'impious *capitula*' from Theodore's writings (nos. 8–10), which were read out; but also counterwritings from the Fathers against him and all heretics; in addition *historiae et leges imperiales illius impietatem ab initio divulgantes* (no. 11), that is, reports and imperial laws which bore witness to Theodore's 'impiety'.

Then the question was discussed whether anybody should be anathematized after death. The Council replied affirmatively to this question, referring to the scriptural passages (Jn 3,18; Gal 1,8–9; Tit 3,10–11; nos. 12–13) and Fathers like Cyril, Augustine, other bishops from Africa and Roman Popes (nos. 13–17). Positive judgements on Theodore by Cyril and Proclus, which his friends adduced, were of no avail,[516] that is, they did not exonerate him, but rather incriminated him. Forgeries and excerpts pieced together from Cyril could not save him either (no. 18).

It was only briefly that Theodoret was reproached with those writings which, in the opinion of the members of the Synod, he had written against right faith, against Cyril's twelve *capitula*, the Synod of Ephesus and in the defence of Theodore and Nestorius. They were read out and included in the *acta*, so that the legitimacy of their condemnation can be investigated (no. 19). The 'alleged' letter of Ibas — this fiction was maintained — was also read out, and its impiety was clear to all (no. 20). Chalcedon had not acknowledged this letter, as the supporters of Theodore and Nestorius claimed (nos. 21–23); rather it had based its definition on the letters of Cyril and Leo of Rome, for which reason the definition was also read out at the Synod (of 553). In this way its contrast to Theodore-Nestorius and to the letter of Ibas was patent (nos. 24–26). By way of recapitulation the confession of the first four synods as the foundation of the catholic Church was highlighted. Whoever did not confess this, like the 'Three Chapters' whose heretical teachings were once again listed to some extent in an even more detailed manner (no. 27), were subjected to the anathema. With the consciousness of having performed a thorough job,[517] the members of the Synod

---

516. ACO IV, 1, p. 212,17: *apparent enim patres non liberantes anathemate Theodorum.*
517. ACO IV, 1, p. 214,35: *his ita cum omni subtilitate dispositis.*

confessed that they had fulfilled their service to right faith in the spirit of the scriptures and the Fathers (no. 28).

Thus from the *Sententia Synodica* as such we can extract no positive contribution to the theological understanding of Christ's person.

(ii) The christology of the canons of 553

Appended to the *Sententia Synodica* were fourteen canons[518] or anathemas, which in part find their explanation from the edict *On right faith*. We shall present a word for word translation for the most important canons only.

Canon I:[519]

This contains a confession of the divine Trinity with the distinction of the concepts *physis–ousia* (*natura–substantia*; the Lateran Council [649] says here: *essentia*) on the one hand, and *hypostasis–prosopon* (*subsistentia-persona*) on the other. The Cyrillian-Severan synonymous use of *physis-hypostasis*, however, is consciously abandoned.[520]

Canon II:[521]

Two births are ascribed to the God-Logos: the eternal, incorporeal one and the birth according to the flesh from the virginal *theotokos* Mary.

Canon III:[522]

The God-Logos who works miracles and the Christ who suffered should not be separated as 'each and other' (*alius et alius*; *allos kai allos*); they are not distinguished as God-Logos (born of the Father) and as 'Christ' (born of the woman); not as one who dwells in another. Rather it is a question of one and the same Jesus Christ, our Lord, the Word, who became flesh and a human being. To him as one and the same belong the miracles and the sufferings voluntarily borne in the flesh.

---

518. ACO IV, 1, 215–20 (Latin); 240–5 (Greek). Cf. CPG 9362 and 9401 (7), according to which *secretarius* IV of the Lateran Council (649) offered another Latin version of the canons. See R. Riedinger, ACO ser. 2, Vol. I, 225–33 (beside the Greek version, 224–32). The fourteen canons of 553 are in part the literal repetition of the thirteen *capitula* of the imperial edict of 551. See the comparative table in J. Straub, ACO IV, 1, XXXII, who is inclined to accept the same author for the Latin rendition of the canons and of Justinian's *capitula* (in Schwartz, *Drei dogmatische Schriften Justinians* (Munich, 1939), pp. 91,16–95,32) (cf. the Greek text, pp. 90,16–94,34).

519. ACO IV, 1, p. 215,9–13 (Latin); p. 240,3–7 (Greek). Translations of the Greek are based on *DEC*, but with modifications.

520. Cf. Justinian emp., *Conf. fidei*: Schwartz, *op. cit.*, p. 86,23–26 and p. 87,24–27 respectively.

521. ACO IV, 1, p. 215,15–18 (Latin); p. 240,8–11 (Greek).

522. *Ibid.*, p. 215,20–24 (Latin); p. 240,12–16 (Greek).

Canon IV:[523]

Both for the rejected Antiochene christology and for the canonized Justinianic christology this canon is highly informative, and for this reason should be rendered verbatim.

> If anyone declares that it was only in respect of grace, or of principle of action (*energeia*, *operatio*), or of dignity or in respect of equality of honour (*isotimia*), or in respect of authority (*authentia*), or of some relation, or of some affection (*schesis, affectus*) or power (*dynamis, virtus*) that there was a unity (*henosis, unitio*) made between the Word of God and the man; or if anyone alleges that it is in respect of good will (*kata eudokian*), as if God the Word was pleased with the man, because he was well and properly disposed (*kalos dokein; quod bene visum est ei de ipso*) to God, as Theodore claims in his madness; or if anyone says that this union is only a sort of synonymity (*homonymia*), as the Nestorians allege, who call the Word of God Jesus and Christ, and even designate the human separately by the names 'Christ' and 'Son', discussing quite obviously two different persons, and only pretending to speak of one person and one Christ when the reference is to his title, honour, dignity or adoration; finally if anyone does not accept the teaching of the holy Fathers that the union occurred of the Word of God with human flesh which is ensouled by a rational and intellectual soul, and that this union is by synthesis or by person, and that therefore there is only one (Latin: composite) person, namely the Lord Jesus Christ, one member of the holy Trinity: let him be anathema.

Explanation:

(a) The negative statement of Canon IV

In this *Kephalaion* (thus the edict) or canon the classical interpretation of Antiochene christology, which was developed in the Nestorian–Cyrillian controversy, is repeated; according to this interpretation the unity of 'Christ' is understood as only accidental and not substantial. The union would then be effected either from above through an act of assuming the (already existing) human being Jesus in grace, or through a continuous directing or leading by God; it remains a unity based on behaviour, whether it be from above (God *vis-à-vis* Jesus) or from below in an affective and ethical *adhaesio* directed completely towards God, of the human being Jesus *vis-à-vis* the Logos. Despite the many citations of Theodore's works in opponents and defenders (Vigilius, *Constitutum* I of 14 May 553; Facundus of Hermiane [547–548] [250 citations] and Pelagius [553]),[524] at the most we may make historico-critical demands only in some details, but in no way for the whole, and we should also not expect any judgement on the Three Chapters which is illuminated by the historical situation.[525]

---

523. *Ibid.*, pp. 215,26–216,15 (Latin); pp. 240,17–241,15 (Greek).

524. CPG 3827–69 give an excellent overview of the evaluation of Theodore's writings in the context of the Council of 553; see also 3871 (inauthentic symbol).

525. On the question of authenticity see above n. 514.

(b) The positive statement of Canon IV

Christ's unity as 'union of the Word of God with human flesh which is ensouled by a rational and intellectual soul' is understood as *secundum compositionem sive secundum subsistentiam facta*,[526] or as *unitio dei verbi ad carnem secundum compositionem ...*, *quod est secundum subsistentiam*.[527] In the combining of both terms, of 'union, *unitio*, *henosis*' and 'composition, *compositio*, *synthesis*', the canon sees the guarantee of excluding both mingling and division. The Council thus appropriated completely Justinian's terminology from 551.[528] We should note that the formula *henosis kath'hypostasin* — in contrast to the usage in Cyril of Alexandria — is not interchangeable with the other formula *henosis kata physin*. It was precisely this latter formula that the moderate Antiochenes had taken umbrage to, because such a 'nature unity' would have expressed the necessity of the incarnation, although this was the free action of God's grace.[529] The synonymous use of *physis* and *hypostasis* in Cyril also caused among the Antiochenes the rejection of the *henosis kath'hypostasin*, even when the *henosis kata physin* was unacceptable to them. The distinction of *physis* and *hypostasis* in Justinian's edict with its consequences should have led the Fathers of 553 to a historical meditation on the time between 431 and 451 when these concepts were used synonymously.

Canon V:[530]

> If anyone understands by the single subsistence of our Lord Jesus Christ that it covers the meaning of many subsistences, and by this argument tries to introduce into the mystery of Christ two subsistences or two persons, and having brought in two persons then talks of one person only in respect of dignity, honour or adoration, as both Theodore and Nestorius have written in their madness; if anyone falsely represents the holy synod of Chalcedon, making out that it accepted this heretical view by its terminology of 'one subsistence', and if he does not acknowledge that the Word of God is united with human flesh by subsistence (*secundum subsistentiam*), and that on account of this there is only one subsistence or one person, and that the holy synod of Chalcedon thus made a formal statement of belief in the single subsistence of our Lord Jesus Christ: let him be anathema. There has been no addition of person or subsistence to the holy Trinity even after one of its members, God the Word, becoming human flesh.

---

526. ACO IV, 1, p. 216,5-6; Greek: p. 241,6: κατὰ σύνθεσιν ἤγουν καθ'ὑπόστασιν γεγενῆσθαι.

527. *Ibid.*, p. 216,12-14.

528. Cf. E. Schwartz, *Drei dogm. Schriften* (Munich, 1939), pp. 86,21-88,3 and 88,15-26.

529. See the evidence in *JdChr* I³, 695-6. The distinction between the concepts *hypostasis* and *physis* in the decree of 551 (E. Schwartz, *op. cit.*, pp. 86,18-88,26; Latin: pp. 87,19-89,26) makes it impossible for Justinian to equate the formulas: *henosis kath'hypostasin* and *henosis kata physin*, and in addition the expressions *hypostasis synthetos* and *physis synthetos*. The section indicated is very significant.

530. ACO IV, 1, p. 216,17-27; Greek: p. 241,16-26.

Explanation:

An old reproach made by the Monophysites maintained that through the assumption of the one *hypostasis* in two natures a *tetras*, a quaternity, was introduced into the Trinity.[531] The like-sounding reproach which is expressed in Canon V does not target this notion, but rather the assumed teaching of two *hypostases* by the two Antiochenes named.[532] In any case the canon conceives the incarnation in a sense which can refute both reproaches, for the incarnation is conceived entirely from the one *hypostasis* of the Son, who is 'one of the Trinity'. The incarnation consists in the union (of the ensouled flesh) with this one subject *secundum subsistentiam*, so that it receives in it for the first time subsistence and existence.

Canon VI:[533]

This canon needs no further analysis. It applied to Theodore what at Ephesus (431) had been said against Nestorius with regard to the *Theotokos* — in contrast to *Christotokos* — but referred to Chalcedon for the heretical nature of this conception.

Canon VII:[534]

> If anyone, when saying 'in two natures', does not confess a belief in our one Lord Jesus Christ, understood in both his divinity and his humanity, so as by this to signify a difference of natures of which an ineffable union has been made, without confusion, in which neither the nature of the Word was changed into the nature of human flesh, nor was the nature of human flesh changed into that of the Word (each remained what it was by nature, even after the union, as this has been made in respect of subsistence); and if anyone understands the two natures in the mystery of Christ in the sense of a division into parts, or if he expresses his belief in the plural natures in the same Lord Jesus Christ, God the Word made flesh, but does not consider the difference of those natures, of which he is composed, to be only in the onlooker's mind, a difference which is not compromised by the union (for he is one from both and the two exist through the one [*di'henos*]) but uses the number to suggest that the natures are separated and have a subsistence of their own: let him be anathema.

Explanation:

Through this canon the Council wants to maintain the confession of the

---

531. And precisely because the one *physis* of the God-Logos is said to be now united with a second *physis* and the *trias* to be changed into a *tetras*.

532. For according to the assumption of the Fathers of 553 Theodore and Nestorius taught that Christ's human nature was also a *hypostasis* in its own right. Thus to the three divine *hypostases* would be added as a fourth the human being Jesus.

533. ACO IV, 1, pp. 216,29–217,5 (Latin); p. 241,27–37 (Greek). See E. Amann, art. 'Théodore de Mopsueste', in *DTC* 15 (1946), 262. *Theotokos* is mentioned in Theodore Mops., *De Incarn.* XV: PG 66, 991B.

534. ACO IV, 1, p. 217,7–16 (Latin); p. 242,1–11 (Greek). Canon VII corresponds to *Keph.* 7–8 of the decree of 551. See E. Schwartz, *Drei dogm. Schriften*, 93.

two natures in the sense of Chalcedon, but from the Cyrillian stock of ideas formulates the conditions for the application of the number two to the two natures, which is not used by Cyril and is detested by Severus. We must note this framework: 'Confession of the number [two] of the natures'. In the Second Letter to Succensus, in contrast, it is a question of defending the *mia-physis* formula against the attacks of those who confess two natures (cf. PG 77, 245A). To explain the relationship of the two natures which results in only one Christ, Cyril used the analogy of body and soul, and thus placed his explanation on the level of a *unio in natura et secundum naturam* (cf. PG 77, 245AB). Justinian's edict and Canon VII of 553 omitted this analogy, introducing in contrast the expression *synthesis*, which had the purpose, as we know, of stating both union and distinction. What really had to be warded off was the *synchysis*, mixing, as the annulment of the distinction which should not be deduced from the '*diaphora* which is there purely according to *theoria*' (ACO IV, 1, p. 242,8) on the one hand, and that in speaking of the number (two), which is permissible, no separation or teaching of two *hypostases* (*idiohypostatos*) results on the other. One should affirm distinction, but deny separation.

Canon VIII:[535]

> If anyone confesses a belief that a union has been made out of two natures, divinity and humanity, or speaks about the one nature of God the Word made flesh, but does not understand these things according to what the Fathers have taught, namely that from the divine and human natures a union was made according to subsistence, and that one Christ was formed, and from these expressions tries to introduce one nature or substance made of the deity and human flesh of Christ: let him be anathema.
>
> In saying that it was in respect of subsistence that the only-begotten God the Word was united, we are not alleging that there was a confusion made of each of the natures into one another, but rather that each of the two remained what it was, and in this way we understand that the Word was united to human flesh. So there is only one Christ, God and man, the same being consubstantial with the Father in respect of his divinity, and also consubstantial with us in respect of our humanity. Both those who divide or split up the mystery of the divine dispensation of Christ and those who introduce into that mystery some confusion are equally rejected and anathematized by the church of God.

Explanation:

If the *mia-physis* formula is introduced here,[536] this is not meant to grant it equal rights with the fundamental Chalcedonian formula or to put it forward as the latter's necessary dialectical correction. It is probably

---

535. ACO IV, 1, p. 217,18–29 (Latin); p. 242,12–23 (Greek). This canon VIII corresponds to *Keph.* 9 of the decree of 551; cf. E. Schwartz, *op. cit.*, 93.

536. The acknowledgement of the 'from two natures', which was rejected at Chalcedon, no longer creates any difficulties, because it goes together with the 'in two natures'.

with respect to Cyril and his followers that its orthodoxy is attested on one important condition, viz., that the duality of the natures remains inviolate.

Canon IX (Summary):[537]
The worshipping of Christ in two natures should not be interpreted as two separate acts of worship, with respect to the Logos on the one hand and with respect to the human being on the other. What, however, is the correct object of the one act of worship? It is not the one *physis* or essence (*ousia*) which would be attained by removing the flesh or by mixing divinity and humanity. Rather the one act of worship is directed to the incarnate God-Logos with his flesh. This is a formula acceptable to Chalcedonians and anti-Chalcedonians. It has to be understood in a manner contrary to that of Theodore.

Canon X:[538]

> If anyone does not confess his belief that our Lord Jesus Christ, who was crucified in his human flesh, is truly God and the Lord of glory (1 Cor 2,8) and one of the members of the holy Trinity: let him be anathema.

Explanation:
'One of the members of the holy Trinity', a consistent theme in Justinian's christology, emerges here (together with *Keph.* 6 of the edict of 551) probably for the last time in one of his texts.

Canon XI:[539]

> If anyone does not anathematize Arius, Eunomius, Macedonius, Apollinarius, Nestorius, Eutyches and Origen, as well as their heretical books, and also all other heretics who have already been condemned and anathematized by the holy, catholic and apostolic Church and by the four holy synods which have already been mentioned, and also all those who have thought or now think in the same way as the aforesaid heretics and who persisted (Latin: or persist) in their error even unto death: let him be anathema.

Explanation:
The phrase 'persisted in their error even unto death' probably intimates the imminent condemnation of a dead person, namely Theodore of Mopsuestia. Canon XI is a brief catalogue of heretics.[540]

---

537. ACO IV, 1, pp. 217,31–218,3 (Latin); p. 242,24–29 (Greek). Nothing corresponds to canon IX in the *capitula* of the edict of 551.

538. ACO IV, 1, p. 218,5–6 (Latin); p. 242,30–31 (Greek). To canon X there corresponds *Keph.* 6 of the decree of 551 (Schwartz, *op. cit.*, 93).

539. ACO IV, 1, p. 218,8–13 (Latin); p. 242, 32–37 (Greek). This is to be compared with *Keph.* 10 of the edict of 551, where the condemnation of Origen is missing.

540. Cf. *JdChr* II/1, 89–93; *CCT* II/1, 78–82.

(iii) The condemnation of the Three Chapters in canons XII–XIV
There now follows in three canons the anathema on the Three Chapters,
on account of whom the whole dispute, the final result of which was
the Council of 553, broke out. Because of the heresiological significance
of these canons, we shall present substantially their unabridged text.

Canon XII:[541]

If anyone defends the heretical Theodore of Mopsuestia, who said that God the Word is
one, while quite another (*allon ... allon*) is Christ, who was troubled by the passions (*pathe*)
of the soul and the desires of human flesh, was gradually separated from that which is inferior
(*cheironon*),[542] and became better by his progress in good works, and could not be faulted
in his way of life, and as a mere (*psilos*)[543] man was baptized in the name of the Father
and the Son and the Holy Spirit, and through this baptism received the grace of the Holy
Spirit and came to deserve sonship and to be adored, in the way that one adores a statue
of the emperor, as if he were God the Word, and that he became after his resurrection
immutable in his thoughts and entirely without sin (*anhamarteton*). [In a long interpolation
further false christological interpretations of Theodore are listed which we can summarize
briefly: (1) comparison of the unity in Christ with the joining together of husband and wife
in marriage in Eph 5,31; (2) the misinterpretation of the confession by Thomas the apostle
in Jn 20,28: he is said to have confessed Christ not as God, but only to have extolled God
on account of Christ's resurrection; (3) in his commentary on the *Acts of the Apostles* Theodore
is claimed to have Plato, Manes, Epicurus and Marcion on a par with Christ as founders
of schools or religions.] If anyone offers a defence for this more impious Theodore, and his
impious books in which he throws up the aforesaid blasphemies and many other additional
blasphemies against our great God and saviour Jesus Christ, and if anyone fails to
anathematize him and his heretical books as well as all those who offer acceptance or defence
to him, or who allege that his interpretation is correct, or who write on his behalf or on
that of his heretical teachings, or who are or have been of the same way of thinking and
persist until death in this error: let him be anathema.

Canon XIII:[544]

If anyone defends the impious writings of Theodoret which were composed against the true
faith, against the first holy synod of Ephesus and against holy Cyril and his Twelve Chapters,
and also defends what Theodoret wrote to support the impious Theodore and Nestorius and
others who think in the same way as the aforesaid Theodore and Nestorius and accept them
or their impiety; and if anyone, because of them, shall accuse of being impious the doctors
of the Church who have stated their belief in the union according to subsistence of God
the Word; and if anyone does not anathematize these impious books and those who have
thought or now think in this way, and all those who have written against the true faith
or against holy Cyril and his twelve chapters, and who persist in such impiety until they
die: let him be anathema.

541. ACO IV, 1, pp. 218,15–219,11 (Latin); p. 243,1–30 (Greek); canon XII corresponds to
Keph. 11 of the edict of 551; Schwartz, *op. cit.*, 92–4 (Greek); 93–5 (Latin).
542. This is an expansion of *Keph.* 11 of the edict.
543. This word is missing in *Keph.* 11 of the edict.
544. ACO IV, 1, p. 219,13–21 (Latin); pp. 243,31–244,6 (Greek); see *Keph.* 12 of the edict
of 551: Schwartz, *op. cit.*, p. 94,14–24 (Greek); p. 95,13–23 (Latin).

Canon XIV:[545]

If anyone defends the letter which Ibas is said to have written to (Latin: the heretical) Mari the Persian, which denies that God the Word, who became incarnate of Mary the holy mother of God and ever virgin, became man, but alleges that he was only a man born from her, whom it describes as a temple, as if God the Word was one and the man someone quite different; which condemns holy Cyril as if he were a heretic, when he gives the true teaching of Christians, and accuses holy Cyril of writing opinions like those of the impious Apollinarius; which rebukes the first holy synod of Ephesus, alleging that it condemned Nestorius without going into the matter by a formal examination; which claims that the twelve chapters of holy Cyril are impious and opposed to the true faith; and which defends Theodore and Nestorius and their impious teachings and books.

If anyone defends the said letter and does not anathematize it and all those who offer a defence for it and allege that it or a part of it is correct, or if anyone defends those who have written or shall write in support of it or the impieties contained in it, or supports those who are bold enough to defend it or its impieties in the name of the holy fathers of the holy synod of Chalcedon, and persists in these until his death: let him be anathema.

(iv) The conclusion of the Sententia Synodica[546]

Such then are the (Latin: correct) assertions we confess. We have received them from holy Scripture, from the teachings of the holy fathers, and from the definitions about the one and the same faith made by the aforesaid four holy synods. Moreover, condemnation has been passed by us against the heretics and their impiety, and also against those who have justified or shall justify the so-called 'Three Chapters', and against those who have persisted or will persist in their own error. If anyone should attempt to hand on, or to teach by word or writing, anything contrary to what we have regulated, then if he is a bishop or somebody appointed to the clergy, in so far as he is acting contrary to what befits priests and the ecclesiastical status, let him be stripped of the rank of priest or cleric, and if he is a monk or lay person, let him be anathema.

(b) Synthesis of the Council's christology

The Second Council of Constantinople belonged to the subsequent history of the Council of Chalcedon, and the adjective 'subsequent' was so strongly stressed that it was only with difficulty that in large parts of the entire Church this Council succeeded in overcoming the barrier of the 'fourfold number' of councils.[547] The history of its reception was just as much interlaced with troubles as its prehistory and its course. It was felt to be a betrayal of Chalcedon. The balancing out of win and loss for this ecclesiastical assembly is not easy to accomplish. In this regard we shall make a distinction between the positive efforts to furnish

---

545. ACO IV, 1, pp. 219,23–220,5 (Latin); p. 244,7–21 (Greek); canon XIV corresponds to *Keph.* 13 of the decree of 551: Schwartz, *op. cit.*, p. 94,25–34 (Greek); p. 95,24–32 (Latin).

546. ACO IV, 1, p. 220,6–14 (Latin); p. 244,22–30 (Greek); abbreviated in the Fourth Lateran Council: Mansi X, 1060AB.

547. See the informative article by R. Schieffer, 'Das V. Ökumenische Konzil in kanonistischer Überlieferung', *ZSavSt.K* 90 (1973), 1–34.

a new expression of Chalcedonian faith and the purely negative, condem-
natory judgements on the Three Chapters. None of the previous councils
used such caustic language with regard to opinions to be dismissed and
the proponents of these. There was no attempt to give an objective
assessment of them. Consequently, no account at all was taken of the
positive significance of these theologians, in particular of Theodore of
Mopsuestia.

(i) The relationship of the Council to the definition of Chalcedon

In the *horos* of Chalcedon one must distinguish between two levels of
statement: the proclamation of the message of God's incarnation in
Christ in the non-technical language of the confessions of the early
Church (Nicaea, Constantinople, the Symbol of Union of 433), and
in conceptually technical language.[548] As we have established, in the
definition of 451 the latter was not intended to be in the foreground,
but was squeezed into the *horos* by the back door, as it were. Nevertheless
the agitation about the Fourth Council occurred precisely because of it:
one *hypostasis* in two natures. Was Chalcedon then secretly a concession
to the dreaded Nestorianism? We have seen what efforts had to be made
at Constantinople to destroy this suspicion definitively. In a certain
regard with relation to language and concepts this should have succeeded,
but perhaps, and this is our question, only with the alteration or at least
the continuation of Chalcedon.

(1) The 'one hypostasis' in Chalcedonian understanding

That the Council of 451 still did not furnish the technical expression
'one *hypostasis* or person' with a profound, speculative content should
be regarded as the outcome of research. What did the Council understand by 'one *hypostasis*' or 'one *prosopon*'? The 'one Christ, the one
hypostasis in two natures' is the end-product — Leontius of Byzantium
had coined the expression *apotelesma* for this — of a process of union,
in which 'one and the same', that is, the eternal, consubstantial Son of
God assumed to his own complete divine being also a complete human
nature so that he is both, although he is both before and after one and
the same — God and human being. Chalcedon calls this 'end-product'
of the process of union the 'one *hypostasis* or the one person' which,
however, maintains both divine and human natures unmingled and
undivided in their unity, these being manifested also in this one concrete

---

548. One is reminded of the distinction between *piscatorie* and *Aristotelice* in the *Codex Encyclius*
of Emperor Leo I; cf. *JdChr* I³, 765–8; *CCT* II/1, 223 with n. 96.

subject; for it is discernible that Christ is at the same time God and human being. The concept *hypostasis* is thus not applied specifically and exclusively to the pre-existent Logos as subject, although for Chalcedon too the Logos is the ultimate subject. What we have just established holds for the technical use of the concept, even if this is still rather indeterminate. On the basis of the fundamental structure of its kerygmatic statement, Chalcedon, as we have said, allows one to see clearly where the one *hypostasis* in Christ is already realized: in the one who 'one and the same' is 'perfect in divinity, but one and the same is also perfect in humanity'. In brief, as we have ascertained, there then arose the custom of identifying the 'one *hypostasis*' in Christ with the *hypostasis* of the pre-existent Logos (Patriarch Gennadius, Diadochus of Photike). In this manner the way was opened for further reflections on what constituted the difference between the 'concept' of *hypostasis* and that of 'nature', and finally on what could lead to the elaboration of a definition of *hypostasis*.

(2) Competing languages

The greatest impediment to a general and untroubled acceptance of this formula of Chalcedon by the entire Church lay in the old-Alexandrian-Cyrillian *synonymous* use of *hypostasis* and *physis* for the *oikonomia*, that is, for the order of the incarnation, in contrast to the *theologia*, for which both terms had another content. It is for this reason that Chalcedon with its two-natures formula was suspected of Nestorianism by the old-Oriental tradition. The Council, however, had already taken a step forward by abandoning the synonymous use of the two concepts *hypostasis* (*prosopon*) and *physis* (*ousia*). There were now two opposed formulas: (1) 'the one incarnate nature (*physis-hypostasis*) of the God-Logos', and (2) 'the one *hypostasis* (or person) in two natures'. The subsequent history of Chalcedon to Justinian's time and even beyond that suffered from the competition between these two linguistic usages. The rift became increasingly deeper.

Where did Justinian and the Council of 553 stand with regard to this problem?

(3) Emperor Justinian

As his edict of 551 shows, Justinian created clarity in two respects.

(I) Terminologically: the Emperor decided clearly for the identical usage of the concepts *physis* and *hypostasis* in both the *theologia* and the *oikonomia*. Both terms were now expressly distinguished. The decisive passage reads:

Thus after we have shown that it is impious to speak of one nature (*physis*) or essence (*ousia*; Latin: *substantia*) of the divinity and flesh of Christ, we shall also say this: it is not possible to speak of the one nature of Christ in a similar way to how we talk of the one subsistence (*hypostasis*) of the divinity and humanity of Christ, because nature (*physis*) and *hypostasis* are not the same.[549]

(II) From this explanation and from the conditions which the Emperor set for tolerating the use of the *mia-physis* formula, if the worst came to the worst, it follows that he himself was not a supporter of the demand for a simultaneous use of the two formulas discussed here. He decided unambiguously for Chalcedon.

(4) Constantinople II (553)

This was also the position of the canons of the Fifth Ecumenical Council.

(I) The members of the Synod did not use *hypostasis* and *physis*, or *subsistentia* and *natura*, synonymously (cf. Canon V).

(II) In Canon VII the Council, like Justinian, distinguished between a *unio secundum subsistentiam*, that is, a 'union according to the *hypostasis*', and a 'union according to the nature' which tended to annul the distinction of the natures (Canon VII, part one; above all Canon VIII). For the use of the formula 'from two natures' too the Council put forward the same demand, that this had to be understood in the sense of 'union according to the *hypostasis*'.

(III) Nowhere in the canons can be found the demand for a simultaneous use of the two formulas of incarnation, the Chalcedonian and the Cyrillian-Alexandrian. As in the decree of 551, *Keph.* 9, in Canon VIII the boundaries were demarcated within which the *mia-physis* formula had in fact to be understood.

(IV) Because of this purified use of formulas the Fifth Ecumenical Council was not a weakening of Chalcedonian terminology, but its logical continuation. With regard to the basic formula 'one *hypostasis* or person in two natures', the canons of 553 belonged to the history of strict Chalcedonianism, because they were not set in competition with the *mia-physis* formula. Nevertheless the use and application of the main concepts were clearer and more unambiguous than at Chalcedon. The one *hypostasis* or *subsistentia* as such was anchored in the pre-existent Logos; to him, as the ultimate subject, Christ's human nature was united *sub ratione subsistentiae*;[550] the assumption into this one *hypostasis* of the human nature which did not exist in itself was formally the event of

---

549. Justinian emp., *Conf. fidei* (CPG 6885): Schwartz, *Drei dogm. Schriften*, p. 86,15–18.
550. Cf. canon V: ACO IV, 1, p. 216,23: *dei verbum carni secundum subsistentiam unitum.*

the incarnation or, seen from above, the self-communication of this Logos hypostatically to the ensouled flesh, by the Logos creating this flesh for himself.

(ii) The 'neo-Chalcedonianism' of 553

In spite of the facts previously established, the Council of 553 has the reputation of representing what, since J. Lebon, is termed 'neo-Chalcedonianism', and because of this having created the christological system that is said to be still ours.[551] We must take into account here that the extreme neo-Chalcedonian synthesis in the sense of M. Richard was no longer attempted. The *mia-physis* formula was discussed briefly, but no longer integrated. However, the Cyrillian renaissance had not yet been nullified. The Council of 553 in fact had recourse to that Cyril who between 431 and 451 gained a hearing from the Fathers, but was not taken into the actual conciliar decisions. In this context two groups of writings have to be distinguished: (1) the twelve anathemas and (2) other 'anti-Nestorian works'.

(1) Cyril's twelve anathemas in Constantinople II[552]

The twelve *capitula*, appended to Cyril's third letter to Nestorius from the year 430, were read out at Ephesus (431) and at Chalcedon (451). From that time on they received as a whole ceremonial recognition from the Council.[553] Individual themes and formulations, however, were also extracted.

Individual formulations:

(i) Cf. A. 12 (*DS* 263) with Canon X (ACO IV, 1, 218; 242; *DEC* 118; *118) in which the contentious so-called theopaschite formula, expanded only by the *unus ex trinitate*, is acknowledged by the Council. On this cf. Canon V, conclusion.

(ii) Cf. A. 2 (*DS* 253) with Canon V (ACO IV, 1, 216; 241; *DEC* 116; *116): *henosis kath'hypostasin*. Through the adoption of this formula the agreement between Chalcedon and Ephesus was stressed. While Cyril, however, was able to replace *henosis kath'hypostasin* by the equivalent *henosis kata physin* (on account of the synonymous use of both words),[554] Constantinople (553) still said only *henosis kath'hypostasin*

---

551. Cf. C. Moeller, 'Le chalcédonisme et le néo-chalcédonisme', in *Chalkedon* I[5], 648.

552. Cf. *DS*, nos. 252–63; *DEC*, 59–61, *59-*61.

553. See the *Sententia Synodica*, no. 19 (condemnation of the works of Theodoret against the twelve *capitula*): ACO IV, 1, 212–13, and no. 27 (summary): *ibid.*, 214.

554. Cf. An. 3: *DS* 254: καθ'ἕνωσιν φυσικήν.

(and rejected a *henosis kata physin*).[555] This linguistic purification was just as much old-Chalcedonian as neo-Chalcedonian, for through it Cyril's language was compared with the Chalcedonian distinction of *hypostasis* and *physis* and was also brought into agreement with the conceptual explanation of the decree of 551.[556] Thus not only was the language of the anathemas clarified by reference to Chalcedon, but Chalcedon too was enriched by Cyril's *capitula*.

(iii) Cf. A. 8 (*DS* 259) with Canon IX (ACO IV, 1, 217–18; 242; *DEC* 118; *118): the one worship of Christ, the incarnate Logos, which is demanded in both texts, should not be justified, however, according to Canon IX on the basis of '*one physis* or *one ousia*'.

(2) Other texts of Cyril and the canons of 553

The concepts θεωρία[557] and ἔννοια pertain to the most important notions which were adopted from Cyril to interpret Chalcedon's teaching of two natures.

(i) 'Only in intellectual vision'

As we have seen (cf. the explanation of Canon VII), Justinian's edict (*Keph*. 8) and Canon VIII of 553 adopted these concepts, but with limitations which Cyril had not yet applied. According to Canon VII the use of the formula 'in two natures' was positively acknowledged as right confession (with the almost verbatim citation of the Chalcedonian text) (ACO IV, 1, p. 242,1–2; *DEC* 117; *117). The 'only according to *theoria* or thought' was intended to exclude the *real* separation or *idiohypostasis* of Christ's humanity.

As *Keph*. 9 of the edict (Schwartz, 92–3) and Canon VIII of the Council show, Justinian's purification of terminology, that is, the distinction of *hypostasis–prosopon vis-à-vis physis* and *ousia*, was essential for the application of this 'according to *theoria*'. If this distinction were not taken into account for Canons VII and VIII, then too much strain would be put on this 'purely according to vision'. The unmingled would be endangered. The command to take the 'duality' only 'according to *theoria*' was related above all to the *hypostasis* (ACO IV, 1, p. 242,17–19). The *henosis kath'hypostasin* no longer fell under the suspicion of *synchysis*, because *mia hypostasis* was placed in opposition to the *mia physis* and the *mia ousia* (ibid., 15–16). Hence we should not relate the 'pure *theoria*' to a nature unity and in this way succumb to a false neo-Chalcedonian mysticism. It is only a new way of rejecting the teaching of two *hypostases*.

(ii) Synthesis *or* compositio

The Christian mystery of the *oikonomia* as the union of God and human being, undivided and unmingled, demanded linguistically the expression 'composition' (*synthesis*, *compositio*). Even in pre-Chalcedonian christo-

555. Or more exactly: *henosis* . . . *kata synthesin* or *kath'hypostasin*. Cf. canon IV: ACO IV, 1, 241.

556. Justinian emp., *Conf. fidei* (CPG 6885): Schwartz, *op. cit.*, pp. 86,29–88,3 (Greek); pp. 87,30–89,3 (Latin). With this is to be compared canon VIII (ACO IV, 1, 217 and 242).

557. Cyril Alex., *Ep. 46 ad Succens.* II (CPG 5346): PG 77, 245A.

logy we find the beginning of the history of this group of words, consisting of verbs and gerundives with the noun *synthesis* at the centre. However, this group of words was extremely suspect and at first remained so even in the post-Chalcedonian period, until it was made presentable at court by Justinian and finally was given a conciliar blessing. We shall classify briefly the major variants of the applications of this group of words in the service of christology.

(A) A first christological use of *synthetos* is found in Origen:[558] the union of the believer with the Lord brings it about that the one so united (*synthetos*) becomes 'one spirit' with him (1 Cor 6,17): 'how much more divine and better will then be the one united to the Logos of God'. Origen means the divinizing union of Jesus' humanity (with body and soul) with the Logos.

(B) *Synthesis* in the heretical Logos-sarx christology[559]
Provided the *acta* can lay claim to authenticity, this history begins as early as the Synod of Antioch against Paul of Samosata.[560] The Arian Eudoxius of Antioch (357-359; from 359 to 369 bishop of Constantinople) speaks of Christ, the human being without a soul, and says: 'the whole is one nature after the composition' (Hahn, *Bibl. d. S.*, § 191).

Apollinarius of Laodicea: Christ is 'a *synthesis* of the human type' (σύνθεσις ἀνθρωποειδής), that is, what the body-soul unity is in the human being is in Christ the exclusive Logos-sarx unity. It is a question of a strict *synthesis* between two incomplete natures, so that a genuine 'nature unity' in Aristotle's sense comes into existence.[561]

(C) Cyrillian usage
Cyril Alex., *Ep. 46 ad Succens*. II (CPG 5346): PG 77, 241BC: 'Unity (*to hen*) is truly expressed not only of simple things according to nature, but also of things which are united according to composition (ἐπὶ τῶν κατὰ σύνθεσιν σύνηγμένων).' He says this in relation to the *mia physis* in Christ and refers to the body-soul analogy.

558. Origen, *C. Celsum* II, 9: Koetschau, p. 137,3. On this see F. Loofs, 'Die "Ketzerei" Justinians', in *Harnack-Ehrung. Beiträge zur Kirchengeschichte* (Leipzig, 1921) (232-48), 239.
559. Cf. *JdChr* I³, Greek index: *synthesis*, Latin: *compositio*.
560. According to M. Richard it is a matter of later Apollinarian forgeries. See *JdChr* I³, 296-9; F. Loofs considers them authentic: *art. cit.*, 239. In a thorough investigation M. Simonetti, 'Per rivalutazione di alcune testimonianze su Paolo di Samosata', *RSLR* 24 (1988), 177-210, now defends with H. de Riedmatten the authenticity of these fragments of this synod of 268. According to H. de Riedmatten, *Les actes du procès de Paul de Samosate* = *Paradosis* 6 (Fribourg, 1952), Malchion defends the *synthesis* in Christ against Paul of Samosata (*op. cit.*, 147, Frag. S, 22): Malchion asks: 'Le Verbe et son corps ne sont pas *composés*? Paul: Qu'à aucun prix il ne soit composé ni mélangé! Malchion: Si tu ne veux pas admettre la *composition*, c'est pour ne pas devoir dire que le Fils de Dieu a été substantifié (οὐσιῶσθαι) dans son corps.' Cf. also Frag. S, 23 (*ibid.*): The Logos is substantially united with his human body, 'étant le même de par la *composition* et l'union substantielle à lui' (while Paul does not consider the Logos as *hypostasis* and does not accept any substantial unity between Logos and body, any *synthesis*). M. Simonetti (197) draws attention to the fact that in fragments 30 and 36 Malchion interprets Christ as a unity of Logos and *sarx* (without Christ's soul); if the fragments are authentic, as Simonetti accepts, Malchion is the first proponent of the strict Logos-sarx schema. The term *synthesis* here gains already the meaning which it would subsequently have in Apollinarius. See H. de Riedmatten, *op. cit.*, 154-5 (Frag. 30); 156-7 (Frag. 36). Simonetti (197-8) stresses, however, that in spite of the same Logos-sarx schema the terminology of the Apollinarians is different from that of Malchion.
561. See I. R. Torrance, *Christology after Chalcedon* (Norwich, 1988), 65 with further examples.

Cyril knows that *synthesis* at the same time also expresses distinction: 'although in the concept of composition the difference of the things, which are brought together *according to nature*, is expressed at the same time' (241C). We must note that (1) the concept *synthesis* is rare in Cyril and (2) in the example adduced he remains in the domain of the *unio in natura et secundum naturam*, which remains the major handicap of the Cyrillian-Severan *mia-physis* teaching.

(D) Severus of Antioch

(1) Letter 25 to the Emesans: PO 12, 222–48: Severus describes the incarnation as a '*synthesis from* two elements', which in the Emmanuel are present unmingled (he speaks in this way to fend off monophysite misunderstandings among some Christians in Emesa).

(2) Against John the Grammarian he still rejects the expression 'one composite nature' (*C. imp. Gr., Or.* II, 10: CSCO 112, p. 81,23–26). He is also opposed to the equation by the Grammarian of 'two united natures' = 'one composite nature' (*mia physis synthetos*). In this he smells the Nestorian division.

(3) The most severe rebuff was suffered by Sergius Scholasticus for his infelicitous idea of the *ousia synthetos*, that is, the composite essence which is called 'Christ'. See *Ep. III ad Sever. Ant.*: CSCO 120, pp. 114,25–115,2 (the main text for *synthesis*).

(4) According to J. Lebon, finally, even if cautiously, Severus did use, however, the formula 'one composite nature and *hypostasis*' (*Le monophysisme sévérien*, 319).

(E) *Synthesis* in its use among the Chalcedonians

(1) Justinian and the Scythians

From the very beginning Justinian comes into contact with the idea of the 'christological *compositio*' through the Scythian monks[562] and their theological sources, to which the *acta* of the Synod of Antioch (268), and additionally Euthymius, belong. For the Scythians (John Maxentius) the main christological formula says: 'composition from two realities'. It is claimed that by this expression both Nestorius and Eutyches are excluded.

In Justinian we have the unhindered adoption of *compositio*, thus of the Latin terminology, but also of *synthesis* and the whole associated Greek semantic field. Does Justinian have other sources?

(2) Leontius of Jerusalem[563]

In the sixth century he is the strongest advocate for the christological application of *synthesis*.

Negatively: he rejects the expression 'composite nature' (PG 86, 1485D3–4) as much as that of the 'composite *hypostasis*'.

Positively: his formula states that 'the natures are composed according to the *hypostasis*' (1485D).

His presupposition is the explicit distinction of the concepts *physis* and *hypostasis*. The two words are no longer synonymous.

His interpretation of Christ's one *hypostasis* before and after the incarnation is strange. Here is an incriminatory element in his christology, with which Leontius in fact remains isolated. Because of this he cannot produce the *Canon of Orthodoxy*, as he claims (PG 86, 1568A8–C10). In Emperor Justinian we do not find this concrete interpretation, based on the Basilian teaching about *idiomata*, of the *enhypostasis* of Christ's humanity in Christ's *hypostasis*, but certainly we do find the frequent use of *synthesis* in the framework of a clear demarcation of the main christological terms. Can Leontius be considered as a source for Justinian? It is not to be ruled out, particularly if we are to assume that Leontius of Jerusalem also wrote in Constantinople.[564]

---

562. See above, Chapter One, pp. 317–43.

563. See above, Part Two, Chapter Three, pp. 271–312 (Leontius of Jerusalem).

564. See P. T. R. Gray, *The Defense of Chalcedon in the East (451–553)* (Leiden, 1979), 122–41. Gray draws attention to the fact that M. Richard considered this Leontius of Jerusalem as a participant in the doctrinal dialogue of 532, in M. Richard, 'Léonce de Jérusalem et Léonce de Byzance', *MSR* 1 (1944), 35–88 = *Op. Min.* III, no. 59; against this position see D. B. Evans, *Leontius of Byzantium: An Origenist Christology*, DOS 13 (Washington, 1970), 156–83. According to Gray, Leontius of Jerusalem wrote between 538 and 550.

This question, however, can remain open. It is important that the true title of the work *Contra Monophysitas* reads: '*Aporiai* against those who say "one composite nature" of Our Lord Jesus, witnesses of the saints, and an analysis of their teaching' (PG 86, 1769).[565]

Summary

Just like Justinian's edict of 551, the christology represented in the canons of the Council of 553 proves to be moderate neo-Chalcedonianism (in the sense delineated above).

Concluding judgement on the Second Council of Constantinople (553)

The Council did not originate from the best of motives, and in various respects it remains historically suspect. In spite of this it is accorded a positive function in the subsequent history of Chalcedon up to the present; this needs to be demarcated clearly.

1. The fact that the Three Chapters dispute was conceived by Theodore Askidas as a 'diversionary manoeuvre' in the face of Emperor Justinian's anti-Origenist action remained concealed from the majority of the members of the Synod; nevertheless it was detrimental to the atmosphere of the Council. Positive christological and theological work was pushed too much into the background in favour of the negative task of expressing condemnations of writings (or persons) from the distant past which, as can be proved, caused no discernible damage in the Imperial Church of the East at that time nor in the Latin West. Development had already passed beyond the weaknesses of a Theodore of Mopsuestia. A neo-Nestorianism within the Imperial Church was not a threat.

2. We should not overlook the fact that the relatively widely spread 'anti-Chalcedonian affect' used the Three Chapters dispute for its own purposes; in particular African and Roman theologians of this time recognized this. For this reason at the Council itself little energy was expended to develop the major christological document of the early Church, namely the definition of Chalcedon, from the potential material and language present in the definition itself, which until then had been too little exploited.

3. Emperor Justinian made the most valuable contribution in this direction by giving prominence in his *Confessio rectae fidei* of 551 to a uniform terminology in the spirit of Chalcedon (with the distinction of

---

565. Cf. P. T. R. Gray, *op. cit.*, 123, n. 91.

hypostasis-person from *physis-ousia* = nature-essence). In this way he also removed from the *mia-physis* formula its innate ambiguity and advanced the guiding principles for an interpretation that a Chalcedonian could also accept.

4. In this interpretation of his the Emperor also excluded that theologically contestable suggestion of the 'neo-Chalcedonians' who, through the simultaneous use of two formulas of different origin and direction of thought, wanted to shut out heresies like Nestorianism and Eutychianism more unequivocally than Chalcedon had already done in all clarity.

5. The Council unfortunately did not address the real task at that time of presenting a definition of *hypostasis*-person in contradistinction to that of nature-essence. Without such a conceptual clarification the tension between the Chalcedonians and non-Chalcedonians could not be eliminated, as long as one still moved on the level of formulas that sounded contradictory. The Council also did not open people's eyes to the necessary distinction between the *unio in hypostasi et secundum hypostasin* on the one hand, and the *unio in natura et secundum naturam* on the other. Justinian's edict on faith could have been of some assistance in this regard.

6. What was incorporated from Cyril's language to ward off Nestorianism and was proclaimed in general as universally valid for the future (Cyril's twelve anathemas) certainly focused the Church's reflection on its faith in the direction of the *henosis* in Christ, but a full integration of these elements was hardly achieved. The best synthesis between Cyril and Chalcedon still remained the definition of Chalcedon itself, especially if it was read against the background of the old Symbols and Cyril's *Laetentur* letter.

7. To set Constantinople II (553) as 'neo-Chalcedonian' over the Council of 451 may generate some advantages ecumenically. It will be only conditionally conducive to a pure, uniform development of Chalcedonian christology.

CHAPTER FIVE

THE FINAL THEOLOGICAL ACTIONS OF EMPEROR JUSTINIAN

With its condemnation of the Three Chapters the Council of 553 did not fulfil what Theodore Askidas had painted for the Emperor as a utopian dream: the restoration of ecclesiastical unity which had been shattered on account of Chalcedon. In the East nothing changed, except that the division consolidated itself in Syria through the building up of an anti-Chalcedonian hierarchy; in the West a part of the Latin Church ended up in schism; the Severan or Julianist South (Egypt) took no notice of the Council of 553. The victims who were most affected were the three accused and condemned teachers. Certainly there were some deficiencies in them which can be explained historically; these were rightly excluded. Through the purely negative and undifferentiated condemnation, however, the positive contribution of these men to the Church's theology in general would from then be discredited. In a palpable manner the relations between the Greek-Chalcedonian and the Persian Churches now suffered.[566] The establishment of their dogmatic and canonical autonomy would only be accelerated by the unbelievably harsh judgements passed on their real teacher, Theodore of Mopsuestia.[567] It is as though the Emperor was conscious of the harshness of the actions against this Church from 543 to 553, which indeed during his reign under the direction of Abraham of Beth Rabban (510–569/570) expanded the school of Nisibis to make it a theological centre, the like of which Byzantium did not possess. All the higher clergy was trained there. Happily the connections of the Old-Oriental Church to Byzantium and to the West were nevertheless not interrupted. One of the most

566. Cf. the important study by A. Guillaumont, 'Justinien et l'Église de Perse', *DOP* 23/24 (1969), 39–66, esp. 54. We shall discuss this study in more detail in the treatment of the christology of the Persian Church.

567. A. Guillaumont, *art. cit.*, 55, n. 75 cites the following as particularly significant from *actio* V: ACO IV, 1, 83, no. 14: 'Il y eut un homme pestilentiel, ou plutôt une bête sauvage, un diable ayant forme humaine, appelé de façon trompeuse Théodore [= Don de Dieu], qui porta le vêtement et le nom d'évêque, caché dans quelque recoin et lieu inconnu de la terre, à Mopsueste, bourg sans importance de la Cilicie seconde.' In any case the beginning of the *Libellus ad Procl. Const.* (CPG 5775) of Basil archim. Const. is involved here. Filled with hatred, Basil had written this document against Theodore (cf. above, p. 414 and n. 388). The Council of 553 incorporated this writing into the *acta*.

significant *catholicoi* of the Persian Church, Aba I (540–552), a convert
from Mazdaism, before his elevation to this office made a long journey
to Palestine, Egypt and Greece in the company of a certain Thomas of
Edessa, his teacher of Greek. In Alexandria he was even allowed to
explain the scriptures using Theodore's commentary. He seems to have
made contact there with Cosmas Indicopleustes, who shortly after 543,
the year of the first condemnation of the Three Chapters, wrote his
Christian Topography and regarded Mar Aba as his teacher.[568] Finally
Mar Aba and his companion Thomas came to Constantinople where,
according to his biographer,[569] he proclaimed 'the true faith'. Emperor
Justinian heard of this and wanted to see the Oriental teacher, who,
however, avoided the encounter and immediately left Constantinople.
According to the 'Chronicle of Se'ert',[570] Justinian wanted to compel
Mar Aba and Thomas to condemn Diodore, Theodore and Nestorius.
When these refused, the Emperor supposedly ordered their mutilation,
but this was not carried out. Nevertheless this (questionable) report,
together with a series of others,[571] shows that Justinian, inspired completely by the Constantinian idea of unity, wanted to extend his religio-
political activity to the Church of Persia as well.

I. THE DOCTRINAL DIALOGUE WITH THE PERSIAN CHURCH IN 561

We have two testimonies from ecclesiastical historians about a doctrinal
dialogue between Justinian and representatives of the Persian Church
which relate to the same event, but differ in their dating.

1. The report of Barḥadbešabba of 'Arbaya (from the end of the sixth century)

According to the report of this Nestorian ecclesiastical historian the
Emperor attempted to move Abraham of Beth Rabban, the head of the

568. See A. Guillaumont, *art. cit.*, 45, n. 26, with reference to the *Christian Topography* II,
2: Wolska-Conus, SC 141, 306–307. The name Patrikios, which appears there, is the Greek
translation of Mar Aba.

569. Cf. *Vie de Mar Aba* in *Histoire de Mar-Jabalaha*, ed. Bedjan (Paris, Leipzig, [2]1895),
221–222; A. Guillaumont, *art. cit.*, 45, n. 27.

570. Chron. of Se'ert: Scher, PO 7, 156. A. Guillaumont, *art. cit.*, 45–6 with n. 29. We should
note that this sojourn in Constantinople is to be assigned to about 532, when Justinian was
dealing with the Severans and did not wish the activity of 'Nestorians' in the capital. In 532
Mar Aba returned to his country.

571. See A. Guillaumont, *art. cit.*, 46–8, where in conclusion he writes: 'Malgré l'autonomie
ecclésiastique et la séparation dogmatique, les rapports restaient donc encore étroits entre les chré-
tiens de Perse et l'Empire byzantin.' We shall return to this.

school of Nisibis, to present himself at court in order to defend his faith there and to answer a series of prepared questions.[572] With reference to his advanced age and his teaching commitments Abraham rejected such a journey, but forwarded a written confession and replied to the questions which had been directed at him. He refused to strike the names of the Three Chapters from the diptychs. In his stead, however, he sent Bishop Paul with some companions to Byzantium. According to Barhadbešabba they appeared before the Emperor, 'defended the faith which they confessed and the Fathers which they preached; they then returned from there in great triumph'.[573]

2. The 'Chronicle of Se'ert'[574]

This chronicle compiled by a Nestorian completes the report of Barhadbešabba:[575]

> It is reported that Justinian, after establishing peace with Khosrau, asked him to send him some Persian sages. Khosrau sent him Paul, the metropolitan of Nisibis, Mari, the bishop of Balad, Barsauma, the bishop of Qardou, Išai, an exegete from Seleucia, Išoʻyahb of Arzoun, who later became *catholicos* of the East, and Babai, the bishop of Shigar. He [Justinian] received them all with honour. The disputation which was written down lasted three days. They [the Persians] made the orthodox faith known. [After stating that the Emperor had questioned Babai about passages from scripture and the Fathers as proof, and the latter had obviously impressed the ruler, the report continues]: They gave him to understand that neither the nature could exist without *hypostasis* nor the *hypostasis* without nature, and that therefore logically the two natures could not be one single *hypostasis*. Justinian listened to them and sent them back overwhelmed with honour. As a consequence, however, he changed his viewpoint by anathematizing Diodore and his companions.

The conclusion of this report of the 'Chronicle of Se'ert' seems to suggest that the doctrinal dialogue took place before or during the Three Chapters dispute. However, there are good reasons for maintaining that the peace settlement alluded to is not that of 532,[576] but is to be placed

---

572. Barhadbešabba of 'Arbaya, *Hist. ss. PP.*: ed. Nau, *PO* 9 (1913), 628–630. Cf. *CCT* II/1, *Ad Fontes*, 37.

573. Barhadbešabba, *Hist. ss. PP.*: *PO* 9, 628–630 at 630.

574. See *CCT* II/1, *Ad Fontes*, 32; I. Ortiz de Urbina, *Patrologia Syriaca* (Rome, 1965), 24.

575. Chronicle of Se'ert: *PO* 7, 187–188; A. Guillaumont, *art. cit.*, 50–1.

576. A. Scher, in *PO* 7, 187, n. 6, and A. Vööbus, *History of the School of Nisibis* = CSCO 266 (Louvain, 1965), 153, wrongly argue for 532. Vööbus considers the Chalcedonian-Severan doctrinal dialogue of 532 (Letter of Innocent of Maronia and the Syrian report), which we have already dealt with, as identical with the conference we are discussing here. Only Nestorians, however, participated in it. Cf. A. Guillaumont, *art. cit.*, 51, n. 58.

in 561.[577] Consequently the Persian mission to the capital can be assigned to 562 or 563. This dating also brings about agreement with the report of Barhadbešabba, in particular with regard to the age of Abraham of Beth Rabban (d. 569). Thus it was Justinian himself, as the 'Chronicle of Se'ert' mentions, who asked the Persian king Khosrau to send Persian theologians — a request which Khosrau met with the delegation of 562/563. How the doctrinal dialogue in Constantinople proceeded is preserved in a fragment of an anti-Nestorian monophysite collection.[578] Its content will be presented later in the depiction of Nestorian christology.

The course of this initiative in making contact with the Persian Church and theology reminds us directly of the doctrinal dialogue of 532. On both occasions it ended in three days.[579] Just like the Severans, the Persian theologians did not condescend to any concession. The anathemas of 553 may have had their share in this negative result.

The fact that it is only the latest research that has produced a relatively complete picture of a further attempt by Justinian to realize his Eusebian-Constantinian ideal of unity of faith in the Imperial Church[580] also creates a prejudice in judging the Emperor's final action which, considered in isolation, seems to tarnish his memory significantly. What is in question is nothing other than a 'heresy' of the aging Emperor, which he allegedly confessed in his reputed 'Edict on Aphthartodocetism'[581] and to which he wanted to commit the Church.

---

577. See the whole argumentation of A. Guillaumont, art. cit., 51–2. The Chronicle of Se'ert: Scher, PO 13, 568 and a note in the 'Catalogue of Christian Writers' of 'Abdišo' Bar Berika (= Ebedjesu) fit in with this. The latter mentions a Disputatio adversus Caesarem (I. S. Assemani, BO III/1, 88), which refers to the conference of 562/563. The Copt Abou'l Barakat confirms this report (Assemani, op. cit., 632; A. Vööbus, The School of Nisibis: CSCO 266, 172).

578. A. Guillaumont, art. cit., 52–3; the fragment is found in B. L. Add. 14535, fol. 16v–20r. Guillaumont (art. cit., 62–6) gives a French translation and a facsimile copy of the Syriac text. Both are reproduced in Amelotti-Migliardi Zingale, Scritti teologici ed ecclesiastici de Giustiniano = Subsidia III (Milan, 1977), 179–192.

579. A. Guillaumont, art. cit., 53, n. 70 (with a further example) highlights this circumstance.

580. This attempt of 562/563, however, now reached beyond the borders of the Imperial Church.

581. The expression 'aphthartodocetism' is just as unsuited to the (allegedly promulgated) decree of Justinian as it is to Julianism, and in particular to the Chalcedonian 'aphthartics' whom Leontius of Byzantium refuted. Hence it is to be recommended that one speak only of 'aphthartics' or of the 'aphthartic' interpretation of Christ's earthly reality.

II. 'HERESY' OR THE EMPEROR'S FINAL INITIATIVE TO RESTORE UNITY OF FAITH

1. The state of research

It has been said that the series of theologico-political actions undertaken by Justinian I, which from beginning to end had been accompanied by many critical qualifications, ended with a document that has been described as 'caprice impérial',[582] namely with the decree which is claimed to have ordered the acceptance of the 'aphthartodocetist' interpretation of Christ's earthly reality. For a century the judgements passed by significant and less significant researchers have pointed in this direction.[583] E. Stein, in contrast, is much more differentiated in his judgement.[584] Indeed he establishes that towards the end of 564 the Emperor promulgated an edict which proclaimed that Christ's body was of an incorruptible and impassible nature.[585] He claims, however, that it was the Emperor's intention and conviction, as it was in his earlier decisions (on the theopaschite question, on Origenism, on the Three Chapters dispute), to remain personally in the framework of the norms of the (four) ecumenical councils. Stein argues that a decree of December 562 (CPG 6890) certainly bears witness to this attitude. A fragment of this decree is transmitted by the *Doctrina Patrum*, in which once again the teaching of the one *hypostasis* in two natures is stressed,[586] although

582. The expression stems from J. Pargoire, *L'Église byzantine de 527 à 847* (Paris, [2]1905), 41-2.

583. They are listed by F. Carcione, 'L' "aftartodocetismo" di Giustiniano: una mistificatione strumentale del dissenso politico-religioso', *StRiOrCr* 7 (1984) (71-8), 71, n. 1. The first is A. Knecht, *Die Religionspolitik Kaiser Justinians I.* (Würzburg, 1896), 140-4. On this cf. R. Haacke, in *Chalkedon* II, 152-3. Then there follow the well-known names: C. Diehl, J. Pargoire, J. B. Bury, J. Maspero, L. Duchesne, L. Bréhier (Fliche-Martin IV, 1937, 480-1), M. Jugie, as the scathing reviewer of the different opinion of W. H. Hutton, *The Church of the Sixth Century* (London, 1897) 303-9, in 'L'empereur Justinien a-t-il été aphthartodocète?', *EO* 31 (1932), 399-402. For all that, Jugie mentions (399-400) that in the third edition of the work of Pargoire (1923) an anonymous editor added a critical appendix to these earlier remarks (41-2). Nevertheless Jugie was still of the opinion that 'ce plaidoyer *pro Justiniano* [by Hutton] ne repose sur aucun fondement solide' (400). For a long time in German theology F. Loofs, 'Die "Ketzerei" Justinians', in *Harnack-Ehrung. Beiträge zur Kirchengeschichte* (Leipzig, 1921), 232-48, was decisive. The article still has value, even if some corrections and additions have to be made.

584. E. Stein, *Histoire du Bas-Empire* II (1949), 685-90.

585. In his treatment of Julianist teaching E. Stein, *op. cit.*, 233-5, presents this in more detail; on 686 he interprets this edict as 'opposed to the spirit, if not indeed the letter of Chalcedonian christology, even if this is interpreted in a Cyrillian sense'.

586. The text is in F. Diekamp, *Doctrina Patrum*, 134; Amelotti-Migliardi Zingale, *Scritti teologici*, 194, Greek and Latin. Here we give the Latin: *si quis, substantialem sive naturalem unitatem in mysterio Christi dicens, hoc modo non intellegit, quod stupenda incarnatio duas substantias* [= ousias] *sive naturas* [physeis] *in unam subsistentiam* [hypostasin] *univit, sed ex hoc unam naturam sive substantiam* [ousian] *Christi factam esse dicit, talis anathema sit.*

the decree on *aphtharsia* would already have been in the drafting stage. The catholic world, it is claimed, should have been prepared 'sur la portée de l'innovation retentissante qui se préparait'.[587] E. Stein rightly establishes that the Severans were not affected at all by the condemnation of the Three Chapters in 553. The Emperor's hopes for union were dashed. His religious politics with regard to the Severans were a failure. Nevertheless he did not abandon his goals. He attempted to realize these now with the final, but very powerful party which regarded Julian of Halicarnassus as its leader. For, in the opinion of E. Stein, the Julianists would have behaved differently with regard to the new edict than the Severans would have done. At least they reacted, even if in a sense that ran counter to the Emperor. Instead of reconciling themselves with the Imperial Church, they took the edict of 562 as an opportunity to choose for their 'sect' a new patriarch by the name of Elpidius,[588] whom the Emperor immediately ordered to be brought bound to Constantinople. The deported patriarch, however, died while being transported to Sigris.

2. Evidence for an 'aphthartic' action by Justinian

The researching and interpreting of the sources[589] are still in a state of flux. According to Michael the Syrian, the occasion that prompted talk of the Emperor's turn to aphthartic teaching was his reception at the court of Constantinople of one of the leading Julianists, the bishop of Joppe (modern-day Jaffa).[590] This is certainly to be placed soon after 560. The first to react against Justinian's new attitude was Eustochius, the Patriarch of Jerusalem, whose subordinate the bishop of Joppe was.[591] In 563/564, however, he was deposed by the Emperor. It was maintained that it was suggested to the Emperor by the new adviser that through the acceptance of the aphthartic teaching a reconciliation with

587. E. Stein, *op. cit.*, 686 with n. 2. Cf. F. Carcione, *art. cit.*, 75.

588. Cf. Theoph., *Chron.* A.M. 6057: de Boor I, p. 241,6–10; J. Maspero, *Histoire des patr. d'Alexandrie*, 214.

589. C. W. F. Walch, *Entwurf einer vollständigen Historie der Kezereien, Spaltungen und Religionsstreitigkeiten, bis auf die Zeiten der Reformation*, 8 (Leipzig, 1778), 550–640, should still be regarded as an overview worthy of note.

590. Michael Syr., *Chron.* IX, 34: Chabot II, 272: 'Un évêque stupide, de la ville de Joppé en Palestine, s'attacha à lui et pervertit son esprit par l'hérésie des Phantasiastes. Il se mit à dire que le corps de Notre-Seigneur n'était pas passible et corruptible.' The Emperor is said to have disseminated this teaching by numerous writings.

591. E. Stein, *Histoire du Bas-Empire* II, 685, says that this bishop, whose name we do not know, became at the end of Justinian's reign 'le théologien le plus écouté de l'empereur'. Theodore Askidas died in 558. It is claimed that it was through the influence of the Bishop of Joppe that the deposition of the Patriarch of Jerusalem happened. Macarius took his place.

the Julianists was possible, even if already no unity with the Severans could be established.[592] According to various historians it was intended that this should happen by means of an 'edict'. According to Theophanes all bishops of the Empire were obliged to subscribe the Emperor's 'edict'.[593] Patriarch Eutychius of Constantinople (like Apollinarius of Alexandria) was said to have opposed this and was taken prisoner on 22 January 565. On 31 January he was deposed after he had refused to appear before a *synodos endemousa* which was completely in the Emperor's hand. Finally he was banished to Amaseia in Pontus, to the monastery from which he had been called in 552 to the patriarchal throne of the capital. His successor was John Scholasticus of Antioch, who for six years had been the *apocrisiarius* of the Patriarch of Antioch.[594]

Eustratius in his *Vita Eutychii* reports in detail on these events.[595] According to him the Emperor's main thesis stated:

The body of our Lord Jesus Christ became incorruptible from the very beginning of the union (ἄφθαρτον τὸ σῶμα . . . ἐξ αὐτῆς ἑνώσεως γεγενῆσθαι).[596]

Eustratius maintains that this teaching almost ruined the whole world. He interprets the Emperor's intention as strict docetism: 'fantasy, not truth, is the becoming flesh and a human being of the God-Logos'.[597] Together with the *Vita Eutychii* of Eustratius, the *Church History* of Evagrius is closest to the course of events in 565. Evagrius reports that Justinian wrote an 'edict' in the Roman mode of expression:

in which he called the body of the Lord incorruptible and unreceptive for the physical and blameless passions; thus he said that the Lord had already eaten before the passion as he did after the resurrection; that he experienced no change or alteration from his formation in the womb onwards, not even in the voluntary and physical passions, just as after the resurrection of his holy body.[598]

---

592. E. Stein, *op. cit.*, 685–6.

593. Theophanes, *Chron.* A.M. 6057: de Boor, pp. 240,31–241,15. Michael Syr., *Chron.* IX, 34: Chabot II, 272.

594. Cf. E. Stein, *op. cit.*, 687–8.

595. Eustrat., *Vita Eutychii* (CPG 7520), V–VIII: PG 86, 2316–2368; on the deposition of Eutychius see also Nicephorus Callistus, *HE* XVII, 29–31: PG 147, 292–301; in addition Michael Glykas, *Annal.* IV: PG 158, 509AB; finally Victor Tunnun., *Chronicon*, a. 565: PL 68, 962; Mommsen II, *MGH* 11, 205.

596. Eustrat. *Vita Eutychii*, IV, 33: PG 86, 2313B.

597. *Ibid.*, PG 86, 2313C. The Emperor's naïveté (*haplotes*) is said to have led him to be deceived by the study of the Origenists (Origen, Evagrius and Didymus) and by the word 'incorruptible' (PG 86, 2316A.C).

598. Evagrius Schol., *HE* IV, 39: Bidez-Parmentier, p. 190,16–23; cf. P. Allen, *Evagrius Scholasticus the Church Historian* (Louvain, 1981), 204–5. Evagrius stresses that the Emperor forced all bishops to subscribe to the edict and that Anastasius of Antioch was the leader of the resistance against this (Bidez-Parmentier, p. 190,23–26).

3. Modern discussion about the Emperor's aphthartic activity

There is great confusion among historians with regard to the Emperor's new development towards aphthartic teaching and a corresponding 'edict'. Up to the present no completely convincing solution has been found. We shall present here briefly two more recent attempts at a clarification.

(a) P. Van den Ven (1965):[599] this scholar begins in particular with a criticism of the chronological ordering of the course of events. He asserts that the major mistake consists in the fact that various phases which Justinian had gone through on the way to extreme measures vis-à-vis the Church are assigned to a time-span which is too short. Van den Ven claims that E. Stein, starting from a false interpretation of Eustratius' *Vita*, assumed that the edict had been promulgated towards the end of 564, but certainly before January, 565. But Stein, he says, did not consider that it was a question of a preparatory document, a χάρτης, which the Emperor had read out before a third party, namely Patriarch Eutychius, in order to be able to judge the reaction of his audience.[600] The Emperor broke Eutychius' resistance by having him brutally driven away from his see on trivial pretexts, not, however, on account of his refusal to subscribe an 'edict' which had not yet been published.[601]

> He [the Emperor] also refrained from any coercive measure with regard to his [Eutychius'] successor, who was more astute than the old monk and from whom he knew that he would not receive (from him) a positive and official assent to his dogmatic ideas. Negotiations in various directions were conducted and pressure was exerted on bishops of the entire Empire, which only ceased with the death of Justinian.[602] L. Bréhier is perhaps not far from the truth when he writes that one is not sure whether the edict, the text of which one does not know at all, was promulgated and then sent to Rome; for one does not know of any reaction on the side of the Apostolic See.[603]

599. P. Van den Ven, 'L'accession de Jean le Scholastique au siège patriarcal de Constantinople en 565', *Byz* 35 (1965), 320–52.

600. *Ibid.*, 342. He refers to his statements on 325–8 and the course of events which he established there. Cf. PG 86, 2316C: ὁ βασιλεύς, ὃν ἐποίησεν χάρτην . . . λέγων. After the reading out of the text, it is claimed that the Emperor demanded that Patriarch Eutychius accept this 'logos'.

601. Cf. *ibid.*, 342–3; 350–1 with 322: the *vita* of Symeon Stylites the Younger also points in this direction. Cf. *idem*, 'Les écrits de s. Syméon le Stylite le Jeune avec trois sermons inédits', *Mus* 70 (1957), 1–57 (cf. CPG 7365–7369).

602. Evagrius Schol., *HE* IV, 39–41: Bidez-Parmentier, pp. 190,23–192,3; P. Van den Ven, *art. cit.*, 343, n. 1, with 336–8.

603. P. Van den Ven, *art. cit.*, 343–4. In such an important matter there would certainly have been a Roman reaction.

An important fact is certainly stressed here, a fact which can also be expanded in a completely different way by the deposed Patriarch Eutychius. The work on the 'Distinction of nature and person'[604] which stems from the time of his exile in Amaseia, in spite of its christological terminology, contains no allusion at all to a text of Justinian and the aphthartic question.[605] Had the deposition of the Patriarch been caused in the main by his refusal to subscribe an edict, a critique of such an edict on the part of the Patriarch would have been expected.

(b) F. Carcione (1984):[606] the author of this article is of the opinion that Justinian's conversion to 'aphthartodocetist teaching' is not to be accepted on objective grounds. This thesis could only arise because the ancient historians confused the dialogue with 'Julianism' really pursued by the Emperor with an actual acceptance of this heresy. On the basis of this interpretation, it is maintained, rested the 'orthodox' complaints about the Emperor when he opened the way for a final undertaking of his religious politics, which were orientated as always towards the restoration of unity of faith in the Empire. According to this scholar, we should note that the Emperor in the last years of his long rule was more and more unpopular and was the butt of repeated criticism. Such criticism could only be successful if it were expressed in religious terms, that is, when it was a question of his religious politics or questions of faith.

We should note in addition that in the last years of his rule Justinian established contact on two sides: with the Nestorians in the East on the one side, and with the Julianists in Egypt on the other. Carcione claims

---

604. Eutychius Const., *De differentia naturae et hypostaseos* (Armenian) (CPG 6940); P. Ananian, 'L'opusculo di Eutichio patriarca di Costantinopoli sulla "Distinzione della natura e persona" ', in *Armeniaca. Mélanges d'études arméniennes* (Venice, 1969), 316–82 (introduction with Italian translation).

605. P. Ananian, *art. cit.*, 355, refers, however, to a text of the Patriarch with the title: 'Anathema against those who characterize Christ's body as incorruptible before the resurrection' (not listed in CPG 6937–6940). Ananian adds: 'probabilmente scritto contro l'imperatore Giustiniano, che, verso la fine del suo regno, aveva emanato un decreto, ove esponeva la dottrina di Giuliano di Alicarnasso circa la incorruttibilità del corpo di Cristo. Eutichio, per aver negato la sua approvazione, fu deposto e mandato in esilio.' Grumel, *Regestes* I², no. 260, nevertheless, places the anathema in the year 577, with recourse to Nicetas Choniates, *Thesaurus* 12: PG 140, 77BC. Ananian thus traces the deposition of Eutychius back to his refusal of the Emperor's decree on *aphtharsia*; he also identifies the Emperor's teaching with that of Julian of Halicarnassus and does not take into account the dating of the anathema to 577, that is, to the second phase of the patriarchate. This date, twelve years after the death of Justinian, would indicate that the *aphtharsia* teaching still had supporters in Constantinople, and that this, and no longer the Emperor, was the stimulus for the Patriarch's anathema. Cf. PG 140, 77D.

606. F. Carcione, 'L'"aftartodocetismo" di Giustiniano: una mistificazione strumentale del dissenso politico-religioso', *StRiOrCr* 7 (1984), 71–8.

that a prospect of addressing contrary groups like this could only have existed if the Emperor preserved the Chalcedonian centre.

Carcione then refers to some special circumstances of Justinian's procedure:

(1) This is the reason for the deposition of Patriarch Eutychius which we have already mentioned. Questions about doctrine were not decisive.

(2) If the Emperor really wanted to engage the Julianists, it was extremely inept to imprison immediately Patriarch Elpidius, newly elected by the Gaianites, and to order his transportation to Constantinople. This must really have jolted the supposed dialogue partners, especially when the prisoner died while being transported. Nicetius, the bishop of Trier, shows just how badly Justinian's final religio-political activity could be misunderstood. In a letter (from the summer of 565) he accused the Emperor of having become at the end of his life a supporter of Nestorius and Eutyches, both of whom denied Christ's human nature.[607]

After all these reflections by researchers on Justinian regarding the Emperor's aphthartism we cannot make a concluding judgement. Nevertheless the following assertions seem to be certain.

(1) The Emperor certainly did not succumb to 'Aphthartodocetism', as this was understood by heresiologists in ancient times as well as in the modern period, that is, as the denial of Christ's humanity. The interpretation which R. Draguet worked out vis-à-vis Julian of Halicarnassus may also be applied mutatis mutandis to Justinian's possible 'aphthartism'.

(2) Justinian certainly remained 'Chalcedonian' in the sense of that sentence transmitted by the Doctrina Patrum from the period of the 'aphthartic' discussion: in this the Emperor denied the mia-physis formula and confessed Christ's two natures.[608]

(3) If he had really been an 'aphthartic', then at the most it would have been in the sense of those Chalcedonians whom Leontius of Byzantium refuted in his writing CA (Contra Aphthartodocetas).[609] Probably it is not to be excluded completely that the word henosis also played a special rôle, as this was the case among the aphthartics that Leontius

---

607. Nicetius of Trier, Ep. II ad Iustinian. (CPL 1063): PL 68, 378–380.

608. See F. Diekamp, Doctrina Patrum de Incarnatione Verbi (Münster, 1907; ²1981), 134. In the second edition 378 there is a comment on the text that Justinian here used the words of Proclus.

609. Cf. above, pp. 217ff.; Leontius Byz., CA (CPG 6813): PG 86, 1316D–1356C; esp. 1317CD: induced by the charm of this word aphtharsia 'some of us' converted to the teaching of Severus and Julian of Halicarnassus and thus surrendered the whole mystery of the incarnation. With regard to Justinian too there is talk of the enticement of this word (cf. PG 86, 2316C).

dealt with who were to be found in Constantinople.[610] In fact this word is mentioned twice in the *Vita Eutychii*,[611] where it is used to establish the continuous *aphtharsia* in the body of the earthly Jesus. Such inferences could also appear in Justinian without his fundamental Chalcedonianism being called into question. Were we also to add the recourse to Cyril of Alexandria, which is apparent in the Three Chapters dispute and the Council of 553 (canons), then the parameters within which Justinian could be considered a 'Chalcedonian aphthartic' are delineated. He would then be at a great distance from that 'Julianism' which the ancient historians and many recent researchers ascribe to the Emperor. This 'Julianism' presupposes the *mia-physis* teaching and formula, which Justinian explicitly excludes in the fragment transmitted by the *Doctrina Patrum*.

EMPEROR AND THEOLOGIAN
CONCLUDING COMMENTS ON JUSTINIAN I

Externally the sixth century received its structure probably more through Justinian's religio-political actions than through the works of theologians, whether they be Chalcedonian or anti-Chalcedonian. From 519 until the end of his reign we find Justinian in action. None of the larger or smaller religious groupings was spared his influence. Admittedly the result was slight; the damage for the whole Church, at least in part of his actions, was considered by many as greater than the benefit. The Three Chapters dispute convulsed the entire Empire. The real goal of restoring unity of faith in the Empire, which was to the fore in all undertakings, was not achieved. In particular he had success only in the insignificant question of the recognition of the formula 'one of the Trinity was crucified'; more significant was the overcoming of Origenism, which as such did not divide the Church, but was extremely confusing. Above all the Emperor foundered in his efforts to win over Severus and his supporters (532), namely that group which went into schism on account of Chalcedon. The condemnation in 536 did not prevent them from organizing their hierarchy and continuing their teaching. The Nestorians too, as the last ones summoned to dialogue, remained unmoved. It was almost as if the conclusion of his actions placed his whole theological work and reputation in question: the attempt to gain

610. Cf. PG 86, 1352CD.
611. Eustratius, *Vita Eutych.*, 33: PG 86, 2313B: the body of our Lord is incorruptible from the union itself; in addition *ibid.*, C.

victory for the teaching of Christ's *aphtharsia* before the resurrection.

Considered more from within, that is, from the christological perspective, in the course of his activity the Emperor without a doubt made considerable advances. His initial uncertainty with regard to the *unus ex trinitate* was quickly overcome. His last great edict, the *Confessio rectae fidei* of 551, is really a balanced document. It served as an introduction to the Council of 553 and offered more good christology than the many hackneyed anathemas of the Fathers of the Council of 553, with which they rejected the Three Chapters. It was only in this main phase of his theologizing that the Emperor developed from a 'Chalcedonian' into a moderate 'neo-Chalcedonian' and committed the Council to this form of the christological dogma. We have made clear that it was one of the merits of this edict of 551 that it officially created terminological clarity for the use of the terms *hypostasis* and *physis*, *ousia* and *prosopon*. Without adopting the *mia-physis* formula, the Emperor acknowledged the orthodox usage of this formula within determined limits, and thus built a bridge of understanding to the Old-Alexandrians, which as a contribution to ecumenical dialogue has continued to have an effect up to the present day.

Which theologians or advisers stood behind his activities can only be recognized obscurely and fragmentarily. His evil spirit must have been Theodore Askidas, who could not hinder the condemnation of Origenism, but who brought on the Three Chapters dispute. Which of the Leontii present in Constantinople influenced the Emperor? There are certain traces and fingerprints of Leontius of Byzantium on the one side, if we look for instance at the letter to Zoilus; on the other and even more intensely are those of Leontius of Jerusalem, whose neo-Cyrillianism appears to correspond exactly to that of the Emperor (the evaluation and interpretation of the *mia-physis* formula; stressing the concept *synthesis*; and other aspects).

Finally there remains a question about the place of the Emperor in the theological structure of the Patriarchate of Constantinople. That he was the leading figure, even *vis-à-vis* the patriarchs, no one can deny in regard to his religio-political activities. The most significant patriarchs were certainly Menas (536–552) and Eutychius (552–565; 577–582). For the Emperor, however, greater authority was vested in the Popes during his reign, Hormisdas (514–523), John II (533–535) and Agapetus I (535–536). In contrast the rôle of Pope Vigilius (537–555) in the contention between imperial and papal duty in questions of faith was a real tragedy. In a ruler such as Justinian the innate obscurity of the Emperor's sphere of competence in the Imperial Church and of the unsolved ques-

tion of Church and state in their reciprocal relationship had its consequences time and again in the whole series of his religio-political actions.
Because of his behaviour *vis-à-vis* the bishops he receives a bad press from
historians.[612]

Thus the Patriarchate of Constantinople in the whole of the sixth
century was not able by its own efforts to achieve that consistency which
Alexandria and Antioch, but Jerusalem too, not to speak at all of Rome,
experienced. If nevertheless the real theological achievement of that
century more or less showed itself as 'Byzantine', then the Ecumenical
Patriarchate owed this to the presence and radiance of an emperor like
Justinian (and his consort Theodora, cf. San Vitale, Ravenna) and to the
attraction of the Imperial City, which, at least for a time, captured the
greatest theologians of the century and drew them to the capital. This
showed itself in several ways. (1) Severus, the monk from Majuma, first
found in the Imperial City the stage which would make him the greatest
theological player of the century, even if he resided there for only a few
years. (2) Controversies like the Origenist dispute in Palestine or the
Agnoetic conflict in Alexandria shifted to the capital and were essentially
decided there. (3) In the monasteries, particularly in the monastery of
the Sleepless Monks, libraries and work possibilities were created which
allowed the historical and theological working out of the individual
phases of the struggle for Chalcedon from the very beginnings, as the
conciliar *acta* of the early Church show. (4) Finally, Constantinople
became a conciliar site, where at the Fifth Ecumenical Council Chalcedon
received those hermeneutical aids which confirmed it as the greatest
theological event in the whole Church after Nicaea. 'Four gospels —
four councils': this statement also retains its validity after 553, if one
looks at the conciliar foundation of the message of Jesus Christ, 'one
and the same in true divinity and true humanity'. It is only from
Chalcedon that the Council of 553 drew its christological content, which
its anathemas alone were not able to offer.

---

612. Cf. H.-G. Beck (ed.), *Byzantinisches Lesebuch* (Munich, 1982), 223: 'Emperor Justinian's
despotism'; M. V. Anastos, *art. cit.*, above, p. 316, n. 4, 'Justinian's despotic control'.

PART FOUR

THE END OF THE JUSTINIANIC ERA AND
AN APPRAISAL OF THE SIXTH CENTURY

With the work of the theologians of Chalcedonian and anti-Chalcedonian orientation and of the politico-religious actions of Justinian I, the christology of the sixth century in Byzantium received more or less its permanent form. Nevertheless it is worthwhile researching the final actions both in the domain of imperial politics and in that of the theologians, and to hear the final witnesses. If we leave aside religious politics and reflective theology, the area of kerygma and piety in Constantinople still has to be incorporated and evaluated in order to complete the picture. In doing this we shall have to consider the entire Justinianic era once again.

CHAPTER ONE

THE END OF THE JUSTINIANIC ERA

I. POLITICO-RELIGIOUS ACTIONS UNDER JUSTIN II

By T. Hainthaler

Justinian's nephew, the *curopalates* Justin, as Justin II (565–578),[1] succeeded his uncle as Emperor. Together with his spouse Sophia, a niece of Empress Theodora, Justin II received a difficult inheritance. The financial and economic situation of the Empire had noticeably worsened through natural catastrophes (beginning as early as the years 543–558),[2] such as earthquakes, floods and starvation, and above all through the Great Plague (542–544),[3] which broke out repeatedly in the following decades, although not to the catastrophic extent of 543. In addition there were conspiracies, and a weakened and demoralized army.[4] Justin seems to have succeeded in giving the throne a new radiance,[5] in particular through religious symbolism: the Emperor as the image of Christ and Christ as *rex regnantium*. This conception of Justin is seen especially in the throne room, the so-called *chrysotriklinos*: the picture of Christ was

---

1. Cf. F. Dölger, *Regesten* I, 1–7. On Justin's religious politics see P. Goubert, 'Les successeurs de Justinien et le Monophysisme', in *Chalkedon* II, 179–92, esp. 182–5; Averil Cameron, 'The Early Religious Policies of Justin II', in *Studies in Church History* 13 (1976), 51–67 = *eadem, Continuity and Change in Sixth-Century Byzantium* (London, 1981), no. X; P. Allen, *Evagrius Scholasticus the Church Historian* (Louvain, 1981) = *SpicSLov* 41, 22–7, 212–14. On the sources concerning Justin II and Tiberius see Averil Cameron, 'Early Byzantine *Kaiserkritik*: Two Case Studies', *Byzantine and Modern Greek Studies* 3 (1977), 1–17 = *eadem, Continuity and Change*, no. IX; cf. E. Stein, *Studien zur Geschichte des byzantinischen Reiches vornehmlich unter den Kaisern Justinus II und Tiberius Constantinus* (Stuttgart, 1919), esp. 19 with 26–9.

2. On this cf. the listing of events in E. Stein, *Histoire du Bas-Empire* II, 756–9. In addition see F. Vercleyen, 'Tremblements de terre à Constantinople. L'impact sur la population', *Byz* 58 (1988), 155–73.

3. Evagrius Schol., *HE* IV, 29; for details of this see P. Allen, *Evagrius Scholasticus*, 190–4. Evagrius reports that as a youth himself he had the plague and at a later outbreak of it he lost his wife, children and servants.

4. Cf. Averil Cameron, 'The Theotokos in Sixth-Century Constantinople', *JTS* 29 (1978), 81, 104–5, = *eadem, Continuity and Change*, no. XIII. In addition see A. Fotiou, 'Recruitment Shortages in VIth Century Byzantium', *Byz* 58 (1988), 65–77.

5. Cf. the building activity and the sponsoring of art under Justin II, which Averil Cameron, 'The Artistic Patronage of Justin II', *Byz* 50 (1980), 62–84 (= *Continuity and Change*, no. XII), demonstrates. It comprises various palaces, also the palace of the Patriarch, churches and social institutions, and testifies throughout to originality in some domains, so that the late sixth century shows itself to be a period of growth and development (*ibid.*, 84).

positioned above the Emperor's throne and thus the Emperor appeared as the embodiment of Christ on earth.[6] On this account Averil Cameron characterizes Justin's reign as 'a turning-point in the imperial ideology'.[7]

1. Efforts to secure unity for the Church

At the beginning of his reign Justin endeavoured to secure unity for the Church 'carefully and eagerly',[8] and for this purpose apparently attempted to be on good terms both with the 'Monophysites' and with the Chalcedonians, if one takes into account the reports of John of Biclar and of Michael the Syrian.[9]

The former reports that he destroyed everything which had been written against Chalcedon, and ordered that the Constantinopolitan Creed, which had been received by Chalcedon, was to be sung at Mass by all the people.[10] The latter indicates that Justin brought back Patriarch Theodosius with honour and, when the Patriarch died shortly afterwards, let him be buried with ceremony. On that occasion Anastasius (a monk from the imperial family) delivered a sermon, during which he openly anathematized Chalcedon. Justin allowed the bishops in Antioch to be free; he gathered the bishops who were in Constantinople into his palace and exhorted both parties to seek the truth and to unite. The dialogues in the palace lasted for a year, but were unsuccessful: 'on account of sins the Church was not pacified.'[11]

The desire for peace and for unity in the Church must have been present without doubt, both in Justin and generally.[12]

According to Averil Cameron, the decree on the introduction of the Constantinopolitan Creed is the background for the laudatory poems on Justin by Corippus and Venantius Fortunatus.[13] In the fourth book of his poem Corippus presents a *credo* which is intended to celebrate the

6. On this see Averil Cameron, 'Images of Authority: Elites and Icons in Late Sixth-Century Byzantium', *Past and Present* 84 (1979), 15–18 = *Continuity and Change*, no. XVIII; see as well the comments on the poem of Corippus on Justin, which gives expression to this thought of *imago Christi: eadem*, 'Corippus' Poem on Justin II', *ibid.*, no. VI, 151–2.

7. Averil Cameron, 'The Artistic Patronage of Justin II', *ibid.*, no. XII, 62.

8. John Ephes., *HE* I, 3: Brooks, p. 2,5.

9. Averil Cameron, 'The early religious policies of Justin II', in *op. cit.*, no. X, 54: '[Justin] was walking a tightrope.'

10. John Biclar, *Continuatio Victoris* (CPL 2261), a. 567?: ed. Mommsen, *MGH* 11, 2, p. 211, 13–17: . . . *qui Iustinus anno primo regni sui ea, quae contra synodum Calchedonensem fuerant commentata, destruxit symbolumque sanctorum CL patrum Constantinopoli congregatorum et in synodo Calchedonensi laudabiliter receptum in omni catholica ecclesia a populo concinendum intromisit, priusquam dominica dicatur oratio.*

11. Michael Syr., *Chron.* X, I: Chabot II, pp. 283b–284b ('à cause des péchés, l'Église ne fut pas pacifiée').

12. John Ephes., *HE* I, 22: Brooks, CSCO 106, 19–20, narrates impressively how much the monophysite bishops were oppressed, because they were reproached for being the ones who were delaying unity.

13. Averil Cameron, *op. cit.*, no. X, 54–6.

Emperor's decree. What is noteworthy in this is that it contains the two-natures formula: *una in naturis extans persona duabus*.[14] Moreover, we also find the formula: *ex tribus una ... persona*, a consistent element of Justinianic christology.

Venantius composed his hymn to Emperor Justin and Empress Sophia[15] on the occasion of the forwarding of a reliquary of the cross to the monastery of Radegundis in Poitiers. In this hymn he lauds the Emperor as a loyal adherent of Chalcedon,[16] and he also mentions that he allowed exiled bishops to return home.[17] Here we have one of the rare testimonies to contact between East and West, which nevertheless does not say very much in support of Justin's orthodoxy.[18]

Close, friendly relations[19] existed between the Emperor and Patriarch John III Scholasticus of Constantinople and the Stylite, Symeon the Younger,[20] both of whom were not on the anti-Chalcedonian side. According to the picture given by John of Ephesus, the Patriarch, who in the meantime had received the function of arbiter in the disputes

---

14. Corippus, *In laudem Iustini*, IV, 303: *MGH* 3, 2, 154.

15. Venantius Fortunatus, *Ad Iustinum et Sophiam Augustos = Appendix Carminum* (CPL 1036), II: *MGH auct. ant.* 4, 1, 275–278; PL 88, 431–434, with the refrain: *Gloria summa tibi, rerum sator, atque redemptor, qui das Justinum, justus, in orbe caput*, or respectively, *quod tenet augustam celsa Sophia gradum*.

16. *Ibid.*, 25–26: *MGH* 4, 276; PL 88, 432B: *reddite vota deo, quoniam nova purpura quidquid concilium statuit Calchedonense tenet*.

17. *Ibid.*, 39–40.

18. Cf. the critical comments of Averil Cameron, 'Early Byzantine *Kaiserkritik*' = *Continuity and Change*, no. IX, 5: 'in part at least merely the expected reaction of a Westerner who saw the Byzantine Emperor making a pious gesture to the Catholic Franks'.

19. On the friendship of the three see P. Van den Ven, 'L'accession de Jean le Scholastique au siège patriarcal de Constantinople en 565', *Byz* 35 (1965), 320–2; *Vita Symeon. Styl. iun.* (CPG 7369), chs. 202–207: Van den Ven, *SubsHag* 32 (Brussels, 1962), 176–9.

20. P. Van den Ven, 'Les écrits de s. Syméon le Stylite le Jeune avec trois sermons inédits', *Mus* 70 (1957), p. 2, n. 9 and p. 3, considers the *Epistula ad Iustinum iuniorem* (CPG 7366) authentic and stemming from Symeon Stylites the Younger, but addressed rather to Justinian. By the *Vita Symeon Styl. iun.*, ch. 207 (ed. Van den Ven, *SubsHag* 32, 178–179), however, it is attested that Justin corresponded with the Stylite on account of the healing of his daughter, who was possessed by a demon. *Sermo* 30 (CPG 7367 [30]): A. Mai, *Patrum Bibliotheca* VIII/3, 148–156 contributes nothing of significance to christology from our point of view. There is no special christological position discernible. *Sermo* 30 is probably also reworked. We shall indicate some of Symeon's thoughts: Jesus Christ is our example in everything, because he lived our life in the body without sin and without deception. *Deitatem praesentem in se habens, et tamquam iudex futuri saeculi, patienter expectat, benignitate utitur, cum ipse solus omnem bonitatem habeat* (no. 7, p. 154). The transformation into the immortal and incorruptible *sponsus* is impending for us who have fallen with Adam after the resurrection of the one who never fell. As God he is *pneuma*, spirit; nevertheless he became a human being. Thus we too should be spiritual (no. 8, p. 154). On the orthodoxy of Symeon Stylites the Younger cf. P. Van den Ven, *SubsHag* 32, Introduction, 167*–170*.

between Severans and Tritheists,[21] was the driving force in the later persecution of the 'Monophysites'.[22]

2. The two 'edicts' of Emperor Justin II

Through Michael the Syrian there are transmitted to us two 'edicts' from Justinian's successor,[23] by means of which the Emperor attempted to reach agreement with the Severans; however, this was done in a completely contradictory manner. Whereas the first 'edict'[24] is a testimony to an extreme concession vis-à-vis the 'Monophysites', almost amounting to the renunciation of Chalcedon, the second can be understood as an endorsement of Chalcedonian christology. What relationship do these initiatives of Justin have to Justinian's christology and religious politics? First of all we shall turn to the content of the first edictum and cite its text verbatim.

> We accept only one unique definition of faith: the one that was promulgated by the three hundred and eighteen Fathers, which was confirmed by the Fathers assembled in Constantinople and Ephesus. We do not know of another definition than: we believe in one God, the Father ... and the rest of the definition. We accept the two births of the God-Logos, that from the Father before time and that at the end of the ages from the virgin Mary. And we confess that he is truly the only (begotten) Logos, that he remained unchanged in his divinity, that he suffered in his flesh and as God worked miracles. (We do not confess) one and another, nor that Christ is one and God another; but (we do confess) one and the same (composed) of two natures, divine and human (natures); one *hypostasis* and one person, not two *hypostases* nor two persons, nor two sons; but one incarnate *hypostasis* of the God-Logos. We anathematize all heresies, above all Arius, Eunomius, Macedonius, Nestorius, who was deposed and anathematized by the Fathers, Celestine and Cyril. In the same way we anathematize Theodore, the letter of Ibas, the writings of Theodoret, and all those who think like them and resemble them in impiety. We accept the holy Patriarch Severus and annul the anathema imposed upon him in iniquity and without reason. We annul the anathemas which have been imposed from Cyril's time to the present.[25]

21. On this see P. Allen, 'Neo-Chalcedonism and the Patriarchs of the Late Sixth Century', *Byz* 50 (1980), 9–10.

22. John Ephes., *HE* I, 11–12: Brooks, CSCO 106, 6–8. Cf. also A. de Halleux, 'Trois synodes impériaux du VIe s. dans une chronique syriaque inédite', in *A Tribute to Arthur Vööbus*, ed. R. H. Fisher (Chicago, 1977), 302–7, who presents the fragment of a report on a synod in Constantinople, at which John of Constantinople anathematized Severus. The synod presumably took place in the early part of 571 and was summoned because the Severans 'did not behave calmly'.

23. Michael Syr., *Chron.* X, II: Chabot II, 289a–290a; and X, IV–V: 295–299. The second is also in Greek in Evagrius Schol., *HE* V, 4: Bidez-Parmentier, pp. 197,28–201,11.

24. The '*edictum*' (Chabot, 289a) was apparently never promulgated, and it is for this reason that P. Allen, *Evagrius Scholasticus*, 212, also rightly speaks of a 'draft of an edict'.

25. Following the translation of A. Van Roey in his article: 'La controverse trithéite jusqu'à l'excommunication de Conon et d'Eugène (557–569)', *OLP* 16 (1985) (141–65), 157, who corrects that of Chabot II (289a–290a).

In this we have the acknowledgement of only the first three councils, whereby Constantinople and Ephesus are understood as an explication of Nicaea. Chalcedon itself is not named. In addition there is the anathema on the Three Chapters and, surprisingly, the recognition of Severus and the annulment of all anathemas that were imposed upon him.[26] The expressions 'from two natures' and the 'one incarnate *hypostasis* of the God-Logos' occur, but the *mia-physis* formula is explicitly missing. Nevertheless this proposal failed because of the resistance of the anti-Chalcedonians, for whom the formulations did not go far enough.

In a petition to the Emperor by the anti-Chalcedonian bishops the following were demanded:[27]

- the addition: 'one single nature or *hypostasis* of the incarnate God-Logos was formed from two natures or *hypostases*', that is the explicit *mia-physis* formula and the synonymous use of nature and *hypostasis*;
- the addition (after 'not two *hypostases*'): 'nor two natures', that is, the formal negation of the two natures;
- the condemnation of all who think otherwise and are of the opinion that is contrary to Cyril's twelve chapters — the 'edict' was seen as a confirmation of Cyril's twelve chapters.

It is interesting that, if these additions were too difficult, the bishops said they would be happy with Zeno's *Henoticon*, because this forbade any change.

These additions of the Severan bishops, however, did not satisfy the 'Monophysite' monks. It was because of their opposition that the Emperor's attempt foundered.[28] The reason for the monks' resistance was that the bishops had not explicitly anathematized Chalcedon, Leo's *Tomus* and all dyophysites.[29]

Michael the Syrian, however, does not let the affair stop there. He writes that the bishops who were distressed by the action of the monks requested Jacob Baradaeus to summon an assembly of bishops once again, and to draft a new *libellus* (concerning the position with regard to the imperial edict). Jacob (allegedly) met this demand. Together with Theodore of Arabia and the Tritheists Eugenius of Seleucia, Aboui and Phocas, he composed a new *libellus* which supposedly turned out not very different from the first (which was torn up). For this reason the reaction of the monks was the same as before. They now threatened to anathematize Jacob Baradaeus himself and to separate themselves from him as their bishop. Michael the Syrian reports that as a result Jacob anathematized this *charta*. Then the *patricius* John departed in great anger. Correspondingly he reported to the Emperor, who immediately replied with new persecutions of the anti-Chalcedonians.[30]

A. Van Roey doubts the historical truth of this report about a second letter from the bishops.

26. J. Maspero, *Histoire*, 168: 'Un pareil édit était purement et simplement la capitulation du catholicisme, représenté et trahi par le basileus.'

27. Michael Syr., *Chron.*, X, II: Chabot, 286b–287b.

28. *Ibid.*: Chabot, 287b–288b, relates that the writing of the bishops was torn up in a tumult by a monk Cosmas ('Bar-Hraniata') when it was read out in the monastery of Mar Zakai. When the Emperor's negotiator, the *patricius* John, learned of this he passed enraged to the other side of the Euphrates.

29. See the report of the archimandrites of the East, Mares of Mar Bassus (at Bītabō), Zenobius of Mar Bīzī (near Seleucia) and Constantine of Mar Eusebius (at Kafr Bartha) and other archimandrites to Jacob Baradaeus: *Documenta ad origines monophysitarum illustrandas*, ed. Chabot (Louvain, 1933) = CSCO 103, 120–123, esp. p. 122,27–29.

30. Michael Syr., *Chron.* X, II: Chabot, 288b.

In any case, he maintains, it did not receive great publicity.[31] For in their writing just mentioned the Oriental archimandrites report to Jacob Baradaeus:

> We know nothing at all of the fact that afterwards [that is, after the destruction of the first *libellus*] another *charta* with the same or a different content from the one torn up was handed over by certain people. Such a writing (*charta*) was not handed over in our name or with our assent, as you also attest.[32]

The Oriental archimandrites also let Jacob Baradaeus know that assent to the imperial edict, as this was expressed in the alleged *libellus*, would mean schism with him. As their writing to Jacob reports, they had a well-founded concern about the collapse of the monophysite front. They state that they had received reports from the imperial city that there some who considered themselves as 'ours' had suggested that Jacob Baradaeus and Mar Theodore should go there, in order to be able to move them to subscribe to the imperial edict under the pretext of a future union.[33] Michael the Syrian also reports that, in order to restore peace and the unity of the Church, the Emperor addressed a document to the *stratelates* Sergōna, to the effect that Jacob Baradaeus and Theodore should come into the residence on account of ecclesiastical matters. Only Theodore obeyed the imperial command; Jacob, however, 'followed the advice of the monks; he did not journey there. The emperor was very annoyed and fell into a rage.'[34]

The first edict of Emperor Justin II thus did not achieve the desired effect. The schism on account of Chalcedon still remained.

The edict of 571[35]

The citation of John 14,27 at the beginning of the edict ('Peace I leave with you; my peace I give to you') indicates that it is an action directed explicitly at ecclesiastical peace. The Emperor immediately gives this interpretation:

> This is nothing other than that those who believe in him come together in one and the same Church, and are of like mind with regard to the right teaching of the Church on the one side, and turn away from those who say or intend the opposite on the other. For correct confession of the faith was presented to all human beings as the highest benefit. Hence we also obey the evangelical commands and the holy *symbolum*, namely the teachings of the holy Fathers, and we request that all come together to one and the same Church and opinion.

On the basis of this call to unity in one and the same Church, which is established in scripture and tradition (teachings of the Fathers and confession of faith), the Emperor then cites verbatim a long excerpt

---

31. A. Van Roey, *art. cit.*, 159.
32. *Doc. monophys.*: Chabot, CSCO 103, p. 123,2–6.
33. *Ibid.*, p. 123,12–15: . . . *praetextu quidem unionis, quam praedicant futuram, sed revera quod cupiunt ut adhaereatis fidei in memorata charta propositae; et sic per vos scopum sibi intentum attingant.*
34. Michael Syr., *Chron.* X, II: Chabot, 289b–290b.
35. According to Dölger, *Regesten* I, no. 19, p. 3. On the dating cf. P. Allen, *Evagrius Scholasticus*, 214. We cite following Evagrius Schol., *HE* V, 4: Bidez-Parmentier, pp. 197,28–201,11.

from the beginning of Justinian's *Confessio fidei* of 551.[36] Into this text he inserts two passages and appends a conclusion.[37] What theological or christological position is expressed there?

In his comment on trinitarian theology Justin adopts Justinian's wording (with insignificant changes),[38] which he clearly regards as still valid in this time, when people were put on their guard by the tritheist dispute.

The christological confession likewise follows Justinian's formulations with some modifications which, however, do not alter the sense.[39]

There is one sentence omitted which contests that another than the God-Logos endured suffering and death, and confirms that the God-Logos assumed human flesh in order to fulfil everything (Schwartz, p. 74,2-3). The soteriological content of the statement, however, is not altered by this, especially when further on Justin adds: 'for the sake of our salvation . . . unchanged having become a human being, he who voluntarily took upon himself suffering and death for us in the flesh' (Bidez-Parmentier, p. 199,17.19-20). Also the omission (*ibid.*, p. 199,23) of three of Justinian's explanatory sentences (Schwartz, p. 74,11-14) does not alter the statement in Justin's edict, but appears more as a redactional abbreviation.

The first of the two longer additions, which Winkelmann explicitly records, renders in other words what was previously omitted.

The first addition in Justin's edict reads:

For when he became a human being for us he did not cease to be God. Certainly he did not refuse to be a human being, because he is God by nature and the similarity to us is not acceptable. As he had remained God in humanity, so he was also a human being in the superiority of the divinity, nothing less, both being in the same, and one God and at the same time human being, the Emmanuel. We confess the same, perfect in divinity and perfect in humanity, from which he is composed.

---

36. Justinian emp., *Confessio fidei* (CPG 6885): Schwartz, *Drei dogmat. Schriften*, pp. 72,13-74,16 and pp. 74,21-27; 76,37-78,1. We owe the observation that Justin's edict takes over parts of the *Confessio fidei* to F. Winkelmann, *Die östlichen Kirchen in der Epoche der christologischen Auseinandersetzungen* (Berlin, 1980), 104-6, esp. 105-6.

37. Evagrius Schol., *HE* V, 4: Bidez-Parmentier, p. 199,26-34 and p. 200,15-25; for the conclusion see pp. 200,26-201,11.

38. In the confession of the Trinity the phrase *logo kai pragmati* is added after the words 'one godhead, namely nature and essence'; furthermore the word *energeia* is added in the listing 'one strength and fullness of power'. The explanation that the properties separate the persons of the Trinity, but the divinity unites them, is omitted; in addition the sentences at the end of the trinitarian part about the rejection of the notion of Sabellius and Arius are absent.

39. Thus in addition Mary is denoted as lady and glorious (Bidez-Parmentier, pp. 199,2 and 200,11-12). The compiler of the edict attaches lines to the title 'one of the Trinity' which in Justinian's edict come later (Schwartz, pp. 76,37-78,1): 'co-glorified with the Father and the Holy Spirit. For the holy Trinity does not add a fourth person as an appendage; incarnate is one of the Trinity, the God-Logos.' This citation concludes with the words: 'but one and the same is our Lord Jesus Christ'.

In the last sentence the phrase 'perfect in divinity and perfect in humanity', familiar from Cyril and Chalcedon, is added. Immediately afterwards 'composed' is additionally expressed of the *hypostasis*, corresponding completely to Justinian's christology. The addition, however, replaces Justinian's sentence:

> and when we discern in each of the two natures, that is, in divinity and humanity, the one Jesus Christ our Lord, the God-Logos become flesh and a human being,

and immediately after that the following sentence is omitted:

> For if we confess the composition, then the parts are discernible in the whole and the whole in the parts. (Schwartz, p. 74,20–21)

Thus the statement about the discernment (*ginoskontes, ginosketai*) of the two natures in the whole of the *synthesis* is dropped. In the addition the discernment is changed into the confession of the one Christ.

Justinian is again clearly adopted, yet with the statement that the God-Logos united himself not to a previously existing human being, but created for himself from Mary a human being 'like us in all things, sin excluded' (cf. Chalcedon) — an addition. No doubt remains that the unity has to be sought in the *hypostasis*. This is clearly expressed in the explanation of the hypostatic union, which is taken over from Justinian:

> The union according to the *hypostasis* is, however, that the God-Logos, that is, the one *hypostasis* of the three *hypostases* of the divinity, did not unite himself with a previously existing human being, but in the womb of the . . . *Theotokos* . . . Mary created [*edemiourgesen*] from her for himself a flesh in the one *hypostasis*, consubstantial with us and like us in all things [in suffering, *homoiopathe*], sin excluded, animated by a rational, spiritual soul.[40]

The second (longer) addition begins with a sentence which has no parallel in Justinian and expresses clearly in a noteworthy way that the *hypostasis* of the incarnate Christ is in the God-Logos:[41]

> For in him he had the *hypostasis* and he became a human being, and one and the same is our Lord Jesus Christ, glorified with the Father and the Holy Spirit.

Then the edict reads practically as a summary.

> Thus when we think of the unutterable union, we rightly confess one incarnate nature of the God-Logos in a flesh animated by a rational, spiritual soul. And when once again we grasp in *theoria* the distinction of the natures, we say that these are two, and in doing so we introduce no separation. For each of the two natures is in him.[42] Hence we can confess

---

40. Bidez-Parmentier, p. 200,8–15.
41. On this cf. similarly Leontius Jer., *CN* I, 49: PG 86, 1512B.
42. In Justinian this sentence occurs earlier as well: Schwartz, p. 74,20.

one and the same Christ, one Son, one *prosopon*, one *hypostasis*, God and at the same time human being.

In this way the *mia-physis* formula is explained as orthodox and the two natures are confessed in *theoria*. Thus in this edict Justin is once again in line with Justinian's (moderate) neo-Chalcedonianism.

We have the following elements of Justinian's christology: the 'one of the Trinity (became a human being)', 'in *theoria* two'; the formula 'in two natures' is missing, and in its place there is 'composed . . . from two natures' (p. 199,24.34), although it is not specially highlighted; 'composite' occurs often; the 'union according to the *hypostasis*' is understood precisely in Justinian's sense, as the act of creating the flesh from Mary in his [i.e. the Logos'] own *hypostasis*. *Mia hypostasis* clearly denotes the *hypostasis* of the Logos, not that of the *apotelesma*.

After the development of the confession in this way, the conclusion expresses the condemnation of all who do not think accordingly, and as well the fact that the customs and stance in the Church should be maintained.[43]

Thus in the edict of Justin II we have a slight shift of Justinian's christology towards the *mia-physis* formula, towards a position where the two natures are no longer stressed so strongly,[44] even though they are, however, expressed in fact. The unity in Christ is emphasized more than the distinction of the two natures, which nevertheless is constantly upheld (in *theoria*).[45] That the concepts *hypostasis* and *physis* are no longer used synonymously is not stated explicitly (as in Justinian), but the non-synonymous use occurs in practice.

In summary, with the excerpts from the *Confessio fidei* of 551 Justin II here takes over the elements of Justinian's christology. The simultaneous use of the two formulas (*mia physis* — *dyo physeis*) is not demanded, but it is certainly established that both can be rightly confessed.

With this edict, however, Justin II was not able to attain the union with the Severans for which he had persistently striven because they held

---

43. An addition which is missing in Michael the Syrian; cf. P. Allen, *Evagrius Scholasticus*, 25. On this as well John Ephes., *HE* I, 19: Brooks, p. 18,2: *et ipsi de suis in fine edicti haeretice inseruerunt 'Ecclesiae consuetudines ei conserventur', quasi propter synodum, ut secundum consuetudinem suam eam proclamarent.*

44. In his edict Justin seems to want to circumvent the expression *physis*: the sentence in Schwartz, p. 74,16–18 (ἐν ἑκατέραι δὲ φύσει . . . γινώσκοντες) is paraphrased without employing *physis* (Bidez-Parmentier, p. 199,33–34), and the clause in Schwartz, p. 74,27 (ὅπερ ἐστὶ φύσις ἀνθρωπίνη) is omitted (Bidez-Parmentier, p. 200,15).

45. The characteristic adverbs in Chalcedon's definition also resonate: no transformation (ἀτρέπτως, p. 199,19), no mingling (σύγχυσιν . . . οὐκ ἐπεισάγομεν, p. 199,26), no separation (διαίρεσιν . . . οὐκ ἐπιφέρομεν, p. 200,1).

out for an annulment of Chalcedon.[46] He turned to coercive measures, and a period of persecution began for the 'Monophysites'. Both 'edicts', essential signposts in the six-year long efforts of the Emperor to restore ecclesial unity by dialogues and negotiations,[47] thus led to a dismal failure. Under the Emperors Tiberius and Maurice who followed Justin II there were no negotiations with the Severans. Dialogues and negotiations were conducted more and more by the Chalcedonian patriarchs.[48]

II. THEOLOGICAL POSITIONS AT THE END OF THE SIXTH CENTURY

1. The testimony of Patriarch Eutychius of Constantinople

The Cyrillian extension of Chalcedonian terminology and of its major formula after 553 appears not to have been taken up everywhere with the same intensity. A writing of Patriarch Eutychius of Constantinople (552-565, 577-582), which is preserved only in Armenian, testifies to this. Eutychius was one of the presidents of the Council of 553 and their head. After his deposition and during his exile from the capital (565), which he spent in his home monastery in Amaseia,[49] he composed the

46. Cf. John Ephes., *HE* I, 19-20: Brooks, 16-18; see also Michael Syr., *Chron.* X, 6: Chabot II, 299-300. The edict was presented to anti-Chalcedonian bishops imprisoned in Constantinople, so that they could make their own improvements. Because of the resistance of the Patriarch of Constantinople and the Chalcedonians, only a few of these corrections were incorporated into the edict, although the additions were said to have pleased the Emperor. From the fear, however, that these *capita* would plunge the Church into great agitation, according to Michael the Emperor succumbed. As a result the 'Monophysites' did not accept the imperial edict. They demanded that Chalcedon be withdrawn so that automatically ecclesial peace would be restored: *causa offensae et perturbationis totius ecclesiae, synodus videlicet Chalcedonis, e medio tollitur* (Brooks, p. 18,24-25). Cf. also John Ephes., *HE* I, 24: Brooks, p. 22,14: *synodum Chalcedonis eicite*. John claims that the edict was written ambiguously, on the one side against, and on the other for the synod (= Chalcedon). According to John Ephes., *HE* I, 24: Brooks, 21-24, it came to the *communio* of the anti-Chalcedonian bishops with John of Constantinople, with the promise that Chalcedon would be anathematized. This promise, however, was not kept.

47. On the Emperor's efforts with regard to the Severans cf. P. Goubert, *art. cit.* Justin II intervened also in order to achieve a union between monophysites and the tritheist Athanasius, and a union in Egypt.

48. Cf. P. Allen, 'Neo-Chalcedonism and the Patriarchs of the Late Sixth Century', *Byz* 50 (1980), 5-17, esp. 8.

49. See R. Janin, art. 'Eutichio', in *Bibl.SS* V (Rome, 1964), 323-4; *Vita*, in *ASS Aprilis* I (Antwerp, 1675), 550-72; PG 86, 2273-2389; Grumel, *Regestes* I², 177-181, 190-192.

writing on the major trinitarian-christological concepts 'nature' and 'hypostasis'.[50]

For his explanation of *physis* and *hypostasis* Eutychius embraces the *theologia* and the *oikonomia*, and elaborates for both the same conceptual content. His starting-point, however, is the *synonymous* use of nature and *hypostasis* by representatives of 'profane science'. His authority for the *distinction* of nature and *hypostasis* is Basil (*Ep.* 210.214.52 and especially *Ep.* 236 to Amphilochius). Naturally letter 38 also plays a special rôle; in the transmission of the text this letter is sometimes ascribed to Basil, and sometimes to Gregory of Nyssa. Eutychius decides in favour of Gregory of Nyssa.[51] The Cappadocian definition of *hypostasis* is adopted without any particular alteration, as is the transposition of trinitarian terminology to teaching about the incarnation.[52] In this way the holistic interpretation of Christ's person is expressed completely according to the state of the christology of 565, but with an emphatic recourse to Chalcedon which is striking.

(1) Eutychius speaks clearly of the insubsistence of Christ's humanity in the *hypostasis* of the Logos.[53] Christ, however, is a *synthesis* from two unequal natures in one person, not a nature unity from (incomplete) partial natures. If the term 'Christ' holds for the Logos only after the incarnation, he is still only one person and *hypostasis*.[54]

(2) Eutychius explained Cyril's *mia-physis* formula by its opposition to Nestorius[55] and his interpretation of the 'two natures' in the sense of 'two *hypostases*'. Eutychius attempted to construct a bridge from Cyril's

50. Eutychius Const., *De differentia naturae et hypostaseos* (CPG 6940): in the Italian translation of P. Ananian, 'L'opuscolo di Eutichio patriarca di Costantinopoli sulla "Distinzione della natura e persona" ', in *Armeniaca. Mélanges d'Études arméniennes* (Venice, 1969), 355–82; for the Italian text see 364–82.

51. Cf. *JdChr* I³, 542–5, on CPG 2900. Eutychius produces a long extract: Ananian, 368–70, who notes the divergences of the Armenian text from PG 32, 325.328–329.336, which are in part considerable.

52. Eutychius Const., *op. cit.*, nos. 6–12: Ananian, 372–8; esp. in no. 8, p. 374, Eutychius investigates the major texts, which from Gregory Nazianzen on were decisive for standardizing trinitarian and incarnational terminology: *Or.* 30: PG 36, 113; *Ep. ad Cledon.* 102: PG 36, 180; *De nativ. Chr.*: PG 36, 328–329.

53. Eutychius Const., *op. cit.*, no. 6: Ananian 372: 'ma fu ordinato che il corpo, preso dalla santa madre di Dio e sempre vergine Maria, sia nell'ipostasi del Verbo'.

54. *Ibid.*, no. 7, p. 373: 'Quindi (Cristo) è uno *nella ipostasi e non nella natura*, colui che viene considerato in due nature ... Quindi Cristo è due nature, ... ed è composto da due nature; però è una l'ipostasi e una la persona di questo composto.'

55. *Ibid.*, no. 9, pp. 374–5.

terminology for *theologia* (where *hypostasis* and nature are clearly divided) to the terminology for *oikonomia*.[56]

What is important is that for Eutychius 'Christ' is not a *tertium quid*, a third product from the addition of two *homoousia*,[57] nor a third composite, as Peter and Paul are *composita* from body and soul.[58] A 'third' could not result from divinity and humanity in Christ, because the ensouled body assumed from the Virgin had its *hypostasis* in that it was in the *hypostasis* of the Logos.[59] The twofold consubstantiality in Christ, to God and to us, relates in contrast to the natures. This 'terzo risultato' should not be inferred from the univocal application of the body–soul analogy to Christ.[60] The result is thus that, corresponding to the Church's tradition, there are many distinctions between 'nature', 'essence' and *hypostasis*.[61] The unity of subject in Christ is clearly recognized and is present in the *hypostasis* of the Logos. This is the concern of Eutychius. The Patriarch had little to say in interpreting how the insubsistence happens. It did not pertain to his theme.

In the second part of his treatise Eutychius discusses the (Cappadocian) teaching on properties (*idiomata*) with reference to Basil, Gregory of Nyssa[62] and the discussion about the formulas 'from two natures' and 'in two natures' which arose at the Synods of Constantinople (448), Ephesus (449) and Chalcedon (451).[63] It is worth noting that the Patriarch here rejects the 'from two natures' of Dioscorus just like the papal and imperial representatives at the Council of Chalcedon. In conclusion he summarizes the whole confession of the Council of 451[64]

---

56. *Ibid.*, no. 9: Ananian 375. Here Eutychius refers to Cyril's *Dialogue*, where he says that against the philosopher Hermias, Cyril stresses his knowledge of the distinction between nature and *hypostasis*. That the *mia physis*, however, is to be interpreted in the sense of 'one *hypostasis*', Eutychius attempts to prove from Cyril Alex., *Ep. 17 ad Nestor.* (III) (CPG 5317): PG 77, 116C: 'Tutte le voci del vangelo sono da attribuire all'unica ipostasi, (cioè) all'unico Verbo incarnato (ὑποστάσει μιᾷ τῇ Λόγου σεσαρκωμένῃ); perché è unico il nostro Signore Gesù Cristo, secondo le sacre scritture.' The fact remains, however, that Cyril also accepts *physis* and *hypostasis* as synonymous for the doctrine of the incarnation. He could also have used φύσει μιᾷ in the passage cited here.

57. *Ibid.*, no. 10: Ananian 375.

58. *Ibid.*, 376.

59. *Ibid.*

60. *Ibid.*, no. 11: Ananian 377. Eutychius cites Ps. Justin (= Theodoret), *Expositio rectae fidei* (CPG 6218) , but as an authentic text of Justin. In the application of this analogy Theodoret distinguishes, as Eutychius comments, between what is pertinent and what is not.

61. *Ibid.*, no. 12, p. 377.

62. *Ibid.*, nos. 13–14: Ananian 378–80.

63. *Ibid.*, nos. 15–16: Ananian 380–2.

64. In this summary the Armenian text exhibits some lacunae, which Ananian (381) fills, not, however, with the text of the synod, but with words from Leo's *Tomus* to Flavian.

by referring to the 'in two natures' of Basil of Seleucia, introduced at the Flavian Synod of 448 and taken over by Chalcedon:[65]

> The Synod of Chalcedon produced this same formula (with one omission) . . . and simply confessed Christ in two natures and in one *hypostasis* and in one person.

The whole is thought of as a justification of the main formula of Chalcedon. Through the sharp contrasting of *physis* and *hypostasis* and the location of the 'one *hypostasis*' in the pre-existent Logos, an interpretation of Chalcedon was arrived at which was beneficial for the Council. There are many elements here which recall Leontius of Jerusalem and Justinian's edict of 551. Not counting the expression *synthesis*, which is already found in the authors named, the Council of 553 left behind hardly any traces.

Did the president of the Council of 553 not return to a pure Chalcedonianism?

2. The Chalcedonian writing *De sectis*

By T. Hainthaler

The author of *De sectis*[66] is, according to the superscription, Leontius Scholasticus of Byzantium, who took notes in the lectures 'of the abbot, dearly beloved of God, and very wise philosopher, Theodore'.[67] The identification of the author of the writing has given rise to many difficulties, and we can also give only a negative response to it.

1. Leontius Scholasticus is not to be confused with Leontius of Byzantium. The hypothesis of F. Loofs that *De sectis* is only the reworking of a lost work (the *scholia Leontiou*) of Leontius of Byzantium can no longer be maintained after the works of Junglas, Richard and Rees.[68]

---

65. *Ibid.*, 381.

66. *Liber de sectis* (CPG 6823): PG 86, 1193–1268. A critical edition is not yet available. On text-critical questions see M. Waegeman, 'The Text Tradition of the Treatise *De sectis* (Ps. Leontius Byzantinus)', *AnCl* 45 (1976), 190–6. We shall cite the text with reference to the number of the *actio* (πρᾶξις) as well as to the number in the Latin translation.

67. According to M. Richard, 'ΑΠΟ ΦΩΝΗΣ', *Byz* 20 (1950), 191–222 (= *Op. Min.* III, no. 60), esp. 200–2, this is the correct interpretation of the title, against Loofs.

68. The 'hypothesis of an original lost writing' proposed by F. Loofs, *Leontius von Byzanz und die gleichnamigen Schriftsteller der griechischen Kirche* = *TU* 3, 1–2 (Leipzig, 1887), 136–63, was already criticized by J. P. Junglas, *Leontius von Byzanz* = *FCLDG* 7/3 (Paderborn, 1908), 5–20. F. Loofs, *ThLZ* 34 (1909), 205–9, esp. 207–8, however, continued to cling to it. In 1939 Loofs' thesis was opposed simultaneously and independently by M. Richard, 'Le traité De Sectis et Léonce de Byzance', *RHE* 35 (1939), 695–723 = *Op. Min.* II, no. 55, and by S. Rees, 'The

We shall briefly give the most important arguments.

(i) The expression ἀπὸ φωνῆς in the superscript must be correctly interpreted, not as 'the σχόλια of Leontius in the reworking [and after the dictation] of Theodorus',[69] but as notes of the lectures of Theodore which Leontius made (proof: Richard; cf. also Junglas).

(ii) The definition of concepts in actio I would not have satisfied Leontius of Byzantium. The concepts enhypostaton and hypostasis (cf. actio VII) are sharply distinguished by Leontius, but in De sectis they are mixed; according to De sectis an accident can be enhypostaton, but not according to Leontius (Richard, Rees).

(iii) De sectis had a detached view of the body–soul comparison (actio VII,VI–VIII; 1245C–1249C), whereas Leontius of Byzantium esteemed it highly (Richard).

(iv) It is striking that Theodore of Mopsuestia was defended by De sectis, while he was strongly attacked by Leontius of Byzantium (Rees).

2. The 'abbot and philosopher Theodore' is not Theodore of Raithu. Junglas was the first to suggest Theodore of Raithu as the author,[70] a thesis which Richard expressly attempted to support, but later, after the publication of the work of Elert, rescinded.[71]

In our opinion the following considerations tell against the hypothesis.

(i) De sectis defends a strict Chalcedonianism, whereas Theodore of Raithu in the Praeparatio is an explicit neo-Chalcedonian.

De Sectis: A Treatise Attributed to Leontius of Byzantium', JTS 40 (1939), 346–60. M. van Esbroeck has recently returned in two articles to Loofs' hypothesis in a modified form: 'Le "De sectis" attribué à Léonce de Byzance (CPG 6823) dans la version géorgienne d'Arsène Iqaltoeli', Bedi Kartlisa 42 (1984), 35–52; idem, 'La date et l'auteur du De sectis attribué à Léonce de Byzance', in After Chalcedon, FS A. Van Roey = OLA 18 (Louvain, 1985), 415–24. M. van Esbroeck advocates a dating of the text to 543–551 and sees in De sectis (by an Abbot Theodore) a continuation of the writings CNE, CA and DTN of Leontius of Byzantium, reworked to address the Gaianites; he suggests that the original form of the work could quite well stem from Leontius of Byzantium. Nevertheless, serious theological doubts (concerning tritheism, the works of John Philoponus, the Gaianites) stand in the way of this thesis. For more details the critical edition is to be awaited.

69. F. Loofs, op. cit., 141–2.

70. J. P. Junglas, op cit., 16.

71. M. Richard, Op. Min. II, no. 55, 700–3. He indicates three similarities to the Praeparatio of Theodore of Raithu. (1) The introduction of the concepts ousia, physis, hypostasis and prosopon at the beginning of De sectis is quite consistent with Praep., ed. Diekamp, 185–222, esp. 207–216. (2) At the end of actio I the position of the Church is characterized as the middle way (μέσον χορεύουσα, 1200A) vis-à-vis the heresies, a conception which is very pronounced in Theodore of Raithu. (3) There is the introduction of Aristotelian scholasticism into theology (although we have to notice that this was previously present in the Leontii, and even more strongly in John Philoponus). S. Rees, art. cit. takes over the hypothesis of Junglas, but in his arguments refutes only the thesis of Loofs that De sectis goes back to Leontius of Byzantium. He brings no positive evidence for the fact that De sectis stems from Theodore of Raithu, whose authorship he nevertheless upholds: idem, 'The Literary Activity of Leontius of Byzantium', JTS 19 (1968), 220–42 (242: 'Theodore of Raithu, author of De Sectis, at the end of the sixth century'). C. Moeller, 'Le chalcédonisme et le néo-chalcédonisme', in Chalkedon I, 664–6, 685–6, continues to distinguish between Theodore of Raithu and the author of De sectis, cf. 699. After the work of W. Elert, 'Theodor von Pharan und Theodor von Raithu', ThLZ 76 (1951), 67–76, Richard, Op. Min. II, no. 55, Append., himself established that this identification had to be abandoned.

(ii) In the *Praeparatio* Theodore of Mopsuestia is unambiguously rejected as a heretic (ed. Diekamp, 188); *De sectis*, however, clearly harbours sympathy for him.

(iii) *De sectis* distinguishes itself by an unusual sense of historical developments, a sense which is certainly not documented in the *Praeparatio*. There, for instance, heretics are depicted purely schematically, and the *mia-physis* formula and the two-natures formula appear in the abstract with no historical anchoring.

Where did this writing originate? Speigl is of the opinion that 'it fits well into the framework of Chalcedonian orthodoxy in the area of Raithu–Pharan–Sinai monasteries at the end of the sixth century'.[72] In favour of this thesis one can adduce the fact that the arguments of the Hebrews and Samaritans against the Christian faith are treated first and in detail. However, that can also be explained satisfactorily by the author's chronological approach, which centres on the history of salvation. Furthermore, one is struck by the author's remarkable knowledge of Egyptian relationships;[73] thus the post-Chalcedonian developments are depicted only for Egypt with the production of a (complete) list of patriarchs. Three heresies receive detailed treatment: Gaianites, Agnoetai (*actio* X) and Tritheists (*actio* V), all of which had their origin in Alexandria. They were then, however, continually discussed in Constantinople and also combated there. We have no clear indications which would enable us to allocate the work to the Sinai region. In addition, on the basis of the christological thoughts expressed, it seems possible that it could have its origin in the Constantinopolitan area. Therefore we have decided to treat this important work at the end of the sixth century in the framework of the Patriarchate of Constantinople.

The dating of the writing, however, seems to be clear: *actio* V, V gives a list of the bishops (τάξις τῶν ἐπισκόπων) of Alexandria, which ends with Eulogius (581–608) (1232C). Accordingly this part of *De sectis* was not written before 581, and thus not after his Patriarchate, for then 'this' would not be the list of patriarchs.

Actio V, V is, however, not a singular piece, but is inserted into the author's plan to sketch the development of the dogmas of the Christians 'to the present' (ἄχρι τοῦ νῦν, *actio* III, I; 1212C).

The writing begins by explaining briefly the four concepts (*ousia*,

---

72. J. Speigl, 'Der Autor der Schrift De Sectis über die Konzilien und die Religionspolitik Justinians', *AHC* 2 (1970), 207–30, here 208. Speigl bases his thesis otherwise only on the arguments which Richard produces for Theodore of Raithu as the author of *De sectis*.

73. M. Waegeman, 'The Old Testament Canon in the Treatise De sectis', *AnCl* 50 (1981), 813–18, particularly on the basis of the Old Testament canon in *De sectis*, declares that the author belonged to the Alexandrian school (*ibid.*, 818).

physis, hypostasis, prosopon)[74] and then proceeds to trinitarian teaching and tells the story of creation (I, II); subsequently it follows biblical chronology: the flood, the story of Joseph, the exodus from Egypt, Moses, the giving of the commandments. After a brief reference to the activity of the prophets, who nevertheless did not move the people to conversion ('They were admonished by many prophets, but they remained the same'), the incarnation is related with an explanation of three attributes: unmingled, true, undivided. The brief characterization of the life of Jesus ends with the confession of Christ's resurrection, ascension and return. We shall render this *regula fidei* verbatim.

> Then the Son and Logos of God dwelt for our sake in the *Theotokos*, clothed with an ensouled body, rational, intelligent, and simply human, united to the human body, *unmingled, true, undivided*. True, because *one hypostasis* resulted [*apoteleo*] from the God-Logos and the human body. Unmingled, because after the union the united are preserved, and have not been changed essentially. Undivided, because their *hypostasis* is one. All this is entrusted to us by holy scripture (for us to believe). For it speaks of one and the same, as if works happened from different natures, now from God, now from the human being. For everything that a human being must endure, he endured. For he was born, and was nourished with milk and reared, and he grew, and when he was thirty years old he was baptized, and after the baptism he began to do signs and to teach the Jews. And at the age of thirty-three he was crucified, and, as crucified, he arose on the third day and was taken up into heaven with his body, and now with it he sits at the right hand of the Father, and he is the one who will judge the living and the dead at the resurrection. This is the faith of Christians.[75]

After this beginning, which is clearly orientated to the history of salvation, a type of history of heresies is offered in *actiones* II–V: as a prelude to this we find at the end of *actio* I a crude confrontation of extreme positions: Sabellius–Arius and Nestorius–Eutyches. Then in connection with the listing and characterization of the books of the Old and New Testaments there follows a depiction and refutation of the 'heresy' of the Hebrews and Samaritans (relating to trinitarian theology and christology). For the period after Christ, on each occasion the teachers and Fathers as well as the heresies are named, divided up into the time between Christ's birth and the beginning of the Constantinian Empire, and from then up to the time of the author, with the last period being once again subdivided by Chalcedon.

That the author is an unreserved defender of the Council of Chalcedon is shown especially in *actiones* VI–VIII, in which he presents and refutes arguments against Chalcedon of a historical (VI), philosophical (VII)

---

74. *De sectis* establishes that both *ousia* and *physis*, as well as *hypostasis* and *prosopon*, are used synonymously by the Fathers. The same argument is also found in John Philoponus, *Diaetetes* 7,21: Sanda 56.

75. Leontius Schol., *De sectis* I, III: PG 86, 1197BD.

and patristic (VIII) nature. Thus a third[76] of his writing is concerned exclusively with the justification of Chalcedon. It is perhaps in the historical part of this justification in particular that 'his feeling for historical developments' is clearly evident, whereby his tone remains 'calm, sober and measured', and hence 'a sense of peace and objectivity' is communicated.[77]

In *actio* VII, which is devoted to philosophical arguments, two objections in particular are discussed, which are proposed from the 'Monophysite' side and which are also to found again in John Philoponus, the Alexandrian philosopher and theologian. Indeed, John Philoponus is named in the *De sectis*, but as an (Aristotelian trained) heresiarch of the Tritheists,[78] not as a Miaphysite. The two objections of Philoponus read:

1. If you speak of two natures in Christ, then you also teach two *hypostases*. If (you teach) two *hypostases*, (you teach) also two persons and two Christs, and two sons, and thus you turn out to have the same opinion as Nestorius.[79]
2. If you speak of two natures, you introduce a separation. For you introduce a number; a number, however, is a discrete dimension.[80]

The author responds to this with a conceptual explanation of *hypostasis* and discusses the claim that number is a discrete dimension.

First of all he points out to the opposition that the proposed conclusion produces more dangerous contradictions for their own mode of expression, viz. Christ is ἐκ δύο φύσεων, than for that of the Chalcedonians. For then there would be actually two *hypostases* and two persons, and it follows that the humanity existed at some time without the divinity, which is absurd and which the opposition certainly does not want to affirm. If one says 'from two natures', then one already presupposes the existence (of those to be united), whereas 'in two natures' speaks of them only after the union.

What is essential, however, is the indication that *hypostasis* can have a twofold meaning: something that exists, and something that exists for itself. Depending upon what the questioner understands by *hypostasis*, one will give a (different) answer to the question about whether Christ's natures are hypostatic or anhypostatic. If *hypostasis* simply means something that exists, then Christ's two natures are to be called

76. Thirteen of the thirty-seven columns in PG 86 are devoted to the discussion of Chalcedon.
77. J. Speigl, *art. cit.*, 230 and 212 respectively. Speigl works out carefully the conception which the author of *De sectis* had of the councils and of Justinian's religious politics.
78. Leontius Schol., *De sectis*, V, VI: PG 86, 1232D–1233B.
79. Cf. John Philoponus, *Diaetetes*, VII, 28–29; X, 35: Sanda 63–64, 70.
80. Cf. *idem, op. cit.*, IV, 17: Sanda 52–53.

hypostatic, for they are real. Should *hypostasis* in contrast characterize something that exists for itself, then one will answer that Christ's natures are anhypostatic, since they do not exist for themselves. One cannot imagine such a conciliatory manner of speaking in Leontius of Byzantium.

With regard to the second question, at first the author directs the opponents' argument again to their formula, and shows that, with their claim that number would separate, they introduce a separation into their own mode of expression (from two natures) in exactly the same way.

Philosophically, however, the author contests that number is a discrete dimension. One can use number both for discrete things as well as for things that belong together (for example, a log five metres long). Again, as in the first objection, he allows a double linguistic usage:

> Number is also a double (meaning) dimension, which is stated both of discrete things and of continuous things. (1244A)

In a second approach, *De sectis* then attempts a new explanation: one must distinguish between whether one affirms the two according to number or according to kind (τῷ ἀριθμῷ, τῷ εἴδει). For this distinction the author refers to Aristotle, who 'openly said that matter and form are one according to number and two according to kind' (1244C). Consequently one can then say of Christ that he is one according to number, and two according to kind. Once again *De sectis* seeks a solution here by distinguishing the different respects under which each statement is made, a solution which admittedly is not participated in by the opponents. In the christological question this was presumably caused by the identification of nature and *hypostasis* (cf. Philoponus), which no longer allowed a distinction.

The body–soul analogy rejected

In *De sectis* the body–soul paradigm is first mentioned by the miaphysites as a reply to the Church's objection that two natures are introduced of necessity, if after the union the united are distinguished.[81] The human being's body and soul are united unmingled, and yet there is *one* nature of the human being. The 'Synodists' (that is, the Chalcedonians), however, also call upon the comparison for their own purposes. *De sectis* nevertheless exhibits a more reserved position.

---

81. *De sectis*, VII, V: PG 86, 1245A. Cf. John Philoponus, *Diaetetes*, X, 36–37: Sanda 70–71, who in justification adduces the body–soul analogy as the first example (X, 37).

The Theodosians are reproached with wanting to apply the anthropological example to Christ in everything (VII, VI; 1245C). In the 'repetition' (from VI, VII) then comes the detailed discussion of the body–soul model. First of all *De sectis* dissociates itself from the reference of the 'Synodists' to the fact that the human being too is composed of two natures: 'the Synodists are driven into the corner by this example' (1248C). In addition Leontius Scholasticus defends the Theodosians against the claim that they for their part must confess 'from three', if they want to force the Synodists to a confession of Christ 'in three natures'. Thus he clearly finds fault with the indication as an excuse that the human being is also said to have two natures. Immediately after this he states that a human being has one nature, but Christ has two. (1248D)

At the end of VII, VI we find a proposition which is central to the christology of *De sectis*:

> For Christ's two [natures] have the same basis [relationship] with regard to the *hypostasis* as the [human being's] one nature has to a human being's *hypostasis*. (1248B)

This proposition forms the background for the entire presentation of VII, VIII and can be heard echoing here. *De sectis* explains that if one remains on the level of the natures and wants to interpret the 'end-product' (ἀποτέλεσμα),[82] Christ, by means of the body–soul analogy, then one cannot maintain the scriptural confession (ὡμολόγηται; 1248D) of true God and true human being. *De sectis* formulates this scriptural confession of faith in the following way:

> It is confessed that he was God and a human being and that he himself was completely God and completely human, and God according to nature and human according to nature, and consubstantial with God and consubstantial with us, and one of the Trinity and one of us, and that the God-Logos vouchsafed to become a human being.[83]

The confession also contains the phrase *unus de sancta trinitate*, but without further addition, simply to express the identity of the second divine person and the human being. Against this *homologia* the teaching of the *mia physis* or the two natures is tested.

Assuming that one takes a body and soul and forms a human being, then this human being is consubstantial neither with the soul nor with the body. If one now wants to apply this paradigm to Christ and puts the divinity in the place of the soul and the humanity in the place of the body, then the *apotelesma* is neither consubstantial with the Father nor consubstantial with human beings, and thus the confession is violated. If in contrast one assumes two natures in Christ, then all the statements of the confession are present. This is because the *hypostasis* allows the concept of two natures.[84]

De sectis rightly sees that the understanding of the unity of divinity

---

82. This word that is used so frequently in Leontius of Byzantium finds application remarkably often in *De sectis*, but it is introduced as a term of the Theodosians, whose formula runs: διάφορα τὰ μέρη, τὸ δὲ ἀποτέλεσμα ἕν (1245C).

83. *De sectis*, VII, VII: PG 86, 1248D–1249A; cf. VII, VIII: 1249BC.

84. *De sectis*, VII, VIII: PG 86, 1249AD.

and humanity in Christ as a *mia physis*, which is then interpreted with the body–soul paradigm, is mistaken. The reason for this is that the unity in Christ is seen as a nature unity and not as a *unio hypostatica et secundum hypostasin*. The similarity of the unity in Christ to the unity in a human being does not consist in the unity of body and soul, but in the unity of human nature and *hypostasis*. *De sectis* rightly and clearly indicates this state of affairs. However, it lacks an exact terminology to express this precisely. *De sectis* contributes nothing to an explanation of how the relationship of *hypostasis* and nature (or two natures) in Christ is to be understood.

The mia-physis *formula*

It is only in *actio* VIII, in the discussion of patristic arguments, that there is talk of the *mia-physis* formula. Then it is used against the charge of the opponents of the Council of Chalcedon that the Council did not mention this formula of Cyril. *De sectis* responds that the formula is Cyril's, but it is not opposed to the Council's teaching. For he does not speak of the one incarnate nature of Christ, but of the God-Logos, so clearly of another nature. And in order to indicate another nature he says precisely 'incarnate'.[85] A confession of the *mia-physis* formula is found again further on (VIII, IV), in connection with an inauthentic citation of Athanasius:

> We do not teach two natures, one of which is adored and the other not, but we say one nature of the incarnate Logos. (1256C)

De sectis shares this understanding of the formula also with Theodore of Raithu,[86] but here nevertheless, in contrast to the *Praeparatio*, it is in no way a tessera of orthodoxy.

The picture of Christ

The christology of *De sectis* gains more profile in the rebuttal of heresies. Against the Gaianites, *De sectis* holds that Christ voluntarily subjected himself to the laws of the body and suffered like us. The difference is only that he was not necessarily subjected to the laws of nature. Christ's body was not incorruptible before the resurrection, and afterwards it was incorruptible through grace and not according to nature (X, I–II; 1260B–1261D). In the position it takes on the Agnoetic question, as we

---

85. In justification *De sectis* offers a long citation from Cyril, *Ep. 46 ad Succens.*: PG 77, 244A1–B11.

86. As well with John the Grammarian, Justinian in *Contra Monophysitas*, Leontius of Byzantium; cf. M. Richard, *art. cit.* (*Op. Min.* II, no. 55), 711.

have already indicated, *De sectis* shows itself remarkably circumspect and completely orientated towards Chalcedon's definition.

How should we define the christological position of the writing characterized by C. Moeller as 'a kind of résumé of the theology of the epoch'?[87]

We are not able to find any re-Cyrillization. Saint Cyril, one of the holy Fathers, appears particularly as the authority to whom the opponents have recourse, and *De sectis* shows that Chalcedon does not stand in opposition to Cyril's main formulas, such as 'union according to the *hypostasis*' and the *mia-physis* formula, if these are understood in the sense of the two natures. How does it stand with regard to the elements which Justinian and the Council of 553 included?

'According to *theoria*' plays no rôle in *De sectis* (cf. VII, I–II); of the two formulas 'from two' and 'in two', the 'in two' receives hefty support in contrast to the 'from two' (cf. VII, I and III). *Synthesis* does not occur. 'Union according to the *hypostasis*' is explained as being in agreement with Chalcedon (VIII, I). 'One of the Trinity' indeed occurs, but without further additions.

On the whole the writing shows a remarkable abstinence *vis-à-vis* typical neo-Chalcedonian terminology. The attitude it displays towards the Council of 553 is also surprising; Constantinople II is not even mentioned by *De sectis*. It represents the Three Chapters in the following way: Justinian condemned (*kat'oikonomian*) Theodoret and Ibas in order to win over the *Diakrinomenoi*.[88] There is no word of the fact that, apart from the condemnation by Justinian's edict of 543, the Council of 553 also explicitly anathematized the three names, Theodore of Mopsuestia, Theodoret and Ibas; nothing is said about the condemnation of Theodore of Mopsuestia.[89]

De sectis demonstrates that it is a persistent defender of the Council of Chalcedon also in the treatment of patristic authorities, as a florilegium in *actio* IX once again underscores.[90]

87. C. Moeller, *art. cit.*, 665.
88. Leontius Schol., *De sectis*, VI, VI: PG 86, 1237CD.
89. This is researched in detail by J. Speigl, *art. cit.*, 224–30.
90. The florilegium accords with nos. 19, 24, 25, 27, 37, 41, 42, 50, 80, 86, 87 of the florilegium in *CNE* of Leontius of Byzantium (ed. Daley). The same numbers appear as in the description by R. Devreesse, 'Le Florilège de Léonce de Byzance', *RSR* 10 (1930), 545–76, apart from: 31 instead of 27, 81 instead of 80, 87 instead of 86 and 88 instead of 87. In detail the contents are:
19: Athanasius (?), *Contra Apollinarem* I, 7: PG 26, 1105A14–B5.
24: Gregory Naz., *Orat.* 38, 15: PG 36, 328C11–14.
25: *Idem, Orat.* 30,7–8: PG 36, 113A6–B10.
27: Gregory Nyss., *Adv. Apollinarem* 40: PG 45, 1213D5–1216A9.
37: Ambros., *De Fide ad Grat.* II, 9,77: CSEL 78, 84,32–85,38; PL 16, 576B13–15.

Because the Chalcedonian 'basic formula' of one *hypostasis* in two natures is clearly highlighted (the two aspects being treated separately, with the *mia hypostasis* occurring in particular in *actio* I in a type of *regula fidei*,[91] and the 'in two natures' in detail in *actio* VII), *De sectis* shows itself to be a strict-Chalcedonian writing.

41: *Idem, Ep. 46 ad Sabinum*, 6: PL 16, 1147B15–C4.

42: *Idem, Expositio Fidei*, frag.

50: Augustine, *Tractatus in Ioannem* 78, 3: PL 35, 1836; CCL 36, 524,4–8.

80: Cyril Alex., *De adoratione in Spiritu et Veritate* IX: PG 68, 637A7–B2.

86: *Idem, Ep. 50 ad Valerianum*, 2: PG 77, 257B11–15; ACO I, 1, 3, pp. 91,31–92,1.

87: *Idem, Ep. 39 ad Joannem Antiochenum*, 5: PG 77, 177A13–B3; ACO I, 1, 4, p. 17,17–20. Thus among these there are four passages from Latin Fathers (Ambrose, Augustine), and three from Cyril. According to CCT II/1, *Ad Fontes*, 58, the numbers are from sections II ('two natures in the one *hypostasis*') and III ('Texts from Cyril' among others 'as witness for the dyophysite position'). Cf. *ibid.*, 60.

91. Cf. PG 86, 1197B: 'one *hypostasis* perfected (ἀπετελέσθη) from the God-Logos and the human body'. The *Regula fidei*: 1197BC, cf. above, p. 496.

CHAPTER TWO

APOTELESMA – *AN APPRAISAL OF THE SIXTH CENTURY*

Time and again in the Justinianic period we have encountered the word *apotelesma* in a christological application. Jesus Christ as the eternal Logos and Son of the Father undergoes the historical process of incarnation and stands in his God-human reality as 'end-product', as it were, before the eyes of believing human beings. An *apotelesma* will be attempted in this final chapter on the christology of the Patriarchate of Constantinople between 500 and 600 — a concluding holistic consideration of the christology of the sixth century in Byzantium. Naturally, reflective theology, that is, the discussion about the Christ of Chalcedon which to a greater or lesser extent works with concepts and formulas, attracted attention.

In the sixth century in Byzantium, however, we have a special opportunity to expand this reflective view by a kerygmatic, hymnodic, liturgical vision of rare consistency, namely by the poems of Romanos Melodos. In terms of chronology, with him we encompass the Justinianic era once again, but now on a more popular, spiritual level, on which as well, and in full union with it, liturgical life is carried out. *Here* we must forgo a separate description of the christology of the Byzantine liturgy, but we shall return to this task and perform it adequately by analysing the Coptic version of Gregory's *anaphora* in the context of Alexandrian christology.[92]

I. THE REFLECTIVE CHRISTOLOGY OF THE SIXTH CENTURY IN BYZANTIUM

Our attempt to depict the development of faith in Jesus Christ in the Patriarchate of Constantinople during the post-Chalcedonian period to roughly 600, despite the many names and an understanding of the extant writings which is as complete as possible, cannot make the claim of offering an evenly developed picture for the Patriarchate as a whole. Naturally the imperial and patriarchal city itself captured our attention, like a brightly lit stage with its players and supernumeraries, while the

---

92. See *JdChr* II/4, 246–56.

audience, that is, the provinces, the *chora*, remained with its own life in the shadows.[93]

We have also accepted a narrowing of content. Our description covers two domains of the history of faith only partially: (1) that of theological reflection on the dogma of Chalcedon in both its affirmative and negative modes, and (2) that of the politico-religious activity of the rulers of the Byzantine Empire during this period. There are many questions which still remain open. Of what type was the Church's baptismal kerygma of Jesus Christ? What did the spiritual life of this period look like in liturgy and asceticism, given that two orientations sought christological dominance in the Patriarchate? At the end we shall attempt to sketch the missing pieces of this picture in broad strokes. But before that we should sum up what we have analysed previously.

The post-Chalcedonian period in Byzantium to the year 600 was not an era of theological awakening or breakthrough, but rather of a tenacious wrestling with a responsible transmission of faith in Jesus Christ. In the Patriarchate of Constantinople in the period up to 600 Chalcedonian faith received a form which it retains to the present. Nevertheless the development in 600 had not yet come to a conclusion; in the seventh century the discussion of Chalcedonian faith would again be taken up anew.

With the two main formulas — 'one *hypostasis* in two natures' and 'the one nature (*hypostasis*) of the incarnate Word' — the two poles of post-Chalcedonian christology were present. Naturally this antithesis demanded a constant discussion which probed ever deeper into the content of the main concepts being used, viz. *hypostasis* and nature. The

---

93. On the development of this relationship, or misrelationship, see H. Ahrweiler, 'L'empire byzantin. Formation, évolution, décadence', *RSJB* 31 (1973), 181–98 = *idem, Byzance: les pays et les territoires* (London, 1976), no. I. That the Asiatic regions of the Patriarchate were not forgotten Emperor Justinian shows in calling the monk John of Amida to carry out missionary work in Asia Minor, with the commission of bringing the newly converted to the acknowledgement of Chalcedon. John loyally carried out this commission, although he himself was an opponent of Chalcedon. For this reason he received the name John of Asia. He is the author of the *History of the Oriental Saints* (E. W. Brooks, PO 17–19) and the *Church History* (E. W. Brooks, *Iohannis Ephesini Historiae ecclesiasticae pars tertia*, CSCO 105.106 [1935/36]; fragments in CSCO 104 [1933]); J. Schönfelder, *Die Kirchengeschichte des Johannes von Ephesus* (Munich, 1862). On the mission of John of Ephesus and his colleagues and their decisive success cf. L. Duchesne, *L'Église au VIe siècle* (Paris, 1925), 276–80. Their base was the monastery of Zooras on the other side of the Golden Horn (*HE* III, 36.37). Critical comments on the actual expansion of Christianity are found in K. Holl, *Gesammelte Aufsätze zur Kirchengeschichte, II. Der Osten* (Tübingen, 1928), 245–6. Furthermore, see E. Honigmann, *Évêques et Évêchés monophysites d'Asie antérieure au VIe siècle* = CSCO 127 (Louvain, 1951), 207–15; F. Winkelmann, *ByzSlav* 37 (1976), 182–3; P. Allen, 'A New Date for the Last Recorded Events in John of Ephesus' *Historia Ecclesiastica*', *OLP* 10 (1979), 251–4.

four familiar adverbs of the Chalcedonian definition had to form the tracks, as it were, along which the movement of thought would have to advance. This happened only slowly, and really haphazardly. We shall summarize the results from a Chalcedonian viewpoint.

1. The question of Christ's one *hypostasis* in the duality of the natures

It is well known that the struggle in the fourth century about the trinitarian formula led to the distinction between the concepts of *hypostasis*-person on the one side, and *physis*, *ousia*, and substance on the other. This was due to the Cappadocians, Basil and Gregory Nazianzen. What they had worked out for the *theologia*, Gregory Nazianzen in particular transferred also to the *oikonomia*, that is, the teaching on the incarnation. In the former one spoke 'theologically' of three *hypostases* in the one *ousia* (*physis*), and in the latter 'economically' of the one *hypostasis* in two natures, to summarize briefly the development up to Chalcedon.

Nevertheless this application of the *theologia* to the *oikonomia* was not accepted either by Cyril of Alexandria and his supporters, among whom the Severans above all counted themselves. Even in the sixth century a Severan says in Leontius of Byzantium:

> There is agreement about the fact that *hypostasis* and *ousia*, or *physis*, are not the same in the *theologia* [trinitarian theology]; in the *oikonomia* [teaching about the incarnation], in contrast, they are identical [i.e. synonymous].[94]

Two linguistic and conceptual systems run side by side. Thus the Chalcedonians had to reflect intensively on the distinction between *hypostasis* and nature, while their opponents could more or less dispense themselves from this.

2. The question about the unity of the natures in Christ

Among all the parties there was unanimity that in Christ divinity and humanity were connected in a way which could be termed undivided and unmingled (*asynchytos* — *adihairetos*) and which continued to exist permanently. If one holds fast to the synonymy of nature and *hypostasis*, then these two concepts are unavailable for an interpretation of the 'unmingled' and 'undivided' in Christ. In any case one could use

94. Leontius Byz., *Epil* (CPG 6815): PG 86, 1921B.

periphrases and stress the perfection of divinity and humanity in the one Christ alternately. Nevertheless the perfection of the humanity seems to be endangered by the formula of the 'one *physis* (*hypostasis*)'. The claim that adding 'incarnate' dispelled this suspicion was either not taken seriously by the Chalcedonian side, or regarded as an implicit recognition of the two-natures formula. In fact, among some supporters of the *mia-physis* formula, the Apollinarian understanding of the Logos and *sarx* as a nature unity continued to shine through repeatedly (as for instance in the Agnoetic question). This is expressed already in the understanding of the concept *hypostasis*. To understand this fact we need to have recourse to the fourth or third century.

(a) *Christ's 'one* hypostasis', *'one* physis', *in Apollinarius*
While in the third century the concept *hypostasis* had been used to express the 'substantial reality' of Father, Son and Holy Spirit in the one God, that is, in the Trinity, Apollinarius in his christology gave this concept a new christological function: *hypostasis* now had the task not of denoting the pre-existent Logos in his substantial reality, but 'of representing the one Christ as composed of divinity and humanity'[95] or, more exactly, as unity 'from Logos and *sarx*'. Christ's one *hypostasis* is the '*synthesis* of Logos and *sarx*'. In this 'anthropological *synthesis*' the divine Logos takes over the spiritual, intellectual and volitional functions which are ascribed to the human soul. The body–soul analogy is thus transferred univocally to the relationship of divinity and carnal nature in Christ. It is precisely for this reason that Christ is only one *hypostasis*, one *physis*, one *prosopon*; in him there is only one *energeia* (activity).[96] The unity in Christ is conceived absolutely as a *henosis* 'in the nature and according to the nature', understood in an Aristotelian sense as a synthesis of incomplete, partial principles which results in one nature-*hypostasis* as a whole.

Accordingly, in the first instance the new content of *hypostasis* does not say 'subject' or 'substantial reality', but the physical unity of the one concrete reality from two natures, which Christ is. To refresh our memory we shall cite as the clearest statement of this a text from the 'speech on faith' which was ascribed to Pope Julius:

95. Cf. M. Simonetti, 'Per la rivalutazione di alcune testimonianze su Paolo di Samosata', *RSLR* 24 (1988) (177–210), 191.
96. Summarized most clearly in the *Kata meros pistis* 30: Lietzmann, 178–179.

... we confess that God the Logos became flesh from the holy virgin Mary, and we do not separate him from his flesh, but he is one *prosopon* and one *hypostasis* and one nature of God the Logos, who became flesh ...[97]

(b) Corrections to the Apollinarian system

Although both Cyril and Severus clearly distinguish themselves from Apollinarius by often stressing the reality of the human soul in Christ, they still take over his *mia-physis-hypostasis* formula. Because both terms were synonymous for them, they were not able to use these same terms to establish the distinction in Christ. Other distinctive terms were not at their disposal.

3. The Chalcedonian way

The Chalcedonian synthesis is based:

(a)   on the Cappadocian acceptance of the trinitarian, theological distinction between *hypostasis* (*persona, prosopon*) and *physis* (*ousia*) for the teaching about the incarnation;

(b)   on the interpretation of the unity and difference in Christ with the help of this new terminology: the unity is on the level of the *hypostasis*, while the difference is on the level of the 'nature'.

Therefore, three things are demanded of Chalcedonian theologians:

(i)   a new definition of the content of *hypostasis*;

(ii)   the contrasting of their understanding of the unity in Christ, which proceeds from the 'subject' to the 'nature', with the Apollinarian 'nature unity'; and

(iii) the interpretation of this event of union, firstly in a concrete way and then conceptually.

(i) What does hypostasis mean?

For Chalcedonian christology after 451 a great deal had already been achieved with the knowledge that the one *hypostasis* was not to be considered as the end-product (*apotelesma*) of the union. Rather it is already present in the person of the Logos who exists in the divine nature, but who now in the incarnation assumes a complete human

---

97. Apollin., *De fide et incarn. contra adversarios*, 3 (CPG 3647): Lietzmann, p. 194,8–12. Cf. the Apollinarian writing *Encyclion* (CPG 3735): Lietzmann, p. 292,19–20: 'one *hypostasis* and one *prosopon* of the God-Logos and the flesh (taken) from Mary'; *Quod unus sit Christus* 3 (CPG 3737): Lietzmann, p. 296,7–8.12; *ibid.*, p. 298,1; *ibid.*, p. 299,9: 'one *hypostasis* of the Logos and the *sarx*'; p. 300,9–10.

nature. What does *hypostasis* of the Logos mean in relation to his human existence, if the dreaded 'Nestorian' teaching of two *hypostases* is to be avoided? Leontius of Byzantium occupied himself intensely with a definition of *hypostasis* in contradistinction to nature, without arriving at a convincing result.[98] He remained trapped in the Cappadocian metaphysics of *hypostasis* which discovered only the *individuum*. On the basis of his formulation Leontius of Byzantium had to deny 'individuality' to Christ's humanity, if he did not want to make it a second *hypostasis*. He did not address this problem quite openly. Hence he did not attain the breakthrough to the solution sought for, though it has often been maintained that he did.

Leontius of Jerusalem advanced a step further than his namesake, although he still had the same starting-point, the Basilian concept of *hypostasis*. He circumvented the barrier against finding a new definition which resulted from that starting-point by considering things concretely. For him incarnation was an event of God's omnipotence, which he described as the 'transposition of one nature into another *hypostasis*'.[99] Furthermore, he was so open that he conceded an individual being for Christ's humanity by which, seen from a Basilian point of view, it would have been *hypostasis*, but was not, because 'the transposition' had happened. For this process he was able to use the expression 'to make or to allow to insubsist'. Hence he left behind Leontius of Byzantium and his *enhypostatos*, which was often not understood. *Hypostasis* thus gained the meaning of independence,[100] or of the final monadic being-oneself.

What Leontius of Jerusalem proposed beyond that as an *ontology* for the explanation of *enhypostasis*[101] was only an application of the Basilian teaching on *idiomata*, but thought through with a good deal of intellectual show. This was forced into a new framework. It would have been much more promising to have thought through the existential start that Leontius of Jerusalem discovered with his idea of the Logos-subject's creatively taking possession of Christ's humanity: in his own *hypostasis* the Logos created for himself his own human being. Emperor Justinian took over this insight almost literally. There were two advantages in this.

(1) The idea of the one subject was clearly highlighted.

(2) For Leontius of Jerusalem there was no more profound possibility

---

98. It was shown that the expression *enhypostaton* should not be used in the search for this definition without further clarification.

99. Leontius Jer., *CN* II, 35: PG 86, 1593C.

100. *Idem*, *CN* II, 13: PG 86, 1561C7-9.

101. For example, in *ibid.*, *CN* I, 20: PG 86, 1485D4-7.

for explaining the *henosis* than the creative intervention in the being of Christ's humanity. This intervention consisted in an act of divine omnipotence which in *one* single action effected two things: the coming into existence (*ousiosis*) and the unification (*synousiosis*) of the human nature with the divine *hypostasis*.[102] In this way a good biblical start was given (cf. Rom 4,17) which far surpassed a constrained ontological interpretation of *henosis*. Only the divine *hypostasis* of the Logos, in unity with the Father and Spirit,[103] could so dispose of created being that it remained utterly created ('unmingled') yet did not belong to itself; it was and remained the 'undivided' existence and being of the divine Logos-subject. Leontius of Jerusalem spoke of *demiourgikon* as the characteristic of God.[104] Thus a valuable element in the interpretation of Christ's unity was recognized: incarnation was only possible to God's creative power.

(ii) Unity in the hypostasis — *as opposed to unity in the nature*
In the sixth century, Leontius of Jerusalem was successful in contrasting most clearly the Chalcedonian sense of a union in the *hypostasis* and according to the *hypostasis* with the nature unity introduced so disastrously by Apollinarius.[105] Through God's creative unifying act a complete human nature becomes the earthly, finite existence of the *hypostasis* of the Logos. The *hypostasis* of the Logos becomes, is and remains a complete human being and at the same time guarantees Christ's inseparable unity. The *mia hypostasis* now has a completely different sense from what it had for Apollinarius. *Hypostasis* is now formally the final subject.

This union 'in the *hypostasis*' permits an undiminished individuality to be awarded to Christ's human nature, as Leontius of Jerusalem explicitly does, although admittedly this is poorly categorized ontologically. Nevertheless it is the human existence of the divine Logos.

(iii) On the interpretation of the event of union
In addition Leontius of Jerusalem attempted to explain the 'singularity' of the *hypostasis* in Christ by means of his Basilian ontology. He could have dispensed with this — in fact he should have — because he then

---

102. *Idem, CN* IV, 17: PG 86, 1684B.

103. In this context the Fathers already emphasized that every creative action of God *ad extra* is common to the three persons. In Justinian's time this was expressed by Romanos Melodos, *Hymn.* 24,19: SC 114, 128 (here related to the multiplication of the loaves).

104. Leontius Jer., *CN* I, 19: PG 86, 1480A.

105. Cf. *idem, CM:* PG 86, 1865B.

falsified the biblical picture of Christ. By overwhelming Christ's human nature with divine *idiomata* in order to prove that it was united with the Logos, he endangered the biblical thought of *kenosis* (Phil 2,5-7). Above all he employed the 'proof in power', that is, the miracle, as indispensable for the revelation of the *henosis*, something that brought Leontius of Jerusalem close to the Chalcedonian aphthartics. If one takes the two main thoughts of Leontius of Jerusalem together, namely (1) the appeal to God's divine creative power and (2) the conception of Christ's humanity as orientated in its very existence to the *hypostasis* of the Logos, then a great deal was achieved for the Chalcedonian understanding of the one Christ.

(1) Because the union happened creatively, but without change for the divinity and the humanity (*atreptōs*), the *kenosis* in the event of the incarnation is finally assured fundamentally. The Julianists (in the traditional interpretation) and the Chalcedonian aphthartics were on the wrong track. The creative union and assumption of Christ's humanity left the latter not in its own hypostatic being, but decidedly in the being of a human nature.

(2) As a result of this the acceptance of a 'theopaschism' was also possible without suffering being ascribed to the divine 'nature', as was the case with Apollinarius. For the human being Jesus who suffers and dies *is* the existence of the divine *hypostasis* of the Logos. God really suffers, in his human nature.

(3) The correct understanding of the Chalcedonian unity of natures in the subject needs no subsequent improvement. Neo-Chalcedonian approaches must guard against falling back into the schema of a 'nature unity' or of adopting individual ideas from it. In particular a 'divinization' of Christ's humanity in a qualitative respect exposes itself to the danger of becoming once again a *henosis* understood naturally.

4. Christ's humanity in the Constantinopolitan christology of the sixth century

'Created for itself' also says that Christ's humanity must be considered as a perfect work of God: 'one and the same, perfect in divinity, the same also perfect in humanity', that is, with the *sarx* and a spiritual, rational and all-human vitality. All parties stressed this against Apollinarius. But how seriously did they take Christ's humanity, especially his rationality, his human knowledge and volition?

We have established that within the fundamental acceptance of Christ's true divinity and true humanity there still existed quite different notions about the relationship of both natures in the one Christ. There were very different 'pictures of Christ', both in the opposition of Miaphysites and Dyophysites, as well as within both groups. Imitating Cyril, Severus of Antioch resolutely constructed his picture of Christ 'from above'. He was followed above all by Theodosius of Alexandria, Anthimus and the Severans in general. Because in Christ there was only one *hypostasis* (*physis*), no 'duality' at all should be accepted in him. There was only one *energeia*, one *thelema*, one knowledge, as it were, only the one flow of energies from above. John Philoponus of Alexandria admittedly reflected on how this 'one *energeia*' also moved Christ's psychic powers.[106] Only in the final effect of the one *energeia* could and should a 'duality' be accepted, thus *outside* the reality of the one Christ, God and human being.

It is also only in individual representatives that the two-natures christology of the Byzantines was successful in considering and acknowledging Christ's human activity in the domains of both intellect and senses. Really it was only Leontius of Byzantium in his discussion with the Chalcedonian aphthartics who took an important step forward.[107] Of all the Greek theologians of the sixth century, he was no doubt the one who understood best the 'consubstantial with us' (*homoousios hemin*) and the 'unmingled' of the Chalcedonian definition.[108] He knew of the distinction between what Christ as a human being can do from his natural powers, which as such he also ascribed to the divine subject, the *hypostasis* of the Logos, and what signifies the supernatural elevation of the natural powers. Here he discovered important facts and formulations for the relationship of nature and supernature, which were to be a model for the Latin Middle Ages. In his writings there were also approaches for a pneumatology of Christ's humanity or for the acceptance of a life of grace in Jesus which is borne by the Pneuma. In the Byzantine theology of the sixth century these insights unfortunately found little response. It was perhaps Emperor Justinian who adopted them the most in his letter to Zoilus. Some Byzantine theologians dared even to refer to Leo I's *Tomus* to Flavian and to speak of a twofold activity in the one Christ.

These approaches to an acknowledgement of Christ's humanity and his powers would have been of the utmost significance for a Chalcedonian soteriology, because this still seemed to reflect Apollinarianism.

106. John Philoponus, *Diaetetes* (CPG 7260), nos. 3–4: Sanda 38–39 (see also T. Hainthaler in *JdChr* II/4, 129–31).
107. Cf. Leontius Byz., *CA*: PG 86, 1336BC, 1336D–1337A.
108. Cf. *CA*: PG 86, 1332D6–1333B5.

The acts which were decisive for the redemption of humanity, that is, Christ's knowledge and freedom, Apollinarius anchored by nature in a divine-spiritual principle and thus arrived at an absolute 'impeccability' of the redeemer (an 'invincible *nous*'). This *nous*, however, was the divinity. What was the purpose, then, of the incarnation? The fundamental soteriological proposition was rightly raised against him: 'what is not assumed, is not redeemed'. This had as well to hold for human knowledge and freedom.

Even though important approaches for a Chalcedonian soteriology can be established, Byzantine christology on the whole was still not successful in developing a convincing appreciation of the knowing and willing of Christ the human being, and of his freedom. In particular with regard to Christ's knowing or not knowing, the Severan-Theodosian reaction to the theses of the deacon Themistius no longer left any scope for the unmingled development of human knowledge and free human willing. The dread of introducing a second person into Christ by such an approach was too great for the anti-Chalcedonians to venture accepting a certain autonomy of Christ's human psychic life.

The Chalcedonian and neo-Chalcedonian interpretation of the human knowledge and its participation in the divine knowledge (Eulogius, Gregory the Great) did not advance in that period beyond the Theodosian approach. The limitation of Christ's human knowledge which had been accepted in the fourth century was no longer gladly called to mind in the struggle against the Agnoetism of Themistius. Fundamentally, up to the present there has been no elaborated teaching on Jesus' human knowledge that is generally accepted and without conceptual contradiction.[109]

Consequently many questions remain open. In the interpretation of soteriology in the sixth century, was Christ's humanity properly seen in its cognitive and volitional power? What task did Christ's human knowledge have as the receiver and mediator of the Father's revelation to human beings? What significance did Christ's human act of obedience before God have? The fear of 'Nestorianism' hindered the utilization of the Leonine *agit enim utraque forma quod proprium est* for soteriology.

The time had still not come to grasp the christological and soteriological questions systematically in their totality. The christologial corpus of the sixth century and of the post-Chalcedonian period in general was

---

109. Cf. R. Moloney, 'The Mind of Christ in Transcendental Theology: Rahner, Lonergan and Crowe', *HeyJ* 25 (1984), 288–300.

still all too much an occasional product of polemical, didactic or also of a politico-religious type. A systematic christology first began to develop embryonically not so much on the ground of speculation, but rather on that of the baptismal kerygma. The *Summa theologica* developed from the *symbolum* which had been formed as the summary of the baptismal kerygma, and to this the sixth century made its own special contribution, but on Latin soil.[110]

II. CONCRETE CHRISTOLOGY: THE MYSTERIES OF THE LIFE OF JESUS IN ROMANOS MELODOS

In the cathedral homilies of Severus of Antioch we have already found access to this way of comprehending Christ's person by way of the life of Jesus.[111] Even if these were not delivered in the capital, they are still a model of the combination of reflection and kerygma which is transferable to the Imperial City, not taking into account naturally the Patriarch's anti-Chalcedonian stance. Through the poetic works of Romanos Melodos the concrete christology in the sixth century is represented much closer to the people than is the case with Severus. These found their inspiration in Syria and Palestine. Romanos offered a relatively comprehensive supplement to the reflective theology that was dominant to a large degree in the sixth century. Without his *kontakia* we would not be able to complete the picture of christological spirituality in the Imperial City; admittedly the liturgy must also be incorporated into this.[112]

Romanos was born towards the end of the fifth century in Emesa in

110. Cf. A. Grillmeier, 'Vom Symbolum zur Summa', in *Mit ihm und in ihm* (Freiburg, [2]1978), 585–636; *idem*, 'Fulgentius' von Ruspe "De Fide ad Petrum" und die "Summa Sententiarum"', in *ibid.*, 637–79.

111. On homiletics in the Justinianic period cf. F. Halkin, *Bibliotheca hagiographica graeca III = SubsHag* 8a ([3]1957) III, Appendix VII: *Orationes et homiliae de festis Christi*, 215–49, no. 1–277. In addition see C. Walter, *Art and Ritual of the Byzantine Church* (London, 1982), 67–72 (homilies).

112. On the following see J. Grosdidier de Matons, *Romanos le Mélode et les origines de la poésie religieuse à Byzance* (Paris, 1977); on this see A. de Halleux, 'Hellénisme et syrianité de Romanos le Mélode', *RHE* 73 (1978), 632–41. In five volumes Grosdidier edited and translated: *Romanos le Mélode. Hymnes* I: SC 99 (Paris, 1964); II: SC 110 (1965); III: SC 114 (1965); IV: SC 128 (1967); V: SC 283 (1981). On the christology of the hymns of Romanos see J. Grosdidier, *Romanos le Mélode* (1977), 247–84: ch. VI, La religion de Romanos. Important for the christology are also the introductions to the individual hymns in the five volumes of the SC. In his work from 1977 Grosdidier presented corrections and expansions to the four volumes which were published before 1977. On Byzantine hymnography see J. Szövérffy, *Guide to Byzantine Hymnography I–II* (Brooklyn, Leiden, 1978–1979).

Phoenicia Libanensis. The exact date of his birth is disputed. He was probably brought up bilingual. For some time he was active as a deacon in Beirut. Under Emperors Anastasius I (491–518), Justin (518–527) and Justinian (527–565) we find him in Constantinople, where he remained to the end of his life. As a deacon in the church of the *Theotokos* in the part of the city called Kyros, he is reported to have had an apparition of the Virgin Mary, who conferred on him the gift of poetic talent.[113] He seems to have died before 565, but after 555, because his famous Hymn 51 on the ten virgins (SC 283) demands this *terminus post quem*.[114]

1. General characterization of the historical significance of Romanos

In all his productivity Romanos was highly receptive with regard to his presentation of Jesus Christ. He did not want to execute an outstanding, historically significant work, but to present the dogma 'in a lively and dramatic form'.[115]

(a) Typical hymns

J. Grosdidier highlights the following hymns as especially typical: (1) the first hymn on Christ's birth (*Hymn*. 10: SC 110, 43–77 with introduction); (2) the *kontakion* on Christ's presentation (*Hymn*. 14: SC 110, 163–197 with introduction); (3) Mary's hymn at the cross (*Hymn*. 35: SC 128, 143–187). In the last-named *kontakion* the poet unfolds a dialogue between Christ and his mother (following Jn 19,25–27 and Lk 23,27–31). Apart from Ephraem the Syrian and Symeon Metaphrastes, this is unique in Oriental hymnody (SC 128, 146). In this *kontakion* the inspiration is highly original; what is striking is the didactic interest and the literary quality of the text. J. Grosdidier (SC 128, 355) highlights in addition *Hymn*. 40, the first on the resurrection (SC 128, 355–421 with introduction); it is an apologetic hymn, which is rare in Romanos; here, however, the subject is the foundation of Christianity (cf. 1 Cor 15,13–14). Hence the poet is at pains to reconcile the differences between the reports of the gospels (cf. the table in SC 128, 357–358).

The form selected in *Hymn*. 40 is found in other very successful *kontakia* (apart from *Hymn*. 10):

(i) the 'temptation of Joseph of Egypt' (*Hymn*. 6: SC 99, 247–293 with introduction; (ii) the beheading of John the Baptist (*Hymn*. 59: yet to be published in SC).[116]

---

113. J. Grosdidier, SC 99, 14. On Kyros see *idem*, *Romanos le Mélode* (1977), 186–7.

114. Cf. W. L. Petersen, *The Diatessaron and Ephrem Syrus as Sources of Romanos the Melodist* = CSCO 475, *Subs.* 74 (Louvain, 1985), 3.

115. J. Grosdidier, SC 110, 325; cf. SC 128, 355–356 on *Hymn*. 40: the peculiarity of Romanos consists in the fact that he is more a preacher than an exegete.

116. Cf. J. Grosdidier, *Romanos le Mélode* (1977), 331–2.

(b) The special character of his poetry

The closeness of homily and hymn is striking. Romanos is a 'real preacher' ('un véritable prédicateur') (SC 128, 57); in many texts, however, he is also a type of pamphleteer, as in *kontakion* 33 on Judas (SC 128, 55–97 with introduction). He relishes moralizing, in part more than the corresponding homilies in Fathers like Chrysostom.[117] The *kontakion* in the sixth and seventh century represented the poetic version of the great Byzantine homily, in narrative and dramatic form.[118] In Romanos, however, the poetic charism seems to be subordinate to his activity as a preacher.[119]

2. The sources of Romanos

(a) The patristic sources

It is striking that J. Grosdidier names the Fathers first and only then the Bible,[120] this procedure being based on the difference in the way Romanos deals with both sources.

Romanos was familiar with two homilies of Basil of Seleucia,[121] who was of particular significance for the formula of Chalcedon. He was inspired by him for his hymns on Elias and on 'Jonah and Nineveh'.[122] He read whole homilies of Basil of Seleucia. Whether apart from these Chrysostom was also used directly cannot be established precisely. Certainly there are reminiscences of Chrysostom, Ps. Chrysostom, but also of Dorotheus of Gaza, Cyril of Jerusalem, Ps. Eusebius of Alexandria, Severian of Gabala and Hesychius of Jerusalem. In short, Romanos did not deny his origin in the Syro-Palestinian cultural circle. He had his roots in a homogeneous tradition which was represented by

---

117. J. Grosdidier, in SC 128, 58–59: 'Romanos n'est pas un coeur tendre, et on ne trouvera guère chez lui les effusions du Chrysostome. L'anathème lui est plus familier que la consolation, et il y a peu d'épisodes évangéliques qui ne lui aient fourni un prétexte à maudire un homme ou une communauté humaine, qu'elle soit juive, païenne ou hérétique . . . Médiocre théologien, médiocre psychologue, il est cependant obligé de dogmatiser et de moraliser . . .' Grosdidier says that the *kontakion* became for him a 'strait-jacket', 'en définitive un genre faux, aussi incommode pour le poète que pour le prédicateur'.

118. Cf. A de Halleux, *RHE* 73 (1978), 633.

119. J. Grosdidier, *Romanos le Mélode* (1977), 247. Romanos adopted the *kontakion* (like the homily), but then popularized it. On the peculiarity of the poetry of Romanos in general cf. H. Hunger, 'Romanos Melodos, Dichter, Prediger, Rhetor — und sein Publikum', *JÖB* 34 (1984), 15–42.

120. J. Grosdidier, *Romanos le Mélode* (1977), 248–55: Sources patristiques; 255: S. scripturaires; he reports that there is still no definitive work on the sources of Melodos (249, n. 7). In his edition of the hymns, Grosdidier takes great pains to give references to the sources where possible. But his concluding judgement states disappointingly (255): 'L'étude de ces sources, dans son état présent, ne nous permet ni d'affirmer, ni de nier l'originalité de l'oeuvre de Romanos.'

121. Basil Seleuc., *Hom.* 39, *In s. deiparae annuntiat.* (CPG 6656[39]): PG 85, 448AB; SC 110, 179, n. 1.

122. Cf. CPG 6656 (10, 11, 12, 13); J. Grosdidier, *Romanos le Mélode* (1977), 244.

the 'Oriental theologians of Greek tongue, but also by the Christian literature in Syriac'.[123] One can contest J. Grosdidier's statement that Romanos evidently had no access to the Syriac works of Ephraem, but that there is evidence of his knowledge of the Greek writings. It is correct that there is a relationship to Ephraem (Greek) in the hymns on the last judgement [124] and on Abraham's sacrifice.[125] Grosdidier's conclusions were corrected by the thorough studies of W. L. Petersen,[126] who showed that Romanos knew the Syriac *Diatessaron* at first hand, and not only through Ephraem the Syrian. Romanos cites the Standard Text of the New Testament forty times, and the *Diatessaron* at least twenty-eight times, probably according to the Syriac text. Romanos also knew the prose commentary on the *Diatessaron* (cited probably nine times verbatim). In short,

Romanos owes a tremendous debt to Syriac literature; it is for others to determine to what — if any — degree the same may be said of the kontakion as well.[127]

(b) Connections with Justinian's politico-religious actions

One source, however, is of particular interest to us: J. Grosdidier established connections with the court and Justinian's writings. The poet probably moved in a circle of ecclesiastics with whom the Emperor was in the habit of discussing theology, although they did not have an official function at the court.

Beyond Constantinople and the court Romanos also had connections with the Latins, who during this period were more numerous in the capital than is usually accepted.[128] With these Westerners and above all with the Emperor himself the poet shared respect for Peter's See in Rome.[129] Romanos belonged to a generation which had experienced much, 'the killing and destruction of the Nika revolt [532], the spec-

123. J. Grosdidier, *Romanos le Mélode* (1977), 254.

124. *Hymn*. 50: SC 283, 209–267 with introduction.

125. *Hymn*. 3: SC 99, 129–165 with introduction; see as well Ephraem's hymn in S. I. Mercati, *S. Ephraem Syri opera* I, 43–83; also in PG 56, 537–541 (Ps. Chrysostom); SC 99, 132–133.

126. W. L. Petersen, *The Diatessaron and Ephrem Syrus as Sources of Romanos the Melodist* = CSCO 475, *Subs*. 74; *idem*, 'The Dependence of Romanos the Melodist upon the Syriac Ephrem: Its Importance for the Origin of the Kontakion', *VigC* 39 (1985), 171–87.

127. W. L. Petersen, *op. cit.*, 200.

128. Cf. Averil Cameron, 'The Theotokos in Sixth-Century Constantinople', *JTS* 29 (1978) = *eadem*, *Continuity and Change*, no. XVI, 83. According to M. Salamon, 'Priscianus und sein Schülerkreis', *Philologus* 123 (1979), 91–6, in the first half of the sixth century in Constantinople a group of Latin speakers, mostly of noble origin, rallied around Priscian, who stemmed from the West.

129. Cf. J. Grosdidier, introduction to *Hymn*. 47, in SC 283, 63–75, esp. from 73, where the various opportunities for contact, but also the friction (Vigilius), are discussed.

tacular success and reversals of Justinian's wars, that had seen the new Hagia Sophia built and then collapsing, that had experienced the trauma of plague and earthquake ...'[130] He acknowledged also, however, the Emperor's encroachments on the Imperial Church as these were presented, for example, in forced baptisms. In these he saw a 'coercion to freedom' of which he approved, because it annihilated the endangerment of salvation which was present with the impending end. [131]

Do we have any concrete allusions to the major christological texts of Justinian? According to P. Maas, the fourth hymn of the resurrection [132] is inspired in certain strophes by the decree of faith of 551.[133] This opinion is endorsed by J. Grosdidier. In strophe 1 Romanos invokes the 'mysterium of the oikonomia',[134] which is 'unutterable and inconceivable';[135] we should 'know (Christ) clearly as from both in unmingledness';[136] for 'he remained what he was and became what he was not';[137] 'he was God in truth, and a human being not only according to appearance, one and the same took suffering on himself in the oikonomia'.[138] Of the further allusions to the Emperor's edict of faith and other documents [139] in this hymn we shall highlight only strophe 4, which seems to betray a special closeness to the formulas most used at that time:

---

130. Averil Cameron, art. cit., 107; on Romanos as 'an established poet' see E. Topping, 'The Apostle Peter, Justinian and Romanos the Melodos', Byzantine and Modern Greek Studies 2 (1976), 1–15.

131. Roman. Melod., Hymn. ad Neoph. 52, 14: SC 283, 360–361: 'Peut-être aussi est-ce par crainte des lois aujourd'hui en vigueur que tu t'es approché du baptême et que tu es devenu ce que tu es devenu, intimidé par le temps présent. Et que t'arrivera-t-il quand viendra le temps du Jugement (ho kairos tes kriseos), et que tout sera dénoncé, et que notre Résurrection rétribuera tous les hommes?' On this see J. Grosdidier, Romanos le Mélode (1977), 282: 'Ce qui signifie: la contrainte présente n'est rien par rapport au risque qu'elle épargne au néophyte.'

132. Roman. Melod., Hymn. 43: SC 128, 485–541 (with introduction).

133. Cf. P. Maas, 'Die Chronologie der Hymnen des Romanos', ByzZ 15 (1906) (1–44), 16–18; J. Grosdidier, Romanos le Mélode (1977), 179.

134. Roman. Melod., Hymn. 43, 1: SC 128, 502; where Grosdidier refers to Justinian emp., Conf. fid.: Schwartz, pp. 88,28 and 92,22: τὸ τῆς θείας οἰκονομίας μυστήριον.

135. Cf. Schwartz, p. 76,16: ἀρρήτως ἀφράστως ἀκαταλήπτως.

136. Roman. Melod., Hymn. 43, 1: SC 128, p. 502,4: εἷς ἐξ ἀμφοῖν ἀσυγχύτως; cf. Justinian emp., Conf. fid.: Schwartz, p. 84,23. The text is from Cyril Alex., Commentary on Leviticus (CPG 5201): PG 69, 576.

137. Justinian emp., C. Orig.: according to Mansi IX, 500B; idem, Conf. fid.: Schwartz, p. 76,3; see the details in SC 128, 503, n. 5.

138. Justinian emp., Conf. fid.: Schwartz, p. 88,20–21, attributes the teaching of 'Christ's humanity as appearance' to Apollinarius and Eutyches; the edict says in addition: 'Being true God he became truly a human being': Schwartz, p. 76,7.

139. J. Grosdidier, in the apparatus of the text and translation of the Hymn. 43: SC 128, 504ff.

CHRIST IN CHRISTIAN TRADITION

When your faith, O human being, is this: the Logos from God the Father was crucified bodily, you do not err at all; for the unity of the natures is not divided . . .[140]

The opinion that Romanos composed a hymn in which the Second Council of Constantinople is mentioned and even defended is not to be accepted. The hymn in question is *The Kerygma of the Apostles*, the quality of which is certainly noteworthy, but it is claimed that it cannot stem from Romanos.[141] In strophe 10 the poet uses the image of the human being's five senses for the five councils between 325 and 553, as earlier the four councils were compared to the four gospels.[142]

(c) The conciliar terminology and problematic in Romanos Melodos

Only a few places can be found in which Romanos refers to the history of christology. He distances himself from the expression 'Christ, mere human being' (*psilos anthropos*), and emphasizes 'not split into two'.[143] The poet hardly investigates the technical language of the councils, and when he does it is mostly in the *theologia*, that is, in the proclamation of the Trinity.[144]

In the teaching of the *oikonomia* Paul of Samosata and above all Apollinarius (doctrine of the heavenly human being, the assumption of the *sarx* without a human soul, even of a mock body)[145] are addressed.

140. SC 128, p. 506,7-9: . . . οὔτε γὰρ διαιρεῖται ἡ τῶν φύσεων ἑνότης. In the apparatus (n. 1) Grosdidier cites from Justinian emp., *Conf. fid.*: Schwartz, p. 86,30: δύο φύσεων ἕνωσιν λέγομεν καὶ μίαν ὑπόστασιν. Cf. *ibid.*, p. 74,22-24. Together with P. Maas, however, Grosdidier considers the verse of 'Romanos' just cited as a later insertion. In the extant texts we do not find explicitly in Romanos himself the whole formula of the 'unity of the *hypostasis* in the duality of the natures'. For the use of the word *physis* for Christ's humanity one can perhaps refer to *Hymn.* 37, 17: SC 128, 254-255: 'Christ is invincible in a vanquished nature'. Here, however, *physis* denotes being human as such, not so much Christ's individual human nature.

141. J. Grosdidier, *Romanos le Mélode* (1977), 209-12, esp. 211; text (Greek), 210 (French): 'A cause de tout cela, la grâce, rassemblant aux temps qu'elle a choisis les cinq conciles des Pères en nombre égal à nos sens, a rendu claire pour eux la connaissance de la vérité.'

142. Cf. *CCT* II/1 336 with n. 49. In the Western fight against the Fifth Council people had recourse to this image; cf. A. Grillmeier, in *Chalkedon* II, 815 (on Isidore of Seville).

143. Roman. Melod., *Hymn.* 36 on the passion, 19: SC 128, 226.

144. See J. Grosdidier, *Romanos le Mélode* (1977), 264-71. In *Hymn.* 20 (on the leper) Romanos distinguishes between *prosopon-hypostasis* and *ousia* in the Trinity: SC 110, 378. Grosdidier indicates a possible reference to the tritheists. However, he finds the use of Basil Caes., *Hom.* 24: PG 31, 605B as a source more probable. In the same *Hymn.* 20 is also found the formula 'one of the Trinity', which is so often employed by Justinian, but here occurs without addition.

145. Cf. *Hymn.* 14, 12 (*Hypapante*): SC 110, 188-190 (*sarx apsychos* — *empsychos*); J. Grosdidier, *Romanos le Mélode* (1977), 333: *Index s.v.* Apollinaire de Laodicée.

It is striking how little reference there is to Nestorius[146] and Severus of Antioch. In the inauthentic hymn *The Kerygma of the Apostles*, the Synod of Constantinople (536) with its condemnation of the Patriarch as 'the enemy of orthodox faith' is mentioned.[147] In spite of his apologetic stance Romanos hardly looks into the christological heresies of the pre- and post-Chalcedonian period.

3. The concrete picture of Christ in Romanos Melodos

According to the logical and systematic division in the Oxford edition of the hymns, Romanos composed thirty-four hymns to the 'person of Christ'.[148] However, it is not so much a question of the person of Jesus in the framework of a two-natures teaching, as of the history of Jesus in the mysteries of his life, as they were celebrated in the Byzantine church year.[149] They are depicted more or less dramatically.

These mysteries of the life and deeds of Jesus begin with the proclamation of his birth (*Hymn.* 9: SC 110; on 25 March). Jesus' infancy is sung in six hymns (10–15: SC 110). *Hymn.* 10 for the feast of 25 December (SC 110) was very famous; it was sung at the imperial table and had been composed as early as 518. *Hymn.* 14 (SC 110) was composed for 2 February (the feast of the *hypapante*) and belonged to the most popular of Romanos' hymns.[150] The depiction of 'Christ's *ministerium*', or of his public life, begins with the hymns for the feast of Epiphany on 6 January and its sequel on 7 January (*Hymn.* 16 and 17: SC 110), in which Christ's baptism is celebrated with recourse to the Gospel of the Ebionites and with the depiction of the turning back of the waters of the Jordan and the appearance of a heavenly light.[151] The arrival of the Magi is already incorporated in detail in *Hymn.* 10 for the feast of Christmas (*Hymn.* 10: SC 110, 50–76).[152] The hymn about the marriage at Cana (*Hymn.* 18: SC 110) opens a series of six poems which deal with Christ's miracles and which are spread over the

146. On Nestorius see *op. cit., Index*, p. 336. To what extent the *Theotokos* title in Romanos is also anti-Nestorian cannot be determined. Here he will have held on to the love of the Byzantines for the *Theotokos*. See Averil Cameron, *art. cit.*; cf. J. Grosdidier, *Romanos le Mélode* (1977), 174–5. According to Grosdidier, the famous *Akathistos-Hymnus* was originally composed to celebrate the old feast of 26 December in honour of the *Theotokos*. See *op. cit.*, 34–5.

147. Cf. J. Grosdidier, *Romanos le Mélode* (1977), 209–11.

148. P. Maas/C. A. Trypanis, *Sancti Romani Melodi Cantica, vol. I: Cantica genuina* (Oxford, 1963), nos. 1–34. See the overview in J. Grosdidier, *Romanos le Mélode* (1977), 330–1.

149. On the *kontakia* of Romanos and the liturgical calendar of the Greek Church see J. Grosdidier, *Romanos le Mélode* (1977), 74–93. On the Byzantine Church year and calendar of feasts see N. Nilles, *Kalendarium Manuale utriusque Ecclesiae Orientalis et Occidentalis* T. I (Innsbruck, 1879): calendar 2–25; further information in T. II (Innsbruck, 1881).

150. On this see J. Grosdidier, SC 110, 164: '. . . un interminable discours théologique où sont définies la dualité des natures du Christ et leur union, où est dressé le répertoire des hérésies qui sont commises à ce sujet'. The expression 'two natures', however, does not occur. The topic is the real divinity and humanity of Jesus, in non-technical language.

151. See SC 110, 271, n. 2.

152. Christ's circumcision on 1 January, as far as I can see, is not dealt with in any of the hymns edited in the SC. Nor do we find a hymn on Christ's transfiguration (6 August).

period between the second week after Easter and the Wednesday before Pentecost. In the hymn about Cana (strophe 8) the poet allows Mary herself to praise the virgin birth of Christ as the greatest of all miracles (SC 110, 308–309). Indeed he alludes to the infancy gospels. For him it is a proof of Christ's divinity, as is stressed in many verses. It is clear that mariologically the dignity of Mary's virginity was highlighted more than her title of *Theotokos*, which nevertheless from 431 played a great rôle in Constantinople and did so again at the end of the sixth century.[153]

Christ's passion is interpreted in five hymns for Holy Week (for Palm Sunday, *Hymn*. 32; the washing of the feet and the betrayal of Judas, *Hymn*. 33; Peter's denial, *Hymn*. 34; Mary's dialogue with the cross, *Hymn*. 35; Christ's trial, *Hymn*. 36: all in SC 128). For the suffering, death and resurrection, J. Grosdidier distinguished two types of description of redemption: (a) with a more historical stance, with an eye to the earthly Jesus of the gospels or of the earthly Jerusalem, and (b) with an action which takes place in the upper (heavenly) world (thus in the hymn for the adoration of the cross [*Hymn*. 39: SC 128]), or in the netherworld (Hades). *Hymn*. 35 represents a middle form (SC 128, 143–144). Christ's descent into the netherworld becomes a favourite theme of Romanos (*Hymn*. 37: SC 128).[154] He develops a far-reaching soteriology, with special emphasis on the rôle of the demon in human history, within which the Jewish people have a very negative share (cf. *Hymn*. 36 and 38) (Grosdidier in SC 128, 236–238).[155]

The theme of Easter begins already with *Hymn*. 37 on the powers of the netherworld, and is then expressed in the hymn about the triumph of the cross (*Hymn*. 38: SC 128) and the adoration (veneration) of the cross (*Hymn*. 39: SC 128); six hymns on the resurrection form a block on its own (*Hymn*. 40–45: SC 128; *Hymn*. 45 has the title: The ten drachmas). To these also, however, belong *Hymn*. 46 (appearance before Thomas) and 47 (sending of the apostles). The series closes with *Hymn*. 48 (ascension) and 49 (Pentecost) (all in SC 283). *Hymn*. 50 (last judgement) (SC 283) describes the end of the history of salvation.

If we attempt to argue from the dramatically depicted event to Romanos' conception of Christ's being, notwithstanding his realistic understanding[156] of the happening, he still retains a christology 'from above'. He is not a Severan, but for him the whole intellectual movement in Christ's humanity has its origin in the Logos. It is there that the free decision to suffer occurs: 'In your voluntary death we have found

153. See Averil Cameron, *art. cit.*

154. On the various depictions of the descent see J. Grosdidier, in SC 128, 566–567 (on *Hymn*. 45). The theory of the contest in Hades (*agôn*) and of Satan's jurisdiction are intended to reinforce the definitive liberation of the human being from the power of the netherworld.

155. According to J. Grosdidier (SC 128, 270–276), one finds in *Hymn*. 38 similar themes (with regard to the descent into Hades) to those in Ps. Eusebius of Alexandria in four of his homilies (CPG 5522–5524, 5526). On this anonymous author at the end of the fifth century or the beginning of the sixth cf. S. J. Voicu, art. 'Eusebio di Alessandria', in *DPAC* I (1983), 1284–5.

156. For example, the statement that Christ ascended into heaven in the body and not in the divinity is important: *Hymn*. 48 in Ascens., 9: SC 283, 154–155. What ascended above was the 'flesh', 'the visible body'. The divinity filled everything; in it there was no movement. Romanos acknowledges the twofold *homoousios* in Christ: *Hymn*. 43, 1: SC 128, p. 502, 3–4.

immortal life, all-powerful, sole God of the universe.'[157] This free acceptance of suffering is a favourite theme of Romanos, however he understands it.[158] Christ's suffering is true suffering, as is expressed particularly in *Hymn.* 35 (Mary at the cross).[159] In this the poet develops his soteriology, which is intended to give an answer to the question *Cur deus homo?* The question: 'Would God have been able to save Adam without Christ's suffering and death?' occupies him in fourteen poems.[160] He takes seriously Christ's *kenosis*, or, expressed in Chrysostom's terms, the συγκατάβασις, God's condescension to us.[161] Nevertheless Romanos systematically avoids speaking of Christ's humanity. The accent is always on the divinity. It is not only Christ's divinity, but also the *Christus triumphans* (against the hellish powers) that is in the forefront. For this reason there is also a heavy emphasis on the miraculous in the life of Jesus.[162] For him it is the pantocrator who freely accepted humiliation and overcame it completely.[163] This way of considering Christ on the basis of his divinity, which, it is clear, alone receives the denotation *physis*, is genuinely Cyrillian, even though Cyril himself or his *mia-physis* formula are not even mentioned.[164]

157. Roman. Melod., *Hymn.* 43, passim: SC 128, p. 500,1. It was the Trinity which decided that the incarnation should take place. Thus J. Grosdidier, *Romanos le Mélode* (1977), 264–5. Romanos strongly insists on this. He combines the *theologia* very closely with the *oikonomia.* It sounds strange when he says in *Hymn.* 35, 14 (Mary at the cross): SC 128, 181: 'c'était dès l'origine mon décret et celui de mon Père, et mon Esprit n'a pas refusé que je me fasse homme et que je souffre pour celui qui a failli'. One can dispute the translation of J. Grosdidier. See *loc. cit.*, n. 3.

158. Cf. Roman. Melod., *Hymn.* 47, 19 (the sending of the apostles): SC 283, 115, with n. 2; J. Grosdidier, *Romanos le Mélode* (1977), 272–3. If the Son of God wanted to become flesh, it was in order to be able to die for human beings. It is, however, the 'death of God'.

159. SC 128, 160–186.

160. Cf. J. Grosdidier, *Romanos le Mélode* (1977), 273. Grosdidier investigates the soteriology of the Melodos in considerable detail. Cf. *loc. cit.*, 271–7.

161. J. Grosdidier, *Romanos le Mélode* (1977), 273; cf. on *Hymn.* 20: SC 110, 357.

162. J. Grosdidier, *Romanos le Mélode* (1977), 268–70.

163. J. Grosdidier, on *Hymn.* 20: SC 110, 357.

164. Romanos is probably to be considered a neo-Chalcedonian, in the same sense as Emperor Justinian. In comparison to him one cannot discern the effort to incorporate more of Cyrillian language. The Emperor carried out this process for him. But more than Justinian he highlights Christ's divinity almost in an Alexandrian manner. The stressing of Mary's virginity or Jesus' birth and of the miraculous in Jesus' life in general reminds one of Leontius of Jerusalem. Was Romanos close to the aphthartics with whom Leontius of Byzantium did battle?

SUMMARY

Without a doubt Romanos Melodos offers an impressive supplement to the reflective christology of the theologians and Justinian's politico-religious decrees. He is the mediator between on the one side the more critical theological discussion based on concepts and formulas, and the celebration of the Church and its people in the Byzantine liturgy on the other, which had its centre in the Hagia Sophia;[165] but he is also the great comforter of all levels of the Imperial City in their great trials, especially since the Nika revolt of 532. Romanos supports a sacralization of everyday life and offers texts for all occasions.[166] Daily life has a series of liturgical acts which accompany the individual hours of the day. The great feasts of the church's year were centred on Christ's person and his work of redemption.[167]

Just how closely membership of the state and the Church were related is expressed by G. Downey as follows:

> To be a member of the orthodox Church was to be a citizen of the empire, and to be a citizen was to be a Christian; and so the participation in the Church's most important service of worship was at the same time an expression of social and political community.[168]

Poetry and music in the liturgy filled the eyes and ears of the Christian with a 'physical radiance';[169] to this Romanos Melodos made a significant contribution. The fine arts, which in the Hagia Sophia had created their greatest work to venerate Christ, the divine Wisdom, became in Constantinople the splendid expression of the content of faith. Here unfortunately we cannot make even the slightest attempt to sense this experience of faith from religious art by the Byzantines, in either its

---

165. See H.-J. Schulz, *Die byzantinische Liturgie. Glaubenszeugnis und Symbolgestalt* (Trier, ²1980), esp. 45–55: the liturgy of Constantinople in the period of the struggle against Monophysitism; 57–90: the liturgy of the Justinianic period and its interpretation by Maximus Confessor. See too G. Downey, *Constantinople. In the Age of Justinian* (Oklahoma Press, ³1980), esp. V: The Emperor as Builder: St. Sophia, 92–113; VI: Empire and Body of Christ: The Divine Liturgy, 114–35.

166. Cf. G. Downey, *Constantinople*, VI, 114: 'In the age of Justinian, every step of human life was blessed, strengthened, and aided by the Church', referring to the sacramental life and the many sacramentals, with which 'the believer's mundane affairs' too were endowed.

167. *Ibid.*, 114–15.

168. *Ibid.*, 117–18. On the liturgy of Chrysostom see *ibid.*, 118. Downey, 120, rightly comments: 'The Divine Liturgy was the same everywhere. The same words, whether in Greek, Syriac or Coptic, would be said or sung in the humblest village in Syria or Egypt, and in St Sophia.' The course of the liturgical day is described on 122–35.

169. *Ibid.*, 121.

possibilities or its realities. It must suffice to refer to some points of access which can introduce one to this spiritual world.[170]

The sacralization of private and public life in Byzantium is still not at its zenith. Even Emperor Justinian could be exceeded in this.[171]

170. See H. Hunger, *Reich der neuen Mitte* (Graz, Vienna, Cologne, 1965), III.5: The fine arts as an expression of the Christian world-view, 202–28. S. Runciman, *Kunst und Kultur in Byzanz. Ein Überblick* (Munich, 1978), esp. 46–82 (on the sixth century); A. Effenberger, *Frühchristliche Kunst und Kultur. Von den Anfängen bis zum 7. Jahrhundert* (Leipzig, 1986), esp. 285–310 (Constantinople and the art of the East).

171. Cf. the increase of religious symbolism under Justinian's successor and the development of a theocratic system; see above on Justin II; Averil Cameron, *art. cit.*

SELECT BIBLIOGRAPHY

Abramowski, L., 'Der Streit um Diodor und Theodor zwischen den beiden ephesinischen Konzilien', *ZKG* 67 (1955/6), 252–87.

'Reste von Theodorets Apologie für Diodor und Theodor bei Facundus' in *StudPat* 1 = TU 63 (Berlin, 1957), 61–9.

Drei christologische Untersuchungen (Berlin, New York, 1981).

'ΣΥΝΑΦΕΙΑ und ΑΣΥΓΧΥΤΟΣ ΕΝΩΣΙΣ als Bezeichnung für trinitarische und christologische Einheit', *ibid.*, 63–109.

'Ein nestorianischer Traktat bei Leontius von Jerusalem' in *III. Symposium Syriacum 1980* = OCA 221 (Rome, 1983), 43–55.

Ahrweiler, H., *Byzance: les pays et les territoires* (London, 1976).

Allen, P., 'A New Date for the Last Recorded Events in John of Ephesus' Historia Ecclesiastica', *OLP* 10 (1979), 251–4.

'Neo-Chalcedonism and the Patriarchs of the Late Sixth Century', *Byz* 50 (1980), 5–17.

Evagrius Scholasticus the Church Historian = SpicSLov 41 (Louvain, 1981).

Altaner, B., 'Der griechische Theologe Leontius und Leontius der skythische Mönch. Eine prosopographische Untersuchung', *ThQ* 127 (1947), 147–65.

'Zum Schrifttum der "skythischen" (gotischen) Mönche', *HistJb* 72 (1953), 568–81.

Amann, E., art. 'Thémistius' in *DTC* 15 (1946), 219–22.

Amelotti, M., 'Giustiniano tra teologia e diritto' in G. G. Archi (ed.), *L'imperatore Giustiniano. Storia e mito* (Milan, 1978), 133–60.

Amelotti, M.–Migliardi Zingale, L., *Scritti teologici ed ecclesiastici di Giustiniano* = Florentina Studiorum Universitas. Legum Iustiniani Imperatoris Vocabularium. Subsidia III (Milan, 1977).

Ananian, P., 'L'opusculo di Eutichio patriarca di Costantinopoli sulla "Distinzione della natura e persona"' in *Armeniaca. Mélanges d'études arméniennes* (Venice, 1969), 355–82.

Anastos, M. V., 'Justinian's Despotic Control over the Church as Illustrated by His Edicts on the Theopaschite Formula and His Letter to Pope John II in 533' in *Mélanges G. Ostrogorsky* II, 1–11 = idem, *Studies in Byzantine Intellectual History* (London, 1979), no. IV.

Atiya, A. S., *A History of Eastern Christianity* (London, 1968).

Bacht, H., 'Die Rolle des orientalischen Mönchtums in den kirchenpolitischen Auseinandersetzungen um Chalkedon (431–519)' in *Chalkedon II*, 193–314.

Bardy, G., 'Sévère d'Antioche et la critique des textes patristiques' in *Mémorial Louis Petit* = Archives de l'Orient Chrétien 1 (Bucharest, 1948), 15–31.

Basdekis, A., *Die Christologie des Leontius von Jerusalem. Seine Logoslehre* (Diss. Münster, 1974).

Baynes, N. H.–Moss, H. S. L. B., *Byzantium. An Introduction to East Roman Civilization* (Oxford, 1948 (1961)).

Beck, H.-G., *Kirche und theologische Literatur im byzantinischen Reich* (Munich, 1959).

'Die frühbyzantinische Kirche' in H. Jedin (ed.), *Handbuch der Kirchengeschichte*, Bd. II/2: *Die Kirche in Ost und West von Chalkedon bis zum Frühmittelalter (471–700)* (Freiburg, Basel, Vienna, 1975), 3–92.

Das byzantinische Jahrtausend (Munich, 1978).

'Geschichte der orthodoxen Kirche im byzantinischen Reich' in B. Moeller (ed.), *Die Kirche in ihrer Geschichte. Ein Handbuch*, Bd. 1, Lfg. D1 (Göttingen, 1980): see D1–2: Bibliograph. Hilfsmittel.

(ed.), *Byzantinisches Lesebuch* (Munich, 1982).

Beierwaltes, W., 'Andersheit. Grundriß einer neuplatonischen Begriffsgeschichte', *ABG* 16 (1972), 166–97.

Proklos, Grundzüge seiner Metaphysik (Frankfurt, [2]1979).

Berger, A., 'La concezione di eretico nelle fonti giustinianee', *Atti della Acc. Naz. dei Lincei* 352 (Rome, 1955), 353–68.

Blum, G. G., *Rabbula von Edessa. Der Christ, der Bischof, der Theologe* = CSCO 300, Subs. 34 (Louvain, 1969).

Bonini, R., *Introduzione allo studio dell'età giustinianea* (Bologna, [3]1979).

Brock, S., 'The Conversations with the Syrian Orthodox under Justinian (532)', *OCP* 47 (1981), 87–121.

Brooks, E. W., *The Sixth Book of the Select Letters of Severus Patriarch of Antioch in the Syriac Version of Athanasius of Nisibis*, Vol. I–II (London, Oxford, 1902–1903).

Browning, R., *Justinian and Theodora* (London, 1971).

Cameron, Alan, 'Demes and Factions', *ByzZ* 67 (1974), 74–91.

Circus Factions. Blues and Greens at Rome and Byzantium (Oxford, 1976).

Cameron, Averil, *Continuity and Change in Sixth-Century Byzantium* (London, 1981).

Procopius and the Sixth Century (London, 1985).

Carcione, F., 'L'"aftartodocetismo" di Giustiniano: una mistificatione strumentale del dissenso politico-religioso', *StRiOrCr* 7 (1984), 71–8.

'La politica religiosa di Giustiniano nella fase iniziale della "seconda controversia Origenista" (536–543). Un nuovo fallimentare tentativo d'integrazione tra monofisismo e calcedonianesimo alla vigilia della controversia sui Tre Capitoli', *StRiOrCr* 8 (1985), 3–18.

'La politica religiosa di Giustiniano nella fase conclusiva della seconda controversia origenista (543–553). Gli intrecci con la controversia sui Tre Capitoli', *StRiOrCr* 9 (1986), 131–47.

Caspar, E., *Geschichte des Papsttums von den Anfängen bis zur Höhe der Weltherrschaft*, Bd. II: *Das Papsttum unter byzantinischer Herrschaft* (Tübingen, 1933).

Charanis, P., 'The Monk as an Element of the Byzantine Society', *DOP* 25 (1971), 61–84.

'On the Question of the Byzantine Church into a National Greek Church', *Byzantina* 2 (1982), 97–109.

Chesnut, R. C. *Three Monophysite Christologies: Severus of Antioch, Philoxenus of Mabbug and Jacob of Sarug* (Oxford, 1976).

Chitty, D. J., *The Desert a City* (Oxford, 1966).

Chrysos, E., *Die Bischofslisten des V. Ökumenischen Konzils (553)* = *Antiquitas* R.1, Bd. 14 (Bonn, 1966).

The Ecclesiastical Policy of Justinian in the Dispute concerning the Three Chapters and the Fifth Ecumenical Council (Thessaloniki, 1969) (Greek).

Claude, D., *Die byzantinische Stadt im 6. Jahrhundert* (Munich, 1969).

Dagron, G., 'La Vie ancienne de saint Marcel l'Acémète', *AnBoll* 86 (1968), 271–321.

'Les moines et la ville', *TravMém* 4 (1970), 229–76.

'Le christianisme dans la ville byzantine', *DOP* 31 (1977), 3–25.

Daley, B. E., 'The Origenism of Leontius of Byzantium', *JTS* 27 (1976), 333–69.

Leontius of Byzantium: A Critical Edition of His Works, with Prolegomena (Diss. Oxford 1978).

'The Christology of Leontius of Byzantium: Personalism or Dialectics' in *Papers from the Ninth International Conference on Patristic Studies 1983*, Oxford, England = Patristic Monograph Series, The Philadelphia Patristic Foundation (typescript).

Darrouzés, J., *Notitiae episcopatuum ecclesiae Constantinopolitanae. Texte critique, introduction et notes* (Paris, 1981).

Delehaye, H., *Les saints stylites* = SubsHag 14 (Brussels, Paris 1923).

Demandt, A., *Die Spätantike, Römische Geschichte von Diocletian bis Justinian 284–565 n. Chr.* = *Handbuch der Altertumswissenschaft* III.6 (Munich, 1989).

Devreesse, R., 'Le Florilège de Léonce de Byzance', *RSR* 10 (1930), 545–76.

Essai sur Théodore de Mopsueste = ST 141 (Vatican City, 1948).

Diekamp, F., *Die origenistischen Streitigkeiten im sechsten Jahrhundert und das fünfte allgemeine Concil* (Münster, 1899).

Doctrina Patrum de Incarnatione Verbi (Münster, [1]1907, [2]1981 ed. by E. Chrysos).

Analecta Patristica = OCA 117 (Rome, 1938).

Dorival, G., 'Athanase ou pseudo-Athanase?', *RSLR* 16 (1980), 80–9.

Dorner, J. A. *Entwicklungsgeschichte der Lehre von der Person Christi* I (Stuttgart, 1845, Berlin [2]1851); II (Berlin, 1853).

Dörrie, H., *Porphyrios' 'Symmikta Zetemata'* = *Monograph. Z. klass. Altertumswissensch.* 20 (Munich, 1959).

Downey, G., *Constantinople. In the Age of Justinian* (Norman, [3]1980).

Draguet, R., *Julien d'Halicarnasse et sa controverse avec Sévère d'Antioche sur l'incorruptibilité du corps du Christ* (Louvain, 1924).

Duchesne, L., *L'Église au VIe siècle* (Paris, 1925).

Elert, W., 'Theodor von Pharan und Theodor von Raithu', *ThLZ* 76 (1951), 67–76.

Engberding, H., 'Zum formgeschichtlichen Verständnis des ἅγιος ὁ Θεός, ἅγιος ἰσχυρός, ἅγιος ἀθάνατος – ἐλέησον ἡμᾶς', *JLW* 10 (1930), 168–74.

Evans, D. B., *Leontius of Byzantium: An Origenist Christology* = DOS 13 (Washington D.C., 1970).

Fedalto, G., *Hierarchia Ecclesiastica Orientalis. Series episcoporum ecclesiarum christianarum orientalium, I. Patriarchatus Constantinopolitanus, II. Patriarchatus Alexandrinus, Antiochenus, Hierosolymitanus* (Padua, 1988).

Fischer, R. H. (ed.), *A Tribute to Arthur Vööbus. Studies in Early Christian Literature and its Environment, Primarily in the Syrian East* (Chicago, 1977).

Flusin, B., *Miracle et histoire dans l'oeuvre de Cyrille de Scythopolis* (Paris, 1983).

Frend, W. H. C., *The Rise of the Monophysite Movement* (Cambridge, 1972).

Frivold, L., *The Incarnation. A Study of the Doctrine of the Incarnation in the Armenian Church in the 5th and 6th Centuries according to the Book of Letters* (Oslo, Bergen, Tromsø, 1981).

Frohne, R., *Agapetus Diaconus. Untersuchungen zu den Quellen und zur Wirkungsgeschichte des ersten byzantinischen Fürstenspiegels* (Diss. Tübingen, 1985).

Gahbauer, F., *Das anthropologische Modell. Ein Beitrag zur Christologie der frühen Kirche bis Chalkedon* = ÖstlChr 35 (Würzburg, 1984).

Galtier, P., 'L'enseignement des Pères sur la Vision béatifique dans le Christ', *RSR* 15 (1925), 54–62.

Garrigues, J.-M., 'La personne composée du Christ d'après saint Maxime le Confesseur', *RevThom* 74 (1974), 181–204.

Gasparro, G. S., 'Il problema delle citazioni del Peri Archon nella Lettera a Mena di Giustiniano' in Lies, L. (ed.), *Origeniana Quarta* (Innsbruck, 1987), 54–76.

Gerhards, A., 'Le phénomène du Sanctus adressé au Christ. Son origine, sa signification et sa persistance dans les Anaphores de l'église d'Orient' in Triacca, A. M./ Pistoia, A. (eds.), *Le Christ dans la liturgie* (Rome, 1981), 65–83.

Gieseler, J. C. L., *Commentationis, qua Monophysitarum veterum variae de Christi persona opiniones inprimis ex ipsorum effatis recens editis illustrantur, Particula I et II* (Göttingen, 1835 (1838)).

Glorie, F., *Maxentii aliorumque Scytharum monachorum necnon Ioannis Tomitanae urbis episcopi Opuscula* = CCL 85A (Turnhout, 1978).

Goubert, P., 'Les successeurs de Justinien et le Monophysisme' in *Chalkedon* II, 179–92. *Byzance avant l'Islam*, I,II/1–2 (Paris, 1952–1965).

Gouillard, J., 'Hypatios d'Éphèse ou Du Pseudo-Denys à Théodore Studite', *RevÉtByz* 19 (1961), 63–75.

Graffin, F., 'La catéchèse de Sévère d'Antioche', *OrSyr* 5 (1960), 47–54.

Gray, P. T. R., *The Defense of Chalcedon in the East (451–553)* = *Studies in the History of Christian Thought* 20 (Leiden, 1979), 105–11.

'Neo-Chalcedonianism and the Tradition: From Patristic to Byzantine Theology', *ByzF* 8 (1982), 61–70.

'An Anonymous Severian Monophysite of the Mid-Sixth Century', *Patristic and Byzantine Review* 1 (1982), 117–26.

'Leontius of Jerusalem's Case for "Synthetic" Union in Christ', *StudPat* 18,1 (Kalamazoo, Michigan, 1985), 151–4.

Art. 'Justinian, Kaiser (ca. 483–565)', *TRE* 17 (1988), 478–86.

Gribomont, J., 'La catéchèse de Sévère d'Antioche et le Credo', *ParOr* 6/7 (1975/76), 125–58.

Grillmeier, A., 'Der Neu-Chalkedonismus', *HistJb* 77 (1958), 151–66 = idem, *Mit ihm und in ihm* (²1978), 371–85.

'. . . Eine Studie zu einer christologischen Bezeichnung der Väterzeit', *Trad* 33 (1977), 1–63.

'Das östliche und westliche Christusbild', *TheolPhil* 59 (1984), 84–96.

'Die anthropologisch-christologische Sprache des Leontius von Byzanz und ihre Beziehung zu den Symmikta Zetemata des Neuplatonikers Porphyrius' in *FS Hadwig Hörner* (Frankfurt, 1987) (typescript).

Grosdidier de Matons, J., *Romanos le Mélode et les origines de la poésie religieuse à Byzance* (Paris, 1977).

Grumel, V., 'L'auteur et la date de composition du tropaire "O . . ."', *EO* 22 (1923), 398–418.

Art. 'Léonce de Byzance' in *DTC* 9 (1926), 400–26.

'Le surnaturel dans l'humanité du Christ viateur, d'après Léonce de Byzance' in *Mélanges Mandonnet* II (Paris, 1930), 15–22.

'La sotériologie de Léonce de Byzance', *EO* 40 (1937), 385–97.

Guillaumont, A., *Les 'Kephalaia Gnostica' d'Évagre le Pontique et l'histoire de l'origénisme chez les Grecs et chez les Syriens* = PatSorb 5 (Paris, 1962).

'Justinien et l'Église de Perse', *DOP* 23/24 (1969), 39–66.

Guillaumont, A. and C., 'Le texte véritable des "Gnostica" d'Évagre le Pontique', *RevHistRel* 142 (1952), 156–205.

Haacke, R., 'Die kaiserliche Politik in den Auseinandersetzungen um Chalkedon' in *Chalkedon* II, 95–117.

Halleux, A. de, 'Le "synode néochalcédonien" d'Alexandrette (ca 515) et l'"Apologie pour Chalcédoine de Jean le Grammairien". A propos d'une édition récente', *RHE* 72 (1977), 593–600.

'Trois synodes impériaux du VIᵉ s. dans une chronique syriaque inédite' in R. H. Fischer (ed.), *A Tribute to Arthur Vööbus* (Chicago, 1977), 295–307.

'Hellénisme et syrianité de Romanos le Mélode', *RHE* 73 (1978), 632–41.

'"Hypostase" et "Personne" dans la formation du dogme trinitaire (ca 375–381)', *RHE* 79 (1984), 313–69, 625–70.

Hanssens, J. M., *Institutiones Liturgicae de ritibus orientalibus*, vol. III (Rome, 1932).

Hefele, Ch.J.–Leclercq, H., *Histoire des conciles d'après les documents originaux*, Vol. 3 (Paris, 1909).

Helmer, S. *Der Neuchalkedonismus. Geschichte, Berechtigung und Bedeutung eines dogmengeschichtlichen Begriffes* (Diss. Bonn, 1962).

Hermann, T., 'Monophysitica', *ZNW* 32 (1933), 287–93.

Hespel, R., *Le florilège Cyrillien réfuté par Sévère d'Antioche. Étude et édition critique* = BiblMus 37 (1955).

Hoffmann, M., *Der Dialog bei den christlichen Schriftstellern der ersten vier Jahrhunderte* = TU 96 (Berlin, 1966).

Hohlweg, A., art. 'Justinian' in *Die Großen der Weltgeschichte*, Bd. II (Zürich, 1972), 748–77 with Bibl. 776–7.

Honigmann, E., *Évêques et Évêchés monophysites d'Asie antérieure au VIᵉ siècle* = CSCO 127 (Louvain, 1951).

Patristic Studies = ST 173 (Vatican City, 1953).

Hunger, H., *Reich der neuen Mitte. Der christliche Geist der byzantinischen Kultur* (Graz, Vienna, Cologne, 1965).

(ed.), *Das byzantinische Herrscherbild* = WdF 341 (Darmstadt, 1975).

Irmscher, J., 'Die geistige Situation der Intelligenz im Zeitalter Justinians' in Altheim, F./Stiehl, R., *Die Araber in der Alten Welt IV* (Berlin, 1967), 334–62.

'Christliches und Heidnisches in der Literatur der justinianischen Zeit', *Revue des Études sudest européennes* 18 (1980), 85–94.

'Paganismus im Justinianischen Reich', *Klio* 63 (1981), 683–8.

Janeras, V.-S., 'Les byzantins et le trisagion christologique' in *Miscellanea liturgica . . .*, FS Lercaro II (Rome, 1967), 467–99.

Janin, R., 'Les monastères nationaux et provinciaux à Byzance', *EO* 32 (1933), 429–38.

Art. 'Eutichio' in *Bibl. SS* V (Rome, 1964), 323–4.

Les Églises et les Monastères des grands centres Byzantins (Paris, 1975).

Jugie, M., Art. 'Gaianite (Controverse)' in *DTC* 6 (1915), 1002–23.

'La béatitude et la science parfaite de l'âme de Jésus viateur d'après Léonce de Byzance', *RSPT* 10 (1921), 548–59.

'Julien d'Halicarnasse et Sévère d'Antioche. La doctrine du péché originel chez les Pères Grecs'. Extrait des *Echos d'Orient* (Paris, 1925).

Junglas, J. P., *Leontius von Byzanz. Studien zu seinen Schriften, Quellen und Anschauungen* = FCLDG 3 (Paderborn, 1908).

Kaegi, W. E., 'The Fifth-Century Twilight of Byzantine Paganism', *Classica et Mediaevalia* 27 (1966), 243–75.

Kornemann, E., *Weltgeschichte des Mittelmeerraumes. Von Philipp II. von Makedonien bis Muhammed*, Bengston, H. (ed.) (Munich, 1967).

Kretschmar, G., 'Neue Arbeiten zur Geschichte des Ostergottesdienstes II: Die Einführung des Sanctus in die lateinische Meßliturgie', *JLH* 7 (1962), 79–86.

Lash, C., 'Saint Athanase dans les écrits de Sévère d'Antioche' in *Politique et théologie chez Athanase d'Alexandrie*. Actes du colloque de Chantilly 23–25 Sept. 1973, Kannengiesser, C. (ed.) = ThéolHist 27 (Paris, 1974), 377–94.

Lebon, J., *Le monophysisme sévérien* (Louvain, 1909).

'La christologie du monophysisme syrien' in *Chalkedon* I, 425–580.

Le Boulluec, A., 'Controverses au sujet de la doctrine d'Origène sur l'âme du Christ' in Lies, L. (ed.), *Origeniana Quarta* (Innsbruck, 1987), 223–37.

Le Quien, M., *Oriens christianus in quatuor patriarchatus digtestus* I (Paris, 1740; reprint Graz, 1958).

Lietzmann, H., *Apollinaris von Laodicea und seine Schule* (Tübingen, 1904).

Loofs, F., *Leontius von Byzanz und die gleichnamigen Schriftsteller der griechischen Kirche* = TU 3, 1–2 (Leipzig, 1887).

'Die "Ketzerei" Justinians' in *Harnack-Ehrung. Beiträge zur Kirchengeschichte* (Leipzig, 1921), 232–48.

Lourdas, B., 'Intellectuals, Scholars and Bureaucrats in the Byzantine Society', *Kleronomia* 2 (1970), 272–92.

McGuckin, J. A., 'The "Theopaschite Confession" (Text and Historical Context): A Study in the Cyrilline Reinterpretation of Chalcedon', *JEH* 35 (1984), 239–55.

Marić, J., *De Agnoetarum doctrina. Argumentum patristicum pro omniscientia Christi hominis relativa* (Zagreb, 1914).

Markus, R. A., *Christianity in the Roman World* (London, 1974).

Maspero, J., *Histoire des patriarches d'Alexandrie* (Paris, 1923).

Meyendorff, J., *Christ in Eastern Christian Thought* (Washington D.C., 1969).

Byzantine Theology: Historical Trends and Doctrinal Themes (New York, 1974).

Moeller, C., 'Le chalcédonisme et le néo-chalcédonisme' in *Chalkedon* I, 670–1.

'Trois fragments grecs de l'Apologie de Jean le Grammairien pour le concile de Chalcedoine', *RHE* 46 (1951), 683–8.

ΑΛΕΞΑΝΔΡΙΝΑ. *Hellénisme, judaisme et christianisme à Alexandrie. Mélanges offerts au P. Claude Mondésert* (Paris, 1987).

Müller, C. D. G., *Geschichte der orientalischen Nationalkirchen* (Göttingen, 1981).

Norris, R. A., 'Christological Models in Cyril of Alexandria', in TU 116 (1975), 255–68.

Orbe, A., *Christología Gnóstica* I (Madrid, 1976).

Otto, S., *Person und Subsistenz. Die philosophische Anthropologie des Leontios von Byzanz. Ein Beitrag zur spätantiken Geistesgeschichte* (Munich, 1968).

Outler, A. C., ' "The Three Chapters". A Comment on the Survival of Antiochene Christology' in Fischer, R. H. (ed.), *A Tribute to Arthur Vööbus* (Chicago, 1977), 357–64.

Pargoire, J., *L'Église byzantine de 527 à 847* (Paris, ²1905).

I Patriarcati Orientali nel primo millennio. Relazioni del Congresso tentutosi al Pontificio Istituto Orientale nei giorni 27–30 Dicembre 1967 = OCA 181 (Rome, 1968).

Pelikan, J., The Christian Tradition 1 (Chicago, London, 1971).

Peri, V., *La Grande Chiesa Bizantina. L'ambito ecclesiale dell'Ortodossia* (Brescia, 1981).

Perrone, L., *La chiesa di Palestina e le controversie cristologiche* (Brescia, 1980).

'Il "Dialogo contro gli aftartodoceti" di Leonzio di Bisanzio e Severo di Antiochia', *CrSt* 1 (1980), 411–42.

Petersen, W. L., *The Diatessaron and Ephrem Syrus as Sources of Romanos the Melodist* = CSCO 475, Subs. 74 (Louvain, 1985).

'The Dependence of Romanos the Melodist upon the Syriac Ephrem: Its Importance for the Origin of the Kontakion', *VigC* 39 (1985), 171–87.

Potz, R., 'Patriarch und Synode in Konstantinopel. Das Verfassungsrecht des ökumenischen Patriarchats' = *Kirche und Recht* 10 (Vienna, 1971).

Prinzing, G., 'Das Bild Justinians I. in der Überlieferung der Byzantiner vom 7. bis 15. Jahrhundert' in *Fontes Minores* VII, Simon, D. (ed.) (Frankfurt, 1976), 1–99.

Rees, S., 'The *De Sectis*: A Treatise Attributed to Leontius of Byzantium', *JTS* 40 (1939), 346–60.

'The Literary Activity of Leontius of Byzantium', *JTS* 19 (1968), 229–42.

Richard, M., 'Le traité "De sectis" et Léonce de Byzance', *RHE* 35 (1939), 695–723 = *Op. Min.* II, no. 55.

'La tradition des fragments du traité Περὶ τῆς ἐνανθρωπήσεως de Théodore de Mopsueste', *Mus* 56 (1943), 55–75 = *Op. Min.* II, no. 41.

'Léonce de Jérusalem et Léonce de Byzance', *MSR* 1 (1944), 35–88 = *Op. Min.* III, no. 59.

'Le Néo-chalcédonisme', *MSR* 3 (1946), 156–61 = *Op. Min.* II, no. 56.

and Aubineau, M. (ed.), *Iohannis Caesariensis Presbyteri et Grammatici Opera quae supersunt* = CCG 1 (Turnhout, Louvain, 1977).

Riedinger, R., *Pseudo-Kaisarios. Überlieferungsgeschichte und Verfasserfrage* (Munich, 1969).

Art. 'Akoimeten', in *TRE* 2 (1978), 148–53.

Pseudo-Kaisarios, Die Erotapokriseis. In Verbindung mit Wolfgang Lackner erstmals vollständig herausgegeben von R. Riedinger (Berlin, 1989).

Rochow, I., 'Die Heidenprozesse unter den Kaisern Tiberios III. Konstantinos und Maurikios', in BBA Bd. 47 = *Studien z. 7. Jh. in Byzanz* (Berlin, 1976), 120–30.

Rondeau, M.-J., *Les commentaires patristiques du Psautier (IIIe-Ve siècles)* = OCA 220 (Rome, 1985).

Rügamer, W., *Leontius von Byzanz, ein Polemiker aus der Zeit Justinians* (Diss. Würzburg, 1894).

Runciman, S., *Byzantine Style and Civilisation* (London, 1975).

Samuel, V. C., 'One Incarnate Nature of God the Word', *GOTR* 10 (1964/65), 37–53.

'The Christology of Severus of Antioch', *Abba Salama* 4 (1973), 126–90.

Savramis, D., *Zur Soziologie des byzantinischen Mönchtums* (Leiden, Cologne, 1962).

Schieffer, R., 'Zur lateinischen Überlieferung von Kaiser Justinians Ὁμολογία τῆς ὀρθῆς πίστεως (Edictum de recta fide)', *Kleronomia* 3 (1971), 285–301.

'Nochmals zur Überlieferung von Justinians Ὁ. τ. ὀ. π. (Edict. de recta fide)', *Kleronomia* 4 (1972), 267–84.

'Das V. Ökumenische Konzil in kanonistischer Überlieferung', *ZSavSt.K* 90 (1973), 1–34.

'Zur Beurteilung des norditalischen Dreikapitel-Schismas. Eine überlieferungsgeschichtliche Studie', *ZKG* 87 (1976), 167–201.

Schönborn, C. von, *Sophrone de Jérusalem: Vie monastique et confession dogmatique* = *ThéolHist* 20 (Paris, 1972).

Schreiner, P., Art. 'Demen' in *LexMA* 3 (1986), 686.

Schubart, W., *Justinian und Theodora* (Munich, 1943).

Schulte, E., *Die Entwicklung der Lehre vom menschlichen Wissen Christi bis zum Beginne der Scholastik* = FCLDG 12,2 (Paderborn, 1914).

Schulz, H.-J., *Die byzantinische Liturgie. Glaubenszeugnis und Symbolgestalt* (Trier, [2]1980).

Schurr, V., *Die Trinitätslehre des Boethius im Lichte der 'skythischen Kontroversen'* = FCLDG 18,1 (Paderborn, 1935), 276–320.

Schwartz, E., *Kyrillos von Skythopolis* = TU 49,2 (Leipzig, 1939).

    Drei dogmatische Schriften Justinians = *ABAW.PH* 18 (Munich, 1939).

    Vigiliusbriefe = *SBAW* 1940,2 (Munich, 1940).

    'Zur Kirchenpolitik Justinians' in *idem, Zur Geschichte der alten Kirche und ihres Rechts* = *Ges. Schriften* IV (Berlin, 1960), 276–320.

Sedlar, J. W., *India and the Greek World. A Study in the Transmission of Culture* (Totowa, New Jersey, 1980).

Sesboué, B., *Traité de l'incarnation. Étude du développement du dogme christologique* (Paris, 1982).

Sieben, H. J., *Die Konzilsidee der Alten Kirche* (Paderborn, Munich, Vienna, Zürich, 1979).

Simonetti, M., 'Alcune osservazioni sul monofisismo di Cirillo di Alessandria', *Aug* 22 (1982), 493–511.

    'La politica religiosa di Giustiniano' in Archi, G. G. (ed.), *Il mondo dell'diritto nell'epoca giustinianea. Caratteri e problematiche* (Ravenna, 1985), 91–111.

    'Per la rivalutazione di alcune testimonianze su Paolo di Samosata', *RSLR* 24 (1988), 177–210.

Speigl, J., 'Der Autor der Schrift De Sectis über die Konzilien und die Religionspolitik Justinians', *AHC* 2 (1970), 207–30.

    'Das Religionsgespräch mit den severianischen Bischöfen in Konstantinopel im Jahre 532', *AHC* 16 (1984), 264–85.

    Art. 'Dreikapitelstreit' in *LexMA* 3 (1986), 1381–2.

Stead, C., *Substance and Illusion in the Christian Fathers* (London, 1985).

Stein, E., *Studien zur Geschichte des byzantinischen Reiches vornehmlich unter den Kaisern Justinus II und Tiberius Constantinus* (Stuttgart, 1919).

    Histoire du Bas-Empire II (Paris, 1949).

Stiernon, D., art. 'Léonce de Byzance', in *DSp* 9 (1976), 651–60.

Stockmeier, P., 'Das anthropologische Modell der Spätantike und die Formel von Chalkedon', *AHC* 8 (1976), 40–52.

    'Die Entfaltung der Christologie und ihr Einfluß auf die Anthropologie der Spätantike' in *Im Gespräch der Mensch*, Balmer, H. P. et al. (eds.) (Düsseldorf, 1981), 248–55.

Straub, J., 'Die Verurteilung der Drei Kapitel durch Vigilius (Vigilii Epistula II ad Eutychium)', *Kleronomia* 2 (1970), 347–75.

Studer, B.–Daley, B., *Soteriologie. In der Schrift und Patristik* = HDG III, 2a (1978).

Suchla, B. R., *Die Überlieferung des Prologs des Johannes von Skythopolis zum griechischen Corpus Dionysiacum Areopagiticum* = *NAWG.PH* 1984, 4 (Göttingen, 1984), 177–88.

    Eine Redaktion des griechischen Corpus Dionysiacum Areopagiticum im Umkreis des Johannes von Skythopolis, des Verfassers von Prolog und Scholien. Ein dritter Beitrag zur Überlieferungsgeschichte des CD = *NAWG.PH* 1985,5 (Göttingen, 1985), 179–94.

    Symposium Syriacum = OCA 197 (Rome, 1974).

Szövérffy, J., *Guide to Byzantine Hymnography* I–II (Brooklyn, Leiden, 1978–1979).

Topping, E., 'The Apostle Peter, Justinian and Romanos the Melodos', *Byzantine and Modern Greek Studies* 2 (1976), 1–15.

Torrance, I. R., *Christology after Chalcedon. Severus of Antioch and Sergius the Monophysite* (Norwich, 1988).

Tuilier, A., 'Remarques sur les fraudes des Apollinaristes et des Monophysites' in Dummer, J. (ed.), *Texte und Textkritik* = TU 133 (Berlin, 1987), 581–90.

Uthemann, K.-H., 'Syllogistik im Dienst der Orthodoxie. Zwei unedierte Texte byzantinischer Kontroverstheologie des 6. Jahrhunderts', *JÖB* 30 (1981), 103–12.

'Das anthropologische Modell der Hypostatischen Union. Ein Beitrag zu den philosophischen Voraussetzungen und zur innerchalkedonischen Transformation eines Paradigmas', *Kleronomia* 14 (1982), 215–312.

Art. 'Byzanz' in *EKL*, 610–16.

Van den Ven, P., 'Les écrits de s. Syméon le Stylite le Jeune avec trois sermons inédits', *Mus* 70 (1957), 1–57.

'L'accession de Jean le Scholastique au siège patriarcal de Constantinople en 565', *Byz* 35 (1965), 320–52.

Van Roey, A., 'Théodose d'Alexandrie dans les manuscrits syriaques de la British Library' in Quaegebeur, J. (ed.), *Studia Paulo Naster oblata*, II: *Orientalia Antiqua* = OLA 13 (Louvain, 1982), 287–99.

'La controverse trithéite jusqu'à l'excommunication de Conon et d'Eugène (557–569)', *OLP* 16 (1985), 141–65.

Vasiliev, A. A., *Justin the First. An Introduction to the Epoch of Justinian the Great* (Cambridge, Mass., 1950).

Verbeke, G.–Moncho, J. R., *Némésius d'Emèse De Natura Hominis. Traduction de Burgundio de Pise. Ed. crit. avec une introduction sur l'anthropologie de Némésius* (Leiden, 1975).

Vian, G. M., *Testi inediti del Commento ai Salmi di Atanasio* = StudEph'Aug' 14 (Rome, 1978).

Vööbus, A., *A History of the School of Nisibis* = CSCO 266 (Louvain, 1965).

Voss, B. R., *Der Dialog in der frühchristlichen Literatur* = Studia et Testimonia Antiqua 9 (Munich, 1970).

Vries, W. de, 'Die Eschatologie des Severus von Antiochien', *OCP* 23 (1957), 354–80.

Waegeman, M., 'The Text Tradition of the Treatise De sectis (Ps. Leontius Byzantinus)', *AnCl* 45 (1976), 190–6.

Walch, C. W. F., *Entwurf einer vollständigen Historie der Kezereien, Spaltungen und Religionsstreitigkeiten, bis auf die Zeiten der Reformation*, 8 (Leipzig, 1778).

Walker, N., 'The Origin of the "Thrice Holy"', *NTS* 5 (1958/59), 132–3.

Walter, C., *Art and Ritual of the Byzantine Church* (London, 1982).

Watt, J. H. I., 'The Authenticity of the Writings Ascribed to Leontius of Byzantium. A New Approach by Means of Statistics' in *StudPat* 7 = TU 92 (1966), 321–36.

Weiss, G., *Byzanz. Kritischer Forschungs- und Literaturbericht 1968–1985* = HistZ Sonderhefte, 14 (Munich, 1986).

Winkelmann, F., 'Kirche und Gesellschaft in Byzanz vom Ende des 6. bis zum Beginn des 8. Jahrhunderts', *Klio* 59 (1977), 477–89.

Die östlichen Kirchen in der Epoche der christologischen Auseinandersetzungen (5. bis 7. Jahrhundert) = Kirchengeschichte in Einzeldarstellungen I/6 (Berlin, 1980).

Wölfle, E., 'Der Abt Hypatios von Ruphinianai und der Akoimete Alexander', *ByzZ* 79 (1986), 302–9.

Zabolotsky, N. A., 'The Christology of Severus of Antioch', *Ekklesiastikos Pharos* 58 (1976), 357–86.

Zettl, E., *Die Bestätigung des V. Ökumenischen Konzils durch Papst Vigilius* (Bonn, 1974).

INDEX OF PERSONS

A. ANCIENT AUTHORS

Tarasis Kodissa (= Emperor Zeno) 236
Tertullian 292, 298
Thalassius 16, 228
Themistius, deacon 68
Theocritus 318, 321
Theoctistus 243
Theoderic I, King 35, 267, 308, 312
Theodora, Empress 14, 47, 328, 330
Theodore of Antinoe 260
Theodore of Arabia 330
Theodore bar Konai 86
Theodore Lector (Anagnostes) 34–6, 237, 243–4, 264–70, 278, 283, 308, 311, 313
Theodore, monk 136
Theodore of Mopsuestia 59, 62, 72, 79–81, 270–1, 279, 285, 287, 329
Theodore of Petra 43
Theodore of Pharan 74
Theodore of Raithu 80, 82, 85
Theodoret of Cyrus 34–5, 37, 45–6, 53, 55, 63, 65, 79–80, 97, 99, 105, 126–8, 192, 234, 270–1, 279, 287, 303, 329
Theodosius I (the Elder) 110, 113, 141–2, 147, 207
Theodosius II (the Younger) 35, 97, 121, 143, 232, 237, 240–1
Theodosius of Alexandria 47, 68, 330
Theodosius, monastic father 262, 334, 336
Theodosius, monk 98–9, 101, 104–5, 115
Theodotus of Ancyra 52, 66
Theophanes the Confessor 30, 36, 115–16, 234, 251, 263–9, 271, 308, 313, 319
Theophilus of Alexandria 64–7, 105–7, 170, 178, 239
Theophylact Simocattes 30
Theophylus of Edessa 32
Theopistus 42
Theopompus 237, 243
Thomas Aquinas 14, 24
Thomas of Arzruni 33
Timotheus IV (III) of Alexandria 67–8, 327
Timothy I, Catholicus 72
Timothy I of CP 279, 282–5, 315

Timothy I, Patr. (Nestorian) 25
Timothy Aelurus 42, 62, 64, 67, 105, 115–17, 148, 158, 172, 180, 190, 192, 194, 196–7, 199, 202–4, 210, 212, 215, 219, 220–1, 226, 232, 234, 236–9, 241–2, 244–8, 254–6, 259–60, 289, 294–6, 304, 307, 310, 312, 324–5, 327, 331
Timothy of Beirut 59
Timothy, presb. 80
Timothy Salophaciolus of Alexandria 249, 258
Tiro Prosper 33
Titus of Bostra 184
Turribius of Astorga 178
Tutus 260

Ursus 179

Valentinian III 176, 178
Valentinus 59, 101, 104, 172–3, 183, 190, 192–3
Verina 237, 247
Victor of Tunnuna 33, 212, 265, 267, 270, 319
Vigilius, Pope 28, 59, 61–2
Vigilius of Thapsus 121–2
Vincent of Lérins 53–4
Virgil 192
Vitalian 311–13, 318, 327
Vitalis 260

Yahbalaha, Catholicus 25

Zacharias Rhetor/Scholasticus 34, 36, 42, 44–5, 55, 82, 98–100, 105, 115–16, 197–9, 202–3, 237–8, 241–5, 247–8, 250, 252, 258, 260–4, 266–70, 273–4, 276–9, 281, 284, 290, 318, 321
Zacharias (Vita Petr. Iber.) 44
Zeno(n), Emperor 24, 28, 31, 44, 55, 65, 70, 141, 236–7, 239, 243–5, 247–9, 251–2, 256–62, 264, 266, 268, 270, 274–5, 279–81, 287, 289–91, 307–8, 314, 325
Zenonis 241
Ze'ora, stylite 48
Zoaras 321
Zoilus 28

B. MODERN AUTHORS

Aalders, G. J. D. 174
Abbeloos, J. B. 31
Abramowski, L. 28, 37, 53, 63, 71–2
Adam, A. 82, 176, 178, 181, 184–5
Ahrens, K. 36, 44, 197, 199
Aland, B. 175–6
Alberigo, J. 24
Allen, P. 34, 36, 237, 271, 311, 318
Alszeghy, Z. 19
Altaner, B. 33, 43, 57, 142
Amalorpavadass, D. 19
Amann, E. 24

Amélineau, F. 42, 252
Ananian, P. 85
Anderson, D. 77
Andresen, C. 17, 53
Arens, H. 128, 149, 153, 156–9, 165, 169, 171
Ashbrook, S. 46
Asmussen, J. P. 82
Assemani, J. S. 37, 48, 270
Assfalg, J. 32–3, 37
Astruc, C. 81–2
Atiya, A. S. 40
Aubineau, M. 56, 80–2, 213

SUBJECT INDEX

INDEX OF BIBLICAL REFERENCES

INDEX OF GREEK AND LATIN TERMS

GREEK

LATIN

INDEX OF PERSONS

A. ANCIENT AUTHORS

Aba I, Catholicos 464
'Abdišo' Bar Berika 466
Aboui 485
Abou'l Barakat 466
Abraham of Beth Rabban 463–4, 466
Abraham, abbot 319
Acacius of CP, Patr. 253, 262, 329–30
Acacius of Melitene 48, 156, 245–6, 415
Achilles, monk 322
Agapetus I, Pope 183, 231, 348–53, 355, 474
Agapetus, deacon 14
Agathias 9–10
Albinos 397
Alexander of Hierapolis 412
Ambrose 44–5, 501–2
Amphilochius 491
Anastasia, deaconess 142
Anastasius I, Emperor 3, 10, 14, 20, 24, 174, 239, 252, 257, 319, 328, 345, 348, 514
Anastasius of Antioch, Patr. 469
Anastasius of Sinai 25
Anastasius, monk 482
Anatolius of CP, Patr. 49, 329
Anatolius, deacon 380
Andrew of Samosata 50, 78, 412
Anicia Juliana 257
Anteonus of Arsenoe 260
Anthemius 10
Anthimus of CP, Patr. 183, 231, 316, 345, 347–53, 355–6, 362–3, 366–8, 374, 377–8, 511
Anthimus of Trebizond 233
Antipater of Bostra 389, 398
Antoninus of Aleppo 113
Apollinarius of Alexandria, Patr. 439, 469
Apollinarius of Laodicea 52, 59, 69, 70, 89, 105, 117, 126–7, 130, 154, 157, 170, 174, 237–9, 300, 358–61, 433, 435, 451, 453, 459, 505, 507, 509–10, 517–18
Appion, patricius 31
Areobindus 257
Aristotle 54, 116–17, 197, 202, 207–9, 459, 498
Arius 135–6, 261, 428, 451, 484, 487, 496
Artemos 342
Athanasius of Alexandria, Patr. 21, 58–9, 70, 78, 91–2, 98–9, 113, 125–6, 168, 172, 220, 237–9, 326, 358, 365, 392, 394–5, 500–1
Athanasius of Antioch 21
Athanasius, tritheist 490

Athenagoras 35
Atticus of CP 11
Augustine 45, 77, 305, 324, 381, 445, 502
Avitus 392, 400

Babai of Shigar 465
Barhadbešabba (of) 'Arbaya 464–6
Barsauma of Qardou 465
Barṣaumā, monk 416
Basil of Caesarea 30, 45, 54–5, 59, 62, 73, 101, 192, 208, 250, 280, 287, 318, 360, 365, 399, 430, 491–2, 505, 518
Basil of Seleucia 29, 244, 493, 515
Basil, deacon 413, 463
Belisarius 10, 346
Blandus 321
Boethius 335–6

Caesarius 374
Calandion of Antioch 256
Carosus, monk 326
Cassiodorus 249
Celestine, Pope 484
Celsus 396
Cethegus, patricius 427
Chrysippus 40
Chosroes I of Persia, King 8, 465–6
Cicero 336
Clement of Alexandria 121
Constantine I, Emperor 6, 14, 344
Constantine of Laodicea 363, 367
Constantine of Mar Eusebius 485
Constantine, deacon 248
Constantine, Roman deacon 324
Corippus 482–3
Cosmas Indicopleustes 464
Cosmas, monk 485
Cumas 413
Cyriacus, Abba 409
Cyril of Alexandria 21–5, 28–41, 44–50, 52, 58–9, 66–9, 71–9, 83–6, 90, 94–5, 99, 101, 109–10, 113–17, 121, 124, 126–7, 130, 137, 148–9, 152–8, 160–2, 164, 169–72, 174, 187, 224–5, 237–8, 240–3, 245–7, 251, 265, 268–70, 272, 289, 294, 303, 318, 321–2, 325–8, 330–1, 333, 336, 341, 348, 357–61, 365–6, 369–71, 373, 379, 383, 413–16, 420–3, 425, 427, 429–35, 439–40, 445,

B. MODERN AUTHORS

INDEX OF SUBJECTS